Cooking Alaskan

Cooking Alaskan

By Alaskans

Alaska Northwest Books™

Anchorage • Seattle • Portland

First printing 1983
Ninth printing 1994

Library of Congress Cataloging-in-Publication Data
  Main entry under title:
  Cooking Alaskan.
    Includes index.
    1. Cookery, American—Alaska. I. Alaska magazine.
  TX715.C7825   1983   641.59798   83-11865
  ISBN 0-88240-237-4

Cover design by Kate L. Thompson
Design by Pamela S. Ernst
Cover photography by Jim Mears
Food styling by Phyllis Bogard and Carrie Seglin
Illustrations by Fred W. Thomas

Alaska Northwest Books™
An imprint of Graphic Arts Center Publishing Company
Editorial office: 2208 NW Market Street, Suite 300,
  Seattle, WA 98107
Catalog and order dept.: P.O. Box 10306, Portland OR, 97210
  800-452-3032

Printed on acid-free paper in the United States of America

Contents

A Note To Our Readers

Regarding current regulations on harvesting wild animals and birds:

Many recipes in **Cooking Alaskan** have come from Native Alaskans who traditionally harvest wild game for subsistence use.

Only individuals who are at least one-quarter Alaska Native are eligible to hunt marine mammals for subsistence use. However, non-Natives can purchase traditional Native foods from special stores in most Alaska communities, including Anchorage.

Alaska Natives may take as many marine mammals as needed for subsistence purposes unless a species is endangered. Gray and bowhead whales are endangered, and the International Whaling Commission determines how many whales Natives in arctic communities may harvest each year.

The numbers of emperor geese, cackling Canada geese, Pacific white-fronted geese, and brant have been declining significantly in recent years, prompting a temporary restriction on harvesting these migratory birds and their eggs.

— From the editor, 1990

Preface

Few things have so much significance to our lives as what and how much Nature provides us to eat and how we use it to nourish body, soul, friendship, ceremony. . . . It is not just hearts that are hidden behind stomachs; it's whole cultures.

Cooking Alaskan is an effort to organize and to share what we have learned about how Alaskan cooks use Alaskan foods . . . plus a little.

For the most part, the major ingredient of its more than 1,500 recipes is Alaskan grown or bred. The great abundance and variety of that home-grown food is represented in the first three books of the volume.

Book One — From The Waters — includes recipes and preparation techniques for what will always be the staple of cooking Alaskan-style, fish and shellfish. In this state, it is a rare settlement that is so removed from either fresh or coastal waters that its people cannot easily take advantage of this resource.

In Book Two — From Field & Forest — are recipes for wild birds and beasts, large and small. And in Book Three — From The Earth — are hundreds of tips and recipes to guide the foragers of wild vegetables and berries and the gardeners of the many tame plants that grow well in Alaskan gardens.

One bit of the "plus a little" is that Book Four — From Cache & Cupboard — includes recipes using items we bring in from Outside — grains, beans, powdered milk — especially if they're used to stir up products that, like sourdough, have become part of the North's traditional fare.

The recipes and "how-to" information come from many, many sources — some never before published; the rest, perhaps printed in books without wide distribution or in magazine or newspaper stories you may wish you'd clipped, but didn't.

In other words, *Cooking Alaskan* is a collection. But another part of the plus a little has been provided by the several people who looked at the collection critically, who chose some recipes in favor of others, helped to organize the rest, say what's missing and fill in the blanks. By this means, the original collection has been selected, edited, and, when we could find expert help, expanded.

It is not complete. There are techniques used by Northern cooks that are nowhere written down so that we could add them to this volume. Others fall into the category of those we, too, only *wish* we'd clipped.

That's why this first collection, big as it is, nevertheless is intended as a beginning that will stimulate supplements in the years to come. We hope those who use it will take an active part in expanding the record of how Alaskans use the foods available to them from the land and waters. You will doubtless think of recipes that are missing, or methods you deem superior to — at least as good as — ones selected for this book. Please let us know about them. If you know about a secret formula you'd like to see written down, send us the name of the creator and let us have a go at convincing him or her to share the secret in print.

How The Book Is Organized

Cooking Alaskan is organized on the assumption that if you're preparing moose steak for dinner tonight, you didn't select the menu by the process most family cooks use. That is, by going to the neighborhood supermarket and wandering up and down the meat counter till you found something that matched your taste and your pocketbook.

No, if dinner is to be moose steak or caribou roast or salmon livers or sheefish, we think that meal got to your kitchen by some other means.

So you have it. Now you've got to fix it.

This book is for you. All the moose recipes are in one section of one chapter, whether the preparation results in appetizer, salad, consomme, main dish or (yes) moose mincemeat pie! This organization becomes especially handy if not just the steak but The Whole Thing arrived in your kitchen at the same time. Or a whole day's berrypicking. Or the result of a week's fishing trip.

So you have it. Now you've got to fix it. *Cooking Alaskan* provides an enormous variety of recipes from cooks all over the state who've been faced with a similar kitchenful of meat or fish or wildfowl or salmonberries, a section for each variety of food rather than each variety of recipe.

But suppose someday it happens that nothing is demanding to be fixed. And it happens to be the first really hot day in a long while, and you happen to think, "Ahhhhhh! I'd like s-a-l-a-d tonight"? Well, then, it also happens you can use this cookbook like a conventional one. With a glance at the salad or soup or stew listings in the index, you may choose from a complete array a menu that matches your taste and pocketbook and the items on your cupboard or supermarket shelves. And have salad tonight. (Moose salad?)

Which brings up the matter of substitutions: Suppose you are fresh out of moose . . . or any wild game . . . can you use the delicious recipes in this book anyhow? Of course. In all sections of the book, substitutions are suggested and encouraged.

Naturally in a book this size, there are frequent occasions to refer to other parts of the book. Besides "see thus-and-so" or a page number, another clue is commonly used. Titles of recipes that are in this book are capitalized. When an ingredients list includes items such as White Sauce, Sage Stuffing, Wild Currant Jelly or Lemon Butter, you know that recipes for those items can be found by referring to the index.

Matters of Taste — Wild Taste

In the process of putting this collection together, we've discovered why it is that most cookbooks authored by more than one person or maybe two very close persons contain little or *no* "how-to" information. They confine themselves to providing only recipes, with maybe a few discordant household hints thrown in.

The reason is not quite what you're thinking. It is a LIE that too many cooks spoil the broth. The fact is, too many cooks would never get around to making the broth. They'd spend all their time arguing about how it was to be done.

Let us illustrate from our own editorial family. One day, the Outdoors Editor (who is usually where he belongs — outdoors — and therefore unavailable for consultation by a cookbook editor) . . . one day,

the excellent Outdoors Editor happened to be within range of one of the cookbook editors (this volume has required several) who was at that moment trying to make sense of several descriptions — several experts' descriptions — of the best way to butcher Dungeness crab. Each expert had written expertly all right, and yet the descriptions jibed not a whit.

"Now, Jim," said this cookbook editor to the Outdoors Editor, "Do you clean crab *before* you cook it or after?" And Jim explained, certainly expertly enough, giving such a precise blow-by-blow illustration of the whole process that the cookbook editor could practically reach out and grab one of the butter-dipped morsels that would be the final result.

At Jim's side during all this and looking increasingly alarmed was another expert, this one the Editor-in-Chief.

Well, you know what happened next . . . or what *might* have happened had the Outdoors Editor not been due back outdoors on the next plane. The potential discussion ended for lack of time and the cookbook editor did not get any crab, cooked before or after cleaning.

What the cookbook editor did get was a convincing demonstration that differing experts may BOTH BE RIGHT when it comes to cooking. And so, in this collection, we have tried to give you a choice where there is a real one to be made.

By that we do not mean to say, however, that good cooking is all a matter of individual taste. It isn't. Good cooking has the obligation to train taste sometimes, too.

One of the biggest controversies reflected in the various recipes considered for this book is whether the wild or gamy flavor is a good thing or a terrible thing. Do you enhance it or hide it?

Quite simply, that is a choice we dismissed almost out-of-hand. We selected recipes we felt would enhance the good flavor of the properly gathered and field- and kitchen-prepared wild foods we hope most Alaskan cooks have to work with. And added a few of the experts' instructions about what that proper preparation must be to preserve the naturally good flavors of the food.

How Measurements Are Handled

The primary measure used in the recipes in this book is the U.S. Customary measure. Metric equivalents are shown in parentheses. As a rule of thumb, we have simply translated whatever measure was given in the original recipe into its metric equivalent. That is, if the recipe calls for so many cups of flour, the metric equivalent is given in liters or milliliters, since cups and liters are both measures of volume. If the recipe calls for pounds of fish, the metric unit is shown in kilograms, both measures of weight.

Because cooks who use the metric system are far more accustomed to measuring by weight than we are in the United States, some of the metric equivalents in the recipes are awkward to measure. For that, we apologize. We feel it is a necessary —but transitional — awkwardness. It is necessary for the moment because many U.S. volume measures do not readily translate to metric weights. We can tell you that a cup of butter weighs 228 grams, but the weight of a cup of sea salt, rock salt, cooked or uncooked Ala, graham cracker crumbs, salmon livers or Parry's wallflower root puzzles us. We only know what a cup-size pile of it *looks* like. Most of our recipes, after all, are still created in that fashion, the cook eyeballing the *volume* of the ingredients.

The awkwardness is transitional, however, because as the metric system becomes more common in the U.S., more chefs will be cooking and creating by weighing ingredients or using liters and milliliters instead of cups and tablespoons to measure volume.

Meanwhile, during the transition, if you're a "metric cook," your best bet is to stick to metric cookbooks! *Or* buy a set of U.S. measuring cups and spoons before they're obsolete.

We do offer something more than apologies and advice, though. At the beginning of Book Three, some U.S. Customary volume measures of common ingredients have been translated to International System of Units (SI) equivalents of weight. In that same section will be found other information about weights, measures and substitutions — for both the metric and the cups-and-spoons cook.

Living Off The Land

What can you eat? How good is it for you? Here are some answers to those questions from the bulletin "Eat Well — Live Well," put out by the Cooperative Extension Service at the University of Alaska. For a graphic portrayal of the answers, you'll find much of interest in the chart on the next page — Food Energy (Calories) & Nutrition in Alaskan Wild Foods — which shows the U.S. Recommended Daily Allowance of certain vitamins and minerals and the percentage of them available in foods that are gathered and fished and hunted from our great land.

Many years ago all the food was from the land. The people who lived in Alaska hunted and fished and gathered wild plants and berries for food. Then explorers, sailors, colonizers, traders and others introduced new foods to Alaskans. The Russians introduced gardening so that potatoes, onions and rutabagas became a part of the diet. Hudson's Bay introduced new foods at their trading posts; and the Americans added many more. We are no longer dependent on the land. But we could be!

Early Alaskans ate a diet high in animal protein. Interior Alaskans ate caribou, moose, bear, beaver, rabbit and fish, while coastal Alaskans ate seal, walrus and whale. In addition to this animal protein, they depended on wild greens and berries to supply other nutrients to their diet. Blueberries, salmonberries and cranberries can be gathered in many areas of Alaska. They were frozen so they could be used as a special treat all year long.

Somehow as more foods were available in stores, the early Alaskans found it was easier to purchase foods than to hunt or gather foods. Newcomers often indicated that the familiar Alaskan foods were not good. And the Alaskans themselves began to doubt the value of the food they had been eating. Some people even said that caribou and moose did not have much food value and that the food grown in Alaska grew too fast to have any nutrients. Both statements were nonsense!

All animal food is a good source of protein . . . beef as well as rabbit, fish, squirrel and bear. Some animal food is higher in fat than others, however. The ground beef you purchase is often 33 percent fat; while caribou and moose flesh are less than 3 percent fat. Of game meats, only beaver and seal have more fat than our familiar ground beef.

A family of four can adequately feed on 700 pounds (315 kg) of moose meat (one good-sized moose) for a year. If the average cost of purchasing meat is figured at $2.00 per pound, that moose is worth $1,400. . . .

How about other nutritional value? Women require 18 milligrams of iron per day to stay healthy. In less than 1/2 cup (120 mL), beaver has 5.9 milligrams of iron; raw seal flesh is an excellent source of iron — almost 20 milligrams. Hamburger has only 2.5 milligrams. One serving of the raw seal flesh would supply the iron needed for one day.

Liver is always a good source of iron no matter what animal it comes from — including fish. Whitefish liver, for instance, has almost 8 milligrams of iron in 1/2 cup (120 mL).

The American diet is now very high in fat. Often more than 40 percent of our calories come from fat. Unfortunately the fat we eat is mostly in the form of vegetable oil. This fat does not carry any other nutrients. The fat in game meats carries fat-soluble vitamins, such as vitamin A and D.

The carbohydrates found in berries and greens are accompanied by vitamins and minerals. The sugar found in soda pop, candy and other synthetic foods is seldom accompanied by nutrients necessary for good health.

From a health standpoint, eating game and edible berries and greens is much more desirable.

Food Energy (Calories) & Nutrition in Alaskan Wild Foods

Showing the Number of Calories and the Percent of the U.S. Recommended Daily Allowance (USRDA) of Eight Nutrients Provided by a 100-Gram Serving of Certain Foods

	Food Energy	Protein	Vitamin A	Vitamin C	Thiamin	Riboflavin	Niacin	Calcium	Iron
U.S. Recommended Daily Allowance (adults)**		65 g	5,000 IU	60 mg	1.5 mg	1.7 mg	20 mg	1,000 mg	18 mg
ALASKAN WILD FOODS (100-gram serving)	(Number of Calories)			Numbers below are the percentage of USRDA (above)					
Beach asparagus†	—	2	40	2	—	8	4	4	4
Bear, black, flesh	148	30	6	—	10	40	15	—	40
Beaver, flesh	150	40	6	—	2	8	10	2	40
Beluga, flesh	107	40	6	—	4	25	30	—	140
air-dried	310	110	10	—	—	—	—	2	505
muktuk	342	30	40	—	15	4	15	—	4
Blueberries†	—	—	2	4	2	10	2	2	6
Caribou, flesh	120	40	4	—	10	30	25	2	15
liver	140	20	570	60*	15*	160*	60*	—	90
Cloudberries	43	2	4	260	2	4	4	2	4
Duck, eider, flesh	109	30	—	—	6*	6*	40*	2*	8*
Eulachon, smoked, frozen†	—	30	80	—	—	70	30	2	70
Eulachon grease†	—	4	110	—	—	—	—	—	—
Fiddlehead ferns†	—	30	30	15	—	20	10	2	4
Fireweed, young leaves	50	4	110	160	2	50	8	2	10
Gumboots†	—	30	30	—	2	20	20	70	4
Herring, flesh, air-dried	270	70	2*	—	—	10*	40	—	6*
roe-on-kelp (giant kelp)†	—	20	2	—	8	10	15	15	20
roe, plain†	—	15	—	—	8	10	10	2	15
roe, air-dried	294	90	—	—	2	10	20	—	—
Huckleberries†	—	—	2	4	—	2	2	2	2
Lingonberries	50	—	2	30	—	4	2	2	2
Mashu, roots	42	10	—	20	6	4	6	—	—
Moose, flesh	123	40	6	—	6	10	—	—	15
Needlefish, whole fish	105	15	25	—	2	80	—	10	30
Octopus†	—	20	—	—	2	2	10	2	30
Oogruk (bearded seal), air-dried	336	130	25	—	8	40	—	—	270
Reindeer, flesh	117	30	—	—	20	40	30	—	30
Rose hips	—	—	—	2670	—	—	—	—	—
Salmon, dried	371	80	25	—	10	20	20	—	—
Salmonberries†	—	2	30	4	2	6	—	2	4
Sea cucumber†	—	20	6	—	2	80	15	2	2
Seal, flesh	143	40	20	—	10	30	—	—	110
Seaweed, kelp	—	—	—	—	—	—	—	110	—
Laminaria, raw	71	4	—	20	4	15	10	6	30
Agarum	—	—	—	—	—	—	—	60	30
black (*Porphyra*), dried†	—	40	90	30	8	190	60	15	60
dulse, dried†	—	30	—	8	4	80	30	20	60
Sourdock, young leaves	47	2	240	110	6	30	6	—	4
Venison (deer) 3 ounces (85.5 g)†	107	30	—	—	—	25	30	—	—
Walrus, flesh, air-dried	246	90	8	—	15	50	50	—	240
Whale, baleen, flesh	134	40	6	—	10	50	40	—	70
Whitefish, flesh	96	20	10	—	6	8	—	—	—
Willow	33	10	370	—	—	—	10	15	15

*Estimates

**USRDA figures have been slightly revised since this comparison was made. Most recommendations have remained roughly the same, although a lower amount of iron is now recommended for males; and for both males and females, the recommended allowance of protein and calcium has been adjusted downward.

†These figures are from the 1980 Southeastern Alaska Native Foods Study. Cooperative Extension Service and U.S. Department of Agriculture cooperating.

Except for figures noted above (†), this chart was prepared by the Cooperative Extension Service, University of Alaska and U.S. Department of Agriculture cooperating. Revised February 1979.

Acknowledgments

About the cooks all over Alaska and how their recipes got into our book: Nobody at Alaska Northwest Publishing Company will admit how long the collecting has been going on. ALASKA® magazine (formerly The ALASKA SPORTSMAN®) has been around for nearly 50 years, and around it there have always been editors interested in how Alaskan cooks prepare the food they gather or hunt from the land, the thousands of lakes and streams, the 30,000-some miles of shoreline and the wide seas beyond.

These editors filled boxes and desk drawers and in baskets with recipes (again, nobody will say how many beyond an indefinite "thousands") that never seemed to go out. Until one day publisher Bob Henning said to one little red hen, "Cull these in baskets and get the Big Alaska Cookbook o-u-t."

And she did. *

Along the way, she needed a whole lot of help. We are especially grateful to five cook-consultants who looked at the original thousands of recipes, helped select the best and tell us what was still missing, in many cases, providing some of the items from their own files. They are Frances ("Bunny") Mathisen of Petersburg; Audrey Rearden of Homer, Mamie Jensen of Juneau; Marguerite Stetson, Nutrition Specialist and Coordinator of the Expanded Food and Nutrition Education Program, University of Alaska Cooperative Extension Service. The fifth consultant is Manya Wik, who lives with her husband Ole and two children in the Bush about 30 miles north of the Arctic Circle, where the family divides its time between several locales, depending on the season's food-gathering chores.

To the sources from which the thousands of recipes were drawn we are also extremely grateful. The food specialties of many Alaskan communities are represented in cookbooks put out by various organizations. The Pioneers of Alaska are responsible for several and other organizations from church groups to State Fair committees to fishermen's auxiliaries have put some fine recipes into print. Some of these books are still available; many more are out of print. At the end of Book Four, you will find a complete list of these community cookbooks and the organizations whose recipes were selected for this volume. Each recipe is credited, too, to the cook, the book and the community.

In many instances, we expect the cook may now be living elsewhere, or has changed names, or may be among the Alaska pioneers who've reached the "End of the Trail®." We've not tried to indicate such changes consistently, but have simply kept the recipes intact since part of the impetus of Cooking Alaskan is to preserve time-honored ways with food.

If we have omitted the name of any contributor, the oversight is entirely unintentional. A good recipe often becomes part of the heritage of many different families.

One long out-of-print volume which has provided much information about time-honored methods is The Alaska Dietary Survey, 1956-1961, which was part of a series on environmental health commissioned by the U.S. Public Health Service in the 1950s. We have quoted from it throughout.

A few of its statements about diet and food preparation in common practice among Native groups are somewhat dated, now, more than 20 years after the study was done. In some instances, we've shared this information for its historical value, but more often, because the old ways still have plenty of merit. We wish we had more to share.

Other government sponsored materials are equally important to this book, particularly the many excellent publications of the Cooperative Extension Service, University of Alaska. But other northern extension services have made wild foods an object of study, too — and we are grateful for material from extension services at the University of Minnesota, the University of Wyoming, Washington State University and the King County Extension Service in Seattle.

Finally, a major source of how-to information and recipes is ALASKA® magazine and its many, many contributors over the years. To these contributors, the heartiest of thanks. You began . . . and sustained . . . Cooking Alaskan.

—Jan Griffeth
one of the cookbook editors

---

*Who is the little red hen? Well, she has long gone by one or another pen name, from "The Old Homesteader" to "from the editors of ALASKA® magazine" and chooses not to turn loose of them now. You will see many evidences of her good cooking throughout this book.

BOOK ONE

From The Waters

Introduction

Of all the "home-grown" foods available to Alaskans, those nurtured by the state's vast waterways are unquestionably the most important. More than 50 species of fish inhabit Alaska's lakes and streams; its marine waters yield even further varieties of fish and shellfish, much in commercially valuable quantity, much that represents the top choice of sport fishermen, cooks and diners everywhere in the world. Other sea creatures, which are nonexistent on most menus, have long been relished fare for Native Alaskans.

Book One consists of two major sections. The first is all about cooking fish — how to treat it from the time it's out of the water, how to clean and dress it, how to prepare it for the table using basic methods and, finally, how Alaska's cooks concoct special dishes using many different species of fish.

The second major section includes similar information and recipes for shellfish and "other sea creatures," large and small, from sea cucumber to whale.

What Book One does not include that its title suggests it might is a chapter on identifying and preparing plant life borne by the sea (also a rich source of nutrients, especially minerals). For a couple of reasons — their similarity to land grown plants as far as preparation is concerned, and the fact that it is sometimes difficult to tell where water ends and land begins in the raising of such

"vegetables" — we've placed information about them in Book Three — From The Earth — along with other wild and garden-grown plant edibles.

Why Eat Fish?

What we choose to eat is our only possible means of obtaining from 45 to 50 nutrients that are essential to health. If we chose "from the waters" — daily — we'd be ahead on many of them. Fish and shellfish contain protein (the amino acids), trace elements (minerals), fatty acids (in varying quantity depending on the fish) and some of the vitamins.

Fish is an especially important protein source. A 4-ounce (114 g) serving, in fact, contains all the essential amino acids. And the quantity of each in that 4-ounce serving is greater than the amount established by the U.S. Department of Agriculture (USDA) as the per-day requirement for a 150-pound (68 kg) person.

Who Eats Fish?

All of us. And the size of this group of recipes is proof positive. But fish and survival have always been linked — even "locked" — companions in

Alaska, since long before there were written recipes. According to *The Alaska Dietary Survey, 1956-1961:*

Fish is the most important year-round food in the Yukon-Kuskokwim Eskimo diet. It is used seasonally, often in considerable quantities by all other Alaskan Eskimos, as well as by Indians and Aleuts. The fishes used in greatest abundance are blackfish [a minnow-sized tundra fish], flounder, grayling, herring, lingcod, needlefish, pike, salmon (king, silver, dog and red), sculpin, smelts, tom cod, trout and whitefish. The individual importance of these fish in the Eskimo and Indian diet depends on the geographic location of the village.

Fish are prepared in a variety of ways. In season they are preferably eaten either boiled or raw-frozen, often dipped in seal or other oil.

The bulk of the salmon (king, dog and silver), whitefish, tom cod, herring and smelt caught during seasonal migration runs is air-dried. Dried fish is preferably eaten after dipping in seal or whitefish oil, but when these oils are not available they are eaten plain. At Hooper Bay and other Norton Sound villages, certain of these fish — silver salmon at Hooper Bay and tom cod and herring at Hooper Bay and other coastal tundra villages — are preferably prepared and eaten as "poke" fish, i.e., partially air-dried and stored in seal oil.

Smoked fish, especially king salmon, is relished as a trail food since it is not only very tasty, but easy to carry.

If we'd been forced to choose, we would have to admit that the main impetus for this book is to gather in one spot what Alaskans have long, long known about preparing fish and shellfish. This record of the banquets, the simple suppers, the campfire meals-on-a-stick that warm the lives of so many different people is meant to help you — each of us — better use and enjoy the priceless bounty that comes from our waters.

There is no other source of food so luxurious.

Chapter 1

How To Prepare Any Fish

IN THE FIELD

Initial Cleaning & Chilling

That 10-pound (4.5 kg) burbot or sculpin or dogfish or king salmon may look and act tough when you pull it from the water, but it isn't. Its flesh is the most delicate invented by Mother Nature for the human palate, and it merits respect.

Because fish bruise easily, don't let them flop around any more than necessary and don't toss them in the bottom of a boat where they will dry out and become coated with slime and dirt. And DON'T store them unrefrigerated in plastic bags. Warmth, plastic and fish make a sure formula for quick spoilage and possible food poisoning.

DO kill fish as soon as they're caught. Cut out the gills and gut them, taking special care to remove the kidney tissue that clings to the backbone. Gills, guts and kidney are fine media for growing the bacteria that cause spoilage or off taste, so removing them quickly after the fish is caught is essential. Salmon and trout ferment especially rapidly, and fish that are caught while feeding tend to become soft and flabby unless tended quickly.

However, fish should not be washed with water until you're ready to cook or freeze them as dry fish last longer. Simply wipe out the cavity with grass or paper towel. All these initial steps, as well as others to be undertaken later in the kitchen, are described in detail as they apply to both round-fishes — such as salmon, trout and rockfish — and the flat ones — flounder, halibut, sole — beginning on page 8.

After the initial cleaning, keep fish as cold as possible and away from sunlight, preferably in an ice chest filled one-quarter full of crushed ice or cooled with dry ice. If you're using crushed ice, pack some inside the fish cavity, too.

If ice isn't immediately available, sprinkle the gutted cavities with salt, wrap the fish in grass to keep them separated, and keep them as cool and ventilated as possible until you can follow one of the procedures for short-term storage — proper refrigeration, brining or field smoking, as described by Ruth Edmondson, beginning on page 6.

A respected catch won't smell or taste "fishy."

If you're not going to clean your fish right away . . .

. . . at least bleed it. Lift up the gill cover and stick your knife down behind the gills into the throat area. This will cut the blood vessels and arteries around the heart. Let the fish bleed freely for 20 minutes or so. Then wipe it as clean as possible and keep it cool and away from sunlight until you can clean it more thoroughly and refrigerate it.

Short-Term Storage

Refrigeration: Some fish will keep up to 10 days held on ice at 32°F (0°C). When the temperature rises to 37°F (3°C), storage time is reduced to five or six days, and a temperature of 45°F (7°C) narrows the time to about two days. The average home refrigerator ranges between 37 and 45°F (3 to 7°C).

Brining or Salting: If immediate icing isn't going to be possible, it's a wise fisherman who carries along a good quantity of salt when he goes fishing. It can be flavored some with pepper if desired — 1 tablespoon (15 mL) pepper to 1 cup (240 mL) salt. As soon as a fish is gutted and wiped clean, rub cavity and skin well with the salt mixture.

Place salted fish in a basket or box and loosely

Smoke-Cure Those "Extra" Fish

"We couldn't eat all the fish we could legally catch. We wanted to take some home." Here's how an especially lucky fishing party smoked some of their catch — rainbow and grayling as well as salmon — to provide a short-term cure that would preserve the fish long enough to transport it to a freezer.

All we really wanted was some restful roaming and perhaps a few fresh fish that we hoped to catch just before the bush plane returned in a week. The fish did not understand the plan.

We arrived in bright sunshine, saluted that beautiful view of Mount McKinley that can be seen from the Petersville mining area, and then greeted our host and hostess. They were summering in a former roadhouse, getting away from the civilization of the lower Susitna Valley.

One day, exploring, we came to a huge boulder

FWT

jutting into the cloudy green stream of rippling white water. The flat-topped rock created an eddy in the river that looked like a perfect salmon rest.

My equipment included salmon eggs, rod, reel and armed escort. Into the middle of the eddy went eggs, hook, line and sinker. As I began to retrieve the bait, there was a jerk. Automatically I let out a little more line to keep from setting the hook in what had to be a snag. But suddenly it wasn't a snag. It felt like a salmon.

It took about three minutes of reel in, slack, and play before the silver tail broke water. After that it was a fight to exhaustion for each of us because the only way to land the fish was to bring him to water's edge where he could be hand-hauled from the stream by the gills.

The next plunk into the eddy brought in a rainbow trout about 12 inches (30 cm) long. Next I hooked a grayling. Each time the hook went into the water it was received by a succession of grayling, rainbow trout and silver salmon. This wasn't a fishing hole, it was an aquatic pantry.

We had plenty of groceries. We didn't expect a plane to pick us up for several days. We couldn't eat all the fish we could legally catch. We wanted to take some home. Three-fourths of our group did not really care for fresh fish, although they admitted that pickled fish, smoked fish, or salt fish were another matter.

By the end of the day we hatched the idea of smoking our catch. A fire bed was dug and forked

pack green leaves around them. Cover the container with several thicknesses of burlap, leaving air space between it and the fish. Moisten the burlap and keep it moist. The constant water evaporation will lower the temperature in the container.

Fish treated this way should stay in good condition for at least 24 hours. At cooking time, rinse the fish thoroughly to remove excess salt. If fish must be held unrefrigerated longer than 24 hours, roll them one at a time in salt and pack them away in the container with as much salt as will cling to them. They should keep for about 10 days. Fish this heavily salted must be freshened before cooking. Soak them about 12 hours in two or three changes of fresh water.

---

stakes driven into the ground to support cross members strung with fish. Firewood was alder, and leafy branches were piled over the entirety to keep the smoke enclosed.

The salmon were filleted and the backbone removed to within 2 inches (5 cm) of the tail. We cut them across to skin depth every 3 to 4 inches (7.5 to 10 cm), sprinkled them with table salt, leaving it on overnight to help toughen the skin and meat.

Rainbow trout and grayling were eviscerated but otherwise left intact, just as you would buy them for fancy prices from gourmet mail order houses.

The fire was started, fish were strung on sticks and placed on stakes. The blaze was damped, and the alder branches heaped around. A plastic sheet spread over the mound helped hold the smoke within our primitive fish preserver.

All was well as long as the fire received continual attention. Fresh wood and water were supplied as necessary to keep the flames and heat down. There was no thought of complete curing; the object was to smoke-dry and seal the outer flesh in order to preserve the catch until it could be returned to the city and the freezer.

The project was the most relaxing two days in memory. I probably remember it that way because mine was only Number Two position — I took orders. The work had a rhythm. It was hunker, think and read, peek into the alder mound, add wood, splash in water, hunker and think or read. It was a peaceful time.

The experiment, for that is really what it was, kept the fish from spoiling, and the alder smoke gave it an added flavor. The primitive smoker was a delicious success. In other, more difficult circumstances, such a technique could be an important survival aid.

1. Cut heads off and gut fish as usual.
2. Split large fish by cutting along either side of the backbone and removing it, so that the fish will lie flat. Small fish leave whole-dressed.

3. Score split fish lengthwise from head to tail, cutting gashes 1/4 inch deep (6 mm) and about 1 inch (2.5 cm) apart.
4. Wash fish thoroughly and wipe dry.
5. Rub inside and out with a mixture of salt and a little pepper for flavor. Use 1 pound (456 g) salt and 1 ounce (28 g) pepper.
6. Store fish overnight in a cool place.
7. Next morning, rinse thoroughly. Spread fish open using several thin, flat sticks with pointed ends that will pierce the skin. Hang the fish in the breeze about three hours or until a thin surface glaze forms.
8. Meanwhile, dig a shallow pit about 3 feet (0.9 m) wide and prepare a bed of red coals, using hardwood fuel such as birch, aspen or alder. Gather enough forked stakes about 4 or 5 (1.2 to 1.5 m) feet tall to serve as props for the fish. Push the unforked end into the ground so that the fork hangs over the fire at an angle. Place stakes far enough apart to keep fish from touching.
9. Around the stakes, make a longer tripod of poles and cover this with a thick layer of green boughs and grass. Leave a hole near the ground.
10. Hang the fish on the stakes. Put green wood on the coals to build up a dense smoke and cover the hole. From time to time add fresh green wood to the fire. Smoke fish 6 to 18 hours, depending on size and degree of smoking desired. Then cool it, wrap it and store it in a dry, cool place. It should keep in good condition two to four weeks.

■ *Ruth D. Edmondson*

Story reprinted from *ALASKA*® magazine, where it appeared under the title, "First Catch a Salmon," September 1971. Step-by-step instructions adapted from *The Fisherman Returns* (see Cooks and Cookbooks . . .).

Scaling — Roundfish or Flat Ones

If you're going to cook a fish with its skin intact, you may have to scrape away tough scales first. If so, you can avoid having a very messy kitchen to clean up afterward in a couple of ways: Either spread out plenty of newspapers that can be thrown away from time to time . . . or scale the fish underwater.

One knowledgeable source, Robert Candy, author of *Getting the Most from Your Game & Fish* [Charlotte, Vermont, 1978], says he likes to scale fish right in the kitchen sink, pressed down under at least 2 inches (5 cm) of cold, sometimes iced, water. "The scales don't fly at all. They just settle to the bottom, and I catch them in the strainer when I let the water out."

His advice about icing the water is also good. Some people suggest dipping a fish into very hot water until the scales curl, making it easier to sluff them off. But since fish is a delicate meat that cooks quickly, hot water at this early stage of preparation is to be avoided. With the convenience of curling scales, you may also invite spoilage, at least of taste. So, with your fish under water or on newspapers:

1. Grab hold of it firmly with one hand.
2. With the other, use the dull edge of a knife, the edge of a heavy spoon or a fish scaler to scrape the fish, working from tail toward head, holding your implement almost at right angles to the fish.
3. Rinse the fish thoroughly and pat dry with toweling.

If you're scaling on newspapers, remember that a wet fish is easier to scale than a dry one. And a slippery fish will be easier to hang onto if you dip your fingers in salt, hold it with a piece of paper towel, or, better yet for some spiny fish particularly, wear a cloth glove on the hand that does the holding.

For an improvised fish scaler that "works great!" take the advice of Mamie Jensen of Juneau and use a steel-bristled paint scraping brush. "Just be sure to hold the fish under water while you scale."

The fine scales on smelt can be removed with a toothbrush, and some fish, such as trouts and smaller salmon, do not require scaling.

Cleaning & Dressing Roundfish

Cleaning a fish is more than just slitting its belly and zapping out its insides. How you do it — and

how soon — is the difference between a good-tasting fish and a spoiled one. Start with:

- A *sharp* knife with a 5- or 6-inch (12.5 to 15 cm) blade and a plastic or other hard-surfaced handle. Wood is more difficult to clean.
- A solid flat cutting surface. Again, stainless steel and plexiglass are easier to keep clean than wood. Wood, however, can be sanitized by scrubbing it with a chlorine solution — 2 tablespoons (30 mL) per gallon (3.8 L) of water. Salt sprinkled on any cutting surface will help cut the slime and sanitize.
- A teaspoon.
- Plenty of clean cold water.

1. Insert the point of your knife into the vent opening, just deep enough to cut through the skin. Then run the cut smoothly the length of the belly to a point just below where the pectoral fins (near the throat) join the body. Keep the cut shallow so you don't damage the flesh or the egg cases or puncture the viscera.
2. Carefully cut the connecting tissues at both ends of the digestive tract (throat and vent) and the viscera will fall right out. Wash the eggs (if there are any), put them in a clean plastic bag and refrigerate to await further treatment. (See page 19 for some general recipes, or check out the special ones for herring sac roe and salmon roe in Chapter 2. Just remember, eggs are, if anything, more perishable than the rest of the fish. So do something about them soon. They're *worth* saving!)
3. Next remove the gills. Reach in under the gill cover. Cut through the connecting tissue at the top of the gill and run your knife around the jaws to the bottom. Then twist the gills out.
4. Now all that is left is the kidney. This looks like a line of clotted blood running along the spine from the head to the vent. Some fishermen simply slit the kidney down the middle and then scrape out the dark material or push it out with a thumbnail. But a better way is to make two long slits through the membrane down either side of the kidney. This makes it easier to remove and also does away with the "ribbons" of membrane (which many processors object to) that are left behind if you cut "fisherman style."
5. Scrape out the kidney blood with a spoon. Get every trace of it. The hardest to reach is the blood in the small bones at the back, called "knuckles." Use the tip of your knife very carefully to pry out this blood, trying not to puncture the flesh.
6. Now wash the fish well, inside and out, with

clean cold water, pat it thoroughly dry and it's **whole-dressed** — ready to be cooked, put on ice or frozen for later or dressed in a slightly different way.

For instance, though it is not necessary, some cooks also like to remove fins before cooking whole-dressed fish. If you want to, cut into the flesh along each side of the fin. Take hold of it and give it a slow steady pull toward the head to remove bony attachments with it.

To fit the frying pan, whole fish are often tailored before being breaded or fried. To **pan-dress** remove head, tail and fins.

Steaks are cross-section slices cut from large whole-dressed fish. Steaks are generally about an inch (2.5 cm) thick and the skin is left on to provide stability during cooking, unless the skin has a very strong flavor.

Fillets are the sides of the fish cut lengthwise away from the backbone. Cut the sides in separate pieces and you have single fillets. Cut so that the two sides remain joined after the backbone is removed and you have a "butterfly" fillet. Some people leave the skin on fillets of some kinds of fish. If you plan to, the fish should be scaled, if necessary, before you fillet it.

Filleting Roundfish

1. Use a knife with a thin, straightedged blade. Place fish flat on cutting board with its back toward you.
2. Hold the knife diagonally close to the head. Cut down and in toward the head to the bones.
3. Then hold the fish by the head and drive the knife away from you, cutting along the backbone toward the tail, keeping the knife edge flat against the bone.
4. Opening the fish with one hand, continue to cut the flesh loose from the spine, using the tip of the blade to clear the flesh from the ribs.
5. Continue the cut through to the belly side of the fish and — voila — the first side is filleted.
6. Turn the fish over, holding the head away from you, to begin the first cut on the other side.
7. Drive the knife toward the tail, still holding the head away from you.
8. Then, holding onto the fillet with one hand, repeat steps 4 and 5, above.
9. To remove the skin, place the fillet skin side down. Cut into the flesh until you reach the skin, then turn the blade nearly flat, grasp the skin in one hand and pull slowly while working the knife with a slight sawing motion.
10. DROP HEAD, TAIL, BONES INTO THE COOKING POT to make a delicious soup to eat right away — or the stock for a soup or sauce for the weeks ahead.

Cleaning & Dressing Flatfish

Fish don't come conveniently packaged in the same sizes and shapes, but besides the generally roundish ones, there's only one other shape so radically different to call for some tailoring of the rather simple rules of dressing.

These are the flatfishes — huggers of the ocean floor whose most startling characteristic is the presence of both eyes on one "side" of the head. It's the topside when the fish is burrowed into the sand, and the eyes bear the same relationship to the backbone that they do in most other creatures. But because flatfish are exactly that — very flat and nearly as broad from dorsal to anal fin as they are long between "nose" and tail —the placement of the eyes seems most peculiar . . . at first glance. There are some 300 species of flatfish worldwide, and they range in size from tiny sand dabs to giant halibut. Naturally, there are a few differences in dressing and cooking techniques that are also dictated by size. (Try finding an oven in which to bake a whole-dressed 800-pound [363 kg] halibut.)

But, with a little adaptation, the following guidelines should suffice for dressing most of them — the various flounders, sole, turbot and halibut. Some special hints about filleting large halibut are with the recipes for halibut in Chapter 2.

1. Cut off the head on a diagonal (to get most recovery of flesh), and gills and some attached viscera will come with the head. Slit the belly pouch and clean thoroughly, removing kidney, and in the case of halibut you will find two lumps of flesh about the size of walnuts or bigger at the tail end of the body cavity lying on either side of a sturdy bone dividing the area into two pocketlike areas. These fleshy items are the gonads and must be removed.
2. Alaska halibut, sole, flounder, and other flatfishes have such minimal scales you can ignore them insofar as any need to scale. Halibut are slimy, however, and washing and scraping away excess slime will make a neater product. In cooking, many cooks like to keep skin on all cuts because much fat of the fish lies under the skin, other cooks believe the skin imparts a "fishy" taste. Whatever, this is a matter of choice. Some may prefer to skin both sides of fillets. Either way, the skin itself is thoroughly edible.

To open up a cavity for stuffing . . .
3. White side up, cut to the backbone along backbone line, leaving a little flesh uncut at head and tail.
4. Then, holding the knife flat and pressed against the bone, slide it underneath the flesh on each side of the backbone to form a pocket large enough for stuffing. Use the fingers of your other

hand to help lift flesh from bone as you cut. (Want an elegant dinner? Try a stuffing that has shrimp as a main ingredient. Bread or rice stuffings are nice, too. You'll find some in the recipe section.)

Filleting Flatfish

The following will describe cutting fillets from sole, flounder, or smaller sized halibut. On page 41 is a description of how to handle a fillet job on really large halibut.

1. One may begin either on the white side or the dark side. Make a diagonal (meat saving) cut with the knife blade angled from head towards the tail end, then laying the knife blade flat along the backbone (flatfishes have basically one flat backbone and ribs system running clear across the fish with no other bones except in the body cavity to be concerned with), begin a long sweeping cut to the tail, allowing the knife blade to ride on the backbone.

2. At this point you can either cut through the bones of the belly wall and remove these afterward, or carefully follow along and over these bones until you are clear of them at the tail end of the body cavity when you can let your knife blade go clear across.

3. Repeat on the opposite side. And remember on halibut there are choice cheeks on the side of the head. For skinning fillets, some people can hold the skin side down and a piece of the skin with a thumbnail or spoon, others use a pliers. Some choose to pull the skin off with the pliers. Others just hold the fillet skin side down and run a flat fillet knife from tail to head between skin and flesh. If there are many fish to handle, a flat nail head driven into the cleaning board and left just above the board a hair makes a handy "hanger-on" to the slippery tail skin piece by simply pressing the skin against the nail head and holding firmly.

:

Basic Fish Cookery

Most fish can be prepared for the table in a variety of delicious ways. And most recipes, no matter what fish is specified, will accommodate a substitute you happen to have on hand, especially if the stand-in is of similar flesh color and texture to the one called for in the recipe.

However you decide to cook fish, the most important rule is DON'T OVERCOOK IT! Until recently, that was the sort of rule everybody talked about and few people followed because "too long" was too vaguely defined. At last definition is at hand.

Several years ago, the Canadian Government's Department of Fisheries and Oceans tested extensively and found that cooking fish quickly at a high temperature, usually 450°F (230°C), preserved its delicate flavor and its juiciness. Because fish, unlike meat, contains very little tough connective tissue that heat must penetrate, it doesn't require long, slow cooking. It is best cooked just to the point where the translucent flesh becomes opaque and flakes or separates easily when tested (gently) with a fork. To determine ahead of time when that point is most likely to be reached, the Canadians came up with a simple, relatively exact rule of thumb:

Measure the thickness of the fish at its thickest point. If the fish is fresh, allow 10 minutes cooking time per inch (2.5 cm) thickness; if frozen, allow 20 minutes cooking time per inch (2.5 cm) thickness.

No more tough dry fish! The Canadian theory is referred to or repeated in a number of places as an excellent gauge, but because the recipes in this book represent many tastes, the cooking times in them don't all conform to it. With the theory as a guide, however, adjustment of individual recipes to your *own* taste becomes a lot easier. Here's how that theory is applied to the basic methods of cooking fish.

Dry Heat Methods

Oven: Baking is a suitable method for cooking whole fish, steaks and fillets — fresh or frozen. To estimate the cooking time:

1. Measure the fish at its thickest point. *If the fish is to be stuffed,* measure after stuffing so that cooking time will be increased proportionately. Stuff loosely, allowing about 3/4 cup (180 mL) for each pound (456 g) of dressed fish. Fasten the opening with small skewers or toothpicks and loop string about them, much as you would lace shoes. Or sew the opening with a large needle and coarse thread.

2. Season fish, place in a greased baking pan and brush it with melted fat or a sauce.

3. Bake at 450°F (230°C). Allow 10 minutes cooking time per inch (2.5 cm) thickness. If fish is frozen, allow 20 minutes per inch.
If fish is wrapped in foil, this really changes the cooking method to steaming rather than baking, but the measurement of cooking time per inch (2.5 cm) thickness remains the same. Then ADD time for the heat to penetrate the foil: add 5 minutes to the total time for fresh fish;

20 minutes for frozen fish. Grease the foil before placing the fish in it; double-fold the edges and crimp to insure a tight seal. The cooking time for fish wrapped in paper is figured the same way.

Broiler: Broil small whole fish, steaks and fillets:
1. Measure thickness of fish as above. Place it on a greased broiler pan and baste it with fat or sauce.
2. Preheat broiler and place broiler pan in the oven so that the fish is 2 to 4 inches (5 to 10 cm) from the heat source. If the fish is frozen, place lower in oven to prevent overcooking the surface before the interior is cooked. Leave oven door ajar unless manufacturer's directions state otherwise.
3. Thin fillets should be broiled without turning. Cuts that are 3/4 to 1 inch (1.8 to 2.5 cm) thick have less tendency to dry out during broiling than do thin cuts. Once thicker cuts are delicately browned, they should be seasoned and turned, basted on the uncooked side and returned to broil. Allow a total cooking time of 10 minutes per inch (2.5 cm) thickness — or fraction thereof — for fresh fish; about 20 minutes per inch (2.5 cm) for frozen fish. The thinner the fillet, the closer the watch must be. Perfection may take *less* than 10 minutes. Many cooks also recommend broiling thin fillets on greased foil to make the transfer to a serving platter easier.

Barbecue:
1. Place fish in greased, hinged wire grill. Baste and season as above.
2. Cook about 4 inches (10 cm) from hot coals, measuring the cooking time as above — about five minutes per side for fish that are cut in serving-sized pieces.

Moist Heat Methods

Poacher: Whole fish, steaks or fillets may be poached in aluminum foil, in court bouillon or fish stock, or in milk. *Foil* is recommended for fish that is to receive further seasoning or brief cooking; that is, for fish you plan to use in salad, casseroles, fish cakes or creamed fish. *Court bouillons* and *fish stocks* are flavorful liquids, often including wine, used for poaching fish that is to be served "as is," either hot or chilled, with or without an accompanying sauce. *Milk*, a bland poaching liquid, is recommended for smoked or other salt-cured fish.
1. *In foil* — Sprinkle fish with salt and place on a large square of greased aluminum foil. Measure thickness of fish at thickest part. Add two or three slices of onion, a stalk of celery or other seasoning as desired . . . just don't overpower the fish. Wrap securely, double-fold the foil and crimp the edges to make the package watertight.

Place in rapidly boiling water and cover the pan. When water returns to boil, begin to time the cooking period: 10 minutes per inch (2.5 cm) thickness for fresh fish; 20 minutes per inch (2.5 cm) for frozen fish. When fish is done, remove package (using tongs if you've got them) and unwrap foil carefully so that you can save the juices inside. This is "fish stock," a good base for a sauce.
2. *In court bouillon or stock* — Wipe fish with a damp cloth, sprinkle with salt and measure thickness. To make it easier to lift out of poacher, wrap the fish in cheesecloth or support it with foil or place it on a greased tray that will fit low enough inside the poaching container to allow the fish to be nearly covered with poaching liquid.

   Small fish or steaks or fillets can be poached in a skillet with a lid. There should be enough liquid to submerge the fish about two-thirds, and it should be brought to the boil before the fish is added.

   Large fish may be poached either in a specially designed poaching pan with a tray or in a roaster or other large container with a lid. Place large fish in the pan before adding the poaching liquid, again, to submerge the fish by about two-thirds. To avoid bursting the skin, the liquid should not be boiling when you pour it in.

   Whether you are poaching "big" or "little," cover the pan, return the poaching liquid to simmer and simmer gently, allowing 10 minutes per inch (2.5 cm) thickness for fresh fish, 20 minutes per inch (2.5 cm) for frozen fish, or until fish just turns opaque. Remove fish and drain well. Save the juices for other poaching or for use in soups and sauces. A variety of poaching liquids is suggested on page 25. Other poaching recipes are in the section on salmon in Chapter 2.
3. *In milk* — Milk poaching is especially suitable for smoked fish. For about 2 pounds (1 kg) of fillets, use 1 cup (240 mL) milk, 1 tablespoon (15 mL) butter and pepper to taste. (Smoked or other salt-cured fish generally should not require further salting.) Measure thickness of fish, then simmer fillets in a covered pan, allowing 10 minutes cooking time per inch (2.5 cm) thickness for fresh fish, 20 minutes for frozen fish. Poaching may be done on top of the stove or in the oven in a covered container at 350°F (175°C), allowing a slightly longer cooking time — 15 minutes per inch (2.5 cm) thickness for fresh fish, 30 minutes per inch (2.5 cm) for frozen fish, or until the fish flakes easily when tested with a fork. The milk may be thickened, seasoned further and used as a sauce.

Steamer: Use a commercially designed steamer or

improvise one from a roasting pan, a deep sauce-pan, a soup kettle or Dutch oven with a tight-fitting lid. A wok with a domed lid is ideal. Commercial vessels have perforated trays or racks on legs or stands, or a separate chamber in which to place the food so that it is above the burbling water in the bottom of the pan and yet the steam circulates around it freely. You can improvise that chamber or tray by using a sieve or the rack from a roasting pan. Fish can even be set on a heat-proof plate that will fit inside a large canner or kettle. Then build any device you can think of to hold that plate up out of the water and allow steam to roll through. The main points to remember about steaming:

1. The water should be boiling rapidly before the fish is lowered into the vessel.
2. Fish should cook *above,* not in, the water. For ease in handling, tie fish in cheesecloth before placing it on the rack or tray.
3. Fill the bottom of the cooking vessel with boiling water, bring it to a rapid boil again, add the tray of fish, making sure the fish doesn't touch the water. Cover tightly. Allow 10 minutes cooking time per inch (2.5 cm) thickness for fresh fish; 20 minutes per inch (2.5 cm) thickness for frozen fish.

Season steamed fish with lemon juice, salt and pepper, and serve with a sauce.

Frying Methods

Skillet: Pan-frying is a popular method for cooking fish steaks, fillets and small, whole or pan-dressed fish. For easier handling, frozen fish may be par-tially thawed in the refrigerator and then cooked immediately. Breading sticks better to fish that has been at least partly thawed and patted dry.

1. Cut fish into serving pieces. Season.
2. Dip in liquid (milk or beaten egg is usually called for) and then in flour or other breading.
3. Heat 1/4 inch (0.6 cm) of fat or oil in frying pan until it is quite hot but not smoking.
4. Fry fish until golden on one side, turn and brown the other side. The total cooking time should be about 10 minutes per inch (2.5 cm) thickness.

Since pan-frying is a favorite method for cooking fish, numerous recipes are in this chapter. And you don't have to bread fish to pan-fry them. Simply season and fry in fat that is hot but not smoking—butter, bacon fat or oil.

Deep-Fryer: Fillets, small fish, fish cakes and some shellfish are delicious when fried in deep hot fat. There are commercial deep-fryers, but this vessel is easy to improvise, too. A wok makes a good deep-fryer because its shape enables a rela-tively small amount of oil to be evenly heated, but a large saucepan and a heat-proof basket or strainer will do. If frozen fish is used in deep-frying, it is preferable to partially thaw it for even cooking throughout since the outside browns so quickly.

1. Cut fillets into uniform size not thicker than half an inch (1.25 cm). If too thick, make several slits in the sides to aid even cooking.
2. Sprinkle with salt. Dip in batter as directed by individual recipes.
3. Place only one layer of fish in the frying basket. Trying to fry too many pieces at once lowers the temperature of the fat too drastically.
4. Fry in deep fat preheated to 375°F (190°C) until golden, about three or four minutes. Drain and serve piping hot.

Serving Raw Fish

Raw fish — used as it is in several recipes in Chapters 1 and 2 — is very healthful: low in calorie, low in fat, high in protein and many essential vitamins and minerals which cooking sometimes destroys or diminishes. In recent years, raw fish has become much more widely used among Ameri-cans swept up by the increasing popularity of *sushi.* Even whole restaurants are devoted to this Japanese method of preparing raw fish delicacies. Nevertheless, there are some cautions for the tyro:

Fish that live in fresh water, or those — like salmon — that spend part of their lives in fresh water (anadromous fishes) may carry tapeworm larvae which can lead to infection in humans. Cooking fish at a temperature of at least 135°F (57°C) for five minutes will destroy the larvae, but that's not "raw" fish.

To eat salmon and other freshwater or anadromous fish raw and still be safe, first FREEZE the fish for at least 24 hours at a temperature of 0°F (-18°C) or, if you must use a higher temperature, freeze longer — 14°F (-10°C) for 72 hours.

Herring, too, sometimes carry roundworm larvae which can cause a different kind of infection in humans if they eat the fish raw. To avoid it, either freeze herring or brine them first.

Using Roe, Milt, Livers, Trimmings

Remember when cod liver oil was prescribed for so many ills? Most fish liver would do as well. The "spare parts" such as roe, milt, livers, fish heads and other trimmings all have special nutritive value, but they are often wasted either because cooks don't know what to do with them or don't get at them soon enough to keep them from spoiling.

All deteriorate rapidly and must be eaten or preserved immediately.

Although many of these items tend to be enormously costly or simply unavailable to people who must depend on supermarkets for supply, Alaskans can afford to indulge — or develop — a taste for them.

Fish roe, when it's called "caviar," is one of the most highly prized and high priced items of the world's cuisine. Though caviar is a term usually reserved for the roe of various members of the sturgeon family — now, unfortunately, not as common a catch in Alaska as they once were — the roe of more available fish species are highly prized by many Native people and by Japanese importers who, in recent years, have paid handsomely particularly for herring roe taken from Alaskan waters. Others of us have long appreciated the red caviar from salmon. Some recipes for both herring and salmon roe are in Chapter 2.

Fish milt, too, is a delicacy for Native Alaskans and other cooks throughout the world, notably the French whose encyclopedia of cooking, *Larousse Gastronomique,* includes no less than a dozen recipes for milt, called "soft roe." A number of recipes for salmon milt, from Alaskan chef Jeanne Culbertson, are in Chapter 2.

Fish livers are cooked whole or mashed or rendered for their oil. According to *The Alaska Dietary Survey, 1956-1961,* "At Unalakleet in times past, and probably in other areas where tom cods were available, the Eskimos used to simmer tom cod livers in a small amount of water. The oil was carefully removed and used in infant feeding. Many of the older women from several of the tundra villages report that in times past fresh fish liver, prechewed by the mother, was one of the first solid foods added to the infant's diet."

Fish heads and other trimmings — backbone, fins, "collar" — should never be discarded unless you're already overloaded with fish soups or stocks and poaching liquids.

A few recipes for these "spare parts" are included in this chapter. For more, see especially the recipe sections for halibut, herring and salmon, in Chapter 2. And don't overlook the wonderful fish head soup, La Salsa de Pez, in this chapter.

Using Cooked or Preserved Fish — Desalting

Leftover, canned, dried, smoked or salted fish can be used in hundreds more ways than we have managed to squeeze into this book — where the emphasis is really on preparing fresh foods to eat now or preserving them for later. Nevertheless, you'll find some unusual and good suggestions in both Chapters 1 and 2.

Fish that are heavily salted as part of the preservation process may need some special treatment before cooking. How vigorously you desalt depends, of course, on your taste buds and on how salty the fish is to begin with. Some smoked fish, such as black cod (sablefish), needs no desalting or can be freshened sufficiently if you simply steam it a few minutes, allowing the saline to dissipate in the curls of steam. Saltier fish can be soaked for an hour or more in cold water or milk that is then discarded before the fish is cooked further. Or you may need to freshen fish up to 12 hours in several changes of water. The rule of thumb — USE your thumb (or an index finger might be easier). Simply rub it lightly over the flesh of the fish and taste it for saltiness.

You may use salted fish in many of the recipes for fresh fish if you adjust the seasonings. The final dish may not need any more salt.

How Much To Serve Per Person

At times most anyone can eat a horse — or at least a small salmon — and at other times 4 ounces (114 g) of fish may be too much. The following portions are only guidelines. The first three weights are for raw fish:

Whole fish	3/4 pound (340 g) per person
Whole-dressed or pan-dressed fish	1/2 pound (228 g) per person
Fillets or steaks	1/3 pound (150 g) per person
Chunks or sticks	1/4 pound (114 g) per person
Canned	1/6 pound (75 g) per person

Arrangement of Recipes

The recipes in Chapter 1 may be used for any variety of fish. Most are "basic" recipes and they are arranged by the kind of dish, from appetizer to main dish. Throughout are tips about cooking fish that you may want to refer to again in preparing the more exotic—and extensive—recipes of Chapter 2.

General information about field care of fish is based on *The Fisherman Returns.* Cleaning & Dressing Roundfish is adapted with few changes from *Alaska Tidelines,* Volume IV, Number 1, "How to Take Care of Your Catch." Basic Fish Cookery is adapted from *The Way To Cook Fish.*

GARNISHES

Garnish can make a beautifully cooked fish even showier at serving time, or it can be made to hide at least a small sin. Once in a while, no matter the precautions, it is not possible to move fish from cooking vessel to platter without breaking it. Don't panic . . . GARNISH. Try:

Beets, cooked whole, sliced or pickled
Butter pats or swirls, seasoned with garlic or chives
   and well chilled
Carrot sticks, curls or shreds, or carrot tops
Celery heart, sticks or curls
Crab Celery Bites (page 116)
Crab Stuffed Eggs (page 116)
Crab Stuffed Mushrooms (page 121)

Cucumber slices or sticks
Green or red pepper rings or sticks
Hard-cooked eggs, in wedges or slices, grated
   or deviled
Herbs, minced
Lemon Relish (see Sauteed Lingcod, page 55)
Lemon slices or wedges
Olives, black or stuffed green ones
Paprika, a light dusting
Parsley, minced leaves or whole sprigs
Pickle slices
Radish roses
Seasoned Crumbs (page 421)
Susan's Egg-and-Olive ''Murres'' (page 89)
Watercress sprigs

SAUCES & STUFFINGS

Sauces and stuffings also enhance the flavor and look of well-prepared fish. Directions for them do not always accompany recipes in which they are mentioned. Capitalized names — such as Lemon Butter or White Sauce — indicate that a recipe for the named item is in the book.

Sauces

APPETIZERS & SALADS

Alaska Ceviche
A raw fish appetizer

Skinned, very fresh raw white-meated fish —
*   halibut and lingcod are best*
Tomato
Onion
Celery
Hot chili peppers
Juice of fresh lemons or limes
Soy sauce
Tabasco

►Cut fish into bite-sized pieces — not too big — and chop tomato, onion, celery and peppers in proportions according to your taste.

Mix vegetables and fish and marinate the mixture in enough lemon or lime juice to cover. (Bottled juice will *not* do.) Add soy sauce and Tabasco to taste.

Marinate in a cool place (a refrigerator if you have one) for five hours or so.

Note to the squeamish: You're right, there's no cooking involved, but the fish changes texture in the lemon or lime juice. It's REALLY good. I dare you to try it!
■ *Susan Ewing, Fairbanks*

Kanarrtuk

►The name means frozen fish. To make it you need a fish, of course. All you have to do next is hang it out to dry on a fish rack and wait until it gets about medium dry (not quite stiff). When it reaches that point, put it in the freezer or somewhere very cold and wait until it is frozen hard. Take it out . . .

Cut it into bite-sized pieces . . .

And eat it with seal oil and salt.
■ *Katherine Groat*
Uutuqtwa
Bristol Bay High School, Naknek

Broiled Seafood Canapes

1 cup (240 mL) cooked seafood, flaked
6 slices white bread
1/4 cup (60 mL) butter
1/3 cup (80 mL) ketchup or chili sauce
1/4 pound (114 g) Cheddar or processed
*   American cheese, grated*

►Toast bread on one side; trim off crusts and cut into rectangles. Butter untoasted sides; cover with a layer of fish, then ketchup and top with cheese. Place canapes on baking sheet under broiler. Broil until cheese melts and canapes are heated through. Makes 12 canapes.

Fisherman's Party Dip

1-1/2 cups (360 mL) cooked, white-fleshed fish
1/2 cup (120 mL) mayonnaise
1/4 cup (60 mL) finely chopped stuffed olives
Salt, pepper, grated onion to taste

►Combine all ingredients and blend well; chill. Serve dip in a bowl surrounded by potato chips or crackers. Makes 1 pint (0.45 L).
■ Seafood Recipes For Alaskans

Basic Seafood Salad

2 cups (480 mL) cooked or canned seafood
1 tablespoon (15 mL) lemon juice
1 cup (240 mL) diced celery
1/3 cup (80 mL) mayonnaise
Salt to taste
Lettuce cups

►Break seafood into bite-sized chunks. Sprinkle with lemon juice. Add celery and toss lightly with mayonnaise. Salt to taste. Serve in lettuce cups.
■ Fish 'n Seafood Salads

Fiskesalat

Any variety cold, cooked fish
Lettuce
1 beaten egg yolk
1/4 teaspoon (1 mL) salt
4 tablespoons (60 mL) cream
1/2 teaspoon (2 mL) mustard
Pepper
Vinegar
Parsley

►Put lettuce in salad bowl with fish. Make a dressing of the egg yolk, salt, cream, mustard, pepper and vinegar to taste. Pour dressing over fish and sprinkle with chopped parsley.
■ *Mrs. O. Wikan*
  PTA Cook Book, *Petersburg*

Summer Fish Salad

2 cups (480 mL) cooked, flaked fish
1/2 teaspoon (2 mL) salt
1/4 cup (60 mL) French dressing
3 cups (720 mL) torn lettuce leaves
1 cup (240 mL) cooked green beans
1/4 cup (60 mL) sliced radishes
1 teaspoon (5 mL) capers or chopped
* sour pickle*

►Sprinkle fish with salt. Pour French dressing over fish and let stand in refrigerator for one hour to blend flavors. Toss gently with lettuce, green beans, radishes and capers or sour pickle. Makes six servings.
■ Fish 'n Seafood Salads

Fisherman's Special Salad

2 cups (480 mL) cooked, flaked fish
1/2 teaspoon (2 mL) salt
1 cup (240 mL) sliced celery
1/4 cup (60 mL) French dressing
1 cup (240 mL) seedless grapes
1/4 cup (60 mL) mayonnaise
1 tablespoon (15 mL) lemon juice
Lettuce cups
1/4 cup (60 mL) toasted slivered almonds

►Sprinkle fish with salt. Add celery and combine with French dressing. Let stand in refrigerator for one hour. Add grapes. Combine mayonnaise and lemon juice. Add to fish mixture and toss gently. Serve in lettuce cups and garnish with almonds. Makes four servings.
■ Fish 'n Seafood Salads

Broiling fish? If you don't have a hinged wire grill, don't try to turn thin fillets. They will cook quickly without turning . . . watch closely. Whole or cut fish may be placed on a large piece of foil to keep basting sauce from dropping into the fire.

SOUPS & CHOWDERS

About Fish Stock: *Using homemade stock as at least part of the liquid in a fish soup will improve its flavor every time. Stocks are quick and easy to make, storable and inexpensive — even if you must buy your fish — and useful in many other dishes besides soup. A good recipe for stock, which is almost a soup in itself, is Helen A. White's Deluxe Wine-Flavored Stock which you'll find with Poaching Liquids and Stocks on page 25.*

But you save almost any liquid in which fish has been cooked to use as an added, concentrated bit of flavor for a soup. One of the best sources of stock is fish trimmings — heads, backbones and fins. Since trimmings spoil very quickly, it's a good idea to turn them into stock right away and then freeze it for later use if you wish.

Start by sauteing chopped onions and celery— 1/4 cup (60 mL) each is about right — in a couple of tablespoons (30 mL) of butter or margarine. Add 1 to 2 pounds (0.45 to 1 kg) fish trimmings and water to cover. Up to 1/2 cup (120 mL) white wine makes a nice addition, too. Just don't overwhelm the trimmings with liquid. Season to taste with salt, pepper and other seasonings. Simmer about 20 minutes.

Don't be tempted to keep fish stock simmering away on the back of the stove as you would a potful of marrowbones. Fish flavor is too delicate. Twenty to thirty minutes' simmering is plenty to capture all of it at its peak.

Basic Fish Chowder

1 pound (0.45 kg) fish fillets
2 slices bacon, chopped
1/2 cup (120 mL) onion, chopped
2 cups (480 mL) water or fish stock
1 cup (240 mL) raw potato, sliced
2 cups (480 mL) milk
1 teaspoon (5 mL) salt
Dash of pepper

►Salmon, halibut, rockfish or cod may be used for the fish. Fry bacon until crisp; add onion and cook until tender. Add water and potatoes and simmer 10 minutes or until potatoes are partially tender. Add fish, which has been cut into 1-inch (2.5 cm) cubes, and simmer again until fish and potatoes are tender. Add milk and seasonings; heat thoroughly and serve immediately. Serves six.
■ Seafood Recipes For Alaskans

Variation: Several cooks suggest varying this basic chowder by adding 2 cups (480 mL) grated Cheddar cheese to the fish broth *before* the milk is added. Stir constantly until cheese is melted. Add milk and heat gently. If desired, thicken with 2 tablespoons (30 mL) flour sauteed in an equal amount of butter. Add to soup, stirring till thickened.

Baked Fish Chowder

►Butter a deep baking dish. Peel and thinly slice three medium potatoes and two onions. In bottom of dish, put half the potatoes and onions. Salt and pepper and dot generously with butter. Cover with a thick layer of fish fillet (or flaked, canned salmon). Season and again butter generously. Layer remainder of onions and potatoes and season again. Pour in enough milk to reach top layer. Sprinkle with paprika and bake one hour at 350°F (175°C).
■ *Mamie Jensen, Juneau*

Wiggling Fish Soup

"During the fishing season I freeze as much fish for later as I can," says cookbook author Gordon R. Nelson. "But fresh fish remains my favorite. A soup made with fish so fresh that it's still quivering, if not wiggling, is the best. I would suggest you prepare some of this recipe ahead so the fresh-caught fish can go right to the pot with as little time loss as possible."

1 tablespoon (15 mL) vegetable oil
1 cup (240 mL) chopped onion
1-1/2 cups (360 mL) chicken stock
1 can (6 oz /or/ 170 g) tomato paste
1 teaspoon (5 mL) minced fresh ginger or
    1/2 teaspoon (2 mL) powdered
1 teaspoon (5 mL) curry powder
1/4 teaspoon (1 mL) cayenne
2 tablespoons (30 mL) creamy peanut butter
3 pounds (1.4 kg) white-fleshed fish,
    cut in 2-inch (5 cm) squares

►Reach for your Dutch oven, add the oil and saute the onions over medium heat. When they are limp, add the stock, tomato paste, ginger, curry, cayenne and peanut butter. Cook five minutes to blend flavors.

At this point you could cool the sauce and wait for the fish to be caught, or take it out on the boat with you. When you have the fish, add it to the pot and simmer it, covered, for 15 to 20 minutes. Turn the fish several times during this period and stop cooking as soon as the fish flakes easily. Serves four to six.
■ *Gordon R. Nelson, Palmer*
Smokehouse Bear —
More Alaskan Recipes and Stories

Fish Soup

►The proportions may be as you wish for this soup. Boil until tender, in water enough to cover, chopped potatoes, celery, onions, garlic, carrots and green pepper. Fry bacon and dice and add to the vegetables, along with some of the bacon fat, minced parsley and bits of pimento. Next, add bite-sized chunks of fresh halibut, black cod, salmon or any kind of fish you like. Simmer gently until fish is cooked; then add minced canned razor clams, oysters, small shrimp and their juices. When heated through, pour in evaporated milk to make enough quantity to serve; heat but do NOT boil. Stir in a generous amount of butter and serve with a dash of paprika on top of each bowl of soup. Teamed with hot garlic bread, this soup makes a whole meal. It is equally good reheated and may be stored in your Deepfreeze. Any size batch can be made, great or small. Try it with as many kinds of fish as you like, whatever you have on hand.
■ An Alaskan Cook Book, *Kenai*

Fiskesuppe

2 quarts (2 L) fish stock
Few carrots
Few stalks of celery
2 tablespoons (30 mL) flour
2 cups (480 mL) milk
1/2 cup (120 mL) sour cream
1 tablespoon (15 mL) butter
1 tablespoon (15 mL) finely grated onion or
    chopped chives
Salt and pepper

►Stock is that saved from boiled fish. Heat it to the boiling point; add diced celery and carrots and cook until tender. Mix flour with two or three spoonfuls of the milk; stir into soup. Add remaining milk and cook until smooth. Remove from fire; add sour cream, butter and chives or onion and serve at once with fish balls.
■ *Mrs. B. Espeseth*
PTA Cook Book, *Petersburg (adapted)*

Fish and Tomato Soup

4 slices lean bacon
3 tablespoons (45 mL) wild chives or
    green onion, minced
1/2 cup (120 mL) celery leaves and stalks,
    minced
2 cups (480 mL) fish stock
1/4 cup (60 mL) rice, uncooked
2 cups (480 mL) tomato juice
2 cups (480 mL) flaked fish
Seasoning to taste
Butter

►Fry bacon until crisp; drain and crumble. Combine bacon, wild chives and celery in a large pan. Add fish stock and simmer for 15 minutes. Add your preferred seasonings next, then the rice. Simmer for 15 minutes longer. Now add to this tomato juice and flaked fish — any lean variety will do. Simmer again until fish and rice are tender. Just before serving drop a small dollop of butter in each bowl and add a light sprinkle of minced chives for garnish.

■ *Helen A. White, Anchorage*
    More About What's Cookin' in Alaska

King Neptune Fish Chowder

"One of my favorite recipes . . . especially if halibut or lingcod is used," says the cook. (Be sure to invite a few neighbors to share it!)

4 pounds (1.8 kg) fish
5 cups (1.2 L) water
1 bay leaf
4 cups (1 L) diced potatoes
3 teaspoons (15 mL) salt
1/2 teaspoon (2 mL) pepper
1/2 cup (120 mL) butter
2 cups (480 mL) chopped celery
4 cups (1 L) sliced onions
4 tablespoons (60 mL) flour
5 cups (1.2 L) milk
1 cup (240 mL) half-and-half
1 cup (240 mL) sour cream

►Combine fish, water and bay leaf. Heat to simmering temperature, uncovered, until fish flakes when tested with fork. Carefully lift fish from stock with slotted spoon. Set aside. Add potatoes and seasoning to fish stock. Cover and cook until potatoes are tender. Meanwhile, melt butter in frying pan. Add celery and onions and saute until tender, about five minutes. Stir in flour, cook and stir over low heat for two minutes. Then stir into fish stock until it thickens. Remove bay leaf.

Scald milk in double boiler, remove from heat and stir in cream and sour cream. Reheat. Combine milk mixture, vegetables and fish stock, adding cooked fish in large pieces. Heat gently five minutes longer, taking care not to boil. Makes 25 servings, 8 ounces (240 mL) each.

■ *Donald E. Kramer, Anchorage*
    Alaska Sea Grant Program

La Salsa de Pez
Fish head soup

1 each — salmon, red snapper and halibut
    heads, collars and tails
Additional belly meat, if desired
1 cup (240 mL) green onion or 1/4 cup (60 mL)
    dry flakes plumped in a small amount
    of water
1 cup (240 mL) green pepper
1 cup (240 mL) celery
3 medium-sized fresh tomatoes or 1-1/2 cups
    (360 mL) canned, drained and
    squeezed tomatoes
2 cloves garlic
1/4 cup (60 mL) olive oil
1/2 to 1 cup (120 to 240 mL) vinegar
3-1/2 cups (a 28 oz /or/ 796 g can)
    stewed tomatoes with juice

►Remove gills and rings of teeth from heads. The collar is the wide bone just behind the gills . . . keep it for the soup. Eyes may be left in or removed* and the sockets stuffed with garlic cloves, as desired. Cut fin from the tail portion, leaving about 3 inches (7.5 cm) of body tail. If fish heads are extra large, split them in half. You may use 1 or 2 inches (2.5 to 5 cm) of belly strips if additional fish is desired. Wash all portions in tepid fresh water. Remove any scales that remain.

Chop the onions, celery, tomatoes, green pepper and garlic very fine and saute them for two or three minutes in hot olive oil. Add vinegar and heat thoroughly. In the bottom of a large kettle, place a layer of fish and spoon a layer of vegetables on top, alternating layers until fish is used. Over the top, pour the can of stewed tomatoes. If more liquid is needed to cover fish, tomato sauce or paste thinned with water or chicken or vegetable broth are good additions. Cover the kettle tightly and cook for 18 to 20 minutes over medium heat. This is a rich dish as these portions of fish contain large quantities of polyunsaturated fish fat and it's rich in calcium, too, from the bony sections.

■ *An "Anonymous transplanted*
    Spanish Basque," FV Donna-Mae
    Seafood Secrets, Sitka

Eskimos — and others they've taught — favor the eye area in most animals and fish for its tasty fat.

SPECIALTIES:
LIVER — MILT — ROE — TRIMMINGS

Please read about using these "spare parts" of the fish on page 12. The basic rule — use or preserve them quickly. They are very nutritious, and they spoil rapidly. Other recipes for fish roe can be found in herring and salmon recipe sections; for milt, in the salmon section; for fish trimmings— throughout. The most common use for the latter is in preparing stock, poaching liquid and soup.

About Fish Roe: *Sometimes a whole skein is used — as in Fried Salmon Eggs on page 71. More often a recipe calls for removing the membrane before further cooking. The ease with which the roe can be separated depends partly on the size and kind of fish.*

In general, the membrane can be picked off larger, mature roe, and the eggs can be separated without too much fuss. If it's difficult, or if a recipe calls for cooked roe, first prick the membrane in several places with a needle. This will keep it from popping during cooking. Cover roe with boiling water, flavored with vinegar or lemon juice — a couple of tablespoons (30 mL) per quart (L) of water — or use a healthy dollop of white wine. Cook roe very gently over low heat, being careful not to let it become hard. Cooking time varies according to the size of the roe and whether or not it's to be cooked further when other ingredients are added —anywhere from 5 to 15 minutes. Using a slotted spoon, lift roe gently out of the water, drain, cool, remove the membrane. Salt to taste — very lightly if salt will be added later.

Tingugtluk or Tingulik or Tungnuchak

This recipe for fish liver creme is a composite of several similar recipes collected by The Alaska Dietary Survey. Tingulik is a mixture of trout livers made by Natives of the Kotzebue area. In the Kuskokwim River basin, a similar fish liver creme is called tingugtluk. At Hooper Bay, it is tom cod livers that are cooked and mashed and mixed with an equal amount of crowberries to produce tungnuchak.

10 to 20 fish livers — trout, whitefish, tom cod or lingcod
3 to 4 cups (720 mL to 1 L) berries — cloudberries, cranberries, crowberries, or a combination of these
1/2 to 1 cup (120 to 240 mL) sugar
2 tablespoons to 1/2 cup (30 to 120 mL) fish oil

►Simmer livers gently in water to cover. Scoop off the oil that forms and carefully reserve it. When livers are soft, remove, mash thoroughly and mix again with the reserved oil. Add berries and sugar.

Sometimes the sugar and oil are added separately at serving time according to individual tastes. And sometimes sugar is not used at all.
■ The Alaska Dietary Survey, 1956-1961 (adapted)

Fish Milt

►Fish milt has iron, calcium and vitamin C in it. Wash the milt in a salt solution and fry it in butter or any kind of vegetable oil. You can cut the milt in little pieces or strips, roll the pieces in flour and cook them for about 5 to 10 minutes or until they are crispy.
■ Uutuqtwa, *Bristol Bay High School, Naknek*

Fish Roe

►Roe from various fish are used in a variety of ways. Herring, salmon, lingcod, tom cod, pike and whitefish roe are considered the most desirable by the Eskimo. It may be eaten fresh raw or cooked in season, or air-dried or otherwise prepared for off-season use. . . .

At Napaskiak a spring soup is made using fresh smelt roe and chopped willow catkins; a summer soup is made using fresh salmon roe and chopped, young, tender willow leaves.

Along the Kuskokwim River fresh or dry king salmon roe is often used in making *agutuk*. . . .

The roe from salmon just about ready to lay their eggs is considered a delicacy by some of the northern Eskimos. The roe has a chewy texture and is called *mupcooleetuk*. In contrast, the roe from early caught salmon — i.e., that from fish which has just entered the river from the ocean — is juicy or watery. This roe is called *cupseeruk* and is rated only second best.
■ The Alaska Dietary Survey

Kapuktuk
Cranberry creme

3 sacs pike, whitefish or sheefish roe, mashed
2 cups (480 mL) very ripe lowbush cranberries
3 tablespoons (45 mL) seal or whitefish oil
3 tablespoons (45 mL) sugar

►These ingredients are stirred or whipped to make a fluffy mixture, which must be eaten immediately

after preparation, since the mixture does not hold its shape or consistency. On the tundra this mixture is called "cranberry creme" or *kapuktuk*. Along the Kobuk River a small amount of baking soda is usually added, and the mixture is called *e-tu-polik*. Koyukuk River Indians call the mixture *unjah*.
■ The Alaska Dietary Survey

Frozen Fish Eggs

►Take fish eggs out and freeze them. They are good to eat like this.
■ *Emma Arey*
  Northern Cookbook

Caviar

►Separate every little egglet. Wash them off with water. Then drain them and put them in a jar with salt and lemon juice. Let stand for about three or four days in a refrigerator. Then you can eat the caviar after it's been cured.
■ *Uutuqtwa*
  Bristol Bay High School, Naknek

Boiled Fish Heads

►Boiled fresh fish heads, especially those of the salmon and whitefish, are highly prized among Northern Eskimos. The cheeks and fat behind the eyes and the soft chewy cartilage are particularly well liked for their very delicate flavor. Occasionally when cooking fresh salmon heads, some of the fresh salmon roe may be added.
■ The Alaska Dietary Survey

Fish Head Oil
Annie Johnson, who grew up in Iliamna, describes how her mother rendered oil from fish heads and some of the uses for it.

►Save the heads from summer fish. String them together and let them rest under water, at the bottom of a lake or stream, until they get real white. Then take ashore, take the string off, and put all the fish heads in a big kettle. Then cook them. As soon as pot starts to boil, and the oil comes to the surface of the big pot, take it off the fire. Let it cool.

My mother would skim all the oil off. It looked just like cod liver oil. When it was fresh, we would eat it with blueberries or blackberries. Just pour the oil over the berries.

My mother would pour extra oil into bottles, and in the winter time, she used it to work into skins to waterproof and soften them.
■ *Annie Johnson, Homer*

MAIN DISHES

Baked Whole Fish with A Choice of Stuffings

3 to 5 pounds (1.4 to 2.25 kg) whole-dressed fish
1-1/2 teaspoons (7 mL) salt
4 tablespoons (60 mL) butter, melted
3 slices bacon (optional)
1/4 to 1/2 cup (60 to 120 mL) milk (optional)

►Place fish in greased baking pan. Brush with melted butter and lay sliced bacon on top. Add milk. Bake in a moderate oven, 350°F (175°C), for 40 to 60 minutes or until fish flakes easily when tested with a fork. Serve immediately. Serves six.
■ The Fisherman Returns

Variations:
• Omit milk and follow hot oven baking instructions on page 10.
• Stuff the fish, using one of the dressings given below. First clean fish and blot dry, inside and out. Rub cavity and skin with a little salt. Stuff fish loosely, using about 3/4 cup (180 mL) per pound (456 g) of fish. Sew or skewer opening shut. Preheat oven to 450°F (230°C). Measure fish at its thickest point and plan baking time—10 minutes per inch of thickness. Brush fish with melted fat or add strips of bacon as suggested in the basic recipe. Bake.

If some fish is left after the meal, remove stuffing before refrigerating each, separately, for later use.

Favorite Rice Stuffing
For a 4-pound (1.8 kg) fish

1/4 cup (60 mL) butter or 2 slices bacon
1/2 cup (120 mL) chopped onion
1 cup (240 mL) sliced mushrooms
3 cups (720 mL) cooked rice
2 tablespoons (30 mL) tomato paste
1/2 cup (120 mL) dry bread crumbs
1 tablespoon (15 mL) lemon juice
2 teaspoons (10 mL) soy sauce
Bouillon or fish stock
Salt and pepper to taste

►Melt butter until bubbly in skillet. Or, fry bacon

until crisp, remove and set on paper towel. Saute onion and mushrooms in hot fat, add rice and tomato paste and stir well. Remove from fire and add remaining ingredients, moistening the mixture with bouillon or fish stock and seasoning as desired. Stuff fish cavity loosely and secure.

A sweeter "Hawaiian-style" stuffing can be made the same way up to the point where the rice is added in. After rice is mixed in, remove from heat, add 3/4 cup (180 mL) well-drained, crushed pineapple, 1/2 teaspoon (2 mL) curry powder, 1 tablespoon (15 mL) soy sauce and 1/2 cup (120 mL) raisins that have been "plumped" first in water. Slivered almonds or sliced water chestnuts are a nice addition if you have them. Bind the mixture with beaten egg.

Clam Stuffing

1/2 cup (120 mL) chopped clams
2 cups (480 mL) fine cracker crumbs
2 tablespoons (30 mL) melted butter
1 teaspoon (5 mL) salt
2 teaspoons (10 mL) chopped pickle
2 tablespoons (30 mL) lemon juice
1/2 cup (120 mL) water

►Mix ingredients in order given. If dressing seems dry, add more water. This will stuff a 3- to 4-pound (1.4 to 1.8 kg) fish. If desired, oyster or clam liquor or fish stock may be substituted for part of the water.

Bread Stuffing
Enough for a 4-pound (1.8 kg) fish

1/4 cup (60 mL) chopped onion
1 cup (240 mL) chopped celery
1/3 cup (80 mL) butter or margarine
1 teaspoon (5 mL) thyme, sage or savory
1 teaspoon (5 mL) salt
Dash pepper
1 quart (1 L) day-old bread cubes

►Cook onion and celery in fat until tender. Add to bread cubes with seasonings; mix thoroughly. If dressing seems very dry, add 2 tablespoons (30 mL) water, milk, fish stock or wine to moisten.
■ Seafood Recipes For Alaskans

Mushroom Stuffing
For a 4- to 6-pound (1.8 to 2.7 kg) fish or a pair of 1-1/2- to 2-pound (0.7 to 2 kg) fillets

1/4 cup (60 mL) finely chopped celery
1/4 cup (60 mL) finely chopped onion
1/4 cup (60 mL) butter or margarine
1/2 pound (228 g) mushrooms, sliced
1 tablespoon (15 mL) minced parsley
2 cups (480 mL) coarsely crushed crackers

1/4 teaspoon (1 mL) poultry seasoning
Salt to taste

►Heat butter or margarine in a large skillet and saute onion and celery until soft, not browned. Add the mushrooms and cook about three minutes, shaking the pan frequently to cook mushrooms evenly. Add parsley and other ingredients and stir to mix well. This recipe can easily be prepared in smaller quantity to stuff a smaller fish.
■ Marine Fish Cookbook (adapted)

Baked Deep-Sea Treat
For a party

25 raw or frozen, breaded fish portions — about 2 ounces (60 g) each
1/2 cup (120 mL) cooking oil
Paprika
1-1/2 pounds (670 g) grated American processed cheese
2/3 cup (160 mL) ketchup
1/4 cup (60 mL) prepared mustard
1/4 cup (60 mL) grated horseradish
25 hamburger rolls, split
1/2 cup (120 mL) soft butter or margarine

►Place fish portions in a single layer on shallow well-greased baking pans. Drizzle oil over fish. Sprinkle with paprika. Bake in extremely hot oven, 500°F (260°C), 15 to 20 minutes or until fish is browned and flakes easily when tested with a fork. Combine and mix cheese, ketchup, mustard and horseradish. Spread rolls with softened butter or margarine. Place one fish portion on bottom half of each roll. Top with cheese mixture and spread evenly over fish. Cover with top roll. Bake in moderate oven, 350°F (175°C) 8 to 10 minutes or until cheese melts. Serve hot. Serves 25.
■ A Seafood Heritage

Charcoal-Broiled Fish

►Pan-dressed fish, fillets and steaks can be charcoal broiled. If possible, use a well-greased, long-handled, hinged wire grill. Brush the fish with a sauce containing a fat such as lemon butter or with plain oil or butter before and while cooking it. To keep the fish moist, broil bacon with it. Another suggestion for salmon is a liberal coating of mayonnaise inside and out.
■ The Fisherman Returns

Pit-Baked Fish
A time-honored campfire method

►Fish can be baked without an oven, too. Dig a hole in the ground about 18 inches (45 cm) deep, and of sufficient size to contain a cleaned fish. Build a fire in the hole and let it burn to coals. Draw off the coals, leaving only the hot ashes at the bottom, upon which place a thick layer of foliage.

Place the fish on top of this and cover with another layer of the same material. Next rake the live coals back along with some loose sand or earth, and rekindle a small fire on top of it.

This method has been used in beach seafood cooking on both coasts. Flavor of the product depends on the nature of the foliage used. Satisfactory materials include lake grass and reeds, tule reeds, non-coniferous tree leaves, berry bush leaves, tender skunk cabbage and many others. To check likable and suitable materials, chew some first to taste for bitterness. Settle for medium-sweet flavors for best results.

■ *J.T. Brown, Port Edward, British Columbia*
   The Cabin Friend
   ALASKA® *magazine, May 1976*

Fish Baked in Sour Cream Sauce

2 pounds (1 kg) fish fillets
2 cups (480 mL) sour cream
5 tablespoons (75 mL) green onion,
   chopped fine
5 tablespoons (75 mL) green pepper,
   chopped fine
4 tablespoons (60 mL) dill pickle, chopped fine
2 tablespoons (30 mL) parsley, chopped fine
1/2 teaspoon (2 mL) dry mustard
1/2 teaspoon (2 mL) basil
1/2 teaspoon (2 mL) salt
1/4 teaspoon (1 mL) pepper

►Mix sauce ingredients and spread on fish fillets. Bake at 350°F (175°C) for 30 to 40 minutes. Serves six.
■ Tsimpshean Indian Island Cookbook
   Metlakatla

Company Fillets in Orange Sauce

1 pound (456 g) white-fleshed fish fillets
1/4 cup (60 mL) orange juice
2 tablespoons (30 mL) melted butter
Salt
Dash of paprika
1 tablespoon (15 mL) grated orange peel

►Place fish on greased broiler pan, 3 inches (7.5 cm) from heat. Combine orange juice and butter; pour half over the fish. Sprinkle fish with salt, paprika and grated orange peel. Broil five minutes and pour remaining sauce over fish. Broil several minutes longer or until fish flakes easily and is golden brown. Makes four servings.
■ *Elody Freeman*
   What's Cookin' in Wrangell

Baked Fish Steaks or Fillets

►Rinse fish in clear water and dry, then arrange in baking dish and sprinkle with salt. To melted butter, add a generous amount of onion powder and lemon juice. Pour this over the fish and baste fish several times during baking period. Bake in a moderate oven, 350°F (175°C), 20 to 30 minutes.
■ *Lee Hardcastle*
   Recipes From The Scrolls of Saint Peter's
   Seward

Fish Fillets Baked in Spanish Sauce

2 pounds (1 kg) fish fillets
1/4 cup (60 mL) chopped onion
1/4 cup (60 mL) chopped green pepper
3 tablespoons (45 mL) butter
2 tablespoons (30 mL) flour
2 cups (480 mL) chopped tomatoes,
   fresh or canned
1 teaspoon (5 mL) salt
Dash of pepper
1 bay leaf
1 whole clove

►Cut fillets into serving-sized portions. Place in a single layer in a well-greased baking pan. Saute onion and green pepper in butter until tender. Blend in flour, add tomatoes and seasonings and cook until thick, stirring constantly. Remove bay leaf and clove. Cover fish with sauce. Bake in a moderate oven, 350°F (175°C), for 20 to 30 minutes. Serves six.
■ Seafood Recipes For Alaskans

Broiled Fish with Magic Potion

2 tablespoons (30 mL) finely chopped onion
2 tablespoons (30 mL) butter, melted
1 tablespoon (15 mL) ketchup
2 teaspoons (10 mL) lemon juice
1 teaspoon (5 mL) Worcestershire
1-1/2 pounds (0.70 kg) fish fillets

►Combine onion, butter, ketchup, lemon juice and Worcestershire in bowl; mix well.

Cover broiler pan rack with aluminum foil and grease with butter.

Cut fillets into serving-sized pieces and arrange on broiler pan. Brush fillets with half of the sauce.

Place under broiler, 2 inches (5 cm) from source of heat and broil three minutes. Turn fillets; brush with remaining sauce. Broil two to three minutes more, or until fish flakes easily with a fork.
■ *Marilyn George, Petersburg*
   Reprinted with permission, Farm Journal
   Copyright May, 1981

Baked Fish and Mustard Sauce

1-1/4 pounds (570 g) fish fillets
3/4 teaspoon (3 mL) salt
Dash of pepper
2 tablespoons (30 mL) butter
1 tablespoon (15 mL) flour
1 cup (240 mL) boiling water
1 tablespoon (15 mL) lemon juice
1 tablespoon (15 mL) prepared mustard
1/2 cup (120 mL) dried bread crumbs

►Cut fillets in six servings. Sprinkle with salt and pepper. Lay in shallow well-greased baking pan. Melt 1 tablespoon (15 mL) butter in a saucepan and blend with flour. Add water, lemon juice and mustard. Stir until thickened, about three minutes. Pour over the fish. Melt remaining butter, add to bread crumbs and sprinkle over fish. Bake in a hot oven, 400°F (205°C), for 20 minutes. Place on hot platter and garnish attractively.
■ *Elsie Coats*
  Pioneer Cookbook, *Auxiliary No. 4, Anchorage*

Baked Smoked Fish

►Freshen smoked fish in cold water for one hour or more before cooking. Dry and place in a greased baking pan, flesh side up. Brush with cooking oil and sprinkle with finely diced onion and carrot. Cover with milk. Bake from 20 minutes to one hour according to the thickness of fish and length of time fish has been smoked. Baste from time to time as milk evaporates. Remove to platter and garnish with parsley.
■ *Smokehouses and the Smoke Curing of Fish*

Broiled Smoked Fish

►Wash and freshen the smoked fish in cold water for one hour, or longer if necessary. Drain, dry and sprinkle well with melted butter or cooking oil. Preheat broiler. Place fish on the rack flesh side up. Broil three minutes on each side. Serve with lemon and/or melted butter. Large fish need a longer period of broiling.
■ *Smokehouses and the Smoke Curing of Fish*

To cut steaks from a large fish without tearing the meat — use a very sharp knife, and instead of "sawing," strike the knife with a hammer to cut quickly through the backbone. If the fish is frozen, don't let it thaw completely. The firmer meat will be easier to cut.

Fish Roast in A Bag

An 8-pound (3.6 kg) fish
Salt and pepper to taste
Fish seasoning
1/2 cup (120 mL) flour
1 onion, chopped fine
2 brown paper bags

►Put one paper bag inside the other. Put flour, salt, pepper and fish seasoning in bag. Shake it around real well. Lay chunk of fish in bag with onion. Roll up so fish is real tight in bag. Tie with cord like wrapping package. Put on cookie sheet and bake at 425°F (220°C) for 1-1/2 hours.* Turn bag once during baking. After taking roast out of oven, let stand 15 minutes before you cut bag away. All skin will be stuck to paper bag.
■ *Marcell Dessell*
  False Island Camp Cook Book

*If you're not cooking such a large fish but want to use this method, measure the fish at its thickest spot and bake it 10 minutes per inch (2.5 cm) thickness at the temperature listed in this recipe. Add five minutes extra to the total cooking time for heat to penetrate bag.

Broiled Fish

►Use any small, whole fish or cuts of larger fish. Clean the fish. Sprinkle it with salt and a few drops of lemon juice or vinegar (except in the case of salmon) and place between the wires of a toast rack. If the fish is dry-meated, sprinkle with a little cooking oil or fat. Place in preheated broiler, cooking the split side first, turning when the fish has "set" and cooking on the other side. Over or under a hot flame or burner, if not too thick, a fish should cook within 10 minutes. The toast rack saves the broiler and makes for easy transfer of the fish from broiler to platter.
■ *Gold Rush Festival Cookbook*
  Whitehorse, Yukon Territory

Herbed Fish Sauterne

1/2 cup (120 mL) butter or margarine
1/2 cup (120 mL) sauterne or other
  white dinner wine
1/3 cup (80 mL) lemon juice
1 clove garlic, chopped
Generous pinch of rosemary
Chopped parsley
Chopped chives or green onions
6 servings salmon, halibut, bass or trout

►Melt butter in a saucepan; add wine and lemon juice; bring to boiling. Add garlic, rosemary, parsley and chives. Use to baste fish frequently while frying, baking, broiling or barbecuing. If desired, marinate fish in the wine about 30 minutes; drain off and combine as above. Personally, I marinate the fish for several hours in the entire sauce,* then barbecue on an outdoor grill basting continually. Turn fish only once for it will be so tender it may break apart if turned too often.

■ *Edie Diver*
Mount Spurr School Cook Book
Elmendorf Air Force Base

If marination lasts longer than 30 minutes, keep the fish refrigerated or in a cool place, 35 to 40°F (1.5 to 4.5°C).

Planked Fish
A method of cooking that has long been used by Pacific Northwest Indians

►Any fish can be planked. A plank or shake board can easily be made with an ax from materials at hand, including your campfire wood supply. Almost any type of non-resinous wood can be used; avoid cedar because of the heavy scent it gives off when heated. Bark can also be used. Length and width of the plank is governed by the size of the fish to be cooked. Sharpen one end of the plank for forcing it into the ground.

Scrape scales off fish and cut out gills. Leave head, fins and tail on. Slit the belly from vent to head. Remove viscera and scrape kidney tissue from backbone. Split the back from the inside so the fish can be opened wide as a book. Wash and pat dry. Wrap fish line around fish and plank to hold fish in place while cooking; have wedges handy for slipping under the lines to keep the fish tight and in place as it begins to shrink somewhat during cooking. Putting the planked fish in campfire smoke for a time before cooking improves the flavor — but keep it away from heat.

Salt and pepper the prepared fish, tuck some thin pieces of bacon or pork under the line at the top of the fish for basting. Onion rings add flavor, too. Force the pointed plank into the ground before a bed of hot coals, but not too close, or fish will scorch. Catch drippings in a spoon and baste if you wish. Meat is done when the flesh starts to curl and separate. Eat right off the plank.

■ *J.T. Brown, Port Edward, British Columbia*
The Cabin Friend
ALASKA® magazine, May 1976

Kabobs on A Stick
A trail treat

2 pounds (1 kg) fish fillets
6 slices bacon, cut in squares

Wedges of onion, green pepper and/or partially boiled potatoes
Salt and pepper
Green sticks or skewers about 30 inches (75 cm) long, sharp at one end
6 wiener buns

►Cut fillets about 1 inch (2.5 cm) wide and 4 inches (10 cm) long. Sprinkle with salt and pepper. Roll up fillets and place on skewers alternately with bacon and choice of vegetables. Hold over hot flame to lightly brown fish, then cook slowly over hot coals, turning constantly. Serve in buttered wiener buns. Serves six.

■ *Seafood Recipes For Alaskans*

Broiled Pizza-Fish
Kids prefer salmon and you're serving hake? Never mind. Spice it up with their favorite Italian flavors.

2 teaspoons (10 mL) margarine or butter
2 tablespoons (30 mL) chopped onion
1 clove finely minced garlic
1 cup (240 mL) tomato sauce
1/2 teaspoon (2 mL) each — oregano and basil leaves, crumbled
2 pounds (1 kg) white-fleshed fish fillets
Oil
Salt and pepper
1/2 cup (120 mL) grated mozzarella cheese
2 tablespoons (30 mL) grated Parmesan cheese

►Heat margarine or butter in a small saucepan till bubbly. Add onion and garlic and saute a minute or two. Add tomato sauce, oregano and basil and blend. When mixture heats through, reduce heat and simmer gently, stirring now and then to prevent sticking, 15 to 20 minutes.

Meanwhile, set fillets in a greased, heat-proof dish, sprinkle with salt and pepper and a little oil. Broil until fish is nearly done. Then spoon sauce over fish, sprinkle evenly with mozzarella and Parmesan and return to broiler till cheese melts and browns slightly. Serves six.

Charcoaled Fish Dinner in A Package
An easy way to serve a crowd at a picnic and leave few dishes to wash afterward

►Place fish fillets, steaks or small, whole fish on greased aluminum foil, preparing as many packages as there are people to be served. Top fish with a slice or two of onion and any two or three of the following, also sliced: green pepper, tomato, potato, zucchini, mushrooms. Salt and pepper the servings and either dot them with butter or arrange pieces of sliced bacon over them. Wrap the fish snugly in the foil, making sure of a good seal. Place packages on a grill, about 3 to 4 inches (7.5 to 10 cm) above hot coals. Turn the packages occasionally with tongs. Grill the fish 30 to 45 minutes, depending on thickness. If you don't have a grill, packages should be double-wrapped. Place them on the hot coals —but not on *flame*; wait till it dies down — turn them frequently, cook 20 to 25 minutes. Serve hot, directly from the foil package.

Poaching Liquids and Stocks

Poaching is a method of cooking whole fish, steaks or fillets in seasoned liquid — nearly to cover. For a complete description of the method, see page 11. Following are several recipes for flavorful broths that may be used as poaching liquids and some complete recipes for the final dish. A few of them call for "boiling" the fish. The process of boiling fish differs from poaching only in the mind of the cook. Few cooks feel their competence threatened when told to boil something, but a surprising number are frightened by what they consider the painstaking process of poaching. So, all right, if you think you can't poach fish, try out the instructions for "boiling" fish. The main thing to remember about boiling fish is that you NEVER boil the fish.

Acid Water
►To each quart (1 L) of water, add 1 teaspoon (5 mL) salt and 3 tablespoons (45 mL) lemon juice or vinegar. This poaching liquid is especially good for preserving the true flavor of the fish.

Wine
►For each pound (456 g) of fish, use 3/4 cup (180 mL) wine and 3/4 cup (180 mL) water as the poaching liquid.

Fish Stock
►To each quart (1 L) of cold water, add 2 pounds (1 kg) fish trimmings (head, bones, skin and tail) and 2 teaspoons (10 mL) salt. Bring liquid to boil, lower heat and simmer for 20 to 30 minutes. Strain before using.

Court Bouillon
1/3 cup (80 mL) diced carrots
1 small onion studded with 2 cloves
1/3 cup (80 mL) chopped celery
2 sprigs parsley
2 tablespoons (30 mL) butter
2 quarts (2 L) water
6 black peppercorns
1 bay leaf

2 teaspoons (10 mL) salt
1/3 cup (80 mL) vinegar or wine

►Bring mixture to a boil, add fish and reduce heat to a gentle simmer until fish flakes easily — 5 to 10 minutes for steaks or fillets. This amount of Court Bouillon will suffice for 3 pounds (1.4 kg) or more of fish.
■ The Fisherman Returns

Deluxe Wine-Flavored Stock
1/4 cup (60 mL) butter
1 cup (240 mL) water
1 large onion, diced
Several sprigs parsley
9 or 10 peppercorns
2 or 3 pounds (1 to 1.4 kg) fish trimmings and bones
2-1/2 pints (1.2 L) cold water
2 pints (1 L) dry white wine
Salt

►Melt butter in saucepan, tilting the pan to coat all sides. Add 1 cup (240 mL) water and onion, parsley and peppercorns (or equivalent in black pepper). Add fish trimmings and bones and cover the pan. Simmer gently for 45 minutes. Uncover and add remaining cold water and white wine; also a liberal dash of salt. Cover pan again and allow to simmer for 30 minutes or so. Strain into storage containers and cool; then cover containers tightly and store in the refrigerator or freeze until needed. Use the stock for poaching fresh fish or as a base for preparing soups, sauces and other fish dishes.
■ *Helen A. White, Anchorage*
    More About What's Cookin' in Alaska

Poached Fish with Olive Sauce
Poaching in milk

1 pound (456 g) fish fillets
1/2 teaspoon (2 mL) salt
1 cup (240 mL) milk
2 tablespoons (30 mL) melted butter or other fat
2 tablespoons (30 mL) flour
1 teaspoon (5 mL) lemon juice
1/4 cup (60 mL) sliced stuffed olives

►Cut fillets into serving-sized portions. Simmer gently in salted milk for 5 to 10 minutes or until fish flakes easily when tested with a fork. Remove from heat. Carefully remove fish to heated platter and keep hot. Combine melted butter and flour. Slowly stir in the hot poaching milk. Cook and stir over low heat until thickened. Add lemon juice and olives. Pour sauce over fish. Makes three to four servings.
■ The Way To Cook Fish

Boil Your Fish Catch #1

2 pounds (1 kg) fish fillets
2 quarts (2 L) water
2 tablespoons (30 mL) salt

►Cut fillets into serving portions. Place fish in a wire basket or on a plate. If a plate is used, tie it and the fish in a cheesecloth bag for easy handling. Lower the fish into the salted boiling water and simmer (never boil) about 10 minutes. Lift basket or cheesecloth bag, remove fish carefully and serve at once with a colorful sauce. Serves six. Boiled fish may be improved in flavor by simmering fish in one of the liquids suggested for poached fish.
■ Seafood Recipes For Alaskans

Boil Your Fish Catch #2

►Cut fish like steak, only 2-1/2 inches (6 cm) wide. Just cover the cleaned fish with water; season with salt and pepper and onions and simmer (never boil). Never stir it or it will fall apart. You can see when it is done; the skin will come off. Drain the water and take the fish out of the pan. Serve with greens and cover fish with Mustard Sauce.
■ Tsimpshean Indian Island Cookbook
   Metlakatla

Fish in Tomato Sauce

Using a skillet as the poacher

2 cups (480 mL) chopped tomatoes
1/2 teaspoon (2 mL) salt
1 bay leaf
1 tablespoon (15 mL) minced onion
2 pounds (1 kg) fish fillets
1 tablespoon (15 mL) butter

►Cook ingredients, except fish, in greased skillet. Add the fish and simmer. Strain off the sauce and pour over the fish as you serve it.
■ Tsimpshean Indian Island Cookbook
   Metlakatla

Pan-Fried Fish

2 pounds (1 kg) fillets or steaks, or 3 pounds
   (1.4 kg) pan-dressed fish
1/4 cup (60 mL) milk
1 egg, beaten
1 teaspoon (5 mL) salt
1/8 teaspoon (0.5 mL) pepper
1-1/2 cups (360 mL) dry bread or
   cracker crumbs
Fat for frying

►Combine milk, egg, salt and pepper. Dip fish in the liquid mixture and roll it in the crumbs. Heat about 1/8 inch (3 mm) fat in the bottom of a 10-inch (25 cm) heavy frying pan. Add the fish and fry it slowly at moderate heat. When the fish is golden brown on one side, turn it carefully. Fry the fish until it is brown and flakes easily when tested with a fork. Cooking will take 8 to 15 minutes, depending on thickness. If desired, drain the fish on absorbent paper. Serve it plain or with lemon wedges or a sauce. Serves six.
■ The Fisherman Returns

Batter-Fried Fish Bits

Cooking oil
1-1/2 pounds (0.70 kg) fish fillets
1-1/2 cups (360 mL) buttermilk baking mix
1 tablespoon (15 mL) sugar
1 teaspoon (5 mL) salt
Water
1 egg, slightly beaten
Tartar Sauce

►Pour cooking oil into 10-inch (25 cm) skillet or electric frying pan to a depth of 1/2 inch (1.25 cm) and heat to 370°F (188°C).
   Cut fillets into 3-1/2 x 3/4-inch (8.75 x 1.9 cm) pieces and coat with 1/2 cup (120 mL) of the baking mix.
   Combine remaining 1 cup (240 mL) baking mix, sugar and salt in bowl. Add enough water to egg to make 1 cup (240 mL). Add egg mixture to dry ingredients. Beat until smooth, using rotary beater. Dip fish into batter, coating well.
   Fry fish in hot oil a few pieces at a time. Cook three minutes, turn, and fry three minutes more, or until golden brown. Drain on paper towels and keep warm in 275°F (135°C) oven. Serve with Tartar Sauce. Makes four to six servings.

Tartar Sauce
1/2 cup (120 mL) mayonnaise or salad dressing
3 tablespoons (45 mL) chopped sweet pickles
2 tablespoons (30 mL) finely chopped onion
1/4 teaspoon (1 mL) Worcestershire

►Combine in a bowl. Chill till serving time.
■ *Marilyn George, Petersburg*
   Reprinted with permission, Farm Journal
   Copyright May, 1981

Dried Fish and Potatoes

►Cut up dried fish into small pieces. Divide eight potatoes in halves and put both dried fish and unpeeled potatoes in a big pot and cover with cold water. Slice seal fat into large chunks and add to the pot along with about 2 tablespoons (30 mL) of salt. Heat to boiling, cover and cook until potatoes are done.
■ *Courtesy, Vivian James, Angoon*

Tempura

3/4 pound (336 g) shrimp or boneless
  fish pieces
3/4 cup (180 mL) sifted flour
1 teaspoon (5 mL) double-acting baking powder
1/2 teaspoon (2 mL) salt
1 egg
1/2 cup (120 mL) water

►Rinse and thoroughly dry fish or shellfish. Sift flour, baking powder and salt together. Beat egg slightly, add dry ingredients and stir until blended. Add water a tablespoon (15 mL) at a time, stirring constantly until batter is smooth and the consistency of a custard sauce. Dip seafood in batter, one piece at a time, and fry in hot fat, 350°F (175°C), until golden-brown, about three minutes. Drain. Makes two to three servings; more if used as an appetizer.
■ The Fisherman Returns

Fish 'n' Chips

1 pound (456 g) boneless fish
1 cup (240 mL) flour
1 teaspoon (5 mL) salt
1 teaspoon (5 mL) poultry seasoning
1 teaspoon (5 mL) baking powder
1 egg with milk to make total of 3/4 cup
  (180 mL) liquid
1 tablespoon (15 mL) melted fat or oil

►Cut fish in finger-size strips. Sift flour, baking powder, poultry seasoning and salt and sprinkle on fish strips. Move floured fish to waxed paper so excess flour mixture may be saved. Beat egg with milk. Add to remaining flour mixture; add fat or oil. Dip floured fish into batter. Fry about one minute, testing a piece to make sure fish is done through. Drain on crushed paper. For dunking fish sticks have ready: mayonnaise, prepared mustard, ketchup, soy sauce and individual bowls for mixing. Serve with chips.
■ *Eleanor Moeser*
  Kitchen Magic, *Ketchikan*

Oven-Fried Fish

2 pounds (1 kg) fillets or steaks less than 1 inch
  (2.5 cm) thick
1 tablespoon (15 mL) salt
1 cup (240 mL) milk
1 cup (240 mL) dry bread crumbs,
  lightly toasted
1/4 cup (60 mL) melted fat or oil

►Cut fish into serving-sized portions. Add salt to milk. Dip fish in milk and roll in bread crumbs. Place on greased, shallow baking pan. Drizzle with melted fat. Place in a very hot oven, 500°F (260°C) and bake approximately 10 to 12 minutes. Serve immediately — plain, with lemon wedges or with a sauce. Serves six. This recipe is especially suited to hooligan or smelt and is also a good basic recipe for clams.
■ Seafood Recipes For Alaskans (adapted)

Fish Potato Cakes
A good breakfast or lunch for campers

1 pound (456 g) skinless fish fillets
3 eggs, beaten
2 tablespoons (30 mL) flour
2 tablespoons (30 mL), or more, grated onion
1 tablespoon (15 mL) chopped parsley
1-1/2 teaspoons (7 mL) salt
Dash of pepper
2 cups (480 mL) finely grated raw potato
Applesauce, warm or chilled
Fat, for frying

►Chop fillets very fine. Combine all ingredients except applesauce and fat and mix well. Place a well-greased heavy frying pan about 4 inches (10 cm) from hot coals, add fat and heat until fat is hot but not yet smoking. Drop fish potato batter by large spoonfuls onto hot pan; flatten cakes with spoon if necessary. Fry three to four minutes or until brown. Turn carefully and fry three to four minutes longer or until well browned. Drain on paper towels. Keep hot. Serve with applesauce.
■ *The Old Homesteader*

Fresh Fish Cakes

Enough raw fish fillets to make 4 cups (1 L)
  ground — about 2 pounds (1 kg)
3 to 4 tablespoons (45 to 60 mL) chopped
  or ground onion
4 teaspoons (20 mL) salt
1 teaspoon (5 mL) nutmeg
4 eggs
4 cups (1 L) ice cold milk
4 tablespoons (60 mL) cornstarch or
  potato flour
1/2 teaspoon (2 mL) additional salt
4 tablespoons (60 mL) butter
Oil and/or butter for frying

►Halibut, salmon or lingcod may be used. Grind the fish three or four times through the fine blade of a meat grinder, cleaning the grinder between times if there are bones to remove. Add onion, salt and nutmeg for the last grinding. You may need more salt. Put the fish in a large mixing bowl. Beat in eggs one at a time; then gradually beat in the milk — starting with 1/2 cup (120 mL) — the cornstarch, additional salt and butter. The mixture will thicken as you beat it. If the fish is dry, you may need more milk.

Form into cakes and boil. Or, drop by spoonfuls into hot butter or oil or some of each, about 1/4 inch (6 mm) deep in a heavy skillet. Flatten the cakes a little, brown, turn and brown again.

This is enough batter for about 20 cakes, and some of it may be refrigerated for later use. It also freezes placed in a container with a tight-fitting cover. Use frozen batter within two months.

■ *Freda Eilertsen*
  Sons of Norway Cook Book, *Ketchikan*

Smoked Fish Cakes

2 tablespoons (30 mL) margarine or fat
1/2 cup (120 mL) chopped onion
2 cups (480 mL) cooked, mashed potatoes
1 cup (240 mL) mashed, canned or smoked fish
1 egg
Salt and pepper
Dry bread crumbs

►Saute onion in hot margarine or fat. Mix with potatoes, fish, egg, salt and pepper. Form patties and roll in fine bread crumbs. Fry in hot fat until golden brown on both sides — about 10 minutes. Serves four to six.

■ Recipes For Canned Fish

Creamed Smoked Fish

1-1/2 cups (360 mL) cooked, flaked smoked fish
1 cup (240 mL) milk
1 cup (240 mL) fish stock
4 tablespoons (60 mL) flour
4 tablespoons (60 mL) fat or oil
1 teaspoon (5 mL) Worcestershire
Salt and pepper

►Make a white sauce of flour, fat, salt, pepper and liquid; stir smooth. Add fish flakes and heat through. Serve on toast, rice or other base. Vary the recipe by adding hard-cooked eggs, carrots, peas, parsley.

■ Smokehouses and the Smoke Curing of Fish

Creamed Fish with Onion White Sauce

1 cup (240 mL) Onion White Sauce
2 cups (480 mL) cooked or canned fish
1/4 teaspoon (1 mL) paprika
1 teaspoon (5 mL) lemon juice
Optional — any of the following:
    1/4 cup (60 mL) chopped pimento;
    1 hard-cooked egg, sliced;
    1/2 cup (120 mL) sauteed
    mushrooms; 1/2 cup (120 mL)
    grated cheese

►In a medium saucepan, make Onion White Sauce. Gently fold in flaked fish, paprika and lemon juice. Add salt and pepper if needed and other optional ingredients desired. Serve over toast, macaroni, potatoes or rice. Or mix with about 1-1/2 cups (360 mL) cooked rice or macaroni and spread in a greased casserole. Top with grated cheese and bake at 350°F (175°C) for about 20 minutes. Serves four to six.

Onion White Sauce
1/2 cup (120 mL) chopped onion
2 to 3 tablespoons (30 to 45 mL) butter
2 tablespoons (30 mL) flour
1 cup (240 mL) milk, or milk and light stock
    (chicken or fish)
Salt and pepper to taste

►Melt 1 tablespoon (15 mL) butter in saucepan. Saute onion until soft but not browned. Remove onion with slotted spoon and set aside. Add enough more butter to the pan to equal 2 tablespoons (30 mL) or more; return to heat. Add flour and cook, stirring, till mixture is foamy. Stir in milk or milk and stock and continue cooking and stirring until thickened. Return onion and heat through, stirring. Use as above or in any recipe calling for white sauce.

Choose-Your-Own Seafood Pie

Filling:
1 can (16 oz/or/456 g) salmon, drained and
    flaked, or 2 to 3 cups (480 to 720 mL) cooked,
    flaked black cod, halibut, rockfish, shrimp or
    crab, or 1 pint (0.47 L) shucked clams
1/3 cup (80 mL) butter
1/3 cup (80 mL) flour
1/2 teaspoon (2 mL) salt
2 cups (480 mL) fish liquor, fish stock or
    diluted mushroom soup
2 tablespoons (30 mL) chopped onion
1 cup (240 mL) cooked vegetables, any
    combination you like

►Melt butter, add flour and salt; cook and blend until bubbly. Add liquid gradually and cook until thick, stirring constantly. Add the onion and cooked vegetables (such as carrots, peas, celery) and seafood. Blend thoroughly.

Crust:
►Prepare 1 cup (240 mL) mashed potatoes or 1 cup (240 mL) pastry. Place filling in a well-greased casserole and top with mashed potatoes or pastry rolled out to fit casserole. Bake in a hot oven, 425°F (220°C), until heated and crust is cooked and browned. Serves six.

■ Seafood Recipes For Alaskans

Fish Balls Petersburg

2 pounds (1 kg) raw fish, any kind
1 tablespoon (15 mL) cornstarch
1 tablespoon (15 mL) flour
1 tablespoon (15 mL) salt
1 egg
Pinch of pepper
Pinch of nutmeg or mace
1 pint (480 mL) milk, fresh preferred

►Bone and skin fish. Cook bones about half an hour in salted water. Put fish through food grinder. Add flour and salt. Put through grinder twice more. Mix in a wooden dish with potato masher, adding milk a little at a time. Mix well after each addition. Add seasoning. Make into small balls. Cook in liquid drained from cooked fish bones. Can be fried and served in brown gravy or cream sauce.
■ *Mrs. Chris Wick*
  PTA Cook Book, *Petersburg*

Fish Balls Ketchikan

1 cup (240 mL) cooked or canned, flaked fish
2 teaspoons (10 mL) salt
1 tablespoon (15 mL) parsley
1 teaspoon (5 mL) horseradish
1/2 teaspoon (2 mL) Worcestershire
1/2 cup (120 mL) water
1 cup (240 mL) mashed potatoes
1 tablespoon (15 mL) grated onion
1-1/2 teaspoons (7 mL) lemon juice
2 eggs, beaten
Bread crumbs

►Mix all ingredients except eggs and bread crumbs. Roll into 1-inch (2.5 cm) balls. Roll in bread crumbs, then in beaten eggs, then again in bread crumbs. Chill. Drop in hot fat, cooking until brown. Serve with sauce or dip.
■ *Doris Dolphin*
  Kitchen Magic, *Ketchikan*

Fish Souffle

2 cups (480 mL) flaked cooked fish
2 tablespoons (30 mL) butter
3 tablespoons (45 mL) flour
1 teaspoon (5 mL) salt
Dash of pepper
Dash of nutmeg
1 cup (240 mL) fish liquor* and milk
3 egg yolks, beaten
3 egg whites, beaten

►Melt butter; blend in flour and seasonings. Add liquid gradually and cook until thick and smooth, stirring constantly. Stir a little of the hot sauce into the beaten egg yolks; add the mixture to the remaining sauce, stirring constantly. Add fish. Fold mixture into beaten egg whites. Pour into a well-greased 1-1/2 quart (1.45 L) casserole or souffle dish. Bake in a moderate oven, 350°F (175°C), for 45 minutes or until souffle is firm in the center. Serves six.
■ Seafood Recipes For Alaskans

*Fish liquor is the juice that forms during cooking or the liquid from canned fish. Fish stock or chicken bouillon may be used.

Fishburgers

2 cups (480 mL) cooked fish
1/2 cup (120 mL) mayonnaise
1/2 teaspoon (2 mL) salt
1/2 teaspoon (2 mL) Worcestershire
2 tablespoons (30 mL) finely chopped onion
2 teaspoons (10 mL) lemon juice
6 buttered, heated (or toasted) hamburger buns
Lettuce leaves
6 slices tomato

►Flake the fish. Combine all ingredients with the fish except for lettuce and tomato. Spread filling on heated (or toasted) buns; add a leaf of lettuce and a tomato slice. Serves six.
■ Marine Fish Cookbook

Custard Fish

1 cup (240 mL) cooked fish
1/2 cup (120 mL) cooked mushrooms
1 cup (240 mL) bread crumbs
2 cups (480 mL) milk
1/3 cup (80 mL) butter
Salt and pepper
Few grains of nutmeg
4 eggs, beaten

►Chop fish into small pieces. Add mushrooms and chop both fine. Cook crumbs and milk in double boiler 10 minutes. Add butter and seasoning, fish and beaten eggs. Pour into greased custard cups. Bake in a moderate oven, 350°F (175°C), about 30 minutes or until firm. Unmold and serve with tomato or Hollandaise Sauce.
■ Tsimpshean Indian Island Cookbook
  Metlakatla

For a little snack . . . burn some smoked fish skins. Just put them on a fork and burn them over a blue flame until they are crispy. Eat them plain or have a little *agutuk* (Eskimo ice cream) on the side.
■ *Marlene Johnson*
  Uutuqtwa
  Bristol Bay High School, Naknek

Fisherman's Casserole

*A blue ribbon winner at the
1976 Southeast Alaska State Fair*

►Layer chopped or sliced vegetables and fish fillets in casserole dish, starting with vegetables such as celery, onion, green pepper, tomatoes — then fish. Season each layer with salt, pepper, lemon juice, Tabasco sauce and butter to taste. Bake at 350°F (175°C) for 35 to 40 minutes. Can be cooked in a double layer of foil over campfire.
■ *Ron Smith*
   Haines Homemakers' Cookbook

Norwegian Fish Pudding

*1 pound (456 g) fish — halibut, cod,
   haddock — finely ground
1 cup (240 mL) softened butter
1 teaspoon (5 mL) salt
1/4 teaspoon (1 mL) white pepper
4 eggs, separated
4 tablespoons (60 mL) flour
2 cups (480 mL) light cream*

►Grind fish at least three times, then work butter and fish together or put in electric blender. Add seasonings, egg yolks, flour and cream. Beat egg whites and fold in gently. Pour into a well-oiled ornate mold. Cover with foil, wrap and steam gently in a covered kettle one hour or less; do not overcook. (Use a trivet so the mold does not touch the bottom of the kettle.) Unmold on a beautiful plate and decorate with radish roses, parsley and a slice of orange on top.
■ *Bunny Mathisen, Petersburg
   "Help Yourself To The Sylta Flesk!"
   ALASKA® magazine, January 1977*

Individual Fish Loaves

Leftover fish dressed up

*2 cups (480 mL) flaked, cooked fish
2/3 cup (160 mL) grated cheese
1 egg, beaten
2 tablespoons (30 mL) melted butter
1 teaspoon (5 mL) salt
2 tablespoons (30 mL) lemon juice
1/2 cup (120 mL) cracker crumbs or
   crushed cornflakes*

►Combine all ingredients except crumbs. Shape into six individual loaves and roll in crumbs. Bake in a moderate oven, 350°F (175°C), 25 to 30 minutes or until brown. Serve plain or with a sauce. Serves six.

Variations:
• *Fishwich* — Omit cheese. Spread remaining mixture on buttered bread or rolls. Top with sliced or grated cheese if desired. Bake in a hot oven, 450°F (230°C), for five minutes.
• *Fishburger* — Omit cheese. Shape mixture into cakes or patties. Fry in a small amount of fat, turning once. Serve on hot buns with ketchup, pickles, relish, onions or other condiments.

Chapter 2

The Cook's Tour

This chapter doesn't tour every fish in the sea. But many favorites are here — from cod to trout—and some fine ways of preparing them. Far and away the largest is the section on salmon, with herring and halibut very distant seconds.

Many of these recipes, too, are basic enough to accommodate substitutions. If you have lingcod, for example, you'll find some excellent recipes for it . . . but, alas, not many of them. Why not also check through the recipes for halibut? They are more numerous and perfectly suitable for lingcod. Other substitutions are just as easy. We've suggested a few along the way. And don't forget — fish and shellfish (all kinds) make good table mates.

COD & COUSINS

Pacific cod, specified in most of the recipes that follow, is a true cod very similar to the renowned Atlantic cod and a favorite of northwest cooks. Two more fish from the same family — pollock and its freshwater cousin, burbot — may be used in recipes calling for cod.

Pollock, sometimes marketed as "whiting," is among the numerous deep-ocean dwellers called "bottomfish" or "groundfish" that are objects of a developing commercial fishery in Alaska.

Burbot, also called freshwater ling, freshwater lush, eelpout or by its scientific name, *Lota lota*, is entirely a freshwater fish. Though it may be the ugliest member of a somewhat homely family, the burbot is an especially good eating fish. It is found throughout Interior Alaska and, though it is supposed to grow to 75 pounds (34 kg), the average size taken by sports and subsistence fishermen in Alaska is much less than a tenth of that. A favorite wintertime way to fish for burbot is through the ice using set lines. Pollock, too, is a relatively small fish, averaging a bit over a foot (30 cm) in length, but Pacific cod commonly grows to around 3 feet (0.9 m).

Taste: All the cod family have mild-flavored white meat, very low in fat and high in protein. The burbot is a superb tasting fish known for firm white meat that flakes nicely when cooked and is nearly boneless. Its liver, like other cod liver, is rich in vitamins A and D.

Preparation Tips: Bake, batter-fry, steam, poach, broil these fish. The cooked meat is a favorite for loaves, burgers and cakes. Cod is also a classic fish for salting.

To use salt cod in recipes calling for cooked, flaked fish, figure 1 pound (0.45 kg) will equal about 2 cups (480 mL) prepared fish. Rinse it thoroughly under running water and then soak it up to 24 hours in several changes of cold water. Rinse again and measure the fish at its thickest point. Then place it in a saucepan with cold water to cover. Add 1/2 cup (120 mL) white vinegar, a diced carrot, two stalks celery, a quartered onion and spices, as desired, tied up in a cheesecloth bag. Half a bay leaf, a few sprigs of fresh parsley or a teaspoon (5 mL) of dried parsley flakes are good ones. DO NOT ADD SALT! Bring the liquid just to the boiling point, lower heat and simmer the fish gently, 10 minutes per inch (2.5 cm) thickness. Then it is ready to skin, bone, flake and use in any recipe for cooked cod.

Favorite Cod Dinner

2 pounds (1 kg) fresh Pacific cod — boiled,
  baked, steamed or poached
1/4 pound (114 g) bacon, diced
8 small carrots, cut in half
6 medium potatoes
6 small white onions
2 cups (480 mL) thin White Sauce
2 tablespoons (30 mL) finely chopped parsley
2 hard-cooked eggs

►Fry bacon until crisp and set aside. Boil carrots, potatoes and onions in salted water until tender. Place fish on a heated platter and surround with cooked vegetables. Scatter bacon bits over fish. Cover with White Sauce and garnish with parsley and egg slices. Serves four to six.
■ Marine Fish Cookbook

Cod Curry

2 pounds (1 kg) fresh cod fillets
1 cup (240 mL) finely sliced celery
1/2 cup (120 mL) sliced onion
1 tablespoon (15 mL) melted fat or oil
1/2 teaspoon (2 mL) curry powder
1 teaspoon (5 mL) salt
Dash of pepper
3/4 cup (180 mL) milk
Paprika

►Place fillets in a layer in a greased baking dish. Cook the celery and onion in fat for five minutes, then blend in seasonings and milk. Spread over fish. Bake at 350°F (175°C) until fish flakes easily. Sprinkle with paprika and other garnishes such as parsley and lemon wedges. Serves six.
■ Marine Fish Cookbook

Broiled Oriental Fillets

1 pound (0.45 kg) cod fillets
1 tablespoon (15 mL) soy sauce
1/4 teaspoon (1 mL) ginger
2 tablespoons (30 mL) brown sugar
3 tablespoons (45 mL) salad oil

►Mix sauce ingredients together and pour over fish fillets. Cover and marinate for two hours in the refrigerator. Remove from sauce and place fish in a flat baking pan. Broil for five minutes or until nicely browned. Do not turn. Serves four.
■ Marine Fish Cookbook

Codfish Casserole

1/4 cup (60 mL) butter
1/4 cup (60 mL) flour
Salt to taste
1/2 teaspoon (2 mL) dry mustard
2 cups (480 mL), or more, milk
4 cups (1 L) cooked cod
1 cup (240 mL) grated cheese
1 cup (240 mL) buttered toast crumbs
  or cracker crumbs

►In a small saucepan, make a white sauce of the first five ingredients. First, melt butter, add flour and cook, stirring, until mixture is frothy. Remove from heat and add seasonings. (If freshened salt cod is being used, go cautiously with the salt shaker here.)

Return saucepan to medium heat and add milk slowly, stirring constantly until mixture reaches desired thickness. Set aside. Grease a 1-1/2 quart (1.45 L) casserole dish and spread half the fish in the bottom, pour on half the white sauce, sprinkle with half the cheese and crumbs. Repeat layers. Bake for about 20 minutes at 350°F (175°C) until browned. Serves six.

Codfish Balls or Cakes

2 cups (480 mL) cooked and flaked Pacific cod
  or other white-fleshed fish
1-1/2 cups (360 mL) mashed potatoes
2 eggs
2 tablespoons (30 mL) undiluted evaporated
  milk or 1 tablespoon (15 mL) melted butter
1/4 teaspoon (1 mL) salt
2 teaspoons (10 mL) grated onion
Paprika (optional)

►Mix flaked fish and mashed potatoes and beat in eggs, one at a time. Beat in evaporated milk or butter and add seasonings. (If salt cod is used, taste before you add salt.) Shape into small balls and fry in hot deep fat — 375°F (190°C) — until golden brown. Or form 2-inch (5 cm) cakes, dip both sides in flour and saute in a mixture of equal parts butter and oil. A sprinkling of paprika during the saute adds a nice color. Serves four.

Sourdough makes a wonderful batter for deep-fried fish. It should be just slightly thicker than you'd use for making pancakes.

DOGFISH

Dogfish — not to be confused with dog salmon — is a variety of small shark more often greeted with epithets than glee when it shows up in the set nets of fishermen who are after salmon in Cook Inlet, at Kodiak, and elsewhere throughout the Gulf of Alaska. Farther south, in the waters of Southeastern, and especially in British Columbia and Washington state, the dogfish is a real pest to both sport and commercial fishermen. But, according to Russ Mohney, who has written a whole cookbook featuring the critter, the little sharks can be turned into quite nice treats for the table if you follow the few simple rules listed as preparation tips below. In this section we share a few of Mohney's recipes. If spiny dogfish are commonly part of your catch, however, you'll probably want the whole book, sensibly enough titled, *The Dogfish Cookbook*.

Taste: Properly marinated in advance of cooking, the dogfish is a tasty enough fish and a good source of protein.

Preparation Tips: Dogfish can be used in most recipes that specify cod and, because it is firm fleshed, it is often prepared "fish and chips" fashion. No matter how it's to be cooked, it must be properly treated beforehand. First, dogfish should be bled immediately on catching, then skinned and filleted as soon as possible, as suggested in these tips from the State of Washington Department of Fisheries:

1. Cool the dogfish immediately, preferably on ice. Many experienced dogfish eaters say the animal should be skinned and cleaned as soon as possible after being landed.
2. Dogfish may be skinned by hooking the whole fish onto a metal spike or hook fastened to a bench or table, belly downwards, hanging over the edge. (A sturdy board with a large nail or hook fixed in one end can be carried aboard an angler's boat.)
3. Trim off dorsal and anal fins. Then, holding the fish — belly down — with one hand, insert the knife near the neck so that the point protrudes on the opposite side. Make a cut down the underside of the backbone, running the length of the fish and ending near the vent. Belly flaps and viscera will fall downwards away from the remainder of the fish, still attached to the head.
4. Make an oblique cut on either side immediately behind the head, and take the side fins, one in each hand, and pull backwards. The skin should come off cleanly within a few inches of the tail, which is then cut off. The skinless body may then be cut away from the head. Some people prefer to use a pair of pliers for removing the skin. Others prefer to cut off the tail before skinning.
5. To avoid color loss, do not wash the body portion of the fish after skinning. Wrap each fish individually in cellophane to protect the color of the meat.
6. Wash the belly flaps and remove the skin from them — an operation similar to the filleting of any large fish. Remove fat from the fillets and from all other dogfish meat.

Before cooking — marinate the fillets overnight in a weak solution of vinegar or lemon juice and water to neutralize urea odor and taste. Russ Mohney suggests, "Place the fillets in a shallow dish and add just enough cold water to cover. To this add 1/2 tablespoon (8 mL) lemon juice or 1 tablespoon (15 mL) cider vinegar for each pound (0.45 kg) fish. This is the single most important step in the proper preparation of dogfish."

Another important step: Don't overcook it. The flavor gets stronger with overcooking. Properly dressed and cooked, dogfish can be used just as you would any other white-meated fish in salads or casseroles.

Dogfish and Chips

2 pounds (1 kg) dogfish meat
Vegetable oil (soybean oil preferred)

Batter:
1 cup (240 mL) flour
1 egg yolk
2 tablespoons (30 mL) beer
1/2 teaspoon (2 mL) onion or garlic salt
3 tablespoons (45 mL) combined milk
    and water
1 egg white, beaten

►Slice dogfish in 2 x 4-inch (5 x 10 cm) pieces. Beat together first five ingredients of batter and fold in beaten egg white. In a deep skillet heat enough oil to cover fish to 350°F (175°C). Dip fish in batter and drop into hot oil. Do not crowd. Fry about two minutes to golden brown. Remove and drain on paper towel. Serve with French fried potatoes, garnished with lemon slices and Tartar Sauce. Serves six.

■ Washington Seafood Recipes
(adapted)

Piccolo Squalo

3 egg whites
2 tablespoons (30 mL) vegetable oil
3 tablespoons (45 mL) flour
Vegetable oil for cooking
1-1/2 pounds (0.70 kg) dogfish fillets
1/4 teaspoon (1 mL) salt
Dash of pepper
Lemon wedges

►Beat egg whites until frothy, blend in oil and 2 tablespoons (30 mL) of the flour to make batter. In heavy skillet heat 1/4 inch (6 mm) oil to about 375°F (190°C). Dip fillets in batter, coating each generously; then dust in remaining flour. Saute in hot oil until light golden brown, usually not more than two minutes on each side. Season lightly with salt and pepper as fish cooks. Serve with lemon wedges. Serves four.
■ *Russ Mohney*
   The Dogfish Cookbook

Deviled Shark Salad

3 whole eggs, hard cooked
1 teaspoon (5 mL) salt
1/4 teaspoon (1 mL) pepper
1/2 teaspoon (2 mL) prepared mustard
1/4 cup (60 mL) vinegar
2 large dill pickles
2 cups (480 mL) dogfish, cooked and diced
3 cups (720 mL) chopped lettuce
Salad oil and vinegar

►Cut eggs in half and scoop out egg yolks. Mash the yolks; mix in salt, pepper and mustard. Heat the vinegar to boiling and pour over egg yolk mixture. Chop the egg whites and pickles; add with dogfish to the egg yolk mixture. Mix well. Chill and arrange on lettuce; dress with oil and vinegar. Serves six.
■ *Russ Mohney*
   The Dogfish Cookbook

Gefilte Fish

1-1/2 pounds (0.70 kg) cooked, flaked dogfish
1-1/2 pounds (0.70 kg) cod or rockfish fillets
1-1/2 cups (360 mL) chopped onion
1 egg, beaten
3/4 cup (180 mL) water
1 teaspoon (5 mL) salt
1/2 teaspoon (2 mL) pepper
1/4 cup (60 mL) soft bread crumbs
1 sliced onion
2 carrots, sliced
Salt and pepper to taste

►Put dogfish, cod and chopped onion through food chopper, set fine. Place fish mixture in large mixing bowl and slowly mix in egg, water, salt, pepper and bread crumbs. In a large saucepan cover onion and carrot slices with water and bring to a boil; season with salt and pepper. Roll the fish mixture into small balls. Drop the balls into saucepan with vegetables. Lower heat and simmer for about one hour. Serve as a fish stew or remove fish and thicken stock with flour and cream as a sauce. Serve with boiled potatoes or over toast. Serves six to eight.
■ *Russ Mohney*
  The Dogfish Cookbook

EULACHON

"Candlefish, smelt, ooligan, hooligan or eulachon . . . a hooligan by any of several names is still an oily, fat, little fish. But in this case fat is beautiful — or at least tasty," says Sean Reid in *ALASKA*® magazine [May, 1981]. In fact the popularity of the little fish can almost be judged by the number of years *ALASKA*® ballyhoos the spring run. It's a popularity well deserved. Eulachon makes good eating and, as the first fish to run up the rivers after breakup, it is as welcome a sign of spring in the North as crocuses in Cleveland.
Taste: Simply put — excellent.
Preparation Tips: Fresh eulachon (called hooligan or smelt in most recipes) should be eaten really fresh, advises Ann Chandonnet in another article from *ALASKA*® [May, 1979], "as their flesh is soft and does not keep well — even when refrigerated — for more than two days. Keep them well wrapped and clean them as soon as possible although some people prefer to cook and eat them whole, without cleaning," a handy preference to develop if you plan to fry your catch and eat it on the spot.

You can bone fresh eulachon if you want. First cut off head and tail. Then slit the full length of the belly, with the point of your knife cutting in as far as the backbone. Clean out entrails, rinse and pat dry. Then, using the back of a spoon or your thumb, press hard all along the backbone, from inside the cavity. Spine and bones should lift free if you start pulling from the head(less) end. Fins can also be pulled away.

Eulachon can be frozen, but because they're small, Chandonnet says, they should be double-wrapped to keep them from drying out in the freezer — first in plastic wrap and then in freezer paper or heavy foil. Or, freeze them in water.

The little fish makes excellent eating, steamed, deep-fried or pan-fried, smoked or broiled. Light salting firms the flesh. Broiling will eliminate some of the oil.

One of the names for eulachon, "candlefish," is particularly well deserved. The fish is so oily that it was once used in candlemaking. That practice belongs to the past, but eulachon oil is still used in a number of Native specialties, two of which are included here. Directions for rendering eulachon oil also follow. It's a practice most of us will have to take up if we wish to use the precious oil which, at last report, was selling — when available — for $50 per 2-quart (2 L) jar!

Pan-Fried Hooligan

1 cup (240 mL) yellow corn meal, or half corn meal, half flour
1 teaspoon (5 mL) salt
Oil

►Clean fish upon catching. Keep cold and covered. At mealtime, remove heads if desired. Coat fish with corn meal and salt (or mixture of corn meal, flour and salt). Heat a heavy cast-iron frying pan and lightly coat it with oil. Fry hooligan three to five minutes on each side until the flesh is opaque and the skin is browned. Be careful not to overcook hooligan or you will lose some of their delicate taste. Serve hot with Tartar Sauce, Lemon Butter, chili sauce or ketchup.
■ *Ann Chandonnet, Chugiak*
  "Hooligan, Sure Sign of Spring in the North"
  ALASKA® magazine, May 1979

Hooligan Beach Fry

2 pounds (1 kg) or more freshly caught hooligan
1-1/2 cups (360 mL) commercial breading mix or a mixture of flour and corn meal seasoned with salt, pepper and paprika to taste

►Don't clean fish. Dip them in salt water to wash them. Drain well and pat dry. Roll in breading or flour mixture. Fry in hot oil in a large skillet over beach fire until brown on both sides. Eat fried hooligan with your fingers, stripping the flesh from the bones, or gobble up bones and all. Especially good served with French bread spread with garlic butter. This amount serves two to four.
■ Marine Fish Cookbook

Rendering Oil From Eulachon

Eagerly awaited every spring is the mid-May run of eulachon. During a short period of time — rarely as much as two weeks — these fish run up into the Chilkat and Chilkoot rivers. Variously written eulachon, eulichan, ooligan, and hooligan, they are called *saak* (as close to the sound as I can manage) in Tlingit, and are still important in the diet of the Chilkat people.

Present-day methods of preparing eulachon oil are much more efficient, but I found the old method fascinating, as it was described to me by a very old lady long ago. A large pit was dug in the ground near the river. The pit was filled with eulachon, which were allowed to ripen in the warm spring sunshine for about two weeks. Then a large fire was built beside the pit to heat rocks and water. Hot water was poured into the pit and the rocks were rolled in to help keep the water hot; the heat rendered out the oil. As more water was poured into the pit, the oil rose to the top and was skimmed off. After the early traders introduced the use of large iron pots, the people reversed the procedure, adding the ripened fish to boiling water, which greatly increased the amount of oil that could be extracted from a given amount of fish.

The eulachon oil, which is as clear as salad oil when properly made, was used for a variety of things. For instance, when poured over berries in a storage box or other container, it sealed out the air and kept the berries from spoiling. This practice, with modern freezing and canning methods available, is no longer used, although oil may be mixed with berries when they are served. Mrs. Mildred Sparks says that when her mother used eulachon oil for frying "Indian doughnuts," the oil did not penetrate the dough, and the doughnuts did not taste fishy. Most important, the oil was, and still is, put into oil dishes into which such foods as dried fish may be dipped before eating, just as some foods are dipped in drawn butter.

Today's rendering vats are rectangular or square metal affairs which can be moved over a trench in which a fire is built to heat the water. There is usually a steam vent near the top and a large wooden plug near the bottom, which can be removed to drain water and fish residue when the rendering process is finished.

When the water comes to a boil, the fish is shoveled from the ripening pit into tubs, carried to the rendering vat and poured into the boiling water. The fish are carefully stirred so that they will heat as evenly as possible. The results are best if the mixture is kept just below boiling. This can be done by regulating the fire below the vat, drawing wood off it or returning it as needed.

As the oil rises to the top of the vat, it is skimmed off — a skillet makes a good skimmer — and put into temporary containers, such as gallon (3.8 L) jugs. When all the oil has been skimmed, the vat is drained of water and residue and fresh water is used for the next batch. The residue is sometimes saved to be used as fertilizer.

Within a day or two of rendering, the oil must be clarified. The thick, cloudy oil is poured into a kettle in which there is a little water. It is stirred and heated to boiling. Then more water is added to help settle impurities out of the mixture.

It takes about half an hour of stirring and settling before the clarified oil can be ladled out and strained into permanent storage containers. Most people prefer to store it in the freezer, where it will remain in perfect condition. In bygone days, it was kept in the coolest, darkest corner of the house, or even partially underground beneath the house. If the oil is not to be frozen, it should be poured into sterilized glass containers and kept cool.

■ *Elisabeth Hakkinen*

Kleown

4 cups (1 L) flour
1/2 teaspoon (2 mL) salt
1 teaspoon (5 mL) baking powder
Little sugar (optional)
1 cup (240 mL) ooligan grease

►Mix all ingredients with a little water and knead it a lot. Press it into greased pan. Bake in oven at 350 to 400°F (175 to 205°C). Bake until brown and hard.

Diaxsh
Indian ice cream

►Mix some of the second fall of snow with melted or heated ooligan grease. Beat it up with the hands until it fluffs. Add a bit of sugar to your taste. Pour some blueberries over this and you have Tsimpshean ice cream. This could be frozen and saved for the summer.

Elisabeth Hakkinen's story, originally titled "Eulachon Run," is adapted from *ALASKA*® magazine, May 1977. The two recipes are from the *Tsimpshean Indian Island Cookbook*, Metlakatla.

Hooligan Spread

►Remove fins, tails and backbones from cooked hooligan. Mashing the fish with a fork, work in enough mayonnaise to make a spreadable paste. Add seasonings to taste — onion powder or minced onion, lemon juice, salt and pepper. This spread is good served on toasted buns with lettuce and sliced tomatoes on the side.
■ *The Old Homesteader*

Whole Hooligan Sandwich

►Fry lightly salted hooligan in a small amount of hot oil until golden brown. Serve either hot or cold between slices of buttered toast. Spread toast lightly with mayonnaise if desired. Two pounds (1 kg) of smelt will make four to six sandwiches.
■ *The editors, ALASKA® magazine*

Hooligan Cheese Pate

1 cup (240 mL) cooked smelt,
*   boned and mashed*
2 packages (8 oz /or/ 228 g, each) cream cheese,
*   softened*
2 teaspoons (10 mL) horseradish
2 tablespoons (30 mL) grated onion
3 tablespoons (45 mL) lemon juice
2 tablespoons (30 mL) chopped parsley
*   (optional)*
1/2 cup (120 mL) crushed potato chips
*   (optional)*
Bread or assorted party crackers and
*   raw vegetable sticks*

►Cream the cheese. Add the seasonings and mashed smelt. Mix thoroughly. Use as a sandwich spread or shape into a mound on a serving plate, combine parsley and crushed potato chips and cover the mound completely. Serve with crackers and raw vegetable sticks as an appetizer. Makes approximately 3 cups (720 mL) of spread.
■ *The editors, ALASKA® magazine*

Smelt Kabobs

1 pound (0.45 kg) smelt
2 tablespoons (30 mL) French dressing
1/4 teaspoon (1 mL) salt
Dash of pepper
12 strips bacon
4 tomatoes, cut in wedges
Melted butter

►Clean and bone smelt. Marinate in French dressing with salt and pepper. Cook the bacon lightly, only about two minutes; drain on absorbent paper. Cut each strip in half, across. Arrange alternately, on skewers — two small, rolled smelt (which have been cut in half lengthwise), two tomato wedges and two folded pieces of bacon. Brush kabobs with melted butter and place in baking pan. Bake at 400°F (205°C) for 10 to 12 minutes. Serves four.
■ Marine Fish Cookbook

Deep-Fried Hooligan
With optional coatings

►Clean fish, leaving tails on to be used as handles (or, don't clean them but dip them in salt water to wash them, per instructions in Hooligan Beach Fry). Wash and pat dry with toweling. Now they're ready to fry in deep fat, heated to 350°F (175°C), three to four minutes, or until browned. Or, dip the towel-dried fish into one of the coatings suggested below and then deep-fry.

Double-Dip Coating
1-1/2 teaspoons (7 mL) salt
Dash pepper
1 cup (240 mL) pancake mix
1/4 cup (60 mL) yellow corn meal
1/2 teaspoon (2 mL) salt
1-1/4 cups (300 mL) milk
1/2 cup (120 mL) flour

►Sprinkle fish lightly with salt and pepper. Combine pancake mix, corn meal and salt. Add milk and stir only until blended. Roll fish in flour, then dip in batter. Deep-fry as directed above.

Variation: Add 2 or 3 tablespoons (30 to 45 mL) sesame seeds to the batter before dipping fish into it. Delicious.

Crispy Coating
1-1/2 cups (360 mL) flour
1/2 cup (120 mL) grated Parmesan cheese
1 can (15 oz/or/425 g) tomato sauce
Cocktail sauce and lemon wedges

►Sprinkle fish with salt and pepper. Combine flour and cheese. Dip fish into tomato sauce and roll in flour mixture. Deep-fry as directed.

Beer Batter
1-1/3 cups (320 mL) flour
1 teaspoon (5 mL) salt
1/4 teaspoon (1 mL) pepper
1 tablespoon (15 mL) salad oil
2 eggs, beaten
3/4 cup (180 mL) flat beer
2 egg whites, beaten (optional)

►Mix first five ingredients well. Add beer while stirring constantly. Allow batter to rest, covered and refrigerated, for 3 to 12 hours. Just before using, you may fold in two stiffly beaten egg whites, if desired. Deep-fry as directed.
■ *The editors, ALASKA® magazine*

Marinated Smelt
An intriguing twist on deep-fried fish

8 smelt
1/2 onion
1 whole red pepper
Cornstarch
Oil
9 tablespoons (135 mL) vinegar
3 tablespoons (45 mL) sugar

3 tablespoons (45 mL) soy sauce
Salt

►Clean and wash smelt. Combine vinegar, sugar and soy sauce and set aside. Dry smelt well and spread cornstarch over them thinly. Fry in deep fat, heated to 350°F (175°C), for seven to nine minutes, until crisp and golden. Drain on paper towels and soak in vinegar mixture. Slice onion thinly and sprinkle salt over the slices. Set aside until moist; then wash and drain thoroughly. Remove seeds from red pepper and cut into round thin slices. Spread onion and red pepper slices over smelt and cover with vinegar mixture. Marinate at least one hour before serving.
■ *Yukari Hosokawa*
   What's Cookin' in Wrangell

THE SMALLER FLATFISHES

The majority of recipes in this section were created for sole, a delicately flavored fish most people know and like. Its mild taste makes it a favorite of cooks who are fond of using herbs and sauces. What many west coast cooks might be surprised to learn is that the "fresh-caught sole" at the local market is likely to be a variety of flounder since no true soles are taken from the Pacific waters of the United States. English sole and Dover sole are perhaps the best known market names for Pacific flounder. Other popular flatfishes are starry flounder, rock sole, sand sole, petrale and turbot (arrowtooth flounder).

Halibut, perhaps the favorite of flatfishes in Alaska, deserves a recipe section all its own, but some recipes are interchangeable, within the limits set by size and texture of the fish.

Taste: Characteristically, the flatfishes have mild-flavored white-fleshed meat, though opinions differ about which possess superior eating qualities. Most people agree that sole — or the Pacific flounder marketed as sole — is top of the line. And the smaller fish are generally preferred because the larger ones have coarser flesh.

Preparation Tips: Filleted, whole-dressed or steaked, flatfishes are cooked in any way that takes account of their rather delicate meat. That is— bake, broil, poach or sauce. Serve the fish in the cooking vessel or bake or broil it on foil to make the transfer to a platter easier. Flatfishes are good candidates for stuffing and baking. Instructions for opening up a "pocket" for stuffing are on page 9. Appropriate sauces and stuffings are listed on page 14. Because flatfish are generally mild-flavored, stuffings and sauces that include shellfish make delicious complements.

Flounder Souffle
2 cups (480 mL) poached and flaked fish —
   flounder, petrale or turbot
3 tablespoons (45 mL) butter
3 tablespoons (45 mL) flour
1/2 teaspoon (2 mL) crumbled rosemary leaves
1/2 teaspoon (2 mL) salt
Dash cayenne
1 cup (240 mL) fish stock or stock and
   milk combined
3 egg yolks, beaten
3 egg whites, beaten

►Melt butter, blend in flour and seasonings. Add liquid gradually and cook sauce until thick and smooth, stirring constantly. Stir a little of the hot sauce into beaten egg yolks and then add this mixture to the remaining sauce, again, stirring constantly. Add fish. Fold mixture into beaten egg whites. Pour into a well-greased 1-1/2 quart (1.47 L) souffle dish or casserole. Bake in a moderate oven, 350°F (175°C), 45 minutes or until souffle is firm in the center. Serves six.

■ *The editors, ALASKA® magazine*

Sauced Petrale

*2 pounds (1 kg) petrale or English or
   Dover sole fillets*
3 tablespoons (45 mL) butter
2 tablespoons (30 mL) lemon juice
1-1/8 teaspoons (5.5 mL) salt
2 slices bacon
1/4 cup (60 mL) chopped green onions
1 clove garlic, finely minced
*1/2 cup (120 mL) mushroom slices,
   fresh or canned*
1 teaspoon (5 mL) flour
1/4 cup (60 mL) ketchup
1/4 cup (60 mL) dry white wine
1/4 cup (60 mL) water

►Arrange fillets in a single layer in a buttered baking dish. Melt 2 tablespoons (30 mL) of the butter and drizzle it and the lemon juice over the fish. Sprinkle with 1 teaspoon (5 mL) of the salt. Broil about 4 inches (10 cm) from heat source until fish flakes easily when tested with a fork. While fish broils, fry bacon until crisp. Drain on absorbent paper and crumble. Add the remaining tablespoon (15 mL) of butter to the bacon drippings and saute onions and garlic until soft. Stir in mushrooms and flour. Add ketchup, wine, water and remaining 1/8 teaspoon (0.5 mL) salt. Cook, stirring constantly, until sauce is slightly thickened. Spoon over fish. Sprinkle with crumbled bacon. Makes six servings.

■ *The editors, ALASKA® magazine*

Variation: Omit the bacon. Increase the amount of butter to saute green onions and garlic and flavor with prepared bacon bits or a pinch or two of a favorite herb, such as tarragon or rosemary.

Fillet of Sole, Anna

8 fillets of sole
Salt, paprika
1/4 cup (60 mL) melted butter
3/4 cup (180 mL) white wine
1 tablespoon (15 mL) lemon juice
1/2 sliced onion
3 tablespoons (45 mL) butter
3 tablespoons (45 mL) flour
1/2 pint (240 mL) cream
*1 large can (8 oz /or/ 228 g) mushrooms,
   drained, reserving liquid*

1 teaspoon (5 mL) Worcestershire
1 teaspoon (5 mL) mushroom ketchup
1 pound (456 g) shrimps
1 pint (480 mL) oysters

►Place fish in buttered baking pan, sprinkle with salt and paprika. Add melted butter, wine, lemon juice and onion. Bake in a hot oven 20 minutes, basting frequently. Remove onion. Make a sauce of the remaining butter, flour, cream and liquid drained from mushrooms. Season with Worcestershire and mushroom ketchup and add cooked shrimps, oysters and mushrooms. Pour the sauce on the fish. Bake five minutes longer.

■ *Evangeline Atwood*
  Alaska's Cooking, Anchorage

Fillets of Sole Florentine

6 fillets of sole, about 2-1/2 pounds (1.2 kg)
Lemon juice
2 tablespoons (30 mL) finely chopped shallot
2 teaspoons (10 mL) dried tarragon leaves
1 teaspoon (5 mL) salt
1 cup (240 mL) dry white wine
*2 packages (10 oz /or/ 285 g, each) frozen
   chopped spinach*

Hollandaise Sauce
3 egg yolks
*1/2 cup or 1 stick (114 g) lightly salted
   butter, frozen*
1 tablespoon (15 mL) water
2 tablespoons (30 mL) lemon juice
1/8 teaspoon (0.5) mL) salt

Wine Sauce
3 tablespoons (45 mL) butter or margarine
3 tablespoons (45 mL) flour
1/2 teaspoon (2 mL) salt
1/8 teaspoon (0.5 mL) pepper
*1 cup (240 mL) fish-wine stock (from
   preparation of fillets)*
1/3 cup (80 mL) light cream
1/2 cup (120 mL) heavy cream

►First make the Hollandaise Sauce by combining egg yolks, frozen butter, water, lemon juice and salt in a heavy saucepan. With a wire whisk, stir over medium heat until butter melts and sauce is smooth. Remove from heat before it becomes too thick. Cool completely.

Rinse fillets under cool water; pat dry with paper towels. Brush both sides with lemon juice. Fold into thirds, dark side inside. Arrange in a single layer in a large skillet. Sprinkle with shallot, tarragon and salt. Pour on the wine. Bring just to a boil. Then reduce heat, cover and simmer 5 to 10 minutes or until fish flakes when tested with a fork; do not overcook.

Meanwhile, cook spinach as label directs. Turn into sieve and drain well, pressing spinach to remove all liquid. Return to saucepan, cover and keep hot.

With a slotted spatula, lift fillets to heated platter; keep warm. Strain liquid from skillet into a 2-cup (480 mL) measure. You should have 1 cup (240 mL) liquid; boil it down if necessary.

Start the Wine Sauce by melting butter in a medium-sized saucepan. Remove from heat and stir in flour, salt and pepper. Then gradually stir in the cup of reserved fish-wine stock and the light cream. Return to medium heat, bring to boil, stirring constantly until mixture thickens. Remove from heat.

Stir 1/3 cup (80 mL) Wine Sauce into thoroughly drained spinach; toss. Spread the mixture evenly into a 12 x 8 x 2-inch (30 x 20 x 5 cm) broiler-proof dish. Arrange fillets in a single layer on spinach. Spoon remaining Wine Sauce over them. Beat heavy cream until stiff. Fold it into Hollandaise Sauce and spoon the mixture over all. Place under broiler two to three minutes or until top turns a golden brown. Serve from dish. Serves six.
■ Seafood Treasures, *Seattle*

Stuffed Fillets of Sole

8 to 10 fillets of sole
A small can (4 oz /or/ 114 g) of mushrooms
1/4 cup (60 mL) chopped onion
1/4 cup (60 mL) margarine
1-1/4 cups (300 mL) flaked crab
2/3 cup (160 mL) coarse cracker crumbs
2 tablespoons (30 mL) snipped parsley
1/2 teaspoon (2 mL) salt

Dash of pepper
3 tablespoons (45 mL) additional margarine
3 tablespoons (45 mL) flour
1/4 teaspoon (1 mL) additional salt
Liquid from mushrooms plus milk to equal
*   1-1/2 (360 mL) cups*
1/3 cup (80 mL) dry white wine
1 cup (240 mL) shredded Swiss cheese
Paprika

►Drain mushrooms, reserving liquid. Saute onion in margarine until onion is soft, add drained mushrooms and heat through. Remove from heat and fold in crab, cracker crumbs, parsley, salt and a dash of pepper. Spread mixture evenly over sole fillets and roll them up, tying them if necessary. Place rolled fillets close together in a well-greased baking dish. Melt additional margarine in a heavy frying pan and blend in flour and additional salt. Stir in mushroom-milk mixture and add white wine. Cook sauce until thickened and pour over fish. Bake at 400°F (205°C) for 25 minutes. Then sprinkle on cheese, add a dash of paprika, and continue baking until cheese melts.
■ *Sharon Snelling*
   The Anchorage Times

Special vinegars — rice, malt, wine or those flavored with garlic, onion or tarragon — make good condiments for fried fish. Serve them at the table alongside the usual ketchup, tartar sauce and lemon wedges.

GRAYLING

Arctic grayling is the major game fish in many parts of central and northern Alaska and is reasonably important as a subsistence fish, too. Sports fishermen like it because it is an active fish that will strike at a wide variety of lures. It is also tasty. Most grayling are 10 to 15 inches (25 to 37.5 cm) long; a 20-incher (50 cm) is a very large fish.
Taste: "First-rate if cooked as soon as caught," says *The Fisherman Returns,* a stipulation the following recipes will help you meet.

Experienced grayling fishermen strongly recommend fishing grayling with a "fly rod in one hand and a frying pan in the other" and avoid holding the fish overnight or expecting to preserve its delicate flavor by freezing. Fresh grayling will intrigue one by an almost intangible odor of thyme, and in fact, its Latin monicker is *Thymallus arcticus.* It should also be mentioned that the gunmetal irridescent blues and bronze or purple and red tones of the grayling's "northern lights" sides are as fleeting as the bright delicate flavor of the flesh, disappearing shortly after death.
Preparation Tips: Pan-fry, broil over coals or gently poach.

Grayling Crisp
A basic pan-fry recipe for almost any stream or lake fish

Pan-size grayling
1 egg, beaten slightly
Yellow corn meal
Vegetable cooking oil
Salt and pepper
Pinch of thyme

►Dress grayling and wipe dry. Dip in beaten egg and roll in corn meal. Put vegetable oil in heavy skillet and heat to moderately hot (not smoking). Place grayling in skillet and sprinkle with salt and pepper and a pinch of thyme. Fry until brown and crisp on each side, turning once, carefully.
■ *The Old Homesteader*

Portage Pass Fish Dish
Another trail special

10 small grayling
2 Sierra cups of Parry's wallflower root*
Small bag of willow leaves*
Corn meal
Seasonings such as parsley, dill,
    salt, pepper, to taste
Oil

►Simmer grayling in water or broth until tender. Cool the fish and remove all bones. While grayling are cooling, cut and boil wallflower root. Saute willow leaves in oil, then add fish, wallflower root, corn meal and seasonings and fry in oil. This is a truly superb meal; the wallflower root adds sweet flavor. Serves two or three.
■ *Jim Greenough and Eileen Helmstetter*
   "The Bush Gourmet"
   ALASKA® *magazine, July 1977*

Both Parry's wallflower root and edible willow leaves are described in the wild vegetable chapter. A "Sierra cup" is a backpacker's drinking cup, holding about 6 fluid ounces (180 mL).

HALIBUT

A premium commercial fish and the largest fish sought by sport fishermen in Alaska, halibut ranks as a favorite seafood for any table. The giant flatfish favors deep, cold water and swims the depths from California to the Norton Sound. sometimes plunging even farther north. Halibut achieves its great size rather slowly, taking about five years to grow to 20 inches (50 cm) in length. Mature females may weigh four or five times as much as males and can reach 8 feet (2.4 m) in length and weigh around 500 pounds (227 kg) after about 15 years of growth.
Taste: Highly prized, firm, flavorful white meat.
Preparation Tips: Any basic method for cooking fish is appropriate to halibut except that few cooks would attempt to bake a whole one! Roasts, however, are delicious, as are steaks, fillets and chunks — baked, steamed, poached, batter-fried, broiled or sauced.

How To Fillet A 200-Pound Halibut

In the fish trade, filleting the "whales," as big halibut are called, is referred to as "fletching." Now, anybody who has ever fletched a big halibut, working on a conventional or larger table area, knows that rolling back and lifting increasing weights of boned out fish can be a chore.

The smart way to do the big ones is to tail-hang them against a building or from a tree or cross-piece, backing up the fish with a sheet of plywood. If you don't have a handy wall backup, the plywood sheet will prevent the halibut from spinning on you, and if you do have a wall, it will make later cleanup easier.

So your fish is now hung by the tail, presumably

the tail around eye level with you or a bit higher. It doesn't matter which side of the fish is to you.

1. First cut to the backbone vertically down the lateral line from tail to throat.
2. Second, begin a cut at the tail from outside, the knife lying flat on the dorsal and backbone fins to the backbone.
3. With a few inches of fillet started, throw a cinch loop around the top end of the fillet and tie it somewhere handily above so when the entire fillet is sliced off, it will remain suspended and not end up in the dirt. That done, keep peeling down the fillet (fletch), cutting flat along the ribs to the backbone.
4. Repeat on the opposite side of the lateral line, then spin the fish around and repeat the procedure . . . the centerline cut and the separation of two giant fletches of boneless halibut. The four resultant big chunks of fish can be readily reduced to handier portions for wrapping and freezing.

Halibut Cebiche
Also known as seviche *and* ceviche, *a raw fish appetizer popular south of the (lower 48) border*

Raw halibut, cut in small squares
Onions, cut in small squares
Green peppers, cut in small squares
Salt and pepper to taste
Lemon juice

►Combine the first four ingredients in quantities to suit the occasion. Cover completely with lemon juice. Refrigerate overnight and serve as an appetizer before meals, or with meals as a salad on lettuce leaves.
■ *Shirley Gunnerson, Anchorage*
  Courtesy, Hazel Vandeburgh

Pickled Halibut
A tidbit for a party or first course at dinner

2 pounds (1 kg) halibut steak
Salt, as directed
1/4 cup (60 mL) mixed pickling spice
2 medium onions, sliced
4 bay leaves
1 cup (240 mL) vegetable oil
1/2 cup (120 mL) red wine vinegar
2 tablespoons (30 mL) capers
2 teaspoons (10 mL) celery seed
Dash of hot pepper sauce

►Thaw halibut if frozen. Cut in 1-inch (2.5 cm) cubes and put in saucepan. Add 1-1/2 tablespoons (23 mL) salt, pickling spice and water to cover. Bring to a boil, drain and cool. In a large bowl alter-

nate halibut chunks with onion slices and bay leaves. Mix 1 teaspoon (5 mL) salt and remaining ingredients and pour over the top. Cover and refrigerate overnight. Serve as a buffet dish or first course. Serves 8 to 10.
■ *Tsimpshean Indian Island Cookbook*
  Metlakatla

Halibut Dip Supreme

2 cups (480 mL) cooked, flaked halibut
2 tablespoons (30 mL) chopped dill pickle
2 teaspoons (10 mL) lemon juice
1/2 cup (120 mL) mayonnaise
1/2 cup (120 mL) sour cream
1/2 teaspoon (2 mL) Worcestershire
1 cup (240 mL) peas, drained*
Salt to taste

►Mix all ingredients and chill at least eight hours before serving as an appetizer with chips, crackers and/or vegetable sticks.
■ *Joan Budai, FV* Supreme
  Seafood Secrets, *Sitka*

For a nice nutlike consistency and flavor, use frozen peas. Don't thaw or cook them. Just put them in a wire basket and toss them a bit to separate them and drain off ice crystals and extra moisture.

Halibut Spread

2 cups (480 mL) poached flaked genuine
  North Pacific halibut
2 tablespoons (30 mL) lemon juice
2 teaspoons (10 mL) minced onion
1/2 cup (120 mL) finely chopped celery
3 tablespoons (45 mL) pickle relish
1 teaspoon (5 mL) Worcestershire
1/2 teaspoon (2 mL) salt
4 dashes Tabasco
1 teaspoon (5 mL) prepared mustard
Mayonnaise or salad dressing to moisten

►Combine above ingredients. Use as a sandwich filling or as a spread for crackers or canapes. Makes 3 cups (720 mL) sandwich spread.
■ Seafood Treasures, *Seattle*

Halibut Popcorn

1 halibut fillet
1 large salt shaker

►Skin the fillet. Using a long, thin-bladed knife, slice the halibut very thin, so thin that the knife blade is visible through the fish. Salt each strip heavily and hang to cure. The dried strips will taste quite a bit like popcorn.
■ *Ginny Shaffer*
  Seafood Secrets, *Sitka*

Halibut Chowder

1 halibut head or small pieces of halibut
4 slices bacon, cut into small pieces
1 large onion, diced
2 cloves garlic, diced
4 quarts (3.8 L) water
Potatoes, cut in chunks
Salt and pepper to taste
1/4 teaspoon (1 mL) cayenne pepper
1/4 teaspoon (1 mL) chili pepper
2 tablespoons (30 mL) flour
1 cup (240 mL) tomato sauce

►Clean head or halibut pieces. If using head, cut into desired pieces. Soak in cold water until ready to use. In a large pot, about 6-quart (5.75 L) size, fry bacon and onions together; add garlic. Now, add about 4 quarts (3.8 L) water to the bacon, onion and garlic. Add potatoes, seasonings and halibut. Cook until potatoes are done. Add a little water to the flour to make a paste; add to the soup to thicken same. Add tomato sauce.

■ Tsimpshean Indian Island Cookbook
Metlakatla

Barbecued Halibut

4 pounds (1.8 kg) thick-cut halibut fillet
1/2 cup (120 mL) soy sauce
1 cup (240 mL) dry white wine
2 tablespoons (30 mL) lemon juice
2 cloves garlic, minced or mashed
1 teaspoon (5 mL) ground ginger
1/2 cup (120 mL) salad oil
2 tablespoons (30 mL) fresh rosemary
6 tablespoons (90 mL) fresh chopped parsley
1 pound (456 g) fresh mushrooms, sliced
1/3 cup (80 mL) butter

►Cut thick — 1 inch (2.5 cm) or more — fillets into 1 x 2-inch (2.5 x 5 cm) pieces. Combine soy sauce, wine, lemon juice, garlic, ginger and oil and pour over fish. Marinate four hours.

Pour off marinade and reserve. Sprinkle fish pieces generously with rosemary and parsley. Skewer carefully or slip inside a hinged wire broiler and place on the grill over low coals. Cook until fish flakes when tested with a fork, about 10 minutes depending on thickness. Baste occasionally with part of the marinade.

In the meantime, saute mushrooms in butter, add the remaining marinade, heat through, and pour over broiled fish at serving time. Serves eight.

■ Kodiak Daily Mirror

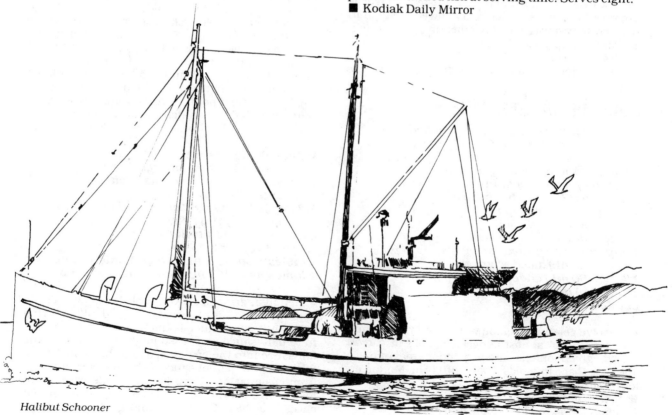

Halibut Schooner

Fish Head Stew

Definitely a full meal served with bread, cheese and maybe a salad

1 medium halibut head
1 quart (1 L) clams in shell
4 medium onions, sliced
2 tablespoons (30 mL) oil or butter
2 teaspoons (10 mL) salt
1/2 teaspoon (2 mL) pepper
1/2 teaspoon (2 mL) sugar
1/8 teaspoon (0.5 mL) thyme
1/4 teaspoon (1 mL) Tabasco
1-1/2 quarts (1.5 L) milk

►Simmer head for 20 minutes in barely enough water to cover. Remove head from broth. Cool and separate meat from the bones. Throw away eyes, skin, bones, etc. Strain broth and reserve. Place whole clams in pan without water. Heat only until clams have fully opened. Reserving liquor, remove clams and snip off necks. Cut up remainder and add to fish. Saute onion in oil or butter about 10 minutes. Add broth from fish and clams, salt, pepper, sugar, thyme and Tabasco. Heat just to boil. Then add fish, clams and milk. Heat but do not boil. When ready to serve, place a pat of butter in each warm soup bowl and ladle in stew. Flavor is improved if stew is cooled and allowed to stand in refrigerator overnight before reheating and serving. Serves six amply. Can be frozen.
■ *Mrs. Robert Ellis*
Sons of Norway Cook Book, *Ketchikan*

Jellied Halibut Salad

1 pound (456 g) halibut fillet, poached or
    steamed, or 2 cups (480 mL) flaked,
    cooked halibut
2 packages (3 oz /or/ 85 g, each)
    lemon-flavored gelatin
1-1/2 cups (360 mL) boiling water
1/4 cup (60 mL) vinegar
1/2 teaspoon (2 mL) salt
4 green onions, chopped fine
1 cup (240 mL) grated carrot
1 cup (240 mL) diced celery
1/4 cup (60 mL) chopped green pepper
1 cup (240 mL) mayonnaise
Lettuce

►Dissolve gelatin in boiling water. Add vinegar and salt. Chill until almost congealed. Fold in carrot, celery, green onions, green pepper, mayonnaise and fish. Place in molds. Chill until firm. Mound on lettuce leaf. Serves six.
■ *Nettie Hansen*
Sons of Norway Cook Book, *Ketchikan*

Halibut Tomato Soup

1 pound (456 g) halibut or other white fish
1/4 cup (60 mL) bacon, chopped
1/2 cup (120 mL) onion, chopped
1/2 cup (120 mL) celery, chopped
2 cups (480 mL) water
1-1/2 teaspoons (7 mL) salt
Dash of pepper
1/3 cup (80 mL) uncooked rice
2 cups (480 mL) tomato juice

►Fry bacon until crisp; add onion and celery and cook until tender. Add water, seasonings and rice; simmer 10 minutes. Add fish, which has been cut into 1-inch (2.5 cm) cubes, and simmer until rice and fish are tender. Add tomato juice; heat thoroughly and serve immediately. Serves six.
■ Seafood Recipes For Alaskans

Baked Halibut with Velvet Shrimp Sauce — New Potatoes with Wild Chives

►Choose a solid chunk of halibut — 2 pounds (1 kg) or more. Sprinkle with salt and pepper and a little lemon juice. Place in the middle of a large piece of foil in a shallow pan. Slice onions in a thin layer over the top of the fish. Fold over the foil to enclose the fish completely. Bake at 375°F (190°C) for 25 minutes. Fold back the foil so that halibut can be browned and bake 15 minutes longer, or until fish flakes easily when tested with a fork. Place fish on a small platter and pour Velvet Shrimp Sauce over it. Garnish with sliced stuffed olives and lemon twists. Serve with New Potatoes with Wild Chives.

Velvet Shrimp Sauce
4 tablespoons (60 mL) margarine
2 tablespoons (30 mL) cornstarch
1-1/2 cups (360 mL) milk
1/2 cup (120 mL) light cream or half-and-half
1 egg yolk, slightly beaten
4 to 8 ounces (114 to 228 g) tomato sauce
Salt and pepper to taste
4 tablespoons (60 mL) grated Monterey Jack
4 tablespoons (60 mL) tiny Alaska shrimp

►Melt margarine in top of double boiler over slowly boiling water. Stir in cornstarch. Add milk, stirring constantly until sauce is thick. Add cream and stir in tomato sauce and seasonings. Stir a little of the hot sauce into the beaten egg and then stir the egg mixture into the hot sauce. (This will keep the egg from coagulating.) Keep hot in double boiler until just before serving time. Then stir in the grated cheese so that it will melt and gently stir in the shrimp. This sauce is good with almost any seafood dish.

New Potatoes with Wild Chives
►Scrape or peel small new potatoes and boil slowly until done. In the meantime snip a handful of wild chive foliage into small bits. Melt sufficient butter or margarine to douse the potatoes well. Squeeze a few drops of lemon juice into the melting butter. Drain potatoes and pour the butter over them. Sprinkle with a generous amount of chives.
■ *The Old Homesteader*

Simple Halibut Pot Roast

A 3-pound (1.4 kg) halibut roast
1 cup (240 mL) flour
1/2 cup (120 mL) fat or oil
6 carrots
6 medium onions
6 medium potatoes
2 cups (480 mL) chopped celery
2 cloves garlic, finely chopped
2 teaspoons (10 mL) salt
1/2 teaspoon (2 mL) pepper
2 cups (0.47 L) water

►Remove skin and bones from roast. Roll in flour and brown in fat on all sides in a large, heavy frying pan or Dutch oven. Place vegetables around fish and season with salt and pepper. Add water, cover and bake in a moderate oven, 350°F (175°C), until fish is done. Remove fish and vegetables to hot platter. Thicken liquid in pan and serve over fish and vegetables. Serves six.

Sea Salad Delight

1 pound (456 g) halibut fillet, poached or
*   steamed, or 2 cups (480 mL) flaked,*
*   cooked halibut*
2 packages (3 oz /or/ 85 g, each)
*   lemon-flavored gelatin*
3 cups (720 L) hot water
1 cup (240 mL) pineapple juice
2 tablespoons (30 mL) lemon juice
1 cup (240 mL) diced pineapple
1/2 cup (120 mL) seedless white grapes
1 cup (240 mL) diced apples
Salad greens

►Dissolve gelatin in hot water and add the juices. Chill slightly, then fold in the fruit and fish and pour into a well-oiled mold. Chill until firm and unmold onto a bed of salad greens. Serve with a dab of mayonnaise or sour cream.
■ *Phyllis Moreland, FV See-Am*
    Seafood Secrets, Sitka

Halibut Caddy Ganty
This famous Alaskan recipe originated with Mrs. Prosper S. [Clara Belle] Ganty. "Caddy," who died in 1980, was a longtime resident of Skagway, Sitka, Hoonah and Pelican and, with her husband, operated mercantile establishments, crab and salmon canneries and cold storage companies. One of them, the Pelican Cold Storage Company, seems to have "given birth" to this recipe that is now regarded as part of the family heritage in many homes in Alaska.

The version here comes from Lena Andree of Dillingham, via Audrey Rearden, Homer. Audrey also says that frozen, thawed fillets can be used in the dish with success. "It also holds well if dinner cannot be served at once and is extra good if there's any left over for next day's lunch."

►The halibut must be very fresh. Take 2 pounds (1 kg) filleted halibut and cut the fillets into a bowl, lightly salting each layer until the fish is all in. Pour into the bowl enough dry white wine to just cover the fish, put a piece of waxed paper over the top of the bowl and set it in a cool place for two hours.

Then drain the chunks of fish and pat them dry as possible with paper towels or a clean cloth. Roll in dry bread crumbs (from homemade bread if possible; sourdough French also can be used as it contributes to the flavor of the completed dish).

Place the crumbed fish in a single layer in a lightly buttered baking dish which can be brought to the table. Cover thickly with a sauce of:

1-1/2 cups (360 mL) sour cream
3/4 cup (180 mL) real mayonnaise
3/4 cup (180 mL) finely chopped onion

►Sprinkle the top with paprika and bake at 500°F (260°C) for 15 to 20 minutes or until light brown and bubbly. Serve at once.

Halibut Fingers
Oven fried

Halibut
Garlic-flavored oil
Finely-grated cheese
Fine bread or cracker crumbs
Paprika (optional)

►Cut halibut into fingers — 2 x 2 x 4 inches (5 x 5 x 10 cm). Dip in garlic-flavored oil, then in finely-grated cheese, and then in fine crumbs. Arrange on a foil-lined cookie sheet. Sprinkle liberally with paprika for added color, if desired. Bake at 500°F (260°C) for 10 minutes.

Stuffed Halibut Fillets

Large thin halibut fillets
Dry bread crumbs
Lemon juice
Salt and pepper
Dash of cayenne pepper
Curry powder
Dill weed
Thyme
Minced dried wild chives
Melted butter

►Mix all stuffing ingredients to your taste, quantities depending on the number of fillets to be stuffed. Use enough melted butter to make the stuffing of spreading consistency. Spread stuffing on fillets and roll up; skewer with a toothpick. Arrange a layer of soda crackers in baking dish. Brush rolled fillets with more melted butter and place on crackers. Crackers will keep the fish from sticking to the dish and are to be discarded. Bake fillets at 350°F (175°C) until fish flakes when tested with a fork.
■ *The Old Homesteader*

Fried Halibut (a la Lille Finne Pete)

►Take several thin pieces of filleted halibut and dip in a sauce consisting of one part Worcestershire and two parts lemon juice. Roll in flour; fry in bacon fat until brown. Or use your favorite shortening. Salt and pepper each side. Dot with butter and simmer in covered pan until fish flakes. Red snapper can be substituted.
■ *Ruth Sandvik*
   PTA Cook Book, *Petersburg*

Halibut a la Norway

Halibut, sliced 3/4 inch (1.9 cm) thick
5 tablespoons (75 mL) flour
1 tablespoon (15 mL) salt
1/2 teaspoon (2 mL) pepper
Butter
1 tablespoon (15 mL) minced onion
Boiling water

►Mix flour, salt and pepper. Heat skillet very hot; put in a generous lump of butter. Dredge the halibut in flour mixture and brown on both sides in hot butter. Sprinkle 1 teaspoon (5 mL) of flour mixture over fish and let brown; add minced onion and 3/4 cup (180 mL) or more boiling water. Simmer a few minutes. Be sure there is a little gravy, after cooking, to put around the fish on the platter.
■ *Agnes Espeseth*
   PTA Cook Book, *Petersburg*

Halibut Steaks Provencale

8 halibut steaks, about 10 ounces (280 g) each
2 tablespoons (30 mL) butter
1 cup (240 mL) sliced onion
4 medium tomatoes, chopped
1 tablespoon (15 mL) minced parsley
1 clove garlic, minced
1 teaspoon (5 mL) tarragon leaves
Salt and pepper to taste
1/2 cup (120 mL) Chablis

►Saute steaks in butter, two or three minutes per side. Add onions and cook another two minutes. Add tomatoes, parsley, garlic, seasoning and wine. Cover and simmer 7 to 10 minutes or more, depending on thickness of steaks. Remove steaks and keep warm. Turn up heat and reduce the liquids in the pan to sauce consistency, stirring frequently. Serve steaks with a large spoonful of the sauced vegetables on each one.
■ The Northern Traveler

Baked Halibut Cheeks

1 pound (456 g) halibut cheeks
2 tomatoes, peeled, seeded and
   coarsely chopped*
1/2 green pepper, chopped
3 green onions, sliced thin
1/4 pound (114 g) mushrooms, quartered
2 to 3 tablespoons (30 to 45 mL) butter
1 can (8 oz /or/ 228 g) tomato sauce*
1/2 cup (120 mL) bread crumbs
1 tablespoon (15 mL) parsley, finely chopped,
   or parsley flakes

►Saute vegetables in butter until soft. Add tomato sauce and heat through. Put half of the hot sauce in the bottom of a baking dish. Place halibut cheeks in a single layer over it and pour remaining sauce on top. Mix bread crumbs and parsley together and sprinkle over sauce. Bake about 20 minutes at 425°F (220°C). Yield: Two or three servings.
*Canned tomatoes may be substituted. Use 1-1/2 cups (360 mL), chopped, with their juice; and, instead of tomato sauce, use half of a small can (6 oz /or/ 170 g size) of tomato paste.
■ *The editors, ALASKA® magazine*

Sweet and Sour Halibut
Chunks of fried fish and other tidbits in sauce

2 pounds (1 kg) halibut, cut into 2-inch
   (5 cm) squares
1/3 cup (80 mL) flour
Salad oil
1 clove minced garlic

1 onion, cut into 1-inch (2.5 cm) squares
Mushrooms, sliced
Celery and green pepper, cut in
    bite-sized chunks
1 or 2 large tomatoes, cut in wedges
Sweet and Sour Sauce

►First, prepare Sweet and Sour Sauce according to directions below. Then, roll fish pieces in flour. Shake off excess. Heat 1/4 inch (0.6 cm) salad oil in skillet over medium-high heat. Add fish pieces and fry until golden on all sides. Drain and keep warm.

In a saucepan, heat 2 to 3 tablespoons (30 to 45 mL) oil over high heat; add garlic, onion, celery, green pepper, and mushrooms, and cook, stirring, for about two minutes. Add tomato pieces and prepared Sweet and Sour Sauce. Heat to boiling, stirring frequently, about two minutes. Add fish just before serving. Spoon over hot rice. Makes four to six servings.

Sweet and Sour Sauce
1/4 cup (60 mL) soy sauce
1/4 cup (60 mL) ketchup
1/2 cup (120 mL) vinegar
1 cup (240 mL) chicken broth
2 tablespoons (30 mL) cornstarch
1/2 cup (120 mL) sugar

►Mix the first four ingredients in a small saucepan over medium heat. Bring just to boil. Blend cornstarch with sugar well and then add into sauce, stirring constantly until thickened and translucent.
■ Nita Prince Rearden, Bethel

Halibut Delmonico

6 halibut fillets
1 onion, sliced
1 pint (0.47 L) milk
2 tablespoons (30 mL) butter or margarine
2 tablespoons (30 mL) flour
2 tablespoons (30 mL) sherry
1 cup (240 mL) fresh, seedless white grapes
Grated cheese
Bread crumbs
Additional butter or margarine

►Place the fish fillets in a large kettle with the sliced onion and just enough milk to cover — about 1 pint (0.47 L). Simmer about eight minutes until fish is tender but not broken. Grease a large, flat casserole and place the cooked fish in it, reserving the milk.

In a small saucepan, over medium heat, mix butter and flour until bubbly and well blended. Gradually add the milk in which the fish was cooked to make a cream sauce. Add sherry and seedless grapes, and pour over fish. Sprinkle

generously with grated cheese and bread crumbs and dot with butter. Bake in a moderate oven, 350°F (175°C), until well heated and crumbs are browned. Serves six. Grayling, black cod and trout are also good fixed this way.
■ Dr. Ernest Gruening
   PTA Cook Book, Petersburg

Halibut Supreme
A casserole that will serve many . . . or a few, with several extra meals for the freezer

1-1/2 to 2 pounds (0.70 to 1 kg) boneless
    halibut chunks
1 large can (29 oz /or/ 826 g) whole tomatoes
    with juice
1 can (8 oz /or/ 228 g) tomato sauce
About 1 pint (0.47 L) milk
1 can (10 oz /or/ 280 g) mushroom soup, diluted
    with 1 can of water
1 can (4 oz /or/ 114 g) mushroom pieces
    and stems
1 can (4½ oz /or/ 126 g) chopped black olives
A handful of dry onion flakes
A handful of parsley flakes
1 can (4½ oz /or/ 126 g) tiny shrimp
Half a dozen stale rolls (sourdough is best),
    broken into pieces
Salt and pepper to taste
Sharp Cheddar cheese
Green pepper rings
Sliced, stuffed olives
Parmesan cheese, grated

►Mix the fish chunks with the next 11 ingredients. Place in a large, greased baking dish. Cover top with thin slices of sharp Cheddar cheese. Bake for 45 minutes at about 350°F (175°C). Then add thin slices of green pepper and sliced, stuffed olives to the top and sprinkle all with Parmesan cheese. Bake another half-hour. Serves at least a dozen. Leftovers freeze well.
■ Bob Henning, Angoon

Peroche Russian

1/2 pound (228 g) halibut fillet
1 tablespoon (15 mL) grated onion
1-1/4 cups (300 mL) cooked rice*
2 hard-cooked eggs
Salt and pepper
Butter, optional
Dough for double-crust pie

►(*The rice should be cooked in salted water and, if you're using raw fish, be sure to salt it well.) Grease pan, spread with bottom crust and add about half the cooked rice. Place halibut fillets on the bed of rice. Grate hard-cooked eggs. You can make a richer mixture — if that's desirable — by adding five or six pats of butter to the eggs. Spread the grated eggs over the fillets together with the balance of the rice and the grated onion. Salt and pepper to taste. Roll out top crust; place over mixture, seal edges and score top to allow steam to escape. If the fish is raw, bake one hour; if canned, half an hour in a hot oven.

■ *Mrs. Al Brookman, FV Ole B*
  Seafood Secrets, Sitka

Fish and Shrimp au Gratin
A poached fish casserole, winner of a Grand Prize at the 1976 Southeast Alaska State Fair

1-1/2 pounds (0.70 kg) halibut fillet
1-1/2 cups (360 mL) Fish Stock
Salt and pepper to taste
Melted butter
Flour
1 egg yolk
1/2 cup (120 mL) cream
1/2 pound (228 g) shelled, deveined shrimp
1 can (10 oz /or/ 280 g) mussels in water, or
  whole clams
Mashed potatoes (for garnish)
1 additional egg yolk
Pat of butter
Fine rusk crumbs

►Fold fish double in an ovenproof casserole and pour strained stock over it. Cover and poach in oven at 425°F (220°C) for 15 to 20 minutes. Leaving fish in casserole, pour off stock into saucepan and reduce volume by cooking rapidly. Salt and pepper to taste. Mix a small amount of melted butter and flour and beat into stock to thicken as desired.

Beat egg yolk and cream together. Remove thickened stock from heat and stir in egg-cream mixture. Add shrimp and mussels and set aside.

Mix mashed potatoes with additional egg yolk and butter. Put this mixture in a pastry tube and squeeze zigzag garniture around the edges of the fish in the casserole, or drop by spoonfuls. Ladle sauce over fillets. Sprinkle with fine rusk crumbs and bake at 450°F (230°C) until potato garnish is lightly browned.

■ *Mimi Gregg*
  Haines Homemakers' Cookbook

Norwegian Fish Balls
The cook says, "This was a recipe given to my mother more than 50 years ago by a Norwegian fisherman living in Douglas."

1 pound (0.45 kg) halibut, ground twice
1 cup (240 mL) milk
1 egg

1 tablespoon (15 mL) cornstarch
1/8 teaspoon (0.5 mL) pepper
1 to 1-1/2 teaspoons (5 to 7 mL) salt

►Place all ingredients except salt in a mixer bowl. Beat at the lowest or next lowest setting for half an hour. Add salt during the last few minutes to thicken the mixture. Drop by soupspoonfuls into boiling water or into vegetable soup. (A soup using chunky vegetables is best.) Cook 10 to 15 minutes.

Fish balls cooked in boiling water can be served in a lemon or tomato sauce, but we like them best served in the same dish with cooked vegetables — such as a mixture of carrots, fresh peas, cut fresh beans, onion and maybe a diced potato or two. Thicken the mixture, if desired, with a little cornstarch dissolved in a small amount of cold water and then stirred in during the last moments of cooking.

Or, instead of making balls, form the uncooked fish mixture into cakes and fry until golden brown. Top with a favorite sauce.

■ *Mamie Jensen, Juneau*

Halibut Fillets with Hurry-Up Sauce

First the sauce:
2 tablespoons (30 mL) fresh, minced onion
3 tablespoons (45 mL) butter or margarine
2 tablespoons (30 mL) cornstarch
1 cup (240 mL) chicken bouillon or stock
1 cup (240 mL) milk or cream
Salt and pepper to taste
Yolks of 2 eggs

►Melt the butter in a heavy skillet and saute minced onions until just golden. Add cornstarch and blend. Add bouillon and milk and cook slowly, stirring constantly, until thickened. You may need more liquid to keep the sauce from being too thick. Set on a back burner to keep barely warm while you prepare the halibut fillets. When fillets are baked, add egg yolks to the sauce per directions below.

Now the fillets:
1 pound (0.45 kg) halibut fillets
1 cup (240 mL) milk
2 teaspoons (10 mL) salt
Bread crumbs
Lemon juice
Pepper to taste

►Combine milk and salt and dip the fillets in this mixture. Roll fillets in the crumbs. (Because of their seasoning, we like to use Salad Crispins, which we first roll between paper towels to crumble them.) Place crumbed fillets in a foil-lined baking dish. Sprinkle with lemon juice and pepper to taste. Bake in an oven preheated to 500°F (260°C). Bake for 15 to 20 minutes, depending on thickness of fillets. The fish should flake easily when tested with a fork. Halibut prepared this way tastes much as if it had been broiled. Place fillets in serving dish. Beat the egg yolks slightly and then beat into them a couple of spoonfuls of the now hot sauce. Combine this mixture with the sauce in the pan and stir to blend. Pour sauce around the fillets in serving dish. Garnish with a few pieces of parsley.
■ *The Old Homesteader*

Molded Halibut

1 pound (456 g) raw halibut
1 cup (240 mL) cream
1 pint (0.47 L) bread crumbs
1/8 teaspoon (0.5 mL) pepper
Salt to taste
4 egg whites

►Finely chop the uncooked fish. Soak bread crumbs in cream until smooth paste. Add fish, pepper and salt. Beat egg whites and add. Line a 1-1/2 quart (1.47 L) mold with buttered waxed paper. Pour fish mixture into mold and place in a pan of hot water. Bake in a moderate oven 45 minutes. Turn out and serve with melted butter or Cream Sauce.
■ *Gudrun Olson*
   Tried and True Recipes, *Juneau*

Halibut Fancy

6 small halibut fillets
1/2 teaspoon (2 mL) salt
1/8 teaspoon (0.5 mL) pepper
1 tablespoon (15 mL) lemon juice
1/2 cup (120 mL) bread crumbs
1 tablespoon (15 mL) minced onion
2 tablespoons (30 mL) butter
1 cup (240 mL) canned milk
2 medium eggs, slightly beaten
1/8 teaspoon (0.5 mL) mustard
1 tablespoon (15 mL) Worcestershire
1 cup (240 mL) flaked crab meat

►Grease a 1-quart (1 L) mold generously. Place fillets in mold; salt and pepper and sprinkle the lemon juice over them. Mix crumbs and onions together with melted butter, milk, and the slightly beaten eggs until creamy. Add mustard, Worcestershire and crab (I much prefer Dungeness) to this creamy mixture and pour over the fillets. Set mold in a pan of hot water and bake at 325°F (160°C) for 35 minutes or until filling is set. Unmold onto a large platter and garnish with asparagus spears and thin orange slices.
■ *Mary C. Owens*
   FV Cape Race
   Seafood Secrets, *Sitka*

Halibut and Rice Casserole
Grand Prize winner, Casserole Division,
1975 Southeast Alaska State Fair

3 cups (720 mL) halibut cubes
2 cups (480 mL) partially cooked long grain rice
1/4 cup (60 mL) butter
1 tablespoon (15 mL) soy sauce
2 tablespoons (30 mL) prepared mustard
1/4 cup (60 mL) honey
1 cup (240 mL) crushed pineapple
1/4 medium green pepper, chopped

►Preheat oven to 350°F (175°C). Put butter in large casserole dish and set in oven to melt. Remove and add honey, soy sauce and mustard. Stir until well mixed. Add remaining ingredients and toss lightly. Cover and bake 45 minutes to one hour.
■ *Polly Hall*
   Haines Homemakers' Cookbook

Hali-Beer Bits

Quantity adjustable to how big the fish, how many the mouths to feed

Halibut
Beer
Buttermilk pancake mix (preferably a brand
    complete except for liquid)
Vegetable oil
Salt
Paprika (optional)

▶Cut skinless halibut into chunks about 1-inch (2.5 cm) square. Heat the oil in a deep-fryer, or a deep pan with a basket, to 350°F (175°C).

While the oil is heating, add beer to the pancake mix until the batter is about the same consistency as for pancakes. Paprika may be added, if desired, for a nice golden color.

Dip halibut chunks into the beer batter and deep-fry until golden brown. Drain on paper towels and sprinkle with salt. The fish cooks rapidly and should be eaten while piping hot. We like to serve Hali-Beer Bits with lemon and a choice of tartar or seafood cocktail sauce.
■ *Daniel A. Wagner*
   "How To Fillet Halibut"
   ALASKA® *magazine, June 1973*

Halibut Fisherman's Pie

2 pounds (1 kg) cooked halibut
1 teaspoon (5 mL) Worcestershire
2 teaspoons (10 mL) chopped onion
2 tablespoons (30 mL) butter
2 tablespoons (30 mL) flour
Dash of pepper
1/2 teaspoon (2 mL) salt
1-1/2 cups (360 mL) milk
3 to 4 cups (0.75 to 1 L) hot, seasoned,
    mashed potatoes
1/4 cup (60 mL) grated cheese

▶Flake fish into greased 2-quart (2 L) casserole. Add onion and Worcestershire. Melt butter, blend in flour and seasonings and cook until foamy. Gradually add milk, stirring constantly until smooth and thick. Pour over fish. Top with mashed potatoes and sprinkle with cheese. Bake at 375°F (190°C) for 25 minutes. Serves six.
■ Marine Fish Cookbook

Halibut Hash

▶This is a good way to use leftovers. All the ingredients and quantities can be varied according to what is on hand. Place a lump of margarine in a heavy skillet and, when it has melted, chop leftover cooked potatoes into it. Add flaked, cooked halibut or other fish and season according to taste. Stir in some minced wild chives or onions, either fresh or dried. Cooked peas, carrots, cauliflower or other vegetables may be added, and the whole cooked and stirred until well heated. The mixture may be put in a greased casserole and cooked in the oven. A little cream or milk added as the hash cooks will keep it from being too dry. Serve with ketchup or other sauce.
■ *The Old Homesteader*

HERRING

"Many Northerners consider herring fit only for catching bigger fish and catch herring only to use as bait for salmon," reports Ann Chandonnet [*ALASKA*® magazine, June 1979]. "However, herring is delicious in its own right and is, in fact, the most widely eaten fish in the world.

"In the not-so-distant past, winter diets were limited to salted or brined meats, salted or smoked fish, dried beans and fruits, greens preserved in pokes of oil and root vegetables that would keep in cold cellars because modern canning and freezing methods had not been perfected. Folks welcomed spring for the change of diet — fresh vegetables, both wild and cultivated — and the return of the herring."
Taste: Delicious — fresh, salted, pickled or smoked — these small silvery fish are an excellent source of protein and fat, though fat content varies at different times of the year. Herring are best for pickling and other general home use in the fall, when their fat content is high, while spring catches are best for smoking.

Preparation Tips: Very fresh herring are good breaded and grilled, but the favorite method of serving herring is marinated or lightly pickled, beginning either with raw fish or salted herring that have been freshened.

"Just-netted herring should be used within two days," Chandonnet says. "If you freeze them, storage time increases to about a year. Salted in brine, herring will keep a week in the refrigerator. Hard-smoked, pickled or kippered herring has a refrigerator shelf life of two to three months." A few short-term pickling recipes are included in this chapter. For long-term preservation methods, see Book Four.

To freshen salt herring, soak them overnight in water or milk to cover. If they are heavily salted, you may wish to change the soak liquid several times.

Herring Roe

Female herring lay an average of 10,000 to 60,000 eggs each spring. How does the saying go? . . . We would be up to our kneecaps, anyway, in herring if we did not also consume some of the eggs. And so we do. Herring roe have long been used by Native Alaskans. It is also an important commercial harvest, marketed chiefly in the Orient in one of two forms. *Sac roe* are the two strips of clustered eggs taken from the bodies of female herring before they spawn. Roe herring are fished by purse seiners or gill-netters to the tune of many tons a day during season. *Roe-on-kelp* are the sticky pearly white eggs females drop or brush against seaweeds (or anything else that is handy) in preparation for fertilization by males. Time is of the essence in gathering both crops, as this excerpt from *Alaska Tidelines* [Volume III, Number 7] makes clear:

> *A huge catch [of roe herring] may turn out to be young fish whose eggs haven't ripened or fish that have already spawned. Worse still, they may spawn in the net while the seiner is waiting for a fish tender, requiring a massive cleanup job. And if a hundred tons of trapped herring decide to dive in deep water, they can take the whole fishing boat down with them. . . . The eggs [on kelp] must be gathered before the larvae begin to form within a week or two [after spawning]. Once the little "eyes" show up, it's all over.*

As *Alaska Tidelines* points out, the roe-on-kelp fishery — or roe on hemlock boughs, as they are often taken for local use in Southeastern—is open to anyone who can find "a good kelp bed, a cooperative school of herring, a low tide, some big plastic buckets. . . ."

Several suggestions for using herring eggs, one for roe-on-kelp, are included in this section. General instructions for preparing and cooking roe are on page 19.

Broiled Herring

►Slit fresh herring along back and sides. Coat with prepared mustard. Season to taste. Sprinkle with fine bread crumbs and broil slowly until done.

Rollmops

6 herring in brine, freshened overnight
Prepared mustard
2 small sour pickles, sliced (dills are fine)
2 onions, thinly sliced
1 tablespoon (15 mL) capers
1 red pepper, coarsely chopped
5 peppercorns
2 bay leaves
5 whole allspice (optional)
2 tablespoons (30 mL) chopped dill weed
  (optional)
1-1/2 cups (360 mL) cider vinegar
1 cup (240 mL) water
5 tablespoons (75 mL) sugar (optional)

►Clean freshened herring, if necessary, and remove heads. Drain. Remove bones and cut fillets into small strips. Drain again. Spread herring with a mixture of prepared mustard, pickle slices, onion and capers. Roll up each "mop" and secure with toothpicks. Place in glass container (do not use metal) with red pepper chunks and seasonings. Boil together vinegar and water and sugar, if you are using any. Cool. Pour over herring and let stand, refrigerated and covered, at least overnight and up to six days. Drain before serving. Serve with sour cream and rye bread as a main dish or appetizer. Makes four to six servings.

■ *Ann Chandonnet*
   "Herring — More Than A Bait Fish"
   ALASKA® magazine, June 1979

Russian Salad

1 pickled herring
1 cooked beet
1 pound (456 g) cooked potatoes
1/2 pound (228 g) cooked carrots
1 raw apple
1/2 cucumber

►Cut up the herring in small pieces and dice other ingredients. Mix with the following dressing:

1 teaspoon (5 mL) prepared mustard
2 tablespoons (30 mL) vinegar
4 tablespoons (60 mL) oil
Pinch of salt
Pinch of sugar

►Rub the serving bowl with a raw onion before putting in the salad.
■ *Anna Blinn*
   Saint Herman's Sisterhood Club, *Kodiak*

Variation: Kippered and smoked herring are also good in potato salads such as this one.

Grilled Herring — British Fashion

Fresh herring
Salt and pepper
Fine oatmeal
Bacon fat, 1 teaspoon (5 mL) per fish
Mustard Sauce or lemon wedges

►Cut heads, tails and fins from washed and gutted fresh herring. Split open along backbone; remove the backbone, including as many bones as possible. Wipe fish dry and sprinkle with pepper and salt to taste. Dip fish into fine oatmeal, coating it inside and out. Place fish on broiler rack. Dot each with bacon fat. Broil 10 minutes on each side or until crisp and golden brown. Serve at once with Mustard Sauce or lemon wedges.

■ *Ann Chandonnet*
"Herring — More Than a Bait Fish"
ALASKA® magazine
Alaska-only edition, June 1979

Sillsallad

Herring salad from the SAS
(Scandinavian Airlines System) smorgasbord

4 small salt herring fillets, soaked
1-1/2 cups (360 mL) diced pickled beets
1-1/2 cups (360 mL) diced boiled potatoes
1/3 cup (80 mL) diced pickles (I use sweet)
1/2 cup (120 mL) diced apple
1/4 cup (60 mL) finely chopped onion
Dressing (below)
1 pint (0.47 L) whipped cream
3 hard-cooked eggs and a sprig of parsley
  for garnish

►Cut herring fillets in tiny pieces and mix with other ingredients. In a small bowl, mix the dressing ingredients and stir gently into salad along with the whipped cream. Pack into a lightly oiled 5-cup (1.2 L) mold and chill in refrigerator for a few hours. Unmold on your prettiest cake plate and garnish with hard-cooked eggs. For the top of the salad, slice the eggs round; for the edge, slice the eggs lengthwise and lean them against the salad. Add a sprig of parsley to the top.

Sillsallad Dressing
4 tablespoons (60 mL) white vinegar
2 tablespoons (30 mL) water
2 tablespoons (30 mL) sugar
Dash of white pepper
■ *Courtesy, Bunny Mathisen*
"Help Yourself To The Sylta Flesk!"
ALASKA® magazine, January 1977

Baked Herring

►Take heads and tails off herring. Roll fish in flour, put them in layers in a baking pan. Bake in a moderate oven for about an hour.
■ *Tsimpshean Indian Island Cookbook*
Metlakatla

Herring in Sour Cream

4 salt herring fillets, soaked in milk for 4 hours
1 cup (240 mL) sour cream
2 tablespoons (30 mL) sherry — the better the
  wine, the better the finished product
A little minced onion

►Mix sour cream, sherry and minced onion. Drain fillets and cut into 1-inch (2.5 cm) pieces. Add to sour cream mixture. Garnish with a bay leaf, snipped chives or parsley. Serves six.
■ *Bunny Mathisen, Petersburg*
"Help Yourself To The Sylta Flesk!"
ALASKA® magazine, January 1977

Adolph's Pickled Herring

12 salt herring, skinned, boned and
  freshened overnight
1/4 cup (60 mL) white sugar
1/2 cup (120 mL) water
1-1/2 cups (360 mL) white vinegar
1 bay leaf
1 teaspoon (5 mL) whole pepper
Whole cloves
Sliced onions
1 lemon slice

►Drain freshened herring. Mix sugar, water, vinegar and spices. Alternate layers of herring and sliced onions in a quart (1 L) jar. Pour vinegar mixture over all and top with lemon slice. Refrigerate a day or so before serving.
■ *Bunny Mathisen, Petersburg*
"Help Yourself To The Sylta Flesk!"
ALASKA® magazine, January 1977

Sildbald

Herring balls, good for any meal of the day

8 salted herring, freshened overnight
  if very salty
8 medium-large potatoes
1 medium-large onion
1/4 teaspoon (1 mL) pepper
3 cups (720 mL) flour

►Clean herring, removing bone and skin. Peel potatoes and onion. Put all three ingredients through food grinder. Add pepper and flour and stir the mixture by hand. Dipping hands into cold water each time, form mixture into balls about the size of a small orange. Place a small piece of bacon or salt pork in the center of each ball. Drop balls into a kettle of rapidly boiling water and cook 45 minutes. Serve with fried bacon or salt pork. If some are left over, they can be sliced and fried in bacon fat the next day. Some people like to serve these fried cakes with syrup.

■ *Mrs. Chris Wick*
   PTA Cook Book, *Petersburg*

Herring Casserole
A good way to welcome herring season

1 pound (456 g) fresh herring
8 to 10 anchovy fillets
3 cooked potatoes, sliced
1 tablespoon (15 mL) prepared mustard
4 tomatoes, sliced
2 tablespoons (30 mL) cracker crumbs
2 tablespoons (30 mL) butter

►Clean, bone and fillet the herring. Rinse well in cold water and drain. Place a piece of anchovy fillet on each herring fillet and roll. Cover bottom of baking dish with potato slices and spread with mustard. Arrange herring rolls on top and cover with tomato slices. Sprinkle with cracker crumbs; dot with butter and bake in a hot oven, 450°F (230°C) for 25 minutes. Makes three or four servings.

■ *Beda Sundell*
   Sons of Norway Cook Book, *Ketchikan*

Herringchova Paste

1 cup (240 mL) herring, pickled, smoked
   or dried
1/4 cup (60 mL) butter
1/8 teaspoon (0.5 mL) cayenne pepper
1/8 teaspoon (0.5 mL) ground clove

►Remove fat, bones and skin from cured fish. Chop fine. Mix in other ingredients and mash to a smooth paste. A jar of this paste, tightly covered, will keep a long time in the refrigerator. Use as an appetizer spread or in any recipe calling for anchovy paste.

■ *Ruth Allman, Juneau*
   Alaska Sourdough

Herring Roe-on-Kelp

►Dip kelp with roe in boiling water briefly. Sprinkle with salt and pepper and dip in melted butter or hooligan grease.

■ *Tsimpshean Indian Island Cookbook*
   Metlakatla

Herring Eggs Two Ways

1. After cooking herring eggs, serve with melted butter, soy sauce or Worcestershire sauce. Most people like them with ooligan grease.
2. Boil little potatoes until they are mushy-done. Take off heat and stir; then stir in herring eggs. Add a little soy sauce.

■ *Tsimpshean Indian Island Cookbook*
   Metlakatla

Scrambled Eggs and Herring Roe

1/2 pound (228 g) herring roe
1 tablespoon (15 mL) vinegar
1 teaspoon (5 mL) salt
1 cup (240 mL) boiling water
2 tablespoons (30 mL) butter
6 eggs
6 tablespoons (90 mL) milk
1/2 teaspoon (2 mL) salt
Dash of pepper

►Add vinegar and 1 teaspoon (5 mL) salt to boiling water. Add roe and simmer 15 minutes; drain and remove skin. Mash roe. Combine eggs, milk, seasonings and roe. Scramble mixture in fat over low heat. Garnish and serve hot. Serves six.

Herring Roe Meuniere

1-1/2 pounds (0.70 kg) herring roe
3/4 teaspoon (3 mL) salt
1/2 cup (120 mL) butter or other fat
2 tablespoons (30 mL) lemon juice
Dash of pepper

►Remove membrane and drain roe on absorbent paper. Sprinkle both sides with salt and pepper. Fry roe in fat at moderate heat until brown; turn carefully and brown other side. Cooking time will be about 12 minutes, depending on thickness of roe. Remove roe to platter. Add lemon juice to brown butter and pour over roe. Garnish and serve hot. Serves six.

Herring Roe The Haida Way

►Herring spawn season in Haida country was during the months of March and April. Fish Egg Island near Craig was a great spawning area. People came from all over the district to harvest the eggs.

   In the early days, several different methods were used in getting the eggs. One way was harvesting different kinds of kelp on which the herring had spawned. The broad-leaf kelp was the most sought after. The hairlike kelp was next. The yellow rock kelp was the least sought after. These three were hung out on lines or poles to dry and cure.

Another way to harvest herring eggs was to secure some young hemlock trees about 6 to 8 feet (1.8 to 2.4 m) tall. These had soft needles for the herring to spawn on. The trees were weighted down by a rock tied on as an anchor. A marked buoy was attached for identification by the owner. This was left out overnight and harvested the next day. The branches were broken or cut off and piled on a boat or canoe. This [harvest] was also dried and cured like the kelp kind.

After drying thoroughly, the eggs were sorted and packed in storage boxes for the winter months. In later years, a large part of the harvest was salted down in barrels. In recent years, much of the harvest was put in the freezer for future use.

Old-timers say that in their day a person could almost walk on the herring. This was true in my time about forty or fifty years ago.

■ *Robert Cogo*
   Haida Food Gathering and Preservation

Herring Roe

►Soak whole fish in 100 percent brine solution* for two or three days to firm up the roe. Remove roe from fish; soak washed roe in 100 percent brine solution for a minimum of 12 hours. Refrigerate it in the brine. Rinse roe and serve with soy sauce or other condiments.

■ Washington Seafood Recipes

This brine is mixed 46.1 ounces (1.3 kg) salt per gallon (3.8 L) water.

LINGCOD

One of several fishes called greenlings, the lingcod — which is neither ling nor cod — is a slender fish with a big head (up to a quarter of its length), a big mouth and very sharp teeth. Sound menacing? Not once it's on your plate!

Because it prefers the intertidal zones among kelp beds and strong currents, the lingcod isn't an easy mark for commercial fishing, but it is a welcome incidental catch because it brings a premium price. The difficulties presented by its habitat do make the lingcod a worthy sport fish which can often foil the catch by darting between jagged rocks and dense kelp fronds.

Taste: The lingcod "must be rated as one of the most palatable of marine fishes, with its white, firm, flaky flesh lending itself easily to cooking, especially to deep oil cookery," says Robert Browning in his magnum opus, *Fisheries of the North Pacific* [Anchorage, 1980 rev]. Sometimes the flesh has a slightly bluish tinge which turns white during cooking, and, in any case, is normal to the species.

Preparation Tips: Breaded and deep-fried, lingcod is almost indistinguishable from halibut and, in fact, is excellently prepared using many other recipes for halibut, as well. Cod, rockfish and sablefish recipes are also quite suitable for lingcod.

German Style Fish Bake

1/2 pound (228 g) lingcod (or snapper or
   halibut) fillet
1/2 tablespoon (7 mL) butter
1/2 onion, chopped
Garlic powder
2 teaspoons (10 mL) dill weed
3/4 teaspoon (3 mL) paprika
3/4 teaspoon (3 mL) caraway seed
Dash cayenne
1 cup (240 mL) sauerkraut
1/2 cup (120 mL) sour cream

►Saute onion sprinkled with garlic powder in butter until soft. Add all remaining ingredients except fish and heat through but do not boil. Place mixture in casserole dish and bake, covered, 15 to 20 minutes at 350°F (175°C). Then place fish on top and continue baking, uncovered, until fish flakes easily when tested with a fork. Serves two.

■ *The editors, ALASKA® magazine*

Oven Barbecued Lingcod

2 pounds (1 kg) lingcod or other firm fish fillets
1/2 cup (120 mL) cooking oil
1 teaspoon (5 mL) salt
Dash of pepper
1 clove garlic, minced
1 cup (240 mL) shredded Cheddar cheese
1 cup (240 mL) fine crumbs — bread, cereal
   or cracker
1 cup (240 mL) Fisherman's Favorite
   Barbecue Sauce, or Spanish Tomato Sauce,
   or a commercial barbecue sauce

►Cut fish into six portions. Combine oil, salt, pepper and garlic. Mix cheese and crumbs. Dip each piece of fish into oil; drain slightly and roll in crumb mixture. Arrange fish in a well-greased baking pan. Bake in hot oven, 450°F (230°C) five to seven minutes.

Meanwhile heat barbecue sauce. Spoon half the

sauce over fillets and continue baking until fish flakes when tested with a fork, about five minutes longer. Keep remaining sauce hot and serve separately. A good way to serve the fish is on split and toasted rolls or hamburger buns.

Sesame Lingcod

2 pounds (1 kg) lingcod or other white fish
3/4 teaspoon (3 mL) salt
6 tablespoons (90 mL) margarine or butter
2 tablespoons (30 mL) minced green onion
*   with tops*
1 teaspoon (5 mL) finely grated fresh ginger
*   or about 1/2 teaspoon (2 mL) freshly ground*
*   black pepper*
3 tablespoons (45 mL) lightly toasted
*   sesame seeds*

►Wipe fish with damp cloth. Season both sides with salt. Arrange in single layer in buttered shallow baking pan. Melt butter and stir in onions, ginger and sesame seed; spoon over fish. Bake in preheated 350°F (175°C) oven until fish barely separates when tested with a dinner knife, 15 to 25 minutes, depending on thickness. Baste occasionally with pan drippings. Makes four servings.
■ *Linda Martinson*
    Seafood Treasures, *Seattle*

Sauteed Lingcod with Lemon Relish

2 pounds (1 kg) lingcod or halibut
Salt and pepper
1/4 cup (60 mL) flour
1/2 cup (120 mL) fine dry bread crumbs
4 tablespoons (60 mL) sesame seed
1 egg, beaten with 2 tablespoons (30 mL) milk
About 2 tablespoons (30 mL) each —
*   salad oil and margarine*

►Cut fish into serving pieces, sprinkle with salt and pepper, dust lightly with flour. Stir together bread crumbs and sesame seed. Dip fish pieces in egg-milk mixture, drain briefly, then coat evenly with crumb-seed mixture.
    Heat oil and margarine in frying pan over medium heat, add fish and cook, turning once, for 8 to 10 minutes or until fish flakes easily with a fork. Place cooked fish on warm serving platter, serve with Lemon Relish. Makes four servings.

Lemon Relish
►Combine:
1/4 cup (60 mL) chopped parsley
1/4 cup (60 mL) fresh-squeezed lemon juice
1/2 cup (120 mL) finely chopped green onion
■ *Linda Martinson*
    Seafood Treasures, *Seattle*

Lingcod Fish and Chips

"A person is wasting good eating if he throws a lingcod back into the ocean," says this cookbook author. "It may look ugly, but it is good eating, especially for fish and chips. When we were in the restaurant business, people often asked if we were serving halibut fish and chips when we used lingcod. The same recipes work for two different fish."

3 pounds (1.4 kg) lingcod
1/2 teaspoon (2 mL) baking powder
2 cups (480 mL) flour
1 teaspoon (5 mL) salt
Dash of white pepper
1 tablespoon (15 mL) seafood seasoning
1-1/2 teaspoons (7 mL) Accent
1-1/2 teaspoons (7 mL) paprika
1 cup (240 mL) or more water

►Cut the fish into strips about 3-1/2 inches (8.75 cm) long. Do not cut the strips too thick. Mix remaining ingredients until smooth. In a deep-fryer, preheat enough oil to cover the fish to 375°F (190°C). Then dip strips of fish into batter and deep-fry for a few minutes until golden. Drain. Sprinkle on salt and other seasonings. Serve with chips.
■ *Kaa T'eix (Mary Howard Pelayo)*
    Kaa T'eix's Cook Book, *Mount Edgecumbe*

Lingcod Cheeks Supreme

"This recipe can be used for either halibut cheeks or lingcod cheeks," according to the cook. "If the halibut cheeks are large, slice them in half. Lingcod cheeks are smaller than halibut cheeks and are considered by some people — like ME, for instance — to be even more of a delicacy."

Lingcod cheeks
2 eggs
1/4 cup (60 mL) oil
1/2 cup (120 mL) flour
1/2 cup (120 mL) fine bread crumbs
1 teaspoon (5 mL) cornstarch
Salt, pepper and paprika to taste

►Whip eggs and oil until thick and smooth, adding water if needed to smooth out the mixture. In a separate bowl, mix flour, bread crumbs and cornstarch (to hold the mixture together). Dip cheeks in egg mixture and then into flour. Sprinkle on salt, pepper and paprika as desired and broil or fry in a pan with a generous amount of hot oil. Turn once and allow about one minute frying on each side.
■ *Phyllis Moreland, FV* See-Am
    Seafood Secrets, *Sitka*

NORTHERN PIKE

This long, slim fish with the large mouth and formidable teeth will feed on practically anything it can catch and swallow. That makes it a somewhat easy fish to hook, but watch out when you trail your fingers in the water alongside the boat! Although the species can reach 50 pounds (22 kg), the average pike caught by sport fishermen in Alaska is probably closer to between 2 and 6 pounds (1 to 3 kg).

Taste & Preparation Tips: "Pike are delicious," says Jim Morrow (*The Freshwater Fishes of Alaska*). "The meat is white, flaky and flavorful. The so-called muddy taste of which some people complain is confined to the skin. If the fish be thoroughly scaled, scrubbed and washed, the muddy taste is eliminated, but it is better and easier to skin the fish." Another common complaint, he says, is against the boniness of the fish. Both matters he remedies for us. On the facing page is an excerpt from his story, "The Guided Guide," from a collection of stories about the legendary master guide, Hal Waugh. In this excerpt, Jim and his son Matt "show [Hal] a trick or two about pike."

Baked Whole Pike
A clever way to part a tasty fish from its less-than-tasty skin

1 whole-dressed but unscaled pike,
   2 to 3 pounds (1 to 1.4 kg)
Salt
Monosodium glutamate
1 medium onion, sliced
2 tablespoons (30 mL) butter
2 tablespoons (30 mL) fresh lemon juice
1/4 teaspoon (1 mL) tarragon

►If possible, the fish should be a very fresh one which was drawn when caught but left unscaled. Wash the fish and pat it damp-dry. Sprinkle flesh with salt and monosodium glutamate. Place slices of onion inside fish. Combine butter, lemon juice and tarragon and sprinkle 1 tablespoon (15 mL) of this sauce on the onion. Reserve remaining sauce. Close fish with skewers or lace with string and measure it at its thickest point to plan cooking time. Then wrap the fish in heavy brown paper and place it in a greased baking dish. Bake it in a hot oven, 450°F (230°C), 10 minutes per inch (2.5 cm) of thickness. Add five minutes to the total cooking time for the heat to penetrate the paper. (If the fish is frozen, double the per-inch cooking time and add 10 minutes to the total for the paper wrapping.) When the fish is done, unwrap it onto a serving platter; the scales and skin will cling to the paper, leaving the tender meat intact. Reheat remaining lemon-butter and pour over fish.

■ Northern Cookbook *(adapted)*

Pitiful Pike Chowder

2 medium northern pike
1 package freeze-dried corn
2 handfuls of bistort leaves*
1 pocketful of brook saxifrage leaves*
Seasonings (salt, pepper, onion, garlic,
   soy sauce)

►Boil the pike and remove all bones. Combine all ingredients in a pot and simmer. How can it miss?
■ *Jim Greenough and Eileen Helmstetter*
  "The Bush Gourmet"
  ALASKA® *magazine, July 1977*

*Both these wild edibles are further described in Chapter 9; bistort (Polygonum bistorta), by the name "pink plume." Brook saxifrage (Saxifraga punctata) is one of two plants which go by the name "wild cucumber."

Camp Cooking — How To Clean, Fillet and Fry Northern Pike

The trip that day was uneventful and we made an early camp at the mouth of the Kandik River. Next morning we went up the Kandik a ways. We caught two nice pike in the slough at the mouth of the river.

"What do you want with those things?" Hal asked. "You can't eat them, can you?"

"Oh, yes," Matt replied. "The way my dad fixes pike, they're real good."

"Well," said Hal, "I've never cared much for them, but if you want to try them, I'm game for anything once."

"That's good," I said, "because I guarantee you that when we stop for the night, I'll whomp up some fried fish that will make your mouth water."

Again it was an uneventful day — warm and sunny — but about the time we reached the mouth of the Charley River, the wind began to blow, and it blew harder and harder, coming straight upstream. By the time we reached Coal Creek, the waves were nearly 2 feet (60 cm) high. The boat was pounding hard even though we were going slowly, and the spray was soaking us. I put in at Coal Creek for the night.

"Now, let me show you a trick or two about pike. The main trouble with pike is, most people don't clean the skin enough. If you are going to eat the fish with the skin on, you must scrape it and scrape it and scrape it. This gets off all the scales and slime and everything else. Most of the muddy taste lies in the skin. Personally, I prefer to skin them, and that's easily done. Take a sharp knife and run a slit just through the skin right down the middle of the back on either side of the dorsal fin. Do the same on the belly side and then make a cut around the fish just behind the head. Now, pick up the corner of the skin with the edge of your knife and your thumb and—one strong pull and your fish is skinned on that side. Do the same on the other and all that bad taste is gone."

"Well, that's a neat trick," said Hal, "but how do you get rid of all the bones?"

"Look, Mr. Waugh," said Matt. "You take a sharp knife and you cut down the back just beside the backbone until you touch the Y-bones. Then you have to work your knife up along those bones right to the end, being careful not to cut through, and not cut off that piece of meat. You can then fold the top part of the fillet back, put your knife against the other side of the Y-bone, work it back to the backbone, twist it a little bit, and work along the main ribs and get a clean piece of meat with no bones in it."

"Well, I'll be plague-taked," Hal said. "I never knew that you could fillet these plague-taked fish without leaving a lot of bones in them. How are you going to cook them?"

"Well, our equipment is kind of limited," I replied. "I think we'll just roll them in flour and sprinkle them with salt and pepper and just a dash of garlic powder. And then we'll fry them. Frying isn't the best way in the world to cook fish, but we don't have enough utensils to do much else."

So that is what we did, and Hal was so impressed that he wrote the recipe in his little notebook.

■ *Jim Morrow*

Excerpted from "The Guided Guide," by James E. Morrow, in *Alaska Game Trails with a Master Guide* [Anchorage, 1977], compiled by Charles J. Keim.

THE ROCKFISHES

Among the best-known saltwater fishes caught by sport fishermen in Alaskan waters are the rockfishes, of which there are many species commonly called by only a few names, some of them misnomers. Both the black rockfish and the rock cod (which is definitely not a cod) are often called black seabass. And the red rockfish is more commonly known as "red snapper" even though there is no true red snapper in our waters. When they are brought to market, most rockfish are sold under two or three names, one reserved for Pacific Ocean perch; the others — "snapper" or "seabass" —hand over to the cook several other species of rockfish. The confusion of names matters not to the final product: rockfishes all provide pleasing meals. Comparatively small as deep-ocean fish go, the rockfishes vary in size according to species, the perch seldom larger than 3 pounds (1.4 kg), others weighing as high as 25 pounds (10 kg), though such weight is exceptional.

Taste: Excellent, mild flavor. The flesh is white to creamy to rosy in color and firm textured.

Preparation Tips: Skinned and filleted or chunked, rockfish can be cooked by most methods appropriate to fillets — baked in sauce, fried, deep-fried, boiled, steamed, poached or broiled. Some

recipes, however, call for simply scraping off the scales and removing the spiny dorsal fins and gill covers before proceeding to steak the fish or use it whole. The head of most rockfishes wins no prize for beauty, either, though it has almost a cartoonist's "classic fish" appeal. Everybody likes rockfish cooked and flaked and casseroled.

Because lingcod, halibut and sablefish (most often known as black cod) are also firm-fleshed fish, they make especially good substitutes in recipes for rockfish . . . and vice versa.

Alaska Fisherman's Stew
A quick and easy full-meal soup

2 pounds (1 kg) rockfish
1-1/2 cups (360 mL) sliced celery
1/2 cup (120 mL) chopped onion
1 clove garlic, minced
1/4 cup (60 mL) butter or margarine
1 large can (29 oz /or/ 826 g) tomatoes,
    undrained
1 can (8 oz /or/ 228 g) tomato sauce
2 teaspoons (10 mL) salt
1/2 teaspoon (2 mL) paprika
1/2 teaspoon (2 mL) chili powder
1/4 teaspoon (1 mL) pepper
1 package (7 oz /or/ 200 g) spaghetti
2 cups (480 mL) boiling water
1/4 cup (60 mL) grated Parmesan cheese

►Cut fish into 1-inch (2.5 cm) chunks. Saute celery, onion and garlic in butter in a large, heavy pan until tender. Add tomatoes, tomato sauce and seasonings. Bring to a simmer, cover and cook slowly 15 to 20 minutes. Add uncooked spaghetti and boiling water, stir and cover. Cook slowly another 10 minutes or until spaghetti is almost tender. Add fish, cover and cook slowly 7 to 10 minutes or until fish flakes easily when tested with a fork. Serve hot with cheese sprinkled over top. Makes six servings.
■ Seafood Moods

A Good Way To Prepare Red Snapper or Rock Cod
A delicious no-fuss soup

►Scrape off the scales with a fork. Cut off the head or you can leave it on. Cut along both sides of the back fin and pull off with pliers. Remove the flippers the same way. Cut fish in crosswise pieces about 2 inches (5 cm) wide and place them in enough boiling water to cover the fish. Add mashed garlic and half a cabbage that has been chopped and fried first. Tomato sauce or whole tomatoes can also be added to this fish soup. Season to taste with salt and chili powder.
■ Tsimpshean Indian Island Cookbook
    Metlakatla

Teriyaki Fish
Marinated and broiled

2 to 3 pounds (1 to 1.4 kg) rockfish fillets
1 cup (240 mL) soy sauce
1/4 cup (60 mL) salad oil
2 teaspoons (10 mL) grated fresh ginger root
1 clove garlic, chopped
1/2 cup (120 mL) sugar (brown sugar is
    especially good)

1 tablespoon (15 mL) sesame seed
Shredded lettuce (optional)

►In a glass dish combine soy sauce, sugar, oil, ginger and garlic. Add fish fillets and turn to coat well. Let fillets stand in this mixture for several hours. Line a shallow baking pan with aluminum foil. Lift fillets from soy sauce mixture and arrange in pan. Broil 5 to 7 inches (12 to 18 cm) from the heat for about four minutes, brushing once or twice with more oil. Turn, brush with oil again and sprinkle with sesame seeds. Broil three to five minutes longer or until fish flakes. Serve on a bed of shredded lettuce, if you like. Serves four to six.
■ *Tsimpshean Indian Island Cookbook*
    Metlakatla

Huachinango a la Veracrusana

1 whole-dressed red snapper, about
    4-1/2 pounds (2 kg)
4 tablespoons (60 mL) olive oil
2 cloves garlic
3 onions, sliced
6 tomatoes sliced
1/2 cup (120 mL) stuffed olives, sliced
Chopped parsley
Lemon juice
Salt and pepper to taste
2 chilies amarillos
Lemon wedges

►Brown garlic cloves in hot oil and then remove garlic. Fry onion slices in the oil until browned. Add tomatoes, olives, parsley, lemon juice, salt and pepper. Cook slightly and pour over the fish in a greased baking dish. Arrange chili strips on top. Bake at 350°F (175°C) until fish flakes. Garnish with lemon wedges. Serves six.
■ *Dolores Stelling*
    Gold Rush Cookbook, Valdez

Rockfish Rockefeller
Baked whole fish with fresh spinach stuffing

1 rockfish, 3 to 4 pounds (1.4 to 1.8 kg)
2-1/2 teaspoons (12 mL) salt
1-1/2 cups (360 mL) thinly sliced celery
1/4 cup (60 mL) sliced green onions
1/2 cup (120 mL) butter or margarine, melted
4 cups (1 L) soft bread cubes
4 cups (1 L) fresh spinach leaves, washed
    and well drained
1 tablespoon (15 mL) lemon juice
1/4 teaspoon (1 mL) pepper

►Clean, wash and dry fish. Sprinkle inside and out with 1-1/2 teaspoons (7 mL) salt. Cook celery and onions in 6 tablespoons (90 mL) butter until celery is tender. Stir in bread cubes and spinach leaves. Cook until spinach is tender. Add lemon juice, remaining salt and pepper; toss lightly. Stuff fish loosely. Close opening with skewers. Place fish in well-greased baking pan. Brush with remaining butter. Measure fish at its thickest point. Preheat oven to 450°F (230°C). Bake fish 10 minutes per inch (2.5 cm) of thickness, or until meat flakes easily when tested with a fork, about 40 minutes. If fish is frozen, double per-inch cooking time.
■ *The editors, ALASKA® magazine*

Rockfish Salad

1-1/2 cups (360 mL) cooked, boned rockfish
1/4 cup (60 mL) mayonnaise
1/4 cup (60 mL) French dressing
1/2 cup (120 mL) chopped tomato
1/4 cup (60 mL) diced celery
Salad herbs and seasonings to taste
1 tablespoon (15 mL) finely chopped onion
1/4 cup (60 mL) pared and diced cucumber
Salt and pepper
Garnishes: 2 hard-cooked eggs and (if you're
    feeling flush) an avocado
Lettuce

►Combine all ingredients except garnishes and lettuce. Chill. Just before serving, slice hard-cooked eggs. Peel avocado, slice and sprinkle with lemon juice to keep from darkening. Toss with a small amount of salad oil. Sprinkle with salt. Place fish salad on lettuce leaves and garnish with egg and avocado slices. Serves four to six.
■ *The editors, ALASKA® magazine*

Rockfish Sea Slaw

1-1/2 pounds (0.70 kg) rockfish fillets
1 quart (1 L) boiling water
1 tablespoon (15 mL) salt
1/4 cup (60 mL) salad dressing
1 tablespoon (15 mL) chopped onion
1 teaspoon (5 mL) sweet pickle relish
1 tablespoon (15 mL) lemon juice
1 teaspoon (5 mL) salt
1 cup (240 mL) shredded green cabbage
1 cup (240 mL) shredded red cabbage
Lettuce cups
Lemon wedges

►Place fillets in boiling water, add salt, cover and simmer up to 10 minutes, but do not overcook. Fish should hold together. Drain. Flake fish. Combine all ingredients except cabbage. Chill for one hour to blend flavors. Add cabbage and toss lightly. Serve in lettuce cups and garnish with lemon wedges. Serves six.
■ *Marine Fish Cookbook*

Savory Seafood Scallop

1/2 cup (120 mL) butter or margarine
1 teaspoon (5 mL) salt
1/4 cup (60 mL) minced green pepper
2 tablespoons (30 mL) minced onion
4 tablespoons (60 mL) flour
2 cups (480 mL) milk
2 teaspoons (10 mL) Worcestershire
3 to 6 cups (0.70 to 1.45 L) cooked chunked or
  flaked fish or shellfish
1 cup (240 mL) fresh bread crumbs
2/3 cup (160 mL) grated cheese

▶Heat oven to 400°F (205°C). Melt butter, add salt, green pepper, onion and cook until tender. Stir in flour. Add milk and Worcestershire. Cook until thickened. Alternate layers of fish and thickened sauce in a greased casserole. Top with combined bread crumbs and cheese. Bake 20 minutes or until browned. Serves eight.
■ *Mamie Jensen, Juneau*

A favorite way of preparing rockfish fillets is breaded and fried. Here are five choices:

Simple Rockfish Fillets

Fillets of rockfish
Egg, beaten well
Fine dry bread crumbs
Salt and pepper
Onion powder
Vegetable oil

▶Have rockfish fillets at room temperature. Press between paper towels to blot all excess juices. Dip in beaten egg, then in very fine dry bread crumbs. Heat oil in heavy skillet and pan-fry fillets. Sprinkle with seasoning; brown well on both sides. A few drops from a "homestead" lemon* on each fillet will enhance the flavor. Serve with a tossed green salad and hot rolls.
■ *The Old Homesteader*

*A homestead lemon is one that comes to you already squeezed — out of a plastic or glass container.

Crispy Fried Perch

2 pounds (1 kg) ocean perch fillets
1/2 cup (120 mL) yellow corn meal
1/2 cup (120 mL) flour
1 teaspoon (5 mL) paprika
1/4 cup (60 mL) evaporated milk
1 teaspoon (5 mL) salt
Dash of pepper

▶Cut fillets into serving portions. Mix flour, corn meal and paprika. In a separate dish, mix milk, salt and pepper. Dip fish pieces in the milk mixture and then in the flour mixture. Fry in hot fat or oil for four to six minutes on each side until the fish is nicely browned. Drain. Serves five.

Succulent Snapper

▶Place about 2 pounds (1 kg) snapper fillets in a flat dish. Pour on enough milk to cover the fish, season it with garlic salt and allow to marinate, refrigerated, for several hours. Remove fish from milk. Salt and pepper to taste and roll in cracker crumbs. Deep-fry quickly.
■ *Bev Stair*
  Seafood Secrets, *Sitka*

Perch 'n' Chips
Oven fried

2 pounds (1 kg) ocean perch fillets
1/2 cup (120 mL) Italian salad dressing
1 cup (240 mL) crushed potato chips
1/2 cup (120 mL) shredded Cheddar cheese

▶Dip fillets in salad dressing. Place in baking pan. Combine crushed chips and cheese. Sprinkle over fish. Bake in a hot oven at 450°F (230°C) for 12 to 15 minutes or until fish flakes easily when tested with a fork. Serves six.

Red Snapper a la Chicken
Northern fried "chicken"

1 red snapper or other rockfish, filleted
Flour
Shortening
1 or 2 onions, sliced
1 clove garlic, minced
Water
Salt and pepper
Nutmeg

▶Red snapper is known as mock chicken by those "in the know." Cut fillets into serving pieces, dredge in flour and brown in hot grease. Place onion slices, garlic and 3 tablespoons (45 mL) water in a large stew kettle. Add the browned fish and salt and pepper to taste.
  In a hot, dry frying pan, brown 1/2 cup (120 mL) flour. Reduce heat, add 3 tablespoons (45 mL) shortening and mix to a paste. Stirring constantly, gradually add enough water to make a thin brown gravy. A pinch of nutmeg will give the gravy that "Norwegian flavor." Pour gravy over fish and cover tightly. Simmer over low heat until the fish flakes easily when tested with a fork. Lift fish carefully to a warmed platter and serve immediately.
■ *Marv Kinberg*
  Seafood Secrets, *Sitka*

SABLEFISH (BLACK COD)

Although it is not one of the primary targets of sport fishermen, the sablefish is a frequent enough catch to be familiar to most cooks. It is perhaps *most* familiar by the name "black cod," but, like a number of fish with the tag, it only looks as if it should belong to the cod family. As the name indicates, too, the skin of sablefish ranges in color from very dark green to black. Average weight, between 8 and 10 pounds (3.6 to 4.5 kg) . . . more than an ample meal.

Preparation Tips: The most popular preparation is smoked sablefish — often steamed and served with a sauce. In the market, smoked sablefish is sometimes sold as "smoked black cod" or "finnan haddie," though it is neither. Sablefish, disregarding its name, does not belong to the cod family; and true finnan haddie is smoked haddock. Fresh sablefish can be steaked or filleted and broiled or baked in a sauce. You'll find plenty of suitable recipes in Chapter 1 . . . besides those that follow here.

Poached Smoked Sablefish

3 pounds (1.3 kg) smoked sablefish
4 tablespoons (60 mL) butter
1 stalk celery, chopped
1 carrot, sliced
1 onion, sliced
Salt to taste
5 whole cloves
5 peppercorns
1 bay leaf
3 quarts (2.85 L) water
1/4 cup (60 mL) vinegar

►Melt butter in a large kettle and saute celery, carrot and onion for several minutes. Tie cloves, peppercorns and bay leaf in a cheesecloth bag and add to vegetables. Add salt if fish is not too salty. Pour in the water and bring it to the boil. Add vinegar and bring to boil again. Cut the fish in serving size pieces and gently lower them into the liquid. Let simmer on low heat — DO NOT BOIL— until fish flakes nicely when poked with a fork, about 10 to 12 minutes. Lift fish carefully to a warmed platter. Serve with boiled potatoes and cream sauce on the side. Serves six.
■ *Mamie Jensen, Juneau*

Steamed Black Cod

►The thick shoulder cuts from large fish are best. If thin tail pieces must be used, steam a much shorter time or the tail will dry out while the thick shoulder portion is still cooking. Do not remove skin. The fish comes to market cleaned and headless, in steaks or whole sides or pieces of sides if smoked. This is the type of cut this recipe is intended for . . . large thick end cuts of smoked sides.

Place codfish skin side down . . . leave skin on (lots of fat on underside and it holds the delicate fish flakes together) . . . in whatever steaming receptable you have that you can equip with a rack to hold the fish up out of the water in the bottom of the pan and still allow steam to circulate around it. Pan must have secure lid to hold in steam.

Let fish steam for about 10 to 20 minutes, depending on thickness of fish, but at any rate, fish is done when it flakes easily and translucent appearance of flakes has *just turned* to opaque . . . repeat, emphasis on *"just turned"* from translucent. Do not continue to cook any longer. It is needless and only dries and eventually toughens the delicate fish.

Serve with small boiled new potatoes and white sauce on the side. White sauce can be made from scratch, but Aunt Penny's little cans of white sauce in the grocery store are excellent. Add thyme, salt and pepper, and a sliced hard-boiled egg.
■ *Bob Henning, Angoon*

Smoky Sablefish Salad

1 cup (240 mL) mayonnaise
1 teaspoon (5 mL) prepared mustard
1/2 teaspoon (2 mL) tarragon leaves
1/2 teaspoon (2 mL) salt
1/4 teaspoon (1 mL) celery seed
3 cups (720 mL) chilled, sliced cooked potatoes
2 cups (480 mL) sliced celery
2/3 cup (160 mL) sliced radishes
1/3 cup (80 mL) sliced green onion
1/2 pound (228 g) smoked sablefish or other
  smoked fish, flaked
Lettuce leaves

►Combine first five ingredients; mix well. Fold in sliced potatoes. Cover and refrigerate several hours to blend flavors. Add celery, radishes, onion and flaked fish; mix carefully. Arrange in center of lettuce lined serving dish. Garnish with additional sliced smoked fish or Pacific pink shrimp. Makes six servings.
■ *Seafood Moods*

SALMON

In all the world where men fish, whether for fun or for money, they fix upon a favorite fish, a fish of substance, such as herring that has started wars and changed kingdoms, or a courageous fish like all of the trouts with their honored history of valiant resistance to the artifices of the fisherman.

Such a fish of the Northeastern Pacific can be none but the Pacific salmon, several sleek fishes that combine the merits of the herring and the trout and all their kind. The salmons have created great wealth, as has the herring; they resist the rod and lure as stoutly as any trout ever has. . . .

Robert J. Browning
Fisheries of the North Pacific

Salmon are without rival among the fishes people like to see waiting on their dinner plates. However, all salmons are not created exactly equal. These five species, important to sport, commercial and subsistence fisheries, spawn in more than 2,000 Alaska streams:

King salmon — also called *chinook* and *spring*— matches its name in many respects. Largest of all salmon, commercially caught kings average between 10 and 30 pounds (4.5 to 13.5 kg), with 80 pounds (36 kg) not an unusual weight, and 125 pounds (56 kg) about the outside limit. It is the king of sport fish in Alaska, too, because of its size, its fighting ability and its delectable taste.

Because they're so large, commercially caught kings are generally marketed as fillets or steaks and are best poached or broiled. Their high oil content makes them ideal for smoking. Smaller kings

Fish wheels have long been used on rivers of the North Country to extract a wealth of fish — mostly salmon. Generally built of spruce, plus a little wire to make the basket, the wheel is floated on logs which are sparred out to allow basket and paddles to turn freely, powered by water current.

are excellent for charcoaling or barbecuing whole. A number of recipes specify the king of salmon, although other salmon may be substituted.

Sockeye — also called *red* or *blueback* salmon—average about 6 pounds (2.7 kg). Though not as abundant as some other varieties, sockeye are prime commercial fish because of their taste. Much of the catch is marketed in cans or frozen for export. Sockeye, too, are rich in oil. The *kokanee*, the landlocked form of the sockeye, is also an excellent food fish, caught mainly by sport fishermen.

Silver — also called *coho* and *medium red*—salmon average 4 to 12 pounds (1.8 to 5.4 kg) and are excellent fish for baking, broiling, poaching—whole-dressed or as steaks — and are also good candidates for mild cure or smoking. Very important as a commercial fish, silver salmon are highly regarded sport fish, too.

Pink — also called *humpback* or *humpy* — salmon are the smallest of the five varieties, averaging 2 to 5 pounds (1 to 2.25 kg). They are also the most abundant of the commercially caught salmon, and most of the catch is canned. Pinks contain very little oil and are not as good as other varieties for smoking.

Chum — called *silver brite* and *dog salmon* — are important subsistence fish, partly because their range is farther north than other Pacific salmon. The catch is often smoked or dried for winter use. The commercial catch in Alaska is very large, but because the chum seldom strikes at a lure — and then in annoyance — sport fishing for them is usually futile. Commercially caught chum average about 9 pounds (4 kg).

Preparation Tips: Despite the variations of taste — king to chum — no salmon can fail to be a distinguished meal — baked, broiled, poached, sauteed, grilled, barbecued or smoked. That Alaskans agree on this point is indicated by the abundance of recipes for this delectable fish.

Smoked, kippered, cooked (leftover) and canned salmon can be used in many ways. Some suggestions are included in Chapter 1. More follow. Smoked and kippered salmon may also be substituted in recipes for canned or cooked salmon to provide a welcome flavor change, though seasonings should be adjusted downward to accommodate the saltier taste of the fish. If you need a substitute for the can liquor called for in a recipe, use fish or chicken stock or bouillon.

Depending on the heaviness of the cure, some smoked salmon may need prior soaking or steaming to remove excess salt. You can tell by rubbing your fingers over the fish and then tasting them for saltiness.

Raw fish — lightly marinated in soy and other sauces — is becoming an increasingly popular dish in the United States, with the emergence of whole restaurants — sushi bars — sporting a complete menu of raw fish preparations in the Japanese style. Raw salmon is a favorite.

Properly prepared raw fish is tasty and good for you. But the Japanese take special precautions with salmon and other fish that spend any or all their time in fresh water. The precautions are simple enough, but they are very important. . . . IF YOU PLAN TO SERVE RAW SALMON, please read about how to pretreat it, page 12.

Gravadlox
The king of King Salmon recipes

7 to 8 pounds (3.2 to 3.6 kg) center-cut of
*   salmon in one piece*
2/3 cup (160 mL) salt (I use mild-cure)
1/2 cup (120 mL) sugar
1 teaspoon (5 mL) whole allspice,
*   coarsely crushed*
1 tablespoon (15 mL) whole white pepper,
*   crushed*
1/2 to 3/4 cup (120 to 180 mL) good cognac
2 large bunches fresh dill weed

►This must be made with fresh salmon and a plentiful supply of fresh dill weed. Wipe salmon with damp cloth. Leave skin on but carefully remove bone so that two big fillets remain. (Be careful not to break fish.) Combine salt, sugar, white pepper and allspice, then rub seasonings carefully on all surfaces of the salmon; sprinkle with cognac. Wash dill and shake dry. Spread one-third of the dill in bottom of glass pan. Place salmon, skin side down, on dill. Spread another third of the dill in the fold. Cover top of salmon with remaining dill. Weight salmon with a heavy plate or board and refrigerate for 36 to 48 hours. (I also turn mine every day.) Drain fish and scrape off dill and spices. Slice on the slant, wafer thin, away from skin. Serve with lemon slices, mustard sauce and freshly ground black pepper. Gravadlox will keep refrigerated about 8 to 10 days only. Do not freeze as it loses the dill flavor.

Variation: In the Scandinavian manner, you may remove skin from fish carefully. Cut the skin into strips and fry in hot butter until crisp. Add a strip of it to each serving. We had this at the Grand Hotel in Oslo, Norway, as a first course with tiny, creamed potatoes. We decided we liked our Gravadlox better, but preferred the hotel's sauce. A discussion with the *maitre d'* resulted in an exchange of recipes.

Sauce Grand Hotel, Oslo
2 tablespoons (30 mL) dry mustard
2 tablespoons (30 mL) sugar
1/2 tablespoon (8 mL) vinegar

2 tablespoons (30 mL) oil
Salt, pepper and dill to taste

Old Scandinavian Recipe
9 tablespoons (135 mL) olive oil
3 tablespoons (45 mL) white vinegar
2 to 3 tablespoons (30 to 45 mL) prepared
    sharp mustard
3/4 teaspoon (3 mL) salt
1/8 teaspoon (0.5 mL) cardamom
1/4 cup (60 mL) sugar

►To make either of the above recipes, combine ingredients and blend thoroughly. Chill sauces for several hours. At serving time, beat smooth with fork or wire whisk — do not use rotary blender. Each makes about 1 cup (240 mL).
■ *Bunny Mathisen, Petersburg*
  "Help Yourself To The Sylta Flesk!"
  ALASKA® magazine, January 1977

Lomi-Lomi
A raw salmon appetizer *

►Cut raw salmon in small cubes and place in glass container. Mix equal amounts of olive oil or salad oil and white vinegar. Add salt and pepper to taste. Cut up green onions into vinegar and oil. Pour mixture over salmon and refrigerate at least six hours before serving.
■ *Belle Sage*
  Haines Homemakers' Cookbook

*Raw salmon fixed this way is a treat, but salmon is one of the fish that must be pretreated before it is safe to eat raw. See page 12.

Kippered Salmon Dip

1-1/2 pounds (0.70 kg) kippered salmon,
    flaked very fine
1 tablespoon (15 mL) grated onion
4 ounces (114 g) cream cheese
1 cup (240 mL) whipped cream
Salt and pepper to taste

►Blend all ingredients together. Chill for a few hours. Serve with potato chips, corn chips or a variety of crackers.
■ Tsimpshean Indian Island Cookbook
  Metlakatla

Smoke-Flavored
Salmon Log Appetizer

2 cups (480 mL) flaked salmon, or 1 large can
    (1 lb /or/ 456 g) salmon, drained
1 package (8 oz /or/ 228 g) cream cheese
1 tablespoon (15 mL) lemon juice
2 teaspoons (10 mL) grated onion

1 teaspoon (5 mL) horseradish, or more
1/4 teaspoon (1 mL) liquid smoke
1/4 teaspoon (1 mL) salt
1/2 cup (120 mL) pecans, chopped fine
Parsley

►Mix everything but pecans and parsley and chill. Shape into a log. Roll in finely chopped pecans and garnish with parsley. Serve as a spread with crackers.
■ *Pat Thomas*
  An Alaskan Cook Book, *Kenai*

Smoke-Flavored Salmon Dip
For A Crowd

2 cups (480 mL) cooked salmon
1 cup (240 mL) mayonnaise
1 teaspoon (5 mL) liquid smoke
2 tablespoons (30 mL) garlic vinegar or minced
    garlic and white vinegar
1 can Cheddar cheese soup
1 cup (240 mL) sour cream
2 tablespoons (30 mL) Worcestershire

►Blend well, using the oil from the salmon (if canned salmon is used). Refrigerate for a few hours to blend the flavors. This can be used as a spread for crackers or toast rounds, too.
■ *Frankie Fitch*
  Haines' Homemakers Cookbook

Smoked Salmon Dip
A good way to use kippered or smoked "tips"

►To 1 cup (240 mL) sour cream, add 1 to 2 cups (240 to 480 mL) smoked or kippered salmon and a little lemon juice if you want. Mix and refrigerate at least one hour before serving with chips, crackers or crisp vegetable sticks.
■ *The editors, ALASKA® magazine*

Potted Salmon
A canape spread for a large party

5 pounds (2.25 kg) cold poached salmon
1/2 teaspoon (2 mL) paprika
1/2 teaspoon (2 mL) thyme
1/2 teaspoon (2 mL) mace
1/4 teaspoon (1 mL) cayenne pepper
1 teaspoon (5 mL) salt
1 cup (240 mL) butter
2 garlic buds

►Scald and drain the salmon; remove skin and bones; put through a food chopper. Combine spices and salt and mix thoroughly. Sprinkle over the salmon; mix well and place in a baking dish. Melt half of the butter, add one garlic bud, mashed or

grated; pour over the salmon and bake in a 350°F (175°C) oven 30 minutes. Remove salmon to a bowl, cool, then rub smooth with a wooden spoon; melt the remaining butter and pour over the fish together with the remaining mashed garlic bud. Mix and blend thoroughly. Chill at least 24 hours before serving. Spread on crackers or toast rounds or raw vegetable slices, such as celery and cucumber. The spread also keeps well stored in the refrigerator in tightly sealed jars.
■ *Bess A. Cleveland*
  Alaskan Cookbook For Homesteader or Gourmet (adapted)

Salmon Flips
Tasty salmon turnovers

1 recipe Cheese Canape Pastry
1 pound (456 g) cooked salmon
4 slices bacon
3/4 cup (180 mL) condensed
    Cheddar cheese soup
1 teaspoon (5 mL) horseradish
1 teaspoon (5 mL) instant minced onion
Dash of pepper

►Prepare Cheese Canape Pastry and chill as directed (see below). Flake salmon and drain, if necessary. Fry bacon until crisp. Drain on absorbent paper; then crumble. Combine with remaining ingredients except pastry. Roll pastry very thin and cut in 2-1/2 inch (6.25 cm) squares. Place 1 heaping teaspoon (about 7 mL) on one-half of each square. Fold over and press edges together with a fork. Place turnovers on a baking pan; prick tops to allow steam to escape. Bake in a very hot oven, 450°F (230°C), for 10 to 12 minutes or until lightly browned. Makes approximately 80 turnovers.

Cheese Canape Pastry
1 cup (240 mL) butter or margarine, softened
1 cup (240 mL) shredded cheese
2 cups (480 mL) flour
Dash of salt
Dash of cayenne pepper

►Cream the butter and cheese. Add flour and seasonings. Mix thoroughly. Shape dough into a ball. Chill at least three hours before using. Makes approximately 2 cups (480 mL) of pastry to be used for Salmon Flips and other fillings.
■ Nautical Notions For Nibbling

Smoked Fish Salad Sandwiches

Smoked salmon, 1-1/2 pint jar (720 mL)
1/2 cup (120 mL) chopped onion
1/2 cup (120 mL) chopped kelp dill pickles
    (or cucumber dills)

1 tablespoon (15 mL) chopped parsley
1/2 teaspoon (2 mL) celery seed
Lettuce
Mayonnaise

►Flake fish. Add onion, parsley, celery seed and pickles. Soften with enough mayonnaise to spread on lightly toasted bread and top with lettuce.
  Or use the mixture for a wonderful salad meal by piling on chunks of lettuce and tomato slices. Top with cottage cheese.
■ *Helen Blanchard*
  "I Smoke Salmon"
  ALASKA® magazine, September 1971

Mark's Alaska Smoked Salmon Spread
"Very often one will receive as a prized gift a can of smoked salmon," Mamie Jensen says. "If you eat it right out of the can — a temptation! — it doesn't go far. Here is what we do to make it s-t-r-e-t-c-h deliciously."

1 can (4 oz /or/ 114 g) smoked salmon
1/2 teaspoon (2 mL) horseradish
2 teaspoons (10 mL) or more lemon juice
Mayonnaise

►Remove peppercorns and bay leaf from the canned salmon (if these are on the fish). Pour off the juice, as this can sometimes be salty. Mash salmon well, add horseradish and lemon juice and enough mayonnaise to make mixture of sandwich spread consistency. This can be spread on crackers or toast rounds.

Variations:
• *For a luncheon sandwich* — Toast slices of bread on one side. Spread untoasted side with the above filling, place a slice of tomato on top and on that put a slice of Cheddar cheese. Or use English muffins. Place under the broiler until cheese is bubbly. Serve immediately.
• *For a dip* — Add to the basic recipe 8 ounces (228 g) sour cream, IMO, sieved cottage cheese or plain yogurt. Serve with assorted crackers and/or fresh vegetable sticks.
■ *Mamie Jensen, Juneau*

Simple Salmon Spread

Cooked salmon, flaked
Pimento stuffed olives, chopped fine
Mayonnaise

►Combine first two ingredients with enough mayonnaise to spread easily.
■ *The Old Homesteader*

Alaska's Best Sandwich

►Chop hard-cooked eggs *very* fine. Add salt and pepper to taste and hold together with Best Foods mayonnaise. Remove crusts from bread, butter it, spread it with egg mixture and put a slice of smoked salmon on top.

■ *Bunny Mathisen, Petersburg*

Fast Cheese Bread Ring with Kippered Salmon

1 roll (10 to 12 oz /or/ 280 to 340 g)
   refrigerator biscuits
1/2 cup (120 mL) dried minced onions
8 ounces (228 g) Cheddar cheese, shredded
1/4 pound (114 g) kippered salmon

►Open refrigerator biscuits. Separate biscuits and place on baking sheet in form of a double ring. Let stand for 10 minutes until dough comes to room temperature. Lightly work the biscuits together to form one piece. Sprinkle onion and half the cheese on the biscuit ring. Very gently work the cheese and onion partly into the dough. Sprinkle half of the remaining cheese on top of ring. Bake in a preheated oven according to temperature listed on biscuit package for about eight minutes. Remove from oven and top with crumbled salmon and remaining cheese. Return to oven for about two minutes longer or until cheese melts and biscuits are golden. Pull apart to serve or serve in wedges while hot.

■ *Marge Welch*
  Seattle Seafoodfest Recipes

Salmon Dill Spread

1 can (7-3/4 oz /or/ 220 g) salmon, drained
1/3 cup (80 mL) minced green onion
1/3 cup (80 mL) chopped fresh dill weed
1/3 cup (80 mL) sour cream
2 tablespoons (30 mL) mayonnaise

►Mix all in a bowl. Use at once or chill and use later as a dip or spread for whole-wheat crackers or toasted English muffin rounds.

■ *Jackie Fonnesbeck*
  Courtesy, Audrey Rearden, Homer

SALMON SALADS & SOUPS

About Salmon Salads: No two are alike, we've found, in looking through dozens of recipes. Some that vary considerably are reprinted complete. From the others, the list of ingredients that can be used to stretch the salmon is as long as your imagination. Try: black olives, some chunks or slices of avocado, banana, apple, pear or orange, salted peanuts, toasted almonds, raw asparagus tips, bean sprouts, shredded cabbage, Sugar Snap peas, cooked or uncooked frozen peas, boiled rice or macaroni, cooked shellfish . . . but not all of them at once! And, first, why not start out with one of these?

Zalivnoie

Jellied fish, a Russian specialty

1 salmon
2 bay leaves
Salt and pepper
1 onion
3 stalks celery
4 or 5 carrots, peeled
2 envelopes (2 Tbsp /or/ 30 mL)
   unflavored gelatin
1 lemon, sliced

►Half fill a large pan with water; place all vegetables and seasonings in it. Cook until vegetables are just tender; add fish which has been cut into chunks. Simmer until fish is done; strain through colander, saving broth. Remove all skin and bones from fish. Flake fish and put in bottom of long baking pan or something similar. Return broth to original cooking vessel and bring to a boil. Add gelatin to 1 cup (240 mL) of cold water and allow to soften a few minutes. Add to hot broth and bring to a boil a second time. Slice carrots quite thin and put on top of fish; add gelatin-broth mixture and decorate with lemon slices. Put in refrigerator to set. Unmold and garnish as desired.

■ *Nadia Kopun*
  Saint Herman's Sisterhood Club, Kodiak

Salmon Stuffed Peppers

A cold or hot luncheon salad

2 cups (480 mL) cooked, flaked salmon
1-1/2 cups (360 mL) chopped cabbage
1/2 cup (120 mL) chopped sweet pickle
1 cup (240 mL) chopped peanuts
1/2 teaspoon (2 mL) salt
1/8 teaspoon (0.5 mL) cayenne pepper
6 green peppers
Mayonnaise

►Combine flaked salmon, cabbage, pickle and peanuts. Mix well and season with salt and pepper. Parboil the green peppers — a few minutes only; they should still be quite green — cut stems off and remove seeds; allow to cool. Fill with salmon mixture, top with mayonnaise and paprika and chill thoroughly if you wish to serve them as a cold salad. Or, if you prefer, the stuffed pepper cups may be baked in a 350°F (175°C) oven for 15 minutes, when tops should be nicely browned.

■ Alaskan Cookbook For Homesteader or Gourmet (adapted)

Salmon Mousse with Cucumber Sauce

2 pounds (1 kg) salmon
2 tablespoons (30 mL) gelatin
1/2 cup (120 mL) cold fish stock
1 cup (240 mL) boiling fish stock
3/4 cup (180 mL) mayonnaise
1 tablespoon (15 mL) Worcestershire
1 teaspoon (5 mL) lemon juice
1 tablespoon (15 mL) onion juice
3/4 pint (360 mL) whipping cream, whipped

►Poach salmon in seasoned vegetable water. (See Court Bouillon.) Soak gelatin in cold fish stock. Add boiling stock and stir until dissolved. Cool. When mixture begins to thicken, add mayonnaise. Beat until frothy; add finely minced salmon and seasonings. Fold in the whipped cream. Turn into a fish mold. Chill until firm. Serve on shredded lettuce leaves with Cucumber Sauce.

Cucumber Sauce
►Peel and grate one large cucumber. Add to it 1 cup (240 mL) mayonnaise, 1/2 teaspoon (2 mL) prepared mustard, 1 tablespoon (15 mL) lemon juice and 1 teaspoon (5 mL) minced chives. Stir to blend.

■ *Edna Ferber*, Alaska's Cooking, *Anchorage*

Quick Salmon Mousse

1 large can (16 oz /or/ 456 g) red salmon
2 tablespoons (30 mL) red wine vinegar
2 envelopes (¼ oz /or/ 7 g, each) plain gelatin
1/2 cup (120 mL) boiling water
1 small onion, quartered
1/2 cup (120 mL) mayonnaise
8 ounces (228 g) plain yogurt
1/4 cup (60 mL) fresh dill, chopped
3/4 teaspoon (3 mL) salt
1/4 teaspoon (1 mL) cayenne

►In a blender, combine the juice from the canned salmon with vinegar and gelatin. Add boiling water and blend 40 seconds. Add onion, mayonnaise,

yogurt, dill, salt, cayenne and salmon and blend 30 seconds longer. Pour into a 4-cup (1 L) shallow mold, chill in freezer for 30 minutes or refrigerate two to three hours. Unmold and serve with Sour Cream Cucumber Dressing.

Sour Cream Cucumber Dressing
1/2 cup (120 mL) plain yogurt
1/4 cup (60 mL) sour cream
1/4 cup (60 mL) chopped green onion
1 small cucumber
1/2 teaspoon (2 mL) salt

►Peel, seed and dice cucumber and mix with remaining ingredients. Chill. Makes 1 cup (240 mL) or more.
■ *Millie DeWitt*
   Frontier Vittles, *Fairbanks*

Salmon Salad

2 tablespoons (30 mL) lemon juice
3/4 cup (180 mL) mayonnaise
1 teaspoon (5 mL) curry powder
3 cups (720 mL) cooked salmon, flaked
1/2 cup (120 mL) celery, chopped
1-1/2 cups (360 mL) cooked peas
1 quart (1 L) cooked rice
1/4 cup (60 mL) Italian dressing
2 hard-cooked eggs
Parsley

►Two hours before serving time combine the lemon juice, mayonnaise and curry powder; stir until well mingled. Add the salmon, celery and peas; toss. Cover this mixture tightly and refrigerate. Now toss the rice with the Italian dressing. Cover and refrigerate this also. At serving time line a large plate with crisp lettuce leaves. Form a ring around the edge with the rice. Fill the center with the fish mixture. Garnish with wedges of hard-cooked egg alternating with sprigs of parsley.
■ *The Old Homesteader*

Valid Salmon Salad
A basic salmon salad that can serve as a first course or become a full meal

►Take the flakes of cold, fried salmon steaks or baked salmon, add three hard-cooked eggs, diced; 1/4 teaspoon (1 mL) Italian Seasoning; salt and pepper; one celery heart, diced; 1/4-head lettuce, shredded; one green pepper, chopped; and half a raw onion, diced. Mix together with any salad dressing to which 1 teaspoon (5 mL) mustard has been added. Garnish with 1-inch (2.5 cm) shoots of fireweed for color.
■ *Margaret G. Mielke*
   Alaska's Cooking, *Anchorage*

Salmon Macaroni Salad

3 hard-cooked eggs, chopped
1 pint (480 mL) canned salmon
1 pound (456 g) macaroni, cooked
3 sweet pickles, chopped
10 ounces (280 g) mayonnaise
2 tablespoons (30 mL) wine vinegar
1 tablespoon (15 mL) lemon juice
1 tablespoon (15 mL) prepared mustard
1 tablespoon (15 mL) brown sugar
1 teaspoon (5 mL) celery seed

►Mix all the salad ingredients in a large bowl and eat it all up!
■ *Ann Thacker, Delta Junction*
   ALASKA® magazine, October 1976

Salmon Stuffed Tomatoes

6 firm, ripe tomatoes
1 package (3 oz /or/ 85 g) lemon gelatin
1 cup (240 mL) boiling water
1/2 cup (120 mL) mayonnaise
1/2 cup (120 mL) seeded and grated cucumber
2 tablespoons (30 mL) lemon juice
1 teaspoon (5 mL) minced onion
1/2 teaspoon (2 mL) Worcestershire
1/2 teaspoon (2 mL) salt, or to taste
1-1/2 cups (360 mL) cooked and flaked salmon,
   or 1 large can (1 lb /or/ 456 g),
   thoroughly drained

►Peel tomatoes. This is easiest done if you scald them first, one at a time, in a full pot of rapidly boiling water. Poke a fork through the stem end of the tomato and plunge it into boiling water for 10 seconds. Still holding it by the fork, run it through cold water very briefly, prick the skin and peel. When tomatoes are peeled, cut slices from the tops and scoop out centers, invert and chill.
   Combine gelatin, boiling water and mayonnaise. Stir well to mix and then chill to about the consistency of egg white. Mix remaining ingredients and fold into chilled gelatin. Chill again until almost firm. Then fill tomato cups and chill thoroughly. Serve on crisp lettuce with additional mayonnaise, sprinkled with paprika. May be served whole as the main course at luncheon for six or cut in crosswise slices and served as a dinner salad to eight or more.
■ Seattle Seafoodfest Recipes *(adapted)*

Salmon Chowder

1 can (1 lb /or/ 456 g) salmon
2 cups (0.47 L) water
1 cup (240 mL) tomato juice
1/2 cup (120 mL) chopped onion
1 cup (240 mL) raw cubed potato
1 teaspoon (5 mL) celery salt
4 tablespoons (60 mL) butter
4 tablespoons (60 mL) flour
3 cups (720 mL) milk
1 teaspoon (5 mL) salt
1 teaspoon (5 mL) dry mustard
1/2 teaspoon (2 mL) Worcestershire

►Combine salmon, water, tomato juice, onion, potato and celery salt in large kettle. Cover and simmer for 40 minutes. In another saucepan melt butter; add flour, salt and mustard; mix until smooth. Add milk, stirring constantly, and cook until thick. Combine with salmon mixture; stir well and serve hot. Serves 10 to 12.
■ *Vera Reynolds*
   PTA Cook Book, *Petersburg*

Prouder Chowder
Waste not . . . and have a good soup

1 backbone from a filleted salmon
1 tablespoon (15 mL) oil
1 chopped onion
1 diced heart of celery
1 diced potato
1 quart (1 L) milk
1 tablespoon (15 mL) butter
Salt and pepper

►Process backbone in a pressure cooker for 10 minutes at 10 pounds pressure (69 kPa) or simmer it 30 minutes in a saucepan in salted water to cover. Cool. Shake meat loose and reserve. Heat oil in a 2-quart (2 L) saucepan and saute vegetables until tender. Add milk, butter and fish pieces reserved from backbone, plus salt and pepper to taste. Heat through and serve as a one-dish meal. Dried vegetable flakes, sauteed green pepper, left-over ham or sausage bits make tasty additions to the chowder. Serves four to six.
■ *Margaret G. Mielke*
   Alaska's Cooking, *Anchorage*

Fresh Salmon Cream Soup
Unusual and worth some effort

1-1/2 pounds (0.70 kg) fresh salmon
2 cups (480 mL) hot water
1 slice onion
1 stalk celery
1 sprig parsley
1 tablespoon (15 mL) green pepper flakes
1 quart (1 L) milk
5 tablespoons (75 mL) butter
5 tablespoons (75 mL) flour
1/2 teaspoon (2 mL) salt
Dash of pepper
1 tablespoon (15 mL) chopped parsley

►Remove skin and bones from salmon and grind twice. Stir into hot water and simmer gently for three minutes, stirring constantly. Add onion, celery, parsley and green pepper to milk. Scald and strain. Melt butter; blend in flour, salt and pepper. Add scalded milk gradually and cook until thick and smooth, stirring constantly. Add the salmon mixture. Heat and serve immediately, topped with chopped parsley.
■ *Lillian Hillman, FV Harold*
 Seafood Secrets, Sitka

Hungarian Salmon Soup
An elegant soup for a special luncheon

1 medium onion, chopped
1 carrot, cut in thin strips
1 stalk celery, thinly sliced
2 tablespoons (30 mL) butter
4 cups (1 L) water
1 sprig parsley
2 tablespoons (30 mL) tomato puree
1 bay leaf
4 peppercorns
1/2 teaspoon (2 mL) thyme
1 clove garlic

2 tablespoons (30 mL) pimento-stuffed
 olives, sliced
1 tablespoon (15 mL) capers
1 can (1 lb /or/ 456 g) salmon, flaked, with juice
Salt and pepper
Sour cream

►Saute chopped onion, carrot and celery in butter for a few minutes. Add water, parsley, tomato puree, bay leaf, peppercorns, thyme and garlic. Bring to a boil and simmer for 15 minutes. Add olives, capers, salmon and salmon juice. Salt and pepper to taste. Garnish with sour cream and sprinkle paprika on each portion. Makes six cups.
■ *Joan Budai, FV Supreme*
 Seafood Secrets, Sitka

Salmon Soup

►Clean fish heads; place in pot large enough to cover with water. Cook until fish is easy to pull away from bones. Add whatever vegetables you have — onions, carrots, peas, cabbage, etc. Cook until vegetables are tender; add salt and pepper to taste. Serve with plenty of hardtack or pilot bread.
■ *Minnie Fisher*

SALMON TRIMMINGS

About Salmon Trimmings: If your salmon is fresh out of the water, you'll appreciate these recipes for parts often discarded for want of techniques that can turn them into meals. Remember, "spare parts," such as livers, roe, milt, salmon "bellies," tips and other trimmings spoil quickly. Plan to eat them or preserve them as soon as possible after the fish is caught.

Leading off are two recipes for salmon caviar that vary enough to make both worth trying. What doesn't vary is the necessity to keep caviar refrigerated — 34°F (1 to 2°C) is ideal. Note that swish restaurants serve caviar on crushed ice. There's a reason for it. Caviar does not keep indefinitely, as some recipes indicate, but stored in an airtight container (don't use metal) in the refrigerator, it will last some time. Most cooks suggest that newly prepared caviar be refrigerated for at least three days before serving. For general information about removing the membrane from roe sacs or parboiling, please see page 19.

Next, more recipes for salmon milt than you're likely to find anywhere else this side of the Mediterranean Sea are shared here, courtesy of the experimental bent of Jeanne Culbertson of Adak.

In keeping with the "spare parts" theme is a recipe for salmon bellies. Just the bellies of salmon (where a lot of fat is concentrated) are salted down by many fishermen by the barrel for a special winter treat. They are most often eaten lightly boiled, after thorough rinsing of excess brine, with boiled potatoes. In some recipes, however, "bellies" are trim pieces, in general, tasty morsels left over when a fillet has been trimmed to a certain shape. We can thank the airlines — and their need to have naturally rounded fillets fit into square meal trays — for one source of leftover "salmon bellies." These small chunks of fillet are ideal for many dishes, such as salads, appetizers and soups, or chunked fish in an elegant sauce. If you are buying them at the market, "bellies" are a good deal cheaper than ordinary fillet.

Another trimming worth saving is the salmon "tip," which is the pectoral fin and the fleshy part around it. This is cut away from the body of a fish that is to be steaked or pan-dressed after the head has been removed. A pair of king salmon tips will yield a good deal of fleshy meat . . . as well as bones. Many markets sell smoked or kippered tips and, because of the bone, they are cheaper than the rest of the smoked fish, worth buying for spreads and other such uses.

The remaining recipes — some excellent ideas among them — are self-explanatory.

Salmon Caviar #1

►Remove egg skein gently from the salmon. A 12- to 14-pound (5.4 to 6.3 kg) female will contain about a half-pound (228 g) egg skein. Freshness is all-important in preparing caviar, so do not keep the roe more than 24 hours. Do not use eggs with any odor of spoilage. Fresh roe has a heavy oily odor, but the prepared caviar will have a light fragrance.

If you cannot process your roe for caviar right away, you may wish to freeze the skeins. This will make the membrane harder to remove, but the resulting caviar should be just as good. To freeze egg skeins, wrap them in wax paper or plastic wrap, then again in freezer paper, covering with several thicknesses and sealing securely. An alternate method is to place the skeins in a plastic freezer container, cover completely with fresh, clean water and freeze at -10°F (-23°C). Using this method you can keep roe frozen indefinitely in good condition.

To prepare the caviar, select a fresh skein of eggs and gently separate the eggs individually from the skein, removing as much of the membrane as possible. For 2 cups (480 mL) of cleaned eggs, stir 1/2 cup (120 mL) salt into 2 cups (480 mL) cold water in a large dish until well dissolved. Add eggs and stir gently. Allow to stand for 30 minutes. The eggs will absorb some of the salt and grow noticeably firmer. Membrane particles will turn white; they are easily seen and should be picked out of the mixture. Pour the mixture through a strainer to drain the water from the eggs. Rinse eggs in a large dish of cold water and strain a second time. Pick out any remaining membrane. Cover tightly and place in refrigerator to chill. Caviar will keep this way for several months. If it develops an off-flavor, discard it.

Caviar should be served ice-cold. It is excellent with unsalted crackers or toast or as an addition to salads with a dollop of sour cream.

■ Washington Seafood Recipes

Salmon Caviar #2

►Place 2 or 3 pounds (1 to 1.45 kg) of salmon eggs in a saucepan. Pour boiling water over the raw eggs to dissolve and drain off the slimy substance which causes the raw eggs to adhere to one another. During this preliminary process, stir the eggs with a long-handled spoon, preferably of wood, or with a stick. Stirring and blanching should continue until the individual eggs float freely in the hot water.

Then pour off the liquid through a colander. By this time the eggs appear partially cooked and have

turned rather white. However, when cold water from tap or stream is sluiced over them to rinse away the last of the slime, the eggs return to their original salmon-egg pink.

After rinsing thoroughly, transfer the mass of eggs to a mixing bowl and sprinkle liberally with pepper. Stir in enough salt to provide the sharp, salty flavor necessary to caviar. Add half an onion, chopped fine, and stir the whole mixture well.

Place the caviar mixture in a cloth bag or nonmetal strainer and place that inside another vessel to catch the drips. Keep the whole thing refrigerated (34°F /or/ 1 to 2°C is ideal) overnight, allowing the last moisture to drain away from the caviar. When this has been done, the caviar may be returned to a bowl and refrigerated again. Cover to prevent drying out.

At the dining table, the Aleuts serve salmon-egg

caviar as a special delicacy spread for bread or crackers. This is rich fare with excellent flavor, as the eggs are filled with vitamin-rich oil. Such a dish can be prepared easily by a fisherman in camp as a tasty highlight of his outdoor menu.

■ *Jay Ellis Ransom*
  "Exotic Aleut Salmon Recipes"
  ALASKA® *magazine, August 1980*

Fried Salmon Eggs

►For size of family, choose the proper number of immature skeins of salmon eggs cut into pieces of convenient size. Roll the cut pieces of skein, with the eggs intact, in corn meal or cracker crumbs, adding salt, pepper and other seasonings to taste.

Fry, browning well on both sides so that the skeins are cooked through. Fry in vegetable oil with a little butter for flavor.

Use a cover with vents to prevent spatter, or pull the cover back from the edge to allow steam to escape. Never use ripe eggs as they explode like popcorn, causing grease and steam to spatter.

■ *Pacific Salmon Cookbook*

Red Caviar with Cream Cheese

►Please have your cream cheese and caviar very cold. Take a block of cream cheese (I use 8 ounces, 228 g) and cover thickly with red caviar. Serve with hot Melba toast attractively arranged. This should serve 25.

■ *Bunny Mathisen*
  "Help Yourself To The Sylta Flesk!"
  ALASKA® *magazine, January 1977*

Salmon Roe Casserole

1-1/2 pounds (685 g) fresh mature salmon roe*
1 cup (240 mL) water
3 peppercorns
1 bay leaf
2 cloves
2 tablespoons (30 mL) grated onion
1 tablespoon (15 mL) parsley flakes
1 cup (240 mL) bread crumbs
1 tablespoon (15 mL) lemon juice
1 cup (240 mL) White Sauce
Pinch of paprika
Salt and pepper

►*Do not substitute roe from any other fish. Combine first five ingredients in a saucepan and bring to a boil. Cover and simmer for 15 minutes. Drain, saving only the roe, breaking it in pieces with a fork.

Place a layer of the roe in a buttered baking dish.

Salt and pepper. Sprinkle lightly with onion, parsley, lemon juice and bread crumbs. Cover with White Sauce. Repeat layers until all roe is used. Dot the last layer of crumbs with butter and sprinkle with paprika. Bake at 350°F (175°C) for 20 minutes or until golden brown.

■ *Joan Budai, FV* Supreme
  Seafood Secrets, *Sitka*

Salmon Backbones

8 pieces salmon backbone, each about 5 inches (12.5 cm) long
1 bottle (8 fl oz /or/ 240 mL) Kraft Casino salad dressing
1 cup (240 mL) corn meal
Salt
Garlic powder

►Line cookie sheet with aluminum foil and spread with a thin coating of Casino dressing. Sprinkle backbones with corn meal, season with salt and a light sprinkle of garlic powder. Place on cookie sheet, each piece overlapping just a bit. Spread generously with the rest of the dressing and bake about 45 minutes on the top rack of the oven, turning when top is lightly browned.

■ *Vi Haynes, Pelican*
  The Alaskan Camp Cook

Versatile Salmon Eggs

►Clean the eggs in water. Cook in boiling water with salt. Cook until medium soft and then mix them with seaweed and a little grease.

Variations:
• After cooking, eat plain with grease or sprinkle with seaweed.
• Mix cooked eggs with mayonnaise and put in salad.
• Or mix cabbage, celery and onions and a little radishes and put cooked fish eggs in it. Add mayonnaise.

■ *Tsimpshean Indian Island Cookbook*
  Metlakatla

Fried Salmon Livers

►Wash livers; slice or cook whole. Dredge in a half-and-half mixture of corn meal and flour, seasoned with salt. Brown two minutes on each side in hot, greased skillet. Allow two or three livers per serving. They are prized for the delicate flavor and are an excellent source of vitamin A. Children, especially, should be encouraged to eat salmon liver.

■ *Ann Mathews, FV* Sultan
  Seafood Secrets, *Sitka (adapted)*

Stink Heads
Tipmuck, to some

►Take a fish that is going up the creek, preferably humpies or pinks. Cut the heads off and either wrap them in wild celery leaves or eel grass or leave them plain. Dig a shallow hole and bury the heads to keep the flies off them. Let the heads ferment for about four or five days. After this time, dig them up and eat them as they are. A couple of things while eating — sit in the tall grass and have a lot of perfume on hand!

■ *Art Johnson*
  Uutuqtwa, *Bristol Bay High School, Naknek*

Baked King Salmon Tips
6 or 8 fresh fish tips
1/2 cup (120 mL) soy sauce
1 cup (240 mL) brown sugar,
*   firmly packed*

What's In A Name?

The French call it laitance *or "soft roe," and the encyclopedia of European cooking,* Larousse Gastronomique, *describes no less than a dozen ways of preparing it. But, alas, in the United States, even people who carefully save salmon roe often throw the milt away. What it needs, says culinary adventurer Jeanne Culbertson, is a "catchy market name and some good PR" . . . plus a few of her kitchen- and market-tested recipes!*

What's in a name? Sometimes a great deal. Gourmets are fond of sweetbreads, which could correctly be called the thymus gland. Who wants to eat a thymus gland?

During the past few years I have been serving guests an unnamed main dish — pieces about 4 inches by 1 inch (10 x 2.5 cm), mild, high-quality protein, usually fried, white and finely textured inside. They generally say, "Hmm, very good. What is it?" When I answer, "Milt," I get either a quizzical, "What's that?" or an uncertain smile and, "Oh, I didn't know you could eat that." Milt, the sperm of a fish, definitely needs a catchy market name and some good PR.

The first year I was on Adak and saw the salmon crowding the streams, I was too overwhelmed to question what the white blobs were along the banks. A year later, while looking through a cookbook given to me 38 years before as a wedding gift, I found a paragraph on milt, explaining that it is the substance in the male fish equivalent to the roe and cooked in the same way.

A few days later my husband caught a good-sized salmon, so I rolled the milt in a little flour and fried it with our salmon steaks. We both liked it right away. I began asking people to save it for me, and when a lot of fish are being caught, I clean other people's fish to get the milt. Among the many guests who've tried it, only one hasn't taken second or third portions. It doesn't have a fishy taste, so it provides variety to menus that already include a lot of fish and also appeals to those who don't like seafood in general. Quite a few friends now save the milt and use it from their own catches. Exceptionally high in protein but with a low fat content, milt also freezes well.

This delicious food makes a great meal with your favorite bread, vegetable, and salad.

Before cooking milt, rinse it and remove the blue vein to make it more attractive and to prevent curling during cooking. Milt averages about an ounce (28 g) for each pound (0.45 kg) of salmon. I figure on at least 3 or 4 ounces (85 to 114 g) of milt for each person.

Quick and Easy Milt

►Dip milt in your favorite batter or roll it in flour and deep-fat fry about five minutes, or slowly brown in butter or margarine. Garnish with parsley and lemon. Serve with Tartar Sauce as a main course with French fries, salad and corn on the cob.

►Arrange tips in a large baking pan so that none overlap. Sprinkle well with the sugar and sauce. Bake at 375°F (190°C) for 45 minutes. No salt is needed. Serves five or six.

■ *Lina Fox*
   Saint Herman's Sisterhood Club, *Kodiak*

Salmon Liver Confection

►Salmon livers are used by Aleuts in a pemmicanlike concoction eaten primarily as a between-meals confection or as a dessert following the main meal.

It is prepared by boiling salmon livers until they turn flour-white. The livers are then thoroughly pulverized and mashed into a paste with the consistency of bread dough.

Into a pan of liver paste, pour about double the volume of berries. Small black mossberries, indigenous to the Aleutian Islands, are a favorite of the Aleuts, but almost any wild berry will do, as well as garden variety currants, cooked and sweetened cranberries, and, in Alaska, any variety of tundra fruit.

Stir and knead the livers and berries. The Aleuts also add seal oil to provide additional flavor. A dollop or two of olive oil may better suit some taste buds. A typical recipe:

1 gallon (3.8 L) berries
8 boiled salmon livers
4 tablespoons (60 mL) seal oil

■ *Jay Ellis Ransom*
   "Exotic Aleut Salmon Recipes"
   ALASKA® *magazine, August 1980*

Steamed Salmon Bellies

This dish uses salted salmon bellies, but fresh or smoked ones would do as well if you have them; just omit the soaking.

►This is a popular company breakfast dish in Alaska. The fish is to be served with melted butter or a rich cream sauce and to be accompanied by plain boiled potatoes. Take as many salted salmon bellies as are needed and soak them for 48 hours, changing the water frequently. On the morning they are to be served, drain the fish and wrap in cheesecloth and steam until fish is tender, at least an hour or two. Remove from cheesecloth and place on hot platter.

■ Out of Alaska's Kitchens

Lena Point "Finnan Haddie"

An excellent use of salmon "scraps"

►Because we are not experts at it, there is quite a bit of fish remaining on the backbone when we fillet salmon for smoking and canning. We salt and smoke the backs, wrap them carefully in plastic bags and freeze them for later use.

To serve, soak smoked backs in cold water to remove excess salt. Cover with milk, add pepper and a piece of butter. Bake until fish flakes from backbone. Either baste occasionally or turn pieces over during baking.

■ *Sally and Clayton Polley*
   Juneau Centennial Cookbook

Even Easier Milt

►Dip milt in salted milk, then into fine bread crumbs; place on oiled baking pan, sprinkle lightly with oil and bake at 400°F (205°C) for 10 minutes.

Milt Casserole

►Grease a casserole with margarine. Alternate layers of milt, frozen peas and bread crumbs (or rice). Cover with a final layer of cream of mushroom soup (or celery soup) and sprinkle with grated cheese. Bake at 375°F (190°C) for 45 minutes.

Luncheon Milt

►Boil milt 10 minutes in salted water. Remove skin and cut into cubes. Make a white sauce with 2 tablespoons (30 mL) butter and 2 tablespoons (30 mL) flour for each cup (240 mL) of milk. Season with salt, pepper, ketchup and Worcestershire to suit your taste. Add the milt and serve on hot buttered toast.

Milt Quiche, Too!

►This is always a hit. For a small casserole, start with this basic recipe and increase as needed. In a blender, put:

2 cups (480 mL) milt
3 eggs
1/2 can cream of onion soup
1/2 cup (120 mL) mayonnaise
2 teaspoons (10 mL) Worcestershire

►Blend thoroughly, pour into a greased casserole or partially baked pastry shell and bake at 375°F (190°C) for 40 minutes. Serve immediately for a delicious luncheon entree with your favorite rolls and a salad.

After blending, you may wish to add 1/3 cup (80 mL) of chopped green onions or a package of chopped broccoli or spinach. Serves three or four.

■ *Jeanne Culbertson*

Reprinted from ALASKA® magazine, August 1980

SALMON MAIN DISHES

Baked Salmon
A basic recipe

►Stuff dressed salmon, if desired. Place in a well-greased or foil-lined baking pan. Brush fish with melted butter or oil inside and out. Bake at 450°F (230°C) allowing 10 minutes baking time per inch (2.5 cm) of thickness measured at its thickest point. Salmon should flake easily when tested with a fork at its thickest part. If stuffing salmon, measure thickness *after* stuffing. Do not turn fish during baking.
■ Alaska Salmon

Variation: Salmon may be baked and served with head, tail, fins and skin intact. Some cooks remove the skin before serving, however, to reveal the delicious, moist meat. Here's a suggestion from Sister Mary Claude, Nulato Mission (via Anita Garnick in *Tried and True Recipes*), about how to make skin removal easy: The fish must be very fresh; that is, right out of the water. Remove head and tail; clean and wipe dry. Pass a sharp knife along the back to cut the skin for later removal. Stuff the fish if desired and bake as directed above. When the fish is almost done, roll off the skin with a knife and rub the meat with a split clove of garlic. Finish baking and serve with lemon juice.

Baked Alaska Red Salmon with Crab Stuffing and Lemon Cream Sauce

1 red salmon, 8 to 10 pounds (3.6 to 4.5 kg)
4 cups (1 L) fresh or frozen spinach,
*   chopped fairly fine*
1 pound (456 g) crab meat
1 teaspoon (5 mL) nutmeg
Juice of 2 lemons
1 teaspoon (5 mL) salt
1/4 teaspoon (1 mL) pepper
Lemon Cream Sauce

►Clean fish and remove all bone, including the backbone, but keep the fish whole; do not split. Mix the remaining ingredients together and stuff the fish. Score the fish lightly about every 2 inches (5 cm) by making diagonal cuts about 1/8 inch (3 mm) deep along its side. Sew up the fish or tie with string about every 3 inches (7.5 cm). Grease baking pan and fish with cooking oil and sprinkle with salt and pepper. Place in a 350°F (175°C) oven for about one hour.
To serve, slice fish with a very sharp knife, being careful to hold the stuffing within the slice. Place a narrow ribbon of Lemon Cream Sauce across the slices and garnish with chopped parsley and lemon wedges.

Lemon Cream Sauce
2 tablespoons (30 mL) butter
2 tablespoons (30 mL) flour
1 cup (240 mL) milk
1 teaspoon (5 mL) lemon juice
Salt to taste
Yellow food coloring

►Melt butter over low heat, add flour and blend for about five minutes. Slowly stir in milk. When sauce has thickened add lemon juice, salt and a dash of yellow coloring to give the sauce a rich, creamy color.
■ Out of Alaska's Kitchens

Salmon Baked in A Jacket

1 whole-dressed sockeye salmon
2 cups (480 mL) flour
1 teaspoon (5 mL) salt
1 teaspoon (5 mL) black pepper
1 cup (240 mL) vinegar

►Mix flour, salt, pepper and vinegar. Add water if necessary to make a thick paste. Spread over one side of fish. Place this side down in foil-lined pan. Spread remaining flour mix on top side of salmon. Bake at 375°F (190°C) until paste cover is hard and brown, about 1 to 1-1/2 hours. Remove from oven. Lift hardened cover off and discard. This is a delicious way to serve salmon that is apt to be dry.
■ Tsimpshean Indian Island Cookbook
    Metlakatla

Islander Salmon
Marinated and baked

1 whole-dressed salmon, 3 to 5 pounds
*   (1.4 to 2.25 kg)*
1 cup (240 mL) soy sauce
1/2 clove garlic, crushed
1/4 cup (60 mL) brown sugar
1 teaspoon (5 mL) dry mustard
Lemon slices
3 or 4 strips bacon (optional)
Dill weed (optional)

►Mix soy sauce, garlic, brown sugar and mustard and pour over salmon in a large plastic bag with a tight seal or in a baking dish. Marinate salmon, turning it frequently, for half an hour at room temperature, or longer, if refrigerated.

Before baking, pour off and reserve marinade to use as a baste during the last 10 minutes or so of cooking. Lay lemon slices and three or four strips of bacon across the fish if desired. Add a sprinkling of dill weed. Bake 15 to 30 minutes at 325°F (160°C), until fish is barely cooked through.*

Garnish with extra lemon and serve with Zesty Salmon Sauce and/or Sauce Verte. Herbed and seasoned cooked rice makes a nice stuffing or side dish to complement this salmon.
■ *David Sykas*
  FV Vernon, Ketchikan

The Canadian hot oven method works well with this fish, too. Just be sure to reserve the basting sauce, as the recipe directs, until the last minutes of cooking, as it has a tendency to burn. Bacon strips, if you want to serve them with the fish, should also be removed after they've done their job of basting . . . and before they singe.

Salmon Grilled in Foil and Zesty Salmon Sauce
For an outdoor grill

1 whole-dressed salmon, 5 to 8 pounds
    (2.25 to 3.6 kg)
Salt and pepper
2 tablespoons (30 mL) softened butter
1/2 medium onion, sliced
1/2 lemon, sliced
Several sprigs fresh parsley
Oil
Zesty Salmon Sauce

►Wash and pat salmon dry. Sprinkle inside with salt and pepper; dot with butter. Arrange overlapping slices of onion, lemon and parsley in cavity. Brush salmon with oil. Wrap well in heavy-duty aluminum foil; seal edges with double fold. Place on grill over medium-hot coals. Carefully turn salmon every 10 minutes. Test for doneness after 45 minutes by inserting meat thermometer in thickest portion. Cook to internal temperature of 160°F (71°C) or until salmon flakes easily when tested with a fork at thickest part. To serve, transfer salmon to serving platter and fold back foil. Cut

---

To give house plants a lift — "Feed" them leftover fish, coffee grounds, water from boiled eggs, crushed egg shells, water from cooked foods and watered milk.
■ *Cooking Up A Storm, Homer*

---

between bone and meat with a wide spatula; lift off each serving. Serve plain or with Zesty Salmon Sauce. Makes 8 to 12 servings.

Zesty Salmon Sauce
1/2 cup (120 mL) butter
3 tablespoons (45 mL) soy sauce
2 tablespoons (30 mL) ketchup
1 tablespoon (15 mL) Worcestershire
1 tablespoon (15 mL) dry mustard
1 clove garlic, crushed

►Combine ingredients in small saucepan; heat gently but thoroughly. Makes 3/4 cup (180 mL).
■ Alaska Salmon

Simple Salmon
Baked in foil

1 red salmon, about 5 pounds (2.25 kg)
Salt and pepper
1 medium onion, sliced
Egg Sauce
Prepared mustard
Lemon wedges, green pepper squares

►Wipe salmon inside and out with paper towels, being sure to get out all blood. Sprinkle inside with salt and pepper or seasoned salt. Put sliced onion inside the fish. Lay enough heavy duty foil in baking pan to completely cover salmon. You may have to use two pieces, one crosswise. Place fish in center of foil and close foil securely. Bake in an oven preheated to 400°F (205°C) for about one hour or until the fish is easily flaked when tested with a fork. Fifteen minutes or so before time for fish to be done, fold back the foil to expose the top of the fish. Lift the baked salmon off the foil onto a warm platter and peel off skin. Add prepared mustard to taste to Egg Sauce and pour over the baked fish. Garnish with lemon wedges and green pepper squares. Garden peas and mashed potatoes are perfect with salmon prepared this way.
■ *The Old Homesteader*

Barbecued King Salmon — Indian Style

►Build fire, not too large, and let it die down to a nice bed of coals. Clean salmon well, split down center, take out backbone (makes two equal halves). If some parts are thicker than others, score the thicker parts lightly so salmon will broil evenly. Cut two straight boughs or willows of medium size and split each down one end. The boughs or willows should be about 2 feet (60 cm) longer than the length of the salmon. Place a side of salmon between each split willow. Whittle some small sticks and place them crossways on both sides of the salmon, between the split willow to hold the salmon flat. Draw the split end of the willow tight and fasten it. This will hold the salmon firmly in place. When the fire coals are right, stick the end of willow into ground alongside fire, with the salmon extending over the coals, but not too close. Baste the salmon with melted butter, a little vinegar, pepper and salt. Turn the salmon when necessary. Broil until well done.

■ *Earl N. Ohmer*
   PTA Cook Book, *Petersburg*

Fish on A Stick

2 pounds (1 kg) salmon steaks
1 green pepper, cut into 1-inch (2.5 cm) squares
10 small onions
1 cup (240 mL) oil
1/2 teaspoon (2 mL) oregano
1/2 teaspoon (2 mL) salt
1/2 teaspoon (2 mL) thyme
1 teaspoon (5 mL) pepper
1/2 teaspoon (2 mL) garlic powder

►Cut salmon into 1-inch (2.5 cm) pieces. Place alternately on a stick — salmon, pepper, onion. Place stick in a shallow dish. Pour oil and seasoning over and let stand for one hour. Drain and put fish over hot coals for four to six minutes. Keep stick turning. Can tell when done; the fish will flake.

■ Tsimpshean Indian Island Cookbook
   Metlakatla

Firepit Baked Salmon

"Living in the Bush means finding ways to cook when you don't have too many conveniences. This way of preparing salmon produces such a tasty dish we would use it even if we had the most modern oven."

2 to 4 half-pound (228 g) salmon steaks
Bread-based stuffing
Onions, sliced in rings

►Put the steaks in a deep baking pan. Cover them with stuffing and top with onion rings. Cover the pan tightly with a double layer of heavy-duty aluminum foil.

Find a sandy spot on the beach or riverbank and dig out a pit about 2 x 3 feet (60 x 90 cm) wide and 18 inches (45 cm) deep. Set the pan in the bottom of the pit and carefully cover it with about 2 inches (5 cm) of sand, not letting any sand trickle into the pan. Then build a fire on top of the sand-covered salmon.

After about 45 minutes, shovel the coals out of the pit and lift out the pan, using oven mitts. Use caution. The sand will be hot, too. Brush it off, peel

back the foil and serve the delicious salmon and stuffing piping hot. Serves two people.

The same method may be used to bake a whole 10- to 15-pound (4.5 to 6.75 kg) salmon for a crowd of people. Just put the stuffing inside the cavity, onions outside and wrap the whole fish in several layers of foil. Bake for 1 to 1-1/2 hours.

■ *Gerald T. Ahnert*
   "From Ketchikan to Barrow®"
   ALASKA® *magazine, October 1982*

Broiled Salmon Fillets
with Herbed Lemon Butter

8 salmon fillets (about 2 lbs /or/ 1 kg)
Salt and pepper
1/4 cup (60 mL) melted butter
2 tablespoons (30 mL) lemon juice
2 tablespoons (30 mL) chopped parsley
1/4 teaspoon (1 mL) dill, rosemary or
*   marjoram, crumbled*
1/4 teaspoon (1 mL) salt
1/8 teaspoon (0.5 mL) coarsely ground pepper

►Line broiler pan with foil and place salmon fillets on the rack. Sprinkle lightly with salt and pepper. Combine remaining ingredients and use to baste the salmon. Place broiler pan 4 inches (10 cm) from heat and broil, allowing 10 minutes cooking time per inch (2.5 cm) thickness. Do not turn salmon. Baste several times during cooking. Serves eight.

■ Alaska Salmon

Barbecued Salmon —
Fisherman Style

►Split a salmon down the back, both sides of ribs. Gut and let flop open. Wipe out cavity with a damp cloth. Do all of this the night before the big barbecue. Throw a handful of brown sugar plus salt and pepper inside the fish and fold together. Keep cool. In the morning open the salmon and shake out.

Use a 50-gallon (190 L) drum, like a garbage can, for a barbecue pit. Use hardware cloth for a grill. Lay fish, skin side down on grill. Place a washtub over it, letting it rest on the mesh. Make a slow fire of alder. It will take a 15-pound (7 kg) salmon 2-1/2 to 3 hours of cold smoke. Baste now and again with melted butter.

■ *The Old Homesteader*

Salmon in Wine Sauce

2 pounds (1 kg) salmon steaks or fillets,
*   1/2 inch (1.25 cm) thick*
Salt and pepper
1 cup (240 mL) sherry
Juice of 1 lemon

Salt and pepper
1/4 cup (60 mL) olive oil

►Place salmon in baking dish and sprinkle on salt and pepper. Combine remaining ingredients and pour over fish. Bake till tender in a hot oven, 400°F (205°C), about half an hour. Serve immediately. Serves six.
■ *Beth Corcoran*
  Alaska's Cooking, *Anchorage*

Salmon in Lemon Sauce

1 red or silver salmon, filleted
1 stick (114 g) butter
Juice of 1 lemon
1 tablespoon (15 mL) Worcestershire
2 to 3 tablespoons (30 to 45 mL) chopped fresh
  or dried chives

►Place salmon fillets on foil and put in shallow dish. Cover tightly and bake at 450°F (230°C) until milk comes to top.* Melt butter, add lemon juice, chives and Worcestershire. Remove cover from fish, pour on sauce and finish baking uncovered, basting occasionally with sauce.
■ *Belva Hamilton*
  Dall Homemakers Cookbook, *Cooper Landing*

Or, measure the fish and time the cooking according to instructions on page 10.

Salmon Baked in Tomato Sauce

2 pounds (1 kg) fresh or frozen salmon
2 cups (480 mL) canned tomatoes
1 cup (240 mL) water
1 large onion, sliced thin
3 cloves
1/2 tablespoon (7 mL) sugar
3 tablespoons (45 mL) butter
3 tablespoons (45 mL) flour
3/4 teaspoon (3 mL) salt
1/4 teaspoon (1 mL) pepper

►Cook tomatoes, water, onion, cloves and sugar in saucepan for 20 minutes. Melt butter, add flour and stir into hot sauce. Add salt and pepper and cook 10 minutes longer, stirring constantly. Pour sauce over split fish (skin side down) in baking dish. Bake in a moderate oven 35 minutes, or until fish flakes easily. Baste often.
■ *Oddveig Johansen*
  Kitchen Magic, *Ketchikan*

Variation: One cook suggests sauteing chopped onion, celery and three or four slices of bacon, cut into pieces, and adding this to the sauce. The sauce is also good over chunks of salmon or halibut steaks and fillets.

Grilled Salmon Steaks with A Choice of Sauces

Salmon steaks
Garlic salt or clove garlic, split
Salt and pepper
Oil

►Marinate salmon steaks in oil seasoned with garlic salt, pepper and salt for about one hour. Place steaks on well-oiled grill. Cook about 4 inches (10 cm) from moderately hot coals for 8 minutes. Turn and cook 7 to 10 minutes longer. Serve with Sour Cream Sauce and/or Lemon Parsley Butter.

Sour Cream Sauce
1 pint (0.45 L) sour cream
1/2 cup (120 mL) chopped green onion
1 medium cucumber, chopped fine

►Combine all ingredients, chill and serve with Grilled Salmon Steaks.
■ *June Sargent*
  Saint Herman's Sisterhood Club, *Kodiak*

Lemon Parsley Butter
1 tablespoon (15 mL) finely minced parsley
2 tablespoons (30 mL) melted butter
2 tablespoons (30 mL) lemon juice
3 sprigs parsley

►Place Grilled Salmon Steaks on serving platter. Sprinkle with minced parsley. Pour melted butter, then lemon juice overall. Garnish with sprigs of parsley and serve.
■ *Bess A. Cleveland*, Alaskan Cookbook
  For Homesteader or Gourmet *(adapted)*

Potlatch Salmon

2 pounds (1 kg) salmon steaks (or other
  fish steaks)
1 tablespoon (15 mL) juniper berries (about 50)
1/4 cup (60 mL) salad oil
2 teaspoons (10 mL) salt
1/8 teaspoon (0.5 mL) pepper
Lemon or lime wedges
Mayonnaise

►Lightly crush juniper berries. Push six to eight berries into each steak. Coat fish with oil to prevent sticking. Sprinkle fish with salt and pepper. Grill over hot coals five to six minutes on each side. (Fish may be broiled or pan-fried for approximately the same length of time.) Garnish with lemon wedges and mayonnaise. Makes six servings.
■ *Ann Chandonnet*
  "Enjoy Eskimo and Indian Cooking"
  Anchorage Daily News

Superlative Broiled Salmon

►Use either steaks or fillet cutlets of king, red or silver salmon. Slices should be about 1 inch (2.5 cm) thick and arranged 1/2-inch (1.25 cm) apart on foil on a broiling pan.

Using Favorite Hot Mustard (page 416), blend 1 tablespoon (15 mL) of it with 1 tablespoon (15 mL) melted butter for each pound (456 g) of salmon. Spread this mixture over salmon and broil for 12 minutes. (If salmon is frozen, broil 15 minutes.) It is not necessary to turn the salmon, as it cooks through and should be served browned side up.

■ *Beth Deisher*
  Recipes From The Scrolls of Saint Peter's
  Seward

Sauteed Salmon Steaks
Simply delicious!

2 salmon steaks, each 1 inch (2.5 cm) thick
1 tablespoon (15 mL) oil
3 tablespoons (45 mL) butter, melted
1 tablespoon (15 mL) soy sauce
Dash garlic powder
4 slices lemon

►Heat oil in medium skillet; add salmon steaks. Combine butter, soy sauce and garlic powder; baste steaks. Cook until browned on one side, about five minutes. Turn, baste, place lemon slices atop steaks and cook until salmon flakes easily when tested with fork. Makes two servings.

■ Alaska Salmon

Baked Salmon a la Fishing Boat
Simple and delicious

1 whole salmon discovered under a bin board
   after delivering to tender
Aluminum foil
Onion
Oleo
Salt
Pepper
Water
Bread

►Clean salmon. Fold a double sheet of foil to line bottom rack and an inch or two (2.5 to 5 cm) of galley stove oven. Make stuffing: tear up several slices of bread; add generous amounts of salt and pepper; cut up onion and add with melted oleo. Dampen with hot water. Salt inside of fish and stuff. Place katty-corner on foil. Bake until tender. Serve to hungry crew.

■ *Rieta Walker*
  Cooking Up A Storm, *Homer*

Salmon Kabobs
For grill or oven

2 pounds (1 kg) salmon fillets
1 cup (240 mL) ketchup
1/4 cup (60 mL) brown sugar
6 tablespoons (90 mL) salad oil
2 teaspoons (10 mL) salt
8 drops Tabasco
1/4 cup (60 mL) vinegar

►Cut salmon into 1-inch (2.5 cm) cubes. Combine remaining ingredients; pour over cubed salmon and marinate for one to two hours. Remove from sauce and place on skewers. Grill over moderately hot coals for about 10 minutes, turning skewers frequently. Or, place skewers across a baking dish and bake in a moderate oven, 375°F (190°C), for about 20 minutes. Baste once during cooking with extra sauce. Serves six.

■ Seafood Recipes For Alaskans *(adapted)*

Salmon in Cream Sauce

2 pounds (1 kg) salmon steaks or fillets
1 tablespoon (15 mL) finely minced onion
1 teaspoon (5 mL) salt
1 teaspoon (5 mL) dried dill weed
1/4 teaspoon (1 mL) white pepper
1 tablespoon (15 mL) butter
1 cup (240 mL) thin cream or half-and-half

►Place steaks in a single layer in a well-greased, shallow baking dish. Sprinkle with onion and spices, dot with butter and pour cream over fish. Bake at 350°F (175°C) for about 20 minutes or until fish flakes easily when tested with a fork. Serves six.

■ Pacific Salmon Cookbook

Sweet and Sour Salmon

2 pounds (1 kg) fresh salmon
1 tablespoon (15 mL) salt
1 cup (240 mL) vinegar
3 cups (720 mL) water
1/2 cup (120 mL) sugar
1 bay leaf
1/3 stick cinnamon
1 lemon, sliced thin
1/2 cup (120 mL) seedless raisins
12 gingersnaps
1/2 to 1 cup (120 to 240 mL) cold water

►Cut raw salmon in 2-inch (5 cm) pieces; dredge with salt and let stand one hour. Combine vinegar, water, sugar, bay leaf, stick cinnamon, lemon slices and raisins and bring to a brisk boil. Rinse the salt from the fish and place the fish in the boiling liquid.

Reduce heat and allow to simmer 30 minutes. Meanwhile, soak gingersnaps in cold water and when dissolved add to the simmering fish. Increase heat and let boil one minute. Remove fish to a platter and pour the liquid with all the ingredients over the fish. This may be eaten either hot or cold but we like it best when cold.
■ *Bess A. Cleveland*
Alaskan Cookbook For Homesteader or Gourmet

About Poaching Salmon: Two recipes for poached salmon are offered here, one large enough to be the centerpiece for a scrumptious smorgasbord; the other, an elegant salmon steak dinner for four. Instructions for poaching salmon and gauging the cooking time are on page 11. Some sauces to try with poached salmon are Quick Herbed Hollandaise, Egg and Parsley and Sauce Verte, all recipes in Book Four — From Cache & Cupboard.

Poached salmon is also excellent served cold. Cool it slightly in the poaching liquid, drain, chill thoroughly.

Emily Marten's Poached Whole Salmon

*1 whole-dressed salmon, about 8 pounds
    (3.6 kg) with head and tail
1/2 gallon (2 L) dry white wine*
5 quarts (4.75 L) water*
2 medium onions, each stuck with
    2 whole cloves
1 tablespoon (15 mL) salt
12 peppercorns
1 teaspoon (5 mL) whole thyme
1 bay leaf
Parsley sprigs*

►(*The proportions of wine and water can suit your taste. I like to use half and half best.) Make a hammock of unfolded cheesecloth, allowing 6 inches (15 cm) at each end for handles. Lay fish on cloth. Combine all other ingredients in a poacher or roasting pan large enough to contain fish. Cover the pan with a lid or heavy aluminum foil; be sure cover is tight to allow no steam to escape. Bring stock to boil and simmer 20 minutes. Lower the salmon into the broth, immersing as much of it as possible. Return broth to a simmer. (If using a pan lid, place it diagonally so it does not rest directly on the head or tail. This is when heavy foil is nice, as you can work it over and under the head and tail to secure the steam.) Allow 6-1/2 minutes cooking time per pound (456 g). Lift salmon by the cheesecloth handles several times during cooking (unless you use poacher with a

rack) to prevent it from sticking to the bottom of the pan. When fish is done, remove from heat and let fish sit in liquid for a few minutes.

Carefully lift fish out by the cheesecloth handles, drain and place on large serving platter. From the sides gently pull out the cheesecloth — the bottom skin will slide out with it. If you are losing too much juice, let fish sit a little longer. Cut the skin around the head and above the tail before you attempt to remove top skin. You will be doing well if you remove the fish fat along with skin. Otherwise, you can remove fat with a spoon or leave it. (The fat is gray and many people like to eat it. I remove the fat as it makes for a more salmon color.)

Decorations — Small gourmet cutters make fancy shapes, but if you're in a hurry, sliced hard-boiled eggs and cucumbers arranged alternately down the center of the fish look nice. Trim everything with lots of parsley; lemon slices also add color. Other good food decorations include canned sliced carrots, black or stuffed olives, celery leaves, chives, pimentos and green peppers. The latter should be parboiled about five minutes to soften them. Use your imagination!
■ *Bunny Mathisen, Petersburg*
"Help Yourself To The Sylta Flesk!"
ALASKA® magazine, January 1977

Skillet-Poached Salmon Steaks with Lemon Butter

*1 cup (240 mL) dry white wine
2 cups (480 mL) water
1 small onion, sliced
1 stalk celery, cut up
1 bay leaf
Parsley sprigs
1 teaspoon (5 mL) salt
4 salmon steaks, about 2 pounds (1 kg)
1/3 cup (80 mL) butter or margarine, melted
1/3 cup (80 mL) lemon juice
3 lemon slices*

►In a large skillet, bring to a boil wine, water, onion, celery, bay leaf, two parsley sprigs and salt. Reduce heat and simmer, covered, 15 minutes. Rinse salmon in cold water, drain well. Place salmon in wine mixture, adding more hot water if needed to just cover salmon. Return to boiling, reduce heat and simmer, covered, about 10 minutes, or until fish flakes easily when tested with fork. Remove salmon from skillet with wide, slotted spoon or spatula; drain. Place on heated serving platter. Combine melted butter and lemon juice. Drizzle mixture over salmon steaks. Garnish with parsley and lemon slices. Serves four.
■ *Mamie Jensen, Juneau*

"Boiled" Salmon Norway Style

►Bring water to boil; add 1 teaspoon (5 mL) rock salt, 2 tablespoons (30 mL) vinegar and then sliced fish. Cook slowly (do not boil) for 20 minutes. Make brine of 1 tablespoon (15 mL) rock salt and fish broth; put pieces of fish on platter. Pour brine over for seasoning. Serve with melted butter.

■ *Arna Hildre*
   Sons of Norway Cook Book, *Ketchikan*

About Piroghi: Piroghi *or* pirozhki, pirok, peroche . . . *all are derived from a Russian specialty that acquired almost as many spellings for its name, when it was translated from Cyrilic to Latin alphabet, as it has acquired varied ingredients from many generations — and several nationalities — of cooks.*

Piroghi *are pies large enough to be cut into serving pieces, while* pirozhki *are tiny pies or tartlets, the sort we all like to serve — or be served — at parties. The filling can be as simple as a dollop of cream cheese or as complicated ("unlikely" is perhaps a better word) as chopped sauteed veal udder . . . seasoned with nutmeg.*

Following are three recipes for the large size pie — piroghi *— one a very large size pie which the cook, Marlene Johnson of Naknek, says is excellent for "Slavi time." During Russian Orthodox Christmas celebrations — "Slavi time" — singers go caroling from home to home, twirling a large Christmas star. Traditionally, they are invited into the homes for something warm to eat or drink, such as hot chocolate or a slice of* piroghi.

Grama Bahrt's Salmon Piroghi
A memorable dish to serve warm for buffet dinner, or to chill and take along on a picnic

Pastry for a 2-crust, 9-inch (23 cm) pie
1 tablespoon (15 mL) melted butter
2 cups (480 mL) rice that has been cooked in
   chicken stock
2 cups (480 mL) cooked salmon,
   coarsely flaked
1 tablespoon (15 mL) lemon juice, flavored with
   an easy dash of nutmeg
4 hard-cooked eggs, sliced
1/4 cup (60 mL) melted butter, mixed with
   2 tablespoons (30 mL) chopped chives
Salt, fresh-cracked pepper, onion salt

Egg Glaze: *blend 1 beaten egg yolk with*
   1 tablespoon (15 mL) milk

►Line a 9-inch (23 cm) pie pan with pastry dough and brush it with 1 tablespoon (15 mL) melted

butter. Bake at 425°F (220°C) just until dough begins to color, five to eight minutes. Pat half the rice on bottom and sides of crust. Add salmon in an even layer and sprinkle it with the nutmeg-flavored lemon juice. Add egg slices and season to taste with salt and pepper. Top this with the remaining rice and pour overall the 1/4 cup (60 mL) butter-chive mixture. Adjust top crust, flute edges, vent crust and paint it with Egg Glaze. Bake at 400°F (205°C) about 35 minutes. If crust browns too quickly, top loosely with foil. Add a light sprinkling of onion salt just before serving and garnish with sprigs of parsley lightly dipped in paprika. Six wedge-shaped servings.

■ *Nadja Kaznakoff Bahrt*
   Courtesy, Elva Bahrt Swenson

Liz's Russian Peroche Pie

Pie dough for 2 crusts
1-1/2 cups (360 mL) cooked rice
Salt and pepper
Butter
2 onions, sliced and sauteed
1 head cabbage, chopped and sauteed
2 cups (480 mL) cooked salmon
5 hard-cooked eggs, sliced
Salmon stock

►Line a baking dish with dough. Then make a layer of rice seasoned with salt and pepper and dotted with butter; then layer with onions, cabbage and fish. Repeat layers and top with seasoned sliced eggs. Moisten with about 1/4 cup (60 mL) salmon stock. Cover with pastry and brush with cream. Bake for 45 minutes at 350°F (175°C). Butter while hot and serve. White king salmon is preferred for the Russian pie recipe.

■ *Elizabeth Randall*
   Seafood Secrets, *Sitka*

Salmon Pirok
For a crowd

Double batch pie crust dough
4 tablespoons (60 mL) vegetable oil
6 cups (1.45 L) cooked rice
1 head cabbage chopped and boiled for
   8 minutes
1-1/2 quarts (1.45 L) canned salmon
1 dozen boiled eggs
2 slices raw onion
1/2 cup (120 mL) butter
Salt and pepper

►Roll out dough to fit a 10 x 13-inch (25 x 33 cm) pan; enough to fit the bottom and sides. Use about two-thirds of the dough. Grease this dough with oil. Add rice, spread evenly; then the cabbage. Spread the fish evenly over rice and cabbage. Quarter the eggs and put them on the fish. Layer onions over the eggs. Add some salt and pepper. Dot with butter. Top it with the remaining crust; perforate the top. Bake at 400°F (205°C) for approximately 45 minutes, or until crust is brown. Serves 20. It is a very good dish for common gathering or freeze it for future use; excellent for Slavi time.

■ *Marlene Johnson*
Uutuqtwa
Bristol Bay High School, Naknek

Salmon Quiche
"An easy-to-make gourmet dish with endless possibilities for variation"

Pie crust:
1 cup (240 mL) flour
1/2 teaspoon (2 mL) salt
1/2 cup (120 mL) shortening
1/4 cup (60 mL) cold water

►Mix flour, salt and shortening until crumbly; then mix in water until dough cleans sides of bowl. Roll out thin and line 9-inch (23 cm) pie plate.

Filling:
1/2 medium onion
2 tablespoons (30 mL) butter
Salt and pepper
Finely minced garlic or garlic powder
Chopped parsley
4 eggs
2 cups (480 mL) milk
1 cup (240 mL) or more drained canned salmon
1 cup (240 mL) grated cheese

►Chop the onion and saute it in butter. Add salt and pepper to taste, a little finely chopped garlic or garlic powder and some chopped parsley. Remove from heat. Beat the eggs and milk together lightly. It is best if half the milk is cream or undiluted evaporated milk. Crumble salmon and stir into onion mixture; then add it all to eggs and milk. Add the cheese and pour mixture into pie shell. Bake at 350°F (175°C) for 20 to 30 minutes.

■ *Marcy Stewart*
Alaska Fisherman's Journal, *Ketchikan*

Alaska Nuggets
Delicious as a main dish or party tidbit

1-1/2 cups (360 mL) canned salmon
1/2 cup (120 mL) mashed potatoes
1 tablespoon (15 mL) minced celery
1 tablespoon (15 mL) minced onion
1 tablespoon (15 mL) butter

Salt and pepper to taste
1 teaspoon (5 mL) Worcestershire
1/2 pound (228 g) Cheddar cheese, cut into 1/2-inch (1.25 cm) cubes
1 egg, beaten
1 cup (240 mL) sifted bread crumbs or flour

►Mix flaked salmon and potatoes. Cook celery and onion in butter until tender; mix with salmon. Add seasonings and shape into little balls the size of a walnut. Push a cube of cheese into each ball; reshape. Dip in egg and roll in crumbs or flour. Fry in enough fat at 375°F (190°C) to cover. Or use less fat and turn balls to brown.

■ Cooking Up A Storm, *Homer*

Variation: *Alaska Doughnuts* — Use all the above ingredients *except* celery and Cheddar cheese. *Add* 1 teaspoon (5 mL) celery salt. Drain and flake salmon. Combine all ingredients except bread crumbs, mix thoroughly and chill for one hour. Roll out and cut with a doughnut cutter. Coat doughnuts with crumbs. Fry in deep fat at 375°F (190°C) for five minutes or until they are golden brown. Drain on absorbent paper and serve plain or with a sauce. Makes 12 doughnuts.

Smoked Salmon Pizza

Dough:
1 package yeast
2 tablespoons (30 mL) warm water
1 cup (240 mL) boiling water
1-1/2 teaspoons (7 mL) salt
2 tablespoons (30 mL) shortening
3 cups (720 mL) flour

►Dissolve yeast in warm water. Pour the boiling water over the salt and shortening and cool. Add yeast and half of the flour to the shortening and beat smooth. Then add the rest of the flour. Divide dough into two parts and pat into rounds about 12 inches (30 cm) across — making a thicker rim around the edge to hold the filling. Place in pie pans or on greased cookie sheet and allow to rise till double in size.

Filling:
1 tablespoon (15 mL) olive oil
1/2 cup (120 mL) grated Parmesan cheese
3/4 cup (180 mL) sharp Cheddar cheese
2 cups (480 mL) drained canned tomatoes, flavored with 1 clove garlic, minced fine
1/2 cup (120 mL) shredded smoked salmon
Oregano
Salt and pepper to taste

►After dough rises brush top with olive oil and sprinkle with Parmesan cheese. Make a layer of Cheddar cheese, cut in small pieces, and then a layer of garlic flavored tomato. Sprinkle with salt and pepper and oregano if desired. Top with shredded smoked salmon and sprinkle with Parmesan cheese and olive oil. Bake in a 450°F (230°C) oven approximately 30 minutes. Cool 5 to 10 minutes before cutting. Serves four. This is an Alaskan variation of a standard pizza recipe.

■ *Mrs. John C. Tower*
   Alaska's Cooking, *Anchorage*

Salmon in A Blanket

2 cups (480 mL) flaked salmon
1 tablespoon (15 mL) lemon juice
3/4 teaspoon (3 mL) salt
2 tablespoons (30 mL) chopped parsley
1/4 cup (60 mL) mayonnaise
1 tablespoon (15 mL) minced onion
1/4 teaspoon (1 mL) pepper
1 recipe biscuit dough

►Roll dough thin in a 7 x 15-inch (18 x 38 cm) oblong. Mix remaining ingredients and spread in middle. Seal edges together on top and slash for steam to escape. Bake at 425°F (220°C) for 12 to 15 minutes.

■ *Oddveig Johansen*
   Kitchen Magic, *Ketchikan*

Double-Crust Salmon Pie

►Line a casserole with baking powder biscuit dough. Into this alternate layers of salmon, hard-cooked eggs, mixed peas and carrots and finely chopped green onions — two layers of each. Over this pour a small amount of White Sauce; then top with biscuit dough. Bake at 350°F (175°C) until biscuit topping is golden brown.

■ *Edna Drinkall*
   Recipes From The Scrolls of Saint Peter's
   Seward

Variations: In both above recipes, a biscuit mix or canned refrigerator biscuits will substitute for homemade dough if you're in a special hurry. Several cooks also suggest adding minced chives, about a teaspoon (5 mL), and grated Parmesan, 1 tablespoon (15 mL) or more, to the biscuit dough.

Salmon Pudding Norwegian Style

1-1/2 pounds (0.70 kg) salmon
2 teaspoons (10 mL) salt
1/4 teaspoon (1 mL) nutmeg
1/4 cup (60 mL) butter or other fat, melted
2 cups (480 mL) milk

►Remove skin and bones from salmon. Grind enough to make 2 cups (480 mL). Place fish, salt and nutmeg in a large bowl and beat 10 minutes with an electric beater. Add butter slowly and continue beating. Add milk, a half-cup (120 mL) at a time, beating after each addition. Beat 15 minutes after final addition, then place in a well-greased casserole. Place in a pan of hot water and bake in a moderate oven, 350°F (175°C), for 1-1/2 hours or until it tests done as for custard. Serves six.

■ *Bob Baade*
   Great Lander Shopping News, *Anchorage*

Gumchalk

►Get smoked salmon or dried fish. Put it in enough water to cover the fish. Boil it until it is tender or your fork goes through the meat and the skin. Eat it with *agutuk* (Eskimo Ice Cream), Sailor Boy crackers (pilot bread) and tea, or dip it in seal oil.

■ *Marlene Johnson*
   Uutuqtwa, *Bristol Bay High School, Naknek*

Baked Smoked Salmon in Cream

1 pound (456 g) smoked or kippered salmon
2 teaspoons (10 mL) flour
1/4 teaspoon (1 mL) pepper
1/2 cup (120 mL) cream
1/2 cup (120 mL) milk

►Generously butter a shallow baking dish and place in it thin slices of smoked or kippered salmon. Dust with flour and pepper. Combine cream and milk and pour over the salmon. Bake at 450°F (230°C) for 15 minutes. Serve with hot buttered toast and a good cup of coffee.

■ *Bess A. Cleveland*
   Alaskan Cookbook For Homesteader or Gourmet

Icy Point Breakfast

1 quart (1 L) White Sauce, medium thick
1 pint (480 mL) smoked salmon, flaked
1 can (16 oz /or/ 456 g) peas and carrots,
   drained, or about 2 cups (480 mL), cooked
Salt and pepper

►Heat White Sauce slowly, gradually add the flaked salmon and peas and carrots. Serve over buttered toast. It is also nice with a garnish of hard-cooked eggs. We like this breakfast on good "catching" days as it can be kept warm and eaten whenever the bite is off.

■ *Mary C. Owens, FV* Cape Race
   Seafood Secrets, *Sitka*

Eileen's Savory Salmon Souffle

5 cold eggs
1/4 cup (60 mL) butter
3 tablespoons (45 mL) flour
1 cup (240 mL) milk

1-1/2 cups (360 mL) flaked salmon
1 teaspoon (5 mL) salt
1/2 teaspoon (2 mL) pepper
1/2 teaspoon (2 mL) thyme
1/2 teaspoon (2 mL) grated lemon rind
1/4 cup (60 mL) bread crumbs

►Preheat oven to 375°F (190°C). Separate *cold* egg whites into a chilled bowl and let stand for 15 minutes.

Melt 3 tablespoons (45 mL) of the butter; stir in flour, making a smooth paste. Gradually stir in milk until it is smooth and thick and cook one minute longer. Remove from heat; add one egg yolk at a time, beating vigorously after each addition. Add salmon and seasonings. Chill for 20 minutes. Grease souffle dish with remaining 1 tablespoon (15 mL) butter. Add bread crumbs and coat dish, shaking out excess.

Beat egg whites to shiny (but not dry) peaks, incorporating as much air as possible. Add one-third of the egg whites to the sauce, mixing thoroughly with an ''up-and-down'' motion. Add remaining egg whites quickly and gently fold and cut them in.

Pour quickly into souffle dish; smooth top. Then run a finger through it to a depth of 1 inch (2.5 cm) in a circle about 1/2 inch (1.25 cm) from the outer rim of the dish.

Bake about 35 minutes at 375°F (190°C) or until a golden brown color and souffle seems firm when shaken slightly.
■ *Eileen Seibert,* FV Moonlight
    Seafood Secrets, *Sitka*

Salmon and Rice Balls

1 pound (456 g) canned salmon
1 cup (240 mL) cooked rice
1/2 cup (120 mL) bread crumbs
1 tablespoon (15 mL) onion, minced
2 teaspoons (10 mL) green pepper, chopped
1 teaspoon (5 mL) salt
2 eggs, slightly beaten
1 can cream of mushroom soup
1/2 cup (120 mL) water

►Mix all ingredients except soup and water. Roll mixture into small balls; place in shallow baking pan. Cover with soup and water mixture. Bake 30 minutes at 350°F (180°C). Very good. Serves six.
■ *Audrey Cox*
    False Island Camp Cook Book

Alaskan Casserole

►Butter baking dish. Place a layer of thin-sliced raw potatoes, layer of flaked salmon, layer of green peas, layer potatoes, layer salmon, layer green peas, layer grated raw carrots mixed with grated onion. Cover with salmon juice from can. Add 1 cup (240 mL) milk, one beaten egg and 3 tablespoons (45 mL) butter. Top with crumbs and a bit of cheese if desired. Season between layers to taste. Bake for 45 minutes at 350°F (175°C).
■ *Mae Ciechanski*
    An Alaskan Cook Book, *Kenai*

Blushing Salmon on Rice

4 tablespoons (60 mL) butter or margarine
1 can tomato soup
2 cups (480 mL) canned or cooked salmon
1/2 pound (228 g) grated cheese

►Melt butter and grated cheese together in double boiler; add tomato soup, stirring until smooth. Add flaked salmon and stir while heating. Serve on boiled rice, buns, bread or toast.
■ Out of Alaska's Kitchens

Salmon Kedgeree

2 cans (7 oz /or/ 200 g, each) smoked salmon
2 cups (480 mL) cooked rice
4 hard-cooked eggs, chopped
1/4 cup (60 mL) butter or other fat, melted
1/4 cup (60 mL) chopped parsley or
    dried parsley flakes
1/2 cup (120 mL) hot milk
Dash of pepper
1/4 teaspoon (1 mL) salt

►Drain and flake salmon, combine all ingredients and heat. Garnish and serve hot. Serves six.
■ The Alaskan Camp Cook

Curried Salmon

1 medium onion, sliced thin
1 tablespoon (15 mL) butter
2 tablespoons (30 mL) flour
1/4 teaspoon (1 mL) curry powder
Milk, about 1 cup (240 mL)
Red or sockeye salmon, about 2 cups (480 mL)
    cooked, or 1 can (16 oz /or/ 456 g)
    salmon, drained

►Cook onion slices to golden brown in butter. Do not let onion become crisp. Add flour and curry powder, stir and cook until bubbly. Add enough milk to make cream sauce of preferred consistency. Add salmon which has been skinned, boned and broken into hunks about the size of a small walnut. Stir lightly in order to keep fish pieces intact. I use fresh cooked salmon and add salt to taste. May be served on rice or toast points.
■ *Marian Earp*
    Good Food A-Plenty, *Fairbanks (adapted)*

Salmon Puffs
Individual souffles

2 cups (480 mL) cooked salmon
1/2 teaspoon (2 mL) salt
1/8 teaspoon (0.5 mL) pepper
1/2 cup (120 mL) soft bread crumbs
1 tablespoon (15 mL) lemon juice
3 eggs, separated

►Chop salmon fine and add salt, pepper, crumbs and lemon juice. Add beaten egg yolks, mixing thoroughly. Then fold in stiffly beaten egg whites. Place in greased custard cups. Set in a pan of hot water and bake in a moderate oven, 375°F (190°C), 30 minutes. Unmold on hot platter, garnish each with a sprig of parsley and serve with a sauce.
■ *Lois Prater*
   Alaska's Cooking, *Anchorage*

Salmon Newburg

1-1/2 cups (360 mL) salmon, cooked or canned
4 tablespoons (60 mL) butter or margarine
4 tablespoons (60 mL) flour
2 cups (480 mL) milk
2 egg yolks, slightly beaten
1/2 teaspoon (2 mL) salt
1/8 teaspoon (0.5 mL) pepper
1/4 cup (60 mL) sherry wine
Dash of Tabasco

►Flake fish in rather large pieces. Melt butter in pan and blend in flour but do not brown. Slowly add milk, stirring constantly and cook over medium heat until slightly thickened and smooth. Add fish. Remove from heat and slowly add the beaten egg yolks. Return to heat and cook two or three minutes longer. Add salt and pepper. Just before serving add the wine and Tabasco. Serve over rice, noodles or toast. Serves four to six.
■ Pacific Salmon Cookbook

Maggie's Casserole

1 can (16 oz /or/ 456 g) salmon
3 tablespoons (45 mL) butter
3 tablespoons (45 mL) flour
2 cups (480 mL) salmon liquor and milk
1 quart (1 L) cooked potatoes, sliced
1/2 cup (120 mL) mayonnaise
1/2 cup (120 mL) grated cheese
1 teaspoon (5 mL) Worcestershire
1 teaspoon (5 mL) mustard

►Drain and flake salmon, reserving liquor. Melt butter, blend in flour. Add liquid gradually; cook until thick and smooth, stirring constantly. Arrange potatoes, salmon and sauce in alternate layers in a well-greased casserole. Mix mayonnaise, cheese, mustard and Worcestershire; spread over top of fish mixture. Bake in a moderate oven, 375°F (190°C), for 30 minutes.
■ *Margaret Schwantes*
   Seafood Secrets, *Sitka*

Salmon Jolly

1 or 2 cans (16 oz /or/ 456 g, each) salmon, drained
1 good-sized onion
1 can cream of mushroom soup

►In a lightly buttered casserole, put a layer of salmon, a layer of thinly sliced onion, then a layer of soup. Repeat, ending with a layer of soup. Bake at 375°F (190°C) till hot through — about 30 minutes. Serve with rice or boiled potatoes and peas.
■ *Hannan Sagmoen, Dillingham*
   Courtesy, Audrey Rearden, *Homer*

Up North Salmon Supper
Winner, Casserole Contest,
1974 Southeast Alaska State Fair

2 cups (480 mL) canned salmon
1 package (10 oz /or/ 285 g) frozen peas
1-1/2 cups (360 mL) cottage cheese
1/2 cup (120 mL) crushed rice cereal
3 tablespoons (45 mL) chopped green pepper
1 tablespoon (15 mL) lemon juice
1 cup (240 mL) crushed saltines
1 cup (240 mL) grated Cheddar cheese
1 tablespoon (15 mL) chopped onion
Salt and pepper to taste

►Precook peas in liquid from salmon can; then mix all ingredients together. Bake at 350°F (175°C) for 45 minutes. Serve with Lemon Almond Butter Sauce.

Lemon Almond Butter Sauce
1/4 pound (114 g) butter
1 tablespoon (15 mL) lemon juice
1/4 cup (60 mL) slivered almonds

►Melt the butter; then add remaining ingredients and heat briefly.
■ *Charlotte Olerud*
   Haines Homemakers' Cookbook

Cold Salmon Loaf

1 envelope (1 Tbsp /or/ 15 mL)
   unflavored gelatin
1/4 cup (60 mL) cold water
Yolks of 2 eggs
1 teaspoon (5 mL) salt

1 teaspoon (5 mL) mustard
1-1/2 tablespoons (23 mL) melted butter
2-1/2 tablespoons (38 mL) lemon juice
3/4 cup (180 mL) milk
2 cups (480 mL) canned salmon or crab

►Soften gelatin in cold water about five minutes. Meanwhile, beat egg yolks in the top of a double boiler and mix with salt and mustard. Add butter, milk and lemon juice. Cook over boiling water, stirring constantly, until mixture thickens. Add softened gelatin to hot mixture and stir until dissolved. Add flaked salmon or crab meat. Turn into mold that has been rinsed in cold water. Chill. When firm, unmold on platter and garnish with parsley, lemon or green peppers or tomato wedges. Serves six.
■ Out of Alaska's Kitchens

Salmon Cakes

A "to taste" recipe for leftovers

Leftover baked salmon
Leftover mashed potatoes
1 or 2 eggs depending on quantity of
**   other ingredients**
Salt and pepper to taste
Flour
Butter or margarine
Leftover Egg Sauce

►Flake the fish; add potatoes and seasoning. Beat the egg lightly and stir into fish-potato mixture. Mixture should not be too moist. Form balls and roll in flour. Flatten into cakes and saute in melted butter in a moderately hot, heavy skillet. Turn once, carefully, so that cakes may be well browned. Serve with Egg Sauce.
■ *The Old Homesteader*

Salmon-Broccoli Casserole

1 can (16 oz /or/ 456 g) salmon
1 pound (456 g) fresh broccoli or 1 package
    (10 oz /or/ 280 g) frozen broccoli
1 onion, sliced thin
2 ribs celery, sliced thin
1/4 pound (114 g) mushrooms, sliced thin
2 tablespoons (30 mL) butter
2 tablespoons (30 mL) flour
1 cup (240 mL) milk
1/2 teaspoon (2 mL) dill weed
1/4 teaspoon (1 mL) pepper
1 teaspoon (5 mL) lemon juice
1/2 teaspoon (2 mL) grated lemon rind
1/2 cup (120 mL) bread or
    cracker crumbs

►Cut broccoli into small pieces. If you're using frozen broccoli, allow it to thaw in a drainer until you can cut it. Blanch the pieces about two minutes and then drain them as dry as possible.

Saute sliced vegetables in butter until onions are soft, then add flour, cook it a little and slowly stir in the milk. Season with remaining ingredients except crumbs. Fold salmon and drained broccoli into this sauce and pour it into a greased baking dish. Sprinkle with bread or cracker crumbs and bake about 20 minutes at 325°F (160°C) until it's bubbly and hot through. Serves three or four.
■ *The editors, ALASKA® magazine*

Corny Salmon Cakes

►Add boned, leftover fish to pancake batter, along with some corn and onion. Fry in a skillet or on a hot griddle.
■ *C. Joe Murray, Angoon*
    "Save Those Salmon Scraps"
    ALASKA® magazine, August 1980

Salmon Pancakes

1 cup (240 mL) pancake mix
1 egg
1 cup (240 mL) milk
1 tablespoon (15 mL) oil
1/2 pound (228 g) canned salmon, drained
  and flaked
White Sauce prepared in advance

►Combine all ingredients except salmon and sauce. Stir the batter until smooth and add half the salmon. Heat the pancake griddle and oil it lightly and fry each cake lightly until golden brown on both sides. Add the remaining salmon to the prepared White Sauce and serve over the hot pancakes. Any favorite sauce may be used or sour cream may be mixed with the remaining salmon. Makes eight medium cakes.
■ Pacific Salmon Cookbook

Fishburgers

►To one tall can of salmon (16 oz /or/ 456 g) add two medium grated raw potatoes, two eggs, one medium minced onion, seasoning to taste. This is a soft batter. Fry the same as hamburgers, allowing sufficient time to cook the potatoes.
■ *Mrs. Clayton L. Polley, Juneau*
  PTA Cook Book, *Petersburg*

SHEEFISH

A member of the whitefish family, the sheefish—also called inconnu — is well regarded as a sport and subsistence fish, even as a commercial fish wherever it is found in large enough quantity. In Alaska, sheefish probably grow to 60 pounds (27 kg) though any over 25 pounds (11 kg) are considered quite large fish. A pretty fish, its body is streamlined and silvery, its color shimmers from light to dark and changes to a purplish sheen when the fish is first pulled from the water.

Taste: In Russia, the sheefish is known as "the white salmon," and this gives a clue to its taste . . . very prized white meat, high in oil content, rich in flavor — described as sweet, almost "comparable to rich cream," says the *Northern Cookbook*.

Preparation Tips: Bake, fry, poach, smoke or pickle; also a good fish for canning.

Pan-Fried Inconnu (Sheefish)

1 medium or small inconnu
1-1/2 teaspoons (7 mL) salt
1/4 teaspoon (1 mL) pepper
2 tablespoons (30 mL) vegetable oil or olive oil
2 tablespoons (30 mL) butter

►Clean, wash and fillet the fish. Cut the fillets in serving pieces or rounds with a biscuit cutter. Season with salt and pepper. Heat oil in a heavy fry pan and when hot add the butter. Fry the fish on one side until nicely browned, then turn and brown the other side.
■ Northern Cookbook

Poached Inconnu (Sheefish)

1 small inconnu, 8 to 10 pounds (3.6 to 4.5 kg)
2 tablespoons (30 mL) butter

1 teaspoon (5 mL) salt
4 cups (1 L) water
1/4 cup (60 mL) vinegar

►Clean the fish and tie it in a cheesecloth bag. Place the bag on a rack in a large pot. In a separate pan, melt the butter, add salt, water and vinegar. Heat to simmer and pour over fish. Cover fish tightly and simmer 10 minutes per inch (2.5 cm) thickness, measured at the fish's thickest point. Serve with lemon juice or a tart sauce.
■ Northern Cookbook *(adapted)*

Baked Sheefish

►Wash, clean and scale a good-sized sheefish. Sprinkle inside and out with green minced onion, salt and freshly ground pepper and paprika. Dot with butter inside and out. Wrap in foil and bake at 400°F (205°C) 40 to 50 minutes.
■ *Edith Bullock, Kotzebue*
  Tried and True Recipes *(Juneau)*

Sheefish Treat

►Cleaned, skinned and frozen sheefish is sometimes cut into paper-thin slices and served with a side dish of seal oil (or olive oil) for dipping.

Roasted Cony Head
(Sheefish or inconnu)

►Cut the head off the cony and split it open so that it will lie flat on the toaster. Shut the toaster well and roast over open fire very slowly. Turn when it is done on one side. A large, roasted cony head will provide a generous meal for several persons.
■ Northern Cookbook

TROUTS & CHARRS

Cutthroat trout, lake trout, Dolly Varden, arctic charr, brook trout, rainbow trout and its sea-going cousin, the steelhead . . . all these members of the trout and charr clans may vary in a good many respects such as size, flesh color and taste, but no group of fish has more avid proponents among anglers and diners.

Taste: Excellent. Trouts and charrs are mild-flavored, the flesh delicate.

Preparation Tips: Depending on size, broil (especially over coals), steam, pan-fry or bake. Though most of the following recipes specify the fish, they are useful for any species, within a limit or two set by size. The best fish for baking are large ones, 3 pounds (1.4 kg) or more, but smaller ones can be baked in a sauce that will keep the meat from drying out. With trouts and charrs *especially* it is important not to overcook.

Arctic Charr: A close relative of the Dolly Varden, the arctic charr inhabits both fresh and salt water and can grow to rather large size — averaging 2 to 10 pounds (1 to 5 kg), with a record fish of 30 pounds (13.5 kg). Smoked, salted, fried, baked,

boiled, the fish is considered a delicacy no matter what the flesh color, but the red-meated ones seem to be preferred over those with pink or white meat.

Dolly Varden: Primarily a saltwater fish — but with some populations that stay in fresh water only, salt water only, or live in both — the Dolly Varden has the widest distribution of any charr in Alaska and, for that reason, is an important subsistence fish. In the past it was much maligned as a predator of young salmon and salmon eggs. But after a number of years of offering a bounty for Dolly Varden tails, authorities in Alaska found that the fish only occasionally fed on salmon eggs and fry and that other predators — even species of salmon — had far more effect on salmon survival rate. The bounty was dropped, of course, but it's still worthwhile collecting the tails as long as you drop them and the rest of the fish into the frying pan or another cooking vessel. The flesh is pink, firm and flavorful, good for smoking, too.

Lake Trout: Rated by many as the best-tasting of all trouts or charrs, the lake trout has a delicate flavor, with flesh color ranging from white to creamy yellow to orange. This very big fish grows to 40 pounds (18 kg) or more — with record fish of whopping size, over 100 pounds (45 kg).

Brook Trout: This is one of the most important sport fish on the continent, and it can grow up to 5 pounds (2.25 kg), though most in Alaska are small. An excellent fish for pan-frying, either breaded or plain, it's, of course, a campfire favorite.

Cutthroat Trout: The body color of the cutthroat varies with its environment. In fresh water, it is black-spotted; in salt water, silvery, with few spots or none at all. The meat is sometimes white, sometimes pink, and of excellent flavor. Fish that have lived in salt water several years may weigh as much as 4 pounds (1.8 kg), occasionally even 6 pounds (2.7 kg) or more.

Rainbow Trout and Steelhead: For its legendary wiliness and fight and its beauty, the rainbow is probably the most sought-after sport fish in North America. It spends all its life in fresh water. The sea-going "rainbow" is called by another name— steelhead. Both are excellent eating, pan-fried, broiled, steamed, poached or baked. The steelhead makes a wonderful fish for barbecuing or smoking. (Special recipes to check: Fisherman's Favorite Barbecue Sauce and Adolph's Cold-Smoked Steelhead, Salmon and Black Cod, both recipes in Book Four.)

About The Recipes: Most of the following recipes — all except those noted — are reprinted from Ann Chandonnet's article, "Lake Trout: Good Fishing, Good Eating," which appeared in the Alaska-only edition of ALASKA® magazine, June 1979.

Although Chandonnet's recipes were designated for lake trout, they are suitable for all charrs and trouts. Since cooking time so very much depends on the size of the fish, Chandonnet warns that you should regard her estimates as approximate — and, then, generally for big fish. Your best bet is to gauge the cooking time by measuring the thickness of the fish (the smaller ones if you have several) at its thickest point and cooking 10 minutes per inch (2.5 cm) of thickness. Then examine to see if the flesh has turned opaque. Stuffed fish should be measured after stuffing. Frozen fish — double the per-inch cooking time; foil- or paper-wrapped fish— add five minutes to the total cooking time.

Simple Baked Trout

►Place fish in shallow baking dish lined with greased waxed or brown paper. Sprinkle with salt, pepper, melted butter or melted garlic butter. Bake at 400°F (205°C), 20 minutes for fillets, 30 minutes for steaks or 10 minutes per inch (2.5 cm) thickness, measured at the thickest point, for cleaned, whole fish.

Baked Trout with White Wine

2 pounds (1 kg) cleaned trout
1 teaspoon (5 mL) salt
Juice of 1 lemon
1 clove garlic, mashed or minced
1 cup (240 mL) white wine
2 tablespoons (30 mL) chopped parsley
2 tablespoons (30 mL) chopped green or
*   white onions*
4 tablespoons (60 mL) melted butter
*   or margarine*
2 tablespoons (30 mL) fine, dry white
*   bread crumbs*

►Wash and dry trout. Rub inside and out with lemon juice and sprinkle with salt. Lay trout in a buttered baking dish and sprinkle with garlic. Pour the wine over the fish. Sprinkle with parsley, onion and bread crumbs. Drizzle with melted butter and bake at 400°F (205°C) for 15 minutes. Test for doneness.

Poached Trout with Dill Sauce

►Make a court bouillon or poaching liquid by mixing three parts water to one part vinegar or dry white wine in a nonaluminum pan. The liquid should be enough to almost cover the fish. Add to it six peppercorns, one bay leaf and 1 teaspoon (5 mL) salt per quart (1 L) of liquid needed. Bring to a boil. Plunge your fresh trout into the boiling liquid. Poach just long enough for the fish to cook through, about four minutes for a 1- to 2-pound (0.45 to 1 kg) fish. Serve hot with melted butter or remove, drain, chill and serve with mayonnaise or Dill Sauce.

Dill Sauce
1-1/2 cups (360 mL) sour cream
1 tablespoon (15 mL) chopped fresh dill weed or
2 tablespoons (30 mL) dried dill weed
1 tablespoon (15 mL) grated onion
1 teaspoon (5 mL) prepared mustard
2 hard-cooked eggs, finely chopped

►Combine ingredients and chill for several hours. Makes enough sauce for six to eight servings of trout.

Fried Trout

►Scale (if necessary), clean and leave fish whole, or skin and fillet. Soak in milk for 30 minutes, wipe dry and roll in corn meal or in a mixture of salt, corn meal and white flour. Fry until golden brown using equal parts butter and oil.

Broiled Trout

►To broil small, whole-dressed fish or fillets, place fish (skin side down) on a preheated, greased broiler pan. Sprinkle with salt, pepper and melted butter. Broil 4 inches (10 cm) from the flame until fish is done; 10 to 12 minutes for boned fillets, longer for whole fish.

Grilled Trout in Wine Sauce

3 pounds (1.4 kg) pan-dressed trout
1 can (15 oz /or/ 425 g) tomato sauce
1/2 cup (120 mL) dry red wine
1/2 cup (120 mL) butter or margarine
2 tablespoons (30 mL) lemon juice
2 tablespoons (30 mL) chopped green onion
*   with tops*
1 teaspoon (5 mL) sugar
1 teaspoon (5 mL) dried herbs — tarragon,
*   shallots, parsley*
1/2 teaspoon (2 mL) salt
A few drops bottled hot pepper sauce (optional)

►In a small saucepan, combine tomato sauce, wine, butter, lemon juice, green onion, sugar, herbs, salt and hot pepper sauce. Simmer, uncovered, 10 to 15 minutes to marry flavors. Meanwhile, grill fish over hot coals 10 to 12 minutes. Test for doneness after eight minutes. Turn fish and grill until done. Brush fish with sauce during final five minutes of grilling. Serve fish with warm sauce.

Baked Stuffed Arctic Charr — with Sour Cream Caper Sauce and Egg-and-Olive "Murres"

1 large arctic charr
Stuffing
1/4 cup (60 mL) butter
Salt and pepper

►Wash and dry the fish, leaving the head and tail on if desired. Sprinkle the cavity with salt. If you don't care for the eyes, remove them with a small measuring spoon and place red or green cherries in the cavities.

Stuff the fish loosely, using about 3/4 cup (180 mL) for each pound (456 g) of dressed fish. Fasten the opening with small skewers or toothpicks and loop string about them as you would lace shoes. Butter the outside of the fish and sprinkle lightly with salt and pepper. Wrap in greased foil, using the drugstore wrap to insure a sealed closure, but leave room for expansion of steam. Measure the fish at its thickest depth and allow 10 minutes cooking time for each inch (2.5 cm) of stuffed thickness, plus 5 minutes for heat to penetrate foil. Bake in a hot oven, 450°F (230°C).

Open foil for the last 10 minutes of baking to crisp the skin. Brush the surface with melted butter once or twice during this period. Transfer the baked fish to a large platter or a board covered with gold or silver foil. Garnish with parsley, lemon slices and "murres" made from peeled hard-cooked eggs and ripe olives. Serve with Sour Cream Caper Sauce. The number of servings depends on the weight of the uncooked fish; figure 1/2 pound (228 g) for each serving.

Sour Cream Caper Sauce
1/2 cup (120 mL) sour cream
2 tablespoons (30 mL) ketchup
1/2 cup (120 mL) mayonnaise
2 tablespoons (30 mL) drained and
*   finely chopped capers*
1-1/2 teaspoons (7 mL) finely chopped onion
1/4 teaspoon (1 mL) salt
1/8 teaspoon (0.5 mL) pepper

►Combine ingredients in order given and mix well. Makes about 1 cup (240 mL).

Susan's Egg-and-Olive "Murres"
A delightful garnish for any dish

4 hard-cooked eggs
10 large, ripe, pitted olives
1 raw carrot, scraped
8 grains cooked rice
Toothpicks

►Slice bottom off large end of hard-cooked eggs so that eggs will stand upright. Fasten a ripe olive to the top with a toothpick. Cut four olives in half lengthwise and fasten two halves to each egg with toothpicks to make the wings. Cut remaining two olives in half lengthwise, then cut each half to make the feet. Fasten feet to front of murres with toothpicks. Cut a piece of carrot into small sticks to resemble beaks. Slit the olive "face" with the tip of a sharp knife and insert the beak. Make slits for eyes and insert grains of white rice.
■ Northern Cookbook *(adapted)*

Zesty Lake Trout

2 pounds (1 kg) lake trout fillets, or other
*   fish fillets*
1/4 cup (60 mL) French dressing
1 tablespoon (15 mL) lemon juice
1 tablespoon (15 mL) grated onion
2 teaspoons (10 mL) salt
Dash of pepper

►Cut fillets into serving pieces and place in well-greased hinged wire grills. Combine remaining ingredients. Baste fish with sauce. Cook about 4 inches (10 cm) from moderately hot coals for six to eight minutes. Baste with sauce. Turn and cook for a few minutes longer or until fish flakes easily when tested with a fork.
■ Over The Coals

Charcoaled Charr

Recommended by the cooks as "the best fish meal" they had during a three-month trip in the back country

1 fresh arctic charr (or Dolly Varden or
    brook trout), about 3 or 4 pounds (1.4 to 2 kg)
1-1/2 to 2 cups (360 to 480 mL) hot, cooked rice
Fish eggs, as available
Seasonings to taste such as onion flakes, salt,
    pepper, parsley, lemon juice

►Mix the hot rice with fish roe and spices and stuff the cleaned fish with the mixture. Wrap the whole works in foil and cook slowly over the coals, turning occasionally. Two of us ate a 3- to 4-pound fish, but it should serve a couple more.
■ *Jim Greenough and Eileen Helmstetter
"The Bush Gourmet"
ALASKA® magazine, July 1977*

Steelhead Skidegate

►Place filleted fish, skin side down, on a sheet of foil on top of your barbecue grill. On top of each fillet, put pats of butter, then a layer of mayonnaise mixed (to taste) with mustard. Top this with slices of lemon. Grill 20 to 30 minutes, or until fish flakes.
■ *The editors, ALASKA® magazine*

Sesame Rainbow Trout

6 pan-dressed rainbow trout or other small fish
1/4 cup (60 mL) melted fat or oil
1/4 cup (60 mL) sesame seeds
2 tablespoons (30 mL) lemon juice
1/2 teaspoon (2 mL) salt
Dash of pepper

►Place fish in well-greased hinged wire grills. Combine remaining ingredients. Baste fish with sauce. Cook about 4 inches (10 cm) from moderately hot coals for six to eight minutes. Baste with sauce again. Turn and cook a few minutes longer or until fish flakes easily when tested with a fork.
■ *Over The Coals*

Dilly Trout

2 pounds (1 kg) pan-dressed trout
1-1/2 teaspoons (7 mL) salt
1/4 teaspoon (1 mL) pepper
1/2 cup (120 mL) butter or margarine
2 teaspoons (10 mL) dill weed
3 tablespoons (45 mL) lemon juice

►Cut almost through fish lengthwise and spread open. Sprinkle with salt and pepper. Melt butter in large fry pan; add dill weed. Place fish in a single layer, flesh side down in hot dill butter. Fry at moderate heat for two to three minutes. Turn carefully. Fry two to three minutes longer or until fish flakes easily when fork-tested. Place fish on a warm serving platter; keep warm. When all the fish have been fried, turn the heat very low and stir in the lemon juice. Pour sauce over fish. Makes five or six servings.
■ *Time For Seafood*

Fisherman's Special

►Choose a big can of either pears or peaches. Also take along a small container of soluble coffee, sugar and dried cream, too, if you use it in your coffee, and a small package of salt and pepper mix. Now, with the above in your pack, pick up your fishin' gear and hike to your own special hard-to-get-at fishin' hole. Build a nice little fire and, while it is getting good and hot, proceed to catch a couple of nice trout. Open the can of fruit (you didn't forget the can opener, did you?) and drink the juice. Wash off a good flat rock and pour the fruit onto it. Rinse the can and fill three-quarters full of fresh creek water and set on fire for your coffee. Cut fish lengthwise in 3/4-inch (1.9 cm) strips. Wrap strips around green sticks and secure with straight pins, fishhooks or small peeled green sticks. Cook over fire for two minutes or until done enough for you. Salt and pepper the morsels and gobble them up. Eat the fruit. And that's a well-balanced meal for any hungry fisherman. No dishes to be washed, and there is nothing to carry back unless you want to catch a string of fish to take home. Oh, of course, you will want to flatten the fruit can and carry it back home, too.
■ *Chuck Thornton*

Best Ever Trout

►In a heavy frying pan put enough cooking fat to cover the fish. The amount will depend on the size of the fish — usually a depth of 2 inches (5 cm) will suffice. Heat the fat until a cube of bread dropped in it will brown while you count to sixty — about 360°F (185°C). Roll the fish thoroughly in prepared pancake mix and drop in the hot fat. When the fish are delicately browned on one side, turn them. When brown on the other side they are ready to serve. The prepared pancake flour will be seasoning enough. The fact that the fish cooks inside and outside at the same time cuts cooking time in half and insures the retention of texture and flavor.

Keep a can of fat for this purpose in the refrigerator all during trout season. After frying trout, strain the fat back into the can and save it for the next occasion.
■ *Out of Alaska's Kitchens*

Chapter 3

Clams, Cockles, Mussels, Oysters & Scallops

*It's early morning in April.
The tide is low and the beach is
washed clean. Wet rocks gleam.
Tide pools sparkle in the spring sun.
And here and there an occasional
spurt from a tiny hole in the sand
lights up like a miniature rainbow.
This is clam country.*

*Where? Almost anywhere along
Alaska's thousands of miles of
shoreline and shallow subtidal
regions.*

*What kinds of clams? Razor
clams. Butter clams. Littlenecks.
Softshells. Pinknecks (sometimes
called surf clams). Alaska has more
than 160 different species of clams,
and you can just about take your pick.*

*How many are there? So many
millions we really don't know. Until
recently the best guess was that
some fifty million pounds of Alaska
clams could be taken each year
without being missed.*

*Alaska Tidelines
Volume I, Number 7, April 1979*

Clams and other bivalves make the shoreline a favorite haunt for thousands of gatherers during the right season.

Most bivalves are easiest to gather during a minus tide. Clams are located by the little dimples they leave in the wet sand as they withdraw their siphons. The shorter the siphon, the closer to the surface the bivalve has to be. That means cockles may rest almost on top, while razors and geoducks and horse clams can be buried deep. Although some clams have a reputation for being very fast diggers, they're not necessarily faster on their "foot" than other clams. It's simply that the long siphon or "neck" may be withdrawn very rapidly to a shell that is already well below the surface.

About The Recipes: We'd like to pretend there is no such thing as paralytic shellfish poisoning (PSP) and that any Alaskan who lives within shouting distance of a good clamming beach won't have much use for recipes that call for canned clams. That's the premise on which we started collecting recipes. . . . Let those poor Lower 48 midwesterners have the canned clams.

But PSP is a reality we can't ignore. Therefore, this book includes more recipes for canned clams than we might otherwise have selected.

You may also use canned clams in any recipe that calls for cooked or minced clams. If drained clam meat is wanted, it will generally take two 7- or 8-ounce (200 to 228 g) cans of clams to equal 1 cup (240 mL) of drained meat, with a little left over. One can will suffice for a recipe that calls for "1 cup (240 mL) chopped clams with liquor."

On the other hand, we are also assuming that this collection will have value far beyond the time when PSP ceases to be a problem — or at least one that is diminished by the discovery of a means of testing for PSP toxicity that any old clam digger can use. And so, we've taken pains to include plenty of recipes for the newly dug bivalves, too.

For now, please read Danger! PSP (page 94) and follow the cautions listed if you plan to harvest shellfish.

CLAMS & COCKLES

Removing Sand

"There is no satisfactory shortcut" to the process of removing sand from clams according to G.S. "Bud" Mortensen of Petersburg. But his method is easy enough. . . . The clams do all the work:

"Put the clams in a burlap bag," he says. "Tie it near the top with a strong rope and suspend it from the boat or float it in salt water for 20 to 30 hours."

If you take your clams away from their natural bathtub, however, a bucket will do for the initial cleaning. First wash off any surface sand with salt water, place the clams in a bucket and cover them with clean sea water (collect it out away from the shoreline). Change this saltwater rinse two or three times over a period of an hour or more. You can duplicate the cleansing effect of sea water by adding salt to tap water — 1/3 cup (80 mL) of salt per gallon (3.8 L) of water.

Some people also swear by the scouring power of corn meal and throw a handful into the water with the clams. But as near as we can tell, the clams ignore it, and as one outraged clam digger says, "It's a waste of good corn meal!" (Maybe they'd like corn bread better.)

Bringing Home The Clams

Clams with unbroken shells will live for one or more days, and you may bring them home in a wet burlap bag or on ice or in a bucket, drained of water and covered with a wet burlap sack. *Shucked* clams must be kept on ice and are "about as perishable as fresh trout," Mortensen warns. If you're going to shuck and clean the clams before you cook them, however, the quality is best if you do so soon after digging.

Shucking Hard-Shell Clams
Method I
Discard any clams with broken shells or any that are dead. (If you touch it and it doesn't clam up, it's dead.) To open a live one:
1. Hold it in the palm of one hand with the shell's hinge against the palm.
2. Insert a slender, strong, sharp knife between the halves of shell and cut around the clam, twisting the knife slightly to pry open the shell.
3. Cut both muscles free from the two halves of shell. If the clams are to be served on the half shell, separate shells and rinse well. For other recipes, remove the meat and rinse it in cold water.

Method II
Clams can be "relaxed" by a brief dousing in boiling water. Since the boiling water may toughen the meat a bit, this method is most suitable for cockles or clams that are to be minced or ground or canned. Clams to be used whole and fresh (or frozen) are best shucked raw.

In any case, the dousing needn't be longer than a few seconds. Place the scrubbed clams in a large washtub or bucket and pour boiling water over them. Stir them around a bit and then drain or pour off the hot water. Immediately pour cold water over the clams to halt the cooking process. The shells will pull away easily.

Shucking & Cleaning Razor Clams

Horse clams, razors and large butter clams can be cleaned similarly. What you want to remember, particularly, is to discard the dark meat — tip of siphon, especially, and dark portion of foot — as these may contain concentrated quantities of PSP:
1. Run a sharp, slender knife blade down the inside of the shell, cutting both adductor muscles on both shells near the hinge. After the clam is free, you'll find that small sharp-pointed scissors are the best cleaning tool.
2. Cut black tip off the neck.
3. Split the neck lengthwise on the side away from the hinges.

4. Cut away the gills.
5. Slit the digger foot from the front side.
6. Cut the gut on the back (hinge side).
7. Remove dark colored materials.
8. Wash off in clean cold water.

Cockles

The name *cockle* refers to a confusing abundance of shelled creatures all popularly called clams. And, for cooking purposes especially, cockles should be considered especially tasty clams. Most familiar in Alaska is the basket cockle which is found in the coarse sand of protected bays along the coast from the Bering Sea to Baja. Averaging about 3 inches (7.5 cm) across, the shell is a pretty one with strong, evenly spaced "ribs" that run from the top of the shell to the bottom. It is sometimes called the heart shell because of its shape viewed from the side. Since the cockle has almost no siphon, you'll find it very near the surface of the sand, sometimes even partly exposed.

Preparation Tips: Cockles are most easily prepared for further cooking by scrubbing them well and then submerging them in boiling water —a few seconds only. Then drain the hot water and cool the cockles quickly with cold water. Shells should open easily. Pick out the meat and prepare it further as you would clams. Cockles are especially good in recipes that call for minced or ground clams. The virtue of the cockle is that it has a large foot, full of flavor, but quite tough . . . making it the choice of many cooks for clam chowder and other minced clam recipes. Others swear by a mix of cockles and butter clams.

Since the shells are pretty, they make nice ones to save for hot appetizers served "on the half shell."

Storing Clams & Cockles

Shucked or unshucked, clams are very perishable. Fresh ones in the shell can be covered with a wet cloth and refrigerated, below 40°F (5°C), for up to 24 hours. Shucked clams can be stored in their liquor in a tightly covered container — refrigerated — up to two days.

To make them last longer than that, freeze them, shucked, in airtight containers. Do not freeze clams in the shell. Always thaw frozen clams under refrigeration . . . not out on the counter.

Mother's Razor Clam Cocktail
A raw appetizer

►Clean clams thoroughly. Then grind them through a medium blade, enough for a half-full cocktail glass per serving. Chill. Make a cocktail sauce for the chilled clam meat by mixing:

1/2 cup (120 mL) ketchup
1 teaspoon (5 mL) sugar
Few drops of Worcestershire
Salt to taste
1 teaspoon (5 mL) vinegar or lemon juice
Dash of pepper or paprika
■ *Enid S. McLane*
 An Alaskan Cook Book, *Kenai*

Variation: Whole raw clams are served as appetizers, too. Littlenecks or small butter clams—up to 2 inches (5 cm) in diameter — are favorites. They must be very fresh and they can be served on the half shell or on a plate of cracked ice after they've been scrubbed, cleaned, and the black tip of the neck clipped and discarded, according to directions at the beginning of this section.

Offer lemon wedges and one or more sauces for dipping. Use the tomato cocktail sauce above, adding horseradish or hot pepper sauce if you like. Plain or seasoned melted butter is another good dip. Season a quarter-pound (114 g) of melted butter with two cloves finely minced garlic, a teaspoon (5 mL) each, of grated onion and lemon juice, a few hours ahead of serving. This will allow flavors to emerge.

King Clam Teasers

►Cut geoduck steaks into long strips about 1/4 inch (6 mm) thick. Cut each strip into thirds. Roll strips in pancake flour and deep fat fry at 350°F (175°C) until golden brown. Serve with dip or sauce.
■ Seas The Opportunity

Clam Nectar

►Take the clam juices from steamed clams; add salt and pepper, butter and a little Tabasco sauce. This is a drink fit for a chief.
■ Tsimpshean Indian Island Cookbook
 Metlakatla

Shellfish notes: A clam's age is judged like a tree's. Count up the annual rings on the shell. If the cockles are too small for best eating this week — wait a bit. They can grow 1/4 inch (6 mm) per week. Hungry for scallops? Follow halibut fishermen. They sometimes find scallops clamped to the longlines.

Deviled Clam Appetizers

Save your cockle shells for this nifty appetizer.

1 pint (480 mL) clams with liquor
1/2 cup (120 mL) chopped celery
2 tablespoons (30 mL) chopped onion
1 clove garlic, finely chopped
1/4 cup (60 mL) melted fat or oil
1 tablespoon (15 mL) flour
1 tablespoon (15 mL) chili sauce
1/2 teaspoon (2 mL) salt
1/4 teaspoon (1 mL) pepper
1/4 teaspoon (1 mL) thyme
3 drops liquid hot pepper sauce

1 egg, beaten
1/2 cup (120 mL) cracker meal
2 tablespoons (30 mL) chopped parsley
1/2 cup (120 mL) dry bread crumbs
2 tablespoons (30 mL) melted fat or oil

►Drain clams and reserve liquor. Chop clams fine. Cook celery, onion and garlic in fat until tender. Blend in flour and seasonings. Add clams and cook until thick, stirring constantly. Stir a little of this hot sauce into the beaten egg and then pour the mixture back into the sauce, stirring constantly. Add cracker meal and parsley. If necessary to moisten, add a small amount of clam liquor.

Fill small, well-greased individual seafood shells

Danger! PSP

"On a good weekend in July when there's an especially low tide expected, there can be three thousand people on the beach at Clam Gulch," reports Ronnie Chappell in the *Anchorage Times* [April 11, 1982]. "They come to enjoy the sun, the air and the breeze that blows off Cook Inlet. They come to walk in the sand with friends and family members. They also come to dig for clams. Few have heard of paralytic shellfish poisoning (PSP) and few are worried about it."

What is PSP? How do you get it? Should you be worried about it? The first two questions, and probably the third, can be answered with one sentence: PSP is a nerve poisoning a thousand times more potent than cyanide, say the experts, and you "get it" by eating shellfish — especially the filter-feeders such as clams, oysters, mussels and scallops — that have consumed large quantities of a microscopic algae, a "dinoflagellate," that produces the poison. Rarely are the shellfish themselves, or even the fish who feed on the shellfish, affected by the toxin. But warm-blooded predators — notably man — who like to dine on shellfish are very much affected.

Unfortunately, there are many wide-spread but false beliefs about how to avoid the poisoning. Perhaps the most dangerous myth is the one that says PSP and "red tides" are synonymous.

They are not. The rust-colored bloom on the water we have learned to shy away from may be caused by many types of harmless one-celled algae. *On the other hand,* shellfish feeding in apparently clear water — even waters that test relatively free of the poison-producing "dinos" — can contain enough of the PSP organism to become poisonous.

For one thing, some shellfish may retain toxic levels of poison long after the rust-colored sea that fed them has turned clear. For another, as Alaska researcher Sherwood Hall has proved in his work at the Seward Marine Center, the cysts that eventually become toxic "dinos" are harbored in deep ocean mud. Hall has discovered several previously unknown forms of the poison by testing a variety of mud samples.

To lay another myth to rest: It is not true that months spelled with the letter *r* offer any magical — let alone scientific — protection. Outbreaks of PSP have occasionally occurred in Alaska during September and October. Can you spell *them* without any *r*'s?

While PSP is found in other parts of the world, its special danger in Alaska is twofold. First is the nearly impossible task of monitoring the state's thousands of miles of shoreline to make certain the shellfish taken from them are safe — no matter what the test. And second, since the waters can look clear and test clear when the shellfish do not, the only conclusive tests are of the shellfish. And so far, the only accepted methods are extremely tricky to perform. One requires grinding the shellfish, extracting and further treating the toxin, injecting it into laboratory mice . . . and waiting to see how they react.

Another dangerous myth is that you can test for PSP by chewing on a little bit of the clam yourself— never mind the white mice — wait a half-hour, and if no numbing occurs, you're safe to eat the rest. Not so, say the experts; you have to *swallow* the poison before the "test" symptoms will appear.

SO WHAT IS A PRIVATE CLAM DIGGER TO DO short of carrying around a sack full of white mice and a hypodermic syringe along with the traditional bucket and shovel?

The only truly safe answer is . . . quit eating shellfish. But then you should probably also quit crossing streets, driving a car and getting out of bed.

Short of absolute safety, there are a few other

with about 2 tablespoons (30 mL) clam mixture. Combine bread crumbs and fat; sprinkle over top of each shell. Bake in hot oven, 400°F (205°C), for 10 minutes or until browned. Makes 36 appetizers.
■ Seas The Opportunity

Smoke-Flavored Razor Clams
If you don't have time to smoke clams, this makes a quick substitute.

1 cup (240 mL) salad oil
3 tablespoons (45 mL) liquid smoke
2 tablespoons (30 mL) Worcestershire
2 tablespoons (30 mL) lemon juice
1 teaspoon (5 mL) flavor enhancer
1 teaspoon (5 mL) garlic powder
1 teaspoon (5 mL) chili powder
1 teaspoon (5 mL) celery salt
1 teaspoon (5 mL) brown sugar
1 teaspoon (5 mL) seasoning salt
2 cups (480 mL) cleaned, chopped frozen or
   thawed razor clams
Paprika

►Mix all ingredients with chopped clams. Include clam liquid. (Frozen clams are easier to chop.) Spread mixture in shallow pan. Sprinkle with paprika and bake at 325°F (160°C) for 1-1/2 hours. Cover and store in refrigerator.
■ *Betty Bennett*, The Anchorage Times

precautions. One can take clams only from the beaches authorized for commercial harvest. At this writing, these are at Polly Creek, Swikshak and Cordova. Or, living a little more dangerously, take clams from areas where periodic tests are run, even though the beaches are not officially open to clamming. By all means check with district offices of the Alaska Department of Fish and Game and the Alaska Department of Health and Social Services to be sure there are no other problems — such as sewage contamination — associated with the area you're about to dig.

One can also be choosy about the variety of clams to take a chance on. Mussels are especially dangerous critters to eat because they accumulate the toxin very rapidly; butter clams are dangerous, too, but for another reason. They retain the toxin long after it's ingested — up to a year. Razor clams appear to be the safest bet if you adhere to the warnings and eat only the white meat. Any poison is likely to be concentrated in the dark parts, especially the tip of the siphon.

So there you have it, a not altogether reassuring answer to the question "Should I worry about it?" but as shellfish biologists continue to work at the problem, one hopes for an early discovery of a safe, simple method of testing for PSP toxicity that every clam digger can perform right at the seashore.

Diminishing The Risk of PSP
If you're going to eat clams ANYway . . . then at least follow this advice outlined by Joe Ferguson of the Alaska Department of Environmental Conservation:
1. Don't eat the digestive organs (dark portions) of any bivalve, the gills of mussels, and the siphons of butter clams. Razor clams are cleaned by removing the tip of the siphons, gills, and digestive tracts. Removal of clam parts should be done **before** steaming, not afterwards. It is easily accomplished by slipping a sharp knife between the shells and cutting the anterior and posterior adductor muscles, then severing the named clam parts.
2. The white meat of the shellfish should be washed thoroughly before cooking.
3. Discard the nectar or broth used in cooking clams; the cooking process concentrates the toxin in the liquid.
4. Remember that drinking alcoholic beverages will speed absorption of the toxin if present. . . .

What To Do If Symptoms Occur
Symptoms may occur within 30 minutes. They include tingling or numbness in tongue and lips, spreading gradually to other parts of the body. This may be followed by nausea, headache and shortness of breath. Death occurs because of respiratory failure.

There is no specific antidote for PSP, so the first thing to do is to seek medical attention immediately. In the meantime, vomiting should be induced. This can be done by sticking a finger down the throat, drinking warm salt water, or taking Syrup of Ipecac. Do not induce vomiting in a semiconscious or unconscious victim. Treat for shock by placing the person in a prone position, elevating the feet, and covering with a blanket. Do not give digitalis or alcohol because these substances will increase absorption of toxin. If breathing problems occur, give mouth to mouth respiration until medical personnel take over.

Diminishing the Risk of PSP and What To Do If Symptoms Occur are excerpted from "Paralytic Shellfish Poisoning — Few Beaches Safe," *Southeastern Log*, Ketchikan, July 1982.

Steamed Clam Nectar

►A couple big buttons of garlic in with the clams changes the nectar from rather bland to highly palatable.

■ *Dick Brennan*
  PTA Cook Book, *Petersburg*

Clam Dip

*4 to 8 ounces (114 to 228 g) cream cheese
  thinned with milk or lemon juice
1/2 pint (240 mL) cottage cheese
Grated onion
Garlic salt to taste
Few drops of Worcestershire
1-1/2 cups (360 mL) minced clams*

►Blend all ingredients well and serve with assorted chips for dipping.

■ Tsimpshean Indian Island Cookbook
  Metlakatla

Variations: Recipes that vary the above ingredients are many. Some suggest using either a large package (8 oz /or/ 228 g) of cream cheese *or* 1-1/2 cups (360 mL) cottage cheese rather than both. Seasoning variations include a few drops of hot pepper sauce and up to a couple of teaspoons (10 mL) lemon juice. Most recipes call for minced or grated onion. Another nice touch is to use cream cheese as the base and thin it some with sour cream and a small amount of clam liquor.

Cordova Clam Relish Spread

*1 can (7 oz /or/ 200 g) minced clams, drained
1 package (3 oz /or/ 85 g) cream cheese
2 tablespoons (30 mL) sweet pickle relish
Tabasco
Salt and pepper*

►Blend clams and cream cheese well to make a smooth paste. Add salt, pepper and Tabasco to taste. Pickle relish gives special zest to this spread, but other things can be substituted for it, if preferred: 2 tablespoons (30 mL) of chopped pickle or minced onion or chives, chopped very fine.

■ *Ruth Allman, Juneau*
  Alaska Sourdough

About Clam Chowder: *"Actually, there are only three authentic recipes for clam chowder,"* says *Bunny Mathisen of Petersburg, whose reputation as a cook — and particularly as a cook whose expertise with fish is unsurpassed — goes far beyond Alaska's borders. "There is Hatteras Chowder for which the clams, potatoes and onions are ground. You add a little water, cook*

lightly, and add cooked, chopped bacon during the last few minutes. Next is Manhattan Chowder, with tomatoes, and lastly, clam chowder with milk. Some people add lots of vegetables to their chowders. Such variations are individual and to the cook's taste, but there are only three true chowders."

Bunny has contributed two of them — her directions for making Hatteras Chowder (just given) and Charliett Daniels's Cream of Clam Chowder, a milk chowder enriched with cream. Besides the third type, Manhattan Chowder, we've included a number "to the cook's taste." You're welcome to experiment on your own, too. That's the way of good soups.

Mamie Jensen, a Juneau expert with fish cookery, says that if a chowder recipe calls for salt pork or bacon sauteed in its own fat, or vegetables sauteed in butter, she likes to add a little thickening, such as flour or cornstarch, so that the fat will not rise to the surface once the saute is added to the soup.

To traditional chowders, she adds color — shredded carrot or parsley or chives — or simply a sprinkle of paprika on top. "A lot depends on what one has on hand," she says. "I think a good cook is innovative and can make substitutions or additions to her advantage."

Audrey Rearden, Homer, who's as good at gathering, hunting or fishing for her supper as she is at cooking it (and that means excellent) says her favorite critter for clam chowder is the cockle. "They're tough, but I put them through the meat grinder. And they sure do have the flavor!"

Basic Clam Milk Stew

2-1/2 quarts (2.4 L) freshly dug clams
1 quart (1 L) cold water
2 tablespoons (30 mL) butter
1 quart (1 L) milk
Salt and pepper

►Wash and thoroughly scrub the clams, using a stiff brush. Rinse well. Put the clams in a large kettle and add the water. Cover tightly. Steam until clam shells open wide. Remove the clams from the kettle and cook the liquid down to half its volume. Remove the clams from the shells and cut off the black tips of the necks. Put the clams through a food chopper, using a coarse blade. Add the clams to the liquid in the kettle and bring to a boil; season to taste and add the butter. Last of all add the milk and heat but do NOT boil. Serve with oyster crackers.
■ *The Old Homesteader*

High Tide Clam Milk Stew

3 cans (7 oz /or/ 200 g, each) minced clams
3 cups (720 mL) milk
Salt and pepper to taste
2 tablespoons (30 mL) butter
1/2 teaspoon (2 mL) onion salt

►Heat clams in their juice until boiling; reduce heat and add other ingredients. Continue heating until milk is steaming or almost boiling but do NOT boil. A few flakes of crushed red pepper in each serving would not be amiss. This is an excellent cold weather soup.
■ *The Old Homesteader*

Clamato Soup

1 onion, diced
2 carrots, diced
1 rib celery, diced
1/2 green pepper, diced
2 tablespoons (30 mL) butter
1 small can (16 oz /or/ 456 g) tomatoes, or an
*   8-ounce (228 g) can of tomato sauce*
2 cups (480 mL) water or fish stock
Salt and pepper
1/4 teaspoon (1 mL) thyme
1/2 teaspoon (2 mL) oregano
1 cup (240 mL) shell macaroni
1 can (8 oz /or/ 228 g) minced clams, with liquid

►Saute diced vegetables in butter. Add tomatoes or tomato sauce, water or fish stock, and the liquid from canned clams. Season, bring to a boil and add macaroni. When macaroni is almost cooked, add clams and heat through. Serves two.
■ *The editors, ALASKA® magazine*

Resurrection Bay Clam Chowder

1 quart (1 L) water
1 teaspoon (5 mL) salt
1 pint (480 mL) diced, unpared potatoes
4 stalks celery, finely chopped
1 medium onion, finely chopped
1 tablespoon (15 mL) diced bell pepper,
*   or equivalent in dried pepper*
6 medium-size bay leaves, whole
1 cup (240 mL) instant nonfat dry milk
1 pint (480 mL) fresh or canned clams,
*   with juice*

►Cook potatoes, celery, onion, bell pepper and bay leaves together in salted water until tender. Remove bay leaves, add milk powder, clams and their juice and cook 10 minutes longer. When serving, garnish with a small lump of butter and a sprinkling of fresh-ground black pepper.
■ *Beth Deisher*
   Recipes From The Scrolls of Saint Peter's
   Seward

Company Clam Chowder
For a crowd

3 quarts (2.85 L) shucked clams with liquor
1/4 pound (114 g) diced salt pork or bacon
2 cups (480 mL) chopped onion
2 cups (480 mL) chopped celery
2 quarts (2 L) diced potatoes
2 cans (29 oz /or/ 826 g, each) tomatoes or
*   2 quarts (2 L) tomato juice*
1 quart (1 L) hot water
1 tablespoon (15 mL) salt
1/2 teaspoon (2 mL) pepper
1/4 cup (60 mL) margarine or butter
1/4 cup (60 mL) chopped parsley, optional

►Drain clams and save liquor. Remove any shell particles and chop clams into 1/2-inch (1.25 cm) pieces. Fry salt pork or bacon until crisp in large heavy pot or saucepan. Add onion and celery and cook until tender. Add potatoes, tomatoes or tomato juice and water. Cover and bring to the boiling point; simmer 20 minutes or until potatoes are tender. Add chopped clams and liquor, salt and pepper, and cook an additional 5 to 10 minutes. Add margarine or butter; melt. Serve, using a large ladle. Garnish with chopped parsley. Serves 25.

Far North Clams

►Partially digested clams obtained from the stomach of freshly caught walrus are considered a delicacy by the Eskimo who hunt this animal. . . .
On Saint Lawrence Island clams, mussels and tunicates [the sea squirt is one], washed up on the

beach after fall storms, are collected and used as food. They are only occasionally available in amounts sufficient to freeze for winter use. These are eaten raw or partially cooked.

Clams are also obtainable in limited quantities at Hooper Bay and other Bering Sea coastal villages.
■ The Alaska Dietary Survey

Pacific Clam and Corn Chowder

8 ounces (228 g) minced clams
1 cup (240 mL) clam nectar and water
3 slices bacon, chopped
1 cup (240 mL) chopped onion
2 cups (480 mL) diced raw potatoes
1-1/2 cups (360 mL) drained whole kernel corn
3 cups (720 mL) milk
2 tablespoons (30 mL) flour
1 tablespoon (15 mL) margarine or butter
1 teaspoon (5 mL) celery salt
1 teaspoon (5 mL) salt
Dash of white pepper
1/2 cup (120 mL) coarse cracker crumbs
  (optional)

►Drain clams; reserve liquid. Add water to clam liquid to make 1 cup (240 mL). Fry bacon until crisp; add onion and cook until tender. Add potatoes and nectar-water. Cover. Simmer gently until potatoes are tender; add corn and milk. Blend flour and butter and stir into chowder. Cook slowly until mixture thickens slightly, stirring constantly. Add seasonings and clams; simmer five minutes. Serve hot. Top with cracker crumbs.
■ Seafood Moods

Cockles

►Cockles are good any time of year where they may be found in sandy beaches. They are good boiled or roasted. When roasting, cook with the valve side next to the fire first. Cool somewhat and then eat.
■ *Frank Johnson*
  Tlingit Survival Practices and Stories

Charliett Daniels's Cream of Clam Chowder

2 to 3 cups (480 to 720 mL) ground clams
2 to 3 cups (480 to 720 mL) diced potatoes
1/2 cup (120 mL) diced onions
1/2 cup (120 mL) diced celery
1 cup (240 mL) water
1 cup (240 mL) milk
1 cup (240 mL) cream
2 to 3 slices bacon
1 teaspoon (5 mL) salt
1 teaspoon (5 mL) pepper

►Cook ground clams, potatoes, onion and celery in water for 20 minutes. Add milk and cream. Chop or dice the bacon and saute. Combine with clams and vegetables, season with salt and pepper.
■ *Courtesy, Bunny Mathisen, Petersburg*

Clam Chowder — Manhattan Style

4 cups (1 L) chopped clams with juice
1/4 pound (114 g) salt pork or bacon,
  chopped fine
1 cup (240 mL) each — chopped carrots, celery
  and green pepper
1-1/2 cups (360 mL) diced raw potatoes
3 quarts (3 L) water
3 cups (720 mL) tomato pulp
Dash of thyme leaves
Dash of Italian seasoning
Dash of salt and pepper

►Saute carrots, celery and green pepper with the salt pork. Add the diced potatoes and water and simmer until potatoes are nearly done. Then add tomatoes, clams and clam juice and seasonings. Let cook for 15 minutes. Serve hot with garlic bread.
■ *John Hanson*
  The Smorgasbord

Variation: Mr. Hanson's chowder gives several "dashes" in honor of one of Manhattan's largest ethnic populations, but thyme and Italian seasonings are optional ingredients in Manhattan Chowder, nevertheless. We know some Norwegian cooks (a couple of generations removed from Manhattan, to be sure) who omit thyme and Italian seasonings and substitute six whole allspice and six whole cloves tied up in a cheesecloth bag. Add the bag to the soup when you add the potatoes and remove it before serving.

Tomato Clam Aspic

1 envelope unflavored gelatin
1/4 cup (60 mL) cold water
1 cup (240 mL) tomato juice
Salt to taste
2 tablespoons (30 mL) lemon juice
1 pint (480 mL) minced clams
2 hard-cooked eggs, diced
2 tablespoons (30 mL) diced cucumber chips
1/2 cup (120 mL) diced celery
Salad dressing
Salad greens

►Soften gelatin in cold water. Heat tomato juice, pour over gelatin and stir until well dissolved. Stir in lemon juice and salt. Chill until slightly thick-

ened. Drain clams and fold in together with diced eggs, cucumber chips and celery. Chill until firm. Unmold onto a bed of salad greens.
■ *Bobbi Krist, FV* Dorinda
   Seafood Secrets, *Sitka*

Razor Clam Aspic

1 can (7 oz /or/ 200 g) minced razor clams
1 tablespoon (15 mL) plain gelatin
1/4 cup (60 mL) cold water
1/2 cup (120 mL) clam liquor
1/2 cup (120 mL) water
1/2 cup (120 mL) celery, chopped
1/4 cup (60 mL) stuffed olives, chopped
1/2 teaspoon (2 mL) Worcestershire
Mayonnaise or salad dressing
Lettuce

►Soften gelatin in 1/4 cup (60 mL) cold water five minutes. Heat clams, remaining water and clam liquor. Add gelatin and stir until dissolved; cool. Add vegetables and seasonings. Pour into six individual molds. Chill until firm. Unmold on lettuce and serve with mayonnaise or dressing.
■ Seafood Recipes For Alaskans

Crew's Favorite Breakfast

►I allow one to two dozen clams per person as we use the tiny butter clams. Using the largest skillet available, cover the bottom with about a half-inch (1.25 cm) of water and fill it with the tiny clams. Bring water to a boil; cover for two or three minutes. When heated through, the clams pop open and are ready to eat. Never use any clams which don't open.

At each place I serve a small dish filled with lemon butter. Melt approximately two cubes of butter (4 oz /or/ 114 g, each) and add 2 tablespoons (30 mL) lemon juice and a dash of salt and pepper. Heat through, then pour into serving dishes. Serve with napkins, toast, milk and a dish of canned fruit. We generally stop serving because I'm tired of cooking rather than because the crew is tired of eating this favorite meal.
■ *Virginia Parrish, FV* N.F.T.
   Seafood Secrets, *Sitka*

The Horse Clams

►Drop horse clams into boiling water until the clams open and you can get the clams out. Squeeze the clams and mash them. Put some ooligan (eulachon) grease to mix with it and serve seaweed on the side. Remember as you mash and squeeze the clams to save the milky juices and mix it all together with a little grease.
■ Tsimpshean Indian Island Cookbook
   Metlakatla

Scrambled Eggs and Gooey Duck

►Clean gooey duck thoroughly. Grind or mince fine. Fry small pieces of bacon until crisp. Add beaten eggs and minced gooey duck and scramble. Use desired amount eggs and gooey duck.
■ Tsimpshean Indian Island Cookbook
   Metlakatla

Clam Souffle

12 square salted crackers, crumbled
1 cup (240 mL) milk
1/4 cup (60 mL) melted butter
1 flat can (7 oz /or/ 200 g) minced clams
Pepper and salt to taste
2 eggs, well beaten

►Pour the milk over the crumbled crackers and let stand about 20 minutes. Add the melted butter (use a little more if you desire a richer souffle), the undrained clams, seasonings and eggs. Minced green pepper and onion may be added for more flavor if desired. Pour into an oiled baking dish and bake in a slow oven, 325°F (160°C), for 30 to 40 minutes, until firm when tested with a knife and delicately brown on top.
■ Out of Alaska's Kitchens

Clambake

►Dig a large hole; line it with wet stones (taken from the water) and build a hot fire in the pit. Let the stones heat for two or three hours. Shovel out the hot coals and place a layer of wet seaweed in the pit. Cover it with chicken wire then add another layer of seaweed. Put in the scrubbed and cleaned clams. Often potatoes and unhusked ears of corn are added to the pit. Cover with seaweed and finally with a tarpaulin. Weigh down the edges of the tarp with stones; then shovel a little sand over the top of the tarp. Allow to steam for approximately two hours.
■ Shellfish Cookbook

Variations: "We used to enclose the clams in a burlap bag and place it over the first layer of seaweed. Then the wire was unnecessary," says The Old Homesteader. "Then we proceeded as in the above. We put the cooked clams, bag and all, on a driftwood plank in the middle of the picnic table and made a long slit in the upper side of the bag so people could help themselves easily." Other items can be added to a "clambake": halves of chicken, for instance, or fish fillets cut into serving portions and wrapped in the outer leaves of corn husks if your bake includes corn. Using some of the clams to make chowder for a first course is also a good idea. A sauce or two to use as a dip for clams can be prepared in advance.

Clam Omelet

1 cup (240 mL) clams
6 eggs, separated
2/3 cup (160 mL) cream or milk
1 tablespoon (15 mL) flour
Salt and pepper to taste

►Saute clams in butter. Add seasoning to egg yolks and beat until light. Add cream and clams and mix thoroughly. Fold in the egg whites that have been beaten stiff and put this mixture into a pan and bake at 350°F (180°C) for about 25 minutes.
■ *Tsimpshean Indian Island Cookbook*
  Metlakatla

Clam Nectar with Steamed Clams

1 gallon (3.8 L) freshly dug clams
2 quarts (2 L) cold water
Pepper
Butter
Onion juice
Buttered toast

►Wash and scrub the clams thoroughly, using a stiff brush. Rinse well. Put the clams in a large kettle with the water; cover tightly and steam until clam shells open wide. Remove the clams from the shells and strain the liquid into mugs, flavoring each serving with a dash of pepper, onion juice and a dollop of butter. Serve the clams with buttered toast and accompany with the mugs of hot nectar.

Bos'n Bill's Clam Shells
Creamed clams on the half shell

2 quarts (2 L) unshucked clams
Water
1 tablespoon (15 mL) olive oil
3 tablespoons (45 mL) butter
3 tablespoons (45 mL) flour
Reserved clam broth, 1/2 cup (120 mL)
1/2 cup (120 mL) milk
1 tablespoon (15 mL) sauterne or sherry
Salt and pepper
Cheddar cheese
Cracker meal
Paprika

►Steam the clams until they open in the olive oil and barely enough water to cover the bottom of the pan. Throw away any that don't open. Strain, reserving clams and liquid.

Melt butter over low heat and stir in flour until well blended. Slowly stir in the half-cup of reserved clam broth, the milk and sauterne or sherry. Add salt and pepper to taste. When sauce is thickened, add shucked clams. Place the clam shells on a bed of rock salt and fill them with the creamed clams. Sprinkle with a mixture of good Cheddar cheese, cracker meal and paprika. Brown in an oven preheated to 350°F (175°C).
■ *Bos'n Bill's Dubious Dutchman*
  Bremerton, Washington
  Pacific Search, *Smorgasbord*

Extra Special Steamed Clams #1

►For the most delicious steamed clams ever, try pouring a can of beer in a large kettle or steamer. Throw a scant handful of celery leaves in the beer and add lots of littleneck clams; boil until the shells open. The liquid makes a delicious nectar served in hot cups with a dash of Worcestershire and a drop or two of Tabasco. Serve the clams in the shell next to dishes of melted butter for dipping.
■ *Gloria Peterson, FV* Kruzof
  Seafood Secrets, *Sitka*

Extra Special Steamed Clams #2

►Needed is a half bucket of small clean butter clams in the shell. In bottom half of steamer combine: one lemon, sliced thin, 1/2 teaspoon (2 mL) garlic powder, 2 tablespoons (30 mL) oil and 1/2 cup (120 mL) water. Put clams in top half of steamer; cover with a tight lid and steam until clams open — approximately 15 minutes. Make a dip for the clams using one cube (4 oz /or/ 114 g) of butter melted together with the juice of one lemon. Serve piping hot.
■ *"Skipper" Barb Workman, FV* Sachem
  Seafood Secrets, *Sitka*

Broiled Clams on The Half Shell

►Use small butter clams. Give them a quick scrubbing with a brush. Starting knife edge at the front, split straight back to hinge. If necks were already well out, cut them off before you scrub and split the clams. Otherwise, snip off the black part of the split neck with a pair of scissors. Wash out the sand under the cold water tap. Then break the hinge, leaving two half-clams in half shells. Leave no water in the shells.

Do this with about three times as many clams as you think those present will eat. Then arrange them on big, shallow baking tins, put a dot of butter and a sprinkle of garlic salt on each half-clam. Place under broiler or in a very hot oven for three to five minutes, until they just start to curl brown at the edges. The smaller ones may get quite browned, which is good for variety. Eat at once and drink the bit of nectar in the shell. Most flavorsome and only really tender cooked clams.
■ *Dick Brennan*
  PTA Cook Book, *Petersburg*

Clams Fried on The Half Shell

►Use medium-sized butter clams in the shell. After scrubbing and soaking them in sea water, cut off one shell. Clean the halves with the clams and set shell side up to drain. Dip clam and shell in beaten egg seasoned with salt and pepper, then into flour. Fry in 1/2 inch (1.25 cm) hot fat or oil until nice and brown. Fry clams with the shell side up.
■ Out of Alaska's Kitchens *(adapted)*

Variations: Many other breadings and batters are popularly used with either this method of frying clams on the half shell or with whole clams out of the shell. Besides the recipe above and the several that follow, please also check breadings and batters in Chapters 1 and 2 with the recipes for Pan-Fried Fish, Oven-Fried Fish, Tempura, French Fried Seafood in Batter and Hali-Beer Bits.

In frying clams on the half shell, some people use the method outlined by Dick Brennan for Broiled Clams on the Half Shell — splitting the clam so that a portion of the meat is left on each half shell. Clams 2 to 3 inches (5 to 7.5 cm) long are suggested for this purpose.

Another way to have good fried clams on the half shell is to skip the breading altogether and simply saute clams, shell side up, in butter or margarine flavored with a little garlic powder or a clove or two of finely minced garlic.

Deep-Fried Clams

1 quart (1 L) fresh clams, shucked
2 eggs, beaten
2 tablespoons (30 mL) milk
2 teaspoons (10 mL) salt
Dash of pepper
3 cups (720 mL) dry bread crumbs
Tartar Sauce

►Drain clams. Combine eggs, milk and seasoning. Dip clams in egg mixture and roll in crumbs. Fry in a basket in deep fat, 350°F (175°C) for one or two minutes or until brown. Drain on absorbent paper. Serve with Tartar Sauce. Serves six.
■ Shellfish Cookbook

Best Ever Razor Clams

►Beat one egg until foamy; beat in enough Bisquick to make a batter of dipping consistency. More than one egg and additional Bisquick may be used if the quantity of razor clams to be fried warrants more batter. Dip the clams in the batter and fry one minute on each side in melted margarine or other fat. A heavy skillet works best. These clams are extra good served with garlic bread and a green salad.
■ *Lois Smith, Olympia, Washington*

Simple Fried Clams

►Dip cleaned clams into beaten egg and roll them in flour seasoned with salt and pepper. Fry quickly in hot oil. Brown for about one minute on one side. Turn and finish frying on the other side, about two minutes longer. Frying too long makes clams tough and chewy. This is our favorite way of fixing clams.
■ *Beverly Wolford, Homer*

Fried Horse Clams

►Remove neck and rim of horse clams. Dip neck in boiling water for two minutes. Split neck and remove dark skin. Pound neck and rim. Dip in beaten egg; roll in cracker crumbs or crushed corn-flakes. Fry in very hot grease (550°F /or/ 285°C) about three minutes per side. Do not overcook.
■ *Bob Bell, FV* Clara III
Seafood Secrets, *Sitka*

Breaded Clams in Pan

►Brown three cloves of garlic in butter in a heavy pan with a lid. Bread clams and brown in another pan. Remove garlic from butter and place browned clams in garlic butter. Cover and cook for a few minutes until tender.
■ Tried and True Recipes, *Juneau*

Fried Gooey Duck

►Shell and clean gooey duck thoroughly. Cut off neck. Pour boiling water over and scrape the skin. Slit one side of neck to open flat. Slice main part of gooey duck in half. Dip gooey duck into beaten eggs with grated onion. Then dip into corn meal. Fry for three minutes on each side.
■ *"Early Day Recipes"*
Tsimpshean Indian Island Cookbook
Metlakatla

Fried Cockles

►Cut up cockle pieces, flour them and fry them in grease. Keep stirring and add enough curry powder to season. Serve with rice on the side.
■ Tsimpshean Indian Island Cookbook
Metlakatla

Sauteed Clams on The Half Shell

►Clean and shuck butter clams, saving and rinsing out shells. Heat olive oil in skillet, brown pieces of garlic and onion diced very small in oil. Add clams and saute on low heat for three minutes. Put this mixture into the clam shells; top with cracker crumbs and dot with butter. Brown under the broiler. Serve with hot garlic bread.
■ *Mrs. Richard Inglima*
Pioneer Cookbook, *Auxiliary No. 4, Anchorage*

Curried Fresh Clams

20 or 30 medium clams, chopped
5 or 6 medium potatoes, sliced or grated
1 onion, chopped
Salt and pepper to taste
Fat
1 tablespoon (15 mL) curry
2 tablespoons (30 mL) flour

►Remove shells, clean and wash clams in several changes of cold water, making sure all sand has been removed. Drain well. Pan-fry potatoes and onions with salt and pepper until potatoes are tender. Add clams. Mix curry and flour and stir in. Simmer 5 to 10 minutes longer, or until clams are tender.

■ Tsimpshean Indian Island Cookbook
Metlakatla

Baked Clams

1 pint (480 mL) shucked clams
1/2 cup (120 mL) salad oil
1 teaspoon (5 mL) salt
1 tablespoon (15 mL) chopped onion
1/2 cup (120 mL) grated Cheddar cheese
1 cup (240 mL) dry bread crumbs

►Combine oil, salt and onion. Place clams in mixture for one minute. Remove and drain; then roll in cheese and then in crumbs. Place in a well-greased baking pan and bake in a hot oven, 450°F (230°C) 12 minutes or until nicely browned. Makes six servings.

■ Shellfish Cookbook

Clam Sylyanka
A Russian dish

3 cups (720 mL) butter clams
Salt and pepper
1/2 cup (120 mL) flour
3 tablespoons (45 mL) oil
2 to 3 cups (480 to 720 mL) water
1 onion, chopped
1 teaspoon (5 mL) dried parsley
1 tablespoon (15 mL) Worcestershire
Hot cooked rice
Fried noodles, for garnish

►Clean and chop the clams into large chunks. Salt and pepper them; then dredge them in flour. Heat oil in large skillet until very hot. Add the floured clams. Keep turning the clams and scraping the bottom of the pan as the clams brown. Continue this procedure until the mixture is a fine golden brown color. Add water, onion, parsley and Worcestershire and simmer on low heat until a

gravy forms. Add water as needed. Serve over hot cooked rice and garnish with fried noodles. This recipe easily converts to a stew with the addition of potatoes.

■ *Natalie Simeonoff*
  Kadiak Times, *Kodiak*

Clam Suey

1 bucket clams in shell
4 to 6 slices bacon
1/2 medium-sized cabbage
1 stalk celery
1 large onion
Soy sauce to taste
Flour
Hot cooked rice

►Steam clams open. Cut clams into small pieces. Fry bacon and remove from pan. Place clams in bacon grease and fry. Add cut up cabbage, celery and onions. Add a small amount of water and simmer. Add soy sauce and flour to make gravy. Serve with rice.

■ Tsimpshean Indian Island Cookbook
Metlakatla

Deviled Clams
This recipe takes time to prepare, but it is so delicious, it's worth the effort.

6 or 8 baking shells*
1 pound (456 g) minced clams
1/2 cup (120 mL) minced onion
1/4 cup (60 mL) minced celery
1/4 cup (60 mL) minced green pepper
1 garlic clove, minced
1 tablespoon (15 mL) chopped parsley
1/2 cup (120 mL) butter
2-1/2 cups (600 mL) soft bread crumbs
1/2 cup (120 mL) heavy cream
2 eggs, beaten
2 hard-cooked eggs, chopped
1 tablespoon (15 mL) white wine vinegar
1 teaspoon (5 mL) Worcestershire
1/4 teaspoon (1 mL) thyme
1/8 teaspoon (0.5 mL) Tabasco
1 teaspoon (5 mL) salt

►Saute the onion, celery, pepper, garlic and parsley in 6 tablespoons (90 mL) butter for about 10 minutes. Set aside to cool. Combine 1-1/2 cups (360 mL) bread crumbs, cream, raw and cooked eggs, vinegar, Worcestershire, thyme, Tabasco and salt. Add to sauteed mixture and mix gently. Add clams and toss lighty. Spoon mixture into lightly buttered baking shells. Melt 2 tablespoons (30 mL) butter and toss with 1 cup (240 mL) bread crumbs. Sprinkle over top of mixture in shells. Place shells in broiler pan or shallow pan; add about 1/4 inch (6 mm) water, just enough to cover bottom of pan. Bake at 450°F (230°C) for 10 to 15 minutes. Remove shells from pan; place on heated serving tray. This recipe may be made early in the day and shells kept in the refrigerator. Remove about 30 minutes before baking. Serves four or five.

■ *Polly Browne*
  Gold Rush Cookbook, *Valdez*

Scallop shells are often used for this dish because they're so pretty, but good-sized cockle or clam shells will do, or ramekins.

Stormbound Macaroni

"One miserable day in Southeastern," as Gordy tells it, "rough seas just outside our 'hole-in-the-wall' harbor kept four of us huddled in the cabin of a small ship. Here's what our skipper served for the evening meal."

4 quarts (3.8 L) boiling water
1 teaspoon (5 mL) salt
1 pound (456 g) macaroni or spaghetti
2 tablespoons (30 mL) oil or bacon grease
2 tablespoons (30 mL) butter or margarine
2 cloves garlic, minced
2 cans (7½ oz /or/ 215 g, each) chopped clams
1-1/2 teaspoons (7 mL) oregano, crumbled
1/4 teaspoon (1 mL) pepper
1 tablespoon (15 mL) fresh snipped parsley, or
   2 teaspoons (10 mL) dried

►Add salt and macaroni (or spaghetti) to boiling water and cook about 12 minutes. Drain and place in a serving dish.

While the pasta cooks, heat oil and butter in a skillet over medium heat and saute the garlic. Add juice from the canned clams, oregano and pepper and simmer 10 minutes. Add clams and simmer another minute. Pour over pasta and toss. Sprinkle on fresh parsley and toss again. Serves four nicely. *Note:* If you use dried parsley, add it to the sauce with the oregano.

■ *Gordon R. Nelson, Palmer*
  Smokehouse Bear

Icy Strait Spaghetti

1 bell pepper, diced
1 onion, diced
2 cloves garlic, minced
2 tablespoons (30 mL) oil
1 pint (480 mL) clams
1 can (6 oz /or/ 170 g) tomato paste
1 can (8 oz /or/ 228 g) tomato sauce
1 large can (29 oz /or/ 826 g) tomatoes
1/4 teaspoon (1 mL) oregano
1 tablespoon (15 mL) sugar

Salt and pepper to taste
Parmesan cheese

►Lightly saute diced pepper, onion and garlic in oil in a heavy cast-iron skillet. Add clams and allow to simmer for a few minutes. Add tomato paste and sauce and tomatoes and stir together. Allow to simmer gently for two to three hours, stirring occasionally to keep it from sticking. Add spices and sugar and allow to simmer for about another half-hour. Serve over freshly boiled spaghetti and sprinkle with Parmesan cheese.

■ *Mary C. Owens, FV Cape Race*
  Seafood Secrets, *Sitka*

Clam Hentze

1-1/4 cups (300 mL) scalded milk and
   clam liquid
1-1/2 cups (360 mL) dry bread crumbs,
   not too fine
2 cups (480 mL) nippy cheese, grated
2 tablespoons (30 mL) butter
Dash each of Worcestershire and
   prepared mustard
4 eggs, well beaten
1/2 teaspoon (2 mL) salt
1 can (7 oz /or/ 200 g) minced clams, drained

►Add crumbs to scalded milk. Stir in cheese, butter, seasonings and eggs. Fold in minced clams. Pour into buttered casserole. Bake at 400°F (205°C) for 10 minutes. Turn oven to 325°F (160°C) and bake until firm, about 40 minutes. Serves four to six.

■ *Jane Hentze*
  PTA Cook Book, *Petersburg*

Clam Frittata

1-1/2 tablespoons (23 mL) margarine
1 tablespoon (15 mL) oil
1/4 cup (60 mL) finely chopped onion
1/2 cup (120 mL) sliced mushrooms
1/4 cup (60 mL) finely chopped green pepper
1 cup (240 mL) cooked, drained corn
1 can (7 oz /or/ 200 g) minced clams, drained
4 eggs
1/2 teaspoon (2 mL) salt
Dash of cayenne
1 tablespoon (15 mL) minced fresh parsley
2 to 3 tablespoons (30 to 45 mL) grated
   Parmesan

►Heat margarine and oil in a 12-inch (30 cm) skillet. Add onion, mushrooms and green pepper and saute until onion is transparent. Add drained corn, then clams and heat through. Beat eggs well, add salt and cayenne and pour over clam mixture. Sprinkle with parsley and cook over low heat until egg is almost set, lifting edges to allow uncooked egg to run into the pan. Sprinkle Parmesan over egg and broil close to heat until lightly browned. Four servings.

Risotto with Clams

1/4 cup (60 mL) cooking oil
1 onion, chopped fine
1 clove garlic, chopped fine
1 cup (240 mL) raw rice
2 cups (480 mL) canned tomatoes (clam broth may furnish part of this quantity)
2 tablespoons (30 mL) chopped parsley (optional)
Pinch of basil (optional)
3/4 teaspoon (3 mL) salt
2 cups (480 mL) minced clams, or equivalent in fresh clams in shell

►Saute onions and garlic lightly in oil, add rice and saute until it turns translucent. Then add remaining ingredients except clams, cover tightly and steam until rice is tender but not soft, about 15 to 20 minutes. Add clams, cover, and heat until flavors are blended.

When fresh clams are used, place well-scrubbed clams on top of rice, cover, then steam until the shells open up.
■ *Eunice and Ray Nevin, Juneau*
   The Alaskan Camp Cook

Billie's Clam Puffs

2 cups (480 mL) ground clams (fresh or frozen if possible)
1-3/4 cups (420 mL) flour
3 teaspoons (15 mL) baking powder
1/2 teaspoon (2 mL) salt
1/8 teaspoon (0.5 mL) pepper
1/2 cup (120 mL) milk
1 egg, slightly beaten
2 tablespoons (30 mL) melted butter

►Conjure up your dry ingredients in a bowl, then add the milk, slightly beaten egg, melted butter and clams — and mix gently. Drop by spoonfuls (you decide the size) into hot deep fat, 385°F (196°C), until nicely browned. If your clams have much juice, you may find it necessary to (1) increase amount of flour, or (2) reduce milk to get a manageable dough. Serve with your own homemade tartar sauce — mayonnaise, pickle relish, prepared mustard and horseradish all mixed up to your pleasure, with the mayonnaise being most prominent. This puff recipe *may* serve four if they aren't too hungry.
■ *Evelyn K. Nowell*
   "A Clam Safari"
   ALASKA® magazine, August 1972

Clam Griddle Cakes

2 tablespoons (30 mL) yellow corn meal
1 cup (240 mL) pancake mix
1 cup (240 mL) minced clams with nectar, or 1 can (8 oz /or/ 228 g) minced clams, undrained
1 egg
1 tablespoon (15 mL) vegetable oil or butter
Applesauce

►Add corn meal to pancake mix. Add clams, egg and oil and mix well. Drop by tablespoonfuls onto hot, greased griddle. Cook, turning once. Serve with butter and hot applesauce. Makes 12 average griddle cakes.
■ *Mamie Jensen, Juneau*

Clam and Cracker Fritters

►For each cup (240 mL) of clams with juice, add one beaten egg and enough freshly rolled cracker crumbs (soda or Saltine crackers) to make a mixture the consistency of pancake batter (not too many crackers, please). Set aside for at least 30 minutes before cooking. Fry in very hot fat until brown; turn and brown other side. Drain on absorbent paper. These fritters are good reheated. Just pop them in the oven for a little while.
■ *Jean McCracken*
   Recipes From The Scrolls of Saint Peter's Seward

Clamburgers

1 cup (240 mL) drained razor clams
1 egg
Seasoned croutons
1/3 cup (80 mL) chopped celery
1/3 cup (80 mL) chopped onion

►Blend in blender until well mixed. Using a large spoon, drop into hot butter and brown well on both sides. Serve plain or on hamburger buns with tartar sauce. To use as an appetizer or buffet dish, simply make smaller burgers.
■ *Betty Bennett*
   The Anchorage Times

Clam Loaf

2 cups (480 mL) minced clams and juice
1 onion, chopped fine
1/2 pound (228 g) pork sausage
1 egg, beaten
Cracker crumbs

►Combine all ingredients thoroughly, adding enough cracker crumbs to form a loaf. No seasoning is necessary as the pork sausage has some spices in it. Bake for 45 minutes at 350°F (175°C).

Serve with baked potatoes, buttered green beans and tossed green salad. Serves four.
■ *Hettie Rodgers, FV* Cheri D
Seafood Secrets, Sitka

Sourdough Clam Fritters

1 cup (240 mL) sourdough starter
2 eggs, beaten
1/2 cup (120 mL) powdered milk
1 cup (240 mL) minced clams
1 teaspoon (5 mL) minced dried onion
1/2 teaspoon (2 mL) salt

1/2 teaspoon (2 mL) baking soda
1 cup (240 mL) all-purpose flour
Vegetable oil for deep-frying

►Add eggs to measured starter in bowl; add powdered milk, clams and onion. Mix dry ingredients and stir into first mixture until all is moistened well. Pour vegetable oil to a depth of 1-1/2 inches (3.75 cm) in a skillet that is at least 3 inches (7.5 cm) deep. Heat oil to 375°F (190°C). Drop batter by the spoonful into hot fat. Fry until a deep golden brown, one to three minutes on each side. Drain on several thicknesses of paper towel.
■ *The editors, ALASKA® magazine*

MUSSELS

Before you move a muscle to eat mussels, read Danger! PSP on page 94. Mussels accumulate the toxin more rapidly than most other shellfish and consequently, until the problem is solved, are the most dangerous shelled critters you can eat.

WHEN there's a solution to the problem of PSP . . . Alaska's delectable blue mussels are a gourmet's treasure. Hunt for them at low tide and you'll find them in clusters clinging to rocks and other surfaces just below tideline. The greatest numbers are along the coast from Norton Sound to Southeastern and throughout the Aleutians. Ideal size to collect are those from 2 to 3 inches (5 to 7.5 cm) long.

Mussels are easily broken loose from their moorage. Clean them by scrubbing off surface sand with fresh sea water, discarding any open or broken shells. A heavy-duty pot scrubber works well. With a knife, scrape off barnacles and remove the "beard" or byssus, the filaments the mussel spins to attach itself to rocks and other solid surfaces.

After that, treat them as you would clams. Put them in a bucket with sea water to cover — or use fresh water with salt added (second best). Change the bath two or three times over the course of an hour or more to allow mussels to clean themselves of sand.

Shucking Mussels

To prepare mussels for cooking or serving on the half shell, remove the fleshy hinges and pry open the shells. Lift out meat or cook in the shell. To steam mussels open, follow directions given by G. S. "Bud" Mortensen in his recipe for Blue Mussel Chowder.

Storing Mussels

Live mussels may be covered with a wet cloth and refrigerated — below 40°F (5°C) — for up to 24 hours. Discard any dead ones (those that don't close up tight when you touch them).

Shucked mussels can be stored in their liquor in tightly covered containers and refrigerated up to two days. They may be frozen for longer storage. Shuck, put meat into a container with an airtight cover and strain the liquor over them. Cover and freeze. Never freeze mussels in the shell. Always thaw them under refrigeration.

Mussels

►These are gathered in spring and summer. They are boiled and served with either melted butter or seal oil.
■ *Aleut Cookbook, Saint Paul Island*

Pan-Fried Mussels

2 quarts (2 L) mussels in the shell
Cracker crumbs
2 eggs, lightly beaten
Salt and pepper to taste

►Clean the mussels by scrubbing thoroughly and taking off the beards. If any are open and fail to close while handling, discard them. Steam briefly in a covered kettle until shells open. Remove meat from shells and discard all dark parts and also discard any shells that have not opened during the steaming. Dip mussel meat in egg and roll in fine cracker crumbs. Pan-fry very lightly in butter or margarine until they are slightly browned. Mussels, like clams, need little cooking or they will be tough.

Steamed Mussels

4 dozen fresh live mussels
Cold water to cover
1-1/2 teaspoons (7 mL) salt
1 onion, sliced
1 green pepper, sliced
1/4 cup (60 mL) olive oil or salad oil
1 cup (240 mL) dry white wine
1/2 bay leaf
1 stalk celery
Dash of Tabasco
2 tablespoons (30 mL) butter

►Place mussels in a heavy kettle; add all ingredients except Tabasco and butter. Cover kettle; place on high heat and shake the pan for about five minutes; continue to heat and shake the pan for another five minutes. Remove and discard top shells; arrange mussels in soup plates. Strain the liquid through several layers of cheesecloth, being careful not to pour out the sand, if any, in the bottom of the kettle. Add Tabasco to the liquid and the butter; then pour over mussels and serve. Serves four to six.
■ Shellfish Cookbook

Blue Mussel Chowder
The aristocrat of seafood chowders

►First clean mussels according to direction. Then place shells only one layer at a time in a shallow pan, season with salt and pepper and barely cover with fresh water. Allow to simmer 20 minutes, or until the shells open up. Cook plenty of mussels, save the cooking water and the meat, discarding the shells and any mussels whose shells have not opened up. Then proceed with the chowder.

(This recipe also makes good clam chowder. If clams are used, you'll need 2 quarts [2 L] *raw*, coarse-cut clams. Add them with the lemon after the potatoes are tender and never, but never, let them cook more than 12 minutes! For the mussel broth, substitute boiling water or ham or other seafood broth.)

1 cup (240 mL) chopped bacon or ham
1/2 cup (120 mL) chopped salt pork
2 cups (480 mL) chopped onions
2 cups (480 mL) chopped celery
1 cup (240 mL) chopped carrots
2 tablespoons (30 mL) butter
2 tablespoons (30 mL) flour
1 quart (1 L) liquid reserved from
*   cooking mussels*

3 cups (720 mL) diced raw potatoes
Salt and pepper
1/2 lemon
2 quarts (2 L) blue mussels, prepared
*   as above and coarse-cut*
Pinch of dried parsley flakes

►Braise ham or bacon and salt pork in a heavy pot until half-fried. Add onions, celery and carrot, stir occasionally, and braise until vegetables are half-cooked. Pour off excess fat, then add butter, let it melt, blend in flour well and add the broth reserved from cooking the mussels. Allow to simmer one hour. Then add the diced raw potatoes and seasonings. When potatoes are tender, add the lemon and mussels. Heat thoroughly but do not cook more than a few minutes. Add parsley flakes and serve. Yield: 1 gallon (3.8 L).

When serving this chowder, put a can of allspice on the table for the individual whim.

For variation, add tomatoes or milk. If tomatoes, omit some of the mussel broth; if milk, use straight canned milk and add it at the very last.
■ *G.S. "Bud" Mortensen, Petersburg*
   The Alaskan Camp Cook

Stuffed Mussels

2 pounds (1 kg) mussels, each about
*   2 inches (5 cm) long*
1-1/2 cups (360 mL) finely crushed
*   dry bread crumbs*
1/2 cup (120 mL) grated Parmesan cheese
1 clove garlic, minced
Sprig of minced parsley
1/4 teaspoon (1 mL) oregano
1/4 teaspoon (1 mL) basil
2 tablespoons (30 mL) olive oil or salad oil

►Remove fleshy hinges joining mussel shells and pry open, discarding empty half. Arrange a layer of mussels on the half shell in a shallow baking pan. Mix all other ingredients and cover the mussels with the mixture. Do not pack. Sprinkle mussel juice over them and bake at 375°F (190°C) for 8 to 10 minutes or until golden brown. Serve at once. Serves four to six.
■ Shellfish Cookbook

Festive Mussels

3 dozen 2-inch (5 cm) mussels
1/2 cup (120 mL) dry wine
1 bay leaf
1/2 teaspoon (2 mL) thyme
1/4 teaspoon (1 mL) parsley
1 large onion, chopped
2 tablespoons (30 mL) butter
2 tablespoons (30 mL) flour

Juice from 1 lemon
Salt and pepper
2 egg yolks, beaten
2 tablespoons (30 mL) heavy cream

►Place cleaned mussels in a large kettle. Add wine, herbs and onion. Then cover and cook for 7 to 10 minutes or until shells open. Discard any unopened shells. Remove mussels from shells and place in a covered dish to keep warm. Now melt the butter in a pan; stir in flour and cook gently for about two minutes. Remove from heat. Strain the liquid from the mussels through cheesecloth and add to the flour mixture, stirring thoroughly to remove any lumps. Add lemon juice, salt and pepper to the sauce and bring it to a boil. Lower heat and gradually add the two beaten egg yolks and cream. Stir until well blended. Pour over mussels; garnish with parsley and serve at once.
■ Shellfish Cookbook

OYSTERS

Although Alaska's clean cold water can grow "what may be the finest, fattest oysters in North America," according to one expert, the same cold usually prevents them from natural reproduction and, consequently, from being bountiful enough to satisfy the casual gatherer. Commercial farming has been tried in Southeastern since 1935, but successful farms have had to import seed oysters each year. After that, it takes three years of tender watchfulness to allow an oyster to reach good eating size.

One Way To Shuck Oysters

For the lucky, the rich, or the traveling (oysters are found in British Columbia and Washington State waters in good quantity), here's the way to shuck raw oysters:
1. Wear a heavy glove on the hand that holds the oyster. Hold it cupped shell downward, flat shell up, with the hinge pointed toward your wrist.
2. Using an oyster knife or a strong blunt-ended knife with a decent cutting edge, locate the single adductor. It is about two-thirds of the distance from the hinge.
3. Keeping the knife blade pressed against the upper shell, move the knife back and forth until the muscle is severed. Twist the knife to pry off the shell.
4. Then probe underneath the oyster to sever the muscle that connects it to the lower shell. Remove meat or prepare it on the half shell.
Throughout the process, try to preserve as much oyster liquor as you can. Leave it in the shell if the oyster is to be served on the half shell or strain it to save for other uses.

Other Methods . . .

There are four more ways to part an oyster from his home:
1. Grill the shells open, following instructions in the recipe Oyster Roast.
2. Steam them open. First, scrub the shells well. Then put them in a kettle with just enough water to cover the bottom of the pan. Steam until shells open, about five minutes. Lift them out of the pan carefully to avoid spilling any of the liquor, which may be used in many recipes or saved for soup stock and sauces.
3. Heat three or four oysters at a time in a microwave oven for about one minute to make shells easier to pull apart.
4. Hold flat side down on a chopping board and "stab" off the tip end of the shells (farthest from the hinge), and a knife can be easily inserted.

Storing Oysters

Oysters in the shell may be kept alive and fresh for many weeks as long as they are stored in the refrigerator, preferably at 34°F (1°C), but at least below 40°F (5°C). Surround them with a damp towel.

Shucked oysters with liquor may be stored up to 10 days, refrigerated in tightly covered containers. The liquor should first be strained through a fine sieve or a double layer of cheesecloth to remove grit. Shucked oysters may also be frozen. Wash them in salt water — 1 tablespoon (15 mL) salt per quart (1 L) of water. Then drain, pack in airtight freezer containers and cover with strained liquor. If the freezer temperature remains constantly below

0°F (-18°C), oysters may be stored up to three months, but because most home freezers are not reliable enough, commercial freezing is advised.

Smoked Oyster Spread or Dip

1 can (2½ oz /or/ 70 g) smoked oysters
2 teaspoons (10 mL) lemon juice
3 drops Tabasco
Few grains pepper
1 large package (8 oz /or/ 228 g) cream cheese
2 tablespoons (30 mL) mayonnaise

►Drain oysters and chop finely. Sprinkle with lemon juice, Tabasco and pepper. Cream the cheese. Blend in mayonnaise and oyster mixture. Beat until fluffy. Use as a spread, or blend in 2 tablespoons (30 mL) of rich milk to make a dip. Makes about 1-1/2 (360 mL) cups.
■ B.C. Pacific Oysters

Oyster Stew

1 cup (240 mL) small oysters
2 tablespoons (30 mL) butter
1 tablespoon (15 mL) grated onion
1 tablespoon (15 mL) minced celery
1/4 teaspoon (1 mL) Worcestershire
2 cups (480 mL) hot milk
Salt and pepper
Paprika and chopped parsley for garnish

►Melt butter in saucepan, and add onion, celery and Worcestershire. Then add oysters in their own juice; heat until oyster edges begin to curl. Add hot milk and seasoning. Serve at once. Garnish with paprika or chopped parsley and additional butter if desired. Yield: two or three servings. For a richer stew, use half milk and half cream.
■Out of Alaska's Kitchens

Broiled Oysters on The Half Shell

►For each serving, prepare:
5 or 6 large oysters on the half shell, with juice
(or about four times that many small ones)
2 or 3 thin slices of bacon, cut in pieces
1/4 cup (60 mL) fine dry bread crumbs
Paprika
Tabasco (optional)

►Anchor the shells in the broiler pan so they won't spill out their juices. A bed of rock salt works, or try setting them in muffin tins or crumpled foil. Sprinkle bread crumbs evenly over each oyster. Add a drop of Tabasco, if you want, and a sprinkling of paprika. Cover each oyster with bacon and broil 3 or 4 inches (7.5 or 10 cm) from the flame until the bacon is crisp, 10 minutes or so.
■ *The editors*, ALASKA® *magazine*

Variation: No bacon? Add a couple of teaspoons (10 mL) softened butter to the bread crumbs before sprinkling the oysters. Broil till the crumbs are browned and the edges of the oysters curl.

Fresh Fried Oysters

1 pint (480 mL) large oysters
2 eggs, well beaten
1 cup (240 mL) cracker crumbs, bread
*   crumbs or corn meal*
Pinch of salt
Butter

►Drain oysters well. Dip in beaten egg, one oyster at a time, and then into crumbs.* Fry in hot butter, turning once, until both sides are a rich brown, about two minutes per side. Serve hot. Makes two or three servings.
■ *Mrs. Anna Elkins*
   PTA Cook Book, *Petersburg*

If oysters are small, dip two together and repeat the egg/crumb dipping to make the binding slightly thicker. This will keep small oysters from frying too done at the center too quickly.

Scalloped Oysters

1 pint (480 mL) oysters, drained
2 cups (480 mL) cracker crumbs
1/2 teaspoon (2 mL) salt
1/8 teaspoon (0.5 mL) pepper
1/2 cup (120 mL) butter or margarine, melted
1/4 teaspoon (1 mL) Worcestershire
1 cup (240 mL) milk

►Combine cracker crumbs, salt, pepper and butter; sprinkle a third of the mixture in a greased casserole; cover with a layer of oysters. Repeat layers. Add Worcestershire to milk and pour over contents of dish. Sprinkle remaining crumbs over top. Bake in a moderate oven at 350°F (175°C) 30 minutes or until brown. Serves four.
■ Seafood Moods

Oysters au Gratin

1 jar (10 oz /or/ 285 g) oysters
4 slices buttered bread
1 cup (240 mL) grated cheese
2 eggs, beaten
1/2 cup (120 mL) milk
1 teaspoon (5 mL) prepared mustard (optional)
1 teaspoon (5 mL) salt
1/2 teaspoon (2 mL) paprika

►Trim bread crusts and quarter each slice of bread. Quarter oysters. In buttered casserole, arrange a layer of bread and cover with a layer of oysters. Sprinkle with grated cheese. Repeat layers. Combine eggs, milk and seasonings and pour over contents of dish, then cover with grated cheese. Place casserole in pan of hot water. Bake at 350°F (175°C) for 30 minutes or until brown. Serves four or five.

■ *Mabel Grytness*
   Kitchen Magic, *Ketchikan*

Pepper Pot Oysters

1 pint (480 mL) oysters
2 teaspoons (10 mL) butter
1/2 green pepper, diced
1/4 cup (60 mL) sliced mushrooms
2 tablespoons (30 mL) ketchup
1/2 teaspoon (2 mL) prepared horseradish
Few drops Worcestershire
1/4 teaspoon (1 mL) salt

►Drop oysters in boiling water for one minute; drain. Saute oysters in butter for one minute. Add diced green pepper and mushrooms and cook one more minute. Add remaining ingredients and cook two minutes longer. Serve over toast or on a bed of hot rice. Makes two servings.

■ B.C. Pacific Oysters

Oyster Roast

36 oysters in the shell
Melted butter or margarine

►Wash oyster shells thoroughly. Place oysters on a grill about 4 inches (10 cm) from hot coals. Roast for 10 to 15 minutes or until shells begin to open. Serve in shells with melted butter. Serves six.

■ Over The Coals

Oysters Alaska

24 oysters in shells
1 tablespoon (15 mL) chopped onion
2 tablespoons (30 mL) chopped parsley
1 tablespoon (15 mL) melted butter
   or margarine
Salt
Pepper
Paprika
3/4 cup (180 mL) cooked, chopped and
   drained spinach
1-1/2 cups (360 mL) finely crushed
   dry bread crumbs
Extra butter or margarine

►Remove raw oysters from shell with a knife, according to directions, page 107. Pour off juice and retain for oyster stew or other uses. Wash and dry shells. Pat oysters dry and place each one in the deep half of a shell. Combine onion, parsley and melted butter and spread over oysters. Season with

salt, pepper and paprika. Top each serving with 1/8 cup (30 mL) chopped spinach and sprinkle with 1/4 cup (60 mL) finely crushed bread crumbs. Dot with additional butter. Brown in a very hot oven, 450°F (230°C), about 10 minutes.

■ *The Old Homesteader*

Oyster Cakes Hollandaise

2 tablespoons (30 mL) finely chopped onion
2 tablespoons (30 mL) butter
2 beaten eggs
3 cups (720 mL) soft bread crumbs
1 pint (480 mL) oysters, drained and chopped
1/2 cup (120 mL) finely chopped celery
1/4 cup (60 mL) milk
2 tablespoons (30 mL) snipped parsley
1 tablespoon (15 mL) lemon juice
1/2 teaspoon (2 mL) salt
1/2 teaspoon (2 mL) paprika
3/4 cup (180 mL) fine dry bread crumbs
2 tablespoons (30 mL) butter
1 envelope Hollandaise Sauce mix or 1-1/2 cups
   (360 mL) freshly prepared Hollandaise

►In saucepan, cook onion in 2 tablespoons (30 mL) butter until tender but not brown. Combine eggs, soft bread crumbs, oysters, celery, milk, parsley, lemon juice, salt, paprika and cooked onion. Chill two hours or until ready to serve. Shape into patties 1/2 inch (1.25 cm) thick. Coat with fine dry bread crumbs. In skillet melt remaining butter and brown cakes. Reduce heat; cook slowly for about six minutes. Prepare Hollandaise Sauce according to recipe or mix directions. Serve over cakes. Makes four servings.

■ *Geraldine S. Davies*
   Kitchen Magic, *Ketchikan*

Hangtown Fry

12 to 18 medium-sized oysters, drained
Cracker crumbs
8 eggs
2 to 4 tablespoons (30 to 60 mL) butter
1/4 cup (60 mL) milk
1 onion, grated
1 clove garlic, minced
6 ounces (170 g) ham, chopped
Tabasco
Celery salt
Crisp bacon bits

►Dip oysters into cracker crumbs, then in beaten egg and again into crumbs. Fry to a golden brown on one side in 2 tablespoons (30 mL) butter in a large frying pan. While oysters brown, beat remaining eggs with milk, and add in grated onion, garlic and chopped ham. Turn the browned oysters over, adding more butter if necessary, and pour the

egg mixture into the pan. Cook slowly until eggs are set and lightly browned. During this cooking, lift the cooked eggs with a spatula to let the uncooked part run underneath. Just before serving, put one drop Tabasco sauce on each oyster and sprinkle celery salt over all. To serve, fold in half and slip onto a hot platter. Garnish with crisp bacon bits. Four to six servings.
■ *Theda Comstock*
Alaska's Cooking, *Anchorage*

Stretched Oysters

1 pint (480 mL) oysters
2 tablespoons (30 mL) butter
4 eggs
4 tablespoons (60 mL) milk
1/4 pound (114 g) cooked ham, diced
Seasoning to taste
Buttered toast triangles
Parsley sprigs

►Chop the oysters coarsely. Melt the butter in a heavy skillet. Beat the eggs slightly with the milk and seasonings. Place oysters and ham in hot butter and pour on egg mixture immediately. Cook slowly until eggs are set, stirring to scramble. Spoon oyster mixture onto toast triangles and garnish with parsley. Serve with a green salad. This is a good way to "stretch" expensive oysters.
■ *The Old Homesteader*

Oyster Stuffing
Enough for a 4-pound (1.8 kg) fish

1 small onion, finely chopped
1 small stalk celery, finely chopped
1/4 cup (60 mL) butter
1 cup (240 mL) oysters with liquid, chopped
4 slices day-old bread, cubed
1/2 teaspoon (2 mL) salt
2 dashes pepper
2 dashes mace
2 dashes poultry seasoning
1/4 teaspoon (1 mL) lemon juice

►Saute onion and celery in butter until tender. Add oysters and saute until edges curl. Add remaining ingredients and mix lightly but thoroughly. Makes approximately 2 cups (480 mL) stuffing.
■ *B.C. Pacific Oysters*

SCALLOPS

Scallops grown in Alaskan waters are excellent, comparable to the best east coast ones. And though the fishery in Alaska (and all along the northwest coast) is an on-again, off-again thing, the 1980s seem to promise an upswing in the commercial take.

Scallops that inhabit shallower waters where they can be taken by beachcombers or divers are to be found in Southeastern and in protected, rocky bays from the Bering Sea southward. The northern scallop, a normally free-swimming type that can sometimes attach itself to a rock for a rest, is easiest to search for with a snorkel — if you can handle the water temperature. An easier prey is the rock scallop which, from early life onward, glues itself to a rock or reef and stays there, growing more and more unscalloplike in appearance. But you can't tell a scallop by its cover; the rock scallop is as tasty as its beautifully packaged cousins.

Shucking Scallops

Scallops are also easy to shuck and are best when they are shucked as soon as they are caught. Detach the muscle that holds the two valves together by inserting a knife between it and the shell on one side. When the shell opens, free the muscle from the underside. It is this tender muscle — white to orangish hue — you will most often be served in a restaurant, at the fish market or at a friend's table. But the body of the scallop is equally edible and can be prepared with the muscle or separately — in dishes where the familiar button shape of the scallop muscle is not necessary for eye-appeal.

Storing Fresh Scallops

Store freshly shucked scallops tightly covered in the refrigerator —below 40°F (5°C) — for up to two days. Or they can be frozen for up to three months at a steady temperature below 0°F (-18°C). First rinse them in a salt water solution — 1 tablespoon (15 mL) salt for each quart (1 L) of water — drain them well and package in airtight plastic containers or freezer bags.

Using Scallops

The scallop muscle is good raw, maybe with a lemon-butter sauce for dipping, or marinated, as in the Scallop Ceviche recipe following. Or simply saute scallops very quickly in butter and serve with a sprinkling of fresh chopped parsley. Change the taste by adding lemon juice and soy sauce to the butter saute.

When recipes call for cooked scallops, plunge raw ones in enough boiling salted water or Court Bouillon to cover. Return to boil, then reduce heat and simmer gently for three or four minutes. If scallops are frozen, increase the cooking time by a few minutes.

Scallop Kabobs

1 pound (456 g) scallops
2 green peppers, cut into 16 pieces
1 large orange, peeled, cut into 12 sections
8 small onions, blanched
16 cherry tomatoes
Marinade

►Wash scallops, drain and pat dry. Mix scallops in a bowl with prepared vegetables and fruit. Add marinade and chill two to three hours. Alternate scallops, vegetables and fruit on four long, well-greased skewers. Broil four minutes. Turn. Baste and broil four minutes longer. Heat marinade and serve with kabobs. Makes four servings.

Scallop Kabobs Marinade
1 can (7½ oz /or/ 200 g) tomato sauce
2/3 cup (160 mL) wine vinegar
2/3 cup (160 mL) water
2/3 cup (160 mL) sugar
1/2 teaspoon (2 mL) paprika
1/8 teaspoon (0.5 mL) allspice
1/4 cup (60 mL) cold water
2 tablespoons (30 mL) cornstarch

►In a saucepan, combine all ingredients and bring to a boil. Cook until thickened and clear, stirring constantly. Cool.
■ Shellfish-A-Plenty

Variation: Change to Hawaiian-style kabobs by using scallops, pineapple chunks, green pepper and button mushrooms. Marinate about 30 minutes in a mixture of 1/4 cup (60 mL) — each — melted fat or oil, lemon juice, chopped parsley and soy sauce, plus a dash of salt and pepper. Meanwhile cut a dozen or so bacon slices in half, fry them until nearly cooked but not crisp. Alternate on skewers and cook as above.

Scallops Ceviche

3-1/2 pounds (1.6 kg) bay scallops
Lime juice
2 large red Italian onions, finely chopped
1 can (4 oz /or/ 114 g) peeled green chilies, chopped
3 cloves garlic, finely chopped
2 green peppers, chopped
Chopped cilantro or sweet basil
2 teaspoons (10 mL) sugar
1/3 cup (80 mL) olive oil
1/4 teaspoon (1 mL) liquid hot pepper sauce
Salt, freshly ground pepper to taste

►Put scallops in a bowl and add lime juice to cover. Cover bowl with foil and refrigerate for eight hours. Drain scallops thoroughly. Mix other ingredients in a separate bowl and taste for seasoning. Add scallops, toss well and refrigerate until serving time. Garnish with additional chopped cilantro or basil and, if desired, sprinkle the top with a little finely chopped orange rind for zest and additional color. Fillet of flounder or any mild white fish may be substituted.
■ *Margaret Clark*
   Good Food A-Plenty, *Fairbanks*

French Fried Scallops

2 pounds (1 kg) scallops
2 eggs, beaten
2 tablespoons (30 mL) milk
1 teaspoon (5 mL) salt
Dash of pepper
1 cup (240 mL) dry bread crumbs

►If scallops are large, cut in half. Combine eggs, milk and seasonings. Roll scallops in crumbs; dip in egg mixture and again roll in crumbs. Fry in deep fat, 375°F (190°C) two to five minutes, or until golden brown. Drain on paper towels. Serve hot with ketchup or Tartar Sauce or lemon.
■ Shellfish Cookbook

Baked Scallops

1 pound (456 g) scallops
1 cup (240 mL) dry bread crumbs
1/4 cup (60 mL) butter or margarine
1 teaspoon (5 mL) Worcestershire
1 tablespoon (15 mL) lemon juice

►Coat scallops with bread crumbs and place on baking sheet. Melt butter and add Worcestershire and lemon juice. Pour over scallops. Bake in a hot oven, 450°F (230°C) for 12 minutes. Makes five or six servings.
■ Shellfish Cookbook

Skillet Scallops

2 pounds (1 kg) scallops
2 cups (480 mL) snow peas in pods, or a
    10-ounce (285 g) package frozen pea pods,
    thawed and drained
1/4 cup (60 mL) butter or margarine
2 tomatoes cut in eighths
2 tablespoons (30 mL) cornstarch
1 tablespoon (15 mL) soy sauce
1/2 teaspoon (2 mL) salt
1/8 teaspoon (0.5 mL) pepper
3 cups (720 mL) hot cooked rice

►Rinse scallops with cold water to remove any shell particles. Cut large scallops in half crosswise. Melt butter in a large frying pan; add scallops and cook over low heat for three to four minutes, stirring frequently. Add pea pods and tomatoes. Combine water, cornstarch, soy sauce, salt and pepper. Add to scallop mixture and cook until thick, stirring constantly. Serve in a rice ring with additional soy sauce. Makes six servings.
■ Time For Seafood

Coquilles Saint-Jacques

1 pound (456 g) scallops
1/2 cup (120 mL) water
2 green onions, sliced
1/2 cup (120 mL) dry white wine
2 celery tops
1 bay leaf
2 sprigs parsley
4 peppercorns
1/4 teaspoon (1 mL) thyme
1/2 teaspoon (2 mL) salt
3 tablespoons (45 mL) melted butter
2 additional green onions, sliced
1/4 cup (60 mL) sliced fresh mushrooms
2 tablespoons (30 mL) flour
1/2 cup (120 mL) table cream
1 egg yolk
1 teaspoon (5 mL) lemon juice
1/4 cup (60 mL) soft bread crumbs
2 tablespoons (30 mL) grated Cheddar cheese

►Wash scallops, drain and pat dry. Simmer with next nine ingredients, five minutes. Drain, reserving broth. Cut large scallops in half. Saute green onions and mushrooms in butter. Blend in flour, slowly add broth and stir until thickened. Mix cream with egg yolk and add to sauce. Fold in scallops and lemon juice. Pour into four greased scallop shells. Bake at 500°F (260°C), five to eight minutes. Sprinkle with bread crumbs and cheese. Broil one or two minutes longer. Makes four servings.
■ Shellfish-A-Plenty

Mystery Salad

2 cups (480 mL) scallops
1/2 cup (120 mL) mayonnaise
2 tablespoons (30 mL) lemon juice
1 teaspoon (5 mL) curry
1/2 cup (120 mL) sliced stuffed or ripe olives
1/2 cup (120 mL) chopped celery
3 cups (720 mL) cold cooked rice
2 tablespoons (30 mL) French dressing
1/2 cup (120 mL) chopped parsley

►Boil scallops for three minutes in water containing 1 teaspoon (5 mL) pickling spices. Drain, cool and grind scallops coarsely in a food chopper. Combine mayonnaise, lemon juice and curry and toss well with ground scallops, celery and olives. Combine rice, French dressing and parsley. Heap rice mixture on serving plate, make a well at the center and add scallops.
■ Rachel Puckett
    Recipes For Alaskan Scallops, Seward

Scallops Baked in Shells

1 pound (456 g) scallops
Salt and pepper
4 tablespoons (60 mL) heavy cream
4 teaspoons (20 mL) fine dry bread crumbs
4 teaspoons (20 mL) melted butter or other fat

►Place four or five scallops in each of four greased scallop shells or custard cups. Season with salt and pepper. Add 1 tablespoon (15 mL) cream to each shell or baking dish. Top each with 1 teaspoon (5 mL) bread crumbs and the same amount of melted butter or fat. Bake in a hot oven, 450°F (230°C) for 10 minutes. Serves four.
■ Shellfish Cookbook

Charcoal Broiled Scallops

2 pounds (1 kg) scallops
1/2 cup (120 mL) melted fat or oil
1/2 cup (120 mL) lemon juice
2 teaspoons (10 mL) salt
1/4 teaspoon (1 mL) white pepper
1/2 pound (228 g) sliced bacon
Paprika

►Combine fat, lemon juice, salt and pepper and pour over scallops. Let stand 30 minutes, stirring occasionally. Cut slices of bacon in half lengthwise, then crosswise. Drain scallops, reserving sauce for basting. Wrap each scallop with a piece of bacon and fasten with a toothpick. Place scallops in well-greased, hinged wire grills. Sprinkle with paprika. Cook about 4 inches (10 cm) from moderately hot coals for five minutes. Baste, turn and cook until bacon is crisp.

Chapter 4

Crab & Shrimp

Several species of crab and shrimp are available in Alaskan waters. The king crab — like sourdough — is almost a symbol for the state. And indeed it may take the stamina of a modern Sourdough to survive this scariest of commercial fisheries.

But many Alaskans besides those who make a living at it fish for these delicious seafoods. Both crab and shrimp (the larger ones) are caught in pots or with ring nets. When fishing is good, several ring nets with buoys on the lifting lines can keep a fisherman in a boat busy baiting and lifting them.

CRAB

The most common species of crab are the king, the Dungeness and the tanner. Procedures for cooking, cleaning and butchering are roughly similar for all, varying most for king crab because of its size (a six-foot span of kicking legs can be difficult to stuff into the cooking pot!) and the enormous quantity of meat in the legs by contrast to a relatively small amount of body meat. Taste varies, too, but the meat is interchangeable in many recipes. An exception again . . . for king crab legs on the half shell, there are no substitutes.

Preparing Live Crab

If you catch crab yourself or buy live ones at the market, there is one rigid rule about preparation: YOU must kill the crab. One that dies of unknown causes is unsafe to eat. For this reason, it's unwise to transport live crab for long distances unless you're commercially equipped to do it. And if you do, don't eat one that dies along the way just because you met it live once.

How you kill it . . . well, you've got several choices, and they do affect taste. You can kill and clean crab before you cook it. Or you can drop it live into boiling water and clean it after. The resulting difference in taste is one of those things that — like buttermilk and chicken liver — divides the world. If you don't know which you prefer, try both. They are each described on following pages.

Method I, Clean First — Cook Later, results in a whiter meat and prevents any chance of contamination by the viscera. Many subsistence fishermen prefer it because they can take care of this part of the task right at shoreline. But the argument for the second method — dropping live (or at least uncleaned) crab into the cooking pot and cleaning it afterward — is equally compelling. Its result is a delectable fat, usually called "butter," that can be scooped to your mouth by the fingerful as you butcher the cooked meat. The fat of Dungeness is a buttery yellow; of the king, white.

There are a couple more delicacies for the cook and butcher of king crab besides the butter. One is the bright red membrane located between body and shell. Its thin outer skin can be peeled off and discarded and the meat popped into the mouth. Another sizable source of meat is the king crab tail. Lift it back and break it off. Then peel away the brown membrane and carefully remove anal material. Rinse and drain the meat. Now, if you can resist eating it immediately, this fine white meat can be prepared a number of ways but is best simply deep-fried.

So experiment away. Whichever method you choose, it's a fairly swift job but a messy one. If you have lots of crab to process or plan on making a habit of it, it's worthwhile to rig up a way to handle both cleaning and cooking outdoors.

Method I: Clean First — Cook Later

1. Put on a large pot of sea water or heavily salted fresh water to boil (see Cooking Crab).
2. *Optional:* Since this is a lively beast you're working with, you may stun it first by holding it under ice water for a few minutes.
3. Scrub off barnacles and seaweed.
4. This is also *optional.* The crab is going to be dead within a few minutes anyway, but if you wish to take care of this task immediately, turn it on its back and incise it with a knife.
5. Grab the legs firmly and pull off the carapace— the "back" — using a sturdy table with a sharp square edge as a pry. Or rest the center of the shell on the corner of the table and pull down sharply to loosen the carapace enough to pull it off.
6. Break the crab in half by bending the two halves like a book.
7. Discard the back, the belly flap, mouth parts and the gray featherlike gills.
8. Wash away the viscera under cold water. Then pop the crab into a pot of boiling water.

Method II: Cook First — Clean Later
(and pass the "butter," please)

Taking crab fresh from cold waters when they are full bodied and fat . . . crackin' it, eatin' it and gettin' some on your shirt front . . . it's livin' you'll never forget. . . .

The cook-'em-live method enriches the meat with all the fine flavors of the crab's natural fat. And if you're a real gourmet, you will like the goop that lies in the center of the body cavity. It's just plain fat, and for the queasy may be a bit hard to stomach, but it does have a rich and unusual flavor. The knowing call it "butter."

Start with crab that has been freshly cooked according to directions below. Then:
1. Begin the procedure of butchering by turning the crab on its back. Lift up and back on the tail and break it off. The tail on a male Dungeness will be pointed; on a female, blunter and rounded.
2. Turn crab right side up and, holding it by the underside in one hand, break the back loose with the other, separating the two.
3. Save the back. Set it upside down to use as a "garbage can" for gills and other trimmings.
4. Peel off the gills. They should come away neatly without trouble.
5. Break off and discard the loosely hinged pieces that are the flaps for the crab's trap door mouth.
6. Once the back and gills have been pulled away, two sharp shell points are revealed. Simply break them off.
7. Then, holding a set of legs firmly in each hand, bend and break the crab in half.
8. Proceed to shake out the meat.

Cooking Crab

1. Fill a deep kettle or cauldron with sea water or salted fresh water to within 6 inches (15 cm) of the rim. You'll need this margin to prevent messy spill-overs. If you must use fresh water, salt it heavily — a standard formula is 1/4 cup (60 mL) salt per gallon (3.8 L) of water.
2. Bring the water to a full rolling boil.
3. Add whole live crab or king crab halves, but do not add more than will be covered by the water.
4. Cook whole crab or large king halves 18 to 20 minutes. Cleaned crab halves may cook a little less time, about 14 or 15 minutes. Then remove crab with tongs.
5. The crab is ready to serve right now, if you want. If you don't plan to eat it right away or shake the meat out of the shell, it is important to cool it immediately. Plunge it into ICY COLD salted water. Then drain well.

   Never put hot crab in the refrigerator to cool. It won't cool fast enough to prevent formation of harmful bacteria that will also spread its odor to other foods.

Shaking Cooked Crab Meat Out of The Shell

King crab legs are easiest to tackle using shears. See the directions for butchering king crab so that all the prime meat is retained — from claws, legs and shoulders — with the recipe, Broiled King Crab Legs on the Half Shell, page 122. For smaller species, use what the pros use — a crab block and mallet and a sturdy container to catch the meat. The meat will fall out more easily if you shake crab while it's hot.

1. To shake the body meat, grasp half a crab in one hand with your thumb folded over the underside of the legs. Then squeeze the body section with the other hand to break up the cartilage. Remove any loose pieces of cartilage. Then sharply rap the body section over a heavy bowl or sturdy container. Most of the meat will then fall out. Tear away cartilage as necessary to shake out the rest of the meat.

2. To shake the leg meat, first separate the legs from each other. Then the trick to extracting whole sections of leg meat is to pull out the cartilage filaments that extend from one section of a leg into the next. To do this, start at the tip section and work back to the largest section:

   Grasp a leg, with the top side up, in one hand. With the other hand, pull up and out on the tip section. Notice the filaments that are pulled out of the next section? Discard tip and filaments. Then lay that first meat section, top side up, over the crab block. Strike it with a quick flick of the mallet to crack the shell but not crush it. Now rap the leg on the edge of the bowl and watch the meat fall out of this first section.

3. Pinching the tip end of the second meat section (to keep the meat inside), twist and pull the now empty first section away, bringing the filaments of the second section away with it. Then rap the second section on the edge of the bowl and the meat should fall out.

   Pull the second section up and out to break loose the empty shell and pull away the third section filaments. Lay this third section on the crab block and strike it quickly with the mallet to split the shell. Shake out the meat. You may have to tear away bits of shell or strike the shell more than once to extract some of the meat.

4. To clean the claw, pull the movable half of the pincer up and out — just as you did the tip section. Then lay the claw on the crab block and strike it quickly. Remove bits of broken shell and shake out the meat.

To prepare crab shells for deviled crab and other "on the half shell" dishes, select large, perfect shells. Wash and scrub with a brush. Be sure to remove all particles of meat from the shells. Place shells in a large kettle with a cover. Add 1 teaspoon (5 mL) baking soda and boil 20 minutes. Remove from soda water; wash with clean water and dry.

■ *Lucy Whitehead*
Pioneer Cookbook, *Auxiliary No. 4, Anchorage*

Now lay the knuckle section on the block and strike it. Pull away broken shell and filaments from the knuckle and shake out the meat. Lay the end section on the block and strike it.

Tear away the empty knuckle and filaments from this section. Then shake out the meat. And there you have it! Now comes the best part . . . eating the crab.

Quantities Per Serving

At the market, you may purchase king crab legs, fresh frozen, cooked in the shell, or you may buy the frozen cooked meat separately, or of course canned. Serving amounts vary greatly from recipe to recipe. If you're serving crab in the shell with few other accompaniments, it's best to count on a whole Dungeness per person or three average size king crab legs. Otherwise:

- 1-1/2 pounds (685 g) of whole crab in the shell yields about one serving.
- An average 2-pound (1 kg) Dungeness will yield half a pound (228 g) of meat.
- 3/4 pound (340 g) of king crab legs in the shell yields one serving.
- 1 pound (456 g) crab meat will equal 2 cups (480 mL).

Storing Crab

Live crab may be stored up to 12 hours in the refrigerator — below 40°F (5°C). Cover them with a damp towel. (Remember that YOU must kill the crab. Ones that die some other way must be discarded.)

Whole cooked crab should be cooled immediately by plunging it into ice water. Then crab may be refrigerated in the shell for up to 24 hours. You may also freeze crab in the shell in airtight freezer bags at a temperature below 0°F (-18°C) for up to two months.

To save freezer space, however, you may shake at least the body meat and store only king crab legs in the shell. Crab meat should be packed into meal-sized containers with airtight seals. Cover the meat with a saltwater solution — 2 teaspoons (10 mL) salt per cup (240 mL) of water, leaving some space at the top to allow for expansion as the water freezes.

Method I adapted from *The Fisherman Returns*. Instructions for cooking crab and shaking the meat adapted from *Seaword*, a leaflet published by the Washington Sea Grant Marine Advisory Program, Seattle, and prepared by Pansy Bray. Method II is excerpted and adapted from "Doing the Dungeness," *ALASKA SPORTSMAN®*, April 1967. Serving amounts and storage information based on *Shellfish-A-Plenty*.

Snappy Crab Stuffed Eggs

1 cup (240 mL) crab meat or 1 can
  (7½ oz /or/ 215 g), drained
6 hard-cooked eggs
1 tablespoon (15 mL) chopped green onion
2 tablespoons (30 mL) lemon juice
1/4 teaspoon (1 mL) salt
Dash of Worcestershire
Dash of Tabasco
Mayonnaise

►Peel cooked, cooled eggs, cut in half lengthwise, remove yolks and set whites on a plate. Combine the yolks with remaining ingredients, adding just enough mayonnaise to moisten. Put mixture back into whites of eggs. Sprinkle with paprika. Remaining filling makes tasty sandwich spread.
■ *Tsimpshean Indian Island Cookbook*
  Metlakatla

Crab Celery Bites

1 cup (240 mL) crab meat or 1 can
  (7½ oz /or/ 215 g), drained
1 tablespoon (15 mL) finely chopped
  green onion
1/4 teaspoon (1 mL) salt
2 dashes Tabasco
3 tablespoons (45 mL) mayonnaise
2 teaspoons (10 mL) lemon juice
Celery stalks, chilled in ice water

►Shred crab meat fine. Combine with remaining ingredients except celery. Drain and dry the celery, stuff with crab mixture and chill well. Cut in 1-inch (2.5 cm) lengths to serve as an appetizer or salad.
■ *Pan Alaska*
  Courtesy, Saint Herman's Sisterhood Club
  Kodiak

Marinated King Crab Tails

A fine cook — bless her or his anonymous heart — has shared this recipe for a delicious smorgasbord dish or appetizer with a number of friends. And the friends, in turn, sent it to other friends who sent it to us attributed to several different names. The friends (or friends of friends) are widely scattered throughout the state, but the original cook, everybody agrees, was from Petersburg. One of the friends, by the way, says she always doubles the amount of marinade used here. You decide.

1 pound (456 g) cooked king crab tails, cut in
  bite-sized pieces
2 medium onions, sliced in rings
3 or 4 bay leaves, broken
Lemon slices

►Place in layers in a quart jar and cover with the following marinade:

1/4 cup (60 mL) salad oil
2 teaspoons (10 mL) sugar
1/2 teaspoon (2 mL) dry mustard
2 tablespoons (30 mL) Worcestershire
1/3 cup (80 mL) ketchup
1/3 cup (80 mL) vinegar
1 teaspoon (5 mL) salt
Dash of Tabasco
Dash of seasoned salt

►Mix the sauce with a wire whip or rotary beater and pour over crab layers. Refrigerate at least 24 hours.
■ *A friend from Petersburg*

Crab Meat Dip

1 large package (8 oz /or/ 228 g) cream cheese
3 tablespoons (45 mL) prepared horseradish
1 cup (240 mL) or 1 can (7½ oz /or/ 215 g)
  crab meat

►Soften cheese with electric mixer and blend in horseradish. Drain crab and flake into mixture with fingers. Then use fork to mix lightly. Do not beat. Chill before using.
■ *Debbie McCune*
  Gold Rush Cookbook, Valdez

Variations: Many cooks add Worcestershire, about 1 tablespoon (15 mL) for this amount of cream cheese, and minced or dried onions to this dip. Other popular additions are lemon juice, mashed avocado, heavy cream or sour cream to thin the mixture somewhat for dipping.

Crab Meat Spread

1 cup (240 mL) finely flaked crab meat
2 tablespoons (30 mL) snipped parsley
1 tablespoon (15 mL) minced onion
3 tablespoons (45 mL) mayonnaise
1/4 teaspoon (1 mL) curry powder
1 teaspoon (5 mL) lemon juice

►Combine all ingredients and mix well. Cover and refrigerate at least 10 hours. Serve with crackers, Melba toast rounds or raw vegetable slices.
■ *An Alaskan Cook Book, Kenai*

Hot Crab Dip #1

1 can (about 10 oz /or/ 285 g) tomato soup,
  undiluted
1 large package (8 oz /or/ 228 g) cream cheese
2 cups (480 mL) or 2 cans (7½ oz /or/ 215 g,
  each), crab meat

►Melt soup and cream cheese together in saucepan. Now, drain and flake the crab and add it in. Serve warm with crackers or chips for dipping.
■ *Wilma Nielson*
  False Island Camp Cook Book

Hot Crab Dip #2

1 cup (240 mL) white crab meat
8 ounces (228 g) cream cheese
3 tablespoons (45 mL) mayonnaise
2 tablespoons (30 mL) white wine
1/2 teaspoon (2 mL) sugar
1 teaspoon (5 mL) prepared mustard
Dash of salt

►Combine ingredients in a double boiler and heat until warm and blended. Serve from a chafing dish with corn chips.
■ *Mrs. Richard Barron*
  Mount Spurr School Cook Book
  Elmendorf Air Force Base

On Hand Crab Dip
Keep some of these ingredients in your larder for unexpected guests.

1 package (1.25 oz /or/ 36 g) sour cream
  sauce mix
1/2 cup (120 mL) milk
3 tablespoons (45 mL) mayonnaise
1/2 teaspoon (2 mL) parsley flakes
2 teaspoons (10 mL) minced onion
1 cup (240 mL) or 1 can (7½ oz /or/ 215 g),
  drained crab meat

►Mix sour cream sauce and milk per package directions. Add remaining ingredients. Serve soon with crackers or chips or raw vegetables for dipping.
■ *Maryanne Stone*
  Cooking Up A Storm, *Homer*

Broiled Crab Canapes

1 pound (456 g) crab meat, diced
3 tablespoons (45 mL) mayonnaise or
  salad dressing
1 tablespoon (15 mL) prepared mustard
1/4 teaspoon (1 mL) salt
Dash of black pepper
1 tablespoon (15 mL) lemon juice
12 slices white bread
1/4 cup (60 mL) grated Parmesan cheese
2 tablespoons (30 mL) dry bread crumbs

►Combine mayonnaise, seasonings, lemon juice and king crab meat. Remove crusts and toast bread. Spread crab mixture on each slice of toast. Combine cheese and crumbs; sprinkle over top of each slice. Cut each slice into six pieces. Place on a broiler pan about 3 inches (7.5 cm) from heat. Broil for two to three minutes or until brown. Makes approximately 72 canapes.
■ *Bertha Carlson*
  Sons of Norway Cook Book, *Ketchikan*

King Crab Cocktail Fritters

1 can (7½ oz /or/ 215 g) king crab
1-1/2 cups (360 mL) buttermilk biscuit mix
1/2 teaspoon (2 mL) salt
1 egg
1/3 cup (80 mL) water
1 tablespoon (15 mL) lemon juice
1 tablespoon (15 mL) melted butter
1/2 cup (120 mL) diced celery
2 tablespoons (30 mL) minced parsley
2 tablespoons (30 mL) chopped onion
Parmesan cheese

►Drain and slice crab. Combine biscuit mix, egg, salt, water, lemon juice and butter. Beat vigorously to blend. Fold in crab, celery, parsley and onion. Drop batter by teaspoonfuls into hot deep fat, 375°F (190°C). Fry until golden. Drain. Sprinkle with Parmesan cheese. Makes about five dozen.
■ Alaska King Crab

Alaska King Crab Kabobs
For a crowd

2 pounds (1 kg) king crab leg meat cut into
  bite-sized chunks
24 tiny cherry tomatoes
24 stuffed olives
6 canned marinated artichoke hearts,
  quartered
24 lemon slices

►Alternate two king crab leg chunks, one cherry tomato and one stuffed olive on 24 skewers. Alternate two king crab leg chunks, one slice artichoke and a slice of lemon on 24 skewers. Makes 48 kabobs.
■ Alaska King Crab

Crab Bites
►Make your favorite baking powder biscuit dough and roll out thinly. Cut into small squares and shape around bite-sized pieces of crab meat. Pinch the edges together to seal. Place on greased cookie sheet, cut side of dough down. Prick a couple of holes in the top of each. Bake at 350°F (175°C) for 12 to 15 minutes or until well browned. Serve hot with a dip.
■ *Helen A. White, Anchorage*
  "Far North Fare"
  ALASKA® magazine, December 1974

Seafood Puffballs

Cream Puff Paste
Chopped crab or shrimp
8 ounces (228 g) cream cheese
2 teaspoons (10 mL) lemon juice
1/3 cup (80 mL) mayonnaise
1 tablespoon (15 mL) finely
  chopped onion

►Make cream puffs very small — bite-sized. Set aside to cool. For filling, mix cheese, lemon juice, mayonnaise and onion. Make a hole in top of each puff; place shrimp or crab in hole. Put filling in with pastry tube. Place a shrimp or small piece of crab on top of each puff. Makes about four dozen.
■ *Maryanne Stone*
  Cooking Up A Storm, *Homer*

Crab-Apple Appetizer

"Esther Johnson," explains Bunny Mathisen of Petersburg, "was a lovely Swedish lady (now a long time dead) and an excellent cook who always told us, when complimented, 'It should be good! It has good stuff in it!'"

1 cup (240 mL) crab meat
1 small jar (2 oz /or/ 56 g) chopped pimentos,
  drained
1 cup (240 mL) chopped tart apple
Mayonnaise
White and dark bread

►Mix the first three ingredients with enough mayonnaise to moisten. Spread on white and dark breads and cut in fancy shapes.
■ *Esther M. Johnson*
  PTA Cook Book, *Petersburg*

King Crab and Grapefruit Cocktail

3 grapefruit
1/2 pound (228 g) king crab meat
1/3 cup (80 mL) tomato ketchup
1/2 teaspoon (2 mL) salt
1/4 cup (60 mL) grapefruit juice
1 tablespoon (15 mL) Worcestershire
3 drops Tabasco
1 tablespoon (15 mL) finely sliced celery

►Peel grapefruit with a sharp knife removing white membrane as you peel. Slide knife blade along membrane of each segment and push the fruit out into a bowl. Drain the segments, saving the juice. Arrange alternate layers of crab and grapefruit in cocktail glasses and chill. Mix together ketchup, salt, grapefruit juice, Worcestershire, Tabasco and celery. If you like a thick cocktail sauce, blend in

1/4 cup (60 mL) mayonnaise. Chill. Spoon cocktail sauce over grapefruit and crab just before serving. Garnish with lemon wedges. Makes six servings.
■ *Mary C. Larsen*
  Alaska's Cooking, *Anchorage*

Avocado-Crowned King Crab Cocktail

King crab in amount desired
Avocado Dressing, about 1/4 cup (60 mL)
  per serving
Lime wedges and salad greens (try parsley,
  watercress, green onion or chives, or finely
  shredded lettuce) for garnish

►Place king crab meat in cocktail glasses or small bowls. Top with Avocado Dressing and garnish. Serve immediately.

Avocado Dressing
2 cups (480 mL) pureed avocado
2 cups (480 mL) sour cream
2 cups (480 mL) mayonnaise
3 tablespoons (45 mL) lime juice
1-1/2 tablespoons (23 mL) horseradish
Tabasco to taste
1 tablespoon (15 mL) sugar
3/4 teaspoon (3 mL) garlic powder
1-1/2 teaspoons (7 mL) salt

►Combine all ingredients and blend until smooth. Chill in covered container until serving time. The yield is 1-1/2 quarts (1.47 L).
■ Alaska King Crab

Crabmeat-Bacon Rolls

1/4 cup (60 mL) tomato juice
1 egg, well beaten
1 cup (240 mL) crab meat
1/2 cup (120 mL) fine dry bread crumbs
1 tablespoon (15 mL) chopped parsley
1 tablespoon (15 mL) lemon juice
1/4 teaspoon (1 mL) salt
1/4 teaspoon (1 mL) Worcestershire
Dash of pepper
9 slices bacon, cut in half

►Mix tomato juice and egg. Add crab, crumbs, parsley, lemon juice and seasonings; mix thoroughly. Roll into 18 fingers, each about 2 inches (5 cm) long. Wrap each roll with half a slice of bacon; fasten with toothpick. Broil 5 inches (12.5 cm) from heat about 10 minutes, turning often to brown evenly. Makes 18 rolls, enough appetizers for six.
■ *Terry Clark*
  Loggin' Camp Cookin' Book, *Dry Pass*

Alaska King Crab Chowder

2 cans king crab or 1 pound (456 g) frozen crab
1/4 pound (114 g) diced bacon
2 medium onions, chopped
1 diced green pepper
1 clove garlic, minced
4 medium potatoes, peeled and diced
2 cups (480 mL) water
1 can (29 oz /or/ 826 g) tomatoes
1-1/2 teaspoons (7 mL) salt
1/4 teaspoon (1 mL) pepper
1/4 teaspoon (1 mL) thyme
1 whole bay leaf

►Drain canned crab or thaw and drain frozen crab, reserving liquid. Slice crab into bite-sized pieces. Cook bacon until crisp in heavy kettle or saucepan. Remove from pan and set aside. In bacon fat, saute onion, green pepper and garlic until golden. Add liquid from crab, diced potatoes, water, tomatoes and seasonings. Cover and simmer 20 minutes. Add crab and bacon and simmer about five minutes longer. Makes six servings.
■ Alaska King Crab
   Courtesy, Saint Herman's Sisterhood Club Kodiak

Crab Soup Rockefeller

3/4 pound (340 g) crab meat
1 pound (456 g) spinach
1/4 cup (60 mL) butter
1/2 cup (120 mL) chopped onion
2 tablespoons (30 mL) flour
1/4 teaspoon (1 mL) salt
2 cups (480 mL) fish stock (adding liquid from canned crab, if you use it)
2 cups (480 mL) light cream (half-and-half)
Pepper and paprika to taste

►Steam spinach until just tender and still bright green. Remove it from the pan with tongs and place it on paper toweling or in a sieve and allow moisture to evaporate. Then chop it coarsely. Flake or slice crab meat . . . a few red chunks add nice color to this soup; guard them. Melt butter in a large saucepan. Saute onion until translucent. Blend in flour and seasonings. Gradually stir in fish stock and continue stirring until the liquid reaches the boiling point. Add cream, crab and chopped spinach. Heat thoroughly and serve. Yields four to six servings.

Crab Bisque

2 hard-cooked eggs
1 tablespoon (15 mL) butter
1 tablespoon (15 mL) flour
1 grated lemon peel
1 quart (1 L) milk
1/2 to 1 pound (228 to 456 g) king crab meat
1/2 cup (120 mL) cream
3/4 cup (180 mL) sherry
1 teaspoon (5 mL) Worcestershire
Salt and pepper

►Mash the eggs to a paste with a fork and add to them the butter, flour, lemon peel and a little pepper. Bring the milk just to the boiling point and pour it gradually on to the well-mixed egg paste. Put over a low fire; add the crab meat and allow to simmer for five minutes. Add the cream and bring to boiling point again. Then add sherry, salt and Worcestershire. Heat sufficiently to serve but do not boil after sherry has been added.
■ *Peggy Goldizen*
   Fairbanks Daily News-Miner

S-t-r-e-t-c-h-e-d Crab Salad

1 loaf sliced white bread
1 cube (¼ lb /or/ 114 g) softened butter
8 or more hard-cooked eggs
1 small onion
3 or 4 ribs celery (about 2 cups /or/ 480 mL), chopped
1 pint (0.47 L) mayonnaise
2 cups (480 mL) flaked crab meat
Garnish

►The night before you wish to serve crab salad, trim crusts from bread, butter the slices and cut them in cubes. Put the cubes in a 2-quart (2 L) bowl and set aside. Mince onion and all but two of the hard-cooked eggs, chop celery and add all to the bread cubes. Toss to mix well. Refrigerate overnight.

Next day, add mayonnaise and crab to the bread cube mixture. Chill again. At serving time, slice the remaining hard-cooked eggs to use as garnish. Spoon salad into lettuce cups. Garnish with egg slices, black olives, radish flowers or other items you like with crab salad.

The bread cubes take on the flavor of the crab and give the impression you have used a lot more crab than you have. Yields 12 servings.
■ *The editors, ALASKA® magazine*

To revive flavor of crab or shrimp that has been frozen, keep it refrigerated an additional eight hours after it has thawed (or overnight).
■ *Audrey Rearden, Homer*

Molded Crab Salad #1

"A recipe I have used for about fifty years, have doubled and tripled for crowds. It is a favorite."

1 package (3 oz /or 85 g) lemon gelatin
1-1/3 cups (320 mL) boiling water
1-1/2 cups (360 mL) mayonnaise
3 tablespoons (45 mL) vinegar
1/2 teaspoon (2 mL) salt
2 cups (480 mL) crab meat
2 tablespoons (30 mL) pimento
1 cup (240 mL) diced celery
6 green onions cut fine, or chives, or
   dry onion flakes

►Dissolve gelatin in boiling water. Cool. Before it sets, whip in mayonnaise and other ingredients. Pour into flat pan, mold or individual molds. Chill. When set, unmold and serve on lettuce leaves. Garnish with more mayonnaise if desired.
■ *Mamie Jensen, Juneau*

Molded Crab Salad #2

2 tablespoons (30 mL) unflavored gelatin
1/2 cup (120 mL) cold water
1 cup (240 mL) chili sauce
1 cup (240 mL) mayonnaise
1 cup (240 mL) cream
2 cups (480 mL) flaked crab meat
3/4 cup (180 mL) minced celery
2 sweet gherkins, minced
1/2 cup (120 mL) grated cheese

►Soften gelatin in cold water. Heat chili sauce in double boiler over boiling water. Then add softened gelatin and stir until dissolved. Let cool and add remaining ingredients. Pour into individual molds and chill. Serve on lettuce with Cheese Dressing. Eight servings.

Cheese Dressing
1 package (3 oz /or/84 g) cream cheese
1/2 cup (120 mL) whipped cream
1/2 cup (120 mL) mayonnaise
1/4 cup ((60 mL) chopped nuts

►Mix and serve on Crab Salad.
■ Out of Alaska's Kitchens

Molded Crab Salad #3

1 pound (456 g) crab meat
1 tablespoon (15 mL) unflavored gelatin
1/4 cup (60 mL) cold water
1 can (8 oz /or/ 228 g) tomato sauce
1 large package (8 oz /or/ 228 g) cream cheese
1 teaspoon (5 mL) grated onion
1/2 cup (120 mL) chopped celery
1/2 cup (120 mL) diced cucumber

1/4 teaspoon (1 mL) salt
Dash of cayenne
Mayonnaise or other salad dressing for garnish

►Cut crab meat into uniform pieces. Soften gelatin in cold water for five minutes. Heat tomato sauce to boiling point; add gelatin and stir until dissolved. Chill until almost congealed. Soften cheese at room temperature; add onion, celery, cucumber, seasonings and crab meat. Fold into gelatin mixture. Place in a 1-quart (1 L) ring mold. Chill until firm. Unmold on salad greens; garnish with mayonnaise. Serves six.
■ *Saint Herman's Sisterhood Club, Kodiak*

Crab Louis

With a choice of dressings

1 pound (456 g) crab meat or 2 cans (7½ oz /or/
   215 g, each), well drained
4 cups (1 L) torn lettuce leaves
2 hard-cooked eggs
4 medium-sized tomatoes, peeled

►Flake crab meat, leaving the large pieces of leg meat unbroken for garnish. Mound the crab meat on lettuce leaves arranged on individual salad plates or in shallow bowls. Quarter the hard-cooked eggs and cut the tomatoes into wedges. Arrange around the crab meat. Decorate with leg meat. Serve with one of the following dressings. Four servings.

Louis Dressing
1/2 cup (120 mL) mayonnaise
2 tablespoons (30 mL) heavy cream
2 tablespoons (30 mL) chili sauce or ketchup
1/2 teaspoon (2 mL) Worcestershire
2 tablespoons (30 mL) minced green pepper
2 tablespoons (30 mL) minced onion
1 tablespoon (15 mL) lemon juice
Salt and pepper

►Mix all ingredients except salt and pepper. Season to taste. Makes 1 cup (240 mL).

Thousand Island Dressing
3/4 cup (180 mL) mayonnaise
1 tablespoon (30 mL) pickle relish or chopped
   sweet pickle
2 tablespoons (30 mL) chili sauce or ketchup
1 tablespoon (15 mL) chopped green pepper
1/2 teaspoon (2 mL) onion seasoning
1 teaspoon (5 mL) sugar
1 hard-cooked egg

►Mix all the ingredients except egg. Chop egg and stir into mixture. Makes 1 cup (240 mL).
■ Shellfish Cookbook

Hot crab salad is a favorite main dish or buffet dish in Alaska. Here are several versions, one that serves a crowd of 30.

Hot Crab Salad #1

2 cups (480 mL) crab meat, flakes and chunks
1 cup (240 mL) soft bread crumbs
6 hard-cooked eggs, diced
1-1/2 cups (360 mL) mayonnaise (Best Foods for best flavor)
1 cup (240 mL) milk ("top" milk is good)
1 tablespoon (15 mL) chopped parsley
1-1/2 teaspoons (7 mL) or more minced onion
1/2 teaspoon (2 mL) salt
Dash of pepper
1/4 teaspoon (1 mL) or more cayenne
Juice of 1/2 lemon
Buttered crumbs for topping (can be mixed with grated Parmesan)

►Mix all ingredients (except topping). Spoon into individual scallop shells to serve as a main course or into one giant shell for a buffet. Sprinkle buttered crumbs and Parmesan on top and bake at 350°F (175°C) until heated through, about 20 minutes.

To use a microwave oven, put about four shells at a time on a round platter, cover with waxed paper and place in microwave set at high for five minutes. Turn platter several times during cooking period to heat food evenly. Do not overcook.

This recipe is a good one to make up early in the day, baking just ahead of serving time. Makes eight main dish servings.

■ *Roberta Herbert, Anchorage*

Baked Crab Salad #2

3 hard-cooked eggs
1/4 pound mushrooms, sliced, or 1 small can pieces and stems, drained
1/2 cup (120 mL) diced celery
1 tablespoon (15 mL) butter
1 cup (240 mL) crab meat or 1 can (7½ oz /or/ 215 g), drained
1 cup (240 mL) crushed Ritz crackers
1 cup (240 mL) mayonnaise
2 teaspoons (10 mL) lemon juice
1 tablespoon (15 mL) onion juice or grated onion
Pinch dry mustard
Salt, pepper, celery salt to taste

►Finely mince the eggs. Saute mushrooms and celery in butter until celery is soft. Mix all ingredients together and spoon into shells or individual casseroles. Bake at 350°F (175°C) for 20 minutes. Serve with green vegetable or tossed salad. Makes four servings.

■ *Mamie Jensen, Juneau*

Baked Crab Salad #3

6 tablespoons (90 mL) chopped green pepper
3 tablespoons (45 mL) chopped onion
1 cup (240 mL) chopped celery
1 cup (240 mL) mayonnaise
1 teaspoon (5 mL) Worcestershire
1/2 teaspoon (2 mL) salt
2 cups (480 mL) or 1 pound (456 g) crab meat
Potato chips, crushed

►Mix all together and top with crushed potato chips. Bake in 350°F (175°C) oven for 30 minutes. Makes six to eight servings.

■ *Helen Ehrendreich*
   Tried and True Recipes, *Juneau*

Broiled Crab-Stuffed Mushrooms

Italian dressing
20 large mushrooms
1-1/2 cups (360 mL) crab meat
2 beaten eggs
1/4 cup (60 mL) Miracle Whip
1 teaspoon (5 mL) lemon juice
1/2 cup (120 mL) bread crumbs
1/4 cup (60 mL) chopped onion
Additional 1/4 cup (60 mL) bread crumbs

►Marinate mushrooms in Italian dressing overnight. Combine remaining ingredients except for the additional bread crumbs. Fill the mushroom caps with the mixture. Sprinkle with remaining bread crumbs. Bake 15 minutes at 375°F (190°C).

■ *The Old Homesteader*

Variation: Omit the first two ingredients and choose four firm ripe tomatoes, instead. Slice in half and scoop out enough pulp to make a shell. Fill with above crab mixture. Sprinkle with bread crumbs or Parmesan. Bake at 350°F (175°C) until browned. Makes eight salad servings.

Hot Crab Salad For A Crowd

1-1/2 cups (360 mL) butter
1-1/2 cups (360 mL) flour
3 large cans (13 fl oz /or/ 385 mL, each) milk
8 cups (2 L) cooked spaghetti
8 cans (7½ oz /or/ 215 g, each) flaked crab
1 bell pepper, chopped
16 hard-cooked eggs
2 cups (480 mL) sliced almonds
1 jar (4 oz /or/ 114 g) pimento
Buttered bread crumbs

►Make the sauce using the butter, flour and milk. Mix in the cooked spaghetti and crab meat. Saute the bell pepper lightly and add to the sauce. Chop the eggs and add. Add almonds and pimentos and

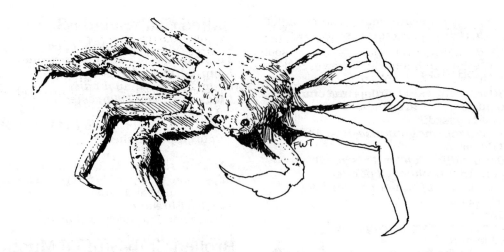

mix all together. Place in a large baking dish and cover with buttered crumbs. Bake until golden brown. Serve on lettuce leaves and garnish with carrot sticks, celery and olives. Serves 30.
■ *Ruth Sylte, FV Ruth & I*
  Seafood Secrets, *Sitka*

Marinated Dungeness Crab
A zesty appetizer or main dish
for a cold supper

3/4 cup (180 mL) oil
3/4 of a small jar of hot mustard
1/2 cup (120 mL) vinegar
2 or 3 teaspoons (10 to 15 mL) paprika
3 chopped green onions
Salt and pepper to taste

►Combine oil, hot mustard, vinegar, paprika and onions and pour over freshly picked crab meat in a bowl. The marinade should cover the crab. Allow crab to marinate 12 hours or more in the refrigerator or a cool place. Serve cold. Freshly cooked Alaskan salad shrimp are also good prepared this way.
■ *G.S. "Bud" Mortensen, Petersburg*
  The Alaskan Camp Cook *(adapted)*

Broiled King Crab Legs on The Half Shell
"In our house — the absolutely best way
to serve king crab"

►A king crab has six legs and two claws, one much heavier than the other, but very little body meat —the glob of meat at the body end of the leg is all the "body" there is and is called a "knuckle."
　Break each section of the leg apart, carefully, and only when fresh or thawed from frozen, using care to pinch between joints and hold meat from pulling out with tendons. (Warning: king crab spines are sharp, and if your hands and gentle handling are not sufficient, don protective gloves when you're butchering.)
　Next, turn bottom side up (the light colored, flattest side) and with a pair of poultry shears or similar — light ones with points are best — cut down each side, and lift off the now upper piece of shell.
　Presto, you have a nice leg section with tendon removed lying in the remaining shell ready for broiling. You'll note that after you have similarly cut each leg section there are three proper leg joints of diminishing size to each leg, plus a knuckle, and the tender little morsel in the very tip of the leg. You may succumb and eat this as you go, but it is a bright piece of red to doll up a salad or cocktail. For that you use the knuckles — the erstwhile "body" meat. By judicious use of the shears you can open the rest of claws (the big one takes a bit of bearing down to break through) for one more split "leg" section and the balance for the bowl of body meat.
　Push out the knuckle meat with a forefinger. Bigger knuckles lend themselves nicely to knocking the meat loose by rapping the knuckle against the lip of the bowl. In either case, you may have to first tear loose a restraining piece or two of shell membrane to make it easier to break the meat free.
　Now the cooking: you have leg sections sitting ready to broil in their own fat, and a bowl full of pure knuckle meat for inclusion in the salad or cocktails, or whatever dish calls for the meat of the crab at this meal or another.
　The leg sections to be broiled call for a simple sauce of melted butter (no oil thinning or additives) with a dash of garlic powder, a touch of lemon juice and a bit of dried parsley flakes. Place leg sections in appropriate broiling tray, brush well with butter

sauce, then place under broiler a few inches away. Leave only a few minutes — most fish and shellfish suffer more often from overcooking — and as soon as the meat begins to bubble and brown, pull the tray out of the oven. The crab is ready to serve simmering in its own juices, on an appropriate platter.

Serve a bowl or two of extra butter sauce at the table . . . and provide a bowl or two for empty shells disposal. Toasted garlic buns, a tossed green salad, a bit of macaroni and cheese, plus a good Chablis or Pinot Chardonnay well chilled makes a meal — if you have enough crab.

In ordering, ask for frozen leg sections (not canned), and let thaw at room temperature for four to five hours. If time is not available, an hour or two in cold water will do the job, but the meat seems better thawing at a slower pace, and use just after it has thawed. Do not refreeze, and hopefully you will get crab that has had continuous frozen storage of not more than three months. For Alaskans near fishing centers, the fresh product is of course that much better — but any good king crab, fresh or frozen, broiled as we have described is true ambrosia.

■ *Bob Henning, Angoon*
  Alaska Fishing Guide (*1979*)

King Crab Legs in Wine Butter

3 king crab legs per person
1 tablespoon (15 mL) snipped parsley

Marinade (enough for 6 to 8 servings):
1/4 pound (114 g) butter, melted
3 tablespoons (45 mL) sherry
3/4 teaspoon (3 mL) salt
1/2 teaspoon (2 mL) fresh cracked pepper
1/4 teaspoon (1 mL) paprika
3 drops Tabasco
Good pinch thyme
Dash cayenne pepper

►Prepare marinade one day in advance so that flavors have a chance to develop.

Next day, heat marinade in chafing dish or a flat pan. Carefully add crab legs and just heat through, basting several times. Sprinkle with chopped parsley and serve as an appetizer or as a main course with rice, salad and other accompaniments.
■ *Elva Bahrt Swenson, Seattle*

Cordova Crab
Marinated in the shell

4 Dungeness crabs
2 cups (480 mL) salad oil
1 cup (240 mL) vinegar
2 tablespoons (30 mL) lemon juice
1 tablespoon (15 mL) soy sauce

1 tablespoon (15 mL) chopped parsley
4 cloves garlic, finely crushed
1 large onion, sliced thin

►Clean the crab. Separate the body and leg sections. Crack legs to allow marinade to flavor the meat. Place crab in a deep bowl.

Mix other ingredients and pour the marinade over the crabs. Use a basting tube to pour the sauce over the crabs for several minutes.

Cover the bowl and refrigerate. Every half hour for four hours, repeat the basting process. Serve cold, as an appetizer or an entree. Makes six to eight servings.
■ *Pansy Bray*, Seaword

Grilled King Crab Legs
For an outdoor barbecue

3 packages (12 oz /or/ 340 g, each) precooked
  frozen king crab legs
1/2 cup (120 mL) butter or margarine, melted
2 tablespoons (30 mL) lemon or lime juice
1/2 teaspoon (2 mL) paprika
Melted butter for serving

►Thaw frozen crab legs. Combine butter, lemon juice and paprika. Baste crab meat with this sauce. Place crab legs on a grill, flesh side down, about 4 inches (10 cm) from moderately hot coals. Heat for five minutes. Turn and baste with sauce. Heat five to seven minutes longer. Serve with melted butter.
■ Over The Coals

Alaska King Crab Legs
Senior Brown

5 ounces (140 g) Alaska king crab legs
1/4 cup (60 mL) olive oil
2 tablespoons (30 mL) onions, finely chopped
1 teaspoon (5 mL) finely chopped garlic
3 ounces (85 g) flour
3 ounces (85 g) dry sherry
1 cup (240 mL) water
Salt to taste
Pepper to taste
1/4 cup (60 mL) parsley,
  finely minced

►Saute onions and garlic in olive oil. Add crab legs and cook five minutes. Remove crab legs and hold. Add flour to pan juices. Cook and stir until thick. Add wine and water. Season with salt and pepper and cook 10 minutes. Adjust consistency and add parsley. Arrange king crab legs in serving casserole; add green sauce and serve very hot. One a la carte serving.
■ Alaska King Crab

Broiled King Crab Legs and Filet Mignon
A "million dollar" lunch!

3 king crab legs, split in shell
1 filet mignon
Melted butter as needed
Lemon wedge
Watercress or parsley

►Place Alaska king crab legs under broiler. Baste with melted butter. Cook five minutes or until heated through. Broil steak as desired. Serve on an oblong platter, place crab legs on one side, steak on the opposite side. Garnish with crisp greens and lemon wedge.
■ Alaska King Crab

Steamed Dungeness Crab Feed

Live crab (at least one per person)
1/2 cup (120 mL) white wine or beer
1/2 cup (120 mL) lemon juice or vinegar
2 tablespoons (30 mL) soy sauce
2 tablespoons (30 mL) salt
3 or more drops Tabasco
Choice of dips: melted butter,
*   Soy-Mayonnaise Dip*
Green salad
Garlic bread

►Stun crab by putting them in a deep tub (sink is fine) and covering with *hot* water (not boiling; just quite hot) briefly. Then scrub crab well and immediately transfer them to a large covered cooking pot to which you've added just enough hot water to cover the bottom. (If you have a rack that fits the kettle, use it to keep the crab above the liquid.) Add wine or beer, lemon juice or vinegar, soy sauce, salt and Tabasco. Cover the pot and steam about 30 minutes. The steaming crab should spew enough juice to keep the pot from running dry. In fact, check now and again to make sure they are still steaming above the liquid rather than stewing in it. If several batches of crab are being prepared, change the steaming liquid from time to time.

Serve hot or immediately plunge crab into icy water, but don't soak them. Drain well and refrigerate until serving time.

At serving time, supply diners with individual bowls of dipping sauce: melted butter, seasoned as you like, and the sauce described below by Dick Brennan. Useful tableware: enough mallets or hammers or other cracking tools to make sharing easy, small forks, knives, "bone" dishes, napkins, and advice, as needed, about how to pry off carapace, remove belly flap, intestines and gills . . . and dig in.

Soy-Mayonnaise Dip
For freshly steamed or boiled crab

►Stir as much soy sauce into mayonnaise as it will take and still retain a good dipping consistency. Add Tabasco, or better, just set the bottle on the table. Serve the Soy-Mayonnaise Dip in individual sauce dishes to accompany a mound of freshly prepared crabs. The sauce is a natural dip for crab. Good for nothing else, not even as a cocktail sauce.
■ *Dick Brennan*
    PTA Cook Book, *Petersburg*

King Crab Paella

1 cup (240 mL) king crab meat
1 frying chicken, cut up
1/2 teaspoon (2 mL) salt
3 tablespoons (45 mL) vegetable oil
1 large onion, chopped
1 clove garlic, minced
1-1/2 cups (360 mL) uncooked rice
1 tomato, chopped
4 cups (1 L) seasoned chicken broth
1/4 teaspoon (1 mL) turmeric
1 package (10 oz /or/ 285 g) frozen peas
2 tablespoons (30 mL) chopped pimento

►Cut crab meat in bite-sized pieces. Cut each chicken piece, bones and all, into two or three pieces. Sprinkle with salt. Saute chicken until golden in oil, using heavy skillet. Remove chicken. Add onions and garlic to skillet. Saute until onion is translucent. Add rice. Cook, stirring, until golden. Add chicken, tomato, chicken broth and turmeric. Bring to boil. Cook rapidly three or four minutes. Reduce heat; continue cooking for 15 minutes or until most of the liquid is absorbed. Add crab, peas and pimentos. Cook five minutes longer. Makes six servings.
■ Alaska King Crab

Sweet and Sour King Crab

1 pound (456 g) king crab meat or 2 packages
*   (6 oz /or/ 170 g, each) frozen king crab meat,*
*   thawed*
1 cup (240 mL) sliced onion
1 small green pepper cut in 1-inch
*   (2.5 cm) squares*
1/4 pound (114 g) mushrooms, sliced (optional)
1/4 cup (60 g) butter or margarine
1 can (20 oz /or/ 570 g) pineapple chunks in
*   heavy syrup*
1/2 cup (120 mL) sugar
2 tablespoons (30 mL) cornstarch
1/2 teaspoon (2 mL) dry mustard
1/4 teaspoon (1 mL) salt
1/2 cup (120 mL) white vinegar

1 tablespoon (15 mL) soy sauce
2/3 cup (160 mL) cherry tomato halves or thin
   tomato wedges
6 servings hot, cooked rice or
   chow mein noodles
Toasted slivered almonds (optional)

►Saute onion, green pepper and mushrooms in butter or margarine until onion is tender, not browned. Drain pineapple; reserve syrup. Combine sugar, cornstarch, mustard and salt. Stir in pineapple syrup, vinegar and soy sauce; mix well; add to onion/green pepper mixture. Cook, stirring constantly, until thick and clear. Fold in pineapple chunks, crab meat and tomatoes. Heat; serve over rice or noodles. Garnish with toasted almonds.
■ Seafood Moods

Hermit Crab/King Crab
Big package or little, it's fresh crab!

►At Point Hope small hermit crabs are caught and eaten, usually raw-frozen. They are left in the shell, set out on the ice to freeze, then the meat is cut out and squeezed to get rid of the salt. Only a few of the people cook crab, a method of preparation learned from Caucasians.

At Diomede, Nome and other Bering Sea points, the king crab is hooked through the ice. It is a staple in the diet in late winter and early spring.
■ The Alaska Dietary Survey

Variation: Hermit crabs are also good sauteed in butter or deep-fried in fat preheated to 390°F (200°C).

Deviled Crab McKinley

2 pounds (1 kg) Alaska king or
   Dungeness crab meat
1/2 cup (120 mL) butter
1 cup (240 mL) minced onions
1 cup (240 mL) minced green peppers
4 drops Tabasco (or more if you like)
Salt to taste
White pepper to taste
1 tablespoon (15 mL) dry mustard
2 cups (480 mL) Thick Cream Sauce
2 ounces (56 g) white wine
1/2 cup (120 mL) bread crumbs
1/2 cup (120 mL) Parmesan cheese, grated
8 crab shells

►Saute onions and green pepper in butter until tender; add seasonings. Then add Thick Cream Sauce and crab meat to mixture, blend, add wine and adjust seasonings to taste. Fill crab shells with

mixture. Sprinkle with bread crumbs and Parmesan. Bake at 400°F (205°C) for 10 to 12 minutes or until golden brown on top. Yields eight servings.
■ The Northern Traveler
   *Reprinted in ALASKA® magazine
   January 1977*

Variations: Omit green pepper and wine and add 2 teaspoons (10 mL) lemon juice, instead. Minced hard-cooked eggs (two for the above amount of crab) are a favorite ingredient in deviled crab. Omit Parmesan and dot bread crumbs with butter instead.

King Crab Newburg

1/3 cup (80 mL) butter
3 tablespoons (45 mL) flour
1/2 teaspoon (2 mL) salt
1/2 teaspoon (2 mL) paprika
Dash of cayenne
1-1/2 cups (360 mL) coffee cream
3 egg yolks, beaten
1 pound (456 g) king crab meat
2 tablespoons (30 mL) sherry
Toast points or hot cooked rice for six

►Melt butter, blend in flour and cook, stirring, until foamy. Add seasonings. Add cream gradually and stir until thick and smooth. Stir a spoonful or two of this hot sauce into the beaten egg yolks and then add the mixture back into the sauce, stirring constantly until it thickens again. Add crab meat, heat, and blend in sherry. Serve at once on toast points or over rice. Makes six servings.
■ Icy Cape
   Saint Herman's Sisterhood Club, Kodiak

Crab Cutlets
"This recipe is 50 years old . . . still delicious!"

2 tablespoons (30 mL) margarine
1/2 cup (120 mL) milk
2 tablespoons (30 mL) flour
1 tablespoon (15 mL) cream (canned cream or
   undiluted canned milk may be used)
1 teaspoon (5 mL) lemon juice
1/2 pound (228 g) crab meat
   (preferably Dungeness)
Salt and pepper to taste
1 egg, beaten
3/4 cup (180 mL) fine dry bread crumbs
Shortening for deep-fat frying

►Make a sauce of margarine, flour and milk. Add cream and lemon juice, seasoning and crab meat. Mix and spread on plate to cool. Shape into flat

cakes, dip in beaten egg and roll in crumbs. Fry in hot deep fat until golden brown. Serve with sliced lemon. Makes two or three servings.
■ *Mamie Jensen, Juneau*

Million Dollar Sandwich
Simple and delicious

1 pound (456 g) crab meat
2 tablespoons (30 mL) finely minced onion
2 tomatoes, peeled, seeded and
    coarsely chopped
Mayonnaise
12 slices white or whole-wheat bread
Butter

►Mix crab, onion and tomatoes and place mixture between paired slices of bread to make six sandwiches. Saute in butter until golden on each side.
■ *Bunny Mathisen, Petersburg*

Crab Fried Rice

1 cup (240 mL) king crab meat
    (chunks are best)
1/2 cup (120 mL) chopped onion
1/4 cup (60 mL) butter or oil
2 cups (480 mL) cooked rice
1 can (4 oz /or/ 114 g) mushrooms
1 teaspoon (5 mL) soy sauce
2 eggs, well beaten
1 teaspoon (5 mL) butter
2 teaspoons (10 mL) chopped green onion

►Saute onion in butter or oil until golden. Add rice and cook over low heat, stirring constantly until golden brown. Add mushrooms; saute briefly. Stir in soy sauce and crab meat. Heat through. While crab is heating, cook eggs in butter in small skillet until set. Cut into strips. Pour crab over rice and garnish with egg strips and chopped green onions.
■ *Maryanne Stone*
    Cooking Up A Storm, *Homer*

Alaska Crab Imperial

1 to 2 pounds (0.45 to 1 kg) crab meat
2 eggs
1 hard-cooked egg, mashed
1/4 cup (60 mL) mayonnaise
3 tablespoons (45 mL) minced green pepper,
    parboiled 5 minutes
3 slices soft stale white bread, crumbled fine, or
    1 cup (240 mL) cracker crumbs
2 tablespoons (30 mL) melted butter
3 tablespoons (45 mL) minced pimento
Chopped tomatoes (optional)
2 tablespoons (30 mL) minced parsley
1/4 cup (60 mL) Worcestershire

Salt
Pepper
2 tablespoons (30 mL) white wine (optional)
1/2 cup (120 mL) additional mayonnaise,
    thinned with a little milk or cream
Paprika

►Handle crab meat carefully; remove any bits of shell and save about a fourth of it, the larger lumps, to decorate the top of the dish. Mix the rest with the raw and cooked eggs, 1/4 cup (60 mL) mayonnaise and all other ingredients except thinned mayonnaise and paprika. Blend well. Pile high in greased crab shells or small ovenproof bowls. Flatten tops and add large lumps of crab. Pour thinned mayonnaise over each mound, letting it run down the sides. Sprinkle with paprika and bake at 350°F (175°C) about 15 minutes or until browned. Makes six or more servings.
■ *Larry Fifer*
    Cooking Up A Storm, *Homer*

Hot Crab Sandwich

4 English muffins or sourdough
    English muffins
2 cups (1 lb /or/ 456 g) flaked crab meat
1-1/2 cups (360 mL) shredded Swiss cheese
1/2 cup (120 mL) sour cream or mayonnaise
3 teaspoons (15 mL) lemon juice
1/2 teaspoon (2 mL) Worcestershire
Dash pepper

►Split muffins and toast them lightly. combine remaining ingredients, reserving 1/2 cup (120 mL) of the shredded cheese. Spread mixture on muffin halves. Top with remaining cheese. Bake at 400°F (205°C) about 10 minutes. Makes four servings for lunch, or divide the muffin halves in wedges and serve as a snack or appetizer with cocktails.
■ *Audrey Rearden, Homer*

Variations: Audrey sometimes uses half crab and half diced shrimp, or mozzarella (a milder cheese) instead of Swiss. Miracle Whip in place of mayonnaise will make a "zippier tasting sandwich," she says. Other cooks vary the sandwich filling by adding a spoonful of chili sauce or a few sliced green olives with pimento.

Crab Omelet
For five hearty appetites

4 cups (1 L) shelled crab meat — minimum
1/4 to 1/2 pound (114 to 228 g) butter
10 eggs (2 per person)
6 green onions
6 radishes
2 tomatoes

1 small can chopped mushrooms
1/2 green pepper
8 slices cheese

►In two cake pans placed on top of stove, melt equal amounts of butter and saute equal amounts of crab meat. As soon as the crab meat is thoroughly heated, place equal amounts of chopped green onions, thinly sliced lengths of green pepper, thinly sliced radishes and chopped mushrooms into each pan with the crab. Stir occasionally but gently until the onions show signs of cooking (two or three minutes). Now pour into each pan equal amounts of well-beaten eggs which have been salted and peppered to taste. Stir each pan briefly to equally distribute the goodies. Lay four slices of cheese (I like sharp Cheddar) on top of the liquid in each pan and on top of each place a thick slice of tomato. Pop this into a moderate oven (350°F or 175°C) for about 30 minutes — depending on whether you like a dry or moist omelet. In my opinion an omelet should be just firm enough to keep from running — same as a good steak — done when it can't move. Serve with hot French garlic bread toast.
■ Jacques M. Norvell
"Let's Go Crab Digging"
ALASKA® magazine, March 1974

Variations: We found many good recipes for crab omelet, but Jacques Norvell's generous one is a hard act to follow. Let us simply say that you *can* get away with less than his "minimum" of crab by filling in with other ingredients such as White Sauce and cheese. A mixture often called "Crab Foo-Yoong" adds bean sprouts and green onion and a teaspoon (5 mL) of soy sauce.

But we'd sure like to have supper at Jacques's house, wouldn't you?

Crab Meat Spaghetti Casserole

8 ounces (228 g) spaghetti
1/4 cup (60 mL) finely minced onion
3 tablespoons (45 mL) butter
1 can (10 oz /or/ 285 g) cream of mushroom
    soup, undiluted
2 cups (480 mL) grated sharp cheese
2 hard-cooked eggs, diced
1 tablespoon (15 mL) chopped pimento
1/2 teaspoon (2 mL) salt
Dash of pepper
1-1/2 cups (360 mL) flaked crab meat
Paprika, dried parsley flakes, grated Parmesan

►Cook spaghetti in boiling, salted water until barely tender. Drain and rinse with cold water. Saute onion in butter until translucent, stir in soup and remaining ingredients and heat thoroughly.

Add drained spaghetti, mix and heat again. Then turn into a buttered 2-quart (2 L) casserole. Sprinkle with paprika and dried parsley and top with Parmesan. Broil a few inches from heat until golden.
■ Dena McKay
Sons of Norway Cook Book, Ketchikan

Lil' Crab Cakes

1/2 cup (120 mL) butter, melted
6 slices bread, trimmed of crusts
3 egg yolks
3/4 teaspoon (3 mL) salt
1/8 teaspoon (0.5 mL) Tabasco
2 teaspoons (10 mL) Worcestershire
1-1/2 pounds (0.70 kg) crab meat
3 egg whites, stiffly beaten
4 tablespoons (60 mL) butter

►Pour the melted butter over the bread and let soak 15 minutes. Then mash the bread and add egg yolks, salt, Tabasco and Worcestershire. Blend in crab meat and fold in egg whites. Shape into about 25 small cakes. Melt the remaining butter in a skillet and brown the cakes on both sides; add more butter if needed. Serve hot.
■ Seattle Seafoodfest Recipes

Crab Meat Rolls

Thin pancakes*:
2/3 cup (160 mL) sifted flour
1/2 teaspoon (2 mL) salt
1 egg
2/3 cup (160 mL) milk
1 tablespoon (15 mL) melted butter
    or margarine

►Combine above and beat until smooth. Using 3 tablespoons (45 mL) batter for each pancake, bake six thin cakes until golden brown. Stack carefully.

Filling:
1 egg
1/2 cup (120 mL) ketchup
1/2 cup (120 mL) soft bread crumbs
2 tablespoons (30 mL) minced onion
1 tablespoon (15 mL) minced parsley
2 teaspoons (10 mL) vinegar
1/8 teaspoon (0.5 mL) hot pepper sauce
1-1/2 cups (360 mL) flaked crab meat
Parmesan cheese
Sour cream

►Combine the egg and ketchup. Add remaining ingredients. Carefully peel off top pancake. Set it on a plate and spoon 1/4 cup (60 mL) crab mixture

over it. Roll up jelly roll fashion and secure with a toothpick or place seam side down on a greased baking pan. Repeat, then sprinkle the rolls with Parmesan cheese and bake at 400°F (205°C) for 10 minutes. Serve hot with a topping of sour cream. Makes six servings.
■ *Nancy Sadusky*
  Recipes From The Scrolls of Saint Peter's
  Seward

This batter is best if you can let it rest a bit — three hours or more —covered and refrigerated. Or make it the night before you plan to bake the cakes. Cakes can also be saved for a while in the refrigerator, but it is easier to peel them apart if you stack them between sheets of waxed paper.

Alaska Crab Fisherman Style

1/4 cup (60 mL) cooking oil
1/2 cup (120 mL) chopped onions
1 teaspoon (5 mL) each — chopped garlic,
  parsley and celery
1 cup (240 mL) drained tomatoes
1 cup (240 mL) tomato sauce
1-1/2 cups (360 mL) water
1 teaspoon (5 mL) pepper
2 teaspoons (10 mL) salt
1/2 teaspoon (2 mL) paprika
1 pound (456 g) crab meat
1 pound (456 g) spaghetti
1/2 pound (228 g) grated cheese

►Cook onions, celery, garlic and parsley in the oil over low heat until they are clear; add tomatoes, tomato sauce, water, pepper, salt and paprika. Simmer this mixture slowly for one hour, then add the crab meat and simmer for 10 minutes. Cook the spaghetti in water until it is tender. Drain and add to the tomato-crab sauce. Pour on a heated platter and sprinkle with grated cheese.
■ Tsimpshean Indian Island Cookbook
  Metlakatla

Fried Crab Legs

2 tablespoons (30 mL) each — flour and
  corn meal
Salt and pepper
1 egg, beaten
1 tablespoon (15 mL) or more water
Pinch of baking powder
Chunks of leg meat

►Shake batter ingredients well in a jar with a tight lid. Dip seafood so that each piece is well coated and fry over medium heat in about 1 inch (2.5 cm) of shortening until golden brown.
■ *Mamie Jensen, Juneau*
  The Alaskan Camp Cook

Crab Sauce For Spaghetti

►In quite a bit of salad oil, saute a button of garlic and a bay leaf. Add crab legs (if crab legs are fresh, cook in oil until pink), lots of black pepper, one can tomatoes, one can tomato paste, one can tomato sauce, a little water. Simmer on low heat for about one hour. Serve over spaghetti.
■ Tsimpshean Indian Island Cookbook
  Metlakatla

Crab Stew

2 to 3 live crabs
5 slices bacon
3 onions, chopped
2 tablespoons (30 mL) butter
Salt and pepper
1 green pepper, chopped
3 tablespoons (45 mL) cornstarch
1 tablespoon (15 mL) soy sauce

►Boil crab for 20 minutes (see page 114). Use claw and body meat in stew. Fry bacon in large cooker. Add onions and green pepper. Fry until onions are clear. Add cornstarch and enough water to thicken into a gravy. Add butter. Place crab in gravy and cook for a few minutes longer. Add salt and pepper to taste. Add soy sauce. Approximately five servings.
■ Tsimpshean Indian Island Cookbook
  Metlakatla

Crab Muffins

3/4 pound (340 g) crab meat
1/4 cup (60 mL) mayonnaise
1 teaspoon (5 mL) chopped onion
1 package (3 oz /or/ 85 g) cream cheese
1 egg
1/4 teaspoon (1 mL) prepared mustard
Salt to taste
3 English muffins
2 tablespoons (30 mL) butter

►Mix crab, mayonnaise, onion, cream cheese, egg, mustard and salt until creamy. Split muffins and toast. Butter toasted muffins and put crab mixture on the muffins. Broil 5 to 6 inches (12.5 to 15 cm) from heat for two to three minutes. Serves three . . . or six light eaters.
■ *Ann Meeks*, An Alaskan Cook Book, *Kenai*

Variation: Omit egg and cream cheese from crab mixture and add any items you like in crab salad, such as pimento and black olive slices. Toast muffin halves or six slices of bread on one side. Spread with crab mixture (if bread is used, spread the untoasted side). Top with a hot cream sauce such as White Sauce or Hollandaise.

Crab Stuffing
For baked whole fish or rolled fish fillets

1 pound (456 g) fresh crab meat or 3 cans,
   6 to 7 ounces (170 to 200 g) each
1/2 cup (120 mL) chopped onion
1/3 cup (80 mL) chopped celery
1/3 cup (80 mL) chopped green pepper
2 cloves garlic, finely chopped
1/3 cup (80 mL) melted fat or oil
2 cups (480 mL) soft bread cubes
3 eggs, beaten
1 tablespoon (15 mL) chopped parsley
2 teaspoons (10 mL) salt
1/2 teaspoon (2 mL) pepper

►Pick over crab meat to remove any remaining shell or cartilage. Saute onion, celery, green pepper and garlic in fat until tender. Combine bread cubes, eggs, parsley, salt, pepper, sauteed vegetables and crab meat. Mix thoroughly. Enough for about 3 pounds (1.4 kg) fish.
■ Over The Coals

To gather Dungeness crab, wait for a minus tide and go out to the grassy beds uncovered by the tide. Be sure you have on hip boots and are armed with a rake. Walk through the grassy beds and the crab will grab your rake and hang on. Pull him up and stuff him in your bag.
■ Tsimpshean Indian Island Cookbook
   Metlakatla

SHRIMP

Five species of shrimp make up the enormous commercial catch from Alaskan waters. Three are sizable enough to catch using pots. The spot shrimp — often called a prawn — is the largest of all, measures up to 12 inches (30 cm) in body length and often weighs as much as a quarter-pound (114 g). The coonstripe and sidestripe, both somewhat smaller, nevertheless may have a body size of about 5 inches (12.5 cm) . . . nothing to spurn from your dinner plate.

Spot shrimp are most often caught in rocky areas where there are underwater ledges or cliffs, often at depths to 40 or 50 fathoms. Coonstripe, probably the most common of the larger prawn-type shrimp in Alaska, like mud bottoms and may be caught in depths from 10 to 30 or more fathoms. Sidestripe shrimp like mud, too, but may also be found where the floor is smooth and sandy.

Two other commercially important species that can be bought in the market are the pink — the so-called "cocktail-size" shrimp — and the humpy.

Heading & Cooking

Shrimp are easy to prepare. Simply snap their heads off and leave the tails, or bodies, to be cooked. Shrimp can be shucked before or after cooking. Alaskan shrimp do not have the iodine taste common to shrimp caught in some southern waters and, for this reason, it is not necessary to devein Alaskan shrimp, but they are tastier and easier to shell if cooked as soon as possible after being caught.

To cook shrimp in the shell, drop the headed shrimp into boiling sea water or heavily salted fresh water. They will immediately sink. When they float to the surface they are cooked and ready to be scooped out and cooled.

Some cooks add seasonings to the boiling water or flavor it with beer.

Storing Shrimp

If fresh-cooked shrimp are to be preserved for later use, freeze them in the shell to retain the best flavor and protect the texture of the meat. When you're ready to use them, thaw them in the refrigerator and allow them to remain refrigerated five or six hours or overnight. This last step is not essential, but it seems to revive the original flavor. If canned shrimp is to be used without further cooking —in salad, for example — the flavor and texture are improved if the shrimp is drained of can juices and placed in ice water for about five minutes. Drain again, thoroughly.

Quantities Per Serving

Uncooked shrimp in the shell are called "green" shrimp. One pound (456 g) of the small variety in the shell will yield about 1/2 pound (228 g) cooked, shucked shrimp — two or three servings. Large shrimp are often served whole and the per-serving amount is judged by how they're going to look on the plate . . . that is, by number rather than by weight. Also, when large shrimp are served whole, the tail is usually left intact as a handle.

Marinated Shrimp

1 pound (456 g) fresh-cooked shucked shrimp
1/4 cup (60 mL) finely minced green onion
1/2 cup (120 mL) finely minced celery
1/4 cup (60 mL) salad oil
1 to 2 tablespoons (15 to 30 mL) lemon juice
2 tablespoons (30 mL) horseradish
1 tablespoon (15 mL) Dijon-style mustard
Tabasco
Paprika
Salt

►Lightly mix shrimp, celery and green onion. Make a sauce of oil, lemon juice, horseradish and mustard and pour over shrimp, lifting mixture gently with a fork to coat shrimp evenly. Add Tabasco, paprika and salt to taste. Marinate, refrigerated, several hours or overnight. Drain shrimp and serve on toothpicks as an appetizer or in lettuce cups for individual salads topped with a garnish of mayonnaise. Serves four to six. You may stretch the salad by adding a cup (240 mL) of cooked, cooled rice to the marinade and increasing marinade ingredients by about half.
■ *The editors, ALASKA® magazine*

Variation: Bobbi Krist, FV *Dorinda*, suggests a simpler marinade [*Seafood Secrets*, Sitka]. She puts a crushed clove of garlic into 1/4 cup (60 mL) salad oil and lets it steep for 30 minutes or more. Then she removes the garlic and tosses a pound (456 g) of shrimp in the oil until it's well coated. Then the shrimp is chilled for at least two hours before serving. A clove of garlic may be added to the marinade above, too, but the flavor will be too strong if it is in the mixture for more than a couple of hours.

Pickled Shrimp

10 pounds (4.5 kg) shucked raw shrimp
8 large onions
3 lemons, halved
1 cup (240 mL) olive oil
3/4 cup (180 mL) wine vinegar
3 dashes Tabasco
3 bottles capers

►Wash shrimp, add two halved onions and lemons and cover with boiling salted water. Simmer for five minutes; strain, remove onions and lemons. Slice six onions thinly. Place layers of shrimp and onion slices alternately in a gallon (3.8 L) jar. Combine remaining ingredients; pour over mixture. Let stand refrigerated for at least 24 hours; shake jar every so often. Will keep for two to three weeks in the refrigerator.
■ *Dolores Wakefield, FV* Success
   Seafood Secrets, *Sitka*

Shrimp Canape Spread #1

2 cups (480 mL) cooked shrimp
1/4 cup (60 mL) ketchup
1/4 cup (60 mL) mayonnaise
2 tablespoons (30 mL) lemon juice
1/2 teaspoon (2 mL) salt
1/8 teaspoon (0.5 mL) dry mustard

►Grind shrimp fine. Combine remaining ingredients with shrimp; mix well. Use as a canape spread or, with the addition of more mayonnaise, for a dip.
■ Seafood Recipes For Alaskans

Shrimp Canape Spread #2

1/2 pound (228 g) cooked, shucked shrimp or
   2 cans (4½ oz /or/ 126 g, each), drained
1/2 cup (120 mL) softened butter
2 tablespoons (30 mL) lemon juice
2 teaspoons (10 mL) horseradish
1/4 teaspoon (1 mL) salt
1/8 teaspoon (0.5 mL) nutmeg
1/8 teaspoon (0.5 mL) liquid hot pepper sauce
Whole shrimp or chopped parsley for garnish
Crackers or breads cut in canape shapes or raw
   vegetable strips

►Mince or grind shrimp. Cream butter, then mix the two together and add seasonings. Mix thoroughly and pack in a 1-1/2 cup (360 mL) mold or two 6-ounce (170 g, each) custard cups. Chill. Unmold and arrange on serving plate, garnish with whole shrimp or parsley, and surround with crackers, breads and/or raw vegetables. Makes approximately 1-1/2 cups (360 mL) of spread.
■ *The editors, ALASKA® magazine*

Shrimp Dip

1 package (8 oz /or/ 22 g) cream cheese
1 pint (0.47 L) sour cream or 1 package
   sour cream mix, reconstituted according to
   package instructions
2 tablespoons (30 mL) A-1 sauce
2 tablespoons (30 mL) lemon juice
2 tablespoons (30 mL) chili sauce
1 teaspoon (5 mL) salt
Dash of Tabasco
Dash of Worcestershire
2 pounds (1 kg) chopped cleaned cooked shrimp

►Soften cream cheese in a bowl; blend in all ingredients except the shrimp. Mix well. Stir in shrimp; chill. Serve with crackers, chips or vegetable sticks.
■ *Candy Dilley*
   Loggin' Camp Cookin' Book, *Dry Pass*

Shrimp Butterflies

Thin-sliced cocktail rye bread
Butter
Cucumber
Fresh-cooked, shucked shrimp
Mayonnaise
Parsley

►Butter thin slices of cocktail rye. If skin of cucumber is a pretty green, score the cucumber unpeeled and then slice it in 1/8-inch (3 mm) slices. Otherwise, peel and slice. Lay slices on top of buttered bread. On each cucumber slice, center two shrimp, "back to back," add a dab of mayonnaise and top with a tiny sprig of parsley.
■ *Bunny Mathisen, Petersburg*

Shrimp Treats

Cheese Canape Pastry (see page 65)
Cheddar cheese, melted
Shrimp, cooked and shucked
Red pepper flakes (optional)

►Make tiny tart shells from Cheese Canape Pastry (or a plain pastry). Melt cheese and add tiny shrimp or larger ones cut into pieces. Stir in pepper flakes. Fill baked and cooled tart shells and chill for a couple of hours or more.

Shrimp Bowl

►Chilled cooked shrimp served with cocktail sauce ranks high in favor as a party appetizer. Arrange shrimp on a large plate and place a small bowl of Cocktail Sauce in the center. The tail may be left on fresh or frozen shrimp for convenience in dipping.

Shrimp Cocktail Sauce
1/2 cup (120 mL) chili sauce
1/4 cup (60 mL) lemon juice
1 tablespoon (15 mL) vinegar
1 tablespoon (15 mL) Worcestershire
2 tablespoons (30 mL) finely chopped celery
2 tablespoons (30 mL) finely chopped onion
1 tablespoon (15 mL) chopped parsley
Few drops Tabasco

►Combine all ingredients and chill. Makes 1 cup (240 mL).
■ Seafood Recipes for Calorie Counters

Shrimp Filled Puffs

2 cups (480 mL) cooked peeled shrimp
1/4 cup (60 mL) butter
1/4 cup (60 mL) flour
1 cup (240 mL) milk
1/2 cup (120 mL) chopped celery

1/4 cup (60 mL) white wine
Salt and pepper to taste
40 tiny cream puff shells (see Cream Puff Paste)

►Melt butter; stir in flour; add milk gradually and stir and cook until thick and smooth. Add remaining ingredients except for cream puff shells; stir to blend. Serve hot in tiny cream puff shells.
■ *Pacific Pearl*
 Courtesy, Saint Herman's Sisterhood Club
 Kodiak

Casey's Shrimp Bisque

1/2 pound (228 g) raw, shucked shrimp
2 large cloves garlic, minced
1/2 medium green pepper, chopped fine
1 bunch green onions, including tops,
 chopped fine
1 stalk celery including leaves, chopped fine
1 teaspoon (5 mL) salt
Black pepper, to taste
1 large bay leaf
Dash cayenne pepper
Dash oregano
Dash marjoram
1/8 pound (56 g) butter
1 cup (240 mL) evaporated milk

►Cover vegetables with water, add salt, pepper, bay leaf, cayenne, oregano and marjoram. Boil until vegetables are tender. Remove bay leaf. Add shrimp and butter; boil two or three minutes longer. Add milk and simmer gently for at least five minutes more. If raw shrimp is not available, canned shrimp may be used. For a different taste treat, try Alaska king crab meat instead of shrimp. Do not overcook vegetables or shellfish.
■ *Casey Cobban*
 Recipes From The Scrolls of Saint Peter's
 Seward

Shrimp Bisque

1/4 cup (60 mL) finely chopped onion
1/4 cup (60 mL) finely chopped celery
1/4 cup (60 mL) butter or margarine
2 tablespoons (30 mL) flour
1 teaspoon (5 mL) salt
1/4 teaspoon (1 mL) paprika
Dash of white pepper
4 cups (1 L) milk or part half-and-half, part milk
2 cups (480 mL) cooked, chopped pink shrimp

►Cook onion and celery in butter until tender. Stir in flour and seasonings. Add liquid gradually; cook until thick, stirring constantly. Fold in shrimp. Heat thoroughly and serve at once. Makes six servings.
■ Seafood Moods

Shrimp and Potato Chowder
A way to stretch shrimp

3 cans (4½ oz /or/ 128 g, each) shrimp
1/4 cup (60 mL) chopped onion
2 tablespoons (30 mL) melted fat or oil
1 cup (240 mL) boiling water
1 cup (240 mL) diced potatoes
1/2 teaspoon (2 mL) salt
Dash of pepper
2 cups (480 mL) milk
Chopped parsley

►Drain shrimp and rinse with cold water. Cut large shrimp in half. Cook onion in fat until tender. Add boiling water, potatoes and seasonings. Cover and cook for 15 minutes or until potatoes are tender. Add milk and shrimp; heat. Garnish with parsley.
■ 'Can-venient' Ways with Shrimp

Smorgasbord Shrimp Salad
"There are so many ways of making shrimp salad I hesitate to tell what I do. However . . ."

8 pounds (3.6 kg) cooked shucked shrimp
1 quart (1 L) Best Foods mayonnaise
1 jar (1 pt /or/ 480 mL) Shedds salad dressing
To taste: chopped celery, green pepper, onion

►Shrimp is the main ingredient no matter what size you make the salad. This amount will serve 75 people at a smorgasbord. But use your judgment for the amount of shrimp and add chopped celery, green pepper and onion. Then make a dressing of Best Foods mayonnaise and Shedds, about three parts to one. Mix lightly and serve well chilled.
■ *Bunny Mathisen*
   "Help Yourself To The Sylta Flesk"
   ALASKA® magazine, January 1977

Shrimp and Fruit Salad

3/4 pound (340 g) cooked shucked shrimp
2 cups (480 mL) fruit — drained pineapple
   chunks, melon balls or diced red apples
   (with skin)
1 tablespoon (15 mL) lemon juice
1/2 cup (120 mL) chopped celery
1 teaspoon (5 mL) salt
1/2 cup (120 mL) mayonnaise
An avocado (optional), cut in chunks and
   sprinkled with lemon juice
Lettuce leaves, nuts (optional) for garnish

►If apples are used, sprinkle them with lemon juice as soon as they are diced to prevent darkening. Then combine all ingredients except lettuce leaves and nuts. Chill. Serve in lettuce cups. Garnish with chopped nuts. Makes six servings.

Shrimp Slaw

3/4 cup (180 mL) French dressing
1/2 cup (120 mL) plain yogurt
2 tablespoons (30 mL) lemon juice
6 to 7 cups (1.5 to 1.7 mL) cabbage, shredded
1 cup (240 mL) cooked, shucked shrimp or
   1 can (4½ oz /or/ 128 g) drained
1/2 cup (120 mL) parsley, chopped
5 green onions, chopped
1/2 cup (120 mL) ripe olives, sliced

►Prepare salad about two hours before serving. With a fork whip French dressing, yogurt and lemon juice in a large bowl until smooth. Add remaining ingredients and toss until evenly coated. Refrigerate until serving time.
■ *Velma Knapp*
   Souvenir Cook Book, *Skagway*

Celery Stuffed with Shrimp Salad

1 cup (240 mL) cooked peeled shrimp
2 cups (480 mL) chilled grapefruit sections
1 package (3 oz /or/ 85 g) cream cheese
3 tablespoons (45 mL) mayonnaise
1/4 teaspoon (1 mL) salt
6 or more crisp pieces of celery
Lettuce
French dressing

►Dice shrimp. Drain grapefruit sections. Mash cheese, add mayonnaise and salt and cream together until smooth. Add shrimp and mix well. Pack grooves of celery with the mixture. Cut into 3/4-inch (2 cm) pieces. Arrange on lettuce with grapefruit sections. Sprinkle with French dressing.
■ *Gladys Langille*
   Kitchen Magic, *Ketchikan*

Tiffany Shrimp Salad

1 pound (456 g) fresh or frozen cooked
   peeled shrimp
1 envelope (¼ oz /or/ 7 g) unflavored gelatin
1/2 cup (120 mL) water
2 tablespoons (30 mL) white wine vinegar
2 teaspoons (10 mL) sugar
1 teaspoon (5 mL) horseradish
1/4 teaspoon (1 mL) salt
1 pound (456 g) cottage cheese
1/2 cup (120 mL) finely chopped celery
1/3 cup (80 mL) finely chopped radish
2 tablespoons (30 mL) minced green onion
1 small cucumber cut into 1/8-inch
   (3 mm) slices

►Cook shrimp and chill. Soften gelatin in water;

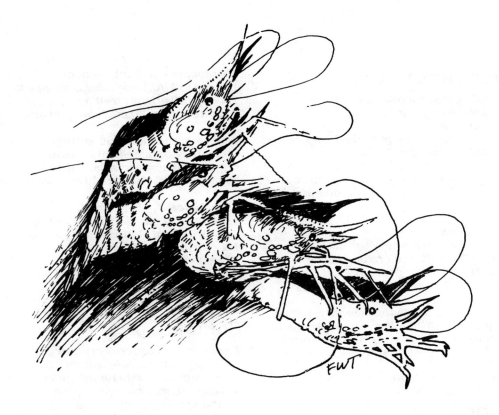

dissolve over hot water. Add vinegar, sugar, horseradish and salt; pour off and reserve half of mixture and add cottage cheese, celery, radish and green onion to remainder. Dip each cucumber slice into reserved gelatin mixture and arrange around the edge of an 8-inch (20 cm) oiled pie plate. Spoon cottage cheese mixture into pie plate; chill until firm. Add shrimp to remaining gelatin and marinate at room temperature until mixture in pie plate is firm. When firm, arrange shrimp atop cottage cheese mixture; spoon any remaining gelatin over shrimp. Chill until firm. Makes five to six servings.
■ The Great Lander Shopping News, *Anchorage*

Seafood Souffle Salad

1 package (3 oz /or/ 85 g) lemon gelatin
Water
1/4 teaspoon (1 mL) salt
1 tablespoon (15 mL) lemon juice
1/2 cup (120 mL) mayonnaise or salad dressing
3/4 cup (180 mL) cooked diced shrimp
1 cup (240 mL) diced avocado
1/4 cup (60 mL) diced celery
1 tablespoon (15 mL) finely chopped onion

►Dissolve gelatin and salt in 1 cup (240 mL) boiling water. Stir in 1/2 cup (120 mL) cold water and lemon juice. Gradually beat gelatin mixture into mayonnaise until smooth. Chill until partially set. Beat until fluffy. Fold in avocado, shrimp, celery and onion. Chill again until mixture mounds when spooned. Turn into a 1-quart (1 L) mold, chill until firm. Makes four to six servings.
■ *Evelyn Sites*
Northern Lites, Tasty Bites, *Fairbanks*

Hearty Shrimp Potato Salad
Also makes delicious supper sandwiches

6 cups (1.45 L) cooked cubed potatoes
6 chopped hard-cooked eggs
1-1/2 cups (360 mL) chopped celery
1 medium onion, chopped fine
2 teaspoons (10 mL) salt
1/2 teaspoon (2 mL) celery seed
2 sweet pickles, diced
Pepper to taste
1/2 cucumber, diced
2 cups (480 mL) tiny cooked shucked shrimp
Mayonnaise to moisten well

►Mix all ingredients except mayonnaise. Add mayonnaise enough to moisten salad well; check to see if more salt is needed. Serve. May be broiled briefly on halved, buttered buns, grated cheese sprinkled on top, for a supper sandwich. Makes 15 or more servings.
■ *Mrs. Vern E. Smith, Wrangell*
PTA Cook Book, *Petersburg*

Shrimp and Rice Salad

2 cups (480 mL) cooked white rice, cooled
2 cans (11 oz /or/ 312 g, each)
    mandarin oranges
1-1/2 cups (360 mL) cooked peeled shrimp
1-1/2 cups (360 mL) chopped celery

►Drain oranges, reserving juice. Toss all ingredients lightly and chill while you make dressing.

Dressing
1/2 cup (120 mL) mayonnaise
1/2 cup (120 mL) sour cream
1-1/2 ounces (42 g) softened cream cheese
1/4 teaspoon (1 mL) curry powder
Dash of salt

►Blend dressing ingredients together with enough juice from the mandarin oranges to make a smooth dressing. Pour over rice mixture and toss gently. Chill two to three hours before serving.
■ *Rhoda Fritz*
    Alaska's Cooking, *Anchorage*

Patio Shrimp

3 cans (4½ oz /or/ 128 g, each) shrimp, or about
    1 pound (456 g) cooked, shucked shrimp
1 large cucumber, sliced
Lettuce
Patio Shrimp Sauce

►Drain shrimp; cover with ice water and let stand for five minutes to revive flavor and texture; drain. Arrange shrimp and cucumber slices on lettuce. Serve with Patio Shrimp Sauce. Makes six servings.

Patio Shrimp Sauce
1 cup (240 mL) sour cream
1 tablespoon (15 mL) horseradish
1 tablespoon (15 mL) grated onion
1/2 teaspoon (2 mL) paprika
1/2 teaspoon (2 mL) salt

►Combine all ingredients and blend well. Chill until serving time.
■ 'Can-venient' Ways With Shrimp

Shrimp and Green Bean Salad

2 cups (480 mL) cooked green beans, drained
1-1/2 to 2 cups (360 to 480 mL) cooked
    peeled shrimp
1 cup (240 mL) raw rice, cooked and cooled
2 tablespoons (30 mL) salad oil
2 tablespoons (30 mL) lemon juice
1 or 2 cloves garlic, minced
1 teaspoon (5 mL) salt

1/8 teaspoon (0.5 mL) pepper
1/3 cup (80 mL) ripe olives, chopped
1/4 cup (60 mL) minced parsley
2 tablespoons (30 mL) chopped green onions

►Make sure beans and shrimp are well drained. Combine all ingredients, tossing well. Chill in serving dish for several hours. Top with Pink Sauce before serving. Makes eight or more servings.

Pink Sauce
1/2 cup (120 mL) dairy sour cream
1/4 cup (60 mL) chili sauce
1/4 cup (60 mL) ketchup
2 teaspoons (10 mL) dill weed

►Blend and chill till serving time.
■ *Mamie Jensen, Juneau*

Shrimp Aspic

1 envelope (¼ oz /or/ 7 g) plain gelatin
1/2 cup (120 mL) cold water
1-1/2 cups (360 mL) tomato juice
1/3 cup (80 mL) chopped onion
1 tablespoon (15 mL) sugar
2 tablespoons (30 mL) white vinegar
1 clove minced garlic
1/3 cup (80 mL) chopped green pepper
1 cup (240 mL) shrimp

►Sprinkle gelatin on cold water to soften. Place over low heat and stir until dissolved. Combine tomato juice, onion, sugar, vinegar, garlic, green pepper and gelatin. Chill until slightly thickened. Fold in crab or shrimp. Pour into six oiled individual molds or a 1-quart (1 L) mold.
■ *Libby Oaksmith*
    Kitchen Magic, *Ketchikan*

Shrimp Steamed Over Beer
With Green Sauce

1 or 2 pounds (0.45 to 1 kg) fresh,
    unshucked shrimp
Beer
3 or 4 whole cloves

►Shuck and clean wiggly, live shrimp fresh off the bottom of Kachemak Bay. Use beer instead of water in the bottom of your steamer. Add the cloves to the beer in the steamer. Place clean shrimp in steamer basket; cover and simmer until shrimp are curly and pink. DO NOT OVERCOOK. Serve at once, dipped in melted butter, dill butter, lemon butter or your favorite sauce. A good sauce follows.

Green Sauce
2 teaspoons (10 mL) finely minced onion

1/4 cup (60 mL) finely chopped chives
2 teaspoons (10 mL) aromatic vinegar, such as
    tarragon, or use lemon juice
1/2 cup (120 mL) mayonnaise
2 tablespoons (30 mL) finely chopped parsley
1/4 cup (60 mL) finely chopped watercress
    (use the wild cress from near Homer streams)

►Mix all together and refrigerate long enough for
flavors to blend.
■ *Patricia L. Nelson*
    Cooking Up A Storm, *Homer*

Shrimp Curry

3 tablespoons (45 mL) butter
3 tablespoons (45 mL) diced onion
3 tablespoons (45 mL) flour
2 teaspoons (10 mL) curry powder
1 teaspoon (5 mL) salt
Pepper
1-1/2 cups (360 mL) milk diluted with 1/2 cup
    (120 mL) water
2 cups (480 mL) cooked shrimp
Toast, patty shells or hot cooked rice

►Melt butter; add onions and cook three minutes.
Add flour, curry powder, salt and pepper and mix
thoroughly. Add milk slowly, stirring, until thick
and smooth. Cook over hot water 10 minutes. Add
shrimp. Heat thoroughly and serve in patty shells,
on toast or over rice. Makes four to six servings.
■ *Mrs. Thure Swanson*
    PTA Cook Book, *Petersburg*

Baked Curried Shrimp

2 pounds (1 kg) large shrimp, peeled
2 eggs, beaten
2 tablespoons (30 mL) water
1-1/2 cups (360 mL) dry bread crumbs
1 tablespoon (15 mL) curry powder
3/4 teaspoon (3 mL) salt
1/8 teaspoon (0.5 mL) pepper
1/4 cup (60 mL) melted butter
Hot Marmalade Dip (see Shrimp Tempura)

►Combine eggs and water. Combine bread
crumbs, curry powder, salt and pepper. Dip shrimp
in liquid and roll in crumbs. Place on a well-greased
cookie sheet. Drizzle butter over shrimp. Bake at
450°F (230°C) 10 to 15 minutes or until golden
brown. Serve with Hot Marmalade Dip.
■ Shellfish-A-Plenty

Ocean Ravager Shrimp

2 parts beer to 1 part water
1 dozen peppercorns
A couple of bay leaves
Raw unshucked shrimp
A pinch of sage
A pinch of thyme
A small palm of salt

►Head shrimp, then wash in cold sea water.
Refrigerate or pack in layers of crushed ice for
several hours prior to using. Shrimp must be fresh
caught to be of good flavor. Place all above ingredients except shrimp in the kettle. When this
reaches a rolling boil, toss in just enough shrimp to
cover the bottom of the kettle. Remove shrimp
when they float to the surface. Large shrimp will
continue to cook after being removed so they must
be carefully watched. Serve with a choice of
dipping sauces.
■ *Ivar Mossback, MV Ocean Ravager*
    Alaska Fish Tails & Game Trails

Boiled Seasoned Shrimp

Salt
Garlic, minced
Soy Sauce
Worcestershire
Dill weed
Parsley
Lemon juice
Raw, peeled shrimp
Cocktail Sauce

►Mix about 1 tablespoon (15 mL) of each of the
first seven ingredients with enough water to cover
shrimp. Bring to a boil. Add shrimp and boil until
they turn pink, about three to eight minutes,
depending on size. Serve with Cocktail Sauce (page
131), dill-flavored mayonnaise or Green Sauce
(page 134).
■ *Barbara Holland*
    Gold Rush Cookbook, *Valdez*

Broiled Seafood

1/2 pound (228 g) each — uncooked medium to
    large shrimp and fresh shucked scallops
1 cup (240 mL) fresh shucked oysters
1/4 cup (60 mL) butter
1 clove garlic, minced
1 tablespoon (15 mL) lemon juice
Salt, pepper, paprika, parsley

►Peel shrimp. Melt butter, add garlic and simmer
three minutes. Add lemon juice and pour over
shellfish arranged in a single layer in a flameproof
dish or in scallop shells. Spoon on half the butter.
Broil 4 inches (10 cm) from heat for about eight
minutes, basting with remaining sauce. Season
and garnish as desired. Serves four.
■ *The editors, ALASKA® magazine*

Shrimp Jambalaya

1/2 cup (120 mL) diced ham
2 tablespoons (30 mL) butter
1/2 cup (120 mL) chopped onion
1 cup (240 mL) chopped green pepper
1-1/2 cups (360 mL) canned tomatoes
1-1/2 cups (360 mL) water
1 cup (240 mL) raw rice
1/4 teaspoon (1 mL) salt
1/4 teaspoon (1 mL) garlic powder
1 bay leaf
1/2 teaspoon (2 mL) thyme
1/4 cup (60 mL) chopped parsley
2 cups (480 mL) cooked peeled shrimp

►Saute ham, onion and green pepper in butter until tender. Add next seven ingredients, cover and cook 25 to 30 minutes or until rice is tender. Add parsley and shrimp. Heat through. Serves six.
■ *Wilma Gregory*
   Cooking Up A Storm, *Homer*

Lemon Parsley Shrimp

2 pounds (1 kg) raw unpeeled shrimp
4 tablespoons (60 mL) olive oil or vegetable oil
2 cloves garlic, minced
1/2 cup (120 mL) fresh parsley
Salt
Pepper
1/2 cup (120 mL) lemon juice

►Peel and butterfly the shrimp by cutting almost through at center back. Heat oil in skillet with garlic. Saute shrimp with garlic until pink — about four minutes. Add salt and pepper and parsley and toss until well coated. Last add lemon juice. Serve for lunch with French bread and salad.
■ *Elsie Lilleness*
   Saint Herman's Sisterhood Club, *Kodiak*

Shrimp Tempura

3/4 to 1 pound (340 to 456 g) raw, peeled shrimp
Assorted vegetables cut in strips, slices or
   bite-sized chunks — such as mushrooms,
   carrots, green pepper, onion
Batter
Oil for frying
Sauces for dipping

►Tempura batter is best made several hours (even a day) in advance and then left covered and refrigerated until meal time. (Commercial tempura batter mixes are available.) The batter can be used to coat almost any food you would deep-fry. The chunks should be small enough to heat through quickly. Crisp vegetables will remain somewhat crisp.

At preparation time, heat oil to 375°F (190°C) in a deep-fryer or wok. Make sure all food pieces are dry as possible so that batter will cling. Then dip them in batter, drain excess, and fry in hot fat, a few pieces at a time, until lightly browned, three or four minutes. Drain thoroughly on absorbent paper. Serve with a choice of dips such as soy sauce, Chinese-style hot mustard and/or the Hot Marmalade Dip which follows.

Tempura Batter
1 cup (240 mL) all-purpose flour
1/2 teaspoon (2 mL) salt
1 teaspoon (5 mL) baking powder
1 egg, beaten
2 tablespoons (30 mL) vegetable oil
3/4 cup (180 mL) flat beer or ice water

►Combine dry ingredients and mix in egg and oil until blended. Add water or beer a little at a time, stirring constantly, until batter is smooth. Cover and refrigerate till cooking time.

Hot Marmalade Dip
1/2 cup (120 mL) orange marmalade
1/4 cup (60 mL) lemon juice
1 tablespoon (15 mL) soy sauce
1 clove garlic, crushed
1/8 teaspoon (0.5 mL) ginger
1 teaspoon (5 mL) cornstarch
1 tablespoon (15 mL) cold water

►Bring to a boil, marmalade, lemon juice, soy sauce, garlic and ginger. Combine cornstarch and water. Add to hot sauce and cook until thickened, stirring constantly. Serve hot with Shrimp Tempura or other seafood dishes.
■ *Shellfish-A-Plenty (dip)*

Shrimp Stuffing
For fish fillets

1 tablespoon (15 mL) butter
2 tablespoons (30 mL) chopped onion
1/4 cup (60 mL) chopped green pepper
1 cup (240 mL) tiny Alaska shrimp
1/4 cup (60 mL) fine bread crumbs

►Melt butter, add onions and green pepper and saute until onion is translucent. Add shrimp and heat through, tossing to mix. Remove from heat and add crumbs. Place a couple of spoonfuls on each fish fillet, roll the fillet and fasten with toothpicks. Fillets should be thin, and it's best to roll *two* per person rather than to put too much stuffing into one. (It looks like more, for one thing.) This amount of stuffing will fill 8 to 10 small thin fillets — enough for four or five servings.
■ *The editors,* ALASKA® *magazine*

French Fried Shrimp

1 cup (240 mL) sifted flour
1/2 teaspoon (2 mL) salt
1/2 teaspoon (2 mL) sugar
1 egg, slightly beaten
1 cup (240 mL) ice water
2 tablespoons (30 mL) salad oil
2 pounds (1 kg) large fresh or frozen shrimp

►Combine batter ingredients and beat well. Peel shell from shrimp leaving last section of tail intact. Butterfly shrimp by cutting almost through at center back. Dip into batter and fry in deep fat, 375°F (190°C) till brown. Serve at once with lemon wedges.
■ Shellfish Cookbook

Fried Shrimp

►Use the large uncooked sidestripe, coonstripe or spot shrimp. Head and shuck but leave tail on. Put flour, salt, pepper and shrimp in a paper bag and shake well to coat shrimp. Pan-fry shrimp as you would chicken in a small amount of fat until golden.
■ *Mrs. Earl Benitz*
  PTA Cook Book, *Petersburg*

Shellfish Sauce
For boiled or steamed fish

2 tablespoons (30 mL) butter
2 tablespoons (30 mL) flour
1/2 teaspoon (2 mL) salt
1/4 teaspoon (1 mL) paprika
1/4 teaspoon (1 mL) dry mustard
1 cup (240 mL) milk
1/4 pound (114 g) shrimp or flaked crab
1 cup (240 mL) lightly cooked peas (preferably fresh or frozen)

►Melt butter; blend in flour and seasonings. Add milk gradually and cook until thick and smooth, stirring constantly. Add shellfish and peas; heat again. Serve over boiled or steamed fish. Serves six.
■ Seafood Recipes For Alaskans *(adapted)*

Sherried Shrimp Sauce
For baked fish

1 small can sliced mushrooms
3/4 cup (180 mL) evaporated milk
1/4 cup (60 mL) water
3 eggs, slightly beaten
1/4 cup (60 mL) butter
1/4 cup (60 mL) flour
1/2 teaspoon (2 mL) salt
1/4 teaspoon (1 mL) pepper

1/4 cup (60 mL) dry sherry
1/4 cup (60 mL) water
1 cup (240 mL) cooked shrimp
1 tablespoon (15 mL) finely chopped chives

►Drain mushrooms, reserving the liquid. Combine liquid with milk, water and eggs. Melt butter in a saucepan; remove from heat and add the flour, salt and pepper, stirring well to make a paste. Gradually add the milk; then cook gently, stirring constantly until smooth. Cook until thickened. Remove from heat; add sherry and water, beating until smooth. Add shrimp, mushrooms and chives. Serve over baked fish.
■ Pacific Salmon Cookbook

Mom's Shrimp Puffs

1/2 cup (120 mL) water
2 tablespoons (30 mL) margarine
1/2 cup (120 mL) flour
2 eggs
1 cup (240 mL) cooked peeled shrimp
1/2 cup (120 mL) grated Cheddar cheese

►Heat water and margarine to rolling boil in saucepan. Stir in flour. Stir vigorously over low heat until mixture forms a ball, about one minute. Remove from heat. Beat in eggs thoroughly, one at a time. Beat until smooth. Stir in grated cheese and shrimp. Heat oil in fryer to 375°F (190°C). Drop by spoonfuls into hot oil and fry until golden, two to three minutes.
■ *Kathie Angerman*
  What's Cookin' in Wrangell

Phyllis's Shrimp Chow Mein

1 cup (240 mL) sliced carrots
1 cup (240 mL) sliced green onions
1 cup (240 mL) sliced mushrooms
1 cup (240 mL) sliced celery
1 cup (240 mL) sliced green pepper
1/4 cup (60 mL) soy sauce
1 cup (240 mL) dry sherry
2 teaspoons (10 mL) cornstarch
1 cup (240 mL) cold chicken broth
2 cups (480 mL) cooked peeled shrimp

►Place the five vegetables in a wok in which there is just enough oil to cover the bottom. Stir to coat vegetables with oil, cover and simmer over moderate heat until vegetables are crisp-done. Then add soy sauce and wine. Mix cornstarch in cold chicken broth and stir into sauce in the wok until thickened. Add shrimp and heat through. Serve with hot boiled rice or chow mein noodles with a fruit salad to accompany.
■ *Phyllis S. Irish*
  Gold Rush Cookbook, *Valdez*

Creole Raisin Rice with Shrimp

1/2 cup (120 mL) chopped green pepper
1/2 cup (120 mL) chopped onion
2 cloves garlic; 1 whole, 1 minced
2/3 cup (160 mL) raisins
1 tablespoon (15 mL) vegetable oil
1 teaspoon (5 mL) salt
1/2 teaspoon (2 mL) pepper
1/4 teaspoon (1 mL) rosemary
1/2 teaspoon (2 mL) paprika
3 drops Tabasco
1 can (1 lb /or/ 456 g) tomatoes
2 cups (480 mL) cooked rice
2 tablespoons (30 mL) butter
1/2 pound (228 g) large cooked peeled shrimp
1/4 cup (60 mL) chopped parsley

►Cook green pepper, onion, the minced garlic and raisins in oil until vegetables soften. Add salt, pepper, rosemary, paprika, Tabasco and tomatoes. Simmer 10 minutes. Combine with rice. Cover and keep warm over low heat. Melt butter; add remaining whole garlic clove and shrimp. Cook, stirring, until heated through. Remove garlic and discard. Stir chopped parsley into rice. Top with shrimp. Makes four servings.

■ *Helen Lee*
Souvenir Cook Book, *Skagway*

Chapter 5

More Shellfish
& Other Sea Creatures

This chapter includes recipes for some of the sea world's smallest — and certainly its largest—edibles. These shellfish and "other sea creatures" have little in common except the marine environment and the fact that fisheries for most of them are severely limited if not unheard of.

The "other sea creatures" are all of them mammals, big ones, and all are protected by federal law against hunting by anyone who is not Aleut, Indian or Eskimo. It would be impossible to exaggerate the importance of these mammals in the Native diet, and we have included a number of recipes for them — seal, sea lion, walrus and whale — beginning on page 154.

The shellfish of this chapter, however, are "open to all." If you haven't tried limpets or gumboots or sea cucumber, you're missing out on the world's easiest "fishery," one that requires nothing more from you than a pleasant stroll on the beach at low tide. Listen:

Limpets we found high up on lavalike rocks, often considerably above high tide line. They live in colonies and seem to favor crevices and the inside edges of rocks. We pried off the largest with our knives. At water's edge, among long, slippery ribbons of kelp, we found gumboots, like soft-shelled limpets, also small snails and a species of bright green algae called ulva.

Placed on a cooking grill shell-side down and broiled over a fire for a few minutes, the limpets and snails cooked in their own juices and loosened from their shells. We sauteed them in butter, flavored them with garlic and ate them whole. Sprinkled with lemon, the limpets were delicious, tasty and tender as clams. The snails, small but fresh, were far superior to any escargot I'd eaten in restaurants. Ulva, crunchy and salty, added color and variety; we blanched it in hot water and ate it with rice. . . .

Next morning we tried our luck at abalone picking. We each took a section of reef, groping about in the slippery kelp that crackled under the diving boots we wore for traction. . . . A shout from Terry alerted me that he had found a colony of abalones. We caught 42, none smaller than 4 inches (10 cm) and many larger than my fist.

We cleaned several of the biggest, wrapped them in the all-purpose muslin cloth we'd brought, and tenderized them between two boards with the flat side of the ax. The rest we cached in a tide pool to keep alive. . . . Sauteed in butter and seasoned with garlic, the abalone were fresh and as tender as a good filet. We ate as many as we wanted and kept the cooked leftovers for snacks. . . .

Terry attached a spear to a long pole and managed to skewer several sea cucumbers and sea urchins with it as I maneuvered the kayak. We cleaned and stripped the long muscles from the cucumber skins and fried them in butter. With knives we pierced the prickly shells of the sea urchins and spooned out their orange roe. That of the small green urchins tasted particularly delicate and nutty when uncooked, and like hen's eggs when fried in butter. . . .

On one of our crab-hunting expeditions, Terry spotted an unusual form lurking on the bottom, hiding in the grasses. He lunged with his spear and lifted 10 pounds (4.5 kg) of writhing octopus to the surface. . . . Although slightly skeptical, I helped scrape the suckers off the legs and peel off the skin as purple and red inks pulsed beneath the surface. We dipped the legs in boiling water for a few minutes, sliced off a few pieces and ate them with lemon juice. Of a chewy, pleasantly rubbery consistency, the octopus tasted very much like crab. We ate it fried in butter and smoked, but liked it best uncooked with a bit of lemon. It became our favorite food, prized more than crab or even abalone.
[Kathryn Morimitsu, "Seashore Gourmets: Living Off Land and Sea," ALASKA® magazine, April 1981]

If you *need* "recipes" after that, simply read on.

ABALONE

Hunting for abalone is very like "trying to cook a seven-course meal after you've waxed the floor with Vaseline," says Diane Zink [ALASKA® magazine, August 1980] whose family nevertheless schedules as many such expeditions as the tide tables will allow. The problem is the habitat chosen by this marine snail with the delectable "foot" or shell muscle. It prefers deep, rock-filled waters that are subject to heavy currents and swells and are almost impossible to reach without diving gear. But during extreme low tides, enough abalone for individual use can be gathered from a boat or searched out by — carefully — crawling over the slippery kelp-covered rocks where abalone are most likely to find "footholds" in cracks or crevices.

Why bother? "The delicate flavor of the abalone is worth all the tumbles and bruises," Mrs. Zink assures.

It is the pinto abalone, one of the smallest of the eight species on the Pacific west coast, that is found in abundance all along the outside coast of Southeastern. Eaten raw, sliced straight out of the shell, pinto abalone tastes "not too unlike a smooth, soft grade of shoe leather," reports James Balog in an ALASKA® magazine story [also August 1980] about the prospects for commercial harvest. But in Tokyo's *sushi* bars, the same single slice of raw abalone "wrapped around a ball of rice and seaweed sells for around $4." And that 1980 price is not adjusted for inflation.

Whether or not you develop the taste for raw abalone, you are missing one of the ocean's finest treats if you've not tried abalone prepared in one of the ways suggested on these pages.

One Way To Clean Abalone

Insert blade of knife on the tapered "low" side of the shell. Holding the blade close to the shell, sever muscles. Cut the edible muscle and foot away from the inedible portions remaining.

At one end of "foot" you will see the abalone's mouth. Cut this away, too, and discard.

Now for the final two steps before cooking: First you take a wire- or plastic-mesh kitchen scrubber such as a Chore Girl and scrub off the black fringe coating the outer edge of the foot muscle.

Next, place the abalone between two boards (plywood which will not split under a blow is best). Rap the board sharply two or three times to break down the tough living abalone muscle. A bigger one will take, maybe, three good stiff raps, smaller ones only a couple. You can feel the meat "relax" under the blow that really does the business.

At that point you have a sweet white piece of meat ready for quick skillet-fry. Use fifty-fifty butter and oil — cracker crumbs or not, whatever you prefer. Saute gently a few minutes on one side, quickly turn to the other and then out before you overcook and toughen. Serve with crisp garden salad and garlic bread, a chilled Chablis — ambrosia! And when is the next minus tide? [Adapted from *ALASKA*® magazine, July 1972]

Other Methods . . .

- To make abalone tender before cooking in any way, you can freeze them overnight in the shell. Next day remove from freezer to thaw. When partly thawed lift abalone from shell and clean under cold water. [*Tsimpshean Indian Island Cookbook*, Metlakatla]
- Boil abalone 15 or 20 minutes in shell. Remove from shell, cover with cold water, then drain. Refrigerate meat in an airtight container for one or two days. This makes the abalone tender and saves the chef from having to pound it. [Chef Ellis C. Bearden, Heritage House, Ketchikan]
- Gather abalone at very low minus tide. You will find them sticking on the rocks like gumboots. Take the abalone and parboil it and the inside will come out. Pound it and roll it in corn meal or flour seasoned with curry powder and pepper. Fry it in deep fat.
- Using an oven rack on an open fire, place abalone on top of rack, shell side down. Keep on fire until tender when poked with a fork. Remove from fire and cool. Cut abalone from shell, eat as is. [These last two suggestions are also from the *Tsimpshean Indian Island Cookbook*, Metlakatla]

Abalone Goma Zu

1 tablespoon (15 mL) sesame seed
1 tablespoon (15 mL) sugar
1/4 teaspoon (1 mL) salt
1 teaspoon (5 mL) cornstarch
Salt
2 tablespoons (30 mL) water
1/2 cup (120 mL) white vinegar or white
rice vinegar
2 small cucumbers
1 pound (456 g) boiled, shelled abalone

►Spread sesame seed on a baking sheet and toast in a 350°F (175°C) oven for five minutes. Blend the sugar, salt, cornstarch, water and vinegar in a saucepan. Add sesame seed. Cool. Peel cucumbers; cut in half lengthwise (removing any large seeds);

then cut in thin crosswise slices and sprinkle with salt. Cut abalone in very thin strips, 2 inches (5 cm) long and 1/2 inch (1.25 cm) wide. Combine cucumbers and abalone with vinegar mixture. Chill. (You can use a boiled octopus, too.) Serves four to eight.
■ Tsimpshean Indian Island Cookbook
Metlakatla

Abalone Stew

►Heat a quart (1 L) of milk together with 2 tablespoons (30 mL) butter. Add chopped abalone and salt and pepper. It couldn't possibly be simpler to prepare or more delicious to eat.
■ *Sammi Sarvela, FV* Myrth
Seafood Secrets, *Sitka*

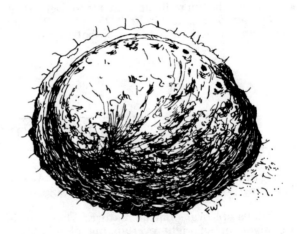

Abalone Provinchae
A dish that keeps this restaurant busy serving about a hundred pounds of abalone a week

►Boil abalone 15 to 20 minutes in shell. Remove from shell, cover with cold water, then drain. Refrigerate in an airtight container for one or two days. This makes the abalone tender and saves the chef from having to pound it.

Slice thinly. Saute quickly in butter with garlic base, adding green onions and tomatoes. Or, to deep-fry, slice as for saute, then dip twice in egg batter and bread crumbs.*
■ *Chef Ellis C. Bearden*
Heritage House, Ketchikan
ALASKA® *magazine, October 1978*

*Egg batter is a beaten egg diluted with a couple of teaspoons (10 mL) of water or milk. Fine bread crumbs can be seasoned as desired. Dip slices in egg, then crumbs. Repeat. Deep-fry in fat heated to 350°F (175°C).

Fried Abalone

►Dip abalones in boiling water; then cut out of shell. Scrape well. Slice thin; place on bread board and pound with something flat such as a cleaver. Dip in beaten, seasoned egg; then roll in fine cracker crumbs. Fry in hot fat — about the same length of time as an egg.
■ Out of Alaska's Kitchens

Abalone Fritters

3/4 cup (180 mL) minced abalone meat
2 eggs
1/4 teaspoon (1 mL) salt
1 cup (240 mL) flour
1 teaspoon (5 mL) baking powder

►Combine the ingredients and blend well. Heat frying pan and place in it 1/2 inch (1.25 cm) shortening. When fat is hot, drop batter into it, a spoonful at a time. Brown fritters on both sides; then serve at once. Abalone should always be served as soon as cooked for delicacy of flavor and tenderness.
■ *Mrs. Helen Hager*
   Sitka's Treasure

Abalone Steak

Abalone steaks
Melted butter
Crumbs, dry, fine

►Be sure abalone is sliced thinly and pound with a meat mallet until it is well tenderized. Abalone will be tough as all get out if not given a good beating. Brush steaks on each side with melted butter and sprinkle lightly with crumbs. Fry quickly in heavy, hot skillet — usually about one minute to each side is enough. Season to suit and serve with lemon wedges.

GUMBOOTS (CHITONS)

This description is excerpted from Alaska Tidelines *[Volume II, Number 8, May 1980].*

Chitons are oval-shaped creatures whose shells are made up of eight overlapping plates. They fasten themselves tightly to rocks and must be pried loose. Chitons live in the middle to lower tidal areas and are often found attached to the underside of boulders or grazing in seaweed-covered rocks. The largest species are the Black Katy chiton and the gumboot chiton, which may reach a length of 10 inches (25 cm) or more. The big gumboot, so called because of a tough, leathery reddish-brown covering which hides its plates — has long been a favorite food of southeast Alaska Indians.
Preparation Tips: Cut out the smooth "foot" on the undersurface, scrape and wash. The meat may be eaten raw, or sliced, then pounded with a rock to tenderize, and fried. Or the whole chiton can be roasted in the fire.

Steamed Chitons or Chiton Patties

1. Steam the animal whole for 15 minutes.
2. Peel off the black skin and remove each of the small bones in the back.
3. Clean out the insides which are found directly under the backbones.
4. Serve the large meaty foot as it is or prepare chiton patties.
■ *Alice Thompson — Ahousat*

Chiton Patties
1. Follow the first three steps for cooking and cleaning chitons.
2. Wash the meaty foot and grind it.
3. Press the ground meat into patties and season with salt and pepper.
4. Fry in oil until browned.
■ *Merle Adams — Haida*
   Indian Food: A Cookbook of Native Foods
   From British Columbia

Several Ways To Prepare Gumboots

►When I was a young girl, we'd build a bonfire on the beach as soon as we were through picking gumboots. Rocks were placed around the fire, and when they were hot, we put the gumboots on them to cook until tender. Using a thumbnail as a pry, we could easily slip off the shells which line the back.

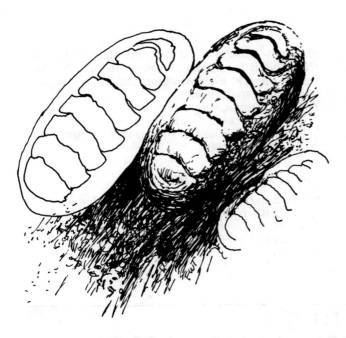

Then we cleaned off the dark parts and ate the rest of the meat with seal oil.

Another way to prepare them is to steam them in a heavy skillet in their own juice for a few minutes. They get hard and rubbery.

They can also be eaten raw. The Tlingits of Southeastern never ate raw fish as the movies indicate, but they do sometimes eat gumboots raw after they have been soaked in fresh water overnight. The meat turns tender and the shells come off easy. These are eaten with seal oil, too.

The white man just recently introduced some modern preparations of this product. The meat can be pounded, like abalone, to tenderize it, sprinkled with seafood seasoning, dipped in beaten eggs and then in cracker crumbs, and fried quickly in hot oil. Or, it may be ground and used in any good recipe for chowder or fish patties. Another good use for ground gumboots is this dish:

Gumboot Fritters
1 cup (240 mL) ground gumboots
2 cups (480 mL) cornflakes
2 eggs, beaten
Seafood seasoning
Monosodium glutamate
Pepper

►Mix all ingredients and drop by spoonfuls into hot, deep fat. Fry quickly until egg coating is golden. Drain and serve.
■ *Kaa T'eix (Mary Howard Pelayo)*
Kaa T'eix's Cook Book, *Mount Edgecumbe*

China slippers or *Chinese slippers or giant Pacific chitons are described by one connoisseur as "an over-sized gumboot found on muddy beaches. They have a covering like felt; scrape them and cut the sides and tongue off and put them into a frying pan and steam them a few minutes." Below are more suggestions, one of which calls for much longer cooking, another that cautions care — "the more you cook them, the tougher they get." Some experiment is in order.*

Steamed China Slippers

►Steam China slippers for an hour or until the outer skin begins to peel off (some people stir China slippers rapidly to rub off the skin).

Remove any remaining skin, the backbones and gills. Leave the girdle and foot for eating.

China slippers may be served after they have been steamed and cleaned or they may be pan-fried with onion.
■ *Ed Hunt; Mary Moody — Bella Bella*
Indian Food: A Cookbook of Native Foods From British Columbia

Chinese Slippers

►Take care, for the more you cook them the tougher they get. Dip them in boiling water and when a knife can scrape the outside skin off, take them out of water and slit the back open. Then drop them into boiling water and when you can see the backbone it is ready for eating. Put it in soy sauce and have a real treat.
■ *Tsimpshean Indian Island Cookbook*
Metlakatla

Gumboot Chop Suey

Gumboots
Onions
Bacon
Salt
Cabbage
Celery
Seal grease
Green pepper

►Steam gumboots and shell. Rinse very well and chop into bite-sized pieces. Set aside for later use. Slice bacon into small pieces and fry over medium-high heat. Add sliced onions, chopped cabbage and celery. Cook or steam until vegetables are almost done. Add chopped or sliced green pepper, gumboots and salt according to your taste. Serve when green pepper is tender. You can also add 2 tablespoons (30 mL) of seal grease for flavor if you like. Serve with rice. Makes six servings.
■ *Barbara George*
Courtesy, Vivian James, Angoon

Pickled Gumboots

Gumboots
2 cups (480 mL) vinegar
2 cups (480 mL) soy sauce
3 tablespoons (45 mL) pickling spice
1/4 teaspoon (2 mL) garlic salt
1 onion, sliced
Lemon juice

►Steam gumboots for one minute in sea water. Remove from heat, drain and cool. Remove shells and clean before adding to pickle brine. In a saucepan, combine vinegar, soy sauce, pickling spice and garlic salt. Boil mixture for one minute. Remove from heat and allow to cool, then add prepared gumboots. Contents should be left refrigerated for 24 hours before using. To spice things up, add a sliced onion and a few drops of lemon juice to the brine.
■ *C. Joe Murray, Angoon*
"Alaska Pickled Treats"
ALASKA® *magazine, Alaska-only edition*
September 1980

Boiled Gumboots

►Put gumboots into rapidly boiling water and punch with a stick till water comes to a boil again. Then rinse gumboots with warm water and peel. Can be eaten with soy sauce or seal grease.
■ *Anon.*

LIMPETS

The following is an excerpt from Alaska Tidelines *[Volume II, Number 8, May 1980].*

Limpet shells look like small pointed Chinese coolie hats. They are found in the high tide zone on rocks that are covered with a film of algae on which they feed.
Preparation Tips: Use your knife to pry them off and cut out the white muscle meat on the underside. This can be eaten raw, simmered in water, or pounded to tenderize and fried. Or if you find a flat rock loaded with limpets, do as the Native people sometimes do: Cover the rock with damp seaweed and lay hot stones from your fire on top. The limpets lose their hold on the rocks as they cook and may be eaten on the spot (along with the cooked seaweed).

Keyhole limpets are found farther down the beach and look very much like other limpets except for the small hole at the peak of their "hats." However, they are more closely related to the delicious abalone which, unfortunately, is usually out of reach in deeper waters. Keyhole limpets are cooked in the same way as true limpets.

Boiled Limpets

►These are small shellfish that resemble Chinese hats. They are fixed the same way as mussels — boiled and served with melted butter or seal oil.
■ Aleut Cookbook, *Saint Paul Island*

Sauteed Limpets

►My family loves to beachcomb during minus tides, and we try to collect enough limpets to saute over a beach bonfire whenever we have the opportunity. We wash the limpets thoroughly, dig them out of their shells and saute them in butter for a few minutes.
■ *Mamie Jensen, Juneau*

MARINE SNAILS

The marine snails in Alaskan waters come in many sizes, and several species make good eating, comparable to clams or to the snail cousin with which we're most familiar — the abalone. The meat or "foot" of the large moon snail — which can grow to 5 or 6 inches (12 to 15 cm) in length — is especially like abalone. Some people compare the taste of it and other marine snails to razor clams. And, indeed, the recipe section you should turn to if you find yourself with buckets of marine snails to prepare is the one featuring clams.
Preparation Tips: If you can catch a large moon snail while it's almost completely extended from its shell, you're in luck. You can wrench the body

loose, clean it and prepare it without boiling. The meat may be sliced thin and pounded, as abalone, rolled in flour and fried. Otherwise, you have the choice of smashing the shell or treating it as you would the smaller snails: Scrub them best as possible and allow them to soak, shell and all, in fresh sea water for several hours, as you would clams. Then drop them into boiling water to simmer 10 to 15 minutes. Some cooking oil added to the water will make the meat slightly slippery and easier to extract. A tool helps, too. Needle-nose pliers and surgical hemostats have been recommended for removing the smaller meats.

Once the meat is removed from the shell, cut away the protective plate on the foot and clean off the soft parts behind the foot. Smaller snails are then ready to dip into butter and pop into your mouth. The larger ones may be ground or minced for other recipes.

Tom's Pickled Snails

Boiled, cleaned whelks
1 pint (0.47 L) water
1 pint (0.47 L) vinegar
1/3 cup (80 mL) brown sugar
2 tablespoons (30 mL) pickling spices

▶Light wine or sherry may also be added to the liquid. Boil these ingredients, then strain the spices off. Pack the snails in jars with onions, lemon or sliced carrots for a variety of color and flavor.

Refrigerate. They will be ready to sample in two or three days.
■ *Tom Wischer, Kodiak*
Courtesy, Kathy Hunter
"Pass the Snails, Please"
ALASKA® magazine, November 1976

Chimkin
(Little snails)

▶Gather in the spring of the year. They can be found on the rocks at low tide. Boil in water. To serve, the meat is picked out and dipped in melted butter, similar to clams.
■ Aleut Cookbook, *Saint Paul Island*

Whelk on Rice

1 cup (240 mL) chopped celery
1 cup (240 mL) chopped onion
1 cup (240 mL) sliced mushrooms
3/4 to 1 cup (180 to 240 mL) ground whelk
Soy sauce

▶Brown the whelk and remove from pan. Steam the onions, celery and mushrooms until tender. Then add whelk and soy sauce to taste. Serve on rice, noodles or toast.
■ *Robert R. Talmadge, Of Sea and Shore*
Reprinted from "Pass the Snails, Please"
ALASKA® magazine, November 1976

OCTOPUS

Surprisingly enough, the octopus is a mollusk, too, along with clams, snails, oysters and other recognizably shelled creatures. Its claim to the family tree is its small, sharp beak, the only part of its being that is not malleable enough to squeeze through very tight spaces. About 30 different species of octopus inhabit Alaskan waters, including the giant Pacific octopus whose stretched tentacles may span 32 feet (9.6 m). It is found in enough numbers to be a potential commercial resource of some value — even if it were never sold for table use. Each year several million pounds of octopus are imported to the state, mostly from Japan, to supply bait for the halibut fishery.

But octopus *is* a superb candidate for the dinner table. Once cooked, the squishy flesh turns firm,

the taste mild, often compared with lobster or crab. Three different methods of preparing octopus are presented on following pages. The first suggests skinning the tentacles *after* boiling them, to make the skinning easier; the second says skin *beforehand,* so that the meat may be pounded and cooked quickly to preserve the tenderness desirable in steaks. And the third suggestion is to start with a *small* octopus, a tenderer beast at the outset.

If any of these methods turns you into a devotee of octopus meat, use the next low tide to look for an octopus den . . . usually a hideaway under or between rocks or in a cave and, luckily for the hunter, well marked with the litter of past meals. Crab shells and other bony debris the fastidious octopus places outside his front door.

Butchering A Large Octopus — Method I

Here is Matthew Dick's blow by blow description of how Walter Metroken of Kodiak prepares and enjoys eating "the whole thing."

I recently acquired a 35-pound (16 kg) octopus and didn't know what to do with it. I had tasted cooked octopus before and found it delicious and tender. Still, it is common knowledge that octopus is as tough as raw leather unless you prepare it correctly. After inquiring around, I found that there is a man in Kodiak whose specialty is octopus, a man who treats octopus with the same affection that a French chef lavishes on filet mignon. Walter Metroken, a long-time Kodiak resident, took the octopus and me to his home and instructed me in the finer points of the creature's preparation. Here is his method of butchering and cooking an octopus.

The animal should be alive, or only dead for a few hours, when you begin. First, open a can of cold beer to put you in the proper, relaxed frame of mind. (Omit this step if you are a minor or Prohibitionist.) Next:

1. Set up a clean sheet of plywood on sawhorses as your work table. (Any large clean cutting surface will work as well.) Sharpen a knife to a fine edge; a dull one simply won't cut octopus. Then spread the animal out on your work table.
2. Cut off each tentacle at the base and remove the last 6 to 8 inches (15 to 20 cm) near the tip.
3. You are now left with the mantle, which contains a good deal of meat, but at this point also contains the viscera. The mantle cavity (the opening is at the base of the head) is divided into halves by a partition, which you must slice through.
4. Then, inserting your hand, grasp the back of the cavity and turn the mantle inside out, exposing the viscera.
5. Cut viscera away from the mantle and skin the mantle, pulling the skin away from the meat and slicing through the fascia, much as you skin seal or deer. It is not necessary to skin the tentacles; this is more easily done after cooking.

   The viscera and most of the skin is now removed from the meat. Be sure to dispose of the wastes, for they will begin to smell terrible if left around in the yard for a day.
6. The next step is to tenderize the meat. Stretch a tentacle out on the cutting board. Using a 2 x 4 about 18 inches (45 cm) long, beat the tentacle until it flattens to approximately half its normal thickness. The muscle fibers are separated during this process, and the tentacle loses its rock hardness. Cut the mantle into 3-inch-wide (7.5 cm) strips and beat these, too.

Cooking Octopus a la Metroken

The meat is now ready to be boiled. Some people prefer to use only salted water, but Walter adds pickling spices, dehydrated mixed vegetables, garlic salt, celery salt, soy sauce and imitation bacon to the boiling water, along with 6-inch (15 cm) segments of tenderized tentacle and mantle. (The proportions of the seasonings are left up to your own taste. Be careful not to overdo it.)

Boil the meat for 30 to 45 minutes, or until tender. When the tentacles are done, cool them, then skin them. Tyros in the art of octopus gastronomy often balk at eating the suction cups, or "buttons," and remove them with the skin. Gourmets like Walter, however, know that the buttons are the tenderest part of the whole animal.

Boiled Octopus: Simply slice the skinned meat and dip in sauces. An Oriental-style sauce can be made by mixing hot mustard and soy sauce to taste. Walter's favorite is a mixture (also "to taste") of mayonnaise, hot mustard, soy sauce, horseradish and ketchup. If you want to make the hot mustard even hotter, add a little beer.

Sauteed Octopus: According to Walter, the best way to eat octopus is to slice the boiled meat thin and saute it in butter. The sauteed meat, too, can be served with sauces or plain, with rice and other accompaniments.

Storing Octopus

If you find too much cooked octopus on your hands, you can freeze it with a little water just as you do any other seafood. It will keep for a year.

Says Walter, "Many years ago, my mother boiled octopus without tenderizing it. It was terribly tough, but we kids liked to chew it, and the flavor was there. Later, when I was gill-netting on Bristol Bay, Greek fishermen would tenderize octopus by whipping the tentacles on shore rocks. This seemed difficult to me, so I perfected the 2x4 method I now use. I have shown many people how to prepare octopus, and the sad thing is that they stop bringing it to me when they find out how good it tastes. Well, I never regret showing them my methods; every one of them breaks down now and then and brings me octopus."

Method II — Octopus Steak

Helen Blanchard decided that given a 40-pound (18 kg) octopus — "for free" — she could afford to throw away the mantle instead of cleaning it.

Method I is adapted from a story by Matthew Dick, "You Have to be Tough to Eat Octopus," which appeared in the Alaska-only edition of *ALASKA*® magazine, September 1977. Method II is excerpted from Helen Blanchard's story, "Octopus for Dinner, in The Cabin Friend, *ALASKA*® magazine, October 1978. Method III is reprinted from *Shellfish Cookbook*.

Below are two ways she prepared the tentacles. Note that she prepares the steaks without the prior boiling recommended by Walter Metroken and Matthew Dick. Instead, she peels the tentacles raw and then pounds the individual steaks to tenderize them. Difficult, but her result makes the effort seem worthwhile at least for a meal or two of steaks, while the rest of a large octopus might be prepared as in Method I.

With a sharp knife, I slit the skin and peeled each arm. Sounds easy, but just try it! Three hours later I had about 10 pounds (4.5 kg) of steaks the size of large scallops. The small arm tips I saved for canning.

Each steak was beaten *hard*. I wrapped the steaks in a cloth while beating to avoid having them all over the kitchen. I tried hitting them once with the hammer as I do abalone to relax the muscle, but they still had the texture of very tough beefsteak. After thorough pounding, I dipped them in flour and pan-broiled them in safflower oil. They came out very tender, delicately textured and quite sweet — every bit as delicious as lobster.

Method III — Start with A *Small* Octopus

For tender meat select a small octopus. The body has an outer layer called a mantle. This will give you a flat piece of tender meat that does not have to be pounded to tenderize. Blanch both the mantle and arms quickly in boiling water for a few seconds. Then peel off the skin; the suckers will come off with the skin. Pound the meat of the arms as you do abalone or beef. Cut into pieces several inches long. Simmer in your choice of seasoning until tender. It may be eaten without further preparation, or, if you prefer, cook it in various sauces, or brown it under the broiler after brushing it with butter.

Octopus Chowder

2 medium octopus tentacles
3 medium potatoes
1 small onion
1 cup (240 mL) water
1 quart (1 L) milk
1/4 cup (60 mL) butter
Salt and pepper to taste

►Cook octopus in boiling salted water for 10 minutes. Remove from heat and peel off tough white skin (similar to skinning a banana, though much tougher skin). Put skinned tentacles through food chopper, using medium fine, very sharp blade. If they escape the chopper blade the first time (and believe me, they will), pull them out and run them through again and again and again until they are well chopped. Peel potatoes and dice; grate onion. Brown both in butter over low heat. Add water and chopped octopus. Simmer until tender. Add milk and season to taste. Bring to eating temperature, garnish with chopped chives and serve. Serves six. Delicious . . . tastes something like extremely rich clam chowder but much better.
■ *Hattie Chase, Wrangell*
  PTA Cook Book, *Petersburg*

Alaska Octopus Gumbo

1/2 cup (120 mL) diced bacon
2 cups (480 mL) water
1 pint (480 mL) canned octopus, or fresh
  octopus steamed until tender
2 cups (480 mL) slightly undercooked
  steamed rice
1 pound (456 g) canned tomatoes
1 can okra
1/2 cup (120 mL) diced onions
1 green pepper, diced
1/4 teaspoon (1 mL) cayenne
1/2 cup (120 mL) diced celery
Salt and pepper to taste

►Boil bacon in water for 15 minutes, then add the rest of the ingredients. Simmer together for 10 minutes. Serve with warm cornbread. Serves four.
■ *Helen Blanchard, Ward Cove*
  "Octopus for Dinner," The Cabin Friend
  ALASKA® *magazine, October 1978*

Octopus Spanish Style

2 large or 4 small octopus tentacles
1 can (15 oz /or/ 425 g) tomato sauce or about
  2 cups (480 mL) whole tomatoes, chopped
1/2 small onion, chopped
1 teaspoon (5 mL) chili powder
Pepper and garlic powder to taste
1 cup (240 mL) raw rice, cooked separately

►Beat legs to tenderize. Boil for about 20 minutes in salted water. Slice. Heat frying pan and just enough fat to cover bottom. Fry onion. Add tomato sauce, chili powder, pepper, garlic powder. Let simmer one-half hour. Then add sliced octopus. Simmer another hour. Cook rice separately to accompany octopus dish. Makes six servings.
■ *Pauline Calugan*
  Island Edibles, *Sand Point*

Deep-Fried Octopus

►Cooking octopus (lots of them in Alaska) — skin the critter, lightly boil it, chunked up, pound it, then roll in egg, cracker crumbs and deep-fry.
■ *Bob Henning, Angoon*

Broiled Octopus

►Prepare in same manner as for deep-frying. Dip in melted butter and roll in fine bread crumbs, being sure to coat all surfaces. Salt and pepper. Broil three to four minutes approximately 5 inches (12.5 cm) from source of heat, turning once to brown evenly on both sides.

■ *Alice Johnstone*
   Seafood Secrets, *Sitka*

Gingered Octopus

►Skin octopus. Save tentacles and hood meat. Freeze meat (muscles relax as they freeze). Cut tentacles in diagonal slices, blot dry; bread, adding 1 teaspoon [5 mL] ginger to breading mixture. Fry in deep fat until brown. Serve with hot sauce, mustard or such.

■ *Janice Taylor*
   Cooking Up A Storm, *Homer*

Devil Fish
(Octopus)

►Dip the devil fish into boiling water until it begins to turn white. Take all the outside skin off. Then if you are going to fry it, cut the length of the legs into 3-inch (7.5 cm) strips and split it flat and pound it. Then roll it in flour that has been mixed with curry powder, salt and pepper. Deep-fry these pieces in grease until golden brown. Serve with potatoes or rice. To boil, just take the full length of legs and boil them in water until they turn red. Take out and serve with rice.

■ Tsimpshean Indian Island Cookbook
   Metlakatla

Marinated Octopus

2 cups (480 mL) octopus meat, sliced thinly
1/4 cup (60 mL) olive oil
1/4 cup (60 mL) lemon juice
1/2 teaspoon (2 mL) salt
1/4 teaspoon (1 mL) pepper

►Mix marinade, place sliced octopus in it and chill for three or four hours before serving.

■ *Gloria Petersen, FV Kruzof*
   Seafood Secrets , *Sitka*

Pan-Fried Ilgatha
(Octopus)

►Dredge with flour after cleaning. Fry lightly in hot fat. Be careful of the buttons as they hold water and will spatter! The flesh turns pink when done. They also can be boiled and served with melted butter.

■ Aleut Cookbook, *Saint Paul Island*

Batter-Fried Octopus

►Cut octopus into bite-sized pieces. Pound to break muscle. Make a batter of:

1 cup (240 mL) flour
2 teaspoons (10 mL) baking powder
1 teaspoon (5 mL) salt
1 egg, separated
1/2 cup (120 mL) lukewarm water
1 tablespoon (15 mL) cooking oil

►Sift dry ingredients into bowl. Drop egg yolk into center. Add water and oil. Fold in stiffly beaten egg white. Dip octopus pieces into batter and fry at 400°F (205°C) until golden brown. The above batter may be used for fried fish, such as halibut, salmon, red snapper, lingcod and rock cod. Cut into bite-sized pieces, fry a few minutes.

■ Tsimpshean Indian Island Cookbook
   Metlakatla

Octopus and Gravy

►Cut tentacles of octopus in small pieces after cleaning. Add onions and fry. Add water and make a gravy. Serve over rice.

■ Tsimpshean Indian Island Cookbook
   Metlakatla

Octopus Italian Style

3 cups (720 mL) sliced octopus
3 tablespoons (45 mL) olive oil
1 onion, diced
1 garlic clove, minced
1 can (6 oz /or/ 170 g) tomato paste
1 can (29 oz /or/ 826 g) tomatoes
2 tablespoons (30 mL) minced parsley
Salt and pepper

►Saute onion and garlic lightly in olive oil. Add tomato paste and tomatoes and stir to break up tomatoes and blend thoroughly. Add seasonings and octopus meat. Cover and simmer gently for at least two hours. Serve over freshly boiled spaghetti.

■ *Alice Johnstone*
   Seafood Secrets, *Sitka*

How inky is octopus ink? "I can do a whole painting with one pure drop of octopus ink," says Alaskan artist Diana Tillion. "It is like stretching a rubber band, it just goes and goes." The ink from four or five octopuses will supply her for a year . . . and the rest of the octopus joins the family for dinner.

SEA CUCUMBER

This story by Richard Dauenhauer is from ALASKA® *magazine ["Stalking Alaska's Yein," Alaska-only edition, July 1975].*

The sheltered coves of Southeastern Alaska abound with many 'incredible edibles,' but few are more incredible than the sea cucumber, known to the Tlingits as yein (rhymes with vein), and to biologists as *Stichopus californicus*.

A denizen of gentle tide pools, the sea cucumber looks like an enormous slug. Its feel is better left to the reader's imagination. The yein lies along the bottom of pools and must be scooped up quickly, brought to the surface, and taken in hand before it stiffens and no longer droops over the stick.

The creature's first line of defense would appear to be its appearance. But, since his average attacker is more concerned with good eating than good looks, the yein has also developed the ability to repulse his enemy by throwing out his internal organs. While the predator is disengaging himself from the disgorged insides of the yein, the prey slips away and, holing himself up, grows a new set of digestive organs.

Preparation Tips: The captured yein is cleaned by cutting the ends, squeezing out the insides, opening the yein and stripping the white fillets from the skin. The fillets make great eating when fried very quickly or cooked up like clam chowder.

Several Ways To Prepare Sea Cucumber

►Collect sea cucumbers at extreme low tide, June, July or August. Cut off ends. Squeeze out insides; wash clean. Split lengthwise and peel off outer skin, leaving the long white muscles. Ways to use:
• Chop for chowder.
• Chop and scramble in omelet.
• Grind for patties, mix with flour and egg batter.
• Dip in egg, then flour or bread crumbs and fry quickly.
• Good in chop suey.
■ *Out of Alaska's Kitchens*

Fried Sea Cucumbers #1

►You need a stick to get a sea cucumber or go out at low tide. They are drying on the beach. To prepare, slit the side jacket and pull the white meat out. It takes 20 to make a good meal. Fry in hot grease with onions and celery. Make a gravy with a little flour. The meat is so white and tender.
■ Tsimpshean Indian Island Cookbook
   Metlakatla

Fried Sea Cucumbers #2

►Blanch the meat in boiling salted water for five seconds to remove the slime and firm the meat. Do not cook it. Remove from water and roll in bread crumbs or corn meal and fry it quickly in hot fat. The cooking should be fast and to a golden brown. Slow frying or overcooking makes it tough and gummy. The meat may also be cut into bits and used in chowder. *Note:* Cleaning sea cucumbers barehanded may turn your hands a reddish brown. This will not wash off but will fade away in a couple of days.
■ Shellfish Cookbook

Secret Ingredient Dip
For "the ultimate in seafood dips"

►Catch a sea cucumber with a dip net, spear it with a pike pole, or jig it with a halibut hook. The flavor is well worth the effort. Rip it open, remove the long, thin white muscles that run lengthwise down the middle, and discard all the rest. Cook muscles for a few minutes until they look done, then mince, grind or whip them in a blender. Drain and use as follows:

1 sea cucumber, prepared as directed
1 cup (240 mL) heavy cream, whipped
1 package (3 oz /or/ 85 g) cream cheese
Salt, pepper and grated onion to taste

►Combine all ingredients. Chill. Serve in a bowl surrounded by potato chips or crackers. If you don't tell your guests what the "secret ingredient" is until they've tasted the dip, they'll wish you had caught two sea cucumbers and doubled the recipe.
■ *Anonymous, Ketchikan*
   The Alaskan Camp Cook

Boiled Sea Cucumber

►Catch. Cut one end off and squeeze the insides out. Then boil it in the skins until it turns dark. It will shrink a lot. It is a chewy delight and is not used for a regular meal but just bites are taken off as a treat between meals.
■ Tsimpshean Indian Island Cookbook
   Metlakatla

Sea Cucumber Fritters

Clara Peratrovich is from the village of Klawock on Prince of Wales Island. Through a school program called Traditional Foods in Science, she hands on her skill in the use of subsistence foods to the village children, and in other demonstrations, such as a workshop sponsored by the Southeast Alaska Native Women's Conference in Ketchikan, she shares her expertise with adults as well. Some of her knowledge has been collected on video-tape and in booklet form by the Ketchikan Indian Corporation.

About 12 large yein (sea cucumber), cleaned and ground
2 eggs
3 stalks celery, ground or chopped
1 small onion, ground or chopped
1-1/2 cups (360 mL) fine bread crumbs or 1 cup (240 mL) pancake mix
1 teaspoon (5 mL) salt
1/2 teaspoon (2 mL) pepper

►Mix ground sea cucumber, eggs, celery, onions, bread crumbs or pancake mix with seasonings. The mixture will be thick enough to spoon onto a hot griddle. Fry until golden brown on one side, turn and fry the other side.

■ Clara Peratrovich, Klawock
  Foods From The Sea

Sea Cucumber Chowder

In his book about how the Haida of past and present generations use nature's food resources, Robert Cogo tells of being on a gas boat anchored in a small cove to wait out a storm. Because provisions in the galley were low, the crew began to look elsewhere for food. . . .

►In just a few minutes, we scooped up about 10 sea cucumbers. We peeled the outer skin away, leaving a strip of white meat much like clam. We diced this into small pieces and soon had enough for a nice chowder. We cut potato, onion and bacon into small pieces and boiled them in water for about 10 minutes, then added the cup of diced sea cucumber and boiled it for another 5 minutes. After serving the chowder in bowls, we mixed in a little canned milk. This chowder cannot be beat for flavor and in my estimation is better than clams.

■ Robert Cogo
  Haida Food Gathering and Preparation

SEA URCHIN

Can't afford "virgin sturgeon" caviar? Never mind. If you live near any of Alaska's 33,904 miles of shoreline, you probably have access to a goodie that some say is more delicious than the finest caviar —the eggs of the sea urchin, a creature which is abundant in the shallow waters of most of Alaska's sea coasts.

And so if you must feed a caviar taste with a cabbage-soup pocketbook, better find out when the sea urchins in your area are carrying full egg sacs. Along both the east and west coasts of the United States, the best gathering time appears to be mid-summer through the end of the year. In Southeastern, the usual spawning time is April.

Preparation Tips: The "caviar" or gonads are the only edible part of the sea urchin, but both male and female gonads are edible. However, the brighter the orange color — as in the female — the better the taste is thought to be. Gathering the roe is rather like shucking a very hard-shelled, hard-cooked chicken egg — easy enough if you have a hammer. Turn the sea urchin on its back, crack the test (the protective skeleton) in several places, pull off the lower part along with the viscera, loosen the egg sac from each of its five points and scoop it out with your finger.

Eat the roe raw, spread on bread or crackers and sprinkled with lemon. Unfortunately, the eggs from one individual will go about as far toward providing a meal as one hen would do feeding daily breakfast to a family of 10. It takes several sea urchins to produce a cupful (240 mL) of roe. But if you've priced sturgeon roe recently, you won't mind the effort. A cupful can go a long way.

Agugnas
(Sea urchins)

►Sea urchins are gathered among the seaweeds whenever there is a low tide. They are opened with a thin stone or a knife. The eggs from the sea urchin are scooped out with the thumb and eaten raw. The sea urchins with light color are the ones which are good eating. Those which have a dark color are not very good to eat. They are said to be skinny.

■ *Moses Dirks and Lydia Dirks*
  Niigugim Qalgadangis — Atkan Food
  Recipe reprinted from Aleutian Wind, *1979*

"Barbecued" Urchin

►Sea urchins are round spiny creatures that look like red, green or purple pin cushions. They live on rocks or kelp in tide pools or shallow waters near the low tide mark. All sea urchins are edible. Their bright orange eggs are considered a delicacy and eaten raw. . . . Or you can throw the whole urchin into your campfire, cook it until the spines burn, then crack it open.

■ *Alaska Tidelines*
  Volume II, Number 8, May 1980

Sea Eggs

►Gather sea urchins in the spring of the year. Scrape out the yellow part from the inside of the shell and serve it raw.

■ *Aleut Cookbook,* Saint Paul Island

SQUID

Squid is another unlikely shellfish that those in the know say "tastes like abalone." Its advantage over many other shellfish with that sought-after taste: it requires no pounding or grinding to make it suitable for the human jaw. Moderate-sized squid are also reasonably easy to clean.

Squid have either eight or ten "arms" or tentacles, two of which are distinctly different from the others, ending in something roughly like fingerless palms which are used to grab hold of prey. Squid range in size from more than 60 feet (18 m) long to less than an inch (2.5 cm). But most are under 12 inches (30 cm). And none, to date, has rivaled Jules Vernes's creation.

Cleaning Squid

To clean a moderate-sized squid, first hold it under running water and pull off the speckled gelatinous skin that covers the mantle or hood. Then, holding tentacles in one hand and mantle in the other, gently pull the two apart. Both are edible after shell structures and viscera are removed.

Inside the mantle is a long transparent piece of shell sometimes called a "pen" or "sword." Pull it out and discard, then rinse away the contents of the mantle, pulling off any parts easily removed. This includes the ink sac — which most Mediterranean cooks leave intact, saying that it adds a richness to sauces in which squid is marinated and cooked. Discard or keep, do as you wish, or save it to supply your own pen. The easiest way to clean the mantle is to turn it inside out, as you would invert the fingers of a rubber glove. Clean, rinse and turn right side out again for cooking.

Cut tentacles away from head and viscera, discarding the latter. Between the tentacles is a hard parrotlike beak which can be popped out or removed with the point of a knife.

Rinse everything again.

Cooking Squid

You may either parboil squid or marinate it several hours in equal parts olive oil and lemon juice (fresh is best) or wine vinegar, adding seasonings such as fresh or dried oregano or dill weed, if you like. After the marination, the mantle may be stuffed with a favorite bread or rice stuffing, the opening secured shut and the whole drizzled with some of the marinade and baked for about 30 to 45 minutes.

Or, slice the mantle into strips or crosswise rings. Dip tentacles and rings into flour and saute with garlic in butter. Squid is also good dipped in batter and deep-fried. Some good batters to try are in Chapter 1.

To parboil squid for use in salads or to prepare for further cooking, slice it, as above, and drop it into rapidly boiling water to cook for no longer than a minute after the water returns to the boil. Scoop out with a slotted spoon and plunge into cold water to stop the cooking. Drain well. To use the meat in salads, marinate it several hours in your favorite oil-based dressing. Adding onion and green pepper rings to the marinade would not be amiss.

And the next time you see "calamary" or *Tantonnet* on the menu of a fancy restaurant, order it . . . and ask for the recipe. It will be dressed up squid.

Storing Squid

Cleaned, raw squid may be stored in the refrigerator in a tightly covered container for one or two days. Or, it may be frozen for up to two months. Pack it in freezer bags, expel air and seal tightly.

Garden Squid Chowder

3 pounds (1.4 kg) squid
2 tablespoons (30 mL) butter
1 cup (240 mL) chopped onion
1 cup (240 mL) sliced fresh mushrooms
1 cup (240 mL) julienne carrots
3 cups (720 mL) chicken bouillon
1 cup (240 mL) sour cream
2 tablespoons (30 mL) flour
1/2 teaspoon (2 mL) dill weed
1/2 teaspoon (2 mL) salt
Dash white pepper
Chopped parsley

►Clean squid, wash, pat dry and cut into small rings. Melt butter and saute squid and vegetables

five minutes. Add bouillon and simmer 30 minutes until squid is tender. Combine remaining ingredients, except parsley, and blend into soup. Cook, stirring constantly, until thickened. Serve garnished with parsley. Six servings.
■ Shellfish-A-Plenty

Squid with Tomatoes

2 pounds (1 kg) squid
3 tablespoons (45 mL) olive oil
2 garlic cloves, finely minced
1/2 teaspoon (2 mL) salt
1/8 teaspoon (0.5 mL) pepper
1/8 teaspoon (0.5 mL) oregano
1/2 cup (120 mL) dry sherry
2 fresh tomatoes, peeled, seeded and finely
    chopped, or 1 cup (240 mL) drained,
    chopped, canned tomatoes
1 tablespoon (15 mL) tomato paste
1 tablespoon (15 mL) chopped parsley
2 cups (240 mL) cooked rice

►Clean squid, wash, pat dry and cut into small pieces. Fry garlic in hot oil one or two minutes. Add squid, cover and simmer five minutes. Stir in remaining ingredients except 2 teaspoons (10 mL) parsley and the cooked rice. Simmer, uncovered, 15 minutes, stirring occasionally, until squid is tender. Serve with rice and garnish with remaining parsley. Four servings.
■ Shellfish-A-Plenty

SEA MAMMALS

Marine mammals — such as seal, walrus, whale and sea lion — provide an essential part of the diet of many of Alaska's Native people. Oils rendered from some of the animals, particularly seal, have long been used as a preservative for foods gathered seasonally, such as berries and wild vegetables, and as a dipping sauce for meats and fish, especially those that have been dried.

Whale steak is said by many to be the most delicious variety of steak, and the organ meats of some marine mammals are prized delicacies.

That these excellent meats are table fare for few other Alaskans is less a function of taste and availability than it is of law. The federal Marine Mammal Protection Act of 1972 made it illegal for any but an Alaskan Eskimo, Aleut or Indian to hunt any marine mammal. While the state may regain management of some species — and some are far from

endangered — the rule for most nonNatives who'd like to sample corned walrus or roast hindquarter of seal is likely to remain a variation of that old step-by-stepper that begins, "First catch a . . ." whatever. Only in this case, Step 1 is "First find a qualified hunter to invite you to dinner."

Polar bear is also protected under the Act. But, as an item for the table, its meat is like other bear, and recipes for it are in Book Two.

Fried Seal Liver

►Dredge pieces of seal liver in flour. Fry lightly in hot fat. Onions may be fried with it if desired. Aleuts like soy sauce with it, too. It is quite a delicacy and tastes better than the finest calves' liver!
■ Aleut Cookbook, *Saint Paul Island*

Sea Lion Soup

1 pound (456 g) sea lion meat
6 cups (1.45 L) water
Salt and pepper
Petruskie (wild parsley)
3 or 4 stalks celery cut up, tops, too
1 onion, chopped
1/2 cup (120 mL) raw rice
1 potato
1 teaspoon (5 mL) Worcestershire
2 tablespoons (30 mL) flour
Water to make a paste with flour

►Boil meat in water for 45 minutes. Add other ingredients except for flour and water and cook another 45 minutes. Make a paste of flour and water; add to soup and cook until meat is tender and soup is thickened slightly.
■ Aleut Cookbook, *Saint Paul Island*

Sea Lion Meatballs and Spaghetti

2 pounds (1 kg) sea lion meat, ground
1/2 cup (120 mL) olive or salad oil
4 medium onions, chopped
4 cloves garlic, minced
2 teaspoons (10 mL) salt
1/2 teaspoon (2 mL) pepper
2 cans (16 oz /or/ 456 g, each) tomatoes or
    4 cans (8 oz /or/ 228 g, each) tomato puree
4 cans (6 oz /or/ 170 g, each) tomato paste
4 teaspoons (20 mL) Worcestershire
1 pound (456 g) spaghetti

►Brown meat in hot oil; add onions and garlic and cook briefly. Then add all other ingredients except spaghetti and simmer over low heat two hours. Pour over spaghetti which has been cooked and drained. Serves 12.
■ Out of Alaska's Kitchens

Roasted Seal Meat

►Remove all fat from seal meat. Rinse meat thoroughly and soak in salted water — 2 tablespoons (30 mL) salt per gallon (3.8 L) of water — for 30 minutes. Drain and let it drip for a few minutes. Cut into pieces with bones; roll every piece in flour — in a pan or bowl, in case you might leave corners without flour. Place in a roasting pan, add onion, chopped or dry flakes, as you prefer, with gravy mix or salt and pepper. Put fresh potatoes alongside the meat in the pan and cover with lid or foil. Roast for 1-1/2 hours in a 375°F (190°C) oven.
■ *Elfie Apatiki*
    Community Education Program Cookbook
    Gambell, Saint Lawrence Island

Curried Seal Roast

1 seal hindquarter
1 teaspoon (5 mL) salt
Mixed pickling spices
1 large onion
3 cups (720 mL) water
1-1/4 cups (300 mL) vinegar
3/4 cup (180 mL) flour
1 teaspoon (5 mL) curry powder
1 teaspoon (5 mL) ginger
1 teaspoon (5 mL) garlic powder

►Place hindquarter in roasting pan and sprinkle with salt and pickling spices. Slice the onion in rings and scatter over the roast. Cover and put into the oven at 400°F (205°C) for two hours or more, depending on size. When the roast is almost done, mix the vinegar, water, flour, curry, ginger and garlic powder like gravy and pour it into the meat juices in the roasting pan and stir well. Then cover roast again and cook for another 15 to 20 minutes. Serve with rice. Six servings.
■ *Mary Duncan, Angoon*

Oknuk
Three versions of a blood soup recipe from Hooper Bay

#1
*4 to 12 cups (1 to 2.85 L) tayahuk**
1 to 2 cups (240 to 480 mL) seal blood
1/4 to 1 cup (60 to 240 mL) seal oil
1/2 to 1 gallon (1.9 to 3.8 L) water or
    cooking broth

#2
1-1/2 sacs fresh lingcod roe
*16 cups (3.8 L) "mouse nuts"***
1 cup (240 mL) seal oil
4 cups (1 L) seal blood
4 quarts (3.8 L) water or cooking broth

#3
3 cups (720 mL) dried tomcod roe
*15 cups (3.6 L) "mouse nuts"***
2 cups (480 mL) seal blood
1/2 cup (120 mL) seal oil
1-1/2 gallons (5.7 L) water or cooking broth

■ The Alaska Dietary Survey

*Tayahuk is the Eskimo name for an aquatic plant which grows in shallow tundra ponds and ditches. Its common English name is mare's-tail.
**Mouse nuts are bits of edible root which rodents collect and bury in underground caches for their winter food supply. The roots of cotton grass are common "mouse nuts."

Early Day Preparation Techniques

More than two decades have passed since The Alaska Dietary Survey was prepared. While some information in it is dated, it remains a valuable record of survival techniques perfected through the centuries. Here is its report of how seal, oogruk (bearded seal), beluga whale and baleen whale and walrus were used "in times past."

Most of the meat from these common sea mammals is eaten either fresh, cooked or raw, frozen or dried. The greater share of the summer catch is air-dried.

Dried meat is usually eaten uncooked with seal oil, the rib meat especially being enjoyed in this way. Half-dried meat is usually cooked; thoroughly dried meat, only occasionally.

Specialty products include the following:

1. The *liver* from the smaller varieties of seal is especially relished. It is eaten either raw-frozen with seal oil or cooked, usually fried, or it may be "soured." This latter process involves placing the liver in a dish and then setting it aside in a cool place for about a month. When sufficiently soured, it is eaten raw with seal oil.

2. Well cleaned *seal stomachs* are sometimes eaten. On Diomede they are sometimes filled with walrus blubber and boiled.

3. *Seal kidneys* may be eaten either fresh, raw-frozen or diced and cooked with liver in seal oil.

4. *Seal heads* are boiled and all parts eaten.

5. The *seal intestines*, well cleaned, are often eaten as *kwak* (raw-frozen). They may also be boiled in water or cooked in oil. They are sometimes dried and eaten either raw or cooked by boiling or frying. The cleaned, chopped *oogruk* intestines are sometimes mixed with berries. Seal oil may be added or not as desired. . . .

6. *Seal oil* is considered by many Eskimos the best of the sea mammal blubber oils for eating purposes. The careful Eskimo housewife stores it in clean barrels or seal pokes in a cold place so that it stays light colored, free from dirt and other extraneous matter.

   Seal oil is used to make "poke" fish or meat; it is used in making *agutuk* and other mixtures; it is used mostly as a condiment or dip for frozen and dried meats and fishes; it is occasionally used medicinally, sometimes taken by the tablespoon for colds or by the cupful as a cathartic.

7. *Seal and beluga flippers* are considered great delicacies by most of the coastal Eskimos. They are enjoyed fresh, raw. They may also be buried in grass-lined ground pits and allowed to sour or putrefy. The usual method is to line the sides and bottom of a 1-1/2- to 2-1/2-foot-deep [45 to 75 cm] pit with grass sufficient to prevent the meat from making contact with the ground. The flippers are thoroughly rubbed with oil and laid in the pit. They are first well covered with plain blubber and then with a strip of blubber and meat from where the two meet on the carcass. This is then covered with grass, next with seal skin and then wood or dirt and left until the skin and hair from the flippers peels off easily.

   Sometimes the clean flippers are laid in a clean *oogruk* skin (hair side on the outside), with plenty of blubber added and then the skin is folded over all. It is then placed in a grass-lined pit and covered to protect from the sun.

   Eskimos emphasize that great care must be taken to protect the flippers from sun and heat both when butchering and during storage in the ground pit. Such care is especially important during a warm dry arctic summer. The pit site must be selected carefully, preferably where there is some shade. Eskimos report that buried flippers can cause fatal illness unless these precautions are taken. . . .

8. *Beluga muktuk* consists of the outside skin of the beluga whale which is about 1/2 to 3/4 inch (1.25 to 1.9 cm) thick with about 1/2 inch (1.25 cm) of attached blubber. It is considered a delicacy by the Eskimos who hunt this animal in the Kotzebue Sound. Long, 3- to 4-inch-wide (7.5 to 10 cm) strips, deeply knife scored, are hung on racks and left to dry a day or two. They are then boiled a long time until the skin is soft. After removal from the cooking water, they are allowed to drain with the blubber side down, and again air-dried on racks for another day or two. In the meantime, the bulk of the blubber is heated in large containers to render the oil. The cooled oil is poured over the properly dried *muktuk*, completely covering it. The *muktuk* is then ready for either immediate eating or storage.

Baleen Whale

The baleen whale is caught more or less regularly at Barrow and Point Hope. Point Hope usually gets one to five animals each year. At Barrow the yearly catch varies from none to 20 or more.

Whale meat is never dried. That not immediately consumed is stored in special underground pits (at

Barrow) or abandoned sod igloos (Point Hope) which remain cold the year round and therefore provide effective storage.

Whale meat is eaten mostly as *kwak* (raw-frozen), but it may also be cooked on occasion. Other parts of the animal cooked and used for human food include part of the *small intestine, the kidneys, the heart,* and *the muktuk* (outside skin with attached blubber). *Whale muktuk,* when fresh, is usually eaten boiled. When a little older, it is generally eaten raw, as the older skin is considered too tough to cook. Part of the blubber may also be used to obtain a clear oil. This is done by cutting the whale blubber into pieces, scoring it with a knife, and packing the blubber in a barrel and letting it stand. The oil, rendered by autolysis, is stored in a cold place.

Whale meat is sometimes made into a special dish called *mikiyuk,* a soured product. This product is made especially for "Nullikituk," the annual whale feast, held every June at both Barrow and Point Hope. . . .

Walrus

At Point Hope and other arctic coastal villages where only a limited number of walrus are caught or where they are only available in certain years, the meat is generally eaten either frozen (*kwak*) or boiled. The blubber is usually cooked and eaten with the cooked meat or skin. But on Diomede, Saint Lawrence and King Islands and at Wales, where walrus is a much more important food, there are naturally many more methods of preparation. . . .

On both Saint Lawrence and Diomede Islands the meat from walrus caught in May and June is cut into strips and air-dried. This dried meat is used throughout the summer, fall and early winter until walrus and seal hunting is again possible, usually in November. Old dried walrus meat is then stored in seal oil. . . .

On Saint Lawrence Island walrus skins not needed or desirable for boat covers are rolled into huge balls, sometimes weighing up to 100 pounds (45 kg), and stored in caches as an emergency food in case the walrus catch during the winter is not sufficient to meet their food needs. If the skins are not needed as an emergency human food, they are eventually fed to the dogs.

One researcher reports that the Eskimos of Diomede Island commonly eat *walrus skin* fresh boiled throughout the season, but skin soured during storage is also relished and is eaten either raw, frozen or cooked.

Sea Lion Hamburger

2 pounds (1 kg) sea lion meat, ground
2 slices bacon (optional) may be ground with
*   the meat*
1 medium-sized onion, chopped
2 teaspoons (10 mL) salt
1/2 teaspoon (2 mL) pepper

►Add chopped onion, salt and pepper to the ground meat. Make patties 1/2 inch (1.25 cm) thick and 3 inches (7.5 cm) in diameter. Broil or fry.

Or, prepare as above; place a slice of cheese on each patty after one side is done and the burger has been turned.
■ Out of Alaska's Kitchens

Two Ways To Fix Seal Liver

►Seal liver is the best of the wild animals that are edible. The liver must be cooked fresh. The seal meat and liver do not taste fishy at all. They have a taste all their own. If you cook them with the right seasoning, they are very good. Here are two ways to fix the liver:
- Slice the liver into small pieces, season with salt, pepper, Accent and seafood seasoning. Fry in butter. Chop up one medium onion and dice some bacon. Add and cook together.
- Slice the seal liver for steaks. Season with salt, pepper, Accent and caraway seed. Let it stand for a while. Then dip the sliced liver into Krusteaz pancake mix and fry in hot fat. Serve with fried bacon or fried onions.

■ *Kaa T'eix (Mary Howard Pelayo)*
   Kaa T'eix's Cook Book, *Mount Edgecumbe*

Seal Liver and Wheat Germ Saute

1 pound (456 g) seal liver, sliced thin and
*   soaked in water to which 1 tablespoon*
*   (15 mL) vinegar has been added*
6 tablespoons (90 mL) vegetable oil
1 onion, sliced thin
1 cup (240 mL) wheat germ
1/3 cup (80 mL) grated Parmesan
Salt and pepper to taste

►Heat 3 tablespoons (45 mL) of oil in skillet and saute onions until clear. Remove to hot platter and set aside. Mix wheat germ, Parmesan, salt and pepper. Heat remaining oil in skillet. Dredge liver in wheat germ mixture and saute over medium heat until blood begins to show on top. Turn carefully and saute on other side. Do not overcook as liver will be dry. Serves four or five.
■ *Mamie Jensen, Juneau*

Salted Seal Meat Stew

2 pounds (1 kg) salted seal meat
Water to cover
1 large can (29 oz /or/ 826 g) tomatoes
2 medium-sized diced potatoes
1 onion, chopped
2 tablespoons (30 mL) butter
Salt and pepper to taste

►Soak meat overnight to wash off salt. Wash in warm water until water is clear. Cut meat into pieces, cover with water and boil. Skim off the blood as it comes to the surface. Drain water, add fresh water and boil 45 minutes. Add other ingredients and cook until potatoes are tender. A spoonful of flour-and-water paste can be added for thickening if desired.
■ Aleut Cookbook, *Saint Paul Island*

Seal Brains au Gratin

►First, wash seal brains thoroughly in salt water, removing loose skin and any blood. Soak the brains in fresh cold water for one hour, changing the water two or three times. Then, place brains in a saucepan, cover with clean water, bring to a boil and boil slowly for 15 minutes. Drain and pat dry with a clean cloth. Proceed:

2 seal brains, cleaned and cooked as directed
3 tablespoons (45 mL) butter, divided
1 tablespoon (15 mL) flour
1 cup (240 mL) milk
1/2 teaspoon (2 mL) salt
1/4 teaspoon (1 mL) pepper
2 tablespoons (30 mL) grated cheese, divided
1/2 cup (120 mL) dry bread crumbs
4 slices hot buttered toast

►Cut the brains in bite-sized pieces. Melt butter in saucepan, stir in flour well. Then add milk and cook and stir over moderate heat until sauce thickens. Add salt, pepper and 1 tablespoon (15 mL) of the grated cheese. Stir until smooth. Add brains, mixing in lightly. Pour into a greased casserole, sprinkle bread crumbs and remaining grated cheese on top. Dot with remaining butter. Place casserole in moderately hot oven, 375°F (190°C), and brown quickly. Serve on buttered toast.
■ Northern Cookbook *(adapted)*

Seal Casserole

Seal meat
Whole-wheat flour
Drippings, bacon
Onion flakes (or fresh onions)
3 whole cloves

Dash of thyme
Water
Salt and pepper

►Select a choice cut of young seal meat and divide into 2-inch (5 cm) chunks. Dredge in seasoned flour after all the natural fat has been removed. Brown the chunks in bacon drippings; then place in a casserole and add the onions, cloves and thyme. Add enough water to almost cover the seal. Cook in a slow oven for two hours — about 300°F (150°C).
■ *Helen A. White, Anchorage*
What's Cookin' in Alaska

Baked Seal Hindquarter

Seal hindquarter
3/4 teaspoon (3 mL) salt
Dash of pepper
1/2 cup (120 mL) water
1 large onion, sliced
3 medium carrots
4 stalks celery

►Put the seal hindquarter into a roasting pan and sprinkle the salt and pepper over it. Pour the water into the pan for steam and cover. Cook in oven for one hour and then add onion, the carrots, sliced in the middle and cut in half, and the celery stalks, halved. Peeled potatoes cut in half can also be added if desired. Put back into the oven and cook for one hour more or until done. Can be served with rice or potatoes. Six or eight servings.
■ *Courtesy, Vivian James, Angoon*

Arctic Muktuk Chowder

1 can (20 oz /or/ 570 g) muktuk, chopped
8 tablespoons (120 mL) olive oil
8 tablespoons (120 mL) diced bacon
2 large onions, chopped
2 leeks, chopped
8 quarts (7.6 L) water
2 teaspoons (10 mL) curry powder
2 teaspoons (10 mL) thyme
4 teaspoons (20 mL) salt
1 teaspoon (5 mL) marjoram
4 bay leaves
8 large potatoes, diced
3 large green peppers, chopped
8 tomatoes, peeled and chopped
1 tablespoon (15 mL) parsley, chopped
1 tablespoon (15 mL) chives, chopped
1 teaspoon (5 mL) Worcestershire

►Place olive oil in a heavy pot, heat and saute the bacon, chopped onion and leeks until golden brown.

Pour the water into the pot, then add curry

powder, thyme, salt, marjoram and bay leaves. Bring to a boil.

Add the diced potatoes, peppers, tomatoes, parsley and chives and boil for about 30 minutes.

Add the muktuk and Worcestershire and let cook another five minutes. Serve with hot biscuits. Serves eight.

■ Northern Cookbook

Kukleetka
(Cutlet)

1-1/2 pounds (0.70 kg) sea lion meat
1 onion, chopped
2 strips raw bacon
1 slice dry bread
1 fresh green pepper or 1 tablespoon (15 mL)
*   pepper flakes*
1/2 cup (120 mL) milk
Salt and pepper
1 tablespoon (15 mL) Worcestershire
1/2 teaspoon (2 mL) parsley flakes
1 egg
Accent, a dash
Meat tenderizer, a dash
1/4 teaspoon (1 mL) garlic salt
1 can (8 oz /or/ 228 g) tomato sauce and
*   1/2 can water*
2 tablespoons (30 mL) flour
Butter

►Soak meat in plain water overnight. Trim off fat. Grind meat together with onions, bacon and bread. Add other ingredients except for flour, tomato sauce, water and butter. Form meat into balls and roll in flour. Place a small piece of butter on top of each meatball. Bake at 350°F (180°C) for 45 minutes. Pour tomato sauce and water over meat while cooking. Good served with rice.

■ Aleut Cookbook, *Saint Paul Island*

Seal Flippers

►The flippers are really a treat when they are cooked in an open fire. You just drop them in hot charcoals and leave them there until they are cooked. Or they can be taken out of the fire when the fur is burned off and boiled with seasoning of salt and pepper. Seal flippers remind me of pickled pigs feet — about the same texture, too.

■ *Kaa T'eix (Mary Howard Pelayo)*
   Kaa T'eix's Cook Book, *Mount Edgecumbe*

Boiled Seal

►Aleuts used to braid the cleaned intestines of the seal with seal meat. Either fur or hair seal was used. It was braided together and then boiled.

Seal stomachs were stuffed with seal meat, rice, onions and spices. When it was cooked, it was sliced and served. Liver and hearts were also cooked this way. When boiling this in a pot, Aleuts tell the story of the stomach coming apart and the contents exploding all over their kitchen!

■ Aleut Cookbook, *Saint Paul Island*

Fried Sea Lion Liver

Sea lion liver
24 bacon slices
2 medium-sized onions
Salt and pepper

►Soak liver overnight in water with small amount of soda added. Drain. Slice thin. Season with salt and pepper. Fry bacon strips. Roll liver in flour and cook in bacon fat until done. Cook onion rings in bacon fat and serve over liver with bacon strips.

■ Out of Alaska's Kitchens

Studen
(Head cheese)

1 sea lion flipper
2 onions
2 carrots
2 stalks celery
1 green pepper
6 tablespoons (90 mL) vinegar
Salt and pepper
6 cups (1.45 L) water
Dash of meat tenderizer
Dash of Accent
2 bay leaves
1 tablespoon (15 mL) Worcestershire
2 dill pickles or 3 tablespoons (45 mL)
*   pickle relish*
1/2 cup (120 mL) pitted black olives
2 hard-cooked eggs

►Skin the flipper, removing the hair. Cut it up and soak overnight in plain water; drain. Place flipper in large pot and cover with water. Add salt. Boil for 1-1/2 hours. Drain meat and run cold water on it to cool it. Grind meat with vegetables; add vinegar, salt, pepper, water and spices. Cook in covered pot for 30 minutes, stirring often. Chop pickles, olives and eggs and add to meat mixture. Place cheesecloth in shallow pan, letting cloth hang over edges. Pour in meat mixture. Tie edges of cloth and drain some of the juice out. Refrigerate until firm. Lift out of pan and remove cheesecloth. Slice while cold and serve with crackers. Lemon juice, vinegar or ketchup may be served with the studen.

■ Aleut Cookbook, *Saint Paul Island*

On Saint Lawrence Island, mukluk *is giant or bearded seal. For both the following recipes, the cook suggests rinsing the meat thoroughly and soaking it in salted water before it is ground. Use 2 tablespoons (30 mL) salt per gallon (3.8 L) of water. Drain well, chop or grind the meat and proceed.*

Mukluk Meat Loaf

1 pound (456 g) chopped or ground
  mukluk meat
1 egg or 3 tablespoons (45 mL) powdered egg
1 cup (240 mL) rolled oats
1/4 cup (60 mL) flour
1 cup (240 mL) canned peas with juice
1/2 teaspoon (2 mL) salt
1/4 teaspoon (1 mL) pepper

►Mix all ingredients thoroughly. Put in greased loaf pan. Bake for 20 to 30 minutes at 450°F (230°C). Walrus meat may be used in the recipe, but it requires longer baking, about 45 minutes.
■ *Elfie Apatiki*
  Community Education Program Cookbook
  Gambell, Saint Lawrence Island

Mukluk Burgers

1/2 pound (228 g) ground or chopped
  mukluk meat
1-1/2 tablespoons (23 mL) onion flakes
1/2 cup (120 mL) rolled oats
1/4 cup (60 mL) flour
1 teaspoon (5 mL) salt
1/4 teaspoon (1 mL) black pepper

►Mix all ingredients very thoroughly in a medium-sized bowl. Make into patties and fry in fat for 10 to 15 minutes. If walrus meat is used, cooking time should be increased to 20 minutes.
■ *Elfie Apatiki*
  Community Education Program Cookbook
  Gambell, Saint Lawrence Island

Rendering Seal Oil

Well-prepared, properly stored seal oil is sweet and clear, a wonderful fat useful in many ways — as a dip for foods such as dried fish; as a cooking oil; as a preservative bath for berries and other foods that protects them from air and retards mold.

Treats such as doughnuts and puff breads that are fried in seal oil come out with crackly sweet edges and not a trace of greasiness on the inside. Fresh seal oil is also a prized ingredient for making agutuk *or Eskimo Ice Cream, as in several recipes to be found in Chapter 11.*

The following methods for rendering the oil come from the childhood memories of several women who now live in Homer, but who grew up in other areas of Alaska — Annie Johnson, in Iliamna; Dolly Spencer, Kotzebue; Felicia Tetpon, at Shaktoolik; Helena Andree, in Dillingham. The most common method is simply to allow the chunks of seal fat to turn to oil almost unaided; that is, without boiling.

Please note that most of the women mention keeping the fat in a cool place during the rendering process and afterward — unless they want oil to use right away. Then they put the fat in a warmer place just until it gives off the amount they need.

While pure fat is not a place where bacteria grows easily, according to the Cooperative Extension Service at the University of Alaska, to be on the safe side, cut all traces of meat off the fat before rendering it. After it is rendered, strain it, boil it to sterilize and pour it into containers that can be closed tightly. Then freeze it or store it in a cool place.

Part of the reason for cutting the meat off before rendering is that it can carry bacteria; but another reason is esthetic; it turns the oil dark and the light, sweet oils are prized.

- Render seal fat when it's very fresh. Cut it into chunks and put it in a low oven. When the fat is fresh, it doesn't smell. When it is rendered, the oil looks just like cod-liver oil. Another way is to put chunks of fat in glass containers, put them in a cool place and let the fat render. All the oil will surface. Done that way, the oil has more flavor, and my family likes it better. When fat is left in a jar too long, however, it starts to get rancid or too strong in flavor. So I keep draining the oil out as soon as it collects. That way, it stays mild. [*Annie Johnson*]
- Cut up the seal fat in chunks, put in jars, stir every day as it renders. As the seal blubber renders, it gets thin, the oil separates and looks pink. [*Dolly Spencer*]
- Cut the seal fat in strips and put in a large container. Let it sit till it renders. When it renders, it starts to smell, but the smell is the natural smell of seal oil. The rendering place shouldn't be too cold, but not too warm either. In Shaktoolik, it is cool enough so you don't have to worry about the seal oil. In Homer, the weather is warmer and some of my seal oil has spoiled. Pour off the oil and store it before all of it is rendered. Remaining fat still renders.

Years ago, my mother put the fat in a seal poke.* My husband and I [ivory carver Eric Tetpon] had to learn how to make our own seal oil. I didn't watch how my mother did it enough. My parents told me to leave a hole in the seal poke

so the air could come in and keep it fresh. Keep the seal poke in a cool place. [*Felecia Tetpon*]

- Strip the fat or blubber of the seal, cut slits in it about a foot long (30 cm), and put the fat in a seal poke. Keep cool, unless you want to use it right away; then keep it in a warmer place until it gives enough seal oil to use. Then put it back into the cool place. If you allow the fat to keep rendering, eventually there is almost nothing left but pure oil. [*Helena Andree*]

A seal poke is sometimes made from seal stomach. Or it can be made from the skin of a seal that has been butchered in such a way as to leave the skin in one piece with holes only where head and flippers have been removed. The skin is turned inside out, hair on the interior, and the openings are sewed.

Seal Oil Dip

▶The rendered seal oil has many uses. The older generation never went without seal oil for cooking. They used it to add flavor to the salmon, seaweed with salmon eggs, or diced clams, dried cockles, and sea ribbons. They even added the oil to desserts like mixed berries. It is especially used with dried fish. Dried fish is what you call a finger food nowadays. You take the roasted dried fish and hold it in your two fingers and dip it into seal oil. This is good eating. . . .

It was probably because the Tlingits dried so many of their edible foods that they usually served seal oil with it. It was easier to eat the food that way and much tastier.

■ *Kaa T'eix (Mary Howard Pelayo)*
Kaa T'eix's Cook Book, *Mount Edgecumbe*

About Cooking Walrus: Some animals have been found to be infested with the parasite that may cause trichinosis in humans who eat meat that isn't thoroughly cooked. Slow cooking is best, but in any case, the meat should reach an internal temperature of 185°F (85°C) to destroy the parasite.

The strong odor of walrus meat can be lessened by soaking the raw meat for 5 to 10 minutes in a solution of 1/4 cup (60 mL) vinegar to 1 gallon (3.8 L) of water.

The meat is easier to grind if the white connective tissue is cut out of it first. Cut walrus steaks from the shoulder meat, slicing across the grain. Steaks are best 1/2 inch (1.25 cm) or more thick. They can be pounded with a meat hammer or an *ulu*, just as you would pound tough round steak, or sprinkle steaks with a commercial meat tenderizer.

Fried Walrus Liver

1 pound (456 g) walrus liver, cut into
*   thick slices*
1 cup (240 mL) flour
Salt, pepper and other dry seasonings to taste
Fat

▶Put liver slices in a paper bag with flour and seasonings and shake until all slices are covered with flour. Fry in hot fat for 15 minutes. Ground liver makes good burgers.

■ *Elfie Apatiki*
Community Education Program Cookbook
Gambell, Saint Lawrence Island

Walrus Steaks with Gravy

4 walrus steaks, 3/4 inch (1.9 cm) thick
Flour
Cooking fat
Salt and pepper to taste
2 tablespoons (30 mL) onion flakes, or
    1 medium onion, chopped fine
1/4 cup (60 mL) ketchup
1 cup (240 mL) water

►Spread steaks on a floured board and sprinkle with flour. Using an *ulu* or meat hammer, pound flour into both sides of the meat until no more flour will cling to it. Heat cooking fat in a frying pan and brown the meat on both sides. Lower the heat, add the remaining ingredients and cover pan. Cook gently from one to two hours, depending on tenderness. Add water from time to time if necessary to keep meat from sticking. Makes four servings.
■ Walrus in the Cooking Pot *(adapted)*

Four-Day Spiced Walrus
Corned walrus — rated very good

1 well-trimmed chunk of walrus meat,
    6 to 8 pounds (2.7 to 3.6 kg)
1 gallon (3.8 L) water to which 1/4 cup (60 mL)
    vinegar is added
1 tablespoon (15 mL) garlic salt
1 tablespoon (15 mL) saltpeter
4 tablespoons (60 mL) plain salt
5 tablespoons (75 mL) allspice
5 tablespoons (75 mL) sugar
1/2 teaspoon (2 mL) cinnamon

►Soak the meat in vinegar-water for about 10 minutes. Then take it out and wipe it dry. Mix remaining ingredients in a bowl. Cut several slits in the meat and put some of the spice mixture down into the cuts. Rub the rest over the outside of the meat. Wrap the meat securely in heavy plastic and store it in a cold place, below 45°F (7°C) but above freezing, for four days.

Then wrap in foil tight enough that meat juices will not escape during cooking. Roast in an uncovered pan in a slow oven, 300°F (150°C), for about four hours.

Let the meat cool before slicing into serving pieces.
■ Walrus in the Cooking Pot *(adapted)*

Boiled Walrus Skin

1 chunk walrus skin with fur and fat*
4 tablespoons (60 mL) salt
Large pot of cold water

►Trim the meat into strips about 1-1/2 x 8 inches

(3.75 x 20 cm), always cutting with the grain in the direction the fur grows. Trim off all but about 1 inch (2.5 cm) of fat. Put in salted cold water and bring to a boil. Cook 15 to 20 minutes until meat is tender. Trim off fur just before serving. For variety, try adding *oogruk* (giant seal) meat, rice, macaroni, onions or potatoes.
■ *Norma Silook, Gambell*
  "Walrus Recipes"
  ALASKA® *magazine, October 1977*

*The size Gambell housewives usually cut is 8 x 6 inches (20 x 15 cm). Chunks are then sewn into furry balls for freezing in underground caches.

Walrus Meat Loaf

2 pounds (1 kg) ground walrus meat
1/4 cup (60 mL) cooking oil
1/2 cup (120 mL) ketchup
1 egg or 1/4 cup (60 mL) evaporated milk
    diluted with water
1 cup (240 mL) oatmeal
1 bay leaf
1/2 teaspoon (2 mL) black pepper
1/2 teaspoon (2 mL) seasoned salt
    (or regular salt)
1 tablespoon (15 mL) soy sauce (optional)

►Mix and put in baking dish. Cover with lid or foil and cook in a slow oven, about 300°F (150°C), for 1-1/2 to 2 hours. Add a little water if dry.
■ *Norma Silook*

Walrus Heart

Walrus heart, sliced 1/4 inch (6 mm) thick
1 cup (240 mL) flour
1 teaspoon (5 mL) salt
1/4 teaspoon (1 mL) pepper
1/4 teaspoon (1 mL) paprika
Fat
1 large onion, chopped
1 large can (29 oz /or/ 826 g) tomatoes

►Combine flour and seasonings in a bowl and roll each slice of meat in the mixture to coat it. Brown meat on both sides in hot fat. Add chopped onion and saute until it is brown. Then add tomatoes and their juice, heat to simmering, cover and simmer gently for 30 minutes. Makes four servings.
■ Out of Alaska's Kitchens *(adapted)*

Broiled Whale Steaks

►Cut whale steaks across the grain of the meat, preferably about 1/2 inch (1.25 cm) thick and pound with the back of a cleaver to insure tenderness. Salt and pepper well; brush with a little cooking oil and broil as any other steak.
■ Out of Alaska's Kitchens

Whale Meat

►TAKE ONE WHALE AND CLEAN WELL. Strip off all of the whale fat and soak meat in vinegar for a few hours. The meat is fine-grained, dark red, and looks as if it should taste like beef. For a quick whale dish, slice meat into thin slices and brown in vegetable oil. Then pour prepared barbecue sauce or mushrooms over the browned meat and simmer until tender. Don't cheat and use garlic — let the full rich whale flavor come through.
■ *Helen Fisher*
An Alaskan Cook Book, *Kenai*

Whale Meat a la Venison

1 pound (456 g) whale meat
Strips of pork
Butter or fat
Pinch of salt
1 cup (240 mL) boiling water
1 cup (240 mL) milk
Sour cream
Pinch of sugar

►Lard the meat with strips of pork. Brown well in butter or fat in iron pan on top of stove or in the oven. Sprinkle with salt. Add boiling water and milk. Cover and simmer until tender. Turn several times during cooking. To make the sauce, brown butter in a skillet and stir in flour. Then strain the gravy from the meat into it and let simmer about five minutes. Add sour cream, if available. Season with a pinch of sugar and salt, according to taste. Dehydrated sour cream mix works nicely, or you may make plain gravy and forget the cream. Serves four.
■ Alaska's Game Is Good Food

Stuffed Whale Roast

5 pounds (2.25 kg) whale meat, sliced
4 tablespoons (60 mL) butter or margarine
Celery salt
4 onions, cut fine
2 cups (480 mL) raw rice
Salt and pepper

►Wash the meat in a solution of 1 tablespoon (15 mL) soda to 1 quart (1 L) water. Then boil the meat in water to cover for about 20 minutes. In a large vessel, saute onions and rice in butter. Add celery salt and salt and pepper to taste. Gradually add in 4 cups (1 L), or more if necessary, of the liquor in which the meat was boiled. Cook until the rice is softened and the mixture is the consistency of poultry dressing. Place dressing on meat slices, roll and tie. Put in a roaster in a moderately hot oven, 375°F (190°C), and cook until well done,

basting occasionally with the juice from the bottom of the pan. Small pieces of salt pork and onion placed on the roast before baking will add to the flavor. Serve whale meat garnished with parsley and fancy cut vegetables.
■ Out of Alaska's Kitchens

Whale Oil Sugar Cookies

1 cup (240 mL) whale oil (or margarine)
2 cups (480 mL) sugar
6 tablespoons (90 mL) milk
2 teaspoons (10 mL) vanilla
3 eggs, beaten
1 teaspoon (5 mL) salt
3 teaspoons (15 mL) baking powder
About 6 cups (1.45 L) flour

►Cream whale oil and sugar together. Add milk and beaten eggs, then add vanilla. Sift dry ingredients together and add to the first mixture until it becomes a stiff dough. Chill. Roll out small portions at a time and cut into various shapes. Roll in small amount of sugar. Place on greased cookie sheet and bake at 375°F (190°C) for about 15 minutes or until light brown.
■ *Helen Fisher*
An Alaskan Cook Book, *Kenai*

Whale Bobotee

4 cups (1 L) cold roast whale
1 large onion
1-1/2 teaspoons (7 mL) salt
1 teaspoon (5 mL) Worcestershire
1/2 teaspoon (2 mL) savory
Pepper
4 cups (1 L) cold mashed potatoes

►Mix coarsely chopped whale meat with finely chopped onion; add salt, Worcestershire, savory and pepper. Put in buttered baking dish. Cover with mashed potatoes and bake in moderate oven, 375°F (190°C), for about 30 minutes, allowing the potatoes to brown slightly.
■ Out of Alaska's Kitchens

Muktuk

►Muktuk is the blubber and skin of whale. The black, thin layer of skin on white, pinkish blubber is muktuk. It is eaten just as it comes off the whale. It is cut in small strips, sliced thin and eaten with salt. Some people use seasoned salt as well. Some say it tastes like coconut, but to me it tastes a lot like salt pork before cooking. The only part used is that skin that covers blubber.
■ *Helen Hickox, former teacher*
Gambell High School
Saint Lawrence Island

Fillet of Whale with Mushroom Sauce

2 pounds (1 kg) whale meat
3 tablespoons (45 mL) butter or margarine
Salt
Pepper

►Cut the meat into small steaks. Melt the butter in a frying pan. Sprinkle the meat with salt and pepper and let stand in the frying pan for one hour, turning the steaks once. Pour melted butter into a saucepan and make sauce as directed below. Then put the frying pan on a quick fire and brown the steaks on each side. Serve the meat hot in the center of the dish surrounded by Mushroom Sauce.

Mushroom Sauce
1 tablespoon (15 mL) flour
1 cup (240 mL) water
1/2 pound (228 g) mushrooms, sliced
2 tablespoons (30 mL) lemon juice

►Make a sauce by adding flour to the melted butter poured from the meat. Stir until well blended and add water and sliced mushrooms. Cook until the mushrooms are done. Add the lemon juice and pour the sauce over the meat.
■ Out of Alaska's Kitchens

Pot Roast of Whale

3 pounds (1.4 kg) whale meat
1 onion, sliced
1 carrot, sliced
Flour
Salt
Pepper

►Wash and wipe the meat thoroughly; rub with salt, dredge with flour. Brown on all sides in a little fat in a frying pan. Place the whale meat in a pot or casserole with onion and carrot slices. Add the fat in which the meat was browned and a little water. Season with salt and pepper. Cover and let cook for two or three hours. When tender, thicken and season the gravy. Serve hot.
■ Out of Alaska's Kitchens

BOOK TWO

From Field & Forest

Introduction

. . . We saw some grouse and ptarmigan in the Kamishak area. Since they relied on camouflage for protection, they would allow us to approach them quite closely. Consequently, we found them an easy food supply.

After a storm, they would often lie under the fluffy snow, invisible to the eye. As we would drive along the trails with our dog team, they would often startle us by popping out of the snowdrifts in a flurry of white flakes, flying right over the bow of our sled.

The natives often rigged nets between trees to catch these birds. Then they would startle the birds with loud noises so they would fly into the nets. . . .

Iva Senft, as told to Mary J. Barry
"Camp Cookery, Trail Tonics and Indian Infants"
ALASKA SPORTSMAN®, July 1964

Many families in Alaska still depend on wild game for their principal winter meat supply, whether they qualify as subsistence or sports hunters. Of moose, alone, the annual harvest is something near two and a half million pounds of meat, which, divided equally amongst us, would amount to about six pounds apiece.

Moose and other members of the deer family are the large game animals most commonly taken by Alaskan hunters, but several species of small game and game birds also are taken in abundance enough to make considerable contribution to the Alaskan diet.

The three chapters of Book Two divide the recipes and how-to information roughly along those lines — between the common, or the ones we cook most often, and the not-so-common — with a chapter on birds; one about moose, elk, deer, caribou and reindeer, or, as the meat is most often called, venison; and finally, a chapter about preparing other game, large and small, from bear to squirrel.

The Hidden Ingredient

Despite the great range of size in the original packaging of these meats — from the pert spruce hen to the ludicrously proportioned moose — the key ingredient in preparing any of these meats for the table is one and the same. And it's not even listed in the recipes. That ingredient is, of course, field care, how the animal is killed and what the hunter does with it immediately afterward. What makes for decent field care is the same for all animals, regardless of size: the quicker the kill, the better; the cleaner the kill, the better; and finally, the faster the meat is cooled after the kill, the better still. Adrenalin that is pumped during a long chase does nothing for the meat. A shot that ruptures the intestines is not much help either. But worst of all is careless handling of the meat afterward. The best cook in the world cannot undo the harm caused by that. . . . But some have certainly tried, which brings us to a fuller discussion of what cooks can and cannot do with wild game.

The Gamy Flavor — Good or Bad?

After looking through the original assemblage of recipes (there were thousands) for the game section of *Cooking Alaskan,* several of our game-loving cook-consultants expressed dismay (or stronger) at the number of recipes that seemed determined to Campbellize the beasts of field and forest. There were excellent recipes in the original collection . . . they are still here . . . but they were quite out-numbered by those that began with the phrase "To avoid gamy flavor . . ."

"I get the feeling that people are afraid to *taste* the meat," said one reader. And so it seemed. But how come? Weren't these good cooks, too?

Probably. And we began to suspect it was not gamy flavor but *off* flavor these recipes were meant to avoid.

For the fact is the quality of game meat destined for human consumption isn't regulated by the United States Department of Agriculture and the Food and Drug Administration. How quickly we would have the Feds out after a commercial rancher who fed herring to his chickens! Or a slaughterhouse whose butcher made a habit of chasing cows all over the feed lot, shooting them in the stomach and leaving the carcasses untended

for several hours in the noonday sun! Or, a step down the line, a grocer who kept meat frozen and for sale well past the pull date.

Exaggerations, maybe. The point is that neither the raising of game meat nor the care of it after it is killed is standardized. Some hunters do everything possible to insure quality. The people they feed enjoy wild game. But some do not and that means cooks wind up with products that vary in quality a great deal more than do frying chickens and rump roasts and center-cut pork chops sold at the meat counter.

Are we pretending there's no difference between wild meats and domestically raised ones — apart from the way they're treated? No. But if we sat down to do it, we and our cook-consultants and the many Alaskans whose recipes are represented here might come up with advice for the *new* Alaskan cook something like this:

First, Alaskans have more reason than most citizens of the United States to enjoy wild game. Here, wild game is more plentiful; domestic meats, more costly. The nutritional value is the same or slightly superior in wild meats because of their lower proportion of fat to protein (see the chart on Preface page x). The taste of wild game most of us will claim is superior as well, particularly to the meats we're used to from Outside.

Second, if you don't now have a taste for wild birds and beasts, by all means use a few of the doctoring methods . . . such as cutting off the fat and substituting fats you like better. Marinating and braising and stewing and spicing meats are other excellent ways to change flavor to suit your taste, whether the meat is beef or muskrat. You will find plenty of recipes to help you in this book.

But, third, tastes change, too. There was a day when you (and I) preferred oatmeal mush to prime rib, though we may not remember it. You may remember the day you learned to like spinach or liver and found, at the same time, that — given quality — it was the cook's touch that made the difference between likes and dislikes nearly as much as the inherent taste of the food.

In Alaska, you have an excellent chance to have good quality game. If you let your taste change to prefer its natural flavors, it's sure to be as rewarding as switching from oatmeal mush.

Chapter 6

Game Birds

IN THE FIELD

The basic rules for handling birds once they've been killed are the same as for *any* wild game: bleed and gut, allow air to circulate in the body cavity, cool the meat quickly and thoroughly and keep it cold and dry till it's cooked.

Big game hunters follow the rules without too much exception, probably because all other action for the day is pretty effectively halted when there is an enormous carcass to be dealt with somehow. The bird hunter can and often does just keep on shooting, counting on cold weather to "take care of the meat."

A casual attitude toward field dressing any warm-blooded (or cold-blooded, for that matter) creature, small or big, risks spoiling the taste if not the safety of the meat.

Gutting & Dressing

After the kill, bleed birds as soon as possible by breaking their necks or cutting their throats and letting the heads hang downward until bleeding stops. Gut them while they are still warm.

To gut, pluck a strip clean of feathers from the end of the breastbone to the vent. Make a shallow incision around the vent to cut an opening large enough to poke your fingers through to remove entrails. Cut only through the skin and the thin layer of meat. Be careful not to cut into the intestines. Reach into the opening with two or three fingers — as far up toward the neck as you can — rotate your hand to loosen all the organs and bring the innards out in one motion. Remove and save the giblets — heart, liver and gizzard — being careful not to rupture the gallbladder which is attached to the liver. Cut the fleshy ends off the gizzard, open it out and discard the material in the center. Wipe off the giblets and wrap them in waxed paper. Store them in a cool place.

If the crop did not come out with the entrails, make a slit on the back of the neck and remove it. While you're at it, this is a good time to figure out how you might cook this bird. Take a look at the contents of the crop. If it's grain or some other vegetarian substance, you're in luck. If fish, well, try out one of the hints for "fish feeders" that follow.

At this time also excise the preen gland, a small double-lobed button affair on the back of the tail. You may have to lift some feathers to find it.

Like the scent hocks on deer and the similar glands on small game, the preen gland secretes an oil that may give an off taste to the meat. So cut well around it and remove it without puncturing.

The gland is full of "hairdressing," or, in this case, feather dressing, which the bird picks at with its beak and then spreads along its feathers to make them shine. We are reminded of a George Orwell story about waiters in the fancy restaurants of Paris who ran their fingers through their carefully pomaded hair, then wiped the oil around the rims of plates to give them an elegant glisten just at serving time.

Cut out the preen gland.

Next, thoroughly wipe the inside of the bird with a clean cloth, paper towel or grass. Unless you're ready to cook it, do not wash the bird, and instead, do what you can to keep it dry since water spreads bacteria that may cause spoiling. Above all, keep the bird cool. Do not wrap tightly in plastic or other material. Cheesecloth is a good meat wrapper to keep meat clean as possible in the field, whether it's skinned birds or large animals.

IN THE KITCHEN

Back at camp or at home, eviscerated ducks may be hung in a cool shaded place (a breezeway is ideal) three or four days. Leave the feathers on to keep off dust, flies and insects or protect with cheesecloth coverings. Giblets, however, should be refrigerated and used or preserved (freezing is easiest) within a day or two. If nothing else, use them to start a camp soup.

Plucking

Birds still warm from their own body heat are easiest to pluck. If you have a refrigerator at hand to protect the meat once it's bare — or the weather is consistently cool enough; that is, not rising above 40°F (4°C) — you can proceed with plucking immediately after eviscerating . . . or even before.

Next best is to have the birds *well chilled* but not frozen. Pluck ducks and geese *dry*, not scalded. Paraffin makes the job easier but isn't essential.

To pluck ducks and geese take small pinches of feathers and pull them out — always pulling in the same direction they grow to avoid tearing the skin. Then roll your hand against the skin to remove the down and pinfeathers. Remove the large guard feathers by twisting them gently but firmly. On small birds, you can save yourself the bother of pulling the large feathers by cutting the wings off at the first joint. Then make a taper of rolled brown paper, light it and singe off the down.

On geese there may be as much as 2 inches (5 cm) of down to pluck once the guard feathers have been removed. Simply peel it off, using a rolling motion of the hand.

SAVE clean dry breast and back feathers for pillow stuffing or for repair jobs to down-filled jackets and sleeping bags. And don't forget the kids. Large goose quills make fun writing instruments. And we know one sizable kid who still saves a Halloween owl mask he made several years ago, using a large, round commercial size ice cream carton which he pasted with duck feathers.

If you have paraffin, the procedure is, again, to have the birds well chilled but not frozen. Pull out the heavy back, tail and wing feathers. Cut off the wings at the first joint. Two pounds (1 kg) of paraffin is enough to "process" four ducks. Melt it in a tall, narrow container — tall enough that the entire bird can be dipped at once. (Hot paraffin can cause the worst imaginable burns. Exercise all due caution with tippy pots, open flames, curious children . . . and yourself.) Holding the bird by its feet, dip it all at once into the paraffin and then immediately plunge it into ice water to harden the paraffin; (the outside air will do it if it's cold). Peel off wax and feathers together. To reuse the paraffin, melt it down and strain out the feathers.

Some hunters don't bother with plucking anything but large ducks and geese. Small ducks and upland birds are often skinned. But, if you want to roast these small birds with the skin on, there's another way of making the plucking somewhat easier. Heat water in a deep pot — not boiling, just hot. A temperature of 150°F (65°C) will do. (Boiling is 212°F or 100°C). Dip the bird in and out of the water several times until the feathers will pull away easily. Then let the bird drip dry a few minutes and pluck the rest. Remaining down may be singed off.

For another ingenious style of plucking, see Kenneth Hughes's recipe, Duck in the Mud.

Whatever the method, check the carcass of your bare bird and trim away shot holes or wounds that may have spread flavor from the entrails. Leg and back seem to pick up off flavors more easily than does breast meat.

Skinning

Small birds — ptarmigan, grouse and other upland birds especially — it is sometimes advisable to skin at the outset if you have a place to keep the meat protected and cool. Skinning is a whole lot quicker than plucking, doesn't seem to harm the flavor of these small birds and may even improve it.

To skin birds, remove the wings close to the body. Cut off the foot at the joint just above it. Slit the skin under the tail and pull it back over the legs and up the body toward the neck. Then break the breast away from the back and cut the legs off close to the back. Save heart, liver, gizzard, breast and legs and throw away back, wings and entrails. Wipe the saved pieces thoroughly (don't wash until cooking time), wrap them in waxed paper and keep in a cool place.

Cooking Game Birds

There are nearly as many controversies about the way to cook game birds as there are about other game meats. Most of them are the direct result of the differing qualities of the meat different cooks have to work with at different times. Cooks tend to make too many hard and fast rules. That it took a bottle of vinegar and a box of baking soda to make one old bird edible does not mean that's the way to cook bird henceforward. Here are some hints to help you be the judge of quality and how to accommodate it.

How Does A Hunter Bag The Best Eating Birds?

"The best bet," says one old-timer, "know what you're shooting and don't shoot fish birds. Concentrate on the seed and grass eaters. Among ducks that means pintails, mallards, teal, widgeon and so on. If you get a mistake bird — golden eye, merganser, old squaw — breast it and marinate in vinegar-water solution for a couple of hours before cooking normally." Some other suggestions for "fish feeders" are given below.

To Age or Not To Age

Aging is the process of hanging killed game in various stages of dress (at least gutted and wiped clean) in a cool place for a period of several days to tenderize and improve the flavor of the meat. Most people agree this is an essential step for game animal meats — moose, caribou and the like.

About birds and the need for aging there is considerable conflict. Which birds should or shouldn't be aged, how long, how they're dressed are all subject to dozens of individual adjustments.

The English (and their cultural descendants, represented in one of America's most widely used cookbooks) recommend bleeding birds immediately after the kill but not drawing or plucking them until just before cooking. Birds in this condition (*i.e.*, with guts intact) may be hung until the legs stiffen and the skin turns green.

That is an extreme few hunters in Alaska — or elsewhere in the United States — favor. Since most "how-to" advice insists that birds be bled immediately and then gutted as soon after the kill as possible, few Alaskan birds are aged in the English fashion.

If birds are to be hung outdoors in camp, many hunters do leave the feathers on — partly so that the plucking job can be handed over to someone at home, we suspect — but also to protect the meat.

Feathered or bare (and protected some other way), birds must be aged at a temperature that does not rise above 40°F (4°C), with a range of 34 to 38°F (1 to 3.5°C) being ideal. If the meat freezes, it doesn't age very rapidly, as any science fiction buff can tell you. And warm weather aging usually has another name — putrefying.

The time recommended by those who favor aging may be anywhere from three days to a week. For a great many people, however, gutted or fully dressed birds, wrapped loosely in waxed paper and refrigerated for 18 to 48 hours, are aged enough.

Roasting Wild Birds

Many recipes suggest placing extra fat such as strips of bacon over the breast of all wildfowl during roasting. Some birds need it; others — well-fed geese, notably — are fat enough to provide excellent self-basting without additional fat. To be sure the breast stays moist, roast birds breast side down until the last half-hour or so of cooking. Then turn the bird and allow the breast to brown, basting frequently with pan juices.

To Stuff or Not To Stuff

Dressing is always a welcome accompaniment for roast wildfowl. Some cooks argue that the dressing should be baked separately because it takes on "too gamy a flavor" cooked inside the bird. Others say that's nonsense — the bird won't have too strong a flavor if it's not a "fish feeder" and the meat was properly cared for in the field. Obviously both opinions have a merit that must be judged by each cook on the spot.

But there is another reason for deciding to bake dressing separately. The length of the cooking time is considerably increased for a stuffed bird, and it is not just the meat that requires additional time. Bird and dressing should reach an internal temperature of 160 to 170°F (70 to 76°C). If the dressing is stuffed inside the bird, it will take longer for it to reach that safe point . . . additional time that risks *over*cooking and thus drying out the bird. For that reason, many cooks stuff the cavity of the bird with onion, carrot or apple, or sprinkle it with herbs for flavoring, and bake heavier stuffings — especially those containing bread — separately, basting the dressing from time to time with juices from the roasting bird. In any case, leftover stuffing should be removed from the bird, stored and reheated separately. A list of dressing and sauce recipes—some of which are hidden within other recipes, some of which are in a separate chapter — is on the following page.

Hot Oven or Slow?

Another controversy amongst cooks about the best way to roast wild birds is whether to use a slow oven or a hot one. Our advice, as usual: experiment to find out what suits your taste, knowing that there are good cooks who swear by each method. Hot oven is most often a recommendation for roasting ducks; slow oven, for geese.

To use the hot oven method, start with an oven preheated to 450 or 500°F (230 to 260°C). Place the duck on a rack in a dry roasting pan and bake it, uncovered, for 20 to 25 minutes. For those who like rare meat, the duck may be sufficiently cooked at this point. If not, reduce the heat to 250°F (120°C) and continue baking an additional half-hour, more or less, depending on the size of the bird.

The slow oven method for roasting a wild goose starts with an oven preheated to 325°F (160°C). Roast, uncovered, about 30 minutes per pound (0.45 kg). Check breast juice with a toothpick; a pink-white color indicates the goose is done. If you have roasted the goose breast side down to prevent drying, turn it during the last half-hour of cooking and baste frequently with pan juices.

Fish Feeders

What to do with a bird that has been eating fish — or any food that may transmit an unwanted taste to the meat — is another question fraught with disagreement. Some cooks say, "Give up. Toss the bird." Others recommend one or another marination. Here are several:

- One way to overcome the fish flavor of wild ducks that have been feeding on fish is to soak the dressed birds a few hours in water to which a little soda and salt have been added. Then parboil them in fresh water with a small carrot and a little onion inside each bird. Throw away carrot and onion, wipe dry and stuff with a sage-flavored dressing. Roast until brown and tender. [Mamie Jensen, Juneau]
- If ducks are inclined to be strong in flavor, stuff dressed duck with peeled onion, apple or potato for a few days before cooking. [F. Marion Smith, *PTA Cook Book*, Petersburg]
- Late in the season, spruce hens go on their winter diet and develop a sprucy flavor. They may be converted into a delicacy, however. Both ptarmigan and spruce hen breasts may be sliced and put to soak overnight in a mixture of sour milk and herbs — a pinch of oregano, marjoram and rosemary. Buttermilk or sweet milk soured with lemon juice or vinegar may be substituted for sour milk. Use 1 tablespoon (15 mL) white vinegar or lemon juice for each cup (240 mL) of sweet milk. The next day, roll the meat in flour, saute it quickly in butter or oil to brown it on all sides, and then simmer it very gently in the sour milk mixture until it's tender.
- Occasionally, a wild goose turned out to be too tough to be roasted in the ordinary manner. By steaming it for 15 to 30 minutes, then roasting it slowly, we made the feathered old-timer into a palatable entree. ["Camp Cookery, Trail Tonics, and Indian Infants," by Iva Senft, as told to Mary J. Barry, *ALASKA SPORTSMAN*®, July 1964]
- Wash and clean the bird thoroughly as you would any fowl. Pour about a half-cup (120 mL) of vinegar into the body cavity and over the breast. Allow this to serve as a mild tenderizer while you prepare a stuffing. . . . If you feel you probably have a tough, old gander to prepare, it is best to forego roasting it. Cut the goose into serving size pieces and parboil them in salted water for 20 to 30 minutes. Then proceed with a recipe that calls for slow cooking in a Dutch oven or covered pot. [Clarence Massey, "To Cook a Wild Goose," *ALASKA*® magazine, March 1973; also see Massey's recipe for Burgundy Gander, page 194.]
- Roasting goose in a brown paper bag saves cleaning the oven afterward. Several holes in the bottom of the bag allow grease to drain out, and the bird browns nicely without basting. [Louise Juhnke, Chugiak, *The Alaskan Camp Cook*]

Dressing and plucking instructions are based on material in *The Hunter Returns After the Kill* (see Cooks & Cookbooks) and Thomas Kean, Mary Darling and Verna Mikesh, *Game Birds From Field To Kitchen* (Agricultural Extension Service, University of Minnesota, Extension Bulletin 346, Revised 1973).

SAUCES — STUFFINGS — OTHER ACCOMPANIMENTS FOR WILD GAME

Sea Gull Egg Cake

Gull eggs, gathered when fresh, can be used much the same as the eggs of chickens. They are smaller and therefore adjustment must be made in quantity used.

3/4 cup (180 mL) shortening or butter
2 cups (480 mL) sugar
1 cup (240 mL) milk
2 sea gull eggs, slightly beaten
3 cups (720 mL) flour
4 teaspoons (20 mL) baking powder
1 teaspoon (5 mL) salt
1 teaspoon (5 mL) vanilla or lemon extract

►Cream together shortening and sugar. Add slightly beaten eggs. Sift dry ingredients. Add milk and flour together. Add vanilla or lemon extract.

Put in greased 13 x 9-inch (32 x 22 cm) pan. Bake at 350°F (175°C) for 25 minutes.
■ Out of Alaska's Kitchens

Sea Gull Egg Pie

Unbaked pie shell
2 sea gull eggs
1 teaspoon (5 mL) vanilla
2-1/2 cups (600 mL) milk
1/2 cup (120 mL) sugar
Dash of salt
Nutmeg

►Beat eggs, sugar, salt and vanilla together. Add milk and beat for five minutes. Place in unbaked pie shell and sprinkle with nutmeg before putting in oven. Bake at 400°F (205°C) about 45 minutes.
■ Out of Alaska's Kitchens

In Times Past

More than 100,000 square miles of marshland and tundra — about a fifth of Alaska — comprise the nesting grounds for millions of ducks, geese, swans and other waterbirds that migrate throughout the Western Hemisphere. Hunting on these lands is subject to international treaty agreement and is carefully regulated by federal agencies. Current U.S. Fish and Wildlife Service policy prohibits harvesting migratory birds and their eggs in the spring. Should numbers increase, the prohibition will be lifted for Native Alaskans who harvest the birds and their eggs for subsistence purposes. Here are some ways wild bird eggs were used in times past.

• During June and July bird eggs are often harvested by the hundreds. Most are served fresh, boiled or scrambled. Occasionally, they are used in making cakes. Duck, goose, murre, cormorant and sea gull eggs are used in greatest abundance, but the people of the tundra villages may also eat the smaller bird eggs too. Bird eggs are used in all stages of incubation. The old method of preservation was to either cook first, or preferably leave uncooked, and store in seal oil.

Another old method of egg preservation practiced by Northeast Cape, Saint Lawrence Island, was to dry the egg yolks on rocks in the sun, then put them in walrus stomachs and store in the cold. . . .

In the Kobuk area bird eggs were preserved by burying them in a mixture of fine sand and gravel, and [then] they were cooked by placing them in a willow bark tube (peeled from a large willow), plugging the ends and laying it in a bed of coals. [*The Alaska Dietary Survey*]

• A long time ago, say some one hundred years ago or so, people would go egg gathering in the month of June, out on the flats along the west shorelines of Alaska. People would save many of these eggs in underground holes covered with mud and moss. They would stake these holes so they would know where to find them.

In this way the eggs would stay fresh all summer. Then the people would come back for the eggs in September or October, just when the weather turns cold. [Milo Minnock, Bethel, *Kalikaq Yugnek*, Volume IV, Number 2, Spring, 1978, Bethel Regional High School]

• The eggs of many types of birds have been gathered by the Aleuts for many years. They were used primarily before fresh eggs arrived in the spring. The eggs were used in puddings, custards and cakes, etc., just like chicken eggs. In order to preserve them, the eggs were put in layers with salt in between. They lasted a long time when fixed in this manner. [*Aleut Cookbook*, Saint Paul Island]

Fresh Sea Gull Eggs

►It's said about the best time of year to pick sea gull eggs is in the early spring or last week in May and the first two weeks in June, because it's about the time when the sea gulls start laying eggs. You can go early in the morning and get quite a few, but then again you can also go in the afternoon which would be after high noon so the sea gulls will lay. But actually you can go out any old time of day just as long as you beat the others.

YOU CAN'T FRY THEM! You can boil sea gull eggs and eat them that way or you can mix them in pancakes and cakes or such. But you can't fry them. If you do your eggs would turn out very rubbery. You probably couldn't cut them. But when you use them in cakes and such they raise about half an inch higher than if you were to use a regular chicken egg.
■ *Roberta Deigh*
Uutuqtwa
Bristol Bay High School, Naknek

GIBLETS

Wild Bird Liver Pate #1

Livers, preferably wild goose
Butter or margarine
Paprika
Parsley flakes
Salt and pepper to taste
Snipped wild chives or minced onion
Eggs, hard-cooked, equal to amount of livers

►Saute livers in plentiful amount of butter or margarine until brown and tender. Sprinkle with paprika, parsley flakes, salt and pepper. Mash the cooked livers and add wild chives or onion and eggs (chopped fine). Mix thoroughly. If pate is too thick, thin it with a little melted butter, bacon drippings or cream. Chill several hours. Roll into balls about the size of marbles. Insert a cocktail toothpick into each and serve with toast triangles or crackers.
■ *The Old Homesteader*

Wild Bird Liver Pate #2

A variation that uses both heart and liver

Livers and hearts from at least 6 wildfowl —
*   more if small*
Dehydrated minced onion or a little grated fresh
*   onion or minced wild chives*
1 or 2 hard-cooked eggs, chopped
2 teaspoons (10 mL) vermouth
1 to 2 tablespoons (15 to 30 mL) softened butter
*   or mayonnaise*
Salt and pepper to taste
Chopped parsley to taste
1/2 teaspoon (2 mL) wild sage

►Boil livers and hearts in water with onions or chives. Cook until tender and then place in blender along with hard-cooked eggs. When blended, remove to bowl and add remaining ingredients. Stir until well mixed. The amount of butter or mayon-naise used will depend on the number of livers and hearts. Chill the pate in refrigerator for at least four hours. Serve with crackers or toast.
■ *The Old Homesteader*

Wild Bird Liver Pate #3

A mild pate even "liver-haters" love

1/2 to 3/4 pound (228 to 340 g) wildfowl livers
1 tablespoon (15 mL) butter or margarine
1/4 cup (60 mL) broth from cooking remaining
giblets and other bird parts (or chicken broth)
1 tablespoon (15 mL) minced onion
*   (can be dried)*
1 teaspoon (5 mL) curry powder, or more
1/4 teaspoon (1 mL) paprika
1 teaspoon (5 mL) seasoned salt
Up to 2 large packages (8 oz /or/ 228 g, each)
*   cream cheese*
1/2 to 1 cup (120 to 240 mL) chopped,
*   toasted nuts*

►With scissors, cut livers into chunks so they will cook quickly and still remain soft. Saute them in butter — adding in onion, curry powder, paprika, salt and broth — until they are tender, no more than 10 minutes. Cool slightly and process in blender until smooth. (Elbow grease and a fork will substitute for the blender.) Soften cream cheese and beat into liver mixture until well blended. Cover and chill several hours. Meanwhile, toast the nuts for a few minutes in a 300°F (150°C) oven. Watch them carefully. Nuts burn quickly, but a slight toasting crisps them and brings up their flavor. Cool. Stir into liver-cheese pate just before serving. The pate is good with crackers, rye bread and/or raw vegetables and is a welcome accompaniment to a simple meal of soup. Put some sliced dill pickles on the serving plate, too.
■ *The editors, ALASKA® magazine*

Pickled Giblets

Giblets from waterfowl or upland birds
Brine to cover, using the following proportions:
2 cups (480 mL) vinegar
1 cup (240 mL) brown sugar
2/3 cup ((160 mL) water
4 tablespoons (60 mL) pickling spice
1 clove garlic, minced
Few mint leaves

►Cut giblets into chunks and steam tender, five to eight minutes. Chill. Combine brine ingredients and boil for one minute. Remove from heat and allow to cool. Then pour over giblets, add one slice onion and a couple of drops of Worcestershire. Stir, then allow to stand in a cool place (about 40°F /or/ 4°C) for 24 hours before serving.

■ *C. Joe Murray, Jr.*
   "Alaska Pickled Treats," Alaska-only edition
   ALASKA® *magazine*
   September 1980

Goose Gizzards and Hearts

►Geese have enormous gizzards, and it takes only a few of these husky giblets to provide a family meal.

Cut gizzards and hearts into small pieces, no larger than half-inch (1.25 cm) cubes. Put them in a Dutch oven or a heavy iron frying pan that can be covered. Sprinkle a package of Wyler's Onion Soup and Dip Mix over the giblets, add 2 cups (480 mL) hot water and stir. Cover with a lid and simmer slowly for about an hour and a half or until tender. Serve over rice, noodles or toast.

■ *Clarence Massey*
   "To Cook A Wild Goose"
   ALASKA® *magazine, March 1973*

Waterfowl Livers with Rice

1 cup (240 mL) wild rice
3 cups (720 mL) boiling water
1 to 1-1/2 cups (240 to 360 mL) waterfowl livers
1/2 stick (56 g) butter or margarine, melted
2 teaspoons (10 mL) minced wild chives or
   minced onion
1 cup (240 mL) sliced mushrooms
Salt and pepper to taste

►Wash rice through two waters. Cover with boiling water and simmer, uncovered, for about 45 minutes or until rice is tender. Stir occasionally. Melt the butter in a frying pan and saute the mushrooms and chives or onions until lightly browned and tender. Add the wildfowl livers and saute a few minutes until they also are browned nicely. Season to taste with salt and pepper; add the rice and stir gently to mix. Serve with toast and a green salad.

SALADS

Chop Suey Salad

1-1/2 cups (360 mL) diced cooked wildfowl
   such as ptarmigan, grouse or duck
1 cup (240 mL) chopped celery
2 tablespoons (30 mL) minced onion
2 hard-cooked eggs, chopped
1/4 cup (60 mL) diced sweet pickles
1/3 cup (80 mL) coarsely chopped nuts
1/2 cup (120 mL) crisp Chinese noodles
1/2 cup (120 mL) mayonnaise
2 tablespoons (30 mL) wine vinegar
1 tablespoon (15 mL) Worcestershire
1 teaspoon (5 mL) salt

►Combine mayonnaise, vinegar, Worcestershire and salt for the dressing. Combine all other ingredients, add dressing and chill. Serve on lettuce. Makes four generous servings.

■ *Mamie Jensen, Juneau*

Cold Duck a l'Orange

A simple salad borrowing the flavors
of a famous recipe

Leftover roast duck or goose
Fresh orange sections
Sliced onion
Torn lettuce greens
Plain French dressing

►Arrange attractively on individual plates and serve.

■ *Bunny Mathisen, Petersburg*

Islander Salad

2 cups (480 mL) diced cooked duck or goose
1 cup (240 mL) pineapple chunks
1 tablespoon (15 mL) chopped wild chives or
   green onion

2 hard-cooked eggs, chopped
2 slices crisp bacon, crumbled
French dressing
Salad greens
Optional garnish: shrimp, avocado
  slices, fresh fruit

►Toss the first five ingredients with French dressing to taste. Serve on a bed of greens. Garnish with shrimp, avocado slices and slices or chunks of fresh fruit. Makes four servings.
■ *Mamie Jensen*
  Juneau

STOCK & SOUPS

Duck Soup #1

►Cut dressed duck into serving pieces as you would a chicken. Place in soup pot and cover with water. Add dry vegetables and salt to taste. Boil for an hour. Then add 1 cup (240 mL) rice and continue boiling until rice is cooked. Soup should not be thick. If not enough broth, cut down on rice. Serve hot with crackers or bread.
■ *Delores Carroll Sloan, Fort Yukon*

Variation: Duck Soup #2 is also provided by a Fort Yukon resident, Doris Ward. She begins the same way, cutting the duck into serving pieces, covering it with water and boiling it for about 45 minutes, but she omits vegetables and seasonings until after this initial cooking period. "Then add 3/4 cup (180 mL) rice, 1 cup (240 mL) macaroni, one large onion and salt and pepper to taste. Continue cooking until rice and macaroni are tender."

Pressed Spruce Hen
Jellied consomme

Legs, wings and necks of game birds
Water
Salt and pepper
Other seasonings

►Cover bony parts of birds with water and seasonings. Boil until meat falls from bones; cool and remove all bones. Pour into loaf pan or can for mold. If it doesn't jell when cooled, add plain gelatin as directed on package and mold again.
■ *Rieta Walker*
  Cooking Up A Storm, *Homer*

Baked Stock

►Good soups, good sauces begin with good stock. The most flavorsome stock or broth is a baked one. Save the bony pieces of fowl in the freezer until you have enough to almost fill your largest enamel, cast-iron or stainless steel kettle. (The handles

must be ovenproof.) Save the giblets in another bag for other uses. This broth or stock should use bony parts — chicken backs, necks, wings and wild bird pieces. Heap these into the pot. Cover them with cold water. Add no seasonings, spices, herbs or vegetables. Just the birds and barely enough water to cover.

Heat slowly on top of the stove until the water begins to steam. Don't boil it. Somehow you lose flavor that way. Then set the pot in the oven, uncovered, and bake it at a low temperature, 300°F (150°C), for at least three hours. Leave it all afternoon, if you want. It won't boil over, and you don't risk scorching the meat that rests on the bottom of the pan. The aroma is wonderful.

When the broth is sufficiently rich, pick out as much of the meat and bone as you can and strain the rest. Skim the fat (or chill the broth until the fat sets on top). Freeze some broth without seasonings to use in sauces, poaching liquids, as the base for next month's soup. (Be sure to mark the containers "unsalted" so you'll remember to correct the seasonings.) The rest you may now season as desired for broth or add whatever ingredients you wish to turn it into soup.

Though other ingredients normally used in making broth — onion, garlic, celery — may be added after the first hour of baking, the richest broth is made from the birds only. Try it that way the first time. Next time, add whole *unpeeled* yellow brown onions after the broth has baked an hour. The onion skins will add a lovely color to the broth.
■ *The editors,* ALASKA® *magazine*

Lazybones Soup

►The carcasses left over from any recipe in which only breast meat is used are the makings of a good soup. Cook them in water — or other liquid — to barely cover. (Too much water will weaken the soup. It's best to start skimpy and add liquid if the soup needs it.) Add dried onion, salt, pepper and other seasonings to suit. A chicken bouillon cube or two adds to the flavor. When the meat is good and tender, remove and discard the bones, chop the meat in smaller pieces and give it back to the soup. Now add raw or leftover rice or barley or noodles and whatever vegetables you wish. Simmer till tender. Correct the seasonings as desired.

■ *The editors, ALASKA® magazine*

Ptarmigan Espanol

►Use the bony pieces of several birds or a whole bird cut into serving pieces. Put them in a soup kettle and add the tomatoes and juice from a large can of stewed tomatoes, plus enough water to cover the meat. Bring to the simmer and cook gently about 30 minutes or until meat falls easily off bone. Cool the soup enough to remove the bones and skim some of the fat. Put it back on the stove and add as many pimento-stuffed green olives as your budget will let you, up to and including the contents of one can. Add some of the juice, too. (We use ''salad'' olives; they're cheaper, and the soup does not know the difference.) Now add a couple of yellow onions, quartered, three or more peeled cloves of garlic and some chunks of potato, peeled or unpeeled. Chopped green pepper also suits the flavor of this soup. Salt and pepper to taste and cook until the vegetables are done. If the result is still too thin to ''eat with a fork,'' you may add noodles during the final minutes of cooking. Last, swirl in a few drops of Tabasco and set the bottle on the table. Sometimes we also offer sour cream to dollop into the soup once it is served.

Such a soup makes a full meal. Serve it with dill bread and a wild bird liver pate.

■ *The editors, ALASKA® magazine*

Teal Mulligan
(and French Onion Soup)

►Skin about six teal. Do not go to trouble of plucking. Fat under skin makes mulligan too greasy. Teal is best . . . never have found a bad teal . . . but any wild duck will do and you only have to cook longer for larger birds.

Cover with water in Dutch oven or similar pot. Season with salt, black pepper, and a little poultry seasoning. Add five (at least) medium-size Spanish onions, quartered. Add 2 cups (480 mL) chopped celery. Cut up four carrots, four small turnips halved, four potatoes, halved. (Allow 45 minutes cooking for turnips and carrots, 30 minutes for potatoes. Teal will take only 45 minutes at low boil . . . larger ducks longer, to two hours.) Put in quartered onions and celery from the beginning.

A few minutes before ready to take off stove and serve, add about a water glass and a half of dry Vermouth and a good dash of Kitchen Bouquet to darken liquid. (Do not thicken . . . the best is to come.)

Dip liquid and onions for soup servings, add handful of garlic croutons with a sprinkling of Parmesan cheese . . . and voila! . . . the best French Onion Soup you ever tasted . . . and the mulligan isn't shabby either.

■ *Bob Henning, Angoon*

DUCK

Roast Wild Duck with Red Sauce

2 wild ducks, pan-ready
2 tablespoons (30 mL) salad oil
1/4 cup (60 mL) grated onion
1/4 teaspoon (1 mL) paprika
2 tablespoons (30 mL) brown sugar
1/2 cup (120 mL) ketchup or tomato sauce
2 tablespoons (30 mL) lemon juice
Salt to taste
1/4 cup (60 mL) cider vinegar
4 tablespoons (60 mL) Worcestershire

►Rub ducks with oil. Mix remaining ingredients and brush half the mixture on ducks. Wrap the ducks in foil and place in a shallow baking pan. Bake at 325°F (160°C) for one hour or until ducks

are tender. Turn foil back and brush ducks with remaining Red Sauce. Bake until brown. Yields four to six servings.

■ *Ann Chandonnet*
  ''Christmas in Alaska''
  ALASKA® magazine, December 1978

Roast Wild Duck — Red Cabbage Stuffing and Cranberry Dumplings

►First prepare dough for Cranberry Dumplings and refrigerate. Cook cranberries per direction and set aside. Then prepare duck for roasting, seasoning well with salt and pepper and a little ground clove. Stuff loosely with Red Cabbage Stuffing and roast until stuffing reaches a temperature of 165°F (73°C), basting frequently with pan juices or other fat and broth. Or bake stuffing separately in a greased, covered casserole. Remove cover during final cooking to brown; baste with pan juices from duck. About half an hour before serving time, roll out and finish preparing Cranberry Dumplings.

Red Cabbage Stuffing

3 cups (720 mL) toasted bread crumbs
1 cup (240 mL) chopped red cabbage
1 medium-sized onion, chopped
Salt, pepper and poultry seasoning to taste
Beaten egg
Warm water

►Mix all ingredients, adding egg and warm water last, just enough to bind the mixture together. Bake as directed above.

Cranberry Dumplings

2 cups (480 mL) lowbush cranberries
1-3/4 cups (420 mL) sifted flour
1 teaspoon (5 mL) salt
2-1/2 teaspoons (12 mL) double-acting
*   baking powder*
1/2 stick (2 oz /or/ 60 g) chilled butter
2/3 cup (160 mL) milk
Sugar and cinnamon

►Cover cranberries with water and cook until berries have burst and water is colored. Drain, reserving liquid.

Mix sifted flour, salt and baking powder. Cut in butter with a pastry blender or a couple of knives until the mixture is a bit smaller than "pea size." Then make a well in the middle, pour in the milk and quickly stir it into the dough just until the mixture clings together. Turn out onto a lightly floured board, knead gently no more than 10 times. Then wrap dough loosely in waxed paper and chill it to make it easier to roll out.

Half an hour before serving time, roll out dough to about 1/4-inch (0.6 cm) thickness and cut into 4-inch (10 cm) squares. Rolling pin and knife may be lightly dusted with flour. Fill centers with cooked cranberries, sprinkled liberally with sugar and a little cinnamon. Fold over and pinch edges of dough well, adding a little water to the edges if necessary to make them stick. Prick tops. Cook in hot cranberry juice for about 15 minutes.
■ Out of Alaska's Kitchens

Roast Duck with Oranges

►Prepare ducks whole for roasting, allowing one-half duck per person. Rub inside and outside well with salt and pepper (I use coarse grind), and a little savory. Fill the cavity with quartered onions and oranges, one each per duck. Close cavity.

Place breast down on a trivet in a roasting pan and place in a hot oven, 450 to 475°F (230 to 245°C), for 30 minutes. Reduce heat to 350°F (175°C) and roast, uncovered, basting frequently with orange juice or very dry sherry. Roasting ducks on a trivet will prevent the fat, which is sometimes strong, from soaking into the bird. Roast until done, two hours or more. During the last half-hour, turn the ducks on their backs to brown breasts. If a glaze is desired, cook 1 cup (240 mL) orange juice with 1 teaspoon (5 mL) corn-starch until thickened and pour over ducks during the last half-hour. Before serving, remove stuffing and discard. Serve with Boiled Oranges.

Roast ducks may be wrapped in foil and frozen for later heating and eating. I find that cooked ducks freeze better than raw ones.

Boiled Oranges for Roast Duck

3 oranges, with skin, cut into thick
*   crosswise slices*
Boiling water
1 cup (240 mL) sugar
1-1/4 cups (300 mL) water
3 tablespoons (45 mL) lemon juice

►Place orange slices in a saucepan and pour over them boiling water to cover. Cook for one hour. Drain well, discarding water. Cook remaining ingredients together for five minutes. Then place the oranges in this syrup and cook until tender, about one hour more. Oranges may be prepared ahead of time and kept in the refrigerator and reheated at serving time.
■ *Mrs. Vic Power*
   Tried and True Recipes, *Juneau*

Roast Wild Duck
An expert's basic — and
beautifully simple — recipe

►Season inside of dressed duck with salt, pepper and poultry seasoning if desired. Stuff with pieces of apple, onion and celery. Place in a roaster and add a little water or consomme. Combine 1/4 cup (60 mL) honey with 1/4 cup (60 mL) orange marmalade and coat the duck. Brush on at least twice during roasting to provide glaze. Roast at 350°F (175°C) for two to three hours or until done.

Alaskan ducks, especially mallards and pintails, are usually nice and fat and do not require covering with bacon or pork strips as is often the case for ducks down south. The fruit and vegetables used for stuffing are enjoyable delicacies for the connoisseur.
■ *Rupe Andrews*
   Alaska Fish Tales & Game Trails

Roast Wild Duck with Bread Stuffing

Another basic recipe

1 cup (240 mL) finely chopped celery
1 cup (240 mL) finely chopped onion
1 cup (240 mL) seeded raisins
4 cups (1 L) soft bread crumbs
2 beaten eggs
1/2 cup (120 mL) scalded milk
1/2 teaspoon (2 mL) salt
2 wild ducks
Bacon strips

►Mix the first seven ingredients well. Stuff ducks and place bacon strips across their breasts. Roast in uncovered pan, 35 minutes per pound (0.45 kg), estimated by the heavier duck. Roast 15 minutes at 500°F (260°C) and remainder of time at 350°F (175°C). Fifteen minutes before removing from oven, mix and pour the following sauce over them.

Chili Basting Sauce
1 cup (240 mL) ketchup
1/2 cup (120 mL) chili sauce
1/4 cup (60 mL) Worcestershire

■ *F. Marion Smith*
   PTA Cook Book, *Petersburg*

Chukchi Pintail with Stuffing

Shishmaref is an Eskimo village situated on an island facing the blustery Chukchi Sea. At the time Joe Rychetnik collected this recipe from Joan Fisher, she and her husband, Fred, were teachers at the BIA school. A typical busy day, Rychetnik says, concluded with a "culinary spectacle . . . a large buffet served around midnight to top off an evening of pleasant conversation or ancient movies shown at the theater in a warehouse next door. . . . The buffet [is] mainly out of cans, with a great deal of Joan Fisher kitchen magic thrown in. Local game has much to do with the menu also. The Serpentine Flats nearby provide ducks of all kinds and my hosts presented a duck dish which would be the pride of any fine restaurant. . . ."

To make Joan Fisher's Chukchi Pintail, prepare one duck per person, taking care to leave skin intact when removing pinfeathers. Thoroughly wash each bird before salting and peppering. Then proceed.

Stuffing (enough for four ducks):
2 cups (480 mL) salted, cooked rice
1 can (6 oz /or/ 170 g) crushed pineapple
3/4 cup (180 mL) raisins

1 medium onion, chopped
1/2 cup (120 mL) chopped celery
2 eggs, lightly beaten
1/4 teaspoon (1 mL) each — ground cloves, thyme, marjoram, savory and paprika
1 teaspoon (5 mL) each — cinnamon, MSG, dried parsley flakes
1/2 teaspoon (2 mL) ground sage

►Mix dressing ingredients together in order given and loosely stuff ducks. Roast in open pan without rack at 400°F (205°C) for 90 minutes. Baste frequently with duck juices or a mixture of cooking sherry and duck juices. Other ducks of similar size may be substituted if pintails are not available.
■ *Joan Fisher*
   Courtesy, Joe Rychetnik
   "Dining Along the Eskimo Coast"
   ALASKA SPORTSMAN®, *April 1964*

Roast Duck with Kraut Dressing

1 large can (29 oz /or/ 826 g) sauerkraut, drained
1 apple, pared and chopped
1/2 cup (120 mL) finely chopped celery
2 good-sized ducks (2 to 3 lbs /or/ 1 to 1.5 kg, each)
1/2 teaspoon (2 mL) salt
Pepper to taste

►Combine kraut, celery and apple. Stuff into cavities of ducks and close with string or skewers. Sprinkle with salt and pepper. Roast at 325°F (160°C) two hours or until ducks are tender.
■ Game Birds from Field to Kitchen

Variation: Chopped onion — raw or first sauteed in butter — and caraway seed, about 1 teaspoon (5 mL) for this amount of kraut, are frequent additions to the above dressing. Or, cut duck in serving pieces and try Mamie Jensen's recipe, Duck 'n' Kraut on the next page.

Roast Duck with Wild Rice Stuffing

►For each mallard, prepare:
2/3 cup (160 mL) boiling water
1/3 cup (80 mL) wild rice
Butter
1 small onion, minced
1/3 cup (80 mL) green pepper, minced
2 tablespoons (30 mL) sherry
1/2 teaspoon (2 mL) salt

►Add rice to boiling water. Reduce heat and simmer gently until rice is done and liquid absorbed, about one hour. In a small amount of butter saute onion, celery and green pepper. Add this mixture together with the sherry and salt to the rice. Sprinkle dressed birds inside and out with salt and pepper. Rub skin with light sprinkling of garlic salt. Stuff birds with rice mixture. Place in shallow pan (without a rack) and put in an oven preheated to 350°F (175°C). Roast until done — two hours, more or less, depending on size and age of ducks. Baste occasionally, more frequently during the last half-hour of cooking, with the following sauce.

Mallard Basting Sauce
(enough for two mallards)
1/2 cube (2 oz /or/ 56 g) butter
1/2 cup (60 mL) sherry
1/4 teaspoon (1 mL) poultry seasoning

►Heat to boiling point and keep warm (stove top will do) while basting duck during last half-hour of roasting.
■ *Mrs. Sam H. Roberson, Douglas*
   The Alaskan Camp Cook

Variation: Wild rice is a classic dressing for duck, but its cost makes most of us think of it only for very special occasions. The distinctive flavor can be s-t-r-e-t-c-h-e-d, however, if wild rice is combined with other rice, brown or white, in about equal parts. Sausage is also a good "stretcher," adding a flavor so complimentary that it's good enough to be included even when money is no object. A combination of hot and mild sausage is especially good. Pan-fry it, crumbling it with a fork while it cooks, before adding it to other dressing ingredients.

Glazed Breast of Wildfowl

►Remove breasts from ducks, grouse or ptarmigan. Skin and clean well. If they require tenderizing, soak in strong salt water solution for several hours. Drain and wipe dry. Rub with salad oil and salt and pepper well. Place in shallow pan on a rack. Broil in very hot oven for 10 to 20 minutes. Glaze with currant jelly and serve with your favorite rice casserole.
■ *Mamie Jensen, Juneau*

Duck and Potatoes

1 wild duck, cleaned
1 unpeeled apple, cut in half
Salt and pepper to taste
4 or 5 large potatoes, diced
1 large onion, chopped
2 to 3 tablespoons (30 to 45 mL)
   dried sage leaves

►Place whole duck in large pot with apple halves and 3 to 4 cups (up to 1 L) water. Cover pot and boil for 30 minutes. Dump water and apple. Add 3 to 4

cups (up to 1 L) fresh boiling water to parboiled duck; salt and pepper to taste. Cover and bake at 350°F (175°C) for 45 minutes. Add potatoes, onion and sage. Bake 45 to 60 minutes longer until duck and potatoes are tender. If necessary, add more water, a little at a time.
■ Tsimpshean Indian Island Cookbook
   Metlakatla

Duck on A Stick

►Hanging ducks to tenderize them and improve their flavor is an absolute "must" . . . unless you're out on a hunting trip and want fresh duck right away. Then use just the breast meat, skewer it on a stick and cook it over a hot fire.
■ *Bunny Mathisen, Petersburg*

Duck 'n' Kraut

1 pint (480 mL) drained sauerkraut
1 pint (480 mL) white wine
   (dry vermouth is good)
2 wild ducks, cut in serving pieces
Flour
Butter or other shortening
1 bay leaf
1 small onion
1 teaspoon (5 mL) salt
3 peppercorns
1 sprig parsley
Additional salt and pepper to taste

►Simmer drained sauerkraut in 1 cup (240 mL) of the white wine for two hours. Meanwhile, rub duck pieces with flour and saute in butter or shortening until lightly browned. Add remaining white wine, the bay leaf, onion, salt and peppercorns. Cover and cook slowly until tender. Then spoon sauerkraut into a baking dish, correct seasonings, and place pieces of browned duck on the kraut. Pour the wine sauce from the duck over all. Cover and bake at 325°F (160°C) for 1-1/2 to 2 hours.
■ *Mamie Jensen, Juneau*

Stikine Duck Casserole

►Cut up four wild ducks as you would chicken fryers. Prepare 4 cups (1 L) bread stuffing seasoned with chopped onion and thyme. Shake duck pieces in paper bag with flour, salt and pepper. Fry in hot oil till lightly browned. Put a ring of fried duck in large casserole. In center make a shallow nest of foil. Place stuffing therein. Put remaining duck around and partially over rest of stuffing. Baste with 1 cup (240 mL) white wine mixed with a little water. Bake at 325°F (160°C) for 45 minutes, covered, and an additional 30 minutes uncovered.
■ *Vern E. Smith, Wrangell*
   PTA Cook Book, *Petersburg*

Braised Duck

Ducks
Salt and pepper
Flour
Fat
Drippings
Onion, minced
Green pepper, minced
Water

►Skin and cut up ducks into serving pieces. Season with salt and pepper and dredge in flour. Brown in hot fat and place in roaster. Brown a generous amount of onion and green pepper in drippings. Add water and pour over all the ducks. Cover and cook in slow oven, 325°F (160°C), until meat is tender tender.
■ *Mrs. Clayton L. Polley, Juneau*
   The Alaskan Camp Cook

Duck Cassoulet

1-1/2 cups (360 mL) dry white beans
1/2 pound (228 g) salt pork, diced
1/3 cup (80 mL) flour
Salt and pepper
2 medium ducks, cut in serving pieces
1 medium onion, chopped
1 clove garlic, crushed
1-1/2 teaspoons (7 mL) salt
1/4 teaspoon (1 mL) pepper
Dash of cloves
1/2 teaspoon (2 mL) mustard
2 peppercorns
1/4 cup (60 mL) ketchup
1-1/2 cups (360 mL) water

►Soak beans overnight; drain. Cook in salted water for about 1-1/2 hours. Drain and place in casserole. Blanch salt pork briefly in boiling water; drain and fry slowly in heavy skillet. Remove pork pieces and reserve both the meat and fat. Season the flour with salt and pepper and dredge the duck pieces. Brown in hot salt pork fat. Remove to casserole. Cook onion and garlic in the same pan about 10 minutes. Add 1-1/2 teaspoons (7 mL) salt and 1/4 teaspoon

(1 mL) pepper and remaining seasonings, reserved pork and water. Bring to a boil and pour over beans and meat, adding hot water as needed to cover well. Bake, covered, in 350°F (175°C) oven for 1-1/2 to 2 hours or until meat is tender and beans are cooked. Serve from casserole with green salad and crusty sourdough bread.
■ *L.W. "Bill" Johnson — Remington's*
   Wild Game Cookbook, ©1968, 1970, 1972
   Published by The Benjamin Company, Inc.

Sherried Duck Breasts

4 mallard breasts, halved
1 cup (240 mL) wild rice
1/3 cup (80 mL) brandy
1/3 cup (80 mL) sherry
1/4 cup (60 mL) currant jelly
1 tablespoon (15 mL) Worcestershire
1/4 pound (114 g) butter or margarine
2 teaspoons (10 mL) cornstarch
2 tablespoons (30 mL) cold water

►Cook rice according to directions on package. In covered skillet melt butter; stir in brandy, sherry, jelly and Worcestershire. Bring to a boil, stirring. Skin duck breasts and add to mixture in skillet. Cover and reduce heat to low. Simmer breasts for 20 minutes, turning a couple of times. Heap wild rice on serving platter and place duck breasts on top; cover and keep warm. Make a paste of the cornstarch and water; slowly stir into liquid in skillet. Cook over low heat, stirring meanwhile, until sauce is thickened. Pour sauce over duck breasts.
■ *The Old Homesteader*

Quick-Fried Breast of Duck

►Prepare this as a topping for hot cakes: Lay uncleaned duck on its back. Slit skin from edge of crop to back end of breastbone. Pull skin sidewise to side of breast meat. Loosen breasts along the breastbone and remove whole.

   Cut breast meat across the grain in strips about 1/2 inch (1.25 cm) thick.

Fry some bacon until nearly done. Place strips of breast in bacon grease and fry to suit. Pour the bacon, duck and drippings on hot cakes and dispose of in the usual manner. (Caution to guides and hunters escorting cheechakos: Don't try this dish on your guests. They'll want it every meal!)

■ *G.R. Gray, Haines, The Alaskan Camp Cook*

Duck Stew

►Clean the meat that is left after you have removed breast meat for another dish. Cut it into suitable pieces, place in stew pot with onions and cover with plenty of water. Salt and pepper to taste. Bring to medium boil and cook about one hour. Add stiff dumplings made of pancake mix and continue boiling for about four minutes in covered pot. (Less time may be needed for dumplings at a fast boil.)

■ *G.R. Gray, Haines, The Alaskan Camp Cook*

Wild Duck Baked in Wine

Breast meat from 2 wild ducks
Seasoned flour
Olive oil
1 onion, chopped fine
1 cup (240 mL) dry red wine
1/2 cup (120 mL) brandy
1 small can (4½ oz /or/ 128 g) chopped
  ripe olives
2 tablespoons (30 mL) chopped parsley
1 tablespoon (15 mL) chopped chives
Salt and freshly ground black pepper

►Dust duck meat with seasoned flour and brown in skillet in olive oil. Remove to baking dish. Saute onion in oil until transparent but not brown. Add remaining ingredients and cook for one minute. Adjust seasoning and pour over duck meat. Bake uncovered at 350°F (175°C) for about 30 minutes, basting occasionally with the sauce.

■ *Mamie Jensen, Juneau*

Broiled Wild Duck

Ducks
Tarragon or rosemary
Soy sauce
Butter, melted

►Split the ducks and rub them well with soy sauce and a little tarragon or rosemary. For rare duck, broil under a hot flame, watching carefully for about six minutes on the bone side and four to six minutes on the skin side. Be sure not to burn the skin. Baste with butter and soy sauce or butter and white wine.

■ *L.W. "Bill" Johnson — Remington's*
  Wild Game Cookbook, ©1968, 1970, 1972
  Published by The Benjamin Company, Inc.

Duck in The Mud

►While you are having breakfast, build up a good campfire in a hollow. Your duck or goose is eviscerated, so wipe it inside and out with a cloth. Rub the inside thoroughly with salt and a little pepper. Stuff cavity with an apple, an onion or both. Fold the feathers to cover all openings and plaster the whole thing with a coat of clay mud (sand or loam will not do) about an inch (2.5 cm) thick. Place the bird in the bottom of your fire among the ashes and cover it well with wood. Go hunting all day, and when you return for dinner, be prepared for the best duck or goose you ever tasted. Dig it out of the ashes (it should still be hot) and break off the clay. The feathers come with it.

■ *Kenneth Hughes, Haines*
  The Alaskan Camp Cook

Barbecued Duck

4 large wild ducks
3 tablespoons (45 mL) lemon juice
2 teaspoons (10 mL) Worcestershire
2 teaspoons (10 mL) prepared mustard
2 teaspoons (10 mL) ketchup
2 tablespoons (30 mL) butter, melted
2 teaspoons (10 mL) salt
1 teaspoon (5 mL) paprika
Brown sugar
2 medium apples, finely grated

►Cut breasts from ducks (eight pieces); broil until brown, about 15 minutes. Baste continuously with barbecue sauce made from lemon juice, Worcestershire, prepared mustard, ketchup and butter. After the meat starts browning, sprinkle with remaining ingredients. Continue broiling 45 minutes for well done meat.

■ Game Birds From Field To Kitchen

Wild Duck with Sour Cream

5 to 6 pounds (2.25 to 2.7 kg) duck, cut up
Flour, salt and pepper
2 tablespoons (30 mL) fat
1 onion chopped
2 tablespoons (30 mL) parsley
1/4 teaspoon (1 mL) each — rosemary
  and thyme
1 cup (240 mL) dry red wine
1 cup (240 mL) sour cream

►Dredge duck pieces in flour, salt and pepper, and brown in fat. Place in Dutch oven. Add all other ingredients except sour cream. Cover and bake 1-1/2 hours at 350°F (175°C). Add sour cream and bake half an hour more at 300°F (150°C).

■ *Ruth H. Smith*
  Alaska's Cooking, Anchorage

Black Coot Ducks

►If you're stuck in the woods or on the beach and the meat supply is nil, try this with "fish" ducks:

Skin out the breasts of three coots. Soak in salt water and vinegar for three hours. Dry and dredge with flour. Brown in bacon fat. Add a large onion chopped up, salt and pepper, and enough water to simmer as for pot roast. Add 1 teaspoon (5 mL) mixed spices. When nearly done, add 1 cup (240 mL) red wine (if available) and let simmer until done. Thicken the liquid for gravy.

■ *Mrs. E.E. Weschenfelder, Fritz Cove*
   The Alaskan Camp Cook

Pickled Duck

1 cup (240 mL) chopped onion
12 cloves
1/2 cup (120 mL) vinegar
1/3 cup (80 mL) sugar
3 bay leaves
Salt and pepper to taste

►Cook duck until tender in a solution made of the above ingredients. This 80-year-old recipe is for one duck only.

■ *Mrs. A.J. Birkenback*
   PTA Cook Book, *Petersburg*

GOOSE

Roast Wild Goose with Apples
A classic recipe

►Singe, clean and wipe dry a young wild goose. Rub inside with salt and pepper. Peel and core four to six firm apples, depending on size. Where the core was removed put one scant teaspoon (4 mL) brown sugar and one whole clove. Stuff the goose with these; sew up both ends, truss and brush with oil. Place breast up in roasting pan. Sear in a very hot oven for 20 minutes; then turn breast down and season with salt and pepper. Cover tightly; reduce heat to moderate and roast 1-1/2 hours, possibly two, or until tender. Baste occasionally with the broth which accumulates in the pan.

The liver, heart and gizzard should be put in a saucepan, seasoned with salt, covered with boiling water and simmered until tender. When done, finely mince these giblets and save them for the gravy. To prepare the gravy, remove the finished goose from the roasting pan and place on a hot dish. Skim off all fat from the broth; then thicken with 2 tablespoons (30 mL) flour creamed to a smooth paste in 2 tablespoons (30 mL) melted butter. If too thick, add hot stock or boiling water to thin. Then add the minced liver, gizzard and heart; season with salt and pepper and serve separately in a gravy boat.

To serve the goose, untruss and garnish with eight small slices of buttered toast that have been spread liberally with spiced apple butter. Sprinkle finely chopped parsley over the breast of the goose and send to the table.

■ Tsimpshean Indian Island Cookbook
   Metlakatla

Variation: Tenderize the meat and vary the flavor, if you want, by first marinating the goose three or four hours in a mixture of: 1-1/2 cups (360 mL) dry white wine; the juice of two lemons and one orange; one onion, sliced; 1/8 teaspoon (0.5 mL) nutmeg; one small bay leaf; a few celery leaves and sprigs of parsley. Then remove goose from marinade and rub cavity with salt and pepper. Stuff with three peeled and quartered apples and three stalks celery; truss goose and place breast side up in roasting pan. Sear in a very hot oven, turn bird, cover pan and continue roasting, all as directed above, basting from time to time with marinade and pan drippings.

■ *Mamie Jensen, Juneau*

Green Olive Marinade
For Wild Goose

3 cups (720 mL) water
1/4 cup (60 mL) brandy
1/2 cup (120 mL) stuffed green olives
2 carrots, grated
1/4 cup (60 mL) olive oil
1 teaspoon (5 mL) salt
1 cup (240 mL) sherry
1 cup (240 mL) chopped onion
1 clove garlic, minced
1/4 cup (60 mL) chopped celery leaves
2 tablespoons (30 mL) lemon juice
1/4 teaspoon (1 mL) pepper
1 wild goose, cut into serving pieces

►Mix the marinade ingredients, pour over meat and marinate, refrigerated, for eight hours or more.

Then place meat and about 3 cups (720 mL) of marinade into a Dutch oven. Cover and cook slowly for about 3-1/2 hours at a low oven temperature, 325°F (160°C), or on top of the stove. Check occasionally to be sure there is sufficient moisture in the pan. Add more marinade or water if needed.

■ Clarence Massey
"To Cook A Wild Goose"
ALASKA® magazine, March 1973

Roast Wild Goose with Apricot Stuffing
A "slow oven" bird with an excellent dressing

1 young wild goose
Juice of 1 lemon
Salt and pepper
1/4 cup (60 mL) butter
1/4 cup (60 mL) chopped onion
1 cup (240 mL) chopped tart apple
1 cup (240 mL) chopped dried apricots
3 cups (720 mL) soft bread crumbs
1/4 teaspoon (2 mL) salt
1/8 teaspoon (0.5 mL) pepper
4 to 6 slices parboiled bacon
Melted butter

►Sprinkle goose inside and out with lemon juice, salt and pepper. Melt 1/4 cup (60 mL) butter in a large saucepan, add onion and cook until tender. Stir in apples, apricots, bread crumbs, salt and pepper. Spoon stuffing lightly into cavity. Close opening with skewers and string. Cover breast with bacon slices and cheesecloth soaked in butter. Place goose breast up on rack in roasting pan. Roast at 325°F (160°C) for 2-1/2 to 3 hours. Allow 30 minutes per pound (0.45 kg). Baste frequently with pan drippings. If age of goose is uncertain, pour 1 cup (240 mL) water in pan and cover during last hour of cooking.

■ Game Birds From Field To Kitchen

Wild Goose in Garlic Cream Sauce

1 wild goose with giblets
2 medium-sized onions
3 carrots, sliced
1 sprig parsley
1 bay leaf
Few celery leaves
4 cloves
8 peppercorns
Butter and/or oil

►Put thoroughly cleaned goose, heart, liver and gizzard in a large kettle and cover with slightly salted boiling water. Bring to boil again and skim carefully. Add vegetables, cloves and peppercorns and simmer slowly until goose is tender. When completely tender, remove from kettle and slice all meat from the carcass.

Heat butter or oil or a combination of the two in a large frying pan and brown the pieces of goose. Place on a large platter, top with Garlic Cream Sauce and serve. Serve remaining Garlic Cream Sauce in a gravy boat.

Garlic Cream Sauce
4 slices whole-wheat bread
3 cups (720 mL) milk
5 small whole cloves of garlic
4 egg yolks, well beaten
1/2 cup (120 mL) cream

►Toast bread until quite dry; crumble finely. Set aside. Heat milk in a small saucepan, add garlic and simmer until garlic is tender; remove garlic. Blend toast crumbs into hot milk. Then strain through a colander or sieve into another saucepan. Blend cream into beaten egg yolks and spoon in about 1/4 cup (60 mL) of the hot milk, blend well and slowly stir into remaining hot milk sauce. Simmer a few minutes, stirring constantly, over a slow fire.

■ Tsimpshean Indian Island Cookbook
Metlakatla

Marinade For Ducks or Geese
An overnight marinade recommended for flavoring "fish feeders" or tenderizing old birds

Mix and beat for one minute:
3/4 cup (180 mL) vinegar
1/4 cup (60 mL) soy sauce
1/8 teaspoon (0.5 mL) pepper
1 teaspoon (5 mL) salt
1/2 teaspoon (2 mL) powdered ginger
4 to 6 cloves of garlic, crushed

►Bathe ducks or geese inside and out in vinegar mix. Let stand in vinegar bath overnight. In the morning, drain and let stand at least one hour before stuffing with your favorite stuffing. Roast at 350°F (175°C) for 35 minutes per pound (0.45 kg) or until done.

■ An Alaskan Cook Book, *Kenai*

Roast (Old) Bird

►Occasionally, a wild goose turned out to be too tough to be roasted in the ordinary manner. By steaming it for 15 to 30 minutes, then roasting it slowly, we made the feathered old-timer into a palatable entree.

■ *Iva Senft, as told to Mary J. Barry*
"Camp Cookery, Trail Tonics,
and Indian Infants"
ALASKA SPORTSMAN®, *July 1964*

Burgundy Gander

"If you feel you probably have a tough, old gander to prepare, it is best to forego roasting it,"
says Clarence Massey. His remedy:

1 wild goose, cut into serving pieces
Salted boiling water
Salt and pepper
Handful of dried onion flakes
1/2 cup (120 mL) Burgundy wine
2 cans (about 10 oz /or/ about 285 g, each)
  cream of mushroom soup

►Parboil goose in salted water to cover for 20 to 30 minutes. Drain pieces, pat dry and place them in a Dutch oven or a heavy iron frying pan with a lid. Season well with salt and pepper and sprinkle over them enough dried onion to equal a good-sized onion. Add wine and one can of soup, plus a canful of water. Put lid on Dutch oven and place in a 325°F (160°C) oven or simmer on top of stove for four to five hours.

When goose is ready to serve, mix the second can of soup with half a can of water in a small saucepan. Heat and pour over goose after it is placed on the serving platter. Garnish the platter with sauteed mushrooms or small, boiled white onions as a finishing touch.
■ *Clarence Massey*
  "To Cook A Wild Goose"
  ALASKA® *magazine, March 1973*

Here are two no-fuss, *no-muss recipes — one for an oven-roasting bag, the other for the slow-cooker, both from The Old Homesteader:*

Orange Wild Goose

1 large wild goose
1/3 cup (80 mL) whole-wheat flour
1 package chicken gravy mix
1 teaspoon (5 mL) salt
2 tablespoons (30 mL) sugar
1 cup (240 mL) hot water
1 can (6 oz /or/ 170 g) frozen orange juice
  concentrate, thawed

►Preheat oven to 375°F (190°C). Put flour in a large oven-browning bag and shake to coat the inside of bag. Mix all other ingredients except goose and pour into bag. Place bag in a deep roasting pan. Place bird in bag and turn gently inside bag to coat all parts of the goose. Close bag with a twist-tie about 2 inches (5 cm) from top. Prick bag in several places on top. Cook goose 2-1/2 to 3 hours or until tender. Remove bird to hot platter and pour sauce into a heavy skillet. Skim off excess fat and thicken gravy to suit.

Slow-Cooked Wild Goose

1 wild goose cut in quarters*
Salt to taste
3/4 cup (180 mL) red wine, not too dry
1 tablespoon (15 mL) grated orange peel or
*   dehydrated orange peel*
2 tablespoons (30 mL) honey
1 tablespoon (15 mL) or less soy sauce

►If bird is fat, prick in several places with a fork. Salt to taste and place quarters, with skin side up, in a slow-cooking pot. Combine the other ingredients and mix. Pour over the bird pieces and cover. Cook on lowest heat for 10 to 12 hours. At serving time, skim off any fat that may have accumulated.

* The original recipe called for an emperor, cackler, or brant. The numbers of these geese have been declining recently in Alaska, so the harvest of these species is currently illegal.

UPLAND BIRDS

Grouse Mulligan

Grouse, cut up
Flour
Salt and pepper
Drippings
1 clove garlic
1 green pepper, chopped
1 good-sized onion, sliced
1 cup (240 mL) hot water

►Cut birds into convenient pieces; roll in flour and brown in hot drippings. Season with salt and pepper and put in covered baking dish. Add sliced onion, chopped pepper, garlic and hot water. Cover and cook at least two hours in a slow oven, about 350°F (175°C). If necessary add more water while cooking. I sprinkle a little flour over the pieces once or twice during the cooking. This is a good way to use old birds. Young grouse should be fried the same as chicken.
■ *Lulu MacKecknie*
  PTA Cook Book, *Petersburg*

Spruce Hens in Foil

4 spruce hens (or ptarmigan)
Whole-wheat flour (or white flour)
Salt and pepper to taste
2 tablespoons (30 mL) butter or margarine
Table wine

►Dust birds with flour and salt and pepper them. Heat butter in heavy skillet and brown the spruce hens on all sides, beginning with skin side down. Prepare four squares of heavy-duty foil and place a bird in the center of each. Add 1 tablespoon (15 mL), or slightly more, table wine to each package. Fold foil over and crimp edges to make a tightly sealed package to keep juices from escaping. Place packages on a cookie sheet in an oven preheated to 425°F (220°C) and bake for about 30 minutes. Open one package and test the thigh with a fork for tenderness. Open packages carefully to save juices which can be poured over the birds for serving.
■ *The Old Homesteader*

Braised Spruce Chicken

Spruce chickens
Salt and pepper to taste
Flour
Butter or bacon drippings
Half-and-half
Cornstarch

►Split spruce chickens in half with the kitchen shears. Sprinkle with salt and pepper; dredge in flour. Brown well in butter or bacon drippings. Add half-and-half to a depth of 1 inch (2.5 cm). Cover and cook over low heat for 45 minutes or until tender. This step may be done in the oven set at 325°F (160°C) if you prefer. Take up the halves of the birds and thicken the juices remaining in the pan with cornstarch stirred to a paste in cold water. Check seasonings and add more salt and pepper if you like; perhaps a dash of paprika, too.
■ *The Old Homesteader*

Variation: Brown a good-sized chopped onion in the drippings before you brown the spruce chickens. Use canned tomatoes and their juice for half the liquid needed to braise the meat.

Grouse Fricassee

Grouse
Salt and pepper
Onion or garlic salt
Flour
Fat
1/2 cup (120 mL) water
2 tablespoons (30 mL) flour
1 cup (240 mL) milk
Salt and pepper to taste

►Cut cleaned grouse into several pieces; salt and pepper and add onion or garlic salt. Roll each piece in flour until heavily coated. Brown the pieces in fat in a heavy skillet. Pour on water, cover and let simmer about an hour or until tender. When ready to serve, remove the meat to serving platter; add flour to pan and stir to blend. Add milk and salt and pepper to taste. Pour over meat.

■ *Gussie and Bill Byington, Juneau*
   The Alaskan Camp Cook

Three Ways To Prepare Upland Birds

►*Stewed* — We generally stewed our grouse and ptarmigan. They have large, meaty breasts and make excellent soup, cooked with carrots, celery or other available vegetables. Rice or soup noodles can also be added to the soup.

Fried — Ptarmigan and grouse may also be fried, by rolling the pieces in flour seasoned with salt and pepper, browning in fat, and steaming until tender in milk.

Roasted — To prepare roast grouse, sprinkle the bird with salt and fill the cavity with bread stuffing or simply place an onion inside. Put the bird breast side up in pan, rub with butter or put bacon strips over the bird, cover, and roast in a slow oven.

■ *Iva Senft, as told to Mary J. Barry*
   "Camp Cookery, Trail Tonics,
   and Indian Infants"
   ALASKA SPORTSMAN®, *July 1964*

Oven-Fried Spruce Hen

►Arrange spruce hens which have been split in half with skin side down in shallow baking pan. Place a generous slice of butter on each piece. Sprinkle with salt, pepper and lots of paprika. Bake in very hot oven until almost tender. Turn pieces and repeat seasoning. Continue baking until well done. Remove from oven and place pieces on hot platter while making gravy. Add 1 cup (240 mL) milk or more to baking pan and heat slowly on top of stove, stirring to loosen bits of meat sticking to pan. Thicken and season to your own taste.

■ *Mamie Jensen, Juneau*

Russian Supper Grouse

Grouse breasts and whatever other
   parts you may have
Bisquick, or any biscuit mix or pancake mix
   (amount depends on how much bird
   you have)
Seasonings from 1 package
   Lipton's noodle soup mix
Grease, for browning
Onions, optional
Whole small new potatoes, or large ones, cut

►Roll grouse in Bisquick seasoned with about half the soup seasoning. Brown in grease in frying pan, turning until well browned. Sprinkle rest of seasoning over browned grouse in pan. (Sliced onions may be placed on top at this time, if desired.) Pour water over all; add more water as needed, keeping about 1/2 inch (1.25 cm) of water in the pan. Cover and cook, heat turned down, until tender — time will depend on the age of the birds. Add potatoes last half-hour of cooking time. When done, remove grouse and potatoes to platter. Thicken gravy with remaining Bisquick (left from first step). Add more water if necessary. Serve in separate bowl. Real good for other types of wild or domestic fowl.

■ *Annetta Gillespie*
   Recipes From The Scrolls of Saint Peter's
   Seward

Spruce Grouse with Blueberries

4 spruce grouse
Salt and pepper
1/4 cup (60 mL) oil
1/4 cup (60 mL) lemon juice
1 teaspoon (5 mL) dried rosemary
2 cups (480 mL) wild blueberries
Sugar
Butter

►Season birds inside and out with salt and pepper. Heat oil and lemon juice just to blend and add crumbled rosemary. Rub this mixture generously over and inside birds. Save any remaining lemon oil to baste birds during final browning. Stuff grouse with blueberries and add 1/2 teaspoon (2 mL) sugar to each after cavity is filled. Sew or skewer shut. Add a small pat of butter to each bird and wrap each separately in aluminum foil, keeping packages loose but tightly sealed so that juices will not escape. Roast, breast down, in a hot oven, 425°F (220°C), for about 30 minutes. Open packages carefully and pour juices into a small saucepan. Turn birds breast side up on foil, leaving foil open, and return birds to hot oven to brown. Baste with lemon oil. Thicken juices if desired, pour over birds at serving time.

■ *The editors, ALASKA® magazine*

The Best Spruce Hen

►Boil pieces of spruce hen. Take out of hot water immediately to drain and cool. Eat with seal oil.
■ *Anon.*

Breast of Grouse

3 grouse
1 each — onion, sliced carrot, celery stalk, bay leaf
Few sprigs parsley
Butter
Flour
Salt and pepper
1 can (4 oz /or/ 114 g) mushroom stems and pieces
Lemon juice or 1/2 cup (120 mL) white wine
1 cup (240 mL) sour cream

►Remove breasts from grouse and set aside. Break the carcasses into pieces and cover with water. Add onion, carrot, celery, parsley and bay leaf, and cook until the liquid is reduced to about 1-1/2 cups (360 mL). Strain and reserve stock.

Meanwhile, roll breasts in flour, salt and pepper, and saute in butter. In another pan, make a sauce of 4 tablespoons (60 mL) butter, 4 tablespoons (60 mL) flour and the reserved stock. Add mushrooms and stir until thick. Season to taste, adding a little lemon juice or the 1/2 cup (120 mL) white wine and the sour cream. Stir together until mixed but do not boil. Place breasts on a platter and surround with sauce. Sprinkle minced parsley over the top and serve.
■ *Marguerite Doucette*
  Governor's House, Juneau
  One Hundred Years in the Kitchen

Grouse, Spruce Hen or Ptarmigan Stew

►If the birds are badly shot, take the good part, cut in pieces, wipe and season with salt. Dip in melted, cooled butter or margarine and let the butter cool on them further, then roll in flour. Fry. Lay each piece in a pan and cover halfway with boiling water. Let simmer. When done, thicken cooking juices with a water and flour paste. If you want, increase the amount of liquid to cover the meat and make dumplings to stew on top. Cover and bake 20 minutes until dumplings are done.
Variation: Butter, flour and brown the pieces as above. Add water and simmer until about done. Mix flour, curry powder to taste and water, and pour over the pieces. Cook a few minutes until juices thicken. Serve over boiled rice.
■ *Mrs. George Foster*
  Recipes From The Scrolls of Saint Peter's
  Seward

Epicurian Grouse

►The breasts are really about all there is to a grouse. Split them in two, season and fry gently in olive oil and you have an epicurian delight. If you really want to show off, try the following:

You will need at least one grouse per person. Slather grouse well, inside and out, with butter and salt and pepper to taste. Pour some lemon and maybe a few lemon wedges, a chunk of onion, a stalk of celery, and a piece of apple inside the cavity. Arrange birds in a shallow pan or foil and set slightly to one side of the main source of heat, either charcoal or wood fire. Now, make a loose-fitting foil tent over this with room for the heat to get up inside and the tent will act as a sort of reflector oven. When the thighs become good and loose when you wiggle them, they're done.

For a final, classic touch, pour a little brandy over and flame . . . this crisps the skin.
■ *Ken Davidson*
  "Moveable Feasts — Cooking Game in the Field"
  BC Outdoors, *September 1981*

Ptarmigan in Cream

►One bird per person is usual. Pluck and clean the birds. Dice the liver, heart and gizzard. Carefully loosen the skin on the breast and insert between it and the body two or three strips of fresh pork on the breastbone. Pull skin back in place. Truss. Put 1/2 teaspoon (2 mL) salt into each bird and then fry on all sides — the breasts first — in butter in a deep heavy skillet. Fry until golden brown. Sprinkle each bird with another 1/2 teaspoon (2 mL) salt. Fry the diced giblets along with the birds. In a saucepan boil half milk and half water — 3/4 cup (180 mL) for each bird — and pour gradually into skillet but not over the birds. Let simmer for about an hour, basting frequently. Now add 1/2 cup (120 mL) sour cream per bird and simmer for another hour. Remove the birds and cut them in two. Season cream gravy with salt if needed. A good hostess will serve the birds with lowbush cranberry jam and boiled potatoes and will let her guests or family pick up the birds in their fingers.
■ *Martha Helmericks*
  Northern Lites, Tasty Bites, *Fairbanks*

For a delicious, rich-tasting gravy that is free from lumps, try this: Gradually stir cold water into WHOLE-WHEAT flour until a smooth paste results. Stir this paste into the hot gravy liquid and simmer gently until thick enough. Or, you can stir the flour into fat that remains in the pan after frying meat, and then add the liquid. Either way, WHOLE-WHEAT flour makes excellent gravy.

Ptarmigan and Dumplings

Breasts, legs and giblets of ptarmigan
Flour
1 onion, minced
Salt and pepper
Garlic powder or thyme
Water

Dumplings
1 cup (240 mL) flour
2 teaspoons (10 mL) baking powder
1/2 teaspoon (2 mL) salt
Liquid

►Use breasts and meaty legs of two or three birds, depending upon number and capacity of people eating. Flour pieces and brown in skillet with giblets and onion. Season to taste. Add water to cover and simmer two hours. Make dumplings with flour, baking powder, salt and liquid enough to make a soft dough. Drop gently on ptarmigan, a teaspoonful at a time, cover and cook 15 minutes more. Good, too, with mashed potatoes or boiled rice, white or brown.
■ *Georgia Griffin, Fairbanks*
   The Alaskan Camp Cook

Ptarmigan Rice Paella

►*The birds:* Use either spruce hen or ptarmigan and allow one per person. Skin and quarter the birds, shake the pieces in seasoned flour and fry in bacon fat or other shortening until tender. Arrange meat around the rice on a serving platter.

The rice:
2 tablespoons (30 mL) butter
1 clove garlic, crushed
1 cup (240 mL) raw rice
2 cups (480 mL) chicken broth or bouillon
1/2 teaspoon (2 mL) saffron
2 teaspoons (10 mL) salt
1 jar (3 oz /or/ 85 g) mushroom buttons
   with juice
1 package (10 oz /or/ 285 g) frozen carrots
   and peas
1 tablespoon (15 mL) monosodium glutamate

►Heat butter in a heavy skillet, add garlic and rice and cook, stirring constantly, until rice turns golden. Add hot chicken broth or bouillon and remaining ingredients and heat to boiling again, stirring occasionally to separate frozen vegetables. Cover, reduce heat and cook until rice is tender and all liquid is absorbed, about 20 minutes.
■ *Joe Rychetnik*
   "Dining Along the Eskimo Coast"
   ALASKA SPORTSMAN®, *April 1964*

Ptarmigan or Spruce Chicken in Wine Sauce

Cut up birds to serve four
Butter
1 large onion, chopped
2 cloves garlic, minced fine
1 bay leaf
4 drops Tabasco
4 whole cloves
1/2 teaspoon (2 mL) salt
1/8 teaspoon (0.5 mL) pepper
Few grains cayenne
1 pint (480 mL) white wine (Sauterne preferred)
1 pint (480 mL) heavy cream
1/4 teaspoon (1 mL) rosemary
1/4 teaspoon (1 mL) marjoram
Hot baked potatoes to serve four

►Heat butter in an electric skillet or heavy iron skillet with a tight-fitting cover. Saute onion in hot butter, add garlic, bay leaf, Tabasco and cloves and stir constantly until onion and garlic are lightly browned. Add salt, pepper and cayenne and saute meat until evenly browned. Add white wine, cover and simmer 30 minutes. Remove meat. Slowly add cream to pan juices, stirring constantly. Then add herbs and return meat to pan. Heat to boiling point but do not boil. Serve at once with baked potatoes.
■ *Leola Anderson*
   Alaska's Cooking, *Anchorage*

Fried or Broiled Grouse or Ptarmigan

A good one for the campfire

Birds
Oil
Salt
Bacon
Barbecue sauce
Paprika

►Split the cleaned birds down the back and press pieces flat. Brush with oil and sprinkle with salt. Place skin side down and broil for 15 minutes, turning once. Place strip of bacon on each bird and broil until bacon is crisp. If desired, baste every five minutes with barbecue sauce or sweet pickle juice. Before serving, sprinkle with paprika.
■ The Alaskan Camp Cook

Upland Bird Casserole

"A favorite way to prepare birds such as ptarmigan and spruce hen"

►Allow about 1 pound (456 g) of bird per person. Cut cleaned bird (or birds) into serving-sized pieces and place in a casserole dish. Pour undiluted cream of mushroom soup over pieces. Cover and bake two to three hours at 350°F (175°C) or until tender, depending on age of bird.
■ *Beverly Wolford, Homer*
   "Cooking Game Meat and Birds"
   Alaska Hunting Guide (1979)

Roast Ptarmigan

►Dress birds (allow at least one to each person) and stuff loosely with your favorite dressing. Place in a heated roaster containing enough vegetable oil to barely cover bottom of pan. Lay a strip of bacon across each ptarmigan and roast in preheated hot oven for 30 minutes with cover on. Baste the birds frequently.
■ *Mamie Jensen, Juneau*

Pot Roast Ptarmigan

►Roll ptarmigan pieces in flour seasoned with salt and pepper. Brown well in olive oil or butter. Place in Dutch oven. Add one chicken bouillon cube dissolved in 1 cup (240 mL) hot water, two or more cloves of garlic and one large onion, sliced. Cover and place in 350°F (175°C) oven for two hours. Add a little more water during cooking; when done, remove to platter in warm oven. Make gravy, adding more water.
■ *Mrs. G.A. Gustafson*
   Alaska's Cooking, *Anchorage*

Breast of Ptarmigan in Sour Cream

Breast meat from 2 ptarmigan
Salt and pepper
Beaten egg
Fine bread crumbs
Butter
1 cup (240 mL) sour cream
2 tablespoons (30 mL) wine
1 clove garlic, minced
Paprika

►Dip breast pieces in beaten egg and roll in fine bread crumbs. Saute until browned in butter or other shortening. Place in a roaster or Dutch oven. Mix sour cream, wine and garlic and spread over meat. Dust generously with paprika. Cover and cook in a 350°F (175°C) oven until meat feels tender when pierced with a fork. The whole bird may be cooked this way, but the breast pieces make a greater delicacy.
■ Out of Alaska's Kitchens

Stuffed Ptarmigan Breasts

►With a sharp knife remove breasts of ptarmigan from the bone. Put together in pairs sandwich fashion, using favorite bread stuffing for filling. Wrap together with strips of bacon and fasten with toothpicks. Bake in an open baking pan for about 45 minutes, basting with orange juice. Serve with Dill Sauce. Make this sauce by preparing Cream Sauce and adding 1/4 cup (60 mL) finely chopped fresh dill.
■ Out of Alaska's Kitchens

Steamed Ptarmigan Breasts

Ptarmigan breasts, boned
Salt and pepper
Garlic salt
2 or 3 drops soy sauce for each piece
1/2 teaspoon (2 mL) oil for each piece
Flour
Oil
Water

►Place breast pieces on a plate; sprinkle with salt and pepper, garlic salt, soy sauce and salad oil or melted shortening. Let meat sit for an hour. Dip breast pieces in flour or a mixture of flour and cracker crumbs. Melt some fat in a heavy skillet; brown ptarmigan breasts on both sides. Add a small amount of water, cover with heavy lid and let steam about 20 minutes or until tender.
■ *Gussie and Bill Byington, Juneau*
   The Alaskan Camp Cook

Braised Ptarmigan

3 ptarmigan, dressed
Salt and pepper to taste
3 tablespoons (45 mL) flour
2 tablespoons (30 mL) vegetable oil
2 cups (480 mL) cream
Paprika to taste

►With a sharp boning knife remove the breast meat from the carcasses of the three ptarmigan. Salt and pepper the meat on both sides and roll in flour. Heat oil in heavy skillet and saute the ptarmigan pieces until well browned on each side. Reduce heat to simmer; pour on cream and sprinkle with paprika. (Half-and-half may be used instead of cream.) Cover the skillet and cook slowly until the meat is tender. This may be done either on top of the range or in the oven. If desired, thicken the sauce with a little cornstarch mixed to a paste with cold water. Serve with a combination of brown and wild rice. Save the rest of the ptarmigan for use in soup.
■ *The Old Homesteader*

Bran-Fried Ptarmigan Breasts

►Skin ptarmigan and separate wings from the breasts. Split breasts in half. Dip breasts in mixture of 1/3 cup (80 mL) bran (or wheat germ) to 2/3 cup (160 mL) seasoned flour. Fry slowly in half butter and half vegetable shortening about 20 minutes, or until done.
■ *Mamie Jensen, Juneau*

Cranberry Baked Ptarmigan

Breast meat of 4 ptarmigan
Salt and pepper
Bacon (optional)
1-1/2 cups (360 mL) cranberry juice

►Sprinkle breast meat with salt and pepper. Place skin side up in a greased baking dish. Or, if meat is skinned, add bacon strips on top. Pour cranberry juice over all. Bake, covered, about 30 minutes at 350°F (175°C). Uncover and continue baking until fork tender.
■ *Sharon Sapp*
  Souvenir Cook Book, *Skagway*

Alaska Game Bird Pie

►Prepare pieces of any wild game bird as you would for frying. Dredge with flour and brown pieces lightly in oil. Use meatier pieces and reserve bony pieces for soup. When well browned, season with salt, pepper, celery and onion salt, and the favorite family seasoning, whatever you prefer. Pour on warm water to twice the depth of fowl, bring to a boil; reduce heat and simmer slowly until meat is almost tender. Add whatever vegetables you like — green peas, diced new potatoes, minced onion, sliced carrots, and so on. Resume simmering until both meat and vegetables are done, then thicken the gravy. Season to taste, add more liquid if necessary and spoon into large baking dish. Make crust of biscuit dough and roll to 1/4-inch (0.6 cm) thickness. Place over meat in baking dish, slash to vent and bake at 450°F (230°C) until biscuit crust is done.
■ *Mamie Jensen, Juneau*

Boiled Murres

►Skin and clean murres. Put birds in a saucepan with 3 quarts (3 L) water or more, as needed. Add 2 tablespoons (30 mL) salt and 1 teaspoon (5 mL) pepper. Boil until tender. Elbow macaroni can be added to broth or enough flour to thicken slightly. If adding flour, mix it with cold water before adding. Old squaw ducks and auklets can be prepared this same way.
■ *Norma Silook, Gambell, Saint Lawrence Island*

Duck-Moose Patties

1 pound (456 g) moose meat or venison
1 pound (456 g) mallard duck meat
2 medium onions, ground fine
3 slices dry bread, ground
2 eggs, slightly beaten
1/2 cup (120 mL) water or juice from the meat
    if it is canned
1-1/2 teaspoons (7 mL) salt
1/2 teaspoon (2 mL) pepper
1/2 teaspoon (2 mL) celery salt
Dash garlic salt

►Grind moose or venison meat and duck meat together. Add remaining ingredients, mix thoroughly and shape into patties. Dip patties in flour and fry in bacon drippings over a hot fire. Makes a good picnic dish.
■ *Mamie Jensen, Juneau*

If you are lucky enough to connect with any ptarmigan while you are hunting this winter, save some of the white feathers — the more fluffy ones. When bird-nesting time comes in the spring, release the feathers to the breezes when you note swallows circling around. There is nothing they like better for nesting material than white ptarmigan feathers.
■ *Chitina Trapper*
  The Cabin Friend
  ALASKA® magazine, *October 1977*

Chapter 7

Antlered Game~Venison

Originally the word *venison* meant the meat of any game — animal or bird. Today most people think of it rather vaguely as the meat of all or at least several members of the deer family, or further defined, as a synonym for deer meat, maybe because that is the most common "venison" to grace the table.

For cooking purposes, we've settled on the second definition. While deer, elk, moose, caribou and reindeer each have distinctive flavors, we figure a cook can't go wrong substituting meat "in hand" for meat that's still in the Bush. It is the rare food locker that contains one of each variety. Therefore, although the recipes may specify the meat of one or another animal, all of them are suitable for *our* favorite venison dishes.

IN THE FIELD

Some excellent information is available for the hunter about how to field dress the large game common to the Lower 48. A photo-book, *After Your Deer Is Down,* by Josef Fischl and Leonard Lee Rue, III [Tulsa, 1981], is one of the clearest, but there are other good ones.

For help with field care of the largest of antlered creatures, Jim Rearden's *ALASKA®* magazine story, "How An Expert Dresses A Moose" [September 1981], details the best way to quickly cool the meat and reduce the carcass to manageable loads for the carry back to camp.

All the experts agree that cooling the meat quickly and keeping it dry are the most important essentials. Most also recommend that the scent hocks be removed carefully and early in the process — whether or not the rut season is in full swing.

Moose meat and other venison that is quickly cooled in the field, kept free of dirt and flies, and properly aged, is almost invariably tender and mild-flavored. Strong flavors come from meat that

has spoiled when hanging because of a lack of air circulation, or from meat that has not been quickly cooled. Even bull moose that are rutting are good eating if the tainted skin is not allowed to touch the meat and if the meat is cooled quickly and properly aged. For the largest animals, skinning first and removing the viscera last is the quickest way to allow body heat to escape. With deer and other smaller game, propping the body cavity open may be sufficient, and leaving the skin on helps to protect the meat.

To prevent blowflies from laying eggs in the meat, put it in large bags made of cotton muslin, old sheets or pillowcases. Such large bags should be part of a hunter's equipment. Liberally coating the meat with pepper also helps, as does smearing the meat with blood, which when dry forms a flyproof glaze.

Never lay the meat on wet or swampy ground. Cut a lot of willow, alder or other brush and pile it high. Then lay the meat on it while you are butchering. This allows air to circulate around the meat so it will cool and a crust will form.

If it is raining, get the meat under cover quickly. Hang it under a thick spruce tree, or put up a pole with a plastic cover over it. Allow the meat to dry as fast as possible. A wet surface in mild weather is likely to spoil. However, a crusted piece of meat, kept dry, will keep a long time.

IN THE KITCHEN

Aging The Meat

At home, field-dressed game meat should be hung in a dry, shaded area where the temperature hovers right around 35°F (1.5°C) and the air circulation is good. Some people keep a fan blowing to keep meat dry because wet surfaces spoil quickly.

The principal reason for aging is to tenderize the meat. The larger the cut, the longer it takes. A mature, well-fleshed moose or caribou should hang one to two weeks; large cuts of meat, about a week. Whereas the smaller pieces, such as the ribs, are best if allowed to age only three days before being cooked and eaten or wrapped for the freezer. Smaller, whole animals — sheep, goat, deer — may be aged about a week. Very lean animals will not improve much with aging.

If you don't have a cool, shaded place to hang the meat while it ages and don't want to tackle the task of butchering, you may hire both tasks done. It is usually best to check with the professional butcher ahead of the hunting trip — whether he has space and whether he wishes to have the animal skinned beforehand. The butcher will cut the meat to your specification and wrap it for the freezer if you want. If you're the butcher, here are the steps.

Butchering at Home

Before you start, consider your family preferences. Decide in advance what cuts you want to keep whole and how much meat you want for burger. If the animal is young and tender, more of the leg meat can be used for steaks. Ground meat takes less freezer space than roasts and stew meat, or meat without bones, but does not keep as well as solid chunks. You can keep one of the quarters fresh for immediate eating if you have a cool place to hang it. Save the bones and clean trimmings for soup stock, which can be canned or frozen.

How To Butcher Elk and Moose

If the carcass has already been split by the

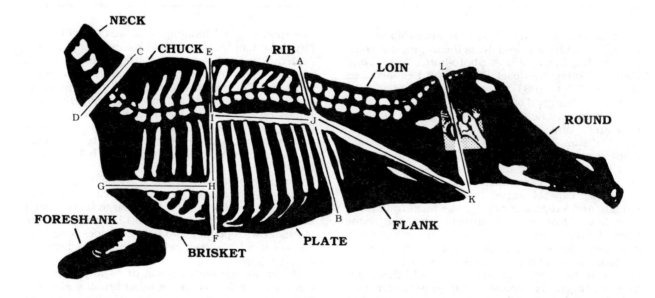

hunter into several manageable chunks, you can skip the "divide and quarter" steps, but they are basically (as shown):

1. Cutting from point A to point B, separate the hindquarters from the forequarters. This is easiest done by inserting a knife between the twelfth and thirteenth ribs, midway between the flank and the backbone (about point J). First cut up to the backbone; then down toward the flank, leaving *uncut* about a 6- or 8-inch (15 to 20 cm) strip that will hold these two huge hunks together while you sever the backbone. Cut through the backbone using a saw; then complete the knife cut through the flank.

2. Forequarters: First remove the neck from the shoulder along the line from C to D. The neck may be boned for ground meat. Then you may either split the forequarters in two, sawing through the backbone or just beside it, or you may first remove front legs, divide the chuck and brisket from the rib cage and then split them in two. Either way, each forequarter is cut as follows:

3. Separate chuck and brisket from the rib and plate by cutting between the fifth and sixth ribs along line E to F. Then separate brisket from chuck — line G to H — cutting just above the elbow joint on a line parallel with the top of the chuck. Armbone and bladebone pot roasts can be cut from the chuck. The portions not suitable for roasts and the entire foreshank and brisket can be set aside to be boned and cut for stew meat or ground for burger.

4. The rib is separated from the plate — line I to J— by cutting 1 inch (2.5 cm) below the scapula (blade bone) on the thick end of the rib and 1 inch away from the loin eye muscle on the small end of the rib. Rib chops, steaks and roasts are excellent pieces of meat for roasting, broiling or barbecuing. The plate supplies short ribs, stew meat and some lean meat to be ground.

5. Now for the hindquarters. Split the hindquarters apart by sawing down the center of the backbone or just alongside it and through the pelvic bone. Then, on each quarter, separate flank and loin, cutting from point K to J. The flank is made into stew meat or ground meat after it is trimmed of inedible areas and fat.

6. The loin is cut from the round about 1/2 inch (1.25 cm) forward of the pelvic bone — line L to K. The loin and round are made into closely trimmed roasts and steaks. Loin cuts are good for dry-heat cooking — frying, roasting or broiling; while cuts from the round are better for braising or other moist-heat methods.

After the basic cuts are made (A through K), all the meat may be boned into roasts and steaks that will take up less space in the freezer. Remember to separate entire muscles and to keep the knife close to the bone. Cut across the grain when making boneless roasts and steaks. The bones are useful, too. Put them in the soup or stock pot.

Cutting Meat — The Alaska Bush Way

Ole Wik describes a different method of butchering which works well for people whose food locker is the outside world . . .

In Alaska's Interior, it is usually cold enough to keep meat naturally frozen from hunting season through spring, so the only real problems remaining are cutting and wrapping. Working with caribou, we find that the best wrapping is the skin the animal comes in. Whenever we need meat, we simply peel the skin off the frozen meat and saw off what we need. If we want to save the hide, we skin the animal right away and allow the skinned meat to freeze. Then we glaze the meat with a half-inch (1.25 cm) layer of ice to seal out the extremely dry winter air. A meat cache partly underground helps us to ride out the occasional midwinter thaw.

As for cutting, the meat saws you see in the butcher shops are intended for bones and they don't work well on frozen meat — especially large chunks. The answer is to use an ordinary bow saw, with the teeth refiled from crosscut to rip. Such a saw will cut through meat of any thickness, no matter how cold or hard-frozen. Fat tends to foul the blade, making it bind, but there is generally a bone somewhere inside the meat that will scrape the fat off the teeth so that you can cut without too much effort. I sharpen the teeth in the fall and again in midwinter, so our bush butchery is a snap . . . even if some of the cuts we end up with would make a professional butcher weep.

How To Butcher Deer, Sheep, Goat

The specific places where cuts are made on the carcasses of smaller large game are also illustrated. The cutting method for one side of the carcass is as follows:

1. Remove neck from shoulder, line A to B. The neck may be boned for ground meat.
2. Separate shoulder and rib section between the fifth and sixth ribs — line C to D. Then the brisket and foreshank are removed just above the elbow joint — line D to E. Bone-in or boneless roast, arm or blade steaks may be cut from the shoulder. The foreshank and brisket may be boned and ground for burger.
3. The hind leg is cut from the loin — line F to G,

leaving one lumbar vertebra on the leg. Sirloin steaks and bone-in roasts are cut first and the shank is trimmed and cut for stew meat or burger.
4. Separate the rib and breast from the flank and loin by cutting between the twelfth and thirteenth ribs — H to I. Then separate rib from breast — J to K — and flank from loin — K to L. The flank and breast are boned for ground meat. The rib and loin are cut into steaks or roasts, excellent cuts for barbecuing, broiling or roasting.

All the basic cuts can be turned into boneless roasts and steaks, if you so desire.

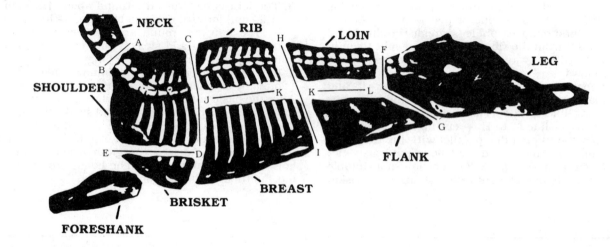

Saving Game Fats

"Different fats from different parts of the animal have very different flavors," says Ole Wik. Here's his advice about how you will want to put them to use if you are butchering an animal with particularly tasty fat.

- The long, triangular ribbon of fat between the shoulder and the ribs is too good to use for anything but the very next meal. Brisket fat is very sweet.
- Bone fats are found where the meat is closest to the bone and the flavor is finest. Marrow is especially good.
- The thick, knobby layer of fat lining the pelvis

needs to be cooked soon due to the possibility of contamination during the gutting process.
- The membranes that enclose the intestinal mass are excellent and we usually hang them to dry for a time, then cook them lightly in a frying pan along with some meat.
- Kidney fat is a harder fat, relatively free of connective tissue, with a mild taste.
- Back fat on a good animal runs an inch or more thick.

There are other deposits of fat on a carcass, but these are the most accessible.

To extract the fat from the larger deposits, cut it into small pieces and render it slowly in a skillet. Allow plenty of time so that the moisture can be drawn from the tissues, and do not overheat. For more dispersed fats — such as those around the bones or in the pelvis — it is better to simmer the meat in a large stock pot for several hours.

Cooking Venison

About Fats

Game animals lead active lives and are most often a good deal leaner than domestically raised ones. The amount of fat on the meat depends on the age of the animal and the time of year when it was killed . . . but in most cases, at least for broiling, roasting and barbecuing, extra fat will be needed.

There are several ways of adding it. You can rub the meat with game fat reserved from another source, or salt pork, butter, margarine, beef suet, bacon fat, vegetable oil, or sweet or sour cream to add moisture and flavor. Or you can baste the meat frequently during cooking, using fat alone or a sauce that contains fat.

Lean roasts may be "larded." Use a skewer or an ice pick to insert slivers of uncooked fat — game, salt pork, bacon or beef suet. If you make your own rolled roasts, cut off some fat to secure around the outside. Or, if you prefer, use pork or beef fat.

Some fats do not freeze well and transmit unwanted taste to the meat during any length of storage. Many say this is true of bear and sheep and excess fat should be removed before the meat is frozen. It is not true of venison, however. If the meat is to be eaten in a few months, leave some fat on it. If it is frozen longer, the fat of most wild game tends to turn rancid. That is one good reason for dating the packages you put in your freezer and planning roughly when you'll use them at the time the meat is trimmed and wrapped.

Moose fat, if it is not kept with the meat itself, is a good one to render and store for other uses. And bear fat is even better . . . see Chapter 8.

Organ Meats

This chapter contains a particularly good selection of recipes for venison liver and some for tongue and heart. Since these are generally the first meats to be used (the rest improve with aging), recipes for them are early in the chapter.

Tough Cuts

Also check the many fine recipes for stewing and braising and for marinated or mildly cured meats, as well as those for mincemeat. These are good ways to use tougher, drier cuts. Some excellent recipes for ground venison are at the end of the chapter and you'll find more ways to use "game-burger" of all kinds at the end of Chapter 8.

Steaks and Roasts

Steaks and roasts from the loin and rib are the premium cuts for dry-heat cooking — roasting, broiling, pan-broiling and barbecuing. The main rule — don't overcook. It will merely toughen the meat.

Sauces and Stuffings

Recipes for sauces, stuffings and other accompaniments good with wild game are scattered throughout the book. Please refer to the listing on page 171.

The sequences on butchering elk and moose, deer, sheep and goat, as well as the illustrations, are adapted with little change from *You and Your Wild Game* B-613, Agricultural Extension Service, University of Wyoming. Information about aging meat as well as guidelines on butchering come from *The Hunter Returns After the Kill* F-41, Cooperative Extension Service, University of Alaska. Ole Wik's description of fats to save during butchering is excerpted from "How To Make Pemmican," *ALASKA*® magazine, April 1979; the other item from Ole Wik, Cutting Meat — The Alaska Bush Way, is an article by the same name, reprinted from *ALASKA*® magazine, November 1974.

ORGAN MEATS

About Cooking Organ Meats: *Some parts of freshly killed venison should not be "aged" as is recommended for the rest of the meat. Brains, heart, liver, tongue and other organ meats spoil quickly and should be eaten or preserved right away.*

Camp Meat

►A good meat to prepare at hunting camp —because it can't easily be preserved — is "backstrap," the narrow strip of meat along the backbone, which may be ripped out with the point of a knife. Cut it into 1/4-inch (0.6 cm) slices. Brush with oil and sprinkle with onion or garlic powder, place on a green "wiener stick" and roast over hot coals. Season to taste and serve between slices of sourdough bread.

■ The Alaskan Camp Cook *(adapted)*

Moose Liver and Onions

►Slice liver thin so it will fry quickly. That way it will taste better and it won't have to be cooked so long or won't dry out. Fry a few pieces of bacon in pan and add sliced onions. Let them cook, covered, while you fry bacon and liver in another pan. Dip liver in flour and fry in hot pan. Salt and pepper when cooked on both sides; place on top of onions and let steam for 5 to 10 minutes, covered.

■ *Bertha Meier*
  Pioneer Cookbook
  Auxiliary No. 4, Anchorage

Venison Liver

►Probably the first used portion of venison is the liver. Here's two ways of cooking it:

• Parboil thick slices of liver in boiling water for about five minutes. Then, either roll in flour and fry in a pan or just sprinkle with salt and pepper, place on wire rack and broil over the coals, turning often.

• Cut thick slices, butter them well and fry as you would a steak. Just before they're done sprinkle liberally with lemon juice and serve with tomato slices and fried bacon.

■ *Ken Davidson*
  "Moveable Feasts —
  Cooking Game in the Field"
  BC Outdoors, *September 1981*

Deer Liver a la Phyllis Henning

►Soak deer liver in sea water (if possible, otherwise salted water) for a few hours or, preferably, overnight. Slice liver as thin as possible and remove all traces of bile duct, membrane and extraneous tissue.

Soak sliced and trimmed liver in milk for approximately one-half hour; throw away milk and add fresh milk and soak for another half-hour. Repeat the milk-soaking process four or five times.

Drain liver, dip in flour seasoned with salt and pepper to taste, and fry very quickly in bacon fat.

■ *Phyllis Henning, Angoon*
  ALASKA® magazine, *December 1980*

Crispy Moose Liver Steaks

1 pound (456 g) moose liver
1 egg, beaten
1 tablespoon (15 mL) water
1 tablespoon (15 mL) lemon juice
1 teaspoon (5 mL) salt
3/4 cup (180 mL) fine cracker crumbs
2 tablespoons (30 mL) bacon drippings

►Blend beaten egg with water, lemon juice and salt. Dip slices of liver in crumbs, then in egg mixture and again in crumbs. Brown for five minutes on each side. Serve with HOT cranberry or tomato ketchup. (Recipes for Cranberry Ketchup are in Chapter 14.)

■ *Anon.*
  Courtesy, Mrs. Aline Strutz

Venison Liver Sauteed in Wheat Germ

1 pound (456 g) venison liver, sliced thin
Cold water to cover, plus 1 tablespoon
  (15 mL) vinegar
6 tablespoons (90 mL) salad oil
1 large onion, sliced thin
1 cup (240 mL) wheat germ
1/3 cup (80 mL) grated Parmesan
Salt and pepper to taste

►Soak liver one-half to one hour in vinegar-water. Drain on paper towel. Heat 3 tablespoons (45 mL) of the oil in a skillet and saute onion until clear. Remove to hot platter and set aside. Mix wheat germ, Parmesan, salt and pepper. Heat remaining oil in skillet. Dredge liver in wheat germ mixture and brown it over medium heat until blood begins to show on top. Turn carefully and brown other side. Do not overcook as liver tends to be dry then. Serve on hot platter garnished with sauteed onion. Serves four or five.

■ *Mamie Jensen, Juneau*

Fried Caribou Liver

►Slice fresh liver in strips 1/4 to 1/2 inch (0.6 to 1.25 cm) thick and 2 or 3 inches (5 to 7.5 cm) long. Dip in a mixture of flour, salt and pepper and fry in bacon fat or butter until golden brown, about five minutes. Fried onions make a good accompaniment, but saute them separately or ahead of the meat, removing them to a warm plate while you cook the liver. Too long cooking makes liver tough. (And, yes, I have to admit dipping little strips of liver in flour is a s-t-i-c-k-y job . . . but the tender, juicy result is well worth the effort.)

■ *Anon.*

Venison Liver Sa Shardo
A "cross-cultural recipe," says the cook,
adapted from a delightfully spicy Philippine dish

2 pounds (1 kg) venison liver
2 cloves fresh garlic, minced
2 tablespoons (30 mL) salad oil
2 tablespoons (30 mL) vinegar
1 teaspoon (5 mL) Accent
1-1/2 teaspoons (7 mL) paprika
1 teaspoon (5 mL) pickling spice
2 stalks celery, diced
1 onion, diced
Sprinkle of soy sauce

►Wash the liver and drain well. Cut into pieces, not too small. In a skillet, saute garlic and other seasonings in the salad oil for a few minutes. Add liver, celery and onions and continue cooking until liver is done. Add a sprinkling of soy sauce.

An excellent accompaniment to this dish is edible wild greens, such as goose tongue, that grow along the tidelands. Wash, drain, steam or fry the greens for a few minutes in butter and add a sprinkle of soy sauce for seasoning.
■ *Kaa T'eix*
  Kaa T'eix's Cook Book, *Mount Edgecumbe*

Caribou Liver Pate

1/4 pound (114 g) bacon, fried crisp and drained
2 tablespoons (30 mL) finely chopped onion or
   wild chives
1 tablespoon (15 mL) fresh or dried parsley
1 pound (456 g) caribou liver, ground
1 egg yolk
1/2 cup (120 mL) fine bread crumbs
Milk
Seasonings to taste (salt, pepper, allspice,
   marjoram and thyme)

►Combine all ingredients with enough milk to make a thick paste. Place the mixture in a casserole and set the casserole in a pan of water. Bake for approximately two hours at 300°F (150°C). Good hot out of the oven, or refrigerate and serve chilled on toast triangles and garnish with quartered tomatoes dipped in French dressing.
■ *Helen A. White*
  "Far North Fare"
  ALASKA® magazine, December 1974

Spanish Liver

►Use either moose, caribou or reindeer liver. Wash 1 pound (456 g) liver in cold water. Drain well and dredge each slice in flour. Have ready a frying pan containing about 1/2 inch (1.25 cm) bacon fat. When fat is hot, add liver and brown well. Season with salt and pepper. Add five medium onions and one large green pepper sliced. Let them brown a bit. Heat and add tomatoes from a No. 2-1/2 can (29 oz /or/ 826 g) and enough hot water to cover the meat. Cover tightly and simmer for about 30 minutes.
■ Out of Alaska's Kitchens *(1947 edition)*

Ways To Cook Venison Heart, Liver and "Towel"

►Venison liver is just as delicious as beef liver. So is venison heart. Use either or both of them in place of bacon for breakfast, with eggs, and you will be surprised how good it is.

To slice liver and heart into serving pieces, cut crosswise, not lengthwise. Both are good rolled in commercial breading mixes, such as Shake 'n Bake or Krusteaz, or in just plain flour mixed with salt, pepper, paprika, and other seasonings to taste. Dip the pieces in beaten egg, if you like, before rolling them in the flour mix. Cook well in butter. Cook a pan of seasoned sliced onions in butter for a side dish.

Venison stomach the Indians call "towel" because it looks like terry cloth. It is good cooked with heart and liver. Clean the stomach inside and out, remove all membrane, and keep cleaning in warm water until all the remains from the stomach are removed. Slice the cleaned stomach in pieces about 1-1/2 inches (3.75 cm) square. Boil the pieces in seasoned water about 45 minutes. Remove from water and drain. Now slice the heart and liver into smaller pieces than the stomach. Set aside while you prepare the following mixture:

Sprinkle-On Seasoning
3 cloves fresh garlic, minced
1/4 cup (60 mL) vinegar
1 teaspoon (5 mL) Accent
1 teaspoon (5 mL) pickling spice
1 tablespoon (30 mL) paprika
Salt and pepper to taste

►Mix all ingredients in a small bowl. Now you are ready to begin the final preparation. First, fry the boiled and drained "towel" in butter until browned. Add the sliced heart and liver and the Sprinkle-On Seasoning and let fry for about 15 minutes more. If you want gravy, sprinkle 1 tablespoon (15 mL) of flour over the mixture and stir in well until the flour disappears. Then slowly add some cold water and let simmer a few minutes.
■ *Kaa T'eix (Mary Howard Pelayo)*
  Kaa T'eix's Cook Book, *Mount Edgecumbe*

Liver Dumplings

1 pound (456 g) deer or moose liver
1-1/2 tablespoons (23 mL) deer suet
2 slices bacon
Salt, pepper and nutmeg to taste
3 slices dry bread
2 eggs, beaten
1 tablespoon (15 mL) chopped parsley
1 small onion, chopped fine

►Soak liver for two hours in 1 quart (1 L) water plus 3 tablespoons (45 mL) vinegar. Drain, wipe dry and slice. Pour boiling water over slices, stirring until liver is grayish; then chill in cold water. Pat dry again, then chop or grind liver, suet and bacon, adding seasonings desired. Soak bread in a little water, squeeze dry and add to liver along with eggs, parsley and onion — plus enough flour to bind mixture. Drop by teaspoonfuls onto hot stew or soup and boil gently 10 minutes. Very good.
■ *Mrs. E.E. Weschenfelder*
  The Alaskan Camp Cook

Liverpostei
(Liver paste)

1 deer liver
Water/vinegar solution
6 eggs
2 cups (480 mL) cream or undiluted
*   canned milk*
1 medium-sized onion, chopped
1-1/2 tablespoons (23 mL) salt
1 teaspoon (5 mL) pepper
1/2 teaspoon (2 mL) cloves
1/2 teaspoon (2 mL) allspice
1/2 cup (120 mL) flour

►The night before, cut the liver into two or three pieces and cover with cold water to which 1/4 cup (60 mL) vinegar has been added. Let stand overnight. Drain liver and grind through meat grinder four times or, the fourth time, mash through a sieve. Beat eggs and cream together; pour into ground liver, add remaining ingredients and stir well. Line greased bread pan with waxed paper; pour in liver paste and bake in a pan of hot water 1-1/2 to 2 hours.
■ *Karen Sund*
   Sons of Norway Cook Book, *Ketchikan*

Hilda's Heart

1 moose heart
3 bay leaves
6 or 8 whole cloves
2 heaping tablespoons (35 mL)
*   prepared mustard*
1 cup (240 mL) cooking wine
Celery, including leaves, as desired
2 teaspoons (10 mL) Worcestershire
1 or 2 onions
1 teaspoon (5 mL) salt
1 clove garlic
Pepper to taste
Water to cover heart

►Boil all together. Cold sliced heart makes good sandwiches.
■ *Hilda Stoltzfus*
   Cooking Up A Storm, *Homer*

Moose Heart with Sage Dressing
A good buffet dish, served hot or cold

►Wash the heart well; remove the muscles from the inside and wash away every particle of blood. Wrap in a cloth, sewing the ends together to keep the heart well shaped. Place in a stewing pan with the point of the heart down; cover with boiling water, cover the pan and let simmer for three hours. Remove the meat from the liquid, but not from the cloth, rinse with warm water and set aside to cool. Delicious sliced paper thin. If you like the heart stuffed; make a dressing like the one suggested below and stuff the cavity before wrapping in cloth.

Sage Dressing for Moose Heart
1 cup (240 mL) bread crumbs
1 tablespoon (15 mL) minced onion
1/2 teaspoon (2 mL) sage
1 tablespoon (15 mL) butter
Salt and pepper to taste

►Mix well. Stuff and bake as directed above.
■ *Bess A. Cleveland*
   Alaskan Cookbook for Homesteader or Gourmet

Roast Moose Heart with Cranberry Stuffing

Moose heart
Lowbush cranberries
Sugar
1/4 cup (60 mL) chopped celery, with leaves
2 tablespoons (30 mL) chopped parsley
4 tablespoons (60 mL) melted margarine
*   or butter*
4 cups (1 L) coarse, stale bread crumbs
Poultry seasoning, salt and pepper to taste
Bacon strips

►Put lowbush cranberries through a food chopper and then add 1/2 cup (120 mL) sugar for each cup (240 mL) of ground berries. Set aside. Saute celery and parsley in melted butter for a few minutes and add to berry mixture. Then add bread crumbs and seasonings to taste.

Spoon the stuffing onto a greased baking surface. Split the heart open and lay it over the stuffing. Add two or three strips of bacon to the top to help keep the heart moist. Cover and roast at 350°F (175°C) until the meat is tender. Remove the bacon strips and return the heart to the oven, uncovered, long enough to brown well.
■ *Helen A. White*
   "Far North Fare"
   ALASKA® magazine, December 1974

Moose Heart Alaska Style

►Take a moose heart and trim off all the fat. Cut it into 1/2-inch (1.25 cm) cubes and brown these in bacon grease in a large frying pan. Then dice a stalk of celery, including the leaves, a handful of mushrooms, one large green pepper and two large onions. Saute until the onions become transparent, stirring constantly. Be careful not to brown the onions.

Add two large cans (15 oz /or/ 425 g, each) of

tomato sauce, one can (16 oz /or/ 456 g) whole tomatoes and salt and pepper to taste. Simmer until done, adding tomato juice if mixture is too thick.

■ *Robert D. Jones*
"Game Plans"
ALASKA® magazine, October 1980

Baked Caribou or Moose Heart

Caribou or moose heart
Salt and pepper
Flour
Bread stuffing
Bacon drippings
Boiling water
1 tablespoon (15 mL) cornstarch

►Clean heart; remove inner membrane and all blood; wash well and dry. Remove any fat and discard. Stuff with your favorite bread stuffing. Sprinkle with salt and pepper to taste; roll in flour. Heat bacon fat in heavy skillet and brown heart evenly and well. Put in a baking dish. Put in a little boiling water and add more water from time to time if the liquid cooks away. Cover. Bake for 1-1/2 to 2 hours at 350°F (175°C). Remove heart to a serving dish and keep warm. Pour the liquid into a small saucepan. Make a paste of cornstarch and a little water. Stir gradually into the broth in saucepan and continue stirring until sauce is thick. Pour around the heart.

■ *The Old Homesteader*

Braised Heart of Venison

1 venison heart
Water
1 tablespoon (15 mL) salt
4 tablespoons (60 mL) flour
1 teaspoon (5 mL) salt
1/4 teaspoon (1 mL) pepper
3 tablespoons (45 mL) bacon fat
1 cup (240 mL) diced carrots
1 cup (240 mL) diced celery
1 medium onion, sliced, or 2 tablespoons
*   (30 mL) dried onion flakes*
2 tablespoons (30 mL) dried parsley

►Wipe heart well with a damp cloth. Soak overnight in enough water to cover, to which a tablespoon (15 mL) of salt has been added.

Remove, drain and pat dry. Slice heart crosswise in 1/2-inch (1.25 cm) slices and remove the tough white membrane. Dredge slices in seasoned flour. Melt bacon fat in a heavy frying pan and saute the slices of heart until lightly browned. Add enough water to cover the meat, reduce heat, cover and let simmer for one hour, adding more water as required. Then add prepared vegetables and con-

tinue simmering until meat and vegetables are tender, adding more water if necessary. Makes four servings.

■ Northern Cookbook

Boiled Tongue
Excellent for cold cuts and sandwiches

►Wash tongue well. Simmer until tender in seasoned water to cover. (Bay leaf, salt, peppercorns and other seasonings to suit.) Figure it will take about one hour per pound (456 g). If the tongue is to be served hot, add quartered onions, potatoes, carrots and/or cabbage wedges during the last half-hour or so of cooking. When the tongue is tender, lift it out of the broth with tongs and hold it under cold running water until you can handle it. Then peel off the tough skin. Trim off gristle and put the tongue back into the broth to reheat if you are serving it hot.

If you want it for cold cuts, allow the tongue to cool in the broth. This makes it juicier. Then drain well, wrap and chill completely. Slice thin to serve.

Serve tongue — hot or cold — with a choice of condiments. The Brown Sauce that follows can be made out of the cooking broth. Raisin Sauce (Chapter 13) is a classic for tongue. Cold tongue can be served with several kinds of mustard (or mix your own variations, using horseradish, capers or chopped sour pickle, a bit of ketchup or A-1 in combinations that suit), horseradish, cranberry relish, dill pickles — all are good accompaniments for tongue, either hot or cold.

■ *Anon.*

Variation: Tongue can be pressure cooked. Place it on a rack in the cooker. Add 2 cups (240 mL) water for a 3-pound (1.4 kg) tongue and seasonings. Cook 45 minutes at 15 pounds (103.5 kPa) pressure.

Brown Sauce
2 tablespoons (30 mL) butter or drippings
1/2 small onion, diced
2 tablespoons (30 mL) flour
1 cup (240 mL) liquid from boiled meat, stock
*   or bouillon*
Salt and pepper to taste

►Heat butter in small heavy skillet over low heat. Add diced onion and saute until light brown. Remove onion. Add flour to butter in skillet and stir until well blended and deep mahogany brown. Remove from heat. Stir in meat stock, stirring constantly, then bring to a boil. Boil one minute. Strain if necessary. Add seasonings to taste and the browned onions if you wish. Makes one cup Brown Sauce.

■ Reindeer and Caribou Recipes

Moose Tongue Stew

1 moose tongue
2 teaspoons (10 mL) salt
1 quart (1 L) stock
1 pint (480 mL) ketchup
1 onion, chopped
1/2 cup (120 mL) celery, chopped
1/2 green pepper, chopped
3 carrots, chopped

1 tablespoon (15 mL) sugar
1 tablespoon (15 mL) cider vinegar
2 tablespoons (30 mL) flour
2 tablespoons (30 mL) butter

►Wash and scrub tongue well. Cook for two hours in enough salted water to cover. Remove skin from tongue. Add remaining chopped vegetables and other ingredients, except flour and butter. Simmer 10 minutes in stock. Thicken with flour and butter

Some Northern Eskimo Specialties

Caribou is an important food for many of Alaska's people. Almost all parts of the animal may be used. All of the following Northern Eskimo specialties are from The Alaska Dietary Survey. *Note that one of them uses "two of the stomach parts." Caribou are ruminants and — like cattle, deer and others — have several "stomachs" through which food is processed and reprocessed.*

Caribou stomach and its contents (partially digested vegetation, including lichens such as reindeer moss) may be frozen immediately after butchering and stored for future use. It is eaten frozen with seal oil.

Sometimes, at butchering, a small amount of the stomach contents is removed, just enough so that the stomach and its remaining contents can be easily handled. The stomach is then set in the snow and covered with caribou skins to prevent freezing. In about two or three days the stomach contents become sweet.

Two of the stomach parts — the rumen (called *knee-oo-kuk* by Northern Eskimos) and the omasum *(muk-pee-rawk)* — are removed, cleaned thoroughly and boiled a short time. They are eaten with or without seal oil as desired.

Caribou intestine — The cleaned small intestines of caribou are stuffed with strips of visceral fat obtained from around the stomach and intestines. The ends are tied and this "sausage" is then boiled a long time. The cooked fat may then be used as a spread or in other ways much like butter.

At the hunting camp, the visceral fat strips may be placed in the cleaned small intestine but left uncooked. At home, these strips are removed and hung up to dry, either indoors or outdoors. The fat is used in making *agutuk.*

The small intestines with the visceral fat left attached are cleaned, thoroughly washed and then cooked in water. The rendered fat is removed, the cooked intestines chopped into lengths of an inch

(2.5 cm) or less and the two are thoroughly mixed together.

The cleaned small intestines with attached visceral fat are ground, chopped and pounded thoroughly and then heated in water. The fat is removed as it is rendered. This fat is then whipped, gradually mixed with seal oil, stirred until it becomes light and fluffy, and one or more of the following is added: blueberries, crowberries, chopped cooked *mashu* [sometimes called Eskimo potato; see Chapter 9], raisins, pilot bread crumbs, cooked dried apples, cooked, chopped or ground caribou meat or cooked whitefish, squeezed dry and thoroughly flaked. Sugar may be added if fruits are used.

Caribou liver may be fried or it may be prepared as *Nay-ru-kuk*, as follows: Short strips of liver and muscle tendon, particularly those found close to the sinews along the back and in the hind and forelegs, are mixed with the stomach contents, put into a cleaned caribou stomach and then set aside in a warm, but not too hot, place for about a week. The mixture becomes sweet. If kept too long it gets too sweet.

Caribou eyes, including the muscle and fat around them, are cooked until soft. Only the muscle and the fat are eaten.

Bone marrow (pa-tik) may be eaten raw or cooked. Marrow differs in consistency depending on the location of the bone. The most solid part is found in the hip and upper thigh bone and is called *ki-nik-nik.* Less solid marrow is found in the lower thigh and upper part of the shank bones. This marrow is called *ah-noa-tuk-suk.* The marrow found in the lower part of the leg is oil-like in consistency and is called *peg-nick.* This is the most preferred.

In times past, but less frequently now, it was a common practice to break up the caribou bones, cover them with water and simmer to render out the fat. Both fat and marrow were then removed from the cooking pot and mixed thoroughly. This mixture was stored in a thoroughly cleaned and

paste. Dice tongue; place in covered baking dish with vegetable sauce. Bake two hours at 350°F (175°C).
■ *Hilda Stoltzfus*
   Cooking Up A Storm, *Homer*

Jellied Moose Nose
Jellied moose nose is a sourdough specialty known and enjoyed only in moose country. It is

dried caribou stomach and then frozen. It was used as a spread or as a condiment with fish and meat. At Shungnak this mixture is called *poing-nik.*

Caribou kidneys are not often eaten and when they are, they are preferred raw right after the animal is killed and the kidneys still "hot and steaming," at which time they are said to have a very spicy taste.

Blood is sometimes drunk raw from the freshly killed animal, but its most common use in aboriginal times was as a soup thickener. It had to be stirred carefully into the hot, but not boiling, liquid to prevent coagulation. Then thin slivers of caribou fat were added and stirred to make a creamy mixture or gravy.
   Fresh caribou blood is sometimes stored in the thoroughly cleaned stomach part, the reticulum, and then frozen. This blood is used in soups or in the preparation of *azeesuk. Azeesuk* is made by chopping lowbush cranberries, adding caribou blood and stirring and whipping the mixture to a fluff.
   Sometimes caribou back fat is dipped into blood and air-dried. It is said the fat inside never gets spoiled or yellow.
   Caribou back fat is sometimes ground, and to it is added blood, flour, pepper, onion and salt. This sausage mixture is stuffed into cleaned caribou intestines, the ends tied and the whole cooked by boiling. This was learned from the Lapps who were brought over in the early days to help with the reindeer industry.

Caribou brains are sometimes eaten raw, especially by the men at hunting camps; sometimes fried, sometimes cooked with tongue to make a stew or used to make *kah-kay-suk*. The latter is made by boiling the caribou brain along with the meat and fat from the jaws and around the eyes and other parts of the head. The meat is separated out, mixed with the melted caribou fat and salted to taste.

not easy to prepare, but, like head cheese, is a worthwhile delicacy.

►Cut the upper jawbone of the moose just below the eyes. Put it in a large kettle of scalding water and boil it for 45 minutes. Remove it and plunge it into cold water to cool. Pick the hairs from the nose as you would the feathers from a duck (the boiling loosens them), and wash the nose thoroughly.
   Put the nose in a kettle and cover it with fresh water. Add a sliced onion, a little garlic and pickling spices and boil it gently until the meat is tender. Let it cool overnight in the cooking liquid.
   In the morning, take the meat out of the broth and remove the bones and cartilage. You will have two kinds of meat: the bulb of the nose is white, and the thin strips along the bone and jowls are dark. Slice the meat thinly, pack it into a high-sided glass dish and cover it with juice. You may add salt, pepper or other spices to the juice if they are needed. Some people add vinegar to suit their own taste. Refrigerate. The mixture will jell, and when it is firm, can be sliced for cold serving.
■ The Hunter Returns After the Kill

Pickled Heart or Tongue
►There are two ways to prepare deer or moose heart and tongue for pickling, and both work equally well. Either saturate the meat in a salt solution for eight to ten hours, or steam diced hearts and whole tongues for 10 minutes. Then prepare a pickle brine as follows:

2 cups (480 mL) vinegar
2/3 cup (160 mL) water
1 cup (240 mL) white sugar
4 tablespoons (60 mL) pickling spice

►Combine ingredients in a saucepan, bring to a boil and boil for one minute. Allow to cool. Place the prepared meat in a glass container, add one large sliced onion, a sprinkle of garlic salt and 1 teaspoon (5 mL) lemon juice. Pour the cooled brine overall. Cover and let stand in a cool place, 35 to 40°F (1.5 to 4.5°C), for 48 hours.
■ *C. Joe Murray, Jr.*
   ALASKA® magazine, September 1980

Before cutting meat, chill it for about 10 minutes . . . or until it's about as firm as a ripe tomato . . . in the freezing compartment of the refrigerator or outside in weather that is below freezing. This chilling is especially useful when thin slices are needed, such as for making jerky. At room temperature, meat is unmanageable.

Caribou Kidneys in Tomato Sauce

3 tablespoons (45 mL) oil, olive or salad
1/2 cup (120 mL) minced wild chives
1 teaspoon (5 mL) salt
1 cup (240 mL) tomato sauce
1 cup (240 mL) mushrooms
Caribou kidneys
3 tablespoons (45 mL) butter, melted
2 cups (480 mL) canned green peas
1/2 teaspoon (2 mL) black pepper
1 tablespoon (15 mL) parsley, minced
1/4 cup (60 mL) dry white wine

►Heat oil in heavy skillet and saute the chives (or onions) for about 10 minutes. Add salt and tomato sauce. Add the mushrooms (dried, fresh or canned). Sliced puffballs are particularly good in this. Cook over lowest heat for 10 minutes. Meanwhile remove the skin and fat from the kidneys; discard the core and slice kidneys thinly. Melt the butter in a skillet and cook the sliced kidneys in it for about three minutes over high heat. Add the peas, pepper, parsley and wine. Continue cooking for another minute or so. Taste test and add more salt if needed. Combine with the sauce and cook for a few more minutes or until the kidney slices are tender. Try serving with fluffy white rice.

■ *Helen A. White, Anchorage*
  What's Cookin' in Alaska

Moose or Caribou Kidneys

►Skin and wash kidneys. Boil with onion and garlic or slice and fry with steak. Don't try to make a whole meal on the kidneys. You will like them if you don't eat too much at a time.

■ *Bertha Meier*, Pioneer Cookbook, *Anchorage*

Moose Suet or Tallow

►Render moose suet or tallow in a slow oven or over low heat in a heavy skillet on top of the stove. A small amount of water may be added, or grind the tallow first to make it render faster without so much waste. When liquid, strain the fat through cheesecloth to remove any meat particles. Can be frozen and used all winter. But in any case, store in a dark, cool place. Mix with bacon grease or oleo and use for frying. To use for shortening in cookies and cakes, beat 1 pint (0.47 L) Wesson oil into 3 pounds (1.4 kg) of tallow and beat until creamy.

■ Pioneer Cookbook, *Anchorage*

Spiced Moose Tongue

►Wash tongue thoroughly and cover with cold water to which has been added a generous handful of mixed pickling spices and several cut up onions. Simmer until tender, then allow to cool in same liquid. Skin cooled tongue and place in refrigerator until ready to use for snacks, sandwiches, or a main dish.

■ Alaska's Cooking, *Anchorage*

Kwak
(Frozen meat or fish)

►Take partially frozen hunk of caribou meat or partially frozen hunk of salmon. Cut into slices and dip in seal oil.

■ *Leona Okaok, Phoebe McDonald and Mary Ann Warden*
Northern Lites, Tasty Bites, *Fairbanks*

STOCK & SOUPS

Game Stock

Long, slow cooking is the key to extracting a flavorful stock from meaty bones. A pressure cooker will shorten the time if you're in a hurry. Another way to heighten flavor — brown the bones briefly in a slow oven before putting them in the stock pot, but be careful not to scorch them. The meat that is strained from the finished stock may be used in mincemeat or other highly seasoned dishes such as sandwich spread. Just remember it has already given most of its flavor to the stock. Save the fat that is skimmed from the stock and use it as a baste for game roasts that are too lean. Reheat solidified fat slowly, strain it to remove meat particles and store it in a cool place or freeze it.

Meaty bones of any wild game and meat scraps
or chunks from tough cuts
Water
1 or 2 onions
2 or 3 carrots
2 or 3 tablespoons (30 to 45 mL) minced
wild chives
Celery leaves
Peppercorns
Herb bouquet
Salt to taste

►When game is butchered there should be a plentiful supply of bones with bits of meat still clinging to them. Saw bones into size to fit a large kettle and crack them to expose the marrow. Place them in the kettle along with any other meat scraps from which the fat has been removed. Cover with cold water. Bring to a boil and simmer slowly for several hours. Allow to stand until cool and remove the meat and bones. Now allow the stock to become completely cold and then skim off fat that has come to the surface. Replace bones in the stock and again bring to a boil. Reduce heat to simmer and add quartered onions, sliced carrots, chives, chopped celery leaves, several peppercorns and an herb bouquet. The bouquet is made by enclosing several sprigs of parsley, bay leaf, celery stalks cut up and a couple of sprigs of thyme and any other herbs you may choose, all in a piece of white cloth and tied into a bag with white thread. Cover the kettle and simmer slowly for at least three hours. Try a spoonful to test for seasoning and add whatever else you think it needs. Remove and discard herb bouquet and allow to cool. Strain; skim off any remaining fat that may have risen. Store in refrigerator in covered containers or freeze until needed. This stock will be the base for many future soups, gravies and sauces and can be used for moistening meat loaves and in stews. It is good economy to keep some on hand at all times.

■ *Helen A. White, Anchorage*
What's Cookin' in Alaska

Chili

►One of the finest things to find on the table after coming in from the cold is a steaming bowl of chili.

And one of the finest ingredients in chili is game meat — moose, caribou, rabbit — anything.

Chili is not made from a recipe, it's made from one's heart, and therein lies the secret of its great popularity. It's never the same and the flavor of each batch depends on the mood you're in while you make it.

We'll give you the ingredients — try not to vary from them — but juggle the proportions to your own taste.

Start with a large kettle, capable of holding slightly more than a gallon (3.8 L). Brown several pounds (1 kg or more) of stew meat in the bottom. (Caribou is fantastic.)

During the browning procedure, start adding other ingredients. Load it down with chopped onion — don't be afraid to get too much as it will eventually cook away, leaving only a subtle flavor. For a gallon (3.8 L) of chili (and there's no point in making less) use at least two large onions.

The secret ingredient for making an unforgettable chili is celery. De-string and chop about half as much celery as you have onion. Celery will give the final product an unidentifiable but marvelous flavor which makes this chili stand head and shoulders above other types. Throw the celery in with the browning meat.

Next comes seasoning. Use chili powder, garlic salt, cayenne pepper, if you wish, and salt and pepper. This is where a good taste sense will help you. Add the seasoning gradually, tasting as you go. When it's seasoned just a little too strong to be easily eatable, you have it just right. You see, the other ingredients you are to add will dilute the strong spices.

Next comes the liquid — by adding canned tomatoes and tomato soup (use both), make it just a little thinner than you want it to be when you eat it. It will boil down during the cooking.

Now, add some canned kidney beans. Put in as many as you like but don't go overboard. Navy beans would be okay except their pale color is a bit repulsive to some.

Simmer the whole mess for a long, long time. The celery is the best indicator of when it's ready to eat. Put the chili in the bowls when the celery is very soft and not before then. Serve with saltine crackers spread with butter. Have some cayenne pepper on the table so those who like it hot can add their own.

The more often chili is reheated, the better it is. And nothing freezes better — pour it into half-gallon (1.9 L) milk cartons.

Chances are you may be tempted to gunk up your chili with other ingredients. Don't. The above items all have their own distinct flavors which are very complimentary to one another.

■ *Ed Martley*
Fairbanks Daily News-Miner

Chili Alaska
Makes 6 quarts (5.7 L) —
total cooking time, two hours

2 pounds (1 kg) dried No. 1 red beans
1/4 pound (114 g) cubed salt pork, bacon or
  moose tallow
3 pounds (1.4 kg) cubed moose, caribou,
  reindeer (or beef in a pinch)
Oil
1 tablespoon (15 mL) dried parsley
1 clove garlic, crushed, or garlic salt to taste
3 cans (8 oz /or/ 228 g, each) tomato sauce
1-1/2 teaspoons (7 mL) salt
1 teaspoon (5 mL) black pepper

1/2 teaspoon (2 mL) oregano
6 chili pequins, crushed
1/2 cup (120 mL) chili powder
1 large can (29 oz /or/ 826 g) whole tomatoes

►Wash beans well, removing any pebbles. Cover with cold water and soak overnight. (Without soaking, dry beans require almost four hours of cooking.)

Simmer beans, covering with same water, in a large pot until they approach tenderness (about one hour). If any water is added, use boiling water.

Saute salt pork (or substitute) briefly and add cubed meat, sauteing an additional 15 minutes. Add contents of skillet to beans.

Saute chopped onions in salad oil until half-tender and add to beans. Add parsley, crushed garlic, tomato sauce, salt, pepper, oregano, crushed chili pequins, and chili powder to bean pot and mix gently.

Cover and simmer for one hour. Break up whole canned tomatoes and add to pot 20 minutes before chili is done. Enjoy!

■ *Robert W. Stevens*
"Fire in the Snow"
ALASKA® magazine
Alaska-only edition, October 1980

Deer Meat Soup

1 package deer meat, cut into chunks
Carrots and potatoes, in chunks
2 small cans tomato sauce
Chili powder to taste
Salt and pepper
3 or 4 beef bouillon cubes
Minced onions
Canned whole kernel corn
Canned peas

►Brown deer meat; put in water to simmer. Add salt, pepper, chili powder, onions, tomato sauce and bouillon cubes. Cook 1 to 1-1/2 hours. Add carrots and potatoes. When they are almost tender, add corn and peas. Guess at the amount you want in your soup. I use enough so that we can eat it two nights in a row. It's even better the second night. Cook a few minutes more and serve.

■ *Dorothy Diamond*
Kitchen Magic, Ketchikan

Caribou Soup
A full meal soup

►First you take a part of the caribou, like the leg or back, and wash it until it is clean. Then cut it into small squares with a sharp knife. Put it in a roaster or heavy pot and add just enough hot water to cover the meat. Let it cook about an hour and a half. Then add 1 cup (240 mL) rice, 1 cup (240 mL) macaroni, a can of tomatoes, and potatoes chopped in squares. Cook about a half-hour longer and when cooked add a can of drained vegetables. (Reserve the juice for other soup or stock.) Then mix it all and serve.

■ *Katherine Peterson*
  Uutuqtwa, Bristol Bay High School
  Naknek

Meatball Soup

4 slices stale bread
Water
1 pound (456 g) ground venison
1 egg, beaten
1-1/2 teaspoons (7 mL) salt
1/8 teaspoon (0.5 mL) pepper
1/4 teaspoon (1 mL) oregano leaves
1/2 teaspoon (2 mL) thyme leaves
2 tablespoons (30 mL) butter
Venison stock, heated
1/2 cup (120 mL) thinly sliced green onion
1/2 cup (120 mL) diced turnip
1 can (29 oz /or/ 826 g) tomatoes
2 medium carrots, slivered
1 stalk celery, sliced
1 can (14 oz /or/ 400 g) whole kernel corn
Salt and pepper
Parmesan cheese, grated

►Cover bread slices with water and let soak up as much as possible. Squeeze dry, break up and combine with ground meat. Add egg, salt, pepper, oregano and thyme and mix well. Form into small balls, about 1 inch (2.5 cm) in diameter. Heat butter in skillet and brown meatballs lightly on all sides. Add to heated venison soup stock. Then add all vegetables, salt and pepper to taste, cover and simmer until vegetables are tender. Serve sprinkled with cheese. Makes about 3 pints (1.4 L).

■ *Mamie Jensen, Juneau*

Pea Soup with Mooseburger Balls

1 package (2 lbs /or/ 1 kg) green split peas
Salt and pepper
1 teaspoon (5 mL) crushed red pepper flakes
2 tablespoons (30 mL) minced dried onions
Cold water
1/2 pound (228 g) mooseburger
Garlic powder to taste
Flour

►Put the split peas in a colander and wash them through several cold waters to get rid of excess starchy material. They may be either cooked all day in a slow-cooker or for four hours on the range, using low heat. Put them in the pot and salt and pepper to taste. Add the red pepper flakes and the dried onions. Cover with cold water about 2 inches (5 cm) above the top of the peas. The peas will swell as they cook so be sure the pot is large enough. Cover the pot and cook as directed above.

About one hour before split peas should be done, prepare tiny meatballs to put in the soup: Mix garlic powder and salt and pepper to taste into the burger. Form tiny meatballs, about the size of marbles. Roll the meatballs in the flour. Drop the balls in the gently bubbling soup and continue cooking for the prescribed length of time. Water should be added from time to time to keep the level of liquid above the peas and the soup should be stirred occasionally, too. Serve with fresh sourdough French bread and plenty of butter.

■ *The Old Homesteader*

Moose Head Soup

►After skinning head, cut off all meat. Cut into bite-sized pieces. Wash. In a large pot put 4 or 5 cups (1 to 1.2 L) meat. Fill kettle with water. Boil about one or two hours. Add 1/2 cup (120 mL) dried vegetables, 1-1/2 cups (360 mL) long grain rice and 1-1/2 cups (360 mL) macaroni. Continue boiling for another 15 or 20 minutes or until rice and macaroni are done. Add salt to taste. Serve hot! If any meat is left over, freeze for future use.

■ *Delores Carroll Sloan*
  Fort Yukon

Before you toss bones into the stock pot, brown them under the broiler about 5 inches (12.5 cm) from the heat source. They'll add a rich brown color to the stock. (But don't scorch them or they add a rich bad taste.)

If you have no refrigerator, place a large pot with an adequate lid outside your kitchen door. Whenever there is juice left from boiling, baking or broiling any foods, put it in the kettle. Add juice from cooked or canned vegetables, any leftover meat — cut in bits — rice and small amounts of leftover vegetables (not many, unless you puree them first; they'll just get mushy). As long as freezeup lasts this mixture will keep well.

When you want to make vegetable soup, just break off a chunk of the frozen mass and thaw it out on the stove, adding whatever you wish — tomato sauce, onions, diced potatoes (or dried) and seasonings to taste. This makes a gourmet soup.

■ *The Old-timer*

Roast Leg of Venison

Leg of venison, 5 pounds (2.25 kg) or more
Salt and pepper
Melted butter or other fat
Flour
Currant jelly, melted

►Wipe leg of venison well; season with salt and pepper and brush with melted butter. Sear in a hot oven, 450°F (230°C), for 30 minutes. Then reduce heat to moderate, 350°F (175°C), and continue roasting, allowing 15 minutes per pound (0.45 kg) for entire cooking time. Dust with flour when half done. When meat begins to brown, brush with melted currant jelly. Add a little water to the pan and baste frequently thereafter until done.
■ *Merle (Pat) Kimes*
   Tried and True Recipes, *Juneau*

Herbed Leg of Game Roast
For venison, Dall sheep or mountain goat

Leg of venison, Dall sheep or mountain goat,
   5 pounds (2.25 kg) or more
1/4 teaspoon (1 mL) garlic powder
1 teaspoon (5 mL) oregano leaves
1/4 teaspoon (1 mL) freshly ground
   black pepper

Herb and Lemon Basting Sauce
1/3 cup (80 mL) olive oil
2 tablespoons (30 mL) fresh lemon juice
1 teaspoon (5 mL) grated lemon rind
1/8 teaspoon (0.5 mL) garlic powder
2 teaspoons (10 mL) oregano leaves

►Wipe the roast with a damp cloth. With a paring knife, cut four or five deep, knife-wide punctures, evenly spaced around the meatiest part of the roast. Divide the 1/4 teaspoon (1 mL) of garlic powder equally amongst these slits, using the knife to hold a slit open while you sprinkle in garlic powder as deeply as you can. Then pinch the slit together so that it is not gaping. Mix oregano and black pepper and rub over the surface of the roast. Heat basting sauce ingredients just to the point of mixing well, then rub over the roast as much as will stay there. Reserve the rest for basting during cooking. Roast the meat on a rack, uncovered, in a slow oven, preheated to 325°F (160°C), 2-1/2 hours or more, until done to taste. Pilaf makes an excellent accompaniment for this pungently flavored roast. Gravy can be made from drippings.
■ *Anon.*

Barrow Reindeer Roast

7 pounds (3.2 kg) reindeer meat
1/4 cup (60 mL) flour
1 teaspoon (5 mL) salt
1/4 teaspoon (1 mL) pepper
1/4 pound (114 g) salt pork
3 medium-sized onions, chopped
4 celery stalks, chopped
4 tablespoons (60 mL) minced parsley
8 tart apples
1 cup (240 mL) sugar
2 cups (480 mL) bread crumbs

►Wipe the meat with a damp cloth. Mix the flour, salt and pepper and rub well into the meat. Dice the salt pork and fry it in a heavy skillet until crisp. Remove from pan with slotted spoon and set aside. Cook the chopped onion, celery and parsley (you may use dried vegetables) in the fat for 10 minutes, being careful not to brown them. Remove these and set aside with salt pork. Core the apples, cut them into eighths and add them to the hot fat. Sprinkle them with sugar, cover, lower heat and cook until tender and candied. Combine bread crumbs with the cooked salt pork, vegetables and then the apples. Pile this stuffing on the meat. Place the meat in a roasting pan and put in a preheated 450°F (230°C) oven for 30 minutes. Reduce heat to 350°F (175°C), cover and continue roasting for three hours. Serve with cranberry sauce. (Several recipes are in Chapter 11.)
■ *Bess A. Cleveland*
   Alaskan Cookbook for Homesteader or Gourmet

Standing Rib Roast of Caribou

1 four-rib roast of caribou
3 small onions
1 tablespoon (15 mL) vegetable oil
1 tablespoon (15 mL) flour
1 teaspoon (5 mL) salt
1/4 teaspoon (1 mL) pepper
1-1/2 cups (360 mL) water

►Select a four-rib roast of caribou. Cut three deep cuts, one between each rib and in each insert one of the onions. Rub the oil well into the meat. Mix the flour, salt and pepper and dredge over the meat after placing it in the roasting pan. Pour the water into the bottom of the pan. Cover and place in a 450°F (230°C) oven for 30 minutes; reduce heat to 350°F (175°C) and continue to cook for two hours.
■ *Bess A. Cleveland*
   Alaskan Cookbook for Homesteader or Gourmet

Pit-Fire Roast Venison

Roast of venison or moose
Salt and pepper
Other desired seasoning

►Keep a good fire going in a pit about 1 foot (30 cm) deep until it is full of red coals. Have at least 4 to 6 inches (10 to 15 cm) of red coals for your roasting. Prepare game roast of venison or moose with salt, pepper and any other seasoning you desire. Place in heavy foil and seal edges carefully by folding them together. Bank coals around roast; cover all with sand and let roast six to eight hours. Remove sand carefully and use care also in opening the foil. Save the juices to serve over the sliced roast meat.
■ *Mark Jensen, Juneau*
  The Alaskan Camp Cook

Braised Venison

3 pounds (1.4 kg) venison
3 slices salt pork
Salt, pepper and flour
1/4 cup (60 mL) fat
1/4 cup (60 mL) hot water
1/2 tablespoon (7 mL) vinegar
1/2 cup (120 mL) chopped celery
1 carrot, diced
1 tart apple, chopped
1/2 tablespoon (7 mL) lemon juice

►Use the less tender cuts of venison for this method. Lard venison with the salt pork and rub with salt, pepper and flour. Saute in hot fat until well browned, turning frequently. Add hot water and vinegar. Cover closely and cook until tender, about 2 to 2-1/2 hours, adding more water as it evaporates. A half-hour before meal is done, add remaining ingredients. Cook until vegetables are tender. Serve with a tart jelly.
■ Tsimpshean Indian Island Cookbook
  Metlakatla

Oven-Barbecued Moose Roast

►Place 3 or 4 pounds (1.4 kg to 1.8 kg) moose roast, cut from the round, in an open roasting pan. A cast iron skillet is good for this. Set the oven at 350°F (175°C). Baste the roast with Smoky Barbecue Sauce and place pan in the oven. Roast for approximately two hours. Turn the meat over a few times and baste until all the sauce is used. When the roast is removed from the pan, pour sauce remaining in pan into a small pitcher and serve with the sliced roasted moose. This is a good recipe to use when the piece of meat is rather small and apt to dry out using ordinary roasting procedures. (And besides, it tastes good.)
■ *The Old Homesteader*

Moose Ribs

►Place 3 or 4 pounds (1.4 to 1.8 kg) moose ribs, bone down, in pressure cooker. Lay strips of fat salt pork over top. Add 1/2 cup (120 mL) water and two or three sliced onions. Cook at medium pressure for 30 minutes. Remove ribs and place in an iron skillet. Mix 1 tablespoon (30 mL) brown sugar and a pinch of dry mustard with fat stock from the pressure cooker and pour over meat. Bake, uncovered, in a moderate oven until crisply browned, basting frequently.
■ *Alaska Department of Fish and Game*
  Wildlife Cookbook

About Pot Roast: Long, slow, moist cooking is probably the favorite way of all to tenderize tougher cuts of meat while preserving excellent flavor. Here are several choice recipes.

Cranberry Moose Pot Roast

4 pounds (1.8 kg) boneless roast
2 tablespoons (30 mL) vegetable oil
2 tablespoons (30 mL) flour
1-1/2 teaspoons (7 mL) salt
Pepper to taste
1-1/2 cups (360 mL) beef or game stock
2 cups (480 mL) chopped onion
2 cups (480 mL) fresh lowbush or bog
  cranberries

►The 6-quart (6 L) Dutch oven is the tool for this job. Set it on medium heat and add the oil. Wipe the meat with a damp cloth and rub on a mixture of flour, salt and pepper. Brown the meat on all sides.

Remove the meat from the pan and discard the pan drippings. Add the stock, onions and cranberries to the pan. Return the meat to the pan, bring to a boil and reduce the heat to simmer for 2-1/2 hours. Turn the meat once or twice during the cooking. When it's tender, remove it from the liquid and onto a platter. Cover and keep warm.

Skim the excess fat off the liquid in the pan. Pour the liquid into a blender, blend one minute; then pour it through a strainer back into the pan. Reheat and add seasoning if needed.

Slice the roast and arrange it on a platter. Pour some sauce over the meat and serve the rest in a gravy boat. Be sure to serve something else with the meat that demands gravy, too. Serves eight or more.
■ *Gordon R. Nelson, Palmer*
  Smokehouse Bear

The gravy made from the juices of wild game is improved by adding a dollop or two of wild currant jelly or a couple of spoonfuls of sweet pickle juice.

Pot Roast Barbecue

4 pounds (1.8 kg) moose rump, round or chuck
1 cup (240 mL) tomato sauce
1/2 cup (120 mL) vinegar
3 teaspoons (15 mL) salt
1/4 teaspoon (1 mL) pepper
2 teaspoons (10 mL) chili powder
1/4 teaspoon (1 mL) paprika

►Brown meat thoroughly on all sides in a heavy skillet or Dutch oven. Mix all other ingredients and pour over browned meat. Cover and simmer gently over low heat until tender, about three hours. Turn meat several times during cooking and add a little water if necessary to keep meat from sticking. Makes six to eight servings.

■ *Teen Cox, Skagway*
   The Alaskan Camp Cook

Caribou or Moose Roast Dinner

1 roast
1 medium potato
1 small zucchini squash
2 medium carrots
1/4 onion
Salt and pepper

Herring Cove Stuffed Deer-ky
Or How I Turned A Small Bag into
A Big Treat For Christmas Dinner

"Deer Season Opens" — a common enough headline on sports pages each year throughout the nation — usually makes hunters dream a common dream . . . *This* is the year I get the Big Buck!

But for those of you who happen to bag a small deer, here's a unique and delicious way to turn it into a big treat for 20 or more people.

You can use this method on deer up to 65 pounds (about 30 kg), field dressed. And all it takes is a standard-sized oven.

Let me tell you how this recipe was born. . . .

It was getting along toward Christmas and the weather, people and people's thoughts and the whole country were getting to look like Ketchikan usually looks around Christmas. I had finished my second year as a packer, wrangler and assistant guide, and was sitting around my Aunt May Torgesen's Arctic Bar listening to the tales of the fishermen, loggers and other Alaskans. My energetic little auntie was tending bar and also trying to decide whether to have turkey or ham for Christmas dinner.

Now this is a big decision for female cooks this time of year, and I was sympathetically working my brain over this turkey-ham thing when I heard a I'd-guess-sober voice say, "May! Invite a lot of people and I'll fix us a deerky!"

Well, I looked around to see who'd make a statement like that, and you know what? Everybody else was looking at me! My Auntie May was kind of squinting at me and asked, "What did you say?" and I heard my voice rising loudly to the occasion, again.

"I'll cook you a whole damn deer, dressing and all!"

Truth was, we had a couple of whole deer aging out at the house in Herring Cove and one was a little small, well pretty small, when you really come down to it. It field dressed at 60 pounds exactly, honest bathroom scale measure.

I'd had this idea kind of loose in my head for over a year. An old-timer up in Sitka, Marv Kinberg, had one time mentioned stuffing a deer and cooking the whole thing. I never thought any more about it till the next hunting season, and then everytime I'd field dress a caribou or moose or sheep, I'd look at that big empty body cavity and think about all the dressing it would hold. Now, I'm a real turkey lover, partly because I like turkey, but mostly because I like turkey with dressing.

Anyhow, here it was the day before Christmas. I had a headache. My aunt was very cheerfully saying something about how nice it was I had volunteered to cook Christmas dinner and how in the world could I get a whole deer in the oven? She'd already invited the guests, however, and I was remembering how I had publicly committed myself to the task.

Well, I cleared the kitchen for action, drank a beer, brought up the deer, and here's how I proceeded:

It's really pretty simple. First thing, take a saw and whack off the neck. Then take a nice sharp knife and separate the shoulders neatly from the ribs (don't poke holes in the ribs). Now. Lay the critter belly down on the table or wherever it is you're working on him. (If you have a headache, like I did, you might have another beer at this point.) With your fingers, feel for the vertebra joint just to the rear of the last rib. Take the point of your knife and cut the muscle over this joint and far enough down to partly separate the bone. Now, move back two vertebrae joints and make another

3 or 4 pats of butter
4 or 5 slices bacon

►Place the roast on a large piece of foil inside a baking dish. Slice vegetables over and around roast. Salt, pepper and spice to taste. Place pats of butter (not margarine) on top and cover with the bacon slices. Close foil tightly and bake in medium oven, 250 to 300°F (120 to 150°C) two to three hours, depending on size of roast. Check for doneness. For frozen roast: add one hour to the cooking time.

■ *Cathy Stingley*
  Cooking Up A Storm, *Homer*

Campfire Pot Roast

►A good chunk of meat makes a grand meal in camp and is handy for sandwiches and snacks the next day. Any cooking process that is self-basting is best for very fresh, very lean meat. Got a Dutch oven? Season your roast with salt and pepper and garlic if you wish. Sear it well on all sides in your Dutch oven. Combine a cup (240 mL) of apple juice (cider will do nicely) with about a quarter-cup (60 mL) flour and pour this over. Put the lid on, set pan in coals and let'er bubble away.

The length of cooking time varies from a couple of hours to longer. Test meat with a fork or cut off a

cut the same way. *Make sure you don't cut all the way through the body cavity.* Then flip the deer on its back and hold one hand on the inside of the backbone right behind the cuts, fold the ribs and neck end up with the other arm. This requires a little effort as you break the remaining tissue of the vertebrae.

You now have the fold points made. With a knife, cut the flanks just along the last rib and up to the loin portion, then with a meat saw, make a cut through short ribs and brisket.

You are almost done, so now fold him over and see how he fits . . . pretty good, huh? . . . or maybe you need to trim a bit more off those ribs so the neck fits down better. Problem now is those darned back legs won't bend up in the air turkey-style, so— knife again — cut a little of the muscle along each side of the backbone and, by golly, it does look like a bird, almost, but you still aren't quite done.

At this point you can very tightly wrap the whole thing and put it in the freezer for a special occasion or, if you're cooking it now, you had better whomp up (a lot of) your favorite dressing.

Here's one I like, and you'd be well off to stick with some kind of sausage dressing as venison of small animals tends to be on the dry side. The sausage dressing will keep it moist and tasty. My recipe:

Sausage Dressing
2 pounds (1 kg) pork sausage
2 medium onions, chopped
1 large green pepper, chopped
3 large cloves garlic, minced
1 teaspoon (5 mL) pepper
2 teaspoons (10 mL) salt
3 teaspoons (15 mL) caraway seed
3 teaspoons (15 mL) chopped parsley

2 teaspoons (10 mL) ground oregano
2 bay leaves
1-1/2 teaspoons (7 mL) rubbed sage
1 cup (240 mL) chopped celery
Approximately 2 quarts (2 kg) dried
  bread crumbs

►Put sausage into large skillet over medium heat. Mix around until you have about a quarter-inch (0.6 cm) of fat in bottom of skillet. Remove sausage. Add chopped onions, green pepper and lightly brown the onions. Put sausage back in skillet and add rest of ingredients except bread crumbs. Stir and cover. Simmer for 15 minutes. Pour whole works in large mixing bowl and, as soon as cool enough to work, use hands to mix in bread crumbs. If too dry, add a little warm water.

To stuff your deerky, first fill bung hole with wad of aluminum foil. With deer folded, bring flanks upward, lap over top and sew together. Now stuff with that delicious dressing. Wad in foil over any holes left by neck. With string, tie leg bones together and forward.

Preheat oven to 350°F (175°C). Put deerky on its side in large pan and cover tightly with a large sheet of foil. Leave in oven two hours, then remove and turn deerky on other side. Cover tightly again and return to oven. Figure about five hours for most deerkies. During the last half-hour remove foil to brown roast. Serve with the rest of your favorite holiday trimmings.

This Herring Cove Stuffed Deerky is the best way I ever heard of to fix and serve a small deer.

■ *Richard H. Krupicka*

Reprinted from *ALASKA SPORTSMAN*®, November 1968

small slice and try it. You'll know when it's ready. Toss in a handful of onion flakes or fresh onion and, when the roast is close to done, add some vegetables. The apple juice and flour make a fabulous gravy and the meat will be tender and sweet.

■ *Ken Davidson*
"Moveable Feasts —
Cooking Game in the Field"
BC Outdoors, September 1981

Norwegian Pot Roast

1 clove garlic
1/4 cup (60 mL) bacon fat
5 to 6 pounds (2.25 to 2.7 kg) moose roast
Salt and pepper
Powdered ginger
Flour
1 cup (240 mL) sour cream
2 bay leaves
1 large onion, finely chopped
1 diced fresh tomato

►Rub an earthenware casserole or Dutch oven with split garlic clove and add bacon fat. Rub the roast with salt, pepper and ginger. Dredge with flour and brown well on all sides in bacon fat. Add sour cream, turning meat until thoroughly covered. Add bay leaves, onion and fresh tomato. Cover and bake in a 350°F (175°C) oven about 2-1/2 hours. Remove cover and continue baking a half-hour longer. Gravy may be thickened or thinned as desired.

■ *Pat Stetson*
Recipes From The Scrolls of Saint Peter's
Seward

Roast Shoulder of Venison
A good remedy for tough meat

Venison shoulder
Seasoned flour
1 cup (240 mL) water
Sliced onions
Celery leaves

►Cut meat from shoulder in serving-sized chunks. Roll in flour, seasoned with salt, pepper and a little sage. Brown all sides of meat in shortening in frying pan. Put browned chunks in roaster; cover with onions and celery leaves. Slowly add water to drippings in frying pan; stir until liquid boils, then pour over meat. Cover roaster and bake at 300 to 350°F (150 to 175°C) about three hours. Baste juice over vegetables two or three times while cooking. Add more water if necessary.

■ *Peggy Larson*
Kitchen Magic, Ketchikan

Curried Caribou Roast

3-pound (1.4 kg) boneless rolled roast of
caribou or other game
1 clove garlic, split
2 teaspoons (10 mL) curry powder
1/4 teaspoon (1 mL) salt
1/8 teaspoon (0.5 mL) pepper
3 tablespoons (45 mL) oil
1 can (16 oz /or/ 456 g) chunk pineapple
2 tablespoons (30 mL) margarine
1 tablespoon (15 mL) cornstarch
Optional:
3 potatoes, peeled and quartered
4 carrots, halved or chunked
3 medium onions, halved
Additional salt and pepper to taste

►One hour before cooking, remove meat from refrigerator. Wipe it with a damp cloth and rub it well with the split garlic. Allow to stand at room temperature for an hour. Then rub well with curry powder, using about as much as will cling, plus the salt and pepper. Heat oil in Dutch oven and brown the roast well on all sides. It will take 15 minutes or more. Then add enough water or stock to cover bottom of pan, lower heat, cover, and cook on top of stove or in a moderate oven for 2 to 2-1/2 hours, adding more liquid from time to time, if necessary. During the last half-hour of cooking, add vegetables and about 1/2 cup (120 mL) more water. When done, remove roast and vegetables to serving platter and keep warm. Pour off pan juices, reserving up to 1 cup (240 mL). Add margarine to the pan and heat, stirring up meat particles at the bottom of the pan. Drain off and reserve 1/4 cup (60 mL) of the pineapple juice. The rest pour into the pan, add pan juices and pineapple chunks and heat to simmering. Add cornstarch to reserved pineapple juice and blend well; then stir into hot liquid and continue stirring until thickened. Spoon over roast or serve in a gravy boat.

■ *The editors, ALASKA® magazine*

Venison Roast in Wine

6 pounds (2.7 kg) venison roast
1 large stalk celery with leaves
2 large carrots, coarsely diced
2 medium onions, quartered
Salt, pepper, crushed bay leaf
1/2 teaspoon (2 mL) rosemary
1/2 teaspoon (2 mL) marjoram
1/2 cup (120 mL) plus a bit more red wine

►Place roast in center of large piece heavy duty aluminum foil. Place in shallow pan and fold foil up to form a vessel to hold juice while roast is browning under the broiler. When roast is well browned, add vegetables and season with salt, pepper and herbs. Add wine. Bring foil up over meat and seal edges well. Place in a 300°F (150°C) oven for about 3-1/2 hours. Remove meat to hot platter and thicken juices for a delectable gravy.

About Long Marination: *A good remedy for roasts that are inclined to be dry or tough is to marinate them in a liquid that usually includes a tenderizer such as vinegar, wine or cider. Several pickly-spicy suggestions follow, each calling for a different length of marination, from two days to two weeks.*

Any marination longer than a couple of hours requires refrigerated temperatures which, in home refrigerators, range between 36°F and 45°F (2°C to 7°C). Ideally, the temperature should be a fairly constant 38°F (3.5°C).

Another caution to remember is that marinades mix badly with metals of various kinds, especially aluminum and copper. Marinate meats in large stoneware crocks, glass or enamelware that has no chips or blemishes. Use stainless steel, glass or wooden utensils to cut, measure and stir.

Weights are often recommended to keep the meat under the marinade. Again, use glass or stoneware or wood. Fill a bowl or jar with something heavy, such as stones, and set it on top of the meat to keep it below the marinade. Then put a covering over the whole thing, plastic wrap or waxed paper or a clean board if the container has no lid of its own. Refrigerate for the specified time.

Seward Peninsula Sauerbraten
Marinate 10 days to two weeks

3 pounds (1.4 kg) well-marbled moose roast
2 quarts (1.9 L) water
2 quarts (1.9 L) cider vinegar
1 small onion, finely chopped
2 bay leaves, crushed
1 tablespoon (15 mL) peppercorns
1 tablespoon (15 mL) MSG
1/4 cup (60 mL) sugar

►Heat all ingredients except meat. Place meat in an enamel pot or crock and weight it. Pour in hot marinade to cover. Cover the container and place in a cool area, about 38°F (3.5°C), for 10 days to two weeks. Turn the meat daily to insure proper marination.

Place moose in heavy pot, adding strained stock from marinade. Cook as pot roast until tender. Thicken stock with flour and, just prior to serving, stir in 1 cup (240 mL) sour cream.
■ *Recipe from Teller Mission*
Courtesy, Joe Rychetnik
"Dining Along the Eskimo Coast"
ALASKA SPORTSMAN®, *April 1964*

Simple Caribou "Pot" Roast

1 small can of mushrooms, drained
1 envelope dry onion soup
1 can cream of mushroom soup
1 hefty caribou roast

►Place a piece of aluminum foil large enough to wrap around roast in a large baking dish. Put roast on foil and spread with cream of mushroom soup. Sprinkle onion soup mix over the meat and top with drained mushrooms. Fold foil over meat and seal securely. Roast in 300°F (150°C) oven for four hours or until done enough for your taste. The drippings in the foil make a delicious gravy. Thicken it as desired.

Bonnet Plume Moose Roti
Marinate 48 hours

1 shoulder roast of moose
2 cups (480 mL) tarragon wine vinegar
1/2 cup (120 mL) water
1/2 teaspoon (2 mL) white pepper
1 teaspoon (5 mL) Atkinsons' herb mustard*
1/2 teaspoon (2 mL) cloves
1/4 teaspoon (1 mL) each — oregano, thyme, rosemary and marjoram
1 teaspoon (5 mL) grated horseradish
1 bay leaf
1 tablespoon (15 mL) onion
1 tablespoon (15 mL) parsley
2 tablespoons (30 mL) salt
3 tablespoons (45 mL) butter
1 clove garlic
8 gingersnaps, crumbled
1 cup (240 mL) sour cream

►In a saucepan, combine all ingredients except meat, gingersnaps and sour cream. Bring just to boiling and let simmer five minutes. Pour over moose and marinate 48 hours in a cool place. Preheat oven to about 450°F (230°C). (On my old camp stove with no gauge I have to judge the amount of heat felt on the palm of my hand held about a foot away from the front of the stove.) Roast moose for 30 minutes, then reduce heat to 325°F (160°C) and continue cooking until done. When done, make a thick gravy by adding gingersnap crumbs to the drippings and mix with sour cream.
■ *Dolores Brown*
"Herbs Are The Difference"
ALASKA SPORTSMAN®, *November 1967*

*We're guessing a Dijon-style mustard will do as a substitute for this mustard made by the herb growers who introduced this cook to the wonders of herb flavoring.

Sour Fleish
(Or Hasenpfeffer)

Call it "Sour Fleish" if the meat is moose (or beef), "Hasenpfeffer" if you use the traditional rabbit meat or substitute chicken. Another recipe for Hasenpfeffer is on page 243.

►Soak meat for two days in two parts vinegar to one part water to cover; turn frequently. Cook in this same marinade, adding onion, celery, bay leaf, carrots and salt to taste. When the meat is tender, drain, reserving cooking liquid, and place in a warm serving dish. Blend 2 tablespoons (30 mL) flour with hot bacon drippings; stir in 1 to 2 cups (240 to 480 mL) of the cooking liquid to make gravy of the consistency you want.

For moose (or other venison), crush eight gingersnaps and add to gravy for proper spice flavoring. Pour gravy over meat and serve.

■ *Edna M. Weir*
  Recipes From The Scrolls of Saint Peter's
  Seward

STEAKS — CHOPS — RIBS

About Cooking Chops and Steaks: *Broiling — in a skillet, under an oven unit or over coals — should be reserved for the tenderest steaks and chops, those from the loin or rib. The main rule: don't overcook. If the meat is tough, choose some other method of cooking or marinate it first. Broiling it a long time will only make it tougher.*

Barbecue or broil chops or steaks about 3 inches (7.5 cm) from the heat source. Maximum broiling time is about ten minutes, five minutes per side, for an inch-thick (2.5 cm) chop or steak.

If you're grilling over coals, confuse the juices by turning the meat frequently. They'll remain inside the meat rather than squandering their precious flavor on the coals. For pan-broiling, the following recipe from the Wild Game Cookbook is a classic, but variations abound. Bastes — butter or a sauce — are popular especially for oven-broiling or barbecuing. Choose from the list on page 171. For a "self-baste," cream some butter with finely minced garlic or wild chives and/or parsley. Then shape the mixture into balls, harden them in the freezer and set one on top of each steak or chop during oven- or pan-broiling.

Whether or not you baste the meat, be sure to use the residue that collects in the skillet or broiler-pan, even if it's dry and crackly. After you've removed the meat to a warm platter, thin these substances with additional butter, wine, water, prepared steak sauce, or a little of each . . . but not *too* much. All you want is a little tasty sauce to pour back over the meat as you serve it. Or, add only butter to the pan juices and saute a few sliced mushrooms and thin onion rings with which to garnish the meat.

What to do with tougher steaks and chops? Fear not. There are some excellent recipes in this section for marinades that help tenderize.

Pan-Broiled Venison Chops

Venison chops cut 1/2 inch (1.25 cm) thick
1 piece bacon

►Heat a heavy cast-iron skillet until it is smoking. Wrap a slice of bacon around tines of a fork and wipe it quickly over the bottom of the skillet. Put the chops in the skillet and sear well, about two to three minutes on each side. Serve immediately on hot plates and season to taste.

■ *L.W. "Bill" Johnson — Remington's*
  Wild Game Cookbook, ©1968, 1970, 1972
  Published by The Benjamin Company, Inc.

Venison Pepper Steak

1-1/2 pounds (0.70 kg) cubed venison
Salt and pepper to taste
1/4 teaspoon (1 mL) powdered ginger
1/4 teaspoon (1 mL) curry powder
1/4 teaspoon (1 mL) sweet basil
1 medium onion, chopped
1 cup (240 mL) celery cut in half-inch
*   (1.25 cm) pieces*
1 tablespoon (15 mL) soy sauce
2 medium peppers, sliced
2 tomatoes cut in medium chunks
2 tablespoons (30 mL) cornstarch

►Brown venison cubes well with the seasoning. Steam until almost tender. Add onions and celery and 1 cup (240 mL) water. Simmer until vegetables are done. Add soy sauce. When onions and celery

are tender, add pepper slices and tomato chunks. Simmer until peppers are semi-firm. Mix cornstarch with 1/4 cup (60 mL) water. Add to pan, mix thoroughly and cook until sauce is clear. Serve on rice, on buttered noodles or plain.
■ Cooking Up A Storm, *Homer*

Marinated Venison Steaks

Marinade:
1/4 cup (60 mL) vinegar
2 tablespoons (30 mL) water
2/3 cup (160 mL) salad oil
1 tablespoon (15 mL) ketchup
1 tablespoon (15 mL) grated onion or dried
*   onion flakes*
1 teaspoon (5 mL) salt
1/2 teaspoon (2 mL) dry mustard
1/2 teaspoon (2 mL) sugar
1/2 teaspoon (2 mL) paprika
1/4 teaspoon (1 mL) pepper
1/4 teaspoon (1 mL) garlic salt

►Measure all ingredients into a jar which has a close-fitting top. Cover and shake vigorously. Pour into a large enamel, glass or earthenware bowl, add steaks and allow to stand for several hours or overnight in a cool place.

To pan-broil:
6 venison steaks cut 1/2 to 1 inch
*   (1.25 to 2.5 cm) thick*
1/2 teaspoon (2 mL) salt
1/4 teaspoon (1 mL) pepper
1/4 teaspoon (1 mL) charcoal seasoning
*   (optional)*

►Remove steaks from marinade and drain well. Season with salt, pepper and charcoal seasoning if desired. Rub preheated heavy frying pan with a piece of fat. Cook steaks quickly at high heat, turning every half-minute until done. Do not overcook. Add only enough fat to prevent meat from sticking to pan. Serve sizzling hot. Yields six servings.
■ Northern Cookbook

Islander Loin Chops
Marinated

4 to 6 venison chops, 1 inch (2.5 cm) thick
1 small can (6 fl oz /or/ 180 mL) pineapple juice
2 tablespoons (30 mL) oil
2 tablespoons (30 mL) soy sauce
2 tablespoons (30 mL) lemon juice
2 cloves garlic, finely minced
1/8 teaspoon (0.5 mL) powdered clove

►Combine all ingredients except chops in a screw-top jar and shake vigorously. Place chops in a glass

baking dish and pour marinade over them. Cover and refrigerate for several hours or overnight, turning from time to time.

Broil over coals or in a small amount of hot fat in a heavy frying pan, five minutes per side, or until done to your taste. The figure-conscious can omit the oil from the marinade with no loss of tenderizing power.
■ *Anon.*

Tamed Game

►Tame your tough game by preparing steaks in this fashion. Dredge steaks lightly with flour. Brown in a little cooking oil in a Dutch oven. Brown sliced onions in oil. When they become transparent, pour them over the meat in the Dutch oven. Add salt, pepper and paprika to taste. For meat enough to serve four people, pour sour cream to suit, plus 3/4 cup (180 mL) water. Add a bay leaf to be removed after cooking. This is a "by guess and by gosh" recipe because you will use onions, seasonings and liquid in amounts to please your own palate. Cook in a 300°F (150°C) oven for two to three hours, adding more liquid occasionally if it seems to be needed. Serve with rice or mashed potatoes.
■ *The Old Homesteader*

Moose Steak Teriyaki

►Marinate moose steak, thinly sliced (1/8 to 1/4 inch /or/ 3 to 6 mm), in sauce for half a day, turning frequently. Sauce is made by combining 1 cup (240 mL) syrup drained from pineapple or cooking sherry, 2 teaspoons (10 mL) fresh ginger root or 3/4 teaspoon (3 mL) ground ginger and two cloves of garlic, chopped fine. When marinated, drain and fry in hot greased pan quickly. Serve with boiled rice and a green salad.
■ Pioneer Cookbook, *Auxiliary No. 4, Anchorage*

Breaded Caribou Steaks or Cutlets

2 to 3 pounds (1 to 1.4 kg) steaks or cutlets
Salt and pepper
Bread crumbs
1/2 cup (120 mL) fat
1/4 cup (60 mL) currant jelly or
*   cranberry relish*

►Rub meat with salt and pepper. Roll in bread crumbs. Melt fat in skillet; fry steaks until well browned on bottom sides. Place on hot platter. Make gravy using drippings in pan and add currant jelly or cranberry relish. Serves four to six.
■ Reindeer and Caribou Recipes

Super Moose Steaks
with Onion Gravy

Moose steaks, 1 inch (2.5 cm) thick, tender and
cut from a well-aged animal
Cooking oil
Salt and pepper to taste
Butter or margarine
Beef soup base or bouillon cubes
Milk
Minced dried onions
Cornstarch

►Select thick, tender steaks that are comparable to beef filet mignon. Put just enough oil in a heavy skillet to barely cover the cooking surface. Heat to medium hot but not smoking. Cook the steaks three minutes and turn and cook three minutes on the other side. Thinner steaks take a lesser time, of course. This produces a medium-rare steak. Salt and pepper to taste. Remove the steaks to a hot platter and keep hot while making the gravy.

Add to the hot skillet 1 tablespoon (15 mL) butter for each serving desired. Stir in soup base or bouillon cubes to taste, usually about 1 teaspoon (5 mL) per serving. Stir cornstarch and milk together (1 cup /or/ 240 mL milk per person is about right, plus enough cornstarch to thicken the amount of fat in the skillet, 1 tablespoon /or/ 15 mL or more). Add milk all at once to skillet, reduce heat to simmer and add onions. Cook until gravy is thick. Serve with steaks.
■ *The Old Homesteader*

Super Flank Steak

1 to 2 pounds (0.45 to 1 kg) flank steak —
moose, caribou, sheep
1/2 teaspoon (2 mL) salt
Generous dash pepper
1/2 cup (120 mL) minced wild chives or onion
1/4 cup (60 mL) cranberry juice
1/4 cup (60 mL) water
Whole-wheat flour
Cooking fat

►Score flank steak diagonally in two directions and on both sides. Place the steak in a large bowl, sprinkle with salt and pepper and chives or onion and add cranberry juice and water. Set in refrigerator, covered, and allow to marinate for four or five hours. Turn the meat in the liquid several times during the marinating process. Remove from marinade and drain thoroughly, reserving marinade. Dredge in whole-wheat flour and brown in a heavy skillet, turning as needed. When the meat is well browned, cut in 2-inch (5 cm) strips, sprinkle lightly with more flour, add the marinade, cover and simmer slowly until most of the liquid

has cooked away. Turn the strips and again sprinkle with flour and add a little water. Bake in a 350°F (175°C) oven until nearly all juice is absorbed. Turn the strips again and add just enough more water to keep from scorching. Bake for about 20 minutes more. The total baking time will be one hour or even more. Flank steak must be cooked long and slowly. You might need to add a little liquid from time to time. This dish has a flavor that can't be beat. One variation that is good is to add a little tomato juice, paste or even cut up fresh tomato. Just enough to give it a bit of tomato flavor.
■ *Helen A. White, Anchorage*
Alaska Wild Berry Trails

Paupiettes de Moose

2 pounds (1 kg) moose steak, 1/4 inch
(0.6 cm) thick
3/4 cup (180 mL) flour
1/2 teaspoon (2 mL) salt
1/4 teaspoon (1 mL) pepper
Dash each — sweet marjoram, rosemary
and thyme
1 cup (240 mL) water
1-1/2 cups (360 mL) Sage Stuffing

►Cut moose into 2 x 4-inch pieces. Mix flour, salt and pepper and pound well into each piece. Next place a mound of Sage Stuffing in the center of each slice, fold the moose meat over the stuffing and fasten with toothpick. Place in roaster, add water and herbs and bake for one hour, letting the meat brown well before serving.

For a vegetable with this dish, we like Russian beets, made with sugar, salt, vinegar, cornstach and a dash of oregano.
■ *Dolores Brown*
"Herbs Are The Difference"
ALASKA SPORTSMAN®, *November 1967*

Chili-Cheesy Moose Steak

2 pounds (1 kg) moose steak, round or chuck,
1 inch (2.5 cm) thick
3 tablespoons (45 mL) flour
2 teaspoons (10 mL) salt
2 teaspoons (10 mL) chili powder
Dash of pepper
1 cup (240 mL) shredded sharp Cheddar cheese
1/4 cup (60 mL) shortening or melted butter
2 cups (480 mL) chopped onions
1 can (1 lb /or/ 456 g) tomatoes

►Cut moose into serving-sized pieces. Combine flour, salt, chili powder and pepper and pound into meat, both sides. Brown well in hot shortening. Remove from pan and brown onions in drippings. Spoon onions into large casserole and arrange steak pieces on top, then undrained tomatoes. Cover and bake 1 to 1-1/2 hours or until meat is tender at 350°F (175°C). Sprinkle with grated cheese and heat five minutes longer to melt cheese. Serves six.

■ Ann Neal
  Cooking Up A Storm, *Homer*

Reindeer Meat Rolls

►Cut thin reindeer round steak into 4 x 5-inch (10 x 12.5 cm) pieces. Pound each piece a little. Put a little salt, pepper, one slice of onion and a half-slice of bacon on each piece. Roll up the pieces and fasten with toothpicks. Roll in flour and brown meat in hot fat. Let meat simmer slowly for about two hours or until tender; also add a little water at times. The gravy can be made more tasty by adding a small can of mushroom stems and pieces.

■ *Out of Alaska's Kitchens*

Caribou Teriyaki

1-1/2 pounds (0.70 kg) caribou sirloin steak
1 tablespoon (15 mL) powdered ginger
1/2 clove of garlic, minced
1 tablespoon (15 mL) sugar
1/2 medium onion, minced
1/4 cup (60 mL) soy sauce
1/8 cup (30 mL) water

►Cut steak into serving pieces. Make a sauce of remaining ingredients. Pour over meat. Let stand one to two hours. Spread out on shallow pan and broil three to five minutes on each side. Serve immediately. Serves four.

■ Reindeer and Caribou Recipes

Round Steak Supper
For the slow-cooker

2 pounds (1 kg) moose round steak, 1 inch
*   (2.5 cm) thick*
1 can (8 oz /or/ 228 g) mushrooms
1/2 cup (120 mL) chopped onion
1/2 cup (120 mL) chopped celery
1/2 cup (120 mL) French dressing
1 package (2½ oz /or/ 70 g) sour cream mix
1/2 cup (120 mL) water
1 teaspoon (5 mL) Worcestershire
Hot noodles

►Slice steak diagonally into 1/8-inch (3 mm) strips. Drain mushrooms and reserve liquid. Put steak in slow-cooker; add onions, celery and mushrooms. Combine French dressing, sour cream sauce mix, water, Worcestershire and mushroom liquid. Pour over mixture in cooker, cover and cook on low for six to seven hours. Serve over hot noodles.

■ *Ruth Hale, Anchorage*

Caribobs with Mushrooms

1 cup (240 mL) cooking oil
1/3 cup (80 mL) lemon juice
2 teaspoons (10 mL) salt
2 teaspoons (10 mL) dry mustard
2 teaspoons (10 mL) nutmeg
Garlic powder
1 tablespoon (15 mL) pepper sauce
1/2 teaspoon (2 mL) crushed red pepper
1 onion, finely chopped
2-1/2 pounds (1.15 kg) caribou steak, chilled
Medium-sized puffballs

►Combine all ingredients except steak and mushrooms in shallow dish. Slice chilled steaks thinly and lay in dish of marinade. Refrigerate overnight. Thread strips of steak accordion fashion on long skewers with mushrooms threaded between folds of steak. Broil kabobs about 4 inches (10 cm) from heat. Brush with marinade several times during broiling. Broil just long enough to suit individual tastes.

■ *The Old Homesteader*

Venison Steak in Mirepoix
Mirepoix is a mixture of vegetables and liquids used to enhance the flavor of meat. In point of fact, after long, slow cooking together, the mirepoix may taste even better than the meat, and it is used as a garnish at serving time.

1 tablespoon (15 mL) butter or margarine
1/2 cup (120 mL) each — diced carrots, celery
*   and onion, cut to 1/4-inch (6 mm) cubes*
1 clove garlic, minced
1/4 bay leaf
2 cups (480 mL) game or beef broth, or broth
*   and Burgundy — 1 part wine to 3 parts broth*
2 pounds (1 kg) half-inch thick (1.25 cm) steaks
Salt and pepper
1/4 cup (60 mL) flour
Additional margarine or bacon fat

►Melt butter or margarine in a small saucepan, add diced vegetables and garlic and saute slowly until onion is translucent. Add bay leaf, broth and wine and simmer gently for five minutes. Set aside. Trim excess fat from meat and slash sides to prevent curling. Sprinkle with salt and pepper and dredge with flour.

In a large skillet with a cover or in a Dutch oven, melt additional margarine or bacon fat — about 2 tablespoons (30 mL) — and brown steak quickly on both sides. Then add the mirepoix, cover tightly and simmer over low heat until meat is tender, about 1-1/2 hours. Serve in large pieces with some sauce spooned over each piece. Serves four to six.

■ You and Your Wild Game *(adapted)*

Dee Mahaffey's
Moose Steak Parmesan

1/2 cup (120 mL) chopped onion
1 pound (456 g) ground moose
2 large cans (29 oz /or/ 826 g, each) tomatoes
1 tablespoon (15 mL) salt or to taste
1 bay leaf
1 can (6 oz /or/ 170 g) tomato paste
2 pounds (1 kg) thinly sliced moose steak
Seasoned bread crumbs
Parmesan cheese
3 eggs, slightly beaten
Olive or salad oil
1 pound (456 g) Monterey Jack or
   mozzarella cheese

►Brown onion and ground moose lightly. Add tomatoes, salt, bay leaf and tomato paste. Simmer at least three hours until mixture thickens. (Can be made ahead and frozen.) Dip thinly sliced moose steaks into mixture of seasoned bread crumbs and Parmesan cheese. Then dip into slightly beaten eggs and into crumbs again. Brown in oil.

Alternate in greased casserole layer of meat, layer of sliced cheese and layer of tomato-meat sauce. Repeat layers until pan is full. Top with sauce. Bake at 300°F (150°C) for 1 to 1-1/2 hours.
■ The Anchorage Times

Barbecued Moose Ribs
Classic open-fire style

5 pounds (2.25 kg) moose ribs (beef can
   be substituted)
2 cups (480 mL) vinegar
1 can (8 oz /or/ 228 g) tomato sauce
1 teaspoon (5 mL) dry mustard
3 tablespoons (45 mL) cooking oil
1 tablespoon (15 mL) garlic salt
Salt and pepper

►Cook ribs over a hot open fire, painting on sauce made of above ingredients frequently. Ribs will be charred on the outside but juicy and tender in the inside. Cook for about 1 to 1-1/2 hours. Serves two hungry people.
■ *Mary Shields*
   AlaskaFest

When cleaning and cutting wild meat, be sure to avoid leaving any hairs on the flesh. Hair will impart an off taste to the meat. A "picker" is the person designated to pick all hairs off the carcass before it is cut into freezer-sized pieces.

Moose Ribs with
Tart Barbecue Sauce
Barbecued on top of the stove

►First rub about 4 pounds (1.8 kg) moose spareribs with charcoal salt and tenderizer. Place in a roaster and add two onions, sliced. Over ribs, pour the following sauce which can be made ahead of time and stored until ready to use.

1 onion, chopped
2 tablespoons (30 mL) oil
2 tablespoons (30 mL) vinegar
3 tablespoons (45 mL) brown sugar or
   2 tablespoons (30 mL) honey
1/4 cup (60 mL) lemon juice
1 cup (240 mL) tomato ketchup
3 tablespoons (45 mL) Worcestershire
1/2 teaspoon (2 mL) prepared mustard
1/2 cup (120 mL) water
1/2 cup (120 mL) celery, diced
Dash of cayenne pepper

►Simmer ribs in sauce for about 30 minutes, adding liquid if needed. Uncover during the last 10 minutes of cooking.
■ *Anon.*
   Courtesy, Mrs. Aline Strutz

Variation: Ribs may be oven-barbecued. First brown them in fat, then place them in a shallow baking pan. Cover with sauce and continue to baste with sauce, turning ribs frequently, during baking. It will take about two hours in a slow to moderate oven, up to 350°F (175°C).

Moose Steaks Supreme
"This recipe is especially suited to moose steaks which have been in a locker all winter and are beginning to dry out."

2 pounds (1 kg) moose steak
1/2 cup (120 mL) flour
1 teaspoon (5 mL) poultry seasoning
1 teaspoon (5 mL) celery salt
1 teaspoon (5 mL) salt
1/2 teaspoon (2 mL) pepper
3 tablespoons (45 mL) fat

►Cut the dried edges and any fat or tissue from the meat. Then cut the meat into elongated strips, about 1-1/2 inches (3.75 cm) wide. Pound these strips once or twice with a meat mallet, then roll the strips in the mixture of flour and seasonings. When thickly coated drop into frying pan containing hot fat. A medium heat is best; however, the fat must be hot when meat is put into it. Then fry as you would fry chicken, slowly, and turning often,

pouring more of the flour mixture on the steaks as the browning proceeds. Fry for about half an hour or until each piece is brown and thoroughly done. The flouring keeps the meat juices in each piece and the result is a tender, well-flavored, juicy piece of meat.
■ Gold Rush Festival Cook Book
  Whitehorse, Yukon Territory

Tender Moose Trophy
"A trophy moose, especially if he has established himself as the king of the herd, is not the tenderest article in the woods, but this recipe will give you an agreeably thick steak that will make for amiable chewing and tasty flavor."

4 pounds (1.8 kg) boneless steak, 1-1/2 inches (3.75 cm) thick, cut from one of the quarters
1/4 cup (60 mL) all-purpose flour
1 teaspoon (5 mL) seasoned salt
1/4 teaspoon (1 mL) paprika
1/8 teaspoon (0.5 mL) freshly ground black pepper
1/2 stick (2 oz /or/ 56 g) margarine

1 cup (240 mL) sliced onions
1 cup (240 mL) double-strength beef bouillon
1/2 cup (120 mL) of your favorite steak sauce
2 tablespoons (30 mL) prepared mustard
2 tablespoons (30 mL) sugar
Small boiled potatoes
Boiled sliced carrots

►Mix flour, salt, paprika and pepper and rub into meat thoroughly. Melt margarine in heavy frying pan over moderate heat, add onions and stir until soft. Brown the meat on both sides.

Add remaining ingredients except potatoes and carrots, cover and simmer over low heat for three hours, or until tender.

Transfer the steak and the onions to a hot platter and surround them with potatoes and carrots. Skim the fat from the liquid and pour the remaining sauce over the meat and vegetables. Such moose meat will increase your stature in what, with wild game cooked at its best, is an enviable world.
■ *Bradford Angier*
  "Moose Can Be The Most"
  ALASKA® *magazine, March 1977*

STEWS — CASSEROLES — OTHER ONE-DISH MEALS

Goulash with A Viennese Accent
6 medium onions, sliced thin
1 clove garlic, minced
1/4 cup (60 mL) butter or margarine
3 tablespoons (45 mL) paprika
2 tablespoons (30 mL) vinegar
2 pounds (1 kg) moose stew meat cut in 1-1/2 inch (3.75 cm) cubes
1-3/4 cups (420 mL) beef broth or 2 bouillon cubes and 1-3/4 cups (420 mL) water
1/4 cup (60 mL) tomato paste
1 teaspoon (5 mL) sugar
1/2 teaspoon (2 mL) caraway seed
Salt and pepper

►Saute onions and garlic in butter in large skillet until golden brown. Stir in paprika and vinegar. Add meat cubes and brown lightly. Add remaining ingredients; cover and simmer about one hour or until meat is tender. Serve over hot cooked noodles or mashed potatoes. Makes six to eight servings.
■ *Ruth Hale*
  Anchorage

Savory Venison Stew
2 pounds (1 kg) lean venison
1-1/2 tablespoons (23 mL) flour
1 generous pinch each — salt, pepper, marjoram and thyme
1 cup (240 mL) red wine
1/2 cup (120 mL) water or meat stock
12 small cubes salt pork
12 small onions
1/2 cup (120 mL) sliced mushrooms (optional)

►Cut venison into 2-inch (5 cm) cubes. Sprinkle with flour and seasonings. Put meat into a heavy skillet or saucepan, add wine and water or meat stock if you prefer. Cook as slowly as possible for four hours. Meanwhile braise salt pork and onions together until browned and add to the stew during the last 45 minutes of cooking. If desired, saute mushrooms in the pork fat and add them to the stew about 10 minutes before serving. The sauce should be dark brown and thick.
■ *Merle (Pat) Kimes*
  Tried and True Recipes, *Juneau*

Venison and Noodles

2 or 3 pounds (1 to 1.4 kg) neck meat or
2 to 4 venison shanks
Cold water
Salt and pepper
1 large onion
Noodles

►Cover meat with cold water and boil until tender. Season with salt, pepper and onion, sliced. Cook until onion is tender. Remove meat and cut into serving portions; keep hot. Add homemade or packaged noodles to rapidly boiling broth. As soon as noodles are done, add meat, reheat if necessary and serve.
■ *Mamie Jensen, Juneau*
   The Alaskan Camp Cook

Sweet and Sour Moose Stew

2 pounds (1 kg) moose meat
1 tablespoon (15 mL) butter or oil
1 teaspoon (5 mL) salt
1 cup (240 mL) onions, chopped
1 cup (240 mL) water
1 clove garlic
1 can (8 oz /or/ 228 g) tomato sauce
1/2 cup (120 mL) ketchup
1/2 cup (120 mL) vinegar
1/2 cup (120 mL) brown sugar
1 tablespoon (15 mL) prepared mustard
About 1 quart (1 L) vegetables (carrots,
**   potatoes, onions, peppers)**
Small can crushed pineapple

►Brown meat in butter in a large Dutch oven. Add salt, chopped onion and cook until light brown. Add water, cover and simmer for one hour. Stir in garlic, tomato sauce, ketchup, vinegar, brown sugar and mustard. Cut the vegetables in chunks; add to meat and cook until tender. Add a small can of crushed pineapple. Serves six to eight.
■ *Audrey Rearden*
   Cooking Up A Storm, *Homer*

Rich Caribou or Moose Stew

1 small onion, chopped
1 or 2 stalks celery, chopped
Shortening
Chopped caribou or moose
1 tablespoon (15 mL) molasses
1 tablespoon (15 mL) flour
Salt and pepper

►Saute onion and celery in shortening, browning the chopped meat at the same time. Simmer together until meat is tender, adding water as needed. Just before serving add the molasses.

Thicken to desired consistency and season to taste. Serve over rice. Soy sauce may be used, too.
■ *Lillian Tackes*
   The Food Cache, *Anchorage*

Pressure Cooker Stew

This convenient device can't quite duplicate the aroma and flavor that comes from long, slow cooking, but if you're in something of a hurry to get a hearty meal on the table — or to carry with you on a camping trip (see the third variation) — the pressure cooker is a great help. All the recipes call for braising or browning the meat first — a must for best flavor and appearance.

1-1/2 pounds (0.70 kg) stew meat
2 tablespoons (30 mL) fat
1 cup (240 mL) minced onion
1 clove garlic, minced
1 teaspoon (5 mL) salt
1/4 teaspoon (1 mL) pepper
1/8 teaspoon (0.5 mL) nutmeg
1 tablespoon (15 mL) sugar
1 tablespoon (15 mL) vinegar
4 potatoes
4 whole carrots
2 cups (480 mL) water

►Heat cooker and melt fat. Cut meat into 1-inch (2.5 cm) pieces and brown. Add remaining ingredients. Close cover securely. Cook 20 minutes at 15 pounds (103.5 kg) pressure. Cool cooker at once. Serve piping hot.
■ Reindeer and Caribou Recipes

Variations:
• If you want firmer vegetables, brown meat and cook all ingredients except carrots and potatoes for 15 minutes at pressure recommended. Cool cooker, add carrots and potatoes and return to pressure for an additional five minutes.
• Another variation (courtesy, Mrs. Aline Strutz) calls for quite different seasoning: Braise 2 pounds (1 kg) cubed moose meat and one large diced onion in 4 tablespoons (60 mL) bacon drippings until meat is well browned. Add 1 teaspoon (5 mL) sweet basil, 1/2 teaspoon (2 mL), each, allspice and chili powder, a pinch of rosemary, two cans (8 oz /or/ 228 g) tomato sauce plus two cans water. Cook at pressure recommended for 15 minutes. Lower pressure, add cubed carrots, potatoes and turnips, three or four each, and a small head of cabbage, quartered or shredded. Return to pressure an additional five minutes.
• Rieta Walker (*Cooking Up A Storm*, Homer) says you can have a hot meal ready the minute you arrive at camp (or somewhere along the way) if

you brown the meat and pressure cook everything except the vegetables at home. Just before you leave, lower the pressure, add desired vegetables and put back on the heat just until cooker returns to pressure. Then take the stew with you in the cooker, with the pressure weight in place. "Stew should be ready to eat on arrival at camp. Reheat if necessary."

Sa-More
(You know, "Gimme sa-more!")

1/2 package (about 2 cups /or/ 480 mL) noodles
Cheese, to taste, cut in chunks or slices
1 can (16 oz /or/ 456 g) pitted olives, drained
*1 large can (16 oz /or/ 456 g) whole kernel corn
    with juice*
1 small can (8 oz /or/ 228 g) tomato sauce
1 medium onion, chopped
1 green pepper, chopped
1 tablespoon (15 mL) butter or other fat
1 pound (0.45 kg) venison, cut in small chunks

►Cook noodles and drain well. Add next four ingredients and set aside. Slowly saute onion and pepper in fat. Add meat and stir-fry until browned. Mix noodles and meat, season to taste and arrange in casserole. Bake in a moderate oven, 350°F (175°C), about two hours.
■ *Tsimpshean Indian Island Cookbook
    Metlakatla (adapted)*

Moose Stroganoff

3 pounds (1.4 kg) moose steak
4 tablespoons (60 mL) olive oil
2 teaspoons (10 mL) salt
*2 cans (4 oz /or/ 114 g, each) mushrooms, or
    about 1/2 pound (228 g) fresh mushrooms,
    sliced and sauteed*
2 tablespoons (30 mL) butter
2 tablespoons (30 mL) flour
1 teaspoon (5 mL) paprika
1 teaspoon (5 mL) pepper
1 pint (480 mL) sour cream
Hot cooked rice or toast

►Trim fat and gristle from meat and cut against the grain into strips about 1 inch (2.5 cm) long and 1/4 inch (6 mm) thick. Heat oil in frying pan and add meat. Cover and cook over low flame, turning meat several times. After a half-hour, add salt and well-drained canned mushrooms or sauteed fresh ones. Cook 10 minutes more or until meat is tender. Add more oil if pan gets too dry.

With a slotted spoon, lift meat and mushrooms from pan and place in the top of a double boiler. Set aside.

Add butter and flour to pan juices and cook and stir until smooth. Mix in sour cream and seasonings and cook slowly until flavors are all properly married, but do not allow to boil.

Pour this sauce over the meat and mushrooms and cook over hot water in double boiler for 10 more minutes. Serve over hot rice or slices of toast. Can be made the day before and reheated in double boiler a few minutes before you are ready to eat. Makes a good dish for buffet suppers. The recipe can be doubled conveniently. If you don't have moose meat, try other venison. If you haven't been that fortunate, try beef!
■ *Mamie Jensen, Juneau
    PTA Cook Book, Petersburg*

Venison Shanks with Parsley Dumplings

►Season the shanks with salt, pepper, celery salt and paprika; brown them in a Dutch oven or similar kettle with a tightly fitting lid. When they are very brown, add 1 cup (240 mL) red wine, cover and simmer until meat is tender. Then add peeled carrots, onions and potatoes and a little water. Let the vegetables steam rather than boil but do not let the meat go dry. When the vegetables are almost done, add one or two cans of cream of mushroom soup, depending on amount of meat and vegetables in kettle. When this comes to a boil, drop in the dumplings, dipping the spoon in the gravy each time so the dumplings will slip off easily. The dumplings should rest on the vegetables and meat and not in the gravy. Cover tightly and cook 15 minutes without lifting the cover.

Dumplings may be made from a biscuit mix. Add 1 teaspoon (5 mL) sugar, pinch of salt and 2 tablespoons (30 mL) dried chopped parsley.
■ *Mrs. Earle L. Hunter
    Tried and True Recipes, Juneau*

Caribou Wild Rice Casserole

*1/2 pound (228 g) caribou, cut in bite-sized
    pieces*
*1/2 pound (228 g) lean pork, cut in bite-sized
    pieces*
1 medium onion, chopped
1 cup (240 mL) chopped celery
Salad oil or other fat
4 cups (1 L) boiling water
1/2 cup (120 mL) raw wild rice
1/2 cup (120 mL) raw white rice
4 tablespoons (60 mL) soy sauce

►Saute caribou, pork, onion and celery in hot fat. Arrange in large covered casserole and add remaining ingredients. Cover and bake for 1-1/2 hours at 350°F (175°C).
■ *Lena Lee, Alaska's Cooking, Anchorage*

FWT

Caribou or Moose Meat Pie

1 pound (456 g) caribou or moose round,
  cut thick
1/2 cup (120 mL) whole-wheat flour
Bacon drippings or other fat
Salt and pepper to taste
Hot water
1 large onion, cut in eighths
8 small potatoes or larger cubed spuds
4 large carrots, cut in quarters
1/2 cup (120 mL) green peas, fresh or frozen,
  or more
1 recipe biscuit dough (or dumpling dough;
  see Variation)

►Cut meat (other game, such as sheep, may be used, too) in large cubes, dredge in flour and brown on all sides in drippings. Use a Dutch oven if possible or other heavy pan. Salt and pepper to suit. Cover meat with water and cook slowly until meat is tender. Add water from time to time to keep the water level constant. When meat is nearly done,

add onions, carrots and potatoes and cook until tender, about 20 or 30 minutes. At the end of this cooking, thicken the gravy with a flour and water paste, and add the peas, fresh or frozen. *

If you did not use a Dutch oven for the browning, now transfer the stew to a large baking dish. Otherwise use the Dutch oven for the last cooking, too. Preheat oven to 400°F (205°C) and roll out biscuit dough to about 1/2 inch (1.25 cm) thick. Cut with biscuit cutter and cover top of stew with biscuits. Bake 10 minutes, reduce heat to 350°F (175°C) and continue baking until biscuits are a rich brown. We usually prepare extra biscuits so that we will have some to use with butter, too.

*Variation: At this point you can change your mind and have stew with dumplings rather than meat pie. Prepare dumpling dough, drop by spoonfuls on top of hot stew, cover and continue cooking on top of stove until dumplings are done.
■ The Old Homesteader

Caribou Hot Pot

Fill a medium-sized casserole with:
A layer of white potatoes, sliced 1/2 inch
  (1.25 cm) thick
A layer of tough lean caribou meat, cut small
A layer of sliced onions

Mix and spread over casserole:
3/4 teaspoon (7 mL) salt
3/4 teaspoon (7 mL) paprika (or more to taste)
1 can (16 oz /or/ 456 g) stewed tomatoes

►Cover and bake in moderate oven, 350°F (175°C), about two hours. Half an hour before the dish will be done, stir in 1/3 cup (80 mL) sour cream or yogurt. Serves six.
■ Alaska's Game Is Good Food

Reindeer Scrapple

Scrapple can be made from almost any boiled meat. Serve it as a hearty breakfast dish, with syrup, or a satisfying supper dish, with green salad and sourdough bread.

►Cook 2 pounds (1 kg) shoulder of reindeer until tender in 2 quarts (1.9 L) water. Remove bone and gristle and cut meat into cubes. Measure 3 cups (720 mL) cubed meat and set aside for scrapple. (Refrigerate any remainder for other uses.) Cool broth and skim off fat. In the top of a double boiler, heat 5 cups (1.2 L) broth and add 1 tablespoon (15 mL) salt, 1/4 teaspoon (1 mL) pepper, 1/2 teaspoon (2 mL) sage and a pinch of allspice. When the mixture boils, slowly stir in 2 cups (480 mL) yellow

corn meal. Then cover and continue cooking over hot water in double boiler for 30 minutes. Add meat and cook 30 minutes longer. Pour into well-greased loaf pan and refrigerate. When cold, slice in 1/4-inch (6 mm) slices, dip in flour and saute in butter or bacon fat until browned on both sides.
■ Out of Alaska's Kitchens

Shepherd's Pie

►Prepare leftover shoulder roast of caribou or reindeer by cutting it into medium-sized pieces. Simmer with vegetables, as for stew, one hour. Thicken the juice with flour mixed with a little cold water. Arrange in a casserole. Pile mashed potatoes on top. Sprinkle with paprika, dot with butter and bake 20 to 30 minutes in a 450°F (230°C) oven or until potatoes are browned.
■ Reindeer and Caribou Recipes

Deer Chop Suey

1 to 2 pounds (0.45 to 1 kg) deer meat
Fat or oil
Water
1 medium green pepper
4 stalks celery
1 medium onion
1/2 cup (120 mL) mushrooms
2 cups (480 mL) bean sprouts, rinsed
*   and drained*
1/2 cup (120 mL) sliced water chestnuts
1/2 cup (120 mL) chopped bamboo shoots
1/4 cup (60 mL) soy sauce, or less
1 tablespoon (15 mL) cornstarch

►Cut deer meat into small pieces and fry over medium-high heat until browned. Then add 1/4 cup (60 mL) water, or less, and steam until meat is tender. Slice green pepper, celery, onion and mushrooms into small wedges and add to meat just about 10 minutes before it is done. Add bean sprouts, water chestnuts and bamboo shoots. Mix soy sauce, cornstarch, and enough water to make a thin paste and add to juices in pan, stirring until the gravy has thickened. Serve with boiled rice.
■ *Vivian James, Angoon*

Venison Pinugbit

A Philippine version of sukiyaki
(via Southeastern Alaska)

2 pounds (1 kg) venison or beef
2 tablespoons (30 mL) salad oil or shortening
3 to 4 cloves fresh garlic, diced
Salt and pepper to taste
1 teaspoon (5 mL) Accent
1-1/2 teaspoons (7 mL) seasoned salt
1 head broccoli, if in season
1 large onion

1 large fresh zucchini
3 stalks celery
1 medium eggplant
1/4 cup (60 mL) soy sauce
1 or 2 tomatoes

►Cut the meat against the grain, slice it thin, about 1-1/4 inches (3 cm) long. The meat is tender when you slice it this way. Next, slice the vegetables, but not too small. Cut the zucchini lengthwise in half, then into pieces about 3/8 inch (0.9 cm) thick. Cut the eggplant into 1-inch (2.5 cm) squares and the onions and celery diagonally as for chop suey. Remove the stem from the broccoli and separate the head into pieces. Cut the tomatoes in eighths, to be added during the very last minutes of cooking. Set all the prepared vegetables aside.

Saute diced garlic in hot oil briefly; then add meat and brown on all sides. Add seasonings. If the meat does not produce its own juice, add a cup (240 mL) of hot water. After this runs dry, add another cup (240 mL) of hot water. After this runs dry, if the meat is tender, add the sliced vegetables. Stir vegetables and meat, add soy sauce, and continue cooking, stirring frequently, until vegetables are lightly cooked but still crisp. Lay the tomatoes on top of the mixture and allow to steam for a few minutes. Makes six to eight servings.
■ *Kaa T'eix (Mary Howard Pelayo)*
  Kaa T'eix's Cook Book, *Mount Edgecumbe*

Bigos
A traditional Polish dish for leftover game and kielbasa (Polish sausage)

2 cups (480 mL) diced sauerkraut
3 tomatoes, diced
4 dried or fresh mushrooms
2 apples, peeled, diced
1/4 pound (114 g) salt pork or slab bacon,
*   diced fine*
1 onion, chopped
Fat
1 to 2 cups (240 to 480 mL) leftover game
*   (bear, game bird, venison), chopped bite size*
1 pound (456 g) kielbasa, peeled and diced
1 tablespoon (15 mL) sugar
1 bouillon cube
Salt and pepper

►Combine sauerkraut, mushrooms, apples and tomatoes. Brown salt pork with onion, adding fat if necessary. Combine with sauerkraut mixture. Mix with remaining ingredients. Simmer one hour on top of stove, or bake one hour at 325°F (160°C). Serve with potatoes. Delicious warmed the next day. Yields six servings.
■ *Ann Chandonnet*
  AlaskaFest

Pirozhki — Little Pies

This excellent recipe for the Slavic specialty, pirozhki, is almost too good to confine to any one section of the book. Anna Blinn's original recipe, we confess, calls for ground beef, and we've substituted venison. We recommend that you come back to this recipe with numerous other fillings, too — flaked halibut or salmon, other ground game meat, cooked and shredded breast of ptarmigan and other wild fowl. Pirozhki are favorites at party time because they can be picked up in the fingers. The larger meat pies, called piroghi (or, among Russian descendants in Alaska, pirok), are made much the same way. Several recipes are in the salmon section, Chapter 2.

Dough:
4 rounded cups (600 g) flour
1 cup (240 mL) ice water
1 pound (456 g) margarine

►Cut margarine into flour as you would for pie crust. Stir water in with fork. Refrigerate overnight or at least one hour.

Meat filling:
2-1/2 pounds (1.15 kg) lean ground venison
1 medium onion, chopped fine
Salt and pepper to taste
2 hard-cooked eggs, chopped fine

►Brown meat in frying pan, using a fork to stir so the meat will be in small particles. Remove from pan. Cook onion in same pan until it is transparent but not browned; add onion to meat and add chopped eggs and season to taste with salt and pepper. Cool.

Assembling:
►Shape one-fourth of dough into a roll about 1-3/4 inches (4.4 cm) in diameter. Cut into 1-inch (2.5 cm) slices and dip edges in flour. Prepare remaining dough in rolls and use as needed.

Roll dough slices into about 3-1/2-inch (8.75 cm) circles. Place a heaping teaspoon (7 mL) of meat filling in the center of each dough circle. Bring edges together and pinch well. Pinch twice to be sure the edge is well sealed. Place on ungreased cookie sheet, pinched edge down. Brush top with beaten egg or evaporated milk. Bake in a preheated 425°F (220°C) oven for 25 minutes. Pirozhki may be frozen after assembling and then baked as needed or can be baked, then frozen and warmed when needed. To bake frozen pirozhki, preheat oven to 450°F (230°C). Place pirozhki on ungreased cookie sheet and brush with beaten egg or evaporated milk. Bake for 10 minutes, reduce heat to 425°F (220°C) and bake for 10 minutes more or until golden brown.
■ *Anna Blinn*
  Saint Herman's Sisterhood Club, *Kodiak*

Alaskan Meat Roll

2 pounds (1 kg) mooseburger
1 cup (240 mL) soft bread crumbs
1/2 pound (228 g) bacon or ham, ground
1 onion, chopped
Salt and pepper
Dry bread crumbs

►Mix everything but the dry bread crumbs in a large mixing bowl. Form into a large roll, 10 inches (25 cm) long. Wrap in waxed paper, then in thin cotton cloth. Tie both ends of the cloth tightly to make sure that roll is securely enclosed. Place the roll in a large pot of boiling water. Bring to a boil again and reduce heat to simmer. Let simmer for three hours —making sure that water level is fairly constant. Allow roll to cool in water, then remove cloth and paper. Roll in dry crumbs and serve, cold and sliced.
■ *Helen A. White, Anchorage*
  What's Cookin' in Alaska

Stuffed cabbage rolls . . . yum! Here are three Russian Alaska versions. For variety, you can use other garden greens as wrappers, too. Some, like spinach and chard, take less blanching time, but otherwise, follow the directions below. Blanch only a few leaves at once to keep the water bubbling and be sure you pull them out when they are at their brightest green.

Russian Style Cabbage Rolls #1

12 large cabbage leaves
1 large onion, chopped
6 tablespoons (90 mL) butter
1 pound (456 g) moose- or elkburger
1/2 pound (228 g) ground pork
1 cup (240 mL) cooked rice
2 tablespoons (30 mL) fresh or dried parsley,
  chopped
1 egg, lightly beaten
Salt and pepper to taste
2 tablespoons (30 mL) flour
1 cup (240 mL) tomato juice or soup
1/2 cup (120 mL) water
1 cup (240 mL) commercial sour cream

Salt
Freshly ground pepper
1/4 cup (60 mL) fresh dill, chopped or
*   2 tablespoons (30 mL) dried*

►*To prepare cabbage leaves:* Choose a fairly large cabbage. Gently pry off 12 large leaves so as not to tear them; pare off the inner bulge of the rib ("stem") of each leaf so that it folds up more easily. Then blanch trimmed leaves in a large pot of boiling water for five minutes. Drain well.

Saute onion in 2 tablespoons (30 mL) butter and combine with meat, rice and parsley. Mix thoroughly; then add egg to bind and salt and pepper to taste. Place a portion of meat mixture on base of each leaf. (Concave side of slightly cup-shaped leaf will be facing up when you do this.) Roll up leaf, tucking sides first, then rolling to end. Secure with string or a toothpick.

Saute stuffed cabbage leaves in remaining butter until lightly browned — about five minutes. Reduce heat to low, cover pan and cook gently for 30 minutes. If rolls stick, add some of the tomato juice during this cooking. Remove rolls from pan and discard string or toothpicks. Arrange on heated platter and keep warm.

Add flour to pan and cook two minutes, stirring constantly. Blend in tomato juice and water. Bring to a boil; blend in sour cream, salt, pepper and dill. Pour over cabbage and serve. Makes six hearty servings.
■ *Ann Chandonnet*
    Kodiak Fish Wrapper and
    Litter Box Liner

Cabbage Rolls #2

Cabbage leaves (1 per person)
1 pound (456 g) mooseburger
1 tablespoon (15 mL) onion flakes or
*   1/2 onion, minced*
1 egg
Dash of pepper
1/2 cup (120 mL) oatmeal or cracker crumbs
1/4 cup (60 mL) ketchup
1 teaspoon (5 mL) salt
1/2 teaspoon (2 mL) oregano or other spices

►Set cabbage leaves out for several hours at room temperature to wilt so they can be rolled without breaking. Mix mooseburger and rest of ingredients. Put some of the mixture on each cabbage leaf and roll up. Secure with toothpick. Place cabbage rolls in baking dish. Cover each roll with either a piece of bacon or ketchup diluted with a little soy sauce. Cover dish and bake at 350°F (175°C) for one hour. Four servings.
■ *Leoda Jenn*
    Cooking Up A Storm, *Homer*

Golubtsy — Stuffed Cabbage Rolls #3

8 large cabbage leaves
1 pound (456 g) ground meat
2 tablespoons (30 mL) Worcestershire
1 egg, slightly beaten
Salt and pepper
1 can tomato soup
1 cup (240 mL) cooked rice
1 small can (8 oz /or/ 228 g) tomato sauce

►Cook cabbage to soften, drain. Combine beef, egg, rice, salt and pepper. Divide the mixture among the cabbage leaves; roll them up, tucking in the sides, and place in a shallow baking dish large enough to hold the rolls and sauce. To prepare the sauce combine tomato soup, tomato sauce and Worcestershire. Mix well and pour over the cabbage rolls, covering them completely. Bake at 350°F (175°C), uncovered, for one hour. About 25 minutes before cabbage rolls are done, place several slices of bacon on the rolls and return to oven for the remaining time. Serves four.
■ *Matushka Kreta*
    Saint Herman's Sisterhood Club, *Kodiak*

Cranberry Meat Loaf

1/4 cup (60 mL) brown sugar
1/2 cup (120 mL) Cranberry Sauce
1-1/2 pounds (0.70 kg) ground moose or caribou
1/2 pound (228 g) ground smoked ham
3/4 cup (180 mL) milk
1/4 cup (60 mL) whole lowbush cranberries
3/4 cup (180 mL) cracker crumbs
2 eggs
1-1/2 teaspoons (7 mL) salt
1/8 teaspoon (0.5 mL) pepper
2 tablespoons (30 mL) diced onion
3 bay leaves

►Spread sugar over bottom of greased loaf pan. Mash Cranberry Sauce and spread over sugar. Combine remaining ingredients except bay leaf. Shape into loaf pan. Place bay leaves on top of loaf. Bake for one hour at 350°F (175°C). Remove bay leaves before serving. Serves 12.
■ *Anon.*
    Courtesy, Mrs. Aline Strutz

A river-washed rock that has been smoothed and flattened over the years makes a good whetstone; as good or better than many you buy.
■ *Henry Corbin, Rogue River, Oregon*
    The Cabin Friend
    ALASKA® magazine, June 1977

well browned. If you have enough mushrooms, saute an additional quantity in margarine quickly and pour over the loaf.

Variations:
- Whole-grain breads (especially wheat) instead of white give a nice taste change to meat loaf. Or use wheat germ instead of bread — 1 to 1-1/2 cups (240 to 360 mL) is about right for this amount of burger.
- Vary the toppings . . . bacon strips cooked over the top of the meat loaf make a good baste. Or, try this mixture, dreamed up by a cook in Kenai (*An Alaskan Cook Book*). Spread it over the top of the loaf and bake loaf covered until almost done, then remove cover for the last 15 minutes:

Meat Loaf Sauce
1/2 cup (120 mL) ketchup
1/3 cup (80 mL) vinegar
1 tablespoon (15 mL) Worcestershire
1 tablespoon (15 mL) chili powder
2 tablespoons (30 mL) chopped onion

Pizza Meat Pie
The meat is the crust!

►Set oven at 350°F (175°C). Combine in a medium bowl:

1 pound (456 g) lean, ground moose or caribou
1/2 cup (120 mL) powdered milk
1/2 cup (120 mL) dry bread crumbs
1 teaspoon (5 mL) salt
1/4 teaspoon (1 mL) pepper
1 clove garlic, crushed
1 cup (240 mL) water

►Mix well and pat into a deep pie pan or casserole. Then combine:

1 cup (240 mL) shredded Cheddar cheese
3/4 cup (180 mL) tomato paste
3/4 cup (180 mL) undrained mushrooms
1 teaspoon (5 mL) oregano
1 teaspoon (5 mL) grated onion or instant minced onion

►Mix well and sprinkle over meat in casserole. On top, sprinkle:

1/3 cup (90 mL) grated Parmesan cheese

►If desired, garnish with cooked sausage, green pepper, mushrooms and black olives. Bake 30 to 40 minutes or until meat is done.
■ *Nedra Evenson*
   An Alaskan Cook Book, *Kenai*

Venison Loaf with Mushrooms

4 slices soft bread, crumbled
1/2 cup (120 mL) milk
2 eggs
1 cup (240 mL) mushrooms, coarsely chopped
1/2 cup (120 mL) tomato sauce
2 pounds (1 kg) ground venison
1/2 cup (120 mL) chopped chives or onions
Water
Seasonings

►Crumble the bread into a large bowl and dampen with milk. Beat eggs and add to softened crumbs together with tomato sauce, onions, mushrooms and seasonings as desired. Stir to blend and then work the venisonburger (or other ground meat) into this mixture evenly. Add as much water as is needed to make a good substantial loaf. Bake at 350°F (175°C) for about an hour or until done and

Reindeer Spaghetti Sauce

1/2 pound (228 g) ground reindeer
2 tablespoons (30 mL) cooking oil
1 medium onion, chopped
1 clove garlic, minced
1 tablespoon (15 mL) parsley, minced
1 teaspoon (5 mL) salt
1/4 teaspoon (1 mL) pepper
Dash of cayenne pepper
1/2 teaspoon (2 mL) sugar
1/4 teaspoon (1 mL) basil
1/4 teaspoon (1 mL) oregano
2 bay leaves
1 tablespoon (15 mL) Worcestershire
1 can (6 oz /or/ 170 g) tomato sauce
1/4 cup (60 mL) mushrooms
1 can (16 oz /or/ 456 g) tomatoes
1 cup (240 mL) water
4 ounces (114 g) long spaghetti

►Brown meat in hot oil; add parsley, onions and garlic. Cook until vegetables are yellow but not brown. Add all ingredients except spaghetti. Cover; simmer over low heat two hours. Cook spaghetti as directed on package. Drain and serve hot with Reindeer Spaghetti Sauce. Serves four.
■ Reindeer and Caribou Recipes

Caribou Agutuk

Agutuk, *spelled various ways when the word is used in English, is often called "Eskimo ice cream." There are many ways of making it. Berries are often incorporated in the fluffy mixture and, instead of the "cheesy" taste ascribed to this recipe, the result is sweet. Several such recipes have been included in the berry section of this volume.*

►Caribou meat, preferably that along the sinews from the back and the hindquarters, is boiled and either chopped into very fine pieces or ground and added to a mixture of fats. Here is a typical Point Hope recipe:

1 cup (240 mL) caribou or edible beef tallow
1 cup (240 mL) seal or whale oil
4 pounds (1.8 kg) caribou meat, cooked
    and ground
1 cup (240 mL) caribou cooking broth

►First, the tallow is thoroughly chopped or hammered; then softened by squeezing in the hands or by warming it slightly on the stove. It is then beaten or whipped to a fluff — using a circular motion of the hand. Seal or whale oil is then added gradually and after each small addition the mixture is whipped until it is light and fluffy. The lukewarm cooking broth is next added, again whipping and stirring thoroughly after each small addition. Lastly, the ground meat is stirred in thoroughly and the mixture set aside to cool. Caribou *agutuk* has a very pleasant delicate cheesy taste.
■ The Alaska Dietary Survey

Slow-Cooker Meatballs

3 pounds (1.4 kg) ground moose
3 cups (720 mL) dry bread crumbs
2 cups (480 mL) canned milk
2 eggs
1 large onion
1-1/2 teaspoons (7 mL) garlic salt
1-1/2 teaspoons (7 mL) seasoned salt
2 teaspoons (10 mL) dill weed
2 teaspoons (10 mL) crushed oregano leaves
1/2 teaspoon (2 mL) allspice
1/4 teaspoon (1 mL) nutmeg
1/4 teaspoon (1 mL) cardamom
1 can cream of mushroom soup
1/2 cup (120 mL) red wine
3/4 cup (180 mL) water

►Soak bread crumbs in milk for 10 minutes. Add ground meat, eggs, onion, garlic and seasoned salt, dill weed, oregano, allspice, nutmeg and cardamom. Mix well and refrigerate for an hour. Shape mixture into 1-inch (2.5 cm) balls and brown lightly under broiler, turning once or twice. Put meatballs in slow-cooking pot. Mix mushroom soup, wine and water and bring to a boil in a small saucepan. Pour mixture over meatballs and cook slowly for six to eight hours in slow-cooker. Check occasionally to see that liquid level is maintained. Add a little more water from time to time if it seems to be needed.
■ *The Old Homesteader*

How to freshen cured meat: Dry-cured or brined meat is usually too salty to be eaten without freshening. You can remove surplus salt by soaking the meat in fresh, cool water for several hours, discarding the brine before the meat is cooked. The time needed will vary with the degree of saltiness, and more than one fresh-water bath may be needed. You can also freshen salted meat by bringing it just to the boiling point in a large volume of water — do this once or twice, discarding the salty broth. This method, though quicker, causes some loss of meat flavor.
■ *Cooperative Extension Service*
    University of Alaska
    The Cabin Friend
    ALASKA® *magazine, July 1977*

Cocktail Meatballs

1 pound (456 g) mooseburger
1/2 cup (120 mL) bread crumbs
1/3 cup (80 mL) minced onion
1/4 cup (60 mL) milk
1 egg
1 tablespoon (15 mL) snipped parsley
1 teaspoon (5 mL) salt
1/8 teaspoon (0.5 mL) pepper
1/2 teaspoon (2 mL) Worcestershire
1/4 cup (60 mL) shortening
1 bottle chili sauce
1 jar grape jelly

►Mix all ingredients except shortening, chili sauce and jelly. Form into 1-inch (2.5 cm) balls and brown in hot shortening. Remove meatballs from skillet and drain off fat. Return skillet to heat and add chili sauce and jelly, stirring until jelly is melted. Stir in meatballs until they are well coated with sauce. Simmer 30 minutes. Serve in chafing dish.
■ *Pat Thomas*
   An Alaskan Cook Book, *Kenai*

Variations:
• How about substituting homemade currant or cranberry jelly?
• Or, omit chili sauce and jelly; make the meatballs exactly the same way and try them with this sauce:

Spicy Meatball Sauce
1/4 cup (60 mL) Worcestershire
1/4 cup (60 mL) molasses
1-1/4 cups (300 mL) ketchup
1/4 cup (60 mL) Grey Poupon mustard

►Mix, heat well, pour over browned meatballs in baking dish and bake in a moderate oven for 30 minutes or so.
■ *Gail McCarthy*
   Great Lander Shopping News, *Anchorage*

Island Meatballs

1/2 cup (120 mL) milk
2 slices bread
1-1/2 pounds (0.70 kg) venison, ground
1 egg, beaten
1 teaspoon (5 mL) salt
Pepper to taste
Dash of garlic salt
Flour for dredging
2 tablespoons (30 mL) oil
2 bouillon cubes dissolved in 1 cup (240 mL) hot water
1/2 cup (120 mL) sugar

1 can (20 oz /or/ 567 g) pineapple tidbits with syrup
1/4 cup (60 mL) wine vinegar
2 tablespoons (30 mL) soy sauce
1 teaspoon (5 mL) Accent
2 tablespoons (30 mL) cornstarch
1/4 cup (60 mL) cold water

►Pour milk over crumbled bread to soften. Add to ground meat, egg, salt, pepper and garlic salt. Mix well with fingers and form walnut-sized balls. Roll in flour and brown in hot oil, being careful that balls keep their shape. Combine bouillon, sugar, pineapple and syrup, vinegar, soy sauce and Accent. Simmer for about 20 minutes. Mix cornstarch in water and stir into boiling liquid. Stir until sauce is clear and thickened. Add browned meatballs. Simmer 15 minutes until flavors are well blended and meatballs are heated. Test for seasoning. Serve on rice. Serves six.
■ Tsimpshean Indian Island Cookbook
   Metlakatla

Game Meat Salad
A good use for leftover meat

2 cups (480 mL) cooked, chopped game meat
1/2 cup (120 mL) mayonnaise
1 cup (240 mL) chopped celery
2 tablespoons (30 mL) minced onion
1-1/2 cups (360 mL) diced cooked potatoes or cooked and drained macaroni
2 teaspoons (10 mL) spicy mustard
1/4 cup (60 mL) chopped sweet pickle
Pickle juice or lemon juice, as desired for moistening
Salt and pepper to taste

►Blend all ingredients and chill thoroughly. Serve on lettuce cups. Garnish, as desired: sliced radishes, chopped olives, hard-cooked eggs and pimento are attractive garnishes. Yields six servings.

Substitutions
• Bear, whale and beaver may be prepared by any pork recipe.
• Moose, buffalo or walrus may be prepared by following directions for beef.
• Rabbit, squirrel and muskrat (after soaking) may be cooked like chicken.
• Caribou, deer and reindeer may be done according to lamb or mutton recipes.
• AND VICE VERSA!
■ Cooking Up A Storm, *Homer*

Swedish Meatballs

1 egg, beaten
3/4 cup (180 mL) milk
4 slices day-old bread, crumbled
1 teaspoon (5 mL) salt
1 teaspoon (5 mL) minced onion
1/2 teaspoon (2 mL) nutmeg
1/2 pound (228 g) ground venison
1/8 teaspoon (0.5 mL) pepper

►Heat oven to 350°F (175°C). Combine egg, milk and bread and let stand five minutes. Beat with a fork until bread is in fine pieces. Stir in next five ingredients. In hot skillet melt fat, drop meat from spoon in rounded balls. Brown quickly. Remove to casserole and cover with cream gravy or cream of mushroom soup, diluted. Bake at 350°F (175°C) for 30 minutes. These are light and delicious.
■ *Mamie Jensen, Juneau*

When making meatballs always dip your fingers in water before rolling. This will prevent stickiness.

REFRIGERATOR "CURED" MEATS

About Cured Meats: If you are going to cure a large quantity of meat, or you want a product that will be safe for long storage outside the refrigerator, or you wish to avoid using nitrites or nitrates in the curing process . . . please turn to Chapter 14, where long-term curing techniques are detailed.

It is possible, however, to have that "home-cured" taste without the longer processing if you stick with small cuts of meat — 4 to 6 pounds (1.8 to 2.7 kg) — "cure" and store in the refrigerator and use the product within a reasonable period of time. To do this you will need to use one of the commercial "curing salts," which are a blend of salt, sugar, and usually, sodium nitrate and sodium nitrite. Two commonly used brands are Morton's Tender-Quick and B. Heller and Company's Complete Cure with Sugar.

All meat curing — including this short-term method — should be done in nonmetal containers. Use glass, stoneware, wood or enamelware that has no chips or blemishes. Utensils for cutting, measuring and stirring should be stainless steel, glass or wood. If a brine cure is used, be sure to weight the meat so that it will remain below the brine. Again, use glass, a heavy plate or bowl — or add something to it to make it heavier; then cover the whole contraption with a plate or board or waxed paper. Refrigerate for the specified time.

Summer Sausage

4 pounds (1.8 kg) venison, ground
1 pound (456 g) fatty hamburger or sausage
5 rounded teaspoons (25 mL) curing salt,
*   such as Morton's Tender-Quick — a must*
2 teaspoons (10 mL) mustard seed
2 teaspoons (10 mL) coarsely ground
*   black pepper*

2-1/2 teaspoons (12 mL) garlic salt
1 teaspoon (5 mL) smoked salt
2 teaspoons (10 mL) liquid smoke — optional
2 teaspoons (10 mL) red pepper seed — optional

►Mix all ingredients together, cover and refrigerate overnight. Once a day for the next three days remix for about five minutes. On the fourth day remix and form into rolls about the diameter of a silver dollar and about 10 inches (25 cm) long. Lay on broiler rack, using foil or cookie sheet underneath to catch drippings. Bake at 175 to 200°F (79 to 93°C) for eight to ten hours. Leave oven door open a crack for moisture to escape. Cool, wrap and refrigerate or freeze.

This sausage is like a salami and is great with crackers or in sandwiches. It will last two to three weeks refrigerated, but it will probably be gone before that!
■ *Courtesy, the Beckham family of Flint,*
  and Terry L. Russler of Tawas City, Michigan
  ALASKA® magazine, October 1980

Alaskan Salami

4 pounds (2 kg) any gameburger
1/2 pound ((228 g) Morton's Tender-Quick
*   curing salt*
2 tablespoons (30 mL) liquid smoke
2 teaspoons (10 mL) garlic powder

►Mix above ingredients thoroughly with the hands. Chill at least 24 hours. Divide into four equal parts. Wrap in nylon net and tie off the ends. Bake for four hours at 225°F (107°C). Place a pan underneath the rolls of salami in the oven as they will drip a great deal. Store in cool, dry place about 38°F (3.5 °C) — or refrigerate.
■ *Lois Smith, Olympia, Washington*

Brine-Cured Tongue

Tongue — moose, caribou or deer
Morton's Tender-Quick
Boiling water
1 large onion, sliced
8 peppercorns
2 cloves garlic
1 tablespoon (15 mL) mustard seed

►Wash tongue well and cut off gristle. Put tongue in a glass bowl or crock large enough that it can be completely covered with brine. To make brine, use 1 cup (240 mL) Morton's Tender-Quick for each 3 cups (720 mL) boiling water it will take to cover the meat. Allow brine to cool before pouring over meat. Then add onion and spices. You will need a weight to keep the tongue completely submerged in the brine. And it must be glass, crockery or wood — not metal. If you want, fill a jar or bowl with stones or something else heavy and set it on top of the meat to keep it below the brine. Then put another covering such as plastic wrap over all and place it in the refrigerator.

The length of the cure will depend on the size of the tongue. For moose tongue, allow two weeks. Deer tongue, about half that.

To cook, remove the tongue from the brine, wash it well with cold water to remove some of the salt and boil it in fresh water to cover, about one hour per pound (456 g).

Remove from boiling liquid and hold under cold running water until you can handle the meat. Then slit the tough skin with a knife and peel off the rest. Tongue is good served hot or, to slice it cold for sandwiches, put the peeled tongue back into the boiling liquid and allow it to cool. Drain, wrap and chill well before slicing thin.

MINCEMEAT MAGIC

About Mincemeat: Since mince pie is one of Alaska's favorite desserts, several recipes for mincemeat made with game are included here. There are almost as many recipes for mincemeat as there are cooks to make it.

The proportions of the various ingredients may differ greatly and still a fine-flavored, full-bodied product will result. So long as there is a base of ground cooked meat, dried fruit and an assortment of spices on hand, a delectable pie filling can be made. Don't hesitate to make up a batch just because you don't have a few of the ingredients. Substitute or even omit them. Some cooks rely on a long, slow cooking process for the flavor. Others prefer to gain piquancy through a more subtle blending of spices and liquors and cook the mincemeat a comparatively short time.

It is a wise practice to make plenty of mincemeat when butchering that moose or caribou. The meat of the neck and other bony pieces can be used. In fact, when making soup stock, pick the meat off the bones and save it for mincemeat.

Many people prefer to add either soaked dried apples, fresh apple slices or applesauce to mincemeat just before making the pies. Any proportion is acceptable. For a richer dessert use fewer apples or none at all.

Mamie Jensen says that she likes to use one of the commercial products, Saucit or Mariani Apples for Sauce, as part of the mincemeat brew. Then, when she is making a pie, she adds fresh unpeeled shredded apples — two will do for 2 cups (480 mL) of mincemeat. She prefers the fresh apples to dried ones because the dried ones usually have a bit of core to be cut out — "a bother."

Besides pies, tarts and turnovers, cookies and other desserts may be concocted by using mincemeat.

Mincemeat can be kept fresh by covering the containers and storing in the refrigerator. If you wish to keep it longer than six weeks, it is better to freeze it or can it under pressure. Instructions for doing so are in Chapter 14.

Mincemeat #1

4 cups (1 L) cooked, then ground meat — deer
*   or moose*
2 packages dehydrated apples or Saucit
*   (enough to make 6 cups /or/ 1.45 L, cooked)*
2 cups (480 mL) seedless raisins, dark or light
1 cup (240 mL) currants
1 cup (240 mL) vinegar
3 cups (720 mL) sugar, or more, to taste
2 cups (480 mL) meat liquor, dark syrup and/or
*   juice from apples*
1 pint (480 mL) tart jelly or leftover sweet pickle
*   juice, or extra apples*
1/4 pound (114 g) butter
2 teaspoons (10 mL) nutmeg
2 tablespoons (30 mL) cinnamon

1 tablespoon (15 mL) cloves
2 teaspoons (10 mL) salt
1/2 teaspoon (2 mL) pepper

►Mix all ingredients in a large kettle. Let simmer slowly, stirring frequently to avoid mixture scorching, and allowing raisins and currants to swell. Simmer about an hour. Then cool slightly, spoon into glass or plastic containers and refrigerate. Will keep several weeks. Mincemeat may also be frozen for longer storage. This recipe makes 5 quarts (4.75 L).

Additions to the mincemeat may be: orange, lemon — either peel or juice — citron, other dried fruits or juices.

Mincemeat Pie

►To make a 9-inch pie, I use 2 cups (480 mL) mincemeat, two or three apples — diced or shredded, peeled or unpeeled — and sometimes add pecans or other nutmeats.
■ *Mamie Jensen, Juneau*

Mincemeat #2

4 cups (1 L) cooked, then chopped venison or
    moose (save the liquor in which meat
    was boiled)
Mix together:
2 cups (480 mL) raisins
2 cups (480 mL) currants
5 cups (1.2 L) peeled and chopped apples
1 cup (240 mL) citron or orange peel
4 teaspoons (20 mL) salt
4 lemons, juice and rind
4 tablespoons (60 mL) molasses
4 tablespoons (60 mL) cider or black tea
4 teaspoons (20 mL) cinnamon
2 teaspoons (10 mL) cloves
2 teaspoons (10 mL) nutmeg
1 teaspoon (5 mL) mace
4 tablespoons (60 mL) vinegar

►Add chopped meat to the mixture and moisten with liquor in which meat was cooked. Cook mincemeat slowly, stirring occasionally, for 1-1/2 hours. Makes 3 quarts (2.85 L). May be stored in the refrigerator for several weeks or frozen. Do not use metal containers. The liquor from boiling the meat may be saved and added to the filling before baking pies.
■ *Helen Allen*
    PTA Cook Book, *Petersburg*

Mincemeat #3

2-1/2 pounds (1.15 kg) caribou, moose or
    other game meat, cooked, then ground
4 cups (1 L) liquid (cider, fruit juice, meat stock)

1-1/2 to 2 cups (360 to 480 mL)
    apricot preserves
1 cup (240 mL) dried wild berries or
    commercial currants
1 pound (456 g) golden raisins
3 cups (720 mL) dried apples, soaked
    (measure after soaking)
1 cup (240 mL) molasses
1 cup (240 mL) white sugar
1 cup (240 mL) brown sugar
1 cup (240 mL) suet, finely chopped
3 tablespoons (45 mL) lemon juice
1 cup (240 mL) lemon or orange peel, diced
1 tablespoon (15 mL) brandy flavoring
1 tablespoon (15 mL) rum flavoring
Spices, your choice and quantity

►Mix all ingredients together in a large preserving kettle in the order given above. If all ingredients are not readily available, make substitutions where necessary, making sure to maintain the correct balance between liquids and solids. Stir only enough to blend well. Bring to a boil and reduce heat to simmer; cook for about an hour or until most of the liquid has boiled away. Stir occasionally to keep from sticking, especially during the last half-hour. Taste test for flavor and add any other seasoning you think it needs. Store in the refrigerator for a few weeks or freeze or can the mincemeat.
■ *Helen A. White, Anchorage*
    More About What's Cookin' in Alaska

About Canning Mincemeat: Information about canning mincemeat is in Chapter 14. As a general rule, the liquid used in making mincemeat that is to be canned should be apple cider rather than meat stock.

Mincemeat #4

1 pound (456 g) ground cooked game meat
2 cups (480 mL) stock
5 cups (1.2 L) shredded apples, firmly packed
3/4 cup (180 mL) candied lemon peel, diced
3/4 cup (180 mL) candied orange peel, diced
3/4 cup (180 mL) candied citron, diced
1 pound (456 g) seedless raisins
1 large orange, grated rind, juice and pulp
1/2 pound (228 g) suet, finely chopped
1 pound (456 g) dried wild berries
1 lemon, juice and rind
1-1/2 pounds (685 g) dark brown sugar, packed
1-1/2 teaspoons (7 mL) each — salt,
    cinnamon, allspice
1/2 teaspoon (2 mL) each — cloves
    and coriander
1-1/2 teaspoons (7 mL) each — mace
    and nutmeg

1 cup (240 mL) brandy or bourbon
1 cup (240 mL) rum or sherry

►Get out your largest preserving kettle and place in it the ground game. Use moose, caribou, venison, sheep or goat — alone or in combination. Then add all the other ingredients in the order given, stirring after each addition — except for brandy and rum. (They should be added after removing from heat.) Blend and bring to a boil; reduce heat and simmer for 1-1/4 hours, stirring frequently to keep the mincemeat from sticking. Remove from heat and add brandy and rum; stir just enough to mingle the flavors. Store in refrigerator. Or, check the canning information in Chapter 14.

■ *Helen A. White, Anchorage*
   More About What's Cookin' in Alaska

Mincemeat Cookies

1 cup (240 mL) evaporated milk
1 tablespoon (15 mL) vinegar
1 cup (240 mL) shortening
1-1/2 cups (360 mL) sugar
1 egg, beaten
2 teaspoons (10 mL) soda
1/4 teaspoon (1 mL) salt
6 cups (1.45 L) sifted flour
Mincemeat

►Combine evaporated milk and vinegar to use as soured milk. Set aside. Cream shortening and sugar until granules are dissolved. Then add the beaten egg and soured milk and mix thoroughly.

Combine dry ingredients and sift again into shortening mixture. Roll dough rather thin. Cut out cookie pairs in any shape. Place a teaspoon of mincemeat in center of half the cookies. Top each with another cookie, pressing edges together. Lift carefully to oiled baking sheet and bake about 10 minutes at 350°F (175°C). Makes 5 dozen cookies.

■ Out of Alaska's Kitchens *(adapted)*

Nectar Mince Pie

Pastry for a 2-crust pie
1/2 cup (120 mL) sugar
1/2 cup (120 mL) corn syrup (or pancake syrup)
1/2 teaspoon (2 mL) salt
1/4 cup (60 mL) shortening
2 eggs, beaten
1/2 cup (120 mL) seedless raisins
1/2 cup (120 mL) mincemeat
1/2 cup (120 mL) walnuts, chopped
1 teaspoon (5 mL) vanilla
1 tablespoon (15 mL) lemon juice
2 tablespoons (30 mL) orange juice

►Combine sugar, syrup, salt and shortening and bring to a boil. In a bowl, combine eggs, raisins, mincemeat, nuts, vanilla and fruit juices and gradually mix in the hot syrup. Cool. Line pie plate with dough, add cooled filling and cover with top crust which has been slit to allow steam to escape. Bake at 425°F (220°C) for 30 to 45 minutes.

■ Out of Alaska's Kitchens

To prevent blackening of the kettle that is to be used over an open fire, cover the outside with a film of moistened scouring powder or soap.

Chapter 8

More Game~Large & Small

In this chapter are recipes and preparation tips for large-game meats that are not common fare for most Alaskans. Bear, bison, mountain goat and Dall sheep — it's a lucky, lucky family that has some of this meat put by. Though various game meats have their champions, sheep seems to have the most, perhaps even outdistancing the popularity of moose. Bear and bison — when it's available — evoke superlatives, too.

Small game represented in this chapter are quite abundant in Alaska, and the meats are used widely, particularly in the Bush. Trappers, especially, have a plentiful supply because many of the animals are valuable for their furs as well as the meat. Muskrats, beavers, rabbits (actually hares) are standby fare for trappers, and they also relish lynx. It has been reported that some trappers and hunters enjoy wolf flesh, fox, and even coyote, though none has shared recipes for us to include here.

Some fur animals may be taken with a hunting license, but unless the hunter also has a trapping license, no hunting is allowed for beaver, marmot, marten, mink, weasel, muskrat, land and sea otter or flying and ground squirrels . . . but we have nice recipes for some, so you might want to apply.

Throughout, we've quoted bits and pieces of information from the *Northern Cookbook* about ways to save both the pelt and the meat of the fur bearers . . . but the instructions for pelt care are by no means complete. They are only meant as an indication that the wise trapper saves and uses *both*, whether or not the pelt has actual sale value.

Last but not least in this chapter are many recipes for the most widely consumed critter in the state — the gameburger. Some recipes suggest a sauce or stuffing, but there are recipes for many more throughout the book. Please see the listing on page 171.

BEAR

Bear meat, by most testimony, is exceptionally tasty if it comes from a young animal — under three years — that has been feeding only on berries and other plant material, rather than fish. If you bag an animal that meets these qualifications, your best bet is to choose simple recipes that won't mask the flavor, such as Jeanne McArthur's Roast Bear with

Yorkshire Pudding or hunter Ralph Hall's instructions on page 232. Meat from older animals or ones taken too early in the season to be sufficiently fat may require more seasoning, long marinating or larding with beef suet to keep meats tender and moist.

One glory of bear meat is its delicious fat which,

for the most part, is concentrated rather than marbled throughout the meat. It can easily be trimmed and rendered. Rendered bear fat or lard "can't be beat" for pastry-making and is highly touted as a cooking oil for doughnuts and other fried foods. Bears taken late in the fall, just before hibernation, are the best for this purpose because they have been storing up nice rolls of fat to see them through the winter.

Young or old, fat or lean, however, bear meat should be thoroughly cooked so that there is no pink tinge to the meat and it reaches an internal temperature of 170°F (77°C). Bear, like the pork of less regulated times, carries a rather high incidence of the parasite that causes trichinosis in humans, and thorough cooking destroys it. Pork recipes, in fact, are recommended as preparations for all cuts of bear. Bear meat should not be used for making jerky or prepared by other curing methods which do not call for cooking.

Another caution applies to polar bear. According to *The Alaska Dietary Survey*, Eskimos have never eaten the liver of polar bear. Their reason, "It makes your hair fall out," is one among the many pieces of folk wisdom substantiated by science. The liver of polar bear contains excessively high — sometimes toxic — levels of vitamin A . . . and should be avoided. However, few people not already "in the know" will ever have the chance to foolishly gorge on a polar bear liver. Under the Marine Mammal Protection Act of 1972, only an Alaskan Native may take polar bear (though polar bears may take any variety of human).

Rendering Bear Fat

The hardest thing about rendering bear fat is . . . getting the bear in the first place. To find out how to do that, you'll have to read the rest of Wes Hallock's story. From it we've excerpted only his clear, simple description of the rendering process. And to that we add only some information about storage: Rendered fat is an unlikely place for bacteria to develop, but to be on the safe side and to keep the fat sweet for months, first strain the rendered oil to remove all particles of meat or other matter — the "cracklings" — then boil it long enough to sterilize (three to five minutes) and pour it into containers with airtight lids. Freeze it or store it in a cool place. Hallock's bear was a small one, he estimated about 150 pounds (68 kg).

. . . I wasn't sure how Cyndi was going to react, this being our first experience at preparing a bear for the table. Dropping the load in front of the cabin, I assumed my most nonchalant tone, "Got a little bear meat here."

"Well, it's not very big," she replied cautiously, avoiding the "meat" comment.

"There should be lots of good fat on him this time of the year," I hinted.

No comment.

But the pioneer spirit was there in action if not in words. The bear was covered with a layer of fat up to three inches thick, and as I skinned and cut, Cyndi was beside me filling pans with large chunks of the thick white stuff. These she cleaned and trimmed of excess meat, rinsed in cold water, and set on the wood stove in a large kettle to simmer slowly.

For about 12 hours the fat bubbled over a low heat with an occasional stirring. There was no offensive odor; if anything there was a slight aroma similar to that of frying bacon. The fat rendered into a clear, amber oil, and a hard residue (cracklings) which settled to the bottom of the kettle.

Cyndi strained the oil, of which there was about two gallons (7.6 L) through a clean cloth into empty coffee cans. As it cooled, the oil thickened and turned an opaque white, much like commercial vegetable shortening.

Since it is easily digestible and of good flavor, Cyndi has become enthusiastic about using bear grease for frying or in any recipe that calls for shortening. . . .

■ *Wes Hallock*
"*Winter Meat*"
ALASKA® *magazine, October 1979*

Garlic Roast Bear

►Use about an 8-pound (3.6 kg) roast off the rump of a young bear. Put in cold water, into which slice three or four medium-sized onions and let soak for about four hours. Remove from water and wipe dry. Force small pieces of garlic deep into the meat, using a sharp knife to make holes. Put pieces of garlic as near bone as possible. Use about one small clove of garlic in all. Season with salt and pepper. Brown in hot bacon drippings. Bake in an open pan for three hours at 350°F (175°C), turning the meat several times while cooking.

■ *Ralph Hall*
PTA Cook Book, *Petersburg*

Bear Steaks

►Cut bear steaks or chops into serving-sized pieces 1 inch (2.5 cm) thick. Mix 1/2 cup (120 mL) flour, 1/2 teaspoon (2 mL) cloves and 1 teaspoon (5 mL) ginger. Pound the mixture into the meat on both sides. Brown in fat in a moderately hot skillet. Salt and pepper after browning. Cover skillet and simmer 10 to 15 minutes. Always cook bear until well done.

■ Alaska's Game Is Good Food

Marinated Roast Bear

►Young bear is delicious roasted as you would pork. Cook it about 30 minutes to the pound (456 g), or longer if you like well-done roast. Select a 3- to 4-pound (1.4 to 1.8 kg) roast, wipe with cloth to clean. Place in a large bowl and cover with half vinegar and half red wine. Let soak in a cool place at least three hours or overnight. Save liquid. Season roast with salt, pepper, allspice, garlic, thyme and marjoram. Sear in a little fat in a Dutch oven. When very brown, add wine and vinegar, about 1-1/2 cups (360 mL). Cook slowly until tender.

■ *Mrs. W.A. Parry, Jr.*
  Alaska's Cooking, *Anchorage*

Roast Bear with Yorkshire Pudding

Roast of young bear
Garlic cloves
Thyme
Salt and pepper

►Stud the roast with garlic cloves; season. Roast at 350°F (175°C) until internal temperature is 170°F (77°C).

Yorkshire Pudding
1 cup (240 mL) sifted flour
1/4 teaspoon (1 mL) salt
3 eggs, beaten
1 cup (240 mL) milk
1/4 cup (60 mL) fat from roast

►Sift flour and salt and add to well-beaten eggs. Add milk and beat well with rotary beater. Pour mixture into warm pan containing fat from roast. Bake at 400°F (205°C) for 30 minutes. Prepare this 30 minutes before roast is done. Delicious meal with potatoes cooked around roast, Alaska peas and carrots and Yorkshire pudding!

■ *Jeanne McArthur*
  Cooking Up A Storm, *Homer*

Oven-Barbecued Bear

►This is for a young black bear. If you've got a brownie or a big old black, admire your trophy but open a can of beans when chow time comes!

First, make up the barbecue sauce. Then place a roasting size piece of bear meat in a 325°F (160°C) oven. When well glazed, baste with sauce. Continue roasting, basting frequently, three to four hours, or until fork tender. Time of course depends upon size of roast and age of animal. Serve with baked potatoes, corn on the cob and crisp salad.

Zippy Barbecue Sauce
1/4 cup (60 mL) vinegar
1/2 cup (120 mL) water
2 tablespoons (30 mL) sugar
1 teaspoon (5 mL) dry mustard
1/2 teaspoon (2 mL) pepper
1-1/2 teaspoons (7 mL) salt
1/4 teaspoon (1 mL) garlic powder
1 tablespoon (15 mL) lemon juice
1 onion, minced
1/4 cup (60 mL) salad oil
1 teaspoon (5 mL) chili powder
5 squirts Tabasco sauce
1/2 cup (120 mL) ketchup
2 tablespoons (30 mL) Worcestershire

►Mix all ingredients except the last two. If you have a blender, blend them in it briefly. Simmer 20 minutes, uncovered. Add ketchup and Worcestershire and bring to a boil. Remove from heat.

■ *Mrs. Sam H. Roberson*
  The Alaskan Camp Cook

Fido food: We find it saves money to prepare our own dog food and this is the way we make it. Mix together 5 pounds (2.25 kg) whole-wheat flour, 2 pounds (1 kg) medium oatmeal and 3/4 cup (180 mL) of fat (bear fat is excellent and so is fat from other game). Gradually stir in 3 quarts (2.9 L) of liquid. The liquid can be all water or milk or a combination. (It can also be partly made up of water that vegetables have been cooked in or any other such broth.) Before adding to the dry ingredients, add 1/2 to 3/4 cup (120 to 180 mL) beef or chicken soup base, or its equivalent in bouillon cubes.

If the mixture is too stiff, work more liquid into it until it is just about right to roll out like pie crust. It should be stiff. Roll out to 1/2- to 3/4-inch (1.25 to 1.9 cm) thickness and bake on lightly greased cookie sheets at 300°F (150°C). Bake until crispy and well browned. Cool and break into small chunks that are right for your dogs.

This is a big batch, so if you have only one dog, you may want to cut it down. Incidentally, you will need a huge container to mix this in if you make the whole recipe. We use a big preserving kettle for a mixing bowl. Store this fido food in a cool, dry place. We always make a lot of this dog food just after hunting season when we can render excess fat from game to use in it.

■ *The Old Trapper*
  The Cabin Friend
  ALASKA® magazine, February 1977

Polar Bear and Onions

Polar bear chunks
Whole-wheat flour
Meat drippings or cooking oil
Onions
Water
Seasonings

►You probably won't have a chance to try this unless you live in the Arctic and perhaps not even then. Polar bear meat is strongly scented because of its diet of seals, and it is advisable to use something equally powerful to counteract the odor. The thing to remember is to be sure to cook any bear meat thoroughly, as you would pork. Cut thick polar bear steaks into sizable chunks, being sure to remove all of the natural fat. Dredge the chunks in the flour and brown well on all sides in a Dutch oven, using the drippings or oil. Add a generous amount of onions, fresh or dehydrated, and water enough to barely cover the meat. Cover and simmer for three hours or more, checking occasionally to be sure the level of liquid is maintained — adding water if necessary. Simmer until the meat is tender. Potatoes or other vegetables may be added the last half-hour if desired.
■ *Helen A. White, Anchorage*
  What's Cookin' In Alaska

Polar Bear Stew

4 pounds (1.8 kg) polar bear meat
Water to cover
3 tablespoons (45 mL) salt
1-1/2 cups (360 mL) dried potato
1 cup (240 mL) celery flakes
1 tablespoon (15 mL) dry onion
2 cups (480 mL) dehydrated carrots
1/2 cup (120 mL) melted butter
1-3/4 cups (420 mL) flour

1 teaspoon (5 mL) garlic powder or garlic salt
3/4 teaspoon (3 mL) pepper

►Cut meat into bite-sized pieces and boil in salted water for 1-1/2 hours or more. Then add dry vegetables; mix melted butter with flour, blend in seasonings and add to meat. Cook 15 minutes longer. The stew is ready. Makes eight to ten servings.
■ *Norma Silook*
  Gambell, Saint Lawrence Island

Tender Kodiak Bear Steak

4 to 5 pounds (1.8 to 2.25 kg) bear loin
1 teaspoon (5 mL) salt
3 crushed peppercorns
1 crumbled bay leaf
1 cup (240 mL) vinegar
1/2 cup (120 mL) each — water and vegetable oil
Butter, lemon juice

►Place bear loin in a large pottery dish or crock. Sprinkle with salt, peppercorns, bay leaf and pour on vinegar, water and oil. The oil will keep the meat from discoloring. Allow to stand in a cool place (refrigerator temperatures) for two days, turning the meat once or twice a day. When ready to cook, wipe the meat dry and cut it into 1-1/2 inch (4 cm) slices. Under the hottest flame of the broiler, sear steaks on one side, dust with salt and pepper and turn. For each steak, have ready a piece of butter the size of a walnut which has been allowed to soak in lemon juice for at least 20 minutes. Place butterballs on the uncooked side, sear under high heat, reduce heat and continue broiling to the desired doneness. Serve on a hot platter.
■ *Bess A. Cleveland*
  Alaskan Cookbook for Homesteader or Gourmet
  (adapted)

BEAVER

The dual use for beaver — as an excellent food for the table as well as the source of one of the most sought-after furs in North America — makes field care of the kill a matter of critical importance. Here is some advice about skinning beaver to save the pelt and about dressing the meat, both reprinted from the *Northern Cookbook*, a publication sponsored by the Government of Canada.

Skinning Beaver

"If the beaver pelt is to be prepared for market, care should be taken in skinning the animal. Lay the beaver on its back in a clean place and cut off the legs at the first joints. Then, with a sharp knife, slit the pelt, starting at the lower lip. Insert the knife in this slit and, with the sharp edge up, cut the pelt in a straight line down the chest and belly to the vent. Work out from this centre line cut and, with short strokes, separate the skin from the flesh. Carefully pull the legs through the skin, leaving four round holes in the pelt. Cut off the tail where it meets the fur. Skin carefully around the eyes and cut the ears close to the skull. Finish removing the pelt, taking as little flesh and fat with it as possible, then lay it on a flat surface, fur side down, and sponge off all blood marks with lukewarm water.''

Dressing Beaver

"Cut the head from the carcass and eviscerate the animal as follows: Make a cut through the thin layer of meat from the breast bone to the vent, encircling the vent, and being careful not to puncture the intestines. Lay the body cavity open, and remove the viscera by grasping them above the stomach and pulling down and out from the body cavity. Carefully cut out the tiny musk glands from under the skin on the inside of the legs and be sure to remove the castor gland under the belly near the tail. . . . Then wash the carcass thoroughly with warm salted water.'' (The recipe section includes some more good suggestions from the *Northern Cookbook*.)

Cooking Beaver

The flavor of very young beaver, says one expert, "reminds us of a fat goose," while others liken it to pork. In either case, the meat is clearly delicious. And yet the contrasting recipes will demonstrate that beaver is another of the critters about which there is quite a bit of controversy over the taste of the fat. Some recipes suggest cutting off "all visible fat" or even parboiling the dressed carcass to render more fat and to tenderize the meat before frying or roasting normally.

Whether or not you "pretreat" quite simply depends on the condition of the meat *you have.* If there is too much fat for your taste, trim off some of it, just as you would trim a very fat pork roast. Save it for other uses. If the animal is old and tough or badly shot up, it may require special tenderizing — a marinade or parboiling. Fat also turns rancid. If the meat has been kept too long in the freezer or refrigerator and it smells strong, trimming off the fat and parboiling the meat will help the flavor.

An exceptional amount of fat is to be found in the beaver tail. For that reason, the tail is considered a delicacy by many. If you don't care for that much concentrated fat, however, the tail is the first item that should go to someone who does. Or, render the fat and save it for other cooking uses.

Several Ways To Prepare Beaver

►When our supply of shortening would run out, we used beaver grease for a substitute. This is rendered by heating, in the same manner as ordinary lard, but stays liquid even after cooling.

The beaver meat was roasted in the same way as any meat roast.

Beaver tail made a rich, flavorful soup broth.

The beaver tail and feet, prepared by pickling, became another wilderness gourmet treat. [First] we would thread the tails and feet on sticks and place them over the fire, taking care not to get them too hot. The beaver is rather oily and can burn if placed too close to the fire. The heat would cause the skin to pop open and fall off.

To preserve the skinned tail and feet, we would pickle them in the same fashion as making pickled pigs' feet.

To preserve the beaver tail and feet by the salt-brine method, combine 4 quarts (4 L) cold water with 2-1/2 pounds (1.15 kg) of [pickling] salt, 1 ounce (28.5 g) of saltpeter and 1 tablespoon (15 mL) of sugar. Heat *to* the boiling point, stirring often, but do not boil. Remove vessel from the heat. After cooling, pour the brine through a very fine sieve or cloth over the meat, which has been placed in a crockery or enamel vessel. [*Refrigerate or put in a cool place, about 38°F or 3.5°C.*] Pickling takes about 10 days.

To pickle them in a vinegar solution, first we skinned and boiled the beaver tail and feet until done. Then we prepared a solution of vinegar, salt, onions and spices, poured it over the cooked meat and let it set for a few days. Pickling spices were made up of whole bay leaves, peppercorns and cloves. Occasionally juniper berries, dry thyme and basil were included in the mixed pickling spices.

We enjoyed pickled beaver tail and feet boiled with sauerkraut.

■ *Iva Senft, as told to Mary J. Barry*
"Camp Cookery, Trail Tonics,
and Indian Infants"
ALASKA SPORTSMAN®, *July 1964*

Barbecued Beaver

1 medium-sized beaver, cut into serving pieces
Salt to taste
2 teaspoons (10 mL) dehydrated minced onion
3 tablespoons (45 mL) brown sugar
1 small bottle beer
1/2 cup (120 mL) chili sauce
1-1/2 teaspoons (7 mL) Worcestershire

►Line a roomy roasting pan with foil and place beaver pieces within. Preheat oven to 350°F (175°C) and roast the meat for half an hour. Mix other ingredients in small bowl. After the initial 30 minutes of roasting, uncover meat and dribble the barbecue sauce over all pieces. Continue to roast, uncovered, for another half-hour, or up to an hour, until tender. Baste occasionally during roasting using sauce accumulated in bottom of roaster.

■ *Anon.*

Beaver Paprika
For a slow-cooker

1 medium-sized beaver cut into
    serving portions
2 tablespoons (30 mL) butter or margarine,
    melted
1-1/2 teaspoons (7 mL) paprika
Salt
4 tablespoons (60 mL) brown sugar
1 small onion, sliced, or equivalent in
    dehydrated minced onion
2 tablespoons (30 mL) lime juice (or lemon)
1 cup (240 mL) water
25 sliced, stuffed olives
Pepper

►Salt and pepper portions of beaver and brown in melted butter. Transfer meat to slow-cooking pot and add all other ingredients except olives. Scatter sliced olives over top of meat. Cover and cook on low for 10 to 12 hours. Additional moisture may be added during the last few hours of cooking if desired.

■ *Anon.*

Atlanta Special

1 beaver, 4 to 5 pounds (1.8 to 2.25 kg)
1 bay leaf
2 medium onions
1 or 2 garlic cloves
Celery leaves, if desired
Flour
Fat
Salt and pepper

►Remove all fat from beaver. Cut up as you do rabbit. Soak overnight in salt water. Parboil until about half cooked in water with bay leaf, onions and garlic. Celery may be added, if desired. Drain meat and roll in flour and brown in hot fat; season with salt and pepper. Bake in a covered pan in a moderate oven until tender. Gravy may be made from the drippings. Plan the same number of servings as from a similar weight of pork. Beaver is very rich.

■ *Alaska's Game Is Good Food*

Beaver Meatballs or Meat Loaf

1 pound (456 g) ground beaver meat
2 eggs

2/3 cup (160 mL) bread crumbs
1/3 cup (80 mL) chopped onion
1 teaspoon (5 mL) dried oregano leaves,
    crumbled
Garlic salt to taste
Dash black pepper

►Mix all ingredients and form into medium-sized meatballs. Place in shallow pan and brown about 20 minutes in a moderate oven, 350°F (175°C). Then meatballs are ready to add to your favorite spaghetti sauce or gravy.

   To make meat loaf, use the same ingredients and add 1 teaspoon (5 mL) ground sage. Then place the mixture in a casserole dish and spread the top with ketchup. Cover and bake at 350°F (175°C) for about one hour.

■ *Beverly Wolford, Homer*

Roast Beaver
To tenderize the meat from an older animal and still enjoy a roast

1 beaver, skinned and cleaned
1/2 cup (120 mL) vinegar
1 tablespoon (15 mL) salt
2 teaspoons (10 mL) soda
1 medium onion, sliced
4 strips bacon or salt pork
1/2 teaspoon (2 mL) salt
1/4 teaspoon (1 mL) pepper

►Wash beaver thoroughly with salt water. Then soak it overnight in water to cover, plus the vinegar and 1 tablespoon (15 mL) salt listed above.

   Next day, drain meat, wash again and cover with 2 quarts (2 L) fresh water, plus the soda. Bring to a boil, reduce heat and simmer 10 minutes.

   Drain again, pat dry and place beaver in roasting pan. Salt and pepper the meat, cover it with sliced onions and strips of bacon or salt pork. Place lid on roaster and bake at 375°F (190°C) until tender. Serve with a tart jelly. About four servings.

■ Northern Cookbook *(adapted)*

Fried Beaver Tail

2 beaver tails
1/4 cup (60 mL) flour
1/2 teaspoon (2 mL) salt
1/4 teaspoon (1 mL) pepper
1/4 cup (60 mL) butter or other fat
1/4 cup (60 mL) sherry or cooking wine
1 teaspoon (5 mL) dry mustard
1 teaspoon (5 mL) sugar
1/4 teaspoon (1 mL) garlic powder
1 tablespoon (15 mL) Worcestershire

►Skin, clean, wash in salt water, and soak beaver

tails overnight in vinegar/salt/water solution; drain and parboil in soda/water solution — all — as directed in the previous recipe. Drain, pat dry and proceed:

Dredge beaver tails in seasoned flour. Melt butter or other fat (such as previously rendered beaver fat) in heavy fry pan and saute tails at low heat until tender.

Mix wine with remaining seasonings, add to beaver tails and simmer gently for 10 minutes, basting often.

■ Northern Cookbook *(adapted)*

Boiled Smoked Beaver

►Smoke the beaver for a day or so. Then cut up the meat and boil in salted water until it is done.
■ Northern Cookbook

Fried Beaver Alaskan

1 beaver
Marinade — per quart (1 L) water, use:
 1 tablespoon (15 mL) salt
 1 tablespoon (15 mL) vinegar
 1/2 teaspoon (2 mL) black pepper
1 or 2 beef bouillon cubes
1 teaspoon (5 mL) onion salt
1 bay leaf
1/2 teaspoon (2 mL) garlic powder
1 tablepoon (15 mL) wild fruit jelly
Seasoned flour
Oil
Leftover gravy, mushroom pieces or
 tomato soup

►Disjoint beaver and remove fat. Prepare marinade as listed, or a marinade of red wine or cranberry juice is equally effective. Soak beaver in marinade for 24 hours, turning a few times during the process.

Drain, place beaver in a large kettle with enough cold water to cover. Add bouillon cubes, salt, bay leaf, garlic powder and jelly. Simmer slowly for three hours.

Rinse meat under hot water faucet, dry with paper towels. Dredge pieces with seasoned flour and fry until crusty brown in hot oil about 1/4 inch (6 mm) deep in the frying pan.

Preheat oven to 350°F (175°C). Place meat in baking dish, cover and bake 30 minutes. When done, pour off excess fat but do not scrape pan. Add about 2 cups (480 mL) leftover gravy or one can of mushroom pieces or a can of tomato soup. Return to oven for another 15 minutes. Serve hot.
■ *Mamie Jensen, Juneau*

Beaver or Porcupine Pot Roast

1 small beaver or porcupine
1 cup (240 mL) flour
1 large onion
4 bay leaves, broken in half
Salt and pepper to taste
Water

►Cut beaver or porcupine into small pieces. Sift flour, salt and pepper together (you may want to add other spices). Roll meat in this flour mixture. Heat shortening in Dutch oven and brown the meat. When the meat is done as desired, add water, bay leaves and onion chopped to desired size. Let simmer over low heat until meat is tender and well done, stirring every so often to prevent sticking.
■ *Uutuqtwa, Bristol Bay High School*
 Naknek

BISON

Since the great herds of American bison were largely killed off before the turn of the century, few living cooks have been called upon to worry up a recipe for the beast. In Alaska, the bison population natural to the area was wiped out some 400 years before that.

Today, however, Alaska has enough animals to allow limited hunting, and from 20 to 50 permits are issued annually. The herds, four of them, are the product of a transplant of 23 animals, brought from Montana and released in the Delta Junction area in 1928. From that herd came three others started at Nabesna, Chitina and near Farewell.

Meat from bison under three years of age is similar to top grade beef and, as some recipes suggest, is quite juicy. Unlike domestic beef, however, meat from older animals is less fat and may require larding with beef suet or long, moist cooking, such as that provided by the Dutch oven or close-wrapped foil.

You'll find the recipe section limited — like the availability of the meat — but if you are lucky enough to have bison meat to prepare for your table, we suggest you also check the recipes for venison — especially moose — for one that teases your palate.

Roast Bison

►Sprinkle salt and pepper all over the roast — top, bottom and all sides. Sprinkle top generously with garlic salt and spread on an equal-parts mixture of Worcestershire and two other favorite steak sauces. The marinade is more for flavor than to tenderize. Do not cover. Roast at 325°F (160°C) until tender. Figure 1/4 pound (114 g) per serving.

■ Alaska's Game Is Good Food *(adapted)*

Bison Swiss Steak

Rump, round or chuck steak, cut 1 inch
*   (2.5 cm) thick*
Salt and pepper to taste
Water
Flour (whole-wheat is best)
Suet
Tomato sauce, 3 tablespoons (45 mL) per pound
*   (456 g) of steak*
Green peppers and/or mushrooms and onions,
*   optional*

►Cut meat in serving portions. Season with salt and pepper; dredge with flour. Pound the flour into the meat with a meat hammer or edge of a heavy plate. Grease a heavy skillet with suet or other grease. Heat skillet and brown the meat on all sides. Add the tomato sauce, peppers and onions, too, if desired. Cover and simmer very slowly until the meat is fork tender (two hours or more). If necessary, add more water from time to time to keep the steak from sticking. If the mushrooms are to be used they should go in during the last half-hour. If the resulting gravy is too thin, thicken it with a paste made of cornstarch and cold water.

■ *The Old Homesteader*

Northern Buffalo Paupiettes

4 buffalo cutlets, 1/2 inch (1.25 cm) thick
1/2 cup (120 mL) finely chopped onions
1-1/2 cups (360 mL) dry red wine
4 strips bacon
4 tablespoons (60 mL) additional
*   chopped onion*
2 pickled cucumbers
4 tablespoons (60 mL) flour
1 cup (240 mL) beef stock
Salt and pepper to taste

►Wipe buffalo cutlets well with a damp cloth. Place meat in a shallow pan, add the 1/2 cup (120 mL) chopped onion and the wine. Marinate for two hours at room temperature. Drain the meat, reserving the marinade, and place it flat on a board.

In a frying pan, saute the bacon and the remaining 4 tablespoons (60 mL) chopped onion, divide in equal amounts and spoon on top of cutlets. Place half a cucumber pickle (sliced lengthwise) across each cutlet and roll cutlet around it like a jelly roll. Fasten with a toothpick.

Dredge these rolls in flour and place them in a casserole. Strain and add the wine marinade and the beef stock. Cover and bake at 350°F (175°C) until tender. Season to taste with salt and pepper. Serve with hot rice and the cooking sauce, thickened if desired. Yields four servings.

■ Northern Cookbook *(adapted)*

Barbecued Bison

Bison roast, 4 pounds (1.8 kg) or more,
*   preferably eye-of-round*
Sliced onions
Small chunk of suet

►Place the meat on a rack in a shallow baking pan without cover. If the bone is left in, no rack will be needed. Preheat oven to 325°F (160°C). Sprinkle the sliced onions over the roast; put in oven and roast from 20 to 40 minutes per pound (456 g) but no more than a total of three hours. After the first 30 minutes, place the chunk of suet on the roast. Bison is sometimes dry and the suet will melt and run down over the roast. Boneless roasts will take the longer time. Roasting time depends on age of animal when killed, the thickness of the roast and general quality. Serve with a good brown gravy or barbecue sauce, commercial or homemade.

■ *The Old Homesteader*

Chopped Sweetgrass Buffalo Cutlets

2 pounds (1 kg) ground buffalo meat
6 slices bread
1 cup (240 mL) red wine
1 cup (240 mL) water
4 tablespoons (60 mL) finely chopped onion
4 teaspoons (20 mL) salt
Dash freshly ground pepper
2 eggs slightly beaten
2 cups (480 mL) fine dry bread, cracker or
*   cornflake crumbs*
4 tablespoons (60 mL) rendered buffalo
*   kidney suet*
Tarragon mustard (English or Dijon)

►Trim crusts from bread and soak it in wine and water. Add onion, salt, pepper, ground meat and eggs and mix well. Form into 12 flat cutlets. Roll cutlets in crumbs and let stand 30 minutes.

Heat rendered suet in a heavy pan and pan-fry the cutlets quickly until brown and crusty on both sides. Serve piping hot with tarragon-mustard.

■ Northern Cookbook *(adapted)*

HARE

One Way To Skin A Hare

Below, Don Cornelius outlines one method for quick and easy skinning of hare. Its advantage— no hair is left on the hare to require time-consuming "picking." If you want to save the pelt, however, it is best to "case" it, pulling it off without slitting the belly. The slit in case-skinning is made along the inside of the hind legs, from feet to anus, and then the skin is pulled off inside out in one continuous piece, like a sweater . . . a hooded sweater. For pointers, see instructions for skinning muskrat, page 249.

Experienced snowshoe hare hunters know it is difficult to pick rabbit hair off a piece of meat. I learned this method from old-time Alaskans Bruce Graham and Vern Donaldson of Palmer. Its greatest advantage is that it keeps hair off the meat, while it is still a fast cleaning technique.

1. First, take a hare — Useful items include one snowshoe hare, knife, ax, rubber gloves and a bucket of water.
2. Ready to skin — After removing feet and head, slit skin of back; dunk entire carcass in water and grasp skin firmly on each side of slit.
3. Easy off — Pull hands in opposite directions to remove hide from hare.
4. Butcher job — Slit belly from neck to anus and remove entrails.
5. No hair — Separate into four quarters and backstrap and the cleaned hare is ready for final washing and cooking. Discard viscera and other unused parts where dogs or other pets cannot get them. Many hares carry tapeworm cysts which, while harmless to man, may be picked up by pets.

Cooking Hare

Immediate field-dressing is essential to the good, mild taste of the meat. All shot-damaged flesh should, of course, be removed. If the animal is badly shot up, it may be soaked in brine for three or four hours — 1 tablespoon (15 mL) salt to each quart (L) of water. Rabbit is quite lean and may need additional fat — such as bacon or salt pork— during dry-heat cooking. All the spices commonly used with chicken are appropriate for rabbit,

Snowshoe hare — or "rabbit" as it is often, but mistakenly, called — is one of the most widely used of all game animals. For that reason, we've tried to assemble many recipes. It is delicious meat, comparable to chicken and just as easily varied with different combinations of herbs and spices.

The snowshoe can weigh up to 3 or 4 pounds (1.4 to 1.8 kg). A much larger but far less common species is the northern or tundra hare, which may weigh 12 pounds (5.5 kg) or more, enough for several meals.

One problem with using the animal is that the disease tularemia — known sometimes as "rabbit fever" — is common enough among Alaskan hares to warrant some precautions. It may be transmitted to humans through the handling of infected animals or by insects, such as the lice, ticks or fleas that may be on fur. Wear rubber or plastic gloves during the skinning and cleaning process. Gloves and utensils should be cleaned afterward with hot soapy water. The meat should be well rinsed in salted water — 1 to 2 tablespoons (15 to 30 mL) salt per quart (L) of water. Vinegar may be substituted for the salt.

One Way To Skin A Hare was written by Don Cornelius for *Alaska Fish Tales & Game Trails.* The item, originally titled "How To Prepare A Hare," was reprinted as a photo-story in *ALASKA®* magazine, March 1976.

various combinations of thyme, rosemary, paprika, marjoram, curry, clove—the full range.

Ann Chandonnet, food editor of the *Anchorage Daily News*, suggests that dressed meat of hare may be tenderized remarkably if it is refrigerated in a covered bowl, at least overnight or up to 24 hours. Some recipes suggest parboiling the meat as the first step in preparation, but we feel this is probably a last resort for tough old animals or ones not immediately dressed after the kill. A better way to tenderize and flavor is a spicy marinade, much as you would use on chicken or any other meat.

Pan-Fried Rabbit

2 rabbits cut in serving pieces
Salt and pepper
Lemon
Flour
Oil
Paprika

►Place portions on plate and rub all surfaces with salt; place in refrigerator for 12 hours. Wash off salt. Rub pieces lightly with cut lemon. Sprinkle with salt and pepper; dip in flour and fry in hot oil or shortening about 1/4 inch (6 mm) deep in frying pan. Brown thoroughly and turn. When both sides are brown, cover, lower heat and cook until tender. Sprinkle with paprika before serving. Serves eight.

Variations:

• Gravy can be made from the drippings of pan-fried rabbit, just as you would make chicken gravy: Pour off all but a couple of tablepoons (30 mL) of fat, heat, rapidly blend in an equal amount of flour and stir until foamy. Slowly add a cup (240 mL) or more of milk, stirring constantly until gravy is the thickness desired. Season to taste with pepper, salt and garlic powder.
• Brown the meat as directed. Then place the pieces in a Dutch oven or covered casserole dish, add 1/2 cup (120 mL) water, cover tightly and continue cooking on low heat or in the oven at 325°F (160°C) for about 45 minutes. The moisture will tenderize the meat. The rabbit won't be "crispy," however.
• Brown the meat as directed. Then place the pieces in a Dutch oven or covered casserole dish, add the juice and tomatoes from a 1-pound (456 g) can, chopped onion and green pepper to taste, and swirl in 1/2 cup (120 mL) sour cream or half-and-half, or a small can of undiluted evaporated milk. Cover and bake in an oven reheated to 325°F (160°C) for about one hour, uncovering the dish for the last 15 minutes.

Roast Rabbit with Potato Stuffing

2 cups (480 mL) mashed potatoes
2 tablespoons (30 mL) butter or margarine
1 teaspoon (5 mL) salt
1/2 teaspoon (2 mL) pepper
1-1/2 teaspoons (7 mL) thyme or sage
1 cup (240 mL) chopped celery, or
    1-1/2 teaspoons (7 mL) celery salt (If using
    celery salt, cut down on table salt)
Bacon or salt pork
1 whole rabbit

►Make dressing by combining all ingredients except bacon or salt pork and rabbit. Dress and wash rabbit, fill body with stuffing and skewer. Place in baking pan with legs folded under body and skewer in this position. Strip back of rabbit with bacon or salt pork to keep it from drying out. Roast at 400°F (205°C) for 10 minutes, then pour on 1 or 2 cups (240 to 480 mL) hot water and cook 35 to 45 minutes. Shortly before the end of cooking time, take off the bacon and let the rabbit brown.

This recipe can be used with Dutch oven and campfire. Just cover the Dutch oven with coals and allow a little more cooking time.
■ *Alma Haik*
The Alaskan Camp Cook

Variation: Cut the rabbit into serving pieces and roll them in seasoned flour. Cut the bacon or salt pork into 1-inch (2.5 cm) slices about 1/4 inch (6 mm) thick, fry a little, remove and set aside. Now brown the rabbit pieces in the hot fat. Spread potato stuffing in bottom of well-greased Dutch oven, lay browned rabbit pieces on top and scatter bacon or salt pork over all. Cook in hot coals as directed or in a moderate oven for about one hour. Add water only if dressing seems to be drying out.

Deep-Fried Rabbit

2 wild rabbits
Juice of 1 lemon
Salt, pepper, nutmeg
Egg, beaten
Bread crumbs
Fat
Parsley
Green peas
Toast

►Disjoint rabbits. Wipe clean and parboil 10 minutes in water containing lemon juice. Drain and pat dry. Season with salt, pepper and a very little nutmeg. Dip in beaten egg, then in very dry bread crumbs. Fry in deep fat. Have the fat hot enough so a 1-inch (2.5 cm) cube of bread is brown in 60 seconds. Drain browned meat free of fat by holding each piece on a fork over the pan until most of the fat drips off. This leaves the meat crispy. Place pieces on a hot dish, garnish with parsley and serve with green peas on toast. Plan to serve as many people as you would from the same weight of chicken.

■ Alaska's Game Is Good Food (adapted)

Roast Arctic Hare

1 large arctic hare*
1 onion, halved
1/2 cup (120 mL) vinegar
Water
1/4 cup (60 mL) butter
1 small onion, chopped
1/2 cup (120 mL) chopped celery
2 cups (480 mL) bread crumbs
1 teaspoon (5 mL) poultry seasoning
1/2 teaspoon (2 mL) salt
1/4 teaspoon (1 mL) pepper
1/2 cup (120 mL) melted butter for basting
2 tablespoons (30 mL) flour

►Skin, clean and wash rabbit thoroughly. Place in a large enameled kettle, add onion, vinegar and enough cold water to cover. Let stand six hours, then remove rabbit and drain.

Melt butter, add chopped onion and celery and saute until translucent. Pour over bread crumbs and seasonings and mix well. Stuff the rabbit, sew up the opening and place rabbit on side in uncovered roaster.

Roast at 325°F (160°C) for 1-1/2 hours or until tender, basting with melted butter every 10 minutes. When rabbit is half cooked, turn it over on other side.

Thicken pan drippings with flour. Add water till gravy is desired consistency. Pour gravy over rabbit before serving.

■ Northern Cookbook (adapted)

*Arctic hares are truly large — 10 to 15 pounds (4.5 to 6.75 kg).

Rabbit Supreme

1 young wild rabbit, disjointed (about 2½ lbs
  /or/ 1.15 kg)
1/4 cup (60 mL) flour
2 teaspoons (10 mL) salt
1/2 teaspoon (2 mL) pepper
1/2 teaspoon (2 mL) garlic salt
1/4 teaspoon (1 mL) paprika
1 egg
4 tablespoons (60 mL) light cream or
  evaporated milk
1/3 cup (80 mL) rolled saltine crumbs
1/3 cup (80 mL) grated Parmesan cheese

2 tablespoons (30 mL) minced parsley
1/4 cup (60 mL) salad oil
1/2 cup (120 mL) water

►Dredge rabbit pieces in mixture of flour, salt, pepper, garlic salt and paprika. Beat egg slightly with cream. Dip floured rabbit in the egg mixture and then in a mixture of the cracker crumbs, Parmesan cheese and parsley. Brown slowly in oil. Remove to a baking pan when browned. Pour the water into the pan drippings and bring to a boil. Pour over the browned rabbit. Bake at 375°F (190°C) for 45 minutes or until rabbit is tender. Serves six.

■ Anon.
  Courtesy, Mrs. Aline Strutz

Rabbit Pie
"My mother's recipe"

1 fat rabbit, about 4 pounds (1.8 kg)
1 stalk celery, chopped
6 small carrots
16 button onions
Pie dough

►Stew the rabbit until tender. Remove the meat from bones. Thicken gravy with flour. Season to taste. Half fill a glass pie plate with rabbit meat; add a few slices of boiled carrot, chopped celery and two or three boiled button onions. Pour over enough gravy to almost cover the rabbit. Roll pie crust, spread on top, crimping it firmly just over edges. Make a slit in center to allow the steam to escape. Bake in hot oven, 450°F (230°C), until done, about 20˙ minutes. One large rabbit will make 12 individual pies.

■ Arlys Johnson
  Frontier Vittles, *Fairbanks*

Tasty Rabbit

2 rabbits, cut up
3 large onions, sliced
1 medium clove garlic, crushed
Bacon drippings
Cracker crumbs
Flour
Salt and pepper

►Soak rabbits in baking soda and water overnight; then put in a kettle and boil for 30 minutes. Wipe rabbit pieces dry and set aside. Saute onions and garlic in bacon drippings. Roll rabbit pieces in cracker crumbs and flour, lay on top of onions. Add about 1 cup (240 mL) water and salt and pepper to taste. Cover and simmer until done.

■ Mary Hall
  Cooking Up A Storm, *Homer*

Braised Rabbit

2 to 3 pounds (1 to 1.4 kg) rabbit,
  in serving pieces
4 tablespoons (60 mL) butter or shortening
1 tablespoon (15 mL) flour
1 cup (240 mL) water
1/2 cup (120 mL) sauterne
1/4 cup (60 mL) chopped parsley
1 bay leaf
1/8 teaspoon (0.5 mL) thyme
1/2 clove garlic, sliced
1 teaspoon (5 mL) salt
1/4 teaspoon (1 mL) pepper
6 small boiling onions

►Blend fat and flour in skillet. Brown rabbit pieces carefully, turning often. Add remaining ingredients; cover and simmer gently for 45 minutes or until tender.
■ *Ann Chandonnet*
  Kodiak Fish Wrapper and Litter Box Liner

Herb-Stuffed Rabbit

"The Alaskan hare can be a dry piece of meat, especially a hare taken in the winter. I've heard it told that you could eat nothing but rabbit, which has no fat, and starve to death. But who wants rabbit that often? A woman in Gakona showed me this way to cook hare; she claimed to have used this method over a campfire on the trail and I see no reason to doubt her. You can even try it with a domestic, from-the-meat-market rabbit."

1/4 teaspoon (1 mL) rosemary
1 teaspoon (5 mL) dried parsley
1/8 teaspoon (0.5 mL) wine vinegar
1/4 cup (60 mL) butter
2 to 3 pounds (1 to 1.4 kg) rabbit, cut in pieces

►In a small dish crush the rosemary and parsley and add the vinegar and butter. Stir and let blend while you wash and dry the rabbit pieces.

With a sharp paring knife make a slit in the flesh of each piece of rabbit. Put a teaspoon (5 mL) of the herb butter in each pocket. Close the pockets with toothpicks or skewers.

Put the rabbit pieces in a pan and place the pan about 4 inches (10 cm) below a broiler. Turn the pieces after 15 minutes and broil another 15 minutes. Baste with the remaining butter mixture as necessary. Yields four servings.
■ *Gordon R. Nelson, Palmer*
  Lowbush Moose* (And Other Alaskan Recipes)

Lowbush moose — to the uninitiated — IS hare; highbush moose is the other kind, the big one. See Gordon Nelson's recipe for highbush moose on page 207.

Sweet-Sour Rabbit

2-1/2 pounds (1.15 kg) rabbit, cut in
  serving pieces
Flour, salt, pepper
2 tablespoons (30 mL) cooking fat or oil
1 cup (240 mL) pineapple juice
1/4 cup (60 mL) vinegar
1/2 teaspoon (2 mL) salt
1 cup (240 mL) pineapple pieces
1 medium green pepper, cut in thin half-slices
1-1/2 tablespoons (23 mL) cornstarch
1/4 cup (60 mL) sugar
1/2 cup (120 mL) water

►Roll rabbit pieces in mixture of flour, salt and pepper. Heat fat or oil in a heavy pan and brown rabbit on all sides over moderate heat. Add pineapple juice, vinegar and salt. Cover pan; cook over low heat for 40 minutes or until meat is tender. Add pineapple and green pepper; cook a few minutes longer. Mix cornstarch and sugar and stir in the water. Stir this mixture gradually into liquid in the pan and cook slowly until slightly thickened, about five minutes. Serves six.
■ The Hunter Returns

Marinated Hare

"Once upon a time there lived a man in the Matanuska Valley who raised rabbits. Rabbits, not hares. He enjoyed eating rabbits and frowned upon the wild hare as less than desirable. Every once in a while one of his rabbits would escape and disappear into the bushes where the hares lived. One day the man saw a hare in its white winter fur, but this one had a large black spot on it. He shot the animal and discovered that it was bigger and fatter than the usual wild hare. He cooked it after marinating it in wine, as he was accustomed to doing, and found it excellent. The story says he opened his cages and turned all his rabbits loose. The man is long gone, but there is a certain place I've heard of where the wild hares are big, fat and tasty even today. Should you find one of the above, or just buy a rabbit in the market, try this method of cooking it."

3 to 4 pounds (1.4 to 1.8 kg) rabbit,
  in serving pieces
1-1/2 cups (360 mL) dry white wine
3 tablespoons (45 mL) vinegar
1/4 cup (60 mL) vegetable oil
1 medium onion, sliced thin
1/2 teaspoon (2 mL) thyme
1 bay leaf
1 teaspoon (5 mL) dried parsley
1/2 teaspoon (2 mL) salt
1/4 teaspoon (1 mL) black pepper

1 tablespoon (15 mL) butter
1/4 pound (114 g) slab bacon, cut in 1/4-inch
   (6 mm) cubes
4 small onions
2 cloves garlic
2 tablespoons (30 mL) flour
1-1/4 cups (300 mL) beef stock

►It is the marinade that is the most important part of this recipe, as that is what turns just plain rabbit into something special. Wash and dry the pieces of rabbit and place them in a shallow glass dish so that all the pieces will be in the marinade.

Combine the wine, vinegar, oil, sliced onion, thyme, bay leaf, parsley, salt and pepper. Mix lightly and pour over the rabbit pieces and refrigerate for 24 hours, turning the pieces at least three times.

When it is time to cook the rabbit, put butter in a frying pan and saute the bacon pieces until most of the fat is rendered. Remove bacon with a slotted spoon and set aside.

Drain rabbit pieces — reserving the marinade — pat dry and fry them in the bacon grease. As the pieces brown, place them in a flame-proof casserole with the four whole onions.

Pour most of the bacon grease out of the frying pan, drop in the garlic and stir-fry for two minutes. Add flour, remove pan from heat, and stir in the beef stock and 1/2 cup (120 mL) of the marinade. Stir constantly at this stage. Return the mixture to the heat and stir until liquid thickens. Pour this sauce over the rabbit, add enough of the remaining marinade to cover the pieces and scatter bacon bits over the top.

Bring to a boil on top of the stove and then bake, covered, at 350°F (175°C) for an hour. Serve right from the casserole. Yields four servings.
■ *Gordon R. Nelson, Palmer*
   Lowbush Moose

Lapin a l'Orange

2 to 3 pounds (1.15 to 1.4 kg) rabbit pieces
1-1/2 teaspoons (7 mL) salt
1/4 teaspoon (1 mL) pepper
1 tablespoon (15 mL) lemon juice
3 tablespoons (45 mL) orange juice
2 teaspoons (10 mL) grated orange rind
4 tablespoons (60 mL) butter
1 tablespoon (15 mL) brown sugar
Dash of nutmeg
Few grains cayenne
Small pinch rosemary
Garlic to taste (optional)

►Rub pieces of rabbit with salt, pepper and lemon juice. Set aside. Mix remaining ingredients and simmer gently for 10 minutes. Place meat in

shallow pan and brush with sauce. Bake at 350°F (175°C) for one hour or until tender. Baste frequently with hot orange sauce, turning rabbit once during the baking.
■ *Ann Chandonnet*
   Kodiak Fish Wrapper and Litter Box Liner

Fruited Rabbit

2-1/2 pounds (1.15 kg) tender young rabbit,
   cut in serving pieces
1-1/2 teaspoons (7 mL) salt
1/4 teaspoon (1 mL) pepper
1-1/4 cups (300 mL) orange juice
2 tablespoons (30 mL) brown sugar
2 tablespoons (30 mL) wine vinegar
1 teaspoon (5 mL) nutmeg
1 teaspoon (5 mL) basil
1/8 teaspoon (0.5 mL) garlic salt
1/2 teaspoon (2 mL) salt
1/4 cup (60 mL) flour
2 tablespoons (30 mL) butter or margarine
1-1/2 cups (360 mL) fresh orange sections
1-1/2 cups (360 mL) fresh grapefruit sections
2 tablespoons (30 mL) snipped parsley

►Sprinkle rabbit with salt and pepper and refrigerate 30 minutes. Meanwhile, combine orange juice, brown sugar, vinegar, nutmeg, basil and garlic salt and set aside. Combine flour with remaining 1/2 teaspoon (2 mL) salt and coat rabbit evenly. Melt butter in a large skillet and saute rabbit on all sides until golden brown. Add orange juice mixture and simmer, covered, one hour, or until rabbit is fork tender, stirring occasionally and turning rabbit once. Now lay orange and grapefruit sections over surface of rabbit; cook, covered, without stirring, until fruit is just heated through. Transfer carefully to large, heated platter, garnish with parsley and serve. Makes six servings.
■ *Mamie Jensen, Juneau*

Hasenpfeffer

2 rabbits, cut in serving pieces
Bacon drippings
1/2 cup (120 mL) vinegar
1-1/2 cups (360 mL) water
2 tablespoons (30 mL) brown sugar
1/4 teaspoon (1 mL) allspice
1 teaspoon (5 mL) cinnamon
1 large bay leaf
2 large onions, sliced
Garlic bud or powdered garlic

►Brown rabbit pieces in bacon drippings. Mix all other ingredients and pour over rabbit. Cover and simmer until meat is tender. Thicken sauce with browned flour.
■ *Mamie Jensen, Juneau*

Curried Snowshoe

2 pounds (1 kg) hare, cut in serving pieces
2 tablespoons (30 mL) Dijon-style mustard
1 tablespoon (15 mL) lemon juice
1 tablespoon (15 mL) honey
3 tablespoons (45 mL) margarine, melted
1 teaspoon (5 mL) curry powder
1/2 teaspoon (2 mL) salt
Paprika
Lemon slices (optional)

►Refrigerate freshly dressed hare in a covered bowl overnight or up to 24 hours to tenderize the meat. At preparation time, grease a shallow baking dish and arrange pieces in a single layer close together. Mix remaining ingredients except lemon slices, adding enough paprika to color the sauce as you wish. Spread evenly over meat. Set lemon slices on top. Bake at 350°F (175°C) for one hour or more until meat is tender. Baste frequently with sauce in pan. Makes four servings.
■ *The editors, ALASKA® magazine*

Snowshoe Hare and Kraut

►Flour and season one or two hares or domestic rabbits, cut into serving portions. In a large covered skillet or Dutch oven, brown nicely in oil or bacon grease. Cover with 2 to 4 cups (0.47 to 1 L) of homemade sauerkraut; put the lid on and simmer slowly for 30 minutes or until meat is tender. Be careful not to let it dry out. Serve the kraut and juices over boiled or mashed potatoes with the meat to the side. This makes the toughest, scrawniest rabbit into an epicurean delight.
■ *Mary Bishop; courtesy, Mary Shields AlaskaFest*

Cookout Rabbit

2 to 3 pounds (1 to 1.4 kg) rabbit, cut in
    serving pieces
1-1/2 teaspoons (7 mL) salt
1/4 teaspoon (1 mL) pepper
1/2 cup (120 mL) sherry
1/2 cup (120 mL) cooking oil
1-1/2 teaspoons (7 mL) seasoned salt

►Season moist pieces of rabbit with salt and pepper. Place pan of rabbit over medium-hot bed of coals. Make sauce by mixing remaining ingredients. Keep rabbit well basted with this sauce, turning the pieces frequently. Cook one hour or until tender. Your own favorite barbecue sauce may be used but some added oil will help keep the rabbit juicy.
■ *Ann Chandonnet Kodiak Fish Wrapper and Litter Box Liner*

Rabbit Stew with Dumplings

1 rabbit, cut in serving pieces
1-1/2 teaspoons (7 mL) salt
1-1/2 cups (360 mL) diced potatoes
1 cup (240 mL) diced carrots
1 medium onion, chopped
1 tablespoon (15 mL) fresh or dried parsley
1 teaspoon (5 mL) salt
1/4 teaspoon (1 mL) pepper
3 tablespoons (45 mL) flour
3/4 cup (180 mL) cold water

►Put rabbit into a pan large enough to hold pieces without crowding. Add salt and enough cold water to cover the rabbit. Cover pan, bring to a boil, then reduce heat and cook over low heat about one hour, or until meat is tender.
    Strain the broth and set aside. With a sharp knife, cut the rabbit meat from the bones and return the meat to the broth. Add diced vegetables and seasonings and simmer over low heat until vegetables are tender. Mix flour and cold water into a paste and add to the stew, stirring constantly to prevent lumping. Make dumplings, add to pan and cook as directed below.

Dumplings
3/4 cup (180 mL) flour
2 teaspoons (10 mL) baking powder
1/2 teaspoon (2 mL) salt
1 egg, slightly beaten
1/3 cup (80 mL) milk

►Sift dry ingredients together, add beaten egg and milk, stirring just enough to moisten all. Drop by spoonfuls on top of finished, hot stew, spacing the dumplings so they will not run together during cooking. Place heavy lid on top and cook for 15 minutes without lifting lid. Serves eight.
■ Northern Cookbook *(adapted)*

Beer-Braised Snowshoe

2-1/2 to 3 pounds (1.15 to 1.4 kg) hare, cut in
    serving pieces
Salt, pepper, paprika
Flour
3 tablespoons (45 mL) bacon drippings
2 cloves garlic, halved
6 onions, sliced
1 can (12 fl oz /or/ 355 mL) beer

►Sprinkle hare with salt, pepper and paprika and roll in flour. Melt bacon drippings in a heavy cast-iron skillet with a lid or in a Dutch oven. Toss in the garlic and stir it around in the hot fat until browned. Remove with a slotted spoon and discard. Add meat pieces a few at a time, to keep heat even, and brown thoroughly. With the last batch, add in the onions and brown lightly. Assemble all the meat in the pan with the onions, add beer, cover tightly and simmer on low heat. Or slide into an oven preheated to 350°F (175°C) for an hour or more, until meat is tender. Yields six to eight servings.

■ *The editors, ALASKA® magazine*

Hare with Sour Cream
A recipe for the slow-cooker

2 pounds (1 kg) rabbit, cut in serving pieces
Salt, pepper and paprika
1/2 cup (120 mL) red wine
1 can (12 oz /or/ 340 g) condensed cream of
    mushroom soup
1 cup (240 mL) sour cream
Dash or two of Worcestershire
2 teaspoons (10 mL) dehydrated onion flakes

►Sprinkle meat with salt, pepper and paprika and place in a slow-cooker or a Dutch oven. Mix remaining ingredients and pour over meat. Cook all day on low heat.

■ *Will — "From the Cabin Wall" (adapted)*
  Alaska Fish Tales & Game Trails
  September 1981

Rabbit Creole Style

1 rabbit, cleaned and skinned
1 large onion, sliced
2 sprigs thyme
2 bay leaves
1/2 cup (120 mL) white wine
1/2 teaspoon (2 mL) nutmeg
1 tablespoon (15 mL) salt
1 tablespoon (15 mL) butter

12 small onions
1 ounce (28.5 g) ham, finely minced
2 tablespoons (30 mL) flour
3 tomatoes, peeled and sliced thin
2 cups (480 mL) consomme or water
1/2 cup (120 mL) red wine

►Cut rabbit in pieces at joints. Marinate in a stone jar for six hours, with the large sliced onion, thyme, bay leaves, white wine, nutmeg and salt. Lift rabbit from marinade, drain well and brown in butter, adding small onions and ham. Let brown 10 minutes; then add flour, stir well and brown a little longer. Add tomatoes and cook 10 more minutes. Then add consomme and red wine; stir until the liquid begins to boil, add salt and pepper to taste, cover and cook 45 minutes longer.

■ *Mrs. W.A. Perry, Jr.*
  Alaska's Cooking, Anchorage

Oven-Barbecued Rabbit

2 to 3 pounds (1 to 1.4 kg) rabbit
1-1/2 teaspoons (7 mL) salt
1/4 teaspoon (1 mL) pepper
3/4 cup (180 mL) barbecue sauce, your own
    or bottled
1/2 cup (120 mL) water

►Season moist pieces of rabbit with salt and pepper. Place in a shallow baking pan and brush generously with barbecue sauce. Pour water in bottom of pan. Cover and bake at 350°F (175°C) for 45 minutes. Remove cover; turn pieces and brush generously with sauce. Bake uncovered for 30 minutes more or until tender, brushing with sauce again to keep surface of meat moist.

■ *Ann Chandonnet*
  Kodiak Fish Wrapper and Litter Box Liner

LYNX

Lynx is an animal to be prized for both fur and meat. Here are some hints about saving the pelt, reprinted from the *Northern Cookbook.*

Case-Skinning Lynx

"Care should be taken in skinning the lynx to protect its deep silky fur. It should be 'cased.' Slit the skin on the inside of the hind legs from the paws to the vent, then work the skin off the legs, the rump and the tail. Tie the hind feet together over a hook or the limb of a tree and then work the skin off, inside out (like peeling off a sweater), using the knife as little as possible. When the forelegs are reached, they should be pushed back and worked out of the skin until the paws are completely skinned out. Take particular care when skinning around the eyes and lips. [These are easy places for tears to begin.] Scrape the pelt to remove any flesh and fat clinging to it, then wash with lukewarm water to remove all bloodstains. Place it on a stretcher, fur side in and let it dry until it can hold its shape. Then turn the fur side out, starting by folding in the nose and working the pelt inwards a little at a time. Replace the turned skin on the stretcher with the fur side out and let it dry thoroughly."

Cooking Lynx

The *Northern Cookbook* describes the meat of the lynx as white and tender, particularly succulent late in the fall when the animal has stored up a good deal of fat for the winter. But, alas, as Beverly Wolford of Homer points out, "Few people realize that lynx is surprisingly tasty," since it is an animal most prized for its fur. She suggests boiling the meat until it is tender, then browning it in butter. The results? "Somewhat like rabbit," she says. Others compare the taste to veal.

Canadian Lynx Stew

2 pounds (1 kg) lynx meat
4 tablespoons (60 mL) fat
1 small onion, chopped
1 teaspoon (5 mL) salt
1/4 teaspoon (1 mL) pepper
1/4 teaspoon (1 mL) summer savory
1/4 teaspoon (1 mL) oregano
4 potatoes, quartered
4 carrots, diced
1/2 cup (120 mL) celery, chopped
2 tablespoons (30 mL) flour
1/2 cup (120 mL) cold water
1 teaspoon (5 mL) Worcestershire

►Wash meat well, pat dry and cut into 2-inch (5 cm) cubes. Melt fat in heavy pot, add meat and cook until nicely browned. Add onions and seasoning. Cover with cold water, bring to a boil; then reduce heat, place a lid on the pot and simmer for 1-1/2 hours. Add potatoes, carrots and celery and continue cooking for a half-hour or until meat and vegetables are tender.

Make a paste of the flour and water and add to the stew, stirring gently until thickened. Just before serving, add the Worcestershire. Serve hot. Yields four servings.
■ Northern Cookbook *(adapted)*

MOUNTAIN GOAT & MOUNTAIN (DALL) SHEEP

Mountain goat makes excellent meat for the table if properly cared for in the field, though the age of the animal will determine, fairly rigidly, how it is to be prepared. The flavor — young animal or old — is mild. But the older the animal, the tougher the meat is likely to be. It is best ground to be used in any of the ways you would use hamburger. Or subject it to slow, moist-heat cooking, as in stew or Swiss steak. Or marinate it overnight in a solution that contains vinegar or wine (or both) as about half the liquid, with water or pineapple juice or bouillon as the other half. Add other flavors as you wish— chopped or dehydrated onion, garlic, powdered clove, soy sauce or Worcestershire or mustard. Oil, 3 or 4 tablespoons (45 to 60 mL) per cup (240 mL) of marinade, is optional, but it, too, adds moisture.

A plus . . . you needn't separate the sheep from the goats in the kitchen. Recipes for either will do nicely for both.

Braised Mountain Goat

►Cut mountain goat round steak into serving size pieces. Roll in flour and season with salt and pepper to taste. Brown well in bacon drippings. Place in ovenproof dish and cover with half-and-half or light cream. Bake in a 325°F (160°C) oven for 1-1/2 hours or until tender when tested with a fork. Remove pieces of meat to a large serving bowl. Make a paste of whole-wheat flour and cold water and stir into the pan juices. Bring to a boil, stirring. Reduce heat and cook gently until gravy is thickened. Pour gravy over the goat pieces in serving bowl. Serve with fresh sourdough bread.
■ *The Old Homesteader*

Sheep Liver

1-1/2 pounds (685 g) Dall sheep liver, sliced
    1 inch (2.5 cm) thick
3 carrots, sliced
2 medium potatoes, sliced thin
1 teaspoon (5 mL) dehydrated minced onion
1 bay leaf (optional)
1 can (8 oz /or/ 228 g) tomato sauce

►Place liver in slow-cooking pot after browning briefly in butter in heavy skillet. Add other ingredients and stir gently to mix. Cover and cook about 9 or 10 hours on low heat.
■ *The Old Homesteader*

Dall Sheep Shish Kabob with Sweet 'n' Sour Sauce

"Top a bed of glowing coals in a natural rock barbecue pit with chunks of fresh Dall sheep meat skewered between mushrooms, tomatoes and onions, and the results will beat any glorious kabob you've ever tried."

►Start a fire and let it burn down to hot coals. You may wish to cover your grill with aluminum foil to hold all the goodies securely and keep them from falling into the fire.

Thread long skewers with alternate chunks of meat, tomatoes, mushrooms and onions using, in all, about 1/2 pound (228 g) meat per person. Each skewer should contain three or four chunks of meat, an onion and two or more tomatoes and mushrooms. Optional additions include a ring of pineapple around the center of each skewer.

Place the shish kabobs over the fire and broil to your liking. Serve on a bed of rice, then top with Sweet 'n' Sour Sauce.

Sweet 'n' Sour Sauce
1 can (16 oz /or/ 456 g) pineapple rings
2 tablespoons (30 mL) cornstarch
3 tablespoons (45 mL) vinegar
2 tablespoons (30 mL) soy sauce
3 tablespoons (45 mL) brown sugar

►Drain pineapple. Use the rings for the kabobs. Add enough water to the juice to make 1-1/2 cups (360 mL) liquid. Mix a small amount with the cornstarch and set aside. Heat remaining juice, vinegar, soy sauce and brown sugar, stir in cornstarch mixture and cook together, stirring, until sauce turns clear.

■ *Sue Entsminger*
  The Cabin Friend
  ALASKA® *magazine, April 1980*

Sheep Skillet

1-1/2 pounds (685 g) sheep meat cut into 2-inch (5 cm) pieces
Flour
2 tablespoons (30 mL) fat
1 tablespoon (15 mL) Worcestershire
1 teaspoon (5 mL) salt
1 cup (240 mL) tomato juice

►Roll sheep chunks in flour and brown in hot fat. When browned on all sides, add Worcestershire, salt and tomato juice. Cover and cook slowly until meat is tender, 1-1/2 to 2 hours. Serve over boiled or steamed rice.

■ *Louis Juhnke*
  The Alaskan Camp Cook

Roast Mountain Goat

A recipe shared by many different cooks

5 or 6 pounds (2.25 to 2.7 kg) roast of young mountain goat
1 or 2 cloves garlic
Salt and pepper

►Clean meat thoroughly. Make small openings with the point of a sharp knife and insert small pieces of garlic. (You can substitute garlic powder—about 1/16 teaspoon or 0.25 mL per slit.) Sprinkle meat with salt and pepper. Put in roaster with small amount of water and roast at 325°F (160°C) until tender, two to three hours. Brown quickly in hot oven or under broiler for a few minutes. Serve with Highbush Cranberry Ketchup (see Chapter 14), or another wild berry sauce of your choosing.

■ *Anon.*

Stuffed Sheep Shoulder

4 pounds (1.8 kg) shoulder roast
1 cup (240 mL) rice
2 tablespoons (30 mL) fat
2 bay leaves
1 onion, chopped
1 green pepper, chopped
1-1/2 cups (360 mL) quartered (or canned)
*   tomatoes*
1 teaspoon (5 mL) salt

►Bone shoulder to make pocket for stuffing. Cook rice in boiling salted water. Drain. Melt fat in heavy pan or skillet, add bay leaves (crushed), chopped onion and green pepper. Cook slowly until tender. Add tomatoes and salt, cook five minutes more, then mix in rice with a fork. Fill pocket in meat with rice mixture, fasten with skewers, place on rack, fat side up, and roast in a slow oven, 325°F (160°C), for 2-1/2 hours. Do not cover.
■ *Anon., Birchwood*
   The Alaskan Camp Cook

Broiled Dall Chops

►Cut ribs into chops 1 inch (2.5 cm) thick. Slash fat to prevent curling. Place on grate or rack about 3 inches (7.5 cm) above hot coals of campfire. Brush chops with French dressing and salt and pepper to taste. Broil 7 minutes on each side, 14 minutes in all.
■ *Anon., Birchwood*
   The Alaskan Camp Cook

Sheep with Vegetables

1-1/2 pounds (685 g) Dall sheep meat, cut in
*   1-inch (2.5 cm) cubes*
Whole-wheat flour
Salt and pepper
Cooking oil
Vegetables

►Dredge the cubed sheep meat in whole-wheat flour and sprinkle lighty with salt and pepper. Heat oil in heavy skillet and brown the meat on all sides. Transfer to stew pot and cover with water. Bring to a boil; reduce heat to simmer and cook gently for three or four hours. About a half-hour before serving time, add vegetables of your choice. Sheep meat has a delicate flavor, so strongly flavored vegetables should be avoided. Add water from time to time as needed. Thicken the gravy a few minutes before serving time with a paste made of whole-wheat flour and cold water. This is especially nice served with hot baking powder biscuits or sour-dough biscuits.
■ *The editors, ALASKA® magazine*

Sheep or Goat Stew

2 pounds (1 kg) meat
1 tablespoon (15 mL) fat
1 quart (1 L) water
1/2 cup (120 mL) pearl barley
1 sliced onion
2 tablespoons (30 mL) chopped parsley
3 tablespoons (45 mL) chopped celery leaves
2 teaspoons (10 mL) salt
6 medium potatoes
1/2 cup (120 mL) old-fashioned oatmeal

►Heat fat in heavy kettle. Cut meat into 2-inch (5 cm) cubes and brown well in hot fat. Add water, barley, onion, parsley, celery and salt. Cook slowly 1-1/2 hours. Add potatoes and oatmeal and continue cooking until potatoes are tender. Serve with crackers and cheese. Serves six to eight.
■ *Louise Juhnke*
   The Alaskan Camp Cook

Sheep Roast
Mountain (Dall) sheep, says hunter Harold Curtis, "is best not kept too long in the freezer. If meat has been stored one to two months, the tallow should be trimmed as close as possible as it absorbs odors and will taste rancid. Sheep can be cooked the same as beef — broiled, fried, roasted or stewed. It is a flavorful meat and does not need heavy seasonings."

►Roll sheep roast in flour. Season with salt and pepper and garlic salt, if desired. Brown in hot fat on top of stove. When nicely browned on all surfaces, place roaster in oven and cover. Roast at 300°F (150°C), allowing cooking time as for rare, medium or well-done beef, as you wish. Remove cover for last 30 minutes of roasting if desired. Or cook in Dutch oven, same as any roast.
■ *Aileen Curtis*
   The Alaskan Camp Cook

Slow-Cooked Mountain Sheep Stew

2 pounds (1 kg) Dall sheep stew meat
4 medium potatoes, cubed
4 large carrots, cubed or sliced
1-1/2 teaspoons (7 mL) salt
1/8 teaspoon (0.5 mL) wild sage or thyme
1-1/2 teaspoons (7 mL) dehydrated minced
*   onion or equivalent in fresh sliced onion*
1 cup (240 mL) apple cider

►Place all ingredients in a slow-cooking pot, pouring the cider on last of all. Cook on low heat for 10 to 12 hours or more.
■ *The Old Homesteader*

Pan-Broiled Sheep Steaks

►Sprinkle salt generously in a heavy skillet. Heat to moderately hot; place the choicest sheep steaks in the skillet and cook until one side is brown. Turn and brown on the other side. Reduce heat and cook until the meat is done to your taste. If any fat accumulates in the pan, pour it off so that the meat is cooked by dry heat.

■ *Anon.*

Dall Sheep Shortcake

1 tablespoon (15 mL) melted margarine
4 onions, sliced thin
3/4 pound (340 g) sheepburger
1 teaspoon (5 mL) salt
1/4 teaspoon (1 mL) pepper
2 eggs, beaten
1 cup (240 mL) sour cream
1/2 teaspoon (2 mL) paprika
1 teaspoon (5 mL) parsley flakes
1/2 recipe, baking powder biscuit dough
Packaged gravy mix, prepared

►Melt margarine over low heat and simmer onions for 10 minutes — until tender but not browned. Add burger, crumbling it with a fork and cook for about five minutes or until meat turns color. Beat eggs, sour cream and seasonings together well and combine with meat mixture. Make half the recipe of your favorite baking powder biscuit dough. Roll on a floured board until about 1/4 inch (6 mm) thick. Press the dough into a lightly oiled, 9-inch (22 cm) pie pan. Place the meat mixture over the pastry and sprinkle with paprika and dried parsley flakes. Bake in a 375° (190°C) oven for 30 to 40 minutes. Cut in wedges and serve hot. Use a packaged gravy mix and serve the gravy with the sheep shortcake.

■ *The Old Homesteader*

Circle Mountain Sheep Chops

6 thick sheep chops
2 tablespoons (30 mL) butter
Salt and pepper
1 tablespoon (15 mL) minced parsley

►The chops should be cut at least 1 inch (2.5 cm) thick. Rub the butter into the meat; sprinkle with salt and pepper. Place under the broiler and broil, turning more often than other meat, until well done. Sprinkle with minced parsley and serve.

■ *Bess A. Cleveland*
   Alaskan Cookbook for Homesteader or Gourmet

Sheep or Goat Rib Barbecue

"Saves carrying out the ribs
and is an excellent camp meal"

►Clean rib cage, which has been separated into two sides. Salt and pepper, how much you like. Prop one on each side of a bed of hot coals. Keep turning until cooked through and very nicely browned. Then have at them. Good!

■ *Buck Moore*
   The Alaskan Camp Cook

MUSKRAT OR "MARSH HARE"

Muskrat is an important food in many rural areas of Alaska and, while the fur is the least valuable of the major furbearing animals, the number of pelts harvested is the largest. Once again, we turn to the *Northern Cookbook* for hints about saving the pelt.

Case-Skinning Muskrat

"The muskrat should be skinned as soon as possible after being trapped [or shot. . . . In Alaska, about 80 percent are taken with .22 rifles]. Slit the skin on the inside of the hind legs from the paws to the vent and cut off both hind and fore paws and the tail. Then work the skin off inside out . . . using the knife as little as possible, taking particular care when skinning around eyes and lips. [The thin skin here tears easily.] The skin should be scraped with a dull knife to remove all flesh and fat, washed with lukewarm water to remove the blood, and placed fur side inward on a wedge-shaped stretching board made of soft wood to dry."

Dressing & Cooking Muskrat

Muskrat is commonly marketed in some parts of the country, sold under the name "marsh hare," probably to separate the quality of the meat— which is high — from the fact that the animal is a rodent nicknamed "'rat."

But the other part of its name is actually more important to its eating quality. The musk of the muskrat is used as an ingredient in perfume but does not taste so good in the mouth. For that reason, the major caution in dressing the meat is to *carefully remove all scent glands without cutting into them* or you risk spreading their off taste to the meat. These glands are light yellow, inconspicuous, fatty "kernels." The larger ones lie just under the skin on the lower abdomen. Smaller ones will be found between front legs and in the groin and between the shoulders on the back. Though rabbit and beaver are equipped with similar glands that should also be removed, the scent of the muskrat is stronger; hence its usefulness in making perfume.

Once the muskrat is skinned, remove the head from the carcass. To eviscerate, insert the knife blade at the tip of the breastbone. Then, cutting from underneath, with the sharp edge of the blade upward, use a couple of fingers to guide the knife safely past the viscera and musk glands without cutting into them. Slit to and around the vent. Then lay the belly open and remove the viscera. Cut out the musk glands and wash the meat thoroughly in salted water.

Muskrat are generally rather lean animals, like rabbit and a cousin-rodent, the squirrel. But there seems to be general agreement amongst cooks that what fat there is has a strong taste. Therefore, most cooks recommend that all visible fat be removed and many suggest parboiling the meat in soda water — 1 teaspoon (5 mL) soda to 1 quart (1 L) water — for 10 to 15 minutes. Or the meat may be soaked two to three hours or overnight in a saltwater brine — 1 tablespoon (15 mL) salt per quart (1 L) of water. In any case, drain the meat and pat it thoroughly dry before proceeding with the cooking.

A dressed muskrat will weigh about 1 pound (456 g), enough for two or three servings. The meat is dark and fine-grained.

Muskrat Chili

3 muskrats, cut in serving-size pieces
1/4 cup (60 mL) red wine
1/3 cup (80 mL) chili sauce
1 teaspoon (5 mL) dehydrated minced onion
2 tablespoons (30 mL) brown sugar
1/2 teaspoon (2 mL) dry mustard
1/2 teaspoon (2 mL) chili powder
1/2 teaspoon (2 mL) Worcestershire

►Sprinkle salt to taste over muskrat pieces and place them in a slow-cooker. Mix remaining ingredients in small bowl and pour over pieces in pot. Cover and cook on low heat for seven to eight hours.

Browned Muskrat with Onion Gravy

2 muskrats
Saltwater solution — 1 tablespoon (15 mL) salt per quart (1 L) water
Water for parboiling and stewing
2 teaspoons (10 mL) salt
1/8 teaspoon (0.5 mL) pepper
1 cup (240 mL) chopped onions
3 tablespoons (45 mL) bacon drippings
6 additional onions, sliced
Flour

►Disjoint two muskrats and soak for an hour in saltwater solution. Drain and cover with fresh water. Boil five minutes and drain again.

Put meat in heavy skillet, add 3 cups (720 mL) fresh water, the salt, pepper, chopped onions and bacon drippings. Cover and simmer for half an hour or until meat is tender. Remove cover. Add sliced onions. Cook 10 minutes longer. Remove meat from pan. For each cup (240 mL) of broth remaining in the pan, make a paste of two tablespoons (30 mL) flour and 1/4 cup (60 mL) water and stir it into the broth. Cook, stirring, until thick. Makes six servings.

■ *Anon.*
Courtesy, Mrs. Aline Strutz

Chicken-Fried Muskrat

Dressed muskrat
Marinade: 1 quart (1 L) water plus 1 tablespoon (15 mL) salt
Salt, pepper, paprika, to taste
Flour
Bacon fat
Sliced onions
1 cup (240 mL) sour cream, or evaporated or reconstituted dry milk soured with 2 teaspoons — (10 mL) vinegar

►Soak muskrat overnight in saltwater marinade. Next day, drain, disjoint and cut into serving pieces. Season with salt, pepper and paprika to taste, then roll in flour and fry in bacon fat until browned on all sides. Cover with sliced onions, salt lightly and pour on sour cream. Cover tightly and simmer or bake in Dutch oven for one hour. Makes two or three servings.

■ *Vernon Haik, Anchorage*
The Alaskan Camp Cook

Variations:
• Muskrat can also be dipped in batter before it's fried. Follow the overnight soak procedure, above, then prepare a batter of one beaten egg, 1/2 cup (120 mL) milk, 1/2 cup (120 mL) flour, 1/4

teaspoon (1 mL) baking powder, 1 teaspoon (5 mL) salt, plus black pepper, paprika and garlic powder to taste. Pat meat pieces dry with paper towel, dip in batter and fry in about 1/4 inch (6 mm) of hot fat till well browned; cover, reduce heat and continue cooking about one hour more.

• Or, once the meat has been fried — either method — transfer the pieces to a heavy casserole, add a sliced onion, some chopped green pepper, a medium-sized can of tomatoes and seasonings as desired. Cover and bake at about 350°F (175°C) for one hour.

Roast Muskrat

▶Wash two muskrats that have been dressed. Stuff with a commercial dressing or your own favorite bread dressing. Bake in oven set at 350°F (175°C) for one hour. Makes four to six servings.
■ *Doris Ward, Fort Yukon*

PORCUPINE

Porcupine is neither hunted nor trapped in Alaska. . . . There's no need! The animal is so slow moving, it can easily be clubbed, and it is therefore regarded as an emergency food that can be obtained even by a lost and hungry soul who has no weapons. It's a tasty meat, nevertheless. Porcupines may be skinned — starting on the stomach side where there are no quills. Then the meat may be eviscerated and cleaned and roasted or boiled. Or try Annie Johnson's method, below, for a quick "one-pot" meal.

Iliamna Boiled Porcupine

▶Find a live porcupine and club it on the head until dead. No need to shoot it — porcupines are slow moving and awkward.

Build a fire, several feet across. Lay several heavy poles across it. Place the whole porcupine on these poles and allow the fire to burn all of the quills and hair.

Remove de-quilled porcupine from the fire and scrape away the charcoaled skin, quills and hair.

Open the porcupine's abdomen and remove the viscera, saving the liver and choice pieces of the intestine.

Cut the porcupine into convenient-sized pieces, wash and put into a pot of boiling water. Include head, tail, feet and body. Throw no part away.

Wash the selected pieces of intestine in water and add to the boiling pot. Cook until tender. Do not salt. Liver may be fried at another time.

Summer porcupines are fat and resemble pork when cooked in this manner. Winter-killed porcupines have less fat.

The meat is tasty and is a favorite with many rural Alaskans. Most people who cook porcupines in this manner also drink the flavorful broth, almost as they would tea.
■ *Mrs. Annie Johnson, Homer*
  "Alaska Mammals"
  ALASKA GEOGRAPHIC®, *Volume 8, Number 2*

Sweet and Sour Porcupine

Legs of porcupine
1 or 2 sliced onions
1 cup (240 mL) cider vinegar
3/4 cup (180 mL) brown sugar
1/2 teaspoon (2 mL) nutmeg
Fat

▶In saucepan, cook onions in vinegar until transparent. Add sugar and nutmeg. Brown porcupine in fat in Dutch oven. Add vinegar mixture to meat. Cover and simmer three hours. Gravy may be thickened with cornstarch. Remove meat from bones and serve with gravy over rice.
■ *Jeanne McArthur*
  Cooking Up A Storm, *Homer*

Make your own bouillon cubes. Boil soup stock down to a concentrate and freeze in ice cube trays. Store in freezer in plastic bags . . . or outside in the deep of winter. Use for gravies and soups.

If your dog has a set-to with a porcupine (quill pig) and gets a mouthful of quills, here is the remedy. Put a couple of cups (480 mL) of vinegar in the dog's mouth and throat. He won't like it but it will soften the quills and they should fall out in a few hours.
■ *The editors, ALASKA® magazine*

"Porky" Liver and Bacon

1 porcupine liver
Salt and pepper
3 slices bacon, cut in half
Hot water

►The unusually large liver of the porcupine is a succulent addition to the bush dweller's or hunter's menu. Slice the liver to 1/2-inch (1.25 cm) thickness and trim out all tubes and such. This will allow the meat to be cooked quickly, preserving its natural tenderness. Fry bacon in a sizzling skillet until crisp. Push it to one side of the pan and place liver pieces in the bacon fat. Fry about one minute to each side or until browned well. Remove bacon and liver slices to a hot serving dish. Pour 1/2 cup (120 mL) hot water into the skillet, simmer for a minute or until reduced in bulk. Pour over the liver and bacon in the serving dish. Serve with French garlic bread and a tossed salad.
■ *The Old Homesteader*

Porcupine Fricassee

►Use porcupine legs only, and trim away all fat. Soak in cold, salted water six to ten hours or overnight. Drain. Roll in flour and brown in hot fat. Put it in a Dutch oven. Make gravy with flour, water and the drippings from the fry pan and pour it over the meat. Simmer slowly for about three hours. Season well with salt, pepper and garlic, onions or other herbs.
■ *Mark Jensen, Juneau*
  The Alaskan Camp Cook

SQUIRREL

Squirrel meat, says the Canadian *Northern Cookbook*, "is tender and has a truly delicious flavour. The slight gamey taste present in most wild game meats is almost absent in the squirrel. No soaking is necessary, and only the toughest animals require parboiling for tenderness."

It is hard to beat that recommendation, and yet there is something about "squirrel" and "Alaskan cookbooks" that seems not to mix. Amongst the many fine game meat dishes perused for this collection, an Alaskan cook's recipes for squirrel turned up only once, in Bess A. Cleveland's estimable *Alaskan Cookbook for Homesteader or Gourmet*, published in 1960.

In fact few hunters *seek* squirrel in Alaska, though one species, the red squirrel, is the most familiar of all Alaskan mammals, and it is listed as legal game.

With permission, some of the Cleveland and Canadian recipes are shared here. Beyond these— as almost any Alaskan who grew up in the Lower 49 can tell you — any recipe for hare, rabbit or chicken is suitable for squirrel meat. Skin and clean squirrel as directed for muskrat, being sure to remove the small scent glands on the inner side of the front legs. But remember, overnight soaking in salt- or vinegar-water, parboiling and other tenderizing methods are generally unnecessary.

Roast Squirrel

Dressed squirrels, about 3
1/2 cup (120 mL) vegetable oil
3 tablespoons (45 mL) lemon juice
2 cups (480 mL) bread dressing
Salt
Pepper
Melted butter
Grated onion

►Wash the cleaned squirrels under running water and wipe dry with a clean cloth. Mix the oil and lemon juice, pour over the meat and let stand one hour. Stuff the squirrels with a good bread dressing, salt and pepper them and roast in a 350°F (175°C) oven two hours. Baste frequently with butter to which a little grated onion has been added.
■ *Bess A. Cleveland*
  Alaskan Cookbook for Homesteader or Gourmet

Squirrel Fricassee

1 squirrel
1/2 teaspoon (2 mL) salt
1/8 teaspoon (0.5 mL) pepper
1/2 cup (120 mL) flour

4 slices bacon, cut up
1 tablespoon (15 mL) diced onion
1-1/2 teaspoons (7 mL) lemon juice
1/3 cup (80 mL) broth

►Skin and clean squirrel, being sure to remove scent glands from forelegs. Wash thoroughly and cut squirrel into serving pieces. Rub with salt and pepper, then dredge with flour. Cook bacon until crisp. Add the squirrel and pan-fry with bacon for 20 minutes, until nicely browned. Add remaining ingredients, cover and simmer for two hours.
■ Northern Cookbook *(adapted)*

Brunswick Stew

3 squirrels, dressed and cut in serving pieces
3 quarts (3 L) water
1/4 cup (60 mL) diced bacon
1/4 teaspoon (1 mL) cayenne
1 teaspoon (5 mL) sugar
2 teaspoons (10 mL) salt

1/4 teaspoon (1 mL) black pepper
1 cup (240 mL) chopped onion
2 cups (480 mL) canned tomatoes
2 cups (480 mL) diced potatoes
2 cups (480 mL) lima beans, fresh or frozen
2 cups (480 mL) corn
1/2 cup (120 mL) dry fine bread crumbs
2 tablespoons (30 mL) melted butter

►Place squirrel pieces in a large kettle. Add water. Bring slowly to boil; reduce heat and simmer 1-1/2 to 2 hours, or until meat is tender, skimming surface occasionally.

Cool enough to remove meat from bones. Return meat to the broth. Add bacon, cayenne, sugar, salt, pepper, onion, tomatoes, potatoes and lima beans. Cook one hour. Add corn and continue to cook 10 minutes. Transfer to a buttered casserole. Add melted butter to bread crumbs, mix well, then sprinkle on top of stew. Bake 20 minutes at 375°F (190°C) till crumbs are golden brown. Serves six.
■ Northern Cookbook *(adapted)*

GAMEBURGER WIZARDRY

And, finally . . . gameburger. Know that animal? Most of the following recipes — all except those noted — are from a fine little book that is now out of print, Helen A. White's, What's Cookin' in Alaska. They are suitable for the ground meat of any game.

Russian Style Meatballs

1 large loaf of white bread
1 cup (240 mL) milk or more
1-1/2 pounds (0.70 kg) gameburger
2 eggs, slightly beaten
1 tablespoon (15 mL) dill, finely cut
Salt
Pepper
2 teaspoons (10 mL) Worcestershire
2 eggs, beaten
1/4 cup (60 mL) water, or less
Dry bread crumbs
Butter
1-1/2 cups (360 mL) sour cream

►Remove crusts from bread and break into chunks. Moisten with milk and allow to stand until soft. Combine burger with two beaten eggs, dill, salt, pepper and Worcestershire. If possible, use several kinds of burger such as moose, caribou and sheep. Add to the softened bread. Form into large loosely-packed balls. Mix the other two beaten eggs with the water. Dip the burgerballs into the mixture and then roll in crumbs. Saute in butter in heavy skillet until well browned. Place balls in a large casserole and pour pan drippings over them, along with the sour cream. Cover the casserole and bake in a 350°F (175°C) oven for 45 minutes.

Scrambled Gameburgers

Cooking oil
2 ounces (57 g) fresh pork or sausage, ground
3/4 pound (340 g) cariburger
Chili peppers, ground
Oregano
A bit of garlic, minced fine
Other seasoning to taste
2 to 3 tablespoons (30 to 45 mL) water
4 eggs, beaten well

►Brown pork and burger together in the oil. Mix in seasonings (in quantity to suit) and water and cook over low heat until all the moisture seems to be cooked away. Pour the beaten eggs over the contents of skillet; stir constantly with pancake turner until the eggs are set. Fine with green salad.

Broiled Gameburger Loaf

Sourdough French bread, 1 loaf
Margarine
1-1/2 pounds (0.70 kg) gameburger, any kind
1/2 cup (120 mL) chopped onion
1 teaspoon (5 mL) Worcestershire
1 teaspoon (5 mL) salt
Sliced onions

►Split the bread lengthwise. If you don't have sourdough French bread, use other French bread. Spread the cut surfaces with margarine. Combine burger with the chopped onion, Worcestershire and salt. Mix well. Spread this mixture liberally on the two half-loaves of bread, building up the edges a bit. Place bread on a cookie sheet 6 inches (15 cm) under the broiler and broil until meat is done. Garnish with raw onion slices.

Tomato Burger Loaf

1-1/2 pounds (0.70 kg) gameburger
2 cups (480 mL) dry bread crumbs
2/3 cup (160 mL) processed American cheese
1 onion, minced
Salt
Other seasonings to suit
1 can (8 oz /or/ 228 g) tomato sauce
2 eggs, beaten
1 green pepper, chopped fine

►Combine all ingredients in the order given, mixing well after each addition. Shape meat into two rounded loaves and place in greased shallow baking pan. Bake about one hour in a 350°F (175°C) oven or until well browned and done clear through. Serve hot with a meat sauce or Lowbush Cranberry Relish.

Stuffed Peppers

Peppers (1 per serving)
1/2 cup (120 mL) chopped onions
Olive oil
Gameburger
Green olives, chopped
Tomato sauce
Kernel corn
2 eggs, beaten slightly
Seasonings

►Remove tops from peppers and scoop out the innards. Chop half the tops with the onions. Saute in oil for five minutes. Remove from heat and mix in burger (moose, caribou, venison) and the remaining ingredients. Stuff the peppers with this and bake in a covered dish at 350°F (175°C) until peppers are tender. Uncover for the last 10 minutes to brown.

Broiled Burgers with Onions

1 large onion
Bacon drippings
2 tablespoons (30 mL) margarine
1 small onion, diced
Parsley
Salt
Pepper
1 egg
1/2 cup (120 mL) soft bread crumbs
1-1/2 pounds (0.70 kg) lean gameburger
Bacon strips

►Peel and slice the large onion. Arrange slices in a shallow baking pan. Pour melted bacon drippings over the slices and bake at 350°F (175°C) for 15 or 20 minutes. Remove from oven and set aside. Melt 2 tablespoons (30 mL) margarine and mix with diced small onion and remaining ingredients. Shape into six plump patties and wrap each with a strip of bacon secured with a toothpick. Brush with drippings and broil to taste, turning when necessary. Serve with onions.

Potato Burger Pudding

3 large potatoes, peeled
1 small onion
1 pound (456 g) gameburger
1/2 cup (120 mL) water
3 tablespoons (45 mL) butter, melted
1/2 cup (120 mL) hot milk
2 eggs, beaten slightly
Salt
Pepper
Bay leaf, crumbled

►Grind the potato and onion together. Add burger which has been crumbled and cooked in the water for 15 minutes. Add the other ingredients and pour into a buttered baking dish. Bake, uncovered, for 1-1/2 hours in a moderate oven — about 325 to 350°F (160 to 175°C).

Burger Steaks

Gameburger
2 tablespoons (30 mL) butter or margarine
1/2 teaspoon (2 mL) rosemary (optional)
1 tablespoon (15 mL) butter
1/4 teaspoon (1 mL) dry mustard
1/4 teaspoon (1 mL) Worcestershire
3 tablespoons (45 mL) cognac

►Form burger into patties of 1/4 pound (114 g) or more — large ones at any rate. Melt 2 tablespoons (30 mL) butter in heavy skillet. Add rosemary, if you have it. Put patties in melted butter and cook to your taste, turning as needed to brown. Remove meat to a hot platter. Add 1 tablespoon (15 mL) of butter to that in the skillet and the remaining ingredients, also. Mix and heat to blend but do not boil. Pour over patties before serving.

Meatballs Burgundy

1 pound (456 g) gameburger, any kind
1 large apple, peeled and shredded
1 egg, beaten
Salt and pepper
Flour
2 tablespoons (30 mL) cooking oil
1 small onion, diced
3/4 cup (180 mL) Burgundy wine
1/4 cup (60 mL) water
2 cans tomato sauce, 8 ounces (228 g), each
Herbs, your choice
1/4 teaspoon (1 mL) sugar

►Combine burger with shredded apples, egg, salt and pepper. Mix lightly and shape into balls; roll in flour. Heat oil in large heavy skillet and add meatballs and diced onion. Cook 10 minutes on fairly low heat or until meat is evenly browned. Mix wine and water and combine with tomato sauce, herbs and sugar. Pour over the meatballs and cover the skillet. Simmer gently for 20 minutes or until the meat is well done.

Layered Game Casserole

1 cup (240 mL) cooked rice
Greens
Salt
Pepper
2 cans (8 oz /or/ 228 g, each) tomato sauce
Water
1 cup (240 mL) chopped onions (or wild chives)
1/2 cup (120 mL) chopped green pepper
Venison, sheep or other game, ground
Bacon strips

►Place the rice in the bottom of a large baking dish. Add a layer of cooked greens such as spinach and sprinkle with salt and pepper. Pour over this one can of tomato sauce mixed with an equal amount of water. Add also the onions and green pepper. Then add a thick layer of ground game meat, either raw or leftover. Sprinkle it with the rest of the seasoning and the remainder of the chopped onions. Pour the other can of tomato sauce blended with a like amount of water over this. Top with several strips of bacon. Cover and bake for an hour at 350°F (175°C). Remove cover and bake for 30 minutes longer. This is an excellent one-dish meal. It is also a good way to use leftovers — rice, greens or meat.

Game-A-Roni
Or, with the right noodles, Alaskan Lasagne

1/4 cup (60 mL) chopped onion
2 cloves garlic, finely chopped
1/4 cup (60 mL) salad oil
2 pounds (1 kg) ground lean game meat
1 large can (29 oz /or/ 826 g) tomatoes
2 cans (8 oz /or/ 228 g, each) tomato sauce
2 teaspoons (10 mL) oregano
2 teaspoons (10 mL) salt (for sauce)
1/2 teaspoon (2 mL) pepper
5 quarts (4.8 L) boiling water
2 tablespoons (30 mL) salt (for pasta)
1 pound (456 g) lasagne noodles or macaroni
2 cups (480 mL) ricotta or creamed
    cottage cheese
1 pound (456 g) mozzarella cheese, sliced thin
1/2 cup (120 mL) grated Parmesan cheese

►Chop onion and garlic, add with meat to heated oil in frying pan. Mix and cook until meat is browned evenly and lightly. Add tomatoes, tomato sauce and spices. Simmer, stirring occasionally, about 45 minutes until mixture is reduced to consistency of sauce.

In a large pot, heat water to rolling boil; add salt and pasta. Cook until tender. Drain well and gently add in a few drops of oil to keep pasta from sticking together.

Grease a large flat pan, spread it with one-third of the meat sauce, then half the lasagne or macaroni, half the cottage cheese or ricotta, half the mozzarella and Parmesan, half the remaining meat sauce, the rest of the pasta; finally, the rest of the cheese topped by the rest of the meat sauce. Sprinkle additional Parmesan over the top. Bake at 350°F (175°C), 20 or 30 minutes or until bubbly. Cool 15 minutes, cut into squares and serve. Makes 12 servings.
■ Alaska's Game Is Good Food

Burger Supreme

2 pounds (1 kg) gameburger
1/4 pound (114 g) salt pork, ground
Salt and pepper
1 small can deviled ham
1/2 cup (120 mL) ground cabbage
3/4 cup (180 mL) dry bread crumbs
2 eggs, slightly beaten
3/4 cup (180 mL) milk
1 small onion, chopped
Bacon drippings

►Blend all ingredients except drippings and shape into plump patties. Fry in bacon drippings over low heat until well done — 45 minutes to one hour.

Sweet 'n' Sour Burgers

1 pound (456 g) burger
2 eggs, beaten
1/2 cup (120 mL) rice, cooked
1 small onion, minced
Sprigs of parsley, minced
Dash of garlic salt
Flour, seasoned with salt and pepper
2 tablespoons (30 mL) butter or margarine
1-1/2 cups (360 mL) mushroom soup, preheated
3 tablespoons (45 mL) brown sugar
1/4 cup (60 mL) vinegar
1 green pepper, diced
1 cup (240 mL) diced celery

►Combine burger, eggs, rice, onion, parsley and garlic salt. Blend and form into meatballs. Dredge with seasoned flour and brown in butter in a heavy skillet. When the meat is browned add to it the remaining ingredients and stir carefully to mix. Cover the skillet and allow to cook slowly for about 45 minutes. Uncover and cook 15 minutes more on low heat. This cooking may be done in the oven if you prefer.

Meat Pie with Potato Crust

3 eggs, hard-cooked
1/4 cup (60 mL) olive oil or other cooking oil
3/4 cup (180 mL) chopped onions
1-1/2 pounds (0.70 kg) gameburger
Chili peppers, ground
Other seasoning to taste
Meat stock
Green olives, chopped
Sprigs of parsley (or dried)
Mashed potatoes
1 egg, slightly beaten

►Heat olive oil in skillet and saute onions for five minutes. Mix in the gameburger and continue cooking until meat is well browned. Add seasoning including a bit of ground chili pepper, a little meat stock, olives and parsley. Spread half the mixture in a buttered casserole and slice the eggs over this. Put in the remaining meat mixture. Leftover mashed potatoes or those made from dehydrated will do. Beat egg into the potatoes and heap them on top of the meat in the casserole. Bake at 400°F (205°C) until the potatoes are nicely browned.

BOOK THREE

From The Earth

Introduction

Ask someone from South Carolina what Alaska's home-grown foods are and the reply is likely to start with "moose" or "salmon" or "king crab" or "I dunno' . . . snow ice cream?"

Nearly always, an Outsider's serious assessment of the food sources indigenous to our state will wind up naming four-legged, winged, finned or shelled creatures and likely overlook the great bounty that is earthbound. Rooted, to be exact.

However, the residents of few other states in the nation can LESS afford to overlook the food plants that grow on home soil than we can. We are a long, costly ways from California's lettuce and Florida's oranges and Iowa's corn and Nebraska's wheat and a Georgia peach (the tree-grown kind).

But cost is not even the primary factor in Alaska's special reason to seek out its own roots. Nutrition, satisfaction and taste are all more compelling ones.

The vegetables you pick from a remote meadow or from the garden plot at the side of the house are fresh, "vine-ripened" . . . not standardized to survive rough handling by mechanical pickers and long storage and shipment; still brimful of maximum flavor and nutrition . . . and not laced with pesticide.

As to Alaska's home-grown fruit, its abundance of berries, there is simply no way of comparing their flavor to that of imported fruit.

What About Nutritional Value?

Recently the National Academy of Sciences (NAS) released a report of their examination of various studies that have linked cancer and diet. The report contains little new information, but it clearly coordinates the message of many different researchers that there is a link: What we eat *does* alter our chances of contracting various kinds of cancer, especially those of the digestive system.

Two of the four major preventive steps we can take are good news to Alaskans who eat home-grown products. One: Lower the amount of fat you eat. Most game animals are leaner than domestic ones; our abundance of fish is also to our tremendous advantage in this regard.

And two: Eat vegetables and fruit and whole-grain products daily. Among the best vegetables are many that thrive in Alaskan gardens, the ones with four-petaled flowers *(Cruciferae)* — broccoli, cabbage, cauliflower, kohlrabi, kale and others. Also important are those loaded with vitamins A and C — carrots, the above-named vegetables and many berries. There is evidence to suggest, in fact, that rose hips increase in vitamin C content the farther north they are grown. Besides A and C vitamins, these plants also provide varying but often substantial quantities of thiamin, riboflavin, iron and potassium.

So collect yourself a year's supply of rose hips this fall and in the spring plant a long row of carrots and kale. And in the summer, well, nobody in Alaska needs much encouragement to enjoy summer's produce of wild greens and sweet berries, but the following chapters may help you identify some you've missed and add to your file of ways to prepare them.

Chapter 9

Wild Vegetables

IN THE FIELD

The plants considered edible are many and varied. Some varieties, however, are limited in quantity and scarcely worth the effort of collecting. Several of them, if available only in small quantities, can be used together to make a delectable salad. Others, such as fireweed, are plentiful enough to use by themselves. Gather these wild vegetables away from roads and dwellings in order to have them clean and dust free. Almost all the wild greens are best picked while young and eaten fresh or as soon as possible.

When harvesting wild plants for food try to get the youngest growth possible on foliage plants such as fireweed, nettles, goosefoot and other similar plants. The young leaves are not so apt to be bitter. Taste a raw leaf and you can tell whether or not they have a good flavor. Edible roots generally are gathered when mature, in the early fall.

Unfortunately, some wild plants are toxic, even deadly poisonous. On the following page is a list of such plants. This chapter is not meant as an identification guide, however. If you plan to do much foraging beyond the most familiar plants, it is wise to consult an extensive guide. Eric Hulten's *Flora of Alaska and Neighboring Territories; A Manual of the Vascular Plants* is the best. The Cooperative Extension Service at the University of Alaska has a handy pocket guide that could be used in conjunction with it — *Wild Edible and Poisonous Plants of Alaska.*

Still there is a relatively small number of poisonous plants — even mushrooms — considering the hundreds that are edible. The poisonous ones are knowable and avoidable, and there is much happy foraging to be found in the hills and dales of Alaska.

IN THE KITCHEN

Most wild greens can be used either raw or cooked. Try using some of them such as fireweed, sourdock or goosefoot cooked as you would wilted lettuce or spinach. (See the recipe Wilted Greens with Bacon Dressing, page 299.)

If your taste test of the leaves reveals that they are somewhat bitter but you still wish to use them, parboil them briefly through one or two preliminary waters first. Drain the greens each time, then finish cooking them to your taste.

Greens that have been gathered from sandy areas may need several rinsings. Lift the leaves from rinsing and cooking waters, rather than allowing the water to drain back through them to redeposit sand.

Use raw greens in various combinations in salads along with other forage items such as herbs, blossoms and seeds. At the end of this section are several salad and cooked greens recipes which share the special concoctions of various cooks.

To try out your own combinations, consider some of these plants as possible partners in a tossed salad: beach greens, birch leaves, cattail shoots, chickweed, chives, young dandelion greens, fiddleheads, fireweed, goose tongue, mushrooms, pink plume, roseroot, scurvy grass, seaweeds, sourdock and sourgrass, spiked saxifrage, strawberry spinach, violets, wild celery, wild cucumber, willow buds and winter cress.

Many wild plants can be preserved by freezing, canning, drying and pickling methods discussed in Chapter 14. Some plant-specific information, however, is included with the plant descriptions.

Alaskans have special reasons for learning to harvest plants that are available in the wild. The corner store is on a corner very removed from many of us, and when we get there, either the price or the quality (and likely both) of the imported produce is disheartening. What's more important yet was best described by C. R. Snow in 1935 (*The ALASKA SPORTSMAN®*):

> There are vegetables in our forests, and good ones, too. No mere desperate hope of the starving man are they, but relishful foods, worthy to share a plate with the fried trout or broiled venison beside any campfire. Test them on your home table this spring and summer. Then, when you unexpectedly prolong an outing beyond the time for which you packed provisions, you will know things helpful in keeping the belt buckle at its old accustomed place.

Good advice even now.

Some Poisonous Plants & Berries

Baneberry

The plants, *Actaea rubra* (red-berried) and *A. eburna* (white-berried), are known commonly as baneberry, snakeberry or mooseberry. They are to be found — and avoided! — along most of the southern coast, in Southeastern, Kenai Peninsula, Kodiak, Bristol Bay and in the upper Yukon valley. The plant is a perennial with a thick rootstock, smooth or slightly hairy stems, 2 to 4 feet (0.6 to 1.2 m) high, with large, thin, coarsely toothed and usually lobed leaves divided into three leaflets. Flowers in spiked clusters are small and white. The fruit is a round, red or white, several-seeded berry on a thick stalk which is red on the white-berried *A. eburna*. A beautiful berry, red or white or candy pink, it is DEADLY POISONOUS.

Narcissus-Flowered Anemone

Anemone narcissiflora, known as the narcissus-flowered anemone, or at least some members of the family, contain anemonine, a mildly poisonous substance. The early spring growth on the upper end of the root is sometimes eaten, but it is not recommended.

Poison Water Hemlock

Cicuta mackenziana, *C. maculata* and *C. douglasii*, or poison water hemlock, can also be deadly poisonous. A small portion of the root will cause death within a few hours; poison is present but not so concentrated in the remainder of the plant. There is some chance of survival if free vomiting can be produced promptly, followed by a cathartic.

The worst thing about poison water hemlock is that the unwary may confuse it with several widely used, edible plants. Please see page 296 for the discussion of the wild celeries (*Angelica lucida*, *Ligusticum scoticum*, *L. hultenii*), cow parsnip (*Heracleum lanatum*) and how they can be differentiated from poison water hemlock.

Wild Sweet Pea

Hedysarum mackenzii, or wild sweet pea, grows up to 1-1/2 feet (45 cm) tall. The stems are erect and minutely hairy; leaves in small, rounded leaflets, smooth above, grayish hairy underneath; flowers rose to purple, showy and fragrant. Reported to be toxic, though it has an edible cousin, *Hedysarum alpinum*, the Eskimo potato, also called *mashu* or *muhzut*.

Nootka Lupine

Lupinus nootkatensis, or Nootka lupine, is a perennial plant with a long taproot which supports clustered and branched stems that may grow up to 3-1/2 feet (1 m). Flowers grow in dense clusters that

BEACH ASPARAGUS

Unfortunately not a common plant, the beach asparagus or glasswort (*Salicornia* species) is found on some Southeastern Alaska beaches.

Preparation Tips: Young plants can be used in salads as you would raw asparagus tips. Or, the plant — all above the roots — may be boiled and served hot with a butter sauce or chilled and served with salad dressing.

■ *C.R. Snow*
"Vegetables of the Alaska Wilderness"
The ALASKA SPORTSMAN®, *April 1935*

A good way to keep mosquitoes from biting is to rub yarrow (*Achillea borealis*) on skin and clothing. Bugs don't like the strong smell.

BEACH GREENS

Also known as Eskimo kraut, seabeach sandwort and sea chickweed, this sprawling, thickly matted plant (*Honckenya peploides* or *Arenaria peploides*) hugs rocky or sandy beaches just above tide line along almost all coasts. Stems may grow up to 2 feet (60 cm) long and are covered with bright green leaves. Flowers are tiny and greenish white.

Preparation Tips: Picked before the plants flower, the leaves are quite juicy and sweet and make an excellent addition to green salads. Use as you would watercress. The best months for gathering young greens are the summer ones. Eskimos sometimes add beach greens to other plants which are cooked, soured and used as one ingredient in Eskimo ice cream. They may also be made into a sort of kraut.

Beach greens may be frozen for later use

---

may be 10 inches (25 cm) long at the end of the stem. Flowers have five petals, blue or shaded pink or white, that eventually produce black, hairy legumes about an inch to 1-1/2 inches (2.5 to 3.75 cm) long. The plant grows on hillsides and open fields in the southern half of the state.

The roots of this plant are gathered by Aleuts in the fall. The skin is carefully scraped off and they are eaten either raw or boiled. But it is said that eating too many can cause discomfort, and some lupines have been known to be fatal to animals that have fed on them.

Locoweed

The plants, *Astragalus* and *Oxytropis*, known as vetch or locoweed, are familiar perennials that grow in fair abundance throughout Alaska — on hillsides, in mountain areas, meadows and tundra. Not all the species are toxic, but it is difficult to distinguish between them and, because a mistake may result in death, it is best to steer clear of all of them.

False Hellebore

This stout-stemmed perennial, *Veratrum eschscholtzii*, or false hellebore, grows up to 8 feet tall (2.4 m). It has a thick rootstock and alternate leaves that are broad and oval-shaped with a quite pointed tip. Small, greenish flowers grow in spike-like clusters with drooping branches. The plant grows in swampy areas in the southern portion of the state. It is known to be fatal to animals who have fed on it. Death results from asphyxia.

Death Camas

Zygadenus elegans, or death camas, is a perennial that grows from a bulb. It somewhat resembles the narcissus, with smooth, leafy stems up to 2 feet (60 cm) high; alternate, long, narrow, flat leaves that clasp the stem and greenish white flowers with three petals that grow in loose terminal clusters. It is found in most of the Interior. All parts of this plant are DEADLY, causing salivation, nausea, vomiting, lowered temperature, breathing difficulty and coma.

Amanita

What is missing from this list are poisonous mushrooms, of which there are several, the deadly *Amanita* species having the most bad press. The *Amanita muscaria*, or fly agaric, is the most poisonous mushroom in Alaska and one of the most attractive, its cap often brilliantly colored red, orange or scarlet. Mushroom gathering requires expert advice. Some guidebooks are suggested in the recipe section.

following the directions for garden greens. The small black seeds can be gathered and used as an extension for flour.

Steamed Beach Greens
A real treat for anyone who likes garden greens

►Use only the leaves and leaf clusters. Rinse with cold water and then steam them by placing in a small amount of boiling water, lightly salted, for two or three minutes. Drain and toss with butter for a delicious vegetable dish.

■ *Nancy J. Torsen, "Beach Greens"*
  Alaskan Edibles series ALASKA® magazine
  Alaska-only edition, July 1980

BIRCH

The white birch (*Betula papyrifera*) thrives throughout southern Alaska and is often planted as an ornamental. Its early spring leaves are edible. They can be dried and made into tea, boiled as a green or made into a salad. Use only the smaller leaves; the larger ones are bitter after cooking. The reproductive catkins (tiny, drooping tassels) may also be eaten when young before they turn brown.

Birch Leaf Salad

1 cup (240 mL) young, tiny birch leaves
1 cup (240 mL) catkins
1 head loose-leaf lettuce, torn in bite-size pieces
6 hard-cooked eggs, sliced
2-1/2 tablespoons (38 mL) red wine vinegar
1/2 cup (120 mL) salad oil
1 tablespoon (15 mL) prepared mustard
Salt and pepper to taste
1 garlic clove, mashed

►Mix leaves, catkins, sliced eggs and lettuce. Mix the remaining ingredients to form a dressing. Just before serving, toss salad with dressing.

■ *Ann Chandonnet (descriptive text*
  and recipe), "Alaska's Plentiful
  (And Tasty) Wild Foods"
  ALASKA® magazine, July 1976

Birch Bark Sandwich

►When the Russians first came to Alaska they found some of the Natives used pieces of the inner bark of birch to make a sort of sandwich with meat. The inner bark is very good to chew at any time of year.

■ *Florence V.J. Thornton, Rabbit Creek*

Birch Juice and Birch Syrup

►Collect birch juice in the spring when the sap begins to run — sometimes as early as mid- to late April. Select a large tree with a low branch about the diameter of your finger. The juice from small trees is quite bitter.

Use a sterilized bottle — liquid shortening, ketchup, juice or another kind with a small neck. Cut the branch you've selected up to the point where the portion left on the tree will be the desired diameter. Push the bottle onto it about an inch (2.5 cm) or so into the neck. Take a small piece of the branch you've cut and whittle a stopper to help hold the bottle securely on the tree limb.

Many bottles may be hung on one tree, but if you live in a well-populated area, you will find that conspicuous bottles are sometimes targets for restless children. A juice hole may also be bored into the trunk of the tree, but this method of using a tree limb will keep the tree living longer.

While the sap is dripping, the bottles should be emptied every 12 hours or oftener. Be sure to sterilize them before returning them to the tree. Do not leave the bottles out in the rain. Even a small amount of rain water in the bottles will quickly sour the juice.

The juice stops dripping the day the leaves unfurl, but it will drip very fast for several days before this.

Strain the juice through a coffee filter or clean

cloth and refrigerate immediately. Sip the juice to enjoy its real flavor. Excess juice may be frozen in ice cube trays and stored in the freezer for later use. Old-timers, prospectors and Natives swear that birch juice is one of the best tonics humans can get in the early spring.

To make birch syrup, boil the juice down to about one/one-hundredth part. This takes a long time and requires careful watching. When the juice begins to thicken, it must be stirred constantly. It takes about 12 hours to boil 25 gallons (95 L) of juice down to 1 quart (1 L) when done outside on a wood fire. The syrup can be boiled down even further to make brown sugar, but most folks do not stir it enough and so burn it. Both birch syrup and sugar have a maple taste and either one makes an excellent "birch sundae" topping.
■ *Florence V.J. Thornton, Rabbit Creek*

Birch Sap

►The sap of the birch tree is known by the Dena'inas as *k'ti, k'ezak'* and *k'eyek'*. It is both their medicine and their spring tonic. Collect the sap in the late spring and summer when it is running well. There are two ways to do it. The old-time way is to peel back the bark and scrape or suck the sap off of the wood. The newer way is to make a small hole in the tree and catch the sap in a bucket as it drips out. Either way the sap tastes delicious. It was especially welcome to the old-timers who didn't have any fresh vegetables to eat all through the winter. It gave them some vitamins they probably needed a lot in the spring.
■ *Dena'ina K'et'una, Tanaina Plantlore*

CATTAIL

This familiar plant, also known as Cossack asparagus, flags or bulrushes, grows in marshes and shallow ponds and along the banks of streams. Cattails *(Typha latifolia)* grow from 3 to 9 feet tall (0.9 to 2.7 m). The leaves are slender, flat and gracefully spiked. Flowers also form in spikes, the lower part — the closely packed female flowers —are at first green, turning in the fall to the familiar dark brown shape that gives the plant its best-known name, cattail. Uppermost flowers — male ones — turn light brown or wheat-colored until they finally drop their pollen as the plants mature.
Preparation Tips: Nearly all parts can be eaten at varying times of the year. During the late fall and winter, cattail roots are a good source of starch and may be cooked just like potatoes, boiled and

mashed, fried or roasted. Season the same way, too.

Along the Don River — Cossack country in southern Russia — the stems are peeled and eaten raw. Pick as far down on the stalk as possible and use only the lower foot (30 cm) or so. Peeled, the stalks are good either raw or briefly steamed or boiled and seasoned with salt or lemon juice. The newest tender shoots are good raw in salads. When the flower spikes are still young — before the pollen begins to show — they can be eaten much like corn on the cob: husk, boil or steam, season with butter and salt.

CHICKWEED

This plant with the pesky reputation belongs to the pink family and is a many-branched plant that grows on creeping stems that root at the nodes (which are also many). According to a weed control booklet put out by the University of Alaska Extension Service, chickweed *(Stellaria media)* is "the most troublesome annual weed in Alaska gardens," and it outlines several ways to kill it. Well, we suggest another way to control it:

Invite it in for lunch.

Here's a couple of recipes. Chickweed can also be made into a medicinal tea. (See How To Brew A Wild Cup of Tea.)

Chickweed Salad

►Chickweed makes a good addition to green salad if the upper, younger and more tender parts of the plant are used.

Creamed Chickweed

►Parboil a nice bunch of fresh chickweed. Strain and chop fine. Heat again, adding a little milk and butter. Salt and pepper to taste and serve hot.
■ *Both suggestions from*
  Cooking Up A Storm, *Homer*

CHIVES

Of all the wild vegetables, perhaps the most widely used plant is wild chives *(Allium schoenoprasum)*. The leaves are used in innumerable ways. They are tubular and similar in appearance to the leaves of green onions. They may be dried and minced or may be used fresh or frozen. They are easily transplanted to the home garden where they will be handy to harvest. They can be used in any dish that calls for onions and they have quite a strong flavor when fresh.

To dry chives, collect the leaves where they are free from dust and will not need washing. With kitchen scissors, snip the leaves into small pieces. Use only the upper portions and do not use the stem which is coarse and tough. Spread the snipped pieces on a cookie sheet or tray and place trays in a barely warm oven with the door slightly ajar. This allows moisture to escape. Dry the chives until the pieces are brittle enough to crush easily between your fingers. Store in small containers with tight covers after chives are completely cooled. Empty spice jars are good for this.

Wild chives that have been transplanted to the home garden may be cut and snipped several times in a season as they will continue to send up new foliage all summer.

Baked Potatoes and Wild Chives

►Cream one stick (114 g) margarine or butter with 2 tablespoons (30 mL) wild chives snipped quite fine. Keep at room temperature for easy handling. Bake potatoes until soft when squeezed. This will take 45 minutes to one hour, depending on size of potatoes. When potatoes are done, cut a cross shape about a third of the way into each potato on the "top" side. Squeeze gently to allow steam to escape and to make a nest for the chive butter. Put a big spoonful of the creamy mixture in the cut. A few bacon bits can be sprinkled on top, if desired.

Scalloped Potatoes and Wild Chives

►Prepare a casserole of scalloped potatoes in your usual way and then stir in a handful of chopped wild chives, fresh or dried. Try using sour cream as part of the liquid in the dish, too.

Biscuits with Wild Chives

►Use your favorite baking powder mix. When prepared, roll out thin to the size of hot cakes. Put a small spoonful of chopped, sauteed wild chives on one side and fold over like a turnover. Seal edges by dampening with milk and pinching together. Bake for 10 to 12 minutes in a 450°F (230°C) oven. May be prepared ahead of time and then heated in foil just before serving.
■ *The Old Homesteader*

Chive Vegetable Dip

1 pint (0.47 L) sour cream
2 teaspoons (10 mL) finely minced chives

2 teaspoons (10 mL) instant beef bouillon
1/4 teaspoon (1 mL) garlic salt

►Use the finely cut hollow leaves of wild chives for this recipe. Mix all ingredients together and let stand for 30 minutes. Stir well before serving as a dip for crisp, raw vegetables or as a garnish for baked potatoes.
■ *Janese Chrystal*
 Gold Rush Cookbook, *Valdez*

Eggs with Wild Chives

Butter
Wild chives
Milk
Ham
Eggs
Seasoning to taste

►Use about a small handful of chives and four eggs to each couple of people. Probably 1 tablespoon (15 mL) of milk to each egg will be about enough. Trim any fat off the ham and put in heavy frying pan to render. When fat is rendered, add butter to make enough to saute ham, cut in small bits. When ham is cooked, add the chopped chives and cook, stirring, until chives are limp. Do not brown them. Beat eggs and milk together and season. I use crushed red pepper flakes, salt and pepper. Pour over ham and chives in skillet and cook over medium heat briefly. When bottom appears to be set, turn so that all parts can set. Cook as much as you wish now. Some people prefer these quite moist; others want them drier. Serve with plenty of hot buttered toast and Wild Currant Jelly.
■ *The Old Homesteader*

COLTSFOOT

Sweet coltsfoot *(Petasites frigidus)* is a coarse plant found in moist tundra and along streams. It abounds in such situations in most of Alaska except for the Kenai Peninsula and Southeastern. Its purplish white flowers form in a head at the top of stout stalks. The shiny green leaves make a thick cluster at the base and are quite large, often attaining a length of 10 inches (25 cm) or more at maturity.

Preparation Tips: The leaves should be collected while small and still young enough to be tender. They are gathered by Eskimos to eat with other greens. It is reported that Siberian Eskimos dig the creeping roots and roast them for a favored dish.

Flavorful Leaves

►The leaves of coltsfoot are among the most tender and subtly flavored of the leaves we tried. We ate these delightful shoots at every opportunity, frequently sauteed with other young buds and mixed with grayling.

■ *Jim Greenough and Eileen Helmstetter*
"The Bush Gourmet"
ALASKA® magazine, July 1977

D A N D E L I O N

Both the descriptive text and the recipe Dandelion Sallet are excerpted and adapted from an ALASKA® magazine story by Ann Chandonnet.

Dandelion *(Taraxacum officinale)* greens must be eaten very young, before any flowers are visible and even before you can see buds in the center of the plant. In an early Alaskan spring, they may be ready the first week in April. In a late spring, gather sometime in May. Dig dandelion greens with a trowel, inserting it beneath the leaves of the plant and severing across horizontally at ground level. The younger the plant, the less bitter the taste.

Preparation Tips: The most tedious part of preparing dandelions is washing them. You may need to soak them six or eight times to remove all the dirt. Pick out the dry brown leaves and grass as you wash. Don't let the water in the sink drain off the greens at each rinse. Lift the greens out, then let the water out; this way the dirt doesn't sift down through the greens as the water drains.

The most common cooking method is to boil dandelions in salted water (with or without salt pork) until tender. Eat hot, with butter, or cold with a little vinegar or ketchup sprinkled on them. Dandelions are high in vitamin A, and the next day you'll see how shiny they have made your hair.

The dandelion is one of a host of weeds (like pigweed, lamb's-quarters, dock, upland cress) that colonials relished as spring tonics after a long winter without fresh foods. Here is a dandelion recipe from the 1700s.

Dandelion Sallet

4 cups (1 L) tender, young dandelion greens, washed
4 slices bacon
3 tablespoons (45 mL) vinegar
2 teaspoons (10 mL) sugar
1/2 teaspoon (2 mL) salt
1/4 teaspoon (1 mL) dry mustard
Black pepper, coarsely ground

►Shred the greens. In a skillet, fry bacon until crisp. Remove bacon, leaving the fat, and drain on paper towels. Crumble the bacon over the drained, raw greens. To the bacon fat, add the vinegar, sugar, salt, mustard and pepper. Heat the mixture and pour over the greens and bacon. Toss until the greens are wilted. Serve at once. Yields six servings.

■ *Ann Chandonnet*
"Alaska's Plentiful (And Tasty) Wild Foods"
ALASKA® magazine, July 1976

Dandelion Fritters

►First thing in the morning pick the blossoms, snapping them off close to the head (stems are bitter). Sprinkle liberally with salt, cover with cold water and let stand for several hours. Rinse to remove salt and bugs. Drain well. Then make a good batter, using a couple of eggs in a pancake mix. Drop a single blossom, covered with batter, into hot fat. Fry until golden brown. Drain, sprinkle lightly with salt. Can be served hot or cold. Try them!

■ *Velma Parks*
Susitna Valley Chronicle
Reprinted from The Cabin Friend
ALASKA® magazine, March 1977

We have found something handier than a trowel for digging wild plants for your garden. We use a dandelion digger. It is especially good among rocks or in rocky soil where many of the little "jewels" seem to grow.

■ *The Old Homesteader*

Dandelions and Salt Pork

►Gather young dandelion leaf rosettes before the blossom stems have formed. Also collect any flower buds of the dandelions. Wash these in several changes of cool water. Place in a large kettle, cover with boiling water and bring to a boil. Cook over medium heat for 10 minutes. Drain and partially cover with salted water. Slice salt pork down almost to the rind and add it to the greens. Cover the kettle and cook on low heat for an hour. Finish cutting the slices of pork and arrange them around the greens in a serving dish. About 2 pounds (1 kg) greens should be used for every 1/4 pound (114 g) salt pork.

Dandelion Omelet

►Gather buds of dandelions before color begins to show. Fry buds in a little butter until they pop. Add four beaten eggs and flavor with salt and pepper. Top with chopped raw, young dandelion leaves before serving.

■ Cooking Up A Storm, *Homer*

ESKIMO POTATO

Caution: There is a look-alike but poisonous cousin.

The Eskimo potato (*Hedysarum alpinum*) makes good eating, but it is not to be confused with another member of the family which it much resembles. The so-called wild sweet pea (*Hedysarum mackenzii*) is reported to be poisonous and the two plants are so similar in appearance that anyone but a botanist might be confused. The territories of the two species are much the same, too, adding to the uncertainty. It is probably best not to collect this plant unless you are sure of the identification. Further confusion results from the fact that the Eskimo potato is known by several names — Indian potato, licorice root, alpine sweet vetch, bear root, *mashu* and *muhzut*.

The Eskimo potato grows in some abundance in many parts of Alaska and may be discovered almost anywhere in the state except the Alaska Peninsula, Aleutian Islands and lower portion of Southeastern. It is found across Canada to the Atlantic. It seems to prefer a varied habitat: rocky slopes, stream banks, fields, gravel bars are all home to the Eskimo potato.

The pealike flowers are rose, aging to purple and the multiple leaves are arranged opposite each other on the stems. It is the root which is an important food item for Native Alaskans. They are sometimes several feet long in a mature plant and often as large as a small carrot.

Preparation Tips: Both Eskimos and Indians once collected the roots by the bushel and some still make good use of them. They are gathered in the fall or spring (they will overwinter in the ground if unmolested). They are eaten raw, roasted or boiled. One good method of preparing them is to dice the roots and boil them with a ham bone, diced ham or bacon.

Mice are said to collect the smaller roots and store them in caches for winter use. Bears dig for them avidly, too.

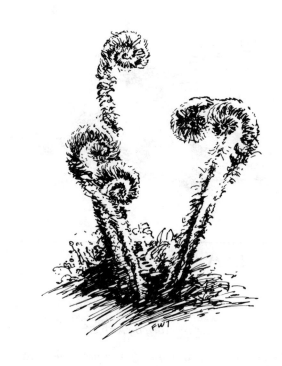

FERN FIDDLEHEADS OR FIDDLENECKS

Caution: Do not eat mature plants — those with fully-opened fronds — of pasture brake or western bracken (Pteridium aquilinum), *known to be poisonous to livestock at this stage. The following information and the recipe Beer and Cheese Dunk are excerpted and adapted from an ALASKA® magazine story by Ann Chandonnet.*

A fiddlehead or fiddleneck is the new leaf or frond of certain edible ferns: ostrich ferns, cinnamon ferns, pasture brake or western bracken, hayscented ferns or evergreen wood ferns. When the new leaves first develop in the spring, they are coiled like the upper part of a bass fiddle or a violin, and, in this young state, are crunchy in texture, sweet in flavor and definitely delicious.

Fern tops remain in the fiddlehead stage for several days and can be found along the edges of northern streams and lakes. They are considered delicacies in Canada.

Preparation Tips: In general, pick when curled, young, tender and about 8 inches (20 cm) tall. Wash thoroughly and serve raw as a salad, dressed with vinegar and/or lemon juice. To steam, barely cover with salted water and boil three to five minutes; serve hot with salt and pepper and desired condiments.

Fiddleheads of the ostrich fern (*Matteuccia struthiopteris*, or *Pteretis pensylvanica*) are much preferred. The largest of the ferns, it reaches a height of 2 to 6 feet (0.6 to 1.8 m) when mature. The leaves grow in dense clumps, looking much like the clusters of plumes worn by circus horses. The best time to pick ostrich fiddleheads is when they are 3 to 6 inches (7.5 to 15 cm) high, while the heads are still curled and firm. Rub the fuzzy brown covering off by hand, then wash. Eat raw on the spot, at home in salad, or saute or steam.

Pasture brake or bracken fern is the most common American fern. In contrast to the ostrich fern, it grows in single fronds spread along an underground stem (rhizome), giving the appearance of scattered plants. Like okra, pasture brake has a mucilaginous quality that can be used to thicken meat stews.

Collect pasture brake when shoots are less than 1 foot (30 cm) high, preferably 6 to 8 inches (15 to 20 cm). Choose fronds that have not completely unfurled. Break off woody base as far up as it will snap off. Rub off woolly covering.

After harvesting fiddleheads, prepare them as soon as possible. If you must hold them for any length of time, cover with crushed ice and refrigerate. Keep ferns dry until you have cleaned them, removing any brown covering and sticks and leaves. If the ferns are wet when gathered, the brown covering and other foreign material can be removed by gently washing the ferns in several changes of cool water.

Fiddleheads are best when eaten fresh, but they can be preserved for a midwinter treat:

- *Freezing* — Blanch cleaned fiddleheads in boiling water for two minutes or less. Cool in ice water several minutes. Drain well, place family-size servings in plastic bags and freeze immediately.
- *Canning* — Blanch as for freezing. Process like other greens, green beans or green vegetables.

- *Steaming* — Don't overcook; two minutes is sufficient for frozen fiddleheads; four to five minutes for tender fresh ones, 10 minutes for ostrich ferns, 30 to 60 minutes for tougher pasture brake. Serve hot with butter and lemon juice, white (cream) sauce, pan drippings or Hollandaise sauce.

Fiddleheads are considered a gourmet food, so count yourself lucky to live in an area where they are free for the taking. Why buy wilted lettuce from California when you can garner both exercise and free, undeniably fresh vegetables by gathering fiddleheads?

Note: Fiddlenecks are sometimes difficult to part from their fuzzy and bitter brown covering. Some cooks try picking it off or scrubbing it away with a bristle brush. Mark White, another connoisseur of fiddlenecks, however, says he tries to find wood ferns (*Dryopteris austriaca* or *D. dilitata*) with a minimum of brown covering to begin with, and he eats them without cleaning them. There is a great variation in the amount of bitter taste, too, he says. Some wood ferns require only a light boiling to make them sweet tasting, while others growing almost alongside are better if treated with two or three changes of boiling water. His recipe for Buttered Fiddlenecks is on the next page.

Beer and Cheese Dunk
For fiddleheads and other fresh raw vegetables

3/4 cup (180 mL) beer
3/4 pound (340 g) sharp Cheddar, diced finely,
  or 3 cups (720 mL) grated cheese
2 teaspoons (10 mL) cornstarch
1 tablespoon (15 mL) beer
8 slices crusty bread, quartered
1 large green pepper, seeded and
  cut into wedges
1 small raw cauliflower, separated into florets
2 dozen cleaned fiddleheads
1 pint (0.47 L) cherry tomatoes,
  rinsed and drained

►In a large saucepan, bring 3/4 cup (180 mL) beer to a boil; add cheese and cook over moderate heat, stirring constantly until cheese melts. In a small cup, blend cornstarch with 1 tablespoon (15 mL) beer; stir this mixture into heated beer and cheese, stirring constantly, and boil until thickened and smooth. Reduce heat to low and simmer one minute longer.

Serve in a heated bowl or chafing dish,

surrounded by fiddleheads, bread squares and other raw vegetables; or divide evenly amongst four servings. Good with more beer.

■ *Ann Chandonnet*
"Fiddleheads: Ferns for the Pot"
Alaskan Edibles series
ALASKA® magazine, June 1977

Fiddleheads with Vegetable Salad

1 cup (240 mL) diced fresh fiddlehead ferns or
*   partly thawed frozen ferns*
1 cup (240 mL) finely shredded carrots
1 cup (240 mL) finely diced celery
1 cup (240 mL) thinly sliced cauliflower
1/2 cup (120 mL) thinly sliced radishes
1/4 cup (60 mL) chopped green onion
1/2 cup (120 mL) French dressing or
*   tart mayonnaise*

►Combine all ingredients with the dressing or mayonnaise, toss lightly and serve in a lettuce cup.
■ The Frontiersman, *Palmer*

Fiddleneck "Bananas"
From the spreading wood fern

►The old leaf stalks on the underground stem of a spreading wood fern *(Dryopteris austriaca)* resemble a bunch of minute bananas. For centuries the Indians of Southeast Alaska and the Eskimos of the Bristol Bay and Lower Kuskokwim region have put them to use. The old stalks are roasted, then the outer shiny brown covering is removed and the inner portion is eaten. They are a source of energy.
■ Wild Edible and Poisonous Plants of Alaska

Buttered Fiddlenecks

►To cook fiddlenecks, we drop them in boiling, lighty salted water for six to eight minutes, drain them quickly and serve them with a side dish of melted butter. They seem to taste better when individually dipped in butter and popped into the mouth. Some folks also boil them lightly and marinate them for a few days, serving them as salad. The taste is somewhere between an artichoke and asparagus.
■ *Mark White*
"We Feast on Fiddlenecks"
ALASKA® magazine, June 1974

Note: This cook also says that "the small pods left from last year's leaf stalks and those clinging to the main root" — the "bananas" referred to in the preceding recipe — are among his favorite parts of the spreading wood fern.

Fiddleheads and Bacon Bits

3 cups (720 mL) fresh or frozen fiddlehead
*   ferns, cleaned*
1/2 cup (120 mL) water
Dash of seasoned salt
1 tablespoon (15 mL) snipped wild chives
2 tablespoons (30 mL) or more bacon bits
Dash of pepper
Dash of lemon juice

►Bring water to a boil and add salt and fiddleheads. Again bring to a boil and boil just four minutes without stirring. Drain and gently stir in the remaining ingredients. Serve with toast points.
■ The Frontiersman, *Palmer*

Baked Fiddleheads

Fiddlehead ferns
2 to 3 tablespoons (30 to 45 mL) butter
3 tablespoons (45 mL) flour
Pinch of salt
1/2 cup (120 mL) cream
1 cup (240 mL) vegetable water
1 egg yolk, beaten
2 tablespoons (30 mL) grated Parmesan
1/2 cup (120 mL) bread crumbs

►Collect fiddleheads in springtime. Wash fern heads and cook in boiling salted water until partly cooked. For the sauce, melt butter, stir in flour, salt, cream and a cup of the water in which the fiddleheads were cooked. Add beaten egg yolk and cheese. Stir until cheese melts. In greased ovenproof dish alternate layers of fiddleheads, sauce and a sprinkle of cheese. Sprinkle final layer with bread crumbs. Bake at 375°F (190°C) for 20 minutes.
■ *Jeanne McArthur*
Cooking Up A Storm, *Homer*

Sauteed Fiddleheads

24 or so fiddleheads
4 tablespoons (60 mL) butter
Salt to taste

►Melt butter in pan. Heat until butter is hot but not yet smoking. Add cleaned fiddleheads. Allow to saute in the butter, turning frequently, until they start to soften. Salt lightly and serve immediately with sourdough biscuits or hot toast.
■ Valdez Vanguard

Fiddleheads with Cheese Sauce

►Cook fiddlehead ferns as you would broccoli or Brussels sprouts. Prepare the cheese sauce as follows: Melt grated cheese very slowly over hot water in the top of a double boiler. Add a few chopped pimentos, black pepper, dash of salt and a little dry mustard. Pour over the fiddleheads at serving time.

■ *Helen A. White*
  "Far North Fare"
  ALASKA® *magazine, December 1974*

Hot Dressing For Fiddleheads

4 slices bacon, cut fine
4 tablespoons (60 mL) vinegar
1 cup (240 mL) thin cream
2 eggs, beaten

►Drop fiddleheads into boiling, salted water and cook without stirring four minutes. Drain. Brown bacon in skillet, add vinegar, stir and keep warm. In the top of a double boiler over hot water, heat cream and eggs together; add bacon mixture gradually. Cook over the hot water until thick. Pour over fiddleheads while still hot and serve.

■ The Frontiersman, *Palmer (adapted)*

FIREWEED

A prolific and showy plant with beautiful purple or rosy to pink flowers, fireweed *(Epilobium angustifolium)* is common along roadsides, in meadows, on open hillsides or recently burned-over forest throughout the North Country. It is also sometimes called great willow herb.

Preparation Tips: Collect in the spring before the plants fully mature, as the leaves eventually become tough and bitter. The newest shoots substitute for asparagus and can be used with other young greens in salad. Peel young stems and eat them raw, as is or chopped up in salad. Or blanch them and serve with dressing. Later on, the leaves can be gathered and prepared as you would spinach. If they are inclined to bitterness, precook them briefly in a small amount of water, pour it off, add fresh water and cook just until tender. Season to taste with margarine or butter, salt, pepper and vinegar or lemon juice. Fireweed is a good source of vitamin C and pro-vitamin A.

Homesteader's Honey
Easy to make and delicious!

2-1/2 cups (600 mL) water
30 red clover blossoms
30 white clover blossoms
18 fireweed blossoms (1 or 2 stalks)

Fireweed

10 cups (2.25 L) sugar
1 teaspoon (5 mL) alum

►Wash blossoms in a colander to remove dust and bugs; place blossoms in large pan with water and bring to a boil. Remove from heat, cover and let steep for 10 minutes, like tea. Bring to boil again, adding sugar and alum; boil for 10 minutes. Strain and pour into small, sterilized jars and seal. Yield is about half a gallon (1.9 L). Run right out in the backyard and get your ingredients!

■ *Laurie Reeve*
  The Willawa, *Reeve Aleutian Airways*
  Reprinted from The Cabin Friend
  ALASKA® *magazine, July 1976*

Fireweed Omelet

►Steam young fireweed leaves until tender. Meanwhile, dice and fry some bacon, then add the drained greens and mix in two beaten eggs. Simmer for five minutes.

■ *Iva Senft, as told to Mary J. Barry*
  "Camp Cookery, Trail Tonics, and
  Indian Infants"
  ALASKA SPORTSMAN®, *July 1964*

How To Brew A Wild Cup of Tea

Pat Monaghan of Fairbanks describes some of the many brews to be made from Alaskan herbs.

In early summer, as arctic shrubs unfold bright new leaves, your thoughts should turn to the dark Alaska winter ahead. For June is the month to gather and dry your collection of Alaska herbs. A couple of afternoons of picking will give you enough to last all winter — and will give pleasure each time you brew a steaming cup that releases delicate summer smells into cold, chapped nostrils.

Easy to find, gather, dry and store, arctic beverage herbs are a boon to the Alaska householder. And there are many more varieties than the familiar tea plant, or Labrador tea. You can buy them, under fancier names and at fancier prices, at any health food store, but save your pennies and enjoy an afternoon in the woods instead.

I've priced packaged versions of the herbs gathered in just one week, and found I'd saved about $20 by picking and drying these plants myself. Some also argue that it's healthier to use local plants for tea because they are fresh.

How To Dry, Store and Brew Alaskan Teas

This is not a definitive list of the useful tea herbs of Alaska. These are, however, widely available and mild in flavor. (It's no good to gather something, however prolific, if it tastes like medicine and you can't bring yourself to drink it.) Most should be gathered before blooms appear. All dry quickly, some within two days; just spread them out on paper towels or cookie sheets, turn them over several times a day, and crumble as you pack to remove extra stems. Store in tightly sealed containers away from heat. To use, brew as you would any tea: boiling water poured over the herb, a few minutes of steeping, some added honey or sugar if you wish.

Bearberry

You'll find this one in health food stores as "uva ursi," which is a shortened form of its Latin name, *Arctostaphylos uva-ursi*. It's known in Alaska as kinnikinnik as well as bearberry; be sure of the identification before you pick, as bearberry is the common name for several Alaska berry plants.

The useful bearberry is a little ground-creeping shrub, easiest to find in fall when its leaves turn a deep russet. In spring, its oval leaves are borne on erect stems 6 to 10 inches (15 to 25 cm) high, changing from reddish green to a shiny dark green as the season progresses. The plants have five-pointed white flowers in little clusters and later will bear bright red berries which, while edible, are not particularly tasty.

The leaves are renowned in herbal manuals as a tonic for the urinary system, said to cleanse the kidneys, bladder and urinary tract. Highly astringent, tea made from bearberry leaves is an effective remedy for chronic cystitis (and cheaper than cranberry juice, the usually prescribed remedy). Somewhat medicinal in taste, bearberry leaves should be gathered in autumn, just before they turn red, for best effect.

Camomile

Herbalists debate whether the "pineapple weed" that grows along Alaska's railbelt is "the real camomile," but unless you're a purist, *Matricaria matricarioides* is real enough to qualify. It's a little ground clinging plant with chartreuse lacy leaves, which produces knobby green buds with a strong pineapple scent.

Gather these buds before they open; be careful to pick from patches as distant as possible from car exhaust. Tea made from the dried buds is intensely flavorful; brew it by infusing the buds with boiling water, rather than boiling the buds themselves. Boiling allows the healthful volatile oils of the plant to evaporate.

These oils are a tonic against colds, as well as settling upset stomachs. Herbalists declare that camomile is useful for almost all ailments, from corns and bruises to sore eyes and gangrene. While that may or may not be so, the plant certainly does seem to be effective in calming digestive irritations.

Cleavers

Some herbalists claim that regular doses of this common weed act like amphetamine, killing the appetite while speeding up the nervous system, and prescribe it for weight loss. We make no promises for that, but *Galium boreale* is said to have a diuretic effect when taken as tea — and it's a light, tangy tea.

The plant, also known as ladies' bedstraw for its sweet-scented flowers, is an erect plant that grows to 2 feet (60 cm); its leaves appear in distinct whorls around its stiff stem, topped in early summer by spiky clusters of white flowers. Cleavers is best gathered while the plant is in flower; pick the blooms, too, for they dry quickly and their smell lasts as long as two years.

Chickweed

The bane of gardeners, *Stellaria media* is a

worldwide plant that takes its name from its alleged appeal to chickens; what you don't feed them, put in the compost heap, for chickweed is one of the richest compost plants. Save enough of this creeper — the one you find springing up before your seedlings, with tiny leaves and stems taking off at right angles from each other — to make a light fresh-tasting winter tea. Herbalists say chickweed, like cleavers, causes weight loss; it is traditionally said to aid digestion. (Fresh chickweed can be taken directly from the garden to the kitchen blender, where it can be mixed with water, ice and honey for a sunshiny drink.)

Red Clover

One of the sweetest wild teas is made from the common red clover, *Trifolium pratense*, whose clustered blossoms rise from ground hugging clumps of leaves throughout the summer. The white blossoms are also suitable for drying, but red clover is tastier: it tastes like a lighter, tangier version of the familiar clover honey.

Highbush Cranberry

In Europe, Asia, and in America, *Viburnum edule* is famed as crampbark, and its antispasmodic properties are recognized. In Alaska, the bush is known for its bitter heavy-scented berries, which are gathered in late summer for jams and juices. But equally useful are the bush's young sprouts, which should be gathered early in summer when their bright green bark distinguishes them from the darker, brownish bark of the older stems. The twigs dry quickly; store them in a tightly covered container.

Then, whenever you have muscle aches, menstrual cramps, or charleyhorses, brew yourself a cup of highbush cranberry bark tea; merely break into pieces a few of the twigs and soak for 30 minutes in boiling water. Though strong tasting, the tea is so effective in calming muscular pains that it's worth gulping it, a shot glass full at a time, every half-hour till the pain disappears.

Labrador Tea

Most Alaskans, when they think of tea plants, think immediately of this piny scented evergreen shrub, *Ledum latifolium* or *Ledum groenlandicum*. It's a real pleasure to gather the brownish, shiny leaves; your hands will smell fragrant for hours. While Labrador tea can be gathered at any time — including winter, as the leaves stay on the stems under snow — the best time is early spring, before the furry umbrellas of white flowers appear.

Labrador Tea

Labrador tea is extremely high in ascorbic acid, second among Alaskan plants only to rose hips. It is also high in tannin, as is black tea; in fact, during the American Revolution, this plant replaced the tea that was tossed into Boston Harbor; also, the spicy tea was a favorite drink of Interior Athabascans. Some will find that excessive use has a laxative effect.

Raspberry

A mild sweet tea comes from the familiar raspberry *(Rubus idaeus)*; it was another common substitute for black tea in Revolutionary America. The deeply notched leaves should be gathered in early summer, when the new leaves are a fresh green color, distinct from the darker old leaves; they dry so quickly that you can be drinking raspberry leaf tea a week after your gathering expedition. Many people find the tea slightly stimulating; it is the old wives' remedy for menstrual cramps.

Wild Rose

Not only the rose hips of this common Alaska plant are useful for tea. The leaves, too, gathered while the flowers are still a handsome pink, make a gentle tasting beverage. Both rose leaf and rose hip tea are commonly seen on health food store shelves; they are even more commonly seen on Alaska roadsides, but be careful not to pick from plants exhausted by car fumes.

While the rose leaves make a pleasantly innocuous tea, something you could serve anyone who enjoys a hot drink, the rose hips produce a

How To Brew A Wild Cup of Tea
(continued)

stronger tasting, more exotic beverage. Rather sweet and somewhat reddish, rose hip tea takes getting used to; but it's well worth it, as it's one of the world's most potent sources of vitamin C.

Yarrow

You've doubtless seen this roadside plant; perhaps you call it old man's pepper, or ladies' mantle, or millefolium. Maybe you've mistaken it for Queen Anne's lace or wild carrot, which it slightly resembles. Yarrow is most easily found by its grayish umbrellas of flowers and by its pungent but pleasant smell.

One of the world's most famous herbs, yarrow has been used as hair restorer by the bald, an intoxicant by drunkards, and a love charm by the lonely. Though it is doubtful that it serves all those purposes equally well, it does make a pleasant tasting spicy tea which is slightly stimulating. It's also said to be a general tonic for the system; use either flowers or leaves for tea, or both.

■ *Patricia Monaghan, Fairbanks*

Other Wild Beverages . . .

Green Drink: Cook equal parts of dandelion greens and chickweed (well washed) each in its own water. Put through sieve and add cider vinegar to the juice to suit your taste. Drink as a tonic.

Dandelion Coffee: Dandelion roots can be roasted and made into a caffeine-free coffee substitute. Dig roots with a trowel or spade, pushing down vertically, then lifting. This is easiest if you can find dandelions growing in sand; otherwise they often snap off. Clean and wash the roots well. Slice and roast at 200°F (93°C) until they are dry enough to snap crisply between your fingers. Grind and store in covered container. May be brewed alone or in combination with coffee.

Spruce Tea: It is possible to find this type of tea through a major part of Alaska where there are spruce trees. Spruce needles are simply boiled in water. This tea was first used by the Russians in the Siberian wilderness to prevent scurvy. Alaskan Natives probably drank it long before the Russians. One way to really "spruce" up this tea is to add a few mint leaves to the brew.

How To Brew A Wild Cup of Tea is reprinted from *ALASKA*® magazine, September 1981. The original title was "An Alphabet of Herbs for Tea." The Other Wild Beverages described come from several sources: Green Drink, from *Cooking Up A Storm*, Homer; Dandelion Coffee, from Ann Chandonnet, excerpted from "Alaska's Plentiful (And Tasty) Wild Foods," *ALASKA*® magazine, July 1976; Spruce Tea, excerpted from C. Joe Murray's "Four Teas for the Cabin Cup," *ALASKA*® magazine, August 1979.

GOOSE TONGUE

Also known as seaside plantain, this perennial seashore plant with a deep root is common throughout Southeastern. One variety or another grows along the Gulf of Alaska, the Alaska Peninsula, Kodiak Island and northward near Norton Sound. Goose tongue (*Plantago maritima* and *P. macrocarpa*) is a welcome green that may be gathered in some areas from early spring to late fall.

Preparation Tips: To avoid as much sand as you can, gather goose tongue greens that are growing from crevices in rocks rather than those on sandy beaches. Cut the taproot well below the surface. Strip the brown sheathing from the root, give the plant a shake to dispel as much sand as you can, pick out withered leaves and douse a small bunch at a time up and down in fresh water to remove more sand. A couple of changes of water may be required. Then cut off the roots.

Gently boil the leaves for about one minute in salted water; lift the leaves out of the pan, change the water, and return the leaves to boil until tender. To serve, again lift the leaves from the water to transfer to a dish. By this means, you'll leave behind as much sand as possible. Cooked goose tongue is good served with butter, bacon fat or Hollandaise Sauce.

The leaves may also be frozen for later use. After washing them well, blanch them in boiling water for one minute. Lift them out and plunge them into cold water to stop the cooking. Then lift out the leaves again, drain and pack in freezer containers. Use within six months.

The youngest plants may also be used raw, as in this salad.

Goose Tongue and Egg Salad

2 quarts (1.9 L) goose tongue
4 hard-cooked eggs
3/4 cup (180 mL) oil
1/4 cup (60 mL) vinegar
1/4 teaspoon (1 mL) white pepper
1/8 teaspoon (0.5 mL) salt
Seasonings — garlic powder and dried kelp

►After washing the spikes of goose tongue thoroughly, mix with oil and vinegar. Chill.

Although you can mix your favorite herbs, I prefer the simple combination of white pepper and salt, with a couple dashes of garlic powder and kelp. These are mixed and sprinkled on sliced hard-

cooked eggs, one per serving. Add to goose tongue. A perfect accompaniment for salmon!
■ *Nathana Rhines*
First Place — "Sourdough Sampler"
Great Lander Shopping News
Anchorage, October 1978

INDIAN RICE

The quoted portion of this description of Indian rice was written for one of the earliest issues of ALASKA® *magazine — then* The ALASKA SPORTSMAN®. *It is excerpted from "Vegetables of the Alaskan Wilderness," by C.R. Snow, April 1935 (Volume 1, Number 4).*

The plant (Fritillaria camchatcensis) *sometimes is called chocolate lily, black lily, Kamchatka lily and sarana, the Russian word for lily.*

"As your native substitute for potatoes or rice, have some 'wild' or 'Indian rice.'

"This dusky lily is no more related to its cereal namesake than the plant called 'Dutchman's breeches' is to a haberdashery in Holland. Yet as soon as you see its bulb and realize that Alaskan Indians have long used it as food, you will heartily approve of the name. The buds of the bulb closely resemble rice grains and provide an even more richly starchy food with an agreeable nutty flavor. In an emergency it may be eaten raw. Boiled and seasoned with butter, pepper and salt it provides a dish that should please even a logger with his stake made.

"The plant is common, and in many places abundant, in the well-drained ground at the edge of woods. In the spring it proclaims its presence by its dark purple, almost black, bell-shaped, drooping flowers and its pointed leaves, distributed on the stem in radiating whorls of four to six. As the summer advances, seed pods become conspicuous in the place of flowers, and they with withered stalks linger late in the fall to tell the woodsman of their whereabouts."

Preparation Tips: "The bulb is the edible part of the plant, and it is available all year. Bulbs grow 2 to 3 inches (5 to 7.5 cm) under ground, usually in a tangle of other roots, so that some care is required in digging them, lest all the rice grains be shaken off and lost."

The best time to dig, however, is early fall, when the bulblets have attained maximum size and all the nutrients from the leaves and stems have descended to them.

Bulblets are most often dried before cooking. They may be added to soups and stews just as other dried vegetables. Or they may be steamed with dried berries or raisins and eaten with cream and sugar as a dessert.

Thoroughly dried bulbs may be crushed and pounded into flour. Chaff that remains may be sifted out. The rice flour may be used as a stretcher for other flour or by itself as a thickening in gravies and sauces.

The seed pods of Indian rice are also edible. Gather them while they are still green before they turn dry and papery. Simmer and use as a vegetable.

Sarana
To boil fresh or to dry

►The month of July is the best time to gather wild rice because this is the time when the wild rice stops growing.

After gathering wild rice, wash it and take the bulbs off. Then fill a pot with cold water and cook the ricelike bulblets.

When the water starts to boil, throw it out and refill the pot with cold water again. Then boil, throw out and refill with cold water again. Then boil it again. When the rice is done, pour the water out and take the lid off the pot. Stick the pot into the oven and let it dry in there. Wild rice is very delicious when served with boiled fish.

If you want to store wild rice for the winter, you gather it and wash it. Then spread it on a cloth. Let the sun shine on the cloth. Whenever there is any sunshine outside, take the wild rice out until it dries. After it dries, store it for winter.
■ *Moses Dirks and Lydia Dirks*
Niigugim Qalgadangis — Atkan Food
Reprinted from Aleutian Wind, *1979*

JUNIPER

Mountain juniper *(Juniperis communis)* is a prickly shrub of subalpine localities. Its berrylike cone takes two or three years to ripen from light green to black. These "berries," when ripe, are choice flavoring agents for game. A few of them tossed into the residue left in the pan in which a moose steak has been sauteed makes a delicious sauce for the steak. For this and other uses, they should be crushed. They can be collected in the fall and dried thoroughly; then stored in a cool dry place until needed. One simply crushes the dry berry and uses it as seasoning on baking roasts or other game dishes.

Juniper berries also make good flavoring agents in marinades for moose and other venison or beef.

Juniper Marinade For Roast Beef or Game
For a 5- or 6-pound (2.25 to 2.7 kg) rib roast

3 cups (720 mL) apple cider
2 medium onions, cut in chunks
1 good-sized carrot, cut in chunks
1-1/2 cups (360 mL) red wine
1/4 teaspoon (1 mL) thyme
1 bay leaf
6 juniper berries*
10 peppercorns
1/4 teaspoon (1 mL) dried parsley

►Put 1/2 cup (120 mL) of the cider, the onions and carrot in a blender and process until you have a liquid. Pour this into a large enamel or stainless steel pan. Add remaining cider and all ingredients except meat. Bring to a boil and simmer for 15 minutes. Cool to room temperature and add meat. Marinate, refrigerated, for 24 hours, turning the meat every few hours.

Remove meat and strain marinade, reserving the liquid. Pat roast completely dry and place on a rack in a roasting pan and roast in an oven preheated to 500°F (260°C). After 20 minutes, baste the meat with 1/2 cup (120 mL) of the marinade and reduce the heat to 350°F (175°C). Baste the roast every 15 minutes. It's done when your meat thermometer reads rare, medium or well done, whichever is your choice. Transfer to a platter and let the meat rest 10 minutes before carving.

■ *Gordon R. Nelson, Palmer*
Lowbush Moose

*If you have forgotten to forage for juniper berries, Gordy says you may substitute 1 tablespoon (15 mL) gin.

LAMB'S-QUARTERS

This information about lamb's-quarters (also commonly known as pigweed) and the recipes for it are excerpted and adapted from "Lamb's-Quarters: Welcome Weed," by Ann Chandonnet, ALASKA® *magazine, Alaska-only edition, August 1979.*

Abundant in various parts of Alaska, lamb's-quarters is found throughout the United States, in sunny, dry places; it especially favors gardens and areas where the ground has been disturbed. There are some two dozen species, but *Chenopodium album* is the most common.

My family is somewhat reluctant to sample all the wild plants I dish up, but they often mistake lamb's-quarters for its botanical cousin, spinach. In fact, we find wild, freshly gathered lamb's-quarters more tasty than much of the supermarket spinach available in Alaska.

Preparation Tips: The small, young leaves are the tenderest, and I recommend that you gather your crop of this delicious wild green during June and July — or before it is more than 6 inches (15 cm) high. These can be cooked whole, seed and all. If you find a crop behind the garage in August, and it is 3 or 4 *feet* (0.9 to 1.2 m) in height, ignore the stems and simply strip the tender leaves for your cooking pot. You'll notice when you wash it that a gray-white dust, or bloom, will come off in the rinse water.

Lamb's-quarters can be preserved for winter meals by freezing; follow any standard directions for freezing greens or spinach.

If you spot lamb's-quarters too late to harvest the leaves, don't forget the seeds. They may be harvested by rubbing the husks between your hands to separate the chaff. You can do this in the field (and thus keep the mess outside) over a sheet of plastic. Then dry and grind. Or dry and cook into a cereal without grinding.

The plant has up to 50,000 tiny, mealy seeds per plant. You can dry them in the sun, grind them in a coffee grinder and make the resulting flour into hoecake or biscuits, mixing half and half with corn meal or an all-purpose flour.

With this many seeds per plant, lamb's-quarters spreads itself very efficiently. Even if you harvest every plant in your garden, more will appear the following year — from windblown or bird-spread seeds.

Steamed Lamb's-Quarters

►Trim off stalks, using just the smallest leaves, gathered before the blossoms appear for most tender greens. Wash well to remove all sand and soil. Steam with just a little water for three to ten minutes; do not overcook. Six cups (1.45 L) of leaves will yield about four servings.

Variation: Steam as above. Then chop and keep hot in double boiler while you make Spanish Sauce. . . . Make a roux of 1 tablespoon each

(15 mL) butter or margarine and flour. Gradually add 1 cup (240 mL) chicken stock. Cook three to five minutes, stirring, until thickened. Add 1 teaspoon (5 mL) salt, 1/4 teaspoon (1 mL) nutmeg, 1 tablespoon (15 mL) finely chopped onion, two whole cloves and pepper to taste. Cook slowly five minutes, stirring; then strain onto greens and serve at once.

Lamb's-Quarters and Feta Tart

Pastry for a deep-dish, 9-inch (22 cm) pie
2 eggs
2 egg yolks
1/2 cup (120 mL) plain yogurt
1/2 cup (120 mL) milk
1 tablespoon (15 mL) chopped parsley
2 tablespoons (30 mL) chopped onion
1/2 teaspoon (2 mL) salt
Dash nutmeg or 1 mashed garlic clove
2 pounds (1 kg) lamb's-quarters, chopped, cooked, drained
1/2 cup (120 mL) crumbled feta cheese
1 tablespoon (15 mL) melted butter

►Line a deep pie plate with pastry. Crimp top edge. Beat together eggs and egg yolks. Then beat in yogurt, milk, parsley, onion, salt, nutmeg (or garlic). Stir in prepared greens and cheese. Distribute evenly in pastry-lined pan and drizzle with melted butter. Bake at 400°F (205°C) for 10 minutes. Then reduce heat to 350°F (175°C) and bake 25 minutes longer or until set. Let cool for five minutes before cutting into wedges. Yield: Six main-dish servings.

MARSH MARIGOLD

Caution: Do not eat raw.

Two subspecies of marsh marigold *(Caltha palustris)* are prevalent in Alaska. One appears on the Alaska Peninsula and north and east through the Yukon Territory and in northern Asia and Europe. The other is a coastal variety found from the Aleutian Islands south to British Columbia. Neither of these are the species found in the eastern part of North America.

This is a lovely plant that can be readily adapted to a position in the home garden. The leaves are bright green and the flowers a vivid yellow. The stems are large and hollow. It is sometimes called cowslip.

Preparation Tips: The whole plant is edible if properly cooked. It contains helleborin, a poison,

and must *never* be eaten raw. Vigorous boiling, through two or even three changes of water, neutralizes the poison.

A dish somewhat like sauerkraut in appearance is obtained by boiling the long white roots. It is served hot with butter, salt and pepper and a dash of minced wild chives if they are available. Young leaves and stems gathered before the flower buds appear are excellent when thoroughly cooked and provide a welcome green vegetable in the spring.

MARE'S-TAIL

Mare's-tail *(Hippuris vulgaris)* is found throughout Alaska — along rivers and streams and in shallow tundra ponds, often growing up out of the water. It is a particularly welcome plant because it can be gathered even in the late fall after the ponds are glazed with ice. Eskimos in the Lower Kuskokwim region call it *tayaruk*, or goosegrass, and use it as in the recipe below.

Tayaruk Soup

►It is time to gather tayaruk when the ponds and lakes freeze over. We use the part that is sticking out of the water. With a stick or a knife we scrape the goosegrass off the ice. Then we pile it on some high ground and store it there for the winter. We make soup with goosegrass. First we boil some water. Then we wash some goosegrass and always cook seal oil with it. Sometimes we mash fish eggs in the soup. Some Eskimos like to cook fresh seal blood in the soup. We use all the goosegrass plant. It has a salty taste.

■ *Anon.*
Wild Edible and Poisonous Plants of Alaska

MOUSENUTS

"Mousenuts" are the root and underground stem portion of tall cottongrass *(Eriophorum angustifolium)* which grows in marshy areas and around tundra lakes and ponds throughout Alaska. The flowers of this tall slender plant eventually go to seed in silky blooms that are called Alaskan cotton. The underground part of the stem and root is gathered by tundra mice to store for winter feed. Hence, the name "mousenuts." Sometimes children search for these caches to garner mousenuts for themselves.

Preparation Tips: In early summer, all the lower part of the young stem may be eaten, up to 4 or 5 (10 to 12.5 cm) inches above ground. Eskimos eat the stems raw with seal oil. Later in the season, the mousenuts may be doused in boiling water to loosen the black outer layer and the interior may be eaten with seal oil or added to soups and stews.

MUSHROOMS

Some 500 species of mushrooms grow in Alaska. Most are edible, many deliciously so, but enough can cause illness or even death that no one should collect them without good background. Rules of thumb are:

- Begin collecting if possible by going with someone very knowledgable who can help with the finer points of identification that even the best guidebooks cannot impart to a reader not already familiar with the subject.
- Unless you plan to become an expert, learn to identify three or four mushrooms really well and stick to those. Good ones to start on are the so-called "foolproof four." These are:

   Shaggy mane *(Coprinus comatus)*
   Sulphur shelf or chicken of the woods
      (Laetiporus sulphureus)
   Conic morel *(Morchella angusticeps)* or
      sponge morel *(Morchella esculenta)*
   Giant puffball *(Calvatia gigantea)* or gem-
      studded puffball *(Lycoperdon perlatum)*

The "foolproof four" were so categorized by C.M. Christensen in the 1940s as edible, readily available mushrooms which are difficult to mistake for any other kinds *once you learn to identify them.* Though Christensen named four mushrooms, two of them have close cousins

which are now included to make it a "foolproof six," a good start for the beginning gatherer.

There are cautions to be learned before even these excellent mushrooms are "foolproof," such as how to identify false morels — which grow in many of the same places as true morels but are poisonous — and how to be sure you're picking a small puffball rather than the button stage of a poisonous *Amanita.*

- In other words, do not attempt to identify mushrooms without a good take-along guidebook. An excellent one is *The Alaskan Mushroom Hunter's Guide* by Ben Guild, illustrated by Jack VanHoesen [Anchorage, 1977]. All the following information about gathering and storing mushrooms and the general cooking instructions are excerpted with little adaptation from the Guide.

Gathering Mushrooms

Always try to gather the youngest or button stages of the edible gilled and fleshy pore fungi, and the early fresh stages of the other edible fungi which are gathered for the table. Positive identification of mature specimens is very important when you are gathering only the button mushrooms. Other pointers to remember:

1. Pick only one kind at a time. If more than one kind is picked on a trip, keep them separated.
2. If you can't identify it, don't eat it!
3. Otherwise, select for eating only the fresh, young, tender mushrooms that are free from wormholes or other obvious damage.
4. Cook and eat only one kind at a time.
5. Test cautiously each kind you have not tried before. Even the best edible mushrooms may contain certain substances to which some people are violently allergic.

Mushrooms should always be "field cleaned"; that is, remove soil, dead leaves and grass as they are gathered. Check mushrooms for insect infestation, discard or cut away infested parts and trim off any animal bites or bruised parts. (Yes, wild animals eat mushrooms.) You may not need to wash mushrooms at all. First try removing any dirt by brushing or gently rubbing it off. If you must wash them, you may do so in a lake or stream near where you collected them. Then shake them as dry as possible, especially before putting them into plastic bags. Moisture clinging to the mushrooms will speed deterioration.

The stems of some mushrooms tend to be tough and unpalatable, and may be discarded or saved to be used for soups and gravy dishes. In others, such as the fleshy pore fungi, the mature tubes tend to decompose faster than the other parts and may be cut away and left for reseeding.

The fleshy pore fungi and some of the gilled types tend to quickly become infested with insect larvae, usually from the base of the stem upward into the cap area. All insect-infested parts should be cut off and discarded. While a little insect protein shouldn't do any harm, it is certainly unpalatable and impairs the mushroom's flavor in cooking.

Cooking Mushrooms

Store mushrooms in the refrigerator. Do not clean if they are to be used within a day. For storing more than one day, clean and cook before storing. To clean, cut off soiled roots, peel if caps are tough and rub off fuzz or scales with a damp cloth. Leave small caps whole. Wash only if necessary, using a quick dip method. Drain and dry on paper towels. Slice stems, if they are tender, and cook with caps.

Shaggy manes and inky caps cannot be stored, even for a day. They mature too quickly and dissolve into ink within a few hours.

Mushrooms can be added to a variety of meats, poultry and fish dishes, and can be added to any of the mild-flavored vegetables, such as peas, spinach, zucchini and green beans. Here are a few tips for using them:

Most edible mushrooms are interchangeable in recipes.

Mushroom recipes frequently include butter, but a good quality margarine may be substituted.

Tender mushrooms will become tough with prolonged cooking.

Mushrooms can be enhanced with a bit of nutmeg. Care should be taken that not too much nutmeg is used — sprinkle just a few grains on the mushrooms.

Large frozen mushrooms often need to be cut up before using. They can be cut more easily while only partially thawed.

Dried mushrooms, either pieces or puree, can be granulated or powdered by crushing with a rolling pin. The powder can be used instead of flour for dredging meat before browning, or can be added to any of a variety of dishes, such as soups and stews — even salad — and other meat dishes.

Favorite Mushroom Soup

►Next to vegetable soup, mushroom soup is perhaps the most popular of all soups with Americans. Alaska has an abundance of edible mushrooms, so it is a good policy to make your own soup. Almost any of the native edible mushrooms may be used in soup but probably puffballs are easier to use than any of the others.

Broil or saute 2 or 3 cups (480 to 720 mL) of mushrooms in butter or margarine or steam them. Make a puree by using the blender or by putting the mushrooms through a sieve. Now make a rich White Sauce using half-and-half instead of whole milk. Add a dash of onion salt or a teaspoon (5 mL) of finely minced dried chives. Carefully blend the puree with the sauce. For a different flavor, use part chicken stock for the liquid or part mushroom stock.

■ Helen A. White, Anchorage
  More About What's Cookin' in Alaska

Cocktail Mushrooms

Mushroom caps
Cream cheese
Ham
Mayonnaise
Seasoning

►Fill perfect mushroom caps with seasoned cream cheese or ham or a mixture of both, moistened with mayonnaise. The mushrooms may be either raw or sauteed.

Basic Mushroom Soup

1 to 2 cups (240 to 480 mL) sliced mushrooms
2 to 4 tablespoons (30 to 60 mL) butter
2 to 3 tablespoons (30 to 45 mL) flour
1 quart (1 L) milk or light cream and milk
Few grains nutmeg
Salt and pepper to taste
Cayenne to taste

►Saute mushrooms in butter for about five minutes, shaking the pan frequently to keep mushrooms from burning. Add flour and stir until sauce foams. Add milk or mixture of milk and cream gradually, stirring gently about five minutes or more until soup is slightly thickened. Add seasonings.

Caution: The emerging "button" stage of the deadly Amanita *mushroom somewhat resembles a puffball. For this reason, be sure to cut all puffballs in half lengthwise to determine whether or not there is an embryo mushroom forming inside. If there is one, throw the mushroom away. The edible puffball is unbroken white inside, similar to the appearance of a cut marshmallow.*

Morels should never be eaten raw as they may contain substances which are poisonous or allergenic. These are dissipated (in true morels) by normal cooking processes.
■ *Ben Guild*
  The Alaskan Mushroom Hunter's Guide

Mushroom Stock

A good way to use stems and pieces
as well as caps

Fresh mushrooms, any edible variety
Water
Wild chives
Salt
Pepper

►If you have collected more mushrooms than you can eat while they are fresh, and don't care to freeze, can or dry them, try this. Mushroom stock can be kept for future use in sauces, gravies and soups. Clean and chop coarsely any of the edible mushrooms — more than one kind can be used. Place the chopped mushrooms in a large kettle and add water in an equal amount. Add also a handful of minced chives and season with salt and pepper. Simmer over very low heat for two or three hours. Strain while still hot. The mushroom pieces may be used in sauce or gravy, meat loaf or the like. They can also be left in the stock if you prefer. When the stock is cool, cover and store in the refrigerator. It will keep well in this manner for several weeks. Of course, it can be frozen, too.
■ *Helen A. White, Anchorage*
   More About What's Cookin' in Alaska

Fresh Puffballs

►Carry a small salt shaker with you when you go collecting so when you find a group of fresh puffballs, you can slice, peel, salt to taste and eat them raw on the spot.
■ *Ben Guild*
   "Stomach Fungi"
   ALASKA® *magazine, September 1978*

True or False? Alaska's morels can be divided into two groups — the true morels (*Verpa* and *Morchella* species) and the false morels (*Helvella* species). False morels are often found at the same time and in many of the same places as the true morels, but as a group they are dangerous and should be left alone.

All species of *Morchella* have one characteristic in common: their caps have a series of ridged pits, as if holes had been punched part way into them. The patterns of the pits vary from species to species, but all *Morchellas* have the pits. *Verpa* and *Helvella* species may be ridged, wrinkled, waved or even quite smooth, but they do not have the hole-like pits.
■ *Ben Guild*
   "The Morels"
   ALASKA® *magazine, June 1978*

Puffball and Rice Soup

2 beef or chicken bouillon cubes
1 cup (240 mL) puffballs, diced in 1/4-inch
   (6 mm) cubes
1 cup (240 mL) quick-cooking rice
3 cups (720 mL) water
Salt and pepper to taste

►Dissolve bouillon cubes in water, salt to taste, add mushrooms and cook five minutes at low boil. Add rice to the boiling mixture, remove from heat, season and eat with hardtack. (Barley may be substituted for or mixed with the rice.)
■ *Ben Guild*
   "Stomach Fungi"
   ALASKA® *magazine, September 1978*

Puffball Salad #1

French dressing
Puffballs
Salt and pepper
Herbs, your choice
Lettuce

►Have French dressing ready in a bowl. Clean and slice firm fresh puffballs into the dressing. This will keep them from discoloring. Season to suit. Herbs that have been found good with this salad include wild chives, thyme and basil. You may wish to experiment with others. Let salad stand in the refrigerator for at least two hours. Drain off any excess liquid and serve salad in a nest of lettuce leaves. Salty crackers are good served with this.

Puffball Salad #2

►Slice freshly gathered puffballs thinly and add to other wild vegetables for a super salad. Dress with a little wine vinegar and a very little oil.

Pickled Mushrooms #1

2 cups (480 mL) small mushrooms
1 teaspoon (5 mL) salt
2 bay leaves
1 clove garlic

►Combine all ingredients and then add 1 cup (240 mL) hot vinegar boiled with a sprig of tarragon. Refrigerate at least three days before using so that flavors can mingle and blend.

Pickled Mushrooms #2

1/3 cup (80 mL) sugar
1/3 cup (80 mL) red wine vinegar
1 teaspoon (5 mL) salt
1 teaspoon (5 mL) whole mixed pickling spice

1 bay leaf
1 to 2 cups (240 to 480 mL) mushrooms

►Nice, fresh, crisp puffballs are the ideal mushroom for this recipe. Combine all ingredients but the mushrooms in a small saucepan. Bring to a boil and remove from heat. Add cleaned mushrooms. If you wish you may also add one small onion that has been thinly sliced and separated into rings. Turn this mixture into a glass jar and cover tightly. Chill overnight to allow flavors to meld. Drain before serving as a relish.
■ *Ann Chandonnet*
    Kodiak Fish Wrapper and Litter Box Liner

Mushroom Spinach Salad

Spinach, fresh and crisp
Mushrooms
Salt and pepper
Oil and vinegar dressing

►Tear spinach into bite-size pieces. Clean mushrooms and slice those that are a bit too large; leave smaller ones whole. Season with a dash each of salt and pepper. Serve with oil and vinegar dressing. One of the wild plants that are rather like spinach also may be used. Try the young leaves of lamb's-quarters or scurvy grass.
■ *The Old Homesteader*

Marinated Shaggy Manes

1/2 pound (228 g) shaggy manes, chopped
    (use stems if mushrooms are scarce)
4 tablespoons (60 mL) olive or vegetable oil
2 tablespoons (30 mL) white wine
2 or 3 green onions, minced
1/2 teaspoon (2 mL) salt
1/8 teaspoon (0.5 mL) pepper

►Combine all ingredients and mix well. Allow to stand for two or three hours before using. To serve, spread on thinly sliced pieces of French bread or on toast rounds. Try this mixture on crackers.
■ *Ben Guild*
    "The Shaggy Mane"
    ALASKA® magazine, June 1978

Continental Mushroom Caviar

1 small onion, sliced and minced
2 tablespoons (30 mL) olive oil
1/2 pound (228 g) mushrooms, chopped fine
Salt and pepper
1 tablespoon (15 mL) lemon juice
Wild chives, chopped
1 tablespoon (15 mL) sour cream

►Fry the onion in the oil until soft and limp. Add mushrooms and cook until just barely soft. Add seasoning and other ingredients. Chill well before serving time. This is nice served with thin tomato slices or spread on crackers.

Pan-Fried Shaggy Manes

►If frozen, thaw partially, until the mushrooms can be easily separated; drain off moisture. Pat dry with paper towels. Dip in beaten egg and then in cracker crumbs. Brown quickly on each side in hot butter. Do not overcook. Serve with steak and green salad, a delicious meal.
■ *Lois Armstrong, Anchorage*

Peas and Shaggy Mane Mushrooms

Shaggy manes, freshly picked
1/3 cup (80 mL) salted water
Peas, fresh or frozen
Butter

►Pick mushrooms, rush home, clean mushrooms. They must be cooked the same day they are gathered. Pick and shell peas or use frozen ones. Bring salted water to a boil. Add peas and mushrooms. Cover and simmer a few minutes. Add a pat of butter and eat.
■ *Rieta Walker*
    Cooking Up A Storm, *Homer*

French-Fried Shaggy Manes

2 eggs
3/4 cup (180 mL) milk
1 cup (240 mL) flour
1 teaspoon (5 mL) baking powder
1/2 teaspoon (2 mL) salt
1 teaspoon (5 mL) melted shortening
Shaggy mane mushrooms (or inky caps)
Onion rings for frying

►Beat the eggs with a rotary beater and then beat in the milk. Sift the dry ingredients together and add to the egg mixture gradually and beat until smooth. Add the shortening and stir until blended into the mix. The batter should be thick enough to coat the rings and mushrooms evenly when they are dipped in it. Select small solid shaggy manes and trim and clean as necessary. Peel and slice onions and separate slices into rings. Dip the rings in the batter and then pop into hot deep fat and fry until golden, turning once. Keep the rings hot in the oven. Now dip the mushrooms in the batter and fry them quickly in the deep fat. This is a "super" recipe.
■ *Marcy White, adapted by*
    Helen A. White for
    More About What's Cookin' in Alaska

Scrambled Eggs and Morels

1 cup (240 mL) morel mushrooms, chopped
2 eggs
2 tablespoons (30 mL) milk
Margarine
Salt
Pepper

►Chop the morel mushrooms coarsely and saute briefly in margarine. Beat the eggs until light and season to taste and add the milk and beat again. Pour the egg mixture over the morels in the skillet and stir gently just until the egg is cooked. Serve with hot toast and jam.

Eggs with Mushrooms

2 tablespoons (30 mL) olive oil
1 tablespoon (15 mL) green onion, minced
1 tablespoon (15 mL) parsley, chopped fine
1 pound (456 g) mushrooms, sliced thin
1 tablespoon (15 mL) flour
1/2 cup (120 mL) dry white wine
Salt and pepper
6 hard-cooked eggs, chopped

►Cook onion and parsley in hot olive oil for two minutes. Add mushrooms and cover; simmer gently over low heat for about 10 minutes. Stir in flour and wine. Again cover and simmer for five minutes more. Season to taste. Add eggs, cover and simmer for five minutes longer, stirring occasionally. Serve with hot garlic French bread.
■ *The editors, ALASKA® magazine*

Mushroom Nuggets

15 to 20 large fresh mushrooms
1/4 pound (114 g) hamburger, browned
*   and drained*
1 packed and heaping cup (275 mL or more)
*   grated Cheddar*
1/2 small onion, chopped
1 tablespoon (15 mL) butter or margarine
3 tablespoons (45 mL) minced parsley
4 tablespoons (60 mL) grated Parmesan
1/2 teaspoon (2 mL) garlic powder
1/2 teaspoon (2 mL) salt
1/4 teaspoon (1 mL) pepper
Dash of oregano
Pinch of basil
Dash of Tabasco
MSG

►Wash mushrooms, take out stems and chop. Set caps aside. Saute chopped onion and chopped mushroom stems in butter until soft. Add browned and drained hamburger and turn heat to low. Add grated cheeses and all spices except MSG.

Cook over very low heat till cheese melts. Sprinkle the inside of each mushroom cap with MSG. Fill with a heaping spoonful of hamburger-cheese mixture. Place filled caps in baking dish or pan so that caps do not overlap. Add just enough water to barely cover the bottom of the pan. Bake uncovered at 350°F (175°C) for 30 to 35 minutes.

These are very hot when they come out of the oven. Spoon onto serving plate and allow to cool slightly before serving. Mushroom Nuggets are also very juicy. Be sure to keep a napkin handy when you eat them.
■ *Rhonda L. Fehlen*
"Sourdough Sampler"
Great Lander Shopping News
Anchorage, October 1978

Buttery Morels

►Cut off the lower part of each stem as you pick morels and brush away any loose soil. Don't wash them unless you absolutely must; and if you must, dry them thoroughly on paper towels.

At cooking time, cut off the stems at the base of the cap and slice the caps in half lengthwise. Melt a generous amount of butter or margarine in a frying pan and add enough morel halves to cover the bottom of the pan. Do not heap. Salt and pepper to taste. Saute about five minutes on each side. Serve immediately on toast or as a side dish. (And don't throw away the stems! Turn them into Mushroom Base — see page 284.)
■ *Ben Guild*
"The Morels"
ALASKA® magazine, June 1978

Variation: Morels are also good dipped in seasoned flour and fried until lightly crisp. Or they may be creamed, stewed or used in most recipes that call for mushrooms. Only one caution: their flavor is delicate and easily overwhelmed.

Baked Shaggy Manes

►Split young and fresh caps lengthwise, discard stems and lay caps with gill side up in a shallow baking pan. Combine butter or margarine, salt and pepper to taste and a dash of garlic (too much will mask the mushrooms' delicate flavor). Dab mixture on the mushrooms and bake at 325°F (160°C) for three to five minutes or broil for one to two minutes.
■ *Ben Guild*
"The Shaggy Mane"
ALASKA® magazine, June 1978

Casserole Supreme

1/4 cup (60 mL) butter or margarine
1 cup (240 mL) finely chopped onion

2 cups (480 mL) shaggy manes
1 cup (240 mL) milk
1 cup (240 mL) homemade Mushroom Soup
2 pounds (1 kg) broccoli
Salt and pepper
2 cups (480 mL) cubed ham
1-1/2 cups (360 mL) commercial stuffing mix

►Saute onions in butter until limp; add mushrooms and saute briefly until tender. Stir in milk and soup. Put one-third of the broccoli in a well-greased casserole dish. Sprinkle with seasonings and put one-third of ham, one-third of sauce and one-third of the stuffing mix on top. Repeat layers until all ingredients are used. Bake at 350°F (175°C) for 30 minutes or until broccoli is tender. (Brussels sprouts or asparagus may be substituted for broccoli.)

■ *Ben Guild*
   "The Shaggy Mane"
   ALASKA® *magazine, June 1978*

Chicken of The Woods

►Chicken of the woods mushrooms — sulphur shelf — may be eaten many ways — fried, baked, boiled, broiled or pickled. Use just the outer 2 inches (5 cm) of the "shelf" margin (one large fruiting body usually will be enough for a meal). The quickest way to cook it is to cut the slabs into 1/2-inch-thick (1.25 cm) pieces and fry them in butter or margarine or vegetable oil. The slabs may be rolled in flour or batter and deep-fried, too, and then the mushroom lives up to its name, for it tastes much like fried chicken.

■ *Ben Guild*
   "Sulphur Shelf Mushroom"
   ALASKA® *magazine, August 1978*

Inky Caps and Shaggy Manes

►Inky caps and shaggy manes are delicious simply steamed for five or six minutes and served with melted butter and any seasoning you wish.

■ *The Old Homesteader*

Rabbit or Chicken Livers and Puffballs

1 slice lean bacon, diced
2 tablespoons (30 mL) butter
1 green onion, diced
1 pound (456 g) rabbit or chicken livers
2 tablespoons (30 mL) whole-wheat flour
1 cup (240 mL) bouillon, chicken flavored
1 teaspoon (5 mL) lemon juice
1/2 cup (120 mL) sliced puffballs
Chopped parsley

►Cook bacon and butter together for five minutes.

Add the diced green onion, tops and all, and cook two minutes more. Add the chicken livers and cook another two minutes. Sprinkle the flour over the mixture and add the bouillon, lemon juice and mushrooms. Cook another two minutes or until slightly thickened. Sprinkle with the parsley, finely chopped.

■ *The Old Homesteader*

Breaded Chicken of The Woods

►Slice chicken of the woods mushrooms. Beat one egg; have on hand butter or oil, bread or cracker crumbs, finely grated cheese and salt. Combine crumbs, cheese and salt. Dip mushroom slices in beaten egg, then in crumb mixture. Fry ·in hot butter or oil until brown.

■ *Ben Guild*
   "Sulphur Shelf"
   ALASKA® *magazine, August 1978*

Broiled Chicken of The Woods

►Cut edge of mushroom into pieces 2 x 3 inches (5 by 7.5 cm), brush with melted butter or margarine and place in shallow pan about 3 inches (7.5 cm) from heat source. Season to taste with salt and pepper and a little nutmeg. Broil eight to ten minutes.

■ *Ben Guild*
   "Sulphur Shelf"
   ALASKA® *magazine, August 1978*

Mushroom Sauce #1

2 cups (480 mL) sliced mushrooms
4 tablespoons (60 mL) butter
3 tablespoons (45 mL) flour
Meat drippings, plus water or bouillon or stock
   to equal 1 or 1-1/2 cups (240 to 360 mL)
   liquid

►Heat butter until frothy, add mushrooms and saute briefly, shaking the pan now and then to cook evenly. Sprinkle flour over the mushrooms. Then stir in liquid gradually until sauce is thickness desired. An excellent sauce for fish, meat, fowl or vegetables.

Mushrooms rank high among foods containing chromium and, believe it or not, chromium is needed badly in our diets. Much refined food has the chromium largely taken out and that is one reason why whole grain foods are more healthful than those made from white flour.

Mushroom Sauce #2

2 cups (480 mL) sliced mushrooms
1 medium onion sliced in thin rings
3 tablespoons (45 mL) butter
1/4 teaspoon (1 mL) paprika
1/2 teaspoon (2 mL) marjoram
Salt to taste or lemon juice

►Heat butter until frothy. Add mushrooms and onion rings and sprinkle paprika and marjoram over all. Saute until onions are lightly browned, shaking the pan frequently to cook mixture evenly. Taste, season with a dash of salt or lemon juice and pour over meat at serving time. This is an especially good garnish for broiled steaks, and the steak juices may be substituted for all or part of the butter.
■ *The editors, ALASKA® magazine*

Mushroom-Herb Stuffing
For mild-flavored fish

4 cups (1 L) half-inch (1.25 cm) bread cubes
1/2 cup (120 mL) butter
1 cup (240 mL) sliced fresh mushrooms

2/3 cup (160 mL) sliced green onions
1/4 cup (60 mL) chopped parsley
4 teaspoons (20 mL) lemon juice
1/2 teaspoon (2 mL) marjoram

►Saute bread cubes in butter until lightly browned. Add mushrooms and onion and cook until tender. Stir in remaining ingredients. Will stuff 3 to 4 pounds (1.4 to 1.8 kg) fish.

Mushrooms with Chicken and Fern Fiddleheads

2 cups (480 mL) boiling water
1 teaspoon (5 mL) salt
2 cups (480 mL) fiddlehead ferns,
    fresh or frozen
3 tablespoons (45 mL) margarine
3 tablespoons (45 mL) flour
1 cup (240 mL) mushroom pieces, sauteed
1 cup (240 mL) chicken broth or stock
2-1/2 to 3 cups (600 to 720 mL) cooked,
    sliced chicken
2 tablespoons (30 mL) parsley
2 tablespoons (30 mL) bread crumbs

►Cook fiddleheads in boiling water for one minute;

More Hints About Cooking Mushrooms

Sauteing Mushrooms — To keep the juices *inside* the mushrooms instead of oozing out into the pan, do not stir them while sauteing in butter. Instead, heat butter until it's bubbly, add mushrooms and *shake* the pan gently from time to time to keep mushrooms from browning or sticking. Add seasonings for the last minutes of cooking. Sauteed this way, mushrooms will absorb the butter and be deliciously juicy.

Mushroom Base — Clean — but *do not wash* unless necessary — firm, fresh mushrooms of any edible species. Cut off bruised or tough lower portions of stems. Chop fine and saute in butter until all moisture is absorbed (see above). Season lightly with nutmeg and onion salt. Add a little Madeira wine. Store in the refrigerator in a covered container to use as a base for sauce or soup or to add as flavoring to sauces, gravies, stews and vegetables. Also useful — and tasty — as a moistening agent in meat loaf or stuffing.

Mushroom Dumplings — Add pulverized dried mushrooms to your dumpling mixture just before dropping spoonfuls into stew or chicken fricasse.

Mushroom Stuffing — Prepare your favorite poultry stuffing and lace it liberally with sauteed mushrooms (or Mushroom Base). Any of the edible kinds will do, but we prefer puffballs.

Raw Mushrooms — Just clean and slice raw mushrooms and add them to salads along with a few drops of lemon juice to keep the color from turning. Raw mushrooms are also excellent marinated for several hours or overnight in a vinegar-and-oil-based dressing to which minced chive, garlic and other seasonings may be added to taste. Don't forget to save the leftover marinade either for the next batch of mushrooms or to be used as part of the dressing for a green salad.

Chanterelles — This variety is especially good sauteed and added to the "center fold" of an omelet. Try it.

Mushroom Rice — Steam long grain and wild rice combination until done and add sauteed mushrooms and chopped wild chives.

Preserving Mushrooms — Mushrooms may be preserved by freezing, drying, pickling and canning. See Chapter 14 for details.

reduce heat and simmer until tender. Mix margarine and flour in saucepan and cook briefly over medium heat, blending well. Stir in the broth and keep stirring until sauce is thick and smooth. Stir in any juice left over from cooking mushrooms. Add mushroom pieces and season to taste. Arrange fiddleheads, drained, in a large casserole and cover with the chicken slices. Pour the sauce over the chicken. Sprinkle crumbs on top and also add a sprinkling of parsley. Bake for 15 to 25 minutes, uncovered, in a 375°F (190°C) oven. When done it should be brown and bubbly. Brussels sprouts, asparagus or broccoli may be used if you have no fiddleheads handy.

■ *The Old Homesteader*

Fresh Mushroom Casserole

1 pound (228 g) fresh mushrooms, sliced
1 can (8 oz /or/ 228 g) pitted ripe olives, chopped
1/2 teaspoon (2 mL) salt
1-1/2 tablespoons (13 g) flour
1/4 teaspoon (1 mL) MSG
1/8 teaspoon (0.5 mL) pepper
1-1/2 tablespoons (23 mL) butter, melted
1/4 pound (114 g) grated Cheddar cheese
1/2 cup (120 mL) half-and-half
1 cup (240 mL) bread crumbs

►Grease a 2 quart (2 L) casserole. Arrange sliced mushrooms, grated cheese, chopped olives in layers. Blend together salt, flour, MSG, pepper, half-and-half and pour over mushrooms. Melt butter and mix with crumbs. Spread over top of casserole and bake, uncovered, at 350°F (175°C) for about 30 minutes. Serves eight.

■ *Debby Novak*, Kitchen Magic, *Ketchikan*

Mushroom Stew Supreme
Excellent served with wild game

1 pound (456 g) sulphur shelf mushrooms,
*   sliced*
1/4 cup (60 mL) oil
1 tablespoon (15 mL) chives, chopped fine
1 teaspoon (5 mL) fennel seed
2 tablespoons (30 mL) chopped parsley
1/2 cup (120 mL) dry wine
Juice of 1 small lemon
Salt and pepper to taste

►Clean and trim mushrooms as needed. Saute in warm oil with chives, fennel seed and parsley for five to eight minutes. Sprinkle lemon juice over mushrooms and cook three minutes longer. Add wine, cover and simmer five more minutes.

■ *Ben Guild*
   "Sulphur Shelf"
   ALASKA® magazine, August 1978

NETTLES

Whenever you handle nettles *(Urtica gracillis)*, it is best to wear gloves. Some people feel the "sting" of nettles much more than others and it is needless to risk nettle rash. Dig the whole plant. Wash and reserve the young and tender leaves and store in the refrigerator for later use as greens. The roots may be used in soup, as suggested below.

If you are unlucky enough to get nettle stings and need an antidote, just look around for some touch-me-nots *(Impatiens noli-tangere)*. Nature often causes nettles and the touch-me-not to grow together, or at least fairly near each other. Crush the leaves of the touch-me-not and gently rub on the affected flesh. Presto! No more itching. (The plant, which grows to 3 feet [90 cm], has yellow flowers and is found in moist soil, often in shady places.)

Nettle Soup

Nettle roots
Thin White Sauce

►Wash and trim the roots and rinse again. Steam or simmer in a little water until tender. Put through a sieve and add the resulting puree to a thin White Sauce which is well seasoned. This is a delicious soup.

■ *Helen A. White, Anchorage*
   (descriptive text and recipe)
   What's Cookin' in Alaska

PARRY'S WALLFLOWER (OR LITTLE CABBAGES)

The Eskimo name for "little cabbages" was given to this plant *(Parrya nudicaulis)* because of the tightly curled appearance of the emerging foliage. The long thick root is used by arctic coast Natives in stews with meat or fish. Bush travelers Jim Greenough and Eileen Helmstetter ["The Bush Gourmet," *ALASKA*® magazine, July 1977] report, "When boiled, the roots were a sweet and palatable addition to our freeze-dried stews." Their recipe, Portage Pass Fish Dish, which uses the root, is on page 41.

PINK PLUME (OR KNOTWEED)

When is a weed "knot" a weed? When it sports a lovely flowerhead of many tiny pink blossoms, the pink plume or knotweed *(Polygonum bistorta)* is definitely more than a weed. It may be said to resemble a "plume" but when it is in tight bud the little rosy buds look more like knots. It grows more or less abundantly over most of Alaska except the Aleutian Islands, the Gulf Coast and Southeastern Alaska. The dainty rosy flowers may be found mainly in subalpine or alpine habitats and even climb to an altitude of 6,500 feet (1.9 km).

Preparation Tips: The roots (rhizomes) are eaten like nuts when small and they are delicious if roasted as you would roast chestnuts. They provide starch in stews and other concoctions. It is said that Eskimos sometimes use them boiled and served with seal oil. The leaves are nutritious, too, but because there are few of them, they are normally tossed with other greens for salads.

ROSEROOT

Roseroot or king's crown *(Sedum rosea)* has succulent, fleshy gray green leaves and stems. Often the leaves are toothed but not always and they are crowded together on the short stems. Small reddish flowers appear at the tips of the stems in a dense cluster. Most of the state except for part of the Arctic and the Aleutian Islands is home to roseroot. The plants make nice subjects for the home rock garden.

Preparation Tips: Roseroot makes a delectable salad with the addition of a few other ingredients. Both stems and leaves can be used and both are best when plucked early in the season before the flowers appear. A few of the first tight buds will do your salad no harm.

The large coarse roots can be dug later in the summer where they grow in some abundance. Scrub the roots and boil slowly until tender. Cooled and chopped they can be added to cooked vegetable salads or they can be served hot with a judicious seasoning of salt, pepper and butter.

Roseroot Seasoning for Fish and Mushrooms

►We used the succulent leaves only a few times, but they were delicious and contributed a sweet,

full flavor when cooked with lake trout and puffballs.

■ *Jim Greenough and Eileen Helmstetter*
  "The Bush Gourmet"
  ALASKA® magazine, July 1977

SCURVY GRASS

Scurvy grass *(Cochlearia officinalis)* is a much branched plant with fleshy leaves. It has the typical arrangement of cross-shaped flowers of other members of the mustard family. Its small white blossoms make it an attractive plant along our beaches. One or the other of our two subspecies can be found growing near the coast of the state from the High Arctic to Southeastern Alaska. They are circumpolar in their range. This plant was often the only source of vitamin C available to crews of early day ships and was used extensively both as a preventative and a cure for scurvy, that scourge of explorers and other northern voyagers. It is also known as spoonwort.

Preparation Tips: Collected in early summer and used either raw or cooked, scurvy grass still makes a nutritious addition to the daily menu. In the fall, collect the young rosettes of new plants. Use scurvy grass raw with a few chopped fresh mushrooms and a simple oil-and-vinegar dressing, and it becomes a good salad to accompany dinner. It is also good added to other salad greens.

Cook it much the way you would spinach. Use only a little water to begin the process and drain that off as soon as it comes to a boil to lessen the tendency of the leaves to be bitter. Add a small amount of fresh water and again bring to a boil; reduce heat and simmer briefly, only until tender. Serve with a dash of salt and pepper and a little vinegar.

SEAWEED & KELP

Saltwater plants called seaweed or kelp come in various shapes, sizes and colors and are tagged with a multitude of common names. Some that you'll find in Alaska's tidal waters are described here. But there are others, nearly all of which are both edible and nutritious. The recipes that follow sometimes indicate which seaweed is preferred and sometimes don't . . . leaving the choice to you. A longstanding survival habit of Native people has been to dry seaweeds of various kinds for later use — to eat as a snack or to add flavor and saltiness to soups and stews.

Washing the sand off plants that grow close to shoreline may take several changes of water. Some advise using sea water for this rinsing so that the salty taste is not washed away. Another suggestion: lift the plants out of rinse water and cooking water rather than letting the water — and sand — drain back through them.

Dulse

This seaweed *(Rhodymenia palmata)* attaches in clusters to rocks at low- to mid-tide mark along the shores of Southeastern, Prince William Sound, Yakutat and Glacier Bays. Another variety *(Palmaria palmata)* can be found around Kodiak Island, throughout the Aleutians and along the Alaska Peninsula. Plants vary in color from rose red to reddish purple and grow from a few inches to a foot (30 cm) in length.

Preparation Tips: Massive quantities of this seaweed are gathered in Southeastern and air-dried for later use. It can be used raw in salads, or quick-fried and eaten like potato chips. Or boiled gently along with fish eggs or other seafood.

Ribbon Kelp

This graceful kelp *(Alaria* species) grows rapidly into a huge plant. It is best to gather it from February through June. The olive brown plants are found near low-tide mark along exposed, rocky shorelines of Southeastern, the Gulf of Alaska and

---

Harvesting & Drying Seaweed

Native Alaskans have long appreciated the taste and nutritional value of seaweeds of many varieties, have harvested each kind at its peak and preserved much of it for later use by drying. Kaa T'eix (Mary Howard Pelayo) of Mount Edgecumbe, tells how it's done:

Here in Southeastern Alaska we have three growths of seaweed. There is also the fake seaweed. It looks like seaweed, but it does not taste like seaweed. The first growth is called the herring-spawn seaweed, and it is harvested in the second week of May. This is considered the best for harvesting because it grows long and is abundant. The second growth is just a month later and is called the budding-of-the-bush seaweed in Tlingit. This seaweed is good for about three weeks only. After that, it starts turning gray. The third growth comes in February and is called the winter seaweed. This is short, but real tasty. The best time to pick this black seaweed is when the tide is out and the wind and sun have dried the seaweed a bit on top. It is rolled off the rocks by hand. Take the one end of the growth and try to form a roll and the seaweed will pull off the rocks.

To proceed with the drying, you do not have to wash it off. It is best to start drying as soon as possible. If it is raining outside, you can spread a tablecloth or sheets in your furnace room. It will dry, but it will take longer than drying in the sun and wind. When it is half-dried, season the seaweed with fresh clam juice. You may also grind the clams and add them to the seaweed. You may also add salt to the clam juice to make it more tasty. Sugar is also a good seasoning. You may add the seasoning after the seaweed is ground. Continue drying, rolling the seaweed so that it dries on all sides. If it is not dry all the way through, the seaweed will mold in storage.

Before the white man introduced the meat grinder, the Tlingits used the pressing method. The seaweed was pressed into squares by placing it in cans — like the modern 5-gallon (19 L) can — and a square board was placed over it with weights on top. It was dried that way in the sun. Before it was used, it had to be cut into pieces with a knife. When it was ready for storage, pine branches were placed between the blocks of black seaweed.

The red seaweed ribbons are dried in the same manner as above, but because the ribbons are a little thicker than the black seaweed, they retain the salt flavor and do not need to be seasoned. Where the black seaweed is almost transparent when dried, the red sea ribbons have a white powder-like substance on them because of the dried salt. The sea ribbons can be eaten as is or can be roasted in the oven. When roasted, they are crispy and just like Cracker Jacks; you can't stop eating the delicious snack.

■ *Kaa T'eix (Mary Howard Pelayo)*

Reprinted from Kaa T'eix's Cook Book, Mount Edgecumbe (see Cooks & Cookbooks . . .)

the Aleutians. It is also called by its generic name, alaria, or ringed kelp, honeyware, wing kelp, bladderlocks and *wakame*.

Preparation Tips: Jeanne Culbertson, a resident of Adak who has made it her business to experiment with this excellent food source from the sea, says that "Overall, the alaria seaweeds are the best and easiest to use. The midrib is cut out, chopped and used fresh in salads or eaten plain like celery. Alaria also dries very well and can be used in many ways. I break it into small pieces or chop it fine in the blender to add to soups and other dishes for flavoring. Or, I sometimes soak dried alaria for about 45 minutes in a mixture of vinegar, soy sauce and water, then add diced cucumbers and sesame seeds for a salad to accompany baked salmon or similar dishes." Several more of her recipes follow. Sometimes the kelp is fried and then tossed with sugar or honey or soy sauce and eaten as a snack. Try out the recipe, Jackie's Seaweed Chips.

Sea Lettuce

This plant *(Monostroma fuscum)* has a bright green color that looks rather like ordinary garden lettuce that has been frozen and thawed. It grows from 5 to 10 inches (12 to 25 cm) long, 7 to 9 inches (17 to 23 cm) wide. It can be gathered from rocks near the low-tide mark from Southeastern to the Aleutians and Saint Paul Island in the Bering Sea.

Preparation Tips: Can be eaten raw, alone, or with other greens in salads. It is also dried, crushed and added as seasoning to fish and meat dishes.

Giant, Bull or Bulb Kelp

This giant marine algae *(Nereocystis leutkeana)* is an annual plant that may grow as much as 100 feet (30 m) in a single season. The base of the plant attaches to rock in waters up to 60 feet (18 m) deep and supports a long, narrow stem or stipe that ends in a large hollow round ball that floats near the surface of the water. Clear waters are the favorite habitat.

Preparation Tips: Gather the kelp during June, July or August and use only the ones that are still rooted — not those that have washed ashore. Wash in sea water; peel the hollow, upper part of the stem and the bulb with a vegetable peeler. Use them as you would green tomatoes or cucumbers. They substitute well for watermelon rind in sweet preserves and are often used in other varieties of pickles. Some recipes are included in the chapter on preserving vegetables and fruits. In the immediately following recipes, however, is one for pickles to enjoy right away; that is, after 48 hours of marination.

Rockweed

This strange little water plant *(Fucus distichus)* goes by many different names. It is a seaweed that pops when it is stepped on; hence, one of its common names is popping weed. It is called rockweed for its habit of clinging to rocks to make up for its lack of a root system. When the plants break free, they sometimes cluster in masses that float near the surface of the water or, when the mass is heavy enough, sink to the ocean floor. Another common name for the plant, leather breeches, calls attention to its growth pattern, always in paired sections. An Indian name for the plant is *Tuhbet'* or "water stomach," a descriptive name rather close to another of the English ones, bladderwrack. Whatever its name, it is found abundantly on Alaska's beaches, an olive brown plant that may grow to 12 inches (30 cm) in length.

Preparation Tips: When it is young and tender, rockweed can be used raw in mixed salads or cooked as a vegetable. Like many other seaweeds, it is dried and used as a seasoning for vegetable and meat dishes. It adds salt as well as flavor. Some people prefer to steam or boil it with meat or vegetables and then discard the seaweed before serving the dish, as they like its flavor better than the texture.

Porphyra

The long, narrow, frilly-edged fronds of porphyra *(Porphyra laciniata)* — also called simply "seaweed" or laver — grow on rocks in the waters along the coast of Southeastern, the Gulf of Alaska and westward to the Aleutians. When fresh, the fronds are very dark green; when dried, black. They are easy to gather at low tide.

Preparation Tips: The favorite preparation for porphyra is drying or drying and toasting. Thoroughly dried and kept in tightly sealed containers in a cool, dry place, it will keep indefinitely. It is eaten as a snack, rather like popcorn, or added to cooked dishes for flavoring. Young fronds, gathered in May and early June, are best for drying. Mature ones, gathered in late summer, can be used in dishes calling for fresh seaweed, though many people prefer the taste of dulse or sugar wrack or ribbon kelp for this purpose.

Sugar Wrack (Kelp)

The palm-leaf shaped sugar wrack *(Laminaria saccharina)* grows very rapidly and is best when picked from February through June. The yellow brown to rich brown plants grow near or below the low-tide mark along coastlines from the Chukchi

Sea to Southeastern Alaska. Mature plants vary in size from 3 to 9 feet long (0.9 to 2.7 m) and 6 to 9 inches wide (15 to 23 cm).

Preparation Tips: As both the common name and part of the Latin name imply, sugar wrack has a sweet flavor. It is one of the favorite species for the herring-roe-on-kelp delicacy. Like other seaweeds, sugar wrack may be eaten raw or cooked in various dishes. Try it in Jeanne Culbertson's recipes, Seaweed Italiano, Sea Beef Stew or Soup and Seaweed Snack.

Fish and Seaweed Chowder

8 slices bacon, minced
4 good-sized onions, diced
1 to 4 pounds (0.45 to 1.8 kg) fish — halibut,
*   salmon, whatever; leftover, fresh or frozen*
1 large can (13 fl oz /or/ 390 mL) evaporated
*   milk, plus enough additional milk to make*
*   4 cups (1 L)*
4 cups (1 L) fresh seaweed, chopped
*   (alaria is best)*
2 stalks celery, chopped
1/2 green pepper, chopped
2 big potatoes, peeled and diced
1 can tomato soup

►If the fish is not cooked and boned, cover it with water and simmer about five minutes. Save the water, cool the fish, then bone and flake it into good-sized pieces.

Put the bacon in a heavy pot over low heat and cook until it begins to brown. Add onions and stir a bit. Add fish stock, milk, celery, pepper and seaweed and cook about 10 minutes. Add potatoes, fish, tomato soup, and simmer until seaweed and potatoes are tender. Stir a little, but try not to break up the fish. The chowder should be thick. Season to taste. Serve with crackers or add cracker crumbs. This chowder is even better the next day.

■ *Jeanne Culbertson*
    "Sea Treasures"
    ALASKA® *magazine, June 1979*

Sea Beef Stew or Soup

2-1/2 pounds (1.15 kg) beef or venison on
*   bones (shank, stew meat, or chuck)*
1 onion, sliced
4 cups (1 L) seaweed, chopped (laminaria,
*   alaria or dulse)*
2 carrots, sliced
1 cup (240 mL) raw rice

►Cut excess fat from beef and melt in heavy iron pot or pressure cooker. Coat meat with flour and brown slowly on both sides. Add onions, cover with water and cook until tender. Remove the meat and bones and measure the beef stock. For stew, you'll need about 2-1/2 to 3 cups (600 to 720 mL) of stock, so add water if necessary. For soup, use any amount of additional water to make the consistency you like best. Add rice and seaweed and cook until tender, about 20 minutes. Take the meat from the bones and cut it into 1/2-inch (1.25 cm) pieces, then add it and the carrots to the stew or soup and cook until the carrots are tender. Add salt to taste.

■ *Jeanne Culbertson*
    "Sea Treasures"
    ALASKA® *magazine, June 1979*

Boiled Fish and Dried Black Seaweed

►Boil about 1 pound (456 g) fillet of salmon or red snapper. Boil for half an hour. Next put in dried, ground or roasted seaweed till the right consistency is reached. Salt to taste. Serve with ooligan grease or milk. Some people prefer soy sauce for seasoning.

■ *Robert Cogo*
    Haida Food Gathering and Preparation

Seaweed Italiano
A sauce for spaghetti or ground meat

4 cans (8 oz /or/ 228 g, each) tomato sauce
1/2 clove garlic
1 tablespoon (15 mL) Worcestershire
1/2 teaspoon (2 mL) oregano
1 cup (240 mL) water
4 cups (1 L) seaweed, chopped (alaria
*   or laminaria)*

►Combine all ingredients. Simmer for one hour. Add water if it is too thick. Serve as usual with spaghetti and meatballs or add browned meat to the sauce.

■ *Jeanne Culbertson*
    "Sea Treasures"
    ALASKA® *magazine, June 1979*

Main Dish Seaweed

►Put whatever meat you have — beef, pork, chicken or game — in a heavy pot with 1/2 teaspoon (2 mL) onion salt and enough water to cover. Cook slowly until almost done. Then add a couple of cups (480 mL) of chopped seaweed, a sliced raw carrot for color, some diced celery and whatever starchy food appeals to you — rice, potatoes or noodles. Cook about 30 minutes more and presto! A complete, delicious dinner.

■ *Jeanne Culbertson*
    Alaska Tidelines, *Volume II, Number 7*

Chung McGuire's Special

2 cups (480 mL) lean, 1-inch (2.5 cm)
  pork cubes
1/2 cup (120 mL) soy sauce
4 cups (1 L) finely sliced seaweed
3 cups (720 mL) water
1/2 teaspoon (2 mL) Accent

►Boil pork cubes in soy sauce until nearly done. Add seaweed, water and Accent and bring to a boil; then turn off heat. Let the mixture sit until the seaweed is tender. Serve as a main dish or lessen the amount of pork and serve as a vegetable side dish.
■ *Courtesy, Jeanne Culbertson*
   "Sea Treasures"
   ALASKA® magazine, June 1979

Clams and Seaweed
A good recipe for dulse

8 fresh clams and juice
1 quart (1 L) boiling water
Seaweed
Ooligan grease

►Dice the clams, saving the juice. Put into a saucepan with boiling water. Add seaweed until it is the consistency you want. Simmer for five minutes. Serve with ooligan grease.
■ *Robert Cogo*
   Haida Food Gathering and Preparation

Jackie's Seaweed Chips
A nice change from popcorn or peanuts

►Rinse seaweed carefully in the sea before bringing it home so that you won't have to rinse it in fresh water, washing away the sea salts. Dry it on a line in the utility room or outdoors if the weather permits. Cut it into 1-1/2-inch (3.75 cm) pieces after it is dry and fry in very hot oil in a deep-fryer for about one second. Mix with sesame seeds or sprinkle with a tiny bit of sugar and serve as a snack.
■ *Jackie Burgess*
   Courtesy, Jeanne Culbertson
   "Sea Treaures"
   ALASKA® magazine, June 1979

Variation: Jeanne Culbertson says that you may also bake seaweed squares at 200°F (93°C) for 15 or 20 minutes. Meanwhile, combine 1/2 cup (120 mL) soy sauce and 1/2 cup (120 mL) honey and mix well. Remove seaweed squares from oven and toss with soy-honey mixture to coat well. Return squares to oven and bake for another 20 to 30 minutes, turning occasionally until crisp.

Rockweed

Seaweed Rolls

Cabbage leaves (enough to make 2 cups
  [480 mL] chopped)
Hot water
1 cup (240 mL) ground pork
1/2 teaspoon (2 mL) Accent
1/2 teaspoon (2 mL) salt
2 teaspoons (10 mL) sesame oil
Alaria, cut into squares as directed

►Soak the cabbage leaves in hot water until they are flexible. Then chop very fine. You should have 2 cups (480 mL). Mix with ground pork, add seasonings and sesame oil. Form mixture into rolls about 1/2 inch (1.25 cm) in diameter and about 2 inches (5 cm) long. Cut alaria into squares large enough to wrap them individually. Steam the rolls about 10 minutes, or until the pork is done and the seaweed is tender.
■ *Jeanne Culbertson, "Sea Treasures"*
   ALASKA® magazine, June 1979

Pickled Kelp

►Cut off the hollow portion of a firm, fresh-looking kelp tube (giant kelp or bull kelp). Wash it in fresh water and cut it into ring slices. Put rings into a glass container along with one large sliced onion, a sprinkle of garlic salt and 1 teaspoon (5 mL) lemon juice. Cover with the following brine and refrigerate for 48 hours or more before serving. (For longer storage, see directions for several varieties of pickled kelp in Chapter 14.)

Brine for Pickling Kelp
2 cups (480 mL) vinegar
2/3 cup (160 mL) water
1 cup (240 mL) white sugar (no substitutes)
4 tablespoons (60 mL) pickling spice

►Combine all ingredients in a saucepan, bring to a boil and boil one minute. Allow to cool before pouring over kelp rings. Beet juice may be added to the brine for color.
■ *C. Joe Murray, Jr., Angoon*
   ALASKA® magazine

Seaweed Chop Suey

1 pint (0.47 L) clams
6 slices bacon, chopped
1 head cabbage, chopped
2 cups (480 mL) dried seaweed
Salt, pepper and soy sauce

►Fry bacon. Add cabbage and enough water to cover. Simmer until cabbage is tender. Add the seasonings, seaweed and clams and heat through. Serve over boiled rice.
■ *Betty Allen, Marine Ways*
   Seafood Secrets, *Sitka*

Seaweed and Fish Eggs

2 cups (480 mL) water
1/4 cup (60 mL) seal oil
1 cup (240 mL) fish eggs — dog salmon or coho
1 cup (240 mL) seaweed*
1 small onion, diced
Salt to taste

►Bring the water and the seal oil to a boil. Add fish eggs and boil for about 10 minutes. Add seaweed and onion and cook for another 15 minutes. Serve with or without rice.

Canned clams may be used in place of fish eggs. Add them with their juice along with the seaweed.
■ *Courtesy, Vivian James, Angoon*

*Various seaweeds are used in similar recipes. For this one, dulse is often used.

I found spruce cones to be as effective as Brillo pads or steel wool to scour my pots.
■ *Dick Proenneke*
   One Man's Wilderness

SILVERWEED

Silverweed (*Potentilla* species) is also called wild sweet potato. It has a long, edible root. There are several subspecies of silverweed but all are much the same in appearance and are cooked in the same manner. The various subspecies together range over most of Alaska except for the Arctic.

The plant has the unusual characteristic of taking root and forming new little plantlets wherever the stolons (runners) touch the ground. In this respect they are much like some species of strawberries. The sunny blossoms are sometimes mistaken for buttercups by the casual observer. The name silverweed comes from the silvery sheen of the undersides of the leaves.

Preparation Tips: The long fleshy roots of the silverweed are used by both Natives and sourdoughs of Southeastern Alaska and are prepared by either boiling or roasting.

SOURDOCK & SOURGRASS

Caution: Some have suggested that any plant of the genus Rumex *used raw should be eaten rather sparingly because of a high potassium oxalate content — which is dissipated when the plants are cooked. It is water soluble.*

Sourdock and sourgrass are common names for a variety of plants so often confused that — for cooking purposes — one may as well treat their various common names as synonyms. In the recipes, when it was clear which plant the cook used, the Latin name has been supplied.

Sourdock — also called wild spinach and Arctic dock — belongs to the genus *Rumex* (part of the buckwheat family). The species found along the Yukon River, on Seward Peninsula from Norton Sound to Nome and Cape Prince of Wales, along the Arctic Coast and in Southeastern is *Rumex arcticus*, native to the North.

Also in the *Rumex* genus are other plants most often called sorrel. *Rumex acetosella* is one that has been introduced successfully in Alaska.

Mountain sorrel, however — also known as sourgrass — belongs to a different genus, *Oxyria*, a plant native to Alaska.

Though the plants differ in appearance, both sourdock and sourgrass are acid tasting; both are good sources of vitamin C; both are prized by

Eskimos; both are eaten either raw — perhaps advisedly in small amounts (see caution) — or cooked, prepared rather like spinach. Sourdock is sometimes mixed with other greens — perhaps sourgrass among them, further adding to the blending of common names — and stored in barrels for the winter.

Preparation Tips: Wash leaves and dry as thoroughly as possible if you wish to use them raw or store them for later use. Store in plastic bags in the refrigerator or a very cool place. Use within a day or two. Raw leaves are good mixed with other leafy greens in salad. Or try them in place of spinach in one of the "Florentine" stuffings for fish (see page 39 for a possibility).

To serve as a cooked vegetable, pack young, washed leaves in a skillet — with a little onion sauteed in butter or margarine or bacon fat, if you wish — cover tightly and steam in the moisture provided by leaves still water-beaded from washing. Season with vinegar or lemon juice.

Bush dwellers, including Natives, use sourdock in soups and stews. The acid content of the greens tenderizes meat when the two are cooked together. Siberian Eskimos are said to relish these leaves chopped, cooked and eaten with sugar and fat.

Mountain sorrel *(Oxyria digyna)*, with its oddly kidney-shaped leaves, is an attractive plant, particularly when in seed; it has a stalk of scarlet seed vessels on the upper third of the stem. Weary hikers often pluck the leaves to chew as they travel, for it has a refreshing acid flavor.

The leaves of mountain sorrel may be cooked as any other green vegetable, and a few of them added to potato soup, along with the chopped leaves of wild chives, make a delectable potage.

Seeds are also edible and can be dried for winter use. Spread them on a tray and dry them in the sun or roast them for about 30 minutes in a moderate oven. Use in breads or cookies or in Sorrel Porridge the breakfast dish on page 294.

Sorrel Stuffed Eggs
(Oxyria digyna)

4 large eggs
1/4 cup (60 mL) mountain sorrel
Salt and pepper to taste
Paprika
3 tablespoons (45 mL) Parmesan cheese
Tomato wedges, salted

►Cook the eggs gently for 15 minutes. Cool quickly in cold water, peel and cut in half lengthwise. Rinse and pat dry with paper towels, some fresh, young mountain sorrel, enough to make 1/4 cup (60 mL) when chopped fine. Remove yolks from egg halves and mash with a fork. Add the mountain sorrel, salt and pepper. Paprika may be added now or sprinkled on later. Fill the whites with this mixture, mounding up the tops. A dab of butter should go on this and then the cheese should be sprinkled over all with another sprinkle of paprika. Run under the broiler long enough for the cheese to melt. Serve on a bed of lettuce and mountain sorrel leaves, garnished with tomato wedges.
■ *The Old Homesteader*

Dock on Toast
(Rumex arcticus)

1 pint (0.47 L) cooked dock greens
1 tablespoon (15 mL) chopped onion
Salt and pepper to taste
1 cup (240 mL) sour cream or a little vinegar
Fried bacon, crumbled

►Mix together and serve on toast. Top with crumbled bacon.
■ Cooking Up A Storm, *Homer*

Stewed Dock
(Rumex arcticus)

3 to 4 cups (0.75 to 1 L) cooked dock greens
2 cups (480 mL) tomatoes, chopped
Onions, chopped, browned in fat
Cheese

►Mix and simmer all but cheese until tomatoes are tender. Serve topped with your favorite cheese.
■ Cooking Up A Storm, *Homer*

A welcome time of the year around Ambler, says Anore Jones, is about the second week of July when somebody announces that it's time to pick qaugaq — sourdock. Anore and her friends pick it by the sackful, enjoy eating some of it fresh, and the rest they pack in barrels to ferment, much as cabbage is treated to make sauerkraut. Below are three of Anore's favorite ways of eating fresh greens. All are excerpted from Anore Jones's article, "Qaugaq — Wild Greens to Eat," which appeared in ALASKA® magazine, August 1979, and are part of the material she is collecting for a book on traditional Eskimo foods.

Hot Supper Greens

►Fill a 1-quart (1 L) pot with chopped greens. Add 1/2 cup (120 mL) hot water, bring to a boil, reduce heat and cover tightly. Cooking time may vary between 2 and 20 minutes. Tougher greens need longer cooking but some people prefer to cook greens as little as possible to preserve more vitamins. When the greens are done to your taste, remove the pan from heat. Stir in butter to taste and serve, accompanied by a small pitcher of vinegar. Although sourdock is already sour, a dash of vinegar further enhances its flavor.

Greens Dessert

►Fill a 1-quart (1 L) pot full of chopped or unchopped sourdock, add 1/2 cup (120 mL) hot water, cover tightly and cook until tender. Remove from heat, cool and serve cold — first stirring in sugar, then seal oil. If you don't ordinarily eat seal oil, try a vegetable oil.

Or, while still hot, stir in honey and butter — about 4 tablespoons (60 mL), each, and serve either hot or cold.

Greens in Akpiks

Akpiks (aqpiks) are cloudberries, or, as they're more often called around Ambler, salmonberries.

►After picking *akpiks*, pick choice sourdock leaves, stems and all. Mix the leaves into the *akpiks* so each leaf is surrounded by berries and there are no air bubbles. When these two acidic foods are stored together, it's the *akpiks* which pickle the greens and give their delicious berry flavor to them. It's a good way to stretch that precious *akpik* flavor. Also, leaves stored this way are probably an excellent source of vitamins A and C.

Sourdock in *akpiks* is eaten just like plain *akpiks* — as a dessert, with sugar and seal oil mixed in, either at the table or ahead of time.

Schav

Jewish sorrel soup

1 pound (456 g) schav (sorrel or sourgrass)
2 onions, minced
8 cups (1.9 L) water
2 teaspoons (10 mL) salt
1 tablespoon (15 mL) fresh lemon juice
1/4 cup (60 mL) sugar, optional
2 eggs
Dairy sour cream

►Wash sorrel and shred. Place sorrel, onions, water and salt in a large, deep saucepan. Bring mixture to a boil, lower heat and simmer, covered, for 45 minutes. Add lemon juice and sugar. Beat eggs and gradually stir into soup. Chill. Serve cold, garnished with sour cream. Yield: 1-1/2 quarts (1.45 L) or six servings, 1 cup (240 mL) each.
■ *Ann Chandonnet*
"Sorrel — Wild Greens for the Bowl"
ALASKA® magazine, Alaska-only edition
September 1978

Dock Soup

(Rumex arcticus)

Cooked dock greens
Milk
Onion
Butter
2 tablespoons (30 mL) flour
Salt and pepper

►Combine all ingredients and cook slowly for half an hour. Vary amounts to please your own palate.
■ Cooking Up A Storm, *Homer*

Maxim's Potage Germiny

2-1/2 cups (600 mL) sorrel leaves
3 tablespoons (45 mL) sweet butter
10 egg yolks, beaten
2 cups (480 mL) heavy cream
4-1/2 cups (1 L) veal or chicken stock
Salt and pepper

►Chop the fresh sorrel leaves into small pieces. Put the butter in a heavy frying pan and gently saute the leaves for three or four minutes. Beat the egg yolks until thick, five minutes. Scald the cream and slowly pour it into the yolks, whisking constantly.

Heat the consomme; season it well with salt and pepper and whisk the egg yolk-cream mixture into it. If not absolutely smooth, strain the mixture. Heat again, but do not boil. Add leaves and butter. Serve immediately accompanied with cheese straws. Yield — 8 cups (1.9 L).
■ *Ann Chandonnet*
"Sorrel — Wild Greens for the Bowl"
ALASKA® magazine, Alaska-only edition
September 1978

Sorrel Brunoise

A delicious garnish or vegetable dish

3 cups (720 mL) sorrel, chopped and prepared
2 tablespoons (30 mL) butter
2 to 3 tablespoons (30 to 45 mL) heavy cream
Salt, pepper and sugar to taste

►Combine the sorrel and butter in a heavy skillet and saute, covered, until liquid evaporates. Then add the cream and season to taste. Use to garnish lamb stew, fillet of sole, veal, sweetbreads or cream soups. Or serve as a vegetable side dish with buttered croutons on top.
■ *Ann Chandonnet*
"Alaska's Plentiful (And Tasty) Wild Foods"
ALASKA® magazine, July 1976

The ABCs of Spruce Gum

All children love gum and mine are no exception. But when my four-year-old announced she was chewing gum one day in spring camp, I was dumbfounded. Gum is not one of the items we pack to our camp. Close questioning disclosed that it was spruce gum and she wouldn't share it with me. But her dad shared his when he came home and gave me very vague directions on how to go about getting more.

"You chew pitch . . . old and hard, not the soft kind."

We set out for a walk among the spruce trees, looking carefully for pitch, which we discovered comes in a wide variety of colors and textures. Old and hard were our guidelines, so I chose such a nubbin and bravely began chewing. It fractured into a vile-tasting powder that caused profuse salivation. I kept chewing and spitting out the saliva and grit, trying to mash something together that could be gum; only a small piece materialized.

Finally we found a piece of whitish pink pitch, so hard I could barely dent it with my fingernail. But it chewed up into nice pink gum with only one mouthful of impurities to spit out. I shared the gum with my daughters. (The only way young children can enjoy spruce gum is to chew ABC — already been chewed — gum.)

Gum became an important part of each day and no walk was complete without it. We got very good at recognizing which pitch would make good gum by its color — pink, white, yellow or brown. Pinkish white pitch ranged from just right to too hard and brittle. It could be softened by mixing in a little bit of softer pitch, raising my body temperature, or chewing only on a warm day. Otherwise it set up hard if I chewed with my mouth open or even talked while chewing. Brown pitch made a good, dark pink gum that usually needed a softener. Hard, dark yellowish pitch chewed up into soft yellow gum, sticky at first, but then chewable and long-lasting.

Wondering how long it took fresh pitch to cure into gum material, we checked along one trail that had been cut about 10 years earlier and found excellent gum pitch.

Chewing is reportedly good for the teeth and gums, and spruce gum seems to have all the good qualities of gum with none of the bad, except that it's not as handy. But then again, sometimes it is even more handy.
■ *Anore Jones, Ambler*

Reprinted from The Cabin Friend, *ALASKA*® magazine, November 1977

Sorrel Porridge
A hot breakfast cereal

1 cup (240 mL) ground, dried sorrel seed (see Preparation Tips, page 292)
3-1/2 cups (840 mL) water
Salt to taste

►Combine ingredients, bring the mixture to a boil and then reduce heat, cover and simmer until tender, about 35 minutes. Serve with butter, brown sugar, cream, applesauce, honey or syrup. Yield: four servings.
■ *Ann Chandonnet*
"Sorrel — Wild Greens for the Bowl"
ALASKA® magazine, Alaska-only edition, September 1978

SPIKED SAXIFRAGE

The upright stems of spiked saxifrage (*Saxifraga spicata*) bear attractive, small white flowers at the top. The thick cluster of large basal leaves makes it an attractive plant even when not in bloom. It is often transplanted to home rock gardens. It inhabits such places as moist subalpine slopes and is sometimes found along mountain streams. It is found only in Alaska and Yukon Territory; the habitats of Norton Sound area and the Kuskokwim and Yukon rivers are notable.

Preparation Tips: Gather the leaves while still young and tender, tear them into bite-sized pieces and use for some of the greens in spring salads.

SPRUCE

Spruce Honey

►The tender, light green tips of the spruce can be gathered in the spring and turned into honey or syrup. Cover tips with water, bring to a rolling boil and cook two hours. Strain the liquid, add an equal amount of sugar and boil again until thick.
■ *Anon.*

Jah

►*Jah* is the Dena'ina name for the kind of spruce pitch used for gum. If you're not used to it, it isn't easy to chew it. First hold it in your mouth awhile

before chewing. This is to make it soft. If you bite down hard on it right away, you'll get it stuck in your teeth. Then it takes a long time to get it out. If you know how, *jah* makes a good chewing gum.
■ Dena'ina, *Tanaina Plantlore (adapted)*

Mama's Spruce Gum

In his autobiography [OSCAR NICTUNE, SR.— Alatna, published in 1980 by Hancock House Publishers, Ltd. for the Yukon-Koyukuk School District] this author describes the spruce gum his mother used to take with her to trade for items brought by others to the great gatherings of far-flung Eskimo groups that occurred in Kotzebue before the year 1898.

►Mother's uncle tell her pick spruce gum to take with her. They come all shapes and sizes. Some like this lollipop candy you got. Different colors, too. Yellow like my butter can to clear like glass.

She only take the kind she can break off. Couldn't chew that clear stuff. Too sticky, it only stretches. That's good for cuts though. Comes from inside those spruce trees we get. Have to split it for that inside gum. It's pure that one, and clean. That's when we put it in our cuts. That's the best. Some of our kids got to know things like this.
■ *Oscar Nictune, Sr., Alatna*

STRAWBERRY SPINACH

The strawberry spinach plant *(Chenopodium capitatum)* — which is also called goosefoot — is neither strawberry nor spinach (and certainly not a goosefoot). It owes its common names to appearance and to use. The clusters of ripe fruit which adorn its long stems at first glance look like strawberries but are much different.

It is a plant that prefers waste places, such as roadsides and gravel bars. Its range covers the Interior and Southcentral Alaska.

Preparation Tips: The fruit of this striking plant is said to be edible but it is not recommended. However, the foliage is good and is prepared like spinach. Wash the leaves through several changes of water before cooking, as the plant grows in dusty surroundings. Bring the leaves to a boil in a small amount of water. Drain immediately; add a little more water and again bring to a boil. Reduce heat, cover and simmer gently until tender. Serve as you would spinach or other greens. Bacon bits sprinkled over the greens add a nice touch.

The first new leaves of spring are a fine addition to tossed salads but they must be picked while young and tender.

(The long, fruit-bearing stems, incidentally, provide a nice color contrast for flower arrangements.)

Goosefoot Salad

►The leaves of goosefoot supposedly resemble the track of a goose. When picked young they can form the main part of a delicious salad. Add other wild greens such as wild celery, fireweed and dandelion but keep the larger proportion as goosefoot. Salt and pepper to taste and chill for a half-hour or so before serving with a generous sprinkling of oil and vinegar dressing.
■ *The Old Homesteader*

VIOLETS

Foraging information about violets is excerpted and adapted from Gretchen Walker's "The Wild Bunch — Alaska's Natural Garden," Alaskan Edibles series, ALASKA® magazine, May 1977.

Several species of violets inhabit Alaska. The northern marsh violet *(Viola epipsela)* is found in wet areas. The plants are often overlooked because they are usually hidden under tall grasses; marsh violets are only a few inches tall and usually have two heart-shaped leaves at the base of the stalk. Alaska violets *(V. langsdorfii)* are similar but are found in less boggy subalpine meadows.

Preparation Tips: Both violets are superior salad material. They are sweeter than most other wild greens. Their flavor is best compared to romaine lettuce. The stalks may be chopped up or removed. The pale purple flowers add sweetness and color to a salad. The leaves may be parboiled and served like spinach. Both leaves and flowers make a delicate aromatic tea if steeped but not boiled.

Wild camomile, also known as "pineapple weed," makes a good deodorant. Rub the raw, fresh plant between your hands to take away a smell like fish.

The Dena'inas (Tanaina Indians) say pineapple weed tea is good for new mothers and infants. It cleans them both out and helps the mother's milk to start. Babies get a very small amount. The tea is used by others as a laxative.
■ Dena'ina K'et'una, *Tanaina Plantlore (adapted)*

WILD CELERY

Caution: *These plants can be confused with the deadly poison water hemlock. Learn to tell the difference!*

Several plants go by the name wild celery, among other common names also given them. They are all members of the parsley family and are often called wild parsley, too. There is seacoast angelica *(Angelica lucida)*, Scotch lovage *(Ligusticum scoticum)*, sea or beach lovage *(L. hultenii)*, and another plant most often known as cow parsnip *(Heracleum lanatum)*. All are tasty plants, especially good with fish. But there's a catch. The plants each look something like poison water hemlock *(Cicuta mackenziana)*. And your most urgent task in planning to use them is to learn to tell the difference because mistaken identity may be deadly. Swallowing even a very small amount of cicutoxin, the poison present in water hemlock, is sufficient to be fatal.

Mary Ford, writing for the *Peninsula Clarion* of Kenai says that "although it is possible to learn to tell them apart by differences in leaf and flower, an easier and surer method is to dig up a root and slice it from top to bottom.

"If you find hollow spaces (horizontal chambering) inside, wash your knife and hands and discard the plant. . . .

"If, on the other hand, you discover no hollow chambers, you know, at least, it is not a water hemlock. All the wild celeries have solid roots."

Try These with Fish

►Beach lovage and other wild celeries are recommended for enhancing the flavor of fish. The peeled, young stalks of wild celery resemble unbleached celery in flavor. They are good eaten raw or cut up and added to salads. Or, they may be boiled briefly in water, the water drained and boiled again until tender. Add this wild celery to stuffing for roasted wild fowl, too. Beach lovage foliage is used like chard or spinach by connoisseurs of wild edibles.
■ *The Old Homesteader*

Poochki

►Pick wild celery — *poochki* or, sometimes, *putchkie* — while young and tender in the spring and early summer. Peel off the outside and then use it as celery. It is sometimes eaten dipped in seal oil.
■ Aleut Cookbook, *Saint Paul Island (adapted)*

Angelica Soup

►Peel and chop 1-1/2 cups (360 mL) angelica or wild celery. Cover with 1 cup (240 mL) boiling water and simmer 20 minutes or until soft. Fish stock may be used instead of water if you have it. Drain and reserve liquid. Mash the vegetable well with a fork or force through a sieve. Add 2 tablespoons (30 mL) margarine, softened and blended with 2 tablespoons (30 mL) flour. Pour in the reserved liquid and 2 cups (480 mL) half-and-half. Heat just to serving temperature and season to taste with salt, pepper and paprika, perhaps with a sprinkling of parsley flakes.

In Siberia, at one time, the root was carried as a charm to keep the polar bears away! Siberian Eskimos also breathed the smoke from roasted angelica roots as a remedy for seasickness.
■ *The Homesteader*

Petruskies

►*Petruskies* — wild parsley — are good in soups. People here dry them to keep them for winter. *Petruskies* grow along the banks of the beach and are green and don't get very big.
■ *Ruth Kudrin*
from "Akutan Food"
Taniisix (To Shed Light)

Scotch Lovage

►Harvest the young stalks of Scotch lovage before the plants bloom so they will still be tender. Cut into bite-sized pieces and bring them to a boil in meat or fish stock or water. Reduce heat and simmer gently until barely tender. Now saute in margarine until lightly browned. Pour on 1/2 cup (120 mL) fish stock. Cook, stirring, for five minutes. Season to taste. A few snips of wild chives would not be amiss on this wild celery. The tender young stems and leaves are good salad material, too.
■ *The Old Homesteader*

Cow Parsnips

►The stalks of the cow parsnip are collected for food while they are still immature and before the blossoms come out. Be sure to peel these stalks

---

To keep insects and bugs away, use any of the mints — catnip is what we use. Just rub catnip on your skin to discourage bugs.

Also place pieces of the mint on your plants to keep the insects away.
■ *Raymond Roadifer, Dayton, Wyoming*
The Cabin Friend
ALASKA® magazine, November 1977

before using. For use in salads they should be thinly sliced and mixed liberally with other salad materials. Their flavor slightly resembles that of licorice. The roots can be used, too. Scrape them and cut into bite-sized sections for adding to soups and stews. They should not be overcooked. Or, alternatively, use them as a vegetable by themselves. After cooking just add butter and a little hot milk, and season as desired.

Creamed Cow Parsnips

Cow parsnip stalks
Water
White Sauce

►Peel the stalks as you would rhubarb and cut into small sections. Cook in enough water to just barely cover them until they are tender and begin to fall apart. Drain and serve with a thin White Sauce or with heated cream and seasoning. Cheese Sauce is also a good sauce to serve with cow parsnips. The peeled stalks may also be sliced very thinly, crisped in the refrigerator and added to salad.
■ *Helen A. White, Anchorage*
What's Cookin' In Alaska

WILD CUCUMBER

Two plants often called wild cucumber look nothing alike, but both make good eating.

The most versatile is *Streptopus amplexifolius,* a member of the lily family that also goes by the names twisted stalk and watermelon berry. The names are all appropriate. The kink in its flower stalk gives it one of them; the shape of its berry provides another; and its distinctive aroma, a third. The plant grows in moist woods and thickets from the Aleutian Islands through Southcentral Alaska and the lower Yukon Territory and south through the Alaska Panhandle to California and the Rockies.

Preparation Tips: The fruit is melon shaped and a clear red, deepening in color until it is dead ripe, when it is extremely juicy, with little pulp.

The tender young shoots should be gathered as early in the spring as you can find them. They are a delicious addition to a green salad. The leaves can also be used this way if collected while they are still tender.

The berries have been reported to act as a cathartic, but that claim is disputed. As a caution, you might not wish to use too many of them at once. In fact, it's rare they can be gathered in enough abundance to use by themselves, and they

are often simply added to other berries in jams or jellies. A lucky gatherer might like to try the Watermelon Berry Syrup recipe that follows.

The other plant called wild cucumber is also known as salad greens to Eskimos and as saxifrage or brook saxifrage after its botanical name *Saxifraga punctata.* It is found in many areas throughout Alaska in moist, rocky and shady places and is especially common along the Bering Sea and Arctic coasts.

Preparation Tips: The leaves of saxifrage should be picked while they are still tender, before the plant flowers. Usually this means early spring, but in areas where the snow is slow to melt, new shoots can be found late in the season. Backpackers who are depending on dried foods to provide most of their tote-along meals will like adding a few of these fresh leaves to a prepackaged stew. They're a good source of vitamins if eaten soon after they are picked. Eskimos eat them raw with seal or walrus oil.

Both recipes below are for the first-mentioned wild cucumber, *Streptopus amplexifolius* . . . or twisted stalk . . . or watermelon berry.

Wild Cucumber Loaf
(Streptopus amplexifolius)

►Cook cucumber sprouts and young leaves as you would any greens in boiling salted water, for 10 to 20 minutes or until tender. Use 1-1/2 cups (360 mL) drained and chopped cucumber greens, 1 cup (240 mL) bread crumbs, one well-beaten egg, 1/2 cup (120 mL) grated cheese, 1 tablespoon (15 mL) lemon juice, 1 teaspoon (5 mL) salt and 1/8 teaspoon (0.5 mL) pepper. Mix well and pour into casserole with cover. Bake in a slow oven, covered, for 30 minutes. Serve alone or with tomato sauce. The young sprouts are good canned as you would any greens, too.
■ *Maxcine Williams*
"*Alaska's Wild Vegetables*"
The ALASKA SPORTSMAN®, *July 1943*

Watermelon Berry Syrup

1 quart (1 L) watermelon berries
1/2 cup (120 mL) water
3/4 cup (180 mL) sugar
Cinnamon, dash

►Crush berries and add the water. Bring to a boil and boil gently for 10 to 15 minutes. Pour the pulp into a moist jelly bag and allow to drain for several hours. Do not squeeze the bag or the juice will be cloudy. Any pulp left over can be combined with other fruit for jam. Pour the juice into a kettle and add the sugar and cinnamon. Bring to a boil and then reduce heat and simmer slowly for 10 minutes. This syrup has a delicate flavor.

WILLOW

There are many species of willow in the state and they are favorite food of moose and other members of the deer family. Willows are eaten to some extent by two-legged animals also. Of the various species available, felt-leaved willow *(Salix alaxensis)* perhaps is more palatable than the others. It is less bitter than some varieties and comparatively sweeter. It is sweetest at breakup time in the spring but is used at other seasons, too. The felt-leaved willow is available in most of Alaska except for the offshore islands and the Aleutians.

Preparation Tips: The inner bark is the part of the willow most relished by those who eat it. The outer bark is first removed and the inner layer then scraped off for food. Eskimos often eat it raw with sugar and seal oil, although it is sweet enough without sugar. Alaska Natives also eat the young shoots in spring but first remove the "yukky" felty layer from the undersides. Willows are a source of early-season green food and, as such, are worthy of a place in bush economy.

Willow Bud Salad

2 double handfuls of willow buds,
*   young and tender*
Oil
Lemon juice
Seasonings

►This is so simple and so good. Other young leaves can be added.
■ *Jim Greenough and Eileen Helmstetter*
*   "The Bush Gourmet"*
*   ALASKA® magazine, July 1977*

WINTER CRESS

Watch for winter cress *(Barbarea orthoceras)* in the spring as it is one of the earliest of our plants that may be used for food. It is found from Southeastern Alaska to the Aleutian Islands and north to the Seward Peninsula. It also grows inland from the coastal areas. It usually inhabits moist places such as riverbanks and pond edges and sometimes ascends to as high as 3,300 feet (990 m). It is also called Barbara cress and poor man's cabbage.

Preparation Tips: The somewhat bitter flavor of the leaves is allayed by soaking them in salted water for 15 minutes or so. Drain and bring to a boil quickly in a small amount of water and drain again. Once more bring to a boil; reduce the heat and simmer slowly until just tender. A few fresh young leaves will not be amiss in a green salad but it is probably best to soak these in salty water briefly, too. The young flower buds — if you can find enough of them — can be simmered until tender and served as you would broccoli.

Cress Soup

►Winter cress was once eaten raw or boiled by Native Siberians and some Alaska Natives, also. Make an excellent soup from young and tender leaves. Sort and wash thoroughly enough such leaves to make about 1-1/4 cups (300 mL); chop fine. Put in the blender together with 3 tablespoons (45 mL) margarine or butter; 3 cups (720 mL) half-and-half or light cream, a few snipped wild chive leaves, 1 teaspoon (5 mL) salt, a dash of black pepper and 1/8 teaspoon (0.5 mL) paprika. Blend until smooth. Remove mixture to saucepan and simmer gently for five to ten minutes. Serve with Sourdough French Bread.
■ *The Old Homesteader*

WOOLLY LOUSEWORT

The woolly lousewort *(Pedicularis lanata)* is indeed woolly, particularly in bud; but how about the second part of its common name? "Wort" means "plant" according to the dictionary. It is said that this plant was once used to ward off lice, hence "lousewort." Never mind the name. This lovely flower has a dense fluorescence of rosy blossoms set quite near the seemingly barren ground on a short thick stem. Its range is wide. It grows in dry, rocky places in the mountains to elevations of 4,500 feet (1.35 km) and over most of the state except for the Gulf of Alaska coast, the Aleutian Islands and has been found only in a restricted habitat in Southeastern.

Preparation Tips: Natives of the Bering Sea coast harvest the flowers as soon as they bloom. They mix them with a little water and allow them to ferment for later use. The large thick roots are often dug in the summer and are prepared either by roasting or stewing.

Ussusaq
Roots "like sweet young carrots"

►Called *ussusaq* by Canadian Eskimos, the woolly lousewort may be used raw in salads or boiled as greens. The roots taste like sweet young carrots and may be eaten raw or boiled and served as a hot vegetable with butter, salt and pepper.
■ Northern Cookbook *(adapted)*

WORMWOOD & YARROW

Two plants that grow wild in Alaska may be used as substitutes for sage. One is prairie sagewort (*Artemisia frigida*), also called wormwood, and the other is yarrow (*Achillea borealis* or *A. sibirica*). The foliage is collected at its peak and air-dried thoroughly. Then it is crumbled and stored in air-tight containers. The foliage should be collected away from roads or it will be full of dust and require washing. Washing destroys much of the savory flavor.

As a seasoning, these wild sages are welcome additions to pork roast or turkey stuffings. They may also be used in sachets to sweeten clothing and sleeping bags that have gotten musty.

The blossoms of yarrow are also used to season meats or meat accompaniments, such as stuffing. They are said to have a flavor similar to rosemary.

No need to waste precious space in your backpack or canoe with commercial scouring pads. Wherever you camp you will be apt to find some natural pot-scouring material. A handful of sand or other soil will get rid of the most determined scorch residue in any kettle or pan. A few pebbles swished around with water in a jug or bottle will do a good cleaning job. And a handful of horsetail (*Equisetum* species) is fine for scouring, too.
■ *Kenai reader*
  The Cabin Friend
  ALASKA® magazine, April 1976

WILD COMBINATIONS

Mix them up! That's among the best ways to use plants gathered from the wild. Following are some suggestions of good partners for tossed salad and mixed cooked greens.

Wild Salad

►When gathering a wild salad, I mix together whatever is in its prime. If you do not like wild greens in bulk, you will be surprised how palatable they are when mixed with lettuce. Try adding 1/4 cup (60 mL) of young willow leaves, 1/2 cup (120 mL) of young fireweed leaves and tips, 1/2 cup (120 mL) sorrel, 2 tablespoons (30 mL) wild chives and a few rose petals to your next spring salad bowl.
■ *Ann Chandonnet, Chugiak*

Wild, Wild Salad

2 cups (480 mL) fresh fireweed shoots
2 tablespoons (30 mL) wild violet leaves
A dozen or so violet blossoms (optional)
A handful of dandelion buds
1 tablespoon (15 mL) wild chives, chopped fine
3 tablespoons (45 mL) young willow leaves
Salt to taste

►Wash all greens in salty water and lift out onto paper towels to dry off slightly. Place in a plastic bag in crisper part of refrigerator for at least two hours. Dress sparingly with oil and vinegar to serve.
■ *The Old Homesteader*

Wilted Greens with Bacon Dressing

►Gather young and tender greens — dandelion, nettle, goose tongue, sorrel, fireweed or other wild greens. Wash leaves thoroughly in lukewarm water. Remove discolored leaves, roots and stems. Wash through at least two waters, lifting greens carefully out of water in order to allow any sand or soil to settle in the pan. Allow greens to dry on thick paper towels. Fry several strips of bacon until crisp. Lift out of fat and crumble. To bacon fat in pan add 2 tablespoons (30 mL) vinegar, 2 tablespoons (30 mL) water, dash of salt and black pepper, and 1 tablespoon (15 mL) brown sugar. Bring to a boil and add crumbled bacon. Pour over greens which have been placed in a salad bowl. Garnish with slices of hard-cooked eggs.
■ *The Old Homesteader*

Spring Salad

►Use fresh greens just coming up in the early spring. Gather a few clover leaves, dandelions, fireweeds, plantain (goose tongue) and a few sprigs of yarrow for flavor. Wash and shake dry. Cut up for salad. Add spices, salt and pepper as desired, and your favorite dressing. Dandelion blossoms, cut fine, will add color.

This same combination is very good sauteed lightly in bacon drippings as you would prepare wilted lettuce.

■ *Florence V.J. Thornton, Rabbit Creek*

Live Off Our Land Wild Salad

10 dandelion plants, with blossoms
10 lamb's-quarters leaves
10 leaves of strawberry spinach or plantain
  (goose tongue)
1 head fresh lettuce, in season, or
  leaf lettuce
Mustard leaves
Watercress, if available

►Cut, trim, wash and cut ingredients into bite-sized pieces. Toss lightly. At serving time toss again with the following dressing.

Wild Salad Dressing
1 cup (240 mL) fresh or canned lemon juice
1/2 cup (120 mL) salad oil
1/4 teaspoon (1 mL) pepper
1/4 teaspoon (1 mL) salt
1 small onion, or 3 green onions with tops,
  chopped fine
Juice and pieces from a crushed tomato
Cubed dry whole-wheat bread

►Mix all but bread cubes together well. Toss with salad greens. Add bread cubes and toss lightly again.

■ *Haines Homemakers' Cookbook (adapted)*

Salted Wild Greens

►Gather dandelion leaves or other wild greens when they are young and tender. Wash them through several waters to be sure all dust and sand is washed away. Blanch the cleaned leaves in boiling water for three minutes or until wilted. Chill

the greens through several cold waters. Weigh them. Using a sterilized crock, layer the greens with pickling salt in the proportion of 1 pound salt to 4 pounds of the green stuff (456 g salt to each 1.8 kg greens). Pack the crock to within 4 inches (10 cm) of the top; cover with a triple thickness of cheesecloth. Place a clean plate on top and a weight on this. Store the crock in a cool place, 38°F (3.5°C), is ideal.

If brine enough to cover the greens has not formed within 24 hours, add more salt solution, using 1 tablespoon salt for each cup of water (15 mL salt to each 240 mL water) needed to cover greens.

To cook, freshen the leaves in cold water for several hours, changing the water a couple of times. Rinse through two or three waters. Then simmer very slowly in just the water clinging to the leaves. Season with a little ham soup base or diced salt pork.

■ *The Old Homesteader*

Emerald Casserole

►Cook about 2 pounds (1 kg) dandelion leaves, lamb's-quarters, fireweed and/or other wild greens until wilted but still bright green. Drain and chop coarsely. Combine with 1-1/2 cups (360 mL) Cream Sauce, 4 hard-cooked eggs, chopped, salt to taste, and 1/2 cup (120 mL) grated cheese and any seasonings you favor. Put in a casserole and sprinkle the top with more grated cheese. Bake at 350°F (175°C) until greens are thoroughly heated and cheese has melted. This is an excellent accompaniment to roast bear or wild fowl.

■ *The Old Homesteader*

Bush Traveler's Wilted Greenery

Pink plume leaves
Willow leaves
Fireweed leaves
Onion flakes and other seasonings
Lemon oil
Oil

►Cut up leaves, saute in oil, add seasonings and enjoy this vegetable supplement to an outdoor dinner.

■ *Jim Greenough and Eileen Helmstetter*
  "The Bush Gourmet"
  ALASKA® magazine, July 1977

Chapter 10

The Alaskan Garden

IN THE FIELD

This chapter is mainly an excuse to use some of the many recipes we've seen for things we don't usually pick from the wild. Two outstanding plants — cabbage and rhubarb — inhabit Alaska gardens so well, often to such monster proportions, that even the Outside world has noticed. Here we are, in the Nebraska farmer's mind's eye, growing cabbages the size of our igloos.

And so, of course, this chapter includes many recipes for cabbage and rhubarb.

Depending somewhat on the locale of the garden, however, a rather vaster range of plants can be grown in Alaska than commonly is imagined even by the Alaska farmer's mind's eye. In the Arctic, in Ambler and Selawik and towns of the Bering Strait and Bristol Bay regions, experiments have proven that residents could support themselves with food production, even to commercial farming of some grains and potatoes.

In milder climates, the variety could be extensive enough to make purchase of imported vegetables unnecessary during season. The list on page 302 indicates what it's possible to grow. To find out more about how to do it, you will want to consult the farm and garden book which The Alaska Geographic Society expects to have available sometime in the near future. The list on page 302 comes from it. We have also collected a little information about transplanting wild edibles to the home garden.

Wild Plants For The Home Garden

You can successfully transplant some wild edibles to your home garden. Many smaller plants, such as wild chives, may either be transplanted or started from seeds gathered when the wild ones mature. Others, such as lamb's-quarters and chickweed, grow unbidden. You might as well eat them and pretend they're part of your plan. Among shrubs and trees that can be transplanted are:

- *Highbush cranberry* — which may grow to 5 or 6 feet (1.5 to 1.8 m).
- *Blueberries*, various kinds — may grow to about 4 feet (1.2 m).
- *Juniper* — a tough little shrub that grows fat rather than tall, may spread out to 12 or 15 feet (3.75 to 4.5 m).
- *Labrador tea* — a beauty that may grow to 2 feet (60 cm) in height; has lovely small creamy flowers.
- *Prickly rose* — which thrives in either sunlight or partial shade, spreads rapidly, and may grow up to 8 feet (2.3 m) in height.
- *Salmonberry* — another shrub that spreads easily and can be (should be) pruned every other year to keep it from growing beyond comfortable harvest height.
- *Willows* — all species — can be grown from seed

if you collect the seeds at the right time and preserve them properly until planting time. Willow cotton puffs — which contain the tiny green seeds — fill the air mid- to late summer (some species, September and October). They die within a few days, but if you collect and freeze them quickly, you can store them till spring. Then spread them on wet soil or paper towels. Presto! Soon you'll have many miniature trees that can be coaxed to greater height in flats or tubs and later in your yard.

Shrubs are not altogether easily transplanted. Try to find small ones that do not have long roots, and be sure to take all the root system. Exercise some caution, too, about where you plant them, not too close together and not where they'll eventually crowd out other valued trees and shrubs.

For digging smaller wild plants to transplant to your garden, The Old Homesteader suggests trying a dandelion digger. It's handier than a trowel, especially if the plants are growing among rocks or in rocky soil, as seems to be the custom of many.

Edibles For The Alaskan Garden

Raise In Open Garden

Well Suited To Alaska Growing Conditions		**Somewhat More Difficult To Grow**
Broccoli*	Onion (sets)	Bean (seldom does well south of Anchorage)
Brussels sprouts**	Parsley**	Beet (many varieties bolt easily)
Cabbage*	Parsnip	Chinese cabbage (early plantings bolt easily)
Cauliflower**	Peas	Garlic
Celery**	Potato	Onion (seed)
Chives	Radish	Shallot
Collards	Rutabaga	Sunflower
Dill††	Spinach†	Apple (some varieties marginally hardy in Southcentral and Southeastern Alaska)
Endive	Swiss chard	Apple-Crabapple Cross
Horseradish	Turnip	Cherry (Southeastern only)
Kale*	Crab apple	Plum (Southeastern only)
Kohlrabi*	Currant	
Leek*	Gooseberry	
Lettuce*	Raspberry	
Mint	Rhubarb	
Mustard	Strawberry	

Raise Through Polyethylene Mulch

Pumpkin**	Sweet corn		
Melon**	Squash**		

Greenhouse Preferred

Cucumber*	Pepper**
Eggplant**	Tomato**

  * Either direct-seeded to garden or greenhouse /or/ grown from transplants

 ** Usually grown from transplants

  † Melody F-1 Hybrid only

†† Luckily this plant thrives in Alaska. Pick leaves as soon as flowers begin to open. Gather seeds when they are ripe — a flat brown color. Both are favorite seasonings for fish and vegetables, especially.

IN THE KITCHEN

Storing Vegetables

Shake or brush off as much garden soil as you can, but otherwise, most vegetables store best if you do not wash them until you are ready to eat them. If you know you are going to use leafy greens within a few days, however, sometimes it's more practical to wash them immediately after you bring them in from the garden.

The best favors you can do for a garden-grown salad (or even a store-grown one) are:
- Clean leafy garden produce, such as leaf lettuce and spinach, through several rinse waters (if garden soil clings).
- Dry the leaves as thoroughly as possible.
- Crisp them by packing loosely into plastic bags with twist-tie seals and storing them in the refrigerator for a few hours.

The best favor you can do for yourself, especially if you're a gardener, is to purchase a vegetable spin-dryer, the kind made of sturdy plastic with a basket inset and a spinner top. Even if you have such limited storage space that you buy new gadgets very reluctantly, a dryer is such a time saver, it's worth spending some space on one.

If you don't dry leafy greens thoroughly, you shorten the amount of time they'll store without going gummy, and you risk watered down, if not soggy, salads and loss of vitamin content.

Head lettuce — which is, alas, for most of us an imported and costly grocery store item — should be given the dry-as-possible storage treatment, too. Discard the outside leaves (that's all the "cleaning" you need to do), grab the head firmly and whack the core end sharply against the sink edge or counter top. That should loosen the core enough that it will pull away easily without the use of a knife. Knife-cut edges turn brown quickly. Refrigerate the lettuce in a plastic bag.

Beans and peas, too, should be stored unwashed in plastic bags and kept at refrigerated temperatures, around 45°F (7°C).

Brush the dirt off root vegetables and cut or twist off the leaves, but don't wash these vegetables either until you are ready to eat them. Some of the leaves make decent eating, but they are no good to the root vegetable once it's been pulled from the garden and, in fact, may draw off nutrients.

Carrots you are going to use within a few weeks may be kept in the refrigerator. For longer storage of large quantities, you need to find another dark cool DRY place, just as is needed for other vegetables such as potatoes, onions, turnips and beets.

In Alaska, the problem is generally finding a dry place that is warm enough rather than cool enough. The best temperature for storing root vegetables is about 55°F (12.5°C).

You may wish to construct a root cellar if you have a very productive garden. Short of that, however, you might try storing root vegetables in sawdust. First, sort them, discarding imperfect ones. Keep like vegetables together . . . some don't mix well in storage. Fill boxes about half full of vegetables. Then pour dampened sawdust over them. Jiggle the box until the sawdust filters down around all the vegetables thoroughly. Add more sawdust to cover to a depth of 2 or 3 inches (5 to 7.5 cm). It may be necessary to pour off the sawdust and inspect the vegetables once or twice during the winter. Sawdust should be dampened again at such times. Store in a cool — again, not too cold — dry place. Potatoes, especially, must be stored away from sunlight to avoid greening of the skins. More information about this is in the recipe section on page 315.

Long-term storage — by freezing, drying, canning — is detailed in Chapter 14.

BEETS

Sour Creamy Beets

2 cups (480 mL) cooked and drained
   julienne beets
1/4 cup (60 mL) sour cream
1 tablespoon (15 mL) vinegar
1-1/2 teaspoons (7 mL) sugar
1/2 teaspoon (2 mL) seasoned salt

Dash garlic powder
Minced fresh chives

►Mix first six ingredients. Heat and stir gently over medium heat until piping hot. Do not boil. Spoon into serving dish and sprinkle with chives. Makes about five servings.
■ *Elva Bahrt Swenson, Seattle*

Syltede Rodbeter
Pickled beets

1-1/2 to 2 quarts (1.5 to 2 L) cooked beets, whole or sliced
1 tablespoon (15 mL) caraway seeds
3 cups (720 mL) vinegar
1/2 cup (120 mL) sugar

►Drain beets and place in large glass jar. Sprinkle layers with caraway seeds. Boil vinegar and sugar and pour piping hot over the beets. Allow to marinate, refrigerated, at least 10 to 14 days before serving.
■ *Bunny Mathisen, Petersburg*
   "Help Yourself To The Sylta Flesk!"
   ALASKA® *magazine, January 1977*

Russian America Borscht
Borscht is one of those soups that may change every time you make it. Serve the soup hot or well chilled. Often the cold version is strained first, and only the flavorful broth is served. Add a generous spoonful of sour cream to the top of each serving and pass a bowl full of it, too. Horseradish is another item that should be on the table for individualized seasoning.

2 strips bacon, cut in 1-inch (2.5 cm) pieces
1 pound (456 g) lean moosemeat or other game
   (beef, in a pinch)
1 large onion, chopped
2 or 3 raw beets, peeled and diced
   (about 1-1/2 cups /or/ 360 mL)
1 large carrot, diced
2 medium turnips, diced
1 teaspoon (5 mL) flour
2 quarts (1.9 L) game or beef stock
1/4 cup (60 mL) vinegar
2 teaspoons (10 mL) sugar
1 cup (240 mL) shredded cabbage
1 potato, cubed
2 tablespoons (30 mL) tomato paste
An additional teaspoon (or more) of flour
Salt and pepper to taste
1 pint (0.47 L) sour cream

►Brown bacon in bottom of Dutch oven or soup kettle until almost crisp. Spoon out bacon and drain on paper towel. Drain off all but about a tablespoon (15 mL) of bacon fat. Chop meat into 1-inch (2.5 cm) cubes, removing as much fat as you can. Brown it and the onions in hot bacon fat. Then add the beets, carrot, turnips and bacon pieces. Sprinkle them with a teaspoon (5 mL) of flour and stir everything around to absorb the fat. Add stock, bring to a boil, cover and simmer until meat is tender, about 1-1/2 hours. If your soup kettle is ovenproof, you may bring the soup to a boil on top of the stove and then set it in the oven to continue cooking at about 325°F (160°C), two hours or more.

When the meat is tender, add vinegar, sugar, shredded cabbage and potato and cook 30 minutes longer, or until potato and cabbage are done.

Measure tomato paste into a larger cup or bowl, add flour and then thin the mixture with several spoonfuls of the hot soup, blending it well and then stirring it into the soup. Add salt and pepper to taste . . . more vinegar, if you want. Serve with sour cream as a garnish. Makes eight servings. Rye bread, dill pickles, a soft spreadable cheese and dark beer make good accompaniments.
■ *The editors, ALASKA® magazine*

Harvard Beets

6 medium beets, cooked and diced
1/2 cup (120 mL) sugar
1/2 teaspoon (2 mL) salt
1/2 tablespoon (7 mL) cornstarch
1/2 cup (120 mL) mild vinegar
2 tablespoons (30 mL) butter

►Mix sugar, salt, cornstarch and vinegar in a small saucepan. Boil five minutes. Pour over beets and let stand in a warm place for half an hour. When serving, dot with butter.
■ *Mamie Jensen, Juneau*

BROCCOLI

Chicken and Broccoli

1-1/2 pounds (685 g) broccoli
2-1/2 cups (600 mL) cooked cubed chicken or other fowl
1 cup (240 mL) mayonnaise
1 tablespoon (15 mL) lemon juice
2 cans cream of chicken soup
1/4 tablespoon (4 mL) poultry seasoning
2/3 cup (180 mL) grated sharp cheese
1-1/2 cups (360 mL) bread crumbs
2 tablespoons (30 mL) butter

►Cook broccoli, drain well and place in a greased

9 x 13-inch (22 x 32 cm) baking dish. Spread cubed chicken over broccoli. Heat together the mayonnaise, lemon juice, cream of chicken soup and poultry seasoning, stirring to blend well. Pour over chicken and broccoli. Sprinkle on grated cheese. In a small skillet, brown the bread crumbs in butter and sprinkle over all. Bake at 325°F (160°C) for one hour.
■ *Mary Dearmin, "Sourdough Sampler"*
Great Lander Shopping News
Anchorage, October 1978

Lemon Broccoli

1 pound (456 g) broccoli spears
1/4 teaspoon (1 mL) salt
1 tablespoon (15 mL) lemon juice

►If broccoli is fresh, blanch in boiling water for three minutes and drain. If frozen, thaw as you would frozen meat. Then, place broccoli in casserole dish, sprinkle with salt and lemon juice and bake at 350°F (175°C) for 30 minutes.
■ *Deane Feetham*
"An Alaskan Dinner Party"
ALASKA® magazine, June 1971

CABBAGE

Palmer Calico Salad
In honor of the Alaska State Fair

1-1/2 cups (360 mL) shredded red cabbage
1-1/2 cups (360 mL) shredded green cabbage
1/4 cup (60 mL) minced onion
1/2 cup (120 mL) Miracle Whip salad dressing
1 tablespoon (15 mL) vinegar
2 tablespoons (30 mL) sugar
1/4 teaspoon (1 mL) salt
1/4 teaspoon (1 mL) celery salt

►In a large bowl combine the cabbages and onion. In a smaller bowl, whip together the salad dressing, vinegar, sugar, salt and celery salt.

Pour the dressing over the cabbage and mix well. Chill. Serves four.
■ *Gordon R. Nelson, Palmer*
Smokehouse Bear

Spruce up stale vegetables by soaking them for one hour in cold water with 1 tablespoon (15 mL) vinegar added.
■ Tried and True Recipes, *Juneau*

Matanuska Cabbage Soup

1 small head cabbage — about a pound (456 g)
3 cups (720 mL) milk
1 cup (240 mL) light cream
3 tablespoons (45 mL) butter
Salt and pepper
Paprika

►Chop cabbage fine, omitting core. Cover with boiling water. Cook seven minutes uncovered. Drain, reserving 1 cup (240 mL) of the liquid. Combine cabbage and liquid with milk and cream. Simmer three minutes. Season to taste with salt and pepper. Pour in hot tureen and top with butter. Sprinkle with paprika. Makes eight servings as a first course.

■ *Ann Chandonnet*
  "Christmas in Alaska"
  ALASKA® *magazine, December 1978*

24-Hour Cabbage Salad

4 pounds (1.8 kg) cabbage, sliced thin
2 carrots, grated

2 green peppers, grated
1 onion, grated

►Combine. Toss well with 24-Hour Dressing and refrigerate 24 hours. This salad will keep several days; the flavor improves as it stands.

24-Hour Dressing
1 tablespoon (15 mL) gelatin
1/4 cup (60 mL) cold water
1-1/2 cups (360 mL) sugar
1 cup (240 mL) vinegar
1 teaspoon (5 mL) celery seed
1/4 teaspoon (1 mL) pepper
1 teaspoon (5 mL) salt
1 cup (240 mL) salad oil

►Soften gelatin in cold water. Heat sugar and vinegar until sugar dissolves. Cool and add celery seed, pepper and salt. Add softened gelatin and chill to the thickness of cream. Add salad oil and toss with salad mixture.

■ *Barbara Shea*
  Recipes From The Scrolls of Saint Peter's
  Seward

Freezer Coleslaw with Vinegar Dressing

*Champion at the 1976 Tanana Valley Fair . . .
and a good way to preserve some of your extra
cabbages for winter use*

1 medium cabbage, shredded or chopped
1 teaspoon (5 mL) salt
1 carrot, grated
1 red pepper, chopped
1 green pepper, chopped
Vinegar Dressing

►Mix salt with cabbage and let stand one hour. Squeeze out excess moisture. Add carrot, peppers and dressing. Toss well and pack into airtight freezer containers. The salad will thaw for use in a short time, and leftover slaw can be refrozen.

Vinegar Dressing
1 cup (240 mL) vinegar
1/4 cup (60 mL) water
1 teaspoon (5 mL) celery seed
1 teaspoon (5 mL) mustard seed
1-1/2 cups (360 mL) sugar, or slightly more
  if desired

►Combine ingredients and boil one minute. Cool to lukewarm before pouring over slaw mixture.
■ *Shirley Boulette*
  Alaska Grown Cabbage —
  More Than Just Sauerkraut

Chow Mein Cabbage

3 cups (720 mL) shredded cabbage
1 cup (240 mL) bias cut celery
2/3 cup (180 mL) green pepper chunks
1 cup (240 mL) chopped onion
2 tablespoons (30 mL) butter or margarine
1/2 teaspoon (2 mL) salt

►Melt butter; add vegetables and salt. Cook five minutes, stirring constantly. Cover and cook until vegetables are tender but still crisp — three to five minutes. Serve immediately. Soy sauce can be added.
■ *Bruth George*
  Alaska Grown Cabbage —
  More Than Just Sauerkraut

Cabbage Salad with Sour Cream Dressing

4 cups (1 L) shredded cabbage
1 green pepper, sliced thin
3 fresh tomatoes, cut in wedges
1 hard-cooked egg, sliced

1/2 cup (120 mL) grated sharp cheese
Sour Cream Dressing

►Toss all ingredients together and garnish with tomato slices and green pepper strips.

Sour Cream Dressing
3/4 cup (180 mL) sour cream
2 tablespoons (30 mL) ketchup
1 tablespoon (15 mL) minced onion
2 tablespoons (30 mL) salad oil
1/2 teaspoon (2 mL) Worcestershire
1 teaspoon (5 mL) lemon juice
1/4 teaspoon (1 mL) ground pepper
1/2 teaspoon (2 mL) celery seed
1/2 teaspoon (2 mL) prepared mustard
1 teaspoon (5 mL) honey

►Beat with a fork or wire whip until well blended. Add to salad ingredients and toss well.
■ *Deane Feetham*
  "An Alaskan Dinner Party"
  ALASKA® magazine, June 1971

Pan-Fried Cabbage

►Heat 1 cup (240 mL) bacon drippings in a heavy skillet over medium heat. Add sliced onions and saute until tender. Shred cabbage; add to skillet with onions (do not add water). Add salt and pepper to taste. Cook over high heat for about 10 minutes, stirring often.
■ *Betty Fletcher*
  Alaska Grown Cabbage —
  More Than Just Sauerkraut

Barrel Cooler: A large, efficient cooler can be made by urethaning a 30-gallon *plastic* garbage barrel. Just remove the handles (if possible) and urethane the garbage barrel with the lid on. Cut the lid off with a pocketknife and replace the handles. To insulate the bottom, we sprayed the urethane on the inside to prevent it from getting torn off when it is moved from place to place. We applied about a 2-inch (5 cm) coating. One inch (2.5 cm) of urethane is equal to about 3 inches (7.5 cm) of fiberglass insulation.

This cooler is much cheaper than a manufactured one of comparable volume. A half-gallon (1.9 L) milk carton of ice will last up to 10 days if the lid isn't removed too often. To hold the lid on, use an elastic tie-down, just hook one end in a handle and stretch it to the other side and hook it.
■ *Jay Rasmussen, Fairbanks*
  The Cabin Friend
  ALASKA® magazine, November 1977

Sweet and Sour Cabbage

5 cups (1.2 L) shredded cabbage (red is nice
    but color is optional)
5 slices bacon
1 large onion, chopped
1/2 cup (120 mL) water
2 tablespoons (30 mL) flour
1/3 cup (80 mL) vinegar
2 tablespoons (30 mL) brown sugar
Salt and pepper

►Brown four slices bacon until crisp in Dutch oven
or large skillet with cover. Drain on absorbent
paper and set aside. Pour off most of the fat and
reserve. Cut fifth piece of bacon in 1-inch (2.5 cm)
chunks and brown slightly but do not crisp. Add
chopped onion and saute until translucent. Add
cabbage, toss until well-coated with fat. Add water
and simmer, covered, over low to moderate heat,
until cabbage is almost tender, about 20 to 30
minutes. Take care not to burn cabbage but don't
drown it with additional water, either.

Mix 2 tablespoons (30 mL) drained bacon fat
with flour, blend in vinegar and brown sugar and
pour over cabbage. Mix well and continue cooking
another 10 to 15 minutes. Salt and pepper to taste.
Just before serving, crumble crisp bacon over top.
■ *The editors, ALASKA® magazine*

Swedish Meat Loaf Roasted With Cabbage

1 medium-sized head of cabbage
1 pound (456 g) ground round steak
1/2 pound (228 g) ground pork steak
1 small boiled potato, mashed, or 1/2 cup
    (120 mL) boiled rice
1 cup (240 mL) bread crumbs
1 egg
1 teaspoon (5 mL) sugar
1 teaspoon (5 mL) salt
1/2 teaspoon (2 mL) pepper
1/2 teaspoon (2 mL) sage
1 cup (240 mL) milk
1 teaspoon (5 mL) grated onion, optional

►Remove outer leaves of cabbage. Cut head in
fourths and remove stalk. Break leaves apart and
cover bottom of roaster. Sprinkle with salt and pour
a little boiling water over. Put on cover and set over
fire to steam until a little wilted. Mix remaining
ingredients well. Form two oblong loaves and place
on top of cabbage. Place in oven and roast for about
two hours. Turn the loaves and stir cabbage
occasionally.
■ *Esther M. Johnson*
    PTA Cook Book, *Petersburg*

Hot Cabbage Slaw

1/2 clove garlic, minced
3 tablespoons (45 mL) salad oil or butter
1/4 cup (60 mL) water
8 cups (1.9 L) finely shredded cabbage,
    well packed
Cream Dressing

►Brown the garlic in fat on low heat five minutes.
Add cabbage and water and cover. Simmer eight to
ten minutes. Pour Cream Dressing over hot cabbage, toss lightly and serve at once. Makes four or
five servings.

Cream Dressing
1 egg
1/3 cup (80 mL) canned milk or cream,
    sweet or sour
1 tablespoon (15 mL) lemon juice
1 tablespoon (15 mL) sugar
1 teaspoon (5 mL) salt
1/2 teaspoon (2 mL) celery seed

►Beat together with a fork or wire whip and pour
over hot cabbage as directed.
■ Alaska Grown Cabbage —
    More Than Just Sauerkraut

*About Sauerkraut: To find out how to turn your
excess cabbage crop into sauerkraut, see Suzanne
M. Hall's instructions in Chapter 14. Below are
several of her recipes for using the tangy
vegetable. All — except those noted — come from
her article, "Alaska Sauerkraut Party,"
ALASKA® magazine, October 1979. She shares
three interesting salads and a recipe for a wonder-
fully moist cake. Let us put our bid in for a
favorite, too: A very unusual kraut recipe is in
Chapter 2 — German Style Fish Bake—
in which lingcod (or another white fish) is baked
on a bed of sour cream and dill-flavored
sauerkraut.*

Applekraut Salad

►Drain a pint (0.47 L) of kraut and put it into a
bowl. Peel and core several apples, slice into thin
wedges and add to the kraut. Add shredded carrots
for a dash of color before tossing, chilling and
serving. A little honey or sugar may be added if the
kraut is especially sour, and commercially canned
kraut and unsweetened pie apples may be used
instead of fresh ingredients.

Spiced Cider Salad

1 package (3 oz /or/ 85 g) lemon gelatin
1 cup (240 mL) boiling sweet cider
1 cup (240 mL) cold sweet cider

1 cup (240 mL) unpeeled red apples, chopped
1 cup (240 mL) drained sauerkraut,
    chopped fine

►Dissolve the gelatin mix in boiling cider, stirring until clear. Add the cold cider. Chill until thick (about consistency of raw egg white). Fold in the apples and kraut. Spoon into serving dish or individual molds. Chill until firm. Makes about six servings.

Coleslaw

►Use drained kraut instead of fresh cabbage, and add canned pineapple tidbits to highlight the tang. Pour a sweetened mayonnaise dressing over the kraut.

Sauerkraut Surprise Cake

1/2 cup (120 mL) butter or margarine
1-1/2 cups (360 mL) sugar
3 eggs
1 teaspoon (5 mL) vanilla
2 cups (480 mL) sifted flour
1/2 cup (120 mL) cocoa powder
1 teaspoon (5 mL) baking powder
1 teaspoon (5 mL) baking soda
1 cup (240 mL) water
1 cup (240 mL) sauerkraut, drained and
    chopped fine

►Cream butter and sugar until light. Beat in eggs one at a time. Add vanilla. Sift next four ingredients and 1/4 teaspoon (1 mL) salt. Add to creamed mixture alternately with 1 cup (240 mL) water, beating after each addition. Snip the kraut or chop it. (I put mine in the blender and chop it until it resembles grated coconut in size.) Stir kraut into cocoa mixture. Turn into a greased and floured 13 x 9-inch (32 x 22 cm) baking pan. Bake at 350°F (175°C) for 35-40 minutes. Cool, then frost with any chocolate frosting. Serves 12 to 16.

It's really a good cake, the kraut adding moisture and a pleasant tang but not obvious as an ingredient. One friend suggested that if people were put off by the cake's name we could call it "Chocolate Surprise Cake," with the surprise remaining a mystery. But when something is so good, why keep it a secret!

Beefrocks

Grand Champion — 1975 Tanana Valley Fair

2 large potatoes
1 packet (¼ oz /or/ 7 g) dry yeast
2/3 cup (160 mL) sugar
1-1/2 teaspoons (7 mL) salt
2 eggs, beaten

2/3 cup (160 mL) oil
7 to 7-1/2 cups (1.7 to 1.9 L) flour
Filling
Glaze (see below)

►Peel and chunk potatoes. Cook, then drain, saving 1-1/2 cups (360 mL) potato water. Mash potatoes. You will need about 1 cup (240 mL). Soften yeast in warm potato water. Add sugar and salt. Allow to dissolve. Stir in potatoes, eggs and oil. Mix well. Add flour until the dough is stiff enough to handle easily. Let stand 10 minutes. Knead until smooth and elastic. Cover and let rise in refrigerator up to 24 hours. Then let stand at room temperature one hour. Divide into thirds. Roll each into rectangle 1/4 inch (6 mm) thick. Cut into 4-inch (10 cm) squares. Place 1 tablespoon (15 mL) filling in each square. Bring up corners and pinch. Heat oven to 350°F (175°C). Let beefrocks rise 15 to 20 minutes on baking sheet. Brush tops with glaze of one egg yolk beaten with 1 tablespoon (15 mL) water. Bake 20 minutes. Makes about three dozen. Can be frozen and reheated in foil at 300°F (150°C) for 20 to 25 minutes.

Beefrocks Filling
1-1/2 pounds (685 g) ground chuck
1 can (16 oz /or/ 456 g) sauerkraut, washed
    and drained
1 envelope dry onion soup mix
1/2 teaspoon (2 mL) salt
Cayenne pepper to taste
1/2 cup (120 mL) pickle relish (optional)

►Cook and drain meat. Add remaining ingredients. Mix.
■ *Deanna Morris*
    Bake-Off Cookbook, 1961-1980, Fairbanks

CARROTS

Another staple of the Alaska garden — and of a healthy diet — is the deliciously sweet carrot, which can be used for any course of a meal, from hors d'oeuvres "chip" to cream soup to cake. Grate about 1/2 cup (120 mL) of carrot to add to your next meat loaf instead of the usual celery for a welcome flavor change. Add grated carrot to almost any salad, vegetable or meat mixture to spark up the color.

As to its healthiness, one raw carrot provides well more than the U.S. Recommended Daily Allowance of vitamin A and is also an excellent source of vitamin C.

About storing carrots for the long-term, The Old

Homesteader says, "Many of us in Alaska do not have the proper storage facilities. Carrots are best stored in a cool place, but if you don't have such a place, they may be frozen as well as any other vegetable. Simply scrub the carrots well with a plastic scouring ball to get off the thin skin and the little hair roots. Then blanch them in boiling water for two minutes (tiny whole carrots, four minutes). The larger carrots may be either sliced or diced. I like to dice them and then blanch them. Dump the carrots into cold water immediately after taking them from the boiling water. Chill thoroughly and drain well before putting them into freezer containers. I usually spread mine on a cookie sheet and quick freeze. Then I put them in large plastic bags. That way they are not frozen into a solid mass and as many as needed can be taken out and the bag resealed. I put a few sprigs of parsley in the bags to enhance the appearance, too."

Combination Salad

1 large carrot, peeled and grated
1/2 large red Delicious apple, chopped
*   and peeled*
1 can (6½ oz /or/ 185 g) crushed pineapple,
*   drained*
1/2 cup (120 mL) chopped raisins
1 tablespoon (15 mL) sugar
3 tablespoons (45 mL) mayonnaise
1 tablespoon (15 mL) wild raspberry jam

►Place first four ingredients in bowl. Sprinkle with sugar. Add mayonnaise and jam and mix well.
■ *Hank Spees*
  Loggin' Camp Cookin' Book, *Dry Pass*

Piquant Carrot Salad

1-1/2 pounds (685 g) carrots (about
*   8 medium ones)*
1 medium onion
1 small green pepper
1/4 cup (60 mL) white wine vinegar
3 tablespoons (45 mL) sugar
3 tablespoons (45 mL) salad oil
1 tablespoon (15 mL) ketchup
1/2 teaspoon (2 mL) seasoned salt
1/2 teaspoon (2 mL) celery seed
1/2 teaspoon (2 mL) Worcestershire
1/2 teaspoon (2 mL) Dijon mustard

►Peel carrots and cut into slanting slices about 1/4 inch (6 mm) thick. Cook, covered, in 1 inch (2.5 cm) boiling salted water, until just tender. Drain and cool quickly in cold water; then drain thoroughly. Cut onion and green pepper into rings. In a serving bowl, layer carrots and vegetable rings.

Combine remaining ingredients, mix well and pour over carrot mixture. Cover and chill for at least four hours or overnight, stirring several times.
■ *Jean Taylor*
  Loggin' Camp Cookin' Book, *Dry Pass*

Carrot-Egg Pirozhki
"Little pies" — A Russian appetizer

Very flaky pastry dough
4 large carrots, cooked
4 hard-cooked eggs
1 tablespoon (15 mL) soft butter
Minced chives and parsley
Salt and pepper
Glaze

►Chop carrots and eggs. Season with butter, chives and parsley, salt and fresh-cracked pepper.
  Roll pastry about 1/8 inch (6 mm) thick. Cut into 3-inch (7.5 cm) rounds. Place one rounded teaspoon (6 mL) filling on side of each round. Fold over to form a half-moon. Moisten edges with cold water and seal with floured tines of fork. Vent crust. Chill about one hour. Place on greased baking sheet and brush with a glaze of one egg yolk beaten with a spoonful of milk. Bake at 375°F (190°C), 15 to 20 minutes. Serve as an appetizer or as an accompaniment to a full-meal soup or salad.
■ *Elva Bahrt Swenson, Seattle*

Buttered Carrots

1/4 cup (60 mL) butter or margarine
2 pounds (1 kg) carrots, quartered and
*   cut in lengths of about 2 inches (5 cm)*
2 teaspoons (10 mL) fresh lemon juice
Snipped parsley
Salt if desired

►Melt butter (or margarine) in medium saucepan until barely bubbly. Add carrot pieces and stir until they are well coated with butter. Turn heat to medium-low and cover saucepan. Check frequently during the first minutes of cooking to make sure carrots are not burning; stir up butter over carrots again. Within a few minutes the carrots will begin to create their own juice, and then you can relax and let them cook gently about 20 to 30 minutes. At the last minute, stir in lemon juice and salt if desired. The lemon juice perks up flavor in the same way light salting does, and this way of cooking will make your carrots as sweet as if you'd added a pinch or two of sugar. Add snipped parsley at serving time. Enough for six people.

Variation: Start the butter as above. In it saute a split clove of garlic and some onion — 1/4 cup (60 mL) or more, to taste. Add three carrots, cut as directed above, stir them around until they are well coated. Lower heat, cover and cook about 10 minutes. Then add chunks of cabbage and turnip, stir to coat, add the lid again and continue cooking until done, about 20 minutes. Season with lemon juice and soy sauce to taste. For a saucepan full of vegetables — about 2 teaspoons (10 mL), each. Delicious.

Harvest (Carrot) Cake
An entry for the Tanana Valley Fair Bake-Off

1-1/4 cups (300 mL) salad oil
2 cups (480 mL) sugar
2-1/4 cups (540 mL) sifted flour
2 teaspoons (10 mL) baking powder
1 teaspoon (5 mL) soda
1/2 teaspoon (2 mL) salt
1 teaspoon (5 mL) cinnamon
4 eggs
3 cups (720 mL) finely grated carrots
Cream Cheese Frosting

►Combine sugar and oil; mix well. Sift dry ingredients together, add half to sugar mixture and blend. Add remaining dry ingredients alternately with eggs, mixing well after each addition. Stir in carrots. Pour into lightly oiled 10-inch (25 cm) tube pan and bake at 325°F (160°C) for 70 minutes.

Or, pour into three 8-inch (20 cm) layer cake pans and bake at 350°F (175°C) for 25 to 30 minutes. (Double the frosting recipe for layer cake.)

Cream Cheese Frosting
1/4 cup (60 mL) butter
4 ounces (114 g) cream cheese
2 cups (480 mL) sifted powdered sugar
1/2 cup (120 mL) chopped pecans or walnuts

►Cream all ingredients together. Add enough milk to spread easily.
■ *Bernice Kinney*
Bake-Off Cookbook, 1961-1980, *Fairbanks*

Homestead Milkshake

Young carrots, prepared as directed to make:
1 cup (240 mL) carrot pulp
1/4 cup (60 mL) brown sugar
2 tablespoons (30 mL) white sugar
Assorted spices (as for pumpkin pie)
Dash of salt
2 eggs
1 to 2 cups (240 to 480 mL) cold milk

►Wash unpeeled carrots thoroughly to get off the garden dirt. Just barely cover them with water and boil gently until soft. Mash with a potato masher or puree them in a blender. Measure 1 cup (240 mL)

into a bowl. Add sugars, spices and salt. Beat eggs until foamy (in the blender if you're using one). Add the prepared carrot pulp and milk as desired. Use the aerate speed on the blender until well mixed —a few seconds should be enough. Lacking a blender, put the mixture in an empty milk carton or container with a screw-top lid, close tightly and shake vigorously for a few minutes. This makes a wholesome beverage, especially if a little rose hip powder is added. It is a good way to use those tiny carrots from the garden. A scoop of vanilla ice cream is fine in this too.
■ *The Old Homesteader*
The Cabin Friend
ALASKA® magazine, March 1977

Carrot Marmalade

1 pound (456 g) carrots
2 lemons
1 orange
4 cups (1 L) sugar
Boiling Water

►Wash and peel carrots. Squeeze juice out of lemons and remove seeds. Put carrots and lemon rind through food chopper. Cut the orange into very thin slices and remove seeds. Combine all ingredients and add 1/2 cup (120 mL) boiling water. Cook until a little of the mixture jells. Pour into glasses and refrigerate.
■ *Elsie Pegues, Fairbanks*
One Hundred Years in the Kitchen, *Juneau*

CAULIFLOWER

Baked Cauliflower

1 cauliflower
1/2 cup (120 mL) tomato sauce
1/2 teaspoon (2 mL) Worcestershire
Minced onion flakes
3/4 cup (180 mL) grated cheese
Salt and pepper to taste

►Remove outer leaves and cut core of cauliflower so that it will stand upright. Boil about 20 minutes, or until tender, in salted water to cover. Lift from water and drain well. Place in shallow casserole upright. Heat tomato sauce, add Worcestershire and onion flakes and stir until flakes swell. Salt and pepper the cauliflower, pour on the tomato sauce to cover well and sprinkle cheese over all. Bake at 350°F (175°C) 10 to 15 minutes or until cheese is lightly browned and bubbly.

Italian Vegetables in Beer Batter

1-1/4 cups beer
1-1/3 cups (320 mL) flour
2 tablespoons (30 mL) grated Parmesan
1 tablespoon (15 mL) minced parsley
1 teaspoon (5 mL) salt
Dash garlic powder
1 tablespoon (15 mL) olive oil
2 egg yolks, beaten
2 egg whites, stiffly beaten
1 medium zucchini, sliced
1 cauliflower, broken into florets
1 green pepper, cut into strips
1 package (9 oz /or/ 255 g) artichoke hearts,
    cooked and drained
Cooking oil

►Let beer stand at room temperature 45 minutes
or until flat. In mixing bowl, combine flour,
Parmesan, parsley, salt and garlic powder. Stir in
olive oil, egg yolks and flat beer. Beat until smooth.
Fold in egg whites. Dip vegetables in batter. Fry in
deep hot fat 375°F (190°C), a few at a time, until
golden, two to five minutes. Drain on absorbent
paper, serve immediately. Makes 3 cups (720 mL)
batter.
■ *Karen Jennings*
    Cooking Up A Storm, *Homer*

CUCUMBER

Jajik
(Cucumber salad)

1 cup (240 mL) yogurt
2 cucumbers, peeled and chopped
1/4 teaspoon (1 mL) salt
1 teaspoon (5 mL) olive oil
1 clove garlic, pressed
1 tablespoon (15 mL) minced fresh mint
2 tablespoons (30 mL) dill seeds

►Combine all ingredients, mixing thoroughly.
Chill at least one hour before serving.
■ *Julia McCray*
    Loggin' Camp Cookin' Book, *Dry Pass*

Cucumber and Bacon

4 cucumbers
3 slices bacon
2 tablespoons (30 mL) tarragon vinegar
1 tablespoon (15 mL) sugar

1 tablespoon (15 mL) flour
Salt
Pepper

►Pare the cucumbers and slice them thinly.
Spread them in a bowl and sprinkle with a tablespoon (15 mL) of salt. Let stand for half an hour to
draw their juice. Drain. Dice the bacon and fry till
crisp. Pour the bacon, with fat, on the cucumbers.
Put on the sugar and some pepper. Simmer,
covered, 25 minutes. Sift flour over them and stir
three minutes. Serve hot.
■ Cooking Up A Storm, *Homer*

Pickled Cucumbers

1/2 cup (120 mL) white vinegar
1/4 cup (60 mL) sugar
1/2 teaspoon (2 mL) salt
2 tablespoons (30 mL) water
2 tablespoons (30 mL) chopped parsley or
    dill weed
2 medium cucumbers

►Mix all ingredients except the cucumbers. Wash
cucumbers, peel and slice thin. Put in bowl and add
vinegar mixture. Refrigerate two to three hours
before serving.
■ *Mamie Jensen, Juneau*

Variation: If the cucumbers have attractive skins,
don't peel them. Wash, dry; then score them,
drawing the tines of a fork the full length of the
cucumber, all the way around. When you slice the
cucumbers, the slices will have pretty "pinked"
(green) edges.

EGGPLANT

Moussaka
*A classic Rumanian dish now claimed
by many countries*

Butter
3 medium onions, diced
1 pound (456 g) ground beef
1 cup (240 mL) tomato paste
3/4 cup (180 mL) water
About 2 pounds (1 kg) eggplant
Oil
3 eggs, beaten
Buttered bread crumbs

►Saute onions in butter until golden. Add ground
beef and cook until it loses its red color. Add tomato
paste and water. Cook on medium heat for 20
minutes. Slice unpeeled eggplant 1/4 inch (6 mm)

thick and fry in very hot oil until the slices turn brown. Place on paper towels to absorb fat. Butter bottom and sides of an ovenproof casserole (souffle type), about 6 inches (15 cm) high and 10 inches (25 cm) in diameter. Make a layer of eggplant in bottom of casserole; top it with a layer of meat and a layer of beaten egg. Repeat until all ingredients are used, ending with a layer of eggplant which will be sprinkled with bread crumbs. Bake at 400°F (205°C) for 45 to 60 minutes and until the top layer is golden.

■ *Matushka Targonsky*
Saint Herman's Sisterhood Club, Kodiak

Variation: Game meat, especially Dall sheep and mountain goat, is good in moussaka. The mold — either the souffle dish described or a large angel food pan or charlotte mold — is often lined with the skins of eggplant. It will take more than called for here, and be sure to grease the mold well before laying them in. The unmolded dish resembles a large purple cake and can be sliced that way, too.

Guido's Stuffed Eggplant

1 large eggplant
4 eggs
1/2 cup (120 mL) half-and-half
2 tablespoons (30 mL) chopped parsley
Salt and pepper
1/2 teaspoon (2 mL) garlic powder
1/4 cup (60 mL) grated Romano or Parmesan
1 cup (240 mL) seasoned bread crumbs
Olive oil
1 pound (456 g) ricotta cheese
1/4 pound (114 g) mozzarella
Simple tomato sauce

►Slice eggplant lengthwise, as thin as possible. In a wide shallow bowl, mix thoroughly two eggs, half-and-half, 1 tablespoon (15 mL) parsley, garlic powder and salt and pepper to taste. In another shallow bowl, mix Romano or Parmesan and bread crumbs. Dip eggplant slices in the bread crumb mixture, then in egg mixture and finally in bread crumb mixture again. Saute in 1 inch (2.5 cm) hot olive oil until golden brown. Drain on absorbent paper.

Chop or shred mozzarella cheese and ricotta cheese. Beat together with electric mixer, adding in remaining eggs, the parsley, and salt and pepper to taste. Place small amount of this mixture on each eggplant slice. Fold over like an omelet. Arrange filled slices in bottom of large well-greased baking dish and cover with simple tomato sauce. Bake uncovered at 350°F (175°C) for 30 to 35 minutes. Garnish with parsley sprigs. Serves four to six.

■ *Jeri Bump*
Frontier Vittles, Fairbanks

Creole Eggplant

1 medium eggplant
1/2 stick (56 g) butter
2 medium onions, sliced
1 can (29 oz /or/ 826 g) tomatoes, drained
1/2 pound (228 g) sharp cheese, sliced
1 teaspoon (5 mL) salt
Pepper to taste
1/2 cup (120 mL) dry bread crumbs

►Peel eggplant and slice into 1/2-inch (1.25 cm) slices. Melt butter in skillet and saute eggplant slowly, about five minutes. Place in buttered casserole with alternate layers of onion, tomatoes and cheese. (Save some cheese for the top.) Season each layer. Top with bread crumbs and cheese, dot with butter and bake in a 375°F (190°C) oven about 30 minutes.

■ *Eunice Fowler*
Frontier Vittles, Fairbanks

GREEN BEANS

Green Bean Soup

1/2 cup (120 mL) butter
2 medium onions, diced
2 cups (480 mL) fresh green beans, cut
1/2 cup (120 mL) flour
5 cups (1.2 L) bouillon
Meat for flavoring: ham hocks, leftover roast, stew or ground beef, and/or mashed potatoes
Salt, pepper, garlic powder, bouquet garni
1 pint (0.47 L) sour cream
Additional flour if necessary

►Melt butter in large saucepan and brown the onions. Add cut green beans and simmer for five to ten minutes. Stir in flour and cook five more minutes. Gradually add bouillon, stirring constantly so that flour does not lump. Reduce heat and simmer for one hour. Add meat and/or mashed potatoes as desired. All are extremely good. Season to taste and continue to simmer slowly.

Just before serving, mix a little of the soup with the sour cream until cream becomes quite liquid. If the soup seems too thin, you may add 2 or 3 tablespoons (30 to 45 mL) more flour to the sour cream mixture. Then stir it into the soup.

Serve with salad and garlic bread and you have a complete meal.

■ *Wilma Carr*
Alaska's Cooking, Anchorage

ONION

Onion Soup

1/4 cup (60 mL) butter
6 medium onions, sliced in rings
5 cups (1.2 L) beef or chicken stock
3 slices French bread or other white bread
Butter
Salt and black pepper
1 cup (240 mL) sherry
1/2 cup (120 mL) grated Parmesan cheese

►In a 3-quart (3 L) saucepan, melt the butter and brown the onions to a golden color. Add the stock and simmer for 20 minutes. During this time, toast the bread, cut it in quarters if it isn't French bread and spread with butter.

Salt and pepper the soup to taste and add the sherry. Pour the soup into wide, deep ovenproof bowls. Sprinkle the pieces of toast with the cheese and float them on the soup. Place the soup bowls in a 350°F (175°C) oven until the cheese melts. Serve in the hot dishes. Makes six servings.

■ *Gordon R. Nelson, Palmer*
   Lowbush Moose

Hunters' Deep-Fried Onion Rings

►Slice up some big onion rings. Dunk into batter of beer (any self-respecting group of hunters should have some beer around) and ordinary pancake mix. Drop into popping hot oil (not smoking) for about one minute, remove with slotted spoon, drain and serve. These onion rings go well with any game or fish. To give the proper credit where it's due, Harry Greenough, a Minneapolis guide and gourmet camp cook, perfected the recipe.

■ *Ken Davidson*
   BC Outdoors, *September 1981*

PARSLEY — PARSNIP — PEAS

Fried Parsley

1/2 cube (56 g) butter
About 2 cups (480 mL) parsley sprigs,
*   removed from stems, rinsed and well dried*

►Melt butter in a skillet and over medium-high heat brown the butter. Add sprigs of parsley and stir constantly. The parsley will become very limp, but continue stirring and parsley will become crisp and chewy. Serve on fish or fried salt pork.

■ *Mrs. Robert Page*
   One Hundred Years in the Kitchen, *Juneau*

Parsnip Fritters

8 parsnips
3 tablespoons (45 mL) butter
1 teaspoon (5 mL) sugar
1/2 teaspoon (2 mL) salt
1/4 teaspoon (1 mL) pepper
1/2 cup (120 mL) cracker crumbs
1 egg, well beaten
Flour
Butter and lard for frying

►Wash and boil parsnips until tender. Plunge into cold water and slip off skins. Mash parsnips with butter, sugar, salt, pepper and cracker crumbs. Mix thoroughly and add well-beaten egg. Shape into little flat cakes, roll in flour and fry in an iron frying pan until golden brown, using half butter and half lard, as little as possible, just to keep from burning.

■ *Elsie Pegues (Fairbanks)*
   One Hundred Years in the Kitchen, *Juneau*

Svenska Artor
Swedish-style peas

2 pounds (1 kg) fresh peas in the pod
1/2 cup (120 mL) boiling water
1/2 teaspoon (2 mL) salt
1/2 teaspoon (2 mL) granulated sugar
1/2 cup (120 mL) melted butter or margarine

►Wash the pea pods well. Cook in a covered saucepan with the boiling water, salt and sugar for about 10 minutes, or until the peas are tender. To test, remove a pod from the boiling water and test the tenderness of the peas. Peas cooked in the pod cook more quickly than shelled peas; overcooking will cause pods to open. Divide the melted butter among six tall cordial glasses or any small slender glasses, which have first been heated or rinsed in

---

It doesn't always pay to keep seeds over from one year to the next. Certain species such as peas, beans, radishes, spinach, carrots and cabbage will keep for perhaps three years. Beets, cucumbers, tomatoes and mustard may keep well up to five years. Others should not be kept beyond the year of purchase if you want to be sure of good germination. Although it is illegal to sell outdated seeds, some firms do, so beware!

■ *The Cabin Friend*
   ALASKA® magazine, *April 1976*

hot water so that the butter will remain melted. Pass the unshelled peas to a large bowl. The pods are to be taken with the fingers, dipped in melted butter, the peas drawn out into the mouth and the pods discarded.* Serves six.
■ Out of Alaska's Kitchens

*This recipe is for "old-fashioned" peas. The new Sugar Snaps should be cooked even less time, and the pod is edible, too.

POTATO

Avoid Green Potato Skins: Be sure to plant potatoes deep and keep the tubers covered with mulch during the growing season to avoid greening the skin by exposure to sunlight. Once potatoes are dug, store them in a dark, cool, dry place. The green shouldn't be eaten. It contains a highly toxic substance called solanine. Don't bake green potatoes. Instead, peel the skins, cutting out all sprouts, quarter potatoes or cut in chunks. If the green goes all the way through — it will be streaky — it's probably best to throw out the potato. If not, however, boil it to remove any remaining solanine. It is water soluble.

Bodenburg Cream of Potato Soup

"I was really into making soup back in the days when our family was living near Bodenburg Butte in the Matanuska Valley," says the cook. "My favorite was clam chowder, but with eight of us in the family, the proportion of potatoes to clams became larger and larger. One son suggested that I rename the soup 'potato chowder,' so I tried leaving the clams out altogether."

2 tablespoons (30 mL) butter or margarine
1 cup (240 mL) chopped onion
3 cups (720 mL) water
4 cups (1 L) potatoes, peeled, diced to 1/4-inch (6 mm) cubes
2 cups (480 mL) carrots, peeled, diced as above
1 teaspoon (5 mL) salt
1/8 teaspoon (0.5 mL) pepper
1 can (13 oz /or/ 370 g) evaporated milk
1/2 teaspoon (2 mL) parsley

►In a Dutch oven, over medium heat, melt the

butter and saute the onions until tender. Add water, potatoes, carrots, salt and pepper.

Bring to a boil and simmer for 20 minutes so that the vegetables are just done, not mushy. Stir in the can of milk and add the parsley. Heat the soup to just under a boil and serve. Makes four to six servings.

If you absolutely must, add a couple of cans of clams.
■ *Gordon R. Nelson, Palmer* Smokehouse Bear

Potato Slices Baked with Onion Butter

1/4 cup (60 mL) melted butter or margarine
1/4 cup (60 mL) onion soup mix (about half a package)
1/4 cup (60 mL) water
4 or 5 medium-sized baking potatoes
Salt to taste

►Start heating oven to 350°F (175°C). Combine butter, onion soup mix and additional salt, if desired. Pour water into a 2-quart (1 L) casserole. Scrub potatoes and cut into 1/4-inch (6 mm) slices but do not peel. Arrange a layer of slices in casserole; spread with a spoonful of onion mixture; repeat, making five layers. Cover and bake 45 minutes to an hour, or until potatoes are fork tender. (If desired, casserole may be baked alongside meat at a temperature of 325°F /or/ 160°C, but cooking time will nearly double at this slower heat.)
■ *Mamie Jensen, Juneau*

Norwegian Potato Balls

12 raw potatoes
1/2 teaspoon (2 mL) nutmeg
2 tablespoons (30 mL) melted butter
1 tablespoon (15 mL) salt
1 large onion, grated
3 or 4 cold boiled potatoes, grated
2 cups (480 mL) whole-wheat flour or 3 cups (720 mL) white flour
Bacon or salt pork, diced

►Grate raw potatoes, place in a small cloth bag and squeeze out most of the starch. Return to a bowl, add nutmeg, butter, salt, grated onion, cold potatoes and enough flour to hold everything together. Mix well and form into balls, placing the salt pork or bacon in the center. Place in boiling, salted water to cover. Boil one hour. Serve with drawn butter or syrup. When cold, may be fried in butter and served with syrup or honey.
■ *Ralph Loken* PTA Cook Book, *Petersburg*

Potato-Vegetable Casserole

3 cups (720 mL) raw potatoes, peeled and cut up
1 tablespoon (15 mL) each — minced raw
   celery, carrots, green pepper, and onion
1/2 cup (120 mL) mayonnaise
1/4 cup (60 mL) butter or margarine
1/4 teaspoon (1 mL) ground pepper
1/2 teaspoon (2 mL) salt
Paprika

►Cook potatoes in water until tender for mashing and drain off water. Then, put potatoes in bowl of electric mixer and add remaining ingredients, except paprika. Whip mixture at high speed until smooth. Turn into casserole dish and sprinkle with paprika. This dish is best when made a day ahead and stored in the refrigerator so the flavors of the minced vegetables will be more prominent. Bake at 350°F (175°C) for one hour if stored in the refrigerator, or for 35 minutes if warm when put into oven.
■ Deane Feetham
   "An Alaskan Dinner Party"
   ALASKA® magazine, June 1971

Scandinavian Potatoes

6 large potatoes, cooked with skin on
1 pint (0.45 L) sour cream
1/2 cup chopped green onions
1-1/2 cups (360 mL) grated sharp Cheddar
Salt and pepper to taste
Paprika

►Cool cooked potatoes and grate them. Mix grated potatoes, sour cream, green onions, 1 cup (240 mL) of the grated cheese, and salt and pepper to taste. Place in buttered casserole dish. Top with remaining grated cheese and a sprinkle of paprika. Place in refrigerator four to six hours. Heat and bake at 325°F (160°C) for 45 minutes.
■ Hank Spees
   Loggin' Camp Cookin' Book, Dry Pass

Cottage Potatoes

4 pounds (1.8 kg) potatoes
3 tablespoons (45 mL) minced onion
Salt and pepper
2 pounds (1 kg) dry cottage cheese
2 cups (480 mL) sour cream, or
   a low-fat substitute

►Peel and cook potatoes until tender. Mash without adding any liquid. Combine other ingredients with potatoes. Turn into a greased 3-quart (2.85 L) casserole. Bake at 350°F (175°C) for 30 minutes. Serves 12. This dish is also delicious when it's been reheated.
■ Mamie Jensen, Juneau

RADISHES

Creamy Sour Radishes

1 cup (240 mL) thinly sliced radishes
1/4 teaspoon (1 mL) salt
1/3 cup (80 mL) sour cream
1/4 teaspoon (1 mL) sugar
1-1/2 teaspoons (7 mL) cream-style horseradish
Freshly cracked pepper

►Crisp radish slices in sugared ice water for several hours. Drain well. Pat dry and sprinkle with salt. Mix sour cream, sugar, horseradish and pepper. Toss in radishes. Serve in lettuce cups with a garnish of radish roses showing a tiny bit of green stem. Sprinkle with paprika. Makes four servings.
■ Elva Bahrt Swenson, Seattle

RHUBARB

About Cooking Rhubarb: Rhubarb is very acidic. When cooking it, use only glass, stainless steel or unchipped enamelware utensils to avoid a possible metallic flavor. Store in glass containers only. Also remember that the leaves of rhubarb are poisonous. They are sometimes used for tanning hides or cleaning aluminum or other metal containers. . . . Imagine what they'd do to your stomach!

Fresh Rhubarb Pie

2-1/2 cups (600 mL) flour
3/4 teaspoon (3 mL) salt
3/4 cup (180 mL) shortening
1/2 cup (120 mL) cold water
3-1/2 cups (840 mL) finely cut rhubarb, or
   rhubarb and strawberries
2 tablespoons (30 mL) minute tapioca
1-1/2 cups (360 mL) sugar
1/4 teaspoon (1 mL) salt

►Sift together the flour and salt. Cut in shortening. Add cold water and knead dough together lightly. Roll out 1/8 inch (3 mm) thick. This should make dough for a 9-inch (22 cm) two-crust pie. Mix together the rhubarb, tapioca, sugar and salt. Pour into the crust. Cover with the top crust; crimp edges. Bake in a 425°F (220°C) oven for 10 minutes. Lower heat to 350°F (175°C) and bake 40 minutes longer, or until crust is brown.
■ Rhubarb Recipes

Strawberry Rhubarb Bars

First place winner,
1979 Tanana Valley Fair Bake-Off

1-3/4 cups (420 mL) flour
2 tablespoons (30 mL) powdered sugar
1/2 cup (120 mL) butter or margarine
1-1/2 cups (360 mL) sugar
1/4 cup (60 mL) flour
1/4 teaspoon (1 mL) salt
6 egg yolks
1 cup (240 mL) whipping cream
4 cups (1 L) shredded fresh rhubarb
1 cup (240 mL) sliced strawberries
1/2 teaspoon (2 mL) lemon juice
6 egg whites
1/2 cup (120 mL) sugar

►Mix 1-3/4 cups (420 mL) flour and powdered sugar in bowl. Cut in butter until mixture resembles coarse crumbs. Press mixture into greased 13 x 9-inch (32 x 22 cm) baking pan. Bake at 350°F (175°C) until golden, 10 to 12 minutes.

Mix sugar, 1/4 cup (60 mL) flour and salt in large bowl. Lightly beat egg yolks. Stir egg yolks and cream into sugar mixture. Stir in rhubarb, strawberries and lemon juice. Spread mixture evenly over crust. Bake until firm at 350°F (175°C), about one hour.

Beat egg whites in large mixer bowl until foamy. Beat in 1/2 cup (120 mL) sugar — 1 tablespoon (15 mL) at a time — until stiff peaks form. Spread over rhubarb mixture. Bake until light brown, 10 to 15 minutes. Cool in pan on wire rack. Cut into bars.
■ *Denise Balliet*
Bake-Off Cookbook, 1961-1980, *Fairbanks*

Raw Rhubarb and Berry Relish

4 cups (1 L) rhubarb
2 cups (480 mL) lingonberries or blueberries
(lingonberries are more colorful)
Sugar

►Cut up and grind the rhubarb and berries. (The rhubarb and berries grind better if they are frozen.) Combine and add as much sugar as pulp, about 4-1/2 (1.1 L) cups, or sugar to taste. This can be stored in the refrigerator for several weeks or can be frozen.

Variation: Wash and grind one orange, peeling and pulp. Remove the seeds and add.
■ Rhubarb Recipes

Baked Rhubarb

►Cut up cleaned rhubarb stalks to the desired amount. Measure. Then measure one-fourth that amount of sugar and layer the two into a buttered baking dish. Cover and bake in a slow oven for 40 minutes. Vary the flavor with spices such as mace, nutmeg or cinnamon or some grated orange or lemon rind.

■ *The Old Homesteader*

Beaver Creek Rhubarb Upside-Down Cake

"One bite . . . pure seduction!"

5 cups (1.2 L) rhubarb, cut into half-inch
    (1.25 cm) pieces
1 cup (240 mL) sugar
2 packages (3 oz /or/ 85 g, each) strawberry-
    flavored gelatin
2 cups (480 mL) miniature marshmallows or
    large ones, quartered
1 package (13 oz /or/ 370 g) yellow or
    white cake mix
Whipped cream

►Grease a 9 x 13 x 2-inch (22 x 32 x 5 cm) baking pan. Spread the rhubarb over the bottom of the pan and sprinkle sugar over it. Now sprinkle the strawberry gelatin, right from the package, over the sugar and rhubarb. Then scatter marshmallows over that.

Prepare the cake mix according to the instructions on the box and pour it over the layers in the pan.

Bake at 350°F (175°C) for 55 minutes. Cool and serve with whipped cream.

■ *Gordon R. Nelson, Palmer*
   Smokehouse Bear

Rhubarb Cream Chiffon Pie

1 9-inch (22 cm) Crumb Crust
1 package (3 oz /or/ 85 g) lemon-flavored gelatin
3/4 cup (180 mL) boiling water
1/3 cup (80 mL) sugar
1 tablespoon (15 mL) lemon juice
1 teaspoon (5 mL) grated lemon rind
1/2 cup (120 mL) heavy cream, whipped
2 cups (480 mL) sweetened cooked rhubarb

►Dissolve gelatin in boiling water. Add sugar, lemon rind and juice. Chill until mixture begins to thicken. Whip the cream until stiff. Fold in cold rhubarb, then fold all into the gelatin mixture. Spread in a pie shell; chill until firm. Garnish with additional whipped cream.

■ Rhubarb Recipes

Rhubarb Punch

1 cup (240 mL) sugar
1 quart (1 L) water
1 quart (1 L) cut up rhubarb
Cracked ice

►Boil sugar and water together two minutes. Pour this syrup boiling hot over the cut up rhubarb. When cold, strain out juice. To serve, pour juice over cracked ice. Makes four glasses of punch. You can also eat the pulp. Stew it, adding about 1/2 cup (120 mL) sugar; then spice as desired.

■ *Courtesy, Audrey Rearden, Homer*

Bessie Billberg's Rhubarb Custard Pie

Pastry for a double-crust 9-inch (22 cm) pie
3 eggs
3 tablespoons (45 mL) milk
2 cups (480 mL) sugar
1/4 cup (60 mL) flour
3/4 teaspoon (3 mL) nutmeg
1/4 teaspoon (1 mL) allspice
1/4 teaspoon (1 mL) salt
4 cups (1 L) cut up, raw rhubarb

►Line pie pan with crust. Beat eggs, milk, sugar, flour and spices and pour into crust. Add rhubarb. Dot with butter and cover with top crust, vented for steam. Bake at 400°F (205°C) for 50 to 60 minutes.

■ *Courtesy, Miki Collins*
   "Rhubarb: Tasty Fruit for Northern Gardens"
   ALASKA® magazine, May 1981

Rhubarb Bread

Grand Champion, Culinary Division,
1975 Tanana Valley Fair Exhibits

1 cup (240 mL) brown sugar
1/2 cup (120 mL) white sugar
2/3 cup (160 mL) oil
2 eggs
1 cup (240 mL) sour milk
1 teaspoon (5 mL) vanilla
1 teaspoon (5 mL) salt
2-1/2 cups (600 mL) flour
2 cups (480 mL) diced rhubarb
1 teaspoon (5 mL) soda
1 cup (240 mL) nuts

►Mix all ingredients and pour into two greased and floured 9 x 5-inch (22 x 12 cm) loaf pans. Bake at 350°F (175°C) for one hour. Glaze with a powdered sugar, water and vanilla glaze, if desired.

■ *Ruth Stratton*
   Bake-Off Cookbook, 1961-1980, *Fairbanks*

Rhubarb Muffins

Second place, 1980 Tanana Valley Fair Bake-Off

1-1/2 cups (360 mL) brown sugar
1/2 cup (120 mL) oil
1 egg
2 teaspoons (10 mL) vanilla
1 cup (240 mL) sour milk
1-1/2 cups (360 mL) diced rhubarb
1/2 cup (120 mL) walnuts
2-1/2 cups (600 mL) flour
1 teaspoon (5 mL) soda
1 teaspoon (5 mL) baking powder
1/2 teaspoon (2 mL) salt
Topping

►Beat together brown sugar, oil, egg, vanilla and sour milk. Add rhubarb and walnuts. In a separate bowl mix flour, soda, baking powder and salt. Add to liquid ingredients, stirring only until moistened. Spoon into greased and floured muffin cups. Sprinkle with Topping. Bake at 400°F (205°C) for 20 to 25 minutes. Test with a toothpick for doneness. Makes about 20 large or 30 medium muffins.

Topping
2 teaspoons (10 mL) melted butter
2/3 cup (160 mL) sugar
1 teaspoon (5 mL) cinnamon

►Mix, scatter over filled cups and lightly press into the batter. Bake as directed.
■ *Martha Thomas*
Bake-Off Cookbook, 1961-1980, *Fairbanks*

Rhubarb Pudding

1 quart (1 L) rhubarb
1/2 cup (120 mL) water
1/3 cup (80 mL) sugar
1/2 cup (120 mL) flour, or 1/4 cup (60 mL) cornstarch

►Stew the rhubarb and water for five minutes. Strain this mixture. Mix together sugar and flour OR cornstarch and add to stewed rhubarb. Cook until thick and clear. Pour into pudding dishes. Sprinkle with sugar to keep the surface moist and free from skin. Chill and serve with cream.
■ Rhubarb Recipes

Rhubarb Sauce

1/2 cup (120 mL) water
1 quart (1 L) rhubarb, cut up
Pinch of salt
1 cup (240 mL) sugar

►Combine the rhubarb, salt and sugar. Heat slowly until the sugar melts. Simmer five minutes or until tender. Yields about 2-1/4 (540 mL) cups.

To vary this recipe, add the water and salt to the rhubarb. Cover and simmer five minutes, or until the rhubarb is tender. Remove from the heat and add sugar to taste.

SPINACH

Green Rice

3 cups (720 mL) cooked short-grain brown rice
1/4 cup (60 mL) grated Parmesan
1/3 cup (80 mL) chopped parsley
1/2 cup (120 mL) minced cooked spinach
2 eggs, well beaten
1/4 cup (60 mL) melted butter
1 cup (240 mL) milk
2 tablespoons (30 mL) minced onion
1 tablespoon (15 mL) Worcestershire
1-1/2 teaspoons (7 mL) salt

►Mix all ingredients and place in a buttered 2-quart (2 L) casserole. Bake at 350°F (175°C) for 45 minutes. Makes six servings.
■ *Mamie Jensen, Juneau*

Spinach Custard Casserole

1 cup (240 mL) finely chopped cooked spinach, beet greens or Swiss chard
1/2 teaspoon (2 mL) salt
1 tablespoon (15 mL) lemon juice
2 tablespoons (30 mL) melted butter
2 eggs, well beaten
1-1/4 cups (300 mL) milk, scalded
Parsley

►Combine spinach, seasonings, butter, eggs, milk; turn into greased loaf pan or mold. Set in pan of hot water and bake in moderate oven, 350°F (175°C), for 30 to 40 minutes, depending on depth of pan. Unmold or serve right from the baking dish. Garnish with parsley.
■ *Mamie Jensen, Juneau*

It's easy to improve the flavor of spinach if you add a clove of garlic to the water while you are cooking it. The extra flavor is delicious and yet does not give the spinach a strong garlic taste. Worth trying!
■ Tried and True Recipes, *Juneau*

Sprouts: The All-Year Kitchen Garden

Two things we sometimes miss during the winters in the bush are sunshine and fresh produce. But in place of the sun, we have crisp, clean air, as refreshing as a drink of cold spring water; and to take the place of wild greens and garden vegetables, we have a rich variety of sprouts.

Even if you don't know mung beans from jumping beans, you have probably eaten bean sprouts in chop suey or some other Oriental dish. More and more persons are sprouting mung beans and other seeds at home, for good reason: the little sprouts are virtual vitamin factories, producing concentrations of essential nutrients from their own stored reserves as they grow.

Besides being super-nutritious, sprouts are tasty, versatile, inexpensive and fun. Best of all, sprouts make it possible for those of us who live in remote areas to enjoy crisp salads and vegetable dishes all year long.

Dry seeds can be ordered by the pound, delivered via parcel post, stored for months without refrigeration and started any time. We keep from 6 to 12 jars of sprouts in various stages of germination all year long, and enjoy fresh stuff every day — even though we may be miles from the nearest trading post.

Many different kinds of seeds are suitable for sprouting, but we find that a half-dozen kinds fill most of our needs. Foremost is alfalfa. Alfalfa sprouts are our equivalent of fresh lettuce, the foundation of any salad. Yellow peas and garbanzos are good in stir-fry vegetable dishes and soups, while lentils and mungs are excellent either in salads or in soups. Kidney beans and others of their family sprout nicely and cook faster than when used dry. Wheat grains are chewy and surprisingly sweet, and are good in soups, salads and bread.

Growing sprouts is easy. Soak your seeds and beans overnight in a jar. Any jar will work, but it is handy to have identical jars so that the lids are interchangeable. Wide-mouth Mason jars are ideal. In the morning cover the mouth of the jar with any waterproof mesh. We use nylon screening cut into 5-inch (12.5 cm) squares and held in place by canning rings, but commercial rinsing tops, made of plastic or stainless steel, are also available. Rinse the seeds with fresh water, drain and set in a warm, dark place so they will sprout.

Rinsing is the most important part of growing sprouts. Twice a day is the minimum, and often we give our sprouts a bonus rinse at midday, especially if they seem a little dry. (If you have to pack your water as we do, you can conserve it by pouring rinsings from one jar to the next, adding more water if necessary. Three or four pints (1.5 to 2 L) of water will rinse a dozen jars of sprouts.)*

When your jar is full or your sprouts have reached the desired length they are ready to eat.

To ensure crispness soak sprouts in their final rinse for 15 or 30 minutes just prior to use.

If you are short on shelf or counter space, you can put the jars in a sack and hang them from the rafters or the ridgepole. (This is particularly handy in a tent.)

If you should think your sprouts have spoiled, smell them before rinsing. Nothing could stay wet in a jar in a warm place for five days and still smell good — except living sprouts. Once you become familiar with the scent of fresh, growing sprouts, you will easily detect any off odor.

Finally, know your supplier and use only seeds you know are intended for sprouting. Seeds sold for planting or for animal feed may have been treated with a fungicide or some other chemical.

People who are hooked on sprouts take them wherever they go. Backpackers grow sprouts in plastic bags in their rucksacks, and we manage to keep sprouts going at spring camp, even though it gets close to freezing in the tent at night.

Not even the full flow of garden produce during our brief summer harvest period can cure the habit. Tender lettuce leaves and succulent home-grown carrots are very welcome additions to our menu, but they still are only supplements to our year-round standby: sprouts.

Basic Salad Sprouts

Sprout together in a 1-quart (1 L) jar:
2 tablespoons (30 mL) alfalfa seeds
1 to 2 tablespoons (15 to 30 mL) mung beans
1 to 3 tablespoons (15 to 45 mL) lentils

►Allow seeds and beans to sprout until the jar is well packed. Experiment with proportions to see what flavors you like best.

Basic Vegetable Sprouts

Sprout together in a 1-quart (1 L) jar:
2 tablespoons (30 mL) mung beans
3 tablespoons (45 mL) lentils
2 tablespoons (30 mL) wheat grains
1 tablespoon (15 mL) yellow peas

►Allow to sprout until the jar is full, or until the individual seeds have reached the length you prefer.

And don't throw the rinse water away if you have any house plants. They like "nutritional value," too!

Sweet Sprout Salad

►In a large bowl combine: 1 quart (1 L) Basic Salad Sprouts with raisins, shredded coconut, nuts (walnuts, almonds, cashews, filberts), dried bananas or other dried fruit and/or sunflower seeds.

All of these are light, easily transported, mailable things you can have on hand all winter without refrigeration, no matter how far out you live. If available, we sometimes also add grated carrots, sliced or grated apple (grated is juicier), sliced oranges and/or canned pineapple or other fruit.

Vegie Salad

►To 1 quart (1 L) Basic Salad Sprouts add grated carrots, chopped celery, chopped wild greens (willow leaves, bluebell leaves, fireweed tips, etc.), sliced tomatoes (fresh or reconstituted), and/or sliced cucumber.

Stir-Fried Sprouts

►Heat 2 tablespoons (30 mL) of oil or fat in a skillet and add 1 small onion, chopped. Saute until half done, then add 1 quart (1 L) Basic Vegetable Sprouts, 2 tablespoons (30 mL) whole almonds, 1 to 2 tablespoons (15 to 30 mL) soy sauce or tamari.

Stir-fry until the sprouts are wilted but still crunchy. Top with cheese and allow to stand, covered, just long enough for the cheese to melt. Serve at once.

Sprouts and Stock

►Melt 2 tablespoons (30 mL) fat or oil in a skillet then add 1 quart (1 L) Basic Vegetable Sprouts and 1 to 1-1/2 cups (240 to 360 mL) stock.

Cover and simmer until the sprouts are wilted but still crunchy. Mix together 1 tablespoon (15 mL) cornstarch, 1 tablespoon (15 mL) soy sauce or tamari and sufficient cool stock to make a thin paste. Add the paste to the mixture in the skillet, stirring well. Allow to simmer long enough for the cornstarch to thicken the broth. Season with freshly grated black pepper. Serve at once.
■ *Ole Wik*

Story and recipes reprinted from "Sprouts — The All-Year Alaskan Kitchen Garden," The Cabin Friend, *ALASKA*® magazine, July 1979.

Tangy-Cool Spinach

1/2 cup (120 mL) water
1/2 teaspoon (2 mL) salt
1 package (12 oz /or/ 340 g) frozen spinach, or about 1 pound (456 g) fresh young spinach
1/4 teaspoon (1 mL) garlic salt
Juice of 1 fresh lemon
2 tablespoons (30 mL) olive oil
Fresh ground pepper

►For frozen spinach, bring water and salt to boil, add spinach and cook until it just comes apart. Fresh leaf spinach, steam briefly over boiling water, until leaves are bright green and barely tender. Do not overcook spinach, whether frozen or fresh. Drain. Spread out on a dinner plate. Place in refrigerator to chill. When ready to serve, sprinkle garlic salt over spinach. Dribble lemon juice and olive oil over spinach, season to taste with freshly ground black pepper. Even spinach-haters like this!
■ *Juli Lederhaus*
"Sourdough Sampler"
Great Lander Shopping News
Anchorage, October 1978

SQUASH

Zucchini

►Saute one chopped dried onion and one clove garlic, chopped. Add pinch of salt and pinch of pepper, and cook until onion is clear.

Add two fresh tomatoes, quartered and a dash of parsley flakes. Then add four (cucumber-size) fresh zucchini, sliced. Put lid on and simmer four to five minutes.
■ Out of Alaska's Kitchens

Zucchini Pancakes

2 cups (480 mL) grated unpeeled zucchini
2 tablespoons (30 mL) diced onion
1 tablespoon (15 mL) parsley
1/2 cup (120 mL) flour
1 egg, well beaten
1/2 teaspoon (2 mL) salt
1/8 teaspoon (0.5 mL) pepper
Olive oil

►Mix all ingredients except oil and beat well. Fry in hot olive oil until golden brown on both sides. Makes 10 to 12 pancakes about 2 to 3 inches (5 to 7.5 cm) in diameter.
■ *Mamie Jensen, Juneau*

Monterey Zucchini
A delicious vegetable to serve
with barbecued meats

4 medium to large zucchini
2 cups (480 mL) soft white bread crumbs
1 cup (240 mL) grated Parmesan
1 teaspoon (5 mL) salt
1/4 teaspoon (1 mL) pepper
1/4 teaspoon (1 mL) oregano
1/4 teaspoon (1 mL) garlic powder
1/2 cup (120 mL) melted butter or margarine

►Trim off both ends of each zucchini. Parboil for five to seven minutes in boiling salted water. Drain and cool a little. Cut each zucchini in half lengthwise and scoop out seeds. Mix all remaining ingredients together in a bowl. Stuff the zucchini with the mixture, dividing it evenly amongst them. Place on broiling rack and broil 5 to 6 inches (12.5 to 15 cm) from heat source until golden. Makes eight servings.
■ *Jeri Bump*
  Frontier Vittles, *Fairbanks*

Winter Squash with Cranberries

4 cups (1 L) cooked, mashed squash
2 eggs, beaten
1/3 cup (80 mL) melted butter
1/4 cup (60 mL) granulated sugar
1-1/2 cups (360 mL) raw lingonberries or
    cranberries (halved if they are large)
1/2 teaspoon (2 mL) salt
Dash nutmeg

►Heat oven to 400°F (205°C). With egg beater, whip squash with eggs and 3 tablespoons (45 mL) of the butter. Stir in sugar, cranberries, salt, pepper. Spoon into 2-quart (2 L) casserole, top with remaining butter, sprinkle with nutmeg. Bake, uncovered, 30 to 40 minutes. Serves eight.
■ *Mamie Jensen, Juneau*

If you are an addict of weaving, try dyeing fabric with carrot tops. Other discards make good dyes, too, and it is fun to experiment.
■ *Anchorage reader, The Cabin Friend*
  ALASKA® magazine, *April 1976*

One good way to keep birds out of your garden is to try what I did. I bought the children two pinwheels made of foil while in Anchorage. After they tired of playing with them I put them in the garden. Just the spinning and glistening does the trick. It also looks attractive.
■ *Jean L. Remington, Alexander Creek*

Heavenly Zucchini

4 medium zucchini, sliced 1/2 inch
    (1.25 cm) thick
2 tablespoons (30 mL) olive oil (no substitutes!)
Salt and pepper to taste
Dry bread crumbs
Grated Parmesan
Paprika

►Cook zucchini, olive oil, salt and pepper in covered saucepan over very low heat until just tender. Place in ovenproof shallow dish. Sprinkle with dry bread crumbs. Add Parmesan and paprika. Place under broiler to brown.
■ *Bea Westover, "Sourdough Sampler"*
  Great Lander Shopping News
  Anchorage, October 1978

Zucchini Casserole

1 pound (456 g) pork sausage
1 small onion, chopped
1-1/2 cups (360 mL) cooked bulgar wheat or Ala
4 to 6 zucchini, sliced
1 can (16 oz /or/ 456 g) whole tomatoes with
    juice, about 2 cups (480 mL)
1/2 cup (120 mL) grated Cheddar cheese

►Saute pork sausage with chopped onion. Pour off grease. Cook bulgar wheat according to package directions until tender. Measure. If there is a little more than 1-1/2 cups (360 mL), include it in the casserole. Wash and slice zucchini. Combine all ingredients in a casserole except cheese. Sprinkle cheese on top and bake 30 minutes at 350°F (175°C).
■ *Marsha Partlow*
  One Hundred Years in the Kitchen, *Juneau*

Spicy Zucchini Pie
If the days grow too short to ripen your pumpkins
for Thanksgiving pie . . . make it from the hardy
and prolific zucchini!

Pastry for a double-crust 9-inch (22 cm) pie
1/2 cup (120 mL) firmly packed light
    brown sugar
1/3 cup (80 mL) cornstarch
1-1/2 teaspoons (7 mL) cinnamon
1/4 teaspoon (1 mL) salt
1/2 teaspoon (2 mL) vanilla
1 tablespoon (15 mL) fresh orange or
    lemon juice
1/2 cup (120 mL) light corn syrup
4-1/2 cups (4.1 L) pared zucchini slices
    (remove seeds if large)

►Combine brown sugar, cornstarch, cinnamon,

salt, vanilla, citrus juice and corn syrup. Add zucchini to the mixture and stir gently.

Pour into unbaked pie shell and cover with top crust in which steam vents have been cut. Bake at 425°F (220°C) for 15 minutes. Reduce heat to 350° (175°C) and bake an additional 45 minutes.

■ *Linda Chizmar*
Bake-Off Cookbook 1961-1980
Tanana Valley Fair, Fairbanks

TOMATOES

"A garden, at season's end, is a forlorn sight," says Catherine Stephenson ["Cooking with Green Tomatoes," *ALASKA*® magazine, September 1979]. "Broken corn stalks double over, rows of wilted leaves stretch out flat and lots of unripe tomatoes are tossed aside."

Toss no more; green tomatoes may be used a number of ways, among them the recipes below; all — except those noted — are from the article by Catherine Stephenson.

Other ways to use green tomatoes — drying, in ketchup, in various kinds of pickles and relishes are detailed in Chapter 14. Chopped green tomatoes may also be used as the base in Availability Bread, Gordon Nelson's spicy rich coffee bread recipe on page 325.

But some green tomatoes do turn red, and to prove Alaskans have nothing against them, a few recipes are provided, plus these hints:

• Tomatoes ripen in the dark. (True. Have you ever noticed that at evening watering time, there are no tomatoes ready for picking, but early the next morning there may be several perfect ones?) *Before the first frost,* pick all your tomatoes. Truly green ones, use as green tomatoes. Those that have the faintest blush can be ripened for the salad bowl. Wrap them individually in newspapers and store them in a dark, well-ventilated, cool but not too cool place. Spread them out in a single layer, not stacked on top of each other. Check every day or two for the ripe ones, and refrigerate them when they've reached eating stage.

• Nothing is better than still firm vine-ripened tomatoes. They can be eaten just like apples, maybe with a hint of salt . . . salad dressing is a nice change but no improvement. Sliced, chilled and served as a side dish at dinner or added to salads, however, they are sometimes improved if the skins are removed. Removing the skin allows tomatoes to accept more flavor from salad dressings, and even tomatoes that are not fully ripe will be excellent if the skins are removed and the slices of tomato are marinated in a small amount of vinegar and oil or other dressing for about 30 minutes before serving. Chopped onion or chives, herbs, cucumber slices and green pepper rings may be added to the marinade if you like, but don't add salad greens. They wilt.

• To peel the skins, there are a couple of methods. *Firm, fairly ripe tomatoes:* Rub or "scrape" the skin all over the tomato with the back edge of your paring knife. This will separate skin and meat somewhat, and you can then turn the knife to the paring edge and peel off the skin in strips. *Less ripe tomatoes:* In a large saucepan, bring water to steaming hot — deep enough to immerse a whole tomato. Poke a fork into the stem end to serve as a handle. Immerse the tomato in hot water for 10 to 20 seconds. Remove, hold tomato under cold running water for a few seconds more. The skin should peel easily. If not, try the hot bath/cold shower treatment a short time longer.

Some recipes call for peeling and seeding tomatoes. *To seed them,* peel first, then cut in half around the "waistline" — that is, across the tomato, not through the stem end. Squeeze each half gently to remove seeds.

Breakfast Fries

►Gather six large firm green tomatoes. Cut each tomato into three slices. Dip lightly into unbleached white flour seasoned with salt and pepper.

Heat 1/4 cup (60 mL) butter in heavy skillet. Fry both sides of slices until brown. Reduce heat. Top with sour cream or cheese and parsley. Heat until topping is hot.

Moosemeat Marmalade
A snappy sauce that goes well with the robust flavor of game

3 cups (720 mL) sliced green tomatoes
Shredded rind of 1 lemon
1/2 teaspoon (2 mL) salt
1 lemon, sliced
1/2 cup (120 mL) honey
1/4 cup (60 mL) diced green pepper
1/4 cup (60 mL) diced onion

►In a kettle combine green tomatoes, rind and salt. Cover with water. Boil 10 minutes. Drain. Add sliced lemon, honey, green pepper and onion. Bring to a boil again, reduce heat and simmer until thick, about 45 minutes, stirring often. This can be served as a warm sauce or may be chilled and served as ketchup. Keep refrigerated.

Fried Green Tomatoes
A good side dish for dinner

2/3 cup (160 mL) flour or corn meal or a mixture
    of the two
2 teaspoons (10 mL) salt
Dash of pepper
1 egg plus 1 teaspoon (5 mL) water
3 pounds (1.4 kg) green tomatoes, cut in
    1/2-inch (1.25 cm) slices
Salad oil

►About 30 minutes before serving, combine flour, salt and pepper in a pie plate. Beat egg slightly with water. Dip tomatoes in egg mixture, then in flour, coating both sides.

Heat about 1/4 cup (60 mL) oil in a large skillet over medium flame. Fry tomato slices a few at a time until golden on both sides and heated through. Drain on paper towels. Add more salad oil as needed. Makes 8 to 10 servings.
■ The Versatile Green Tomato *(adapted)*

Stuffed Tomatoes

Onions, chopped
Mushrooms, chopped
Cooked spinach, drained and chopped
Garlic salt
Grated Parmesan
Olive oil
Firm ripe tomatoes

►Saute chopped onions and mushrooms until just soft. Mix with the drained cooked spinach and garlic salt. Add grated Parmesan cheese to taste. Cut a slice off the stem end of tomatoes and scoop out most of the pulp. Discard all seeds. Sprinkle tomatoes inside with salt. Turn upside down and allow to stand for half an hour. Stuff the tomatoes with the mixture and put in a buttered pan. Sprinkle with bread crumbs if desired. Bake at 400°F (205°C) for 20 minutes.
■ *The Old Homesteader*

Green Tomato Pie
Enough for two 9-inch (22 cm) pies

Pastry for 2 double-crust pies
3 cups (720 mL) minced green tomatoes
3 cups (720 mL) minced apples
1/2 cup (120 mL) raisins
1/2 cup (120 mL) honey
3 tablespoons (45 mL) vinegar
2 tablespoons (30 mL) lemon juice
2 tablespoons (30 mL) water
1 tablespoon (15 mL) cinnamon

1/2 teaspoon (2 mL) salt
1 teaspoon (5 mL) ground cloves

►Place tomatoes and apples in a large kettle. Add remaining ingredients and bring to a boil, stirring often. Reduce heat and simmer until thick.

Line two 9-inch (22 cm) pie plates with pastry. Fill with mixture. Adjust top crusts. Cut slits for steam to escape. Bake at 350°F (175°C) for 50 minutes or until done.

VEGETABLE MEDLEYS

Vegetable Soup
►When you wish to serve vegetable soup all you need do is to measure the required amount of stock into the kettle and add any vegetables and seasonings you desire. These may be leftovers, fresh or frozen, and in any combination you wish. Add noodles, rice or tiny dumplings. Cook until all ingredients are tender. The secret of good vegetable soup is in the long slow simmering of the bones when you make stock. With your already prepared stock* you won't need to spend that time when you decide to have vegetable soup for lunch.
■ *Helen A. White, Anchorage*
  What's Cookin' in Alaska

See various stock recipes on pages 16 and 25, (fish); 175 (wild bird); 203 (game).

Balkan Vegetable Casserole
A delicious dish for a buffet supper

6 potatoes, peeled and sliced thin
4 tomatoes, chopped
3 carrots, sliced thin
1/4 cup (60 mL) chopped celery
2 onions, chopped fine
2 cloves garlic, minced
3 tablespoons (45 mL) chopped parsley
1-1/2 teaspoons (7 mL) salt
1/2 teaspoon (2 mL) pepper
2 cups (480 mL) water
1/4 cup (60 mL) oil — olive oil preferred

►Place potatoes in shallow buttered baking dish. Mix tomatoes, carrots, celery, onion, garlic, parsley and seasonings together. Spread over potatoes and add water. Bake at 375°F (190°C) for 45 minutes, lightly covered with foil. Remove foil, add the oil over the vegetables and continue baking for 15 minutes longer. Can be served hot or cold.
■ *Mamie Jensen, Juneau*

Availability Bread

"In my files are dozens of recipes for breads using fruits, nuts and even vegetables . . . 10 recipes for zucchini bread, alone," claims Gordon Nelson. "But Harry T., the chef, taught me how to whip out every one of them using one basic recipe. His instructions were to use any fruit or vegetable that sounds good and that can be grated or mashed to measure 2 cups (480 mL). Try it yourself."

3 cups (720 mL) all-purpose flour
1/2 teaspoon (2 mL) baking powder
1 teaspoon (5 mL) salt
1 teaspoon (5 mL) baking soda
2 teaspoons (10 mL) cinnamon
1 cup (240 mL) chopped nuts
3 eggs
1-1/2 cups (360 mL) sugar
1 cup (240 mL) vegetable oil
1 teaspoon (5 mL) vanilla
2 cups (480 mL) chopped, grated or mashed
    fruit or vegetable pulp (suggestions below)

►In a mixing bowl combine the flour, baking powder, salt, baking soda, cinnamon and nuts. In a second bowl, beat the eggs and blend in sugar and oil. Add vanilla and the 2 cups (480 mL) fruit or vegetable pulp.

Combine both mixtures and stir until batter is evenly moist. Divide between two well-greased 9 x 5-inch (22 x 12 cm) loaf pans. Bake in a preheated oven at 350°F (175°C) for one hour. Test by inserting a toothpick in the center of the loaves. If it comes out clean, the bread's done. Remove loaves from the oven and let stand 10 minutes. Then remove from pans to finish cooling on a wire rack. You now have the makings of two delicious mug-ups.*

Some suggestions for a variety of breads:

Zucchini bread — Shred the zucchini coarsely and pack tightly into a 2-cup (480 mL) measure.

Orange bread — You'll need four large oranges. Grate a tablespoon (15 mL) of peel and place it in a 2-cup (480 mL) measure. Peel the oranges, discarding the white membrane and seeds. Finely chop the orange meat and pack it into the measure.

Apple bread — You'll need three or four large apples. Peel, core and shred apples to fill 2-cup (480 mL) measure. Add 1 teaspoon (5 mL) lemon juice to keep apples from darkening.

■ *Gordon R. Nelson, Palmer*
Smokehouse Bear

A mug-up, Nelson explains, is the Alaskan version of the high tea or coffee klatsch ceremony. In his cookbooks, he describes several memorable mug-ups.

Other Variations: In Nelson's bread, try 2 cups (480 mL) seeded and chopped green tomato, or 2 cups (480 mL) shredded carrots — or half and half carrots and drained crushed pineapple.

Garden Medley Supper

2-1/2 to 3 pounds (1.15 to 1.4 kg) bony meat —
    short ribs, chicken or turkey wings or wild
    fowl wings if there's meat on them
2 tablespoons (30 mL) margarine and
    1 tablespoon (15 mL) oil (for wings) or
    2 tablespoons (30 mL) bacon fat
    (for short ribs)
1 clove garlic, split
1 large onion, sliced in thin rings
2 cups (480 mL) coarsely chopped ripe tomato
1/4 cup (60 mL) chopped fresh parsley
1 tablespoon (15 mL) chopped fresh tarragon or
    1/2 teaspoon (2 mL) dried leaves, crushed
Salt and pepper to taste
3 cups (720 mL) or more mixed vegetable
    chunks — zucchini, carrots, unpeeled
    potatoes, cauliflower or cabbage wedges
Dash cayenne or Tabasco
A squeeze of lemon juice (optional)

►Cut meats into serving pieces if necessary. Heat fat in a Dutch oven or heavy skillet with lid. Saute garlic about five minutes, stirring. Discard. Saute meat quickly, turning frequently until well browned. Set aside. Add onion to skillet and saute lightly, then add tomatoes, parsley and tarragon, stirring as they heat for about five minutes. Return meat to skillet, salt and pepper to taste. Then cover, reduce heat and simmer 45 minutes to 1-1/2 hours, depending on kind of meat and tenderness. Then add cut vegetables and continue cooking 20 to 30 minutes longer. Season with lemon juice, cayenne or Tabasco, stir and serve. Makes four to six servings — infinitely extendable if you have a good garden.

■ *Anon.*

You have no refrigerator in your cabin, but you do have a supply of potatoes, carrots and onions which will be ruined by freezing. To avoid vegetable loss from freezing when you must leave the cabin for a long period, place in an airtight metal or glass container. Attach a rope and cut a hole in the lake or river ice. Weight the container so it will sink below the ice level. You can come back a month later and your vegetables will be fresh and crisp.

■ *Bernadina Vogel, Anchorage*
The Cabin Friend
ALASKA® magazine, April 1975

Freezeup Salad

"In the fall that worst of all days arrives — the first hard freeze that will kill all the goodies in the garden. Since I can't let that happen without a fight, I pick as many vegetables as I can ahead of time for salads. One like this uses quite a number."

3 carrots, thinly sliced
3 zucchini, 6 to 8 inches (15 to 20 cm) long, sliced thinly
4 green onions, chopped well into the green
1/2 cup (120 mL) vegetable oil
2 tablespoons (30 mL) lemon juice
1/2 teaspoon (2 mL) salt
1/4 teaspoon (1 mL) pepper
1 teaspoon (5 mL) curry powder

►In a medium bowl combine the carrots, zucchini and onions. In a smaller bowl whip together the oil, lemon juice, salt, pepper and curry powder. Pour the dressing over the vegetables and toss to coat. Chill for at least two hours before serving.

To save even more goodies from freezeup (and make a still tastier salad) add some of the following:
8 broccoli florets
8 cauliflower florets
8 Sugar Snap peas, pod and all
Get the idea?
■ *Gordon R. Nelson, Palmer*
Smokehouse Bear

Alaska Garden Vegetable Soup

3 to 4 cups (0.7 L to 1 L) diced onion
2 cloves garlic, minced
1/4 cup (60 mL) vegetable oil

3 cups (720 mL) grated cabbage
1 cup (240 mL) grated carrots
1 to 2 teaspoons (5 to 10 mL) dill weed
1/2 cup (120 mL) grated potato
1/2 teaspoon (2 mL) celery seed
2 tablespoons (30 mL) raw sugar
1/4 cup (60 mL) tomato puree
1 teaspoon (5 mL) salt
1 or 2 teaspoons (5 to 10 mL) beef seasoning
1/2 teaspoon (2 mL) oregano
1 pound (456 g) sauerkraut, including juice
1 cup (240 mL) diced fresh tomato
1-1/2 quarts (1.4 L) water

►Saute onion and garlic in oil in a large kettle until lightly browned. Add cabbage, carrots and dill. Cook five minutes, stirring constantly. Add remaining ingredients. Cook, covered, for 20 minutes over low heat. Serve piping hot. Makes six servings.
■ *Joy (Mrs. Ed) Baker, Douglas*
One Hundred Years In The Kitchen, *Juneau*

If you forget to wash your lettuce until just before dinner and it is still drippy, try this: Put the loose lettuce leaves in a pillowcase, fasten at the top with a "twistem" or rubber band. Place the pillowcase in the washing machine and set for the spin or damp-dry cycle. The lettuce will come out dry and crisp, and it takes only a few seconds.
■ *The Cabin Friend*
ALASKA® magazine, June 1976

Chapter 11

Mostly Berries

The wild berries of Alaska are various and plentiful — if one knows where the best patches are. Undoubtedly there are many good picking areas that no one ever finds. Don't be content with a patch near the road. The berries there will be dusty and probably picked over already, too. Try to get back a good distance from any highway or habitation. Don't ask your friends where to pick berries; that is like asking a pirate where he hid the treasure.

The lowbush cranberry or lingonberry is probably the most popular and can be used in more ways than any other. It is also one of the easiest to store and can be kept fresh throughout the winter.

Other favorites are the succulent blueberry and its close cousin the red huckleberry; the bog cranberry, which is delicious but rather hard to retrieve; nagoonberries, which are somewhat time-consuming to pick but worth the effort to eat just plain, without enhancement from sugar or other treatment; currants, strawberries, raspberries, cloudberries . . . the list goes on.

Plenty are good by the handful; others are best for jams and jellies or mixed with other berries for better flavor; some are downright tasteless, such as timberberry, silverberry and kinnikinnick, and not really worth the gathering.

Another plant that provides a worthwhile fruit is the wild rose, from which petals and hips — the fruit left after petals fall — are both usable. The latter can give a real boost to your vitamin C intake if you use the juice to make jelly or, better yet, add it to that from other berries or use rose hip pulp with other berries in jams and marmalades, at a ratio of about one part rose hip juice or pulp to 20 parts other berries.

Alaska's only tree-grown fruit is the crab apple, well worth picking if you find them in enough abundance. They can also be used as a source of pectin in jelly making. Moose love crab apples, too.

Unfortunately, one of Alaska's most poisonous plants — the baneberry or snakeberry *(Actaea rubra)* — bears a beautiful bright scarlet berry. It is even lovelier before it is ripe, a real candy pink. There is also a white form of the berry *(A. eburna)*, sometimes called doll's eyes. The quality of this berry isn't debatable: DON'T EAT IT! More information about it is on page 262.

Cleaning Berries

Soft fruits such as raspberries and salmonberries should be cleaned and processed as soon as possible. The softer the fruit, the closer it will pack and the more apt to get moldy. If you have gathered berries away from roads and other sources of dust, you can get away with very little (or no) washing.

How to clean fairly firm berries is a subject handled by Ole Wik along with information about picking berries using a *qallutaq* (page 330). Another suggestion is to place a piece of turkish toweling or fuzzy blanket on a sloping drainboard or in a wheelbarrow. Then gently pour the berries onto it at the high end so they roll slowly down the towel into the sink or wheelbarrow. Leaves, stems and other debris will adhere to the towel.

Storing Berries

Lowbush cranberries, blueberries and huckleberries may be left out of doors to freeze if you live in the right climate for it. Clean berries and be sure there are no imperfect ones or berries that are overripe. If you have a mesh bag such as onions once were sold in, you are in luck. Otherwise improvise by using an old pillowcase or other cloth bag. It is essential that the berries get air circulation so don't use plastic or other such bags. Perhaps you could use several thicknesses of cheesecloth to make a bag. One thickness is not strong enough. Do not put more than a couple of quarts (2 L) of the berries in one bag. Hang them up out of doors and under the eaves of the house, perhaps within easy reach. You don't want to wade through deep snow to reach them later on. The berries will stay in excellent condition as long as the weatherman provides freezing temperatures, a long time in some parts of Alaska!

When berries freeze, their skins burst, allowing the juices to seep as they thaw, so it's best to use these berries before they are fully thawed. Other freezing and storing methods are outlined in Chapter 14.

Good printed information is readily available on Alaska's berries. The *Alaska Wild Berry Guide and Cookbook,* from the editors of *ALASKA®* magazine, identifies and pictures more than 40 different berries and includes several hundred recipes. The University of Alaska Cooperative Extension Service also provides useful material that is updated from time to time, the latest, *Collecting and Using Alaska's Wild Berries and Other Wild Products,* P-120.

All in all, berry picking and eating just might be the best part of an Alaskan summer.

BLUEBERRY & HUCKLEBERRY

Blueberries and huckleberries belong to the same genus *(Vaccinium)* that includes several others of Alaska's most delicious berries — such as the lowbush and bog cranberries — but they are distinct enough in flavor to be treated separately, at least in print if not in your fruit salad bowl.

What's the difference between a blueberry and a

huckleberry? Technically, it is that a huckleberry has 10 large seeds while a blueberry has many small ones, but most people distinguish by color — red for huckleberry, and blue for blue whether true blueberry or not.

Preparation Tips: In Southeastern, blueberry season is long and the berries abundant. But some varieties are common on the tundra of the Interior, around the Gulf of Alaska, the Alaska Peninsula and in the Aleutians. In Southeastern it's possible to have "blueberry pie by the Fourth of July," but if your season is not so lucky, there's a pie in this collection for impatient berry lovers — made of green blueberries. See page 331. Blueberries and huckleberries are interchangeable in most recipes.

"Southeastern Alaska's mid-season (August) blueberries are sometimes hosts to tiny green worms," *The Alaskan Camp Cook* advises. "Huckleberries are less often affected. Some people avoid the worms by avoiding the berries. Others ignore the worms ('just converted blueberries'). To have wormless berries even in August, soak them at least half an hour in salt water — about 1 tablespoon (15 mL) salt to 1 gallon (3.8 L) of water. This does not detract from the quality of the fruit, but it brings the worms out so they are easy to see, and the wormy berries can be removed with leaves and other debris. By September the wormy berries have withered and fallen."

In your haste to try all the wonderful dessert and sweet bread recipes that follow, don't overlook the delicious eating blueberries make by the bowlful. Add cream if you want, or mix them with other less abundant berries or imported summer fruits such as cantaloupe or honeydew. If you want to sweeten the fruit slightly, or enhance the flavor of not-quite-vine-ripened imports, add a delicate sauce that starts with a couple of spoonfuls of honey, thinned to taste with lime juice. Toss the mixture gently with the fruit and chill. Lemon juice will do in a pinch, but the lime flavor lends unusual tang to summer fruit without overpowering it.

Molded Blueberry Salad

1 quart (1 L) unsweetened* canned blueberries
1 can (about 16 oz /or/ 456 g) crushed pineapple
1 package (6 oz /or/ 170 g) cherry-flavored
  gelatin
2 bananas, sliced
1/2 cup (120 mL) chopped pecans or walnuts
1 red Delicious apple, shredded without peeling
1/2 cup (120 mL) mayonnaise
1/2 cup (120 mL) cherry-flavored yogurt

▶*I use unsweetened berries because the gelatin and pineapple add enough sweetness to make a delicious, tart salad, but, of course, sweetened berries could be used.

Drain pineapple, reserving juice. Drain blueberries, pouring the juice into a 4-cup (1 L) measure. Add enough of the reserved pineapple juice to equal 3-1/2 cups (840 mL). Heat juice and dissolve gelatin in it. Chill to the consistency of unbeaten egg white. Fold in drained pineapple, banana, nuts and shredded apple. If bog blueberries *(Vaccinium uliginosum)* are used, the drained berries can be folded in also. (Southeastern blueberries are very seedy, so I do not fold them into the salad.) Pour into a flat pan, mold or bowl and chill. Serve on lettuce with mayonnaise-cherry yogurt dressing. Makes 8 to 10 servings.
■ *Mamie Jensen, Juneau*

Blueberry Muffins

2 cups (480 mL) sifted flour
3 teaspoons (15 mL) baking powder
3 tablespoons (45 mL) sugar
1 teaspoon (5 mL) salt
1 egg, slightly beaten
1 cup (240 mL) milk
1/4 cup (60 mL) vegetable oil
1 cup (240 mL) fresh blueberries

▶Heat oven to 400°F (205°C). Sift flour, baking powder, sugar and salt. Combine egg, milk and oil; pour into flour mixture and stir enough to moisten flour. Fold in berries. Fill paper-lined muffin tins with batter. Bake 20 to 25 minutes. Makes one dozen.
■ *Paula Nichols*
  Dall Homemakers Cookbook, *Cooper Landing*

Susie's Orange Nut Blueberry Muffins

A blue ribbon winner at the
1971 Southeast Alaska State Fair

2 cups (480 mL) flour
3/4 teaspoon (3 mL) salt
1/4 cup (60 mL) sugar
2 teaspoons (10 mL) baking powder
1/2 cup (120 mL) Tang
2 eggs
4 tablespoons (60 mL) butter, melted
3/4 cup (180 mL) milk
1/2 cup (120 mL) chopped nuts
1/2 cup (120 mL) blueberries

▶Stir all together just until moist, folding in nuts and blueberries last. Fill greased muffin cups two-thirds full. Bake at 400°F (205°C) for 25 minutes.
■ *Suzanne Butz*
  Haines Homemakers' Cookbook

Blueberry Kuchen
A rich yeast coffeecake

1/3 cup (80 mL) shortening
1/2 teaspoon (2 mL) salt
1/4 cup (60 mL) sugar
1 cup (240 mL) hot milk
3/4 cake compressed yeast
1 egg
1/4 teaspoon (1 mL) mace
3 cups (720 mL) all-purpose flour
Blueberries
1/3 cup (80 mL) additional sugar
Few grains salt
1 egg yolk, beaten
3 tablespoons (45 mL) cream

►Scald milk, add shortening, salt and the 1/4 cup (60 mL) sugar. Cool to lukewarm and add yeast, well-beaten egg and mace sifted with flour. Stir until mixed. Cover and let rise until double in bulk. Spread as thin as possible into oiled 9-inch (22 cm) pie pans. Work dough gently with fingers. Make sure that it extends well up around rim of pan. Cover each kuchen with a thick layer of blueberries. Sprinkle with remaining sugar and salt. Mix beaten egg yolk and cream and drizzle over all. Bake 30 to 35 minutes.

■ *Mrs. Robert Reid*
  PTA Cook Book, *Petersburg*

Blueberry Delight

►Prepare muffin batter in the usual manner, adding 2 tablespoons (30 mL) extra melted butter and 4 tablespoons (60 mL) brown sugar. Pour batter in a greased, square, shallow baking pan.

Using A Qallutaq . . . and Other Berry Rakes

Berry picking was serious business for the ancient Eskimos and the presence of good berry patches helped determine the location of subsistence campsites during late summer. The women gathered great quantities of blueberries, not only to eat but to use in preparation and preservation of other foods. The gradual fermentation of the berries provided an effective and prized pickling medium.

The blueberry season is short, but while it lasts the fruit is available in incredible abundance. Modern-day Eskimos take advantage of the harvest as their ancesters did; pickers speak in terms not of quarts or gallons, but barrels. To collect berries in this quantity, the women rely on an ancient tool that vastly increases their picking power — the *qallutaq*. A *qallutaq* is simply a large, flat, short-handled wooden spoon, usually carved from spruce root. It is used to beat alpine blueberries off the plants and into a waiting receptable such as a birch bark basket. Because of the spoonlike shape of the bowl, the berries are "reflected" toward a common focal point — the basket. The edge of the lip opposite the handle is sometimes left a bit long to assist in raking the fruit off the plants. The lip is also useful in scooping up crowberries from especially thick patches. The two kinds of berries are often mixed in the same basket and eaten together.

Blueberries gathered by *qallutaq* are always mixed with twigs and leaves, so the women periodically winnow the fruit by pouring it into a second vessel, letting the breeze carry away the chaff. If there is no natural breeze, they may winnow in the boat on the way home, taking advantage of the breeze set up by the boat's motion, or they may set the fruit aside in hopes the wind will pick up later.

Blueberry picking trips may be postponed in wet weather purely because the leaves and fruit stick together and can't be winnowed. But a simple blueberry cleaner can easily be made from a bath towel fastened between two parallel sticks to form a shallow, gently sloping chute. As the fruit is slowly poured into the top of the chute, the berries roll all the way down to a second basket while the leaves and twigs stick to the towel. This method works well until the first frost, but after that collecting with a *qallatuq* ruptures the skins of the berries, smearing them with sticky juice and destroying their spherical shape so they won't roll. The only answer for the rest of the season is to pick on a frosty morning while the berries are still frozen.

Berry-beating is a much more active pursuit than hand-picking; one is always on the move from bush to bush and patch to patch. If you have a chance to use a *qallutaq*, sooner or later you are bound to discover its one disadvantage. Once you've picked blueberries by beating, you'll find that picking by hand seems kind of fruitless.

■ *Ole Wik*

Or, Try A Lance Packer Berry Rake

For the serious picker who wants to preserve several dozen jars of berries, hand-picking enough berries is very time-consuming. Well, take heart, pickers — there is a faster way. With my berry rake I can collect 6 quarts (5.7 L) of blueberries or huckleberries in an hour and enjoy myself, too.

To make my rake I soldered 10 galvanized nails,

Sprinkle blueberries generously over the top. Bake in a moderate oven, 350°F (175°C), until well browned. Cut in squares while still warm and serve with cream. Sliced bananas may be sustituted for part of the berries if you wish. A few chopped nuts sprinkled on just before baking add a nice touch.

■ *Helen A. White, Anchorage*
Alaska Wild Berry Trails

Alaska Blueberries Kaznakoff

2 cups (480 mL) fresh blueberries
Brown sugar
Sour cream

►Clean and drain fruit very well; pat dry. Serve berries in a glass compote sprinkled with brown sugar and topped with thick sour cream and additional brown sugar. Garnish one side of the bowl with a small blueberry twig — leaves, berries and all.

Raspberries and strawberries fixed this way are also highly recommended.

■ *Nadja Kaznakoff Bahrt*
Courtesy, Elva Bahrt Swenson

Green Blueberry Pie
A great pie for impatient berry lovers

►Line a pie tin with pie crust and fill about half full of green blueberries. Make a custard of two eggs, 1 can (13 oz /or/ 370 g) evaporated milk and 1 cup (240 mL) sugar. Beat well and pour over berries in crust. Sprinkle nutmeg on top and bake in moderate oven until custard is set.

■ *Emma McKinnon*
Past Presidents' Parley Cook Book, Anchorage

---

leaving a 3/8-inch (about 1 cm) gap between each, along one edge of a store-bought steel funnel, 6-1/2 inches (16 cm) in diameter and 10 inches (25 cm) long, so that the nails extended 1-5/8 inches (4 cm) beyond the lip of the funnel. The long funnel spout serves as a handle and I plug it with leaves to prevent the berries from falling out while I pick.

It is usually best to start at the bottom of a bush and work your way up. If possible, work only those bushes that have the most berries and fewest leaves. In Sitka we collect mainly blueberries and huckleberries, although the rake will work on any bushy plant.

Rake the nails along the branches in a short, brushing motion. Don't force the rake as this will squash the berries and just add more leaves. Hold the branch and then stroke the rake along the underside of it where the berries hang. Bend and twist the branches so the berries are exposed to the rake. Sometimes it is necessary to grasp the lip of the funnel and reach it around to the backside of a bush in order to get all the berries; don't worry about the branches, this doesn't hurt them a bit.

I really like using a metal rake because it is easy to clean, doesn't absorb water when I'm working wet bushes, and the spout on the funnel allows water to drain from the wet berries. I also carry a metal bucket and plastic bags so I can separate the berries as I pick them. A scoopful of these and a scoopful of those, each dumped quickly in its bag, really makes the work go fast. A year's supply is quickly gathered, leaving me with more time to enjoy the great Alaska summer.

■ *Lance Packer*

Commercial berry rakes are also available, most of them imported from Scandinavian countries. Not everyone is as positive about the virtues of "raking" as Ole Wik and Lance Packer, however, so you might want to borrow a rake before you commit yourself to buying or making one.

For one thing, they should not be used on the soft berries, such as raspberries and salmonberries. These berries are far too delicate if fully ripe . . . and who wants to pick them green?

For another, rakes pick up a lot more debris than the fingers do and it must all be winnowed out, one way or another. For the firmer berries, if you're picking large quantities, raking and winnowing ultimately saves time. To make a nice pie or two, not so.

Finally, one confirmed berry picker we know — an "edict" (actually, it is The Old Homesteader, if you really must know) — describes the raking task as, "Scoop and dump, scoop and dump — endlessly — and endlessly boring. Well, not nearly so much fun, anyway."

Suit yourself, judging a rake's utility mainly by the kind of berries being harvested and the quantity you will use.

Ole Wik's description of the *Quallutaq* is reprinted from "Beating Around The Blueberry Bushes," *ALASKA®* magazine, July 1976. Lance Packer's invention is from The Cabin Friend, *ALASKA®* magazine, September 1978.

Blueberry Nuggets

"These little gems are too fat for cookies and too thin for muffins so I named them nuggets. In spite of the peculiar assortment of ingredients, they are really good snacks. They can be wrapped in plastic film, then in foil and frozen for later use. They are good shippers, too. Just wrap with several layers of newspaper for insulation and mail them while still frozen."

2 cups (480 mL) flour
1 teaspoon (5 mL) baking soda
1/2 teaspoon (1 mL) salt
1 cube (114 g) margarine
1 cup (240 mL) sugar
2 eggs, slightly beaten
1 cup (240 mL) ripe bananas, mashed
1 tablespoon (15 mL) orange rind or
    dried orange bits
1/4 cup (60 mL) milk
1 teaspoon (5 mL) vanilla
1 teaspoon (5 mL) almond flavoring
1 cup (240 mL) shredded coconut
1/2 to 1 cup (120 to 240 mL) nuts, chopped
1 to 1-1/2 cups (240 to 360 mL) wild
    blueberries, frozen

►Mix and sift flour, soda and salt; set aside, reserving a little flour with which to dredge the frozen berries before using. Cream margarine until light and fluffy; gradually add sugar and beat until light. Add eggs, bananas and orange rind; blend. Combine milk and flavorings. Add dry ingredients alternately with liquid, beginning and ending with dry ingredients. Blend well after each addition; stir in coconut and nuts. Remove berries from the freezer and dredge with reserved flour; add to batter. Fill paper-lined muffin pans one-fourth full and bake in an oven that has been preheated to 350°F (175°C). Nuggets should be baked about 25 minutes or until well browned and the surface springs back when touched with a fingertip.
■ Helen A. White
    "Alaska: Land of Wild Berries"
    ALASKA® magazine, August 1979

Blueberry Squares

1/3 cup (80 mL) butter
1 cup (240 mL) sugar
2 eggs, unbeaten
1-3/4 cups (420 mL) sifted flour
2 teaspoons (10 mL) baking powder
1/2 teaspoon (2 mL) salt
2/3 cup (160 mL) milk
1-1/2 cups (360 mL) blueberries, dusted with
    a mixture of:
    2 tablespoons (30 mL) flour and
    1 tablespoon (15 mL) sugar

►Cream butter and sugar until fluffy. Beat in eggs, one at a time. Sift flour, salt and baking powder together and add to creamed mixture alternately with milk. Mix blueberries with additional flour and sugar and stir into batter. Bake at 375°F (190°C) for 35 or 40 minutes. Cut into squares while hot and serve with butter. Makes two dozen squares.
■ Tried and True Recipes, *Juneau (adapted)*

Bush Cream on Blueberries

►I like mine fresh . . . a bowl of good ripe blueberries sprinkled with sugar, nonfat dry milk and some commercial dried coffee "cream." Stir them up for a real feast. Out in the bush we don't have access to cream from the dairy, but this way is just fine.
■ *Dick Proenneke, Twin Lakes*
    The Cabin Friend
    ALASKA® magazine, March 1975

Blueberry Oatmeal Bread

2 cups (480 mL) flour
1 teaspoon (5 mL) baking powder
1 teaspoon (5 mL) baking soda
1 teaspoon (5 mL) salt
1/2 teaspoon (2 mL) nutmeg or mace
1 cup (240 mL) oatmeal
1/3 cup (80 mL) shortening
1/2 cup (120 mL) light brown sugar
2 eggs
1 cup (240 mL) buttermilk
1-1/2 cups (360 mL) blueberries
1 cup (240 mL) nuts, chopped

►Sift all dry ingredients together. Cream shortening and sugar in separate bowl. Add eggs and buttermilk. Gradually add dry ingredients and mix well. Add blueberries and nuts. Bake for one hour at 350°F (175°C).
■ *Mary Jane Hanousek*
    Souvenir Cook Book, *Skagway*

Blueberry Nut Bread

2 cups (480 mL) sifted flour
3 teaspoons (15 mL) baking powder
1/4 teaspoon (1 mL) salt
1 cup (240 mL) sugar
1 cup (240 mL) blueberries
1/2 cup (120 mL) chopped nuts
2 well-beaten eggs
1 cup (240 mL) milk
3 tablespoons (45 mL) melted butter
    or shortening

►Sift dry ingredients into a large bowl. Add blueberries and nuts. Add eggs mixed with milk and shortening. Stir slightly. Pour into paper-lined loaf pan. Let stand 30 minutes. Bake at 350°F (175°C) for one hour. A double recipe will make three nice loaves.

■ *Mrs. Frank Shellhorn*
  Pioneer Cookbook
  Auxiliary No. 4, Anchorage

Blueberry-Coconut Chews

1 cup (240 mL) all-purpose flour
1 teaspoon (5 mL) baking powder
1/2 teaspoon (2 mL) salt
1 cup (240 mL) sugar
2 tablespoons (30 mL) orange-flavored instant
  breakfast drink powder
1/2 cup (120 mL) margarine
1 egg
2 tablespoons (30 mL) water
1-1/3 cups (320 mL) coconut, flaked
1 cup (240 mL) blueberries or
  lowbush cranberries
Flour

►Mix 1 cup (240 mL) flour with baking powder and salt; sift. Combine sugar and instant breakfast mix. Cream margarine and blend in sugar mixture gradually. Add egg and water and beat until smooth. Fold in flour mixture and stir in coconut. Dust berries with remaining flour and fold into batter. Line a rectangular pan with foil. Press batter with fingers into a thin layer in pan. Bake at 350°F (175°C) 35 to 45 minutes or until batter draws away from sides of pan and is a good brown. Cool in pan for 15 minutes. Cut into squares and immediately peel off the foil from the chews.

Blueberries and Cake

1 package white cake mix
Frozen blueberries, partially thawed
Sugar to taste

►Fix cake according to package directions. When cake has cooled a bit, gently spoon sugared partially thawed blueberries on top of the cake. As berries thaw the juice will seep into the cake. Let stand a couple of hours before serving.

■ *Pat Rogge*
  Northern Lites, Tasty Bites, *Fairbanks*

Blueberry Shortcake

4 cups (960 mL) self-rising flour
1/2 cup (120 mL) butter
1-1/3 cups (320 mL) milk
2 to 3 cups (480 to 720 mL) blueberries
Melted butter
Sugar

►Sift and measure flour. Cut in the butter. Add the milk and mix lightly with a fork. Turn a bit more than half the dough into a well-greased shallow pan and press out to the edges. Brush with melted butter and cover with waxed paper extending over the sides of the pan. Grease the paper and place rest of dough on top, patting it out to within 1/2 inch (1.25 cm) of sides of pan. Brush with melted butter and sprinkle lightly with sugar. Bake in a hot oven, 450°F (230°C), 25 to 30 minutes. Lift off top layer by paper. Slip lower crust onto a hot platter and cover with sweetened berries. Place top crust over berries and cover with more berries. Serves eight persons. Serve plain or with cream.

■ Out of Alaska's Kitchens

Blueberry Dessert

2-1/2 cups (600 mL) fresh blueberries
1/2 cup (120 mL) sugar
1/4 teaspoon (1 mL) orange peel
Dash of mace
1/8 teaspoon (0.5 mL) cardamom
1 cup (240 mL) pie crust mix
1 tablespoon (15 mL) butter
2 teaspoons ((10 mL) lemon juice
1/2 teaspoon (2 mL) vanilla

►Place blueberries in buttered shallow baking dish. Combine sugar, grated orange peel, mace and cardamom. Sprinkle sugar mixture and pie crust mix in alternate layers over berries. Continue until all are used. Dot with butter. Drizzle lemon juice and vanilla over all. Bake in 350°F (175°C) oven 45 minutes. Serve with whipped cream if desired. Serves four to six.

■ *Henny Collins*
  What's Cookin' in Wrangell

Blueberry Pudding
An old-fashioned delicious dessert

4 cups (1 L) blueberries
1 to 1-1/4 cups (240 to 300 mL) sugar
1/2 cup (120 mL) water
8 slices white bread (or whole-wheat)
Softened butter
Cream or ice cream

►Bring berries, sugar and water slowly to a boil and simmer for 10 minutes. Remove crusts from bread and spread each slice with softened butter. If a small loaf pan — 8 x 5 inches (20 x 12 cm) — is used, the bread will just fit, two pieces to each layer. Place the bread in the pan, buttered side down and cover with hot berries. Continue these layers, ending with berries. Let stand until cool, then chill in refrigerator. To serve, unmold on a platter and slice, or slice right out of the loaf pan. Serve with cream or ice cream.

■ *Mamie Jensen, Juneau*

Blueberry Bomb
A steamed pudding

2-1/2 cups (600 mL) flour
2 teaspoons (10 mL) baking powder
3/4 cup (180 mL) sugar
3 eggs, beaten
2 cups (480 mL) milk
1 teaspoon (5 mL) salt
1-1/2 cups (360 mL) blueberries

►Mix first six ingredients together; then add the blueberries. Pour into bowl. Then steam in double boiler until done —about 1-1/2 hours. Serve with Blueberry Sauce or Syrup.
■ *Doris Ward, Fort Yukon*

Blueberry Buckle

1/2 cup (120 mL) sugar
2 cups (480 mL) flour
2-1/2 teaspoons (12 mL) baking powder
1/4 teaspoon (1 mL) salt
1 egg
1/2 cup (120 mL) milk
1/4 cup (60 mL) melted fat
1 pint (0.47 L) blueberries
1 tablespoon (15 mL) lemon juice

Topping:
1/2 cup (120 mL) sugar
1/3 cup (80 mL) flour
1/2 teaspoon (2 mL) cinnamon
1/4 cup (60 mL) melted butter

►Sift together sugar, flour, baking powder and salt. Beat egg, milk and fat together and pour into dry ingredients. Stir just enough to mix. Spread into a well-greased shallow glass baking dish, 9 x 9 x 2 inches (22 x 22 x 5 cm).

Cover with berries and drizzle on lemon juice. Mix topping ingredients and sprinkle over all. Bake 50 to 60 minutes at 350°F (175°C).
■ The Alaskan Camp Cook

Campfire Blueberry Pie

1 rainhat full of plump blueberries
1 package vanilla pudding
Pie crust (whole-wheat flour, a little Bisquick,
  oil, honey, water and powdered milk)

►Mix the crust and bake in reflector oven or with hot rocks. Fill with vanilla pudding and smother in blueberries.
■ *Jim Greenough and Eileen Helmstetter*
  "The Bush Gourmet"
  ALASKA® magazine, July 1977

Blueberry Cream Cheese Delight
Crust:
16 crushed graham cracker crumbs
1/4 cup (60 mL) sugar
1/4 cup (60 mL) melted butter or margarine

Filling:
1 package (8 oz /or/ 228 g) cream cheese
1/2 cup (120 mL) sugar
2 eggs
1 teaspoon (5 mL) vanilla

Topping:
2 cups (480 mL) cooked or canned blueberries
  with juice
2 tablespoons (30 mL) cornstarch
1/2 cup (120 mL) sugar
Juice of 1 lemon

►Mix crust ingredients and pat into a 9-inch-square (22 cm) cake pan or large pie tin. Mix cream cheese, sugar, eggs and vanilla until thick and smooth. Spoon on top of crust. Bake at 300°F (150°C) for 30 minutes. Drain cooked berries, pouring juice in a saucepan. To the saucepan add cornstarch and remaining 1/2 cup (120 mL) sugar. Cook until thick. Add the lemon juice and the blueberries. Pour over the top of cheese filling, spread; cool and put in refrigerator. The pie is best if refrigerated 24 hours before serving. Cut in squares and serve with whipped cream. Double the recipe if you use a large cake pan.
■ *Alta Bloom*
  "More Good Eating," *Tokeen Cove*

Blueberry Fudge

4 cups (1 L) blueberries
1 cup (240 mL) raisins
1 cup (240 mL) sugar, more or less to taste,
   or honey
1 tablespoon (15 mL) cornstarch
1 cup (240 mL) nuts

►Blend blueberries, raisins, sugar and cornstarch in blender. Add nuts and blend briefly. Put in a heavy kettle and cook down until thick. Pour into pan and dry in slow oven until firm enough to cut. Use as a candy treat for children in lunches.
■ *Sue Butz*
   Haines Homemakers' Cookbook

Alaska Blueberry Cobbler

1 quart (1 L) blueberries
1/2 cup (120 mL) sugar
1 tablespoon (15 mL) cornstarch
1/2 teaspoon (2 mL) grated lemon peel
1 teaspoon (5 mL) lemon juice
1/4 teaspoon (1 mL) cinnamon
1 cup (240 mL) flour
2 tablespoons (30 mL) additional sugar
1-1/2 teaspoons (7 mL) baking powder
1/4 teaspoon (1 mL) salt
3 tablespoons (45 mL) butter or margarine
1/3 cup (80 mL) milk or half-and-half
1 egg, beaten

►Combine first six ingredients and cook over medium heat, stirring constantly, until mixture just begins to bubble. Lower heat and simmer five minutes, stirring frequently, until mixture is thick. Pour into 2-quart (2 L) baking dish and keep warm. Combine flour, additional sugar, baking powder and salt. Mix milk and egg and pour all at once into dry ingredients, stirring just until moistened. Spoon batter over hot berries. Bake at 400°F (205°C) about 20 to 25 minutes until topping is golden brown. Serve plain or with cream or ice cream. Makes four to six servings.
■ *The editors, ALASKA® magazine*

Pop-in-A-Pan Pie Filling

4 quarts (3.8 L) fresh blueberries
3-1/2 cups (840 mL) sugar
3/4 cup (180 mL) quick-cooking tapioca
6 tablespoons (90 mL) lemon juice
1 teaspoon (5 mL) salt

►This recipe makes enough filling for four 9-inch (22 cm) pies;* fillings can be stored for up to six months before use. To prepare filling, wash and drain berries, then mix well with sugar, tapioca, lemon juice and salt. Line four 9-inch pie pans with heavy-duty foil, allowing the foil to extend 5 inches (12 cm) beyond the rim of each pan. Pour filling equally into foil-lined pans. Fold foil loosely over the tops and freeze until solid. Remove frozen filling from pans, fold foil tightly and return to freezer.

To bake a pie, prepare pastry and line 9-inch (22 cm) pie pan with bottom crust. Take filling from freezer and remove foil. Do not let filling thaw. Pop frozen filling into a pastry-lined pie pan and dot with butter. Add top crust, seal edges and cut slits in crust for vents. Bake at 425°F (220°C) until syrup boils up with heavy bubbles that do not burst.
■ Alaska Wild Berry Guide and Cookbook

You can mix up all four pie crusts at the same time if you want, too. Check out the Master Mix for pie crust on page 402.

Blueberry Meringue Pie

3 cups (720 mL) blueberries
1 cup (240 mL) sugar
2 tablespoons (30 mL) flour
1/4 teaspoon (1 mL) salt
1 tablespoon (15 mL) lemon juice
2 eggs, separated
1 baked pie shell
2 tablespoons (30 mL) powdered sugar

►Mix together berries, granulated sugar, lemon juice, flour, salt and egg yolks. Cook over boiling water 10 minutes or until thick, stirring constantly. Cool slightly. Turn into pie shell. Cover with meringue made by beating the powdered sugar into stiffly beaten whites. Bake in a moderate oven about 15 minutes or until delicately browned.
■ Out of Alaska's Kitchens

Basic Red Huckleberry Sauce

1 cup (240 mL) red huckleberries
1/4 cup (60 mL) sugar
3 tablespoons (45 mL) cold water
2 tablespoons (30 mL) light corn syrup
1 tablespoon (15 mL) cornstarch
2 teaspoons (10 mL) lemon juice

►Wash berries and place in a saucepan. Add sugar, 2 tablespoons (30 mL) cold water and syrup. Bring to a boil. Blend cornstarch and 1 tablespoon (15 mL) cold water, stirring gradually into berry mixture. Cook until thickened, stirring constantly. Stir in lemon juice and remove from heat. Chill. This topping is especially good on ice cream, Swedish pancakes or waffles. I like it as a topping for cheesecake, too.
■ *Karen Hofstad, Petersburg*
   Alaska Wild Berry Guide and Cookbook

Alaskan Blueberry Pie

1 cup (240 mL) sugar
2-1/2 tablespoons (38 mL) cornstarch
2/3 cup (160 mL) cold water
1/2 cup (120 mL) blueberries
1 tablespoon (15 mL) butter
1 tablespoon (15 mL) lemon juice
1 teaspoon (5 mL) grated lemon rind (optional)
2 cups (480 mL) additional fresh or
  frozen blueberries
Baked and cooled pastry shell or
  graham cracker crust

►Mix the first seven ingredients in a saucepan and cook until very thick. Fold in the 2 cups (480 mL) remaining berries and pour into baked pie shell. Let the pie cool, top with whipped cream and serve.
■ *Twila K. Palmatier*
  "Sourdough Sampler"
  Great Lander Shopping News
  Anchorage, October 1978

Variation: Make a rich pastry and bake tart shells over muffin tins or custard cups. Prepare filling as above but cool for an hour before folding in the 2 cups (480 mL) frozen or fresh berries. Fill tart shells and chill for at least one more hour. Top with whipped cream.
■ *Helen A. White, Anchorage*
  Alaska Wild Berry Trails

Blueberry Ice Cream
For an ice cream maker

1 quart (1 L) half-and-half
1/2 cup (120 mL) honey
Dash salt
3/4 cup (180 mL) crushed blueberries

►Scald cream in a pan over medium heat. Remove from stove and stir in honey and dash of salt. Pour into ice cream container and stick in the refrigerator until completely cooled. Add blueberries and then freeze according to ice cream maker's instructions. Makes about 1-1/2 quarts (1.45 L).
■ *Alaska Department of Fish and Game*
  Wildlife Cookbook

Huckleberry Pie
A good basic baked-in-the-shell recipe
for any berry

2-1/2 cups (600 mL) huckleberries
1-1/4 cups (300 mL) sugar*
3 tablespoons (45 mL) cornstarch or 1/3 cup
  (80 mL) flour
Pinch of salt

1 tablespoon (15 mL) lemon juice or a sprinkle
  of green huckleberries
Pastry for 2-crust pie

►Combine all ingredients except pastry and mix well. Fill a 9-inch (22 cm) pastry-lined pan. Cover with top crust that has been vented for steam. Pinch top and bottom crusts together around pan. Bake at 450°F (230°C) for 10 minutes; reduce heat to 350°F (175°C) and continue baking for 35 minutes.
■ *Tsimpshean Indian Island Cookbook*
  Metlakatla (adapted)

*Adjust the amount of sugar if the berries are quite sweet.

Sugarless Blueberry Pie

1 can (6 fl oz /or/ 177 mL) frozen apple juice
1 can water
4 cups (1 L) fresh or frozen berries, uncooked
3 tablespoons (45 mL) cornstarch
2 teaspoons (10 mL) lemon juice (optional)
Baked pie shell

►Mix juice and water, reserve 1/2 cup (120 mL) and pour the rest in a saucepan. Add 1 cup (240 mL) of the berries and simmer to release the berry juice into the water. Smashing some of the berries helps hurry this along, and the shorter the cooking time, the better the flavor. Mix cornstarch in reserved juice, add to berry mixture and stir constantly until it thickens.

Add lemon juice and remaining berries to thickened sauce and place in a baked pie shell.
■ *Shirley Smith*
  Courtesy, Lael Morgan
  "Sugarless Cooking in the Wild"
  ALASKA® magazine, April 1978

Blueberry Syrup

2 quarts (2 L) blueberries
1 quart (1 L) sugar
3/4 cup (180 mL) cold water

►Pick over and mash fruit. Sprinkle with sugar, cover and let stand overnight. Add water, bringing slowly to boiling point and cook 20 minutes. Force through a double thickness of cheesecloth. Again bring to boiling point; then fill small glass jars or bottles that have been sterilized. Adjust covers and seal.* Use as foundation for beverages, ices or sauces. Good on pancakes and waffles, too.
■ *An Alaskan Cook Book, Kenai*

*This syrup will keep for some time refrigerated. For longer storage in a cool place besides the refrigerator, consult Chapter 14.

Best Ever Sundae Sauce

►When you bring in a picking of blueberries, here is the way to make a super sundae sauce.

Combine 1 quart (1 L) of blueberries and 8 cups (1.9 L) sugar in a crock (a large pottery bowl or a big glass jar will do). Allow this mixture to stand for about one week, stirring several times each day. Turn into sterilized jars and seal. It will keep well (but not indefinitely) if the jars are stored in the refrigerator.

■ ALASKA® magazine, January 1977

Blueberry Rum Sauce

►In a saucepan combine 1/3 cup (80 mL) sugar, 1-1/2 tablespoons (23 mL) flour and 1/4 teaspoon (1 mL) salt. Place over moderate heat and stir in gradually 1 tablespoon (15 mL) lemon juice and 1 cup (240 mL) hot water. Stir until smooth and beginning to thicken. Add 1 cup (240 mL) blueberries and continue to cook until sauce is thick. Remove from fire and beat in 2 teaspoons (10 mL) butter and 2 tablespoons (30 mL) of rum. Strain. Excellent on ice cream or pudding.

■ Mrs. H.L. Faulkner
 Tried and True Recipes, Juneau

Blueberry Hot Cake Sauce

1/2 cup (120 mL) sugar
Dash of salt
2 tablespoons (30 mL) cornstarch
1 cup (240 mL) Blueberry Juice
1 cup (240 mL) water
2 tablespoons (30 mL) lemon juice
3 tablespoons (45 mL) butter or margarine

►Combine sugar, salt and cornstarch in a saucepan and mix until smooth. Add the juice and water gradually and keep stirring. Simmer over low heat until thick and clear. Remove from heat and stir in lemon juice and butter. Wonderful on waffles or blueberry hot cakes.

■ Alaska Wild Berry Guide and Cookbook

Alaska Blueberry Syrup

►The ultimate topping for a pagoda of rich brown sourdoughs is made from our wild Alaska blueberries. In the fall, take a 10 to 20 gallon (38 to 76 L) whiskey keg, knock out one end and, without washing it, put in a layer of sugar about 2 inches (5 cm) deep. Follow this with about 3 inches (8 cm) of big, juicy Alaska blueberries. Repeat this layering until the keg is full. Cover and store away in a cool corner of your cabin. Without mashing or a disturbance of any kind, a mild fermentation takes place. Those busy little enzymes are working again. In a short time the skins and the seeds have settled to the bottom and the balance of the keg is filled with a rich, purple cordial. Spread some of this over your stack of sourdoughs. You are in for a treat. The bouquet is heady and the flavor something out of this world.

■ Ruth Allman, Juneau
 Alaska Sourdough

CLOUDBERRY

Cloudberries *(Rubus chamaemorus)* or baked-apple berries, as they are also called, grow in greatest abundance in the Kuskokwim River basin and on the Seward Peninsula around Norton Sound. They favor sphagnum bogs and other wet places of the arctic and subarctic tundra. Many Natives of northern and western Alaska refer to the berries as ''salmonberries'' because the coloring of the two berries is similar. Although the two plants belong to the same genus, there is considerable difference between the cloudberry plant and the salmonberry found in greatest abundance in Southeastern and around the Gulf of Alaska. The cloudberry grows from low, sprawling rootstock that is rather like the strawberry plant. It is rarely more than 8 inches (20 cm) tall. The salmonberry, on the other hand, grows on a shrub which may attain a height of 8 feet (2.3 m).

Preparation Tips: Eskimos gather large quantities of cloudberries when they are available, usually in late August and early September, and freeze a great many for later use, storing them in ice cellars or in kegs or barrels buried in the frozen tundra.

Cloudberries may be eaten any of the ways one might fix fresh strawberries — with cream, spooned over shortcake, and so on. A favorite Native dish mixes fermented greens with cloudberries. (See Greens in Akpiks, page 293.) Another favorite use is in *agutuk*, or Eskimo ice cream, a specialty that has many variations of ingredients. A number of different recipes — including one that uses cloudberries — are on pages 363 and 364. Cloudberries

---

You can make your own luscious and healthy fruit-mixed yogurts (better than ''store bought''). Just mix plain yogurt with any berry sauce or topping or simply mashed berries, sweetened to taste. Experiment with one or more extra flavorings — cinnamon, vanilla, almond extract or a small amount of lemon or orange pulp.

---

also make yummy pie. Use the recipe for Basic Wild Berry Pie, page 362. Or try this Cloudberry Chiffon Pie for a dessert that looks as heavenly as its name.

Cloudberry Chiffon Pie

Graham cracker crust for 9-inch (22 cm) pie
2-1/4 cups (540 mL) cloudberries
1/2 cup (120 mL) sugar
1 envelope (1 Tbsp /or/ 15 mL)
*   unflavored gelatin*
1/4 cup (60 mL) cold water
1/2 cup (120 mL) hot water
1 tablespoon (15 mL) lemon juice
Dash of salt
1/2 cup (120 mL) whipping cream
2 egg whites
1/2 cup (120 mL) sugar

►Prepare graham cracker crust and press into pie pan. Bake at 350°F (175°C) for 10 minutes. Chill. Crush berries and sprinkle with 1/2 cup (120 mL) sugar. Allow to stand for 30 minutes. Soften gelatin in cold water, then dissolve in hot water. Allow to cool. Add the sweetened berries, lemon juice and salt to the berry mixture. Beat egg whites until peaks form when beater is removed. Beat 1/2 cup (120 mL) sugar into egg whites and continue beating until peaks hold form. Carefully fold berry mixture into the egg whites and sugar. Pour into cooled crumb crust. Chill until firm. Garnish with extra berries.
■ Alaska Wild Berry Guide and Cookbook

CRAB APPLE

The western crab apple *(Malus fusca)* is Alaska's only tree-grown fruit. And, actually, this plant can be rather more shrub than tree, too. It grows anywhere from 6 to 16 feet (1.8 to 4.8 m) tall and the fruit is tiny, less than 1 inch (2.5 cm) long, and oblong in shape. It ripens during the height of berry season and makes a good source of pectin for jelly-making. Here are some more good ways to use it, all reprinted from the *Alaska Wild Berry Guide and Cookbook.*

Crab Apple Sauce

1 quart (1 L) crab apples
1/2 cup (120 mL) water
Sugar
Cinnamon

►Stem the crab apples and rinse in lukewarm water. Drain, then place the apples in a saucepan with the water. Bring to a boil and reduce heat to simmer. Cook slowly until the fruit is soft. While still warm, put through a sieve to remove seeds and skins. Add the sugar and cinnamon to suit your taste. This Crab Apple Sauce is especially good in cake, cookies and bread and can be used wherever regular applesauce is called for.

Crab Apple Sauce Cake

2 cups (480 mL) flour
2 tablespoons (30 mL) cocoa
1/2 teaspoon (2 mL) baking soda
1/2 teaspoon (2 mL) salt
1-1/2 teaspoons (7 mL) baking powder
1-1/2 teaspoons (7 mL) cinnamon
1/4 teaspoon (1 mL) cloves
1/2 teaspoon (2 mL) nutmeg
1/2 teaspoon (2 mL) allspice
3/4 cup (180 mL) coarsely chopped nuts
1/2 cup (120 mL) soft butter or margarine
1-1/2 cups (360 mL) sugar
2 eggs
1-1/2 cups (360 mL) Crab Apple Sauce
1 teaspoon (5 mL) vanilla

►Preheat oven to 350°F (175°C). Oil a 9 x 13-inch (22 x 32 cm) pan and line with waxed paper. Sift together flour, cocoa, baking soda, salt, baking powder and spices. Add nuts and toss to coat with the flour. In a large bowl, cream the butter and sugar until light. Add eggs, one at a time, while beating. Add flour mixture, alternating with apple sauce; add vanilla. Turn into prepared pan and bake for 50 to 60 minutes or until cake tests done. A coffee or mocha frosting is particularly nice with this cake.

Crab Apple Nut Loaf

3/4 cup (180 mL) Crab Apple Sauce
1 tablespoon (15 mL) dried orange peel
2 tablespoons (30 mL) butter or margarine
1 egg, slightly beaten
1 cup (240 mL) sugar
1/2 to 1 cup (120 to 240 mL) chopped dates
1/2 to 1 cup (120 to 240 mL) coarsely
*   chopped nuts*
1 cup (240 mL) white flour
1/2 teaspoon (2 mL) salt
1/2 teaspoon (2 mL) baking soda
1/2 teaspoon (2 mL) baking powder
Choice of spices
1 cup (240 mL) whole-wheat flour

►Heat Crab Apple Sauce, orange peel and butter together and set aside to cool. Blend egg and sugar together, adding dates and nuts. Combine with first mixture. Sift white flour with salt, baking soda, baking powder and spices. Gradually add this, with the whole-wheat flour, to the first mixture. Preheat oven to 325°F (160°C). Spoon batter evenly into an oiled loaf pan lined with waxed paper. Bake 45 to 60 minutes or until well done. Filberts are especially good in this loaf, but any nuts will do. Dried wild berries or raisins may be substituted for the dates.

Apple Horseradish Sauce

1 cup (240 mL) Crab Apple Sauce
1/2 pint (0.25 L) whipping cream
1 jar (4 oz /or/ 228 g) horseradish

►Whip the cream. Combine all three ingredients and stir gently to blend. This is delicious with ham or other pork. (And wild game.)

CRANBERRY

Lowbush and Bog Cranberries

If recipes could be invented before the ingredients were given names, this berry would have to be called the versatileberry. Described on following pages are dishes for every part of the meal — from soup (albeit a sweet one which we've included with "beverages") to Cranberry Baked Beans to pie and, of course, many other desserts.

Most of them start with lowbush cranberries *(Vaccinium vitis-idaea)*, or, as they're also called in English and other languages common to Alaska— mountain cranberry, lingonberry, partridgeberry, *tytebeer, nutlut, keepmingyuk, keepmik* and *toomalgleet*. Regardless of the name, most Alaskans "generally regard this berry as the best there is," says *The Alaskan Camp Cook*.

Lowbush cranberries — as the name implies— grow on low evergreen plants that are usually no more than 6 inches (15 cm) tall. They are abundant in many parts of the state. Another member of the family — unfortunately less abundant — is the bog cranberry *(Oxycoccus microcarpus)* which grows on a creeping evergreen vine that selects moss and bogs and other wet places as its habitat. Where the two berries grow side by side, they can be picked and used together, each improving the flavor of the other.
Preparation Tips: High in acid content, the lowbush cranberry has excellent keeping qualities, on or off the bush. Though they are best picked right after first frost, they'll keep on the bush till early spring. Picked, they will also keep well stored

in a cool place. One suggestion is to put the berries in a cloth bag (so they can "breathe") and hang the bag outdoors under the eaves.

Both berries are similar to commercial cranberries — only much better — and can be used just as you would commercial berries.

Lowbush Cranberry

Highbush Cranberry

The other cranberry, the highbush cranberry *(Viburnum edule)*, neither looks nor tastes nor smells like the *Vaccinium* species. It is a small, waxy red or orange red berry with a single large, flat seed. And it grows, of course, on a high bush, 8 or 10 feet (up to 3 m) tall.
Preparations Tips: The highbush cranberry has a strong woodsy odor and flavor that some people don't like, but it is prized by others as an accompaniment to game meats. It makes a beautiful jelly and is used in fruit ketchup, chutney and some beverages, but because of the large seed, it is not good in pies, sauces or jams. In other words, it is *not* interchangeable in any way with bog or lowbush cranberries.

Again, most of the recipes following are for lowbush or bog cranberries. Where highbush berries are wanted, the name will be used. More recipes for them will be found in Chapter 14.

Refreshing Snack

►Highbush cranberries, plucked directly from the bush and consumed on the spot are refreshing to hikers, hunters and campers. They are excellent when frozen and taken from the plant then; they melt on the tongue like a spot of sherbet.

Raw Cranberry Salad

2 packages (3 oz /or/ 85 g) lemon gelatin
3 cups (720 mL) boiling water
1/2 cup (120 mL) sugar
1 cup (240 mL) crushed pineapple, drained
1 cup (240 mL) finely chopped celery
2 apples, diced
1 orange, diced
Juice and rind of 1 lemon
1/2 cup (120 mL) chopped nuts
4 cups (1 L) lowbush cranberries

►Pour hot water over gelatin and add sugar; stir until dissolved. Chill until it begins to jell; then add remaining ingredients. Chill until completely jelled.
■ The Alaskan Camp Cook

Variation: For a sweeter salad, several cooks recommend allowing the cranberries — ground or whole — to stand in sugar ''to taste'' — some use as much as 1 cup (240 mL) for this amount of cranberries — while the gelatin is prepared and chilled to the ''unbeaten egg white'' stage.

Raw Cranberry Relish

1 pound (456 g) lowbush cranberries
1 orange, ground
1 pound (456 g) sugar

►Grind orange, rind and all; mix with cranberries and sugar and stir until sugar is dissolved. Let stand overnight. Stir well again and pack in sterilized jars. No cooking necessary as fruit will jell without cooking. Store in a cool place.

Variations: Grind the cranberries and orange together, adding other fruits — two or three unpeeled apples, half a lemon — as desired. Add chopped nuts and/or tiny marshmallows. Mix and store in refrigerator.

Simple Cranberry Sauce

Lowbush cranberries
Sugar
Water

►Measure cleaned cranberries into saucepan. Measure half as much sugar as cranberries into the pan. Add 1 tablespoon (15 mL) cold water for each cup (240 mL) of fruit. Stir gently. Allow to stand for an hour; then place pan over medium heat until the sauce comes to a boil. Reduce heat to simmer and cook for four or five minutes. May be stored in the freezer or refrigerator in jars. Longer it cooks, the thicker it becomes.
■ *The Old Homesteader*

Frozen Cranberry Salad #1

2 packages (3 oz /or/ 85 g, each) cream cheese
3/4 cup (180 mL) mayonnaise
1 cup (240 mL) heavy cream, whipped
1 cup (240 mL) cubed Jellied Cranberry Sauce
1 can (9 oz /or/ 255 g) crushed pineapple, drained
1/2 cup (120 mL) chopped ripe olives
1/4 cup (60 mL) chopped celery

►Blend cream cheese and mayonnaise together. Fold in whipped cream. Then fold in the Cranberry Sauce cubes, crushed pineapple, ripe olives and celery. Pour into a refrigerator tray and freeze three to four hours. Makes five or six servings.
■ *Donna Fontaine*
   The Food Cache

Frozen Cranberry Salad #2

1 quart (1 L) raw cranberries
6 apples, peeled and cored
1-1/4 cups (300 mL) sugar
1 small can crushed pineapple
1 pound (456 g) miniature marshmallows
1/2 cup (120 mL) chopped walnuts
2 cups (480 mL) heavy cream, whipped

►Run apples and cranberries through a grinder, using fine blade. Add sugar, pineapple and marshmallows. Stir thoroughly and set aside to ''ripen'' for 15 minutes. Then add nuts and fold in whipped cream. Spoon into containers and freeze immediately. This will keep for weeks if frozen.
■ *Jacqueline Soter*
   Mount Spurr School Cook Book
   Elmendorf Air Force Base

Molded Cranberry Sauce or Salad
Using cooked berries

2 pounds (1 kg) lowbush cranberries
2 cups (480 mL) water
1 cup (240 mL) sugar
1 family-size package (6 oz /or/ 170 g) wild raspberry gelatin
1 can (8 oz /or/ 228 g) crushed pineapple
1 cup (240 mL) coarsely chopped walnuts

►Combine berries, water and sugar. Boil for 10 minutes. Add gelatin to hot mixture and remove from heat, stirring well to dissolve gelatin. Cool and add pineapple and walnuts. Chill. Serve as a molded salad or in a side dish to accompany game meats.
■ *Gloria Houp*
   What's Cookin' in Wrangell

Campfire Game Sauce

►Put a couple handfuls of lowbush cranberries in a pan or skillet. Add just enough water to cover the bottom of the pan, allowing the tops of most of the berries to stick out. Heat until all of the berries pop out of their skins. Add sugar (this will take a little sampling on the part of the cook) and continue stirring over the fire until the desired consistency is obtained. If the sauce gets too thick, just add a little more water.

■ *Gladys M. Wilson*
"Lowbush Cranberries"
ALASKA SPORTSMAN®, *October 1968*

Jellied Cranberry Sauce

2 quarts (1.9 L) lowbush cranberries
1 quart (1 L) water
4 to 5 cups (1 to 1.25 L) sugar

►Boil berries and water together until the skins pop. Mash berries and juice through a colander or medium-fine sieve. Add sugar to taste, return to heat and boil until a little of the sauce will jell on the spoon. You may either store this sauce in the refrigerator or pour it hot into hot, sterilized jelly jars and seal as you would any jelly (see directions in Chapter 14).

Variations:
• Add a spice bag to the second boiling, following proportions given in the last variation to Whole Berry Cranberry Sauce top of next column.
• Add 1 tablespoon (15 mL) orange juice and an equal amount of grated orange rind to the second boiling.

Whole Berry Cranberry Sauce

6 cups (1.45 L) lowbush cranberries
4 cups (1 L) sugar
3/4 cup (180 mL) water

►Blend all ingredients in a saucepan and bring to a full, rolling boil. Boil until a little of the juice will jell on the spoon, approximately 25 minutes. Cool. Store in the refrigerator.

Variations:
• Substitute 1/2 cup (120 mL) honey for the same amount of sugar and reduce the amount of water used by 2 tablespoons (30 mL).
• Add slivered, crystallized ginger and/or a bit of grated orange rind.
• Substitute a portion of orange juice for an equal amount of water.
• To 2 cups (480 mL) Whole Berry Cranberry Sauce, add 1/4 cup (60 mL) butter, 1/4 cup (60 mL) brown sugar or maple syrup and cinnamon to taste. Serve hot on waffles or pancakes.
• Spice up the sauce by adding the following whole spices tied up in a cheesecloth bag — eight whole cloves, eight whole allspice, three cinnamon sticks. Allow spices to cook with the sauce; remove bag before storing in refrigerator.

■ Alaska Wild Berry Guide and Cookbook

Cranberry Glazes for Ham, Chicken or Game

• An *ALASKA*® magazine suggestion from Helen A. White: Trim excess fat off ham (with bone in, is best) and place in baking pan. The ham should be placed in the pan with the fat side up and on a rack. Melt cranberry jelly and stir in the spices of your choice. With a sharp pointed knife, make deep holes all over the ham. Force the jelly mixture into the holes and pour more of it over the ham. Reserve part of the jelly to pour over it at intervals as it bakes. Also good on smoked game.
• Jelly makes a wonderful glaze for baked ham. Take 1 cup (240 mL) melted ham or bacon fat, 1/2 cup (120 mL) melted Lowbush Cranberry Jelly (or Currant Jelly), add 1/4 cup (60 mL) prepared mustard and heat together. Pour over the ham and bake as usual. Excellent on game.
• And this one from the *Alaska Wild Berry Guide and Cookbook:* Mix 2/3 cup (160 mL) Lowbush Cranberry Juice, 1/2 cup (120 mL), each, prepared mustard and honey, 1/4 cup (60 mL) melted butter or margarine in a saucepan or bowl and use it as a basting sauce for broiled or baked chicken, spruce hens or duck. This is enough for two moderate-sized birds cut into serving pieces. Brush with sauce before placing in oven or broiler and continue basting as needed until birds are done, 40 to 60 minutes.

Cranberry Corn Bread Stuffing

1 cup (240 mL) lowbush cranberries
1/4 cup (60 mL) sugar
1/4 cup (60 mL) chopped celery
2 tablespoons (30 mL) chopped parsley
1/2 cup (120 mL) diced ham or bacon
4 tablespoons (60 mL) butter or margarine
3 cups (720 mL) stale bread crumbs
1 cup (240 mL) corn bread crumbs
Poultry seasoning to taste

►Run the cranberries through a food chopper and add sugar. Cook celery, parsley and diced ham in butter for five minutes. Add the bread crumbs, seasoning and berries and blend lightly. This is particularly good with baked moose heart, wild duck or poultry.

■ Alaska Wild Berry Guide and Cookbook

Cranberry Barbecue Sauce

1 cup (240 mL) Lowbush Cranberry Juice
1 cup (240 mL) ketchup
1/2 cup (120 mL) water
1/4 cup (60 mL) Worcestershire
1 large tomato, chopped
1/4 to 1/2 green pepper, chopped
1/2 tablespoon (7 mL) minced, dried onion
1 tablespoon (15 mL) horseradish
1-1/2 teaspoons (7 mL) dry mustard

►Combine all ingredients in a saucepan and simmer for 10 minutes or so. This makes a good barbecue basting sauce for wild game, beef, lamb or pork. Or serve it warm as a dip for tiny cocktail meatballs.
■ Alaska Wild Berry Guide and Cookbook

Wild Cranberries
The delicious, hard-to-come-by,
easy-to-eat bog cranberry

1 pair hip boots for kneeling in swamp
1 bail bucket slipped over strong belt

►Dig into wet moss and select cranberries — not too ripe. Pick over. Wash in cold water and let dry on paper. Grind in food chopper. Add 1 cup (240 mL) sugar to 1 cup (240 mL) berry pulp. Place in stone jar, stir occasionally until sugar dissolves. Keep in cool dry storage. Serve with turkey or other fowl or meat. DO NOT COOK.
■ *Crystal Snow Jenne*
    Tried and True Recipes, *Juneau*

Cranberry Baked Beans

1-1/2 cups (360 mL) dried beans
2 cups (480 mL) Lowbush Cranberry Juice
2 cups (480 mL) water
1/3 cup (80 mL) onions, chopped
2 tablespoons (30 mL) molasses
1 teaspoon (5 mL) dry mustard
1/8 teaspoon (0.5 mL) ginger
1/4 cup (60 mL) ketchup
2 tablespoons (30 mL) dark brown sugar,
    packed
1-1/2 teaspoons (7 mL) salt
1/4 pound (114 g) salt pork, sliced

►Wash beans and soak overnight in combined cranberry juice and water. Bring beans to a boil in the soaking liquid. Cover the pan and lower the heat; simmer just until beans are tender. If necessary, add more water to keep beans from sticking. Drain beans and place in a large bowl, reserving the cooking liquid. Add onions, molasses, mustard, ginger, ketchup, brown sugar and salt to the beans and mix well. Turn half the mixture into a bean pot. Arrange half the salt pork slices over the beans. Add remaining beans and top with remaining pork. Pour 1-1/2 cups (360 mL) of the reserved liquid over all. Cover and bake in a slow oven, about 250°F (125°C) for six to eight hours. Uncover for the last hour and add more of the reserved liquid to keep the beans from drying out. Serve with a green salad.
■ *Vera Kirkwood,* Atlin News Miner
    Reprinted from ALASKA® magazine

Cranberry Cookies

1 stick (114 g) margarine
1 cup (240 mL) sugar
3/4 cup (180 mL) firmly packed brown sugar
1 teaspoon (5 mL) vanilla
1/3 cup (80 mL) milk
1 egg
3 cups (720 mL) sifted flour
1 teaspoon ((5 mL) baking powder
1/4 teaspoon (1 mL) baking soda
1/2 teaspoon (2 mL) salt
1 cup (240 mL) candied fruit
1 tablespoon (15 mL) orange peel
2-1/2 cups (600 mL) fresh lowbush cranberries,
    chopped

►Cream margarine, sugar and vanilla. Beat in milk and egg. Mix and sift flour, soda, baking powder and salt; stir into creamed mixture. Blend well. Stir in candied fruit, orange peel and cranberries. Drop in mounds on well-greased cookie sheet. Bake at 375°F (190°C) for 15 to 18 minutes. Makes about 3-1/2 dozen.
■ *Phyllis Sinclair,* Kitchen Magic, *Ketchikan*

Brandied Cranberries

1 pound (456 g) lowbush cranberries
2-1/2 cups (600 mL) sugar
5 tablespoons (75 mL) brandy

►Place berries in shallow baking pan in one layer. Sprinkle with sugar. Cover tightly with heavy duty foil. Bake at 350°F (175°C) for one hour. Cool. Mix in brandy, a little at a time, until you have enough for your taste. These cranberries make a good garnish for holiday foods.

Cranberry Rollups

►Place 2 cups (480 mL) of pancake mix in bowl; add 1 cup (240 mL) of evaporated milk and one egg, slightly beaten first. Beat until smooth; then add a cup (240 mL) of apple which has been finely chopped. Have griddle hot and well greased. Pour 1/4 cup (60 mL) batter for each pancake. Brown, turn and brown on other side. Have lowbush cranberry jelly ready, which has been previously beaten to a spreading consistency. Remove cakes from griddle and immediately spread with jelly. Roll up and sprinkle with powdered sugar. Serve while warm.

■ *Helen A. White, Anchorage*
  Alaska Wild Berry Trails

Cranberry Pudding

2 cups (480 mL) biscuit mix
1 cup (240 mL) sugar
3 tablespoons (45 mL) melted butter
2/3 cup (160 mL) milk
1 egg
2 cups (480 mL) lowbush cranberries

►Add sugar, butter, milk and egg to biscuit mix. Fold in cranberries. Bake in 8- or 9-inch (20 to 22 cm) square pan for 40 to 45 minutes at 350°F (175°C). Serve with Butter Sauce.

Butter Sauce
1/4 cup (60 mL) butter
1/2 cup (120 mL) sugar
1/3 cup (80 mL) cream or evaporated milk

►Heat together for five minutes and serve as a topping for Cranberry Pudding.

■ *Nancy Warren*
  Good Food A-Plenty, Fairbanks

Cranberry "Sour Cream" Coffeecake

"My favorite coffeecake"

1 cup (240 mL) butter
1-1/2 cups (360 mL) sugar
2 eggs
1 cup (240 mL) Alaska "sour cream"*
3-1/2 cups (840 mL) flour
1/2 teaspoon (2 mL) baking powder
1/2 teaspoon (2 mL) baking soda
1 tablespoon (15 mL) vanilla

Topping:
1/2 cup (120 mL) chopped nuts
1/2 cup (120 mL) lowbush cranberries
2 teaspoons (10 mL) sugar
1-1/2 teaspoons (7 mL) cinnamon

►Cream butter and sugar. Add eggs and beat well. Sift flour, baking powder and soda together. Add flour and "sour cream" alternately, beating well after each addition. Blend in vanilla. Put half the mixture into a well-greased tube pan. Mix the nuts,

cranberries, 2 teaspoons (10 mL) sugar and cinnamon and sprinkle half over the batter in the pan. Add remaining batter and sprinkle on remaining nut mixture.

Place in a COLD oven, turn it to 350°F (175°C) and bake for 55 minutes.

■ *Polly Kallenberg, Chugiak*
  Courtesy, Audrey Rearden, Homer

*Alaska "sour cream" is made by placing 1 tablespoon (15 mL) vinegar in a measuring cup, then filling the balance of a 1-cup measure (240 mL) with undiluted canned milk. Allow it to "sour" for a few minutes.

Cheechako Sherbet

►Beat 1-1/2 cups (360 mL) Lowbush Cranberry Jelly with an egg whip; add juice and grated rind of one orange and one lemon and continue beating until frothy. Freeze to mush consistency and then fold in two stiffly beaten egg whites or 1/2 pint (240 mL) heavy cream, whipped. Finish freezing. This is really a dessert but it also makes a wonderful accompaniment to wild birds or other poultry. Try it with roasted ptarmigan. *

■ *Helen A. White, Anchorage*
  Alaska Wild Berry Trails

*The Italians have a nice habit of serving a small scoop of sherbet between the courses of a heavy meal to ready the taste buds for what's next.

Snow Berry Cake

2-1/2 cups (600 mL) sifted flour
3 teaspoons (15 mL) baking powder
1 teaspoon (5 mL) salt
2/3 cup (160 mL) shortening
1 cup (240 mL) sugar
1 teaspoon (5 mL) grated lemon peel
3/4 cup (180 mL) milk
4 egg whites, beaten stiff
1/2 cup (120 mL) additional sugar
1 cup (240 mL) Jellied Cranberry Sauce, cubed

►Combine sifted flour, baking powder and salt and sift these together. Combine shortening, the 1 cup (240 mL) sugar and lemon peel and cream well together. When thoroughly blended, begin adding dry ingredients and milk, a little at a time, alternately. If electric mixer is used, beat at low speed. Beat egg whites until they hold a soft peak, then begin adding the 1/2 cup (120 mL) sugar a little at a time until meringue holds peaks which are shiny but not dry. Fold this gently into the batter and then carefully fold in Jellied Cranberry Sauce cubes. Pour into two well-greased and lightly floured round layer pans. Bake in a moderate oven at 375°F (190°C) 30 to 35 minutes. Cool and frost.

■ *Mrs. Fred Cox*
  Sitka's Treasure

Cranberry-Banana Nuggets

2 cups (480 mL) all-purpose flour
1 teaspoon (5 mL) baking soda
1/2 teaspoon (2 mL) salt
1 stick (114 g) margarine
1 cup (240 mL) sugar
2 eggs
1 cup (240 mL) mashed ripe bananas
1 tablespoon (15 mL) grated orange rind
1/4 cup (60 mL) milk
1 teaspoon (5 mL) vanilla
1/2 teaspoon (2 mL) almond extract
1 cup (240 mL) shredded coconut
1/2 cup (120 mL) or more chopped nuts
1 cup (240 mL) lowbush cranberries

►Mix and sift flour, soda and salt and set aside, reserving a little of the flour with which to dredge the cranberries. Cream margarine until light and fluffy; gradually add sugar and beat until light. Add eggs, bananas and orange rind; blend well. Combine milk, vanilla and almond extract. Add dry ingredients alternately with the milk mixture to the margarine mixture beginning and ending with dry ingredients. Blend well after each addition. Stir in coconut, nuts and berries that have been dredged in the reserved flour. Pour into paper-lined muffin cups, filling one-quarter to one-half full. The thinner nuggets will be crisper. Bake at 350°F (175°C) until well browned and the surface springs back when tested with a fingertip — from 15 to 30 minutes, depending on thickness. Makes about three dozen.

■ *The Old Homesteader*

Spicy Cranberry Orange Bread

Juice of 2 oranges and enough water to make
* 1-3/4 cups (420 mL) total liquid*
2 tablespoons (30 mL) grated orange rind or
* dried orange bits*
6 tablespoons (90 mL) margarine
3 cups (720 mL) white flour, sifted
1 cup (240 mL) whole-wheat flour
1 teaspoon (5 mL) each — salt and baking soda
1-1/2 teaspoons (7 mL) baking powder
2 cups (480 mL) sugar
1 teaspoon (5 mL) each — cinnamon
* and nutmeg*
1/2 teaspoon, (2 mL) each — cloves, allspice
* and ginger*
2 eggs, slightly beaten
1/2 cup (120 mL) white flour
3 cups (720 mL) lowbush cranberries
2 cups (480 mL) coarsely chopped walnuts

►Bring water and orange juice to a boil; add margarine and orange rind. Set aside to cool. Sift white flour and measure out 3 cups (720 mL). Sift again with all other dry ingredients except the rest of the flour. Place sifted materials in large bowl and stir in whole-wheat flour; make a "well" in the center. Pour cooled liquid into well and stir just enough to moisten. Add beaten eggs and again stir gently until eggs are blended into mixture. Sprinkle the 1/2 cup (120 mL) white flour on the cranberries and chopped nuts. Roll them around to coat well with the flour. Add the floured ingredients to the batter, stirring no more than necessary. Gentle handling is needed for this step to keep from breaking the berries. It does no real harm to break the berries but the finished product looks better if the berries retain their shape. Add more flour, if it is indicated, in order to make a stiff dough.

Line two 4 x 8-inch (10 x 20 cm) loaf pans with strips of foil. Or use paper cups in muffin tins. Bake at 350°F (175°C) for up to 1-1/2 hours, depending on size of pans. Be sure the loaves are well done. It is so easy to underbake them. Allow baked bread to stand on rack for 15 minutes before removing from pans and peeling off foil. Be certain loaves are completely cold before wrapping for the freezer.

I like to slice this bread immediately after I remove it from the freezer. It slices like a dream. I make up six to eight batches each fall and use the loaves for gifts. It ships to the Lower 48, too. I always freeze the loaves and allow them to remain frozen for some weeks before shipping; then I wrap them in plastic film and foil and several layers of newspaper before packing in the shipping box.

■ *Helen A. White, Anchorage*
   "Alaska: Land of Wild Berries"
   ALASKA® *magazine, August 1979*

Cranberry Muffins

2-1/2 cups (600 mL) sifted flour
2-1/2 teaspoons (12 mL) double acting
* baking powder*
1/2 teaspoon (2 mL) salt
1/2 cup (120 mL) sugar
1 cup (240 mL) cranberries
2 eggs, well beaten
1 cup (240 mL) milk
4 tablespoons (60 mL) melted butter or
* other shortening*

►Sift flour once, measure; add baking powder, salt and sugar and sift again. Combine berries with 1/3 cup (80 mL) of flour mixture. Combine eggs, milk and shortening; add to flour mixture, beating only enough to dampen flour. Fold in berries and bake in greased muffin pans (or muffin pans with paper liners) in hot oven, 425°F (220°C), for 25 minutes or until done.

■ Out of Alaska's Kitchens

Magic Fruit Pudding

1 cup (240 mL) honey
1/2 cup (114 g) butter
1/2 teaspoon (2 mL) salt
1 teaspoon (5 mL) cinnamon
1/4 teaspoon (1 mL) nutmeg
1 cup (240 mL) lowbush cranberries
1 cup (240 mL) raisins
2 cups (480 mL) water
6 cups (1.45 L) toasted whole-wheat bread
    cubes, packed

►In a saucepan, mix together honey, butter, salt, spices, cranberries, raisins and water. Bring to a boil over medium heat, stirring. Boil gently five minutes or until cranberries are soft. Butter a 2-quart (2 L) pudding pan; add bread cubes. Pour prepared fruit sauce over cubes. Allow mixture to stand 15 minutes to blend flavors. Bake, uncovered, at 350°F (175°C) for 45 minutes. Serve warm with honey-sweetened dairy sour cream or your favorite holiday sauce. Makes 10 servings.
■ *Mrs. Keith Jones*
   The Food Cache

Cranberry Cheese Frosting

1 small package (3 oz /or/ 85 g) cream cheese
4 tablespoons Jellied Cranberry Sauce
1/8 teaspoon (0.5 mL) salt
1 pound (456 g) powdered sugar

►Soften cream cheese and mix with Jellied Cranberry Sauce and salt. Gradually stir in powdered sugar until frosting is creamy in texture. This is not only a good cake icing, but it is wonderful spread on graham crackers for an after-school treat.
■ Alaska Wild Berry Guide and Cookbook

Cranberry Cake

1 cup (240 mL) shortening
1-1/2 cups (360 mL) sugar
4 eggs
2-1/2 teaspoons (12 mL) baking powder
3 cups (720 mL) sifted flour
Dash of salt
3/4 cup (180 mL) milk
1/4 cup (60 mL) orange juice
1/2 cup (120 mL) chopped walnuts
1 cup (240 mL) chopped dates
2 cups (480 mL) lowbush cranberries
2 tablespoons (30 mL) grated, dried orange peel
1 teaspoon (5 mL) chopped, crystallized ginger
Jewel Cake Frosting

►Preheat oven to 350°F (175°C). Cream the shortening, add sugar. Add eggs, one at a time. Beat well. Sift the baking powder, flour and salt together. Combine milk and orange juice and add to the shortening mixture, alternating with the dry ingredients. Fold in nuts, dates, berries, orange peel and ginger. Pour into a well-oiled and floured 10-inch (25 cm) tube pan and bake for 1 hour and 20 minutes or until well browned. When cake is almost cool, top with frosting.

Jewel Cake Frosting
3-1/2 cups (840 mL) sifted powdered sugar
1/2 cup (120 mL) softened butter or margarine
2 egg yolks
1 teaspoon (5 mL) grated lemon rind
1 tablespoon (15 mL) lemon juice
1/8 teaspoon (0.5 mL) salt
1/2 cup (120 mL) finely chopped nuts
Red food coloring (optional)
3/4 cup (180 mL) lowbush cranberries
Whipped topping

►Mix sugar, butter, egg yolks, lemon rind, lemon juice and salt until light and fluffy. Stir in nuts, 1/2 cup (120 mL) cranberries and a few drops of red food coloring. Fill and frost the cake. Garnish with a whipped topping and the remaining cranberries.
■ *Florence Thornton, Rabbit Creek*
   Alaska Wild Berry Guide and Cookbook

40-Below Cranberry Dessert

1 package vanilla wafers
1/2 cup (120 mL) margarine
1 cup (240 mL) confectioners' sugar
2 eggs
2 cups (480 mL) ground lowbush cranberries
2/3 cup (160 mL) sugar
2 bananas
1/2 cup (120 mL) chopped nuts
1 bottle whipping Avoset*

►Crush vanilla wafers and line pan with half of crumbs. Cream margarine, confectioners' sugar and eggs well and spread over crumbs. Add sugar and sliced bananas to cranberries and spread over egg mixture. Sprinkle chopped nuts over cranberry mixture. Spread whipped Avoset over chopped nuts. Sprinkle remaining crumbs over whipped cream. Refrigerate overnight. Serve with whipped cream. Serves 12.
■ *Mrs. Jack Cook*
   Good Food A-Plenty, *Fairbanks*

Avoset is the brand name for a sterilized whipping cream that will keep in the refrigerator for a long time. You may use a pint (0.47 L) of regular whipping cream as a substitute. There are other long-lasting products now on the market, such as Stayfresh whipping cream, which does not require refrigeration.

Basic Cranberry Pie

Pastry for 9-inch (22 cm) lattice-topped pie
3 cups (720 mL) lowbush cranberries
1 tablespoon (15 mL) flour
1-1/2 cups (360 mL) sugar
1/4 teaspoon (1 mL) salt
1 tablespoon (15 mL) water
1 teaspoon (5 mL) vanilla
Butter or margarine

►Line a 9-inch (22 cm) pie pan with crust. Mix all remaining ingredients except butter and pour into pan. Dot with butter. Weave strips of pastry to make a lattice top, sealing edges carefully. Bake in a hot oven, preheated to 450°F (230°C), for 15 minutes. Reduce heat to 350°F (175°C) and bake about 30 minutes longer.

Variations:

• Use 1-1/2 cups (360 mL) cranberries and 1-1/2 cups (360 mL) apples, peeled and chopped, or the same amount of dried apples, plumped in water before measuring. Drizzle apples with about 1 tablespoon (15 mL) lemon juice.
• Fresh pears, peeled and quartered, also make a good addition to this pie. If they are especially juicy, you may need extra flour.

Christmas Cranberry Eggnog Pie

For some of those lowbush cranberries you've got hanging out under the eaves (see page 328)

►You will need a large, deep pie crust. Do not prebake; flute crust around the edges. Put 1-1/2 cups (375 mL) whole raw lowbush cranberries in bottom of crust. Cover them with 3/4 cup (180 mL) sugar. Do not stir. Bake in a preheated oven, 425°F (220°C) for 12 to 15 minutes or until edges of crust are lightly browned. Now stir berries lightly until sugar is absorbed, being careful not to pierce the crust.

Cheese-Eggnog Topping
1 package (8 oz /or/ 228 g) cream cheese, softened
1 tablespoon (15 mL) flour
3 tablespoons (45 mL) sugar
1-1/2 cups (375 mL) eggnog
3 eggs

►Cream together the cream cheese, flour and sugar. Add in eggnog gradually, a small amount at first, and beat well with rotary beater until smooth. Beat eggs well and add. Cover hot berries with Cheese-Eggnog mixture — full to the brim. Reduce the oven temperature to 350°F (175°C) and bake for 30 to 40 minutes, until set. Let cool completely and serve. This is best if cooled and then chilled in

refrigerator before serving. Keeps well several days. The combination of flavors is superb and it is a beautiful pie — golden in color with the red berries all through it.

■ *Esther McDaniel*
Alaska's Cooking, *Anchorage*

Prize-Winning Mock Cherry Pie

Pastry for 2-crust 9-inch (22 cm) pie
1 egg, beaten
1 teaspoon (5 mL) salt
1 cup (240 mL) sugar
1 teaspoon (5 mL) vanilla
1 rounded tablespoon (20 mL) flour
1/2 cup (120 mL) water
1 cup (240 mL) lowbush cranberries
1 large apple, chopped, or 1/2 cup (120 mL) raisins
Whipped topping

►Line a 9-inch (22 cm) pie pan with pastry. Mix egg, salt, sugar, vanilla, flour and water until smooth and pour into unbaked shell. Add cranberries and apple or raisins. Cover with top crust, sealing edges well and cutting vents for steam. Bake at 400°F (205°C) for about 45 minutes. Serve with your favorite whipped topping. This pie, originating from the early days of Dawson, has won me many prizes.

■ *Beverly I. Poirier, Whitehorse, Yukon Territory*
The Cabin Friend
ALASKA® magazine, *December 1980*

Cranberry Yum Dessert

1 pound (456 g) lowbush cranberries, ground
1 pound (456 g) miniature marshmallows
1-1/2 cups (360 mL) sugar
1 can (20 oz /or/ 567 g) crushed pineapple, well drained
1 pint (0.47 L) whipping cream, whipped with 1/2 cup (120 mL) sugar
3/4 cup (180 mL) chopped nuts

►Combine and chill overnight — the cranberries, marshmallows and 1-1/2 cups (360 mL) sugar. The next day, mix in the pineapple. Whip the cream, beating in sugar toward the end. Add nuts and fold into cranberry mixture. Freeze.

■ *Connie Purvis*
"More Good Eating," *Tokeen Cove*

Easy-Does-It Cranberry Tarts

►Mix 2 cups (480 mL) lowbush cranberries, 3/4 cup (180 mL) water and 1-1/2 cups (360 mL) sugar. Stir until sugar is dissolved. Pour into a covered casserole and bake in a very slow oven until berries are tender. It may be necessary to stir the fruit now and then. Avoid cooking too long. Cool slightly and pour into prepared tart shells made from your favorite pastry.

Mini Cranberry Cupcakes

1 stick (114 g) margarine
1-1/2 cups (360 mL) brown sugar, packed
1 egg
1-1/2 cups (360 mL) cottage cheese
1 cup (240 mL) raisins
2 cups (480 mL) fresh or frozen lowbush
   cranberries, drained
2-1/2 cups (600 mL) flour, unsifted
1 teaspoon (5 mL) salt
1/2 teaspoon (2 mL) baking soda

►Cream margarine in a bowl until light and fluffy. Stir in sugar, egg, cheese. Fold in raisins and cranberries. Stir in flour, salt and soda. Spoon batter into paper-lined muffin cups, filling each about three-quarters full. Bake in preheated 350°F (175°C) oven for 30 to 35 minutes or until puffed and browned. Serve sprinkled with confectioners' sugar if desired.
■ The Anchorage Times, *Christmas 1976*

Cranberry Crisp

2 cups (480 mL) fresh lowbush cranberries
3/4 cup (180 mL) sugar
1 cup (240 mL) chopped pecans
2 eggs
1 cup (240 mL) sugar
1/2 cup (120 mL) margarine
1/4 cup (60 mL) melted shortening or oil
1 cup (240 mL) flour

►Sprinkle first three ingredients on bottom of 10-inch (25 cm) greased pie pan. Mix and spread over cranberry mixture the remaining ingredients. Bake at 325°F (160°C) for one hour. Serve warm with whipped cream or other topping.
■ *Bessie Willburn*
   Dall Homemakers Cookbook
   Cooper Landing

Berry Red 'n' Green Fudge

1 package (8 oz /or/ 228 g) cream cheese
2 pounds (1 kg) confectioners' sugar
1 teaspoon (5 mL) almond extract
Green food coloring
1 cup (240 mL) almonds, chopped
1 cup (240 mL) fresh or fresh frozen lowbush
   cranberries, drained

►In a bowl mash cheese until light and fluffy. Gradually beat in confectioners' sugar. Beat in

almond extract and enough green food coloring to make a bright green. Knead in almonds. Line a 9-inch (22 cm) square pan with foil and press half of the fudge into an even layer in the pan. Place berries evenly over fudge. Cover with remaining fudge and press until level. Chill for several hours. Cut into 1-inch (2.5 cm) squares with a sharp knife. Store in refrigerator until ready to serve.
■ The Anchorage Times, *Christmas 1976*

Cranberry Sauce Drops

1 cup (240 mL) shortening
1-1/2 cups (360 mL) sugar
3 eggs
1/2 teaspoon (2 mL) salt
1 teaspoon (5 mL) baking soda
1 teaspoon (5 mL) cinnamon
3 cups (720 mL) sifted flour, plus 1 cup
   (240 mL) more
1-1/3 cups (320 mL) Simple Cranberry Sauce
1 teaspoon (5 mL) orange peel
1 cup (240 mL) nuts, chopped

►Cream shortening, gradually adding sugar. Blend well. Add eggs; beat until smooth. Add measured salt, soda and cinnamon to 3 cups (720 mL) of the sifted flour. Gradually add this to the creamed mixture. Gently stir in cranberry sauce and orange peel so that berry pulp will retain its bulk. At this point cookie batter will be moist. Stir in additional flour, (approximately 1 cup or 240 mL), to make a stiff dough; fold in nuts. Preheat oven to 400°F (205°C). Drop batter by teaspoonfuls on greased cookie sheets, about 2 inches (5 cm) apart. Bake for 12 minutes or until nicely browned. *Note:* You may need to drain excess juice from the cranberry sauce. It can be added later if needed.
■ *Elsie Tourville*

Candied Cranberries

2-1/2 cups (600 mL) sugar
1-1/2 cups (360 mL) water
1 quart (1 L) lowbush cranberries

►Stir sugar and water in saucepan until sugar is dissolved. Bring to a boil. Have cleaned berries ready in a bowl. Pour boiling syrup over berries. Place in a steamer for 45 minutes to an hour. Remove and cool without stirring. Leave in a DRY room for three or four days, stirring now and then.

Nuts grow in Alaska? Why, shore! But they grow on bushes instead of trees. Try this: Next time you make banana bread, substitute lowbush cranberries for the nuts. Dust them with sugar first and then fold them into the batter just before baking.

Cranberry juice will save a long time, bottled, stored in the refrigerator or a cool place or, of course, frozen in airtight plastic containers, it will keep even longer. Keep it on hand, unsweetened, to become the base for these drinks or others of your own concoction. An Alaskan Cook Book, from the Kenai Historical Society, suggests that rhubarb juice is a good one to add to the cranberry "stock." To find out how to extract these juices, see page 468.

Hot Spiced Punch

1 cup (240 mL) water
3/4 cup (180 mL) brown sugar
Dash of salt
1/4 teaspoon (1 mL) nutmeg
1/2 teaspoon (2 mL) cinnamon
1/2 teaspoon (2 mL) allspice
3/4 teaspoon (3 mL) cloves
3 quarts (2.85 L) Lowbush Cranberry Juice
1 quart (1 L) pineapple juice
2 cups (480 mL) water
Cinnamon sticks
Butter

►Bring to a boil 1 cup (240 mL) water, sugar, salt and ground spices. Add juices and 2 cups (480 mL) water to hot spiced syrup and heat to boiling. Serve in mugs with a small bit of butter floating on top of each. Use cinnamon sticks as stirrers. May be kept hot in double boiler.
■ *Helen A. White*
  "Far North Fare"
  ALASKA® magazine, December 1974

Hot Spiced Cranberry Tea

8 cups (1.9 L) lowbush cranberries
8 cups (1.9 L) water
1-1/2 cups (360 mL) sugar
2 or 3 sticks of cinnamon
15 to 20 whole cloves
1 lemon, sliced
2 cups (480 mL) freshly brewed tea

►Cook cranberries in water until all the skins pop open. Strain through cheesecloth. Do not stir or press. To the juice add sugar, cinnamon and cloves. Cook for five minutes. Add lemon slices and tea and pour into punch bowl. Sprinkle with nutmeg. Serve piping hot.
■ Out of Alaska's Kitchens

Cottey Wassail

2-1/2 gallons (9.5 L) apple cider
1 quart (1 L) grapefruit juice
1 quart (1 L) Simple Syrup
3 quarts (2.85 L) orange juice

1 quart (1 L) Lowbush Cranberry Juice
  (page 468)
3 quarts (2.85 L) Spiced Tea

►Blend all ingredients and let stand overnight. Heat and add more sugar if necessary. Serve warm.

Simple Syrup
Combine and bring to boiling 1 quart (1 L) water and 1 quart (1 L) sugar.

Spiced Tea
►Put in cloth bag or tea container 2 teaspoons (10 mL) whole cloves and two sticks of cinnamon. Add 3 quarts (2.85 L) prepared tea; heat to boiling and simmer a few minutes.
■ *Mae Huffman*
  What's Cookin' In Wrangell

Hot Rendezvous Punch
Try this on your friends at Fur Rendezvous time

4 cups (1 L) Lowbush Cranberry Juice
4 cups (1 L) apple juice
2 sticks cinnamon
Several whole cloves
2 cups (480 mL) orange juice
4 tablespoons (60 mL) or more sugar
Thin orange slices

►Heat all ingredients except orange slices slowly until piping hot but DO NOT BOIL. Pour into mugs of ample size and float a thin slice of orange on top of each.
■ *The Old Homesteader*

Highbush Cranberry Rhubarb-Ade

2 cups (480 mL) Highbush Cranberry Juice
2 cups (480 mL) Rhubarb Juice
2 cups (480 mL) water
1-1/2 cups (360 mL) sugar

►Simmer juices and water. Add sugar and simmer until dissolved. Chill before serving. Or, pasteurize to boiling point, pour into sterilized jars, seal and process in boiling water bath for 15 minutes (see Chapter 14). This cranberry-rhubarb juice is also good mixed half and half with a carbonated beverage of your choice, such as lemon-lime soda.
■ An Alaskan Cook Book, *Kenai (adapted)*

Use one of the thicker types of cranberry sauce to spread on top of meat loaf. Wait till meat loaf is almost done, add sauce and bake an additional 5 to 10 minutes to set the topping.

Lowbush Cranberry Soup

1 cup (240 mL) lowbush cranberries or canned
   lingonberries or large fresh cranberries from
   the Lower 48, measured after cooking
3 thin orange slices
3 thin lemon slices
2 tablespoons (30 mL) lemon juice
1/4 cup (60 mL) raisins
1/2 stick cinnamon
1 cup (240 mL) water
1 can (16 oz /or/ 456 g) grapefruit sections or
   sections of 1 fresh grapefruit
1/2 cup (120 mL) sugar
Salt
2 teaspoons (10 mL) cornstarch
8 fluid ounces (240 mL) heavy cream, whipped

►Simmer the cranberries, orange and lemon slices, lemon juice, raisins and cinnamon for 20 minutes in 1/2 cup (120 mL) water. Now add the grapefruit, sugar and a dash of salt. Bring to a boil.

Mix the cornstarch in the remaining 1/2 cup (120 mL) water and add to the mixture, stirring constantly until it thickens. Check the soup for sweetness and add more sugar if needed. Remove from the heat and chill.

Serve cold on a hot afternoon, topping each serving with a gob of freshly whipped cream. Makes two or three servings.
■ *Gordon R. Nelson, Palmer*
Lowbush Moose

CURRANT

In this section, both the descriptive text and recipes — except those noted — are excerpted from Ann Chandonnet, "Currently, The Crop Is Currants," ALASKA® magazine, July 1978.

A week before to two weeks after Labor Day, gatherers of wild edibles in Alaska can scarcely spare a minute for coffee klatsches or board meetings because there are so many native crops ripe and ready to be gathered. The most fragile ones are berries and, of those, raspberries and currants must be consumed or preserved immediately.

Recipes can be found almost everywhere for raspberries, but currants are a subject not so well covered in standard cookbooks.

The name "currant" is applied to two totally different fruits — one a berry, the other a dried grape. It's the berry (*Ribes* species), a member of the gooseberry family, that grows in Alaska. Both red and black currants grow in profusion in shaded forests. During wet years pickers should wear boots when setting out to gather currants because there are likely to be puddles beneath their spreading bushes. It is easy to recognize currant bushes. They resemble wild grape vines in many ways, with the same dangling fringes of old bark, the same flat leaves, with three to five fingers. The berries are translucent and have faint lines running from top to bottom. They glisten in the dim thickets almost as if lit from within.

Preparation Tips: Red currants are eaten fresh as a fruit, as well as cooked in jams and jellies. Black currants are used primarily in jams, jellies and beverages. To store for later processing, sort them to pick out debris, cover and refrigerate; use within two days at most. You'll find more uses for wild currants in Chapter 14.

Creamy Currant Salad Dressing

1 package (3 oz /or/ 85 g) cream cheese
3 tablespoons (45 mL) Wild Currant Jelly
2 teaspoons (10 mL) lemon juice
1/3 to 1/2 cup (80 to 120 mL) whipping cream

►Whip the cream. Carefully blend in remaining ingredients until evenly mixed. This dressing is good on almost any combination of fruits.
■ Alaska Wild Berry Guide and Cookbook

Currant Game Sauce

1/2 cup (120 mL) red Currant Jelly
Grated rind of 1 orange
1/8 teaspoon (0.5 mL) salt
1/8 teaspoon (0.5 mL) cayenne pepper
1 tablespoon (15 mL) prepared mustard
2/3 cup (160 mL) orange juice

►Break up jelly with the tines of a fork. Add remaining ingredients and beat well. May be served hot or cold. Makes six servings.

Madeira Sauce For Wild Game

►Cut the rind of an orange into slivers the size of a spruce needle and cook with 1 cup (240 mL) Madeira or port wine. Simmer gently until reduced by two-thirds. Now add the juice of the orange, 1 tablespoon (15 mL) lemon juice, 1/2 cup (120 mL) Wild Currant Jelly and a dash of ginger. Continue to simmer only until jelly is melted. Superb with grilled or roasted venison, caribou or moose.
■ *The editors, ALASKA® magazine*

Currant Sponge

1 envelope (1 Tbsp /or/ 15 mL)
    unflavored gelatin
2 cups (480 mL) orange juice
1 cup (240 mL) sugar
4 egg whites, at room temperature
1 cup (240 mL) fresh, raw currants

►Soak the gelatin in 1/2 cup (120 mL) of the orange juice for five minutes, then stir over low heat until dissolved. Mix with sugar and remaining juice. Refrigerate until mixture is the consistency of unbeaten egg white; then beat. In a separate bowl, beat the room-temperature egg whites until stiff. Fold into orange-gelatin mixture. Then fold in currants; do not mash berries. Turn into a mold or serving dish and chill until set, about four hours. Serve plain or with whipped cream. Makes four to six servings.

Currant Gravy For Wild Game

3 tablespoons (45 mL) flour
1 teaspoon (5 mL) beef seasonings
2 tablespoons (30 mL) bacon fat
1/3 cup (80 mL) Wild Currant Jelly
1 cup (240 mL) hot water
2 tablespoons (30 mL) sherry
Salt and pepper to taste

►Brown flour in hot skillet, add seasonings and bacon fat, stirring until well blended. Gradually add water, stirring constantly until thickened. Melt jelly in sauce, stir in wine and thicken again. Salt and pepper to taste.
■ The Old-Timer

Currant-Chili Sauce

1 glass Wild Currant Jelly
3/4 to 1 cup (180 to 240 mL) chili sauce
3 tablespoons (45 mL) prepared horseradish
Dash of pepper

►Break up jelly into small pieces with a fork. Add remaining ingredients and beat to consistency you prefer. This is a flavorful accompaniment to moose or caribou tongue and good with other game, too.
■ The Old Homesteader

Currant-Mint Sauce
For Dall Sheep

1 glass Wild Currant Jelly
Grated orange rind
Mint sprigs

►Break up the jelly with a fork, into small pieces, but do not beat. Put in serving dish and sprinkle with orange rind. Dehydrated orange rind may be used if fresh is not available. Tuck in several sprigs of mint and serve with any game meat, but the sauce is particularly fine with wild sheep roast.
■ The Old Homesteader

Wild Currant Syrup

►Quite by accident I discovered how to make this delicious syrup. I had cooked currants briefly to get the juice flowing and then had strained the resulting liquid and added the sugar for jelly. Something distracted me for a few hours and when I was finally ready to cook the juice I found it already thickened, so I just left it alone.

Use equal parts currant juice and sugar. Stir in sugar well and allow to stand for an hour or so. Stir again and again allow to set. Repeat this process for four or five rounds and then bottle the syrup or store it in jelly glasses in a cool place. No paraffin is necessary.

This makes an excellent sauce for ice cream and puddings and it is superlative on hot cakes, toast or poured over slices of pound cake. Sometimes it thickens sufficiently to be jelly, and that is good, too!

The syrup is also a good additive for summertime lemonade or punch like the following:

Currant Cooler

1 large can orange drink concentrate
3 cans cold water
1/4 cup (60 mL) lemon juice
1/2 cup (120 mL) Wild Currant Syrup

►Combine ingredients and chill for an hour or so. Makes 10 small servings. Ingredients can be varied to suit the taste.
■ Both recipes, Helen A. White
   "Alaska: Land of Wild Berries"
   ALASKA® magazine, August 1979

"Tea" Leaf Syrup

►Steep currant leaves in boiling water. Strain. Sweeten with honey and simmer to reduce into a syrup. This is good for coughs or over sourdough hot cakes.

Fresh Currant Pie

1 quart (1 L) fresh currants
1 cup (240 mL) plus 6 tablespoons (90 mL)
    sugar
3 tablespoons (45 mL) quick-cooking tapioca
1/4 cup (60 mL) water
1/8 teaspoon (0.5 mL) salt
8-inch (20 cm) pie shell, baked
3 egg whites
1/4 teaspoon (2 mL) salt

►Wash currants and drain. Combine currants, 1 cup (240 mL) of the sugar, tapioca, water and 1/8 teaspoon (0.5 mL) salt. Cook for 15 minutes, stirring occasionally, or until tapioca is transparent. Cool. Pour into pie shell. Make a meringue with the egg whites and the remaining 1/4 teaspoon (2 mL) salt and 6 tablespoons (90 mL) sugar, adding the latter gradually and beating until egg whites are stiff and glossy. Spread over pie, making sure meringue clings to edges of crust. Bake at 300°F (150°C) for 25 minutes, or until meringue is firm. Makes six servings.

Currant-Apple Pie

Pastry for a 2-crust 9-inch (22 cm) pie
1 pound (456 g) apples, peeled, cored, sliced
1 teaspoon (5 mL) grated orange or lemon peel
1 cup (240 mL) brown sugar
1 teaspoon (5 mL) cinnamon
1 cup (240 mL) fresh currants
1 teaspoon (5 mL) ground clove
Juice of 3 lemons

►Line a 9-inch (22 cm) pie plate with half the pastry. Mix apples, citrus peel, sugar, cinnamon, currants and clove. (Add 2 or 3 tablespoons [30 to 45 mL] flour or tapioca to thicken, if you wish.) Put mixture evenly into the bottom crust. Sprinkle with lemon juice. Top with second crust, seal and cut steam vents. Bake for one hour at 400°F (205°C). Makes eight servings. *Note:* A pound (456 g) of apples equals about 3 cups (720 mL) apple slices.

Berry Red Ice Cream

4 cups (1 L) heavy cream
3/4 cup (180 mL) red Wild Currant Jelly
3/4 cup (180 mL) red raspberry jam
1/8 teaspoon (0.5 mL) almond extract
1/2 teaspoon (2 mL) red food coloring (optional)
3 tablespoons (45 mL) kirsch

►Scald cream. Melt jelly and jam together, stirring until absolutely smooth. Stir cream into jellies and cool. Add almond extract and coloring, strain into bowl, cover and chill 12 to 24 hours. Add kirsch, churn in crank-type ice cream maker according to directions that come with. maker. Freeze as directed. Makes 1-1/2 quarts (1.45 L).

No need to be burdened with a rolling pin. An empty bottle will serve as well. It will do to roll cookies, pie crust or biscuits just fine. The bottle doesn't even have to be empty if the top is secure.
■ *The Old Homesteader*
The Cabin Friend
ALASKA® magazine, June 1977

NAGOONBERRY

Information about nagoonberries is excerpted and adapted from Carol Beery Davis, "The Nagoon Berry," ALASKA SPORTSMAN®, September 1961.

In Alaska, if you are ever offered a gift of nagoonberry jelly, you should know that you are being accorded a favored treatment reserved only for the best of friends.

The nagoonberry *(Rubus stellatus, R. arcticus* and *R. alaskensis)* is relatively rare, it is hard work for the picker, and its juice has such a wonderful, delicate flavor, the giver of nagoonberry jelly alone knows what sacrifice it is to give it away. Unless you actually visit or live in Alaska, this berry may be totally unknown to you.

Sometimes it is misnamed "lagoon berry," probably because it is found in muskeg or swamp, but it's *nagoon*, a Tlingit word meaning "bubbling fresh spring," an item that is also part of its characteristic habitat. It belongs to the same genus as the raspberry and cloudberry, and it inhabits marsh and tundra alike. The *stellatus* species is a coastal variety, while *R. arcticus* is circumpolar and may be seen also in the British Columbia Rockies and eastward to northern Minnesota. The *alaskensis* berry may be collected in Southcentral Alaska and in Southeastern. Plants grow from a spreading root stalk, generally one stem to a plant, always one berry to a stem and low to the ground, usually about 6 inches (15 cm) tall, though the Southcentral variety may grow on woody stems that are up to 20 inches (50 cm) in height.

Preparation Tips: Even if you are not lucky enough to find enough berries for jelly, they should be picked — in whatever quantity you find them — and combined with something else. This clear, sparkling red fruit is very soft and juicy and must be handled with a gentle touch. Unless dead ripe — when it is very pleasing to the taste — the berry can be almost bitter.

Nagoonberry Pie

Baked 9-inch (22 cm) pie shell
3 beaten egg yolks
1 scant cup (220 mL) sugar
Pinch of salt
1 cup (240 mL) nagoonberry juice
1 envelope (1 Tbsp /or/ 15 mL)
*   unflavored gelatin*
1/2 teaspoon (2 mL) cream of tartar
3 egg whites
Whipped cream

►In a double boiler mix egg yolks, 1/2 cup (120 mL)

sugar, salt and 1/2 cup (120 mL) berry juice. Place over boiling water and cook until mixture thickens (about 10 to 12 minutes), stirring gently as it cooks. Soften gelatin in the remaining 1/2 cup (120 mL) juice. Remove egg mixture from heat and stir in gelatin. Chill. Mix together the remaining sugar and cream of tartar. Beat the egg whites until foamy, then gradually beat in the sugar and cream of tartar. Continue beating until stiff. Fold the two mixtures together and pour into baked pie shell. Chill. Serve topped with whipped cream.

■ *Maxcine Williams*
Alaska Wild Berry Guide and Cookbook

RASPBERRY

The following is excerpted and adapted from Ann Chandonnet, "Alaska's Plentiful (And Tasty) Wild Foods," ALASKA® magazine, July 1976.

The red raspberry (Rubus idaeus) is native to Europe, was introduced to North America by the early 1800s and spread quickly due to its popularity with birds. High in vitamin C, the berry is easily recognized even by toddlers and it is probably the most succulent of Alaska's wild foods. Raspberries grow wild in thickets and begin ripening the week before Labor Day, although you may happen upon ripe berries anytime after the middle of August.

A black raspberry (R. leucodermis), similar to the ordinary red one but ranging in color to almost black, may be found in some places in Southeastern, but nowhere abundantly.

Preparation Tips: Unless really dusty, do not wash, as this tends to leach away their delicate flavor. Eat the day they are picked. A ripe raspberry is deep red, firm but soft, juicy but not mushy, and falls readily away from its white-green core when you pick it. If it falls into your hand when you brush the cane and is losing its shape, it is overripe.

One of the most delicious ways to eat fresh raspberries is with sugar and milk or cream. Or try the summer coolers that follow.

Raspberry-Mint Ade

3 sprigs fresh mint or 2 tablespoons (30 mL)
  dried mint
1 cup (240 mL) fresh raspberries, crushed
1/2 cup (120 mL) boiling water
1-1/2 quarts (1.45 L) fresh lemonade

►Wash mint and cook it with the boiling water for five minutes. Strain and cool. Then add the crushed berries. Add the mixture to the lemonade. Refrigerate for at least an hour to allow flavors to blend. Serve in tall glasses with ice. Makes six servings.

■ *Ann Chandonnet*
"Alaska's Plentiful (And Tasty) Wild Foods"
ALASKA® magazine, July 1976

Wild Raspberry Punch

2 cups (480 mL) Raspberry Juice
1 teaspoon (5 mL) cornstarch
1/4 cup (60 mL) sugar
5 cloves
1 stick cinnamon
1 cup (240 mL) orange juice
3/4 cup (180 mL) grape juice

►Boil raspberry juice mixed with sugar, cornstarch and spices. Cool. Add other juices and swirl to mix. Serve over cracked ice.

■ *Helen A. White*
"Far North Fare"
ALASKA® magazine, December 1974

Raspberry Shrub

►Fill a large jar with ripe wild raspberries and press them down slightly. Fill the jar with vinegar. After a month, strain the juice and seal in sterilized bottles. Dilute with cold water and sweeten to taste to make a refreshing drink.

■ *Minnie Fisher*
The Frontiersman, *Palmer*

Hope Raspberry Stir

1 quart (1 L) fresh wild raspberries
1 quart (1 L) granulated sugar

►Stem the berries and stir together with the sugar in a clean jar or crock. Store in a cool place (refrigerator or cellar). Continue to stir each morning for 14 days. This delicious topping will keep all winter. It will not ferment if stirred without fail as directed and stored in a cool place. It is a colorful, fresh, tasty topping for ice cream, shortcake or pancakes.

■ Out of Alaska's Kitchens

Wild Raspberry Syrup

Wild raspberries
Rose hips (one-quarter the amount of berries)
Lemon juice
Water
Sugar

►Clean the fruit but avoid washing the berries as some of their rare flavor will be washed away. Put fruit in a good-sized saucepan and crush. Add 1 cup

(240 mL) water to each quart (L) fruit. Bring to a boil; reduce heat and cook for about 15 minutes or until rose hips are soft. Pour hot fruit into a damp jelly bag and drain overnight without squeezing. Measure juice into saucepan; add a few drops of lemon juice if available and add half as much sugar as berry juice. Bring to a boil; reduce heat and simmer gently until the liquid is slightly thick. Store in refrigerator or pour into plastic containers and freeze. To keep unrefrigerated, the hot syrup may be poured into hot, sterilized jars, sealed and processed in a boiling water bath for 15 minutes (see Chapter 14).

Not only is this syrup great on breakfast dishes, it is also excellent as a dessert topping, served either hot or cold.

■ *The editors, ALASKA® magazine*

Raspberry Squares

Cake:
1 cup (240 mL) sifted all-purpose flour
1 teaspoon (5 mL) baking powder
1/2 cup (120 mL) butter or margarine
1 tablespoon (15 mL) milk
1 egg
1/2 cup (120 mL) wild raspberry jam

Topping:
1/4 cup (60 mL) butter or margarine
1 egg
1 cup (240 mL) sugar
1 can (4 oz /or/ 114 g) coconut
1 teaspoon (5 mL) vanilla

►Start your oven at 350°F (175°C), or moderate, and grease an 8-inch (20 cm) square baking pan. Sift flour and baking powder together into bowl. Cut in butter or margarine with two knives or pastry blender until mixture looks mealy. Beat the egg slightly and stir into flour mixture along with the milk. Mix well. Spread dough over bottom of baking pan. Cover with layer of jam.

Make up the topping: Melt butter or margarine. Beat the egg until frothy, then beat in sugar and melted butter thoroughly. Chop coconut into small pieces and mix with sugar-egg combination. Flavor with vanilla and spread on top of the raspberry jam. Bake 15 minutes. Cool and cut into squares.

■ *Mary Ann Dehlin*
   Alaska's Cooking, *Anchorage*

Bridge Tease

1 package (6½ oz /or/ 180 g) vanilla wafers, crushed
1/2 cup (120 mL) butter
1 cup (240 mL) powdered sugar
2 eggs, separated

1/2 cup (120 mL) toasted almonds
1 pint (0.47 L) fresh raspberries
1/2 cup (120 mL) sugar
1/2 pint (240 mL) whipping cream, flavored with sugar and vanilla

►Put half of the wafer crumbs in bottom of an 8 x 10-inch (20 x 25 cm) pan. Cream butter and powdered sugar until fluffy. Add beaten egg yolks, then fold in beaten whites. Spread this fluffy hard sauce over crumbs. Sprinkle most of the almonds on top of this, reserving some for top layer. Crush berries and mix with sugar. Spread on top of other layers. Add 1 teaspoon (5 mL) sugar and 1/2 teaspoon (2 mL) vanilla to whipped cream and spoon atop berries. Sprinkle on remaining almonds and crumbs. Cover with waxed paper. Chill for 12 hours. Cut into serving pieces and lift out one piece at a time to serve. Do not try to unmold all at once.

■ *Mertie Baggen, Fairbanks*
   PTA Cook Book, *Petersburg*

Plain raspberry pie probably can't be beat. If you're lucky enough to have 3 cups (720 mL) firm, ripe berries, try the recipe on page 362 for "any berry" pie. Or, here's a couple of fancier ones:

Venetian Pie

1 cup (240 mL) crushed raspberries
1 cup (240 mL) sugar
1 tablespoon (15 mL) quick-cooking tapioca
Pinch of salt
Baked 9-inch (22 cm) pie crust
1-1/2 to 2 cups (360 to 480 mL) firm, ripe raspberries, well chilled
1 pint (0.47 L) whipping cream, whipped
2 egg whites
Additional sugar

►Cook first four ingredients together until thick. Then chill thoroughly. Shortly before serving, spread the mixture over the bottom of baked crust and place fresh berries over it. Sprinkle on a little sugar. Over that spread whipped cream, sweetened to taste. Beat egg whites until stiff and gradually beat in 1/2 cup (120 mL) sugar. Spread meringue over whipped cream and slip under broiler long enough to brown slightly. Be sure berries and cream are very cold for this recipe.

■ Out of Alaska's Kitchens *(adapted)*

Berries or raisins coated with flour will not sink to the bottom of your batter. In cake or sweet bread recipes, try dusting them with sugar.

Raspberry Ice Cream Pie

►Make a graham cracker crust by crushing 16 graham crackers fine. Work in 1/4 cup (60 mL) sugar and 1/4 cup (60 mL) soft butter. Press into bottom and sides of lightly greased 8-inch (20 cm) pie plate. Bake in hot oven 400°F (205°C), 8 to 10 minutes. Chill. Fill completely cooled shell with 1 quart (1 L) softened vanilla ice cream. Place in freezer until ready to serve. Serve with crushed wild raspberries over the top.
■ *Goldie Hukill*
  Souvenir Cook Book, *Skagway*

WILD ROSE

Three species of wild rose are found in Alaska. The prickly rose *(Rosa acicularis)* is the most common, but one or another of the three flourish from Cook Inlet to the Brooks Range, from the Seward Peninsula throughout the Yukon, and elsewhere in Canada and the Lower 48.

Practically all parts of the plant are useful for food, as many birds and animals besides the two-legged kind have discovered. Even the large, less-than-dainty moose will browse on the bush ignoring the thorns.

Preparation Tips: The part most used for consumption is the rose hip, the seed pod of the plant. Seeded and dried, the hips make fine snacks as is or can be turned into "leather" or jam, syrup and jelly. Rose hip powder sprinkled on cereal or buttered toast lends unique flavor and a healthy dose of vitamin C. The seeds need not be wasted either. Pulverize them and use the resulting pulp to add to many dishes; they are reported to be rich in vitamin E.

Removing the seeds from rose hips can be tedious business, but there are a couple of ways to avoid it if you are going to dry them for later use. To use rose hips fresh, clean them and snap off the "tails." Then remove the large seeds with the point of a knife. To dry rose hips, either partially dry them first, split them and then remove the seeds (see Rose Hip Candy #1), or make a puree of rose hips, dry the puree and crush *it*. Complete directions for the puree method of drying berries are in Chapter 14, along with recipes for leather, jelly and other preserves made of various parts of the wild rose. (See Purees, page 458.)

There is some disagreement about when it's best to gather the hips, whether just before or just after the first frost. In any case, you *can* use them almost any time of the year, but they are generally plumpest and reddest right around Labor Day. Petals are picked at their prettiest, in summer. Here are some pointers about gathering them, condensed from an *ALASKA®* magazine article by Dianne K. Davis ["Tasty Petal Pickin' " June 1975]:

- Long sleeves, long pants, sturdy shoes (no rubber thongs!) help protect you from thorns.
- If you can, pick from bushes off the beaten path. The petals will be cleaner and you'll be leaving pretty roses for others to enjoy in the more traveled areas.
- Carry a small container for freshly plucked petals and empty it from time to time into a large one left at a convenient spot. A small spill is less annoying than a big one.
- Dry petals are easier to collect than wet ones; prime picking time is just after the morning dew has thoroughly evaporated.
- Wash (only if absolutely necessary) and pick through petals as soon as possible after gathering.
- Immediate cooking produces the best flavor, but petals may be stored in the freezer for several weeks. One or the other treatment is a must, however, since petals deteriorate rapidly.

June's Salad

►Some summers I make a delicious salad using fireweed shoots, nasturtium leaves, flowers from my garden, wild rose petals, lettuce and the last of the young dandelions. This is a good June combination.
■ *Ann Chandonnet*
  "Alaska's Plentiful (And Tasty) Wild Foods"
  ALASKA® magazine, July 1976

Candied Rose Petals

1 egg white, beaten
1 tablespoon (15 mL) water
Granulated sugar
Wild rose petals

►Snip off white bases of petals (these are bitter). Dip each petal in a mixture of the egg white and water. Place on a towel to drain. When barely damp sprinkle both sides with sugar and let stand 12 hours on waxed paper. Refrigerate in covered container. Keeps about one month.
■ Cooking Up A Storm, *Homer*

Wild Rose Petal Cupcakes

1 cup (240 mL) sugar
1/2 cup (120 mL) butter
3 eggs
Grated peel of 1 lemon

3 cups (720 mL) cake flour
2 teaspoons (10 mL) baking powder
1/2 teaspoon (2 mL) salt
1 cup (240 mL) milk
1 cup (240 mL) fresh wild rose petals
1 teaspoon (5 mL) lemon juice

►Cream together the sugar and butter; add eggs and beat well. Then add the grated peel. Sift together the flour, baking powder and salt. Add to the creamed mixture alternately with the milk. Cut the rose petals into bits. Add the petals and the lemon juice and stir just enough to blend nicely. Line muffin tins with pink paper baking cups and fill each half full of the cake batter. Bake at 375°F (190°C) for 12 to 15 minutes. Cool and spread with frosting. Yields about three dozen cakes.
■ *Florence Thornton, Rabbit Creek*
   What's Cookin' in Alaska

Rose Petal Honey

►Bring 2 pints (1 L) honey to a boil; add 1 pint (0.47 L) wild rose petals that are clean. Allow to rest for four or five hours. Again bring to a boil. Remove from heat and pour at once into sterilized jars and seal.

Rose Hip Syrup

4 cups (1 L) rose hips
2 cups (0.47 L) water
1 cup (240 mL) sugar

►Wash rose hips thoroughly. Remove stems and flower remnants. Boil hips and water for 20 minutes in a covered saucepan. Strain through a jelly bag. Return clear juice to kettle. Add sugar, stir well and boil five minutes. Refrigerate until used.
■ An Alaskan Cook Book, *Kenai*

Rose Hip Nut Bread

Juice of 1 orange plus water to make 1 cup
   (240 mL)
1/2 cup (120 mL) chopped raisins
3/4 cup (180 mL) seeded and chopped wild
   rose hips
2 tablespoons (30 mL) melted butter
1 teaspoon (5 mL) vanilla
1 egg, beaten
1-1/2 cups (360 mL) flour
1 cup (240 mL) sugar
1 teaspoon (5 mL) baking powder
1/2 teaspoon (2 mL) baking soda
1/4 teaspoon (1 mL) salt
1/2 cup (120 mL) nuts or sunflower seeds

►In a large bowl, mix the first six ingredients. Sift together and then add the dry ingredients. Mix until well blended but do not overmix or bread will be dry and heavy. Gently stir in nuts or sunflower seeds. Spoon batter into a well-greased 5 x 8-inch (12 x 20 cm) loaf pan and bake at 350°F (175°C) for one hour.
■ Cooking Up A Storm, *Homer (adapted)*

Rose Hip Tea

►Pour boilng water over 1 teaspoon (5 mL) dried rose hips in a teacup. Steep three to five minutes and enjoy! Or soak 2 tablespoons (30 mL) dried hips a few hours in 1 quart (1 L) water. Remove rose hips from water and heat the water until it almost comes to a boil, but do not boil. For a sweetener, use honey.
■ Cooking Up A Storm, *Homer*

Kodiak Rose Hip Tea

1 tea bag
1 tablespoon (15 mL) dried rose hips
3 or 4 whole cloves
Sugar or honey to taste
1 cup (240 mL) boiling water

►Steep tea bag, rose hips and cloves in boiling water for five minutes. Remove hips and cloves. Reheat if desired. Sweeten to taste with sugar or honey. Makes one serving.
■ *Ann Chandonnet*
   ALASKA® magazine, December 1978

Rose Hip Crumble Pie

Pastry for single-crust 9-inch (22 cm) pie
1 cup (240 mL) dried rose hips
1/4 cup (60 mL) milk
1-1/2 cups (360 mL) sifted flour
2 teaspoons (10 mL) baking powder
Dash of salt
1/2 cup (120 mL) shortening
1-3/4 cups (420 mL) brown sugar
2 egg yolks, beaten
2 egg whites
Pecan halves (optional)

►Prepare pastry and line a pie pan. Soften rose hips in milk. Sift together flour, baking powder and salt. Cream in shortening and brown sugar, mixing well. This makes a crumbly mixture — reserve 1 cup (240 mL) for topping. To the remainder add the egg yolks, milk and rose hips. Beat the egg whites until peaks hold form. Fold into the berry mixture. Spoon into pie pan and sprinkle with the crumbly topping. Garnish with pecan halves, too, if you wish. Bake at 350°F (175°C) for 35 to 45 minutes or until pie appears well done.
■ Alaska Wild Berry Guide and Cookbook

Rose Hip Pie

Pastry for double-crust 9-inch (22 cm) pie
1-1/2 cups (360 mL) rose hips (best if not
*   quite ripe)*
1-1/2 tablespoons (23 mL) cornstarch
1 cup (240 mL) sugar
1/4 pound (114 g) butter, melted
2 eggs, beaten
1 cup (240 mL) light corn syrup
Dash of salt
1 teaspoon (5 mL) vanilla
Lemon juice, about 2 teaspoons (10 mL)

►Prepare pastry and line a pie pan with bottom crust. Clean and seed rose hips. Mix cornstarch and sugar and blend in melted butter. Add the eggs, corn syrup, salt and vanilla; mix. Stir in the rose hips. Pour into the pie shell, sprinkle with a little lemon juice and cover with a lattice crust. Bake at 350°F (175°C) until pastry is nicely browned.
■ Alaska Wild Berry Guide and Cookbook

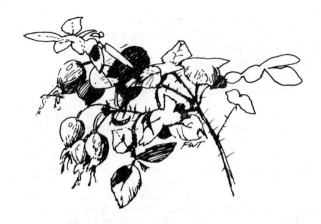

Rose Hip Candy #1

►Gather a lot of good clean rose hips while you are berry picking. (Just after frost is the best time to get them.) Snap off the "tails" as you pick, or later when you reach home. This is a good job for the kids. Spread the hips out on a clean surface and allow to dry partially. When the skins begin to feel dried and shriveled, split the hips and take out the large seeds — all of them. If you let the hips dry too much it will be difficult to remove the seeds. If not dry enough, the inside pulp will be sticky and cling to the seeds. After the seeds are removed allow the hips to dry completely before storing or they will not keep well. Then store in small plastic bags with a twist seal. These will keep indefinitely in the freezer or for several months in the refrigerator. They are packed with vitamin C and are good to munch on anytime you need extra energy . . . or a moderately sweet nutlike "candy."
■ *The Cabin Friend*
  ALASKA® magazine, April 1975

Rose Hip Candy #2
A winner of two blue ribbons at the
Southeast Alaska State Fair

►Wash the rose hips with a spray or under running water. Drain and pat dry gently with paper towel or a clean cloth towel. Remove the seed from each rose hip with a small coffee spoon or pointed knife.

For each 1 cup (240 mL) rose hips, dissolve 1/3 cup (80 mL) sugar in 2 tablespoons plus 2 teaspoons (40 mL) water.

Add rose hips to the sugar-water and cook over medium heat. Be sure all hips are coated on the

inside. This is easiest done by tilting the pan and spooning the syrup over and around them. Shake pan occasionally. Cook until rose hips are just about to burn, about 5 to 10 minutes. Remove hips as quickly as possible from pan — but individually, if you can — dropping each onto a sheet of waxed paper that is covered with granulated sugar. (I use two forks for this process.) Separate any nested hips. Sprinkle sugar over them, then roll in the sugar until the hips are well coated on all sides.

While they are drying, break off any hard bits of sugar. Add more sugar and toss the hips gently with two forks. Store in a glass jar.

It is not advisable to try more than 1-1/2 cups (360 mL) rose hips at one time. For that amount, use 1/2 cup (120 mL) sugar and 1/4 cup (60 mL) water. It is best to have the hips only one layer deep in the pan to avoid nesting of hips. Also, the syrup thickens fast while you are removing the hips from the pan.
■ *Janet Woodring, Haines*
  One Hundred Years in the Kitchen, *Juneau*

Prickly Rose Soup

2 cups (480 mL) fresh or 1-3/5 cups (385 mL)
*   dried rose hips*
5 cups (1.2 L) water
1 to 2 tablespoons (15 to 30 mL) sugar
3/4 to 1 tablespoon (11 to 15 mL) cornstarch
12 almonds, shredded (optional)

►Rinse the fresh or dried rose hips. If using dried ones, crush them. Simmer in the water until soft; fresh rose hips, 30-40 minutes and dried rose hips, about one hour. Strain them through a colander.

Bring the puree to a boil. Add the sugar. Mix the

cornstarch with about 2 teaspoons (10 mL) of cold water and add it to the soup, stirring constantly. Boil several minutes.

Add shredded almonds, if desired.

The dish may be served warm or cold for dessert. Offer cream, whipped cream, cottage cheese or ice cream as a garnish. In Sweden this easy-to-prepare dish is so popular that it's commercially packaged as a powdered mix and is a special favorite of backpackers.
■ *Mary Beth Buza*
"Prickly Rose Soup"
ALASKA® magazine, July 1973

S A L M O N B E R R Y

"This is another in the same family of plants as the red raspberry," reports Helen A. White [*Alaska Wild Berry Trails*], "but not quite as abundant or as well known. The salmonberry [*Rubus spectabilis*] resembles the raspberry in general appearance. The bushes are somewhat larger and stronger growing and the fruit also is larger. The salmonberry has a rose red blossom and its fruit runs the gamut of color from yellow, through orange, to red. It is usually ripe enough to pick during all three color stages. These handsome plants seem to prefer a forested mountainside where there is plenty of rain or snow in the winter and spring. They occur in great abundance in certain parts of Southeastern, the Aleutians, Kodiak and other coastal areas."

Some Natives of northern and western Alaska refer to another berry as "salmonberry" because it is colored similarly. That berry, however, is more often known as the cloudberry or baked-apple berry. It, too, is a cousin of the raspberry, but the plant it grows on is quite different. While raspberries and salmonberries develop on shrubs that may grow 6 feet (1.8 m) or more in height, cloudberry plants hug the ground like a strawberry.

Preparation Tips: Like other members of the raspberry family, salmonberries are soft, delicate fruit and should be handled with care. They are good by the handful or sweetened and served with cream or, as Helen White says simply, "used in the same ways red raspberries are used."

Alaskan Flan

2 tablespoons (30 mL) sugar
3 whole eggs, beaten
3 egg whites, beaten

1 can (13 oz /or/ 370 g) evaporated milk
1 can (14 oz /or/ 400 g) sweetened condensed milk
2 tablespoons (30 mL) vanilla extract
2 cups (480 mL) sweetened crushed salmonberries

►Preheat oven to 350°F (175°C). In a saucepan, cook the sugar, stirring constantly until it turns into a dark, caramel substance. Pour into a covered baking dish. Blend together the beaten whole eggs, egg whites and both milks. Add vanilla, then pour over carameled sugar. Cover the dish and place it in a shallow baking pan that is half-filled with hot water. Bake for two hours. Serve cold with crushed berries spooned over each serving.
■ Alaska Wild Berry Guide and Cookbook

Salmonberry Cream Pie

Baked 10-inch (25 cm) pie shell
6 cups (1.45 L) salmonberries
Water
2/3 cup (160 mL) sugar
3 tablespoons (45 mL) cornstarch
Dash of salt
Whipped cream

►Crush 2 cups (480 mL) berries and force through sieve. Add enough water to make 1-1/2 cups (360 mL). Mix together sugar, cornstarch and salt and add to berries. Cook, stirring constantly, for five minutes or until the mixture is well thickened. Allow to cool. Place remaining 4 cups (1 L) berries in pie shell, then pour on cooked mixture. Chill for several hours. Serve with whipped cream and garnish with a few perfect, whole salmonberries.
■ Alaska Wild Berry Guide and Cookbook

Shishmaref Salmonberries Glace

►This frozen berry dessert is a delicious treat. Mix together 1 quart (1 L) salmonberries* with 1 cup (240 mL) granulated sugar, using a wooden spoon and a nonmetal container. Place mixture in freezer. Before serving, thaw berries to precise point where they still retain a frozen center and the sweetened juice is thick and cold. Serve into dishes with wooden spoon and top with sweetened whipped cream or the bush equivalent — sweetened whipped evaporated milk.
■ *Joe Rychetnik*
"Dining Along the Eskimo Coast"
ALASKA SPORTSMAN®, April 1964

Judging from the locale, this "salmonberry" may well be the ground-hugging one, known by others as the cloudberry or baked-apple berry. The distinction is completely academic, however. If you have one or the other berry in enough quantity to try in this nice ice, go ahead!

Salmonberry Cake

2 cups (480 mL) flour
1 teaspoon (5 mL) baking soda
1/2 teaspoon (2 mL) salt
1 teaspoon (5 mL) allspice
1 teaspoon (5 mL) cinnamon
1 teaspoon (5 mL) nutmeg
1/4 cup (60 mL) butter or margarine
1 cup (240 mL) sugar
3 eggs
1 cup (240 mL) salmonberry jam
3/4 cup (180 mL) sour milk

►Preheat oven to 375°F (190°C). Sift together the flour, baking soda, salt and spices. Cream butter and sugar until fluffy. Beat eggs until light and add to the sugar mixture. Blend jam and sour milk and stir into the egg mixture, alternating with the dry ingredients. Pour batter into two greased and floured cake pans. Bake 20 to 25 minutes. Ice with your favorite frosting.
■ Alaska Wild Berry Guide and Cookbook

SOAPBERRY

The soapberry (*Shepherdia canadensis*) is a colorful orange-red berry that grows rather abundantly from Southeastern to the Interior. It is called "soapberry" after the frothy dessert made from it. Eaten plain, it has a quite astringent flavor that might also be confused with some kinds of soap. It is not a berry most people like to eat in quantity unless it is mixed with sweeter berries or turned to sweetened fluff, as in the two recipes here.

Soapberry Dessert

►This particular berry grows around Icy Strait. They are called soapberries because when you start whipping them by hand they produce a sudslike substance which gradually turns into a foam and then into whipped cream. The Native people used large stock pots to make soapberry dessert. Half a cup (120 mL) of berries will produce about 5 gallons (19 L) of soapberry dessert. The more water you add, the more it will produce. The more water you use, the more the tangy taste will disappear. Then you add sugar to taste. For extra pleasure, add diced apples or sliced bananas. You have to keep on beating this as long as your guests are eating, or it will dissolve into water. The old-timers used to say that you should pop it in and out of your mouth. It was to let the air come in and out of the foam. It always turned out to be fun when everyone had had

enough and started playing with the foamy substance. For example, they would try to throw it at one another, but it is weightless and wouldn't go very far.
■ *Kaa T'eix (Mary Howard Pelayo)*
  Kaa T'eix's Cook Book, *Mount Edgecumbe*

Ash-and-Hash

"Ash-and-hash" is how the Tsimpshean word sounds to English ears.

►Take some soapberries and add a little water at a time as you beat it. In the early days they did this with their hands, today you can use an egg beater. When it starts to foam up put in a bit of fireweed which has been scraped from the insides of the stem and add a bit of sugar to taste. Then dish it up. It is sheer delight. When available any and all fruits like bananas can be added for variety.
■ Tsimpshean Indian Island Cookbook
  Metlakatla

STRAWBERRY

The well-known, well-loved beach strawberry (*Fragaria chiloensis*) is thought to be the forerunner of all commercial and domesticated strawberries. In general, the fruit is smaller than the garden-grown types but can grow up to an inch (2.5 cm) long, nevertheless. It grows throughout Southeastern, the Gulf of Alaska coast, the Seward Peninsula and the Aleutians. Its somewhat smaller cousin, the Yukon strawberry (*F. virginiana*), grows in some areas of Interior Alaska. The fruit ripens in midsummer.
Preparation Tips: Nobody needs "tips" on how to eat strawberries! By the handful, that is, uncooked, they are a rich source of vitamin C. . . . Even a moderate-sized hand can hold enough to equal the C value of an orange. Here are a few of the many ways to enjoy strawberries.

Strawberry Jubilee

1 quart (1 L) strawberries
1 teaspoon (5 mL) cornstarch
1/2 cup (120 mL) brown sugar
2 tablespoons (30 mL) lime juice
1/4 cup (60 mL) rum*
Ice cream

►Pick out the best 3-1/2 cups (840 mL) of strawberries. Slice them and set to one side. Smash the remaining berries.
  In a saucepan stir together the cornstarch and

brown sugar. Add the crushed strawberries and the lime juice. Place the pan over low heat and stir until the mixture is bubbly. Remove from heat.

Dish the ice cream into six dessert bowls and top with the sliced strawberries.

In a small saucepan pour the rum and light it with a match. Pour the flaming rum into the bubbly strawberry mixture while stirring constantly. When the flame dies, the sauce is ready to serve. Pour it evenly over the six dishes of strawberries and ice cream.

If you practice, you can perform the entire ceremony at the table using a chafing dish.

■ *Gordon R. Nelson, Palmer*
  Smokehouse Bear

*Kirsch makes a nice flavor change — and is just as flammable.

Strawberry Ice Cream

3 eggs
1-1/2 cups (360 mL) confectioners' sugar
2-1/2 cups (600 mL) milk
1 tablespoon (15 mL) vanilla
2-1/2 cups (600 mL) heavy cream
1/8 teaspoon (0.5 mL) salt
2 to 4 cups (0.47 to 1 L) berries

►Beat eggs and sugar lightly. Stir in milk and add vanilla, cream and salt. Whip until stiff in a cold bowl. Fold in berries. If there is a lot of juice on berries, drain well first. Put in freezer until firm. Makes 4 quarts (3.8 L).

■ *Diana M. Benson*
  Haines Homemakers' Cookbook

Jordberfromge — Strawberry Creme

2 cups (480 mL) strawberries
1/2 cup (120 mL) sugar
2 teaspoons (10 mL) unflavored gelatin
2 cups (480 mL) cream, whipped

►Cover the berries with sugar and let stand a few minutes. Melt the gelatin by sprinkling it over a small amount of cold water in a saucepan, then heating until completely dissolved. Cool and fold into whipped cream along with strawberries. Let stand until firm.

■ *Mrs. Pete Knutsen*
  PTA Cook Book, *Petersburg*

Variations:
• Prepare a small package (3 oz /or/ 85 g) of wild strawberry gelatin according to package directions. Cool to "unbeaten egg white" stage. Then

whip the gelatin and fold in 2 cups (480 mL) strawberries, 1 cup (240 mL) whipped cream and about a dozen large marshmallows, diced. [Mrs. A. Fenswick, *PTA Cook Book.*]
• Prepare wild strawberry gelatin as above. Then spoon in 1 cup (240 mL) sour cream and beat with hand beater until blended. Stir in 3/4 cup (180 mL) crushed wild strawberries with juice. Chill until set. Or pour into a prepared (baked and chilled) graham cracker crust and chill until set. This is called "Strawberry Yum-Yum" by Audrey Myers, *What's Cookin' in Wrangell.*
• Prepare wild strawberry gelatin as above. When it is partially set, beat in 1 pint (0.47 L) vanilla ice cream and 1 cup (240 mL) strawberries or raspberries. Serve at once or refreeze. Makes six to eight servings. [Wilma Gregory, *Cooking Up A Storm,* Homer.]

Strawberry Butter
Turn hot rolls into a special treat!

1 pound (456 g) sweet butter
3/4 cup (180 mL) finely chopped
  fresh strawberries
3 to 5 tablespoons (45 to 75 mL)
  powdered sugar

►There are no substitutes for butter in this recipe. Soften and whip it, then combine with remaining ingredients and whip until light or process in a blender or food processor. Keep in refrigerator. Can be put in microwave oven a few seconds before serving, then stir. Serve with hot rolls. Makes 2-1/2 cups (600 mL).

■ *Mrs. Jack Randolph, Golden Heart*
    Homemakers Club (adapted)
  The All-Alaska Weekly, *Fairbanks*

Sunkissed Strawberry Jam

►This is the "best ever" strawberry jam but you must have sunlight and plenty of it. Clean and crush wild strawberries. Avoid washing if they are clean enough. Gently stir in an equal amount of sugar and pour into large platters in a thin layer. Do NOT use metal containers. You may use several platters. Place a clean sheet of clear glass over each platter and set outdoors in the sun. You must bring them indoors at night [midnight sun won't do!] and take them out again when the sun is warm. It will take about three days of good sunlight to "cook" the jam. Take samples after the first day and a half and you will be able to tell when it is "cooked" enough. Delightful taste, isn't it? Pack in sterilized jam jars, and store in the refrigerator. You may find it hard to resist eating it at once.

■ *Helen A. White, Anchorage*
  Alaska Wild Berry Trails

Strawberry 'n' Cream Smoothie

*1/2 cup (120 mL) frozen pink lemonade
   concentrate, thawed
1 cup (240 mL) vanilla ice cream
2 cups (480 mL) frozen wild strawberries,
   partially thawed*

▶Combine all ingredients in blender container, blend until smooth. Serve immediately in stemmed glasses. Makes two or three servings.
■ The Anchorage Times

THE ANY BERRY

Any berry, your choice, can be used in most of the recipes in this chapter. However, here's a few recipes for which even the cook couldn't decide which berry was best.

Dressing For Fruit Salad

*1/2 cup (120 mL) your choice berry juice
1/2 cup (120 mL) mayonnaise
Sugar*

▶*Carefully* mix the berry juice and mayonnaise or the dressing may curdle. Taste a sample and add sugar to suit your preference. This makes a lighter dressing than pure mayonnaise and is more suitable for fruit salads.
■ Alaska Wild Berry Guide and Cookbook

Enhancing Dressings For Salads

▶Start with 1 cup (240 mL) mayonnaise and blend in any of the following variations for fruit salad dressing:
• 1 cup (240 mL) chopped lowbush cranberries and a few drops orange juice.
• 1 cup (240 mL) Wild Currant Jelly and 1 cup (240 mL) whipped cream.
• Raspberry puree.
• 1 cup (240 mL) crushed strawberries and 1 tablespoon (15 mL) powdered sugar, 2 tablespoons (30 mL) lemon juice and 1 cup (240 mL) whipped cream.
• 6 tablespoons (90 mL) crushed strawberries or raspberries, 4 tablespoons (60 mL) toasted shredded almonds, 2 tablespoons (30 mL) berry juice and 2 tablespoons (30 mL) white wine.
■ Alaska Wild Berry Guide and Cookbook

Easiest Berry Sauce

*1 cup (240 mL) berry juice
1 cup (240 mL) water
1/2 cup (120 mL) sugar
1 tablespoon (15 mL) cornstarch*

▶If the berry juice is already sweetened, you will not need additional sugar. Otherwise, heat juice and water together. Mix sugar and cornstarch with a small amount of the liquid, then return all to the hot juice. Cook, stirring, until the sauce is thick and clear. This sauce is excellent served on Jelly Roll or other berry desserts.
■ Alaska Wild Berry Guide and Cookbook

Fruit Juice Sauce

*1 cup (240 mL) sugar
Dash of salt
1 tablespoon (15 mL) cornstarch
1/2 cup (120 mL) boiling water
2 tablespoons (30 mL) lemon or orange juice
1 cup (240 mL) juice of blueberries, raspberries
or strawberries*

▶Mix sugar, salt and cornstarch in a saucepan and slowly add boiling water. Boil five minutes and then add the juices. Cool and stir in a few whole, fresh berries if available.
■ Alaska Wild Berry Guide and Cookbook

Berry Glaze

▶Measure 1/2 cup (120 mL) of juice from any thawed frozen berries and add 1/2 teaspoon (2 mL) grated lemon or orange rind and 1 tablespoon (15 mL) lemon or orange juice. Heat on low heat slowly and just to the boiling point. The juices will boil away if this is done too rapidly. Add a little cold berry juice, drop by drop to 1 tablespoon (15 mL) cornstarch until a thin paste is formed. Stir this paste into the hot mixture and continue cooking until thick and clear. This glaze makes a good topper for fruit pie, cake, coffeecake, muffins, cookies and hot cakes.

North Star Scones

*Red sugar (optional)
3/4 cup (180 mL) wild berry jelly or jam
1/2 cup (120 mL) finely chopped apple slices
3 tablespoons (45 mL) brown sugar
1/2 teaspoon (2 mL) cinnamon
1/4 cup (60 mL) chopped walnuts
2 cups (480 mL) flour
4 teaspoons (20 mL) baking powder
1 tablespoon (15 mL) white sugar
Dash of salt*

5 tablespoons (75 mL) butter or margarine
Egg white or milk

►Prepare red sugar by stirring a few drops of red food coloring into granulated sugar. Prepare filling by combining jelly, apple slices, brown sugar, cinnamon and nuts. Blend lightly until mixture reaches spreading consistency. In separate bowl, sift dry ingredients together and blend in butter, as for pie dough. Roll out on waxed paper to about 10 x 20 inches (25 x 50 cm). Spread filling over half the dough and carefully fold the other half over it, pressing edges together firmly with a floured fork. Transfer to ungreased baking sheet, waxed paper and all. Trim off excess paper and brush top of scone with egg white or milk. Sprinkle the red sugar on top for a gala touch. Bake at 450°F (230°C) until golden brown. Cut into squares and serve warm.
■ Alaska Wild Berry Guide and Cookbook

Jelly Roll

4 eggs, separated
3/4 cup (180 mL) sugar
1 teaspoon (5 mL) vanilla
2 tablespoons (30 mL) milk
3/4 cup (180 mL) flour
Salt
1 teaspoon (5 mL) baking powder, level or
   slightly less
Wild berry jelly

►Cream egg yolks, sugar and vanilla. Add milk and dry ingredients. Cream well. Whip egg whites and add last. Blend in thoroughly. Grease heavily and then flour a jelly roll pan or cookie sheet. Spread batter in pan evenly. Bake in a hot oven, 375 to 400°F (190 to 205°C), for 10 minutes. After baking, place cake on a towel or cloth that has been dusted with powdered sugar. Put jelly on and spread quickly. Roll up in towel to keep fresh.
■ *Mrs. Carol Mulhall*
   Mount Spurr School Cook Book
   Elmendorf Air Force Base

Tutti Frutti

►No one likes to throw away good fruit during the picking season just because it is left over from other recipes. Here is a way to store the fruit and make a delicious sauce at the same time. As you get the extra berries, place them in a covered crock. The more types of berries the better. Include peaches or apricots, too, to equal one-quarter of the total fruit. With each addition of fruit, add about half as much sugar. Add brandy or rum to suit your taste. Keep

the crock in a cool, dry place — the refrigerator or the cellar work perfectly. Let the concoction stand 10 days or so after the last addition. This thick sauce makes an excellent topping.
■ Alaska Wild Berry Guide and Cookbook

Cloo Kloo

►Clean berries (blueberries or lowbush cranberries may be used). In large kettle cover berries with water and bring to a boil. In frying pan, brown moose fat or bacon cut in small pieces. Add to berry mixture and continue boiling. Mix flour and water in small bowl for a thin gravy and add to berry mixture. Mix and stir well. Cinnamon and sugar to taste may be added at this time. Continue boiling on low heat until thickened. Serve as a dessert or with meat. Good hot or cold.
■ *Delores Carroll Sloan, Fort Yukon*

Alaska-Hawaii Salad

►Carefully clean your choice of Alaska wild berries for this salad. Sprinkle with powdered sugar. Combine 1 package (3 oz /or/ 85 g) cream cheese, 2 tablespoons (30 mL) finely chopped walnuts, 1/4 cup (60 mL) salad marshmallows (or the larger ones, diced) and the berries. Place a slice of Hawaiian pineapple on a crisp lettuce leaf and put a mound of cheese-berry mixture in the center. Garnish with a spoonful of dressing made by mixing mayonnaise and whipped cream in equal portions. Top with a perfect berry or two.
■ *Helen A. White, Anchorage*
   Alaska Wild Berry Trails

Eskimo Berry Pie

►Make a meringue of four egg whites beaten stiff with 6 tablespoons (90 mL) powdered sugar. Sweeten your choice of berries. Place a layer of very hard vanilla ice cream in a baked pie shell. Spread the fruit over the ice cream and top with the meringue, being careful to spread it clear to the edges to insure completely sealing in the fruit and ice cream. Place in a very hot oven, 450°F (230°C), and brown until topping is golden (a few seconds should suffice). Serve at once.
■ *Helen A. White, Anchorage*
   Alaska Wild Berry Trails

Bake lots of pies? Check the Master Mix for pie crust on page 402. If you're a now-and-then pie maker, recipes for many other pastries are in the same chapter. There's even a crust made from sourdough described on page 397.

Jam Buns

2 cups (480 mL) flour
3 teaspoons (15 mL) baking powder
2 tablespoons (30 mL) sugar
1/4 teaspoon (1 mL) salt
1 cup (240 mL) shortening
1 egg, slightly beaten
1/2 cup (120 mL) milk
1 teaspoon (5 mL) vanilla
Wild berry jam

►Mix sifted flour, baking powder, sugar and salt together. Cream shortening and egg together. Gradually add the milk and vanilla. Slowly add the dry ingredients; mix lightly but thoroughly. Roll out the dough on a floured board and cut in 3-inch (7.5 cm) squares. Drop a spoonful of any wild berry jam (or jelly) in the center of half the squares. Cover with remaining squares; pinch the edges together to seal. Place in muffin tins that have been slightly oiled. Bake in a moderate oven, 375°F (190°C), for 15 minutes or until well browned. These are goodies for after school snacks; especially when still warm.

■ *Helen A. White, Anchorage*
  Alaska Wild Berry Trails

Basic Wild Berry Pie

Pastry for double-crust 9-inch (22 cm) pie
1 cup (240 mL) sugar
1/4 cup (60 mL) sifted flour
Dash of salt
3 cups (720 mL) wild berries
2 tablespoons (30 mL) butter or margarine
1/4 cup (60 mL) cold water

►Prepare pastry and line a pie pan with bottom crust. Sift together the sugar, flour and salt and sprinkle over the berries in a bowl; toss lightly to mix. (Tart berries may require more sugar.) Turn berry mixture into the pan. Dot with butter. Pour the cold water over the ingredients in the pan. Add top crust and crimp the edges to seal. Prick the crust to vent steam. Bake at 450°F (230°C) for 10 minutes. Reduce heat to 375°F (190°C) and bake for another 30 minutes or until pie appears well done.

Most berry pies boil over. You can foil a mess in the oven by cutting a sheet of foil somewhat bigger than the pie pan. Place it on the oven rack below the one holding the pie to catch the drips.

■ Alaska Wild Berry Guide and Cookbook

Alaskan Wild Berry Cobbler

1 cube (114 g) butter or margarine
1 cup (240 mL) flour
1 cup (240 mL) sugar

2 teaspoons (10 mL) baking powder
Dash of salt
1 cup (240 mL) milk
3 cups (720 mL) wild berries
1/2 cup (120 mL) additional sugar
2 cups (480 mL) warm water*
Cinnamon, sugar, butter for topping

►Place cube of butter in large baking dish, 9 x 13 inches (22 x 32 cm). Cut cube a few times to make melting faster; set in oven to melt, meanwhile preheating it to 425°F (220°C). Mix flour, 1 cup (240 mL) sugar, baking powder and salt and add enough milk to make a thin batter, about 1 cup (240 mL). Pour by spoonfuls over the butter melted in the baking dish. Spread wild berries — raspberries, lowbush cranberries, blueberries or huckleberries — over this dough and sprinkle them with the additional sugar. Pour warm water over berries, place dish in preheated oven and bake about 30 minutes. After a few minutes in the oven, the dough will rise to the top. When this happens, remove from oven and sprinkle sugar and cinnamon over it generously. Dot with butter. Return dish to oven and finish baking. Serve warm with cream.

■ *Freda Hering*
  Northern Lites, Tasty Bites, *Fairbanks*

*The amount of water probably should be adjusted depending on the juiciness of the berries.

Eskimo Fried Pies

►Use either pie crust or biscuit mix for these delectable pies. If you use biscuit mix it would be wise to enrich the dough with a little vegetable oil. Roll prepared dough lightly to about 1/8-inch (3 or 4 mm) thickness between sheets of waxed paper. Remove top paper. Using a canister lid for a cutter, cut 5-inch (12.5 cm) rounds. Use your pet berry filling. Any of the wild berries are fine for these and you may try endless variations by adding chopped nuts, coconut flakes, lemon juice, spices, raisins and the like. Just be sure that the fruit is cooked and thickened before filling the pies. It must be thick or it will ooze out the sides of the little pies in spite of all you do. The amount of sugar and other ingredients is up to you. Most people like these quite tart so don't use too much sugar. Now you are ready to build your pies. Put a large spoonful of the thick, cooled filling on each piece of pastry. Fold over and seal edges securely with a fork dipped in flour.

While you were making the pies the oil should have been heating. Use a deep cast-iron skillet or Dutch oven. Use any good cooking oil and be sure to have it at least 1 inch (2.5 cm) deep in the pan. It should heat to 350°F (175°C) or until a cube of

bread fries brown in five minutes. Unless your pan is quite large, only one pie can be fried at a time. Fry for four or five minutes and turn carefully, so as not to puncture the crust. Cook until the other side is well browned, too. Drain on paper towels and serve warm. Sprinkle with powdered sugar just before serving. Make these ahead of time and warm in a slow oven before serving.
■ *The Old Homesteader*

Aleut Berry Pudding

1-1/2 cups (360 mL) water
1/2 cup (120 mL) evaporated milk
1/3 cup (80 mL) sugar
Dash of salt
4 tablespoons (60 mL) flour
4 teaspoons (20 mL) seal oil
3 cups (720 mL) berries

►Bring water and milk to a boil. Add sugar and salt. Add flour that has been mixed with a little cold water to make a paste. Cook over low heat until thickened, stirring constantly. Cool and add berries and seal oil. Good to eat with boiled seal meat as a relish or can be eaten as a dessert.
■ Aleut Cookbook, *Saint Paul Island*

Agutuk *or* akutaq *or* ackutuk . . . *or "Eskimo ice cream" . . . in the past always began with tallow from big game and seal oil as the base for whipping various kinds of berries into a fluffy dessert. Now that these things are not always available, beef tallow and vegetable oil are used when necessary.*

Also in the long ago days, no sugar was used, but that is another ingredient that has come into use in recent years. The methods varied, but as a rule, the fat was broken up by beating with the hands, then the seal oil and other ingredients — berries in season — were added while the mixture was constantly worked with the hands to achieve greater lightness.

The following recipes represent both old ways and new. Because each one uses berries as a major ingredient, all are sweet-tasting products, even without sugar. *Agutuk* made with tallow and oil, alone, is said to have a cheesy flavor. A recipe for that variety is on page 225.

The first three recipes below are reprinted from *The Alaska Dietary Survey*. While these are rather short on directions, read on . . . you'll get the hang of it!

Agutuk with Cloudberries

1 cup (240 mL) beef, caribou or moose fat
1/2 to 1 cup (120 to 240 mL) seal oil
(sometimes oogruk oil)

1/2 cup (120 mL), more or less, water or snow
10 to 12 cups (2.4 to 2.8 L) cloudberries
0 to 2 cups (0 to 480 mL) sugar

Crowberry Agutuk with Sourdock

1-1/4 cups (300 mL) beef or caribou tallow
1 cup (240 mL) seal oil
1 cup (240 mL) sugar
1/2 cup (120 mL) water
5 cups (1.2 L) sourdock, cooked
6 cups (1.45 L) crowberries
1 cup (240 mL) raisins, softened
1/2 pound (228 g) dried apples, cooked

Cranberry Agutuk

1 piece moose fat, about 4 x 1 x 1 inch
(10 x 2.5 x 2.5 cm)
1/2 cup (120 mL) hydrogenated fat
1/2 cup (120 mL) seal oil
1 cup (240 mL) sugar
4 cups (1 L) lowbush cranberries
2 cups (480 mL) crowberries

Akutaq
. . . and now some directions!

►If you use fresh seal oil you don't get the strong taste. Put a handful of Crisco in the bowl. Work it with your hand and add a little cold water. Put in the seal oil and work it more. The real Eskimo way was to make it with reindeer fat, chopped in small pieces. They put it on the stove to melt it. They never used to put sugar in. They used no sugar, just berries. Then later we used to put sugar in. Stir in the sugar. If you keep your hand working it a long time all the sugar melts, it dissolves. It will just fluffy up, now watch. You keep adding water, more water. Every time you put sugar in it will fluff more. Keep working it and you can't smell the seal oil. Then put in the salmonberries. There should be blackberries, too. And then I put it up in my little freezer up there, let it cool off and eat it. If you just want to have a little spoonful now, you may.
■ *Alice Smith, Mekoryuk*
  Tundra Drums

Berry Cream-y

►Add sufficient granulated sugar to 1/2 pound (228 g) sweet cream butter to make a stiff paste. Stir in 1 cup (240 mL) tart fresh or cooked wild berries such as raspberries or blueberries. (Cranberries and strawberries are not suitable.) Let "brew" in refrigerator for at least 24 hours. Serve as a dessert.
■ *Mrs. Michael Petrov*
  An Alaskan Cook Book, *Kenai*

Real Eskimo Ice Cream

2 cups (480 mL) seal oil
1 to 1-1/2 pounds (0.45 to 0.70 kg) reindeer fat
Berries

►Boil the oil and reindeer fat together for two or three minutes. Cool until lukewarm. Take a bowlful of loose snow (not too powdery) and add oil; beat well to avoid lumps. Let freeze a bit. Fold in wild berries.
■ Out of Alaska's Kitchens

Our Favorite Eskimo Ice Cream

Shortening, about 1/2 to 3/4 cup
(120 to 180 mL)
Sugar, about 1 cup (240 mL), or sweeten to taste
Berries, about 1 scant quart (0.85 L)

►We use salmonberries, blueberries, blackberries. Cream shortening until fluffy. You can add a little of the berry juice to make this softer. Add berries, a small amount at a time, until you use up the berries. Serve with smoked salmon strips.
■ *Audrey Rearden*
  Cooking Up A Storm, *Homer*

Cranberry and Whitefish Agutuk

1 cup (240 mL) shortening
2 to 2-1/2 cups (480 to 600 mL) sugar
Few drops of water
Desired amount of lowbush cranberries
2 cups (480 mL) boiled and shredded whitefish

►Wash your hands and let them remain wet. Cream the sugar and the shortening. Add a few drops of water and mix well with hands until fluffy. Add desired amount of cranberries alternately with whitefish. Don't worry about it being too sour; the fish and sugar take away the bitterness. Serve as a dessert.
■ *Carol Hester*
  Uutuqtwa, *Bristol Bay High School*
  Naknek

BOOK FOUR

From Cache & Cupboard

Introduction

. . . Then I got ready for morning. I uncovered the jar of sourdough starter, dumped two-thirds of it into a bowl, put three heaping teaspoons of flour back into the starter jar, added some lukewarm water, stirred and capped it. If I did this every time, the starter would go on forever. To the starter in the bowl I added five tablespoons of flour, three tablespoons of sugar and a half cup of dry milk, mixing it all together with a wooden spoon. Lukewarm water was dribbled in until the batter was thin. Then the bowl was covered with a pan. It would work itself into a hot cake batter by morning.

Next morning: Time now to put the finishing touches to the sourdough batter. I gave it a good stirring and folded in a beaten egg; sprinkled half a teaspoon of baking soda, scattered a pinch of salt and dripped in a tablespoon of hot bacon fat. When these additions were gently folded into the batter, it seemed to come alive. I let it stand for a few minutes. Then I dropped one wooden spoonful of batter, hissing onto the skillet. When bubbles appear all over it's time to flip. Brown, thin and light . . . nothing quite like a stack of sourdough hot cakes, cooked over a wood fire in the early morning.

■ One Man's Wilderness:
  An Alaskan Odyssey
  by Sam Keith from the Journals
  of Richard Proenneke

No Alaska cookbook would be complete without acknowledgment of the culinary wonders to be performed with the legendary yeast, sourdough. Since cooks of the stuff are as productively lively as the yeast itself, the topic won't ever be exhausted. In Chapter 12, we have collected plenty of information to get a cheechako started, plus a fine sampling of recipes to please and surprise beginner and expert. Sourdough may be the floury product most associated with the Far North in the popular imagination, but other baked goods are as typically Alaskan. Chapter 13 begins with a selection of them, then moves on to other concoctions from cupboard supplies.

And, finally, in Chapter 14, are techniques for stocking the cache by preserving the foods taken from land and waters during seasons of plenty.

"Cooking Alaskan" has always required ingenuity . . . not only in dreaming up ways to serve the unusual range of wild foods available here, but also in figuring out how to "cook around" what is not in the cupboard.

Our cupboard door opens with a list of suggested substitutions you can make if your cupboard suddenly is bare of certain staples.

Making Substitutions

If you're out of this . . .	Use this
1 square (1 oz /or/ 28 g) unsweetened chocolate	About 3 tablespoons (45 mL) cocoa, plus 2 teaspoons (10 mL) shortening
1 cup (240 mL) whole milk	4 tablespoons (60 mL) dry milk powder, plus 1 cup (240 mL) water OR . . . 4 tablespoons (60 mL) *nonfat* dry milk powder, plus 2 teaspoons (10 mL) margarine or butter, plus 1 cup (240 mL) water OR . . . 1/2 cup (120 mL) each — evaporated milk and water
1 cup (240 mL) sour milk	Place 1 tablespoon (15 mL) vinegar or lemon juice in bottom of measuring cup. Fill to 1-cup line (240 mL) with sweet milk.
1 cup (240 mL) sour cream	Place 1 tablespoon (15 mL) vinegar or lemon juice in bottom of measuring cup. Fill to 1-cup line (240 mL) with undiluted evaporated milk.
Sweetened condensed milk	Mix until dissolved: 1 cup plus 2 tablespoons (270 mL) instant dry milk powder, 3/4 cup (180 mL) sugar and 1/2 cup (120 mL) very warm water. †
1 teaspoon (5 mL) baking powder	1/4 teaspoon (1 mL) baking soda, plus 1/2 teaspoon (2 mL) cream of tartar
1 cup (240 mL) sugar *When using starred substitutions, reduce liquid in recipe by 1/4 cup (60 mL).	1 cup (240 mL) corn syrup* OR . . . 1 cup (240 mL) honey plus 1/4 to 1/2 teaspoon (1 to 2 mL) baking soda* OR . . . 1 cup (240 mL) maple syrup, plus 1/4 teaspoon (1 mL) baking soda* OR . . . 1/2 cup (120 mL) maple syrup plus 1/4 cup (60 mL) corn syrup* OR . . . 1 cup (240 mL) firmly packed brown sugar OR . . . 3/4 to 1 cup (180 to 240 mL) molasses, plus 1/4 to 1/2 teaspoon (1 to 2 mL) baking soda*
Brown sugar	Mix well: 1/2 pound (228 g) white sugar, plus 4 to 5 teaspoons (20 to 25 mL) dark corn syrup, plus two drops maple flavoring. †
Eggs	Mix egg powder to be used in a recipe by putting measured water in bowl, sprinkling powder on top and beating until smooth: *For 1 egg in recipe* mix 2-1/2 level tablespoons (38 mL) egg powder, plus an equal amount of lukewarm water; *2 eggs in recipe* . . . 5 tablespoons (75 mL) each — egg powder and lukewarm water; *3 eggs in recipe* . . . 1/2 cup (120 mL) each — egg powder and lukewarm water.
1 tablespoon (15 mL) flour for thickening	1/2 tablespoon (8 mL) cornstarch OR . . . 2 tablespoons (30 mL) rice OR . . . 1 egg OR . . . 1 tablespoon (15 mL) egg powder
1 cup (240 mL) sifted cake flour	1 cup less 2 tablespoons (210 mL) all-purpose flour
1 cup (240 mL) all-purpose flour	Mix 1/2 cup (120 mL) all-purpose flour with up to 1/2 cup (120 mL) whole-wheat flour, bran or corn meal for variety in baking.

†These suggestions are from Peggy Goldizen, *Northern Lites, Tasty Bites*, Fairbanks. Others are from Betty Lou Murray, "Camp or Cabin Baking," *ALASKA®* magazine, July 1972.

WEIGHTS & MEASURES

What Does A Meter Measure?

length	Name	Symbol	Approximate Size
length	meter	m	39½ inches
	kilometer	km	0.6 mile
	centimeter	cm	width of a paper clip
	millimeter	mm	thickness of paper clip
area	hectare	ha	2½ acres

	Name	Symbol	Approximate Size
weight	gram	g	weight of a paper clip
	kilogram	kg	2.2 pounds
	metric ton	t	long ton (2240 pounds)
volume	liter	L	one quart and 2 ounces
	milliliter	mL	1/5 teaspoon
pressure	kilopascal	kPa	atmospheric pressure is about 100 kPa

Units of **time** and **electricity** will not change.

How To Convert From One Measure To Another

Symbol	When You Know Number of	Multiply By	To Find Number of	Symbol
LENGTH				
in	inches	2.54	centimeters	cm
ft	feet	30	centimeters	cm
yd	yards	0.9	meters	m
mi	miles	1.6	kilometers	km
AREA				
in²	square inches	6.5	square centimeters	cm²
ft²	square feet	0.09	square meters	m²
yd²	square yards	0.8	square meters	m²
mi²	square miles	2.6	square kilometers	km²
	acres	0.40	hectares	ha
WEIGHT (mass)				
oz	ounces	28	grams	g
lb	pounds	0.45	kilograms	kg
	short tons (2000 pounds)	0.9	metric tons	t
VOLUME				
tsp	teaspoons	5	milliliters	mL
Tbsp	tablespoons	15	milliliters	mL
in³	cubic inches	16	milliliters	mL
fl oz	fluid ounces	30	milliliters	mL
c	cups	0.24	liters	L
pt	pints	0.47	liters	L
qt	quarts	0.95	liters	L
gal	gallons	3.8	liters	L
ft³	cubic feet	0.03	cubic meters	m³
yd³	cubic yards	0.76	cubic meters	m³
PRESSURE				
inHg	inches of mercury	3.4	kilopascals	kPa
psi	pounds per square inch	6.9	kilopascals	kPa
TEMPERATURE (exact)				
°F	degrees Fahrenheit	5/9 (after subtracting 32)	degrees Celsius	°C

Common Temperature Readings

	°C	°F
Freezing point of water	0	32
Boiling point of water	100	212
Normal body temperature	37	98.6
Comfortable room temperature	20-25	68-77

Common U.S. Customary Measures

3 teaspoons	=	1 tablespoon
4 tablespoons	=	1/4 cup
5-1/3 tablespoons	=	1/3 cup
8 tablespoons	=	1/2 cup
10-2/3 tablespoons	=	2/3 cup
12 tablespoons	=	3/4 cup
16 tablespoons	=	1 cup

2 cups	=	1 pint
4 cups	=	1 quart
2 pints	=	1 quart
4 quarts	=	1 gallon

To equal one pound, it takes approximately:
4 cups powdered cocoa
5 cups ground coffee
3 cups corn meal
3 cups cornstarch
4 cups all-purpose flour
4-1/2 cups cake flour
2 cups shortening or butter
2-1/2 cups brown sugar
2 cups granulated sugar
3-1/2 cups powdered sugar

The Weight in Grams of Common Baking Ingredients

Ingredient	U.S. Customary Volume Measures						
	1 cup	3/4 cup	2/3 cup	1/2 cup	1/3 cup	1/4 cup	1 tsp
Bread crumbs, dry	100 g	75 g	66 g	50 g	33 g	25 g	—
Butter and margarine	226	169	150	113	75	56	—
Cake flour, enriched	96	72	66	48	33	24	—
Cocoa, dry	86	64	56	43	28	21	—
Corn meal	148	111	98	74	49	37	—
Flour, sifted all-purpose	116	87	78	58	39	29	—
Flour, unsifted all-purpose	140	105	94	70	47	35	—
Milk, instant dried	68	51	46	34	23	17	—
Nuts, chopped	119	87	80	59	40	28	—
Oatmeal, dry	71	53	48	35	24	18	—
Peanut butter	251	187	168	125	84	62	—
Raisins	143	106	95	71	47	35	—
Rice, uncooked long grain	198	150	132	99	66	50	—
Shortening	226	169	150	113	75	56	—
Sugar, packed brown	220	165	146	110	73	55	—
Sugar, granulated white	200	150	134	100	67	50	—
Sugar, unsifted powdered	123	92	82	61	41	31	—
Powdered ginger or mustard	—	—	—	—	—	—	1.5 g
Ground allspice, cinnamon, cloves	—	—	—	—	—	—	1.7
Nutmeg	—	—	—	—	—	—	1.9
Black pepper	—	—	—	—	—	—	2.3
Active dry yeast	—	—	—	—	—	—	2.5
Cream of tartar or baking powder	—	—	—	—	—	—	3.2
Salt	—	—	—	—	—	—	6.0
Baking soda	—	—	—	—	—	—	4.0

Excerpted from Fact Sheet — Food Science and Nutrition No. 28 — revised 1976, Mary Darling and Debora Wardle, Agricultural Extension Service, University of Minnesota, "Metric Measure for Home Recipes."

All About Sourdough

IN THE KITCHEN

Although some Sourdoughs talk about sourdough as if the rules of success were baked in loaves of stone, our reading of the recipes is that sourdough cookery is both fun and practical because it leaves room for creativity and, within a few limits, even downright error.

It's a good thing. Trying to follow the advice of sourdough authorities can be somewhat perplexing. Terms used religiously by all sourdough cooks — "starter," "batter," "sponge," "sourdough" —are flung about interchangeably by some and describe specific — but varying — steps recommended by others. To boot, some cooks successfully *begin* "starters" with ingredients others swear should n-e-v-e-r touch a sourdough pot.

To the beginner, we offer the following rules of thumb. (The expert can go on about his or her business of breaking them.)

Starting A Starter

Sourdough starter is a slow-developing yeast with a distinctive flavor. It can be used in most products that call for yeast. Commercial starters, usually granulated for long storage and easy packaging, are available, but many cooks prefer to make their own, or, if they're lucky enough to know someone who has a special culture going, borrow

the initial half-cup (or less) that is required to establish another sourdough pot.

The end products — hot cakes, bread, doughnuts and so on — require no more fuss than those made from other yeasts. But the starter itself calls for planning ahead (a) to develop the characteristic sour taste that has attracted so many fans, and (b) to keep the yeast alive and well for repeated use.

This initial step, developing the starter, can take anywhere from 24 hours to several days. Most of the starter recipes in this chapter recommend three days or longer. One is ready for use after only 24 hours though it, too, improves with some additional souring time.

Once the starter has fermented sufficiently the first time, however, it can be preserved almost "at the ready" indefinitely. Simply remember that the night before you wish to bake, "set the sponge" for the next day's baking.

Setting The Sponge

Sourdough yeast or starter is a living critter in the sense that it thrives on regular feeding. . . . It needs to be refueled before it will work; and, each time it "eats," it likes to have six or eight hours in a nice cozy spot to digest its food before you ask it to raise any doughs. All this is called "setting the sponge." You *could* set the sponge one morning and be ready for baking by mid-afternoon, but most cooks prefer to set the sponge at night so the sourdough is ready for work bright and early in the morning.

To set the sponge, place in a large bowl or crock equal parts sourdough starter and flour, and add about an equal amount of warm water, or a little less. Or:

> *1 cup (240 mL) sourdough starter*
> *1 cup (240 mL) flour*
> *3/4 to 1 cup (180 to 240 mL) warm water*

Beat the mixture with a wooden spoon (a night of digestion will absorb any leftover lumps). Then set the bowl in a warm — not hot — place for six to eight hours or overnight. Cover the bowl with a loose foil lid that will keep out foreign objects but still allow air circulation. Sourdough borrows its yeast-building organisms from its surroundings.

The next morning, before you add other ingredients, reserve about a cupful (240 mL) of this sponge for your sourdough pot. (See Replenishing the Pot.) The remaining sponge is ready to be used as the yeast for hotcakes, doughnuts, cakes, pie dough . . . your heart's desire.

Some cooks add more flour and water per cup of starter during sponge setting. A standard ratio is:

> *1 cup (240 mL) starter*
> *2-1/2 cups (600 mL) flour*
> *2 cups (480 mL) warm water*

We say — that depends. If yours is a young starter and you're planning to make a product calling for raised dough, go cautiously. Don't feed the starter more than equal its volume of flour and water. When yours is an effervescent, reliable old starter, the larger ratio of flour and water to sourdough can be used quite successfully.

OR, if you are setting the sponge to make pancakes or waffles, adding the larger amount of flour and water is quite all right — in fact desirable — since the sponge *is* most of the batter and it doesn't have to do a significant amount of "rising."

What do you do if you're up against a recipe that calls for more starter than you have? Just keep setting the sponge until you have the required amount, allowing each batch to "digest" (most cooks call this "work"), if possible, six to eight hours before you feed it again. If you're planning a hot cake breakfast for five hundred, this is exactly how you would proceed to obtain enough sourdough.

Replenishing The Sourdough Pot

Once a sourdough starter is in work, it can be preserved at the ready indefinitely. People who have hot cakes every morning or use the sourdough at least two or three times a week in various baking activities, keep the sourdough pot on the back of the stove, or perhaps hanging in a warm corner of the room or in a warm cupboard. "Setting the sponge" the night before they use it is as much a habit with them as letting the cat out or feeding the dogs or washing up after dinner.

But you don't have to bake every day or even once a week to make it practical and fun to keep a sourdough pot going. And it isn't very difficult. Sourdough starter can be kept somewhat dormant stored in the refrigerator, or in a cool place, about 38 °F (3.5 °C). There it will stay alive and healthy on a reduced feeding schedule of once a week.

Store the sourdough starter in a sterilized glass or earthenware container (not metal) with a lid. This is your "sourdough pot." It should be large enough to allow some expansion of the yeast. People who keep large amounts of sourdough going swear by the commercial size mayonnaise jar, but the quart size (1 L) is adequate for 2 cups (480 mL) or more of sourdough.

Then, once a week, whether or not you plan to bake, "set the sponge" as directed above and allow it to "digest" or "work" overnight in a warm place. If you put it in a different bowl, this will allow you to clean the sourdough pot . . . but that isn't necessary every week.

The next morning, as usual, reserve the amount you want for your sourdough pot. What you do with the remaining sponge is up to you. Use it for baking, make pancakes for the dogs, give it away, dry some of it to send to friends in the Lower 48 (along with some directions, of course) . . . or . . . (shhhhhhhhhh!) simply throw the extra away. The pot won't mind as long as it has a full belly.

You see? That's not even as difficult as maintaining a houseplant, is it? When you run onto compulsive cooks who claim they've been driven batty by the demands of sourdough, teach them to chant to themselves, "I do NOT have to bake every week to keep a happy sourdough burbling away in the refrigerator." All it needs is a little Saturday night merriment of food, drink and warmth.

Why Bother?

Why bother to keep a sourdough going when a new one can be started on a few days' notice? Age improves the power and flavor of sourdough, and in a very real sense, sourdoughs become a part of the family, borrowing special character from their individual surroundings. And, *old* sourdoughs are guaranteed to keep you from getting lonely by jumping up to hug you whenever you feed them. (At least they bubble a lot.)

That means, when someone offers you a half-cup (or even a spoonful) of sixty-year-old sourdough, take it. However small the amount, feed it with an equal amount of flour, thin it with nearly an equal amount of water and start it growing.

Signs of Sourdough Sickness

Sourdoughs don't get sick very often, but sometimes they become a little tired. If yours loses its ability to bubble away after a feeding, that's easily treated. Some people sprinkle a little sugar over the dough to liven it up; others add a small amount of another yeast. Soften a teaspoon (5 mL) or so of dry yeast in 1/4 cup (60 mL) very warm water and add it to the pot when you feed it.

If a clear liquid forms on top (and it will if you store it in the refrigerator), simply stir it back into the starter. It's perfectly healthy.

About *other* colors that may appear on top of your sourdough, old-timers — old Sourdoughs — disagree. One says, "If an orange liquid develops, discard the whole works and start over." Another, "If the starter turns orange, it is not spoiled; but if it turns green, it must be discarded." And more than one claims a black film over the top isn't harmful. Their advice is roughly the same regarding discoloration: Remove it carefully. Scoop up some untainted starter, put it in a sterilized container and start the growing process again. Scrub and sterilize the old pot before reusing it.

However, we favor the assumption of the University of Alaska Cooperative Extension Service that "Modern Alaskans do not use discolored starters . . . "!

Long-Term Storage of Sourdough

"Don't let sourdough freeze!" is a common piece of advice, backed up by tales of how the old Sourdoughs used to carry the precious yeast inside their clothing to insure that it stayed warm enough. But several authorities maintain that freezing is the best way to keep sourdough indefinitely.

Both are right. Some cultures survive freezing; some do not. If you wish to find out about yours, test a small amount of it.

Freeze, then thaw it in the refrigerator (or in the cool air), add equal parts flour and water, set it in a warm spot and watch for bubbles. Coax it a few hours later with a little more flour and water. If bubbling appears, your culture freezes successfully. Drying is a more versatile and common long storage method, however. Again, testing with a small amount of your culture is in order.

To Dry Starter

Either drop starter by teaspoonfuls onto waxed paper, letting the daubs spread out to thin circles, or spread a larger amount thinly on a cookie sheet lined with waxed paper. (Don't let it touch the metal.) When they are dry enough to handle, the circles should be turned frequently until they are completely dry. In Interior Alaska that will take about 24 hours. The sheet may require longer.

When it is thoroughly dry, break it into pieces as you would peanut brittle. You may crush the pieces or circles to a powder, using a rolling pin, but this is not necessary. Store the dry culture in airtight plastic bags or jars in a cool, dry place.

To Reconstitute Dry Starter

To reconstitute, crumble two or three pieces or circles or sprinkle two or three spoonfuls of powder into about a half-cup (120 mL) of warm water. Let stand overnight or until bubbly. Add a half-cup (120 mL), each, of water and flour and, again, let it stand overnight or until it is bubbly. At that time it is ready to be used in a recipe or stored in the refrigerator until the next regular feeding time. It may not be as good as the original at first, but in time, it will improve.

Cold Kitchen — Warm Hearth

Like other yeasts, sourdough requires warmth to grow (though you'll find it isn't entirely dormant even in the refrigerator), but it stops growing entirely if there is too much warmth. For developing a starter, setting the sponge, raising doughs, a spot free of drafts and a temperature somewhere between 65 and 80°F (18 to 27°C) is recommended. Different cultures work best at different temperatures, and some are slower than others to react even when conditions are ideal.

During the day, especially when the kitchen is in use, a sourdough's need for warmth is easily accommodated. It's the long cold night that can be a problem. A banked fire in a wood stove, a stove or heater with a pilot light, even placing the sourdough near a lighted medium-wattage electric bulb, will generally serve. In fact, some caution is in order to keep the dough from too much warmth.

Or, try insulating the sourdough. A cupboard above the stove will retain heat even after it is turned off. A large kettle or box lined with inch-thick foam rubber or some other insulating material also makes a good bed for the sourdough pot, but the chamber should not be airtight.

Using Other Yeasts and Leavenings

Most recipes for sourdough products call for the addition of baking soda. Soda sweetens the sour taste somewhat and makes a lighter batter.

NEVER add soda to the sourdough starter itself, however, and BE CAUTIOUS about the amount of soda and how you add it to the recipe. Too much soda will make breads and other products brown too much and may destroy more sour flavor than you wish.

Add soda to batters and doughs just before baking time. Some recipes suggest combining salt, sugar and soda and stirring them together until all lumps of soda have been broken up before sprinkling the mixture over a batter.

Another way of handling soda is to reserve a tablespoon (15 mL) of the liquid in any recipe and dissolve the soda in it. Either way, the soda mixture is folded gently into batters at the last minute before baking or can be kneaded into bread dough after the initial rising.

In stipulating the use of other yeast, most recipes call for it by the "package," by which is meant the smallest unit commercially available. That means the 5/8-ounce (18 g) cake of compressed yeast or the 1/4-ounce (7 g) packet of dry active yeast, usually sold in a set of three packets.

Though compressed yeast is preferred by many cooks for its extra flavor, even refrigerated it has such a short shelf life that it has been replaced in many kitchens (and stores) by the longer lasting dry granulated yeast.

Package for package, the two yeasts are equal in leavening power. The difference is the temperature needed to activate them. The "warm water" called for in recipes needs to be only 80°F (27°C) for compressed yeast, but it must be between 110 and 115°F (43 to 45°C) to soften and activate dry yeast.

If you are using a recipe that does not call for softening dry yeast, either follow the directions on the packet about how to add it to other dry ingredients, OR decrease the amount of liquid in the recipe by whatever warm water it will take to soften the yeast — at least 1/4 cup (60 mL) per packet. Sprinkle the yeast over the water and allow it to sit for about five minutes before proceeding with the recipe.

Dry yeast also comes in jars — sensible if you do quite a bit of baking. To measure a "package" of dry yeast from a jar, use a generous 2 teaspoons or a scant tablespoon (between 11 and 14 mL).

Do not confuse active dry yeast with brewer's yeast. The latter has nutritional value but no leavening power.

Hints From Sourdoughs

• To convert a yeast-bread recipe to sourdough, take half the flour and all the liquid of any recipe, plus 1/2 to 1 cup (120 to 240 mL) starter, mix and set in a warm place overnight. Then add the remaining ingredients, minus the yeast, plus a little extra flour, knead, let rise and bake according to the original recipe. The same applies to pancakes and other recipes. [Gretchen Walker, "Sourdough Cookery — Life in A Crock Pot," ALASKA® magazine, June 1978.]

• If by accident all the sourdough is used — do not panic! Just add flour and water and scrape down sides of the sourdough pot. There will be enough enzymes to start the sourdough to bubble again. [Ruth Allman, Alaska Sourdough.]

• To tan small hides such as mink, rabbit, ermine, or muskrat, first wash the hide with lukewarm soapy water, using a mild soap. Lay the skin on a flat board, hair side down. Cover it with a thick batter of sourdough. When dough begins to dry, start working the skin. Rub it with a circular motion against the palm of the left hand. Rub and knead the skin until it is dry and soft. [University of Alaska Cooperative Extension Service, Sourdough, Publication No. 61, July 1974.]

• Secret for Crisp, Crunchy Sourdoughs: Stir the soda with the little finger of your left hand, as it is cleaner than the right — and you will eat — 50% Baked Hot AIR! [Ruth Allman, Alaska Sourdough]

SOURDOUGH STARTERS

These sourdough starters were selected for variety. The first is from a sourdough iconoclast (popular species in this state) who says a 24-hour starter is plenty old enough for him. Others suggest fermenting the yeast three days or more before using it in a recipe. We still cherish our belief that sourdoughs (and Sourdoughs) improve with age. To maintain your starter supply indefinitely, be sure to reserve 1 cup (240 mL) of it for your sourdough pot before starting to make bread or hot cakes or other products from the remaining sponge.

Sacrilegious Sourdough Starter

"They tell me that there are sourdough starters in Alaska that are over a hundred years old. Well, mine isn't over a week old. It's just too much bother to keep a starter going when it's so easy to start a batch with today's yeast. A friend of mine has the same feeling. She compares keeping a starter alive to keeping a bird. You're always feeding it, watering it, and cleaning up after it. I'll buy that!

"I keep my starter in the refrigerator in a gallon mayonnaise jar, but a nice neat crock with a cover would be fine, too. Okay, let's start a batch of sourdough."

2-1/2 cups (600 mL) warm water
1 package active yeast
3 cups (720 mL) all-purpose or
*   whole-wheat flour*

►Pour the water into a large bowl, sprinkle the yeast on top of the water, and wait five minutes. Gradually add the flour, stirring in a little at a time. When all the flour is in, beat the mixture vigorously until it is smooth. Pour the batter into your jar or crock and cover lightly with aluminum foil. Set in a warm place for 24 hours. If the yeast is active, you'll have a good, bubbling starter. You can now claim it is a hundred years old and who's to question you?

■ *Gordon R. Nelson, Palmer*
  Lowbush Moose

Deluxe Thick Sourdough Starter

This starter is especially suited to Maxine Reed's Deluxe Sourdough Hot Cakes and Waffles. To maintain the thick consistency, the cook recommends this method of setting the sponge each time: "For every 2 cups (480 mL) of flour to be used, add to the starter mixture — in addition to the 2 cups (480 mL) of flour — 1 cup (240 mL) warm water and 1 tablespoon (15 mL) sugar. Good idea to dissolve sugar into solution before adding flour. This mixture must stand in a 65 to 70°F (18 to 21°C) room at least overnight — longer is better."

1 cake compressed or 1 package dry yeast,
*   dissolved in 1/4 cup (60 mL) warm water*
2 cups (480 mL) warm water
2 tablespoons (30 mL) sugar
4 cups (1 L) or more unsifted all-purpose flour

►Into a large jar or stone crock put warm water, dissolved yeast and sugar. (The 1 gallon /or/ 4 L wide-mouthed restaurant mayonnaise jars are excellent.) Stir until in solution. Add flour and stir well. The amount of flour ⸏ vary with dryness of flour. Cover loosely so sourdou⸏ allow to stand in a warm ⸏ stirring down occasionally, ⸏ the jar. When dipping into t⸏ with a CLEAN SPOON. The ⸏ ⸏ain only flour-sugar-water and ye⸏ ⸏ep without spoiling. This starter is ready ⸏or use, but always reserve some for future use, setting the sponge a day ahead of baking, per directions.

■ *Maxine M. Reed*
  Alaska's Cooking, *Anchorage*

Mashed Potato Starter

2 cups (480 mL) thick potato water
2 tablespoons (15 mL) sugar
2 cups (480 mL) flour (more or less)
1/2 teaspoon (2 mL) yeast (optional)

►To make rich potato water, boil potatoes with jackets on until they fall to pieces. Lift skins out; mash potatoes, making a puree. Cool. Add more water, if necessary, to make sufficient liquid. Richer the potato water, richer the starter. Put all ingredients in sourdough pot. Beat until smooth creamy batter. Cover. Set aside in warm place to start fermentation. *Use optional yeast only to speed action.*

Sourdough starter can be used after three days, providing those little enzymes have started working. But it is better to wait a few more days. Toss in extra fuel for the sourdough to work on — a spoonful of sugar along with a couple spoonfuls of flour. Add water if batter too thick. Mix well. Cover. Put in warm spot to work more. After a week, starter will be effervescing with a million bubbles. Looks like sour cream — smells like sour cream — but is rich luscious sourdough.

■ *Ruth Allman, Juneau*
  Alaska Sourdough

Grated Potato Starter

2 raw potatoes, peeled, then grated in bottom of
*   sourdough pot*
1 yeast cake, diluted in 2 cups (480 mL)
*   warm water*
2 tablespoons (30 mL) sugar
Flour enough to make a smooth, creamy batter.

►Beat well. Get all lumps out at this time so it is not necessary to remove any flour lumps later when ready to use the starter. Cover. Place sourdough pot on the shelf in a warm spot free from drafts. This starter takes longer to start working than some, but in a week it will be bubbling.

■ *Ruth Allman, Juneau*
  Alaska Sourdough

Otto's Sourdough Starter

This starter makes the huge amount called for in Otto's Sourdough Bread

4 cups (1 L) flour
1 tablespoon (15 mL) salt
2 tablespoons (30 mL) sugar
3-1/3 cups (840 mL) warm potato water (water in which peeled potatoes have been boiled)

►Sift the flour into a large earthen pot or crock. Mix in salt and sugar, then slowly stir in the potato water. Mix thoroughly, cover crock loosely, and leave it in a warm place for three days. The mixture will smell sour as it ferments.

■ *Pauline McClellan*
  "Otto's Sourdough Bread"
  ALASKA® magazine, December 1980
  Alaska-only edition

Whole-Wheat Sourdough Starter

By combining a portion of this starter with additional yeast, Diana Scensy Greene has developed a whole-wheat bread that has a spongy texture, keeps well and is quicker to rise than those that depend entirely on sourdough leavening. See her recipe, Sourdough Whole-Wheat Bread — Plus.

2 cups (480 mL) warm water
2-1/2 cups (600 mL) whole-wheat flour
1 tablespoon (15 mL) honey
1 tablespoon (15 mL) active dry yeast

►Combine starter ingredients in a glass bowl, large jar or earthenware crock. Let mixture stand, uncovered, in a warm place about five days, or until it ferments and smells sour.

■ *Diana Scesny Greene*
  "Sourdough Plus For Better Bread"
  ALASKA® magazine, April 1977
  Alaska-only edition

Tin snips and a pair of pliers are all you need to make a good cookie sheet from a 5-gallon (20 L) gas can. A little more ingenuity is required but you can make pie pans and cake tins, too.

■ *Former Wasilla homesteader*
  The Cabin Friend
  ALASKA® magazine, October 1977

SOURDOUGH HOT CAKES & WAFFLES

About Setting The Sponge: *Please read about preparing sourdough at the beginning of the chapter. The night before you plan to bake hot cakes, always "set the sponge." Use a large bowl, big enough for more hot cake ingredients. Generally, the sponge for hot cakes and waffles combines about twice the amount of flour and water as sourdough starter. (Bread sponges are often about one-to-one.) Unless otherwise directed in a recipe, use these proportions. For each batch of hot cakes or waffles, combine:*

1 cup (240 mL) starter
2 cups (480 mL) warm water
2-1/2 cups (600 mL) flour
1 tablespoon (15 mL) sugar (an optional ingredient many cooks favor)

As usual, set the sponge in a warm place, cover it loosely and allow it to work overnight or at least six to eight hours.

Next morning, remove 1 cup (240 mL) to return to your sourdough pot. Use the remaining sponge to make batter.

Few recipes tell you how *much* sponge is needed. You simply use what you have left and adjust other ingredients to suit your own taste in thin or thick hot cakes. Figure a batch of sponge will make enough hot cake batter to serve three to five people, depending on the thickness of the hot cakes . . . and the waistlines.

Bake sourdough hot cakes on a lightly greased, moderately hot griddle — hot enough to make a drop of water dance, but not hot enough to smoke.

As most of these recipes indicate, mix hot cake and waffle batter with a light touch . . . especially after you add soda. If sourdoughs are tough, you've probably mixed the batter too much, maybe because it was too thick to mix lightly.

Next time, try a little more liquid in the batter and mix it in with as little stirring as possible. Then let the batter rest about 10 minutes (same as you would bread dough) before you start spooning it onto the griddle.

Basic Sourdough Hot Cakes or Waffles

►Set the sponge the night before you wish to bake. In the morning, remove 1 cup (240 mL) of the sponge for your sourdough pot. Use what is left in this recipe.

Sourdough sponge
2 eggs, well beaten
2 tablespoons (30 mL) oil or bacon drippings
1/4 to 1/2 cup (60 to 120 mL) evaporated milk or
   reconstituted dry milk
1 teaspoon (5 mL) salt
1 teaspoon (5 mL) baking soda
2 tablespoons (30 mL) sugar

►Lightly combine sponge, beaten eggs, oil or drippings and milk enough to make a batter as thin or thick as you like. In a small bowl, combine salt, soda and sugar, stirring well to remove any lumps. Sprinkle over the batter and fold in gently. Let batter rest 10 to 15 minutes. Bake on a hot, lightly greased griddle until golden brown. Serve at once with plenty of syrup and butter. Don't throw the leftover pancakes out. You will be happily surprised when you eat them cold!

Use a little imagination with mixing your pancakes. Blueberries, grated apple and crumbled bacon make nice additions to sourdoughs.

For sourdough waffles — Use the basic pancake recipe but add two extra tablespoons (30 mL) of oil or bacon drippings and more sugar and eggs if desired.

■ *Ouida Johnson*
"More Sourdough Recipes"
ALASKA® *magazine, March 1970*

Variations:

• *Granola Waffles* — Use the Basic Hot Cakes or Waffles recipe, increasing the number of eggs to three. Increase the amount of oil or bacon drippings to 1/4 cup (60 mL). Proceed as directed. When soda, salt and sugar have been folded in, spoon batter onto a preheated and lightly greased waffle iron, and immediately sprinkle it with about 1/4 cup (60 mL) granola. Bake for five to six minutes until waffle is crispy. Repeat.

• *Berry Good Hot Cakes* — Dust a cupful (240 mL) of blueberries with flour and a sprinkling of sugar. Let them sit a few minutes, then fold them into the batter. Or sprinkle blueberries over the cakes while they are baking on the griddle. Softer berries may be sprinkled on top of finished cakes.

• *Nutty Hot Cakes* — A handful of nuts makes an interesting addition to the batter, too. Or try adding 1/2 cup (120 mL) whole-wheat flour, corn meal, wheat germ, cracked wheat or bran flakes to the batter for added flavor and nutrition.

Sourdough Waffles For Two
A basic recipe

►The night before you wish to bake waffles mix in a quart (1 L) bowl:

1 cup (240 mL) all-purpose, unbleached
   white flour
1 cup (240 mL) warm water
1 cup (240 mL) sourdough starter

►Stir well, then replace 1 cup (240 mL) of the newly fed starter back into your sourdough pot. Cover the bowl and the sourdough pot lightly and set them both in a warm place to work overnight. Next morning, put the sourdough pot in the refrigerator for future use. To the batter in the bowl, add all the following *except the soda/water mixture:*

1 egg
1/2 teaspoon (2 mL) salt
1 to 2 teaspoons (5 to 10 mL) sugar
1/4 cup (60 mL) salad oil
1/4 cup (60 mL) wheat germ
1 teaspoon (5 mL) soda dissolved in
   1 tablespoon (15 mL) warm water

►Mix well. Then gently fold the soda solution into the batter. Spoon batter onto hot waffle iron and bake until steaming stops and waffle is golden brown. Serve hot with maple syrup, fruit syrup, strawberries and strawberry yogurt, or blueberries and blueberry yogurt.

To increase the amount of batter to serve eight people, set the sponge the night before, using 3 cups (720 mL) flour, 3 cups (720 mL) warm water and 1 cup (240 mL) sourdough starter. Triple all other ingredients except soda, which is increased only to 1-1/2 teaspoons (7 mL).

■ *Mamie Jensen, Juneau*

Deluxe Sourdough
Hot Cakes or Waffles

The starter designed for this recipe is Maxine M. Reed's Deluxe Thick Sourdough Starter, at the beginning of this chapter. If you plan to use a different starter, thicken it when you set the sponge the night before baking:

To 1 cup (240 mL) starter, add 2 cups (480 mL) flour and 1 cup (240 mL) warm water in which 1 tablespoon (15 mL) sugar has been dissolved. "This mixture must stand in a 65 to 70°F (18-21°C) room at least overnight — longer is better."

1 egg, separated
1 teaspoon (5 mL) soda
1 teaspoon (5 mL) salt
1 tablespoon (15 mL) sugar
1 tablespoon (15 mL) salad oil
About 1/2 cup (120 mL) undiluted
   evaporated milk
2 cups (480 mL) sourdough sponge

►Separate egg, putting white and yolk into separate medium-sized mixing bowls. Beat the white until stiff but not dry. Set aside. To the yolk, add soda, salt, sugar, salad oil and evaporated milk and beat well. Beat sourdough starter until bubbly and then blend it with yolk mixture as rapidly as possible. Care must be taken not to break the bubbles, now or later, as they are the leavening. Never beat or stir the batter once it is complete. As soon as the yolk mixture and sourdough are blended, pour the bubbling batter over the beaten egg white, folding together carefully to avoid breaking bubbles. Bake on a hot, greased griddle.

To make waffles — Use two eggs instead of one, and increase the amount of salad oil to 1/4 cup (60 mL), or use cooled, melted shortening.

To serve a crowd — The starter should be built up over a period of several days, dividing and redividing the starter to add more flour, sugar and water each morning, according to proportions for setting the sponge.
■ *Maxine M. Reed*
   Alaska's Cooking, *Anchorage*

Leftovers — Good!

- **Hot Cake Cookies** — To the leftover batter in the bowl, add some honey or brown sugar, cinnamon, nutmeg and enough whole-wheat flour and oatmeal to make a drop cookie dough. A little soda mixed with the flour gives the batter an extra boost. Add some raisins, sunflower seeds or nuts or even chocolate chips and drop by spoonfuls onto lightly greased cookie sheets. Bake at 350°F (175°C) for 10 to 15 minutes. These store well in a coffee can [cool them completely, first] and seem to get better with age, though we eat them right up, they're so good! [Faith Smith, Gold King Creek, The Cabin Friend, *ALASKA®* magazine, May 1977]

- **Cocktail Waffles** — These are a wonderful substitute for toast or crackers for hot canapes. Make them ahead of time, label with the special spice of the waffle before putting in the freezing unit. Keep a variety on hand for spur of the moment needs. Store whole waffle. Do not cut until ready to use. Excellent way to utilize leftover batter from morning sourdoughs. Add to the batter — a dash of curry powder — or a dash of chili powder —or mustard and horseradish. Use only enough for a hint [of flavor] rather than overpowering use of these pungent spices. [Ruth Allman, *Alaska Sourdough*]

- **Packboard Treat** — Breakfast over and being sure of extra sourdough left in the crock, dash in three shakes from the cinnamon and mace cans, one shake from the clove and nutmeg cans. Add 1-1/2 cups (360 mL) mixed pancake "trimmings," such as syrup, jellies, sauces, fruit juice, and so on. Toss in as many raisins as you can spare and thicken the batter with flour to barely pouring consistency. Beat in 1 teaspoon (5 mL) soda and 1/3 cup (80 mL) liquid shortening. Pour batter into oiled and floured square or loaf cake pan. Bake slowly until a finger touched to the top of the cake does not leave a print.

   Cool while preparing for day's hike. Wrap ample portions in foil and tuck into pack. It will survive the roughest trail and go well with campfire coffee. [Mary Willets, *An Alaskan Cook Book*, Kenai]

- **Sourdough Pizza** — Cook one 8-inch (20 cm) sourdough cake for each person to be served. Place in broiling pan to crisp over on top. Mix one can chili sauce without beans, one can sandwich spread and 1/2 pound (228 g) Polish sausage. Spread chili mixture on sourdoughs and serve immediately with Alaskan Cranberry Sauce or any, sweet, tart jam. [Margaret J. Mielke, *Alaska's Cooking*, Anchorage]

Russian America Blintz

This creation, a specialty of Ruth Allman of the House of Wickersham in Juneau, is another variation of Basic Sourdough Hot Cakes.

To the basic batter add an extra egg. This will make batter very thin, as you want paper-thin, 7-inch (17 cm) cakes. If you have time, allow the batter to rest from one to three hours before baking.

Bake blintz cakes one at a time by pouring a small amount of batter into a hot, lightly greased 7-inch (17 cm) cast-iron skillet or crepe pan. Tilt the pan quickly to spread the batter paper thin and evenly over the bottom. Bake the cakes only on one side until blistered with bubbles and very lightly browned around the edges.

To remove cakes from the pan, lift edges gently with a spatula, and the rest of the cake should peel away easily. Lay cakes, baked side up, in a single layer on a damp tea towel, or stack them with waxed paper between. Then you're ready to continue with Ruth's recipe.

Blintz Filling
2 cups (480 mL) dry cottage cheese
1 egg yolk
1 tablespoon (15 mL) sugar
2 teaspoons (10 mL) melted butter
2 teaspoons (10 mL) grated orange rind
1/4 teaspoon (1 mL) cinnamon
Salt to taste
Blintz cakes, baked as directed
Garnish — sour cream or fruit

►Mix filling thoroughly and then place a spoonful in the center of each blintz cake, on the baked side. Fold all four sides over the filling, envelope fashion, and seal with a dab of sourdough. At this point blintzes may be held, chilled, in a covered dish, for several hours or overnight if you wish. When you're ready to serve them, place blintzes seam side down on a hot griddle (or a large skillet) greased well with equal parts butter and oil. Turn once to brown both sides. Serve immediately with sour cream or fruit.

■ *Ruth Allman, Juneau*
Alaska Sourdough

SOURDOUGH BREADS — ROLLS — DOUGHNUTS

Please read about preparing sourdough at the beginning of this chapter. The night before you plan to bake bread or rolls, always "set the sponge," according to the formula suggested by the recipe you plan to use, or, use a ratio of one part sourdough starter to one part flour to almost one part warm water. A typical sponge mixture is:

1 cup (240 mL) starter
1 cup (240 mL) all-purpose flour
3/4 to 1 cup (180 to 240 mL) warm water

Stir this mixture well, set it in a warm place, cover it loosely and allow it to work overnight or at least six to eight hours. When you're ready to bake, remove about a cup (240 mL) of it to replace in your sourdough pot. Use the remaining sponge in the recipe. Some recipes specify an amount of starter to be used; others only say "use what's left" after you reserve starter for the next time.

By the way, if you find yourself using almost all of your starter supply in a batch of bread, don't panic. Practically any amount, down to the spoonful of leavings on the side of the jar or sourdough pot is enough to build on again. See Setting The Sponge, Replenishing The Pot, early in this chapter.

Forming Loaves

Most recipes make enough dough to fill two 5 x 9-inch (12 x 22 cm) loaf pans or make one quite large French loaf. To form 5 x 9-inch loaves, divide dough into the number of portions suggested by the recipe. Roll out one to a thick oblong. The width of the oblong should be about 9 inches (22 cm) — or the length of the loaf pan. You want to form a loaf that will touch the ends of the pan, so that most of the expansion will go upward as the dough rises to double its size. Roll up the oblong, pressing the dough together with the heels of your hands as you turn it. Go gently but firmly enough so that air spaces will easily be filled in with the rising of the bread. The seam should be sealed a little more carefully. Then, seam side down, seal the ends of the loaf by pressing down about 1/2 inch (1.25 cm) of the dough; fold it under and press to seal, shaping as you go. Place in the pan, grease the top lightly, cover with a damp cloth and allow dough to rise in a warm place until doubled. Bake as directed.

French loaves may be formed the same way, but the oblong is much wider. Or roll out the oblong about the length you want the loaf to be, then fold each side in to meet at the middle, seal, turn seam side down and shape the ends to have the narrower French loaf look. Place loaf seam side down on a greased cookie sheet. Using a razor blade, a very sharp knife or very pointy scissors, cut shallow, diagonal slits across the top. Allow to rise as directed.

Round loaves are fun to build, too. Using your hands or a few deft touches of the rolling pin, form a circle of the dough and fold all the edges under until you shape a smooth, plump slightly flattened ball. The top may be slit or not, as desired.

Glazing

Sourdough breads are often not glazed, but if you want the glossy French bread look, mix one beaten egg white with 1 tablespoon (15 mL) cold water. When the baking bread reaches its peak of golden color, about five minutes before you take it from the oven, brush it with the egg white mixture and return to the oven for glaze to set.

To test for doneness, remove loaf from pan and thump the bottom with your fingers. It should make a hollow sound.

A harder crust can be achieved by setting a pan of warm water on the rack below the baking bread.

Basic Sourdough White Bread
A hearty, fine-grained bread that can be varied with spices and herbs

►Set the sponge the night before by adding 2 cups (480 mL), each, warm water and flour to the starter in your crock. Next morning, set aside a half-cup (120 mL) of starter for your next baking effort. To the remaining sponge, add the following, as directed below.

2 tablespoons (30 mL) cooking oil
4 cups (1 L) white flour
1 teaspoon (5 mL) salt
2 tablespoons (30 mL) sugar
1/4 teaspoon (1 mL) baking soda, dissolved in a
   scant tablespoon (13 mL) warm water

►Add cooking oil to the sourdough sponge and mix well. In a large bowl, combine dry ingredients (except soda, which is added later) and form a "well" in the center. Pour sponge into the well and mix thoroughly. If necessary, add more flour until you have dough suitable for kneading. Knead on a floured board for about 10 minutes. Put dough in a greased bowl, turn it to grease all sides, cover it with a towel and put it in a warm place for about three hours. Then punch down dough and let it

rest, covered, on a floured board for about 10 minutes.

Dissolve 1/4 teaspoon (1 mL) soda in a scant tablespoon (13 mL) warm water and knead it into the dough. Shape dough into one long, heavy loaf, French style, or two smaller ones and set in bake pans to rise. When dough doubles in size, bake at 375°F (190°C) for about 55 minutes.

■ *Clarence Massey*
   "Sourdough Bread Is Better
   Than Store-Bought"
   ALASKA SPORTSMAN®, *March 1968*

Variations:
• Raisin Bread — The night before baking, set the sponge as usual, then separate out the amount you will be using for raisin bread. To it add 3/4 to 1 cup (180 to 240 mL) raisins and allow the mixture to work overnight. Make sure you use a good-sized bowl. Raisins cause the sponge to rise faster than usual. Next day, follow the above bread recipe, adding extra sugar to sweeten the dough slightly.
• *Raisin-Nut Bread* — At the time you knead in the soda, also knead in 1/2 cup (120 mL) brown sugar, up to 1 cup (240 mL) chopped nuts, if you have them, and 1 cup (240 mL) raisins that have first been plumped in an equal amount of boiling water and then drained thoroughly.
• *Cinnamon Bread* — After dough has risen, punch down. Press or roll dough to 1/2-inch (1.25 cm) thickness. Sprinkle generously with cinnamon and brown sugar. Dot with butter. Roll up and cut in half. Place each half in a warm, well-greased loaf pan. Let double in bulk and bake as white bread.
• *Bacon-Cheese Bread* — After the soda has been kneaded into the bread, roll dough into a large rectangle (or two small ones). Sprinkle with 3/4 cup (180 mL) grated Cheddar cheese and 3/4 cup (180 mL) fried and crumbled bacon or commercial bacon bits. Roll into a loaf and allow to rise; bake as directed.
• *Herb-Cheese Bread* — Combine 1/3 cup (80 mL) melted butter, 2 tablespoons (30 mL) dried parsley flakes, 1 teaspoon (5 mL) instant minced onion and 1/2 teaspoon (2 mL) instant minced garlic. Spread mixture on rectangle of dough and sprinkle with 1/2 cup (120 mL) grated sharp cheese. (Parmesan, Romano or Cheddar in the can works well.) Form loaf and continue as directed.
• *Sourdough Bread Sticks* — After the first rising, when soda has been kneaded into the dough, divide it into two large lumps. Roll out each lump on a floured board to 1/2-inch (1.25 cm) thickness. Slice into strips 1/2 inch (1.25 cm) wide and 6 inches (15 cm) long. Roll these gently with your fingers to make rounded sticks. Brush

with water and place 1 inch (2.5 cm) apart on lightly greased cookie sheets. Bake at 400°F (205°C) for 20 minutes or until well browned. This recipe may be varied by kneading in dried minced onions, parsley flakes or other herbs, or rolling the sticks in corn meal or sesame seeds before baking.

San Francisco Sourdough French Bread

Added yeast makes this a somewhat lighter, faster rising bread than Basic Sourdough.

1-1/2 cups (360 mL) warm water
1 package yeast
1 cup (240 mL) sourdough starter
6 cups (1.4 L) flour
2 teaspoons (10 mL) salt
2 teaspoons (10 mL) sugar
1/2 teaspoon (2 mL) soda

►Pour warm water into large bowl and stir in yeast until dissolved. Add starter, 4 cups (1 L) flour, salt and sugar; stir vigorously about three minutes with a wooden spoon. Turn dough into greased bowl and let rise in a warm place until doubled in bulk, 1 to 1-1/2 hours. Mix soda with 1 cup (240 mL) flour and stir into dough. Dough will be very stiff. Turn dough out onto floured board and begin kneading, adding remaining flour and more if necessary, so that the dough is not sticky. Knead dough for at least eight minutes until satiny. Shape into two long loaves or one large round loaf and place on a slightly greased cookie sheet, cover and let rise in a warm place until double in size, about 1 to 1-1/2 hours. Just before baking, brush top with water, then make diagonal slashes across top of loaves with a sharp knife. Place a shallow pan of hot water in bottom of oven and place baking sheet on center rack. Bake bread at 400°F (205°C) for 45 minutes for two small loaves, 50 minutes for a large loaf.

■ *Carolyn Hieb*
  Good Food A-Plenty, *Fairbanks*

Honest-To-Goodness Sourdough Bread

►Here's a simple, honest sourdough bread recipe. . . . Set your sponge out the night before, as much as you want. In the morning remove the amount you want to use, and to it add flour — part rye, part whole-wheat and part white is a good combination. Add so much flour that you can barely stir the stiff dough with a wooden spoon. It should be very stiff and not sticky. *Your arm should be sore from trying to stir!* Now fill each bread pan about two-thirds full of this dough. Dip your hand in white flour and pat and shape the dough into a loaf

in the pan. The pans should seem very heavy — and you'll be thinking ''Good grief, this dough will *never* rise!'' But, if you started with a good, active starter, it will. Cover the pans with a cloth and set them in a very warm place. It may take up to four hours for the dough to rise — but let it take its time and when it's about doubled in bulk, bake in a 375°F (190°C) oven for about 1-1/4 hours. Remove from pans to cool. This is *very* dense bread and never falls apart when you slice or butter it. You really have to *chew* this bread — it's delicious!

■ *Faith Smith, Gold King Creek*
  The Cabin Friend
  ALASKA® *magazine, April 1976*

Sourdough Potato Bread

First Place, 1976 Tanana Valley Fair

1 package dry yeast
Approximately 5-3/4 cups (1.4 L)
    unbleached flour
1/4 cup (60 mL) sugar
2 teaspoons (10 mL) salt
Instant mashed potato flakes for 2 servings
3/4 cup (180 mL) milk
1/4 cup (60 mL) melted margarine
2 eggs
1 cup (240 mL) starter
1 egg white, beaten with 2 tablespoons
    (30 mL) water

►In large bowl, combine yeast, 2 cups (480 mL) flour, sugar and salt. In a saucepan, prepare two servings instant mashed potatoes according to directions on package. Then stir in the 3/4 cup (180 mL) milk, melted margarine, eggs and starter. Stir until blended.

Add potato mixture to dry ingredients; beat two minutes at medium speed. Add 1-1/2 cups (360 mL) flour and beat two minutes longer. With heavy spoon, stir in enough remaining flour to form a stiff dough. On floured board, knead dough with floured hands, about eight minutes. Place in greased bowl, turn, cover and let rise until double (1-1/2 to 2 hours). Punch down and divide in half.

Shape dough into smooth balls, then lift up and smooth each top by pulling down and pinching a lengthwise seam underneath. Cover loaves lightly with clear plastic wrap and let rise until almost double, about 45 minutes. With a razor blade or sharp knife, cut 1/2-inch-deep (1.25 cm) slashes on tops of loaves. Brush loaves with egg white mixture and bake at 350°F (175°C) for about 35 minutes, or until richly browned. You may brush loaves again with egg white mixture after they have been baked 20 minutes.

■ *Mrs. E.E. Sisson*
  Bake-Off Cookbook 1961-1980
  Tanana Valley Fair, Fairbanks

Onion-Chive Sourdough Bread

1 cup (240 mL) sourdough starter
2 tablespoons (30 mL) dry yeast
1/4 cup (60 mL) warm water
2 cups (480 mL) scalded milk
1/2 to 1 pound (228 to 456 g) grated cheese
1/2 teaspoon (2 mL) baking powder
2 tablespoons (30 mL) cooking oil
2 tablespoons (30 mL) sugar
1 package dry onion soup mix or 1/2 cup
(120 mL) minced wild chives
6 to 7 cups (1.4 to 1.7 L) all-purpose flour

►Dissolve yeast in warm water. To sourdough starter in large bowl add scalded milk, cheese, baking powder, oil, sugar and onion soup or wild chives. Add dissolved yeast and beat in 1/2 cup (120 mL) flour at a time. Dough should be stiff and should "clean" the bowl by pulling away from the sides. Turn onto lightly floured board and knead well, adding more flour as necessary. Put in a greased bowl and turn to coat with grease. Cover with a tea towel and put in a draft-free, warm — not hot — place and let rise until double in bulk. Punch down. Shape into two loaves and place in well-greased loaf pans. Cover and let rise again for approximately two hours or until doubled in bulk. Bake at 375°F (190°C) for 40 minutes or until done.
■ *The Old Homesteader*

Pressure-Steamed Sourdough Sesame Bread

1 cup (240 mL) Whole-Wheat Starter
1/2 cup (120 mL) corn meal
1/2 cup (120 mL) rye grits
1/3 cup (80 mL) whey powder
1/2 cup (120 mL) sesame seeds
1/2 cup (120 mL) brown sugar
1/2 cup (120 mL) milk
1 teaspoon (5 mL) baking soda

►Mix all ingredients. Put in a greased straight-sided can. Let rise about one hour in a warm place. Cover with foil and put in pressure cooker. Cook 15 minutes without pressure and then 30 minutes at 15 pounds (103.5 kPa).
■ *Gretchen Walker*
   "Sourdough Cookery — Life in A Crock Pot"
   ALASKA® magazine, June 1978

French Bread with Mixed Herbs

French bread, 1 loaf
1/2 cup (120 mL) wild chives, minced
1/2 pound (228 g) butter or margarine, softened

►This is all that is really necessary to make that delicious homemade sourdough French bread even better. Split the bread lengthwise and spread with the butter or margarine which has been blended with the chives. For variety you may also add all or any combination of the following: chopped parsley, crushed garlic, grated Cheddar or Swiss cheese, toasted sesame seeds, minced fresh marjoram, tarragon or basil. Now put the split loaf back together and wrap loosely in heavy foil, closing securely so that it is airtight. Put on warm (not hot) part of grill until well heated through or heat in the oven. If you desire, individual packages may be prepared.
■ *Helen A. White, Anchorage*
   What's Cookin' in Alaska

Otto's Sourdough Bread

4 cups (1 L) Otto's Sourdough Starter
6 cups (1.45 L) sifted flour, divided
1 teaspoon (5 mL) baking soda
1 teaspoon (5 mL) salt
3 teaspoons (15 mL) melted lard

►To the sourdough starter add 1 cup (240 mL) of flour that has been sifted with the soda and salt. Add melted lard, stir, and add three heaping cups (750 mL) of flour, then stir some more. Next knead in two more cups (480 mL) sifted flour until dough is smooth. Divide into three parts and knead into three loaves. Place side by side in a big, well-buttered bread pan and let rise 30 minutes. Bake in moderate oven until loaves are light brown on top. Remove from oven and from bread pan and spread butter or margarine lightly on top of loaves. Let cool before serving.
■ *Pauline McClellan*
   "Otto's Sourdough Bread"
   ALASKA® magazine, December 1980
   Alaska-only edition

Basic Whole-Wheat Sourdough Bread

1 package dry yeast
1-1/2 cups (360 mL) warm water
3 cups (720 mL) whole-wheat flour
1 cup (240 mL) starter
1/4 cup (60 mL) dark molasses
2 teaspoons (10 mL) salt
3 tablespoons (45 mL) butter, softened
2-1/2 to 3 cups (600 to 720 mL) all-purpose
   white flour
1/2 teaspoon (2 mL) baking soda

►Soften yeast in the water in a large mixing bowl. Blend in whole-wheat flour, starter, molasses, salt and butter. Combine 1 cup (240 mL) white flour with soda and stir into yeast mixture. Add enough of remaining flour to make a fairly stiff dough. Turn onto floured board and knead 6 to 10 minutes or until smooth and elastic. Shape into a ball and place in a well-greased bowl. Turn ball once to coat completely with grease. Cover with cloth. Set in draft-free, warm place and allow to rise until doubled in bulk, about two hours. Punch down and divide in half. Allow to rest for 10 to 15 minutes. Shape into loaves and place in well-greased pans. Cover and let rise until it again doubles in bulk — about one hour. Bake at 375°F (190°C) for 35 to 40 minutes. Remove from pans to cool.

■ *The Old Homesteader*

Fried Sourdough Sandwich

►Spread your favorite brand of peanut butter on sourdough whole-wheat bread; sprinkle generously with chopped fresh wild chives and close the sandwich. Now spread the outside of the sandwich thinly with butter and saute quickly in a very hot, heavy fry pan, turning once to brown each side.

■ *The Old Homesteader*

Sourdough Whole-Wheat Bread— Plus

If you already have an active sourdough pot, you may want to use your own starter in the following recipe. If not, use the recommended Sourdough Whole-Wheat Starter, which you will find with other starter recipes at the beginning of the chapter. Notice that the directions below call for two "sponge settings" — one, the usual overnight period; the other for a brief time the next morning before all the flour has been added. This method was developed by the cook to produce whole-wheat bread that is quicker to rise than others that depend on sourdough leavening.

Sourdough Whole-Wheat Sponge
►The night before you plan to bake bread, combine:

*1 cup (240 mL) Sourdough Whole-Wheat Starter
2 cups (480 mL) warm water
2-1/2 cups (600 mL) whole-wheat flour
1 tablespoon (15 mL) honey*

►Let the mixture stand overnight in a warm place. The next morning, remove 1 cup (240 mL) of the sponge to return to your sourdough crock to store for another day's baking. The rest, use as directed below.

Sourdough Whole-Wheat Bread — Plus
*1 tablespoon (15 mL) active dry yeast dissolved
   in 1/4 cup (60 mL) warm water*

*1/4 cup (60 mL) evaporated milk
1/4 cup (60 mL) water
1/4 cup (60 mL) honey
Sourdough Whole-Wheat Sponge
1/4 cup (60 mL) oil
1 cup (240 mL) whole-wheat flour*

►Heat milk, water and honey in a small saucepan until the mixture is warm and blended. Then combine this mixture with the dissolved yeast and the Sourdough Whole-Wheat Sponge. Add oil and flour and beat with a wooden spoon until bubbles form. Let this mixture rise in a warming oven for 45 minutes. Then add to it:

*2 teaspoons (10 mL) salt
3-1/2 cups (840 mL) whole-wheat flour*

►Mix well. Turn the dough onto a floured board and knead for five minutes. Return dough to a greased bowl and let rise, covered, for one hour. Punch down and let rise again for 30 minutes. Divide the dough in half and shape into two loaves. When loaves have doubled in size, bake for 50 minutes in an oven preheated to 350°F (175°C).

■ *Diana Scesny Greene, author*
   Sunrise — A Breakfast Cookbook
   Using Natural Foods and Whole Grains
   (recipe adapted from ALASKA® magazine)

Sourdough Rye Bread
*Department Champion —
1975 Southeast Alaska State Fair*

►Combine the following ingredients and beat until smooth:

*1-1/2 cups (360 mL) warm water
1 cup (240 mL) sourdough sponge
1/2 cup (120 mL) molasses
2 teaspoons (10 mL) salt
2 packages yeast
1 to 2 tablespoons (15 to 30 mL) caraway seeds
2 cups (480 mL) rye flour
2 cups (480 mL) whole-wheat flour*

►Let rise until doubled and bubbly. Sift together 1 cup (240 mL) white flour and 1/2 teaspoon (2 mL) soda. Add to first mixture. Knead until elastic. Shape into two round loaves or put in greased shortening cans. For special hors d'oeuvres, use greased juice cans; fill one-half full. Let rise until almost doubled. Bake at 400°F (205°C) for 20 to 25 minutes. Large loaves may require 10 to 15 minutes longer and covering with a foil "tent" to prevent further browning.

■ *Gayle Oram*
   Haines Homemakers' Cookbook

Whale Oil Sourdough Bread

2 cups (480 mL) thick sourdough sponge
1/4 cup (60 mL) whale oil
2/3 cup (160 mL) powdered milk
1 cup (240 mL) warm water
1 tablespoon (15 mL) salt
1/4 cup (60 mL) sugar
1 teaspoon (5 mL) soda
2 teaspoons (10 mL) sugar

►Mix first six ingredients together; then add soda mixed with sugar. Slowly stir in enough flour to make a stiff dough. Knead lightly and put into oiled pan to rise. Form into loaves and rolls and let rise again. Bake at 375°F (190°C) until brown and crusty.
■ Helen Fisher
    An Alaskan Cookbook, Kenai

Sourdough Dark Rye Bread and Onion Rye Dinner Rolls

This excellent First Place winner makes either four loaves of bread and a pan of dinner rolls or five loaves of bread. Caraway seeds are added while the dough is being prepared, and could be added in smaller quantity to only a portion of the dough if you wish. Onions are added to the rolls when loaves and rolls are being shaped, but could also be added to loaves, of course. Adjust the amount of onion you prepare accordingly.

1 cup (240 mL) sourdough starter
2 cups (480 mL) warm water — 100 to 110°F
    (38 to 43°C)
2-1/2 cups (600 mL) white flour
4 cups (1 L) white flour
5 teaspoons or 2 packets (25 mL) dry yeast
3 cups (720 mL) hot water — 120 to 130°F
    (49 to 54°C)
3/4 cup (180 mL) molasses
4 cups (1 L) rye flour
5 teaspoons (25 mL) salt
1 box (1-3/4 oz /or/ 50 g) caraway seeds
1/4 cup (60 mL) oil
4 cups (1 L) white flour
2-1/2 ounces (70 g) chopped onion

►The day before making bread and rolls, set the sponge by mixing the first three ingredients — the sourdough starter, warm water and 2-1/2 cups (600 mL) white flour. The next day, set aside one cup (240 mL) of sourdough for future batches and use the remaining, about 3-1/2 cups (840 mL), for this recipe.

Mix the next 4 cups (1 L) white flour and dry yeast. Set aside. Heat mixing bowl by rinsing with hot water. Add molasses, 3 cups (720 mL) hot water and the white flour and yeast mixture. Mix with beater on low speed for one minute. Scrape down sides of bowl. Add the 3-1/2 cups (720 mL) of sourdough sponge. Mix on medium speed 1 to 1-1/2 minutes.

Mix the 4 cups (1 L) rye flour and salt. Add all at once to the above mixture. Then add caraway seeds and oil. Mix on low. As soon as flour mixture is wet enough, mix on medium for three minutes.

Reduce speed to low and add, a spoonful at a time, 3 cups (720 mL) of the 4 remaining cups (1 L) white flour. When dough is stiff enough, place any remaining flour on breadboard and knead the dough 10 minutes, adding in as much of the flour as it will take to make a stiff dough. Put dough in greased bowl. Place bowl in a cold oven with a pan of boiling-hot water under it until dough doubles in size — about 60 to 70 minutes. Punch down dough, fold over and let rest for another 30 minutes.

Weigh dough and divide into five portions of 1 pound, 6 ounces (630 g) each. Reserve one-fifth for rolls, if desired. The remaining mounds may be formed into round loaves or placed in 9 x 5-inch (22 x 12 cm) loaf pans. Cover with plastic wrap.

Note: Chopped onion may also be added to loaves. Roll out dough into rectangles, sprinkle onion over all but an outside edge of about 1/2 inch (1.25 cm). Roll and form loaves as usual.

To form rolls — Roll out dough and spread onions over half. Fold dough over and let rest 10 to 15 minutes. Shape rolls as desired and place in a round 8-inch (20 cm) cake pan.

Let rolls and bread rise until double — about 50 to 60 minutes if placed in a cold oven with boiling-hot water beneath them. Remove from oven about 15 minutes before ready for baking and preheat oven to 350°F (175°C). Again, place a pan of boiling-hot water on the lowest oven rack to provide steam. Brush top of bread very lightly with warm water and make three slashes in the loaves with a sharp knife. Bake 40 to 50 minutes or until nicely browned. Cool on wire racks — about two hours for loaves. When completely cool, wrap in plastic wrap and freeze. Next day, remove bread and put in freezer bags. Seal and return to freezer.
■ Max LeLande
    Prize-Winning Baked Goods
    Anchorage Fur Rendezvous, 1982

Sourdough Pumpernickel

2 cups (480 mL) sourdough sponge
2 packages yeast
1/4 cup (60 mL) warm water
1/2 cup (120 mL) molasses
2 tablespoons (30 mL) oil
1 teaspoon (5 mL) salt
2/3 cup (160 mL) corn meal in a 1-cup (240 mL)
    measure; fill with boiling water

4 cups (1 L) rye flour
1 cup (240 mL) whole-wheat flour

►Dissolve yeast in warm water; mix into sourdough with molasses, oil, salt and corn meal (semi-solid consistency). Work in rye and whole-wheat flour. Add extra if necessary. Place dough in well-greased bowl. Cover with damp cloth and let stand for three hours. Poke down. Knead two times. Form in loaf. Keep warm until double in bulk. Bake in 350°F (175°C) oven for 1-1/2 hours. Remove from pan. Rub with melted butter. Return to oven for 20 minutes — making tender crust.

■ *Ruth Allman, Juneau*
   Alaska Sourdough

Pauk

This Swiss recipe makes fine use of sourdough bread (or any bread) that is no longer fresh enough to serve plain.

16 slices stale bread
6 eggs, beaten
1-1/2 to 2 cups (360 to 480 mL) milk
1 teaspoon (5 mL) salt
Butter
Maple syrup

►Cut stale bread into squares, leaving crusts on. Beat eggs to make a rich egg batter. Thin down with milk. Add salt. Pour over bread and toss as you would a salad. Fry until golden brown in butter or bacon fat. Serve with butter and pitchers of syrup. Serves eight. Can be kept warm for late breakfasters.

■ *Mamie Jensen, Juneau*

Basic Sourdough Dinner Rolls

►Early in the morning mix:

1 cup (240 mL) sourdough starter
1 cup (240 mL) warm milk
1-1/2 cups (360 mL) flour

►Mix together until all lumps are gone. Cover and set in warm place to rise. One and one-half hours before dinner stir dough down. Combine in a small bowl:

1 tablespoon (15 mL) sugar
1 teaspoon (5 mL) salt
1 teaspoon (5 mL) baking powder
1/2 teaspoon (2 mL) baking soda
Flour
Oil or bacon drippings

►Be sure all lumps are out of this mixture. Sprinkle over dough and stir in gently. Turn dough onto

board which has a cup of flour on it. Knead lightly until all the flour is used up. Use more flour if dough does not feel right. Shape into rolls, dipping each one in warm oil or bacon drippings. Place in a warm pan and let rise until double in bulk or about 45 minutes. Bake at 350°F (175°C) about 30 minutes or until golden brown. Serve at once.

■ *Ouida Johnson*
   "More Sourdough Recipes"
   ALASKA® magazine, March 1970

Variation: Before blending the flour into the first mixture, add to it 1 scant teaspoon (4 mL) dried minced onion or wild chives, 1/2 teaspoon (2 mL) wild sage or dried thyme and 1 teaspoon (5 mL) dried parsley flakes. Blend in herbed flour and one beaten egg. Continue as directed, mixing well until lumps are gone.

Jim and Jinnie's Super Sourdough Bread

1 cup (240 mL) sourdough starter
5 cups (1.2 L) warm water
5 cups (1.25 L) whole-wheat flour

►Combine starter, water and flour. Let grow for at least 12 hours. Blend in approximately:

2 tablespoons (30 mL) yeast softened in
   1/2 cup (120 mL) warm water
1 cup (240 mL) honey
1 cup (240 mL) dry milk
1/2 cup (120 mL) peanut oil
2 tablespoons (30 mL) salt
2 to 3 tablespoons (30 to 45 mL) brewer's yeast
1 cup (240 mL) soy flour
1/2 cup (120 mL) millet
1 cup (240 mL) wheat germ
1/2 cup (120 mL) 4-grain or 7-grain cereal
1/2 cup (120 mL) corn meal

►Add flour to the above combination. We use half whole-wheat and half unbleached white flour. Add enough to make the dough "kneadable." Turn onto board and knead about 10 minutes, adding flour if necessary. Place in oiled bowl and let rise until doubled in bulk. Punch down and let rise again. Turn onto board and cut into four parts. Knead each part a few times and shape into loaves or rolls. Bake at 350°F (175°C) for about 45 minutes. Remove from pans and brush tops with melted butter. Makes four loaves, one or two of which will be gone in about 10 minutes. Also, sometimes we add other ingredients like rolled oats, sunflower seeds, nuts, and so on.

■ *Jinnie Thompson*
   Goldrush Cookbook, *Valdez*

Sourdough-Yeast Refrigerator Rolls

1 cup (240 mL) sourdough starter
1 cup (240 mL) warm water
1 cup (240 mL) flour
2 packages dry yeast
1/3 cup (80 mL) warm water
1/2 cup (120 mL) oil
3 eggs, beaten
3/4 cup (180 mL) warm water
1/2 cup (120 mL) sugar
2 teaspoons (10 mL) salt
4-1/2 to 5-1/2 cups (1 to 1.3 L) flour
Melted butter

►Mix starter with 1 cup (240 mL) flour and 1 cup (240 mL) warm water and let stand overnight. Remove 1 cup (240 mL) for reserve starter. Soften yeast in 1/3 cup (80 mL) warm water; set aside. In large bowl combine remaining starter, oil, eggs, 3/4 cup (180 mL) warm water, sugar and salt. Stir in the softened yeast and enough flour to form a ball. Cover with a cloth and set in warm place until doubled. Punch down, cover with plastic wrap and refrigerate overnight. Three hours before baking, form dough into rolls, brush with melted butter, put in greased muffin pans. Cover and let rise two to three hours. Bake at 400°F (205°C) for 12 to 15 minutes. Makes two to three dozen.

■ Mary Dunkelburg
   Bake-Off Cookbook 1961-1980
   Tanana Valley Fair, Fairbanks

Variation: Berry Rolls — When you remove dough from the refrigerator, turn it onto a lightly floured board and divide it into about two dozen pieces. Roll each of these with the palms of your hands (as you would clay) until they form long, pencil-thin rolls. Shape on greased baking sheet by holding one end of piece firmly in place and winding around loosely to form a coil; tuck end under well. Place 2 inches (5 cm) apart and cover with tea towel. Let rise as directed above until doubled in size. Make an indentation at the center of each roll, pressing fingers clear to the bottom. Fill indentation with a wild berry sauce or jam. Bake as directed; cool for 30 minutes on wire racks. Drizzle with a glaze of powdered sugar, milk and vanilla. [The Old Homesteader]

Cinnamon Coffee Bread

2 cups (480 mL) sourdough starter
4 cups (1 L) sifted flour
1 teaspoon (5 mL) salt
2 tablespoons (30 mL) sugar
2 tablespoons (30 mL) melted fat or
   vegetable shortening
1/4 teaspoon (1 mL) soda added during
   second kneading
1 cup (240 mL) raisins
Butter, cinnamon and sugar for filling

►Sift dry ingredients into a bowl and make a well in the center. Add fat to the starter and mix well. Pour this into the well in the dry ingredients. Add enough flour to make a soft dough and knead on a floured board for 15 minutes. Grease a bowl and place kneaded dough into it. Cover with a towel. Allow to rise until doubled. This is usually from two to four hours in a warm place.

Dissolve the 1/4 teaspoon (1 mL) soda in a tablespoon (15 mL) warm water and knead it into the dough. Knead in raisins. Divide the dough in half and roll each half into a rectangle about 12 x 15 inches (30 x 38 cm). Spread generously with softened butter, sprinkle with cinnamon and about 3/4 cup (180 mL) sugar. Roll up tightly and put in a warm place to rise. When the two loaves have doubled in size, bake at 375°F (190°C) for 50 to 60 minutes.

■ Clarence Massey
   "... More Sourdough"
   ALASKA® magazine, October 1969

Frosted Cinnamon Rolls or Butterscotch Pecan Rolls

2 cups (480 mL) sourdough starter
1 cup (240 mL) lukewarm milk
3 cups (720 mL) all-purpose flour, added in
   3 portions
2 eggs
1/4 cup (60 mL) oil
1/2 cup (120 mL) sugar
1 teaspoon (5 mL) salt
1/2 teaspoon (2 mL) baking soda

Filling:
Melted butter, brown sugar, cinnamon, raisins
   and chopped nuts, as desired

Frosting:
1 cup (240 mL) sifted powdered sugar
2 tablespoons (30 mL) milk
1/2 teaspoon (2 mL) vanilla

►Mix together sourdough starter, milk and 2 cups (480 mL) of the flour. Beat until smooth. Add eggs and oil and beat again thoroughly. In a small bowl, blend another 1/2 cup (120 mL) of the flour and the soda and salt. Sprinkle this mixture over dough and stir gently. Turn dough out onto the remaining 1/2 cup (120 mL) flour on a breadboard. Knead lightly, working in most of the flour. This is a very soft dough. Put dough in a well-greased bowl and turn once to grease both sides. Cover with waxed paper and set in a warm place to rise until double in bulk. Turn dough onto board dusted with an additional 1/2 cup (120 mL) flour. Cut in half. Roll half the dough out to a rectangle 1/4 inch (0.6 cm) thick. Brush with melted butter. Sprinkle with brown sugar and cinnamon, as desired, and then with raisins and chopped nuts. Roll up jelly-roll fashion and cut into 1-inch (2.5 cm) lengths. Place in a warm, well-buttered pan, cut side down. Pan should be at least 2-1/2 inches (6 cm) deep. Cover and set in a warm place to rise until double in bulk. Bake at 375°F (190°C) 40 minutes, or until rolls are golden brown and shrink slightly from the sides of the pan. Turn rolls out of pan at once. Turn right side up. Blend frosting ingredients and drizzle over the rolls while they are still warm.

Butterscotch Pecan Rolls
►Prepare rolls the same way, but put each cut piece in a muffin-cup which is well buttered and contains 1 teaspoon (5 mL) brown sugar and two pecan halves. Bake the same as cinnamon rolls. Turn out at once and leave upside down.
■ *Ouida Johnson*
 "More Sourdough Recipes"
 ALASKA® *magazine, March 1970*

Sugared Doughnuts

2 cups (480 mL) sourdough starter
1 cup (240 mL) lukewarm milk
3 to 3-1/2 cups (720-840 mL) flour, added in
 3 portions
2 eggs
1/4 cup (60 mL) oil
1/4 cup (60 mL) sugar
1 teaspoon (5 mL) salt
1/2 teaspoon (2 mL) soda

►Mix together sourdough starter, lukewarm milk and 1-1/2 cups (360 mL) of the flour. Beat until smooth. Add eggs and oil and beat again well. In a separate small bowl blend sugar, salt, soda and another 1/2 cup (120 mL) of the flour. Add this mixture to the dough and blend well. Sprinkle a breadboard with 1 cup (240 mL) flour and turn dough onto it. Knead lightly, working in most of the flour. The dough will be very soft. Place it in a well-greased bowl and turn once to grease top. Cover with waxed paper and set in warm place to rise until double in bulk. When double in bulk, turn out onto 1/2 cup (120 mL) flour sprinkled on the breadboard. Pat or roll out to 1/2 inch (1.25 cm) thick. Cut with a doughnut cutter. Place cut doughnuts on a well-floured board or cookie sheets, about 1 inch (2.5 cm) apart. Do not cover. Let rise until double in size. Fry in hot grease and put only three or four doughnuts in at one time so the fat won't cool down. Fry the raised side (top side) first, turning only once. When golden brown on both sides, drain on paper towels or brown paper. While doughnuts are still warm, shake them in a bag with granulated sugar to coat them. Makes about four dozen.
■ *Ouida Johnson*
 "More Sourdough Recipes"
 ALASKA® *magazine, March 1970*

Blueberry Sourdough Bread

1 cup (240 mL) sugar
1/2 cup (120 mL) margarine
2 eggs, slightly beaten
1 cup (240 mL) sourdough starter
1-1/2 cups (360 mL) all-purpose flour
1/2 teaspoon (2 mL) salt
1 teaspoon (5 mL) baking soda
3 tablespoons (45 mL) milk
1 cup (240 mL) mashed bananas
1/2 teaspoon (2 mL) vanilla
3/4 cup (180 mL) chopped walnuts
3/4 cup (180 mL) blueberries

►Cream sugar and margarine together; beat in eggs and add starter. Mix flour with salt and baking soda and add to sourdough mixture. Combine milk, bananas and vanilla; mix thoroughly and add to first mixture. Beat well after each addition; add nuts. Fold in blueberries carefully so as not to crush them. Pour batter in a well-greased loaf pan and bake at 350°F (175°C) for one hour or until well done. Cool in pan on rack for 10 minutes before removing from pan.
■ *The Old Homesteader*

Whole-Wheat Spice Doughnuts

3 tablespoons (45 mL) margarine
2/3 cup (160 mL) brown sugar
1 egg, beaten
2 tablespoons (30 mL) powdered orange peel
1 teaspoon (5 mL) nutmeg
2 cups (480 mL) sourdough starter
3 cups (720 mL) whole-wheat flour

►Cream margarine and brown sugar and add egg, powdered orange peel and nutmeg. Beat in sourdough starter and whole-wheat flour. Place in a large greased, nonmetal bowl and brush the top of the dough with salad oil. Cover with a cloth and let rise in a warm place until doubled in bulk. Punch down and roll out on a lightly floured board to a 1/2-inch (1.25 cm) thickness. (Do not flour or handle any more than necessary.) Cut with a doughnut cutter and deep-fry.
■ *Gretchen Walker*
 "Sourdough Cookery — Life in A Crock Pot"
 ALASKA® *magazine, June 1978*

Sourdough English Muffins

First Prize winner —
1975 Southeast Alaska State Fair

1 package dry yeast
1 teaspoon (5 mL) sugar
1/4 cup (60 mL) warm water
1/2 cup (120 mL) scalded milk
1 cup (240 mL) water
1/2 cup (120 mL) sourdough starter
1/4 teaspoon (1 mL) soda
1 rounded teaspoon (6 mL) salt
4 cups (1 L) sifted flour
3 tablespoons (45 mL) melted shortening

►Sprinkle yeast and sugar over 1/4 cup (60 mL) warm water. Cool milk to lukewarm; add water, sourdough starter, soda, salt and yeast which has been allowed to get bubbly. Add half the flour and beat well with either electric beater or wooden spoon. Let rise to double in bulk. Add melted shortening and remaining flour. Beat and knead thoroughly. Let rise until double in bulk. Place on board dusted slightly with corn meal and flour. Flatten with rolling pin to 3/4-inch (2 cm) thickness. Let stand until light. Cut with a 2-1/2-inch (6.5 cm) diameter cutter. (A can with both ends cut out works well.) Bake 15 minutes on a hot, buttered griddle — about 340°F (172°C) in an electric skillet — turning several times during cooking. When ready to serve, split in half, toast and serve hot with butter and jam. Yields 12 muffins.

■ *Mimi Gregg*
Haines' Homemakers Cookbook

SOURDOUGH "QUICK" BREADS

Sourdough is never a "quick" bread in the same way other doughs can be, but because most of the following recipes for biscuits, dumplings, muffins and corn bread include baking powder, the rising time required is less than for plain sourdough or sourdough combined with another yeast.

Note: Several of the recipes list special ingredients to be added to the sourdough starter when you set the sponge the night before baking. And often all of this sponge is used in the recipe. That means the reserve starter for your sourdough pot should be "fed" separately.

Doughboys

A "breakfast-on-the-trail" treat kids appreciate for any meal of the day

►The night before (or six to eight hours before) you plan to make doughboys, be sure to set the sponge* for your favorite sourdough biscuit recipe. Next morning (if doughboys are for breakfast), when the campfire is getting started, send the troops out to gather up a dozen or so long sticks of non-resinous wood, such as willow or alder. The toasting end of the stick needs to be about an inch thick (2.5 cm) and should be peeled. Meanwhile, make up biscuit dough and roll it out a bit more than 1/4 inch (about 1 cm) thick. Cut rounds about 2-1/2 inches (5 to 6 cm) in diameter. Fold doughboys around the peeled ends of the sticks, pressing edges together firmly to make a good seal. Let rise in a warm place 20 to 30 minutes, and then toast over hot coals, turning the sticks to brown the dough evenly. Remove doughboys from the sticks and fill the center of each with wild berry jam or jelly. Peanut butter, chocolate squares and grated cheese are also good fillings in varying combinations, but not all at once.

■ *The editors, ALASKA® magazine*

Pinched for time — or sourdough — any soft biscuit dough or raised, plain bread dough will work.

Sourdough Honey Biscuits

1 cup (240 mL) sourdough starter
1 cup (240 mL) milk
2-1/2 cups (600 mL) flour
3 tablespoons (45 mL) cooking oil
1/2 teaspoon (2 mL) salt
1/2 teaspoon (2 mL) baking soda
1 teaspoon (5 mL) baking powder
3 tablespoons (45 mL) honey
2-1/2 cups (600 mL) more flour

►Mix starter, milk, and 2-1/2 cups (600 mL) flour in a bowl the night before. Cover and let stand overnight. The next day, add remaining ingredients and mix well. Knead about three minutes. Add more flour if dough is too sticky to handle. Roll out dough about 1/2 inch (1.25 cm) thick and cut into 2-inch (5 cm) biscuits. Place on a greased baking sheet and let rise one hour. Brush with melted butter and bake in 375°F (190°C) oven for 35 minutes or until light brown. Bake early and reheat to serve. Makes about 16 biscuits. Serve the biscuits with butter, honey and wild berry jam.

■ *Deane Feetham*
"An Alaskan Dinner Party"
ALASKA® magazine, June 1971

Basic Sourdough Biscuits

►Set the sponge by mixing the following ingredients in a large bowl, cover it loosely with a foil or waxed paper lid and allow the mixture to work overnight in a warm place:

1/2 cup (120 mL) sourdough starter
1 cup (240 mL) lukewarm water
1 cup (240 mL) all-purpose flour

►When you are ready to bake, assemble these ingredients:

1-1/2 cups (360 mL) all-purpose flour, to be
  added in two portions
3/4 teaspoon (3 mL) salt
1 tablespoon (15 mL) sugar
1 teaspoon (5 mL) baking powder
1/2 teaspoon (2 mL) baking soda
1 tablespoon (15 mL) cooking oil
1 tablespoon (15 mL) margarine, melted
2 tablespoons (30 mL) corn meal (optional)

►Beat 1 cup (240 mL) of the flour into the sponge which has been working overnight (or at least six to eight hours). In a small bowl combine the remaining 1/2 cup (120 mL) flour with the salt, sugar, baking powder and soda and sprinkle this mixture over the dough. Blend quickly with a fork. Turn dough onto floured board and knead lightly about 10 times or until it is springy. Roll out to 1/2-inch (1.25 cm) thickness. Cut with a biscuit cutter (a can with both ends cut out makes a good one) and dip in a mixture of oil and margarine. If you wish, sprinkle half the optional corn meal in bottom of baking pans and the rest on top of the biscuits. Place biscuits in pan close together. Cover with a clean cloth and set in a warm, draft-free place to rise until doubled in bulk — 30 to 40 minutes. Bake at 375°F (190°C) until golden brown, about 25 minutes. Makes a baker's dozen good-sized biscuits.
■ *The Old Homesteader*

Sourdough Dumplings

►In the morning mix:

1/2 cup (120 mL) sourdough starter
1/2 cup (120 mL) warm milk
1/2 cup (120 mL) flour

►Cover and set in warm place to rise. Forty-five minutes or so before you wish to serve the dumplings, add to the above batter:

1 egg
1 tablespoon (15 mL) oil

►Beat vigorously. Blend together until all the lumps are gone:

3/4 cup (180 mL) flour
1/2 teaspoon (2 mL) salt
1/2 teaspoon (2 mL) baking powder
1/4 teaspoon (1 mL) baking soda

►Add to batter and beat well. Cover and set in warm place to rise for about 30 minutes. Drop by tablespoonfuls into hot stew or soup. Cover pot tightly and cook for 12 minutes. Serve at once.
■ *Ouida Johnson, "More Sourdough Recipes"*
ALASKA® *magazine, March 1970*

Sourdough Corn Bread

1-1/2 cups (360 mL) corn meal
1-1/2 tablespoons (23 mL) sugar
1-1/2 teaspoons (7 mL) salt
1-1/2 cups (360 mL) milk, scalded and cooled
  to lukewarm
1-1/2 cups (360 mL) sourdough starter
1-1/2 teaspoons (7 mL) cream of tartar
1-1/2 teaspoons (7 mL) baking soda
2 eggs
6 tablespoons (90 mL) soft margarine

►Combine corn meal, sugar, salt and milk. Add remaining ingredients and mix well. Pour into a well-greased square baking pan and bake at 425°F (220°C) for 40 minutes.
■ *Ruth Parsons*
An Alaskan Cook Book, *Kenai*

Sourdough Cinnamon Biscuits

1-1/4 cups (300 mL) all-purpose flour
2 teaspoons (10 mL) baking powder
1/2 teaspoon (2 mL) salt
1/4 teaspoon (1 mL) baking soda
1-1/2 tablespoons (23 mL) sugar
1/4 cup (60 mL) vegetable shortening
1/2 cup (120 mL) finely chopped walnuts
  or pecans
1 egg, beaten slightly
1 cup (240 mL) sourdough starter
2 tablespoons (30 mL) additional sugar
1/2 teaspoon (2 mL) cinnamon

►Mix together well the first five ingredients. With a pastry blender or a couple of knives, cut in the shortening until the mixture is crumbly. Stir in nuts. Add beaten egg to sourdough and add all at once to first mixture, stirring with a fork. Drop by small spoonfuls onto greased cookie sheet. Combine sugar and cinnamon and sprinkle over tops of biscuits. Bake at 425°F (220°C) for 10 to 12 minutes or until a deep golden brown.
■ *The Old Homesteader*

Basic Sourdough Muffins

2 cups (480 mL) sourdough starter
1-1/2 cups (360 mL) whole-wheat flour
1 teaspoon (5 mL) salt
1 teaspoon (5 mL) soda
1/2 cup (120 mL) melted bacon drippings or oil
2 eggs
1/2 cup (120 mL) sugar

►Sift the dry ingredients into a bowl. Mix fat and eggs with the starter. Make a well in the center of the dry ingredients and add the mixed starter. Stir just enough to moisten all the flour. Grease the muffin tins and fill about three-fourths full. Bake at 375°F (190°C) for 30 minutes. Raisins or chopped nuts or wheat germ may be added to the batter if desired. Makes 12 or more large muffins.
■ *Clarence Massey*
   ". . . More Sourdough"
   ALASKA® magazine, October 1969

Sourdough Granola Muffins

1 cup (240 mL) sourdough starter
1/2 cup (120 mL) milk
1 egg
1/4 cup (60 mL) cooking oil
1/2 cup (120 mL) honey
1 cup (240 mL) applesauce
1/2 teaspoon (2 mL) salt
1-1/2 cups (360 mL) whole-wheat flour
1 cup (240 mL) granola cereal
1 teaspoon (5 mL) baking powder

►Measure sourdough into large bowl and add the next five ingredients. Mix well. Add dry ingredients and fold in the granola. Stir just enough to moisten well. Fill paper-lined muffin cups two-thirds full. Bake at 400°F (205°C) for 15 to 20 minutes or until well done. A good variation: Dredge 3/4 cup (180 mL) wild blueberries with flour and fold in with granola.
■ *Anon.*

Sourdough Corn Muffins

1 cup (240 mL) all-purpose flour
1 cup (240 mL) yellow corn meal
2 teaspoons (10 mL) baking powder
1/4 teaspoon (1 mL) baking soda
1 teaspoon (5 mL) salt
1 teaspoon (5 mL) sugar
1/2 cup (120 mL) sourdough starter
1 egg, slightly beaten
1/4 cup (60 mL) vegetable oil
1 cup (240 mL) milk

►Mix dry ingredients together and make a well in center. In another bowl, mix starter, egg, oil and milk. Add all at one time to dry ingredients; mix lightly. Grease muffin tins or line with paper muffin cups and fill two-thirds full of batter. Bake in a 400°F (205°C) oven for 15 to 20 minutes. For crustier muffins use more muffin tins and don't fill them so full.
■ *The Old Homesteader*

Oatmeal Muffins

1 cup (240 mL) rolled oats
1 cup (240 mL) milk
1 cup (240 mL) all-purpose flour
1-1/2 teaspoons (7 mL) baking powder
1/8 teaspoon (0.5 mL) baking soda
1/2 teaspoon (2 mL) salt
1/2 cup (120 mL) brown sugar, packed
1/3 cup (80 mL) vegetable oil
1/2 cup (120 mL) sourdough starter
1 egg, slightly beaten
1/2 cup (120 mL) seedless raisins (optional)

►Allow oats to soak in milk for an hour or more. Mix together flour, baking powder, soda, salt and brown sugar in a large mixing bowl. Make a well in center. Now mix together oil, starter, egg and raisins and combine with oats. Add to dry ingredients all at one time and mix until just moistened well. Grease muffin pans or line with paper cups and fill to about two-thirds full. Bake at 400°F (205°C) for 20 to 30 minutes or until a deep golden brown. Serve hot with butter and plenty of honey.
■ *The Old Homesteader*

Super Sourdough Berry Muffins

1-1/2 cups (360 mL) all-purpose flour
1/4 cup (60 mL) sugar
2 teaspoons (10 mL) baking powder
1/2 teaspoon (2 mL) salt
1/2 cup (120 mL) sourdough starter
3/4 cup (180 mL) milk
1/3 cup (80 mL) vegetable oil
1 egg, well beaten
1/2 cup (120 mL) mashed bananas
3/4 cup (180 mL) wild blueberries

►Measure flour into large mixing bowl, reserving a little to dredge the berries. Add sugar, baking powder and salt. In a separate bowl combine sourdough starter, milk, oil, egg and mashed bananas. Add this mixture to the dry mixture all at one time, stirring just until all is moistened. Fold in berries that have been cleaned and dredged with flour. Grease muffin tins or line with paper muffin cups and fill two-thirds full. Bake at 400°F (205°C) 20 to 25 minutes or until a light golden brown.
■ *The Old Homesteader*

Variations:

- *Cranberry-Nut Muffins* — Substitute 3/4 cup (180 mL) orange juice for the milk. Substitute 3/4 cup Wholeberry Cranberry Sauce for the blueberries. Substitute 1/2 cup (120 mL) chopped walnuts for the mashed bananas. *Add* 1 tablespoon (15 mL) grated orange peel. Follow directions in main recipe, folding in cranberry sauce, walnuts and orange peel just before filling muffin cups. (Omit dredging.)

- *Date-Nut Muffins* — Increase sugar to 1/2 cup (120 mL). Increase milk to 1 cup (240 mL). Substitute 1 cup (240 mL) finely chopped dates for the blueberries. Substitute 1/2 cup (120 mL) chopped walnuts or pecans for the mashed bananas. (Omit dredging.)

SOURDOUGH CAKES — COOKIES — OTHER DESSERTS

When Duncan Hines and his relatives packaged up cakes that are quick to prepare, good to eat and relatively cheap, they did us a favor of the same magnitude as the invention of no-iron clothes.

However, if you yearn to duplicate the surprise and pleasure experienced by that legendary baker who accidentally whomped up the very first cake . . . try making one from sourdough.

It's a wholly new and wonderful treat, not just in taste — though sweetened sourdough provides moistness and rich flavor — but even better is the fun of putting together docile elements that suddenly leap to a life of their own.

Unless they tell you otherwise, the following recipes presume you are familiar with all the terms of the sourdough trade. If you are not, please read about preparing sourdough at the beginning of this chapter.

If you do not already have a sourdough pot going, start one. Meanwhile, try Fast Start Sourdough Cake. It comes complete with a recipe for starter which is ready for use in 30 minutes.

The "other desserts" include pudding, cobbler, Baked Alaska and even Sourdough Pie Crust.

Note: Recipes for most of the icings and glazes suggested for these sourdough cakes are to be found in the next chapter, beginning page 413.

Sourdough Chocolate Cake #1

►Two or three hours in advance of baking, combine:

1/2 cup (120 mL) thick sourdough starter
1/4 cup (60 mL) nonfat dry milk

1-1/2 cups (360 mL) flour
1 cup (240 mL) water

►Mix well and allow to ferment two to three hours. Then proceed with recipe.

1/2 cup (120 mL) shortening
1 cup (240 mL) sugar
1/2 teaspoon (2 mL) salt
1-1/2 teaspoons (7 mL) baking soda
1 teaspoon (5 mL) vanilla
1 teaspoon (5 mL) cinnamon
2 eggs
3 squares melted chocolate

►Cream shortening, sugar, salt, soda and flavorings. Add the eggs one at a time and beat well. Add slightly cooled melted chocolate and creamed mixture to the sourdough mixture. Mix at low speed until well blended. Pour into two well-greased round 8-inch (20 cm) pans or a 9 x 13-inch (22 x 32 cm) pan and bake at 350°F (175°C) for 30 or 40 minutes. Add frosting if you must, but I prefer mine plain.

■ *Clarence Massey*
"*. . . More Sourdough*"
ALASKA® *magazine, October 1969*

If you're ever out camping and use milk out of a can, then wonder how to keep it from spilling between uses, the holes can be sealed effectively by smearing butter over the openings.

■ *R. McCauley, Whitehorse, Yukon Territory*
The Cabin Friend
ALASKA® *magazine, September 1977*

Sourdough Chocolate Cake #2

2/3 cup (160 mL) shortening
1-2/3 cups (400 mL) sugar
3 eggs
1 cup (240 mL) sourdough starter
1-3/4 cups (420 mL) all-purpose flour
2/3 cup (160 mL) cocoa
1/2 teaspoon (2 mL) baking powder
1-1/2 teaspoons (7 mL) baking soda
1 teaspoon (5 mL) salt
3/4 cup (180 mL) water
1 teaspoon (5 mL) vanilla

►In a large mixing bowl, cream shortening and sugar. Add eggs, one at a time, beating well after each addition. Blend in starter. Sift dry ingredients together and add to shortening mixture alternately with water and vanilla, mixing at low speed. Pour into two greased and floured 9-inch (22 cm) layer pans. Bake at 350°F (175°C) about 35 minutes. Allow cakes to cool 10 minutes, then invert on cooling racks. Cool thoroughly and frost.
■ *Jacie Smith*
  Kitchen Magic, *Ketchikan*

Applesauce Cake
A rich, moist cake with good storage qualities (under lock and key, that is)

1/2 cup (120 mL) shortening
2 cups (480 mL) sugar
2 eggs
1-1/2 cups (360 mL) sourdough starter
1-1/2 cups (360 mL) applesauce
1 teaspoon (5 mL) cinnamon
1/2 teaspoon (2 mL) cloves
1/2 teaspoon (2 mL) allspice
1-1/2 teaspoons (7 mL) salt
1-1/2 teaspoons (7 mL) baking soda
2 tablespoons (30 mL) additional sugar
2 cups (480 mL) flour
1 cup (240 mL) raisins
1/2 cup (120 mL) chopped walnuts

►Cream together shortening and 2 cups (480 mL) sugar. Beat in eggs. Stir in sourdough starter, applesauce, cinnamon, cloves and allspice. In a separate bowl, blend salt, baking soda and the 2 tablespoons (30 mL) additional sugar until all the lumps are gone. Sprinkle this mixture over the cake batter and stir in gently. Add flour and stir until smooth. Add raisins and walnuts and stir well. Pour into two well-greased and lightly floured 9-inch (22 cm) round cake pans. Bake at 350°F (175°C) for 30 minutes or until cake springs back to touch. Cool 10 to 15 minutes before removing to racks.

The rounds may be drizzled, warm, with Lemon or Vanilla Glaze and used as coffeecakes. Or cool completely and ice as a layer cake. Cream Cheese Icing is excellent with this cake. If you wish, the cake may be baked in loaf pans and sliced like bread — no icing required to be delicious. Cool completely before wrapping and storing. Keeps longest under refrigeration.
■ *Ouida Johnson*
  "More Sourdough Recipes"
  ALASKA® magazine, March 1970

Sourdough Streusel Coffeecake

1/2 cup (120 mL) sourdough starter
3/4 cup (180 mL) sugar
1/4 cup (60 mL) vegetable shortening
1 egg
1/2 cup (120 mL) milk
1-1/4 cups (300 mL) sifted flour
1/2 teaspoon (2 mL) baking powder
1/2 teaspoon (2 mL) salt
Streusel

►Measure starter into a large mixing bowl. In another bowl, cream sugar, shortening and egg together. Add to sourdough starter together with milk, flour, baking powder and salt. Spread half the batter in a greased, 9-inch (22 cm) square pan. Sprinkle batter with half the streusel mixture. Pour in remaining batter and sprinkle top with the rest of the streusel mixture. Bake at 375°F (190°C) for 25 to 30 minutes or until well done and browned.

Streusel
1/2 cup (120 mL) brown sugar, firmly packed
2 tablespoons (30 mL) flour
1-1/2 teaspoons (7 mL) cinnamon
2 tablespoons (30 mL) margarine, melted
1/2 cup (120 mL) finely chopped pecans
  or walnuts

►Mix well. Sprinkle over coffeecake as directed.

Fast Start Sourdough Cake
A sourdough starter that requires only a 30-minute notice

Starter:
2/3 cup (160 mL) warm milk
1-1/2 teaspoons (7 mL) vinegar*
1 package active dry yeast
1 cup (240 mL) all-purpose flour
1/8 teaspoon (0.5 mL) salt

►(*Note: If you wish, omit the vinegar and let this sourdough starter "work" overnight.) In a small mixing bowl, combine milk and vinegar. Stir in yeast to dissolve. (Mixture will look curdled.) Stir in flour and salt to form a smooth batter. Cover and let stand in a warm place for 30 minutes. Stir well before mixing in other cake ingredients.

Cake:
1/2 cup (120 mL) butter or margarine
1-1/2 cups (360 mL) sugar
2 eggs
Sourdough starter
1-1/2 cups (360 mL) all-purpose flour
1 teaspoon (5 mL) baking soda
1 teaspoon (5 mL) salt
1-1/2 teaspoons (7 mL) instant coffee
1/2 cup (120 mL) milk
1/2 cup (120 mL) finely chopped walnuts

►In large mixing bowl, cream butter and sugar until light and fluffy. Add eggs and sourdough starter; beat well. Combine flour, soda, salt and instant coffee; add to creamed mixture alternately with the milk, and mix in at medium speed. Stir in walnuts. Pour batter into a well-greased, 10-inch (25 cm) tube or bundt pan. Bake at 350°F (175°C) for 50 to 55 minutes or until a toothpick inserted in center comes out clean. Cool 10 minutes; remove from pan. Drizzle with Coffee Glaze if desired. Sprinkle with additional walnuts. Serve warm or cold.
■ *Mary Mack*
    Saint Herman's Sisterhood Club, *Kodiak*

Carrot-Raisin Sourdough Cake

1 cup (240 mL) flour
1 teaspoon (5 mL) baking powder
1/2 teaspoon (2 mL) salt
1/2 teaspoon (2 mL) baking soda
1 teaspoon (5 mL) cinnamon
4 eggs, separated
1/2 cup (120 mL) light brown sugar,
    tightly packed
1/2 cup (120 mL) vegetable oil
1/2 cup (120 mL) sourdough starter
1 cup (240 mL) coarsely-grated carrots
1/2 cup (120 mL) seedless raisins
2 tablespoons (30 mL) grated lemon peel

►Combine dry ingredients and set aside. Beat egg whites in small bowl until soft peak forms. Set aside. In a large mixing bowl combine egg yolks, sugar, oil and starter. Mix in carrots, raisins and lemon peel. Blend in dry ingredients; then fold in beaten egg whites. Turn batter into well-greased and lightly floured 2-quart (2 L) ring mold. Bake at 350°F (175°C) for 30 minutes or until cake springs back immediately when tested with finger tip. Cool on rack for 10 to 15 minutes before turning out. Drizzle with Lemon Glaze while still warm.
■ *The editors, ALASKA® magazine*

Sourdough Gingerbread

1/4 cup (60 mL) margarine
1/2 cup (120 mL) sugar
1 egg, beaten slightly
1/2 cup (120 mL) dark molasses
1 cup (240 mL) sourdough starter
1 teaspoon (5 mL) cinnamon
1 teaspoon (5 mL) ginger
1/4 teaspoon (1 mL) cloves
1/4 teaspoon (1 mL) nutmeg
1/2 teaspoon (2 mL) salt
1/4 teaspoon (1 mL) baking soda
1/2 teaspoon (2 mL) baking powder
1 cup (240 mL) flour
1/2 cup (120 mL) milk

►Cream margarine and sugar together until fluffy; add egg and stir well. Add molasses, starter, spices, salt, baking soda and baking powder and mix. Add flour and milk alternately and beat well after each addition. Bake in a well-greased 9-inch (22 cm) square pan at 350°F (175°C) for 45 to 55 minutes or until bread springs back immediately when top is pressed with a finger tip.
■ *The Old Homesteader*

Alaska's Easter Sourdough Coffeecake
A Sourdough's version of Kulich

4 cups (1 L) sourdough starter
2/3 cup (160 mL) fireweed honey
1 teaspoon (5 mL) salt
1 envelope dry yeast, dissolved for 5 minutes in
    1/4 cup (60 mL) very warm water
3 cubes (340 g) butter
Flour, as directed below
1 cup (240 mL) halved, blanched almonds
1 teaspoon (5 mL) grated lemon peel
Green citron, to taste
6 eggs

►Blend first three ingredients — starter, honey, salt. Add dissolved yeast and mix well. Work in butter. Then add flour until dough is as thick as can be beaten with a wooden spoon. Add almonds, lemon peel and green citron, to taste. Work in the six eggs and again add enough flour that dough is soft but not sticky. Toss dough with a whipping motion of the hands, kneading to center of bowl. Put into a 9-inch (22 cm) square baking pan. Let the dough gently smooth itself into shape. Cover. Let rise to double in bulk or more. Top with melted butter and honey. Bake in a 425°F (220°C) oven until golden.
■ *Ruth Allman, Juneau*
    Alaska Sourdough

Carrot-Pineapple Sourdough Cake

1-1/2 cups (360 mL) vegetable oil
2 cups (480 mL) sugar
1 cup (240 mL) sourdough starter
3 eggs
1 small can crushed pineapple
2 cups (480 mL) carrots, grated
1/2 cup (120 mL) chopped walnuts
2 teaspoons (10 mL) vanilla
2-1/2 cups (600 mL) flour
2 teaspoons (10 mL) cinnamon
1/2 teaspoon (2 mL) salt
1 teaspoon (5 mL) baking soda
1/2 cup (120 mL) shredded coconut

►Mix oil and sugar; add starter and eggs, one at a time, beating after each addition. Fold in pineapple, carrots, nuts and vanilla. Sift dry ingredients together and stir into sourdough mixture. Fold in coconut last of all. Bake in greased and floured 9 x 13-inch (22 x 32 cm) cake pan at 350°F (175°C) for 45 minutes or until cake springs back immediately when tested with a finger tip. Frost with your favorite icing. Cream Cheese Icing is good with this.
■ *The Old Homesteader*

Sourdough Fruitcake
A scrumptious holiday treat that can — and should — be baked ahead

►A day or more before you plan to bake (about the time you "set the sponge" or a little earlier), prepare this fruit mixture as directed:

1-1/2 cups (360 mL) raisins
1-1/2 cups (360 mL) currants
3 cups (720 mL) mixed candied fruit and peels
1 cup (240 mL) hard cider

►Rinse, drain and coarsely chop the raisins; rinse and drain currants. Chop candied fruit and peels. Combine all fruits with hard cider and let stand overnight or longer. Next day, proceed with the recipe.

2/3 cup (160 mL) shortening
1 cup (240 mL) granulated sugar
1 cup (240 mL) brown sugar, packed
1-1/2 teaspoons (7 mL) cinnamon
1 teaspoon (5 mL) nutmeg
1/2 teaspoon (2 mL) allspice
2 eggs, well beaten
1 cup (240 mL) sourdough starter
1 cup (240 mL) sliced almonds
4 cups (1 L) sifted flour
1 teaspoon (5 mL) baking soda

2 teaspoons (10 mL) salt
Additional hard cider

►Cream shortening, sugars and spices together until fluffy; beat in eggs. Stir in sourdough sponge. Combine batter with fruit mixture and almonds. Sift flour, soda, salt together into batter and mix thoroughly. Turn into two loaf pans, 9 x 5-inch (22 x 12 cm), which have been lined with well-greased heavy brown paper. You may also make cupcakes from this batter using silicon-treated papers to line cupcake tins. Bake below oven center in very slow oven, 275°F (135°C), for about 2-1/2 hours or until firm to touch; about 40 minutes for cupcakes. Remove from pans; cool on wire racks before removing paper. Spoon 2 or 3 tablespoons (30-45 mL) additional cider over each cooled loaf before storing. Wrap in foil and refrigerate.
■ *Deanna Morris*
    Northern Lites, Tasty Bites, *Fairbanks*

Hurry Up Sourdough Cupcakes

1 cup (240 mL) sugar
1 egg
1/2 cup (120 mL) cocoa
1 cube (114 g) margarine, softened
1-1/2 cups (360 mL) flour
1 teaspoon (5 mL) vanilla
1/2 cup (120 mL) milk
1/2 cup (120 mL) sourdough starter
1/2 teaspoon (2 mL) baking soda
1/2 teaspoon (2 mL) baking powder
1/4 teaspoon (1 mL) salt
1/2 cup (120 mL) chopped walnuts

►Measure all ingredients together into a large bowl. Do no mixing until everything is in the bowl. Beat vigorously and pour paper-lined muffin cups two-thirds full. Bake at 400°F (205°C) for 18 to 22 minutes or until surface springs back immediately when tested with a finger tip. May be served "as is" or frosted with your favorite icing.
■ *The Old Homesteader*

Honey-Glazed Orange Drops

1/2 cup (120 mL) thick sourdough starter
1/3 cup (80 mL) sugar
1 egg
2 tablespoons (30 mL) cooking oil
2 tablespoons (30 mL) grated orange rind
1 teaspoon (5 mL) nutmeg
2 teaspoons (10 mL) baking powder
1/4 teaspoon (1 mL) soda
1/2 teaspoon (2 mL) salt

►To the sourdough, add sugar, egg and oil. Mix well. Add dry ingredients with orange rind. Blend but do not overbeat. Dough should be soft and easy to drop from a spoon. To prevent dough from sticking, dip spoon in hot oil before dipping into dough. Use another teaspoon to push dough into deep fat heated to 375°F (190°C). Fry to golden brown. Drain. Dip in Honey Glaze and roll in coconut.

Honey Glaze
1/2 cup (120 mL) fireweed honey
4 teaspoons (20 mL) boiling water
1 cup (240 mL) powdered sugar
1 cup (240 mL) shredded coconut

►Mix ingredients in a saucepan and bring to a boil. Boil three to five minutes.
■ *Ruth Allman, Juneau*
Alaska Sourdough

Sourdough Jelly Treats

1 cube (114 g) margarine
1/4 cup (60 mL) brown sugar, firmly packed
1 egg, separated
1/2 cup (120 mL) sourdough starter
2/3 cup (160 mL) sifted flour
1/2 cup (120 mL) finely chopped pecans
Wild berry jelly or jam

►Cream margarine and sugar together until fluffy. Beat egg yolk well and add; stir in starter, then gradually stir in flour which has been sifted. Chill dough for an hour or two. Pinch off small pieces of chilled dough, about an inch each (2.5 cm) and roll into balls. Beat egg white until foamy. Dip balls into egg white and then into chopped pecans. Place on cookie sheets. Make a dent in each ball with your thumb. Bake at 350°F (175°C) for 12 to 15 minutes. Remove from oven and fill the dents with wild berry jam or jelly.
■ *The Old Homesteader*

Soft Sourdough Ginger Cookies

1/2 cup (120 mL) sourdough starter
1/2 cup (120 mL) shortening
3/4 cup (180 mL) sugar
1/2 cup (120 mL) blackstrap molasses
1 egg
2 teaspoons (10 mL) grated orange peel
3-1/2 cups (840 mL) flour
2 teaspoons (10 mL) ginger
2 teaspoons (10 mL) cinnamon
1 teaspoon (5 mL) cloves
1/2 teaspoon (2 mL) cardamom
1 teaspoon (5 mL) soda

►Cream shortening and sugar. Add molasses, egg and orange rind. Mix in sourdough starter. Add dry ingredients. Use enough flour to make a soft dough. Chill the dough. Roll out on floured board. Cut into cookie shapes desired. Bake on greased cookie sheet at 375°F (190°C) for 10 minutes.
■ *Ruth Allman, Juneau*
Alaska Sourdough

Sourdough Coconut Drop Cookies

1 cup (240 mL) evaporated milk
1/2 cup (120 mL) sourdough starter
2 cups (480 mL) all-purpose flour
2 cubes (228 g) margarine
1-1/4 cups (300 mL) brown sugar, packed
1 egg, slightly beaten
1/2 teaspoon (2 mL) salt
1/2 teaspoon (2 mL) baking soda
3 cups (720 mL) cornflakes, crushed
1 cup (240 mL) chopped walnuts
1 cup (240 mL) shredded coconut

►Mix together in a large bowl the milk, starter and 1-1/2 cups (360 mL) of the flour. Allow to rest for 2 to 2-1/2 hours. In another bowl cream margarine with sugar and blend in egg and a mixture of remaining 1/2 cup (120 mL) flour, salt and soda. Stir in cornflakes, nuts and coconut. Blend this into the starter mixture carefully. Drop by small spoonfuls onto cookie sheet lined with waxed paper, about two inches apart. Bake at 375°F (190°C) for 12 to 15 minutes.
■ *Anon.*

Sourdough Squash Brownies

1/2 cup (120 mL) vegetable shortening
1-1/4 cups (300 mL) granulated sugar
2 eggs, slightly beaten
1/2 cup (120 mL) sourdough starter
2/3 cup (160 mL) winter squash or pumpkin,
cooked and mashed, or raw zucchini,
peeled and grated
1 teaspoon (5 mL) vanilla
1/4 cup (60 mL) milk
1 cup (240 mL) all-purpose flour
1 teaspoon (5 mL) baking powder
1/2 teaspoon (2 mL) salt
1 teaspoon (5 mL) cinnamon
1/2 teaspoon (2 mL) nutmeg
1/2 teaspoon (2 mL) ginger
1/2 cup (120 mL) nuts, chopped

►Cream shortening and sugar. Beat in eggs, sourdough starter and squash in that order. Stir in vanilla and milk. Mix and sift dry ingredients and stir into creamed mixture; stir in chopped nuts. Pour into greased baking pan and bake at 350°F (175°C) for 25 minutes or until well browned. This is a nice, moist brownie. Brown sugar may be used instead of white.

Sourdough Brownies

4 squares (4 oz /or/ 114 g) sweet
  baking chocolate
1/2 cup (120 mL) hot water
1 teaspoon (5 mL) baking soda
2 cubes (228 g) margarine
2 cups (480 mL) sugar
2 eggs
2 teaspoons (10 mL) vanilla
1 cup (240 mL) chopped walnuts or pecans
1-1/2 cups (360 mL) flour
1/2 teaspoon (2 mL) salt
1-1/2 cups (360 mL) sourdough starter

►Place chocolate in small pan and add hot water; bring to a boil, stirring meanwhile. Add soda and mix well. Mixture will be foamy. Set aside until lukewarm. In a large bowl, cream margarine and sugar together until fluffy. Add eggs, one at a time, and beat well after each. Add vanilla and cooled chocolate mixture and nuts. Gradually add flour that has been sifted with salt. Last of all add the starter. Beat well after each addition. Grease and flour a 9 x 13-inch (22 x 32 cm) pan and pour batter into it. Place pan in a warm spot for half an hour. Preheat oven to 350°F (175°C) and bake for 35 to 40 minutes.

Sourdough Chocolate Balls

1 cup (240 mL) sourdough starter
1-1/2 cups (360 mL) sugar
1/2 cup (120 mL) vegetable oil
1-1/2 teaspoons (7 mL) vanilla
1/3 cup (80 mL) chocolate bits
3 eggs
1/4 cup (60 mL) powdered milk
2-1/2 cups (600 mL) flour
1/2 teaspoon (2 mL) baking soda
1/4 teaspoon (1 mL) salt
1 cup (240 mL) chopped walnuts
Powdered sugar

►Measure starter into large bowl and add sugar, oil, vanilla, chocolate bits, eggs and powdered milk. Sift together flour, soda and salt. Stir into sourdough mixture and add walnuts; chill for at least one hour. Shape into balls, using a small spoonful per ball. Roll in powdered sugar. Place on greased cookie sheets and bake at 375°F (190°C) for 10 to 12 minutes. While still warm, roll again in powdered sugar. A good variation is to use half brown sugar in place of part of the white.

Sourdough Oatmeal Cookies

1 cup (240 mL) vegetable shortening
1 cup (240 mL) white sugar
1/2 cup (120 mL) brown sugar, packed

1 egg, slightly beaten
1/4 cup (60 mL) water
1 cup (240 mL) sourdough starter
1 teaspoon (5 mL) vanilla
1/2 teaspoon (2 mL) baking soda
1 teaspoon (5 mL) salt
1 cup (240 mL) all-purpose flour
2-1/2 cups (600 mL) rolled oats, uncooked
1 cup (240 mL) raisins (optional)
1/2 cup (120 mL) chopped nuts (optional)

►Cream sugars and shortening together until light. Add beaten egg and water and beat until light and fluffy. Add starter, vanilla, salt, soda and flour. Mix until dry ingredients are well moistened. Add rolled oats, raisins and nuts, if desired. Dough will be very thick. Drop by small spoonfuls onto greased cookie sheet, leaving about 2 inches (5 cm) between cookies. Bake at 400°F (205°C) for 10 to 12 minutes or until nicely browned. Cool on pan for five minutes, then cool on rack.

Sourdough Baked Alaska

Items needed:
Sourdough waffle — crisp
Ice cream — brick or bulk
Meringue (see below)
Wooden plank (never use metal or crockery
  for this)

►Preheat oven to 500°F (260°C). Place crisp, crunchy waffle on board. A breadboard is excellent to use. For oblong waffle, top with a slab of ice cream that will leave a 1-inch (2.5 cm) border of waffle all around. Completely seal in ice cream with swirls of glossy, dry meringue. Since the egg whites are an insulation, make certain that meringue tightly prevents any heat getting in to melt the ice cream. Place the Baked Alaska in very hot oven. Leave door open just a crack. Remove from oven when meringue is delicate brown. Quickly slip onto chilled plate or platter and serve immediately.

Baked Alaska Meringue
6 to 8 egg whites
1 cup (240 mL) sugar

►Beat egg whites until stiff and dry forming peaks that will stand alone. VERY SLOWLY add the sugar, beating constantly, until smooth and glossy. If not beaten enough before sugar is added, the meringue will not get stiff enough to hold shape regardless of later beating.

Variation: *Individual Baked Alaskas* — Cut crisp sourdough waffles in desired segments — square, oblong, round, diamond. Place segments on top of wood board. Top with scoop or slab of ice cream.

Hollow out a well in the ice cream. Fill with fresh or preserved fruit — peach or pineapple preserves, strawberries or blueberries. Completely seal with swirls of meringue and bake as above, two to five minutes, until delicately brown.

■ *Ruth Allman, Juneau*
Alaska Sourdough

Sourdough Cobbler

3 cups (720 mL) wild berries
1-1/4 to 2 cups (300-480 mL) sugar, divided
1/4 cup (60 mL) margarine
1 cup (240 mL) sourdough starter
3/4 cup (180 mL) milk
1 cup (240 mL) flour
1 teaspoon (5 mL) baking powder
1/2 teaspoon (2 mL) salt

►Cook berries slowly with 1/4 to 1 cup (60-240 mL) of the sugar, depending on how sour the berries are. Bring to boil and boil gently for five minutes; set aside to cool slightly. Melt margarine in deep casserole. Mix together the starter, milk, flour, baking powder, salt and remaining 1 cup (240 mL) sugar. Pour this mixture over the melted margarine. Add the cooled berries. Bake at 350°F (175°C) for 45 minutes or until cobbler is well done. The batter should rise to the top as it cooks and should be nicely browned.

Sourdough Carob Pudding

2 cups (480 mL) sourdough starter
1 cup (240 mL) milk
1 cup (240 mL) whole-wheat flour
2 cups (480 mL) brown sugar
2 teaspoons (10 mL) baking soda
1/2 cup (120 mL) carob or unsweetened
   chocolate powder

►Add milk, whole-wheat flour, brown sugar, soda and carob or chocolate powder to sourdough sponge. Mix thoroughly and pour into greased tube pan. Bake at 300°F (150°C) until firm enough that a knife blade inserted will come out gooey but not drippy. Cool some before spooning into bowls. Serve warm or chilled.

■ *Gretchen Walker*
   "Sourdough Cookery — Life in A Crock Pot"
   ALASKA® magazine, June 1978

Beewack

Beewack (sourdough beer) isn't really dessert, but reading about it is definitely a treat.

►Sourdough beer is simple to make but disagreeable to drink. But, if consumed in quantity, will produce any desired degree of intoxication.

All one needs is a barrel, flour, and some water. Into this pour some sourdough and Dame Nature takes its course from there. A little sugar will speed up matters, but even without it, those smelly little ascomycetes will soon acquaint your neighbors with the fact you have brew in the making.

After the solids have sunk to the bottom, all that remains is for the imbibers to gather around with tin cups and dip deep into the malodorous liquid. Beewack is never bottled. Only a fool would carry a live bomb.

Care should be exercised, however, when one nears the bottom of the barrel. Not many years ago a man from down Dutch Harbor way slipped while dipping deep and drowned in his own barrel. His drinking companions were all too befuddled to drag him out.

■ *Ruth Allman, Juneau*
Alaska Sourdough

Sourdough Paste Pie Crust

2 cups (480 mL) sifted flour
1/2 cup (120 mL) sourdough starter
3 tablespoons (45 mL) water
3/4 teaspoon (3 mL) salt
2/3 cup (160 mL) shortening

►Sourdough is more flavoring than leavening for pie crust and does not need warming overnight. Because the crust will be "sour" and doughy, it is especially good with meat or fish pies, or fruit pies that combine well with a slightly sour flavor. It is excellent for Eskimo Fried Pies, page 362.

Combine 1/2 cup (120 mL) of the sifted flour, the

starter and water, and set in a warm place for an hour or more. To the remaining flour, add salt and shortening, mixing well. If a slightly sweeter dough is desired, add 1/4 teaspoon (1 mL) soda to the dry flour.

Combine the two mixtures, adding enough more flour to make a dough that will roll out on a floured board. Shape, fill and bake as usual. Makes two 9-inch (22 cm) crusts.
■ *The editors, ALASKA® magazine*

Blueberry Sourdough Dumplings

3 cups (720 mL) blueberries
1/2 cup (120 mL) boiling water
1 cup (240 mL) sugar
1/2 teaspoon (2 mL) nutmeg
1/2 teaspoon (2 mL) cloves

►Boil above mixture five minutes in a heavy skillet or saucepan with a tight lid before dropping in small dumplings made from the following batter:

1/2 cup (120 mL) sourdough starter
1 tablespoon (15 mL) sugar
1 tablespoon (15 mL) cooking oil
1 teaspoon (5 mL) grated lemon rind
1 egg
1 cup (240 mL) flour
1/2 teaspoon (2 mL) baking soda
1/2 teaspoon (2 mL) baking powder

►Mix lightly but well and drop by teaspoonfuls into boiling berry mixture. Replace lid tightly and return to boil. Turn down heat and continue cooking for 12 minutes. Do not lift lid during cooking period. Serve in bowls, warm. Top with whipped cream, if desired.
■ *Ruth Allman, Juneau*
Alaska Sourdough

Chapter 13

More Northern Wonders

In this chapter are recipes for many dishes other-than-sourdough that also are concocted of items from the cupboard — staples such as flour, sugar, powdered milk, even tea leaves.

Leading off are more baked goods. There are homemade Master Mixes to save you time and money, recipes for treats, such as bannock, fry bread and *kulich*, which are as traditionally Alaskan as sourdough, plus a selection of brews for the teacup to be served alongside.

The chapter concludes with numerous recipes for frostings and glazes, main dish sauces, relishes and stuffings which are suggested accompaniments for dishes described in all parts of the book.

HOMEMADE MASTER MIXES

Mixes are a boon to people whose very own dining table is the favorite place to "eat out." Mixes allow most of the benefits of home cookin' without exacting the long hours usually required. The toll is the additional cost of prepackaged mixes. The solution? Make your own mixes. The following recipes (except as noted) are adapted from bulletin P-60, "Make Your Own Mix," Cooperative Extension Service, University of Alaska.

Ingredients For Master Mixes

Shortening — Generally, use the kind that does not need refrigeration. Or, if lard is used, reduce the amount. About 1-2/3 cups (400 mL) of lard equals 2 cups (480 mL) of other shortening. Mix made with lard should be refrigerated.

Flour — If Mix is to be used mainly for cakes and cookies, use a box of cake flour (the 2-3/4-pound size /or/ 1.2 kg) and sift it with 1/2 cup (120 mL) baking powder, 1-1/2 tablespoons (23 mL) salt, 1/4 cup (60 mL) sugar, 1 cup (240 mL) dry skim milk to 1 pound (0.45 kg) shortening.

Eggs — Powdered eggs should not be added to mixes that will be stored. When making up recipes, however, reconstituted powdered eggs may be substituted for the fresh eggs called for in the recipe. Measure carefully. (See Making Substitutions, page 368.)

Storing Homemade Master Mixes

Each Master Mix is sufficient to make from four to six — or more —of the recipes that accompany it.

You may want to decide in advance which recipes you're likely to use and store at least some of your mix premeasured in recipe quantities. Label each package with the quantity and directions for finishing it, such as:

3-1/2 cups (840 mL) Quick Mix for
  Peanut Butter Cookies
Add: *1-1/3 cups (320 mL) sugar, 1 cup (240 mL)*
  peanut butter, 2 eggs
Bake: *375°F (190°C) — 6 dozen*

Cookie recipes are especially useful stored this way to encourage children to make up their own after-school snacks.

Store mixes unrefrigerated (unless you use lard as the shortening), tightly wrapped in aluminum foil or plastic bags or cartons with close-fitting lids. If the container is transparent, keep it in a dark cupboard.

Quick Mix *(Master Mix I)*

8 cups (1.9 L) sifted all-purpose flour, or
  10 cups (2.4 L) sifted soft wheat or cake flour
1/3 cup (80 mL) double-acting baking powder
1 tablespoon (15 mL) salt
2 cups (480 mL) nonfat dry milk
1 teaspoon (5 mL) cream of tartar (optional)
1/4 cup (60 mL) sugar
2 cups (480 mL) shortening

►Stir baking powder, salt, milk, cream of tartar and sugar into flour. Sift three times into a large bowl. Cut in shortening until Mix is consistency of corn meal. Store in covered containers at room temperature. To measure the Master Mix, pile it lightly into the measuring cup and level off.

Quick Mix Biscuits
3 cups (720 mL) Quick Mix
About 1/2 cup (120 mL) water

►Put Mix into bowl. Add water and stir just enough to blend. Turn onto a lightly floured board and knead a few times. Pat or roll to about 3/4-inch (2 cm) thickness. Cut with floured cutter. Bake 12 to 15 minutes in hot oven, 400°F (205°C). Makes 18 biscuits.

Variation: *Chive Turnovers* — Roll cut rounds of biscuit dough thin, about the thickness of pancakes. Put a small spoonful of chopped and sauteed wild chives on one side of each round and fold it over like a turnover. Seal edges by dampening with milk and pinching together. Bake as directed. May be prepared ahead and reheated in foil. [The Old Homesteader]

Quick Mix Muffins
3 cups (720 mL) Quick Mix
2 tablespoons (30 mL) sugar
1 cup (240 mL) water
1 egg, beaten

►Add sugar to Mix. Combine water and beaten egg. Add to Mix. Stir only until flour is moistened — about 15 times — as mixture should be lumpy, not smooth. Bake in greased muffin pans about 20 minutes in a hot oven, 425°F (220°C). Makes 24 small muffins.

Quick Mix Griddle Cakes or Waffles
3 cups (720 mL) Quick Mix
1-1/2 cups (360 mL) water
1 egg, beaten

►Stir combined water and beaten egg into the Mix until blended. Bake on hot griddle or waffle iron. Makes 10 griddle cakes or 6 waffles.

Quick Mix Corn Bread
1-1/2 cups (360 mL) Quick Mix
3/4 cup (180 mL) corn meal
1/2 teaspoon (2 mL) salt
2 tablespoons (30 mL) sugar
1 cup (240 mL) milk
1 egg, beaten

►Stir corn meal, salt and sugar into Mix. Combine milk and beaten egg. Add to Mix, stirring until blended. Bake about 20 minutes in greased 8 x 8-inch (20 cm) pan in a hot oven, 400°F (205°C). Makes about 12 servings.

Variation: *Trapper Creek Corn Bread* — Add to the finished dough 2 tablespoons (30 mL) chopped wild chives and four strips crisp, fried and crumbled bacon (or about 2 tablespoons /or/ 30 mL commercial bacon bits). Grease an oblong pan (even a cookie sheet will do) and spread the batter thinly and evenly. Bake in a hot oven until well browned. Cut or break into large slabs and butter generously. This is perfect with baked beans. [The Old Homesteader]

Quick Mix Scones
2 cups (480 mL) Quick Mix
1 tablespoon (15 mL) sugar
1/2 cup (120 mL) water
1 large egg

►Put Quick Mix and sugar in a bowl. Reserve 1 tablespoon (15 mL) or so of the beaten egg. Mix the rest with the water and stir quickly into the dry ingredients, handling the dough as little as possible. Turn out onto lightly floured board and pat to about 3/4-inch (1.9 cm) thickness.

Cut into diamond shapes or squares. Brush with egg, sprinkle with additional sugar and bake at 400°F (205°C) 10 to 12 minutes.

■ *Anon.*

Quick Mix Plain Cake
3 cups (720 mL) Quick Mix
1-1/4 cups (300 mL) sugar
1 cup (240 mL) milk
2 eggs, beaten
1 teaspoon (5 mL) vanilla

►Stir sugar into the Mix. Combine milk, eggs and vanilla. Stir half the liquid into the Mix and beat two minutes by hand or by electric mixer at low speed. Scrape bowl occasionally. Add remaining liquid and beat two minutes longer. Pour into two 8-inch (20 cm) round pans or a 13 x 9-inch (32 x 22 cm) oblong pan, lined with waxed paper. Bake in a moderate oven, 375°F (190°C) about 25 minutes.

Variations:
• *Coffeecake* — Vary the Plain Cake recipe by decreasing the sugar to 1/2 cup (120 mL), the milk to 2/3 cup (160 mL); use only one egg and omit vanilla. Combine dry and liquid ingredients separately; then mix together just until moistened. Spread into a greased 9-inch (22 cm) square pan. Sprinkle with a topping made of 1/2 cup (120 mL) brown sugar, 1 tablespoon (15 mL) flour, 1/2 teaspoon (2 mL) cinnamon and 1 tablespoon (15 mL) butter. Bake at 400°F (205°C) about 25 minutes.
• *Chocolate Cake* — Increase sugar to 1-1/2 cups (360 mL); increase milk to 1-1/4 cups (300 mL). Add 1/2 cup (120 mL) cocoa to other dry ingredients. Use all other ingredients listed.

Quick Mix Oatmeal Cookies
2-1/4 cups (540 mL) Quick Mix
1-3/4 cups (420 mL) brown sugar
1 teaspoon (5 mL) cinnamon
1/3 cup (80 mL) water
1/2 cup (120 mL) shortening, melted
2 eggs, beaten
1/2 cup (120 mL) chopped nuts
3 cups (720 mL) rolled oats

►Stir sugar and cinnamon into Mix. Combine water, beaten eggs and shortening. Stir into Mix until well blended. Add oats and nuts. Drop by teaspoonfuls onto greased baking sheet. Bake about 12 minutes at 375°F (190°C). Makes six to seven dozen.

Quick Mix Peanut Butter Cookies
3-1/2 cups (840 mL) Quick Mix
1-1/3 cups (320 mL) sugar
1 cup (240 mL) peanut butter
2 eggs, beaten

►Stir beaten eggs, peanut butter and sugar into the Mix until well blended. Roll dough into small balls, place on baking sheet and flatten with fork, making a crisscross. Bake at 375°F (190°C) until lightly brown. About six dozen.

Quick Mix Drop Cookies
3 cups (720 mL) Quick Mix
1 cup (240 mL) sugar
1/2 cup (120 mL) raisins
1/3 cup (80 mL) water
1 beaten egg
1 teaspoon (5 mL) vanilla

►Stir sugar and raisins into the Mix. Combine water, egg and vanilla. Stir into the Mix until well blended. Drop by teaspoonfuls onto greased baking sheet. Bake at 375°F (190°C) 10 to 12 minutes. Makes six to seven dozen.

Quick Mix Raisin Bread
3 cups (720 mL) Quick Mix
1/2 cup (120 mL) sugar

Who hasn't experienced the frustration of trying to bake a cake or gingerbread in the warped oven of a camp stove? It comes out 1/2 inch (1.25 cm) thick on one side and 3 inches (7.5 cm) thick on the other! Here's a simple solution: Just take a raw potato, cut some wedges from it and shim up the baking pan until it's level. It works!

■ *Howard Ballew, Jackson Hole, Wyoming*
The Cabin Friend
ALASKA® magazine, August 1976

For those who hand-grind their own grains, here is a hint that seems to make the work of grinding a little bit easier. When you have ground, say wheat, to the fineness you want (this usually takes at least three grindings), go ahead and crack another batch before you quit. The cracked wheat keeps indefinitely in a cool, dry place, and the next time you run out of flour and have to grind, the first grinding is already done, which makes the subsequent run-throughs seem much easier; your flour is fine-ground in no time. Also the cracked grain is on hand for a nutritious hot cereal on a cold winter's morning.

■ *Faith Smith, Gold King Creek, Alaska*
The Cabin Friend
ALASKA® magazine, April 1977

1/2 cup (120 mL) raisins or nuts (or a mixture)
1 cup (240 mL) water
1 beaten egg

►Stir sugar and raisins or nuts into the Mix. Combine egg and water. Add to Mix, stirring until well blended. If mixture seems too dry, add a little water. Bake in a greased 5 x 8-inch (12 x 20 cm) loaf pan at 350°F (175°C), about one hour.

Quick Mix Dumplings
3 cups (720 mL) Quick Mix
3/4 cup (180 mL) water

►Add water to Mix all at once and stir about 30 strokes. Drop by tablespoonfuls on top of cooked and boiling meat and vegetable stew. Cover and boil gently 12 minutes without removing cover.

Quick Mix Meat Pie Topping
2 cups (480 mL) Quick Mix
1 cup (240 mL) water

►Add water to Mix and stir well. Fill a baking dish two-thirds full of hot, cooked meat and vegetable stew. Pour topping over meat and bake in a hot oven, 450°F (230°C), about 20 minutes.

Pie Crust Mix (Master Mix II)

1 pound (0.45 kg) lard (about 2 cups /or/
    480 mL) or other shortening (about
    2-1/2 cups /or/ 600 mL)
7 cups (1.7 L) sifted all-purpose flour
4 teaspoons (20 mL) salt

►Mix flour and salt thoroughly; cut in cold lard or shortening, using pastry blender, two knives, or tips of fingers, until fat particles are no larger than small peas. Store in tightly covered containers — in the refrigerator if lard is used.

One 9-Inch (22 cm) Crust
1-1/2 cups (360 mL) Pie Crust Mix
2 to 3 tablespoons (30-45 mL) cold water

►While blending with a fork, sprinkle cold water over Mix a little at a time, using just enough water to make dough adhere and form a ball but not be sticky. Let stand five minutes before rolling and shaping crust. If you wish to bake the crust before filling it, bake 10 to 12 minutes at 425°F (220°C). Cool completely before filling.

Double Crust for 9-Inch Pie
2-1/2 cups (600 mL) Pie Crust Mix
4 to 6 tablespoons (60-90 mL) cold water

►Combine according to directions for one crust.

Flour Mixture For Campers
(Master Mix III)

10 pounds (4.5 kg) white flour
10 pounds (4.5 kg) whole-wheat flour
5 pounds (2.25 kg) yellow corn meal
4 pounds (1.8 kg) soy flour
4 pounds (1.8 kg) wheat germ

►Mix thoroughly in a large container. Pack in heavy pliofilm bags. This mixture can be used for all flour requirements in camp and is wholesome and nourishing.
■ *Mardy Murie, Moose, Wyoming*
   The Alaskan Camp Cook

Homemade Granola (Master Mix IV)

1/3 cup (80 mL) instant cream of wheat
    (prepared)
3-1/2 cups (840 mL) quick oats
1 teaspoon (5 mL) vanilla extract
2 teaspoons (10 mL) cinnamon
Small pinch nutmeg
1 cup (240 mL) applesauce
1 teaspoon (5 mL) salt
1/2 cup (120 mL) melted butter or margarine
1/2 cup (120 mL) chopped nuts
1 cup (240 mL) raisins
1/2 pound (228 g) brown sugar

►Mix all the ingredients; spread mixture evenly on a large cookie sheet and bake at 350°F (175°C) for 20 minutes, stirring with a fork to brown evenly. Reduce heat to 300°F (150°C) or 325°F (160°C) and continue baking until brown and fairly dry. Store at room temperature in a covered container.
■ *Mary Ellen Wurm, Fairbanks*
   The Cabin Friend
   ALASKA® magazine, June 1976

Pudding Mix (Master Mix V)

1-1/2 cups (360 mL) sugar
1 cup (240 mL) flour
2-1/2 cups (600 mL) nonfat dry milk
1 teaspoon (5 mL) salt

►Mix well and store in a covered container.

Vanilla Pudding
1 cup (240 mL) Pudding Mix
2-1/2 cups (600 mL) water
4 tablespoons (60 mL) butter or margarine
1 teaspoon (5 mL) vanilla

►Combine Mix and water. Cook, stirring constantly until mixture boils. Add margarine and let boil two minutes. Remove from heat and add vanilla extract. (If desired, one beaten egg may be added at this time: beat egg, add some hot pudding to it and blend into the mixture in the pan. Cook for an additional minute after adding egg.) Chill until set. Serves six.

Variations:
• *Chocolate Pudding* — Add 3 tablespoons (45 mL) cocoa to the dry Mix. Proceed as directed.
• *Lemon Pudding* — Omit vanilla; substitute 3 tablespoons (45 mL) lemon juice.
• *Pineapple* or *Apricot Pudding* — Omit water; substitute pineapple juice or syrup or diluted apricot nectar. Also omit vanilla; substitute an equal amount of lemon juice.

Vanilla Pudding with Eggs
1-1/3 cups (320 mL) water
3/4 cup (180 mL) Pudding Mix
2 egg yolks (or reconstituted powdered eggs;
see Making Substitutions page 368)
1 teaspoon (5 mL) vanilla

►Heat water to boiling, beat in Mix. Cook until

flour is thoroughly blended. Beat egg yolks, add a little of the hot mixture; blend, then combine with pudding. Cook two minutes longer. Add vanilla. Cool.

Variations:
• *Floating Island* — Beat the two egg whites until stiff enough to stand in peaks. Continue beating and add 1/4 cup (60 mL) sugar, slowly. Drop spoonfuls into six sherbet glasses and pour hot pudding over each.
• *Chocolate Mint Fluff* — Melt eight chocolate mints in the water called for. Then make pudding as directed. Beat two egg whites until stiff, adding in 1/4 cup (60 mL) sugar. Fold into pudding. Chill.
• *Chocolate Dot Pudding* — Stir 1/2 cup (120 mL) chopped nuts into cooked Vanilla Pudding with Eggs. Pour into shallow baking dish. Make a meringue with the remaining egg whites, adding in 1/4 cup (60 mL) sugar. Then fold in 1/2 cup (120 mL) chocolate chips. Pile meringue on top of pudding. Bake at 350°F (175°C) for 15 minutes, or until meringue is browned.

TRADITIONAL BREADS & SWEETS

Many of the recipes in this section grew out of one or another of the state's numerous ethnic heritages. Some recipes don't bother with exact measures and some have no exact counterpart among the recipes of "the old country." Alaskan cooks — Native, Scandinavian, Russian or Iowan — all learned to use the sometimes limited, sometimes unique, goods at hand, often in ways not prescribed by "the old country."

And a few cooks, over a period of several generations, simply forgot what their moms taught them, did something else, and called it by the same name. Or reversed names. That's why *kulich*, a Russian Easter bread, is sometimes called by the name *paskha*, also served traditionally at Easter time, but a quite different treat, one in which cheese is the major ingredient rather than flour. The English, or English-Aleut, names of these delicacies are also spelled many different ways. For the most part, we've left the cook's spelling intact. And we haven't often tried to identify *which* heritage a dish comes from either. There's one called *Rosky*, for example, which was probably someone's way of saying "Russian," but who knows if the original cook was Russian, Aleut or Swede?

We only know that one of the originals was Alaskan.

Hardtack
2 level teaspoons (10 mL) baking powder
Pinch salt
1-1/2 cups (360 mL) flour
2 cups (480 mL) sugar
4 eggs, well beaten
1 jelly glass orange marmalade
1 pound (448 g) finely chopped walnuts
1 pound (448 g) finely chopped dates

►Sift dry ingredients together. Add the remainder of ingredients; mix well. Bake about 1 inch (2.5 cm) thick on a cookie sheet in a moderate oven, 375°F (190°C), about 45 minutes. Cut into squares while warm.
■ *Elaine Talbot Johnson*
Kitchen Magic
Ketchikan

Pupootnee
Natalie Simeonoff (Mrs. Kelly Simeonoff) grew up on Woody Island, just off the east coast of Kodiak. The two recipes following are ones she learned from her mother and, in turn, taught to a large family of her own. "Pupootnee," she explains, "is a Russian version of the English muffin," which was made by her mother whenever

shortening was scarce enough to prevent her making regular bread. Alahdickys, *delicious breakfast cakes, have long been a favorite of the Simeonoff grandchildren. Because she has never measured the ingredients she uses to make the breads, she warns that you may have to experiment a little to discover the right proportions for you.*

2-1/2 cups (600 mL) warm water
2 packages yeast
1 tablespoon (15 mL) honey
6-1/2 cups (1.6 L), or more, all-purpose flour
2 teaspoons (10 mL) salt
1 tablespoon (15 mL) melted shortening
Farina or corn meal

►In a large bowl, mix water, honey and yeast. Let stand for a few minutes. Mix in 2 cups (480 mL) of the flour and add salt and melted shortening. Gradually stir in remaining flour. The mixture should have typical bread dough consistency. Knead well, 10 minutes or more. Place in a greased bowl, turn to grease top, cover with a towel and set in a warm place to rise. The dough must rise and be punched down three times. After the third, roll the dough out on a floured board to a thickness of about 1/2 inch (1.25 cm). Cut in large circles and set aside, covered, to rise for about 30 minutes.

Preheat griddle to medium heat. Sprinkle the surface with farina or corn meal. Place the *pupootnee* on the griddle and bake first one side, then the other. It may be necessary to turn it a few times to achieve a *pupootnee* that is lightly browned and baked through.

Serve split with melted butter and jam or use for hamburger buns. Any good bread recipe can be used to make *pupootnee*. Simply use water for the liquid and less sugar and shortening.

■ *Natalie Simeonoff*
  Courtesy, Kadiak Times, *Kodiak*

Alahdickys
(Also called Aladniks)

►Use the same recipe as for *pupootnee*, but add 1 cup (240 mL) nonfat dry milk powder to the water mixture and 1 more tablespoon (15 mL) honey. Use 5 cups (1.2 L) or less flour to make a sticky dough.

Let dough rise once to twice its original size. Preheat a frying pan with oil two fingers deep to medium-hot, 375°F (190°C). Dip out heaping tablespoons of the dough and carefully drop into hot oil. Use two spoons to spread the dough so that it doesn't fry in a big blob. Fry till golden brown on one side, turn and brown the other side. Serve with honey-butter or jam or any syrup.

■ *Natalie Simeonoff*
  Courtesy, Kadiak Times, *Kodiak*

Bachelor Bannock
A recipe as generous as the size of your hand

3 handfuls whole-wheat flour
1 handful wheat germ
1/2 handful bran
1/2 to 3/4 handful corn meal
1/4 to 1/2 handful rolled oats (Easy now.
  Too much will hold moisture and make the
  bannock soggy.)
Baking powder — approximately 1 teaspoon
  (5 mL) per cup (240 mL) of the above
  ingredients
2 to 3 tablespoons (30 to 45 mL) milk powder
1 egg
Water
Nuts, raisins, dates (and so on) to taste
Oil or shortening

►Mix the first five ingredients in a medium bowl, using proportions to suit your own taste. Estimate the number of "cups" in the bowl and add baking powder accordingly. Mix well. Add milk powder and egg and mix again. Add enough water to produce a batter which is slightly wet, sticky and light. It should fall slowly from spoon in a sticky mass. Then add nuts, raisins and other goodies as desired.

Put enough oil in the fry pan to completely cover the bottom. (Bear fat is the very best shortening to use. Corn oil is good. Soya oil is bad.) Heat oil until a tiny amount of water dropped in the pan spatters and crackles.

Pour in batter and fry until done. All the bannock mixture should be used at one frying or the baking powder gases will quickly escape and the remaining batter will lie lifeless in the pan.

■ *Dick Person*
  Carcross, Yukon Territory

Hyortetak
(Small doughnuts)

4 eggs
1-2/3 cups (400 mL) sugar
1 cube (114 g) butter, melted
1/4 teaspoon (1 mL) cardamom
3 cups (720 mL) flour
1 teaspoon (5 mL) baking powder

►Beat eggs and sugar until thick; add melted butter and remaining ingredients. Roll out the size of a pencil; cut off in 2-1/2-inch (6.2 cm) lengths. Shape into small rings, lapping the ends over each other and pinching them together. Drop in hot lard and cook like doughnuts.

■ *Karen Sund*
  Sons of Norway Cook Book, Ketchikan

Indian Bread
Little yeast breads

1 envelope dry yeast
1/4 cup (60 mL) very warm water
1 cup (240 mL) milk
1/4 cup (60 mL) sugar
1/4 cup (60 mL) shortening
1 teaspoon (5 mL) salt
1 egg
3-1/2 cups (840 mL) flour
1 cup (240 mL) raisins
About 6 cups (1.4 L) cooking oil for deep-frying

►Sprinkle dry yeast into warm water — 110 to 115°F (43 to 45°C) — in a small bowl and let stand while mixing other ingredients. In a saucepan, over medium heat, mix milk, sugar, shortening and salt until dissolved and blended. Let mixture cool. Then add egg and yeast and stir in flour and raisins gradually until it forms a soft dough. Place in a greased bowl and lightly grease the top of the dough. Cover and let rise until doubled in size — about 1-1/2 hours.

Place on a floured surface and knead air bubbles from dough. Pinch off small pieces and stretch them to oval shapes, being careful not to stretch them too thin. Make a hole in the center of each and place them on a clean, floured surface. Allow them to rise again until doubled in size. Heat oil in frying pan at high heat until it is bubbling hot. Deep-fry the little breads, a few at a time, turning them until both sides are golden brown. Place them on napkins or other absorbent paper to drain grease.
■ *Courtesy, Vivian James, Angoon*

Squaw Bread
"A few pieces tucked away in a pocket make a delicious snack on the trail."

3 cups (720 mL) all-purpose flour
1/2 cup (120 mL) sugar
1 teaspoon (5 mL) salt
Milk or canned milk, as directed
Raisins (optional)
Oil or melted fat

►Mix dry ingredients in a bowl and add enough milk or canned milk to make a thin, but not watery, batter. Canned milk may be thinned with an equal amount of water. A handful of raisins may be added to the batter, if desired.

Then get out the old cast-iron skillet and put in enough oil or melted fat until it is about 3/4 inch (1.9 cm) deep. The grease should be hot, but not smoking. Drop the batter in by large spoonfuls. As the circles of dough cook, they will rise from the bottom. Blisters will form on top if the temperature

is right, and when they turn golden brown on the bottom, carefully roll them over with a fork and cook the other side.

Drain the cooked pieces of bread on a rack with paper towels or a brown bag underneath to catch the drippings. One batch yields about 20 pieces. When completely cooled, they may be stored in a plastic bag or an old bread wrapper. This method of storage gives the bread its characteristic chewy texture.

Many other ingredients may be added or substituted to vary the bread. Try brown sugar and whole-wheat flour, for instance. Or add blueberries, rose hips, candied fruit, apples — anything at hand. But you will not be disappointed with the plain variety, which has gone to the woods with trappers, miners and woodcutters for many years. I received my recipe from the late Lucy Crow, of Circle. As a little girl growing up in Circle, I knew her parents, Chief William Moses and his wife, Sarah.
■ *Lee Alder*
"Baking in a Skillet"
ALASKA® magazine, October 1982
Alaska-only edition

Dutch Pancake
A giant-sized popover

1/2 cup (120 mL) sifted flour
1/2 teaspoon (2 mL) salt
1/2 cup (120 mL) milk
3 eggs, well beaten
2 tablespoons (30 mL) shortening, melted
    and cooled

►Add flour, salt and milk to beaten eggs. Add shortening. Pour batter all at once into a greased cast-iron skillet and bake in a preheated oven at 450°F (230°C) for 10 minutes. Then reduce heat to 350°F (175°C) and bake 30 minutes more. Makes one large pancake to serve two or three. Serve with syrup or golden honey whipped with butter.
Note: This recipe also may be used for individual pancakes (about six of them). Drop batter from spoon onto a hot, lightly greased griddle.
■ *Mamie Jensen, Juneau*

Grease Bread
Leave the salt and baking powder at home?
Try this camp bread.

3 cups (480 mL) flour
1/2 cup (120 mL) sugar
2 cups (480 mL) water, or more

►Mix ingredients, adding enough water so that batter will spread like pancakes when dropped into hot grease. Fry until golden brown.
■ *Doris Ward, Fort Yukon*

Potato Doughnuts

1 cup (240 mL) hot mashed potatoes
4 tablespoons (60 mL) butter
3 eggs
1-1/4 cups (300 mL) sugar
1 cup (240 mL) milk
4 cups (1 L) flour
6 teaspoons (30 mL) baking powder
1 teaspoon (5 mL) salt
1/2 teaspoon (2 mL) vanilla
1/4 teaspoon (1 mL) nutmeg

►Add butter to potatoes and beat well. Beat eggs with sugar and stir into potatoes. Add remaining ingredients. Mix well. Let stand in a cold place for one hour. Roll out and cut and fry. The dough may take a little more flour.
■ *Carol Smith*, Island Edibles, *Sand Point*

Rye Bread in A Can

"This bread can be made without an oven — maybe in camp, using an open fire, or on a simple gas stove in a camper. You will need three tins with tight-fitting lids. I use tobacco tins and burn them out to clean them thoroughly. Some tins have a thin coating inside and this might come off in bits on your bread. This recipe is for three tobacco-tin loaves."

6 cups (1.4 L) rye flour
1 tablespoon (15 mL) salt
6 teaspoons (30 mL) baking powder
3/4 cup (180 mL) molasses
1/4 cup (60 mL) honey
3 cups (720 mL) water

►Mix flour, salt and baking powder in a large bowl. In a smaller container, mix honey and molasses and add 1 cup (240 mL) of the water to make them thinner and easier to handle. Then add this liquid mixture to the flour and stir well. Add a second cup (240 mL) of the water and mix again. Add the last cup gradually since you may not need the entire amount to make a moist but not "wet" dough.

Grease the three tins well and divide dough equally between them, pushing the dough down into each tin so your bread won't have air holes in it. Grease the lids, too, and put them on the cans. Set them in a large pan with a lid, fill the pan with water to 1/2 inch (1.25 cm) below the can lids. Put the lid on the pan and turn on the heat. Bring water to a boil and boil slowly for three hours. Check the water level every hour and add water when necessary. After three hours, take the tins out of the water, remove lids and shake the loaves out. (Don't pry them out; a few minutes of cooling in the can will probably do the trick.) When cold, the loaves may be stored in a plastic bag in a cold place. The next day you may start tasting. Always slice the bread fairly thin — it tastes better that way. For variety, try making the steamed bread using equal parts rye and whole-wheat flour, or add a cup of raisins.
■ *Mickey Lammers, "Rye Bread in A Can"*
ALASKA® magazine, July 1977
Alaska-only edition

Rosky

6 cups (1.4 L) flour
1 teaspoon (5 mL) salt
4 teaspoons (20 mL) sugar
1 pound (456 g) margarine or other shortening
1 cup (240 mL) sour cream
1/2 cup (120 mL) milk
6 eggs
1 cake compressed yeast softened in
    2 tablespoons (30 mL) sour cream

►Sift flour, salt and sugar. Cut in shortening. Add sour cream, milk and eggs and blend. Add softened yeast to mixture. Put in refrigerator two hours or more. Roll out on a board that has been sprinkled with sugar. Roll about 1/2 inch (1.25 cm) thick; cut in 2-inch (5 cm) squares. Place 1 teaspoon (5 mL) Rosky Filling on each square, fold over and shape as crescents. Bake 15 minutes at 400°F (205°C).

Rosky Filling
1 pound (456 g) ground walnuts
1 cup (240 mL) sugar
3 egg whites, stiffly beaten
1 teaspoon (5 mL) vanilla

►Mix and use as directed above.
■ *Anne Kerndrat*
Saint Herman's Sisterhood Club, *Kodiak*

Survival Grub

"Almost like candy . . . but more nourishing"

1 tablespoon (15 mL) honey
1 tablespoon (15 mL) water
3 cups (720 mL) oatmeal (or barley flakes or
    wheat flakes)
2-1/2 cups (600 mL) powdered milk
1 cup (240 mL) white sugar
1/2 package (3 oz /or/ 85 g size)
    citrus-flavored gelatin

►Put honey and water in a small pan and bring to a boil. While this is heating, combine the dry ingredients — except gelatin — in a mixing bowl. Dissolve the gelatin in the hot honey-water, then add it to the dry ingredients. After mixing well, add more water, a teaspoonful at a time until the mixture is barely moist enough to be molded. Pack into a baking dish or other mold and place in an oven and dry under very low heat. Cut into bars and wrap in aluminum foil and store until needed.

This recipe makes two bars about the size of a kitchen matchbox, and each contains about 1,000 calories, or enough food for survival for a day. It can be eaten dry, or cooked with about two-thirds canteen cup of water. The addition of dried fruit —raisins or apricots — makes a good variation.

I take a couple of these bars under the seat of my plane at all times. Sometimes the bars are the only thing I carry for food, if it is to be a short trip, but most of the time they are for emergency use. The bars have a long shelf life and freezing doesn't hurt them. They require no preparation to use. I have kept some of the bars more than a year, and they remained palatable.

■ *Richard V. Underwood, "Survival Grub"*
ALASKA® magazine, October 1969

Grama Bahrt's Kulich

A regal Russian bread traditionally served on Easter morning, Kulich is baked in tall cans so that the loaves will represent the domes of the old cathedrals. "Grama Bahrt," Nadja Kaznakoff Bahrt, emigrated to Sitka from Russia about the time of the Alaska Purchase.

1/4 cup (60 mL) white rum
1 cup (240 mL) seedless raisins
1 tablespoon (15 mL) grated lemon peel
1 teaspoon (5 mL) vanilla
1 teaspoon (5 mL) ground cardamom (optional)
1/2 teaspoon (2 mL) ground mace
2 packages active dry yeast
1 tablespoon (15 mL) sugar
1 cup (240 mL) lukewarm water
1 cup (240 mL) diluted evaporated milk
6 tablespoons (90 mL) butter
1/2 cup (120 mL) additional sugar
1 teaspoon (5 mL) salt
About 7 cups (1.7 L) sifted, all-purpose flour
3 medium eggs, well beaten
1/2 cup (120 mL) lightly toasted almond slices
A secret ingredient*

►Combine white rum, raisins, lemon peel and mace and set aside to "plump" and develop flavor. Dissolve yeast and 1 tablespoon (15 mL) sugar in lukewarm water. Set aside. Scald diluted milk and pour into a large mixing bowl. Add butter, sugar and salt and cool to lukewarm. Stir in 2 cups (480 mL) of the sifted flour to make a soft batter; then add yeast mixture and well-beaten eggs. Beat well. Stir in rum-raisin mixture and almonds. Now add just enough more flour to make a soft dough.

Place dough on a lightly floured pastry cloth and knead with the heel of the hand until smooth and satiny, about 10 minutes. Then put the kneaded dough in a well-buttered mixing bowl. Turn the dough to coat it well with butter. Cover with a clean towel and let rise in a warm place until double in bulk, about 1-1/4 hours. (If your kitchen is cold, place the covered bowl on the top shelf of an unheated oven. On the shelf beneath, put a pan of hot water, directly beneath the bowl. Keep oven door closed while dough rises.)

When light, punch dough down and let it rest about 10 minutes. Turn out onto a lightly floured pastry cloth and shape into logs large enough to half fill well-greased tins of the size you want. Don't forget to bake some dough in small tins for your "little people." Small baking powder tins or juice cans are good for the small loaves; 1- and 2-pound (0.45 and 1 kg) coffee cans are appropriate for medium and large loaves. Use tall, slender cans to make the traditional shapes.

Cover the filled tins with a towel and let dough rise until double in bulk.

Bake on lowest oven rack in a preheated 350°F (175°C) oven. One-pound (0.45 kg) tins will require about 35 minutes; a 2-pound tin (about 1 kg), 45 minutes; smaller tins, 15 to 20 minutes.

Remove "towers" of bread from tins immediately and place on wire racks. Frost and decorate while still warm.

Lemon Kulich Glaze
2 cups (480 mL) powdered sugar
4 teaspoons (20 mL) fresh lemon juice
4 teaspoons (20 mL) cold milk
Fresh grated lemon peel

►Beat ingredients together, adding sugar or liquid, if needed, for a good "drizzle" consistency. While bread is still warm, spoon glaze over top and let drizzle down sides. Decorate breads with tiny candy Easter eggs, a fresh flower, or other Easter decorations such as chicks or bunnies. Use your imagination and plenty of the Secret Ingredient. I like to make Kulich at Christmastime, too, decorating small breads for the children with tiny Santas or whatever.

To serve, slice off the frosted top and place it on a doily in the center of a serving platter. Cut slices of bread, crosswise, from the remaining "tower." Cut slices in half again. Then toast, butter them well and arrange these half-moon slices around the frosted top. Accompany with well-brewed tea flavored with lemon and whole cloves.

*Now for the Secret Ingredient: Throughout baking and serving, add plenty of TLC (tender loving care) and you will have true Grama Bahrt Kulich.

■ *Elva Bahrt Swenson, recalling*
"from taste memory" the recipe of
Nadja Kaznakoff Bahrt

Weinbroe

2 pounds (1 kg) prunes
4 eggs
1 cup (240 mL) shortening
2 cups (480 mL) sugar
4 cups (1 L) flour
4 teaspoons (20 mL) baking powder
1 teaspoon (5 mL) salt
1-1/2 cups (360 mL) milk

►Cook prunes. Remove seeds and mash. Mix all other ingredients and enough more flour to make a stiff dough. Roll it out thick, like cookie dough. Spread on the prunes. Fold dough over. Bake at 350°F (175°C) for 35 minutes. Frost with powdered sugar frosting. Makes about four small prune rolls if you wish to divide the dough before rolling it out.
■ *Lena Hunt*
   Island Edibles, *Sand Point*

Boalotchkee
(Russian buns)

1 pound (456 g) butter
5 eggs
2 cups (480 mL) sour cream
3/4 teaspoon (3 mL) baking soda
2 pounds (1 kg) flour
1 pound (456 g) sugar
Nuts
Beaten egg yolk

►Cream butter and eggs. Mix sour cream and soda; combine with butter-egg mixture. Sift flour on board and mix with sugar. Make a hole in the middle and add the egg mixture. Knead the dough with hands, constantly sprinkling the board with flour. Shape into round buns, place in lightly oiled shallow pan, brush with beaten egg yolk and sprinkle with any kind of chopped nuts. Bake at 350°F (175°C) until done, about 18 to 25 minutes.
■ *Ann Lewis*
   Saint Herman's Sisterhood Club, *Kodiak*

Paskha

An unusual use for cottage cheese, this Russian dish is traditionally served with Kulich at Easter time.

1 pound (456 g) cottage cheese
Pinch of salt
1/4 cup (60 mL) butter
1 egg, beaten
1/3 cup (80 mL) sugar
1/2 cup (120 mL) whipping cream
3/4 cup (180 mL) crushed pineapple, drained
1/4 cup (60 mL) chopped nuts
1 teaspoon (5 mL) vanilla

►Drain cottage cheese. Add pinch of salt. Soften butter and combine with sugar, stirring until mixture is smooth. Add egg and continue beating. Add cheese. Whip the cream and stir it in. Add drained pineapple, nuts and vanilla. Wet a piece of cheesecloth and put it in the bottom of a colander or strainer. Pour in cheese mixture. Gather up ends of cloth and twist to remove excess moisture. On top of the cheese put a saucer with a heavy object in it to weight the cheese. Place this in the refrigerator to continue draining and firming. May be kept overnight or up to two days in refrigerator. Slice and serve with Kulich. Usually made on Good Friday to serve on Easter Sunday.
■ Aleut Cookbook, *Saint Paul Island*

Variation: Substitute sour cream for the whipped sweet cream. Omit pineapple and add 2 teaspoons (10 mL) grated lemon rind or 2 to 3 tablespoons (30 to 45 mL) seedless raisins. Decorate finished Paskha with berries, nuts or candied fruit.

Ginger Crisps
"These are my favorites of all the cookies I have ever tried. They take a little more time than many others . . . because they must be rolled and cut but they are worth the time. This recipe is actually for gingerbread boys and can be used for that if rolled to about 1/4 inch (6 mm) thick and then decorated after baking."

1/2 cup (120 mL) molasses
1/4 cup (60 mL) granulated sugar
3 tablespoons (45 mL) margarine
1 tablespoon (15 mL) milk
2 cups (480 mL) flour
1/2 teaspoon (2 mL) each — soda, salt, nutmeg,
   cinnamon and cloves
3/4 teaspoon (3 mL) ginger
1 tablespoon (15 mL) lemon juice
Icing

►Heat molasses to boiling point; add sugar, margarine and milk. Sift remaining ingredients together and stir into first mixture, adding more flour if needed to make thick enough dough to roll out. Put dough in covered bowl and chill for a couple of hours. Dust board lightly with flour or powdered sugar. Put no more than a cup (240 mL) of dough on the board at one time; keep the rest

---

Favorite Popcorn: Fry some herring in a skillet. Use the same pan to pop corn.

---

chilled. Roll to about 1/8 inch (3 mm) or less in thickness. Cut desired shapes and put 1 inch (2.5 cm) apart on ungreased cookie sheet. Bake five to seven minutes at 350°F (175°C) or until firm. Remove from pan and cool before frosting.

Frost with a very thin icing made of a bit of soft margarine, one egg yolk and powdered sugar. Moisten further with milk to make it of good spreading consistency. Colored sugar may be sprinkled on top.

■ *Helen A. White, Anchorage*
  A Christmas Cookie Collection

So-Good-For-You Bar

"A good lunch for campers or young ones"

1 cup (240 mL) peanut butter
1 cup (240 mL) honey
1 cup (240 mL) carob powder
1 cup (240 mL) sunflower seeds
1/2 cup (120 mL) toasted (or regular)
  sesame seeds
1/2 cup (120 mL) chopped walnuts (omit if
  using crunchy peanut butter)
1/2 cup (120 mL) raisins or dates
1/2 cup (120 mL) wheat germ

►Heat peanut butter and honey slowly, stirring until smooth. Remove from heat and add remaining ingredients. Form into rolls. Makes four 12-inch (30 cm) rolls. Slice as needed. Can be served cold.

■ *J. and Curt Lund*
  "Sourdough Sampler"
  Great Lander Shopping News
  Anchorage, October 1978

Tin Can Ice Cream

►First, make an ice cream freezer from a 3-pound (1.4 kg) shortening can. Cut a 1-inch (2.5 cm) hole in the center of the plastic lid, and put a large wooden spoon up through the hole. Then mix the ingredients.

1/2 cup (120 mL) sugar
1/8 teaspoon (0.5 mL) salt
4 egg yolks, slightly beaten
2 cups (480 mL) scalded milk
1 cup (240 mL) heavy cream, or undiluted
  evaporated milk
1 tablespoon (15 mL) vanilla

►Mix sugar, salt and egg yolks. Add scalded milk, stirring constantly. Cook over hot water until the mixture coats a spoon. Cool. Add cream (or evaporated milk) and vanilla. Place the mixture in the can, insert the spoon and close the lid. Set the can into a bucket of ice, and put a few handfuls of rock salt, water softener salt or ordinary table salt onto the ice. (Salt is what produces the low temperatures needed for freezing the mixture, so don't skimp on it.) Allow the mixture to chill by itself until a test stir with the spoon reveals that ice crystals are just beginning to form on the inside of the can (about 20 minutes). Now stir very slowly until the mixture becomes too thick to stir any more. You can then let the ice cream chill further without stirring (it will get even harder), or you can go ahead and start eating.

■ *Ole and Manya Wik*
  "Try Our Alaskan Bush Ice Cream"
  ALASKA® magazine, July 1974

Blueberry Snow Ice Cream

2 eggs
1 cup (240 mL) undiluted evaporated milk
3/4 cup (180 mL) sugar
1 teaspoon (5 mL) vanilla
1 cup (240 mL) blueberries
Snow, new-fallen is best

►Beat eggs, add milk, sugar and vanilla. Fold in snow until mixture is the consistency of ice cream, then fold in berries. You may have to put it in freezer for a short time to get the proper consistency.

■ *Ann Chandonnet*
  "Cooking with Snow"
  ALASKA® magazine, Alaska-only edition
  November 1977

Eggless Snow Ice Cream

2 cups (480 mL) whole powdered milk
1 teaspoon (5 mL) vanilla
1/4 cup (60 mL) honey
1/4 cup (60 mL) light cooking oil
1 cup (240 mL) water, approximately
1 bucket clean fluffy snow

►Place powdered whole milk into a large bowl and make a well in the center. Add the honey, vanilla, oil and enough water to form a paste without lumps as you stir. Continue to add water, a little at a time, until the mixture has the consistency of thick pancake batter. Fold in the snow, a few cups at a time, until the ice cream has the consistency and taste you like. Be careful not to add too much snow, or the ice cream will be too weak. If desired, top with canned or fresh fruit, toasted coconut, chopped nuts, raisins, wheat germ or your favorite sauce.

■ *Ole and Manya Wik*
  "Try Our Alaskan Bush Ice Cream"
  ALASKA® magazine, July 1974

Cross-My-Heart Absolutely No-Fail Pie Crust

Do friends laugh when you sit down to slice homemade pie? Here's help. We don't guarantee the exact words of praise — "This is the best pie I e-v-e-r tasted!" or "What wonderful crust!" — but close. This is enough for a two-crust 10-inch (25 cm) pie or two shells.

3 cups (720 mL) all-purpose flour
1/2 teaspoon (2 mL) salt
1-1/2 cups (360 mL) vegetable shortening
1 egg, slightly beaten
5-1/2 tablespoons (83 mL) water
1 teaspoon (5 mL) cider vinegar

►Mix flour, salt and shortening with forks or pastry blender until mixture is pea-sized. In a separate

Camp or Cabin Baking

Many recipes in this volume — and in this chapter — are suited for camp or cabin cooking. But here are some special recipes for baking "bush style" collected by one experienced cook.

Cooking and baking in camp or cabin seem to bring out creative instincts. Lack of modern kitchen facilities or a few ingredients should not prevent creation of delicious meals and desserts — with the help of common sense plus lots of ingenuity.

Economy of space and time are also essential when living in a tent, cabin in the bush, small apartment, or trailer in the city. With these thoughts in mind I have collected some useful recipes that call for minimal basic ingredients and need only a few simple utensils. These recipes are especially handy because they call for ingredients normally included in any camper's list of supplies.

Eggs, usually the most important ingredient in cakes and cookies, are not easily come by when living in remote areas. When they are obtainable, they are more appreciated fried or poached, and they are not apt to be used for desserts. That's no reason to go without desserts on special occasions or just for a boost in morale on a cold or rainy indoor-type day.

Following are some recipes that require no eggs.

Eggless White Cake

1/4 cup (60 mL) shortening
1 cup (240 mL) sugar
2 cups (480 mL) sifted all-purpose flour
1/2 teaspoon (2 mL) soda
1/2 teaspoon (2 mL) baking powder
1 teaspoon (5 mL) salt
1 cup (240 mL) buttermilk
1 teaspoon (5 mL) vanilla

►Cream shortening with sugar. Sift together flour, soda, baking powder and salt. Add to shortening mixture alternately with buttermilk; blend in vanilla. Pour into greased, floured 8-inch (20 cm) square pan. Bake 30 to 35 minutes in moderate oven, 350°F (175°C).

Variation: *Eggless Spice Cake* — Sift with the dry ingredients 1 teaspoon (5 mL) cinnamon, 1/2 teaspoon (2 mL) nutmeg and 1/4 teaspoon (1 mL) cloves.

Wacky Cake

Mix this cake right in the baking pan

1-1/2 cups (360 mL) sifted all-purpose flour
1 teaspoon (5 mL) salt
3 tablespoons (45 mL) cocoa
1 teaspoon (5 mL) baking soda
1 cup (240 mL) granulated sugar
1 teaspoon (5 mL) vinegar
1 teaspoon (5 mL) vanilla extract
5 tablespoons (75 mL) salad oil
1 cup (240 mL) water

►Start heating oven to 350°F (175°C). Sift together — into an ungreased square 8-inch (20 cm) pan — the flour, salt, cocoa, soda and sugar. Make three holes in these ingredients. In the first hole, put the vinegar; in the second, vanilla extract; and in the third, the salad oil. Over the whole thing, pour the water. Mix well. Bake for 25 to 30 minutes or until tester comes out clean.

Eggless, Milkless, Butterless Cake

1 cup (240 mL) brown sugar
1-1/4 cups (300 mL) water
1/3 cup (80 mL) lard or other shortening
2 cups (480 mL) raisins
1/2 teaspoon (2 mL) nutmeg
2 teaspoons (10 mL) cinnamon
1/2 teaspoon (2 mL) cloves
1 teaspoon (5 mL) salt
1 teaspoon (5 mL) soda, dissolved in
   2 teaspoons (10 mL) water
2 cups (480 mL) sifted all-purpose flour
1 teaspoon (5 mL) baking powder

►In a saucepan mix brown sugar, water, lard, raisins, nutmeg, cinnamon and cloves. Boil for

bowl, blend beaten egg, water and vinegar. Add to flour mixture and blend. The result will be GUMMY. Your grandma will never believe it's pie dough. Divide it in half, flatten some, wrap each half in plastic wrap or bags. Refrigerate *at least* 12 hours before you roll out the crusts. Don't cheat. This is the key to the No-Fail guarantee.

When the dough is thoroughly chilled, its original gumminess will have hardened enough

three minutes. Let cool. Then add salt and dissolved soda. Mix baking powder and flour and blend into batter. Pour into greased, floured 8-inch (20 cm) square pan. Bake about 50 minutes in a slow oven, 325°F (160°C). Delicious without icing.

Eggless Chocolate Cake

3 tablespoons (45 mL) shortening, melted
1 cup (240 mL) sugar
6 tablespoons (90 mL) cocoa
1-1/2 cups (360 mL) sifted all-purpose flour
1 teaspoon (5 mL) soda
1 teaspoon (5 mL) salt
1 cup (240 mL) buttermilk

►Melt shortening, then blend in sugar and cocoa. Sift together flour, soda and salt. Add to cocoa mixture alternately with the buttermilk. Pour into greased and floured 8-inch (20 cm) square pan. Sprinkle broken nuts over top, if desired. Bake about 30 minutes in moderate oven, 350°F (175°C).

No Bake Cookies

1/2 cup (120 mL) milk
2 cups (480 mL) white sugar
1/2 cup (120 mL) margarine or butter
6 tablespoons (90 mL) cocoa
3 cups (720 mL) quick oats
1 cup (240 mL) coconut, nuts or raisins,
*   cut up*

►Put milk, sugar, cocoa and margarine in pan and bring to full rolling boil. Remove from heat and fold in oats while still hot. Add coconut, nuts or raisins. Drop from spoon on wax paper (or lightly buttered pan) and allow to cool. When cold they are ready to eat. Wrapped in heavy foil and stored cold they keep a long time and are handy to carry on a hike.
■ *Betty Lou Murray*

Excerpted and adapted from a story by the same title in *ALASKA*® magazine. July 1972.

that you can roll out the dough without too much additional flour on the board. Bang on the dough with the rolling pin to soften it some, lift and turn the dough as you roll to make sure it does not stick. Pinch together any cracks that appear (they'll hold) and continue rolling and shaping dough to about 1/8 inch (3 mm) thickness.

If the dough is too sticky, you may flour the board as heavily as you need to (oops — your grandma fainted!) without harm to the No-Fail crust. Pie dough should not be handled more than necessary. But this unconventional dough will tolerate quite a lot of amateur fiddling around and still turn out a very respectable product.

A few more No-Fail tips: Roll out the bottom crust a couple of inches (2 cm) larger than the dimension of the pie pan. Fold the dough — gently —in quarters and lay it into the pan with the corner of the fold in the middle of the pan. Unfold and ease the dough downward to fit snugly against bottom and sides, leaving no air space. The dough should be pressed — again, gently — toward the center of the pan while you're doing this, *not* stretched from the center outward.

Trim outer edge to about 1/2-inch (1.25 cm) overhang. If you are making a one-crust shell, fold this extra dough under to meet the edge of the pan; then flute it or press it down firmly with a fork. For a two-crust pie, leave the overhang as is. Fill the pie according to recipe, cut top crust to fit just to the edge. Prick it well with a fork or slash a design in it with a sharp knife to allow steam to vent during baking. Then place the top crust over the filling, fold the overhang up over it like an envelope and finish the edge by fluting or pressing with a fork.

Many one-crust pies need a *prebaked shell.* To keep an unfilled shell from shrinking during baking, line it snugly with a buttered foil basket. Fill the foil with clean pebbles or dried beans to serve as a weight. (Whatever material you use can be saved in the foil basket and used again and again for the same purpose.) Bake in a hot oven, 400°F (205°C), for about 15 minutes until the pastry is set in shape. Then carefully remove the foil basket, prick the crust all over with a fork and put it back in the oven for further crisping. If the pie is to be baked again after it is filled, don't brown the shell much more, perhaps two or three minutes, until very lightly colored. Otherwise, continue baking to desired color, 10 to 15 minutes after foil is removed. Thoroughly cool a pre-baked shell before adding filling.

An *extra flaky No-Fail crust* may be made using half butter and half lard as the shortening. The dough will be gummier, the crust flakier and yummier . . . as well as higher in calorie, cholesterol and cost. But it's a wonderful special-occasion crust.
■ *The editors, ALASKA*® *magazine*

Crumb Crust For A 9-Inch Pie

A shortcut to pie baking, crumb crusts can be made of crushed graham crackers, zwiebach, cornflakes, gingersnaps, chocolate cookies or vanilla wafers —depending on which goes best with the filling you plan. The recipe calls for sugar which may be omitted if cookies are used.

1-1/3 cups (320 mL) fine crumbs
1/4 cup (60 mL) sugar
6 tablespoons (90 mL) soft or melted butter
   or margarine

►Mix together until evenly moistened, then press mixture evenly on bottom and sides of a well-greased 9-inch (22 cm) pie pan. Chill well before filling. If the filling contains a lot of liquid or is not to be baked, the crust may be baked first to further strengthen it and add flavor. Use a slow oven, 300°F (150°C). Bake until crust is firm and slightly browned, about 10 minutes. Cool completely before adding filling.
■ *The editors, ALASKA® magazine*

Plum Pudding Eska

This pudding and its accompanying sauce are two of the glories described in "An Oldtime Alaskan Christmas Dinner," a menu prepared by Ann Chandonnet for the December issue of ALASKA® magazine, 1978. Both recipes were specialties of Bronwen Jones, who came to the town of Eska — 20 miles northeast of Palmer — in 1917.

1 cup (240 mL) sifted flour
1 teaspoon (5 mL) soda
1 teaspoon (5 mL) salt
1 teaspoon (5 mL) cinnamon
1 teaspoon (5 mL) nutmeg
1-1/2 cups (360 mL) dried currants, plumped*
1-1/2 cups (360 mL) raisins, plumped*
1/2 cup (120 mL) chopped nuts
1-1/2 cups (360 mL) coarse soft crumbs from
   white bread
3/4 cup (180 mL) finely diced candied fruit
2 cups (480 mL) ground suet (8 oz /or/ 228 g)
1 cup (240 mL) brown sugar
3 beaten eggs
6 tablespoons (90 mL) red Wild Currant Jelly
1/4 cup (60 mL) grapefruit or orange juice,
   brandy or sherry

►*This amount of dried fruit equals 1/2 pound (228 g). Sift together flour, soda, salt, cinnamon and nutmeg. Mix in raisins, currants, nuts, bread crumbs, candied fruit.

   Mix together the suet, brown sugar, eggs, Currant Jelly and fruit juice or brandy. Then mix with the flour-raisin mixture. Pour into a well-greased 2-quart (2 L) mold or two 1-quart (1 L) molds or clean coffee cans. Cover cans with doubled waxed paper, tied on. Steam on racks for six hours, replacing water as necessary so that water level stays at bottom of molds.

   Serve piping hot with Vanilla Sauce Bronwen Jones.

Vanilla Sauce Bronwen Jones
1/2 cup (120 mL) butter
1-1/2 tablespoons (23 mL) cornstarch
2 cups (480 mL) hot water
Vanilla extract to taste

►Melt butter, blend in cornstarch. Remove from heat and stir in hot water gradually. Return to heat and cook until thickened, stirring constantly. Season to taste with vanilla.

Tarkun

"Stropen" or little tarts

2 cups (480 mL) flour
3 teaspoons (15 mL) baking powder
2 teaspoons (10 mL) salt
1/4 cup (60 mL) shortening
3/4 cup (180 mL) water or milk
Jelly for filling

►Sift flour with baking powder and salt. Cut in shortening and add water. Pat or roll out on a floured board, about 1/4 inch (6 mm) thick. Cut half the dough as biscuits and half with a hole in the middle as doughnuts. Place the ones without the holes on a cookie sheet. Dip the "holed" ones in milk, both sides, and place on top of biscuit. The milk serves to brown the tops and to make them stick together. Bake in a hot oven, 400°F (205°C), for 12 minutes. When done, fill holes with your favorite jelly.
■ *Aleut Cookbook, Saint Paul Island*

Paris-Brest

*Culinary Division Grand Championship,
1979 Tanana Valley Fair*

2 cups (480 mL) Cream Puff Paste
1 cup (240 mL) Pastry Cream (flavored with
   vanilla, chocolate or rum)
1/2 cup (120 mL) Apricot Glaze
2 cups (480 mL) whipped cream
1/4 cup (60 mL) slivered toasted almonds
Powdered sugar

►On an ungreased cookie sheet make a ring of Cream Puff Paste 8 inches (20 cm) in diameter and about 1-1/2 inches (3.75 cm) thick. Use a pastry tube or spoon it out. Bake at 425°F (220°C) for 30 minutes. Reduce heat to 375°F (190°C) and continue baking for another 10 minutes. Split ring horizontally. Dry in oven with heat off for 5 to 10 minutes. Fill bottom with flavored Pastry Cream. Top with whipped cream. Replace top of ring. Spread with Apricot Glaze. Sprinkle with almonds, then with powdered sugar.

Cream Puff Paste *
1 cup (240 mL) water
6 tablespoons (90 mL) butter, cut in pieces
1 teaspoon (5 mL) salt — omit if salted butter is used
1 teaspoon (5 mL) sugar, if puffs are for a sweet filling
1 cup (240 mL) sifted flour
4 large eggs, at room temperature
Pinch of nutmeg

►In a 1-1/2 quart (1.45 L) saucepan, bring the water to a boil with the butter and seasonings. Boil slowly until the butter has melted. Remove from heat and immediately pour in all the flour at once. Beat vigorously with a wooden spoon to blend thoroughly. Then beat over moderately high heat for one or two minutes, until mixture leaves the sides of the pan and forms a smooth mass. Transfer quickly to an electric mixer; beat the eggs in one at a time until they are completely absorbed. Use the paste at once. *Note:* Never double or alter this basic recipe.

Pastry Cream
2 cups (480 mL) milk
4 egg yolks
1/2 cup plus 1 tablespoon (135 mL) sugar
1/2 cup less 1 tablespoon (105 mL) flour
1 teaspoon (5 mL) vanilla
1 tablespoon (15 mL) butter

►Scald the milk. Beat egg yolks with sugar until mixture is pale yellow. Beat in flour. Gradually pour on the hot milk, continuing the beating. Pour into a saucepan and cook, beating constantly with a wire whisk until smooth and thick. Remove from heat, stirring in vanilla and butter. Makes about 2 cups (480 mL) cream filling for Paris-Brest or cream puffs. May be kept refrigerated one week or frozen for longer.

Apricot Glaze
1/2 cup (120 mL) apricot preserves, forced through a sieve
2 tablespoons (30 mL) sugar

►Stir the strained preserves with the sugar over moderately high heat for two to three minutes until thick enough to coat the spoon and the last few drops are sticky as they fall from the spoon, 225 to 228°F (107 to 108°C) on a candy thermometer.

While the glaze is still warm, use a pastry brush to apply it to the top of Paris-Brest or filled cream puffs. If you are in a hurry, a glaze of 1/2 cup (120 mL) apricot jam warmed with 2 tablespoons (30 mL) hot water is very good, but it will not have the waterproofing quality of the cooked glaze.

■ *Lynne Hightower*
   Bake-Off Cookbook 1961-1980
   Tanana Valley Fair, Fairbanks

*Cream Puff Paste may also be used to make individual puffs, eclairs or other shapes. This recipe will make about two dozen 3-inch (7.5 cm) puffs. For eclairs, lay the paste in ribbons about 3 inches (7.5 cm) long and an inch (2.5 cm) wide. For bite-size puffs — popular containers for a variety of appetizer fillings — make teaspoon-size globules (about an inch or 2.5 cm around). The larger the glob, the larger the puff. For a moderate 3-inch (7.5 cm) puff, use a rounded tablespoon (about 17 mL).

This prize-winning cook says to bake cream puffs at 425°F (220°C) for about 20 minutes (less for small puffs), remove them from the oven and make slits with a sharp knife where filling can be inserted later. Then turn them over and dry them out another 10 minutes in oven with heat turned off.

FROSTINGS & GLAZES

Cream Cheese Frosting
1/2 pound (228 g) powdered sugar
3 ounces (85 g) cream cheese, softened
3 tablespoons (45 mL) margarine
1/2 cup (120 mL) chopped nuts

1 teaspoon (5 mL) vanilla
1/2 teaspoon (2 mL) milk

►Mix together, spread on cake when cool.
■ *Barb Schmidt*
   Northern Lites, Tasty Bites, *Fairbanks*

Chocolate Frosting

1 cube (114 g) butter
1 square (1 oz /or/ 28 g) unsweetened chocolate
2 tablespoons (30 mL) water
4 tablespoons (60 mL) evaporated milk
1 pound (456 g) powdered sugar,
    approximately
3/4 cup (180 mL) chopped nuts
1 teaspoon (5 mL) vanilla

►Bring to boil for about one minute the butter, chocolate, canned milk and water. Remove from heat and add powdered sugar, beating with a mixer. Add nuts and vanilla. If cake is firm enough not to crumble, this frosting is best used on a warm cake. If cake is cooled, you may need to add extra milk to the frosting or spread it with a knife that has been dipped in water.
■ *Virginia Steiner*
    Kitchen Magic, *Ketchikan*

Vanilla or Lemon Glaze

1-1/2 cups (360 mL) sifted powdered sugar
2 tablespoons (30 mL) melted butter
1 to 3 tablespoons (15 to 45 mL) evaporated
    milk or cream
1 teaspoon (5 mL) vanilla

►Mix to a rather thin sauce that will drizzle and spread easily over a warm cake.

Variation: *Lemon Glaze* — Omit milk and vanilla in above recipe. Add 1 to 3 tablespoons (15 to 45 mL) lemon juice.

Coconut Frosting

1 cube (114 g) margarine
1/4 cup (60 mL) evaporated milk
3/4 cup (180 mL) sugar, brown or white
1/2 teaspoon (2 mL) vanilla
1 cup (240 mL) coconut
1 cup (240 mL) chopped pecans or other nuts

►Place all ingredients in a pan; bring to boil. Remove from heat. Beat slightly; pour on warm cake. Place under broiler for a few minutes.
■ *Linda Wells*
    Northern Lites, Tasty Bites, *Fairbanks*

Wild Strawberry Jam Frosting

2 tablespoons (30 mL) wild strawberry jam
1 teaspoon (5 mL) water
Butter
1 cup (240 mL) confectioners' sugar

►Melt the jam and dilute with the water. Remove from heat and add a small piece of butter. When butter melts in the jam, combine with sugar added gradually. Beat until smooth and creamy. Add a little more sugar or water if needed for proper consistency to spread.
■ *Florence Thornton, Rabbit Creek*
    What's Cookin' in Alaska

Coffee Glaze

1 to 2 tablespoons (15 to 30 mL) hot water
1 cup (240 mL) powdered sugar
1/2 teaspoon (2 mL) instant coffee
1 tablespoon (15 mL) butter
    or margarine

►Mix and drizzle over warm cake. This glaze is especially good with Fast Start Sourdough Cake.
■ *Mary Mack*
    Saint Herman's Sisterhood Club, *Kodiak*

RUSSIAN ALASKA TEAS

Kodiak Russian Tea

"During the time my family lived in Kodiak, my mother was fascinated with the Russian ideas and ways that are still alive from the days of the early settlers of the community. Making Russian tea was a serious business to her even though we did not use a samovar."

►This ritual requires a teakettle, boiling on the stove, and two teapots on the table:
First, heat the number one pot by filling it with boiling water to the brim. When the pot is hot, dump the water.

Add to the warmed teapot 1 measured teaspoon (5 mL) of tea leaves for each teacupful of water to be poured into it, plus an extra teaspoonful (5 mL) "for the pot."

Then refill the number one pot with boiling water and let it steep for exactly four minutes.

During the time lapse, heat the second teapot with boiling water, too. Empty that water and add to this pot one bay leaf, one whole clove and a light pinch of thyme.

Now strain the tea from the first pot into the second pot and cover.

Serve at once and make a sweetener available. Mother always used currant jelly — one spoonful per teacup.
■ *Gordon R. Nelson, Palmer*
Smokehouse Bear

Variations: The sweetener may also be a spoonful of raspberry jam or a "splash" of rum. Serve the tea in heated glass cups.

Georgian Tea*

6 tablespoons (90 mL) green tea
2 quarts (1.9 L) boiling water
1 tablespoon (15 mL) grated lemon or
    orange rind, or mix the two

►Steep until very strong; strain. Sweeten with honey or sugar and serve very hot.

Russian Tea with Fruit Juices*

1/2 cup (120 mL) sugar
1 cinnamon stick
1-1/2 teaspoons (7 mL) orange rind
1/4 cup (60 mL) pineapple juice
1 teaspoon (5 mL) lemon rind
1/4 cup (60 mL) orange juice
1/2 cup (120 mL) water
3 tablespoons (45 mL) tea
3 cups (720 mL) boiling water from samovar

►Combine sugar, water, cinnamon stick, lemon rind and orange rind in a saucepan and boil five minutes. Remove cinnamon stick and add fruit juices. Pour hot water over tea and steep five minutes. Combine spicy fruit mixture with tea and serve it hot in tea glasses.

Russian Tea*
(Great Russia)

6 tablespoons (90 mL) Orange-Pekoe tea
4 whole cloves
1/2 cup (120 mL) sweet cider
1/2 teaspoon (2 mL) red food coloring
2 quarts (1.9 L) boiling water
Sugar, honey or strawberry jam

►Steep tea, cloves, cider, food coloring in boiling water for 10 minutes. Strain and sweeten with sugar, honey or strawberry jam.
■ *All three recipes are from the
    Alaska State Museum
    Reprinted from* One Hundred Years
    In the Kitchen, *Juneau*

Instant "Russian" Tea

2 cups (480 mL) Tang
3/4 cup (180 mL) instant tea — without sugar
    or lemon flavoring
1 cup (240 mL) sugar
1 package Twist, or 3 ounces (85 g)
    Country-Time instant lemonade mix
1 teaspoon (5 mL) cinnamon
1/2 teaspoon (2 mL) cloves
1/2 teaspoon (2 mL) allspice

►Mix all ingredients together and store in a glass jar with a tight cover. Use 2 heaping teaspoons (12 mL) per teacup. Fill with boiling water.
■ *Mid McLay, Homer*

MAIN DISH ACCOMPANIMENTS

Many of the salad dressings, fish, vegetable and meat sauces, basting mixtures, flavored butters and stuffings detailed in this section are called for in recipes throughout the book. It's a collection worth studying for accompaniments to many of your favorite dishes.

Polynesian Baste or Marinade
For fish or game meat

1 small can (6 fl oz /or/ 177 mL) pineapple juice
2 tablespoons (30 mL) oil
2 tablespoons (30 mL) lemon juice

2 tablespoons (30 mL) soy sauce
1 clove finely minced garlic
1/8 teaspoon (0.5 mL) powdered clove

►Mix well with a wire whisk. Use as a baste for fish during broiling or baking. Also makes a tenderizing marinade for moose or other game meat steaks or shish-kabob chunks. Allow meat to marinate four hours or more in the refrigerator. Drain meat well before broiling, using the reserved marinade as a baste only during the last minutes of cooking. Left-over marinade may be saved in the refrigerator.
■ *Anon.*

Schuler's Herb Butter

Serving fish to a crowd? Here's the sauce.

2 cups (480 mL) softened margarine or butter
1/4 cup (60 mL) finely chopped parsley
1/4 cup (60 mL) finely chopped chives
1/4 cup (60 mL) lime juice
2 teaspoons (10 mL) salt
1/2 teaspoon (2 mL) liquid hot pepper sauce
1/8 teaspoon (0.5 mL) freshly ground
   black pepper

►Cream margarine until smooth and fluffy. Beat in remaining ingredients. Serves 25 as an accompaniment to fish.
■ A Seafood Heritage

Parsley Butterballs

1/4 cup (60 mL) butter
1 teaspoon (5 mL) lemon juice
1 teaspoon (5 mL) chopped parsley

►Cream butter, add remaining ingredients. Form into small balls and chill well. Serve with fish, setting one on top of each steak — either during broiling or after, just at serving time. Makes six butterballs.
■ Seafood Recipes For Alaskans

Variation: Change the lemon juice to Worcestershire and you have a similar baste or garnish for moose steak.

Thyme Butter

For fish or shellfish

1/4 cup (60 mL) butter
1 tablespoon (15 mL) lemon juice
1 tablespoon (15 mL) chopped parsley
1/2 teaspoon (2 mL) basil
1/2 teaspoon (2 mL) thyme
1/4 teaspoon (1 mL) salt
Dash pepper

►Melt butter and add remaining ingredients. Makes about 1/3 cup (80 mL) sauce.
■ Time For Seafood

Wild Chive Sauce For Salmon

1/2 cup (120 mL) wild chives
1/2 stick (56 g) margarine (or more)
1/2 cup (120 mL) water
1/2 teaspoon (2 mL) crushed dried red pepper
Salt and pepper to taste

►Saute snipped chive leaves in margarine until tender. Add water and simmer until reduced con-

siderably in volume. Add the dried red pepper, salt and pepper as the concoction simmers. This is delicious poured over pan-fried or broiled salmon steaks. May be made ahead of time, refrigerated and then reheated.
■ The Old Homesteader

Quick and Easy Yogurt Dressing

Salad dressing or sauce for fish

1 cup (240 mL) yogurt
1 tablespoon (15 mL) nonfat milk powder
1 teaspoon (5 mL) dried onion flakes
1 to 2 teaspoons (5 to 10 mL) dry seasonings
   from a packet of your favorite buttermilk or
   milk salad dressing mix

►Mix and chill for an hour or so (if possible) to plump onion flakes. If you're short of time, omit the onion flakes and increase dry seasonings to taste. Excellent with cold white fish fillets (especially if they've been rolled and baked with Wheat Bread Stuffing).
■ Anon.

Hot Sauce For Crab

1 cup (240 mL) ketchup
2 teaspoons (10 mL) vinegar
1 tablespoon (15 mL) horseradish
3 drops Tabasco
1 tablespoon (15 mL) chopped celery
1 tablespoon (15 mL) chopped onion
1 teaspoon (5 mL) Worcestershire

►Mix all ingredients together well and store in refrigerator.
■ Phyllis Zehe
   Saint Herman's Sisterhood Club, *Kodiak*

Favorite Hot Mustard

Especially good with broiled or baked salmon

8 ounces (228 g) dry mustard
4 tablespoons (60 mL) flour
1 teaspoon (5 mL) cayenne
1/2 teaspoon (2 mL) garlic puree
1 tablespoon (15 mL) dehydrated horseradish
1/2 cup (120 mL) salad oil
1 cup (240 mL) tarragon vinegar

►Combine dry ingredients and salad oil. Then add vinegar and mix well. More vinegar may be added to turn this spread into a sauce, as desired. Store in a plastic container. Keeps indefinitely in the refrigerator.
■ Beth Deisher
   Recipes From The Scrolls of Saint Peter's
   Seward

Peppy Chive Sauce
For meat, fish or vegetables

1 cup (240 mL) plain yogurt
2 teaspoons (10 mL) lemon juice
1 teaspoon (5 mL) salt
1 tablespoon (15 mL) snipped chives

►Combine ingredients in a bowl. Refrigerate to blend flavors. Serve cold or heated.*
■ *Mamie Jensen, Juneau*

*Note: *If you heat this sauce, barely heat it. . . . Do not boil! To make it more stable, before you heat it, mix 1 teaspoon (5 mL) cornstarch into the yogurt.*

Creamy Mustard Sauce
For fish

1/2 cup (120 mL) yogurt
1 teaspoon (5 mL) cornstarch
2 tablespoons (30 mL) nonfat milk powder
1-1/2 tablespoons (23 mL) prepared mustard
2 teaspoons (10 mL) margarine
1 teaspoon (2 mL) minced parsley
1/8 teaspoon (0.5 mL) salt

►Combine yogurt, cornstarch and powdered milk in a small saucepan. Mix in remaining ingredients and heat, stirring constantly. Makes about 2/3 cup (160 mL) sauce. Add more color, if you wish, with a dash of paprika.

Yogurt-Cucumber Dressing
A good dressing for all salads — especially fish

1 or 2 medium cucumbers — enough to make
   1-1/2 cups (360 mL), chopped
1-1/2 cups (360 mL) yogurt
1-1/2 cups (360 mL) sour cream, sour
   half-and-half, or imitation sour cream
1 tablespoon (15 mL) lemon juice or white
   wine vinegar
1 tablespoon (15 mL) chopped wild chives
1 tablespoon (15 mL) sugar
1 teaspoon (5 mL) dry mustard
Cayenne pepper to taste
1 teaspoon (5 mL) salt

►To remove excess moisture from cucumbers, peel, chop and spread out on a plate. Sprinkle lightly with salt and let rest for 20 minutes or so. Drain well, blotting dry with paper toweling. Combine remaining ingredients, fold in cucumbers and chill before serving. Makes 1 quart (1 L).

Variation: If you wish to use all yogurt instead of combining it with sour cream, first combine the

3 cups (720 mL) yogurt with *either* 1/4 cup (60 mL) salad oil *or* 1/2 to 3/4 cup (120 to 180 mL) instant nonfat milk powder. Mix well before proceeding with recipes.

Quick Horseradish-Mustard Sauce
For smoked meats or pot roast

1 cup (240 mL) sour cream
2 tablespoons (30 mL) prepared horseradish
2 teaspoons (10 mL) dry mustard

►Combine ingredients in a small bowl. Cover and chill.
■ *Mamie Jensen, Juneau*

My Favorite Horseradish Sauce
A cold sauce for roast meats, ham, corned venison

1 can (14 oz /or/ 396 g) Eagle brand
   condensed milk
1/2 cup (120 mL) cider vinegar
1/2 cup (120 mL) salad oil
2 egg yolks
1 teaspoon (5 mL) salt
2 teaspoons (10 mL) dry mustard
1 jar (3-1/2 oz /or/ 100 g) prepared horseradish
Dash cayenne pepper

►Mix all together in a blender or electric mixer. Keep in container in refrigerator. Keeps a long time.
■ *Mamie Jensen, Juneau*

Quick Herbed Hollandaise
Especially for poached salmon

1/4 pound (114 g) butter
1-1/2 tablespoons (23 mL) fresh lemon juice
1/4 teaspoon (1 mL) dried tarragon, dill or
   basil leaves, crushed
Generous dash white pepper
3 egg yolks, well drained of whites
1 tablespoon (15 mL) chopped fresh parsley

►In a small saucepan, heat butter with lemon juice, choice of herbs and pepper until bubbly. Add slowly to egg yolks, beating constantly with wire whisk. Stir in parsley. Makes about 3/4 cup (180 mL) sauce.
■ *Alaska Salmon*

Variation: If you have a blender, this quick sauce can be quicker. Heat butter until foamy. Put all remaining ingredients in blender. Set the blender at lowest speed, add butter in a thin stream. Blend until thick, about 15 seconds.

Egg Sauce
For seafood

4 tablespoons (60 mL) butter or margarine
3 tablespoons (45 mL) flour
1/2 teaspoon (2mL) salt
Dash white pepper
3/4 cup (180 mL) poaching liquid, fish or
   chicken stock
3/4 cup (180 mL) milk or cream
3 hard-cooked eggs, sliced or chopped
1/3 cup (80 mL) minced parsley (optional)

►Melt butter, add flour, salt and pepper. Cook and stir until smooth. Combine poaching liquid or stock and milk; gradually stir into flour mixture. Cook and stir until thickened. Cook five minutes. Add chopped eggs. Decorate with parsley if desired. Makes 2 cups (0.47 L).
■ Alaska Salmon *(adapted)*

Creamy Lemon Sauce
For fish or shellfish

2 tablespoons (30 mL) butter
2 tablespoons (30 mL) flour
1/2 teaspoon (2 mL) salt
1/4 teaspoon (1 mL) paprika
1-1/4 cups (300 mL) milk
1/2 cup (120 mL) mayonnaise
1 tablespoon (15 mL) lemon juice

►Melt butter in saucepan. Stir in flour, salt and paprika and cook until frothy. Add milk; cook until thickened and smooth, stirring constantly. Blend in mayonnaise and lemon juice; heat through. Makes about 1-3/4 cups (420 mL) sauce.
■ *Mamie Jensen, Juneau*

Variation: Flavor with 1 teaspoon (5 mL) dill weed and/or 2 teaspoons (10 mL) capers or chopped sour pickle.

Creamy Hollandaise
A special topping for broiled fish
or a sauce for vegetables

3 egg yolks
1/2 cup or 1 stick (114 g) lightly salted butter,
   frozen
1 tablespoon (15 mL) water
2 tablespoons (30 mL) lemon juice
1/8 teaspoon (0.5 mL) salt
1/2 cup (120 mL) heavy cream (optional)

►Combine egg yolks, frozen butter, water, lemon juice and salt in a heavy saucepan. With a wire whisk, stir over medium heat until butter melts and sauce is smooth and thickened as desired. Sauce may be used "as is" to accompany vegetables or fish.

   Or, to make topping for broiled fish, cool the sauce completely. When fish is broiled, beat cream until stiff and fold into cooled Hollandaise. Spoon over fillets and return to broiler until topping is golden brown, about two minutes.
■ Seafood Treasures, *Seattle*
   (adapted from the recipe, Fillets of
   Sole Florentine, page 39)

Sauce Verte
For seafood

1/3 cup (80 mL) sour cream
1/3 cup (80 mL) mayonnaise
1 tablespoon (15 mL) chopped parsley
2 teaspoons (10 mL) chopped green onion
   or chives
1/4 to 1/2 teaspoon (1 to 2 mL) salt
1/4 teaspoon (1 mL) dill weed
Generous dash bottled hot pepper sauce

►Combine ingredients; mix thoroughly. Chill at least one hour to blend flavors. Delicious served with hot or cold salmon. Makes 2/3 cup (160 mL) sauce.
■ Alaska Salmon

Variation: Mix in 1/3 cup (80 mL) finely chopped fresh spinach; increase mayonnaise and sour cream to 1/2 cup (120 mL) each. Proceed with recipe.

Devil Sauce
For poached, broiled or baked fish fillets or steaks

2 tablespoons (30 mL) oil
1 clove garlic, peeled and split
1 tablespoon (15 mL) Worcestershire
2 teaspoons (10 mL) Dijon mustard
1/4 cup (60 mL) lemon juice
2 teaspoons (10 mL) sugar
A few grains cayenne or drops of Tabasco —
   to taste
3/4 cup (180 mL) finely chopped green onion or
   2 tablespoons (30 mL) dry onion flakes
   "plumped" in a little water
Lemon wedges and parsley

►Heat the oil in a small skillet or saucepan, adjust heat to medium and add the garlic. Brown it briefly, swirling it around in the oil constantly to keep it from burning, and then discard it. If plumped dry onion flakes are used, add them now, saute them until they are soft and slightly colored but not browned. Add the remaining ingredients — except green onions — and stir until sauce begins to boil. Devil Sauce can be used for any white-fleshed fish. You may wish to brush on a small amount during the last few minutes of broiling or baking. Remove fish to a heated platter, sprinkle on the green onions if you have them and pour remaining sauce over all. Garnish with lemon wedges (and a sprinkling of minced parsley, for color, if you're not using green onion). Sauce for four to six servings, or about 3 pounds (1.5 kg) of fish.

White or Cream Sauce (Bechamel)
For meats, vegetables, fowl and fish

2 tablespoons (30 mL) butter
1-1/2 to 2 tablespoons (23 to 30 mL) flour
1 cup (240 mL) milk
Seasonings

►Melt butter in small saucepan, sprinkle in flour and stir with a wire whisk until the mixture cooks and becomes quite frothy, three to five minutes. Add milk in a steady stream, stirring constantly until the sauce is thickened and smooth. This makes 1 cup (240 mL) basic White Sauce. You may season it to taste with salt and white pepper and use it as is, or increase the amount to suit your needs.

The variations, however, are limitless. *For the liquid,* substitute stock, or a combination of stock and milk, or use any of the liquids suggested in the basic sauce until it is thickened; then stir in 2 tablespoons (30 mL) or more of cream or sour cream until heated through and blended.

Seasonings vary the basic sauce, too. When you use them, however, be sure to add salt last of all and only if needed. Many seasonings, such as lemon juice and garlic powder, substitute for it— or, such as soy sauce and Worcestershire, already contain salt. Good flavor changes to basic White Sauce come from 1 to 2 teaspoons (5 to 10 mL) lemon juice (especially for fish or fowl); up to 1 teaspoon (5 mL) Worcestershire (for meats); a sprinkling of onion powder or juice; minced chives; a teaspoon or two (5 to 10 mL) of wine.

More Variations:
• *Cream Sauce* is the same as White Sauce except that the liquid used is always milk — no choice. After the milk has been blended in and the sauce thickened, salt to taste and then flavor, if desired, with a pinch of nutmeg and a few small cooked onions. (Steam them with their jackets on about 20 minutes; then peel and add to sauce when ready to serve.)
• *Heavy or Thick Cream Sauce* is made by increasing the ratio of flour and butter to milk.

Use 3 tablespoons (45 mL) each of butter and flour to 1 cup (240 mL) of milk. A small amount of cream or undiluted evaporated milk may be added once the sauce is thickened. Bring the sauce just to the boiling point, stirring to incorporate cream.
• *Extra-Thick Cream Sauce* is often used to hold ground fish or meat cakes together to saute or deep-fry them. Simply increase the proportion of flour in the basic sauce. For 2 tablespoons (30 mL) butter, use 4 tablespoons (60 mL) flour to 1 cup (240 mL) liquid.
• *Cheese Sauce* is easy, too. Just stir 3/4 cup (180 mL) grated Cheddar or a white cheese (avoid the stringy ones such as mozzarella) into the finished sauce. Heat and stir slowly until cheese blends.
• *Seasonings* of chopped hard-cooked egg, a tablespoon (15 mL) of sherry, capers or chopped sour pickle, horseradish or whipped cream each vary the flavor, too.

Orange Sauce For Wild Duck

1 cup (240 mL) orange juice
1 tablespoon (15 mL) cornstarch, dissolved in a
    little cold water or additional orange juice
1 tablespoon (15 mL) grated orange rind
3 tablespoons (45 mL) sugar
2 tablespoons (30 mL) curacoa or
    Grand Marnier (optional)

►Heat orange juice, thicken it with dissolved cornstarch. Add rind, sugar and curacoa or Grand Marnier. Serve hot with sliced roast duck.
■ *Mamie Jensen, Juneau*

Spiced Tomato Sauce
Poaching liquid or sauce for fish

2 cups (480 mL) canned tomatoes
2 sprigs parsley
1/4 cup (60 mL) chopped onion
1 teaspoon (5 mL) salt
2 whole peppercorns
2 whole cloves
1 whole allspice
3 tablespoons (45 mL) fat
3 tablespoons (45 mL) flour

►Simmer tomatoes, onion, parsley and seasonings together for 10 minutes. Remove whole spices and discard. Melt fat; blend in flour and gradually add the tomato mixture. Cook until thick, stirring constantly. Use as a sauce in which to bake or poach fish or use separately as an accompaniment to fish. Serves six.
■ Seafood Recipes for Alaskan

Fisherman's Favorite Barbecue Sauce

This recipe was created by a very successful fisherman especially for charcoal-grilling steelhead. It's excellent for other fish and game meats, too.

1/2 pound (228 g) margarine
1 cup (240 mL) water
1 teaspoon (5 mL) dry mustard
1-1/2 cups (360 mL) tomato juice
3/4 tablespoon (12 mL) salt
3/4 tablespoon (12 mL) sugar
3/4 tablespoon (12 mL) chili powder
1/4 teaspoon (1 mL) red pepper
1/2 tablespoon (8 mL) Worcestershire
1/4 cup (60 mL) vinegar
1/2 tablespoon (8 mL) Tabasco
3/4 tablespoon (12 mL) black pepper
1 tablespoon (15 mL) paprika
1 grated onion
1 clove garlic

►Combine all ingredients and simmer 30 minutes. Use to baste steelhead (and other fish) as it grills on foil over a charcoal fire or bakes in the oven. Extra sauce freezes well for future use.
■ *The editors, ALASKA® magazine*

Raisin Sauce For Tongue

1 cup (240 mL) raisins
2 cups (480 mL) broth from cooked tongue
2 tablespoons (30 mL) cornstarch, dissolved in
 2 tablespoons (30 mL) cold water
1/8 teaspoon (0.5 mL) dry mustard
1/8 teaspoon (0.5 mL) horseradish
Salt and pepper, if needed

►Put raisins and broth in saucepan and simmer until raisins are puffed — about 15 minutes. Add dissolved cornstarch and stir until thickened. Add mustard and horseradish. Salt and pepper if desired. Serve hot with sliced deer or moose tongue.
■ *Mamie Jensen, Juneau*

Cumberland Sauce

A recipe from the SAS (Scandinavian Airlines Service) smorgasbord, especially good with cold cuts of game meats

2 cups (480 mL) red currant jelly
1/2 cup (120 mL) port wine
1/2 cup (120 mL) red wine
2 tablespoons (30 mL) orange juice
1 tablespoon (15 mL) lemon juice
1/2 teaspoon (2 mL) French mustard

1 to 2 teaspoons (5 to 10 mL) cinnamon
1 tablespoon (15 mL) thin strips orange peel
1 tablespoon (15 mL) thin strips lemon peel
Cayenne pepper and ground ginger to taste

►Put red currant jelly through sieve and add wines and fruit juices. Stir and add mustard, cinnamon, cayenne pepper and ginger. Scald orange and lemon peel twice and fold into sauce. Serve well chilled as an accompaniment to game meats, hot or cold.
■ *Courtesy, Bunny Mathisen*
 "Help Yourself To The Sylta Flesk!"
 ALASKA® magazine, January 1977

Wheat Bread Stuffing For Fish Fillets

3 slices whole-wheat bread — or any dark, moist bread such as "seven-grain" or pumpernickel
2 teaspoons (10 mL) margarine
2 tablespoons (30 mL) minced celery
2 tablespoons (30 mL) minced onion
1/2 cup (120 mL) sour cream or yogurt, or a mixture
4 teaspoons (10 mL) lemon juice
Fish fillets

►With a fork, pull bread apart into coarse crumbs. Heat margarine in a skillet and saute celery and onion until soft — not brown. Mix into crumbs and sour cream or yogurt in a bowl. Spread over white-fleshed fish fillets. Roll fillets and anchor with a toothpick. Sprinkle evenly with lemon juice and bake about 20 minutes at 400°F (205°C). Enough stuffing for four good-sized fillets — 6 to 8 ounces (170 to 228 g) each. Serve hot with Quick Herbed Hollandaise — or chilled and topped with Quick and Easy Yogurt Dressing.
■ *Anon.*

Smoky Barbecue Sauce For Meat

3 tablespoons (45 mL) tomato sauce
2 tablespoons (30 mL) butter or margarine
2 tablespoons (30 mL) salad oil
1 tablespoon (15 mL) brown sugar
1 tablespoon (15 mL) Worcestershire
1-1/2 teaspoons (7 mL) liquid smoke
1 tablespoon (15 mL) minced dried onion
1 teaspoon (5 mL) salt
Few drops of Tabasco

►Combine above ingredients and bring to a boil. Reduce heat to simmer. Cook slowly for five minutes; add 1 cup (240 mL) hot water and cook gently for 10 minutes more.
■ *The Old Homesteader*

Wiener Sauce

1 glass Wild Currant Jelly
1 bottle chili sauce
1 drop Tabasco
1 drop Worcestershire
1 package wieners, cut up, or use cocktail size

►Combine and simmer gently until blended and heated through.

■ *Vera Slaymaker*
   Alaska's Cooking, *Anchorage*

Red Relish

1 clove garlic, minced fine
1/2 cup (120 mL) olive oil
3/4 cup (180 mL) ketchup
1 cup (240 mL) chili sauce
1/4 teaspoon (1 mL) dry mustard
3 tablespoons (45 mL) lemon juice
1/2 teaspoon (2 mL) mixed pickling spices
1 cup (240 mL) peeled and sliced carrots
1 cup (240 mL) sliced cauliflowerets
1 can (16 oz /or/ 456 g) artichoke hearts
1 small can tiny corn on the cob
1/2 cup (120 mL) drained cocktail onions
1/2 cup (120 mL) drained salad olives
   with pimento
3/4 cup (180 mL) dill pickle chunks

►Combine garlic, oil, ketchup, chili sauce, dry mustard, lemon juice and pickling spice in a saucepan. Bring to a boil. Place carrots and cauliflower in a bowl. Drain well and add the canned ingredients. Pour piping hot sauce over all. Mix well, cover and chill at least two days before serving. Makes a little over 1 quart (1 L) relish. Serve it with any meat, fish or chicken dish. It also makes an excellent first course for dinner, served with garlic bread or crackers. It is too soupy to eat as "finger food," but if you add small plates and forks to the layout, it makes a very popular nibble at cocktail time.

■ *Anon.*

Hot Fruit Compote
A delicious accompaniment for game meat or birds

2 or 3 large cans of fruit
Bananas
1/2 cup (120 mL) brown sugar
1/3 cup (80 mL) melted butter
2 teaspoons (10 mL) curry powder

►To serve eight people at dinner — or a crowd for a buffet — you will want about 1-1/2 quarts (1.45 L) of drained fruit. And for this dish you want large fruit — the "mixed fruit cocktail" size gets lost. If you can find mixed fruit for salads — and the picture shows pear or peach *halves* on the outside —that's fine. Get two of the 29-ounce (826 g) cans or three of the 1-pound (456 g) cans.

Or, you can make up your own mixture, choosing pear halves, peach halves, pineapple chunks and one other, if you wish, either plums or large sweet cherries. Fresh bananas are also excellent in this compote. Use one or two, as needed, cut into chunks.

Drain the canned fruit well (reserve the syrup for gelatin salad or something). Place it in an ovenproof serving dish. Add banana chunks, if you have them, and brown sugar, melted butter and curry powder. Mix gently until fruit is coated.

Allow this mixture to stand at room temperature for two hours or more. Then bake, uncovered, in a moderate oven for about 20 minutes. Serve as a hot side dish with smoked meats, roast pork, game meat, chicken, turkey or wild birds. With rice pilaf, this makes an elegant dinner needing very little else to complete.

■ *Anon.*

Savory Jelly Sauce

1/4 teaspoon (1 mL) dry mustard
1/4 teaspoon (1 mL) powdered clove
1/4 teaspoon (1 mL) cinnamon
2 tablespoons (30 mL) vinegar
1 cup (240 mL) Wild Currant or Crab Apple Jelly

►Mix all together in small saucepan and heat until jelly is melted, stirring constantly. Serve over hot baked, sauteed or broiled ham. Very good!

■ *Frieda Lidgren*
   Sons of Norway Cook Book, *Ketchikan*

Seasoned Crumbs
Sprinkle on salads, fish, vegetables, casseroles — you name it!

2 cups (480 mL) fine dry bread crumbs
1/4 cup (60 mL) grated Parmesan or
   Romano cheese
1/4 teaspoon (1 mL) salt
1/4 teaspoon (1 mL) pepper
1/4 teaspoon (1 mL) garlic salt
1/4 teaspoon (1 mL) monosodium glutamate
   (optional)
1/4 cup (60 mL) crushed parsley flakes

►Combine all ingredients, mixing well. Pack loosely in jars. Cover airtight and store at room temperature up to two weeks — or freeze in airtight container. Makes 3 cups (720 mL).

■ *Pearl Judd*
   Frontier Vittles, *Fairbanks*

Marinade For Spareribs

1-1/2 cups (360 mL) Lowbush Cranberry Juice
1/2 cup (120 mL) tomato puree
1/4 cup (60 mL) tarragon vinegar
2 tablespoons (30 mL) Worcestershire
1 tablespoon (15 mL) prepared mustard
2 teaspoons (10 mL) chili powder
1/2 cup (120 mL) honey
1 large onion, chopped
2 cloves garlic, peeled and split
2 teaspoons (10 mL) salt
Tabasco, a dash
2 teaspoons (10 mL) oregano

►Combine all ingredients in a large flat dish and marinate the ribs for 24 hours in the refrigerator. Turn the ribs frequently to insure that all meat has been marinated well. This should be enough marinade for five or six pounds (2.2 to 2.7 kg) of spareribs. Use the liquid for basting the ribs while barbecuing. This is particularly good for bear spareribs.

Pepper Relish
For any wild game

12 green peppers
12 red peppers
12 medium onions
2 cups (480 mL) vinegar
2 cups (480 mL) sugar
2 tablespoons (30 mL) salt

►Put the vegetables through a food chopper. Combine with remaining ingredients in a saucepan and boil for 10 to 20 minutes. Cool and store in glass jars in refrigerator, or process in boiling-water bath as directed for other relishes in Chapter 14.
■ *Elsie Clausen (adapted)*
  PTA Cook Book, *Petersburg*

Hot Wine Sauce For Venison (or Lamb)

1 tablespoon (15 mL) butter
1/2 glass currant wine
Juice of 1/2 lemon
Pinch of cayenne pepper
1/2 cup (120 mL) water

3 cloves
1 teaspoon (5 mL) salt
1/2 cup (120 mL) port wine

►Simmer all ingredients except wine for five minutes. Strain and add wine. Also add a little of the meat gravy and stir to blend.
■ *Lulu MacKecknie*

Gourmet Sauce For Moose Steaks

1 cup (240 mL) wild chive leaves, snipped into
    small pieces
1/4 pound (114 g) margarine
1/4 cup (60 mL) sherry

►Melt margarine in small heavy skillet. When the margarine begins to turn brown, put in the snipped chives. Cook gently until tender. Pour in the sherry; simmer one minute longer. Delectable on moose steaks just out of the broiler.
■ *The Old Homesteader*

Sage Stuffing For Wild Birds
Enough for 4 to 6 pounds (1.8 to 2.7 kg) of bird

1 cup (240 mL) hot water
2 tablespoons (30 mL) butter or margarine
2 chicken bouillon cubes
2 tablespoons (30 mL) minced dried onion
3 cups (720 mL) stale bread, cubed
Salt and pepper
Wild sage or commercial sage
1/4 cup (60 mL) bacon bits or crisp fried bacon,
    crumbled
1 egg

►Put hot water in small saucepan and bring to a boil. Add butter, bouillon cubes and onion. When butter is melted pour half the liquid over the bread cubes. Sprinkle with salt, pepper and sage. Use less sage if the wild variety is at hand — it is strong. Stir in bacon bits and the egg, unbeaten. Add as much more liquid as you will need to make the stuffing of a consistency to suit your taste. We like it rather moist, and we pack it into the birds tightly. You may pefer a drier dressing and may pack it loosely.
■ *The Old Homesteader*

Chapter 14

Stocking The Cache

The art of preserving the bounty of one season to provide at least survival through the next has to be as old as the first winter people inhabited these northern climes. It is an art we have not given up, for good reason. We have learned a thing or two about sanitation and temperature control and the affect of air and dampness and bacteria, but the techniques of food preservation and the reason for it have remained much the same.

This chapter is divided roughly the same way the book is. The first section describes ways of preserving fish — freezing, salting, smoking, pickling and canning.

In the second section, on game meats, you'll find techniques for making sausage, curing and smoking meats, making jerky and pemmican and a few directions for canning some of these products.

Finally, in the last section, is information about preserving the production of the earth — berries, mostly, and wild and garden produce — the key techniques being freezing, drying and canning, but with some interesting suggestions for other processes.

The process that requires the most special equipment and strict attention to the very latest "how to" information is canning. The general principles are explained here; how they apply to specific foods is discussed in each section.

CANNING — GENERAL PRINCIPLES

Canning is the best method we have of preserving seasonal foods for a long time when storage temperatures cannot be strictly controlled. It is also relatively inexpensive, unless you count your time as an expense.

It is safe *only* if it is done correctly. And it is one of the few ways with food for which many "time-honored traditions" ought to be discarded.

If you have been using the "open-kettle" method of canning for anything but jelly, stop.

Yes, "open kettle" is the method your grandmother used — loading a deep kettle with prepared fruit or vegetables or pickle relish or mincemeat; heating it to a good boil; scrupulously washing and sterilizing the jars; dipping the hot food into hot jars; clapping on the lids . . . and presuming that they sealed safely.

If you are saying, "My grandmother [aunt, uncle, cousin, brother . . . I] *always* put up green tomato relish that way. She *never* had any trouble!" . . . she was lucky. And so are you. So far.

For canning anything but jelly, there are only two ways. And, there is only one appropriate way for some types of food.

For high acid foods — fruits, barely ripe tomatoes and pickled vegetables — you may use either a boiling-water-bath canner or a pressure canner.

For all common vegetables except tomatoes; for

all fish, all poultry, all meats — use a steam-pressure canner. To process these low-acid foods safely in a reasonable length of time takes a temperature higher than that of boiling water. That can be achieved only under pressure. It is not safe to use a boiling-water bath, an oven, a steamer without pressure or the open kettle.

The reason: A very high heat is needed to kill many harmful organisms — chiefly *Clostridium botulinum,* which can cause the deadly illness called botulism. If the product being canned does not become hot enough to kill the spores (240°F or 116°C is required; boiling is 212°F or 100°C), they will grow in the airtight, low-acid conditions created in the sealed can or jar. As they grow a toxin is formed which, if eaten, causes the illness.

Canning Instructions

The best sources of canning information include recent bulletins published by the U.S. Department of Agriculture, Agricultural Extension Service (such as the University of Alaska Cooperative Extension Service), and major manufacturers of home-canning equipment. Toss out any instructions written before 1976, even the official ones. Of "unofficial" instructions, even current ones are often in error. If you have doubts, check with an agent of the Cooperative Extension Service. What follows is a shortened compilation of — but not a replacement for — the current official information. If you can foods, you should put yourself "on the mailing list" to receive updated materials from government sources.

Canning Equipment

Water-Bath Canner

The boiling-water-bath canner is used for processing high-acid foods such as fruits, tomatoes, pickles and preserves. Canners are readily available on the market. But any big metal container may be used *if it is deep enough* so that the water is well over the tops of the jars and has space to boil freely. IF YOU ARE PURCHASING A NEW CANNER, MEASURE FIRST. Not all canners are correctly represented as to size. There must be enough space above the jars to allow for 1 or 2 inches (2.5 to 5 cm) of water, plus 1 or 2 inches for brisk boiling. The canner must have a tight-fitting cover and a wire or wooden rack. If the rack has dividers, all the better, the jars will not tip during processing. A steam-pressure canner may be used for water-bath processing if it is deep enough. Cover it, but do not fasten. Leave petcock wide open so that steam escapes and pressure does not build.

Steam-Pressure Canner

The pressure canner increases the temperature at which water boils from 212°F (100°C) to 240°F (116°C). The higher temperature is required for safe preservation of low-acid foods — vegetables (except barely ripe tomatoes), all meats, all poultry, all fish.

There are presently two types of pressure canners available — the dial-gauge type and the weighted-gauge or weight-control pressure canner.

The dial-gauge canner must be checked every two years to make certain that the gauge is working correctly. Contact your local Extension office if you have questions on testing the dial gauge.

The weighted-gauge or weight-control pressure canners do not need to be checked for accuracy. There are no mechanical parts to get out of order.

The essential parts of the pressure canner include the rack, rubber gasket, safety valve and vent (petcock or steam valve). The rack prevents jars from coming in direct contact with the canner. A rubber gasket helps to seal the canner. It should be checked prior to each canning season and replaced when it becomes hard, cracked or stretched. The safety valve is a metal alloy plug located in the canner lid which melts or blows out if the temperature gets too high or the canner boils dry. The vents (petcock or steam valve) need to be cleaned after each use to allow steam to escape properly.

Pressure Saucepan

A pressure saucepan may be used for canning under pressure, but *increase the processing time by 20 minutes.*

Containers

Jars

Use only jars that are made for home canning. Jars that once contained a commercially canned product are not tempered to stand up under the time and temperature used in home canning. Also, the threads on such jars do not match canning rings and may cause an unsafe seal. Wash glass jars in hot, soapy water and rinse well. Wash and rinse all lids and bands. Metal lids with sealing compound may need boiling or holding in boiling water for a few minutes — follow manufacturer's instructions. If you use rubber rings, have clean, new rings of the right size for the jars. Don't test by stretching. Wash rings in hot, soapy water. Rinse well.

Tin Cans

Plain tin cans are satisfactory for most foods. Enameled cans are recommended for some in order to avoid discoloration of the food. Follow the manufacturer's instructions on using the sealer and preparing the cans. Of course, use only those cans which are in good condition. Cans may not be reused. Cans should be washed with hot soapy water prior to use and checked for dents and imperfections, but the lids should not be washed, since doing so may damage the seal.

Because tin cans are sealed before processing, the temperature of the food inside the cans must already be 170°F (77°C) or higher when the cans are sealed. If you are using a "hot-pack" method, check the temperature of the food again before you seal the can. If you are packing raw foods — or if the temperature has dropped below 170°F — you must "exhaust" air from the food before sealing. (See Exhausting.)

Packing into Jars & Cans

Methods

Foods packed into jars or cans may be raw or already cooked — "raw pack," "hot pack." Directions for canning individual foods usually indicate "raw pack" or "hot pack."

The Hot-Pack Method is best for meats, poultry and fruits like applesauce and, of course, jams and jellies. One Extension Service bulletin reports that its testing concludes that *all meat* is "satisfactorily canned only by the hot-pack method," though USDA information continues to list both ways. Precooking food makes it more pliable, allowing a tighter pack and requiring fewer jars. Generally, the food is precooked in water, syrup or juice. Then food and cooking juice are packed into clean hot jars.

The Raw-Pack Method is used for foods which are delicate once they are cooked and more difficult to handle — such as fish and tomatoes. Foods packed raw should be packed firmly but not crushed. Shrinkage will occur during processing. Then boiling syrup, juice or water is added to food.

Head Space

Head space is the room between the top of the food (and the juice it is packed in) and the lid. Most recipes indicate how much head space is desirable. Some foods expand during processing. Giving them too little head space can mean spillovers and, of course, an improper seal. Too much can also result in an imperfect seal because the processing time may be too short to exhaust all the excess air.

Sealing Cans and Jars

Before applying lids, wipe rims of jars and cans with a clean, damp cloth. Particles on the rim may prevent an airtight seal. Air must be exhausted from any raw fish or meat packed in either jars or cans; and from all foods packed in cans.

Exhausting Air From Tinned Foods & Raw-Packed Meats & Fish

Because tin cans are sealed before processing, the temperature of the food inside must be brought up to 170°F (77°C) or higher to expel air before the cans are sealed. Meats and fish that are packed raw — into either jars or cans — also require "exhausting" to expel air from the tissues of the food.

If you are packing hot foods into cans, simply check the temperature again before you seal the can. If it is 170°F (77°C), the can may be sealed. Otherwise . . .

To exhaust, place open, filled cans (or jars containing raw fish or meat) in the canner on a rack. Add boiling water to the canner to about 2 inches (5 cm) below the tops of the jars or cans. Do not put lids on the cans or jars. Cover the canner (any large kettle may be used). Bring water back to boiling. Boil until a thermometer inserted into the jars or cans — with the *bulb at the center of the food* — registers 170°F (77°C), or for the length of time given in the directions you are following.

Check temperatures and remove cans or jars from the water one at a time, and add boiling packing liquid or water if necessary to bring head space back to the level specified for the product. Seal cans, adjust lids on jars according to manufacturer's instructions and process.

The Steps of Boiling-Water-Bath Processing

Use the boiling-water bath for canning foods with a high acid content — fruits (most of them), tomatoes (the best are just barely ripe — *not* over-ripe and *not* green), and pickled vegetables.

Have the water ready in the canner — boiling for hot-pack and hot for cold- or raw-pack. Lower the filled jars into the water quickly. The bubbling around the rim of each jar is caused by air being forced out of the jar. Add more boiling water if needed to bring the level to an inch or two (2.5 to 5 cm) above the containers. Don't pour boiling water directly on glass jars, however. Cover the canner. When water comes to a rolling boil, start to count the processing time. Boil gently and steadily for the time recommended. Add boiling water during processing if needed to keep containers covered.

Adjusting Processing Times For Altitude

Follow times carefully. If you live at an altitude of 1,000 feet (300 m) or more above sea level, you will need to adjust processing times given in the instructions for individual foods. For boiling-water-bath canning at altitudes above sea level, adjust processing times as follows:

Boiling-Water-Bath Canner
Altitude Adjustment Chart For Canning Food

Altitude	If timetable recommends processing at 20 minutes or less, add:	If timetable recommends processing at more than 20 minutes add:
Sea level	0	0
1,000′ (300 m)	1 minute	2 minutes
2,000′ (600 m)	2 minutes	4 minutes
3,000′ (900 m)	3 minutes	6 minutes
4,000′ (1,200 m)	4 minutes	8 minutes
5,000′ (1,525 m)	5 minutes	10 minutes
6,000′ (1,830 m)	6 minutes	12 minutes
7,000′ (2,135 m)	7 minutes	14 minutes
8,000′ (2,440 m)	8 minutes	16 minutes
9,000′ (2,745 m)	9 minutes	18 minutes
10,000′ (3,050 m)	10 minutes	20 minutes

The Steps of Steam-Pressure Processing

Water Level
Use enough water in the steam-pressure canner to heat jars or cans at a steady rate and to insure against boiling dry. Water 2 or 3 inches (5 to 7.5 cm) deep is usually enough, although more may be needed for a long processing period in a canner with a weight gauge, because the weight permits a little steam to escape regularly.

Venting Steam
This is a critical step. (Don't confuse it with "exhausting" air. That is explained on page 425.) Arrange the jars or cans on the rack in the canner. Do not let them touch each other. Stagger containers so that steam can flow around them. Fasten the cover on the pressure canner securely, but do not close the vent on the lid. That is, leave the petcock open or weight gauge off. Begin heating until steam comes out the vent in a steady stream. Allow the canner to vent steam for 10 minutes. Then close the vent by placing a weight or weighted gauge over it or by closing the petcock.

Maintaining Pressure
Heat the loaded canner rapidly until the desired pressure is reached (according to directions for food you are canning). Then start the timing. *Write down* your starting time and calculate the finish time. Watch the canner during processing and regulate the heat to make sure the pressure remains constant. *If the pressure drops below the number of pounds indicated, the timing must begin again.*

Adjusting Pressure for Altitude
The recommended pressure (usually 10 or 15 pounds — 69 or 103.5 kPa) in all recipes is given for processing at sea level. If you live above sea level, process for the same length of time, but increase the pressure — 1/2 pound (3.45 kPa) for each 1,000 feet (300 m) above sea level.

Pressure Canner
Altitude Adjustment Chart For Canning Food

Altitude	Using recommended times, process at pressure of:
2,000′ (600 m)	11 pounds (75.9 kPa)
4,000′ (1,200 m)	12 pounds (82.8 kPa)
6,000′ (1,830 m)	13 pounds (89.7 kPa)
8,000′ (2,440 m)	14 pounds (96.6 kPa)
10,000′ (3,050 m)	15 pounds (103.5 kPa)

(Do not raw pack vegetables or meats at altitudes above 6,000 feet.)

Cooling The Pressure Canner
When processing time is up, turn off heat or remove canner from range. *If jars have been used,* let the canner cool until the pressure is Zero. Then wait one minute more. Open petcock or remove weight slowly to prevent a sudden change of pressure that might cause liquid to be lost from jars. Never try to hurry the cooling of any canner by putting it in cold water or by wrapping wet cloths around it. Unfasten the cover and tilt the far side up so that the steam escapes away from your face.

Take the jars out and put them on a cloth-covered table away from drafts. If some liquid in the jars has boiled away, do not open to add more. Plan to use those jars sooner than the others. Cool jars right side up. Do not cover with a cloth or try to hasten cooling. When cool — label, date and store in a dark, cool place.

If you used tins, release steam in canner as soon as the processing time is up, following the method outlined in your canner directions. After pressure reaches Zero, wait one minute and then unfasten the cover, tilting the back side toward you, so that steam will flow in the opposite direction. Cool tins in cold, clean water, changing the water as it gets warm. Take the cans from the cold water while still a little warm and they will dry themselves. Label, date and store in a dry place.

All Canning — Testing For A Good Seal
Cans and jars do not seal completely until after

they have cooled. Test the seal after the containers have cooled 12 hours.

Tap jar lids with a metal spoon. A ringing metal sound is caused by a vacuum inside the jars. The center of the lid should be pulled down (concave). It should not move when pressed with a finger. The contents should not leak when the jar is inverted.

Tin cans may be tested the same way or by immersing them in water. If any bubbles appear, they are not sealed.

If the cans or jars are not sealed, refrigerate them and use within a week or freeze the contents in other containers.

Storing & Serving Canned Foods

Cool, dry, dark, but not too cool are the rules for storing canned goods. A constant temperature of about 65°F (18°C) is ideal. Freezing does not cause canned foods to spoil, but it may damage the seal so that spoilage begins anyway. In an unheated storage area, cover canned goods with an old blanket or wrap them in newspapers. Straw is good insulation, too. The insulation should also keep cans dry. Check the seals from time to time. *Before tasting* home-canned food once it is opened, boil the product 20 minutes. (An oven method for delicate food is outlined on page 439.)

Substitutes For Salt & Sugar in Canning

Sugar

Recipes for canning fruit usually contain sugar or sugar syrup. Sugar is added for flavor and helps hold the texture, shape and color of the fruit, but is not needed to prevent spoilage.

Honey and corn syrup can be substituted for part of the sugar in preparation of syrups. Use 1 cup (240 mL) corn syrup or 3/4 cup (180 mL) honey for 1 cup (240 mL) of sugar. A mild-flavored honey is recommended to prevent masking of the fruit flavor.

There are no particular health benefits to be achieved from substituting honey for sugar. The only benefit would be cost reduction . . . if you raise your own bees!

However, all fruits may be safely canned *without* sugar (or honey or corn syrup). Simply substitute water or fruit juice for syrup or sugar pack.

To prevent fruits from softening, use only high quality fruit when canning without sugar. Prevent darkening of light colored fruits by placing them in a lemon juice and water solution — 1 tablespoon (15 mL) juice per quart (L) of water — or use a commercial ascorbic acid mixture.

Salt

With the exception of pickles and cured or smoked foods, salt is not necessary for safe processing of home canned foods. It does help retain natural color and texture of food, but it is primarily added for flavor.

To can foods without salt, follow reliable canning directions, but omit salt. The flavor of saltless vegetables can be improved by adding 1/2 to 1 tablespoon (8 to 15 mL) of lemon or orange juice to each pint (0.47 L) of carrots, beets or asparagus. Try adding 1/4 teaspoon (1 mL) mace, nutmeg or curry powder per pint (0.47 L) of green beans or peas. The use of salt substitutes is not recommended in canning as they can contain additives which may react with the foods, imparting off-flavors or colors or clouding the brine.

In making pickles and cured or smoked foods, the amount of noniodized salt specified in the recipe should always be added. Salt is generally essential for safe preservation of these foods.

FREEZING FISH & SHELLFISH

Some instructions for freezing individual species — many of the shellfish, for example — will be found in Book One recipe sections.

A good quality frozen product requires the same careful handling you give to fish you intend to eat fresh. Clean fish immediately after they are caught, keep them iced or cold until you can further treat them, freeze within 24 hours if at all possible.

Small Fish

Small fish such as smelt, may be frozen in water to keep them from drying out in the freezer. Arrange cleaned fish in a bread pan or an empty milk carton, fill the container with water and freeze. Once it is frozen remove the block of ice and wrap it in a double layer of freezer wrap.

If you have too much fish to devote freezer space to blocks of ice, wrap the fish in plastic film (see Drugstore Wrap, page 442), then in freezer wrap or heavy-duty foil.

Large Fish

You may cut large fish into steaks and fillets before freezing, if you wish, but bear in mind that the larger pieces and whole fish will keep better than small cuts.

Whole-dressed fish may be treated a couple of ways, each satisfactory. (1) Quick-freeze the fish on a tray without wrapping. Then put it in a Ziploc bag, fill the bag with water and freeze. Or (2) lay the cleaned fish on a cookie sheet or tray. Set it in the freezer, uncovered, until the fish is frozen solid. Then *glaze* the fish. Dip it into water, making sure it is completely coated, inside the cavity and outside. Return it to the freezer. Repeat this process several times. The more coats of glaze, the longer the fish will keep well. When you're finished, wrap the glazed fish carefully in freezer wrap or in a Ziploc bag, press out excess air and seal well.

Shellfish

Fresh crab should be cooked, the meat picked as soon as possible and packed in serving-size plastic containers with airtight lids. Leave 1/2-inch (1.25 cm) headroom. Many people freeze cleaned and cooked Dungeness crab halves and king crab legs in the shell, but it takes plenty of freezer room and lower steady temperatures than most home freezers can maintain when a large quantity of unfrozen food is put in at one time. If you can have them commercially frozen, first, a home freezer can maintain them.

Shrimp may be frozen raw or cooked. To freeze raw, head the shrimp, wash it in a mild salt solution — 1 teaspoon (5 mL) salt to each quart (L) of water. Drain well and pack snugly in rigid freezer containers without any headroom. Seal tightly. *To freeze precooked,* head, wash in salt solution and drop in salted boiling water until they rise to the top again. Dip them from the water, cool quickly and pack snugly in rigid containers without headroom. Seal tightly.

Storage Time in The Freezer — Fish & Shellfish
0°F (-18°C) or Less

9 to 12 Months	5 to 9 Months	3 to 4 Months
Halibut	King salmon	Chum salmon
Sole	Red salmon	Pink salmon
Flounder	Silver salmon	Clams
King crab	Rockfish	Cooked shrimp
Dungeness crab	Ocean perch	Oysters
Cod	Raw shrimp	Trout
	Large white fish	Grayling
	Sablefish	Lake trout
	Sheefish	Dolly Varden
		Small white fish

Clams and scallops are very perishable and must be frozen within hours of the time they are caught. Clams should be frozen raw; cooked ones toughen in the freezer. To freeze them in the shell, clean, scrub and place them in a heavy freezer bag. Submerge the bag in a bucket of water to force air out. Seal. For extra wrap, use a second bag, forcing the air out the same way.

Shucked clams may be wrapped tightly in several layers of plastic wrap, and then several of these packages may be put inside a freezer bag. Shucked clams and scallops may also be covered with their own juices and a weak brine — 1 teaspoon (5 mL) salt per cup (240 mL) of water. Pack meat in rigid containers, cover with juice and brine, leaving 1/2 inch (1.25 cm) headroom. Seal tightly.

SALTING & DRYING FISH

Brine-salting, dry-salting and drying are simple and cheap methods of preserving fish. They are less expensive than canning or freezing, and they do not require much equipment. All preservation methods require patience and care. These are no exception. Both brine-salted and dry-salted fish may be freshened for table use. "Good salt salmon," claims Robert Browning in *Fisheries of the North Pacific*, "soaked out, steamed or poached, teamed with a white sauce and served with boiled potatoes, makes a better country Sunday breakfast than any salt cod." Both varieties of salt-preserved fish may also be used in another popular cure — pickled fish. Brine-salting is also the first step in smoking fish, but the cure is sometimes a milder, shorter one than is required to preserve fish without freezing or canning.

Brine-Salting

The family salting 50 pounds (22.5 kg) or less of salt fish needs no special equipment except a sharp knife and a 2 to 4 gallon (8 to 16 L) container. This may be a stone crock, a wooden barrel or a tub or a food grade plastic container with a lid. Garbage cans are not food grade.

Salt Quality

Salt should be as pure and as clean as can be purchased. It should be free from carbonates or magnesium. A high-grade medium-coarse pickling salt is both inexpensive and good for all curing and canning, but dairy salt or other noniodized salt is also suitable for salt-curing. Do NOT use "free-flowing" or iodized salts, which contain chemicals that may cause off-flavor and color.

Preparing The Fish

Lean fish are salted more easily than oily fish. The salt brine penetrates better and it doesn't become rancid so easily. However, if oily fish are well salted, they are of the finest quality. Both saltwater and freshwater fish can be brine-salted.

The method of brining is the same for all varieties. Smaller fish are split down the back so as to lie flat. Large fish are split into two fillets, removing the backbone. The gills are always removed but the collarbone just below is not cut away. The collarbone is needed to support the weight of the piece when handled, especially if the brined fish is to be smoked. Without this, the piece will drop from the smokehouse hangers during the smoking.

For good penetration of salt, the flesh of the thickest pieces may be scored lengthwise to a depth of 1/2 inch (1.25 cm) and about 1 or 2 inches (2.5 to 5 cm) apart. Cut carefully so as not to penetrate the skin. The pieces should be cut no larger than will lie flat on the bottom of the crock or container you have prepared.

Saturated Brine

After the fish is cleaned, draw off diffused blood by soaking the fish in saturated brine — 6 cups (1.45 L) salt per gallon (3.8 L) of water. Then drain the pieces while you prepare the salt.

Salting Down The Fish

The amount of salt to be used depends on the season of the year, the size and fatness of the fish and the probable length of storage time. A general rule is to use one part of salt to three parts fish. Add more salt for especially fat fish and for preserving a long time without refrigeration, smoking or in hot weather. Remember, however, that excess salt may "burn" the fish and lower the quality.

In any case, find a convenient container for the salt — a pasteboard box or dishpan that you can dip into easily and will hold salt to a depth of several inches. Fill it with salt. Then scatter a thin layer of the salt on the bottom of the container you have designated as your "fish barrel." Dredge each piece of fish with salt and rub some salt into the scored places in the heavier pieces. Pack fish into the container skin side down and arrange so the pieces make an even layer. Scatter a thin layer of salt over each layer of fish and repeat the dredging of fish. Arrange each succeeding layer of fish at right angles to the layer below.

With large fish, the pieces with the backbone are placed next to the wall of the container. An extra piece may be placed in the middle to level the layer, if needed. The pieces should overlap each other as little as possible. Small fish are packed in a ring with the tip of the head touching the walls of the container. It may be necessary to lay one or two fish across the center to keep the layer level. Stagger successive layers so that each fish rests across two fish of the layer below. Scatter salt between each layer. *The top layer of fish, both large and small, should be packed skin side up.*

Place a loosely fitting wooden cover or china plate on the top layer of fish and weight the cover down with fair-sized rocks or bricks — well washed for this purpose. The fish will form its own brine. Small fish will be completely brined in 48 hours. Thicker and fatter fish will require a week or slightly longer.

Final Storage

At the end of this time, the fish are removed, scrubbed in fresh saturated brine (proportions given earlier) with a stiff brush and then smoked or repacked with a very light scattering of salt between the layers. Fill the crock or container with a fresh saturated salt brine and store in a cool, dark place. After three months, or at the first sign of fermentation, change the brine again. *Do not keep longer than nine months.*

Dry-Salting

The initial steps of dry-salting fish are exactly like those for brining, the difference being that the salted fish are stacked on a rack so that the brine will run off, rather than accumulating.

Dry-salting takes a little more effort and equipment. You need a place where the salted fish can be stacked to let the brine run off, and you need a shaded drying rack or a method of hanging the fillets to dry where they will get good ventilation but be protected from sun. The reward is that dry-salted fish will generally last longer than brine-salted ones.

Initial Steps

Prepare fish as directed for brine-salting: Split smaller fish, fillet and score larger ones, clean and drain the fish; then dredge the pieces with salt.

After salting, stack the fish in rows on a rack, choosing a place where the brine formed can run away. First, scatter a thin layer of salt on the place where the fish are to be stacked. Alternate each layer, head to tail, so that the layers remain even, and scatter salt between each layer. Pile the fish flesh side up except for the final layer, which is laid skin side up. Overall, use about one part salt to four parts fish.

Removing Excess Salt

The fish are taken out of salt after 48 hours or in one week, depending upon their size and the weather. In damp or stormy weather, they are allowed to remain in salt longer. Less time is required for salting in warm weather.

When the fish are ready for drying, they should be scrubbed in brine to remove all excess salt. No traces of salt should be visible. Drain for 15 or 20 minutes before arranging on the drying racks.

Drying

Drying racks are frames made of wood and covered with chicken wire or wooden slats about 2 inches (5 cm) apart. The frames are placed on legs about 4 feet (1.2 m) high to allow good air circulation. The racks are roofed over to protect the drying fish from rain and direct sun, but the sides are left open.

Fish should be kept shaded at all times during drying. A breezy location should be chosen if possible. If only a few fish are being dried, they may be hung from the rafters of a shed or barn where there is good cross ventilation. The pieces may also be hung on hooks or dowels as you would hang them in a smokehouse.

If placed on racks, the fish are laid skin side down but should be turned three or four times the first day. The fish are gathered up and stored each night to prevent molding and decay where dew is heavy. At night, the fish are stacked, as during salting, on floor racks and covered with a weight at least as heavy as the fish, to press out further moisture. No stack should be more than 2 feet (60 cm) high. If at any time the weather is unfavorable and the fish cannot be put out to dry, repile each day with the top fish at the bottom and the bottom fish at the top of the pile. If several days are bad for drying, added salt may be needed.

A smoke or smudge under the drying racks may be necessary, for the first day at least, to keep the flies away. The smudge should always be of "green" deciduous leaves and branches to make a heavy smudge. Evergreens give off a resinous smoke.

Testing Dryness

The usual test for dryness is to press the thick part of the flesh with the thumb and forefinger. If no impression can be made, the fish are sufficiently dried. The cured fish are wrapped in waxed paper, packed in a wooden box, tightly covered, and stored away in a cool, dry place. At the first sign of rust, mold or reddening, scrub the fish off in a saturated brine and dry in the air for a day or two, before storing again in a cool, dry place.

Drying Fish Without Salt

Fish may be dried without salting to provide a food much like jerky. Because the salt acts as a preservative and speeds the process of drawing off moisture, drying fish without it takes even more care. Many of the same principles apply, however.

Start with very fresh fish. Clean and fillet them as suggested earlier, leaving skin on or not, as desired. Skin gives stability to smaller fillets.

If you air-dry the fish — rather than using a heated dryer — good ventilation is essential, but the fish should also be protected from direct sunlight. An open frame that will allow you to stretch a wood or canvas roof over the racks is ideal. Do not use plastic, however, as it traps hot moist air — enemies of successful drying.

Cover the fish with cheesecloth to protect it from insects — or build a smudge as suggested above. After the first day or two, the fish develops a glaze that helps protect the meat.

Check the drying fish frequently, turning it so that all areas dry evenly. Where flesh hangs over a wood drying pole or folds over itself, air circulation is not adequate to dry properly. It's also wise to give fish the "nose test" frequently. Fish should remain sweet smelling throughout the drying. Off odors mean spoiling fish.

"As your fish dry," says Ole Wik ["How to Dry Fish," *ALASKA*® magazine, May 1979], "they will slowly change color, just as meat does. Whitefish, for example, go from translucent gray white to a light, chalky yellow. At the same time, the flesh shrinks greatly in volume — by perhaps two-thirds — and the fish become progressively stiffer. . . . Like meat jerky, the fish will continue to dry for some time after getting hard. The flavor will change, too. . . . When the fillets resemble little sheets of leather, they are ready to take down. . . . To store the fish, you can just put them loosely into a cloth sack and hang them in a dry place."

SMOKING FISH

Since the advent of freezers, smoking has become more a technique for adding special flavors to fish than it is a means of long-term preservation. All smoked fish requires storage at cool — 38°F (3.5°C) — temperatures. And, for storage longer than several weeks, all but the most thoroughly smoke-cured (smoke-*dried*) fish should be frozen or canned.

If your end purpose is mainly to preserve delectable *taste*, however, smoking or kippering part of your catch is rewarding and relatively effortless. It is also a technique open to immense creativity. The strength of the brine, added ingredients, the length of brining, drying time without smoke, the kind of wood used, the length and temperature of the smoke — all these elements are varied in many ways to achieve different tastes and textures.

What Kinds of Fish To Smoke

In Alaska, the fish most often used for smoking is salmon, but many species are suitable. Some people swear the technique was developed especially for steelhead. Sablefish, or black cod, is also a popular fish for smoking, as are grayling and whitefish and lake trout. In fact, smoking them right on the riverbank may be the only way to bring home a catch of grayling, their flavor is so delicate.

Whatever the kind, the fish must be top quality. It should have been cleaned and gutted immediately when caught and kept cool and shaded. If the fish isn't good enough to eat fresh, it won't be good smoked.

Frozen or completely brine-cured fish may also be used for smoking. Thaw frozen fish in the refrigerator. Then treat it as you would fresh fish. Soak out brine-cured fish in several changes of water for up to 12 hours, or until it is no longer too salty.

Methods of Hanging Fish For Smoking

The way you plan to hang fish in the smokehouse — or on the racks of a smaller smoker — determines how you cut them before brining.

Small fish may simply be gutted to be hung whole on S-shaped hooks. Or string several gutted fish on a round wooden stick that is inserted under the gill flap and through the mouth. Smaller dowels may be inserted in each cavity to hold it open for even smoking. Or split small fish so that the meat may be hung on two rods run through the flesh just beneath the bony neckplates.

A large fish may be split along the back and boned so that the meat opens in one piece, leaving the belly solid. To do this, first remove tail and gills. With a sharp knife, make a crosswise cut down to the backbone on each side of the head. Then make two lengthwise parallel cuts on each side of the backbone through to the stomach cavity. After some practice, you will learn to lift out head, backbone and entrails in one piece. Clean the cavity thoroughly.

If the split sides are quite thick, slash the flesh with several lengthwise parallel cuts (not through to the skin) so that the smoke will penetrate. These splits may be hung open across poles, or they may be propped open with dry cedar sticks placed across the fish and inserted into the flesh at each side. A longer stick may be inserted all the way through the skin near the tail end of the fish to act as a rod from which to hang the fish. If the fish is heavy, a second rod may need to be inserted behind it for additional support.

Another method useful for both small and large fish is to remove the head and split the fish down both belly and back, leaving the tail section unsplit to act as a hanger.

Or simply fillet the fish and smoke the two sides or cut them in strips or pieces. Strips run the length of the fillet and are usually about 1-1/2 to 2 inches (3.75 to 5 cm) wide. They may be hung or set on trays. Chunks are generally smoked on trays and should be about 2 inches (5 cm) wide and no more than 1 inch (2.5 cm) thick.

In preparing the fish, always keep them as cool and tidy as possible. After the pieces are cut, soak them for about 30 minutes in a cleansing brine of 1 cup (240 mL) salt per gallon (3.8 L) of water to draw off blood.

Salting The Fish

Salting is an essential feature in smoking fish. Unsalted fish will usually sour or spoil if kept at smoking temperatures for any length of time. The strength of the brine and the amount of time the fish is left in it and some of the ingredients are all matters of preference.

One method of determining the ratio of water to salt is to just keep adding salt to the amount of water it will take to cover the fish until no more salt will dissolve in it. Some people also swear by the efficacy of dropping a raw potato or egg into the water and adding salt until the object floats.

Or you can be conventional and measure. Try using 1 pound (456 g) of salt for every 5 quarts (4.75 L) of water.

If you're new at it, you can leave discretion entirely to someone else and pick one of the recipes that comes complete with brining instructions. (Most do.)

Brine ingredients — always water and salt, of course — may also include brown sugar and/or some spices. The length of the brining also varies, from 25 minutes to 8 or 10 hours. Because of that, by the way, grayling is better simply sprinkled with salt rather than brine-soaked prior to smoking.

Desalting & Air-Drying

Once fish is removed from brine, rinse or scrub it well to be sure all visible particles of salt are gone. If the brining has been more than a few hours, it may be necessary to soak the fish under running water or in several changes of fresh water to remove saltiness. You may cook a small piece to see how salty it is, or run your fingers over the flesh and then taste them for saltiness.

It is also important to air-dry the fish enough to glaze the meat before smoking begins. Choose a shaded, breezy location and protect the fish from insects by covering it with cheesecloth. The temperature should be below 40°F (4.5°C). If the meat is not sufficiently dry before smoking begins, it will tend to steam and soften instead of becoming firm once heat is applied, and white spots may develop on the flesh. The drying may take several hours, overnight, or up to two days in damp weather. Fish may be hung in the smokehouse during this period if ventilation is good. A blower or fan may be used to speed the process.

Making The Smoke — Hot or Cold?

The choice of wood leaves still more room for personal preference. It should NOT be evergreen because the resinous smoke transmits an unpleasant taste. Alder is the most popular choice in Alaska, but hickory chips, crab apple, cottonwood and sawdust are other possible selections. Many of the recipes indicate the cook's choice.

The temperature of the smoke also makes a difference in the final product. Most processes begin with an initial period of cool drying when the temperature in the smokehouse is about 90°F (32°C). Then smoke is introduced and the heat is adjusted so that the *internal temperature of the fish* is brought up to about 85°F (29°C) for "cold-smoked" fish and to about 150°F (65°C) for "hot-

smoked" or "kippered" fish. In other words, kippered or hot-smoked fish is *cooked*, ready to eat as soon as it comes from the smokehouse and subject to more rapid spoilage; while cold-smoked fish has been moderately preserved — still in need of refrigeration but able to retain safe quality for a period.

The length of time the fish are smoked depends on how dry you want them. A light (that is, shortened) cold smoke is recommended for fish that is to be canned, since the canning process brings up smoke flavor.

Flavor and texture is also regulated by how close the fish are hung to the heat. For cold smoking, it stands to reason, the fish are hung farther from the heat source than those being kippered.

For all these matters — choosing the wood, controlling heat and smoke, Adolph Mathisen's directions — Adolph's Cold-Smoked Salmon, Steelhead and black Cod — contain excellent advice.

Storing Smoked Fish

After smoking, allow the pieces of fish to cool for a short time while they are in the smokehouse. Cold-smoked fish may be left to cool a longer time than kippered or hot-smoked fish.

After that smoked fish may be wrapped tightly and stored in the refrigerator. Cold-smoked fish will generally keep about three weeks. Kippered fish, a much shorter time.

To retain the best flavor, however, do what the commercial packers do — freeze or can smoked fish immediately, unless you plan to use it right away.

Smoke-Cured Fish — "Indian Style"

Only thoroughly smoke-cured fish — the "Indian" style prepared by Eskimos, Indians and other bush dwellers as the winter supply for themselves and their dogs — may be kept successfully unfrozen for longer than about three weeks.

Preparing this product is tricky. It is actually smoke-drying. It requires from four days to a week of continuous fire, and the resulting product is only about one-third its original weight, is quite firm and has a very glossy surface. Fish and fire must be tended very carefully or the fish simply cooks to a tasteless shrivel rather than drying slowly. This dehydrated fish will keep for an undetermined period (not "indefinite"), but it, too, must be stored tightly wrapped, in a dry place, at a temperature that does not rise above 40°F (4.5°C). It is boiled 10 minutes before being eaten.

Adolph's Cold-Smoked Steelhead, Salmon and Black Cod

►It is important that you smoke fish only in cool weather. The ideal temperature is between 30 and 40°F (-1 to 4.5°C). This keeps the smoke cool.

The ideal fish for smoking is steelhead. The steelhead has a flavor all its own, and the oil content in the fleshy part of the fish is perfect for a good, moist smoked product.

Prepare your fish for salting — steelhead or king salmon, whichever you prefer or happen to have — by splitting the fish lengthwise. Then remove the backbone so that there is none on either side. Use a very sharp knife.

Set the fish on a tray, fleshy side up, and just cover the surface with a medium grind noniodized salt. Lift and shake the fish lightly to remove excess salt. The salt should be evenly distributed on the fleshy side of the fish.

Now you need a tub with a rack that fits inside. Set the fish, fleshy side down on the rack so that it is not resting on the bottom of the tub. It is important to vary according to the size of the fish the length of time that it stays in the brine that forms. A 6- to 8-pound (2.7 to 3.6 kg) fish should stay 14 hours. A 10- to 12-pound (4.5 to 5.5 kg) fish, I would leave there about 18 hours. If the fish is over 18 pounds (8 kg), leave it 24 hours.

After that time, I remove the fish and rinse it lightly. Then I put it in a tray and allow it to drain for about two hours.

Then the fish is ready to hang. I use stainless steel tuna hooks because they do not mar or discolor the flesh. They have two prongs; each one is a hook with an eye in it. Using the cotton-type line made for wrapping meat, I hang the fish on 8-inch (20 cm) loops threaded through these prongs.

I hang the fish in the smokehouse and allow it to air-dry for a day or two before I start the smoke. (Again, the temperature should be 40°F — 4.5°C— or cooler.) This removes as much of the moisture on the outside of the fish as possible. The drier the flesh, the brighter the color the smoked fish will be. This is the big secret of getting good color.

For cold smoke, the fish must be hung as close to the top of the smokehouse as possible. Keep it far away from the heat, so that the smoke will be cool by the time it reaches the fish.

A lot depends on the quality and condition of the smokehouse. Number one, you should be able to control the ventilation. The smoke has to pass through your smokehouse and be vented through the top. Mine has a pitched roof covered by a plywood sheet I can raise and lower to control the amount of smoke going out the top.

Then, of course, you must have a pit in which to build the fire for making smoke. Again, it is desirable to be able to control the amount of heat and air that go into the burner.

For cold smoke, start the fire with dry wood and then feed it green alder for the long smoke, but be sure to remove all the bark. If you don't, your fish will have a bitter taste.

I start with a very small fire, adding to it when the logs burn down to coals so that the added wood will ignite without smoldering too much. If the fire isn't burning properly, it will give off gray smoke. You must have enough draft to make sure the smoke is blue.

Continue this process for a minimum of six days. Smoke the fish until oil begins to show on the outside. The fish can be taken out or at least sampled at this time, but leaving it a while longer will give it more color.

Black Cod (Sablefish)

►On an 8- or 9-pound (3.6 to 4 kg) black cod, split and remove backbone, cover with salt (same as for salmon or steelhead), shake off surplus and place on a rack for 12 hours. Use the same method for smaller fish but reduce the number of hours in proportion to the size of the fish. Hang in the smokehouse, keeping a low fire as cold as possible, until the fish are a very pale yellow. Too much color makes the fish bitter.

To cook smoked cod, put it in boiling water, allow it to simmer 12 to 15 minutes without covering, or until the fish flakes. Do not overcook or it all falls apart.

■ *Adolph Mathisen*
Courtesy, Bunny Mathisen
Petersburg

Cold-Smoked White Fish Fillets

►Any white-fleshed, "lean" fish which will produce fillets weighing more than 1 pound (456 g) may be used. Cut the fish in fillets, removing the backbone and skin. Cover with a saturated brine and hold for two hours. Remove and drain for 10 to 15 minutes and air-dry for two hours. Hang fish and cure over a fire with a fairly light smoke for eight hours at a temperature not higher than 90°F (32°C). (If any of the flesh is resting against a stick or pole, turn the fillets after the first four hours so that the smoke penetrates evenly.)

After the first eight hours, smother the fire so that a dense cloud of smoke is obtained and continue smoking until the fillets are a deep straw yellow, turning them as necessary to color evenly. This operation should take about six hours. Cool the fillets thoroughly and wrap each separately in waxed paper. Store in a cool, dry place. They will keep about 10 days.

■ Smokehouses and The Smoke Curing of Fish *(adapted)*

Smoky Joe Salmon
No smokehouse? Try this recipe for a small amount of salmon that may be processed in a portable smoker.

10 pounds (4.5 kg) salmon fillets
Brine #1 — Water to cover, plus 1-1/2 cups (360 mL) rock salt
Brine #2 — 1/2 cup (120 mL) each — noniodized salt and brown sugar— per 1 quart (1 L) water needed to cover fish
Seasonings: pepper, garlic powder, maple flavoring, honey (optional)

►Soak fish in Brine #1 about 30 minutes (no longer) to draw off any remaining blood. Rinse and cut into chunks about 1 inch (2.5 cm) thick and 2 inches (5 cm) wide. Place in Brine #2 and refrigerate or keep in a cool place about eight hours or overnight.

Remove fish from brine, rinse in cold running water, drain and pat dry with paper towels. Allow fish to air-dry until the surface looks shiny and is tacky to the touch. Sprinkle fish with pepper and garlic or other seasonings — such as flavored salts — and brush with maple-flavored honey, if desired. If the skin has been left on, pierce it in several places.

Allow about 15 minutes to preheat smoker, using hickory or alder chips. Oil racks to keep fish from sticking and arrange fish, allowing space between pieces for smoke to circulate and placing smaller pieces on top racks farthest from heat.

The length of smoke depends on your taste (and the manufacturer's instructions if you are using a commercial smoker). Check the fuel every hour or so. When smoking is finished, allow fish to cool thoroughly at room temperature, up to two hours. Then wrap well in plastic wrap and store in refrigerator or freeze.
► *Anon.*

Smoked Brown-Sugar Cured Salmon

►Clean and fillet salmon. Prepare a salt mixture by combining 2 cups (480 mL) salt, 1 cup (240 mL) brown sugar, 2 tablespoons (30 mL) white pepper, 1 tablespoon (15 mL) each — crushed bay leaves, allspice, crushed whole cloves and mace. Dredge salmon in salt mixture to collect as much as will cling to the flesh. Leave for six to eight hours. Rinse and scrub under running water to remove all traces of salt. Soak salmon in running or frequently changed water four to six hours. Dry in fresh air for six hours. (If the day is damp, dry up to 10 hours.)

Start fire and let it burn down to coals; smoke temperature should not be over 90°F (32°C).

Smoke fish for eight hours, then build up a dense smoke, keeping temperature below 100°F (38°C) and using a spray of water when necessary. Continue smoking for 16 hours. It is best to keep fire going continuously for the 24 hours, but if you must let fire die at night, start again in the morning. When finished, the fish is almost tender enough to spread with a knife.

If fish is to be canned after smoking, limit the dense smoke to four to seven hours, or until the flesh surface is light brown. The canning process will intensify the smoke flavor.
■ The Fisherman Returns *(adapted)*

Crab Apple Smoked Salmon
"Some people use alder to smoke salmon, but we use wood from crab apple trees that are plentiful on Gravina Island near Ketchikan, where our homestead is located. I like the sweet, mild, fragrant smoky odor and taste we get from it."

►Fillet salmon (any species) or steelhead. Cut it into 4-inch (10 cm) squares, about 2 inches (5 cm) thick. This way all the fish will be uniform in flavor. Fish halves can be smoked if preferred. Use uneven pieces and backbone for canning.

For each 5 pounds (2.25 kg) fish, sprinkle with the following mix, adjusted to suit individual taste:

5 teaspoons (25 mL) salt
3 teaspoons (15 mL) raw sugar
1/4 teaspoon (1 mL) black pepper

►Let the fish stand overnight. Drain. Place fish chunks on racks in smokehouse, skin side down, over glowing coals and charred wood in order to dry and glaze. This takes about an hour. Then smother the glowing coals to a heavy smoke with green chunks of apple wood or peeled alder.

For quick kippered fish, ready in about eight hours, use low rack, 18 inches (45 cm) from the fire.

For longer smoking, use middle rack, 30 inches (75 cm) from fire. After the first eight hours, smoke about two hours each day for 7 to 10 days. The fish will become dry and hard-smoked.

To cold smoke for canning, use the top rack, 48 inches (1.2 m) from fire, three to four hours.
■ *Helen Blanchard*
"I Smoke Salmon"
Alaska Fishing Guide *(1979)*

Norwegian Smoked Pressed Salmon

►After cleaning as usual, cut off tail and head. Then cut along spine and remove backbone. Spread flat and hold down edges of back skin with wooden picks. Cover with salt and sugar — 1 quart

(1 L) salt to 1 cup (240 mL) sugar. Press between two wide boards with a small weight on the top for two to three days, depending on the size of the salmon.

Remove the salt mixture with a cloth. Wash fish with 1 teaspoon (5 mL) saltpeter dissolved in 1/4 cup (60 mL) of brandy or water. Smoke for eight hours in cool alder smoke. Let salmon hang for about six days before use. (The temperature should be cool, about 38°F — 3.5°C).

■ The Fisherman Returns

Kippered Salmon

Kippered fish is dried in cool smoke, then cooked in hot smoke for a short period. It is a quick-to-spoil product and must be kept refrigerated or frozen. But it is ready to eat without any further cooking when it comes from the smokehouse, and there are many people who like it as well or even prefer it to cold-smoked salmon. The dark orange or red coloring of commercially kippered salmon comes from a very short (30-second) dip in food coloring right after the fish has been drained of brine. Home-kippered fish has a browner sheen. "Any kind of salmon may be kippered," says Robert Browning [Fisheries of the North Pacific], "but white king salmon and fall-run chum salmon are the species most commonly kipper-processed. First-quality kippered salmon consists of choice, evenly shaped and sized pieces of the side. But odd pieces [such as collar tips or tail chunks] are extensively used, too, turning into human use perfectly good salmon that otherwise might be discarded entirely or made into animal food or meal." Other species of fish may be kippered, too. Herring — slit along the back so that it will open in one piece, leaving the belly solid — is especially popular. Adjust brining and smoking times depending on the size of the fish.

►Halve salmon lengthwise and cut into chunks. Soak pieces in a brine solution of 2-1/2 cups (600 mL) salt dissolved in 2 quarts (1.9 L) of water for 30 minutes to two hours, according to thickness. Be sure the chunks are well covered in brine. Rinse the pieces thoroughly in running water and lay out on a rack to air-dry for an hour or two. If flies are present, protect fish with a covering of cheesecloth or a light smudge of smoke. When the fish has dried sufficiently, the surface will be shiny and dry to the touch.

Start the fire and let it burn down to coals; smoke temperature should be about 80 to 90°F (27 to 32°C). Smoke fish a total of 12 to 15 hours until a good glossy skin has formed. During the last two hours, increase the temperature gradually — up to 250°F (121°C).* If the temperature rises rapidly to 250°F, the smoking time is decreased 40 to 60 minutes. Cool and eat.

■ The Fisherman Returns

*The internal temperature of the fish itself should not go above 150°F (65°C). That's cooked.

PICKLING FISH

Curing fish with vinegar (acetic acid) is one of the easiest food-preservation techniques known.

Pickled fish may be cooked or uncooked and requires no further processing under pressure, *but it must be refrigerated or kept at a steady temperature of about 38°F (3.5°C) during pickling and afterward.* And, while many old — and otherwise very good — recipes claim "indefinite" storage life for their product, pickled fish should be used within four or five months. Pickled fish MAY be canned, if desired. A recipe for Pressure-Canned Pickled Herring begins on page 440.

The best fish for pickling are those with high oil content — king and sockeye salmon, herring, smelt, black cod, for example. Although they can be pickled without prior salting, the salt cure— even a short one — firms the flesh and kills undesirable bacteria. Since heavy salt curing does preserve fish for extended periods without refrigeration and pickling does not, your best bet for storing a large quantity of fish is to keep it salted, pickling only amounts you can easily refrigerate and use within a short period. Once salt-cured fish is freshened and placed in pickle brine, it needs to be refrigerated.

Preparation

Either start with fish that has already been dry-salted or brine cured (see page 428) for at least five to eight days. Or, if you want to pickle a small amount of fresh fish, use one of the shorter-term salt cures suggested in many of the recipes that follow. *Refrigerate the fish during this short cure.*

Fresh fish should be cleaned as usual, heads and scales removed, backbone removed if the fish is large. After salting, surface brine may be removed by rinsing the fish in fresh water or soaking it in several changes of water — not longer than a day —if the fish has been heavily salted. The skin may be removed, if desired, the fish cut into bite-sized pieces or strips which are placed loosely in glass jars or crocks (never metal). Cover the fish with a pickling solution and cure it under refrigeration until the bones soften — one to two weeks.

Ingredients

Pickling recipes are many and varied — and sometimes secret. The safe ones must use at least as much vinegar as water. Additions such as sugar, salt, spices and onions add flavor, but it is the vinegar that preserves the fish (along with refrigeration).

If *fresh fish* is used, choose the same high quality fish you would broil or bake for your next meal. Pickling will not improve bad fish. By the same token, salted fish should have been cured under proper conditions.

Vinegars must have an acetic acid content of at least 4 percent. (Forty grains means the same thing.) This will be listed on the label. Most general purpose vinegars are 5 percent acetic acid and quite suitable for pickling. Distilled white vinegar is the most generally used.

The *water* used in pickling solutions should not be hard water. Especially avoid water that has a high iron, calcium or magnesium content as it may cause off-flavor and color. The *salt* should be high grade, pure canning or pickling salt because it does not contain calcium or magnesium compounds. *Whole spices* give the best taste results, although ground ones may be used.

One gallon (3.8 L) of solution will pickle 6 to 7 pounds (2.7 to 3.2 kg) of fish and make about 2 gallons (7.6 L) of pickled fish. Maintain these ratios to pickle safely.

Mustard Fish Pickles

1 gallon (3.8 L) fresh herring or hooligan
(or any oily fish)
2 quarts (1.9 L) vinegar
1 quart (1 L) water
1/2 cup (120 mL) sugar
1/2 teaspoon (2 mL) cardamom
3 tablespoons (45 mL) dry mustard
3/4 teaspoon (3 mL) white pepper
1 teaspoon (5 mL) mace
1 teaspoon (5 mL) cloves
1 teaspoon (5 mL) allspice

►Wash and clean fish. In a container that is not metal, place alternate layers of cleaned fish and curing salt — not iodized. (Large fish should be filleted first; smaller fish may be brined whole.) Put a plate or glass utensil on fish to weight it and it will make its own brine. Keep cool — about 38°F (3.5°C) — or refrigerate.

Rinse fish well. (Fish salted longer than 24 hours in brine should be soaked in cold fresh water before pickling.) Cut into chunks about 1 to 1-1/2 inches (2.5 to 3.75 cm) long, discarding tails, fins, and heads.

The remaining ingredients combine in a

saucepan and simmer about 20 minutes. Cool and pour over prepared fish. Keep refrigerated.

■ *E.V. Roberts, Cougar, Washington*
   The Alaska Sportsman®
   ALASKA® *magazine, August 1972*

Spiced Herring

5 salted herring
2 large onions, sliced thin
Equal parts of milk and water, enough to
   cover herring

►Clean herring and soak in equal parts of milk and water for two or three hours. Cut in pieces, any size desired. Alternate layers of sliced onion and herring in a jar and cover with the following sauce:

1 cup (240 mL) vinegar
1/3 cup (80 mL) salad oil
1/3 cup (80 mL) water
6 tablespoons (90 mL) sugar
3 bay leaves
1/2 teaspoon (2 mL) whole pepper
Pinch of nutmeg

►Combine sauce ingredients and bring to a rolling boil. Allow to cool before covering the herring. Keep refrigerated. If this recipe is made in the morning, it can be eaten in the evening.

■ *Mrs. Knud Stenslid*
   PTA Cook Book, Petersburg

Cordova Pickled Salmon

►*Step 1:* Cure salmon fillets retrigerated overnight in a salt brine, or use salted fish. Old-timers recommend that the salmon be salted down in the keg for 15 days for the best curing, and they use fine or medium salt rather than rock salt because there is less pitting of the flesh.

Step 2: Cut flesh from skin and slice fish into approximately 1-1/2-inch (3.75 cm) pieces, boning what you can.

Step 3: Rinse the brine from the fish or, if it is heavily salted, soak in clear water about 10 hours, or to taste, changing the water frequently. (You can test the saltiness by rubbing your fingers over the fish and then tasting them.)

Step 4: Per quart (1 L) of picklng brine desired, mix in a 4-cup (1 L) measure:

1/2 large box (box size — 1¼ oz /or/ 35 g)
   pickling spices
1 tablespoon (15 mL) bay leaf or 3 whole leaves
1/4 cup (60 mL) brown sugar, or more to
   suit taste
White vinegar diluted with an equal amount of
   water to make 1 quart (1 L) pickle brine

►Taste the brine. If it's too "vinegary," add a little more sugar, but always use as much vinegar as you do water in the brine. Pour solution into a saucepan, bring it to a boil and boil five minutes. Cool completely and strain.

Step 5: Layer loosely into a large jar:

Prepared fish chunks
1 lemon, sliced
1 white onion, sliced
Whole red peppers, as desired
1/4 to 1 cup (60 to 240 mL) white wine,
   depending on size of jar

►Other ingredients suggested by Bob Gill of Cordova are: sliced stuffed green olives, pickled canned carrots, tiny canned corn on the cob, hot peppers, pimento and other pickle pieces. His additions are rated "Super good!" by my husband.

Cover ingredients of jar with pickling solution and allow to pickle at least four days before using. Keep under refrigeration or in a cool place that doesn't get above 38°F (3°C) during pickling and afterward. If you find you like a spicier fish, you can save the pickling spices from the brine, tie them in a cheesecloth bag and place them at the bottom of the jar before you layer in other ingredients. Tilt the jar of fish now and then during pickling.

■ *Rose Arvidson, Cordova*

Pickled Smelt

Brined smelt
4 cups (1 L) white vinegar
1 cup (240 mL) brown or white sugar
1 cup (240 mL) dry sherry or water
2 large onions — one chopped, one sliced thin
2 bay leaves, crumbled
4 teaspoons (20 mL) mixed pickling spices
2 large lemons, sliced, or equivalent in
   lemon juice

►*Note:* White sugar gives a product with a lighter color; brown sugar may be preferred for flavor.

In an enamel or stainless steel pot, bring vinegar, sherry or water, sugar and spices to boil. Reduce heat and barely simmer for about five minutes, stirring to dissolve sugar. Set aside to cool. When cool, add lemon.

Wash, drain and dry the salted smelt. (If it is heavily salted, it may require soaking in several changes of fresh water.) Cut fish into 1-inch (2.5 cm) pieces, removing tail and fins.

Layer fish and onions in a sterilized gallon (3.8 L) jar. Pour in enough cold pickling liquid to cover. Allow to stand refrigerated 48 hours before eating. Pickled fish will keep refrigerated up to three months.

■ Smelt

Pickled Herring

12 salt herring, skinned
1/2 cup (120 mL) brown sugar
1/2 cup (120 mL) water
1 teaspoon (5 mL) whole pepper
Few whole cloves
Few bay leaves
1-1/2 cups (360 mL) vinegar
Lemon slices
Onion slices

►Skin, bone, and put herring to soak overnight. Drain. Boil sugar, water, cloves, peppers, and bay leaves for five minutes, then cool. Add 1-1/2 cups (360 mL) vinegar. Alternate layers of herring, sliced onion, lemon slices, until all herring is used. Top with slices of onion and lemon. Pour the vinegar and spices over the mixture. Let stand a day or so before serving. Keep refrigerated. Makes two pints (0.47 L).

■ *Mrs. Thomas Lande*
PTA Cook Book, *Petersburg*

CANNING FISH & SHELLFISH

Before you begin, please read the general information about canning, beginning on page 423. Canning is the best way we have of preserving foods for long storage when the temperature of storage cannot be entirely controlled. But good quality — and safety — exact a price. Canning requires particular attention to "the rules." THE ONLY WAY TO CAN FISH IS IN A PRESSURE CANNER. Be sure you understand the kinds of pressure canners that are acceptable, how to check the gauge for accuracy, how to prepare the containers, how to adjust the times given in recipes if you live above sea level and all the steps of the canning process itself.

Before you can clams and other bivalves, read Danger! PSP, beginning on page 94. Canning does NOT destroy the toxin.

Preparing Fish & Shellfish For Canning

The quality of fresh fish and shellfish deteriorates rapidly. To prevent spoilage, follow the same procedures for gutting, cleaning and chilling as those recommended for fish that are to be eaten fresh. Then can them as soon as possible afterward, or soon after processing by smoking or pickling.

Shellfish to be canned should be soaked or cooked in water containing salt, acid, or both, as directed in the recipes that follow. Either lemon juice or white vinegar can be used to prevent discoloration of light-colored shellfish. Citric acid, sometimes recommended, can be purchased from pharmacies.

Packing into Containers

Containers for pressure canning fish may be glass or tin, but NO LARGER THAN 1 PINT (0.47 L). Safe processing times for quart (1 L) jars have not been determined.

One-half pint (240 mL) or pint (0.47 L) jars may be used or half-pound (228 g) flat or No. 2 tins can be used. Check rims for chips or cracks.

Plain tin cans may be used for fish, but "C" enamel (seafood formula) cans should be used for shellfish and smoked salmon to minimize sulfide discoloration of the container and the product. The use of regular tins is not harmful, but does affect the appearance of the product. In general, use the container specified by individual instructions.

Number of Containers Needed

As a rule of thumb, for each 25 pounds (11.3 kg) of fish, you will need 12 No. 2 cans or pint jars; 24 half-pint jars or flat tins.

Packing

Another rule of thumb is to pack raw fish flush to within 1/4 inch (6 mm) of the top of the can or jar. Specific instructions are given in most recipes.

Wipe rims carefully with a clean cloth before sealing with a lid. Any fat or food particles may prevent a proper seal.

IF THE FISH OR SHELLFISH IS PACKED RAW — OR — IF IT IS PACKED IN CANS (either raw or cooked), you will need to exhaust air from it before lids are applied. See page 425 for instructions. Don't confuse "exhausting" with "venting." *Exhausting* is the process of expelling air from the contents of the jar or can itself. Fish needs extra help with that if it is packed raw. All foods packed into cans must be exhausted because cans are completely sealed before processing begins. *Venting* is the process of expelling air from the pressure canner, so that it will be steam — not air pressure— that completes the canning process.

The remaining steps of canning fish are as outlined in the general instructions for canning (see page 423) and in the following recipes.

Halibut, Gray Cod, Rockfish, Large Flounder or Sole

►Fillet fish and remove the dark, fatty portions. Cut the fillets into can or jar size pieces. Prepare a brine of 1-1/2 cups (360 mL) salt to 1 gallon (3.8 L) of water. Add the cut pieces to the brine solution and soak for 10 minutes. Remove and drain for five minutes — OR — if brine is not used, add salt to each container, 1/2 teaspoon (2.5 mL) per pint (480 mL). Pack tightly in containers, leaving 1/4-inch (6 mm) head space.

Exhaust containers (see page 425) until the center of each container reaches 170 °F (77 °C). Remove containers from the canner. Drain off the liquid and add salad oil: 1 tablespoon (15 mL) for half-pint (240 mL) jars or half-pound (228 g) flat tins; 2 tablespoons (30 mL) for pint (480 mL) jars or No. 2 tins.

Clean rims of containers and seal according to manufacturer's directions for the lids. Vent pressure canner; add gauge or weight and bring pressure up to 10 pounds (69 kPa). Then begin timing. Process half-pint (240 mL) jars and half-pound (228 g) flat tins at 10 pounds pressure (69 kPa) for 90 minutes. Process pint (480 mL) jars and No. 2 tins for 100 minutes.
■ The Fisherman Returns

Whole or Minced Clams

►Keep live clams cool until ready to can. Wash shells and steam to open. Discard any that don't open. Remove meat, saving the juice.

Wash the meat thoroughly in a weak salt brine— 1 to 3 tablespoons (15 to 45 mL) salt per gallon (3.8 L) of water.

Then blanch the meat by dropping it into boiling water that contains 2 tablespoons (30 mL) vinegar or lemon juice — OR — 1/2 teaspoon (2 mL) citric acid per gallon (3.8 L) of water. Boil one to two minutes.

Drain* and pack the hot clams into half-pint (240 mL) or pint (480 mL) jars, leaving 1 inch (2.5 cm) head space. Cover with hot clam juice. Add boiling water if necessary, leaving 1 inch (2.5 cm) head space. Adjust caps. Process half-pints (240 mL) for 60 minutes, pints (480 mL) for 70 minutes at 10 pounds pressure.

*Variation: *Minced Clams* — After blanching and draining the meat, grind the clams. Then pack 7 ounces, or about 1-1/2 cups (200 g or 360 mL), into pint (480 mL) jars — OR — 3/4 to 1 cup (180 to 240 mL) into half-pint (240 mL) jars, leaving 1 inch (2.5 cm) head space. Cover with hot clam juice, adding boiling water, if necessary, and leaving 1 inch (2.5 cm) head space. Process as for whole clams.
■ Canning Seafood *(adapted)*

Salmon

►Remove fins and head. Clean and wash thoroughly. Leave backbone in. Cut into can-length pieces. Soak in brine — 1 cup (240 mL) salt to 1 gallon (3.8 L) water — for one hour. Drain for several minutes — OR — if brine is not used, add salt to each container — 1/2 teaspoon (2 mL) per pint (480 mL). Pack solidly but do not crush.

Exhaust containers until the center of each container reaches 170 °F (77 °C). Remove containers from the canner. Check food level, clean rims of containers and seal according to manufacturer's directions for lids.

Vent pressure canner; add gauge or weight and bring up to 10 pounds (69 kPa) pressure. Then begin timing. Process pint jars (480 mL) and No. 2 tins 100 minutes.
■ The Fisherman Returns

For Safety's Sake
Heat Home Canned Fish Before Eating!

Here's how:
- **Open the jar or can of fish. Check the contents. If it smells bad or has gas bubbles, THROW IT AWAY! DO NOT TASTE!**
- **If it smells and looks good, insert a meat thermometer upright into the jar, with the tip at the center of the fish.**
- **Cover the jar or can loosely with foil.**
- **Place in an oven that has been preheated to 350 °F (175 °C).**
- **Remove from the oven when the meat thermometer registers 185 °F (85 °C). This will take about 30 minutes.**
- **Allow the jar or can to stand at room temperature for about 30 minutes. This allows heat to distribute evenly.**
- **Serve the fish hot or chill for later use.**
- **Wash the lid in hot soapy water before placing it back on the jar.**

Crab

►Keep live crabs cool until ready to use. An acid brine helps to prevent discoloration of crab meat. Prepare the brine by adding 1/4 cup (60 mL) lemon juice or white vinegar and 1 cup (240 mL) salt per 1 gallon (3.8 L) of boiling water needed to cook crab. Remove the back shell and thoroughly clean the crabs. (Chapter 4 contains a full description.) Wash the bodies with several changes of cool water. Boil 20 minutes in the acid brine.

Meanwhile, add 1 cup (240 mL) salt and 2 cups (480 mL) lemon juice or white vinegar to 1 gallon (3.8 L) *cool* water. Drain the cooked crabs. Remove the meat from body, legs and claws and rinse in cool brine. Squeeze the crab meat to remove some of the liquid.

Pack into half-pint (240 mL) or pint (480 mL) jars, leaving 1 inch (2.5 cm) head space. Cover with boiling water, leaving 1 inch (2.5 cm) head space. Adjust lids. Process at 10 pounds (69 kPa) pressure — 70 minutes for half-pint jars, 80 minutes for pint jars.
■ The Fisherman Returns

Halibut Cheeks Canned in Jelly

►Get the halibut cheeks from select halibut. Avoid those that have been gaffed, bruised or clubbed. The coagulated blood will spoil the delicate flavor. Fresh halibut cheeks are best, but select frozen cheeks may be canned if they have been carefully frozen without darkening.

Can in half-pound (228 g) flat C-enamel cans. Prepare halibut cheeks as for canned fillets of halibut. After draining off hot liquid, add 1 ounce (28 g) or 2 tablespoons (30 mL) Jelly Solution, sufficiently hot to run through the fish. Seal and process as indicated for halibut, gray cod and rockfish fillets (page 439).

Jelly Solution
1-1/2 teaspoons (7 mL) powdered agar-agar
8 level teaspoons (40 mL) plain gelatin
1 cup (240 mL) hot water

►Powdered agar-agar may be obtained from a drugstore. Dissolve it and the gelatin in hot water. Heat again and pour over fish. Proceed.
■ The Fisherman Returns

Oysters

►Keep live oysters cool until ready to can. Wash shells and steam open. Remove meat. Wash meat in weak salt brine — 1/2 cup (120 mL) salt per gallon (3.8 L) of water.

Drain meat and pack into jars, leaving 1 inch (2.5 cm) head space. Cover with a weak salt brine—about 1 tablespoon (15 mL) of salt per quart (1 L) of water.

Adjust lids and process pints (480 mL) and half-pints (240 mL) for 75 minutes at 10 pounds (69 kPa) pressure.
■ Canning Seafood

Shrimp

►Remove heads as soon as shrimp are caught. Chill until ready to can. Wash and drain shrimp. Cook shrimp 8 to 10 minutes in boiling acidic brine — 1/4 to 1 cup (60 to 240 mL) vinegar per gallon (3.8 L) of water. Rinse in cold water and drain.

Peel shrimp.

Pack into jars, leaving 1 inch (2.5 cm) head space. Cover with boiling salt brine — 1 to 3 tablespoons (15 to 45 mL) salt per gallon (3.8 L) of water.

Adjust lids and process half-pints (240 mL) and pints (480 mL) for 45 minutes at 10 pounds (69 kPa) pressure.
■ Canning Seafood

Smoked Salmon

►Smoking followed by canning is a favorite method of preserving salmon. Cut smoked fillets in can lengths. Pack in the can. It is recommended that smoked salmon be canned in C-enamel (seafood formula) cans. Seal containers according to the manufacturer's directions for the lids. Vent pressure canner. Add gauge or weight and bring pressure up to 10 pounds (69 kPa). Then begin timing. Process 95 minutes for half-pint (240 mL) jars; 90 minutes for half-pound (228 g) C-enamel tins; 100 minutes for No. 2 C-enamel tins.
■ The Fisherman Returns

Trout, Smelt and Perch

►Remove fins, head and insides. Clean and wash thoroughly. If large, cut in slices. Pack vertically. Add salt — 1/2 teaspoon (2 mL) per pint (480 mL)—if desired, but no water.

Exhaust containers until the center of each container reaches 170°F (77°C). Remove containers from the canner. Check food level, clean rims of containers and seal according to manufacturer's directions for the lids. Vent pressure canner; add gauge or weight and bring pressure up to 10 pounds (69 kPa). Then begin timing. Process pint (480 mL) jars or No. 2 tins, 100 minutes.
■ The Fisherman Returns

Pressure-Canned Pickled Herring
A pickle that need not be refrigerated

►Use strictly fresh herring. Scrape off scales, remove fins and heads; clean and wash the fish thoroughly, but do not remove backbones. Cut fish into jar-length pieces and soak in a brine of 1/2 pound (228 g) pickling salt to 1 gallon (3.8 L) of water for about one hour. Drain fish for 10 minutes. Pack into half-pint (240 mL) or pint (480 mL) jars, rather loosely. Fill each with half-strength Spiced Vinegar Sauce. (Dilute finished recipe below with water, half and half). Place jars in cold water up to a level of 2 inches (5 cm) below rims and bring to a boil. Let boil 20 minutes.* Invert jars over a wire screen and drain well.

Place a slice of raw onion, a bay leaf, a few mixed pickling spices and enough *fresh* full-strength Spiced Vinegar Sauce to cover the fish in each jar. Seal according to the type jar being used. Process in a pressure canner at 10 pounds pressure (69 kPa) for 90 minutes for 1/2-pint (240 mL) jars; 100 minutes for pint (480 mL) jars.

Full-Strength Spiced Vinegar Sauce
2 quarts (1.9 L) distilled white vinegar
1 quart (1 L) water
4 tablespoons (60 mL) sugar
1/4 ounce (7 g) whole black peppercorns
1/4 ounce (7 g) mustard seed
1/4 ounce (7 g) whole cloves
1/8 ounce (3.5 g) cracked cardamom seed
1/8 ounce (3.5 g) cracked whole ginger
1/8 ounce (3.5 g) bay leaves

►Add sugar and water to the vinegar; add spices tied loosely in a cheesecloth. Let simmer for one hour. Strain and use clear liquid.
■ *Courtesy, Dr. Donald E. Kramer*
Sea Grant Program
University of Alaska, Anchorage

*It is best to check the temperature of the fish at the center of the can by inserting a thermometer. Exhaust until it reads 170°F (77°C). This recipe is also suitable for salmon, shad, mackerel, trout and lake trout.

Garlic Sauce For Canning Salmon

1 pint (0.47 L) ketchup
1/2 pint (240 mL) salad oil
1 heaping tablespoon (17 mL) salt
1 teaspoon (5 mL) white pepper
1/2 cup (120 mL) cider vinegar
10 large, fresh, crushed garlic cloves

►Heat sauce ingredients to boiling. When canning any salmon except king, add 1 tablespoon (15 mL) sauce to each half-pint (240 mL) jar after exhausting and draining. Seal and process as directed. Do not open for a month or more. . . . Gets better all the time.
■ *Dory Wingard and Bunny Mathisen*
Petersburg

Tomato Sauce For Canning Hooligan
Enough for 6 pounds (2.7 kg)
cleaned hooligan, heads removed

2 cups (480 mL) barbecue sauce
3/4 cup (180 mL) oil
1/4 cup (60 mL) vinegar
2 teaspoons (10 mL) salt

►Pack fish into jars as directed (Trout, Smelt and Perch), leaving 1/2-inch (1.25 cm) head space. Exhaust containers until fish at center reaches 170°F (77°C). Meanwhile, heat sauce ingredients to boiling. Remove fish containers from the canner and drain. Add enough Tomato Sauce to cover fish, leaving 1/2-inch (1.25 cm) head space. Adjust caps. Process as directed.
■ *Ann Chandonnet*
"Hooligan, Sure Sign of Spring in the North"
ALASKA® *magazine, May 1979*

FREEZING GAME MEAT

The specific techniques of aging and butchering of game meats are discussed in Chapter 7. The main essential: Chill meat as quickly as possible after the animal is killed and keep it chilled — 33 to 36°F (0.5 to 2°C) — until it is wrapped for the freezer. Meat should be hung for chilling and aging.

When you are ready to package butchered meat for the freezer, prepare the packages in the quantities you're likely to use them. (There's an exception to this; bush dwellers who use an outdoor cache as the freezer sometimes find it better to freeze meat in large chunks, using the animal skin as protective wrapping. If that's your situation, please see Ole Wik's advice on butchering — Cutting Meat The Alaska Bush Way — page 193. In order to use the outdoors, game should be killed after you can be certain of steady below 0°F [-18°C] temperatures. Ole lives at the foot of the Brooks Range and faces few doubts about his ability to keep meat frozen.)

Wrap the meat in moisture-vapor-resistant coverings to make the package airtight. This will help to prevent drying out in the freezer. Place a couple of layers of waxed paper between individual chops and steaks. This will also help retain moisture and make it easier to thaw pieces evenly.

The Drugstore Wrap

To wrap an airtight package, first wrap the meat in plastic wrap, pulling it tight to drive out air. Then wrap in foil or freezer paper, using what's usually called "the drugstore wrap." Cut foil or paper sufficiently large to have 2 or 3 inches (5 to 3.75 cm) of paper left over at each end. Bring these edges up around the package to meet evenly. Then fold — once, twice or more — to snug the paper tightly around the meat. Fold ends similarly and seal ends and seams of paper packages with freezer tape. Foil is usually crimped enough to seal without tape. Label the packages — date, what's inside, weight or number of servings.

Loading The Freezer

Freeze quickly at 0°F (-18°C) or colder. Turn the temperature control to the coldest position to speed up freezing and to prevent warming of already-frozen foods. To freeze a maximum load, wait 24 hours before returning the control to its normal position (which should maintain the 0°F [-18°] temperature). Smaller quantities take less time.

If possible, limit the amount of food frozen at any one time to about 2 pounds (1 kg) per cubic foot (30 cm) of total storage space. Place the unfrozen packages against a refrigerated surface — not on top of other frozen food. If necessary, use a board or heavy cardboard — such as corrugated carton material —between the frozen and unfrozen packages to prevent them from coming in contact with each other.

In the following chart of recommended storage limits, note that the smaller the cut of meat, the shorter the storage time generally. Hence, flank and other cuts often used as stew meat might be best frozen whole to be cut after thawing. Stew meat, steaks and chops may be cut most easily from meat that is still partially frozen.

Thawing Meat

Most frozen meat may be cooked either with or without thawing first. But extra cooking time must be allowed for meats not thawed. Large frozen roasts may take as much as one-and-one-half times as long to cook as unfrozen cuts of the same weight and shape. Small roasts and thin cuts, such as steaks and chops, would, of course, require less increased time.

If you prefer to thaw meat before cooking, thaw it in the refrigerator without unwrapping it. A 3-pound (1.4 kg) roast will require about 24 hours to thaw in the refrigerator.

Freezing Cured Meats

Frozen cured meat loses quality quickly and *should be used as soon as possible after it is thawed.* If you freeze it, be sure you can remove it from the freezer in meal-sized quantities.

Storage Time in The Freezer — Game Meats
0°F (-18°C) or Less

6 to 12 Months	5 to 9 Months	3 to 4 Months	1 to 2 Months
Venison roasts	Sheep/goat roasts	Ground Venison	Fresh sausage (up to 3 mo)
Venison steaks	Sheep/goat chops	Venison stew meat	Cured meats (1 mo preferred)
		Sheep/goat ground meat	
		All organ meats	

For best quality, use within the shortest recommended time, rather than the longest.

MAKING SAUSAGE FROM GAME MEATS

One of the best uses for tough cuts of meat, scraps and trimmings is sausage. Almost any game is suitable — deer, elk, antelope, moose, caribou or smaller game which has been trimmed of fat.

Different kinds of meat may be mixed together in sausage. Caribou or moose with fat pork makes an excellent combination.

Preparing The Meat

Lean meat from any part of the carcass may be used. Most often, the meat from the back and hind legs is saved for roasts and steaks. But trimmings and boneless, fat-free lean meat from other areas of the carcass are excellent for sausage.

Because fresh or cooked sausage has a short "shelf life," lengthen it as much as you can by preparing it as soon as possible after the kill. The next day is best. The rest of the meat may be left for aging, but prepare sausage right away. If possible, briefly freeze the meat to be used for sausage to destroy live parasites which are sometimes found in game meat.

Speed and cleanliness in sausage making is a must to avoid bacterial growth. Keep the meat at 38°F (3.5°C) or colder while you prepare everything else you need. The quality of the sausage is almost directly proportional to the length of time meat has been thawed or left to stand before being used.

Mixing The Ingredients

Cut the meat and fat into 1-inch (2.5 cm) squares and sprinkle with seasonings. Mix well and then grind. Fat or suet should be kept thoroughly chilled for easier grinding. People who make a lot of sausage develop special spice combinations that are a unique "trademark," but basically there are four kinds of sausage: the raw bulk kind (see Country Style Sausage); fresh sausage that is cooked in the casings or in loaf form (see Moose Meat Bologna); sausage cured in casings (see Summer Sausage and Hard Salami); and specialty sausages that are made from organ meats (Head Cheese).

Using Commercial Cures

Several of the sausage recipes suggest using a commercial cure. Most of them contain sodium nitrate and/or sodium nitrite which gives a red, "cured" color to the sausage after heating. Sausages which do not contain cure will be browned after processing. Cures such as Modern Cure or Prague Powder can sometimes be purchased from small commercial sausage makers. Complete cures such as Morton's Tender Quick are also available in grocery stores or locker plants. Follow the instructions on the container if complete cures are used. They often replace most of the salt

and sugar called for in these sausage recipes. A couple of recipes for "refrigerator cured" meats, using the Morton mixture, are in Chapter 7.

Shaping The Sausages — Using Casings

Fresh sausage may be made into patties and frozen that way for later use (or frozen in bulk, just as you would hamburger). Or it may be cooked in loaf pans if you don't want to bother with casings. If so, the mixture should contain at least 5 to 10 percent binder of some kind — bread crumbs, soy protein concentrate or another — in order to keep the meat from separating.

The most common way to store sausage is in casings. Pork casings, pickled or preserved in dry salt, may be obtained from some locker plants. Beef casings, sheep casings and artificial casings are also available where sausages are made commercially.

Casings preserved in dry salt must first be soaked in lukewarm water for about 30 minutes before use. Flush each case by putting the end of it over the cold water tap and running water through it. Unused casings may be drained, covered again with fine salt and frozen.

Some artificial casings should be soaked in hot tap water — 100°F (38°C) — at least 30 minutes, but not more than four hours, before use. Then they must be punctured with a knife point before the sausage is stuffed inside to eliminate air pockets in the finished sausage.

You may also MAKE casings from strips of muslin. To form casings about 1-1/2 inches (3.75 cm) in diameter, cut strips about 6 inches (15 cm) wide and 16 inches (40 cm) long. Fold lengthwise and stitch edges together to form tubes.

Stuffing The Casings

It's easy . . . if you have access to a commercial sausage stuffer! Or if you plan to make sausage very often, an attachment for your meat grinder is a reasonable investment. But it is not an overwhelming job without such equipment, especially if two people perform it — one manning the stuffing implement, the other holding the casing.

A reasonably adequate set of tools can be homemade. For larger casings, get a piece of plastic or stainless steel pipe of a diameter that will fit snugly into one end of the casing. Then you need a baseball bat, sawed off so that it will fit into the pipe. You need to be able to push it all the way through, but it should be a tight fit. (If your children object, another dowel might substitute for their baseball bat, as long as it's the appropriate diameter.)

First you stuff the sausage into the pipe, tamping it well to remove air. Then attach the casing to one end of the pipe. Tie off the open end of the casing. Then force the meat into the casing by pushing it through the pipe with the baseball bat or other tight-fitting rod.

Processing Cooked Sausage

Sausage that is cooked during processing must be heated to an internal temperature of 152°F (67°C). A thermometer is an absolute must for accuracy. Insert the bulb to the center of the meat.

Smoking Sausage

Sausages may be smoked in their casings after they are cooked. See instructions on page 451, Smoking Cured Game. Hang sausages to drip thoroughly dry before applying smoke. Use a light, cold smoke from a small fire of peeled green alder or willow — three to five days. Cold-smoking is most thoroughly described in the section on Smoking Fish, beginning on page 431.

If you use a smoke chamber in which the coals are directly beneath the meat, protect the fire from meat drippings by inserting a metal or aluminum foil baffle between meat and fire. (Be sure smoke can circulate around it to the meat.) This will prevent the wood from catching fire or emitting smoke that is produced from the meat drippings.

Storing Sausage

Fresh or fresh cooked sausage is readily perishable and has a short shelf life of four or five days at refrigerator temperature. It should be frozen if it is to be kept longer. In the freezer, either cooked or fresh sausage will keep two to three months, stored at 0°F (-18°C), or slightly longer at colder temperatures.

If you won't use it in that length of time, it is best to freeze the meat unseasoned — ground or in chunks. Mark the packages "meat for sausage making." Then thaw, grind and season it as you use it.

Fully cured sausage (such as Hard Salami, which is dried enough to lose 35 percent of its weight in moisture reduction) may be wrapped in locker paper or foil and hung in a cool, dry, well-ventilated place. Keep it away from sunlight. Or it may be kept frozen, either dipped in wax first or wrapped in foil or locker paper. Lightly seasoned sausage may also be canned. See page 454.

Serving Sausage

To keep fresh sausage patties from falling apart while frying, add up to 1/2 cup (120 mL) of cold water for each 4 pounds (1.8 kg) of sausage and mix meat and water together well (use your hands) until the mass becomes sticky and doughlike.

Fresh uncooked sausages and cooked sausages may be pan-fried, baked in an oven, simmered, pan-broiled or grilled. However, some cooked sausages are usually eaten cold — such as salami and liver sausage.

Country Style Sausage

15 pounds (6.75 kg) lean meat
10 pounds (4.5 kg) pork or beef fat
3/4 cup (8 oz /or/ 228 g) salt
6 tablespoons (90 mL) ground black pepper
5 tablespoons (75 mL) rubbed sage

►Cut lean meat and fat into 1-inch (2.5 cm) squares or grind through a coarse — 1/2- to 1-inch (1.25 to 2.5 cm) plate. Season by sprinkling the ingredients over the meat and hand mix. Grind through a smaller plate — 3/16 inch (4.5 mm). Sausage may be frozen in packages, made into patties or stuffed into casings. This recipe produces a mild sausage. For more seasoning, increase the amount of pepper and add other spices such as nutmeg, ginger or mace — about 1 tablespoon (15 mL).
■ You and Your Wild Game

Fresh Cooked Sausage
Two styles — both made the same way

Moose Sausage
15 pounds (6.75 kg) moose meat, one-fourth to one-third pork fat or suet
3 tablespoons (45 mL) sausage seasoning
5 teaspoons (25 mL) salt
2 heaping teaspoons (12 mL) sage (if desired)
6 chili peppers, crushed

Moose Meat Bologna (Italian Style)
15 pounds (6.75 kg) moose meat, one-fourth to one-third pork fat or suet
1 cup (240 mL) commercial smoked salt (follow directions on package)

3-1/2 tablespoons (53 mL) salt
4-1/2 tablespoons (68 mL) black pepper
1 tablespoon (15 mL) mace

►For either recipe, follow the same procedure. The meat and suet should be kept chilled for easier grinding. Put them through the grinder with a coarse blade. Spices may be sprinkled on the meat before it is ground, or afterward, as preferred. Mix the meat by hand for at least 15 minutes; a small amount of water in the mixture helps keep the meat from sticking to the hands. Pack the ground meat into a pan and chill it overnight before grinding again with a fine blade.

Stuff the mixture into casings, and boil them in plain water until they float.

The sausages may be refrigerated or frozen for use as is or smoked, using a cold smoke, three to five days.

■ The Hunter Returns

Variation: *Summer Sausage* is drier and harder than regular cooked sausage and keeps longer. It is made in the same way, except that the chunks of meat are first cured for three days in a pickle or corning solution before grinding. DO NOT ADD SALT to the sausage. Meat cured previously can be mixed into this recipe if you have some on hand.

Cooked Salami

19 pounds (8.5 kg) lean meat
6 pounds (2.7 kg) pork or beef fat
1 cup (240 mL) salt
1/2 cup (120 mL) sugar
1 quart (1 L) cold water
4 tablespoons (60 mL) ground black pepper
3 tablespoons (45 mL) garlic powder
3 tablespoons (45 mL) coriander seed
4 teaspoons (20 mL) ground mace
4 teaspoons (20 mL) ground cardamom
2 teaspoons (10 mL) cure (optional)

►Cut lean meat and fat into 1-inch (2.5 cm) pieces or grind through a coarse blade. Season by sprinkling the ingredients over the meat and hand mix. Grind through a 1/4-inch (6 mm) plate while adding water; then regrind through a 1/8-inch (3 mm) plate. Stuff into casings 2 or 3 inches (5 to 3.75 cm) in diameter. Place in a smokehouse and heat at 180°F (82°C) until the internal temperature of the sausage reaches 152°F (67°C). Move to a cold-water bath until the internal temperature lowers to 100°F (38°C). Rinse briefly with hot water to remove grease and hang sausage at room temperature for two or three hours before refrigerating. Chill overnight before serving.

■ You and Your Wild Game

Hard Salami

You should be thoroughly familiar with drying and smoking processes before trying this recipe — rewarding, but more exacting than others.

22 pounds (9.9 kg) lean meat
3 pounds (1.4 kg) pork fat
0.87 pound (0.39 kg) salt
0.37 pound (0.17 kg) sugar
3 tablespoons (45 mL) ground white pepper
2 teaspoons (10 mL) cure
1 teaspoon (5 mL) garlic powder

►Grind meat and fat through a 1/2-inch (1.25 cm) plate and mix all ingredients. Regrind through a 1/8-inch (3 mm) plate. Store the mix in 6-inch-deep (15 cm) trays for seven days at 45°F (7°C). Stuff in fibrous or natural casings. Hold stuffed product for 35 days at 45°F (7°C). Fully dried sausages lose 35 percent of their weight during this drying period, which takes approximately 90 days. If the product molds in the drying room it should be wiped with an oiled rag. At the end of the 90-day drying period, hard salami can be smoked as long as the smoke-house temperature stays below 90°F (32°C).

■ You and Your Wild Game

End-of-Season Sausage

An old-time Alaskan has developed the following recipe for using the meat still left in his outdoor cache when spring breakup comes. When you need space in your freezer for a new season's kill, use his flavorful formula.

40 pounds (18 kg) game meat
10 pounds (4.5 kg) smoked ham or bacon*
1-1/4 cups (300 mL) black pepper
1/2 cup (120 mL) white sugar
2-1/2 tablespoons (38 mL) salt
1 ounce (28 g) coriander
5 tablespoons (75 mL) mustard seed
Garlic (if desired)

►Let the meat thaw. Grind the cuts into burger. *In place of smoked ham or bacon, you may use ordinary bacon fat; or use 2 pounds (1 kg) of ham or bacon and about 7-1/2 pounds (3.4 kg) of pork trim. Grind it. Add seasonings to the burger and work in with the ground pork. The garlic may be light if you do not like the flavor, but don't leave it out entirely as it helps cover the "end-of-season" flavor of meat that has been frozen all winter. Spread the meat in trays or dishpans and mix thoroughly. Stuff the mixture into casings and boil the sausages until they float. Hang them and let drip until thoroughly dry. Then smoke for three to five days in a light, cold smoke.

■ The Hunter Returns *(adapted)*

Kielbasa or Polish Sausage

25 pounds (11.25 kg) deer meat, ground
10 pounds (4.5 kg) pork sausage, unseasoned
2-1/2 tablespoons (38 mL) sage
1 tablespoon (15 mL) thyme
8 teaspoons (40 mL) garlic juice
6 teaspoons (30 mL) cracked black pepper
6 teaspoons (30 mL) seasoned pepper
12 ounces (340 g) Tender-Quick
2 tablespoons (30 mL) dried onion flakes
1/3 ounce (10 g) mustard seed

►Combine all ingredients in a large dishpan and mix well with hands. Stuff into sausage casings, using a meat press. Now smoke in smokehouse at 180°F (82°C) until internal temperature of sausage reaches 152°F (67°C) and a smoked color is obtained. Then immediately cool the sausage in cold water until the internal temperature falls to 100°F (38°C). Rinse briefly to remove grease and allow to dry one or two hours at room temperature. Store in the refrigerator. Polish sausage is also sometimes made with cured meat.
■ *Pat Challender*
  False Island Camp Cook Book

Head Cheese

Head cheese can be made from the head of any game animal. Hearts, tongues and trimmings may be included with the head meat in this recipe.

6 pounds (2.7 kg) chopped meat
3 tablespoons (45 mL) salt
4 teaspoons (20 mL) pepper
2 teaspoons (10 mL) red pepper
2-1/2 teaspoons (13 mL) allspice
3 teaspoons (15 mL) cloves
2 quarts (1.9 L) of the broth in which the meat
  is boiled

►Clean the head by removing the eyes, ears, brains, and all the skin. Trim off any fat. Cut the head into pieces to fit your largest kettle. Soak the pieces of head in salt water — 1/2 cup (120 mL) salt to 1 gallon (1 L) water — for three to five hours, to draw out all the blood. Drain the pieces and wash them well in clean water. Cover the pieces of head, and other trimmings, with hot water and cook slowly until the meat can be removed from the bones. Strain the broth and boil to evaporate until only 2 quarts (1.9 L) of liquid remain for each 6 pounds (2.7 kg) of meat.

Remove the meat from the bones, and chop all meat fine. Add salt, pepper, and spices, add the broth to the mixture and stir it thoroughly. Heat the mixture and let it boil for 15 minutes. For immediate use, pour the mixture into a shallow pan, cover it with cheesecloth, press the contents under a weight. Keep in a cool place. It will cool into a firm jell that may be sliced for serving.
■ The Hunter Returns

Louis Seversen's Rullepulse

►Use the outside casing of deer ribs for rullepulse casing. Cut up miscellaneous strips of meat approximately 1 x 6 inches (2.5 x 15 cm), or smaller, from various parts of the deer. Place enough meat strips inside casing to make a sausage. Add 1/2 cup (120 mL) chopped onion, salt, pepper, anise seed, whole allspice, ginger and bay leaves to season. (If desired, add saltpeter for coloring.) Sew up sausage with butcher string and large darning needle to make a round roll.

Make a brine of rock salt and water, using enough salt to float a potato with an eightpenny nail in it. Brine the rullepulse in a cool place —38°F (3.5°C) — for about two weeks. Soak out in fresh water for 48 hours. Boil and simmer slowly for two to three hours. Place hot rullepulse between two boards and add weight to compress meat. Refrigerate or return to cool place until well chilled, 24 hours or more. Slice to serve with other cold cuts along with Cumberland Sauce (page 420).
■ *Bunny Mathisen*
  "Help Yourself To The Sylta Flesk!"
  ALASKA® magazine, January 1977

Caribou Wieners

20 pounds (9 kg) caribou or moose meat
10 pounds (4.5 kg) fat pork
1 pound (0.45 kg) Tender-Quick
1-1/2 ounces (43 g) mace or sage finely ground
Garlic or onions (can be added if desired)

►Above is for making 30 pounds (13.5 kg) of frankfurters. Mix the Tender-Quick and seasoning together; then mix thoroughly with the meat and run through the grinder, using fine plate. Grind two or three times to make sure the seasoning is evenly distributed and meat is ground very fine. After grinding, stuff in sausage casing.

Hang in a smokehouse and smoke until a rich, orange color. Then cook in water heated to 155°F (68°C) until they float. Cooking time depends upon the thickness of the frankfurters. Do not have the water over 155°F (68°C) or the casings will burst. After cooking, rinse in hot water to remove grease. Store in Deepfreeze.
■ An Alaskan Cook Book, *Kenai*

To prevent bacon from molding, wash it with a clean cloth dipped in vinegar.
■ Cooking Up A Storm, *Homer*

MAKING JERKY &
OTHER DRIED MEATS

Jerky can be made from almost any very lean game meat. Some pains should be taken to remove as much fat as possible before the drying process begins. Fat does not dehydrate and simply turns rancid when it is held at the low drying temperatures required for making jerky. While the Indians who perfected the technique first used the loin or tenderloin, muscle from any place on the carcass may be used.

"All you need to begin is a cutting board and a sharp knife," says Ole Wik ["How to Make Jerky," The Cabin Friend, *ALASKA*® magazine, March 1979]. "First I skin the animal, separate it into quarters and then separate out the large muscles one by one.

"I place the individual muscles into dishpans, buckets and similar containers as I remove them from the carcass and end up with a fairly bare skeleton."

Then the tough, membranous sheaths on the outside of each individual muscle are trimmed away and the meat is cut —with the grain — into 1/4-inch-thick (6 mm) strips.

"Large muscles can be cut much like bread, in good-sized strips that are easy to handle. Smaller muscles treated this way would yield a bunch of very small strips, which would be a nuisance to keep balanced on the drying ropes." Other pointers to remember:

- Use fresh lean meat — free of fat and connective tissue. Aged meat may be used, but it is not recommended by most experienced jerky-makers.
- Since the process of making jerky does not heat meat sufficiently to kill parasites sometimes present in any game, a wise precaution is to freeze the meat, first. This has a second advantage besides ridding the meat of parasites. Meat that is only partially thawed is far easier to cut into the thin slices required for drying. After cutting, if there are still ice crystals in the meat, refrigerate it again to thaw completely before beginning the drying process.
- Do not make jerky from bear, walrus or pig — all of which may carry the parasite that causes trichinosis, killed only when the meat is thoroughly cooked.
- Slice the meat with the grain, not crosswise. Always slice well-chilled meat. Limp fresh meat is unmanageable.
- If you cure the meat first, do so at refrigerator temperatures.

- The following recipes all suggest various combinations of spices, but meat may be dried without them. The choice depends on intended use. Ole Wik and his family depend on jerky for whole meals.

"You begin to appreciate the absence of spices and salt and all the other window dressing that goes into jerky intended as a snack or appetizer only," Ole says.

If you dry meat without curing or salting it, however, controlled temperatures and low humidity become especially important. For drying outdoors, the Wiks choose spring, when temperatures are between 25 and 55°F (-4 to +13°C). But even for indoor drying where the temperature may be quite warm, they prefer cold weather because it is more likely to be accompanied by low humidity.

The Wiks use various oils and fats to provide seasoning variety. "With our jerky, we have eaten dried caribou and moose suet or more mundane substances such as warmed bacon fat, salad oil, margarine, cooked suet or peanut butter. We eat the harder cold fats much like cheese and the soft ones like a dip — a little fat, a little meat. . . . With a variety of fats it is possible to live on jerky for a long time without getting tired of it."

- If you are drying meat in the oven or in the smokehouse, be sure to keep the temperature at 120°F (49°C) or below. Use a thermometer. Gas ovens usually maintain the proper temperature when the pilot light alone is on.
- If an oven is used, line the sides and bottom with aluminum foil to catch drippings. Open the door to the first or second stop to allow moisture to escape and to lower oven temperature when necessary.
- Use any hardwood for smoking. Do not use pine, fir or conifer.
- Remove the jerky from the smokehouse or oven before it gets too hard for your taste.
- Five pounds (2.25 kg) of fresh meat should weigh approximately 2 pounds (1 kg) after drying or smoking.
- Store jerky in clean jars with tight lids or plastic bags with an airtight seal; or wrap it tightly in plastic wrap, then foil or freezer paper, and freeze. Dryness is more important to maintaining jerky than temperature. It will last almost indefinitely at any temperature, but you should expect the quality to deteriorate after a few months.

Simple Oven-Dried Jerky

5 pounds (2.25 kg) lean meat
3 tablespoons (45 mL) salt
1 teaspoon (5 mL) ground pepper
2 tablespoons (30 mL) sugar

►Trim as much fat as possible from the meat. Cut it with the grain into strips 1/2 inch (1.25 cm) thick, an inch (2.5 cm) wide and up to a foot (30 cm) in length. Spread out meat and sprinkle on salt, pepper and sugar. Then put the meat in a pan or dish and let it stand 24 hours in a refrigerator. If desired, the meat may be dipped in liquid smoke for a couple of seconds to add flavor.

Spread out meat in the top half of a kitchen oven on a rack to dry. Open the oven door to the first or second stop. Heat at 120°F (49°C) — the lowest temperature — for 48 hours or until the desired dryness is reached. Use an oven thermometer to make sure the oven does not get hotter than 120°F. Higher temperatures will result in hard, brittle jerky that crumbles when it is eaten.
■ You and Your Wild Game

Pickle-Cured Jerky

5 pounds (2.25 kg) lean meat
1 gallon (3.8 L) water
3/4 cup (180 mL) salt
1/2 cup (120 mL) sugar
2 tablespoons (30 mL) ground pepper

►Cut meat into strips as directed in Simple Oven-Dried Jerky. Make a brine of the remaining ingredients and refrigerate the meat strips in it overnight. Pour off the brine and let cold tap water run on the meat in a container for an hour. Hang the strips of meat in the smokehouse at 80 to 120°F (27 to 49°C) until the jerky is the desired texture. (An oven may also be used, but the smoke flavor will be lacking.) Some people add other spices to the brine such as 10 bay leaves, a teaspoon (5 mL) of cloves or sage — or all three.
■ You and Your Wild Game

Moose or Caribou Jerky

1-1/2 pounds (685 g) very lean frozen meat
4 teaspoons (20 mL) salt
1/4 teaspoon (1 mL) liquid smoke
1 teaspoon (5 mL) pepper
1 teaspoon (5 mL) chili powder
1 teaspoon (5 mL) garlic powder
1 teaspoon (5 mL) onion powder
1/4 teaspoon (1 mL) Tabasco or cayenne
1/2 cup (120 mL) water

►Thaw meat to a half-frozen state. Remove all fat and slice it into 1/8-inch-thick (3 mm) strips. Slice across the grain for crunchy jerky and with the grain for chewy jerky. Mix remaining ingredients. Put sliced meat in this marinade for 2 to 12 hours. Line large cake pan with foil. Place cookie-cooling racks on foil. Lay meat strips across rack. Dry in 150°F (65°C) oven for 8 to 12 hours. Or, dry in oven for one hour and then dry over wood or oil stove for two to three days. Wipe off any grease with a towel before storing.
■ *Pat Oakes, Courtesy of Mary Shields*
  AlaskaFest

Venison Bacon Bits

10 pounds (4.5 kg) venison
6 tablespoons (90 mL) salt
3 tablespoons (45 mL) brown sugar
1 tablespoon (15 mL) black pepper
1 tablespoon (15 mL) hot red pepper

►Slice meat from hams across the grain, 1/4 inch (6 mm) thick. Let stand in the cure overnight. Hang or lay on racks in smokehouse to drain well. Then smoke for 8 to 10 hours with alder or apple wood. Place in baskets above the airtight heater or over the register of a furnace until very dry and brittle. Store in cans with airtight lids. Crumble into scrambled eggs, over salads and in corn or clam chowders, or leave in pieces to cook in bean recipes calling for smoked ham. This is a good staple food that will keep a long time, if it is kept dry and cool.
■ *Helen Blanchard*
  "Old-Fangled Venison"
  ALASKA® magazine, June 1978

Ground Meat Jerky

1 pound (456 g) lean ground meat
3 tablespoons (45 mL) soy sauce
1 tablespoon (15 mL) Worcestershire
1/4 teaspoon (1 mL) freshly ground pepper
1/4 teaspoon (1 mL) powdered onion (not salt)
1/8 teaspoon (0.5 mL) powdered garlic (not salt)
1/8 teaspoon (0.5 mL) freshly ground nutmeg
1/8 teaspoon (0.5 mL) ground ginger

►Fat does not dehydrate and will turn rancid. Extra-lean meat is needed for this jerky. Cover a large flat cookie sheet with clear plastic wrap. Tape the plastic to each corner of the tray. Set aside. In a bowl, thoroughly mix all ingredients. Place the mixture between two large sheets of waxed paper. Using a rolling pin, roll it about 1/8 to 1/4 inch (3 to 6 mm) thick, in a rectangle about 10 x 14 inches (25 to 35 cm). Then remove the top sheet of waxed paper. Invert the meat onto the lined cookie sheet and remove the other sheet of waxed paper.
Drying Method A: Place cookie sheet in a 120°F (49°C) oven. Leave the door open a few inches to lower the heat and to allow moisture to escape. Dry

for two hours. Remove meat from cookie sheet, discard lining and return meat to cookie sheet. Place a piece of coarse brown paper toweling (the soft kind sticks) on the meat and roll out as much excess fat as possible. Using kitchen shears, cut into sticks about 5 inches (12.5 cm) long and 1/2 inch (1.25 cm) wide. Continue to dry in oven. Blot fat occasionally until meat is dry, like jerky, about two hours more.

Drying Method B: Place meat on cookie sheet in a gas oven with pilot light on and the oven door open 4 or 5 inches (10 to 12.5 cm). Let dry overnight. Next day, discard plastic wrap and blot fat from meat. Cut the meat into pieces. Return to oven for a few more hours of drying.

Store jerky in airtight containers in a cool place or freeze. This recipe yields about 50 sticks.

■ *Matanuska-Susitna District
Extension Service, June 1980*

Pemmican

*Here's a way to turn jerky into a storable
flavor-base for some excellent meals.*

►To make pemmican, you'll need a supply of good jerky, some suitable fat, a grinder and a few kitchen utensils.

First, select the meat. You must be able to powder it, so select jerky as free as possible of connective tissue. Be sure the jerky pieces are absolutely dry. Crisp by hanging them over the stove for a day or two, if necessary. Remove the sinews. Break each piece into small pieces, about the size of a postage stamp. Peel any fibers away from the meat and set them aside for your next stock pot.

Then powder the meat. The Indians used to pulverize it using a mallet and some sort of anvil, but a grinder is far easier to use. A meat grinder with large holes is more efficient than a food grinder. (This powder, incidentally, may be stored as is in airtight containers and used as flavoring in soups and gravies.)

Then select the fat. If you butcher your own game, there are many deposits on the carcass to choose from. [See Ole's discussion of them on page 194.] Or, store-bought fat may be used. Avoid lard or other soft fat which is too greasy for pemmican. You may use tinned beef tallow, or you may buy your own suet from the butcher and render it fresh. Ask for large, round chunks. Trim and discard the outer layer as it tends to pick up a moldy flavor. Then render the rest. Cut it into small pieces and render slowly in a skillet. Strain to remove any meat particles.

Use 3 cups (720 mL) firmly packed meat powder and 1-3/4 cups (420 mL) melted fat for a good batch of pemmican.

Heat the fat to 140°F (60°C). Place the meat powder in a baking tin or other suitable container, making sure it is not so cool it will chill the fat before it can coat all the meat particles. Pour the hot fat into a well in the center of the powder and stir with a fork. Press and knead the mixture with the fork to distribute the fat throughout the powder, then press the mass flat in the tin to exclude any air bubbles, forming a slab about an inch (2.5 cm) thick. Score the slab into blocks right in the pan before the fat hardens and the pemmican becomes brittle.

Allow to cool, then remove from the pan. This is easiest done by heating the pan very slightly, just until the blocks can be lifted out.

To store pemmican, wrap each block in waxed paper and put it in a cloth sack — to hang in a dry, cool place — or in a jar with a tight lid. Pemmican seems to keep better than plain jerky.

The plain pemmican blocks can be dropped into hot water as the base for quick, hearty soups, or they can be combined with tomato sauce to make dishes such as Spanish rice or spaghetti. Or, use pemmican as the Indians did — for trail food. Carry a few blocks in your vehicle, rucksack or jacket pocket, and you'll always have a delicious meat meal, ready to go.

■ *Ole Wik
"How To Make Pemmican"
ALASKA® magazine, April 1979*

Variation: Raisins, berries, dried fruit and nuts may also be added to the mixture, but Ole suggests using a little more fat to bind the blocks together. Or try Sourdough's Pemmican.

Sourdough's Pemmican
*A delicious blend of powdered jerky,
dried fruits, sugar and spices*

4 cups (1 L) powdered meat*
1-1/2 cups (360 mL) suet or bear fat
*3/4 cup (180 mL) lowbush cranberry jam, or
    Wild Currant Jelly*
1/2 cup (120 mL) soup stock
1/2 cup (120 mL) brown sugar
*1/2 cup (120 mL) dried and finely ground
    blueberries, raisins or currants*
*1/2 teaspoon (2 mL) each — savory, allspice,
    garlic powder, onion powder*
1 teaspoon (5 mL) dried minced wild chives
3/4 teaspoon (3 mL) black pepper

►*To make the meat powder, start with jerky that has been made without seasoning, or cut long strips of lean meat — moose or caribou — as thin as possible and dry or dehydrate completely. When the meat is thoroughly dried, it must be pounded until it becomes powdered. If this sounds like too much work, simply run it through the meat grinder a couple of times, using the finest blade.

Melt the suet or bear fat and start to cook slowly, adding the jam or jelly as it simmers. In the meantime, blend the meat powder with soup stock, brown sugar, ground dried fruit and spices and add this mixture gradually into the melted fat, stirring constantly all the while. Do NOT add salt unless the pemmican is to be used immediately. Cover tightly and place in the oven which has been preheated to 300°F (150°C). Let bake for 3-1/2 hours. Remove from oven, pour into shallow pans to cool and set. A little more hot soup stock may be added if the mixture seems too thick when it is poured.

Ideal pans for cooling are individual foil pie pans, as this size cake of pemmican is a good size to pack.

Muffin tins make smaller blocks and can be filled to make thicker blocks. When thoroughly cooled and set, the cakes should be individually foil wrapped and stored in cool, dry place until needed. Put several small ones in your pocket when you start out for a day in the Bush. You will find these make mighty good eating. It is also good emergency food to carry on any kind of a trip. It can be eaten "as is," fried like steak or used in stew. Quite a versatile food, isn't it? When you wish a hearty meal in camp just open a can or two of beans, toss in a few cakes of pemmican and stew until pemmican is dissolved in bean liquid. Make a batch of hot biscuits and you have a real feast.

■ *Anon.*
   Courtesy, Mrs. Aline Strutz

CURING & SMOKING GAME

The three most important factors in successful curing are — high-quality meat, salt and temperature control.

Dry-salting and brining are no longer thought of as the solution to all food storage problems, but in combination with cool temperatures, curing does provide protection for meat kept outside the freezer, and it certainly adds nice variety to the diet, especially in combination with smoking.

The choice between dry-salting and brining may depend on climate. Dry-curing is faster and is said to produce a tastier product with better keeping qualities than brining. Brining, however, is recommended for climates of extreme dryness and cold temperatures which naturally dehydrate the meat.

For either process, select top-quality, fresh meat. Cut it into "wholesale" cuts such as ham and shoulder or into family-size pieces. The bone may be left in or removed.

Ingredients

Curing can be done with salt alone. Be sure to use noniodized salt — coarse to fine pickling salt or dairy salt. It is recommended by some sources that the water used in brine solutions be purified by boiling and straining. If you have any doubts about your water supply, or it is heavily chlorinated and you wish to dissipate some of the taste, follow the directions for purifying water found with the basic directions for Brine-Salting on page 452. A different method of purifying is with the recipe for Corned Bear. Sugar is also a common ingredient in both dry-salting and brining. It is not necessary as a preservative, but it mellows the flavor. Various spice combinations also may be added.

Many recipes call for sodium or potassium nitrate (saltpeter) or commercially mixed "complete cures," which are likely to contain saltpeter or sodium nitrite plus sugar and salt and other chemical preservatives. If you use a commercial cure, follow package directions carefully about adding other ingredients, especially salt and sugar, because it probably contains much of what you need.

There is considerable controversy about the health hazards of using nitrates and nitrites. In any case, they are poisonous substances if used improperly. *Store them away from food,* and, of course, from children and pets. They are not necessary for the curing process, but meats cured without them will not have the "typical" pink color.

The bible of food preservation techniques, *Putting Food By* [Brattleboro, Vermont, 1975], suggests the use of *pure crystalline ascorbic acid,* or vitamin C, as a substitute which will at least slow down if not stop color loss from the meat during curing. The amount recommended is 1 gram of crystalline ascorbic acid for every 4.5 pounds [2 kg] of meat, which rounds off as follows:

1/4 teaspoon (1 mL) for 5 pounds (2.25 kg)
1/2 teaspoon (2 mL) for 10 pounds (4.5 kg)
1 teaspoon (5 mL) for 20 pounds (9 kg)

Equipment

For dry-salting, you need clean, roomy counter

space for spreading the meat out and rubbing in salt. Containers for curing meat must be clean wooden, crockery, glass, porcelain or plastic ones large enough to hold the meat being cured. Do NOT use galvanized metal, plastic garbage cans or any container in which pesticides have been mixed. Off-flavors and colors may develop with metal containers. Plastic garbage cans are not "food grade" plastic. Pesticides can leach from apparently clean containers into the curing mix. Dry-salting doesn't require watertight containers; in fact small holes at the bottom are an advantage to drain off excess fluid. Clean, nonmetal weights to press the meat under the brine and lids for the containers are also needed. A meat thermometer is also an essential, and household scales which will measure small amounts accurately are very helpful.

Temperature Control

During curing, meat must be held between 35 and 40°F (1.5 to 4.5°C). Warmer, the meat spoils; cooler, the process slows; and below 32°F (0°C), curing stops. Allowing the meat to freeze is not a complete disaster, though it will affect quality. You must compensate for it by increasing the curing time by whatever time the meat was frozen. Frozen meat should be returned to 38°F (3.5°C) before you start counting the curing time again.

Storing Cured Meats

Present-day (since the 1970s) government bulletins are very hedgy about the length of time cured meat may be stored. There is general agreement that brined meats such as Corned Moose are protected for several months if they are stored below 38°F (3.5°C) and the brine is watched carefully, overhauled when needed. Or fully cured meats may be removed from the brine, freshened in clear water, the surface allowed to dry thoroughly and then smoked with a cold smoke. The smoked meat is then wrapped in cotton stockinette and hung in a dry, cool, well-ventilated area. Of course, meat that is to be used right away may be taken from the brine sooner than meat that is to be smoked and stored.

Dry-salted meat, too, may be smoked to add flavor and storage time.

Overhauling Brine Solutions

Watch the meat in a brine solution closely. If at any time the sweet-pickle corning solution turns sour, ropy or syrupy, throw it away. Scald the barrel, lid and weights. Scrub the meat in hot water. Rechill it thoroughly. Then repack and cover it with a newly-made brine, mixed with slightly more purified water than the original. To make the new solution, combine 5-1/2 gallons (21 L) of pure water with the Basic Formula salt mixture for 100 pounds (45 kg) of meat. Follow directions as outlined for Brine-Salting, page 452.

Freshening & Cooking Cured Meats

Because most of the commercially packed smoked meats are "fully cooked . . . ready to eat" when we buy them from the grocery, there is some confusion about what curing and smoking accomplish. Curing and cold-smoking do not bring meat up to the internal temperature required to cook even meat that is commonly eaten rare. When meat is hot-smoked on the other hand, it *is* cooked and cannot be stored much longer than ordinary fresh cooked meat.

Cured meat must be freshened before cooking. You can remove some surplus salt by soaking the meat in fresh cool water for several hours. Discard the resulting brine and cover the meat with fresh water to cook it. Sometimes even that water may be too salty after it comes to a boil. If so, empty it and begin again. After the preliminary cooking by boiling, a large piece of meat that has been cured and smoked may be drained well, placed in a hot oven for about 30 minutes and glazed with a favorite brown sugar or currant jelly glaze.

Smoking Cured Game

All kinds of cured meat — dried, brined or corned — may be smoked for better keeping and improved flavor. When the curing time is ended, soak the cured meat for two hours in cold fresh water and scrub it well with a stiff brush to produce a better color and milder flavor.

Hang the chunks in the smokehouse so they do not touch and let them drip for 24 hours before starting a fire. Use nonresinous wood (preferably peeled alder or willow) to produce a light fog of smoke, not hotter than 100°F (38°C). This is a cold smoke. Keep the ventilators open at first to let the moisture escape. Smoke for two or three days for a good flavor and a dark, rich color.

To store smoked meat, be sure the surface is thoroughly dry, wrap the piece in cotton stockinette, attach a cord to the cloth (not the meat), apply a tight wrapper of paper and hang the meat in a dry, cool, well-aired place away from direct light. Or wrap in moisture-vapor-proof paper and freeze.

Because bacteria in meat grow fastest between 70 and 100°F (21 to 38°C), you should smoke meat in fairly cold weather, in late fall or early spring when temperatures are between 30 and 50°F (-1 to +10°C) during the day. Really cold weather —down to 0°F (-18°C) — should be avoided unless your smokehouse and your techniques are well-equipped to handle it.

Smoke should be kept as continuous as possible, but you can sleep at night if the weather is cool but not freezing, leaving the meat in the smokehouse until you start the smoke again in the morning.

About The Recipes: Many of these recipes are not complete cures. Follow their directions about storage and cooking times.

Basic Formula
For dry-salting or brine-salting

For 100 pounds (45 kg) meat:
8 pounds (3.6 kg) noniodized coarse pickling or dairy salt
2 pounds (1 kg) sugar — brown, white, syrup or honey
2 ounces (56 g) saltpeter — optional

►Mix well and use as directed for Dry-Salting, Brine-Salting or Corned Moose.

Dry-Salting

►Mix the Basic Formula in a large pan, being careful — if you use it — to blend the finely powdered saltpeter thoroughly. Rub one-third of this mixture into the chunks of meat. On large pieces with bone, insert the mixture into the interior by opening up joints or incising along the bone with a thin-bladed sharp knife and pushing the salt in well.

Pack the pieces in nonmetal containers with the skin side up on the top layer. Keep in a cool place for three days. On the third day, remove the meat from the crock and rub in half of the remaining salt mixture.

Replace the chunks in reverse order, with bottom pieces on top. This is called "overhauling the pack." Let the meat stand for seven days, then rub in remaining mixture and cure for the remaining period.

Curing time for larger and thicker pieces — 3 inches (7.5 cm) or more through — is 1-1/2 days per pound (0.45 kg) from the day of the first salting. For example, a 10-pound (4.5 kg) piece would take 15 days. Smaller pieces or slabs like bacon — or a lighter cure for meat that is to be used immediately — may be left in the cure a shorter time. In any case, allow at least one day per pound.

Liquid will collect as the salt draws moisture from the meat. This should be poured off or drained through holes in the bottom of the container. Do not let the containers rest directly on the ground or floor. Raise them on supports.

■ The Hunter Returns

Variation: To add a special flavor to meat that will be smoked after curing — try this mixture of spices. For 100 pounds (45 kg) of meat:

2 cups (480 mL) or more mixed pickling spice
20 to 30 cloves of garlic
2 ounces (56 g) coriander seed
Several dried red peppers

►Mix these together and sprinkle them between the layers of meat at the first salting. Redistribute the spices as evenly as possible each time the pack is overhauled.

FWT

Brine-Salting

►Game meat may be quick-cured in a sweet-pickle solution which takes 28 days. Fit chilled, smoothly trimmed cuts into a clean wooden barrel or crock— skin side up on the top layer. Using the Basic Formula, make a brine by adding 4-1/2 gallons (17 L) of water to the salt-sugar mixture for each 100 pounds (45 kg) of meat.

The water used for making the curing pickle should be pure. *To purify water,* boil more than you expect to use and let it cool. Strain it or pour it off slowly to leave sediment behind. Heat the purified water again to boiling, add the curing ingredients and stir until ingredients are dissolved. Skim the surface and let the solution cool to 40°F (4.5°C) or less before pouring it over the packed meat. Cover the meat completely with the brine and weight it down. If any of the meat rises out of the brine, the entire cure may spoil quickly.

Overhaul the pack about the seventh day, reversing the order of the packed meat. Cover again with the same mixture, unless it has begun to spoil. (See Overhauling Brine Solutions.) The curing time for larger, thicker pieces is 3-1/2 days per pound (0.45 kg), and proportionately less for smaller pieces. Minimum brining time for all cuts is 28 days.

■ The Hunter Returns

Brine Cure For Poultry

►For 25 pounds (11.25 kg) of meat, prepare:

6 quarts (5.7 L) water (boiled and cooled
* to lukewarm)*
2 pounds (1 kg) pickling salt
1 pound (0.45 kg) granulated or
* light brown sugar*
1-1/2 ounces saltpeter, optional
1 bay leaf
1/4 ounce (7 g) black pepper

►Eviscerate birds, remove head and feet. Pluck and clean thoroughly. Mix brine ingredients and cool to 35 or 40°F (1.5 to 4.5°C). Pack birds in container. Cover with brine. Weight down to keep submerged. Cover. Place in refrigerator or cool place between 35 and 40°F. Soak birds in brine for 48 hours.

Remove from brine and soak in cold water for one hour. Drip dry. Truss and tie in stockinette. Hang in smoker, legs up. Smoke large birds six to eight hours at 160°F (71°C) or 8 to 10 hours at 120°F (49°C). Smoke smaller birds at 180°F (82°C) with as dense smoke as possible for one hour; reduce temperature to 130°F (54°C) and continue smoking for an additional four to six hours.

After this hot smoking, birds should be fully cooked and eaten or stored in the refrigerator.

■ Curing and Smoking Meat, Poultry,
  and Fish at Home

Corned Bear

►For 50 pounds (22.5 kg) of meat, prepare:

2-1/2 gallons (9.5 L) pure water
* (non-chlorinated)*
2-1/2 pounds (1.15 kg) plain noniodized salt
1 pound (0.45 kg) brown sugar
2 pints (1 L) red wine
6 cloves crushed garlic or 4 tablespoons
* (60 mL) liquid garlic*
4 ounces (114 g) mixed pickling spices

2 tablespoons (30 mL) whole black peppercorns

►To get pure water, either boil it according to directions under Brine-Salting or allow it to stand 24 hours in an open container. Strain through several thicknesses of clean cloth.

Boil the spices in a small amount of the water — 1 quart (1 L). Combine spice-water, remaining pure water and all other ingredients in a tall, narrow crock or enameled pan. Do not use a metal or wood container. Check the salinity of the brine to see if it will float an egg. Add more salt until it will. Place the meat in this solution, weighing it down so that it is completely submerged. Refrigerate or keep the meat at 35°F (2°C) for 15 to 30 days. Turn and stir thoroughly every two days.

After curing, rinse meat in clear water and can in glass jars. (See Canning Game Meats.)

Special pointer — If the above corning solution does not cover the meat, prepare additional brine by adding salt to pure water until it will float an egg.

■ *Cheri Jensen, Juneau*
  One Hundred Years in the Kitchen

Corned Moose

Fine for lean caribou or tough cuts of any game

►For 100 pounds (45 kg) of meat prepare:

Basic Formula (page 452)
8 cups (1.9 L) sugar
5 tablespoons (75 mL) baking soda
3-1/2 tablespoons (53 mL) saltpeter, optional
4 gallons (15.2 L) water, previously boiled,
* cooled and strained of sediment*

►Prepare the meat as for brining, packing it in a barrel or crock with 8 pounds (3.6 kg) of salt for each 100 pounds (45 kg) of meat. Sprinkle a half-inch-thick (1.25 cm) layer of salt on top. Let stand overnight.

Then make a solution of the sugar, baking soda, saltpeter and 1 gallon (3.8 L) of the purified water and pour it over the meat. Add the remaining 3 gallons (11.4 L) of water by pouring it down the inside edge of the container. Keep the meat cool, and keep it pressed entirely under the brine with a weighted board. Take the same precautions to prevent spoilage as for the sweet pickle. Watch the meat closely and overhaul it at the slightest sign of spoilage or fermentation. Corned meat may be ready for use in 10 days, but has a better flavor after 30 days. After 40 days, remove it from the brine and prepare it for dry storage or can it under pressure. (See Canning Game Meat & Birds.)

To cook it, freshen and boil as you would corned beef — with cabbage, carrots and other vegetables.

■ The Hunter Returns

Mama's Corned Venison

5 to 6 pounds (2.25 to 2.7 kg) venison brisket
1/4 teaspoon (1 mL) saltpeter
1/4 cup (60 mL) warm water
2 tablespoons (30 mL) sugar
2 cloves garlic, minced
2 teaspoons (10 mL) paprika
1 tablespoon (15 mL) pickling spice
3/4 cup (180 mL) noniodized salt
2 quarts (1.9 L) water

►Place meat in crock, cutting meat in half or thirds to fit crock if necessary. Dissolve saltpeter in warm water. Add sugar, garlic, paprika and spices. Dissolve salt in remaining water. Stir in saltpeter mixture, cool completely and pour over meat. Cover meat with plate and weight down to keep meat covered with liquid. Keep cold three weeks. Turn occasionally. To eat, freshen in water and cook according to your favorite corned beef recipe.
■ *Jody Clift*
  False Island Camp Cook Book

Corned Venison Spread

1/2 cup (120 mL) minced corned venison
  (leftover)
1/2 cup (120 mL) minced sweet potatoes
  (cooked)

2 tablespoons (30 mL) butter

►Mix and blend to a paste. Spread on crackers or slices of sourdough bread and serve as an appetizer.
■ *Ruth Allman, Juneau*
  Alaska Sourdough

Variations:
• *Baked Corned Moose* — After freshening it thoroughly, cook a family-sized portion of the corned meat in a slow oven set at 300°F (150°C). Place the meat in a covered roaster (or wrap it tightly with foil), add a small amount of water, enough to cover the bottom of the pan well, cover tightly and place in the oven for three hours or more. Then use this juice to cook the vegetables you want on top of the stove, adding the corned moose back in just long enough to reheat it.
• *Pressed Corned Moose* — Remove the corned moose from the corning brine and wash it in warm water. Simmer in a kettle for two hours, keeping the meat just barely covered with water at all times. Remove the meat and pack it in pans or in a cold meat press. Strain the broth through a cheesecloth or muslin several times to remove all sediment. Boil the broth to one-half its original volume and pour it over the meat. Allow it to chill in a cool place until it holds the shape of the pan.

CANNING GAME MEAT & BIRDS

In this section we have included only a few recipes promised in other parts of the book. Before you use them, please read the general information about canning at the beginning of this chapter. Especially see the information about exhausting meats that are packed raw or in tins.

Game meat and birds are canned at the same pressure and times used for domestic meat and poultry. If you plan to do much canning of game, keep yourself supplied with the latest government guide. At present, that is U.S. Department of Agriculture Home and Garden Bulletin No. 106, "Home Canning of Meat and Poultry." The directions below are adapted from it. Some USDA-sponsored testing (not Bulletin 106, however) indicates that *all* meat should be hot-packed. The meat is precooked before it is packed in jars or cans. Then boiling broth or boiling water is poured over it before the containers are processed in a pressure canner. The temperature of hot-packed food should be at least 170°F (77°C) at the time jars are closed and cans are sealed. Directions for returning cooked meat to that temperature if it has cooled slightly in packing are the same as those for Exhausting.

Canning Ground Meat & Sausage

Use seasonings sparingly in making sausage that is to be canned. Measure spices, onion and garlic carefully, perhaps using less than the recipe calls for. Omit sage altogether. It becomes bitter in canning.

►Shape ground meat or sausage into fairly thin patties that may be packed into jars or cans without breaking. Precook the patties in a slow oven —325°F (150°C) — until medium done. When cut at center, patties should show almost no red color.

Skim fat off the drippings; the fat should not be used in canning.

Glass Jars — Pack hot patties leaving 1 inch (2.5 cm) of head space. Cover with boiling meat juice leaving 1 inch (2.5 cm) head space. Adjust jar lids. Process in a pressure canner at 10 pounds pressure (69 kPa), 75 minutes for pint (480 mL) jars, 90 minutes for quart (1 L) jars.

Tins — Pack hot patties to 1/2 inch (1.25 cm) from top of cans. Check the temperature at the center of the meat. It should be 170°F (77°C). If not, bring it up to that temperature by following the directions for Exhausting. Then cover with boiling meat juice to fill cans to top; seal. Process in a pressure canner at 10 pounds pressure (69 kPa), 65 minutes for No. 2 cans; 90 minutes for No. 2-1/2 cans.

Canning Corned Bear or Other Corned Game

►Wash corned meat thoroughly to scrub away some salt. Drain well. Cut into pieces or strips that will fit in canning containers.

Cover the meat with cold water and bring to a boil. If broth is very salty, drain meat; boil again in fresh water. Pack while hot.

Glass Jars — Leave 1 inch (2.5 cm) of head space. Cover hot meat with boiling broth or boiling water. Leave 1 inch of head space. Adjust lids. Process in pressure canner at 10 pounds pressure (69 kPa), 75 minutes for pint (480 mL) jars; 90 minutes for quart (1 L) jars.

Tin Cans — Pack meat hot, leaving 1/2-inch (1.25) head space. Check temperature at center of meat. It should be at least 170°F (77°C). (If not, reheat per instructions for Exhausting at the beginning of this chapter.) Fill cans to top with boiling broth or boiling water. Seal. Process in a pressure canner at 10 pounds pressure (69 kPa), 65 minutes for No. 2 cans; 90 minutes for No. 2-1/2 cans.

Moose Mincemeat

5 cups (1.2 L) ground, cooked moose or caribou
1 quart (1 L) ground suet
3 quarts (2.85 L) chopped, pared tart apples
1/3 cup (80 mL) finely chopped orange peel
1-1/2 cups (360 mL) chopped orange pulp
1/4 cup (60 mL) lemon juice
2 pounds (1 kg) currants
3 pounds (1.4 kg) seedless raisins, light and dark
8 ounces (228 g) chopped, candied citron
2 pounds (1 kg) brown sugar
1 tablespoon (15 mL) each — salt, cinnamon and allspice
2 teaspoons (10 mL) nutmeg
1 teaspoon (5 mL) cloves
1/4 teaspoon (1 mL) ginger
1 quart (1 L) sweet cider or grape juice

►Mix all ingredients in a large kettle and simmer for one hour, stirring frequently to prevent sticking. Pack hot into hot jars, leaving 1-inch (2.5 cm) head space. Adjust caps. Process pints (480 mL) and quarts (1 L) 20 minutes at 10 pounds (69 kPa) pressure. The recipe yields about six quarts.

FREEZING ALASKA FRUITS & VEGETABLES

Mostly Berries

Select full-flavored, ripe berries, preferably with tender skins. Sort, leaving in a few underripe berries as they contain more pectin than the fully ripe ones. If berries have been picked far from dusty roads and paths, they may need no washing. If they do, run a light spray of water over them, draining immediately. Do not soak. Rolling berries (gently) down Turkish toweling helps to remove some of the debris.

Spread berries one layer deep on a tray or cookie sheet and place them in the freezer. When they are frozen hard, pour them into moisture-vapor-proof containers or bags and seal. Leave 3/4-inch (1.9 cm)

head space in pint (480 mL) containers (twice that for quarts and liters) and express air from bags before sealing.

Blueberries and huckleberries profit from blanching before freezing. Lower them into rapidly boiling water — one minute only — then plunge into cold water to stop the cooking. Drain well and freeze as above. This will keep the skins from toughening in the freezer.

If freezer space is limited or berries are overripe, make some into puree (see page 458) for use in sauces and jams and butters or in Fruit Leather. Four cups (1 L) of berries will generally make about 2 cups (480 mL) of puree.

Berries may also be frozen packed in sugar or

syrup, but they are not nearly so versatile as those packed without. Plain ones may be used almost as if they were fresh, "as is" or in recipes.

Freezing has special advantages besides the obvious one of preserving seasonal produce. Jelly-makers will note that frozen berries release more juice, and freshly made berry relishes have better taste than those fully processed and stored several months. Best of all, you can enjoy your summer berry picking without having to put up all the jams and jellies and relishes you want immediately.

Crab apples may be stored whole or as applesauce, sweetened or unsweetened.

Rose hips — Freeze as berries, whole or in puree.

Rhubarb — Choose firm stalks with good flavor. Wash, trim and cut into 1- or 2-inch (2.5 to 5 cm) pieces. Blanch for one minute in boiling water, drain and plunge into cold water to stop the cooking. This will set good color and flavor. Pack unsweetened as you would berries or in Medium Syrup (see Canning Alaska Fruits & Vegetables), allowing 1/2 cup (120 mL) per pint (480 mL) of rhubarb and leaving 1/2-inch (1.25 cm) head space. Rhubarb may also be pureed.

Serving Frozen Berries

Thaw berries in unopened containers at room temperature or in the refrigerator. All fruits tend to darken and lose flavor once they are thawed, so use them as soon as possible, preferably while a few ice crystals still remain. Berries to be used in pies or cobblers need to be defrosted only enough to separate the fruit.

Vegetables

Wash and sort vegetables as for table use. Blanch them before freezing to inactivate enzymes which might cause flavor change and vitamin loss. There are two methods.

Blanching in Boiling Water

Allow 1 gallon (3.8 L) water for each pound (456 g) of vegetables, except leafy greens — wild or garden-grown — which need twice as much water. Bring water to a rolling boil. Immerse vegetables in a wire basket or tied loosely in cheesecloth. Cover kettle and boil at top heat the amount of time listed for each vegetable. Begin counting as soon as vegetables are in the water. Cool immediately by plunging into cold running water for the same amount of time used in blanching. Drain and pack in moisture-vapor-proof containers. Expel air from

Steps For Freezing Specific Vegetables

Beans—Wax, Green, Snap:
Wash, snip off tips and sort for size. Cut or break into suitable pieces or freeze small beans whole. Blanch 3-1/2 minutes. Cool.

Beets:
Select small or medium beets. Remove tops and wash. Cook until tender. Chill. Remove skins. Slice or dice large beets.

Broccoli:
Discard off-color florets or ones with flowers. Remove tough leaves and woody ends. Cut to fit container. Cut through stalks lengthwise, leaving heads 1 inch (2.5 cm) in diameter. Soak 1/2 hour in salt brine — 1/2 cup salt to 1 quart water (120 mL to 1 L). Rinse and drain. Blanch four minutes in water or steam-blanch five minutes. Cool.

Cabbage:
Use solid heads. Trim coarse outer leaves. Cut into medium to coarse shreds or thin wedges or separate into leaves. Blanch in boiling water for 1-1/2 minutes. Cool. Drain well. (Frozen cabbage is suitable only as cooked vegetable.)

Carrots:
Use tender carrots harvested in cool weather.

Top, wash and scrape. Dice or slice 1/4 inch (6 mm) thick. Blanch 3-1/2 minutes. Cool.

Eggplant:
Precook by peeling and cutting into 1/4- to 1/2-inch (6 mm to 1.25 cm) slices, or dice. To retain light color, drop pieces immediately into cold water containing 4 tablespoons (60 mL) salt per gallon (3.8 L) of water. Blanch 4-1/2 minutes in same strength salted boiling water. Cool. Package in layers separated by freezer paper.

Herbs — wild and garden:
Wrap sprigs or leaves in foil and seal in film bags and store in carton or glass jar. Wash leaves only if necessary. Don't scald.

Mushrooms — wild and commercial:
Sort according to size. Pieces should not be larger than 1 inch (2.5 cm) across.

To steam — Soak mushrooms for five minutes in a solution of 1 pint (480 mL) water to 1 teaspoon (5 mL) lemon juice or 1/2 teaspoon (2 mL) citric acid powder. Drain and steam-blanch five minutes for larger pieces, 3-1/2 minutes for smaller ones. Cool.

To blanch — Dip small quantities of mushrooms briefly in boiling water treated with

bags; leave 1/2-inch (1.25) head space in rigid containers. Seal tightly.

Steam Blanching

Put 1 inch (2.5 cm) of water in a kettle; bring to a rolling boil. Suspend a thin layer of vegetables in a wire basket or loose cheesecloth over rapidly boiling water. Cover and process for the time listed for each vegetable. Plunge into cold water, drain and pack as above.

Specific blanching times for many Alaskan vegetables are listed below.

DRYING FRUIT

Berries with thick or tough skins — blueberries, serviceberries, crowberries —should be blanched or "checked" before drying. Otherwise only the skin will dry and the inside of the berry will remain moist. Place a small amount of the berries at a time in a colander or cloth bag and dunk in rapidly boiling water for one minute. Drain thoroughly as the berries should harbor no excess moisture when they are spread to dry.

There are two basic ways to dry out wild berries. They may be dried whole or pureed and then dried.

If you add sugar to the puree, you have Fruit Leather, but the puree may be dried without it.

It is possible to make your own dryer with several shelves for holding the berries as they dry. There are commercial dryers for home use on the market, too. However, unless you plan to go into drying in a big way, the sun- or oven-drying methods will do well enough. Sun-dried fruit seems to have the best flavor; probably that is natural. Sun-dried fruit should be pasteurized before storing. (See page 459.)

---

citric acid or lemon juice as above. Cool immediately in cold water. Drain well and pack.

To broil —Select large mushrooms, dot with butter and broil until almost done.

To batter-fry — Cut each mushroom in half lengthwise — even large ones do well this way — dip each half in beaten egg, then in seasoned flour. Fry in oil, turning once, until golden on both sides. Drain on paper toweling several hours or overnight. Pack in rigid plastic.

To serve batter-fried mushrooms — Warm a few minutes in an oven or microwave.

Onions:
Peel, wash, chop and blanch 1-1/2 minutes. Cool. (Will keep three to six months.)

Peas:
Shell small amount at a time. Blanch 1-1/2 to 2 minutes. Cool.

Peas with edible pods:
Remove stems, blossom ends and any string. Leave whole. Blanch 1-1/2 minutes. Cool.

Potatoes:
Wash, peel, remove eyes, bruises and any green surface coloring. Cube to 1/4 to 1/2 inch (6 mm to 1.25 cm). Blanch five minutes. Cool.

For hash browns — Cook in jackets until almost done. Peel and grate. Form in patties or other shapes and freeze.

French fries — Peel and cut in thin strips. Fry in deep fat until very light golden. Drain and cool. Freeze on cookie sheet spread out. Then pack in bags, expel air and seal.

To serve French fries — heat 20 minutes in 400°F (205°C) oven, stirring frequently.

Spinach and other wild or garden greens:
Sort and remove tough stems. Wash. Blanch most greens two minutes. Collards and stem portion of Swiss chard, blanch three to four minutes. Blanch very tender greens (young wild greens and spinach) 1 to 1-1/2 minutes.

Squash — summer, zucchini:
Wash, peel and cut in pieces. Blanch 1/4-inch slices three minutes; 1-1/2-inch (3.75 cm) slices, six minutes. Cool. Zucchini for breads may be grated and frozen without blanching. (Color loss will be covered by spices.)

FREEZE AND STORE ALL FRUITS AND VEGETABLES AT 0°F (-18°C) OR LOWER

Oven-Drying Whole Berries

Whole berries may be dried this way. Set oven at lowest heat. Line a cookie sheet with a single layer of paper towels and spread out the berries on this. Put in the oven and leave the oven door ajar a bit to allow moisture to escape. Drying will take about four hours. Dry until berries are hard and rattle when shaken on the tray.

Storing Dried Berries

Put dried berries into airtight plastic bags or screwtop jars and store in a cool, dry place. Inspect occasionally for mold.

Using Dried Berries

Whole dried berries may be used like raisins or commercially dried currants; or they may be reconstituted by adding a little water and allowing to soak for an hour or so, then simmering gently for a few minutes. Purees may be reconstituted in similar fashion; or crush purees with a rolling pin and add the powder to puddings, pies and other berry dishes.

Purees, Fruit Leathers & Chips

Fruit leathers are dried leathery sheets of pureed fruit. Fruit chips are made from crisp fruit leather that breaks easily. Both have tangy, concentrated fruit flavor that makes them a favorite snack for anyone, especially handy to pack in a lunch or rucksack. Much of the following information about making purees, fruit leathers and chips and the individual recipes are excerpted and adapted from University of Alaska Cooperative Extension Service Bulletin P-228, "Fruit Leather."

Making Purees

Rose hip puree: Use soft ripe rose hips (the riper they are the sweeter they are). It takes about 4 cups (1 L) of rose hips to make 2 cups (480 mL) of puree. Remove stalks and blossom ends. Rinse berries in cold water. Put them into a pan and add enough water to almost cover. Bring to a boil and simmer 10 to 15 minutes. Press through a sieve or strainer. All that does not go through the sieve is placed in the pan again. Add a little water, enough to almost cover, if you want a thicker puree, add slightly less. This time heat but do not boil so vigorously. This will dissolve a little more of the fruit so that it will go through the sieve. Press again and then repeat the process one more time. By now, most of the fruit should have gone through the sieve leaving only seeds and skin to discard.

Rhubarb puree: Wash and cut about 1 quart (1 L) of rhubarb into small 1/2-inch (1.25 cm) pieces. Put 1/4 cup (60 mL) water in a saucepan and add rhubarb. Cook only until rhubarb starts to soften. Let cool slightly; put in blender and make into puree. This should make about 2 cups (480 mL) puree.

Berry puree: To make berry purees, rinse berries, drain, put in a blender and blend until the consistency of thick puree. Most berries do not need to be cooked. Salmonberries and highbush cranberries have larger seeds and should be put through a sieve after blending to remove seeds.

Drying Puree and Fruit Leather

Line a cookie sheet — 12 x 17 inches (30 x 42 cm) — with plastic wrap. This size cookie sheet holds approximately 2 cups (480 mL) of puree. Spread puree or fruit leather evenly over the plastic but do not push it completely to the sides. Leave a bit of plastic showing for easy removal. Place on a card table or picnic table in the hot sun to dry. If the plastic is bigger than the cookie sheet and extends up the sides, anchor it with clothes pins so it will not flop down and cover the edges of the leather. Puree should dry in the sun six to eight hours. The heat of the sun and the humidity make drying time variable.

Puree and fruit leather may be dried in an oven set at 140°F (60°C). Too high a heat will disintegrate the plastic. Leave the oven door ajar so moisture can escape. It takes about six hours in the oven.

It can also be placed in the back window of a car and dried. Leave the car windows open about 1 inch (2.5 cm).

To make sure the fruit leather is completely dried, pull from the plastic wrap or touch to see if the fruit leather is "tacky." Purees without sugar will be much drier and more brittle. If it is not completely dry it will mold during storage. When the fruit leather becomes too dry, it will crack and crumble and won't roll, but it is still good to eat . . . call it "fruit chips."

Storing Puree and Fruit Leather

Roll fruit leather loosely in plastic wrap and store in the cupboard. To store puree without sugar for other uses, break it into small pieces and store in plastic bags in a dry, cool place or in the freezer.

Rose hip powder may be made by crushing dried puree with a rolling pin until it is fine enough to suit you. This may be stored in small jars in a cool, dry

Did you know? The farther north you collect rose hips, the higher the content of vitamin C. Good news for a place where oranges are so expensive! Harvest them and do your health a favor. Rose hip powder can be added to other fruit dishes.

place. It is good to sprinkle over cereal and to include in hot cakes and other dishes.

Rose Hip/Blueberry Fruit Leather

►Combine 1 cup (240 mL) rose hip puree and 1 cup (240 mL) blueberry puree. Add 2 tablespoons (30 mL) honey and spread on plastic wrap. Dry as for fruit leather. The dominant flavor in this fruit leather is rose hips; if you like, you can change the proportions to have more blueberry flavor.

Salmonberry Fruit Leather

►Combine 2 cups (480 mL) salmonberry puree (put through sieve to remove large seeds) and 2 tablespoons (30 mL) honey. Spread on plastic wrap and dry as for fruit leather.

Rhubarb-Strawberry Fruit Leather

►Combine 1 cup (240 mL) rhubarb puree and 1 cup (240 mL) strawberry puree. (Strawberries may be fresh, frozen or frozen with sugar added.) Add 1-1/2 tablespoons (23 mL) honey, unless you use frozen strawberries with sugar already added. Spread on plastic wrap and dry as for fruit leather.

Blueberry-Applesauce Fruit Leather

►Combine 1 cup (240 mL) blueberry puree and 1 cup (240 mL) unsweetened applesauce. Add 1 tablespoon (15 mL) honey and spread on plastic wrap. Dry as for fruit leather. This makes a tart fruit leather, so if you like it sweeter, add one more tablespoon (15 mL) of honey.

Rose Hip Fruit Leather

►Combine 2 cups (480 mL) rose hip puree and 1 tablespoon (15 mL) lemon juice. If the rose hips were not extremely ripe, add 1 tablespoon (15 mL) honey. Spread on plastic wrap and dry as for fruit leather.

Rhubarb Leather

►Combine 2 cups (480 mL) rhubarb puree and 3 tablespoons (45 mL) sugar. Spread on plastic wrap and dry as for fruit leather.

DRYING VEGETABLES

Most vegetables benefit from blanching (see directions on page 456) a few minutes before drying begins. How long is listed on the following chart, Steps for Drying Specific Vegetables.

Before drying, remove any excess moisture by placing vegetables on paper toweling or clean cloths. Then arrange on drying trays, usually not over 1/2 inch (1.25 cm) deep. Successful drying depends on having enough heat to draw out moisture but *not* enough to cook the food, plus dry air and good circulation to carry moisture away.

For vegetables, controlled-heat drying (as in the oven) is usually faster than sun-drying . . . but it costs more. If you use the oven, be sure trays are at least 1-1/2 inches (3.75 cm) smaller than the width and depth of the oven; separate trays by about 2-1/2 inches (5.25 cm) and leave 3-inch (7.5 cm) clearance between trays and top and bottom of oven.

The best temperature for drying is 140°F (60°C). Keep the oven door ajar to allow moisture to escape.

Testing for Dryness

Dried vegetables should be hard and brittle. Most vegetables take 4 to 12 hours to dry in the oven. To test, let a few pieces cool before you try to break them. The hot ones may seem soft but won't be after they cool.

Pasteurizing

Certain dried foods need to be heated briefly again before storage to prevent spoiling. Sun-dried foods, vegetables cut in small pieces and foods allowed to stand exposed to air after drying should all be pasteurized. Sun-dried foods and those allowed to stand for a while after drying may be contaminated by insects or other airborne bacteria, while small vegetable pieces require such a short drying time that it may not be sufficient to destroy unwanted bacteria. There are two ways to pasteurize either fruits or vegetables:

- Heat dried food on trays in a 150°F (65°C) oven for 30 minutes.
- Heat in a 175°F (80°C) oven — fruits, 15 minutes — vegetables, 10 minutes.

Using Dried Vegetables

Use dried vegetables "as is" to add to soups and other dishes with a lot of liquid or as "crunchies"

Steps For Drying Specific Vegetables

Cabbage:
Remove outer leaves; quarter and core. Cut into strips 1/8 inch (3 mm) thick. Steam-blanch until wilted, about 2-1/2 to 3 minutes; or blanch in boiling water, 1-1/2 to 2 minutes. Drain on toweling. Sun-drying will take about seven hours; oven, one to three hours; dehydrator, one to two hours.

To cook — 2 cups (480 mL) dried cabbage, cover with 4 cups (1 L) boiling water; add 1/2 teaspoon (2 mL) salt. Lower heat, cover, boil gently 10 to 15 minutes or until tender. Makes about 3 cups (720 mL).

Carrots:
Select crisp, tender carrots, free from woodiness. Wash and trim root and top. Cut into slices or strips about 1/8 inch (3 mm) thick. Steam-blanch 8 to 10 minutes. Arrange in a thin layer on trays. Dry until tough and leathery.

Corn:
Select tender, sweet corn. Husk. Sort ears on basis of maturity. Young corn requires longer blanching time. Steam on cob 10 to 15 minutes or until milk is set. Cut from cob after cool enough to handle. Spread kernels 1/2 to 3/4 inch (1.25 to 1.9 cm) deep on trays. Stir frequently during drying to prevent lumping. Drying time — six to eight hours in controlled heat. Dry until hard and brittle.

Herbs:
Gather when leaves are mature but before flowers develop. Wash if necessary, remove excess water. Hang small bundles of stems in warm, dry, airy place. (May be enclosed in a large brown paper bag.) OR, dry leaves on a cookie sheet in a warm oven. Dry until leaves become brittle and crumble easily.

Mushrooms:
Cut large mushrooms in 1/2-inch (1.25 cm) slices; discard tough stems. Leave small mushrooms whole. Spread on sheet pan not more than 1/2 inch (1.25 cm) deep. Dry until mushrooms are leathery.

To puree for drying — Cook unseasoned cleaned mushrooms, including stems if you wish, by simmering gently for an hour in a small amount of water. Drain and put through food mill, blender or fine sieve to make puree. Spread on plastic-wrapped cookie sheet (see Fruit Leather) no more than 1/8 to 1/4 inch (3 to 6 mm) thick. Dry in sun or oven. When thoroughly dry, break into pieces and pasteurize. Excellent flavoring for gravy, soups, stews, sauces, meat loaf . . . you name it. Dried mushrooms must be stored in cool, dry, insect and rodent-free environment.

Onions:
Select pungent varieties. Peel. Remove outer discolored layers and cut uniform slices 1/8 to 1/4 inch (3 to 6 mm) thick. Spread thinly on trays. Dry in oven 6 to 10 hours until brittle and light-colored.

For onion powder — crush slices after drying and cooling.

Peas:
Select young, tender peas of sweet variety. Shell. Steam-blanch 8 to 10 minutes or dip in boiling water three to four minutes. Spread thinly on trays. Dry in oven 6 to 10 hours or until hard and shriveled. Peas should shatter when hit with a hammer.

Squash — summer, zucchini:
Wash, trim, cut into 1/4 inch (6 mm) slices. Steam-blanch six minutes. Spread in a thin layer on trays. Dry until brittle.

Tomatoes for stewing:
Steam or dip in boiling water to loosen skin and then chill in cold water. Peel. Cut large tomatoes into 3/4-inch (1.9 cm) sections or slice. Cut small tomatoes in half. Steam-blanch three minutes. Spread in single layer on trays. Dry four to eight hours in controlled heat.

Wild greens:
Leafy plants such as goosefoot, willow and fireweed can be dried rather like herbs. Wash if necessary and drain on toweling. With kitchen scissors, snip the leaves into small pieces. Do not use coarse stems. Spread on trays and dry until brittle enough to crush between the fingers.

for salads. To use dried herbs — 1/3 to 1/2 teaspoon (2 mL) or slightly more will equal about 1 tablespoon (15 mL) of fresh herbs.

Vegetables may also be reconstituted to very nearly their original form, size and appearance if they have been dried well, and they retain much of the original flavor. One cup (240 mL) of dried vegetables reconstitutes to about 2 cups (480 mL). Soak dried vegetables in cold water just to cover for 20 minutes to two hours. Cover greens with boiling water. To cook, bring vegetables to a boil and simmer until done. Remember, dried vegetables are partially cooked and do not need as long a cooking time as fresh ones.

Storing Dried Vegetables

Dried foods should be thoroughly cooled before packaging. Pack as tightly as possible without crushing into clean, dry, insect-proof containers. Metal cans or boxes with fitted lids, glass jars or moisture-vapor-proof freezer cartons or heavy gauge plastic bags make good containers for either fruits or vegetables. Herbs dried on the stem may be stored on the stem in plastic or paper bags. Or, store only the leaves whole or crushed. Store containers in a cool, dry, dark place. The quality will be affected by heat and dampness. Check from time to time. Moldy food should be discarded, but slightly damp foods may be reheated to dry and repackaged. Storage time is usually six months to a year.

A dryer can be made in about 10 minutes. Using log poles or 1 x 1-inch lumber, frame out a rectangle that covers the surface area of your heating stove. At each corner attach a length of cord that will enable you to suspend the dryer from ceiling or rafters over your stove. The reason for suspending the dryer instead of building a platform on top of the stove is to be able to raise or lower the dryer so it can be at a temperature of 110°F (43°C) or cooler. Attach a nylon (washable) screen to bottom surface of frame. You're done.
■ *Sally Eichelbarger*
Susitna Sentinel
Reprinted from ALASKA® magazine
March 1977

BUSH SPECIALTIES — "OIL CAPPING" & FERMENTING

"Oil Capping" Blueberries
A way of preserving raw blueberries without sugar and without a refrigerator

►The peak of the blueberry harvest in our part of Northwestern Alaska hits in mid-August, when the daytime temperatures are still quite warm. But the Great Outdoor Refrigerator doesn't get cold enough to freeze the berries until the end of September, so it is necessary to find some way of protecting the harvest from mold and fermentation for about six weeks. Here is the system we use.

Manya puts the berries into containers (we use ordinary glass jars) and presses them down to release the juice. Then she pours enough cooking oil onto the surface to form a layer 1/4 inch (6 mm) thick. Peanut oil is our favorite because it congeals at just the right temperature, but any cooking oil will do.

Then we put the closed containers in a hole in the ground (our natural refrigerator) and lay an insulated cover over the opening. We keep the fruit chilled by storing it at the very bottom of our cold hole, nearest the permafrost, because even with the air completely excluded by oil, the berries can still ferment if they are too warm.

Later in the fall, when the air begins to get colder than the ground, we take the lid off the cold hole and let the berries start to freeze.

Whenever we want blueberries during the winter, we just bring in a container, let it warm a bit, lift off the semisolid oil cap (the oil is still usable for other things, by the way) . . . and eat! Cold-hole blueberries give us a little taste of summer right through the cold, dark months.
■ *Ole Wik*
"Preserving Raw Blueberries"
The Cabin Friend
ALASKA® magazine, September 1979

How To Make Sauerkraut

"Our Great Alaskan Sauerkraut Party began several years ago when my friend Lynn brought some of his homemade kraut to Alaska from Wisconsin," explains Suzanne Hall. "After it was tested, tasted and raved about, plans were made to fill the 20-gallon (75 L) crock again the following year." Several of her recipes for using kraut — including one for cake — are in Chapter 10. Here she describes Lynn's lesson in kraut-making.

►The ideal kraut container, according to Lynn, is a big ceramic crock, or a white oak whiskey barrel. Avoid plastic buckets or cans because they will affect the flavor.

Lynn says to prepare the kraut, "Slice the cabbage as fine as you can, about as thin as a dime, and that's a lot of work. Sometimes you can buy a kraut slicer, a blade on a board, and that works best. When you have a layer in the crock about 2 inches (5 cm) deep, pour some salt over it, maybe a handful." Lynn says he uses a pound (0.45 kg) of salt — or 1-1/2 cups (360 mL) — for each 40-pound (18 kg) head of cabbage. Use pure pickling salt — not iodized salt. Iodine inhibits fermentation.

Layer cabbage and salt in the crock and pound with a wooden mallet after each new layer — cabbage, salt, *pound*, cabbage, salt, *pound*. "Why let valuable space go to waste?" Lynn says. "You want to get as much kraut out of the crock as possible. Pound the heck out of it, but be careful you don't break the bottom out of the crock!"

Leave a little space at the top for the lid and future expansion of the contents, then fold a piece of sterilized white cloth over the cabbage, so that no ends stick out. (You can sterilize a clean cloth by boiling it for five minutes.) Lynn emphasizes *white* cloth, because the kraut mixture is so potent that it could easily pull the dye right out of colored fabric. At this point some doubts crossed my mind about this stuff we were concocting! "And don't let the cloth hang out because it'll act as a wick and draw out moisture that you want to stay in the crock," Lynn cautions.

On top of the cloth, place a round lid of wood that fits loosely into the crock. "Don't make it from pine or spruce," Lynn warns. "There's too much sap in them and this will get into the kraut and give it a bad flavor."

A heavy stoneware plate will do, too. The main things to remember are: don't use metal or plastic; and you want something heavy enough to keep the kraut below the brine which will begin to form within several hours. If you need it, on top of this lid, put a heavy, clean rock. Once this is in place, the crock is ready to hibernate while the cabbage ferments.

The best kraut temperature is about 60°F (15°C). Fermentation will progress faster with warmth, and frequent temperature changes will result in fluctuating expansion and shrinkage and some variation in taste and texture. The temperature should not go above 70°F (21°C).

As it "works," the kraut should be inspected every day. If, after 24 hours, the salted cabbage hasn't released enough brine to cover it, add enough salted water to bring the level up. Use a ratio of 2 teaspoons (10 mL) pickling salt for each cup (240 mL) of cold water needed to cover the cabbage.

Scum that forms on the cabbage should be skimmed off. And, each day, the cloth should be rinsed out and boiled again before being replaced. Rinse the lid and scald it with boiling water, too.

Wondering how long it would be before these strange rituals paid off, I learned it would be six weeks. (A smaller amount of kraut can be done in as little as two weeks.)

"Some folks add sugar to their kraut after it's done working, but I never do," Lynn says. "Mine doesn't get very sour, so I don't need sugar." He pointed out one advantage of regular inspection and skimming: the kraut can and should be tasted to see how fermentation is coming along. The process is completely done when there is no gas being produced and bubbles cease to rise to the top when the crock is tapped. He said he often doesn't wait for the mixture to ferment completely. Whenever the maker decides he likes the taste, the process can be interrupted and the canning will prevent further fermenting.

Or, if you can store kraut at a steady temperature

Sauerkraut By The Jar

►Sauerkraut can be made in smaller quantities, too, if your garden doesn't produce dozens of 40-pound (18 kg) cabbages, or you simply don't want that much kraut.

Take the quantity you have, trim off the outer leaves and grate it as Suzanne and Lynn suggest. Then weight it and combine it with noniodized salt in the ratio of 3-1/2 tablespoons (53 mL) salt to each 5 pounds (2.25 kg) of cabbage, layering it into sterilized jars. Pack as tightly as you can, leaving about 2 inches (5 cm) of expansion space at the top. Into this pack the sterilized white cloth — as described. And then over that you can crisscross plastic spoons to hold the cabbage and cloth in place as the brine develops, or fill small plastic bags with water, seal and place them on top of the cloth.

Packing the cabbage in smaller amounts may result in much faster fermentation. Check every day and follow the rest of the directions outlined in this article.

around 38°F (3°C), it will keep without further fermentation. Be sure to continue to weight the kraut below the brine. If you can't be sure of steady temperature control, you should freeze or can it.

To freeze — pack it into meal-sized airtight containers and freeze. At serving time, cook it at least 10 minutes to reduce its gas content.

To can it — heat the kraut to simmering — above 185°F (85°C) but *below* boiling temperature, 212°F (100°C). Then pack the hot kraut in hot, sterilized pint (480 mL) or quart (1 L) jars and ladle in boiling-hot brine to cover it, leaving 1/2 inch (1.25 cm) of headroom.

If you run short of brine or the fermenting brine seems too sour and you wish to freshen it some, create more, using the ratio of pickling salt to water suggested earlier.

Wipe off jars with a clean cloth, adjust lids and process in boiling-water bath 25 minutes for pint (480 mL) jars, 30 minutes for quarts (1 L).

I had never listed sauerkraut among my favorite foods, but after tasting Lynn's, I decided I could easily eat it two or three times a week. I think Lynn's secret is to stop fermentation before the cabbage becomes unbearably sour and to drain off most of the fermented brine before canning.

■ *Suzanne M. Hall*
Excerpted and adapted from
"Alaska Sauerkraut Party"
ALASKA® *magazine, October 1979*

MAKING PICKLES, RELISH, CHUTNEY, MARMALADE & KETCHUP

Cranberries, blueberries and huckleberries are favorites for making relish, chutney, ketchup and other sauces to accompany meat dishes. Fruit sauces and relishes are best made fresh from either frozen or fresh berries. You will find most of these recipes in Chapter 11. In this chapter are a few that may be further processed in a boiling-water bath and sealed for longer storage outside the refrigerator.

The Alaska garden yields rhubarb and several vegetables for pickly-spicy products, and the prime wild vegetable pickle is kelp. Any firm-textured fruit or vegetable is suitable. (Wish we had a crab apple pickle to share. There must be an Alaska recipe we overlooked.) Pick them in their prime and process quickly. Classic dills from the Alaska garden start with green tomatoes or zucchini.

Ingredients

Salt — It must be noniodized, but don't use the table variety that is treated so it will not lump or cake during damp weather. Use pure pickling or dairy salt without any additives.

Water — Soft water is preferred. Iron in hard water will cause pickles to darken.

Vinegar — Use a high-grade cider or white distilled vinegar of 4- to 6-percent acidity (40 to 60 grain). Vinegars of unknown acidity should not be used. Cider vinegar gives a nice taste but may darken light-colored fruits and vegetables. White vinegar is sharper in flavor but is useful when light color is important — with cauliflower and onions, for example. Do not dilute the amount of vinegar called for in a recipe. If you want a sweeter product, add more sugar.

Sugar — Either white granulated sugar or brown sugar may be used, again, depending on color and taste requirements.

Spices — Whole spices give the best flavor. Powdered ones may cause clouding. Tie whole spices in a cheesecloth bag and then remove it before the pickle product is canned. The fresher the spices (dried ones, too), the better the pickle.

Equipment

For heating pickling liquids, you may use unchipped enamelware, stainless steel, aluminum or glass. (Do NOT use copper, brass, galvanized or iron utensils.)

For fermenting and brining, however, avoid metal altogether. Use lead-free crockery or stoneware, large glass jars, bowls or unchipped enamelware. You will also need a weight of similar material — a heavy plate or large glass lid that will fit inside the pickling container. Or a heavy-duty plastic bag may be filled with water, sealed carefully and used as a weight to keep pickling produce under the brine. It should be a kind that is intended for use with food.

Besides these, you need all the standard cutting,

peeling and scrubbing equipment, plus a water-bath canner, jars and lids specifically designed for home canning.

The Pickling Process

Some pickles are kept in brine for several weeks before further processing, but many recipes call for a short brine treatment — overnight or slightly longer. And some products — relishes, chutney, ketchup — are completely cooked before processing in a canner.

The Need for Canning in Boiling-Water Bath

Many, many people still "put up" relishes, sauces, ketchup and chutney using the "open-kettle" method. This is fine for short-term storage *under refrigeration.* It is not "canning." Nor will brine keep pickles indefinitely. They must be processed in a boiling-water bath to destroy yeasts and molds in the jar and to preserve good texture and flavor for several months.

Please read the general information about canning at the beginning of this chapter.

Pickled Beets

About 7 pounds (3.2 kg) beets
1 cup (240 mL) water
2-1/2 cups (600 mL) sugar
3 cups (720 mL) vinegar
1 teaspoon (5 mL) salt
2 teaspoons (10 mL) allspice
3-inch (7.5 cm) stick cinnamon
1/2 teaspoon (2 mL) whole cloves

►Wash beets. Leave 2-inch (5 cm) stems and taproots. Cover with boiling water and cook whole until tender. Drain, peel and slice. Should be 3 quarts (2.6 L).

Combine all remaining ingredients and bring to a boil. Turn heat down; simmer 15 minutes. Add the sliced beets and simmer five minutes longer. Pack beets hot into hot pint (0.47 L) jars. Bring syrup back to a boil and pour over beets, leaving 1/2-inch (1.25 cm) head space. Process in boiling-water bath for 30 minutes. Makes 6 pints (2.9 L).
■ *Mamie Jensen, Juneau*

Kelp Relish

6 pounds (2.7 kg) kelp
1 cup (240 mL) water

4 large onions
3 heads cabbage
3 green peppers
2 red peppers
1 small jar pimentos
1/3 cup (80 mL) salt
1/2 teaspoon (2 mL) powdered alum*
2 tablespoons (30 mL) mustard seed
2 tablespoons (30 mL) whole allspice
6 cups (1.45 L) sugar
4 cups (1 L) vinegar
2 tablespoons (30 mL) whole turmeric

►Select kelp that is rooted. Use the bulb kelp that floats in shallow bays or channels. Cut kelp into 6-inch (15 cm) pieces, peel and cut in strips. Soak eight hours in fresh water, making sure all kelp is covered; this makes the kelp crisp.

Drain and grind in food chopper, using medium blade. Put into large enameled kettle or canner and add 1 cup (240 mL) water; cook half an hour, stirring constantly; then set aside to cool.

Grind onions, cabbage, peppers and pimentos and add to the cooled kelp. Add 1/3 cup (80 mL) salt and mix well; let stand for eight hours.

Mix other ingredients — alum, mustard seed, allspice, turmeric, sugar and vinegar. Boil for three minutes. Meanwhile, drain kelp-vegetable mixture and add the hot liquid to it. Cook for 20 to 25 minutes. While it is still boiling hot, pack loosely into hot sterilized jars. Adjust caps and process five minutes in a boiling-water bath.
■ *Augusta Clements, Elfin Cove*
The Cabin Friend
ALASKA® magazine, August 1976

*Powdered alum is a crisping agent. Use it sparingly. You may omit it and instead try soaking the 6-inch (15 cm) pieces of kelp in salted water rather than fresh. Follow proportions in Pickled Bull Whip Kelp recipe.

Pickled Bull Whip Kelp
The brine recipe below makes about 7 pints (3.3 L). Each pint jar (480 mL) will hold about one 20-inch (50 cm) kelp stipe, or stem, the amount varying with the diameter of the stipe.

Pickle Brine
1 to 2 quarts (1 to 1.9 L) vinegar*
1 quart (1 L) fresh water
2/3 cup (160 mL) salt
1/4 cup (60 mL) sugar
Per pint jar — 1/2 clove, 1/2 teaspoon (2 mL) dill seed, 1/2 teaspoon (2 mL) whole mustard seed, 2 peppercorns
Onion slices, 1 for each pint jar

►(*Two quarts of vinegar makes a very tart pickle, but do not use less vinegar than water.) Wash kelp well and cut in 12-inch (30 cm) lengths. Peel away outer brown skin with a vegetable peeler. Soak peeled pieces in salt solution — 1 cup (240 mL) salt to 2 gallons (7.6 L) water for eight hours. Keep all kelp covered with brine.

Remove kelp from brine and wash thoroughly in cold water. Cut kelp in rings, slices or cubes and place in an enamel kettle. Cover with boiling water and cook until kelp can just be pierced with a fork.

Meanwhile, prepare pickle brine, adding desired amount of vinegar to the 1 quart (1 L) of fresh water. Add salt and sugar. Tie whole spices in a cheesecloth bag and add those. Heat to boiling.

Drain kelp thoroughly. Pack hot into clean, hot pint (480 mL) jars. Divide spices from brine equally between jars, add a slice of onion to each and cover with boiling pickle brine to within 1/2 inch (1.25 cm) of jar rim. Adjust lids. Process in boiling-water bath for 10 minutes.

■ *1983 Cooking Edition (adapted)*
Ketchikan Daily News

Alaska Sweet Kelp Pickles

►Pick six to eight giant bulb kelp. Prime kelp is available during June, July and August. Use only the ones attached to the bottom. Soak overnight in sea water. Be sure it covers the kelp. Peel with potato peeler and wash in cold water.

4 pounds (1.8 kg) bulb kelp
1/2 teaspoon (2 mL) alum
2 quarts (1.9 L) water
3-1/2 cups (840 mL) sugar
1 pint (480 mL) white vinegar
1/2 teaspoon (2 mL) oil of cloves
1/2 teaspoon (2 mL) oil of cinnamon
1/2 teaspoon (2 mL) green
*   food coloring*

►Cut kelp to bite size. Then soak in alum solution — 1/2 teaspoon (2 mL) alum powder to 2 quarts (1.9 L) water for 15 minutes. Drain and wash in cold water; drain again. Place kelp in kettle and cover with boiling water. Cook only until kelp can be pierced with a fork. Drain.

Combine sugar, vinegar, oils and food coloring and boil two minutes. Pour over cooked kelp. Let stand overnight. In the morning, drain off and save the syrup. Cover kelp with water again and reheat to boiling. Drain. Pour syrup back over kelp and allow to stand 24 hours. The third morning, heat both kelp and syrup to boiling point. Pack hot kelp in hot pint jars and cover with boiling syrup. Adjust caps and process in boiling-water bath 10 minutes; or, simply seal and store in refrigerator. Makes 3 pints (1.45 L) total.

■ *Jeanne Norheim and Irma Lind*
*   Petersburg*

Here are some pickly-spicy products made from the versatile green tomato, all from the University of Alaska Cooperative Extension Service booklet called . . . The Versatile Green Tomato!

Green Tomato Relish

3/4 cup (180 mL) salt
2 quarts (1.9 L) chopped green tomatoes
1 teaspoon (5 mL) pepper
1-1/2 teaspoons (7 mL) each — mustard,
*   cinnamon, allspice, cloves*
1/4 cup (60 mL) white mustard seed
1 quart (1 L) vinegar
2 red or green peppers, sliced
1 chopped onion

►Add salt to tomatoes, cover and let stand 24 hours. Drain. Add other ingredients. Bring to boiling and cook 15 minutes. Pour hot into hot jars, leaving 1/2-inch (1.25 cm) head space. Process in boiling water bath for five minutes. Makes 4 pints (1.9 L total).

Green Tomato Ketchup

12-1/2 pounds (5.67 kg) green tomatoes
2 medium onions
1 teaspoon (5 mL) cayenne pepper
2 cups (480 mL) cider vinegar
1-1/2 tablespoons (23 mL) broken
*   stick cinnamon*
1 tablespoon (15 mL) whole cloves
3 cloves garlic, finely chopped
1 tablespoon (15 mL) paprika
1 cup (240 mL) sugar
2-1/2 teaspoons (12 mL) salt

►Wash tomatoes, then chop in blender. Boil about 15 minutes or until soft. Slice onions into another kettle, cover with water and simmer until tender. Mix tomato and onion pulp. Add the cayenne pepper. Boil the mixture rapidly until it has been reduced to about one-half the original volume.

Place the vinegar in an enamel or stainless steel pan; add spice bag containing cinnamon, cloves and garlic. Allow this to simmer for about 30 minutes. Cover and remove from heat.

After the tomato mixture has cooked down to about half the original volume, add the vinegar — of which there should be 1-1/4 cups (300 mL). Add the paprika, sugar and salt and boil rapidly until desired consistency is reached. This should require about 10 minutes of rapid boiling. At this point add enough red food coloring to change the green color to a brown red — about 1 teaspoon (5 mL). Pour into hot jars leaving 1/2-inch (1.25 cm) of head space. Process in boiling-water bath for 10 minutes. Makes 3 pints (1.45 L total).

■ *Joy McDougall*

Green Tomato Dills

Green tomatoes — enough to fill six 1-quart
   (1 L) jars
6 stalks celery
2-1/2 sweet green peppers, seeds removed
6 cloves garlic
2 quarts (1.9 L) water
1 quart (1 L) vinegar
1 cup (240 mL) salt
Dill — fresh if possible; or 3 tablespoons (45 mL)
   dill seed

►Use small, firm green tomatoes. Pack into hot, clean jars. Add to each quart (1 L) jar a bud of garlic, a stalk of celery and one-fourth of a green pepper, cut into strips. Make a brine of the water, vinegar and salt. Boil with dill for five minutes. Pour the hot brine over the pickles to within 1/2 inch (1.25 cm) of the top of the jar. Put on cap; screw band firmly tight. Process in boiling-water bath for 15 minutes. These will be ready to use in four to six weeks.

Green Tomato Pickles

3 pounds (1.4 kg) green tomatoes
2 cups (480 mL) white vinegar
2 tablespoons (30 mL) salt
3 cloves garlic, peeled and split
5 fresh dill sprigs or 2-1/2 teaspoons (13 mL)
   dried dill

►Wash tomatoes. Remove stems. Cut each tomato into six wedges; set aside. Sterilize five pint (480 mL) jars; leave in hot water until ready to fill. In a small saucepan, combine vinegar with 1 cup (240 mL) water and the salt; bring to boiling. Reduce heat and simmer uncovered for five minutes. Add tomatoes; bring just to boiling. Remove from heat. With slotted spoon, quickly ladle tomatoes into hot jars. To each jar, add one-half clove garlic and one dill sprig or 1/2 teaspoon (2 mL) dried dill. Fill with vinegar mixture to within 1/2 inch (1.25 cm) of top. Process 10 minutes in boiling-water bath. Makes 5 pints (2.37 L total).

Green Tomato Marmalade

2 quarts (1.9 L) sliced, small green tomatoes
4 cups (1 L) sugar
1/2 teaspoon (2 mL) salt
4 lemons, peeled (save the rind)

►Combine tomatoes and salt in a cooking vessel. Chop lemon rind fine and add. Cover with water and boil 10 minutes. Drain well. Slice the peeled lemons very thin, discarding seeds but reserving all juice. Add chopped lemon rind, lemon slices, juice and sugar to the tomato mixture. Stir over moderate heat until sugar melts. Bring to boiling, reduce heat and simmer until thick, about 45 minutes. Stir frequently. Pour into hot jars leaving 1/4-inch (6 mm) head space and process in boiling-water bath 10 minutes. Makes 2 pints (1 L total).

Dilled Zucchini
Zucchini no larger than 2 inches (5 cm) in
diameter are best for pickles.

6 pounds (2.7 kg) zucchini, trimmed and sliced
   thin (about 16 cups)
2 cups (480 mL) thinly sliced celery
2 large onions, chopped
1/3 cup (80 mL) salt
Ice cubes
2 cups (480 mL) sugar
2 tablespoons (30 mL) dill seeds
2 cups (480 mL) white vinegar
6 cloves garlic, halved

►Mix zucchini, celery, onions and salt in large bowl; place a layer of ice cubes on top; cover. Let stand three hours; drain well. Combine sugar, dill seeds, and vinegar in a kettle; heat to boiling, stirring constantly. Stir in vegetables. Heat, stirring several times, just to a full rolling boil. Ladle into hot sterilized jars and place one or two pieces of garlic in each. Process for five minutes in boiling-water bath. Makes 12 8-ounce jars or 16 6-ounce jars (2800 mL total).
■ Zucchini From A to Z

Crisp Pickle Slices

4 quarts (3.8 L) zucchini
6 medium onions
2 green peppers
3 cloves garlic
1/3 cup (80 mL) salt
5 cups (1.2 L) sugar
1-1/2 teaspoons (7 mL) each — turmeric and
   celery seed
2 tablespoons (30 mL) mustard seed
3 cups (720 mL) vinegar

►Do not pare zucchini. Slice them into a stainless steel or enamel pan. Add onions, peppers and whole garlic cloves. Add salt, cover with cracked ice and mix thoroughly. Let stand three hours. Drain thoroughly. Combine remaining ingredients. Pour over zucchini mixture. Heat just to boiling. Ladle hot mixture into hot sterilized jars and cover with boiling liquid. Process for five minutes in boiling-water bath. Makes 6 to 8 pints (3 to 3.8 L). (Note: This recipe is a little large. Making only half the recipe results in a crisper pickle.)
■ Zucchini From A to Z

Blueberry Ketchup

2-1/2 quarts (2.4 L) blueberries
7 cups (1.7 L) sugar
3 cups (720 mL) white vinegar
1 tablespoon (15 mL) cinnamon
1 teaspoon (5 mL) allspice
2 teaspoons (10 mL) ground cloves

►Mix all ingredients in a large saucepan and bring to a boil over medium heat. Lower heat and simmer gently until mixture is smooth and thick, about two hours. Stir from time to time during cooking to prevent sticking. Ketchup may be stored, refrigerated, for several weeks. For longer storage, pour boiling hot mixture into hot jars, leaving 1/2-inch (1.25 mm) head space, adjust lids and process in boiling-water bath for 15 minutes. Yields about 4 pints (1.9 L). Excellent served with roast game meats and birds or brushed on as a glaze for kabobs, meat loaf and other meats during last 10 minutes of baking or broiling.
■ *Jeanne Gray, Anchorage*

Alaska Apple Butter

►Soak together one hour:

1 pound (456 g) dried apples
2 quarts (1.9 L) warm water

►Add 2 quarts (1.9 L) lowbush cranberries and cook until soft. Put pulp through food saver. Reheat and add:

3/4 as much sugar as pulp
1 teaspoon (5 mL) cinnamon
1/4 teaspoon (1 mL) salt
1/2 teaspoon (2 mL) cloves

►Cook until clear. Add juice of one lemon. Spoon hot into hot sterilized jars. Add lids. Process for 15 minutes in boiling-water bath. Yields 4 pints (1.9 L total).
■ *Tsimpshean Indian Island Cookbook (adapted)*

Cranlili

Extra good on hotdogs, hamburgers and cold meats

2 large peppers
2 teaspoons (10 mL) salt
3 medium-sized onions
1 cup (240 mL) vinegar

2 cups (480 mL) fresh lowbush cranberries
1/2 cup (120 mL) granulated sugar

►Put peppers, onions and berries through course blade of food chopper. Put into saucepan. Add remaining ingredients and simmer gently 20 to 30 minutes. Pack in hot sterilized jars. Add lids. Process for 15 minutes in a boiling-water bath. Yield: 3-1/2 cups (840 mL).
■ Collecting and Using Alaska's Wild Berries

Highbush Cranberry Ketchup

6 pounds (2.7 kg) highbush cranberries
1-1/4 pounds (570 g) sweet white onions
3 cups (720 mL) water
3 cups (720 mL) mild vinegar
6 cups (1.45 L) sugar
1 tablespoon (15 mL) cloves
1 tablespoon (15 mL) cinnamon
1 tablespoon (15 mL) allspice
1 tablespoon (15 mL) salt
2 tablespoons (30 mL) celery salt
1-1/2 teaspoons (7 mL) pepper

►Cook berries and onions in the water until soft. Put through a sieve and return the pulp to saucepan. Add remaining ingredients. Bring to a boil, reduce heat and cook until thick and ketchup-like in consistency. Stir frequently to keep from sticking. Pour into sterilized canning jars and seal immediately. Process 10 minutes in a boiling-water bath. Use your Highbush Cranberry Ketchup just like regular tomato ketchup.
■ Alaska Wild Berry Guide and Cookbook

Lowbush Cranberry Ketchup

1 pound (456 g) lowbush cranberries
1/2 cup (120 mL) mild vinegar
1/2 cup (120 mL) water
1 cup (240 mL) brown sugar
1/2 teaspoon (2 mL) cloves
1/2 teaspoon (2 mL) ginger
1/2 teaspoon (2 mL) paprika
1 teaspoon (5 mL) cinnamon
1/4 teaspoon (1 mL) pepper
1/2 teaspoon (2 mL) salt
2 tablespoons (30 mL) butter or margarine

►Boil the berries in the vinegar and water until they are soft. Put through a sieve. Add the sugar, spices and salt and cook slowly for four or five minutes. Add the butter. Pour into sterilized jars. Adjust lids and process 10 minutes in a boiling-water bath. Serve with pork or poultry.
■ *Anna Marie Davis, Anchorage*
   Alaska Wild Berry Guide and Cookbook

Cranberry-Apple Chutney

4 cups (1 L) lowbush cranberries
12 tart apples
3 red peppers
3 green peppers
12 ripe medium-sized tomatoes
6 medium onions
1 cup (240 mL) diced celery
2 ounces (56 g) crystallized ginger
2 quarts (1.9 L) cider vinegar
3 cups (720 mL) sugar
2 teaspoons (10 mL) salt

►Cut peppers in half and remove seeds. Pare apples and remove core. Force vegetables, cranberries, apples and ginger through food chopper. Combine all ingredients and cook until thick and clear, about one hour. Stir frequently. Mixture should be reduced in volume about one-half. Pack boiling-hot chutney into hot sterilized pint (480 mL) jars, leaving 1/2-inch (1.25 cm) head space. Adjust lids and process in boiling-water bath for five minutes. Makes 7 or 8 pints (3.3 to 3.8 L total).
■ *Mamie Jensen*
  Juneau

MAKING JAMS & JELLIES

Because Alaska has so many berries suitable for making jams and jellies, everyone has favorite recipes. Printed sources of recipes abound, too. There is Alaska Northwest Publishing Company's new one, *Alaska Wild Berry Guide and Cookbook*, an updated edition of the University of Alaska Cooperative Extension Service Bulletin, *Collecting and Using Alaska's Wild Berries and Other Wild Products* (from which several of the recipes below are taken) and many others.

That's why — in this section of the book — we've been conservative.

To Extract Juices For Jelly-Making & Other Uses

Blueberries: For better flavor, half the berries should be ripe, half slightly green. Simmer them with just enough water to keep from scorching. Strain overnight through a moistened jelly bag or several layers of wet cheesecloth. Do not squeeze the bag or the juice — and jelly — will be cloudy. The juice will keep, stored in the refrigerator, for several weeks. Huckleberry juice may be extracted the same way, but to substitute huckleberries for blueberries in jelly or jam making, make the proportion of juice or pulp to other ingredients slightly higher. e.g.: Use 5 cups (1.2 L) huckleberry juice or pulp rather than 4 cups (1 L) of blueberry juice or pulp.

Chokecherries: The seeds, stems and leaves of this plant are toxic. Be sure stems and leaves don't become part of your brew and, when you are mashing the berries to extract the juice, take care not to crush the seeds. This means chokecherries are NOT suitable for blender preparation. To extract the juice, remove and discard stems from 1 quart (1 L) chokecherries. Wash and drain. Add 1 cup (240 mL) water, place over low heat and simmer until fruit is tender, stirring occasionally. Mash berries gently in order not to crush the seeds. Strain through dampened jelly bag.

Crab Apples: It will take about 2-1/2 to 3 pounds (1.15 to 1.4 kg) to make 4 cups (1 L) of juice. Wash and stem crab apples and put in a large saucepan with water enough to cover fruit completely. Simmer until apples are soft. Strain overnight through a damp jelly bag. Don't squeeze or the resulting juice and jelly will be cloudy. Sweeten to taste or follow directions for jelly making.

Highbush Cranberries: For 2 cups (480 mL) juice, add 1 cup (240 mL) water to 4 cups (1 L) berries. Mash berries, place on medium heat and simmer, covered, for about 10 minutes. Strain through dampened jelly bag. When it's cool enough to handle, the bag may be squeezed to extract juice. Discard pulp.

Lowbush Cranberries: Use half as much water by volume as lowbush cranberries. Mix water and berries and boil gently for five minutes or a bit less. Crush and strain the mixture through a wet jelly bag to obtain a clear juice. Reserve the pulp for use in jams or desserts. Seal the juice in sterilized bottles or canning jars for later use in beverages, jellies and sauces. Keep in a cool place or refrigerate.

Currants: Crush currants and warm to 165°F (74°C) over low heat. Drain through jelly bag.

Raspberries: Add 1 cup (240 mL) water to 1 quart (1 L) berries, mash berries and simmer over low heat, covered, for about 10 minutes. Strain through dampened jelly bag overnight. For a clear juice and jelly, do not squeeze jelly bag.

Rhubarb: Add 1 cup (240 mL) water to 2 quarts

(1.9 L) cut up rhubarb stalks. Simmer until fruit is soft, about five minutes. Strain through cheese-cloth. Store refrigerated or frozen to add to other fruit juices and sugar in making punch.

Rose Hips: If possible, gather rose hips before the first frost. Clean and remove tails. Place hips in a kettle with enough water to completely cover the fruit. Bring to a boil slowly, reduce heat and simmer for 15 minutes, or until the fruit is soft. Strain the hips through a wet jelly bag overnight. Pour juice into a container you can cover, then store in the refrigerator, where it will keep for several weeks — ideal for having on hand throughout the preserving season. It can add a healthy dollop of vitamin C to the preparation of other berries into jellies and beverages.

To obtain rose hip pulp to stretch other fruit in jam making and to raise the vitamin C content, proceed as above, then force the mixture through a sieve to remove seeds and skins. Place everything that doesn't go through back into the cooking pot; add water and cook again gently. Force through sieve. The steps can be repeated once or twice again to obtain the maximum amount of pulp. The pulp is best combined with other fruits.

Testing Fruit Juice For Pectin

If you are stuck wondering if the berries you have picked have enough natural pectin to jell, test their juice by either of these two simple methods provided by Robbie Jayne Johnson of Anchorage:

Method I — To 1 teaspoon (5 mL) of cooked juice, add 1 teaspoon (5 mL) of grain alcohol and stir slowly. You can discover the berries' natural jelling ability by keeping in mind that juices rich in pectin will form a large amount of bulky, gelatinous material; those moderately rich in pectin will form a few pieces of gelatinous material; and juices poor in pectin will form small, flaky pieces of sediment.

Method II — Mix 2 teaspoons (10 mL) sugar, 1 tablespoon (15 mL) Epsom salt and 2 tablespoons (30 mL) cooked juice. Stir well and let stand for 20 minutes. If the mixture forms a semi-solid mass, the juice contains sufficient pectin to jell.

The Sheet Test for Jelly

If you do not have a jelly thermometer to tell you when the boiling juice has reached the jelly stage, use the "sheet" test. Dip a cold, metal spoon into the boiling liquid and then hold it from 12 to 18 inches (30 to 45 cm) above the pan but out of the path of the rising steam. Turn the spoon so the jelly runs off the edge. If two or more drops form and run together before dripping off the edge of the spoon as

separate drops, the jelly stage has been reached. It usually takes from 8 to 15 minutes to reach the sheet or jelly stage.

Processing & Sealing Jams & Jellies

Jelly is the only product everybody still agrees Grandma knew how to "put up" to perfection. The old-fashioned "open-kettle" method and sealing with paraffin are perfectly proper.

Jam, on the other hand, must be processed and sealed using a boiling-water-bath canner. Please read about the method, beginning page 425.

Sealing Jelly with Paraffin

Always melt paraffin over simmering water, rather than on direct heat. It ignites very easily. Melting it in an old teakettle gives a handy pouring device.

Pour boiling hot jelly mixture into hot sterilized glasses, leaving 1/2-inch (1.25 cm) head space. Cover with hot paraffin. Use only enough to make a layer 1/8 inch (3 mm) thick. A single thin layer—which can expand or contract easily — gives a better seal than one thick layer or two thin layers.

To be a good seal, paraffin must touch all sides of the glass. Prick air bubbles. They may cause holes as paraffin hardens. Allow glasses to stand until paraffin hardens. Cover with metal lids to keep top free from dust.

Sealing Jelly without Paraffin

Use jars with two-piece lids. Pour jelly immediately into hot, sterilized jars, leaving 1/8-inch (3 mm) head space. Place lid on jars, screw band on tightly; invert. Repeat with all jars. When all are sealed, stand them upright. Cool.

Raspberry Jelly

2 cups (480 mL) wild raspberry juice
1 cup (240 mL) highbush cranberry juice
1 cup (240 mL) wild blueberry juice
Juice of 2 limes
7-1/2 cups (1.9 L) sugar

►Boil one minute and stir in one bottle commercial pectin. Bring to a boil again; remove from fire; skim and pour into sterilized jars. Cover with paraffin.
■ Gold Rush Festival Cook Book
  Whitehorse, Yukon Territory

Crowberry Jelly

2 cups (480 mL) crowberries
4 cups (1 L) water
2 boxes (1-3/4 oz /or/ 50 g, each)
  powdered pectin
1/2 cup (120 mL) lemon juice
3/4 cup (180 mL) water
7-1/2 cups (1.8 L) sugar

►Put crowberries and 4 cups (1 L) water in blender and process until berries are pureed. Pour the mixture into a heavy saucepan with pectin, lemon juice and 3/4 cup (180 mL) water. Boil rapidly, then add sugar. Boil hard for one minute; be careful, for it boils over easily. Strain or skim and pour into sterilized jars and seal.
■ *Patricia Monaghan*
  "A Berry To Crow About"
  ALASKA® magazine, August 1979

Nagoonberry Jelly

►Pick over berries but do not attempt to remove hulls. Put into large kettle and add water until it is two-thirds as deep as the berries. Boil for 20 minutes, mashing and stirring occasionally. Strain through jelly bag. Make juice into jelly 1 quart (1 L) at a time. Boil in a jelly kettle for five minutes; then add 4 cups (1 L) sifted sugar, stirring until dissolved. Boil until mixture sheets when poured from the edge of a spoon. This should take only two or three minutes. Pour at once into sterilized jelly glasses and seal.
■ *Mrs. Louise Shattuck*
  Tried and True Recipes, *Juneau*

Highbush Cranberry Jelly

4 pounds (1.8 kg) highbush cranberries
2 cups (480 mL) water

►Crush berries in water and bring to a boil. Simmer 10 minutes. Strain through a jelly bag or several layers of cheesecloth. Measure juice.

5 cups (1.2 L) highbush cranberry juice
7 cups (1.7 L) sugar
1/2 bottle liquid pectin

►Mix sugar and juice in saucepan. Place over high heat and bring to a boil stirring constantly. At once stir in liquid pectin. Bring to a full rolling boil and boil hard one minute, stirring constantly. Remove from heat. Skim off foam with metal spoon and pour quickly into hot sterilized jelly glasses. Yield: 8 cups.
■ *Marguerite Stetson, Nutrition Specialist*
  Cooperative Extension Service
  University of Alaska

Wild Currant Jelly

4 pounds (1.8 kg) ripe, fresh currants
  (about 3 quarts)
1 cup (240 mL) water
7 cups (1.7 L) sugar
1/2 bottle fruit pectin

►Crush currants with a potato masher. Add water, bring to a boil and simmer, covered, for 10 minutes. Put in jelly cloth or bag and strain out juice. Measure 5 cups (1.2 L) of juice into a very large saucepan. Add sugar and mix well. Put over high heat and bring to a boil, stirring constantly. Stir in pectin at once. Then bring to a full rolling boil and boil hard one minute, stirring constantly. Remove from heat, skim off foam with a metal spoon, and pour quickly into hot, sterilized glasses. Seal with paraffin. Yields 11 medium glasses.
■ *Ann Chandonnet*
  "Currently The Crop Is Currants"
  ALASKA® magazine, July 1978

Rose Petal Jelly

1 cup (240 mL) rose petals, packed down
1 cup (240 mL) water
2 tablespoons (30 mL) lemon juice
Sugar
1/2 bottle liquid pectin

►Simmer the first three ingredients together until the petals have lost their color. Strain the liquid to remove the petals. Measure the strained liquid and add three-quarters as much sugar as there is liquid. Add pectin and boil the mixture rapidly for one minute.

To use the jelly immediately, I pour it into a clean jar with a lid and place it in the refrigerator. For longer storage, seal with paraffin and store in a cool, dark place.

Here are some things you can do for the birds at holiday time (or anytime):
• String cranberries on fine wire and make a circle, leaving enough wire to form a loop to hang on a tree branch.
• String cranberries and popcorn on heavy-duty thread, make a loop of the stringed goodies and hang on a tree.
• Form tiny boxes of heavy cardboard and make hanging loops from pipe cleaners. Fill the boxes with birdseed or table scraps and hang.
• Loop colored ribbon through the holes in several doughnuts and hang for the birds' Christmas tree.
■ *The Old Homesteader*

I've read claims of rose petals curing everything from sore throats to Black Plague. Speaking from experience, I can verify that rose petal jelly cures hunger in a most delightful way, and I soon forget the few thorns I encounter during the gathering.

■ *Dianne K. Davis*
  "Tasty Petal Pickin'"
  ALASKA® magazine, June 1975

Crab Apple Jelly

Crab apples to make 4 cups (1 L) of juice —
  about 2-1/2 to 3 pounds (1.15 to 1.4 kg)
1/4 teaspoon (1 mL) cinnamon (optional)
Water
3 cups (720 mL) sugar

►Wash and stem wild crab apples and put in a large saucepan with water enough to cover fruit completely. Simmer until apples are soft. Extract juice by draining through a damp jelly bag overnight. Return juice to pan and add sugar and cinnamon. Boil rapidly until juice reaches the jelly stage. Skim off foam, if any forms, and pour jelly into hot, sterilized glasses. Seal immediately with paraffin. Crab apples are good combined with almost any of our berries which will help to stretch the yield if you are short on quantity.

■ Alaska Wild Berry Guide and Cookbook

Uncooked Berry Jam

Easy as powdered pectin . . . this one must be stored in refrigerator or freezer.

2 cups (480 mL) crushed berries
1 package (1¾ oz /or/ 49 g) powdered pectin
1 cup (240 mL) water
4 cups (1 L) sugar

►Mix berries and sugar. Let stand 20 minutes, stirring occasionally. Combine pectin with water, bring to a boil and boil one minute, stirring constantly. Add pectin mixture to the berries and sugar and stir about two minutes more. Pour into clean sterilized jars and cover with a lid or aluminum foil. Let stand at room temperature for 24 hours until it congeals. Then refrigerate until it is set. Store in refrigerator or freezer until used. Makes 1-1/2 pints (0.72 L).

■ Collecting and Using Alaska's Wild Berries
  (adapted)

Rhubarb-Strawberry Jam

►Slice thin about 1 pound (456 g) rhubarb. Add 3/4 cup (180 mL) water and simmer, covered, until rhubarb is soft. Measure into saucepan mashed strawberries and cooked rhubarb to equal 3-1/2

cups (840 mL) total. Add 6-1/2 cups (1.6 L) sugar. Bring to full rolling boil and boil hard one minute, stirring constantly. Remove from heat and add 1/2 bottle or one pouch Certo, stirring well. Stir about two or three minutes. Pour into hot, sterilized jars, adjust caps and process in boiling-water bath 15 minutes.

If no fresh strawberries are available, use one package frozen strawberries and rhubarb to make the amount needed.

■ *Mamie Jensen, Juneau*

Short-Cooked Berry Jam

6 cups (1.45 L) crushed berries
8-1/2 cups (2 L) sugar
3 ounces (85 g) liquid pectin

►Measure crushed berries into a large kettle. Add sugar and stir until dissolved. Place on high heat, stirring constantly until it comes to a full boil. Boil hard one minute, stirring constantly. Remove from heat; at once stir in liquid pectin. Skim off foam with metal spoon. Then stir and skim for five minutes to cool slightly. Pour into hot sterilized jars. Add lids. Process for 15 minutes in boiling-water bath. Makes 3 to 4 pints (1.45 to 1.9 L).

■ Collecting and Using Alaska's Wild Berries.

Rhubarb Strawberry Jelly

1 quart (1 L) of rhubarb, cut very fine
2 quarts (1.9 L) ripe strawberries
6 cups (1.45 L) sugar
6 ounces (170 g) pectin

►Crush strawberries, add to rhubarb and bring to a boil. Strain juice through a jelly bag. Use 3-1/2 cups (840 mL) juice. Combine with sugar and bring to a boil. Add one bottle pectin and boil one minute. Remove from heat and skim. Pour into jelly glasses and pour on a 1/8-inch (3 mm) layer of paraffin. Yields 6 to 7 half-pints (1.45 to 1.7 L total).

■ Rhubarb Recipes *(adapted)*

To prevent the disappointment of losing handpicked berries during a stumble in the berry patch, use an empty plastic lard bucket with the lid attached. Cut a hole in the middle of the lid large enough to easily drop berries in. The lid left attached by the corners will prevent excessive loss during a spill.

What to do with the lard? Well, it makes delicious pie crust.

■ *Karen Parrish Zollman, Sterling*
  The Cabin Friend
  ALASKA® magazine, November 1977

Long-Cooked Berry Jam

The long-cook method has no added pectin and relies on the natural pectin in the fruit to form a jam. Use firm, ripe berries — three-quarters should be fully ripe; one-quarter, underripe, because they contain more pectin. Make jams in small batches. Cook rapidly after the sugar or other sweeteners have dissolved.

8 cups (1.9 L) crushed berries
6 cups (1.45 L) sugar

►If berries are very seedy, part of the pulp may be put through a sieve. Heat berries thoroughly in a large kettle. Add sugar to the heated berries. Cook, stirring constantly, until mixture has a thick, jelly-like consistency. (Some cooks do this in the oven at 300°F — 150°C.) You can test for jell by pouring a small amount of boiling-hot jam on a cold plate and putting it in the refrigerator a few minutes. If the mixture jells, it should be done. While you're making the test, remove jam from heat.

If it's done, return mixture to heat just long enough to make sure it is very hot, then pour into hot sterilized jars. Add lids and process 15 minutes in boiling water bath. Yields 3 to 4 pints (1.45 to 1.9 L).

■ Collecting and Using
  Alaska's Wild Berries
  (adapted)

Don't forget to use rose hip powder or juice in practically everything. The powder will replace a like amount of dry ingredients and the juice can be used in place of part of the liquid in almost any recipe.

■ Alaska Wild Berry Trails

CANNING ALASKA
FRUITS & VEGETABLES

The timetables in this section give the minimum information you'll need to preserve berries and some of the more common garden produce by canning methods. First, please read Canning Foods — General Principles at the beginning of this chapter. Especially be sure you know how to exhaust foods processed in tin cans, how to adjust processing times or pressures if you live above sea level and all the steps of boiling-water-bath and pressure processing.

Nearly all vegetables, except those that are pickled or cured, must be canned under pressure. Tomatoes and tomato juice — which we think of as "vegetable" — are safely canned by the boiling-water-bath method only if the tomatoes are "slightly underripe to ripe." Otherwise they, too, are lacking in sufficient acidity and are best canned under pressure.

Berries may be canned in the boiling-water bath and may be put up as whole fruits (raw pack, hot pack, with or without sugars in varying degrees of sweetness); pureed fruit or juice.

Syrups For Sweetening Fruits
For use in canning or freezing

Types	Cups of Sugar	Cups of Water	Yield: Cups of Syrup
Very light syrup	1	4	4-3/4
Light syrup	2	4	5
Medium syrup	3	4	5-1/2
Heavy syrup	4-3/4	4	6-1/2

Bring required amounts of sugar and water to a boil and boil gently for five minutes. Use as a canning or freezing syrup or as a sweetener for fruit beverages.

Other Sweeteners
Light corn syrup or mild-flavored honey may be used to replace half the sugar called for. Do not use brown sugar, sorghum or molasses.

Canning Unsweetened Fruit
You may can fruit without sweetening — in its own juice, in extracted juice, or in water. Sugar is not needed to prevent spoilage; processing is the same for unsweetened fruit as for sweetened.

TIMETABLE 1 — Steps For Canning Fruit, Tomatoes and Cured Vegetables

See page 423 for complete processing instructions. Prepare foods as directed. Have water ready in boiling-water bath — boiling for hot pack, hot for cold pack. Add boiling water to bring water 1 or 2 inches over tops of jars but don't pour boiling water directly on glass jars. Cover canner. Count processing time when water returns to rolling boil, unless otherwise directed. *The times and pressures listed are for sea level. If raw pack directions are not given, raw pack is not recommended.

Product	Preparation	Boiling-Water Bath*		Pressure Canner 5 pounds pressure* (34.5 kPa)	
		Pints	**Quarts**	**Pints**	**Quarts**
Berries: (Yield— 1½-3 lbs = 1 qt)	**Raw Pack —** Wash, stem and drain. Fill jars, shaking berries down gently. Cover with boiling syrup or water leaving 1/2-inch head space.	10 min.	15 min.	8 min.	8 min.
	Hot Pack — Best method for very juicy fruit. Wash and drain. Add 1/2 cup sugar to each quart fruit. Cover pan and bring to a boil. Pack berries and juice, leaving 1/2-inch head space.	10 min.	15 min.	8 min.	8 min.
Fruit juice:	**Hot Pack —** Stem, wash and remove seed if desired. Crush fruit. Heat to simmering. Strain through dampened cloth bag. Add sugar if desired — about 1 cup per gallon of juice. Reheat to simmering and fill jars, leaving 1/2-inch head space.	10 min.	10 min.	5 min.	5 min.
Fruit puree:	**Hot Pack —** Crush fruit. Simmer with a little water to keep from sticking. If the fruit is juicy, no water may be necessary, but stir the pulp frequently in any case. Put through strainer or food mill, adding sugar to taste. Heat again to simmering. Pack while hot in glass jars to within 1/2 inch of the top.	10 min.	10 min.	—	—
Jams, jellies, marmalades, relishes, pickles:	See individual instructions, Chapter 14.				
Rhubarb:	**Hot Pack —** Remove leaves, wash and cut into 1/2-inch pieces. Add 1/2 cup sugar to each quart rhubarb and let stand to draw out juice. Bring to boiling. Pack hot, leaving 1/2-inch head space.	10 min.	10 min.	5 min.	5 min.
Sauerkraut:	**Hot Pack —** Heat sauerkraut to simmering — 185°F to 210°F (85 to 98°C). Do not boil. Pack hot sauerkraut into hot jars and cover with hot juice to 1/2 inch from top. Start to count processing time as soon as jars are placed in actively boiling water.	15 min.	20 min.	—	—
Tomatoes: (Yield— Bushel = 15-20 qts 2½-3½ lbs = 1 qt)	**Raw Pack —** Use only slightly underripe to ripe tomatoes. Scald just long enough to loosen skins; plunge into cold water. Drain, peel and core. Leave tomatoes whole or cut in half. Pack leaving 1/2-inch head space, pressing gently to fill spaces. Add 1 teaspoon salt per quart if desired.	40 min.	50 min.	10 min.	10 min.
	Hot Pack — Quarter and peel. Bring to boil and pack, leaving 1/2-inch head space. Add 1 teaspoon salt per quart if desired.	35 min.	45 min.	8 min.	8 min.
Tomato juice: (Yield— Bushel = 12-16 qts 3-3½ lbs = 1 qt)	**Hot Pack —** Use underripe to ripe tomatoes. Wash, remove stem ends, cut into pieces. Simmer until softened and put through strainer. Add 1 teaspoon salt to each quart juice if desired. Reheat just to boiling. Fill jars with juice leaving 1/2-inch head space.	35 min.	35 min.	5 min.	5 min.

1 bushel = about 34 L
1/2 inch = 1.25 cm
1 inch = 2.5 cm
Quart = 0.95 L
Pint = 480 mL

Half-pint (1 cup) = 240 mL
1 tablespoon = 15 mL
1 teaspoon = 5 mL
1 pound = 456 g
1 pound pressure = 6.9 kPa

TIMETABLE 2 — Steps For Canning Alaska Vegetables

For adjustments and other pressure canning procedures, see page 423. Prepare food as directed. If desired, add 1 teaspoon salt per quart. Place jars on rack in pressure canner containing 2 to 3 inches of boiling water. *Pressure listed is for sea level; time is for pressure canner. If raw pack time is not listed, raw pack is not recommended.

Product	Preparation	Pressure Canner: 10 pounds pressure* (69 kPa)	
		Pints	**Quarts**
Beans, snap: (Yield— Bushel = 12-20 qts 1½-2½ lbs = 1 qt)	**Raw Pack** — Wash. Trim ends and cut into 1-inch pieces. Pack tightly in jars. Cover with boiling water, leaving 1/2-inch head space.	20 min.	25 min.
	Hot Pack — Prepare as for raw pack. Cover with boiling water and boil five minutes. Pack jars loosely. Cover with hot cooking liquid and water, leaving 1/2-inch head space.	20 min.	25 min.
Beets: (Yield— Bushel = 15-24 qts 2-3½ lbs = 1 qt)	**Hot Pack** — Sort for size. Cut off tops, leaving 1-inch stem. Wash. Boil until skins slip easily. Cool, skin and trim. Cut into 1/2-inch cubes or slices; halve or quarter large slices. Pack into jars. Cover with boiling water leaving 1/2-inch head space.	30 min.	35 min.
Cabbage:	*Cabbage may be canned but other food preservation methods give a better product. In canning, leaves tend to discolor and flavor becomes strong. However, to can, use . . .*		
	Hot Pack — Remove outer leaves, quarter, core and cut into thin wedges. Cover with boiling water and boil five minutes. Pack jars loosely. Cover with hot cooking liquid and water, leaving 1/2-inch head space.	30 min.	35 min.
Mushrooms:	**Hot Pack** — Trim stems and discolored parts of mushrooms. Soak mushrooms in cold water for 10 minutes to remove adhering soil; drain, wash in clean water and drain again. Leave small mushrooms whole; cut larger ones in halves or quarters. Steam four minutes or heat gently for 15 minutes without added liquid in covered saucepan. Pack into pint or half-pint jars only, leaving 1/2-inch head space. Add 1/4 teaspoon salt to half-pints; 1/2 teaspoon to pints. For better color, add crystalline ascorbic acid — 1/16 teaspoon to half-pints 1/8 teaspoon to pints. Add boiling hot cooking liquid or boiling water to cover, leaving 1/2-inch headroom at top of jar. Of wild mushrooms, orange delight and meadow mushrooms are best for canning.	30 min.	Do not use quarts
Peas, green: (Yield— Bushel = 5-10 qts 3-6 lbs = 1 qt)	**Raw Pack:** Shell and wash. Pack loosely in jars. Cover with boiling water, leaving 1-inch head space	40 min.	40 min.
	Hot Pack — Prepare as for raw pack. Cover with boiling water and **bring to boil. Pack peas loosely in jars. Cover with cooking liquid and boiling water, leaving 1-inch head space.**	40 min.	40 min.
Squash, summer & zucchini: (Yield— Bushel = 10-20 qts 2-4 lbs = 1 qt)	**Raw Pack** — Wash. Trim ends. Cut squash into 1/2-inch slices; halve or quarter to make uniform pieces. Pack into jars leaving 1-inch head space. Cover with boiling water, leaving 1/2-inch head space.	25 min.	30 min.
	Hot Pack — Prepare as for raw pack. Add water to cover. Bring to boil. Pack hot squash loosely to 1/2 inch from top. Cover with boiling cooking liquid and water. Leave 1/2-inch head space.	30 min.	40 min.
Spinach & other greens (Yield— Bushel = 3-8 qts 2-6 lbs = 1 qt)	**Hot Pack** — Sort and wash thoroughly. Cut out tough stems and midribs. Place about 2-1/2 pounds spinach in cheesecloth bag and steam about 10 minutes or until well wilted. Pack loosely. Cover with boiling water, leaving 1/2-inch head space.	70 min.	90 min.

---

1 bushel = about 34 L
1/2 inch = 1.25 cm
1 inch = 2.5 cm
Quart = 0.95 L
Pint = 480 mL

Half-pint (1 cup) = 240 mL
1 tablespoon = 15 mL
1 teaspoon = 5 mL
1 pound = 456 g
1 pound pressure = 6.9 kPa

WINE & OTHER
BOTTLED BEVERAGES

Raspberry Vinegar

"It sounds awful, doesn't it? Like some kind of curiosity for salad fiends. But Raspberry Vinegar is an old French Canadian treat, a sort of sweet-sour soda pop. It's a good recipe for other sweet berries, too: blueberries and strawberries, for instance."

1 quart (1 L) raspberries
1 quart (1 L) cider vinegar (white vinegar can also be used; flavor is milder)
8 cups (1.9 L) sugar

►Soak raspberries overnight, or longer, in vinegar. Blend well in blender to mash thoroughly. Then strain seeds from berry puree.

Pour berry puree into large enamel pan and add sugar. Heat to rolling boil and boil hard for three minutes.

Pour hot into hot sterilized jars and seal; process in boiling-water bath 10 minutes.

To use: Mix 3 tablespoons (45 mL) Raspberry Vinegar with one glass of water; add ice and serve. For a sparkling drink, more delicious than any raspberry pop on the market, add club soda or charged water.

■ *Pat Monaghan, Fairbanks*

Northern Comfort

3 pounds (1.4 kg) wild cranberries or lingonberries
1 fifth Everclear
6 cups (1.45 L) sugar
3 cups (720 mL) water

►Crush berries and let stand for 24 hours. Then add Everclear and let stand another 24 hours. Then put the mixture through a juicer or ricer and strain the juice so that it is entirely clear. Boil sugar and water for five minutes. Cool. Add to juice mixture. Should stand three to six months before being used as it is much smoother after aging. We have also used blueberries and presumably any tart berry would do.

In the absence of Everclear, vodka could be used but it is only about half the proof of Everclear,* and to bring the final product up to the same proof as the recipe, you get more liquid and a different flavor.

We have also made it of domestic berries. Even bottled cranberry juice would do, I suppose. In that instance, I suggest starting with the juice and adding syrup and alcohol to taste. We have never tried the juice, but it should work.

The recipe, with slight variations, has been around a long time and is not anything exclusive with me.

■ *Anon.*

Our anonymous Northern Comfort connoisseur points out that Everclear is an astonishing 190 proof pure grain alcohol . . . illegal in many states.

Dandelion Wine**

1 quart (1 L) blossoms, packed solid
3 quarts (2.9 L) boiling water

►Pour water over blossoms and let cool. Let stand in crock 24 to 48 hours, pushing blossoms down, seeing that they are kept covered with water as much as possible. After desired time, strain. To each gallon (3.8 L) of liquid add:

1 orange, diced or sliced
1 lemon, diced or sliced
3 pounds (1.4 kg) sugar

►Bring liquid to a boil and let bubble good. Strain and put in crock or barrel. Let ferment about three weeks in warm place. Strain carefully (don't squeeze) and pour into bottles. Store in cool place.

Rhubarb Wine**

►For every 7 pounds (3.2 kg) rhubarb crushed, add 1/2 gallon (1.9 L) boiling water. Let stand 12 hours. Strain. Add 4 pounds (1.8 kg) sugar to the gallon (3.8 L). Mix in crock, let ferment, then bottle and cork tight. Half a package of winemaker's yeast, dissolved, may be used if desired.

Currant Wine**

►Cover berries with cold water. Crush well with wooden masher. Let stand 24 hours. Strain. To 1 gallon (3.8 L) juice, add 3 pounds (1.4 kg) brown sugar, pour in crock, let ferment. Skim daily. When fermentation stops, strain and funnel into cask or suitable container. Let stand about eight months. Strain again and bottle.

■ **All three recipes (dated 1916) are from the files of Marie Weschenfelder
Courtesy, Mamie Jensen, Juneau*

Birch Wine

When Ann Baltzo and her husband Howard first began tapping trees to gather birch sap for winemaking, they drilled holes at a 45° angle into the trunks of trees with an 8-inch (20 cm) diameter. Into the holes, they inserted rubber tubing and, with nails, hung 1-pound (456 g) coffee cans to catch the drips. After a while they found this method slow going and discovered that a much faster way was to draw the sap off freshly cut stumps. To do this, they fell larger trees — 14 inches (35 cm) or more in diameter —with a slanting cut. Then they groove the slanted surface of the fresh-cut stump and attach a metal trough to the down-slant to drain the sap into a No. 10 can lined with a plastic bag. The Baltzos have found that they can cut trees for firewood in the winter and prepare the stumps at that time by chiseling the groove and attaching the trough. Then they cover the stump with plastic to await warmer weather and sap-flow time. Collection occurs when night temperatures are around 30°F (-1°C) and days reach 55°F (12.7°C).

6 gallons (22.8 L) birch sap
15 pounds (6.75 kg) corn sugar
5 Campden tablets, crushed
2-1/2 pounds (1.15 kg) raisins
Juice of 1 lemon
1/2 ounce (14 g) citric acid
1/2 cup (120 mL) strong tea
1/2 ounce (14 g) tartaric acid
2-1/2 teaspoons (12 mL) yeast nutrient
1 envelope Montrachet yeast

►Heat sap to 120°F (49°C). Add sugar and stir to dissolve. Add next six ingredients. Let stand 12 hours or overnight. Add yeast nutrient, also the Montrachet yeast, prepared as instructed on envelope. (These yeasts are not like that used in bread making and should be obtained from a winemakers' supply store.)

If you do not have a stove-top container large enough to hold the full amount of birch sap, no doubt you could get away with heating only the amount of sap necessary to dissolve the sugar.

When this primary fermenter is placed before a sunny window, we note that raisins float to the surface and a fine bottom fermentation gets started by evening or, at the latest, the next morning. Ours is a closely watched fermentation since my husband scrutinizes and stirs daily to be sure all's well.

When we use this recipe, we can progress from straining into a 5-gallon (19 L) carboy two weeks after gathering, through two subsequent rackings, using a jug for any excess, and then racking to the final, fully clear carboy to age the balance of the year after we bottle it.

Each year's adventure produces an alcoholic content varying 'twixt 12 and 14 percent. Special vintage samples are sequestered to be tried five years hence. Friends agree that it's a most pleasing white table wine. It's always a surprise that our source of supply is a tree!

■ *Ann Baltzo*
"Capturing Birch Spirits"
ALASKA® magazine
Alaska-only edition, April 1975

Rose Petal Wine

1 quart (1 L) wild rose petals
1 gallon (3.8 L) boiling water
3 pounds (1.4 kg) sugar
1 ounce (28 g) winemaker's yeast
2 lemons

►Pour 1/2 gallon (1.9 L) of the boiling water over the rose petals in a large crock. Cover tightly and leave for 48 hours, stirring occasionally. Boil half the sugar in 1 quart (1 L) of water for two minutes, cool and add to the rose petals and ferment for three days. Strain through a jelly bag and wring out the bag to obtain all juice. Return the liquid to the crock and allow to ferment for 10 days more. Pour the liquor into a gallon jar being sure to leave all sediment behind. Boil the rest of the sugar and water as before and when cool, add to the first mixture with the juice of the lemons. Cover and leave until all fermentation has ceased. Pour into sterilized bottles and cap at once. Store in a cool place for several months before sampling.

■ *ALASKA® magazine*

The text in Chapter 14 is based on many sources. General canning information is compiled from Pacific Northwest Extension Service (PNW) publications and the University of Alaska Cooperative Extension Service (UAX), P-27, *The Fisherman Returns.* Information about preserving fish is from PNW publication, *Canning Seafood* (reprinted September 1981); from Washington Department of Fisheries, *Smokehouses and the Smoke Curing of Fish,* 1971; and U.S. Department of Agriculture (USDA), Home and Garden Bulletin No. 93, *Freezing Meat and Fish in the Home,* slightly revised August 1980.

Information about preserving game is compiled from Agricultural Extension Service, University of Wyoming (UWX) Publication B-613, *You and Your Wild Game,* revised 1983; USDA Home and Garden Bulletin No. 106, *Home Canning of Meat and Poultry,* slightly revised, June 1977; Cooperative Extension Service, Washington State University (WSU) Publication E.M. 2030, *Curing and Smoking Meat, Poultry, and Fish at Home,* revised July 1975; UAX F-41, *The Hunter Returns After the Kill,* reprinted 1963.

Preservation methods for fruit and vegetables are based on material from the *Alaska Wild Berry Guide and Cookbook,* Alaska Northwest Publishing Company, Anchorage, 1983; WSU Cooperative Extension Bulletin 658, *Home Freezing of Fruits and Vegetables,* reprinted September 1978; USDA Home and Garden Bulletin No. 92, *Making Pickles and Relishes at Home,* Revised July 1978; WSU Cooperative Extension Bulletin 0700, *Drying Fruits and Vegetables;* USDA Home and Garden Bulletin No. 56, *How to Make Jellies, Jams, and Preserves at Home;* UWX Publication B-783, *Home Canning of Fruits, Vegetables, and Meats,* reprinted June 1982, as well as a number of UAX publications: P-64, *Rhubarb Recipes,* revised September 1978; P-120, *Collecting and Using Alaska's Wild Berries,* rev. August 1980; P-169, *Alaskan Grown Cabbage,* revised July 1981; P-6, *Know Alaska's Mushrooms* (no date).

Cooks & Cookbooks In This Collection

The Cookbooks

Most of the Alaska "community" cookbooks were published to share much more than good cooking. The sponsoring organizations nearly always had in mind helping to finance one or another project with proceeds from the sale of the book. Profits from Alaska's Cooking went toward a club building for the people of Anchorage. The Aleut Cookbook helped to fund the Aleut Arts and Crafts Club of Saint Paul Island, while the various Homemakers' clubs dedicated their books to "promoting good hospitals, schools, roads, libraries, churches, government and all the things that make better homes and better communities."

Many of these books are still in print ... and the projects are ongoing. If you have found recipes to your liking in Cooking Alaskan, *bear in mind there are more where these came from!*

THE ALASKAN CAMP COOK: Trail-tested Recipes from the Kitchens of Alaskan Big Game Guides; illustrations by Rie Munoz; published in 1963 by Alaska Northwest Publishing Company

AN ALASKAN COOK BOOK, compiled by the Kenai Historical Society; published in 1975 by Cookbook Publishers, Inc. (formerly the Bev-Ron Company), Lenexa, Kansas

ALASKAN COOKBOOK: For Homesteader or Gourmet, by Bess A. Cleveland; published in 1960 by Howell-North Books, San Diego, California

THE ALASKAN MUSHROOM HUNTER'S GUIDE, by Ben Guild; illustrations by Jack VanHoesen; published in 1977 by Alaska Northwest Publishing Company

ALASKA'S COOKING, compiled by the Anchorage Woman's Club and published in 1959

ALASKA SOURDOUGH: The Real Stuff by A Real Alaskan, by Juneau resident Ruth Allman; published in 1976 by Alaska Northwest Publishing Company, Anchorage

ALASKA WILD BERRY GUIDE AND COOKBOOK, by the editors of *ALASKA®* magazine; published in 1983 by Alaska Northwest Publishing Company

ALASKA WILD BERRY TRAILS (With Recipes), by Anchorage resident Helen A. White; illustrated by Virginia Howie; published in 1973

ALEUT COOKBOOK, compiled and edited by Miriam LoPinto; printed in 1966 at Saint Paul Island

BAKE-OFF COOKBOOK, 1961-1980: Best Baking Ideas For A Golden Harvest, collected by the Bake-Off Cook Book Committee and published in 1981 to celebrate the Fiftieth Anniversary of the Tanana Valley Fair in Fairbanks and the Twentieth Anniversary of the Bake Off

COMMUNITY COOKBOOK, by Elfie Apatiki, published by the Community Education Program of Gambell, Saint Lawrence Island

COOKING UP A STORM: Favorite Recipes of Homer Cooks, compiled by Homer Homemakers and published in 1972

DALL HOMEMAKERS COOKBOOK: Recipes Ewe Will Enjoy, collected by the Dall Homemakers' Club, Cooper Landing, and published in 1974

DENA'INA K'ET'UNA: Tanaina Plantlore, compiled by Priscilla Russell Kari; illustrations by Kathleen Lynch; published in 1977 by the Adult Literacy Laboratory, University of Alaska, Anchorage

THE DOGFISH COOKBOOK, by Russ Mohney; drawings by the author; published in 1976 by Pacific Search Books, Seattle, Washington

FALSE ISLAND CAMP COOKBOOK, compiled by the Wives of the Clear Creek Loggers, False Island Camp (Sitka); published in 1974 by Cookbook Publishers, Inc.

FOODS FROM THE SEA: A Videotape Teacher's Guide with Native food recipes from Clara Peratrovich; prepared by Carol Hendrickson, Curriculum Development Specialist, and a student production crew; sponsored by Tlin Tsim Hai News, NEH Youth Project, Ketchikan Indian Corporation, Ketchikan

FRONTIER VITTLES: A Book of Favorite Recipes, compiled by the Amaranth Social Club, Polaris Court #2, Order of the Amaranth, Masonic Temple, Fairbanks; published by Circulation Service, Shawnee Mission, Kansas

GOLD RUSH COOKBOOK, compiled by the 1976 Gold Rush Days Committee, Valdez; published in 1976 by Cookbook Publishers, Inc.

GOLD RUSH FESTIVAL COOK BOOK, compiled by the Whitehorse Diocesan Council, Catholic Women's League, Whitehorse, Yukon Territory, Canada

GOOD FOOD A-PLENTY, compiled by the Memorial Hospital Auxiliary, Fairbanks,

Alaska; published in 1974 by Cookbook Publishers, Inc.

HAIDA FOOD GATHERING and PREPARATION, by Robert Cogo; published in 1979 by Ketchikan Indian Corporation as part of Southeast Alaska Native Materials Development Project

HAINES HOMEMAKERS' COOKBOOK: *Featuring Recipes from the Southeast Alaska State Fair;* compiled by the Chilkat Valley Homemakers' Club, Haines

ISLAND EDIBLES, general editor, Lee Bullington; published by Sand Point High School Press, Sand Point

JUNEAU CENTENNIAL COOKBOOK, written by Jane Stewart and Betty Harris; edited and designed by Phyllice Fallah Bradner, Juneau

KAA T'EIX'S COOKBOOK, by Kaa T'eix (Mary Howard Pelayo); sponsored by Alaska Native Brotherhood, Mount Edgecumbe; printed in 1977 by General Publishing and Binding, Iowa Falls, Iowa

KITCHEN MAGIC, compiled by Pioneer Auxiliary No. 7, Pioneers of Alaska, Ketchikan; published in 1975 by Circulation Service

LOGGIN' CAMP COOKIN' BOOK, compiled by Dry Pass Community Club, Ketchikan; published by Cookbook Publishers, Inc.

LOWBUSH MOOSE *(And Other Alaskan Recipes),* by Palmer resident Gordon R. Nelson; published in 1978 by Alaska Northwest Publishing Company

MORE ABOUT WHAT'S COOKIN' IN ALASKA, by Anchorage resident Helen A. White

"MORE GOOD EATING," compiled by the Sunshine Society, Tokeen Cove, with the participation of Bloom Logging Camp, Roger Gildersleeve Logging Camp, Murray Gildersleeve Logging Camp; published in 1976 by Cookbook Publishers, Inc.

MOUNT SPURR SCHOOL COOK BOOK, compiled by Mount Spurr Elementary School Student Council, Elmendorf Air Force Base; published in 1975 by Cookbook Publishers, Inc.

NORTHERN COOKBOOK, edited by Eleanor A. Ellis; original illustrations by James Simpkins; issued in 1977 by the Minister of Indian Affairs and Northern Development; recipes and other materials reproduced by permission of the Minister of Supply and Services Canada

NORTHERN LITES, TASTY BITES, compiled by the women of the First Presbyterian Church, Fairbanks; published in 1976

ONE HUNDRED YEARS IN THE KITCHEN, an anthology of recipes compiled by Mary Scott Peter; illustrations by Richard and Mary Peter; published in 1976; Juneau

OUT OF ALASKA'S KITCHENS, compiled by members of the Easter Seal Society for Alaska Crippled Children and Adults, Inc.; published in 1961; Anchorage

PAST PRESIDENTS' PARLEY COOK BOOK, compiled by American Legion Auxiliary, Jack Henry Post #1, Anchorage

PIONEER COOKBOOK, compiled by Auxiliary No. 4, Pioneers of Alaska, Anchorage; first edition, 1966

PRIZE-WINNING BAKED GOODS: *A Collection of 1982 Prize-Winning Recipes;* compiled by Anchorage Fur Rendezvous and published in 1982

PTA COOKBOOK, compiled and published by the Petersburg Parent-Teachers' Association; first edition, 1932

RECIPES FOR ALASKAN SCALLOPS, compiled by the Boosters Club, Seward

RECIPES FROM THE SCROLLS OF SAINT PETER'S, compiled by Episcopal Churchwomen and Their Friends, Seward; published in 1966

SAINT HERMAN'S SISTERHOOD CLUB (cookbook); published in 1976 at Kodiak

SAINT PETER'S EPISCOPAL CHURCHWOMEN'S COOKBOOK, Sitka; published in 1975 by Cookbook Publishers, Inc.

SEAFOODFEST RECIPES: *Prize-winning recipes used in Seattle Seafoodfest Recipe Contest,* edited by Arthur Martin, Seattle

SEAFOOD SECRETS, ©South East Alaska Troller's Ass'n. Aux. 1970; Sitka

SEAFOOD TREASURES and *Selected Restaurant Recipes,* compiled by the wives of members of the Puget Sound Gillnetter's Association, Seattle; published in 1978 by Cookbook Publishers, Inc.

SITKA'S TREASURE of *personal recipes,* compiled by the American Legion Auxiliary Unit No. 13, Sitka; published in 1961 by Cookbook Publishers, Inc.

SMOKEHOUSE BEAR: *More Recipes and Stories,* by Gordon R. Nelson; published in 1982 by Alaska Northwest Publishing Company

THE SMORGASBORD, by John Hansen; printed in 1976 by Ed's Quality Printing, Anchorage

SONS OF NORWAY COOK BOOK, compiled by members and friends of Midnatsol Lodge No. 32, Ketchikan; published in 1973 by Cookbook Publishers, Inc.

SOUVENIR COOK BOOK, compiled by American Legion and Auxiliary Post and Unit No. 7, Skagway

TLINGIT SURVIVAL PRACTICES and STORIES, by Frank Johnson; published in 1979 by Ketchikan Indian Corporation

TRIED AND TRUE RECIPES: *by the Best People in the World (B.P.W.),* compiled by the

Business and Professional Women's Club, Juneau

TSIMPSHEAN INDIAN ISLAND COOKBOOK: A Book of Favorite Recipes, compiled by the Ladies Aid of the William Duncan Memorial Church, Metlakatla; published in 1971 by Circulation Service

WHAT'S COOKIN' IN ALASKA, by Helen A. White

WHAT'S COOKIN' IN WRANGELL, compiled by the Women's Civic Club and the American Cancer Society, Wrangell; published in 1975 by Cookbook Publishers, Inc.

WILD GAME COOKBOOK: A Remington Sportsmen's Library Book; published by The Benjamin Company, Inc., One Westchester Plaza, Elmsford, New York 10523

WILDLIFE COOKBOOK: Favorite Recipes from the Alaska Department of Fish and Game Folks; compiled for the 1982 Association for Conservation Information Conference, Sitka/Juneau, 1982

Some Cooks Who Shared Recipes From Their Files

Helena Andree, Homer
Lois Armstrong, Brookings, Oregon
Rose Arvidson, Cordova
Mary Duncan, Angoon
Warren Ernst, Mukilteo, Washington
Susan Ewing, Fairbanks
Jackie Fonnesbeck, Surrey, B.C.
Barbara George, Angoon
Shirley Gunnerson, Anchorage
Ruth Hale, Brookings, Oregon
Bob Henning, Angoon
Katy Huston, Seattle, Washington
Vivian James, Angoon
Mamie Jensen, Juneau
Annie Johnson, Homer
Polly Kallenberg, Chugiak
Donald E. Kramer, Anchorage
Irma Lind, Petersburg
Frances ("Bunny") Mathisen, Petersburg
Mid McLay, Homer
Jeanne Norheim, Petersburg
Dick Person, Carcross, Yukon Territory
Audrey Rearden, Homer
Nita Prince Rearden, Bethel

Delores Carroll Sloan, Fort Yukon
Lois Smith, Tumwater, Washington
Dolly Spencer, Homer
Marguerite Stetson, Fairbanks
Aline Strutz, Anchorage
Elva Bahrt Swenson, Seattle, Washington
David Sykas, Ketchikan
Felicia Tetpon, Homer
Florence V.J. Thornton, Anchorage
Elsie Tourville
Doris Ward, Fort Yukon
Beverly Wolford, Homer
Noreen Zeine, Edmonds, Washington

Newspaper, Magazine and Book Contributors

AlaskaFest, a magazine for Alaska Airlines, published by Seattle Northwest Publishing Company, Seattle, Washington

Alaska Fisherman's Journal, a monthly newspaper published in Seattle, Washington

ALASKA FISHING GUIDE, ALASKA HUNTING GUIDE, ALASKA® magazine (formerly ***ALASKA SPORTSMAN®*** and ***The ALASKA SPORTSMAN®***), all published by Alaska Northwest Publishing Company, Anchorage

Alaska Fish Tales & Game Trails, a publication of the Alaska Department of Fish and Game, Juneau

Alaska Tidelines (now called ***Alaska Earthlines/Tidelines***), a newsprint magazine published by The Alaska Geographic Society, Anchorage

Aleutian Wind, the yearbook of the Aleutian

Region School District (quoted materials are from the 1979 edition)

The All-Alaska Weekly, Fairbanks

Anchorage Daily News

The Anchorage Times

B.C. Outdoors, a monthly magazine, Vancouver, British Columbia, Canada

Fairbanks Daily News-Miner

Farm Journal, Philadelphia, Pennsylvania

The Frontiersman, Palmer

Great Lander Shopping News, Anchorage

Kadiak Times, Kodiak

Ketchikan Daily News

Kodiak Daily Mirror

Kodiak Fish Wrapper & Litter Box Liner

The Northern Traveler, published by the University of Alaska Travel Management Program

Oscar Nictune, Sr, an autobiography sponsored by the Yukon-Koyukuk School District and published in 1980 by Hancock House Publishers, Ltd., Surrey, British Columbia, Canada

Pacific Search (now called *Pacific Northwest*), a monthly magazine published in Seattle, Washington

Southeastern Log, a monthly newspaper published in Ketchikan

Taniisix ("To Shed Light"), a journal published by the Aleutian Region School District

Tundra Drums, Bethel

Uutuqtwa ("I go home"), a magazine produced by the students of Bristol Bay High School, Naknek

Valdez Vanguard, a weekly newspaper

Government Offices and Marketing Services

Alaska King Crab Marketing and Quality Control Board, Juneau: *Alaska King Crab*

Alaska Seafood Marketing Institute, Juneau: *Alaska Salmon*

Fisheries and Oceans Canada: *Fish'n Seafood Salads,* 1977; *Seafood Recipes for Calorie Counters,* 1978; *Shellfish-A-Plenty,* 1978; and *The Way To Cook Fish,* 1980. Material from these booklets was reproduced by permission of the Minister of Supply and Services Canada

Pacific Northwest Extension Service, Seattle, Washington: *Canning Seafood,* August 1979; *Canning Vegetables,* May 1980; *Fish Pickling For Home Use,* January 1978

University of Alaska Cooperative Extension Service, Fairbanks: *Alaska Grown Cabbage: More Than Just Sauerkraut* (P-169), revised July 1981; *Alaska's Game Is Good Food* (P-126), revised July 1974; *Collecting and Using Alaska's Wild Berries and Other Wild Products* (P-120), revised August 1980; *The*

Fisherman Returns (P-27), revised July 1980; *The Hunter Returns After The Kill* (F-41), reprinted 1963; *Know Alaska's Mushrooms* (P-6), by Virginia L. Wells and Phyllis E. Kempton; *Make Your Own Mix* (P-60), revised July 1974; *Recipes For Canned Fish* (P-220B), reprinted 1972; *Reindeer and Caribou Recipes* (P-68), October 1973; *Rhubarb Recipes* (P-64), revised September 1978; *Sausage From Alaskan Game* (P-125) October 1975; *Seafood Recipes For Alaskans* (P-57), reprinted 1965; *Smelt* (P-25), reprinted May 1980; *Sourdough* (P-61), revised July 1974; *The Versatile Green Tomato* (P-63), August 1979; *Walrus In The Cooking Pot* (RP-66), reprinted 1973; *Wild Edible and Poisonous Plants of Alaska* (P-28), reprinted 1976; *Zucchini From A to Z* (P-260), revised June 1979

University of Minnesota Agricultural Extension Service: *Game Birds From Field To Kitchen* (B-346), July 1973; *Home Canning — Fruits, Vegetables, and Meats* (B-413), 1978; *Game Animals From Field To Kitchen* (B-345), 1968

University of Wyoming Agricultural Extension Service: *Home Canning of Fruits, Vegetables and Meats* (B-783), reprinted 1982; *You and Your Wild Game* (B-613), revised 1983

U.S. Department of Commerce, National Marine Fisheries Service: *Seas the Opportunity; Fish and Shellfish Over the Coals* (Test Kitchen Series No. 14); *Nautical Notions for Nibbling,* 1976; *A Seafood Heritage*

U.S. Department of Health, Education and Welfare: *The Alaska Dietary Survey, 1956-1961,* Christine A. Heller, Ph.D. and Edward M. Scott, Ph.D., U.S. Public Health Service Publication No. 999-AH-2, Environmental Health Series: "Arctic Health"

U.S. Department of the Interior, Fish and Wildlife Service, Bureau of Commercial Fisheries: *'Can-venient' Ways with Shrimp* (Fishery Market Development Series No. 2); *Seafood Moods* (FMDS No. 14); *Let's Cook Fish* (FMDS No. 8); *Time for Seafood* (FMDS No. 12)

Washington (State of) Department of Fisheries: *Marine Fish Cookbook,* by Iola I. Berg, Editorial Assistant, July 1969; *Salmon Cookbook,* by Iola I. Berg, 1971; *Seafood Potpourri,* by Elaine Shaw, 1974; *Shellfish Cookbook,* by Iola I. Berg, 1974; *Smokehouses and the Smoke Curing of Fish,* compiled by Iola I. Berg, 1971; *Washington Seafood Recipes,* 1977

Washington State University Cooperative Extension Service: *Curing and Smoking Meat, Poultry, and Fish at Home* (EM 2030, rev.), July 1975

Index